이번 시험에 나온 문제가
다음 시험의 적중률을 보장할까요?

파고다 어학원 토익 전문 연구진 108인은
다음 시험 적중률로 말합니다!

..

이번 시험에 나온 문제를 풀기만 하면,
내 토익 목표 점수를 달성할 수 있을까요?

파고다 토익 시리즈는
파고다 어학원 1타 강사들과 수십 만 수강생이
함께 만든 토익 목표 점수 달성 전략서입니다!

파고다 어학원 1타 토익 강사들의
토익 목표 점수 달성 전략 완전 정리

토익 개념&실전 종합서
700~800점 목표

내 위치를
파악했다면
목표를 향해
나아갈 뿐!

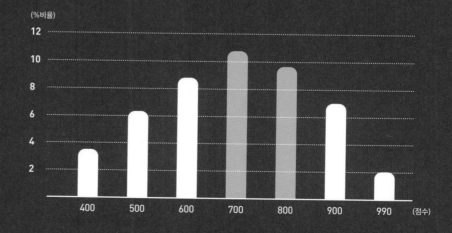

파고다 토익 프로그램

독학자를 위한 다양하고 풍부한 학습 자료

세상 간편한 등업 신청으로 각종 학습
자료가 쏟아지는
파고다 토익 공식 온라인 카페
http://cafe.naver.com/pagodatoeicbooks

교재 Q&A
교재 학습 자료
나의 학습 코칭
정기 토익 분석 자료
기출 분석 자료
예상 적중 특강
논란 종결 총평

| 온라인 모의고사 2회분 |
| 받아쓰기 훈련 자료 |
| 단어 암기장 |
| 단어 시험지 |
| MP3 기본 버전 |
| MP3 추가 버전(1.2배속 등) |
| 추가 연습 문제 등 각종 추가 자료 |

매회 업데이트! 토익 학습 센터

시험 전 적중 문제, 특강 제공
시험 직후 실시간 정답, 총평 특강, 분석 자료집 제공

토익에 푹! 빠져 풀TV

파고다 대표 강사진과 전문 연구원들의
다양한 무료 강의를 들으실 수 있습니다.

600

기본 완성 RC
토익 문법·독해·어휘 입문서
토익 초보 학습자들이 단기간에 쉽게 접근할 수
있도록 토익의 필수 개념을 집약한 입문서

700

실력 완성 RC
토익 개념&실전 종합서
토익의 기본 개념을 확실히 다질 수 있는
풍부한 문제 유형과 실전형 연습문제를 담은 훈련서

800

고득점 완성 RC
최상위권 토익 만점 전략서
기본기를 충분히 다진 토익 중고급자들의
고득점 완성을 위해 핵심 스킬만을 뽑아낸
토익 전략서

3rd Edition

토익 개념&실전 종합서

RC 실력완성

초　　판 1쇄 발행	2016년	4월	29일
개정 2판 1쇄 발행	2016년	12월	26일
개정 3판 1쇄 발행	2019년	1월	5일
개정 3판 13쇄 발행	2024년	7월	12일

지 은 이 | 파고다교육그룹 언어교육연구소, 장진영, 천성배
펴 낸 이 | 박경실
펴 낸 곳 | **PAGODA Books** 파고다북스
출판등록 | 2005년 5월 27일 제 300-2005-90호
주　　소 | 06614 서울특별시 서초구 강남대로 419, 19층(서초동, 파고다타워)
전　　화 | (02) 6940-4070
팩　　스 | (02) 536-0660
홈페이지 | www.pagodabook.com

저작권자 | ⓒ 2019 파고다아카데미, 파고다북스

ISBN 978-89-6281-821-5 (13740)

파고다북스	www.pagodabook.com
파고다 어학원	www.pagoda21.com
파고다 인강	www.pagodastar.com
테스트 클리닉	www.testclinic.com

Ⅰ 낙장 및 파본은 구매처에서 교환해 드립니다.

3rd Edition

토익 개념&실전 종합서

RC 실력 완성

목차

PART 5 GRAMMAR

PART 5 VOCA

PART 6

PART 7

이 책의 구성과 특징

>> **PART 5** GRAMMAR 토익 중급자들을 위한 토익 핵심 문법과 문제 유형을 학습한다.
VOCA Part 5, 6 필수 동사, 명사, 형용사, 부사 어휘를 핵심 어휘 문제로 정리한다.

>> **PART 6** Part 5에서 학습한 어법 적용 문제, 어휘 문제, 글의 흐름상 빈칸에 알맞은 문장을 고르는 신토익 문제
에 충분히 대비한다.

>> **PART 7** 문제 유형별 해결 전략과 지문의 종류 및 주제별 해결 전략을 학습한다.

OVERVIEW

본격적인 학습의 준비 단계로, 각 Part별 출제 경향 및 문제 유형,
변경된 신토익 소개 및 그에 따른 접근 전략을 정리하였다.

🧠 기본 개념 이해하기

Part별 문제 풀이에 앞서, 해당 Part의 기본 개념을 예문과 함께 익힐 수 있게 구성하였다.

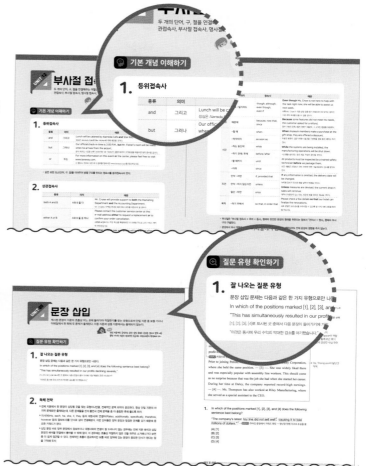

🔍 지문·질문 유형 확인하기

본격적인 학습에 앞서, 최신 토익 출제 경향과 문제풀이 전략을 제시하여 보다 효율적으로 학습 전략을 세울 수 있도록 구성하였다.

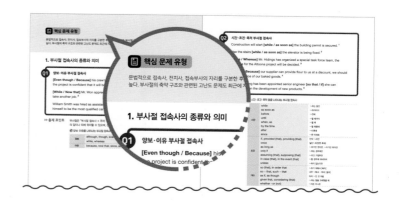

📘 핵심 문제 유형

토익 핵심 문제 유형과 출제 포인트에 대해 알아보고, 학습한 내용을 문제에 적용해 볼 수 있도록 확인 문제들을 제시하였다.

이 책의 구성과 특징

Practice

다양한 토익 실전 문제를 접할 수 있도록 핵심 빈출 유형과 고난도 문제를 각 Part별로 골고루 구성하였다.

PART 5 GRAMMAR : 20문항
　　　　　VOCA : 20문항
PART 6 : 16문항
PART 7 문제 유형별 : 3~4지문
　　　　　지문 유형별 : 3~4지문

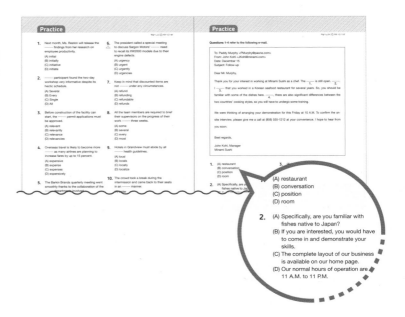

REVIEW TEST

각 Part별 학습한 내용을 마지막으로 체크할 수 있도록 정기 토익 시험과 동일한 유형과 난이도로 구성하였다.

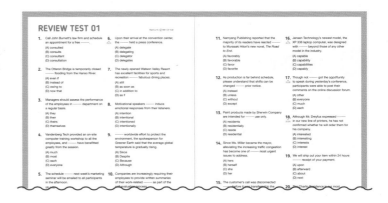

HALF TEST

5회분의 풍부한 연습 문제를 통해 전반적인 실력을 파악할 수 있도록 구성하였다.

PART 5 : 20문항
PART 6 : 8문항
PART 7 : 6지문 / 22문항

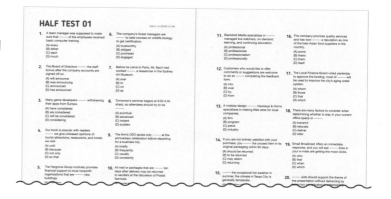

ACTUAL TEST

토익 시험 전 학습한 내용을 점검할 수 있도록 실제 정기 토익 시험과 가장 유사한 형태의 모의고사 1회분을 제공하였다.

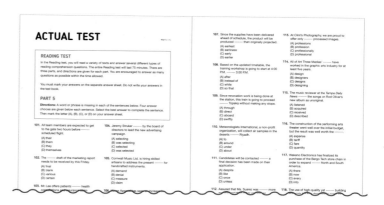

해설서

실력완성을 위한 정·오답 분석과 문제 풀이에 필요한 어휘를 제시한 상세한 해설로 구성하였다.

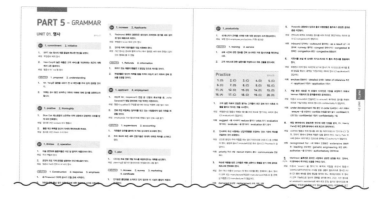

토익이란?

TOEIC(Test Of English for International Communication)은 영어가 모국어가 아닌 사람들을 대상으로 일상생활 또는 국제 업무 등에 필요한 실용 영어 능력을 평가하는 시험입니다.

상대방과 '의사 소통할 수 있는 능력(Communication ability)'을 평가하는 데 중점을 두고 있으므로 영어에 대한 '지식'이 아니라 영어의 실용적이고 기능적인 '사용법'을 묻는 문항들이 출제됩니다.

TOEIC은 1979년 미국 ETS(Educational Testing Service)에 의해 개발된 이래 전 세계 150개 국가 14,000여 개의 기관에서 승진 또는 해외 파견 인원 선발 등의 목적으로 널리 활용하고 있으며 우리나라에는 1982년 도입되었습니다. 해마다 전 세계적으로 약 700만 명 이상이 응시하고 있습니다.

>> **토익 시험의 구성**

	파트	시험 형태		문항 수	시간	배점
듣기 (LC)	1	사진 문제		6	45분	495점
	2	질의응답		25		
	3	짧은 대화		39		
	4	짧은 담화		30		
읽기 (RC)	5	단문 빈칸 채우기		30	75분	495점
	6	장문 빈칸 채우기		16		
	7	독해	단일 지문	29		
			이중 지문	10		
			삼중 지문	15		
계				200	120분	990점

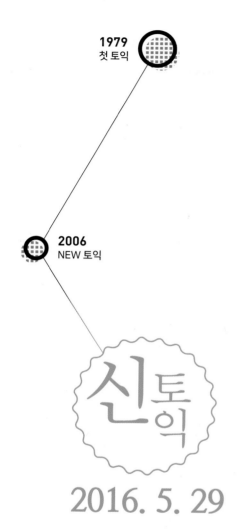

1979
첫 토익

2006
NEW 토익

신토익

2016. 5. 29

토익 시험 접수와 성적 확인

토익 시험은 TOEIC 위원회 웹사이트(www.toeic.co.kr)에서 접수할 수 있습니다. 본인이 원하는 날짜와 장소를 지정하고 필수 기재 항목을 기재한 후 본인 사진을 업로드하면 간단하게 끝납니다.

보통은 두 달 후에 있는 시험일까지 접수 가능합니다. 각 시험일의 정기 접수는 시험일로부터 2주 전까지 마감되지만, 시험일의 3일 전까지 추가 접수할 수 있는 특별 접수 기간이 있습니다. 그러나 특별 추가 접수 기간에는 응시료가 4,000원 더 비싸며, 희망하는 시험장을 선택할 수 없는 경우도 발생할 수 있습니다.

성적은 시험일로부터 16~18일 후에 인터넷이나 ARS(060-800-0515)를 통해 확인할 수 있습니다.

성적표는 우편이나 온라인으로 발급 받을 수 있습니다. 우편으로 발급 받을 경우는 성적 발표 후 대략 일주일이 소요되며, 온라인 발급을 선택하면 유효 기간 내에 홈페이지에서 본인이 직접 1회에 한해 무료 출력할 수 있습니다. 토익 성적은 시험일로부터 2년간 유효합니다.

시험 당일 준비물

시험 당일 준비물은 규정 신분증, 연필, 지우개입니다. 허용되는 규정 신분증은 토익 공식 웹사이트에서 확인하기 바랍니다. 필기구는 연필이나 샤프펜만 가능하고 볼펜이나 컴퓨터용 사인펜은 사용할 수 없습니다. 수험표는 출력해 가지 않아도 됩니다.

시험 진행 안내

시험 진행 일정은 시험 당일 고사장 사정에 따라 약간씩 다를 수 있지만 대부분 아래와 같이 진행됩니다.

>> 시험 시간이 오전일 경우

AM 9:30 ~ 9:45	AM 9:45 ~ 9:50	AM 9:50 ~ 10:05	AM 10:05 ~ 10:10	AM 10:10 ~ 10:55	AM 10:55 ~ 12:10
15분	5분	15분	5분	45분	75분
답안지 작성에 관한 Orientation	수험자 휴식 시간	신분증 확인 (감독교사)	문제지 배부, 파본 확인	듣기 평가(LC)	읽기 평가(RC) 2차 신분증 확인

* 주의: 오전 9시 50분 입실통제

>> 시험 시간이 오후일 경우

PM 2:30 ~ 2:45	PM 2:45 ~ 2:50	PM 2:50 ~ 3:05	PM 3:05 ~ 3:10	PM 3:10 ~ 3:55	PM 3:55 ~ 5:10
15분	5분	15분	5분	45분	75분
답안지 작성에 관한 Orientation	수험자 휴식 시간	신분증 확인 (감독교사)	문제지 배부, 파본 확인	듣기 평가(LC)	읽기 평가(RC) 2차 신분증 확인

* 주의: 오후 2시 50분 입실 통제

파트별 토익 소개

PART 5

INCOMPLETE SENTENCE
단문 빈칸 채우기

Part 5는 빈칸이 있는 문장이 하나 나오고, 4개의 선택지 중 빈칸에 가장 적합한 단어나 구를 고르는 문제로써 총 30문항이 출제된다.

문항 수	30문항 (101번 ~ 130번)
문제 유형	**[어형 문제]** 문제의 빈칸이 어떤 자리인지를 파악하여 네 개의 선택지 중에 들어갈 적절한 품사 및 형태를 묻는 문제이다. 보통 10문항 정도가 출제되는데 어형 문제는 품사에 관한 기초만 탄탄히 하면 쉽게 풀 수 있는 비교적 난이도가 낮은 문제이다.

[어휘 문제] 어휘의 정확한 용례를 알고 있는지 묻는 문제로 같은 품사의 서로 다른 어휘가 선택지로 나온다. 어휘 문제는 다른 Part 5 문제들보다 어려운 편인 데다가 전체 30문항 중 절반가량이 어휘 문제일 정도로 출제 비중이 점점 높아지고 있다.

[문법 문제] 문장의 구조 파악과 구와 절을 구분하여 전치사와 접속사 또는 부사 자리를 구분하고, 접속사가 답인 경우는 접속사 중에서도 명사절, 형용사절, 부사절을 구분하는 문제가 출제된다. 보통 6~7문항이 출제되는데 쉬운 문제부터 상당히 어려운 문제까지 난이도는 다양하다.

어형 문제
>>

101. If our request for new computer equipment receives -------, we are going to purchase 10 extra monitors.

(A) approval
(B) approved
(C) approve
(D) approves

어휘 문제
>>

102. After being employed at a Tokyo-based technology firm for two decades, Ms. Mayne ------- to Vancouver to start her own IT company.

(A) visited
(B) returned
(C) happened
(D) compared

문법 문제
>>

103. ------- the demand for the PFS-2x smartphone, production will be tripled next quarter.

(A) Even if
(B) Just as
(C) As a result of
(D) Moreover

정답 101. (A) 102. (B) 103. (C)

PART 6

TEXT COMPLETION
장문 빈칸 채우기

Part 6은 4문항의 문제가 있는 4개의 지문이 나와 총 16문항이 출제된다. 각각의 빈칸에 가장 적절한 단어나 구, 문장을 삽입하는 문제로 Part 5와 Part 7을 접목한 형태로 볼 수 있다.

문항 수	4개 지문, 16문항 (131번 ~ 146번)
지문 유형	설명서, 편지, 이메일, 기사, 공지, 지시문, 광고, 회람, 발표문, 정보문 등
문제 유형	[어형 문제] 빈칸의 자리를 파악하여 네 개의 선택지 중에 들어갈 적절한 품사 및 형태를 묻는 문제로 Part 5와 같은 유형의 문제들이다. 전체 16문항 중 3~4문항 정도가 출제된다.
	[어휘 문제] 네 개의 선택지 중 의미상 가장 적절한 어휘를 고르는 문제로, 전후 문맥을 파악하여 풀어야 하므로 Part 5의 어휘 문제들보다 어려운 편이다. 보통 5~6문항이 출제된다.
	[문법 문제] 구와 절, 즉 문장 구조를 파악하는 문제로 Part 6에서는 출제 빈도가 낮은 편이지만 Part 5보다 상당히 어려운 문제들로 출제된다. 전체 16문항 중 1~2문항 정도가 출제된다.
	[문장 삽입 문제] Part 7처럼 전반적인 지문의 흐름을 파악하여 4개의 선택지 중에 가장 적절한 한 문장을 선택하는 가장 난이도가 높은 문제이며, 지문마다 한 문제씩 총 4문항이 출제된다.

Questions 131-134 refer to the following e-mail.

To: sford@etnnet.com
From: customersupprt@interhostptimes.ca
Date: July 1
Re: Your Subscription

Congratulations on becoming a reader of *International Hospitality Times*. --131.-- the plan you have subscribed to, you will not only have unlimited access to our online content, but you will also receive our hard copy edition each month. If you wish to --132.-- your subscription preferences, contact our Customer Support Center at +28 07896 325422. Most --133.-- may also make updates to their accounts on our Web site at www.interhosptimes.ca. Please note that due to compatibility issues, it may not be possible for customers in certain countries to access their accounts online. --134.--. Your business is greatly appreciated.

International Hospitality Times

문법 문제 >> 131. (A) Besides
(B) As if
(C) Under
(D) Prior to

어휘 문제 >> 132. (A) purchase
(B) modify
(C) collect
(D) inform

어형 문제 >> 133. (A) subscribe
(B) subscriptions
(C) subscribers
(D) subscribing

문장 삽입 문제 >> 134. (A) We have branches in over 30 countries around the globe.
(B) We provide online content that includes Web extras and archives.
(C) We are working to make this service available to all readers soon.
(D) We would like to remind you that your contract expires this month.

정답 131. (C) 132. (B) 133. (C) 134. (C)

PART 7 READING COMPREHENSION
독해

Part 7은 지문을 읽고 그에 해당하는 각각의 질문(2~5개)에 알맞은 답을 고르는 문제이다. 지문의 종류가 다양하며 그 형태도 1개의 지문으로 된 것과 2개, 3개의 지문으로 된 것이 있다.

문항 수	54문항 (147번 ~ 200번) → 단일 지문: 10개 지문, 19문항
	이중 지문: 2개 지문, 10문항
	삼중 지문: 3개 지문, 15문항

지문 유형	편지, 이메일, 광고, 공지, 회람, 기사, 안내문, 웹페이지(회사나 제품소개, 행사 소개, 고객 사용 후기), 청구서 또는 영수증, 문자, 온라인 채팅 대화문 등

문제 유형	- 주제·목적 문제
	- 세부사항 문제
	- 암시·추론 문제
	- 사실확인 문제
	- 동의어 문제
	- 화자 의도 파악 문제
	- 문장 삽입 문제

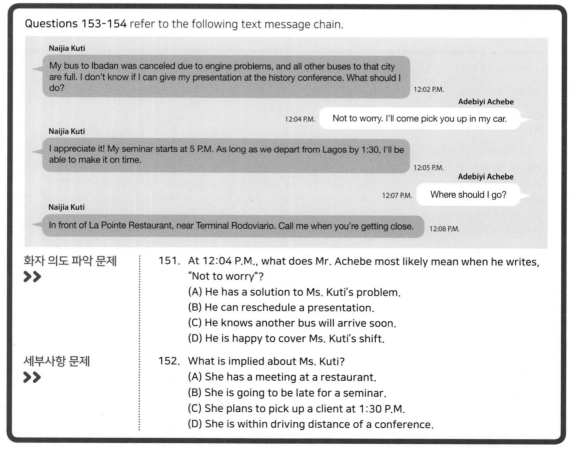

Questions 153-154 refer to the following text message chain.

Naijia Kuti
My bus to Ibadan was canceled due to engine problems, and all other buses to that city are full. I don't know if I can give my presentation at the history conference. What should I do?
12:02 P.M.

Adebiyi Achebe
12:04 P.M. Not to worry. I'll come pick you up in my car.

Naijia Kuti
I appreciate it! My seminar starts at 5 P.M. As long as we depart from Lagos by 1:30, I'll be able to make it on time.
12:05 P.M.

Adebiyi Achebe
12:07 P.M. Where should I go?

Naijia Kuti
In front of La Pointe Restaurant, near Terminal Rodoviario. Call me when you're getting close. 12:08 P.M.

화자 의도 파악 문제 ▶▶

151. At 12:04 P.M., what does Mr. Achebe most likely mean when he writes, "Not to worry"?
(A) He has a solution to Ms. Kuti's problem.
(B) He can reschedule a presentation.
(C) He knows another bus will arrive soon.
(D) He is happy to cover Ms. Kuti's shift.

세부사항 문제 ▶▶

152. What is implied about Ms. Kuti?
(A) She has a meeting at a restaurant.
(B) She is going to be late for a seminar.
(C) She plans to pick up a client at 1:30 P.M.
(D) She is within driving distance of a conference.

정답 151. (A) 152. (D)

Questions 158-160 refer to the following Web page.

http://www.sdayrealestate.com/listing18293

Looking for a new home for your family? This house, located on 18293 Winding Grove, was remodeled last month. It features 2,500 square feet of floor space, with 5,000 square feet devoted to a gorgeous backyard. Also included is a 625 square feet garage that can comfortably fit two mid-sized vehicles —[1]—. Located just a five-minute drive from the Fairweather Metro Station, this property allows for easy access to the downtown area, while providing plenty of room for you and your family. —[2]—. A serene lake is just 100– feet walk away from the house. —[3]—. A 15 percent down payment is required to secure the property. —[4]—. For more detailed information or to arrange a showing, please email Jerry@sdayrealestate.com.

세부사항 문제
»

158. How large is the parking space?
(A) 100 square feet
(B) 625 square feet
(C) 2,500 square feet
(D) 5,000 square feet

사실확인 문제
»

159. What is NOT stated as an advantage of the property?
(A) It has a spacious design.
(B) It has been recently renovated.
(C) It is in a quiet neighborhood.
(D) It is near public transportation.

문장 삽입 문제
»

160. In which of the positions marked [1], [2], [3], and [4] does the following sentence best belong?

"A smaller amount may be accepted, depending on the buyer's financial situation."

(A) [1]
(B) [2]
(C) [3]
(D) [4]

정답 158. (B) 159. (C) 160. (D)

학습 플랜

4주 플랜

DAY 1	DAY 2	DAY 3	DAY 4	DAY 5
[PART 5 GRAMMAR] Unit 01. 명사 Unit 02. 대명사 Unit 03. 형용사	Unit 04. 부사 Unit 05. 전치사 REVIEW TEST 01	Unit 06. 동사의 형태와 수 일치 Unit 07. 능동태와 수동태 Unit 08. 시제	REVIEW TEST 02 Unit 09. 동명사 Unit 10. to부정사	Unit 11. 분사 REVIEW TEST 03 Unit 12. 부사절 접속사

DAY 6	DAY 7	DAY 8	DAY 9	DAY 10
Unit 13. 명사절 접속사 Unit 14. 형용사절 접속사 REVIEW TEST 04	Unit 15. 비교·가정법·도치 REVIEW TEST 05	[PART 5 VOCA] Unit 01. 동사 Unit 02. 명사 Unit 03. 형용사	Unit 04. 부사 REVIEW TEST	[PART 6] Unit 01. PART 6 유형 분석 Unit 02. 실전 연습 01 Unit 03. 실전 연습 02

DAY 11	DAY 12	DAY 13	DAY 14	DAY 15
Unit 04. 실전 연습 03 REVIEW TEST	[PART 7] Unit 01. 주제·목적 Unit 02. 상세정보 Unit 03. 사실확인	Unit 04. 암시·추론 Unit 05. 문장 삽입 Unit 06. 동의어	Unit 07. 문자 대화문과 화자 의도 Unit 08. 편지·이메일 Unit 09. 광고	Unit 10. 공지·회람 Unit 11. 기사 Unit 12. 양식

DAY 16	DAY 17	DAY 18	DAY 19	DAY 20
Unit 13. 이중 지문 Unit 14. 삼중 지문	REVIEW TEST HALF TEST 01	HALF TEST 02 HALF TEST 03	HALF TEST 04 HALF TEST 05	ACTUAL TEST

8주 플랜

DAY 1	DAY 2	DAY 3	DAY 4	DAY 5
[PART 5 GRAMMAR] Unit 01. 명사 Unit 02. 대명사	Unit 03. 형용사 Unit 04. 부사	Unit 05. 전치사 REVIEW TEST 01	Unit 06. 동사의 형태와 수 일치 Unit 07. 능동태와 수동태	Unit 08. 시제 REVIEW TEST 02

DAY 6	DAY 7	DAY 8	DAY 9	DAY 10
Unit 09. 동명사 Unit 10. to부정사	Unit 11. 분사 REVIEW TEST 03	Unit 12. 부사절 접속사 Unit 13. 명사절 접속사	Unit 14. 형용사절 접속사 REVIEW TEST 04	Unit 15. 비교·가정법·도치 REVIEW TEST 05

DAY 11	DAY 12	DAY 13	DAY 14	DAY 15
PART 5 GRAMMAR 다시보기 - 필수 문법 및 어휘 되새기기	[PART 5 VOCA] Unit 01. 동사 Unit 02. 명사	Unit 03. 형용사 Unit 04. 부사	REVIEW TEST PART 5 VOCA 다시보기 - 필수 어휘 되새기기	[PART 6] Unit 01. PART 6 유형 분석

DAY 16	DAY 17	DAY 18	DAY 19	DAY 20
Unit 02. 실전 연습 01	Unit 03. 실전 연습 02	Unit 04. 실전 연습 03	REVIEW TEST	[PART 7] Unit 01. 주제·목적 Unit 02. 상세정보

DAY 21	DAY 22	DAY 23	DAY 24	DAY 25
Unit 03. 사실확인 Unit 04. 암시·추론	Unit 05. 문장 삽입 Unit 06. 동의어	Unit 07. 문자 대화문과 화자 의도 Unit 08. 편지·이메일	Unit 09. 광고 Unit 10. 공지·회람	Unit 11. 기사 Unit 12. 양식

DAY 26	DAY 27	DAY 28	DAY 29	DAY 30
Unit 13. 이중 지문	Unit 14. 삼중 지문	REVIEW TEST	HALF TEST 01	HALF TEST 01 다시보기 - 틀린 문제 다시 풀어보기 - 모르는 단어 체크해서 암기

DAY 31	DAY 32	DAY 33	DAY 34	DAY 35
HALF TEST 02	HALF TEST 02 다시보기 - 틀린 문제 다시 풀어보기 - 모르는 단어 체크해서 암기	HALF TEST 03	HALF TEST 03 다시보기 - 틀린 문제 다시 풀어보기 - 모르는 단어 체크해서 암기	HALF TEST 04

DAY 36	DAY 37	DAY 38	DAY 39	DAY 40
HALF TEST 04 다시보기 - 틀린 문제 다시 풀어보기 - 모르는 단어 체크해서 암기	HALF TEST 05	HALF TEST 05 다시보기 - 틀린 문제 다시 풀어보기 - 모르는 단어 체크해서 암기	ACTUAL TEST	ACTUAL TEST 다시보기 - 틀린 문제 다시 풀어보기 - 모르는 단어 체크해서 암기

GRAMMAR

▲

RT5

▼

단문 빈칸
채우기

OVERVIEW

Part 5는 빈칸이 있는 문장이 하나 나오고, 4개의 선택지 중 빈칸에 가장 적절한 단어나 구를 고르는 문제로써 총 30문항이 출제된다.

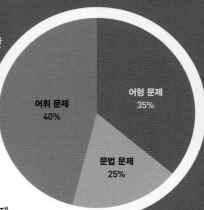

어형 문제
35%

어휘 문제
40%

문법 문제
25%

문제 유형

어형 문제 ㅣ 빈칸의 자리를 파악하여 선택지 중 알맞은 품사나 형태를 고르는 문제
어휘 문제 ㅣ 같은 품사의 네 개 어휘 중 정확한 용례를 파악하여 알맞은 단어를 고르는 문제
문법 문제 ㅣ 문장의 구조 파악과 구와 절을 구분하여 접속사나 전치사, 부사를 고르는 문제

출제 포인트

- 문법적 지식과 어휘력을 동시에 묻는 문제들이 증가하고 있다.
  ⋯ 명사 자리인데 선택지에 비슷하게 생긴 명사가 두 개 이상 나오는 문제가 출제된다.

- 두 가지 이상의 문법 포인트를 묻는 문제들이 출제되고 있다.
  ⋯ 동사의 문장 형식을 이해하고 태를 결정하는 문제가 출제된다.

- 다양한 품사의 선택지로 구성된 문제들이 출제되고 있다.
  ⋯ 부사 문제이지만 전치사, 접속사, 관용 표현 등으로 선택지가 구성된다.

PART 5 이렇게 대비하자!

- 무조건 해석부터 하지 말고 선택지를 보고 [어형 문제/어휘 문제/문법 문제] 중 어떤 문제인 지부터 파악한다. 어형 문제는 해석 없이도 답이 나오는 문제가 대부분이므로 최대한 시간을 절약할 수 있는 방법으로 풀어나가야 한다.

- 고득점을 얻기 위해서는 한 단어를 외우더라도 품사, 파생어, 용법을 함께 암기해야 한다. 예를 들어, announce와 notify를 똑같이 '알리다'라고 외워두면 두 단어가 같이 선택지로 나 오는 어휘 문제는 풀 수 없다. notify 뒤에는 사람만이 목적어로 나온다는 사실을 꼭 알아 두어 야 한다.

단계별 문법 학습 전략

(1) 문장의 구조를 결정하는 5형식 동사와 품사별 문장 성분 역할과 문법을 학습한다.

(2) 구와 절을 연결하여 문장을 확장시켜주는 전치사와 접속사의 역할을 학습한다.

(3) 동사의 시제와 태, 가정법, 분사 구문 등의 다소 까다로운 문법 지식을 습득한다.

PART 5 문제 유형별 문제 풀이 접근법

1. 어형 문제

아래 문제처럼 한 단어의 네 가지 형태가 선택지로 나오는 문제를 어형 문제 또는 자리 찾기 문제라고 한다. 어형 문제는 빈칸이 [주어, 동사, 목적어, 보어, 수식어] 중에 어떤 자리인지를 파악해서 선택지 중 알맞은 품사나 형태를 고르는 문제이다.

> Billy's Auto Repair has ------- with 15 different parts suppliers.
>
> (A) contracting   (B) contracts
> (C) contractor   (D) contract

빈칸은 이 문장의 목적어 자리로 명사가 들어갈 자리인데 명사가 보기에 (B), (C), (D) 이렇게 세 개나 나와 있다. 이런 문제들은 자리만 찾는 것으로 끝나지 않고 한 단계 더 나아가 명사의 특성을 알고 있어야 풀 수 있는 문제이다. 한정사 없이 가산 단수 명사는 쓸 수 없으므로 복수명사 (B)가 답이 되는 문제이다.

2. 어휘 문제

아래 문제처럼 같은 품사의 네 가지 다른 단어가 선택지로 나오는 문제를 어휘 문제라고 한다. 어휘 문제는 최소한 빈칸 주변을 해석해야만 풀 수 있고, 어려운 문제의 경우에는 가산/불가산 명사의 구분, 자/타동사의 구분과 같은 문법 사항까지 같이 포함되어 출제되기도 한다.

> I have enclosed a copy of my résumé for your ------- and look
> forward to hearing from you soon.
>
> (A) explanation   (B) participation
> (C) reference   (D) consideration

빈칸은 전치사 for의 목적어 자리에 어떤 명사 어휘를 넣으면 가장 자연스러운지를 고르는 문제인데 '당신의 고려를 위해 제 이력서를 첨부합니다' 정도는 해석해야만 정답 (D)를 고를 수 있는 문제로 어형 문제보다는 훨씬 난이도가 높다.

3. 문법 문제

아래 문제처럼 종속접속사, 등위접속사, 전치사, 부사 등이 선택지에 같이 나오는 문제를 문법 문제라고 한다. 문법 문제는 그 문장의 구조를 파악하여 구와 절을 구분하고 절이라면 여러 가지 절 중 어떤 절인지를 파악해야 하는 어려운 문제들로 대부분 해석까지도 필요하다.

> We need more employees on the production line ------- production
> has increased by 60 percent.
>
> (A) although   (B) since
> (C) because of   (D) so

빈칸은 전치사 두 개의 절을 연결하는 종속접속사 자리이다. 전치사인 (C)와 등위접속사인 (D)는 답이 될 수 없고, 접속사 (A)와 (B) 중에서 '생산이 증가했기 때문에 추가직원을 고용해야 한다'는 의미에 맞는 (B)를 답으로 고르는 문제이다.

명사

동사는 그 의미에 따라 완전한 내용을 전달하기 위해 목적어나 보어를 취한다. 문장의 형식은 목적어나 보어에 따라 결정되며, 명사는 주어, 타동사나 전치사의 목적어, 보어 역할을 한다.

Tip! 가산 명사와 불가산 명사를 구분하는 게 많이 어려워. 토익에서는 사람 명사가 가산 명사임을 활용하는 문제가 자주 출제되고 있어.

🧠 기본 개념 이해하기

1. 문장의 형식과 명사의 자리

> **1형식: 주어(명사) + 동사**
>
> The company's **profits** have been declining recently. 그 회사의 수익이 최근 들어 하락하는 중이다.
>
> **2형식: 주어(명사) + 동사 + 주격 보어(명사)**
>
> Mr. Lee became the new Chief Executive **Officer** of the company. Mr. Lee는 그 회사의 새로운 최고경영자가 되었다.
>
> **3형식: 주어(명사) + 동사 + 목적어(명사)**
>
> The manager made a **presentation** on the safety regulations. 매니저는 안전규정에 대한 발표를 했다.
>
> **4형식: 주어(명사) + 동사 + 간접목적어(명사) + 직접목적어(명사)**
>
> The new advertisement will bring the **company** better **results**. 새 광고는 회사에게 더 좋은 결과를 가져다 줄 것이다.
>
> **5형식: 주어(명사) + 동사 + 목적어(명사) + 목적격 보어(명사)**
>
> A special lunch menu made our **restaurant** a famous **attraction**. 특별 점심 메뉴는 우리 식당을 명소로 만들어 주었다.

- **4형식 동사:** give, hand, lend, offer, bring, grant, award, send 등 '무엇을 주다'라는 기본 의미를 가진 4형식 동사 뒤에는 간접목적어('누구에게')와 직접목적어('무엇을')에 해당하는 명사가 온다.
- **5형식 동사:** 4형식 문장의 간접목적어와 직접목적어는 서로 다른 대상을 나타내지만, 5형식의 목적어와 목적격 보어는 동일한 대상을 나타내며 목적격 보어 자리에는 명사 또는 형용사가 올 수 있다.

2. 명사의 종류와 한정어

명사는 보통 관사 등의 한정사나 형용사 등의 수식어와 결합된 구 형태로 쓰인다.

	가산 명사 단수형	가산 명사 복수형	불가산 명사
불특정 명사	an employee	(무관사) employees	(무관사) information
	one employee	some/any employees	some/any information
특정 명사	the/this/your employee	the/these/your employees	the/this/your information

- **명사의 특정성과 수:** 명사는 특정 대상 지칭 여부나 단수/복수에 따라 관사, 소유격, 수량형용사와 같은 한정사를 통해 표시한다.
- **불특정 명사:** 정해지지 않은 '새로운' 대상을 가리킬 때 가산 명사 단수형 앞에 a/an을 쓴다.

  가산 명사 복수형과 불가산 명사는 앞에 a/an을 쓸 수 없고, 관사 없이 단독으로 쓰거나 some, any 등의 수량형용사와 함께 자주 쓰인다.
- **특정 명사:** '서로 알고 있는' 정해진(definite) 대상은 가산 명사의 단수형이나 복수형, 불가산 명사 앞에 the를 쓴다. 지시형용사(this, these)나 소유격(your, his, her) 등도 명사의 대상을 구체화시킨다.

문장의 구조상 빈칸이 명사 자리일 때, 선택지에 하나 또는 두 개 이상의 명사가 제시된다. 주어, 목적어, 보어 역할을 하는 명사 자리를 파악한 후 명사의 종류(가산 명사/불가산 명사)를 고려해서 문맥상 알맞은 명사를 선택해야 하는 문제가 출제된다.

해설서 p.2

1. 명사의 형태와 역할

Q1 관사·소유격 + (형용사) + [명사 vs. 다른 품사]

BRT, Inc. has shown an unwavering **[commitment / committed]** to its product quality. [1]

Hex-Corp's high sales resulted from its recent **[initiative / initialize]** to improve customer service. [2]

>> 출제 포인트

❶ 명사는 그 앞에 의미를 한정시켜 주는 관사, 소유격, 형용사의 수식을 받는다.

❷ 명사형 어미: -tion, -sion, -ness, -ity, -ance, -ence, -ment, -sis, -th, -sm 등으로 끝나는 단어는 대부분 명사이다.

addition	추가	extension	연장	competitiveness	경쟁력
productivity	생산성	preference	선호	payment	납부
analysis	분석	growth	성장	enthusiasm	열의

❸ -al, -ive 등과 같이 형용사형 어미를 지닌 명사나 -ing로 끝나는 명사 등에 주의해야 한다.

-al	approval	승인	appraisal	평가
	disposal	처분	proposal	제안
	removal	제거	rental	대여 [형] 대여의
	renewal	갱신	original	원본 [형] 원본의
	withdrawal	인출	potential	잠재력 [형] 잠재적인
	referral	추천	individual	개인 [형] 개인적인
	arrival	도착	professional	전문가 [형] 전문적인
-tive	initiative	계획	objective	목적 [형] 객관적인
	perspective	관점	executive	중역 [형] 중역의
	alternative	대안(책) [형] 대안의	adhesive	접착제 [형] 접착성의
	representative	대표자 [형] 대표하는		
-ing	planning	계획 수립	marketing	마케팅
	accounting	회계	spending	지출
	funding	자금[재정] 지원	understanding	이해
	dining	식사	boarding	탑승
	opening	공석, 개막, 개업	housing	주택
	training	훈련	widening	확장
기타	remainder	나머지	characteristic	특성
	architect	건축가	assembly	조립
	critic	비평가	delegate	대표자

1. Mr. Yang will review my **[proposal / proposed]** carefully before making a decision.

2. We would like to express our appreciation for your **[understand / understanding]** during the construction.

Q2 **[형용사 vs. 부사] + 명사와 동사의 형태가 동일한 단어**

The owner of the Blue Oak Restaurant was pleased to receive **[positive / positively]** reviews in the local newspaper. [1]

Please make sure you **[thorough / thoroughly]** check the inventory list. [2]

>> 출제 포인트 ❶ 명사와 동사의 형태가 동일한 단어들이 문장에서 어떤 품사로 쓰였는지 파악할 수 있어야 이와 관련된 문법(형용사나 부사 선택, 대명사나 관계대명사의 격 선택 등) 문제를 해결할 수 있다.

access	접근, 이용; 접근하다, 이용하다	manufacture	제조; 제조하다
check	점검; 점검하다	order	주문; 주문하다
contract	계약; 계약하다	purchase	구매; 구매하다
delegate	대표자; 위임하다	research	연구; 연구하다
document	문서; 기록하다	stay	체류; 머물다
feature	특징; 특징으로 하다	volunteer	자원봉사자, 자원자; 자원하다
increase	증가; 증가하다	charge	요금; 청구하다
offer	제안; 제안하다	decline	감소; 감소하다
plan	계획; 계획하다	discount	할인; 할인하다
refund	환불; 환불하다	experience	경험; 겪다
review	검토; 검토하다	gain	증가; 얻다
visit	방문; 방문하다	need	필요, 요구; 필요로 하다
work	일; 일하다	outline	개요; 개요를 설명하다
change	변경; 변경하다	record	기록; 기록하다
damage	손상; 손상시키다	request	요청; 요청하다
demand	수요, 요구; 요구하다	support	지원; 지원하다
estimate	견적서; 추정하다	wish	바람, 의도; 원하다, 바라다
function	기능, 행사; 기능하다		

Q3 주어 역할: [명사 vs. 다른 품사] + 동사

[Entries / Enter] for the art contest must be submitted by the end of the month. [1]

목적어 역할: 타동사 + [명사 vs. 다른 품사]

There is an instruction manual that describes the **[operation / operational]** of the plant's assembly machine. [2]

>> **출제 포인트** ❶ 명사는 주어, 타동사나 전치사의 목적어, 보어 역할을 한다.

❷ 명사는 타동사와 전치사의 목적어 역할을 한다. 또한, 타동사 to부정사나 동명사의 뒤에서 목적어로 사용된다.

> • **전치사의 목적어**
>
> Delivery was delayed as a result **of confusion** about the recipient's address.
> 수취인의 주소에 관한 혼동으로 인해 배송이 늦어졌다.
>
> • **to부정사의 목적어**
>
> The interviewers expect you **to give** details of your work experience.
> 면접관들은 당신이 업무 경력의 상세 정보를 주기를 기대한다.
>
> • **동명사의 목적어**
>
> The lecturers can be contacted directly by **calling the numbers** provided.
> 제공된 번호로 전화하면 강사들에게 직접 연락을 취할 수 있다.

+ check

1. [Construct/ Construction] of the new Pinewood train station will begin in early December.

2. In [respond / response] to your teller job posting, I have sent a résumé to HR.

3. By placing a heavy [emphasis / emphasize] on fast delivery, Poco has become an industry leader.

2. 가산 명사와 불가산 명사

> **Q4** a/an + [가산 명사 단수형 vs. 복수형]
>
> The management at Redmond Chemicals attributed a 20 percent **[increase / increases]** in productivity to the newly installed equipment. [1]
>
> **무관사 + [가산 명사 단수형 vs. 복수형]**
>
> **[Applicant / Applicants]** for the researcher position should apply in person. [2]

>> 출제 포인트 ❶ 가산 명사는 셀 수 있는 명사이므로 앞에 부정관사 a/an, 소유격, 수량형용사 등의 한정사와 함께 쓰거나 복수형으로 써야 한다. 따라서 선택지에 가산 명사의 단수와 복수가 제시되고 그 앞에 한정사가 없다면, 반드시 복수형이 답이 되어야 한다는 점에 유의한다.

✓ 명사의 종류와 관사

- a/an + 가산 명사 단수형
- 무관사 + 가산 명사 복수형/불가산 명사
- the + 가산 명사 단수형/가산 명사 복수형/불가산 명사

✓ 빈출 가산 명사

사람	representative	대표자, 대리인	official	공무원
	applicant	지원자	attendant	참석자
	employee	직원	critic	비평가
금융·돈	discount	할인	bonus	보너스
	sale	할인	salary	급여
	refund	환불	account	계좌
	price	가격	cost	비용
	rate	요금	profit	이익
주로 복수형	specifics	세부사항	standards	기준
	proceeds	수익	procedures	절차
	funds	기금	measures	조치
	regulations	규정	belongings	소지품
	precautions	예방 조치	goods	상품
	instructions	지시 사항	valuables	귀중품
	guidelines	지침	earnings	수익
기타	increase	증가	decision	결정
	reduction	감소	benefit	혜택
	change	변화	reservation	예약
	place	장소	arrangement	준비(계획)
	request	요청(사항)	resource	자원
	complaint	불만(사항)		

❷ 불가산 명사는 셀 수 없는 명사이므로 그 앞에 단수를 나타내는 부정관사 a/an이 올 수 없고, 뒤에 -(e)s를 붙여 복수형으로도 쓸 수 없다.

☑ 빈출 불가산 명사

information	정보	knowledge	지식	news	뉴스
advice	충고	access	접근	money	돈
cash	현금	approval	승인	consent	허가
assistance	보조	potential	잠재력	equipment	장비
merchandise	상품	baggage	수하물	luggage	수하물
clothing	의류	furniture	가구	stationery	문구류

＋check

1. [Refund / Refunds] for defective products will be processed within three business days.

2. The interviewers will ask for [detail / information] about your work experience to see if you are eligible for the position.

3. 명사 어휘

Q5 [사람 명사 vs. 사물 명사]

Of the 12 candidates Mr. Hopkins interviewed last week, Julia Sarawati is the most qualified [applicant / application] for the sales management position. [1]

무관사 + [사람 명사 단수형 vs. 사물 명사]

The annual career fair will offer numerous resources for people seeking [employee / employment]. [2]

>> 출제 포인트　❶ 명사 자리 문제에 한 어근에서 파생된 사람 명사와 사물 명사가 보기로 제시되면, 해석을 통해 문맥에 어울리는 명사를 선택해야 한다.

❷ 해석상 사람 명사와 사물 명사의 구분이 어려운 경우, 사람 명사는 가산 명사이지만, 사물 명사는 가산 명사도 있고 불가산 명사도 있다는 점에 유의한다. 즉, 사람 명사는 가산 명사이므로 단수일 때 반드시 관사와 함께 쓰거나 복수형으로 써야 한다는 점에 착안하여 문제를 푼다.

☑ 동일 어근 사람 명사와 사물·추상 명사

사람 명사		사물·추상 명사	
accountant	회계사	accounting	회계
		account	계좌
assistant	보조자	assistance	도움
applicant	지원자	application	지원(서)
architect	건축가	architecture	건축학
attendee	참석자	attendance	참석(자 수)
authority	권위자, 당국	authority	권한
		authorization	승인
commuter	통근자	commuting	통근
consultant	자문위원	consulting	자문
contributor	공헌자, 기고자	contribution	공헌, 기고
competitor	경쟁자, 경쟁 업체	competition	경쟁
correspondent	통신원, 기자	correspondence	서신, 왕래
delegate	대표자	delegation	대표단, 위임
distributor	배급 업자	distribution	분배
employee	직원	employment	고용
employer	고용주		
facilitator	협력자	facilitation	편리화
financier	자본가	finance	재정
founder	설립자	foundation	설립
investigator	조사관	investigation	조사
instructor	강사	instruction	지시사항
investor	투자자	investment	투자
journalist	언론인	journal	학술지, 신문
manufacturer	제조업자, 제조사	manufacture	제조
producer	생산자, 생산 업체	productivity	생산성
		production	제작
		product	제품
		produce	농산물
professional	전문가	professionalism	전문성
		profession	직업
resident	거주자	residence	주거, 주택
retailer	소매상인[업체]	retail	소매
rival	경쟁자	rivalry	경쟁
sponsor	후원자, 후원 업체	sponsoring	협찬
successor	후임자	success	성공
		succession	계승
supervisor	상사	supervision	감독
supplier	공급자, 공급 회사	supply	공급

+ check

1. Workers must report to their immediate **[supervision / supervisors]** after completing a task.

2. All of our tax specialists have graduate degrees in **[accountant / accounting]**.

26

의미가 비슷한 [가산 명사 vs. 불가산 명사]

The CEO has approved a **[plan / planning]** to offer free professional development courses. [1]

>> 출제 포인트   비슷한 의미의 명사들이 함께 제시되어 해석으로 판단하기 어려운 경우, 한정어의 유무나 종류를 통해 가산 명사 자리인지 불가산 명사 자리인지를 파악한다.

☑ 의미가 비슷한 가산 명사와 불가산 명사

가산 명사		불가산 명사	
alternative	대안(책)	alternation	교대
approach	접근 방식	access	접근, 이용
certificate	증명서, 자격증	certification	증명
description	설명	information	정보
detail	세부 사항		
estimate	견적서	estimation	견적
guide	안내인[서]	guidance	안내
permit	허가증	permission	허가
potentiality	잠재력	potential	잠재력
product	상품	merchandise	상품
survey	조사	research	연구

☑ 의미에 따라 달라지는 가산 명사와 불가산 명사

가산 명사		불가산 명사	
business	회사	business	사업
room	방	room	공간
work	작품	work	일
purchase	구매품	purchase	구매 행위
establishment	설립한 회사	establishment	설립 행위

☑ 동일 어근 가산 명사와 불가산 명사

가산 명사		-ing형 불가산 명사	
account	계좌	accounting	회계
advertisement	광고	advertising	광고업
clothes	옷, 의류	clothing	옷, 의류
diner	식사하는 사람, 간이식당	dining	식사
fund	자금	funding	자금[재정]지원
house	집	housing	주택
market	시장	marketing	마케팅
plan	계획	planning	계획 수립
process	과정, 절차	processing	처리
ticket	티켓	ticketing	티켓 발급
trainer	훈련시키는 사람	training	훈련
screen	스크린	screening	검열
seat	좌석	seating	좌석 배치
writer	작가	writing	글쓰기

가산 명사		불가산 명사	
opening	공석, 개막, 개업	boarding	탑승
		restructuring	구조 조정
		spending	지출
		understanding	이해
		catering	음식 납품
		pricing	가격 책정
		staffing	직원 채용

+ check

1. [**Approach / Access**] to this facility is not permitted unless you hold an authorized pass.

2. A recent [**survey / research**] has shown that the number of employees using the company's fitness center has decreased dramatically over the past six months.

3. The advertising conference will recognize those who have demonstrated innovation in [**market / marketing**] and design.

4. Any questions about obtaining a [**certificate / certification**] to be a welder should be directed to Cindy Wong.

Q7 복합 명사: 명사 + [분사 vs. 명사]

Since the new manager started working, employee [**producing / productivity**] has significantly increased. [1]

>> 출제 포인트

❶ 두 개 이상의 명사가 「명사 + 명사」 형태로 하나의 단어처럼 쓰이는 것을 복합 명사라 한다. 복합 명사의 가산/불가산, 단수/복수 여부는 마지막 명사에 따라 결정된다. 따라서 복합 명사의 복수형은 마지막 명사가 가산 명사인 경우 그 명사에 -(e)s를 붙여 표현한다.

❷ 복합 명사의 첫 번째나 두 번째 자리에 명사의 수식어인 형용사나 분사가 아닌 명사를 넣어 복합 명사를 완성하는 문제가 출제된다. 따라서 시험에 자주 출제되는 복합 명사들을 하나의 단어처럼 익혀 두어야 한다.

account information/number	계좌 정보/번호
application form	신청 양식
attendance record	출석 기록
awards ceremony	시상식
boarding pass	탑승권
business expansion strategy/plan	사업 확장 전략/계획
clearance sale	재고 정리 할인 판매
contingency plan	비상 대책
customer service/satisfaction/complaint	고객 서비스/만족/불평
earnings growth	수익 성장
electronics company	전자 회사
employee productivity/performance	직원 생산성/실적
enrollment/entrance fee	등록비/입장료
expiration date	만기일
information packet	자료집
growth/interest/exchange rate	성장률/이자율/환율
job opening/performance/description/fair	공석/업무 성과/업무 설명/취업 박람회
keynote speaker/address	기조 연사/연설
maintenance work	정비 작업
meal/food/hiring preference	식사/음식/고용 선호
office supplies	사무용품
parking structure	주차 건물
performance evaluation	직무 평가
product availability/description/manual	제품 입수 가능성/설명/설명서
production schedule/facility/plant/line	생산 일정/시설/공장/라인
reference[recommendation] letter	추천서
replacement product	대체품
retirement celebration	은퇴식
safety regulations/standards/guidelines/precautions/procedures/equipment	안전 수칙/기준/지침/예방책/절차/장비
sales division/promotion/figure	판매 부서/촉진/매출액
savings account	예금 계좌
submission deadline	제출 마감일
training session	교육 시간
tourist attraction	관광 명소
travel arrangement/expenses	여행 준비/경비
water usage	물 사용(량)

+ check

1. For complete details on the [trainable / training] session, check our Web site.

2. Please complete the questionnaire about our customer [served / service] to receive a free gift.

Practice

해설서 p.3 / ⏱ 제한 시간 6분

1. A careful ------- of the consumer survey data suggests that customers are reducing their spending following the recent economic crisis.

(A) evaluative
(B) evaluate
(C) evaluated
(D) evaluation

2. ------- of the HR Department include recruiting new employees and communicating the organization's goals.

(A) Priority
(B) Prioritizing
(C) Priorities
(D) Prioritized

3. The customers who received damaged products must contact the ------- directly to get a product replacement or a refund.

(A) manufacture
(B) manufactured
(C) manufacturer
(D) manufactures

4. ------- will receive a convention schedule and two meal vouchers.

(A) Participant
(B) Participation
(C) Participate
(D) Participants

5. Inbound and outbound flights at the Roseville Airport are often delayed as a result of ------- on its runways.

(A) congests
(B) congested
(C) congestion
(D) congestive

6. When sending an -------, you should enclose a detailed cover letter and two letters of reference.

(A) applying
(B) applicant
(C) application
(D) apply

7. The new design of the car model under development was shown to only a few executives of Verman Motors in order to ensure -------.

(A) confide
(B) confident
(C) confidential
(D) confidentiality

8. Recognized for his extensive research in the field, Dr. Henry Park is the world's leading ------- in genetic engineering.

(A) authorization
(B) authorized
(C) authority
(D) authoritatively

9. 고난도 Marlinson Solution has been experiencing considerable growth in the online marketplace, and is seeking additional ------- in this field.

(A) assistant
(B) assist
(C) assisted
(D) assistance

10. According to the new policy, all interoffice ------- will be delivered to each department's mail box rather than to each employee.

(A) correspondent
(B) corresponds
(C) correspondence
(D) corresponding

11. Sales representatives of Tyler Medical Equipment are encouraged to subscribe to multiple clinical ------- to become knowledgeable about new medical appliances.

(A) journals
(B) journalism
(C) journalists
(D) journaling

12. 고난도 Parents who have children under the age of six are advised to use ------- when they allow their children to watch TV.

(A) cautious
(B) cautiously
(C) cautioned
(D) caution

13. The Sales Department still has several outstanding ------- related to the Enco project, whose profits have been decreasing consistently.

(A) expends
(B) expense
(C) expended
(D) expenses

14. The official ------- of the new airport at South Port will take place in the presence of the city mayor.

(A) open
(B) openness
(C) opened
(D) opening

15. 고난도 The ------- of Colonial Drive from two lanes to four lanes will take six months.

(A) width
(B) wide
(C) widest
(D) widening

16. Please visit the Ministry of Transportation Web site to review the requirements before applying for a ------- or license.

(A) permit
(B) permission
(C) permitted
(D) permitting

17. As part of its business expansion -------, ST Apparel will begin selling men's and women's formal clothing.

(A) strategize
(B) strategic
(C) strategy
(D) strategically

18. 고난도 It is very unfortunate that there have been ------- about the inappropriate behavior of our sales representatives.

(A) complaining
(B) complained
(C) complaint
(D) complaints

19. If the package has already been opened or has been damaged by the carrier, refuse ------- of the package and the item will be sent back for exchange.

(A) receive
(B) receiving
(C) receipt
(D) recipient

20. 고난도 It is our company's policy to offer ------- of up to 10 percent to every new customer when they visit a new branch.

(A) discount
(B) discounted
(C) discounter
(D) discounts

대명사

대명사는 앞에 나온 명사의 반복을 피하기 위해 대신 쓰는 품사로 명사와 마찬가지로 주어, 목적어, 보어 역할을 한다. 가리키는 대상에 따라 인칭대명사, 재귀대명사, 지시대명사, 부정대명사가 있다.

Tip!
토익에 가장 많이 나오는 대명사는 소유격 인칭대명사야.
by oneself는 최근에도 여전히 단골로 출제되고 있어.

🗨 기본 개념 이해하기

1. 인칭대명사의 격과 수

앞에 나온 사람·사물 명사를 대신하여 쓰는 인칭대명사는 문장에서 어떠한 성분으로 쓰이는지에 따라 격을 결정한 후, 대신하는 명사의 수나 성과 일치시켜야 한다.

2. 소유격과 소유대명사

소유격	my	your	his	her	its	our	your	their
소유대명사	mine	yours	his	hers	없음	ours	yours	theirs

• 소유격은 '~의'라는 뜻이고, 소유대명사는 '~의 것(= 소유격 + 명사)'이라는 의미이다. it은 소유대명사가 없다.

3. 목적격과 재귀대명사

목적격	me	you	him	her	it	us	you	them
재귀대명사	myself	yourself	himself	herself	itself	ourselves	yourselves	themselves

• 「목적격 인칭대명사 + -self/-selves」 형태로, 목적어가 주어와 의미상으로 동일한 대상을 나타낼 때 '~자신'이라는 의미를 가진 재귀대명사를 쓴다. 목적어가 주어와 동일하지 않은 대상을 의미할 때는 목적격 인칭대명사를 쓴다.

4. 지시대명사

특정 사람이나 사물을 지칭하는 대명사인 지시대명사에는 this, that, these, those가 있으며 that과 those는 뒤에 수식어(전치사 of + 명사/관계대명사)를 동반할 수 있다.

5. 부정대명사

수량을 나타내는 형용사 one, some/any, many/much, all, most, each 등은 뒤에 「of the 명사」를 수반하여 불특정한 사람이나 사물 전체 중 일부('하나', '일부', '다수·다량', '모두', '대부분', '각각')를 가리킨다.

핵심 문제 유형

인칭대명사의 소유격과 목적어 자리에 올 수 있는 목적격, 재귀대명사, 소유대명사의 구분에 대한 출제 비중이 가장 높다. 수식어구의 수식을 받는 지시대명사 those와 다양한 부정대명사 관련 문제가 고난도 문제로 출제된다.

1. 인칭대명사

Q1 **[주격 vs. 재귀대명사] + 동사**

Once Ms. Lane booked Mr. Kim's flight, **[she / herself]** sent him the travel itinerary. [1]

[소유격 vs. 목적격] + (부사) + (형용사) + 명사

James Lennon decided to stay in Europe to collaborate with a famous writer for **[his / him]** next novel. [2]

[소유격 vs. 재귀대명사] + own + 명사

With 20 years' experience in an Italian restaurant, Jason has finally opened **[his / himself]** own restaurant. [3]

[주격 vs. 소유격] + 동사와 명사 형태가 동일한 단어

Mr. Lin asked when the design would be ready for **[he / his]** review. [4]

>> 출제 포인트

❶ 주격은 주어 자리에 온다.

❷ 소유격('~의')은 명사 앞에 오며, 그 앞에 관사나 한정사가 올 수 없다. 소유격과 함께 쓰는 own은 형용사('자신의')와, 대명사('~의 것')로 소유격을 강조한다.

one's own + 명사 = 명사 + of one's own	~자신의 명사
on one's own = by oneself	혼자서

❸ 소유대명사('~의 것')는 「소유격 + 명사」를 대신하므로, 뒤에 명사가 올 수 없다는 점에서 소유격과 구별된다.

❹ 빈칸 뒤에 동사와 명사 형태가 동일한 단어가 제시된 후, 인칭대명사의 주격과 소유격을 선택하는 유형의 문제가 자주 출제된다. 따라서 인칭대명사의 격을 선택할 때는 빈칸 뒤의 단어가 문장 내에서 어떤 품사로 쓰였는지에 특히 유의해야 한다.

Q2 타동사 + [목적격 vs. 소유격]

If your order is defective, you can send **[us / our]** the product within a week of receiving it. [1]

전치사 + [목적격 vs. 소유격]

Ms. Schmitt and her colleagues requested the deadline to be extended, but the manager wants to talk with **[them / their]** first. [2]

[소유대명사 vs. 목적격]

Although Ben submitted his proposal much later than Jane, the manager chose his idea instead of **[hers / her]**. [3]

>> 출제 포인트　❶ 목적격은 타동사나 전치사의 목적어 자리에 온다.

　　　　　　　　❷ 소유대명사는 격변화 없이 주어, 목적어, 보어 자리에 모두 올 수 있다.

2. 재귀대명사

Q3 재귀 용법: [재귀대명사 vs. 목적격 대명사]

During the presentation, Mr. Brown proved **[himself / him]** to be knowledgeable. [1]

강조 용법: 타동사 + 목적어 + [재귀대명사 vs. 목적격 대명사]

The architect oversaw the construction of the building **[himself / him]** to make sure that it would be completed by the end of July. [2]

관용 용법 - 혼자서: by [재귀대명사 vs. 목적격 대명사]

Ms. Anais will be attending the senior management workshop by **[herself / her]** as Mr. Conrad is currently on vacation. [3]

>> 출제 포인트　❶ 재귀 용법('자기 자신'): 주어와 목적어가 동일한 대상을 의미할 때 목적어 자리에 재귀대명사를 쓰며, 이때 재귀대명사는 생략할 수 없다. 목적어 자리에 쓰이는 목적격과 재귀대명사의 구분에 유의해야 한다.

> 의미상 주어 = 목적어 ⋯▸ 재귀대명사
>
> 의미상 주어 ≠ 목적어 ⋯▸ 목적격 대명사

❷ 강조 용법('~가 직접'): 주어나 목적어를 강조하기 위해, 강조하는 말 바로 뒤나 문장 끝에 재귀대명사를 쓴다. 이때 재귀대명사는 문장 성립의 필수 요소가 아니므로 부사처럼 생략할 수 있다.

❸ 관용 표현

| by oneself(= on one's own) | 혼자서 | of itself | 저절로 |
| for oneself | 혼자 힘으로 | in itself | 그 자체로 |

3. 지시대명사

 Q4

[that vs. those] of

TPR, Inc.'s current sales figures are remarkably similar to **[that / those]** of last year. [1]

[anyone vs. those] who + 복수 동사

Once all applications are reviewed, **[anyone / those]** who are qualified will be contacted for an interview. [2]

≫ 출제 포인트 ❶ **that / those**: 주로 비교하는 문장에서, 뒤에 수식어구를 동반하여 앞에 나온 명사를 대신할 때 지시 대명사 that/those를 쓴다. 이때, 앞에 나온 단수 명사를 대신하면 that('~의 것'), 복수 명사를 대신 하면 those('~의 것들')를 쓴다.

❷ 지시대명사 those가 사람들(people)의 의미로 쓰일 때 관계대명사 who, 분사구, 전치사구 등의 수식 을 받는다. 이때 those는 복수 동사로, anyone/everyone은 단수 동사로 수를 일치시키는 점에 유의 한다.

that of/those of 참고 it/them/this of ❌	~의 것/것들
those who + 복수 동사 those + V-ing/p.p./전치사구	~한 사람들
anyone/everyone who + 단수 동사 anyone/everyone + V-ing/p.p./전치사구 참고 they/them/themselves/these + who/V-ing/p.p./전치사구 ❌	~한 사람은 어느 누구나

+ check

1. We at Istanbul Dissiz Hospital make our best effort to meet with patients at **[they / their]** booked times.

2. Library members are requested not to shelve items **[theirs / themselves]**.

3. We need help contacting artists and arranging for **[themselves / them]** to donate work.

4. Ms. Park has proven **[her / herself]** to be a loyal and innovative member of the R&D team.

4. 부정대명사

Q5

[many vs. every] + of the + 복수 명사

[Many / Every] of the managers found your suggestion very useful and decided to implement it next month. [1]

[neither vs. most] + of the + 가산 복수 명사 + 단수 동사

Unfortunately, **[neither / most]** of the two venues has the capacity to hold the anniversary party. [2]

[few vs. little] + 동사

Of the interns who worked during summer, **[few / little]** received better evaluations than Mr. Lee in the Accounting Department. [3]

[any vs. none]

We cannot order more strawberries because our local supplier has **[any / none]** in stock. [4]

>> 출제 포인트 ❶ 「부정대명사 + of + the/소유격 + 명사」 형태로 특정 명사의 일부나 전체를 나타낸다. 이때, of 뒤에 오는 명사는 이미 정해져 있는 대상에 해당하므로, 그 앞에 the나 소유격 등의 한정사가 반드시 있어야 한다.

부정대명사	of the/소유격 + 명사의 종류와 수	동사의 수
both 둘 다 ǀ few 거의 없음 ǀ fewer 더 적음 ǀ a few 약간 ǀ several 여럿 ǀ many 많음	of the/소유격 + 가산 명사 복수	복수 동사
little 거의 없음 ǀ a little 약간 ǀ much 많음	of the/소유격 + 불가산 명사	단수 동사
one 하나 ǀ each 각각 ǀ either (둘 중) 하나 ǀ neither (둘 중) 어느 것도 아니다	of the/소유격 + 가산 명사 복수	단수 동사
half 반 ǀ some 몇몇 ǀ any 몇몇 ǀ most 대부분 ǀ all 모두 ǀ none 어느 것(누구)도 아니다	of the/소유격 + 가산 명사 복수	복수 동사
	of the/소유격 + 불가산 명사	단수 동사

참고 every/everyone/everybody/everything of the + 명사 ❌

❷ 부정대명사가 단독으로 주어, 목적어로 쓰일 수 있다. 알맞은 부정대명사 선택 문제는 문맥과 가리키는 명사의 단수/복수를 고려하여 결정한다.

✓ 부정대명사의 종류

단수 또는 복수	all	most	some	any	none	
항상 복수	both	many	(a) few	ones	others	several
항상 단수	each either	much neither	(a) little	one	the other	another

· 부정대명사는 복수 명사를 대신하면 복수, 단수 명사나 불가산 명사를 대신하면 단수 취급한다.
· all, most, some, any, none은 복수 명사 또는 불가산 명사를 대신한다. no one은 단수 명사를 대신한다.

Q6 **[other vs. the others] + 동사**

Of the conference attendees, some preferred morning classes, but **[other / the others]** preferred evening classes. [1]

[other vs. one another]

Employees should work collaboratively with **[other / one another]** in the office. [2]

>> 출제 포인트

부정형용사		부정대명사	
another + 가산 명사 단수	또 다른 하나의	another	(이미 언급한 것 이외의) 또 다른 하나
other + 가산 명사 복수/불가산 명사	다른	the other	(정해진 수 중에서) 나머지 하나
		the others	(정해진 수 중에서) 나머지 전부
		others	(특정되지 않은 막연한) 다른 것들/사람들
		each other	(둘 사이에) 서로
		one another	(셋 이상에서) 서로

❶ 부정대명사 another 와 the other는 단수, the others 와 others는 복수를 의미한다.

❷ other는 부정형용사이므로 반드시 뒤에 가산 명사 복수나 불가산 명사와 함께 써야 한다. 즉, 부정형용사 other는 뒤에 명사 없이 단독으로 주어나 목적어 자리에 쓸 수 없다.

❸ 부정대명사 each other/one another는 타동사나 전치사의 목적어로 쓰이며, 주어로는 쓰지 못한다.

해설서 p.5 / ⏱ 제한 시간 6분

1. Langan's has been voted the best Latin American restaurant, and its chef has been praised for ------- unique recipes.

(A) himself
(B) his
(C) him
(D) he

2. ------- who is interested in joining the biochemistry study should email Ms. Hall at Glen Medical Hospital.

(A) Anyone
(B) Yourself
(C) One another
(D) Those

3. Before taking the highway, please make sure that ------- of the passengers fasten their seatbelts.

(A) every
(B) all
(C) each
(D) one

4. After Mr. Marshall completes the annual earnings report next week, ------- will be sent to Mr. Byeon for the meeting.

(A) itself
(B) other
(C) it
(D) them

5. Visa applicants can complete the form by ------- without depending on travel agents or others to perform this task.

(A) they
(B) them
(C) themselves
(D) their

6. Discover for ------- why London's reputation as a theater town is known all over the world.

(A) yourself
(B) myself
(C) itself
(D) themselves

7. The new accounting program will allow ------- to process payroll much faster and more efficiently.

(A) yourself
(B) your
(C) yours
(D) you

8. ------- who have worked for more than five years in the International Trade Department are eligible for positions abroad.

(A) Anyone
(B) They
(C) Every
(D) Those

9. Although many tourists who come to Hasselhoff Point go on guided tours of the town, ------- simply want to relax at the beach.

(A) another
(B) anyone
(C) other
(D) some

10. New employees are encouraged to refer to ------- company manuals to learn about the company regulations.

(A) theirs
(B) their
(C) them
(D) they

11. Most senior managers approved of the plan for the head office's relocation, although ------- expressed concerns about the expenses.

(A) one
(B) one another
(C) each other
(D) other

12. If you are interested in this position, please call us to get directions to ------- conveniently located office.

(A) our
(B) ourselves
(C) ours
(D) us

13. Klamore Tech employees should seek assistance from the maintenance manager instead of removing items from the equipment closet -------.

(A) themselves
(B) their own
(C) them
(D) their

14. Since its acquisition of Gallagher Autos, Mando Automobile has become ------- of the largest auto-component manufacturers in the world.

(A) some
(B) one
(C) this
(D) more

15. 고난도 Through his hard work and dedication to his research, Mr. Trilby has shown ------- to be a valuable asset to SLS Biotex.

(A) he
(B) him
(C) himself
(D) his

16. 고난도 Invitations to the fundraising party were sent to all 20 city council members, but ------- will be able to attend.

(A) little
(B) few
(C) whoever
(D) so

17. After ------- review the performance evaluations of all the interns, managers of each department will decide who will be offered the permanent position.

(A) their
(B) themselves
(C) they
(D) them

18. 고난도 Although the initial cost of installing them on the roof was large, the solar panels have already paid for -------.

(A) its
(B) itself
(C) their
(D) themselves

19. 고난도 For ------- with dietary restrictions, Aringston Airline provides special in-flight meals if requests are made in advance.

(A) those
(B) them
(C) whose
(D) which

20. 고난도 ------- of the conference participants was given an information packet that provides schedules and summaries of each presentation.

(A) Most
(B) All
(C) Every
(D) Each

형용사

형용사는 명사 앞에서 대상이나 수, 특성 등을 나타내는 수식어 역할을 하거나 2형식 동사 뒤나 5형식의 목적어 뒤에서 주어나 목적어의 상태를 설명해 주는 보어 역할을 한다.

Tip! 토익은 뒤에 오는 명사의 단수/복수를 결정하는 형용사 each, every, various 문제를 좋아해. 목적격 보어 자리에 오는 형용사를 고르는 고난도 문제도 자주 등장하고 있어!

기본 개념 이해하기

1. [관사/소유격/지시형용사/수량형용사] + [특성 및 상태 형용사] + 명사

a, an, the, your, this, these, etc. ····› 관사/소유격/지시형용사	
some, any, many, much, a few, a little, one, two, etc. ····› 수량형용사	+ 명사
informative, spacious, etc. ····› 특성 및 상태를 나타내는 형용사	

- 형용사들이 나열될 때 특성이나 상태를 나타내는 형용사는 한정사 뒤에 위치한다.

  Authorized managers have access to this information. [형용사 + 명사]
  인가를 받은 매니저들은 이 정보에 접근할 수 있다.

  A few authorized managers have access to this information. [수량형용사 + 형용사 + 명사]
  인가를 받은 몇몇 매니저들은 이 정보에 접근할 수 있다.

  The authorized managers have access to this information. [관사 + 형용사 + 명사]
  인가를 받은 그 매니저들은 이 정보에 접근할 수 있다.

2. 2형식 동사 + 주격 보어

be, become, look, remain, stay, seem, appear, prove	+ 형용사(주격 보어)

- 주어를 설명하는 역할을 하는 주격 보어 자리에 형용사가 온다.

  Most items in this catalog are **available** at no additional cost.
  이 카탈로그에 있는 대부분의 물품들은 추가 비용을 들이지 않고 이용할 수 있다.

  cf be, become + 명사(주어=주격 보어): be, become 뒷부분이 주어와 동일한 의미를 나타내는 경우 명사가 주격 보어로 올 수 있다. 그러나 토익 시험에서는 거의 형용사 보어를 고르는 문제만 출제된다.

  The firm has quickly become **a threat** to its competitors.
  그 회사는 금세 경쟁사들에게 위협이 되었다.

3. 5형식 동사 + 목적어 + 목적격 보어

make, find, leave, consider, keep	+ 명사(목적어) + 형용사(목적격 보어)

- 목적어를 설명하는 역할을 하는 목적격 보어 자리에 형용사가 온다.

  Many customers found the new Web site **user-friendly**.
  많은 고객들이 새로운 웹사이트가 사용하기 쉽다고 생각했다.

  cf consider, name, call, elect + 목적어 + 명사(목적어=목적격 보어): 5형식 동사의 목적어 뒷부분이 목적어와 동일한 의미를 나타내는 경우 명사가 목적격 보어로 올 수 있다.

  They elected him to be **the temporary captain** of their company.
  그들은 그를 회사의 임시 수장으로 선출했다.

핵심 문제 유형

명사 수식이나 보어 역할을 하는 형용사 자리를 묻는 문제와 명사의 수를 한정하는 수량형용사 관련 고난도 문제가 출제된다.

1. 형용사의 형태와 역할

Q1

[형용사 vs. 다른 품사] + 명사

The award is intended to recognize workers who provide **[exceptional / exceptionally]** service to customers. [1]

According to Tersla's **[recent / recently]** announcement, it will release a new product. [2]

This handbook was written to help new employees resolve technical problems in a **[timely / time]** fashion. [3]

명사 + [형용사 vs. 명사]

Ms. Leman is the technician **[responsible / responsibility]** for upgrading the company server. [4]

>> 출제 포인트 ❶ 형용사의 형태

✓ **-al, -ive, -ant(-ent), -able, -ful, -less, -ous, -ic로 끝나는 단어는 대개 형용사**

exceptional	뛰어난	managerial	관리의
innovative	혁신적인	significant	중요한, 상당한
sufficient	충분한	affordable	(가격이) 알맞은, 저렴한
successful	성공적인	useless	쓸모없는
previous	사전의	strategic	전략적인

✓ **분사형 형용사**

-ing로 끝나는 형용사		-ed로 끝나는 형용사	
challenging	어려운	accomplished	뛰어난
demanding	힘든	complicated	복잡한
existing	기존의	customized	맞춤형의
leading	선도적인	detailed	상세한
outstanding	두드러진	experienced	노련한
rewarding	보람 있는	qualified	자격을 갖춘

✓ **유의해야 할 형태의 형용사 「명사 + -ly」**

hourly	매시간의	weekly	매주의	monthly	매달의
quarterly	매 분기마다의	yearly	매년의	timely	시기적절한
costly	비싼	orderly	질서 정연한	friendly	친절한

❷ 형용사가 명사 앞에서 수식할 때 「관사/소유격 + (부사) + 형용사 + 명사」의 어순을 취한다.

Prices on all FOS cameras were lowered in response to a sales promotion by **a leading** competitor.
한 주요 경쟁업체의 판촉 활동에 대한 대응으로 모든 FOS 카메라의 가격이 인하되었다.

❸ 주로 -able/-ible로 끝나는 형용사가 전치사구나 to부정사 등의 수식어구와 함께 쓰여 길어질 때, 명사를 뒤에서 수식한다.

The abundance of quality electronics **available in stores or online** makes it difficult to make quick purchase decisions.
상점이나 온라인에서 양질의 전자제품이 넘쳐나는 것이 빠른 구입 결정을 어렵게 만든다.

Q2 **2형식 동사 + [형용사 vs. 명사]**

The market for slim laptops has recently become very **[competitive / competition]**. [1]

5형식 동사 + 명사 + [형용사 vs. 부사]

Many users have found the new software quite **[beneficial / beneficially]**. [2]

>> **출제 포인트** 형용사는 주어의 상태를 설명하는 주격 보어와 목적어의 상태를 설명하는 목적격 보어로 쓰인다.

❶ 2형식 동사의 주격 보어로 주어의 성격이나 상태를 나타내는 형용사가 주로 출제된다. 하지만, 주어와 동일한 인물이나 사물을 나타낼 경우에는 주격 보어로 명사를 쓴다.

☑ **주격 보어를 취하는 2형식 동사**

be ~이다	seem, appear ~인 듯하다	+ 주격 보어(주로 형용사)
become ~되다	look ~처럼 보이다	
remain, stay 여전히 ~이다	prove ~임이 판명되다	

❷ 5형식 동사의 목적격 보어로 목적어의 성격이나 상태를 나타내는 형용사가 주로 출제된다. 하지만, 목적어와 동일한 인물이나 사물을 나타낼 경우엔 목적격 보어로 명사를 쓴다.

☑ **목적격 보어를 취하는 5형식 동사**

make ~하게 하다	consider ~라고 여기다	+ 목적어 + 목적격 보어(주로 형용사)
find ~라고 여기다, 생각하다	keep 계속 ~하게 하다, 유지하다	
leave ~인 채로 두다		

+ check

1. The exhibit will be **[available / availability]** to the public on August 15.

2. These frames are designed to keep interior temperatures **[comfortably / comfortable]**.

2. 수량형용사

Q3

[every vs. all] + 가산 명사 단수

Once a month, managers from **[every / all]** branch meet at the head office. ¹

various + [가산 명사 단수 vs. 가산 명사 복수]

In order to minimize risk, investors should maintain a diverse portfolio by putting their money in various industry **[investment / investments]**. ²

[many vs. much] + 불가산 명사

Campaigns to reduce fuel consumption have not had **[many / much]** impact on the public. ³

[another vs. other] + 가산 명사 복수

The exceptional service at Cape Motors sets the company apart from **[another / other]** competitors. ⁴

[another vs. other] + 불가산 명사

[Another / Other] information, including store driving directions, can be found online. ⁵

>> **출제 포인트** ❶ 수량형용사는 수식하는 명사의 종류와 수를 결정한다.

☑ 수량형용사 뒤에 오는 명사의 종류와 수

a(n), one, a single 하나의 either 둘 중 하나의	each 각각의 neither 둘 중 하나도 아닌	every 모든 another 또 하나의	+ 가산 명사 단수
a few, several 몇몇의 many, numerous 많은 a (wide) variety of 다양한 each of the ~중 각각	a number of 많은 a range[selection] of 다양한 one of the ~중 하나	few 거의 없는 both 둘 다의 various 다양한	+ 가산 명사 복수
a little 약간의 a large amount of 많은	less 더 적은 a great deal of 많은	little 거의 없는 much 많은	+ 불가산 명사
some 몇몇의 a lot of, lots of 많은	most 대부분의 plenty of 많은	other 다른	+ 가산 명사 복수 + 불가산 명사
any 어느 ~든지, 모두	no 어떤 ~도 없는		+ 가산 명사 단수/복수 + 불가산 명사

❷ every와 another는 뒤에 둘 이상의 수와 함께 하면 복수 명사와 쓰인다.

every + 둘 이상의 수 + 복수 명사	~마다	every two years 2년마다
another + 둘 이상의 수 + 복수 명사	~더	another four books 책 4권 더

Q4 **[all vs. whole] + the + 가산 명사 복수**

To avoid more issues, we need to keep **[all / whole]** the sales representatives regularly informed of customer feedback. [1]

[all vs. any] + 가산 명사 단수

The warranty states that the manufacturer will repair **[all / any]** product that is defective. [2]

>> 출제 포인트 ❶ single / entire / whole은 한정사와 함께 쓰여야 하며, 가산 명사 단수를 동반한다. all은 한정사 앞에 위치할 수 있으며, 가산 명사의 복수나 불가산 명사와 쓰인다.

> • 한정사 + single / entire / whole + 가산 명사 단수
> • all / both / half + 한정사 + 가산 명사 복수 / 불가산 명사

❷ any / the / 소유격 / no 뒤에 오는 명사는 수의 제약을 받지 않으므로, 그 뒤에는 가산 명사 단수, 가산 명사 복수, 불가산 명사가 모두 올 수 있다.

+ check

1. The committee consists of staff from various **[departments / department]** of the company.

2. **[All / Whole]** business suites are fully furnished and have wireless internet.

3. 혼동하기 쉬운 형용사

Q5
Please be **[considerate / considerable]** of others, and dispose of all garbage in marked trash bins. [1]

Our customers' personal details are kept strictly **[confidential / confident]**. [2]

>> 출제 포인트

형태가 유사하나 의미가 완전히 다른 형용사들이 보기에 제시된 후, 문맥상 알맞은 형용사를 선택하는 문제가 출제된다.

✅ 유사한 형태의 형용사

Tip!
'완료된'의 의미인 형용사 complete은 명사 앞에 사용 안 해!

argumentative	논쟁을 좋아하는	arguable	논란의 여지가 있는
considerate	사려 깊은	considerable	상당한
confident	확신하는	confidential	기밀의
complete	완전한, 완료된	completed	완료된, 작성된
complimentary	무료의, 칭찬하는	complementary	보충의
comprehensive	종합적인, 포괄적인	comprehensible	이해할 수 있는
extensive	광범위한	extended	연장된
favorite	가장 좋아하는	favorable	우호적인
forgetful	잘 잊어버리는	forgettable	쉽게 잊혀지는
impressive	인상적인	impressed	감명받은
informative	유익한	informed	잘 아는
managerial	관리의	manageable	처리하기 쉬운
persuasive	(주장이) 설득력 있는	persuadable	(사람이) 설득되는
reliable	신뢰할 만한	reliant	의존하는
respective	각각의	respectful	공손한
responsible	책임 있는	responsive	반응하는
sensitive	민감한	sensible	분별 있는
successful	성공적인, 합격한	successive	연속적인
various	다양한	variable	변동이 심한
weekly	매주의	weeklong	일주일간 지속되는

+ check

1. No one could predict how **[successful / successive]** the restaurant would become.

2. Successful candidates for this job must have **[reliable / reliant]** transportation and a driver's license.

Practice

1. Next month, Ms. Reston will release the ------- findings from her research on employee productivity.

(A) initial
(B) initially
(C) initiative
(D) initiate

2. ------- participant found the two-day workshop very informative despite its hectic schedule.

(A) Several
(B) Every
(C) Single
(D) All

3. Before construction of the facility can start, the ------- permit applications must be approved.

(A) relevant
(B) relevantly
(C) relevance
(D) relevancies

4. Overseas travel is likely to become more ------- as many airlines are planning to increase fares by up to 15 percent.

(A) expensive
(B) expense
(C) expenses
(D) expensively

5. The Barkin Brands quarterly meeting went smoothly thanks to the collaboration of the ------- departments involved.

(A) various
(B) variety
(C) variation
(D) variable

6. The president called a special meeting to discuss Sargon Motors' ------- need to recall its XW2000 models due to their engine defects.

고난도

(A) urgency
(B) urgent
(C) urgently
(D) urgencies

7. Keep in mind that discounted items are not ------- under any circumstances.

(A) refund
(B) refunding
(C) refundable
(D) refunds

8. All the team members are required to brief their supervisors on the progress of their work ------- three weeks.

(A) some
(B) several
(C) every
(D) most

9. Hotels in Grandview must abide by all ------- health guidelines.

(A) local
(B) locals
(C) locally
(D) localize

10. The crowd took a break during the intermission and came back to their seats in an ------- manner.

(A) order
(B) orders
(C) ordering
(D) orderly

11. Human Resources plans to provide a revised employee handbook which will be especially ------- for recently hired employees.

(A) using
(B) use
(C) user
(D) useful

12. During the performance, the audience is not allowed to use ------- electronic recording equipment.

(A) any
(B) another
(C) one
(D) many

13. Of all the interviewees, Mr. Hernandez has the most ------- background in telecommunications business operations.

(A) impressive
(B) impressed
(C) impresses
(D) impressively

14. Mr. Jacob will be ------- to attend the 고난도 supervisor meeting tomorrow morning due to a flight cancellation.

(A) doubtful
(B) impossible
(C) unable
(D) remote

15. The recently implemented software made it ------- to process the large amount of customer information in a relatively short time.

(A) possible
(B) possibility
(C) possibly
(D) possibilities

16. ------- employee working late in the office 고난도 must remember to lock the door before leaving.

(A) Several
(B) Others
(C) Any
(D) Few

17. The editor-in-chief revised the article as the language in it was too -------.

(A) repetitive
(B) repeating
(C) repetition
(D) repetitively

18. The advertising consultant suggested hiring local celebrities since it has turned out to be an ------- marketing strategy.

(A) effectively
(B) effectiveness
(C) effect
(D) effective

19. If you have any ideas during the 고난도 brainstorming session, do not be afraid to shout them out, no matter how ------- they may seem.

(A) ridicule
(B) ridiculous
(C) ridiculously
(D) to ridicule

20. South Palm Hospital has a ------- range of 고난도 positions available for volunteers to match their skills and working hours.

(A) various
(B) several
(C) wide
(D) prolonged

부사

부사는 명사를 제외한 형용사, 동사, 부사, 구, 절, 문장 전체를 수식할 수 있다.

Tip! 동사를 수식하는 부사와 숫자 앞에 오는 부사 문제가 가장 많이 나와! since는 보통 전치사나 접속사로 쓰이지만, 현재 완료 사이에 위치해서 '(앞에 언급된 특정 시점) 이후에'라는 뜻의 부사도 출제돼.

🧠 기본 개념 이해하기

1. 동사 앞뒤에 오는 부사

동사 + 부사	She quit **unexpectedly**. 그녀는 갑자기 그만두었다.
동사 + 목적어 + 부사	She quit her job **unexpectedly**. 그녀는 갑자기 일을 그만두었다.
부사 + 동사 + 목적어	She **probably** failed the test. 그녀는 아마도 시험에 떨어졌을 것이다.
조동사 + 부사 + 본동사 + 목적어	She has **unexpectedly** quit her job. = She has quit her job **unexpectedly**. 그녀는 갑자기 일을 그만두었다.
be동사 + 부사 + 현재분사: 현재진행형	They are **patiently** waiting for the announcement. = They are waiting for the announcement **patiently**. 그들은 참을성 있게 발표를 기다리고 있다.
be동사 + 부사 + 과거분사: 수동태	Ms. Bradley's talk show is **nationally** broadcast. = Ms. Bradley's talk show is broadcast **nationally**. Ms. Bradley의 토크쇼는 전국적으로 방송된다.

2. 부사 + 형용사/부사/전치사구

한정사 + 부사 + 형용사 + 명사	Ms. Lee is an **exceptionally** valuable client of our hotel. Ms. Lee는 우리 호텔의 굉장히 귀중한 고객이다.
2형식 동사 + 부사 + 형용사	He was **largely** responsible for the increase in expenses. 그는 비용 증가에 대한 주된 책임이 있다. They looked **hugely** impressed by the chef's superb cuisine. 그들은 주방장의 훌륭한 요리에 크게 감명받은 듯 보였다.
부사 + 부사	You should compare all the benefits **extremely** carefully. 당신은 그 모든 혜택들을 굉장히 신중하게 비교해봐야 합니다.
부사 + 전치사구	Some of the equipment broke down, **reportedly** due to poor maintenance. 전하는 바에 따르면 정비 불량으로 인해 일부 장비가 고장 났다고 한다.

3. 문장 앞에 오는 부사

문장 앞	**Unfortunately**, the model is no longer manufactured. 유감스럽게도, 그 모델은 더 이상 제작되지 않는다.

부사의 역할 중 동사를 수식하는 부사의 다양한 위치를 파악하는 문제의 출제 비중이 가장 높다. 명사구를 강조하는 부사와 문법적으로 고유한 특성을 가진 개별 부사들과 관련된 고난도 문제가 자주 출제된다.

해설서 p.10

1. 부사의 역할

Q1

주어 + 타동사 + 목적어 + [형용사 vs. 부사]

All candidates should email their job applications **[direct / directly]** to hr@elvira.com. [1]

주어 + 자동사 + [형용사 vs. 부사]

The printing job proceeded **[slow / slowly]** due to technical issues. [2]

be동사 + [형용사 vs. 부사] + 현재분사 / 과거분사

Bex Construction is **[aggressive / aggressively]** trying to acquire Herman Architecture. [3]

be동사 + 과거분사 + [형용사 vs. 부사]

The budget proposal must be reviewed extremely **[careful / carefully]** before it is approved. [4]

조동사 + [형용사 vs. 부사] + 본동사

Based on their performance appraisals, the interns will **[short / shortly]** be assigned to suitable positions. [5]

>> 출제 포인트 ❶ 부사가 동사를 수식하는 경우 다양한 자리에 위치한다.

- 동사 앞: 부사 + 자동사/타동사
- 동사 사이: 조동사 + 부사 + 동사원형 | have + 부사 + p.p. | be + 부사 + V-ing/p.p.
- 동사 뒤: be + p.p. + 부사 | 자동사 + 부사 | 타동사 + 목적어 + 부사

1. Hankens Oil Company is confident that high prices of crude oil will not **[adverse / adversely]** affect its net profit in any case.

2. Since Hidy Norman was appointed CEO, productivity at Cordin Manufacturing has **[signification / significantly]** improved.

3. The basketball championship games will be broadcast **[nation / nationally]**.

Q2 [형용사 vs. 부사] + 동명사

Management emphasized the need to increase productivity by **[efficient / efficiently]** redistributing workloads. [1]

to + [형용사 vs. 부사] + 동사원형

It is important to **[thorough / thoroughly]** review all the terms of the contract before you sign it. [2]

>> **출제 포인트**   부사는 동사의 성질을 가지는 준동사(동명사, to부정사, 분사)를 수식한다.

• to + 부사 + 동사원형	• to 동사원형 + 목적어 + 부사
• 부사 + 동명사	• 동명사 + 목적어 + 부사

1. If you cannot attend a client-hosted event, make sure to decline the invitation **[polite / politely]** in advance.

2. The company succeeded in increasing productivity by **[efficient / efficiently]** managing employees.

Q3 관사 + [명사 vs. 부사] + 형용사 + 명사

Mr. Kong started work as an accountant, but now he is a **[nation / nationally]** renowned financial analyst. [1]

[형용사 vs. 부사] + 전치사구

As of today, a music streaming service is provided **[exclusive / exclusively]** to our subscribers at no cost. [2]

[형용사 vs. 부사], 문장

[Unfortunate / Unfortunately], the marketing director will not be present at the meeting due to a scheduling conflict. [3]

>> 출제 포인트 ❶ 부사는 형용사, 부사, 전치사구, 절, 문장 전체를 수식하며, 동사를 수식하는 경우를 제외하고는 수식하는 어구 앞에 위치한다.

❷ 전치사구 앞에 자주 나오는 부사

largely, primarily, mainly	주로	particularly, especially	특히
exclusively	오로지, 오직	currently	현재
immediately, promptly	즉시		

largely due to its low price 주로 낮은 가격 때문에
currently out of stock 현재 재고가 없는
promptly at 10 A.M. 오전 10시 정각에

❸ after 앞에 관용적으로 붙는 부사

immediately, promptly 즉시	
soon, shortly 곧	+ after ~한 직후에
just, right, directly 바로, 즉시	

immediately[right, just, shortly, directly] after a job interview 면접 직후에

2. 유의해야 할 부사

Q4 **형태가 비슷하나 다른 의미의 부사**

Although the analyst worked incredibly **[hard / hardly]**, his application for a pay raise was not granted. [1]

숫자와 양을 수식하는 부사

It takes **[approximately / somewhat]** five business days to receive your order. [2]

be + [former vs. formerly] + 명사구

Five office complexes recently opened in the Greenwood district, which was **[former / formerly]** a residential area. [3]

[still vs. yet] + have not p.p.

The work request was sent, but maintenance **[still / yet]** has not responded. [4]

unless + [otherwise vs. 다른 부사] + p.p.

Unless **[otherwise / however]** stated, all content on this Web site is the exclusive property of Nomukon Pharmacy. [5]

수식에 제한이 있는 부사

Although the movie is educational, the director thinks viewers will **[still / quite]** find it entertaining. [6]

>> 출제 포인트 ❶ 형태가 비슷하나 다른 의미의 부사

hard	혱 근면한 ₉ 열심히	hardly	₉ 거의 ~않다
near	혱 가까운 ₉ 가까이	nearly (= almost)	₉ 거의
high	혱 높은 ₉ 높게	highly (= very)	₉ 매우
late	혱 늦은 ₉ 늦게	lately (= recently)	₉ 최근에
close	혱 가까운 ₉ 가깝게	closely	₉ 면밀하게, 밀접하게

❷ 숫자와 양을 수식하는 부사

nearly, almost	거의	approximately, about, around, roughly	대략
more than, over	이상	less than, under	미만
up to	~까지	at least	최소한, 적어도
just	딱	only	오직

❸ 「a/the + 명사」 형태의 명사구 앞에 위치하여 명사구를 수식하는 부사

formerly, previously once originally	이전에 한때 원래	clearly arguably mainly, largely only, simply, just	분명히 (주로 최상급 앞에서) 아마도, 틀림없이 주로 단지

❹ already, yet, still

> • already: 벌써, 이미(긍정문); 혹시라도(부정문)
> • still: 아직도, 여전히, 그런데도(긍정문, 부정문, 의문문 구분 없이 사용 가능)
> • yet: 아직(부정문); 이미(의문문)
>   ⋯➡ 긍정문에서는 have[be] yet to부정사(아직도 ∼하지 못하다) 형태로만 쓰임
> 참고 부정문에 쓰일 때 yet은 부정어 뒤에(not yet), still은 부정어 앞에(still not) 쓰인다.

❺ otherwise

> • 일반부사
> (1) 그와는 다르게, 달리: unless + otherwise + p.p. 그와 다르게 p.p.되지 않는다면
> (2) (앞의 내용) 외에는
> Visitors check out the Espen House, one of the few historic buildings in the **otherwise** modern town of Sprava.
> 방문객들은 몇 안 되는 역사적 가치가 있는 건물들을 빼고는 현대적인 도시인 Sprava에서 그 중 하나인 Espen House를 구경한다.
>
> • 접속부사
> (1) 그렇지 않으면: 주어 + 동사 ; otherwise, 주어 + 동사
> In order to complete the transaction by phone banking, customers should enter their password within 30 seconds; **otherwise**, they will have to try it again.
> 폰뱅킹에 의한 거래를 완료하기 위해 고객들은 30초 이내에 비밀번호를 입력해야 하며, 그렇지 않으면 다시 시도해야 할 것이다.

❻ well

> • 잘, 만족스럽게(동사 수식)
> • 훨씬, 아주(전치사구 수식)
> **well** below[above] the price 그 가격 훨씬 아래로[위로] | **well** ahead of time 예정보다 매우 빨리
> This year's sales figures for Talos Corporation are **well** below the industry average.
> Talos 사의 올해 매출액은 업계 평균보다 훨씬 낮다.

❼ 수식에 제한이 있는 부사

✔ 형용사나 부사만 수식하는 부사 (동사 수식 불가)

so, very, fairly, quite extremely, exceptionally, incredibly, overly relatively	꽤 몹시, 극도로 비교적

✔ 동사만 수식하는 부사 (형용사나 부사 수식 불가)

well	잘	further	(정도가) 더

Practice

1. Much time and effort has been invested in developing the new product line, and the company expects it to be launched ------- next month.

(A) succession
(B) succeed
(C) successful
(D) successfully

2. Although the global economy has begun to recover from the 2008 financial crisis, the housing market has ------- to recover.

(A) often
(B) already
(C) afterwards
(D) yet

3. Monday's client meeting was ------- cancelled because some of our consultants had to deal with other urgent cases.

(A) abrupt
(B) abruptness
(C) abruption
(D) abruptly

4. All department managers were required to work ------- on the task to ensure a smooth transition to the new system.

(A) collaboration
(B) collaborate
(C) collaborative
(D) collaboratively

5. After confirming how many employees will attend the company dinner, the event coordinator will determine the menu -------.

(A) accordance
(B) accordingly
(C) according
(D) accord

6. Many consumers expect a new hybrid electric vehicle to be available soon, even though a recent news report indicates -------.

(A) somehow
(B) otherwise
(C) below
(D) else

7. The sales director was very pleased that the profit for the last quarter was ------- higher than originally forecast.

(A) signified
(B) significance
(C) significant
(D) significantly

8. Employees of Newport Electronics are ------- in favor of the new vacation policy.

고난도

(A) overwhelming
(B) overwhelms
(C) overwhelm
(D) overwhelmingly

9. The Customer Service Department used to get ------- 60 letters of complaint every month, but the number has been decreasing.

(A) roughness
(B) rough
(C) roughen
(D) roughly

10. Sales staff are asked to respond ------- to requests from vendors for product catalogues.

(A) promptly
(B) prompting
(C) prompted
(D) prompt

11. Everyday Tour introduced ------- priced tour packages to promote tourism in Woodstock beyond the peak season.

(A) competitively
(B) competitive
(C) competed
(D) competition

12. ------- opened as a small local theater 50 years ago, Tretiak Hall is now a world-famous performing arts center.

(A) Originally
(B) Original
(C) Originality
(D) Originals

13. Applicants will be interviewed ------- following a short test to assess their basic knowledge of computer science technologies.

(A) immediately
(B) immediate
(C) immediateness
(D) immediacy

14. Airline passengers must observe the regulation that ------- limits their baggage by weight.

(A) strictness
(B) strictly
(C) stricter
(D) strict

15. All the applicants for the senior accountant position are instructed to read the guidelines for the interview -------.

(A) meticulousness
(B) meticulous
(C) meticulously
(D) meticulosity

16. The organic vegetables you wish to order are ------- out of stock, but we will notify you as soon as we get a new shipment.

(A) temporary
(B) temporize
(C) temporal
(D) temporarily

17. The news that consumers are dissatisfied with our product's packaging is ------- the most valuable finding of the study.

(A) arguable
(B) arguing
(C) argument
(D) arguably

18. Companies can have their monthly utility bill ------- charged directly to their corporate account.

(A) automatically
(B) automatic
(C) automates
(D) automate

19. Customers were surprised to learn how ------- the software lets them find and store all the information they need.

(A) effortful
(B) effortless
(C) effortlessly
(D) efforts

20. Mr. Tal began working in the Research and Development Team ten years ago and has ------- become the manager.

(A) ever
(B) yet
(C) so
(D) since

전치사

전치사는 절(주어 + 동사)을 이끄는 접속사와 달리 명사 앞에 쓰여 시간, 장소, 이유, 목적, 양보 등을 나타낸다. 전치사구(전치사 + 명사)는 형용사나 부사와 같은 수식어 역할을 한다.

Tip!
전치사 문제는 매회 많게는 6문제나 나오기도 해. given은 전치사와 접속사가 모두 가능한데, 최근 들어 전치사로 2회 연속 출제되었어. 주제를 나타내는 regarding, concerning, pertaining to 등은 토익이 여전히 좋아하는 표현이야.

기본 개념 이해하기

1. 전치사구의 형태

전치사 + (관사, 형용사) + 명사	전치사 + 대명사(목적격)	전치사 + 동명사
in the nearby area	about them	by visiting the Web site
가까운 곳에	그들에 대해	웹사이트를 방문해서

• 절(주어+동사)이 아닌 명사 상당어구(명사, 대명사, 동명사, 명사구) 앞에는 전치사를 쓴다.

2. 전치사구의 역할

동사 수식의 부사 역할	The meeting is scheduled to begin **at 3 o'clock** this afternoon. 회의는 오늘 오후 3시에 시작될 예정이다. [시간]
	The company banquet will take place **in the grand ballroom** of the Midas Hotel. 회사 연회는 Midas 호텔의 대연회장에서 열릴 것이다. [장소]
	There were several car accidents **due to its faulty brakes**. 브레이크 결함으로 인한 자동차 사고가 몇 건 있었다. [이유]
명사 수식의 형용사 역할	Detailed explanations **of the courses** are available online. 과정에 대한 자세한 설명은 온라인에서 확인할 수 있다.

• 전치사구는 '언제, 어디서, 어떻게, 왜' 등 동사의 의미를 구체화하는 부사 역할과 명사를 수식하는 형용사 역할을 한다.

3. 관용 표현

자동사 + 전치사	University students **account for** 15 percent of our customer base. 대학생들이 우리 고객층의 15%를 차지한다.
명사 + 전치사	Sunflowers Industries announced an **increase in** net profits to $400 million. Sunflowers 산업은 순이익이 4억 달러로 증가했다고 발표했다.
형용사 + 전치사	Customers will be **subject to** fines for any lost, overdue, or damaged materials. 고객들은 모든 분실, 연체 또는 파손된 물품에 대해 벌금을 물어야 한다.
전치사구	**In addition to** occasional overtime hours, the team will sometimes work on the weekend. 가끔씩의 초과 근무 외에, 그 팀은 때때로 주말 근무를 할 것이다.

시간, 시점, 기간, 장소, 위치, 방향 등 전치사의 기본적인 의미와 용법을 묻는 문제와 특정 동사, 명사, 형용사와 함께 쓰이는 전치사 관용 표현을 묻는 문제가 출제된다.

해설서 p.12

1. 시간 전치사

Q1 [in vs. on] + 특정한 날

The conference attendees are advised to arrive early at the venue [in / on] Saturday evening. [1]

>> **출제 포인트**　시간(때)를 나타내는 전치사

at + 시각/구체적인 때	at 4 P.M., at midnight, at the end of this fiscal year 오후 4시에, 자정에, 이번 회계연도 말에
in + 아침/점심/저녁/월/계절/연도	in the morning, in August, in summer, in 2017 아침에, 8월에, 여름에, 2017년에
on + 날짜/요일/특정한 날	on May 10, on Friday, on Christmas Day 5월 10일에, 금요일에, 크리스마스에

Q2 동작 완료 동사 + [by vs. until] + 시점

The construction of our headquarters building is scheduled to finish [by / until] the end of this year. [1]

현재완료 + [since vs. after] + 시점

Mr. Kensmore has worked abroad [since / after] his graduation from university. [2]

[prior to vs. within] + 시점

Cristal Sky Airlines advises that passengers arrive at the airport at least one hour [prior to / within] their scheduled departure time. [3]

>> 출제 포인트　특정 시점을 나타내는 전치사

by + 시점	~까지	완료 의미 동사(finish, submit, return, deliver 등) + by five o'clock 5시까지
until + 시점	~까지	계속 의미 동사(postpone, last, continue, remain, stay 등) + until five o'clock 5시까지
from[as of, effective, starting] + 시점	~부터	from May to August 5월부터 8월까지 as of July 1 7월 1일부로
since + 과거 시점	~이후로	since last Friday 지난주 금요일 이후로
past + 시점	~지나서	past midnight 자정이 지나서 past retirement age 정년을 지나서
before[prior to] + 시점	~전에	before delivery 배달 전에 prior to the scheduled departure time 예정된 출발 시간 전에
after[following] + 시점	~후에	after the expiration date 만료일 이후에 following a coffee break 커피 마시는 휴식시간 후에
참고 after는 기간 명사와도 쓰일 수 있다.		after a six month trial period 6개월간의 시험기간 후에

Q3

[for vs. during] + 특정 사건 기간

Mr. Lane was asked to call back [for / during] normal business hours. [1]

[for vs. since] + 기간

The management at Lukas Corporation has shown commitment to improving employee productivity [for / since] the last 10 years. [2]

[within vs. into] + 기간

We will deliver your order [within / into] three days of the purchase date. [3]

[throughout vs. since] + 기간

Except for one minor setback, sales have steadily increased [throughout / since] the year. [4]

>> 출제 포인트　❶ **for vs. during**: 「for + 소요 시간」은 '얼마 동안'을 나타내고, 「during + 특정 사건 기간」은 '어떤 사건이 진행되는 동안'을 의미한다.

❷ 기간을 나타내는 전치사

during + 기간	~동안에(사건 기간)	during the conference, during business hours 회의[학회] 동안, 영업 시간 동안
for + 기간	~동안에(소요 시간)	for three years 3년 동안
throughout + 기간	~내내	throughout the year 일년 내내

in + 기간	~후에[이내에]	in two weeks 2주 후에[이내에]
within + 기간	~이내에	within 24 hours 24시간 이내에
참고 over[for, during, in] the last[past] 3 years 지난 3년 동안		

2. 장소 전치사

 Q4 **[along vs. between] + 장소 명사**

The city offers scenic boat rides **[along / between]** the Ran River. [1]

[throughout vs. among] + 장소 명사

After years of research, we have finally developed a new innovative product that is becoming popular **[throughout / among]** the world. [2]

[past vs. over] + 장소 명사

The community center is located slightly **[past / over]** the movie theater on West Street. [3]

>> **출제 포인트** ❶ 장소를 나타내는 전치사

at + 지점	~에	비교적 좁고 구체적인 장소	at the corner, at a restaurant, at the party
in + 공간의 안	~안에	비교적 넓은 장소나 장소의 내부	in Seoul, in Asia, in the theatre, in the kitchen
on + 접촉하는 표면	~위에	도로, 교통수단 등	on the table, on Main Street, on the bus/train/plane

❷ 방향/위치를 나타내는 전치사

to	~로(도착점)	from	~로부터(출발점)
through	~을 통해	along	~을 따라
into	~의 속으로	out of	~밖으로
across	~을 건너, ~곳곳에	past	~을 지나서
above	~위쪽에	below	~아래쪽에
over	~바로 위에	under	~바로 밑에
near	~가까이에	opposite	~의 맞은편에
beside/by/next to	~옆에	around	~주위에
between	둘 사이에	among	셋 이상 사이에
within	(장소, 범위) ~이내에, 안에	throughout	~곳곳에
in front of	~앞에	behind	~뒤에

1. Tourists can join a guided tour [**between** / **along**] 9 A.M. and 6 P.M.

2. We have enclosed the application form [**in** / **on**] the return envelope for your convenience.

3. Ms. Park is often late for meetings although she lives [**between** / **within**] walking distance of the office.

4. Kenneth Motors's market research team conducted a customer satisfaction survey on their new model [**onto** / **through**] interviews and questionnaires.

3. 기타 빈출 전치사

Q5 의미에 유의해야 할 전치사

Ashai Kitchen has been voted the best restaurant in Boston five years in a row [**as to** / **due to**] its excellent customer service. [1]

Please contact Technical Support for any problems [**regarding** / **regarded**] your software program. [2]

[**Instead of** / **Except for**] selecting outside applicants, the CEO has appointed Mr. Roman to Operations Director. [3]

Please contact Customer Support [**for** / **as**] a refund within 30 days of your order date. [4]

Please remember that you should send the original receipt [**along with** / **between**] the defective item. [5]

>> 출제 포인트 ❶ 비슷한 의미의 전치사

due to, because of, owing to, on account of, thanks to	~때문에, ~덕분에 [이유]
despite, in spite of, notwithstanding	~에도 불구하고 [양보]
without, except (for), aside from, apart from	~을 제외하고 [제외]
in addition to, besides, plus, on top of	~뿐만 아니라 [부가]
along with, together with	~와 함께, ~와 더불어
considering, given	~을 고려(감안)할 때
regarding, concerning, as to, as for, with regard[respect] to, on, over, about, pertaining to	~에 관하여

❷ 의미에 유의해야 할 빈출 전치사

for	~을 위해서	the training program for new sales staff 신입 영업 사원을 위한 연수 프로그램
with	~와 함께, ~을 가지고 있는, ~인 채로	a designer with at least three years of experience 적어도 3년 이상의 경력을 지닌 디자이너
of	~의	effectiveness of work procedures 업무 절차의 효과
as	~로서	work as a financial advisor 재정 고문으로 일하다
alongside	~의 옆을 따라, ~와 함께	run alongside the road, work alongside one another 길을 따라 달리다, 서로 함께 일하다
according to	~에 따르자면	according to the meeting agenda 회의 의제에 따르면
like unlike	~처럼 ~와 달리	like/unlike other banks 다른 은행들과 같이/달리
such as	예를 들어 ~와 같은	sports games such as soccer and baseball 축구와 야구 같은 스포츠 경기들
including excluding	~을 포함하여 ~을 제외하고	all merchandise including/excluding shoes 신발을 포함/제외한 모든 상품
regardless of	~와 관계없이	regardless of price changes 가격 변동을 막론하고
on, upon	~하자마자	upon receipt of the books 책을 수령하자마자
under	~중인, ~의 영향 하에 있는	under construction, under the direction/supervision/guidance of 공사 중인, ~의 감독/지도 하에
without, barring	~없이	without permission[approval] 허가 없이
instead of	~대신에	instead of the service 서비스 대신에
beyond, above	~를 넘어서는	beyond[above] one's expectation 기대를 넘어서는

+ check

1. WRB Industries has maintained its incentive program **[in spite of / except for]** the recent decline in profits.

2. **[Such as / In addition to]** good writing skills, fluency in Korean is required for the editor position.

3. Garrix Financial will offer more benefits **[according to / such as]** bonuses and longer vacations.

4. Our company selects applicants for interviews **[regardless of / such as]** their educational backgrounds.

5. They announced yesterday that they would make every effort to reorganize the company **[without / during]** laying off employees.

4. 전치사 관용 표현

Q6 동사 + [전치사]

To comply **[to / with]** new safety regulations, the company will replace some old equipment. [1]

명사 + [전치사]

The position requires a university degree and experience **[in / about]** a retail environment. [2]

be + 형용사 + [전치사]

The assistant manager was absent **[at / from]** yesterday's meeting. [3]

>> **출제 포인트** 기출 전치사 관용 표현

❶「동사 + 전치사」

account for	~을 설명하다	dispose of	~을 처리하다
agree to[with]	~에 동의하다	enroll in, register for	~에 등록하다
allow for	참작하다, 고려하다	fill in[out]	~을 작성하다
apologize for	~에 대해 사과하다	interfere with	~을 방해하다
apply for/to	~에 지원하다/적용되다	keep track of	~을 기록하다
benefit from	~로부터 혜택을 입다	lag behind	~에 뒤쳐지다
check A for B	B에 대해 A를 점검하다	make up for	~을 보상하다
collaborate[cooperate] with/on	~와/~에 관해 협력하다	participate in	~에 참여하다
come into effect	효력이 발생하다	prevent A from B	A가 B를 못하도록 하다
comment on	~에 대해 언급하다	proceed with	~을 진행하다
compensate for	~에 대해 보상하다	protect A from B	A를 B로부터 보호하다
complain about	~대해 불평하다	put up with	~을 참다
comply with, adhere to	(규정, 법) 등을 준수하다	refrain from	~을 삼가다
concentrate[focus] on	~에 집중하다	respond[reply, react] to	~에 응답하다
consist of	~로 구성되다	sign up[put in] for	~을 신청하다
contribute to	~에 공헌하다	subscribe to	~을 구독하다
correspond with	~와 부합하다	succeed in/to	~에 성공하다/계승하다
deal with	~을 다루다	take advantage of	~을 이용하다
depart from	~에서 출발하다	talk about/with/to	~에 관하여/함께/ ~에게 이야기하다
depend[rely] (up)on	~에 의존하다		

❷「명사 + 전치사」

access to	~에 접근, 이용	approach to	~에 대한 접근법
advances in	~의 진보	business with	~와의 거래
advantage over	~이상의 장점	concern over[about]	~에 관한 우려
agreement with	~에 대한 합의	contribution to	~에 대한 기여

damage to	~에 대한 손상	problems with	~의 문제
decrease[drop] in	~의 감소	question about	~에 대한 질문
demand for	~에 대한 수요	reaction to	~에 대한 반응
dispute over	~에 관한 토론	reason[cause] for	~의 이유
experience in	~에 대한 경험	request for	~에 대한 요구
increase[rise] in	~의 증가	respect for	~에 대한 존경
influence[effect, impact] on	~에 대한 영향력	solution to	~의 해결책
information on	~에 대한 정보	standard for	~에 대한 기준
interest in	~에 대한 관심	tax on	~에 부과되는 세금
lack of	~의 부족		

❸ 「be + 형용사 + 전치사」

be absent from	~에 결석하다	be equal to	~와 동등하다
be affiliated with	~와 제휴되다	be equipped with	~을 갖추고 있다
be appreciative of	~을 감사하다	be faced with	~에 직면하다
be associated with	~와 연관되다	be familiar with	~에 정통하다
be aware[conscious] of	~을 인식하다	be famous for	~으로 유명하다
be capable of	~을 할 수 있다	be ideal for	~에 적합하다
be compared with[to]	~과 비교되다	be involved in	~에 연관되다
be concerned about	~을 염려하다	be relevant to	~와 관련되다,
be concerned with	~와 관계되다		~에 적절하다
be consistent with	~에 일관되다	be responsible for	~을 책임지다
be dedicated[devoted, committed] to	~하는 데 헌신하다	be satisfied[contented] with	~에 만족하다
		be similar to	~와 유사하다
be different from	~와 다르다	be subject to	~하기 쉽다
be eligible for	~에 대한 자격이 있다	be superior to	~보다 뛰어나다
be entitled to	~에 대한 자격이 있다	be used[accustomed] to	~에 익숙하다

❹ 구전치사

according to	~에 의하면	in excess of	~을 초과하여
ahead of	~에 앞서	in exchange for	~의 대신으로
as of, effective, starting, beginning	~부로	in favor of	~을 찬성하여
		in honor of	~을 기념하여
as part of	~의 일환으로	in light of	~을 고려하여
at one's convenience	~이 편리할 때에	in recognition of	~을 인정하여
at the conclusion of	~이 끝날 때에	in reference to	~에 관하여
by means of	~의 방법에 의하여, 통하여	in regard to	~에 관하여
contrary to	~와 반대로	in response to	~에 응답하여
depending on	~에 따라	in terms of	~의 관점으로
for use	사용을 위한	in the event of	만약 ~의 경우에
in accordance[keeping] with	~에 따라서	in use	사용 중인
		on account of	~때문에
in advance of	~에 앞서서	on behalf of	~대신에
in celebration of	~을 축하하여	prior to	~이전에
in charge of	~을 책임지고 있는	regardless of	~와 관계 없이
in comparison with	~와 비교하여	until further notice	추후 공지가 있을 때까지
in cooperation with	~와 협력하여	with the exception of	~을 제외하면
in detail	상세하게		

Practice

1. Extra equipment will be available to the development team at Hung Motor's Shanghai plant ------- the duration of the project.

(A) between
(B) behind
(C) upon
(D) throughout

2. ------- most other comparable systems from its competitors, Hisakawa's recording system can be easily installed.

(A) Along
(B) Unlike
(C) Moreover
(D) Unless

3. Kitt National Park offers daily ferry tours ------- the city's scenic waterfront.

(A) between
(B) along
(C) below
(D) apart

4. Personal information should not be shared ------- customers' approval.

(A) except
(B) besides
(C) among
(D) without

5. In order to guarantee that you receive this promotional discount for the advertised items, please place your order ------- 24 hours.

(A) within
(B) into
(C) since
(D) about

6. The majority of participants who completed Walmont Employment Center's questionnaire stated that they plan to continue working ------- retirement age.

(A) still
(B) past
(C) pertaining to
(D) at last

7. Rojanho project team members are invited to a dinner ------- the company president on September 10th to celebrate their success.

(A) off
(B) with
(C) throughout
(D) among

8. The president will be out of the office ------- Thursday, as he is currently attending the international business conference in Singapore.

(A) since
(B) along
(C) between
(D) until

9. ------- the completion of one year of employment, employees at Finnerman Technologies are eligible for a one-week paid vacation.

(A) Following
(B) Because
(C) Moreover
(D) Except

10. Any employees who enter new customers' data should contact Ms. Ahn in the Customer Service Department ------- further instructions.

(A) onto
(B) within
(C) along
(D) for

11. The KD Beverage Company has issued a statement to address concerns ------- the ingredients in its drinks.

(A) excluding
(B) during
(C) following
(D) regarding

12. Questions ------- to paychecks should be directed to Ms. Avilia of the Accounting Department, who is in charge of payroll duties.

(A) regarding
(B) receiving
(C) similar
(D) pertaining

13. The remodeling of the reception area should be completed by Thursday if everything goes ------- plan.

(A) in addition to
(B) agreeing with
(C) relating to
(D) according to

14. The representatives from Volgasy Solutions and Xerman Chemicals reached an agreement to work ------- one another.

(A) jointly
(B) collaborating
(C) together
(D) alongside

15. Walton Technologies is ------- the leading manufacturers of automobile seats in Asia with more than 10 production plants in China and Vietnam.

(A) around
(B) along
(C) toward
(D) among

16. The applicants are required to submit their résumés ------- letters of recommendation to Ms. Lynn no later than this Friday.

(A) along with
(B) except for
(C) additionally
(D) on behalf of

17. Bektal Construction is planning to open branch offices in Europe in an effort to broaden its market ------- the Asia-Pacific region.

(A) before
(B) between
(C) beyond
(D) behind

18. Many of the photographs ------- Alma Roberto's new book help the readers to understand the changes in fashion trends.

(A) among
(B) throughout
(C) during
(D) toward

19. ------- 25 years in the tourist industry, Always Loving Tour is widely recognized as the leading company in this field.

(A) Ahead of
(B) Until now
(C) With
(D) Past

20. ------- the popularity of the annual music festival, those interested in attending should purchase tickets well in advance.

(A) Since
(B) About
(C) Given
(D) Upon

REVIEW TEST 01

해설서 p.15 / ⏱ 제한 시간 10분

1. Call John Burnett's law firm and schedule an appointment for a free -------.

(A) consulted
(B) consults
(C) consultant
(D) consultation

2. The Otteron Bridge is temporarily closed ------- flooding from the Hanso River.

(A) even if
(B) instead of
(C) owing to
(D) now that

3. Managers should assess the performance of the employees in ------- department on a regular basis.

(A) they
(B) their
(C) theirs
(D) themselves

4. Vandenberg Tech provided an on-site computer training workshop to all the employees, and ------- have benefitted greatly from the session.

(A) much
(B) most
(C) each
(D) everyone

5. The schedule ------- next week's marketing seminar will be emailed to all participants in the afternoon.

(A) into
(B) over
(C) for
(D) at

6. 고난도 Upon their arrival at the convention center, the ------- held a press conference.

(A) delegate
(B) delegating
(C) delegator
(D) delegates

7. The newly opened Watson Valley Resort has excellent facilities for sports and recreation ------- fabulous dining places.

(A) still
(B) as soon as
(C) in addition to
(D) as if

8. Motivational speakers ------- induce emotional responses from their listeners.

(A) intention
(B) intentional
(C) intentioned
(D) intentionally

9. ------- worldwide effort to protect the environment, the spokesperson for Greener Earth said that the average global temperature is gradually rising.

(A) Since
(B) Despite
(C) Because
(D) Although

10. Companies are increasingly requiring their employees to provide written summaries of their work-related ------- as part of the self-evaluation process.

(A) accomplishing
(B) accomplishes
(C) accomplishments
(D) accomplished

11. Namyang Publishing reported that the majority of its readers have reacted ------- to Murasaki Hitori's new novel, *The Road to End*.

(A) favorably
(B) favorable
(C) favor
(D) favorite

12. As production is far behind schedule, please understand that shifts can be changed ------- prior notice.

(A) instead
(B) unless
(C) without
(D) except

13. Paint products made by Sherwin Company are intended for ------- use only.

(A) residents
(B) residentially
(C) reside
(D) residential

14. Since Ms. Miller became the mayor, alleviating the increasing traffic congestion has become one of ------- most urgent issues to address.

(A) hers
(B) herself
(C) she
(D) her

15. The customer's call was disconnected ------- before it was transferred to the Technical Support Department.

(A) accident
(B) accidents
(C) accidental
(D) accidentally

16. 고난도 Jensen Technology's newest model, the XP 336 laptop computer, was designed with ------- beyond those of any other model in the industry.

(A) capable
(B) capability
(C) capabilities
(D) capably

17. 고난도 Though not ------- got the opportunity to speak during yesterday's conference, participants were able to post their comments on the online discussion forum.

(A) other
(B) everyone
(C) much
(D) each

18. 고난도 Although Mr. Dreyfus expressed ------- in our new line of printers, he has not confirmed whether he will order them for his company.

(A) interested
(B) interesting
(C) interests
(D) interest

19. We will ship out your item within 24 hours ------- receipt of your payment.

(A) upon
(B) afterward
(C) about
(D) next

20. 고난도 The Charlin Residence is our most spacious villa and ------- the best choice for the whole family to have a great time.

(A) definite
(B) definitive
(C) defined
(D) definitely

UNIT 06
동사의 형태와 수 일치

문장이 성립하려면 주어 뒤에 주어의 행위나 상태를 설명하는 동사가 있어야 한다. 한 문장 안에 추가로 동사를 쓰기 위해서는 접속사와 같은 연결어가 필요하며, 주어와 동사 사이에 전치사구, 분사, to부정사, 관계사절 등의 수식어가 들어가 주어와 동사를 분리하기도 한다.

 기본 개념 이해하기

 Tip!
동사와 관련된 문제는 태, 시제를 먼저 따지기 전에 주어와 동사의 수 일치를 확인 하는 것을 잊지 않도록 하자!

1. 주어 뒤에 오는 수식어

전치사구	The employees / **in the conference room** / are going to attend the ceremony. 회의장에 있는 / 직원들은 / 식에 참석할 예정이다.
현재분사구	The employees / **wishing to attend the training session** / need to contact Mr. Kim. 교육 세션에 참가하고자 하는 / 직원들은 / Mr. Kim에게 연락해야 한다.
과거분사구	The employees / **interested in attending the training session** ~. 교육 세션에 참가하는 데 관심이 있는 / 직원들
to부정사구	The employees / **to help us with this project** ~. 이 프로젝트를 도와줄 / 직원들
관계사절	Employees / **who park their vehicles on campus** / are required to register with the security office to obtain access cards. 캠퍼스에 차를 주차하는 / 직원들은 / 출입카드를 받기 위해 경비실에 등록해야 한다.

• 주어 + [전치사구, 형용사구, 분사, to부정사, 관계사절] + 동사: 주어와 동사 사이에 위치한 수식어구는 주어와 동사의 수 일치에 영향을 주지 않는다.

2. 주어 자리의 명사구와 명사절

동명사구	**Recovering** lost files is not an easy job. 손실된 파일들을 복구하는 것은 쉬운 일이 아니다. ⋯▶ 동명사
to부정사구	**It** is recommendable **to visit one of our authorized service stations**. 저희 공인 서비스 센터 중 한 곳을 가시는 걸 추천합니다. ⋯▶ It(가주어) ~ to부정사(진주어)
that절	**It** is obvious **that he is an excellent employee**. 그가 훌륭한 직원인 것은 분명하다. ⋯▶ It(가주어) ~ that절(진주어)
what절	**What is important to us** is that the consumer is satisfied with our products. 우리에게 중요한 것은 소비자가 우리 제품에 만족하고 있다는 것이다. ⋯▶ what절

• 명사구(동명사, to부정사)와 명사절(that절, what절 등)은 주어, 목적어, 보어 역할을 하며, 명사구나 명사절이 주어 자리에 오면 단수 취급한다.

문장 내에서 동사 자리인지를 확인한 후, 수식어가 포함된 복잡한 구조의 문장에서 주어를 정확히 찾아 동사의 수를 일치시키는 문제가 출제된다. 동사 관련 문법 문제에서 첫 번째로 확인할 것이 주어와 동사의 수 일치이며, 최근에는 태/시제와 연계하여 풀어야 하는 복합 문제가 고난도 문제로 자주 출제되고 있다.

해설서 p.17

1. 동사의 기본 형태

Q1 (Please) [동사원형 vs. 동사 변화형]

Please [**welcome / welcomed**] Ms. Goro to the Marketing Department. [1]

조동사 + (부사어) + [동사원형 vs. 동사 변화형]

According to Gloria Claughton's survey, television advertisements do not necessarily [**boost / to boost**] sales. [2]

요청·제안 동사 + that + 주어 + [동사원형 vs. 동사 변화형]

The board asked that the budget proposal [**be / was**] submitted by Friday. [3]

>> 출제 포인트 한 문장에는 반드시 하나의 동사가 있어야 하며, 다음의 경우 동사원형을 쓴다.

❶ 명령문은 주어를 생략하고, 동사원형으로 시작한다.

❷ 조동사 뒤에는 동사원형이 와야 하고, 그 사이에 부정어 not이나 다른 부사어가 위치할 수 있다.

❸ 요청·제안 등을 의미하는 동사 또는 이성적 판단을 나타내는 형용사 뒤에 오는 that절이 문맥상 당위성(~해야 한다)을 나타내면 그 뒤 that절의 동사는 should가 생략된 동사원형을 쓴다.

요청 동사	ask 묻다 ι request 요청하다 ι require 요구하다 ι demand 요구하다
제안 동사	suggest 제안하다 ι recommend 권하다
명령 동사	order 명령[지시]하다 ι urge 권고[촉구]하다 ι insist (~해야 한다고) 고집하다
이성적 판단 형용사	necessary 필요한 ι imperative 반드시 해야 하는 ι essential 필수적인 ι important 중요한 ι crucial 결정적인

● check

1. After reviewing it, please [**contact / contacts**] your supervisor with any further questions you may have.

2. A copy of the guide should [**arrives / arrive**] in the mail this week.

3. The manager requested that Mr. Kim [**will examine / examine**] all possible ways to lower expenses at the Tokyo facility.

Q2 be + [동사원형 vs. 분사]

All employees are **[require / required]** to complete travel expense reports immediately after returning from a business trip. [1]

have + [동사원형 vs. 과거분사]

The president has **[promise / promised]** to upgrade the company cafeteria. [2]

>> 출제 포인트 ❶ be동사 뒤에 동사가 올 경우 과거분사나 현재분사 형태로 바꾸어 태를 나타낸다.

❷ 조동사 have 뒤에 동사가 오는 경우 과거분사로 바꾸어 완료형 시제를 나타낸다.

- 능동 진행형(be + V-ing): 주어 + am/are/is/was/were + 동사원형-ing
- 수동형(be + p.p.): 주어 + am/are/is/was/were + 동사원형-ed
- 완료형(have + p.p.): 주어 + have/has/had + 동사원형-ed

2. 주어와 동사의 수 일치

Q3 고유명사 + [단수 동사 vs. 복수 동사]

Cal Appliances **[is / are]** dedicated to providing quality items at low prices. [1]

동명사/to부정사/명사절 + [단수 동사 vs. 복수 동사]

Preventing accidents in advance **[is / are]** the best way to maximize the company's profits. [2]

복수 선행사 + 관계대명사 + [단수 동사 vs. 복수 동사]

The line of furniture is designed for customers who **[resides / reside]** in small residences. [3]

there + [단수 동사 vs. 복수 동사] + 복수 주어

Brooks Auto has been recalling its TX301 model because there **[was / were]** several car accidents due to its faulty brakes. [4]

>> **출제 포인트** ❶ 동사는 반드시 문장의 주어와 수를 일치시켜야 한다.

❷ 주어가 회사명 등의 고유 명사나 to부정사/동명사구, 명사절일 때는 단수 취급하여 단수 동사를 쓴다.

❸ 주격 관계대명사 who, which, that 뒤의 동사는 수식하는 선행사에 수를 일치시킨다.

❹ 「There + 동사(be/remain/exist) + 명사」 구문의 동사는 뒤에 오는 명사에 수를 일치시킨다.

+ check

1. There has been a growing need for editors who **[possesses / possess]** technical knowledge.

2. Sencomp Electronics **[requires / require]** the use of a new ID verification system.

3. I'm afraid there **[is / are]** no more seats for the Toronto session you asked about.

Q4 **each of the + 복수 명사 + [단수 동사 vs. 복수 동사]**

Each of the new employees **[is / are]** required to take training courses before starting work. [1]

a number of + 복수 명사 + [단수 동사 vs. 복수 동사]

A number of safety inspectors **[is / are]** coming next week to verify the company's compliance with safety regulations. [2]

most of the + 불가산 명사 + [단수 동사 vs. 복수 동사]

Most of the information on our products **[is / are]** available on our Web site. [3]

>> 출제 포인트 ❶ 단수 동사를 써야 하는 주어 형태

• every/each + 단수 명사 ('모든'/'각각의')
• everything/everyone/everybody ('모든 것'/'모든 사람')
• one/each/either/neither of + the 복수 명사   ┐
('~중 하나'/'각각'/'둘 중 하나'/'어느 것도 아님')   ├ **+ 단수 동사**
• the number of + 복수 명사 ('~의 수')   ┘

❷ 복수 동사를 써야 하는 주어 형태

• a number of/lots of/many + 복수 명사 ('많은~')   ┐
• a variety of + 복수 명사 ('다양한~')   ├ **+ 복수 동사**
• a range of + 복수 명사 ('다양한~')   ┘

❸ of 뒤의 명사에 수 일치 하는 주어 형태

숫자 + percent 퍼센트 ǀ three-fourths 분수 ┐	단수 명사 + 단수 동사
part 부분 ǀ half 절반 ǀ some/any 몇몇 ├ **+ of the [소유격] +**	복수 명사 + 복수 동사
most 대부분 ǀ the rest 나머지 ǀ all 모두 ┘	

+) check

1. One of the issues our firm has **[is / are]** a shortage of funding.

2. The number of people using public transportation **[has / have]** increased sharply because of the rise in oil prices.

3. Most of the candidates **[was / were]** well qualified for the position.

Q5 주어 + 수식어 + [단수 동사 vs. 복수 동사]

Executives from the company **[is / are]** expected to make an important announcement. [1]

The suggestions made by the analysts **[is / are]** summarized in the company newsletter. [2]

The proposal that Ms. Borgen submitted at the planning meeting **[was / were]** interesting. [3]

>> 출제 포인트   주어(명사)를 뒤에서 수식하는 수식어구(전치사구, 분사구, to부정사구, 관계대명사절, 동격어)는 수 일치에 영향을 주지 않는다. 수식어구의 일부를 주어로 혼동하지 않도록 수식어구를 하나의 의미 단위로 묶고 문장 구조를 파악한 후, 주어와 수 일치시켜야 한다.

+ check

1. Some receipts not yet approved by the accounts manager **[was / were]** left on the counter.

2. Customers applying for a store loyalty card **[needs / need]** to fill out an online application form.

3. Ms. Yoo, the front-desk assistant, **[orders / order]** office supplies every Friday.

Practice

해설서 p.18 / ⏱ 제한 시간 6분

1. The seminars featuring Dr. Johnson and other distinguished professors ------- scheduled for 7:30 P.M. on Saturday in Maylor Auditorium.

(A) is
(B) has
(C) does
(D) are

2. 고난도 The fact that celebrities appear in advertisements ------- not guarantee a product's success.

(A) are
(B) has
(C) being
(D) does

3. ------- to the municipal museum in Lindsey Park is free for children six years of age and under.

(A) Admission
(B) Admits
(C) Admit
(D) Admissions

4. Please ------- this letter if you have already paid the additional charge for the late return of our book.

(A) disregarding
(B) disregarded
(C) disregard
(D) disregards

5. Customers ------- enthusiastically to the desserts that the café added to its menu.

(A) responding
(B) responses
(C) responsibly
(D) responded

6. ------- three to five days for delivery of any Chaikrabi Skin Care product.

(A) Allows
(B) To allow
(C) Allowing
(D) Allow

7. Queen's Electronics ------- a variety of electronic home appliances such as TVs and refrigerators.

(A) produce
(B) produces
(C) product
(D) producing

8. In her weekly online article, *Eastern Exchange*, Maria Nguyen ------- stock market trends in Asia.

(A) analysis
(B) analyzer
(C) analyzes
(D) analyzing

9. Approximately half of the employees at Greensville Company ------- to work alone in a personal car.

(A) commute
(B) commutes
(C) is commuting
(D) has commuted

10. 고난도 The *Current Business Journal* reported that the number of merger and acquisition deals in the pharmaceutical industry ------- consistent for the last five years.

(A) remaining
(B) has remained
(C) remain
(D) have remained

11. A revised proposal for Goodwill Finance Bank ------- that it increase its interest rates as other local banks have done.

(A) suggest
(B) suggesting
(C) suggestion
(D) suggests

12. 고난도 The Degas' Island Restaurant requests that reservations for a table ------- at least a week in advance.

(A) make
(B) be made
(C) to make
(D) making

13. Toronto has a well-developed underground system that ------- most of the major buildings.

(A) connecting
(B) connection
(C) connects
(D) connect

14. The impressive ------- that will become Orlando University's Center for the Arts was designed by renowned architect Carmen Olsen.

(A) structural
(B) structure
(C) structures
(D) structured

15. All of the ------- for the upcoming research project have to observe the application guidelines in order to achieve an acceptable level of quality.

(A) application
(B) applies
(C) applying
(D) applicants

16. Sales of Rubber Lovers' popular rain boots ------- expected to dramatically increase its second quarter's profits.

(A) are
(B) having
(C) being
(D) has

17. 고난도 We are ready to take responsibility for ensuring that each of our customers ------- completely satisfied with our service.

(A) is
(B) were
(C) being
(D) to be

18. To save time and costs, RTA Industries recommends that any associates who travel for business ------- the amount of luggage they carry.

(A) to minimize
(B) minimize
(C) have minimized
(D) minimizing

19. 고난도 The product manual the Sales Department had asked for ------- by express mail yesterday.

(A) arriving
(B) arrival
(C) arrive
(D) arrived

20. Survey ------- analyze the composition of the ground and evaluate its suitability for construction.

(A) technicians
(B) technically
(C) technical
(D) technicality

능동태와 수동태

대부분의 태 문제는 목적어로 쓰이는 명사의 유무에 따라 태를 구분할 수 있는 3형식 동사가 출제되지만 뒤에 명사가 있더라도 수동태를 쓸 수 있는 4·5형식 동사도 출제되므로 정확한 해석을 기반으로 문제에 접근해야 한다.

> **Tip!** 동사의 태는 해석을 통해 의미상으로 능동/수동을 결정해야 해. 하지만 토익의 태 문제로 출제되는 동사가 대부분 타동사니까 해석으로 애매하다면 목적어가 있으면 능동, 없으면 수동을 선택하면 돼.

기본 개념 이해하기

1. 능동태와 수동태의 개념

능동태	The flight attendant **discouraged** the use of electronic devices. 승무원은 전자 기기를 사용하지 못하게 했다. 주어 = 행위의 주체ㅣ목적어 = 행위의 영향을 받는 대상
수동태	The use of electronic devices **was discouraged** by the flight attendant. 전자 기기 사용은 승무원에 의해 저지당했다. 주어 = 행위의 영향을 받는 대상ㅣby + 목적격 = 행위의 주체

• 행위의 주체가 문장의 주어이면 능동태를, 행위의 영향을 받는 대상이 주어이면 수동태를 쓴다.

2. 수동태의 형태: be동사 + 과거분사 ~ (by 행위자)

단순 시제 수동태	The Eiffel Tower **is visited** by a large number of tourists. 많은 관광객들이 에펠탑을 방문한다. ⋯ 현재형 「am/are/is + 과거분사」 The Eiffel Tower **was designed** by Gustave Eiffel. 에펠탑은 Gustave Eiffel에 의해 고안되었다. ⋯ 과거형 「was/were + 과거분사」 The Eiffel Tower **will be given** a new coat of paint next month. 에펠탑은 다음 달에 새롭게 페인트칠이 될 것이다. ⋯ 미래형 「will(조동사) + be + 과거분사」
진행 시제 수동태	The bread **is being baked**. 빵이 구워지고 있다. ⋯ 진행형 「be동사 + being + 과거분사」
완료 시제 수동태	A room **has been booked** for you. 당신을 위해 방이 하나 예약되어 있습니다. ⋯ 완료형 「have + been + 과거분사」
by + 행위자	The safety regulations will be revised. 안전 수칙이 개정될 것이다. ⋯ by them 생략 We were advised **by the analyst** that property prices might increase next quarter. 분석가는 우리에게 다음 분기에 부동산 가격이 오를지도 모른다고 조언했다. ⋯ 수동태의 행위자는 주로 생략되지만, 필요한 경우 「by + 행위자(목적격)」 형태로 나타냄

목적어로 쓰이는 명사의 유무로 태를 구분하는 3형식 동사의 출제 비중이 가장 높다. 뒤에 명사가 있더라도 수동태가 정답이 될 수 있어 혼동하기 쉬운 4·5 형식 동사의 태 관련 내용이 고난도 문제로 출제된다.

해설서 p.19

1. 능동태와 수동태 구분

Q1 [주어(행위의 주체)가 ~하다 vs. 주어(행위의 대상)가 ~되다, 당하다]

The bank will contact you in writing as soon as your loan application is **[approving / approved]** by a manager. [1]

>> 출제 포인트　**해석에 의한 태 구분:** 주어가 행위의 주체가 되어 행위를 '~하면' 능동태를, 주어가 행위의 대상으로서 행위를 '~당하면' 수동태를 쓴다. 수동태는 「be + 과거분사」의 형태를 취한다.

Q2 3형식 동사의 [능동태 vs. 수동태] + 명사

The Marketing Department **[has conducted / has been conducted]** a thorough survey to develop new marketing strategies. [1]

3형식 동사의 [능동태 vs. 수동태] + 전치사

Safety regulations for the assembly line **[had revised / will be revised]** in response to the inspection. [2]

>> 출제 포인트　**목적어 유무에 의한 태 구분:** 대부분 3형식 타동사가 출제되기 때문에 동사 뒤에 목적어(명사)가 있으면 능동태, 목적어(명사) 없이 전치사나 부사가 오면 수동태를 쓴다.

✓ **3형식 동사의 수동태**

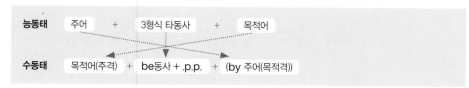

능동태	주어	+	3형식 타동사	+	목적어
수동태	목적어(주격)	+	be동사 + .p.p.	+	(by 주어(목적격))

＋ check

1. Tripfolio **[was provided / provides]** an easy way to track all your business vehicle expenses.

2. A change will be **[made / making]** to our subscription package prices beginning next year.

Q3 **4형식 동사의 [능동태 vs. 수동태] + 명사**

Candidates with sales experience will **[give / be given]** the chance to interview for the job. [1]

>> 출제 포인트

목적어를 2개 취하는 4형식 동사는 수동태 뒤에도 명사가 올 수 있기 때문에, 4형식 동사의 태를 결정할 때는 우선적으로 해석에 의해 판단한다.

☑ **4형식 동사(give, offer, award, send, issue, charge 등)의 수동태**

능동태	주어 + 수여동사 + 간접목적어(명사 1) + 직접목적어(명사 2)
수동태	명사 1 + be + 수여동사의 과거분사 + 명사 2 + (by 주어(목적격))

Q4 **5형식 동사의 [능동태 vs. 수동태] + 명사**

Wheelers Corporation, a medical consulting company, has **[named / been named]** Boston's Best Workplace by Best Biz, a business research organization. [1]

5형식 동사의 수동태 + [형용사 vs. 부사]

Emergency fire doors are located on every floor of the building and must be kept **[clearly / clear]** of any obstacles. [2]

5형식 동사의 [능동태 vs. 수동태] + to부정사

Commuters are strongly **[advising / advised]** to take public transit today. [3]

>> 출제 포인트

5형식 동사는 명사나 to부정사를 목적격 보어로 취하기 때문에 수동태로 바뀌면 뒤에 명사나 to부정사가 남는다.

☑ **명사를 목적격 보어로 취하는 5형식 동사(appoint, name, call, elect 등)의 수동태**

능동태	주어 + 5형식 동사 + 목적어 + 목적격 보어(명사)
수동태	목적어(주격) + be + 5형식 동사의 p.p. + 목적격 보어(명사) + (by 주어(목적격))

☑ **형용사를 목적격 보어로 취하는 5형식 동사(make, consider, keep, leave, find 등)의 수동태**

능동태	주어 + 5형식 동사 + 목적어 + 목적격 보어(형용사)
수동태	목적어(주격) + be + 5형식 동사의 p.p. + 목적격 보어(형용사) + (by 주어(목적격))

☑ **to부정사를 목적격 보어로 취하는 5형식 동사의 수동태**

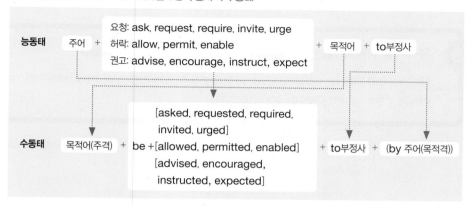

☑ **to부정사를 목적격 보어로 취하는 5형식 동사들과 수동태**

- **ask** A to do: A가 ~하도록 요청하다
  → be **asked** to do ~하도록 요구받다

- **request** A to do: A가 ~하도록 요청하다
  → be **requested** to do ~하도록 요청받다

- **require** A to do: A가 ~하도록 요구하다
  → be **required** to do ~하도록 요구받다

- **invite** A to do: A가 ~하도록 요청[초대]하다
  → be **invited** to do ~하도록 요청[초대]받다

- **urge** A to do: A가 ~하도록 권고하다
  → be **urged** to do ~하도록 권고되다

- **allow** A to do: A가 ~하도록 허용하다
  → be **allowed** to do ~하도록 허용되다

- **permit** A to do: A가 ~하도록 허락하다
  → be **permitted** to do ~하도록 허락받다

- **enable** A to do: A가 ~하는 것을 가능하게 하다
  → be **enabled** to do ~하도록 가능하게 되다

- **advise** A to do: A가 ~하도록 권고하다
  → be **advised** to do ~하도록 권고되다

- **encourage** A to do: A가 ~하도록 권장하다
  → be **encouraged** to do ~하도록 권장되다

- **instruct** A to do: A가 ~하도록 지시하다
  → be **instructed** to do ~하도록 지시받다

- **expect** A to do: A가 ~할 것으로 기대[예상]하다
  → be **expected** to do ~할 것으로 기대[예상]되다

+ check

1. Your personal information is kept [**confidentially / confidential**] by Farisys.

2. All staff members are [**expecting / expected**] to maintain an appropriate level of professionalism when interacting with clients.

2. 유의해야 할 수동태

Q5 목적어를 취하지 않는 자동사의 태

Ms. Kovac has requested your presence at the regional meeting that will **[take place / be taken place]** on Thursday. [1]

>> 출제 포인트 ❶ take place는 행위의 대상인 목적어를 취하지 않는 자동사이므로 수동태로 쓰이지 않는다.

✓ 수동태로 잘못 쓰기 쉬운 자동사

remain	남아있다	arrive	도착하다
seem	~인 것 같다	exist	존재하다
take place	개최되다	occur, happen	발생하다
rise	오르다	proceed	진행되다
last	지속되다	expire	만료되다

❷ 「자동사 + 전치사」 형태의 구동사는 타동사처럼 뒤에 목적어를 취하기 때문에 수동태로 표현할 수 있다.

Normally this training would **be carried out** by your supervisor, Ms. Elly Park.
평소대로라면 이 교육은 당신의 상사, Ms. Elly Park이 진행했을 것입니다.

✓ 자동사 + 전치사

account for	~을 설명하다	deal with	~을 다루다
refer to	~을 참고하다	carry out	~을 실행하다
rely on	~에 의존하다	take care of	돌보다
interfere with	방해하다		

> **cf** '구성되다'의 consist of는 「자동사 + 전치사」 형태이나 구성된 상태를 표현하므로 수동으로 쓰지 않으며,
> be made up of, be composed of와 같은 수동 표현으로 '구성되다'라는 동일한 의미를 표현한다.
>
> A special task force team which consists of[= is made up of/is composed of]
> representatives from relevant divisions will be organized.
> 관련 부서에서 대표자들로 구성된 특별 대책반이 조직될 것이다.

+ check

1. All orders placed online will be **[arrived / shipped]** from our Busan warehouse within 48 hours.

2. Please remember that your Terryvale Children's Zoo membership **[will expire / has been expired]** on July 31.

Q6 수동태 + by 이외의 전치사

The store manager was pleased **[in / with]** the positive responses to the sales event. [1]

>> **출제 포인트** ❶ 감정을 나타내는 동사는 주어가 감정을 느끼는 사람이나 단체일 때 수동태를 쓴다.

❷ 행위의 주체를 나타낼 때 수동태 뒤에 「by + 명사」를 쓰는 게 일반적이지만, by 이외의 다른 전치사를 쓰는 표현에 유의해야 한다.

☑ **by가 아닌 다른 전치사를 쓰는 수동태**

감정 동사의 수동태	

be concerned about	~에 대해 걱정하다
be disappointed with	~에 실망하다
be frightened[alarmed, surprised, astonished, shocked] at	~에 놀라다
be interested in	~에 관심 있다
be satisfied[pleased] with	~에 만족하다
be accustomed[used] to	~에 익숙하다
be acquainted with	~을 알고 있다
be assigned to	~에 배정되다
be associated with	~와 관련되다
be based on[upon]	~에 기초하다
be committed[dedicated, devoted] to	~에 전념하다
be composed of	~로 구성되어 있다
be divided into	~로 나눠지다
be engaged in	~에 종사하다
be equipped with	~을 갖추다
be exposed to	~에 노출되다
be faced with	~에 직면하다
be involved in	~에 관련되다
be known as	~로 알려져 있다(자격)
be known for	~때문에 알려져 있다(이유)
be limited to	~로 제한되다
be related to	~와 관계가 있다

Practice

1. All requests for reimbursement ------- to a department manager for approval before the end of the week.

(A) will submit
(B) has been submitted
(C) should be submitted
(D) had been submitting

2. A luxury suite with a view overlooking the river ------- for the board of directors meeting this weekend.

(A) reserving
(B) has been reserved
(C) has reserved
(D) reserve

3. Please use the other photocopier in the corner until a new ink cartridge ------- next week.

(A) were installing
(B) would be installing
(C) have installed
(D) has been installed

4. A routine check of the exterior lighting on campus is ------- by the maintenance staff on a weekly basis.

(A) conducted
(B) conductor
(C) conducting
(D) conducts

5. Once the decision on hiring new sales representatives -------, the Personnel Department will place an advertisement.

(A) approve
(B) has been approved
(C) approved
(D) will approve

6. Funds from Bowson Tech's budget surplus ------- primarily for improving its company Web site and updating office equipment.

(A) allocated
(B) has been allocating
(C) allocation
(D) are allocated

7. The court hearing on the ownership of the property ------- now that the parties have reached a settlement.

(A) to cancel
(B) cancel
(C) has canceled
(D) will be canceled

8. The processing speed of the WTX smartphone is ------- to that of any mobile device within the same price range.

(A) compare
(B) comparable
(C) comparison
(D) comparing

9. At today's workshop, Dr. Ikeda will ------- ways to achieve particular marketing objectives.

(A) addressed
(B) be addressed
(C) address
(D) addressing

10. All the residents who are ------- about the proposed water rate increase will be invited to a public hearing next month.

(A) concerns
(B) concerned
(C) concerning
(D) concern

11. Everyone who signed up for the symposium on the Effects of Global Warming ------- a letter regarding the schedule.

(A) was sending
(B) would send
(C) sent
(D) was sent

12. Everyone attending tomorrow's marketing seminar at the Lygon Hotel ------- to sign in at the registration desk.

(A) will invite
(B) is inviting
(C) can invite
(D) is invited

13. Those who are looking for jobs are ------- to bring at least 10 résumés to the job fair and to be prepared for short interviews.

(A) advised
(B) criticized
(C) monitored
(D) excused

14. Procedures for claiming business travel expenses ------- since many employees complained that the paperwork was too complicated.

(A) streamlining
(B) have been streamlined
(C) streamline
(D) to be streamlined

15. Jefferson Company announced that its annual operating expenses ------- steady compared to those of last year.

(A) is remaining
(B) have remained
(C) to remain
(D) were remained

16. The number of people who have registered for the event ------- to be more than 200.

(A) estimation
(B) is estimated
(C) estimated
(D) were estimating

17. At last night's retirement party, Charles Choi ------- for his 30 years of hard work and dedication to the company.

(A) honored
(B) had honored
(C) to be honored
(D) was honored

18. Due to the recent price increases, purchase of nonessential lab equipment ------- until further notice.

(A) has deferred
(B) is deferring
(C) will be deferred
(D) have been deferring

19. Since it has such faithful customers, Cotter's Market ------- the fierce competition from new supermarkets in the region.

(A) withstanding
(B) is withstood
(C) to withstand
(D) has withstood

20. The Bridgeport-Tech Company ------- a two-year contract since it offered a bid at a very competitive price.

(A) awards
(B) has been awarded
(C) awarded
(D) awarding

시제

상태나 동작이 일어난 시점을 동사의 다양한 시제 형태로 표현한다. 동사는 주어와의 수 일치, 태, 시제 등이 반영되어 문장에서 쓰인다.

시제 문제는 제일 먼저 시간을 나타내는 부사구를 파악하는 것이 관건이야. 부사구가 등장하지 않는다면 시간 접속사에 의해 연결된 동사의 시제를 활용하여 시제를 일치시켜 주면 돼.

 기본 개념 이해하기

1. 단순 시제

과거 시제	The accounts manager **submitted** next year's budget proposal yesterday. 회계 담당자가 어제 내년도 예산안을 제출했다.
현재 시제	Ms. Kim **attends** the staff meeting every Monday. Ms. Kim은 매주 월요일마다 직원 회의에 참석한다.
미래 시제	Mr. Jones **will be** transferred to the headquarters in London next month. Mr. Jones는 다음 달에 런던에 있는 본사로 전근 갈 것이다.

- 단순 시제는 현재, 과거, 미래 시점의 상태나 동작을 나타낸다.
  (1) **과거 시제:** 이미 끝난 일 또는 과거의 사실이나 습관
  (2) **현재 시제:** 반복적인 일이나 현재의 일반적인 사실
  (3) **미래 시제:** 아직 일어나지 않은 앞으로의 일을 예상하거나 앞으로 할 일

2. 진행 시제

과거 진행 (was/were + V-ing)	The accounts manager **was preparing** next year's budget proposal last week. 회계 담당자는 지난 주에 내년도 예산안을 준비하고 있었다.
현재 진행 (am/are/is + V-ing)	Mr. Jones **is attending** the staff meeting this week. Mr. Jones는 이번 주 직원 회의에 참석한다.
미래 진행 (will be + V-ing)	Ms. Pollock **will be working** as a sales manager in London next month. Ms. Pollock은 다음 달부터 런던에서 영업 매니저로 일하게 될 것이다.
현재 완료 진행 (have/has been + V-ing)	The marketing team **has been working** on the project for a month. 마케팅 팀은 한 달 동안 그 프로젝트 작업을 진행하고 있다.

- 진행 시제는 (현재, 과거, 미래의) 특정 시점의 한시적인 기간 동안, 일시적으로 일어나고 있는 일을 나타낸다.
  (1) **과거 진행 시제:** 과거의 특정 시점에 진행되었던 일
  (2) **현재 진행 시제:** 지금 현재 시점에 진행되고 있는 일 또는 이미 예정된 가까운 미래
  (3) **미래 진행 시제:** 미래의 특정 시점에 진행될 일
  (4) **현재 완료 진행 시제:** 과거부터 계속되어 현재 시점에도 진행되고 있는 일

3. 완료 시제

과거 완료 (had + p.p.)	Mr. Jones **had worked** here for five years before he was transferred to London. Mr. Jones는 런던으로 전근 가기 전에 이곳에서 5년 동안 일했다.
현재 완료 (have / has + p.p.)	The accounts manager **has already submitted** next year's budget proposal. 회계 담당자는 이미 내년도 예산안을 제출했다.
미래 완료 (will have + p.p.)	By that time, Ms. Keith **will have finished** setting the marketing strategies. 그때쯤이면 Ms. Keith는 마케팅 전략 개발을 완료했을 것이다.

- 동작이 발생한 특정 시점에 초점을 맞추는 단순 시제와 달리 완료 시제는 말하는 시점(현재, 과거, 미래)과의 관련성에 초점을 맞춘다.
  (1) **과거 완료 시제:** 과거시점에 발생한 어떤 일보다 먼저 일어난 일
  (2) **현재 완료 시제:** 과거에 발생해 현재에 영향을 끼치는 일
  (3) **미래 완료 시제:** 과거나 현재부터 시작된 일이 미래의 어느 시점까지 계속되어 완료되는 일

핵심 문제 유형

특정 시점을 나타내는 단서 표현을 찾아 동사의 알맞은 시제를 고르는 문제와 시간·조건 부사절에서 현재 시제가 미래 시제를 대신하는 문제가 가장 많은 출제 비중을 차지한다. 두 개의 절로 구성된 문장에서 해석을 통해 시제를 파악하는 문제와 현재/미래 시제를 주고 해당 시제와 어울리는 부사를 선택하는 문제가 최근에 자주 출제되고 있다.

1. 단서로 파악하는 시제

Q1 단순 시제[과거·현재·미래 시제]와 시간 부사어구

Management **[implemented / would implement]** a policy to conserve energy yesterday. [1]

The manager **[holds / held]** a regular staff meeting every Friday morning. [2]

The director of finance **[has attended / will attend]** a conference in London next week. [3]

Safety inspections at the manufacturing facility are **[shortly / normally]** conducted by city officials. [4]

>> 출제 포인트 ❶ **과거 시제:** 과거 특정 시점에 일어난 일을 나타낸다.

☑ **과거 시제와 어울리는 부사(구)**

시간 + ago	~전에	last + 시점	지난 ~에
yesterday	어제	recently, lately	최근에

❷ **현재 시제:** 일반적인 사실이나 반복되는 일을 나타낸다.

☑ **현재 시제와 어울리는 부사(구)**

normally, typically, usually, ordinarily, generally, commonly	보통, 일반적으로
regularly, routinely, periodically	정기적으로
every/each + 시간	~마다
often, frequently	자주
currently	현재 (현재 진행형과 자주 쓰임)

특히, 현재 시제를 나타내는 단서가 없더라도, 공연 일정, 대중교통 시간표, 계약서, 품질 보증서, 할인 등 이미 정해 놓은 일이 미래까지 일정기간 지속적으로 적용되는 경우 현재 시제를 사용한다는 점에 유의한다.

The contract with our current vendor for bottled water delivery **expires** in 90 days.
생수 배달을 위한 현재의 판매상과의 계약은 90일 후 만료된다.

The promotional discount offer **ends** on November 10.
판촉 할인 제공은 11월 10일에 끝난다.

❸ **미래 시제:** 미래에 일어날 사건이나 상황에 대한 예상·추측을 나타낸다. 「will / may / can + 동사원형」, 「be going to + 동사원형」, 「be to + 동사원형」, 명령문 모두 미래를 의미하는 표현이다.

✓ **미래 시제와 어울리는 부사(구)**

next + 시점	다음 ~에
tomorrow	내일
soon, shortly	곧, 머지 않아
in + 미래연도	~후에
starting / beginning / as of + 미래 시점	~부터, ~부로

❹ **보기에 제시되는 동사의 시제 파악:** 앞으로 일어날 미래의 내용을 나타내는 「조동사 + 동사원형」과 과거의 일에 대한 추측을 나타내는 「조동사 + have p.p.」가 보기에 자주 제시되므로, 각각의 의미와 시제의 차이를 정확히 구별할 수 있어야 한다.

조동사 + 동사원형		조동사 + have p.p.	
would + 동사원형	~할 것이다	would + have p.p.	~했을 텐데
should / must + 동사원형	~해야 한다	should + have p.p.	~했어야만 했는데
could + 동사원형	~할 수 있을 것이다	must + have p.p.	~했음에 틀림없다
might + 동사원형	~일지도 모른다	could + have p.p.	~할 수 있었을 텐데
		might + have p.p.	~였을 수도 있는데

┌→ 미래에 일어날 일에 대한 내용
The innovative advertising campaign <u>would contribute</u> to the success of our new books.
혁신적인 광고가 우리 신간도서의 성공에 기여할 것이다.

┌→ 과거에 일어난 일에 대한 내용
The Westfield project <u>must have been cancelled</u> due to a shortage of funds.
자금 부족으로 Westfield 프로젝트가 취소되었음에 틀림없다.

Q2 현재 완료 시제와 시간 부사어구

The company **[will expand / has expanded]** its business over the past two years. [1]

Employee productivity **[has improved / improved]** significantly since the factory purchased some new equipment last year. [2]

>> 출제 포인트 「have / has + p.p.」 형태의 현재 완료 시제는 과거부터 지금까지 계속되거나 최근에 완료된 일을 나타낸다.

✓ **현재 완료 시제와 어울리는 부사(구)**

for[during, over, in] the past[last] + 기간	지난 ~동안
since + 과거 시점 명사 (since가 전치사) since + 주어 + 과거 동사 (since가 접속사)	~이래로
up to now, so far	현재까지
recently, lately	최근에 **참고** recently는 과거 시제와도 쓰임

2. 문맥으로 파악하는 시제

Q3 두 개의 절로 구성된 문장의 동사 시제

Lucky Mart **[had conducted / will have conducted]** a survey before they decided to open another location. ¹

The results of the clinical trials were made public after the head of the research center **[approves / had approved]** the release. ²

By the time the merger was announced, Roxy Co. **[will suffer / had suffered]** from profit loss for a long time. ³

>> 출제 포인트

❶ 두 개 이상의 절이 접속사로 연결된 문장의 동사들은 서로 시제 일치를 이룬다. 특히, 시간 접속사 (before, after, when, while, as soon as, by the time)가 두 개의 절을 연결한 문장에서 동사의 시제를 묻는 문제가 자주 출제되는데, 이 경우 문제에서 제시된 시간 부사절의 동사의 시제를 기준으로, 해석을 통해 주절 동사의 시제를 파악한다.

❷ 과거에 발생한 두 사건이 선후 관계가 있을 때, 그 중 먼저 완료된 일을 과거완료 시제(had + p.p.)로 표현한다. 따라서, 과거의 어느 시점보다 먼저 일어난 일을 나타내는 과거 완료가 쓰인 문장에는, 항상 비교되는 과거 시점이 언급된다.

┌→ 비교되는 과거 시점   ┌→ 앞에 언급된 과거보다 먼저 일어난 일
Before participants of the conference **left** the hotel, they **had completed** the evaluation forms.
학회 참가자들은 호텔에서 나가기 전 평가 양식을 작성했다.

❸ By the time이 이끄는 부사절의 동사가 과거 시제면 주절에는 과거 완료가, 현재 시제면 주절에는 미래완료가 쓰인다.

> • **By the time** + 주어 + **과거**, 주어 + **과거완료(had p.p.)**: ~했을때, (이미) ~했었다
> • **By the time** + 주어 + **현재**, 주어 + **미래완료(will have p.p.)**: ~할때쯤, (이미) ~했을 것이다

┌→ 기준이 되는 과거   ┌→ 기준이 되는 과거 전에 완료된 일
By the time the interns **arrived** at the hotel, some of their rooms **had been assigned** to other guests.
인턴사원들이 호텔에 도착했을 때쯤 그들의 방 중 일부는 다른 투숙객들에게 배정되어 있었다.

┌→ 기준이 되는 미래 대신 쓰인 현재   ┌→ 기준이 되는 미래 전에 완료될 일
By the time you **get** approval from the manager, she **will have finished** setting the marketing strategies.
당신이 매니저의 승인을 받을 때쯤이면 그분이 마케팅 전략의 수립을 끝내놓았을 것입니다.

Q4 시간·조건 부사절의 시제 일치 예외

After all résumés **[will be / are]** reviewed, the two-stage interview process will start. [1]

If you are hired, you **[have helped / will help]** me develop marketing campaigns. [2]

Once the speech ends, guests **[will be / were]** able to enjoy snacks in the lobby. [3]

>> 출제 포인트 ❶ 시간·조건의 접속사가 이끄는 부사절이 미래를 나타낼 때는 미래 시제 대신 현재 시제를 쓴다.

> • 시간 부사절을 이끄는 접속사: when ~할 때 | while ~하는 동안 | as soon as ~하자마자 |
> before ~하기 전에 | after ~한 후에 | until ~할 때까지 | by the time ~할 때쯤
> • 조건 부사절을 이끄는 접속사: if ~라면 | once 일단 ~하면 | unless ~아니라면

❷ 시간, 조건의 접속사가 이끄는 부사절의 현재 시제 동사는 주절 동사의 시제가 미래임을 파악하는 단서가 된다.

┌ 시간 부사절 접속사   ┌ 시간 부사절에서 미래(will find) 대신 쓰인 현재 시제 ┄→ 주절의 시제가 미래임을 알려주는 단서

As soon as we **find** a suitable place for the workshop, further details **will be** provided.
적절한 워크숍 장소를 찾는 데로 더 자세한 세부사항을 알려드리겠습니다.

┌ 조건 부사절에서 미래(will be made) 대신 쓰인 현재 시제
┄→ 주절의 시제가 미래임을 알려주는 단서   ┌ 조건 부사절 접속사

The lease with The Hawthorn Group **will be continued** **if** modifications to the existing offices **are** made.
기존 사무실에 대한 변경이 이루어진다면 Hawthorn 사와의 임대 계약이 지속될 것이다.

❸ 시간·조건 부사절이 미래 시점을 의미하면 미래 대신 현재 시제를 쓰나, 과거 시점을 의미하면 원래대로 과거 시제를 쓴다.

When the supervisor **attempted** to install the new software, she **encountered** a small problem.
감독관은 새 소프트웨어의 설치를 시도했을 때 작은 문제에 맞닥뜨렸다.

Practice

해설서 p.23 / ⏱ 제한 시간 6분

1. Next year, a refined version of GKM Motors' bestselling car model ------- in its spring advertising campaign.

(A) will introduce
(B) has been introduced
(C) will be introduced
(D) introduces

2. Production at Nelson Manufacturing was suspended while safety inspections -------.

(A) were being conducted
(B) to conduct
(C) will be conducted
(D) have conducted

3. Last year, Harington Computers' Quality Control Department ------- several new policies to improve production efficiency.

(A) implementation
(B) implements
(C) implemented
(D) implementing

4. If the construction director ------- the building plans, construction will begin on the new library next week.

(A) will approve
(B) approve
(C) will have approved
(D) approves

5. Cherub Bank will retain its current name even after it officially ------- with a rival company.

(A) will merge
(B) merges
(C) merge
(D) merged

6. 고난도 After we have reviewed the details of your contract, we ------- you to arrange a meeting.

(A) was contacting
(B) has contacted
(C) contact
(D) will contact

7. Luky Star Corporation ------- expanding its operation before it was named one of the best small businesses in the home appliance industry.

(A) has not considered
(B) was not considered
(C) will not consider
(D) had not considered

8. We are confident that your test drive of Beuve's new TXL 430 model next week ------- your expectations.

(A) has exceeded
(B) exceeding
(C) will exceed
(D) exceeded

9. Timberlake Golf Club ------- among the best golf clubs in New Zealand over the last five years.

(A) has ranked
(B) is ranking
(C) had ranked
(D) would rank

10. According to our customer service policy, the company ------- free repair service for a year at no additional cost.

(A) providing
(B) provides
(C) is provided
(D) has been provided

11. Accidents at the Gonyang Apartment construction site have been substantially reduced since the revised safety regulation procedures -------.

(A) have been implemented
(B) were implemented
(C) had implemented
(D) will be implementing

12. Mega Construction ------- gives free estimates for commercial renovation projects.

(A) routinely
(B) previously
(C) recently
(D) formerly

13. Poet Hakim Gomez ------- his new poem in last month's edition of *The Bostonian Review*.

(A) was presented
(B) present
(C) will present
(D) presented

14. By the time the Purchasing Department is ready to place another order, Startrack Office Supplies ------- a new price list.

(A) published
(B) publishing
(C) had published
(D) will have published

15. All candidates are asked to indicate which licenses they ------- before their interviews.

(A) had possessed
(B) possess
(C) possessing
(D) will possess

16. This is to remind everyone that our building ------- major construction work starting next week.

(A) to undergo
(B) will be undergoing
(C) undergoing
(D) would have undergone

17. The Vice President ------- the press conference last Thursday, but he had a scheduling conflict.

(A) can attend
(B) must have attended
(C) should attend
(D) would have attended

18. The researchers at the Davies Laboratory have ------- developed a medicine plaster comparable in quality to the best-selling brand in Europe.

(A) usually
(B) recently
(C) soon
(D) highly

19. Shanghai International Airlines ------- a press conference once the management has decided whether or not to merge with Hong Kong Air.

(A) is held
(B) hold
(C) will hold
(D) has held

20. The company is very pleased to announce that sales have significantly increased ------- the launch of its new model last April.

(A) after
(B) since
(C) for
(D) during

REVIEW TEST 02

1. Financial analysts ------- that the housing market will begin to improve after interest rates are cut.

   (A) predict
   (B) predicting
   (C) predictive
   (D) prediction

2. Those freight companies serving the national market must ------- to pick up and deliver anywhere in the country, anytime.

   (A) prepared
   (B) preparing
   (C) be prepared
   (D) being prepared

3. The musician's world tour ------- on hold for three days due to production delays.

   (A) is putting
   (B) has put
   (C) being put
   (D) has been put

4. Katarina Volgaskaya recently ------- positive reviews for her role in the film, *In Sight*.

   (A) will receive
   (B) received
   (C) is received
   (D) receives

5. The sudden decline in stock markets in South America ------- most investment firms.

   (A) surprising
   (B) surprise
   (C) have surprised
   (D) has surprised

6. Over the weekend, flights departing from L.A. ------- between 10 P.M. and 6 A.M. while the runway is being checked for maintenance needs.

   (A) will be suspended
   (B) was suspended
   (C) is suspending
   (D) to suspend

7. The Lafayette Art Association has asked that city council members ------- the closing of the public museum.

   (A) reconsider
   (B) to reconsider
   (C) reconsidering
   (D) reconsidered

8. SG announced it ------- its e-book reader and smartphone products, and may restructure its PC division.

   (A) discontinuing
   (B) will discontinue
   (C) to discontinue
   (D) have discontinued

9. Local business owners have been satisfied with the ------- rate of growth in sales over the past few years.

   (A) steadily
   (B) steady
   (C) steadies
   (D) steadiness

10. The conference fee ------- admittance to various lectures and networking events.

    (A) include
    (B) includes
    (C) is included
    (D) including

11. Boden Carpeting ------- a special sale next month to celebrate its 20th year in business.

(A) will be run
(B) have run
(C) ran
(D) will be running

12. Candidates who ------- need to inform the committee before September 25 if they do not wish to run for election.

(A) nominated
(B) will be nominating
(C) have been nominated
(D) have nominated

13. A dedicated social worker, Ms. Annan has worked ------- volunteers in a variety of age groups.

(A) with
(B) about
(C) from
(D) onto

14. ------- return the defective item with the enclosed form, and a replacement product will be delivered to your home address.

(A) By
(B) Just
(C) Toward
(D) Quite

15. Despite the accumulated evidence on climate change, ------- of the recommendations related to sustainable development have been implemented.

(A) any
(B) none
(C) whoever
(D) someone

16. Ms. Martin worked with a manager who believed strongly that he ------- the skills required to be a top-level leader.

(A) is mastering
(B) has mastered
(C) masters
(D) had mastered

17. It is imperative that computer passwords ------- confidential.

(A) keep
(B) were kept
(C) be kept
(D) had kept

18. Maria Fuentes will be taking over as Director of Customer Service ------- Gerald Monard retires next month.

(A) soon
(B) after
(C) until
(D) rather than

19. Many in the sector worry that the recent ------- could cause a wave of price cuts which could see smaller firms going out of business.

(A) discount
(B) discounts
(C) discounted
(D) discounters

20. A number of employees have complained that the noise from the construction has been ------- to their work.

(A) disruptive
(B) disruptions
(C) disrupt
(D) disrupted

동명사

「동사 + -ing」 형태로 문장에서 명사처럼 쓰이는 것을 동명사라 한다. 명사 역할을 하지만 본래 동사에서 비롯되었으므로 명사와 달리 목적어나 보어를 동반할 수 있으며, 부사의 수식을 받는다.

Tip!
토익에서는 동명사와 명사 중 하나를 선택하는 문제가 많이 나와. 전치사 중에 동명사와 함께 잘 쓰이는 「by / before / after + 동명사」 구조도 자주 등장하니 기억해 둬.

🗨 기본 개념 이해하기

1. 동명사의 명사 역할

주어	**Finding** a job isn't easy for many young people. 많은 젊은이들에게 직장을 구하는 일은 쉽지 않다.
타동사의 목적어	Ms. Meller is considering **buying** one of Goldwave's products. Ms. Meller는 Goldwave 제품 중 하나를 사는 것을 고려하고 있다.
전치사의 목적어	Jim will be responsible for **arranging** shifts for employees. Jim은 직원들의 교대 근무 일정을 짜는 일을 맡게 될 것이다.
보어	Byte Tech's main objective is **helping** you to grow your business. Byte 전자의 주된 목표는 당신이 사업을 성장시키는 일을 돕는 것입니다.

• 동명사는 명사 역할을 하여, 문장에서 주어, 목적어, 보어로 쓰일 수 있다.

2. 동명사의 동사 성격: 동명사의 의미상 주어

Aeroi Corp's scientists have been working on **developing** a vaccine for the disease.
Aeroi 사의 과학자들은 이 질병에 대한 백신을 개발하기 위해 노력해 왔다.
⋯→ 의미상의 주어: 문장의 주어와 일치해서 생략

The editors really appreciate **your informing** us of the errors. ⋯→ 의미상의 주어: 동명사 앞의 소유격
편집자들은 당신이 오류에 관해 알려주신 데 대해 정말 감사하고 있습니다.

• 동명사의 의미상 주어가 문장의 주어와 일치하거나 문맥 속에서 파악할 수 있는 경우, 별도로 표시하지 않는다. 동명사의 의미상 주어를 밝혀야 할 경우, 동명사 앞에 소유격의 형태로 의미상의 주어를 나타낸다.

3. 동명사의 동사 성격: 동명사의 태와 시제

능동형 (V-ing)	The company increased sales by **expanding** its market globally. 그 회사는 시장을 전 세계적으로 확대하여 매출을 상승시켰다.
수동형 (being p.p.)	Mr. Hampton has a good chance of **being promoted**. Mr. Hampton은 승진할 가능성이 크다.
완료형 (having p.p.)	Catherine got a reward for **having developed** a multifunctional printing process. Catherine은 다기능 인쇄 공정을 개발한 것에 대해 포상을 받았다.

• 문장의 본동사보다 이전에 일어난 일임을 밝히기 위해 동명사의 완료 형태를 쓰고, 의미상 주어와 수동 관계일 경우 동명사의 수동 형태를 쓴다.

핵심 문제 유형

전치사의 목적어 자리에 동명사를 선택하는 문제와 명사와 동명사를 구분하는 문제의 출제 비중이 가장 높다. 타동사의 목적어나 주어 자리에 사용되는 동명사와 동명사 관용 표현을 묻는 문제가 출제된다.

1. 동명사의 명사 역할과 동사 성격

Q1 **주어 역할**

[Assisting / Assist] customers promptly is how we keep them satisfied. [1]

타동사의 목적어 역할

The sales team recommends [enhancement / enhancing] service quality to attract more customers. [2]

전치사의 목적어 역할

The city set a goal of [reducing / reduction] the number of unemployed residents. [3]

보어 역할

The purpose of offering extra vacation days is [improvement / improving] productivity while reducing stress. [4]

>> **출제 포인트** ❶ 「동사 + -ing」 형태의 동명사는 명사 역할을 하며, 문장의 주어, 동사나 전치사의 목적어, 보어로 쓰이며 '~하는 것'으로 해석한다.

❷ 「동사 + -ing」 형태로 동명사와 동일한 형태인 현재분사는 형용사 역할을 하며 '~하는'으로 해석된다는 점에서 동명사와 다르다.

❸ 동명사가 주어로 쓰일 경우 단수 취급하며 단수 동사를 쓴다.

Q2 **동명사의 동사 성격: 의미상의 주어**

[You inform / Your informing] an associate of your hotel experience will help us improve our services. [1]

>> **출제 포인트** 동명사는 동사의 성격이 남아 있어 주어를 표현할 수 있다. 문장의 주어와 동명사의 주어가 다른 경우, 동명사의 의미상 주어(행위의 주체)는 동명사 앞에 소유격으로 나타낸다. 하지만, 문맥상 의미상 주어가 누구인지 분명하거나 일반인인 경우는 따로 표시하지 않는다.

Q3 동명사의 동사 성격: 태와 시제

Mr. Walker was given a bonus after **[having sold / being sold]** 11 cars in just one week. [1]

>> 출제 포인트 동명사는 동사의 성격이 남아 있어 태와 시제를 반영하여 나타낼 수 있다.

❶ 동명사의 태: 동명사와 의미상 주어가 수동 관계일 경우 수동형(being + p.p.)을 쓴다.

❷ 동명사의 시제: 동명사의 시제가 본동사보다 더 과거(이전)에 일어난 일을 나타낼 때 완료형(having + p.p.)을 쓴다.

The managing director proposed a newly designed environmental policy shortly after **being appointed** last month. ⋯→ '임명된 후에' 라는 의미의 수동 동명사
상무 이사는 지난달 임명된 직후 새롭게 짜여진 환경 정책을 제안했다.

The installation of security updates will prevent employees' computers from **being accessed** by unauthorized parties. ⋯→ '직원 컴퓨터들이 접속되는 것'이라는 의미의 수동 동명사
보안 업데이트의 설치는 직원들의 컴퓨터가 권한 없는 자들에 의해 접속되는 것을 예방해줄 것이다.

2. 동명사와 명사 구분

Q4 [동명사 vs. 명사] + 목적어 / 보어

The security department is in the process of **[establishing / establishment]** a new set of safety guidelines for the office. [1]

According to a recent report, **[demanding / demand]** for portable fans has increased by 50 percent this year. [2]

>> 출제 포인트 동명사는 동사의 성질이 남아 있기 때문에 뒤에 목적어나 보어를 취할 수 있으나, 명사는 목적어나 보어를 취할 수 없다. 즉, 동명사 뒤에 오는 구조는 자동사, 타동사와 같이 동사의 종류에 따라 목적어나 보어를 수반하는 동사 뒤의 구조와 동일하다.

+ check

1. Thank you for **[renewing / renewal]** your membership for another year.

2. A personal identification number is necessary for **[access / accessing]** to your account information.

Q5 **[부사 vs. 형용사] + 동명사**

Install the program after **[carefully / careful]** reviewing the instructions. [1]

[형용사 vs. 부사] + 명사

All employees must receive **[adequate / adequately]** training in the use of delicate equipment. [2]

관사 + 형용사 + [동명사 vs. 명사]

The contract will not be signed without the final **[approving / approval]** from the CEO. [3]

>> 출제 포인트 **❶** 명사는 형용사의 수식을 받고, 동명사는 부사의 수식을 받는다.

❷ 명사 앞에는 관사(a/an/the)가 올 수 있으나, 동명사 앞에는 관사가 올 수 없다.

❸ 「동사 + -ing」 형태로 되어 있어 얼핏 보기엔 동명사처럼 보이지만 관사나 형용사의 수식을 받을 수 있는 -ing 형태의 명사들에 유의해야 한다.

☑ -ing로 끝나는 명사

accounting	회계	boarding	탑승
advertising	광고업	catering	출장 연회 서비스
cleaning	청소	clothing	의류
dining	식사	funding	자금[재정]지원
housing	주택	mailing	우편물 발송
marketing	마케팅	writing	글쓰기
planning	계획 수립	processing	처리
restructuring	구조조정	screening	검열
seating	좌석 배치	spending	지출
staffing	직원 채용	ticketing	티켓 발급
training	훈련	understanding	이해
opening	공석, 개막, 개장		

+ check

1. Legislators were able to reach **[unanimous / unanimously]** agreement on the new policy.

2. Thanks to **[careful / carefully]** planning, the construction project will be finished under budget.

3. 동명사와 함께 쓰이는 표현

Q6 타동사 + [동명사 vs. to부정사]

Some board members suggested **[honoring / to honor]** the founder of the company at the annual reception. [1]

타동사 + [동명사 vs. 명사]

A pharmacist's duties include **[confirming / confirmation]** a patient's prescription with a doctor. [2]

>> 출제 포인트 ❶ 동명사를 목적어로 취하는 타동사

고려·제안	consider	고려하다	suggest	제안하다
	recommend	추천하다	include	포함하다
	enjoy	즐기다		
중단	stop	멈추다	quit	그만두다
	discontinue	중단하다	finish	마치다
회피	avoid	회피하다	mind	꺼려하다
	dislike	싫어하다	give up	포기하다
	postpone, delay	미루다	deny	부인하다

❷ 의미 변화 없이 to부정사와 동명사를 모두 목적어로 취하는 동사

begin, start	시작하다	prefer	선호하다
continue	지속하다	like, love	좋아하다

Q7 전치사 to + [동명사 vs. 동사원형]

Nex Innovation is committed to **[lowering / lower]** your monthly utility bills. [1]

The firm is looking forward to **[hiring / hire]** accountants with extensive experience. [2]

Guests should register at the front desk prior to **[attending / attend]** the lecture. [3]

>> 출제 포인트　명사나 동명사를 취하는 전치사 to와 동사원형을 취하는 to부정사의 to를 구분해야 한다.

☑ be + 형용사 + 전치사 to

be accustomed[used] to	~에 익숙하다
be committed[devoted, dedicated] to	~에 전념하다
be entitled to	~할 자격이 있다
be opposed to	~에 반대하다
be related to	~에 관련되다
be subject to	~에 영향받기 쉽다, ~에 달려 있다

☑ 동사 + 전치사 to

consent to	~에 동의하다	look forward to	~을 고대하다
contribute to	~에 기여하다	object to	~에 반대하다
lead to	~을 초래하다	respond/reply to	~에 대응하다

☑ 구 전치사

according to	~에 따라	prior to	~ 전에
in addition to	게다가		

Q8 동명사의 관용 표현

The company is having difficulty **[to attract / attracting]** overseas clients. [1]

The construction manager spent weeks **[to design / designing]** a plan to renovate the building. [2]

Should you experience any problems upon **[receiving / to receive]** your purchase, please call our customer service center at 555-3000. [3]

>> 출제 포인트   동명사의 관용 표현

be busy (in) -ing	~하느라 바쁘다
be capable of -ing	~할 수 있다
cannot help -ing	~하지 않을 수 없다
be worth -ing	~할 가치가 있다
feel like -ing	~하고 싶다
go -ing	~하러 가다
have difficulty[a hard time] -ing	~하는 데 어려움을 겪다
keep (on) -ing	계속해서 ~하다
on[upon] -ing	~하자마자
prevent[prohibit] A from -ing	A가 ~하는 것을 막다
refrain from -ing	~하는 것을 삼가다
spend 시간/돈 (in) -ing	~하는 데 시간/돈을 쓰다

Practice

1. Because the estimated cost was reasonable, the department decided to have the printer repaired instead of ------- a new one.

(A) purchase
(B) purchased
(C) purchasing
(D) purchases

2. Our president has considered ------- Ms. Myer as chief editor to succeed Mr. Jason, who is retiring next month.

(A) appointment
(B) to appoint
(C) appointed
(D) appointing

3. Employees must submit a vacation request form to receive official ------- for their time off.

(A) approval
(B) approved
(C) approve
(D) approving

4. By ------- displaying cultural artifacts in a modern setting, the curator of the Lenningrad Museum created a special exhibit.

(A) innovated
(B) innovational
(C) innovative
(D) innovatively

5. ------- shifts for employees is one of a manager's most important responsibilities.

(A) Arranges
(B) Arranging
(C) Arrangement
(D) Arrange

6. It would be better for Stylish Footwear to discontinue ------- running shoes and focus on hiking boots instead.

(A) produce
(B) would produce
(C) producing
(D) to produce

7. Extreme Sportswear's R&D team has been working on ------- a new fabric which can withstand extreme temperatures.

(A) development
(B) developed
(C) developing
(D) to develop

8. High Point Ferry management reserves the legal right to change departure times without ------- passengers in advance.

(A) notifies
(B) notified
(C) notifying
(D) notification

9. The largest bus company in Manila has decided to reduce its fares as a way of ------- customers.

(A) attractive
(B) attraction
(C) attracts
(D) attracting

10. Daily Stock Exchange Broadcasting is dedicated to ------- accurate investment information.

(A) providing
(B) provide
(C) provided
(D) provision

11. Please keep in mind that all outdoor
고난도 activities are subject to ------- without
notice.

(A) cancellation
(B) canceling
(C) canceled
(D) cancel

12. Indigo Technologies offers innovative
software that is ------- of maximizing an
organization's efficiency.

(A) able
(B) capable
(C) possible
(D) responsible

13. The Daubert Center can be most quickly
고난도 reached ------- taking subway line 5.

(A) into
(B) to
(C) by
(D) at

14. Upon ------- the notebook, the expert
found that the protective seal had been
broken.

(A) examining
(B) examination
(C) examine
(D) examined

15. ------- company policies has been the
Legal Department's main responsibility for
the last two months.

(A) Updates
(B) Updated
(C) Updating
(D) Update

16. Speed Lending Services has provisionally
고난도 approved your loan application, but we
await ------- of the items listed in this
document.

(A) receiving
(B) to receive
(C) receipt
(D) recipient

17. Staff members at Greenbaum General
Hospital are ------- to satisfying their
patients' needs.

(A) expressed
(B) scheduled
(C) committed
(D) designed

18. The consultant offered some suggestions
for ------- introducing change in the office.

(A) succeeding
(B) successful
(C) successfully
(D) succeed

19. Jane's Books has a good reputation for
고난도 being very ------- to its customers, so it
has been named the best bookstore in
Boston.

(A) attention
(B) attentive
(C) attentively
(D) attentiveness

20. Before ------- to rent an apartment in
고난도 Greenville, Mr. Weber asked his coworkers
about the area.

(A) decide
(B) decision
(C) decides
(D) deciding

to부정사

「to + 동사원형」 형태로 쓰이는 to부정사는 동사를 명사, 형용사, 부사로 전환하여 문장에서 다양하게 쓰인다.

Tip! to부정사 문제 중 가장 많이 출제되는 유형은 바로 목적을 나타내는 「(in order) to부정사」야. 꼭 기억해두자!

기본 개념 이해하기

1. to부정사의 명사, 형용사, 부사 역할

명사 역할	**To maintain** positive relations with Heron Spa's guests is essential for the position. ⋯→ 주어 Heron Spa의 손님들과 긍정적인 관계를 유지하는 것은 이 직책에 필수적이다. We sincerely hope **to hear** from you in the near future. ⋯→ 타동사의 목적어 가까운 시일 내에 당신으로부터 소식을 듣기를 진심으로 바랍니다. Her job is **to supervise** manufacturing and packaging. ⋯→ 주격 보어 그녀의 일은 제조와 포장을 감독하는 것이다. Team members asked the director **to extend** the deadline. ⋯→ 목적격 보어 팀원들은 부장에게 마감일을 연장해 달라고 요청했다.
형용사 역할	Mr. Brown has the authority **to choose** the raw material supplier. ⋯→ 명사 수식 Mr. Brown은 원자재 공급처를 선택할 권한이 있다.
부사 역할	Please send us a deposit of $50 by Friday **to secure** your reservation. ⋯→ 동사 수식 예약을 확보하기 위해 금요일까지 50달러의 보증금을 보내 주십시오. We are happy **to provide** you with a replacement at no cost. ⋯→ 형용사 수식 우리는 당신에게 무료로 대체품을 제공해드리게 되어 기쁩니다.

2. to부정사의 동사 성격: 의미상 주어

Ms. Davis would love **to visit** our branch in Paris next time. ⋯→ 의미상의 주어: 문장의 주어와 일치해서 생략
Ms. Davis는 다음에 파리에 있는 우리 지점을 방문하고 싶어할 것이다.

It is necessary **(for people) to exercise** regularly. ⋯→ 의미상의 주어: 일반인이므로 생략
(사람들은) 규칙적으로 운동할 필요가 있다.

It is necessary **for her to exercise** regularly. ⋯→ 의미상의 주어: for her
그녀는 규칙적으로 운동할 필요가 있다.

- to부정사의 의미상 주어가 문장의 주어와 일치하거나, 일반인인 경우 별도로 표시하지 않는다.
- to부정사의 의미상 주어를 밝혀야 할 경우, to부정사 앞에 「for + 목적격」 형태로 의미상의 주어를 나타낸다.

3. to부정사의 동사 성격: 태와 시제

능동형 (to 동사원형)	It is necessary **to decline** the invitation respectfully in advance. 미리 초대를 정중하게 거절할 필요가 있다.
수동형 (to be + p.p.)	The schedule for the seminar is **to be distributed**. 세미나 일정이 배포될 예정이다.
완료형 (to have + p.p.)	It was inconvenient for the passengers **to have waited** for so long. 승객들은 그렇게 오래 기다리는 것이 불편했다.

- 문장의 본동사보다 이전에 일어난 일임을 밝히기 위해 to부정사의 완료 형태를 쓰고, 의미상 주어와 수동 관계일 경우 to부정사의 수동 형태를 쓴다.

목적을 나타내는 부사적 용법의 to부정사 관련 문제의 출제 비중이 가장 높다. 타동사의 목적어나 목적격 보어 자리에 사용되는 to부정사, 의미상의 주어, 부정사 관용 표현을 묻는 문제가 출제된다.

해설서 p.29

1. to부정사의 특징

Q1

2형식 자동사의 to부정사 + [형용사 vs. 부사]

Mr. McConnell suggested focusing on developing additional products to remain **[competitive / competitively]**. [1]

3형식 타동사의 to부정사 + [명사 vs. 부사]

The new laptop prototype was only shown to senior management to ensure **[confidentiality / confidentially]**. [2]

>> **출제 포인트** 자동사의 to부정사 뒤에는 보어나 부사가 올 수 있으며, 타동사의 능동형 to부정사 뒤에는 목적어가 온다. 즉, to부정사 뒤에 오는 문장 구조는 자동사, 타동사와 같이 동사의 종류에 따라 목적어나 보어를 수반하는 동사 뒤의 구조와 동일하다.

Q2

to부정사의 동사 성격: 의미상의 주어

It is important **[for / that]** employees to respond promptly to customer complaints. [1]

>> **출제 포인트** to부정사는 동사의 성격이 남아 있어 주어를 표현할 수 있다. 문장의 주어와 to부정사의 주어가 다른 경우, to부정사의 의미상 주어(행위의 주체)는 to부정사 앞에 「for + 명사」나 「for + 대명사의 목적격」으로 나타낸다. 하지만, to부정사의 의미상 주어가 문장의 주어와 일치하거나, 일반인인 경우는 따로 표시하지 않는다.

Q3 **to부정사의 동사 성격: 태와 시제**

The articles for the magazine need **[to have reviewed / to be reviewed]** by Friday. [1]

In order for the new flooring to **[install / be installed]**, the office will close on Tuesday. [2]

>> 출제 포인트 동사의 성격이 남아 있는 to부정사는 태와 시제를 반영하여 표현할 수 있다.

❶ to부정사의 태: to부정사가 의미상 주어와 수동의 의미를 나타낼 때, 수동태 「to be + p.p.」로 표현한다.

❷ to부정사의 시제: to부정사가 주절보다 한 시제 앞선 일을 나타낼 때, 완료형 「to have + p.p.」로 표현한다.

2. to부정사의 명사 역할

Q4 **주어 자리: [동사원형 vs. to부정사] ~ + 동사**

[Submit / To submit] a marketing proposal by tomorrow is impossible. [1]

가주어 it ~ 진주어 to부정사 구문: [it / there] + be + 형용사 + to부정사

[It / There] is necessary to work collaboratively with colleagues in order to increase productivity. [2]

>> 출제 포인트 ❶ to부정사가 명사적 용법으로 쓰일 때는 '~하는 것'으로 해석되고, 문장의 주어, 목적어, 보어 역할을 한다.

❷ 가주어 it/진주어 to부정사: to부정사가 주어 역할을 할 때 가주어 it을 쓰고, 진주어인 to부정사를 뒤로 보내는 경우가 일반적이다.

❸ 가목적어 it/진목적어 to부정사: to부정사가 5형식 동사[consider, make, find, think 등]의 목적어 역할을 할 때는 가목적어 it을 쓰고 진목적어인 to부정사를 뒤로 보낸다.

┌ 가목적어 it   ┌ 의미상의 주어   ┌ 진목적어 to부정사

The sales manager considers **it** important **for** employees **to learn** to treat customers with respect.

영업부장은 직원들이 고객들을 공손히 대하는 법을 배우는 것이 중요하다고 생각한다.

Q5 보어 자리: be동사 + [과거분사 vs. to부정사]

The goal of the Customer Service Department is **[resolved / to resolve]** all customer complaints in a timely manner. [1]

>> 출제 포인트 be동사 뒤에 to부정사가 오는 경우 다양한 의미를 갖는다.

> **• ~하는 것이다**
> The purpose of this training **is to help** employees learn company regulations.
> 이 교육의 목적은 직원 여러분이 회사 규정을 알도록 도와드리는 것입니다.
>
> **• ~할 것이다 (예정)**
> The construction **is to begin** on April 1 and **to be** finished by August 1.
> 공사는 4월 1일에 시작해서 8월 1일에 마무리될 예정이다.
>
> **• ~해야 한다 (의무)**
> The total amount of the bill **is to be** paid by the end of this month.
> 청구서의 총액은 월말까지 지불되어야 합니다.

Q6 목적어 자리: 타동사 + [to부정사 vs. 동명사]

Should your client wish **[revising / to revise]** their order, let me know before the end of the day. [1]

The design team has been working overtime since the supervisor **[avoided / refused]** to extend the deadline. [2]

>> 출제 포인트 to부정사를 목적어로 취하는 동사

희망	want, wish, hope	바라다	would like	~하고 싶다
의지	intend aim plan	의도하다 목표로 하다 계획하다	try promise, pledge	~하려고 노력하다 약속하다
결정	decide refuse	결정하다 거절하다	choose	선택하다
부정	hesitate	망설이다	fail	하지 못하다
기타	need manage	필요로 하다 그럭저럭 ~하다	afford	여유가 있다

Q7 **5형식 동사 + 목적어 + [to부정사 vs. 동명사]**

The urgent project deadline will not allow Ms. Liou to **[attending / attend]** the conference. [1]

Employees are reminded **[to turn off / turning off]** their desktop computers before leaving the office. [2]

help + 목적어 + [동사원형 vs. 동사]

Company workshops help employees **[strengthen / would strengthen]** working relationships. [3]

>> 출제 포인트

❶ to부정사를 목적격 보어로 취하는 동사의 능동태: '누가 ~하도록 ...하다'라는 의미를 갖는 5형식 동사가 능동태로 쓰일 때, 목적격 보어로 to부정사를 취한다.

☑ to부정사를 목적격 보어로 취하는 동사

요청	ask	요청하다	invite	요청하다	
	request	요청하다	require	요구하다	
권장·제안	encourage	권장하다	urge	촉구하다	**목적어 + to부정사**
	persuade	설득시키다	advise	충고하다	~가 ~하도록
	convince	납득시키다	remind	상기시키다	
지시·강요	instruct	지시하다	force	강요하다	
	obligate	강요하다			
기타	enable	가능하게 하다	expect	기대하다	
	allow	허락하다	cause	야기하다	

❷ 위에 열거한 to부정사를 목적격 보어로 취하는 동사가 뒤에 목적어 없이 to부정사를 바로 취하면, '목적어 + be p.p. + to부정사'의 수동태로 파악한다.

All staff members **are encouraged to** get in touch with the personnel office whenever they have problems with their coworkers.
모든 직원들은 동료간에 문제가 생길 때는 언제든지 인사과에 연락하도록 권장된다.

❸ 「help + 목적어 + (to)부정사」: '누가 ~하는 것을 돕다'라는 의미를 갖는 help는 목적격보어 자리에 원형부정사와 to부정사를 모두 쓸 수 있다.

This course will **help** you **(to) develop** the skills to negotiate successfully.
이 수업은 여러분이 성공적인 협상의 기술을 개발하도록 도와드릴 것입니다.

> **cf** 「help + (to) 동사원형」: help는 '~하는 것을 돕다'는 의미로 목적어 없이 원형부정사나 to부정사를 바로 취하는 구조로도 자주 쓰인다.
>
> Flexible work hours will **help (to) reduce** traffic congestion, particularly in metropolitan areas.
> 탄력근무제는 특히 대도시 지역에서 교통혼잡을 감소시키는 데 도움이 될 것이다.

1. The government urged the National Lottery **[withdraw / to withdraw]** their exaggerated advertisement.

2. Mr. Pak asked his assistant **[to type / was typing]** the meeting minutes.

3. All employees working in the assembly area will be required **[to take / taking]** a course on machine operation.

3. to부정사의 형용사 역할

Q8 특정 명사 + to부정사: the right / effort + [to부정사 vs. 분사]

Pinnacle Airlines reserves the right **[to refuse / refusing]** boarding of any passenger without valid identification. [1]

Sales associates will make an effort **[to respond / responding]** to customers' inquiries within 24 hours. [2]

>> 출제 포인트   to부정사는 특정 명사 뒤에서 '(~해야) 할, ~할 수 있는, ~하기 위한"의 의미로 명사를 수식하는 형용사 역할을 한다. to부정사의 수식을 받는 특정 명사에 유의해야 한다.

✔ **to부정사의 수식을 받는 명사**

effort	노력	right	권리
opportunity, chance	기회	ability	능력
time	시간	authority	권한
way	방법	means	수단
plan	계획	need	필요
decision	결정	attempt	시도
failure	~하지 못함	proposal	제안서

4. to부정사의 부사 역할

Q9 목적을 나타내는 to부정사

To + [동사원형 vs. 동명사]~, 주어 + 동사

To **[accommodate / accommodating]** a wide range of schedules, we offer a variety of times and dates for the workshop. [1]

[For vs. To] + 동사원형~, 주어 + 동사

[For / To] update your contact information, log on to your account. [2]

[분사구문 vs. to부정사] ~, 주어 + 동사

[Being / To be] eligible for the sales manager position, candidates must have a university degree in marketing. [3]

>> 출제 포인트

❶ to부정사의 부사 역할 중 '～하기 위해서'라는 의미의 목적을 나타내는 to부정사는 문장 맨 앞, 중간, 맨 뒤 등 다양한 위치에 올 수 있다. 목적의 의미를 강조할 때 「in order to부정사」나 「so as to부정사」 형태로 쓸 수 있다.

✓ 목적을 나타내는 to부정사

in order[so as] to 동사원형 ~, S + V	～하기 위하여, S가 V한다

❷ 분사구문도 목적을 나타내는 to부정사와 동일하게 문장 앞에 위치할 수 있다. 따라서, 문맥을 통해 시간, 조건, 양보, 이유 등의 의미를 나타내는 분사구문인지, 목적의 의미를 나타내는 to부정사인지 구분할 수 있어야 한다.

✓ 분사구문

V-ing/p.p. ~, S + V	～하는 때에/～이라면/～임에도 불구하고/～때문에, S가 V한다

+ check

1. [To apply / Apply] for this opening, applicants should have more than three years of experience.

2. [In order to / As to] complete construction of the new shopping center on time, the project director decided to hire 10 additional workers.

3. All proceeds from the charity event will be used [for / to] the renovation of the local medical center.

4. [Being / To be] a general manager, Mr. Simpson is in charge of the overall branch operations.

Q10 형용사 + [to부정사 vs. 동사]

Leisure Bistro is pleased **[announce / to announce]** the opening of a new location. [1]

to부정사의 관용 표현

During its tour of Chicago, the delegation from the Ministry of Education is **[likable / likely]** to visit the city's distinguished educational centers. [2]

It is too costly **[to store / store]** old files in off-site warehouses. [3]

The new hiking shoes are durable **[enough / well]** to withstand harsh weather conditions. [4]

>> **출제 포인트**   형용사와 함께 쓰이는 to부정사의 관용 표현은 형용사 뒤의 동사 형태를 묻거나 어휘 문제로 출제된다.

✅ **be + 형용사 + to부정사**

be able/unable to부정사	~할 수 있다/없다 **cf** be capable of ~을 할 수 있다
be about to부정사	막 ~하려고 하다
be designed[intended] to부정사	~하도록 의도되다
be eager to부정사	~하기를 열망하다
be eligible to부정사	~할 자격이 있다 **cf** be eligible for + 명사 ~에 대해 자격이 있다
be expected to부정사	~할 것이 예상되다
be hesitant to부정사	~하는 것을 망설이다
be likely[liable, apt] to부정사	~할 가능성이 있다(할 것 같다)
be pleased[delighted] to부정사	~하게 되어 기쁘다
be ready to부정사	~할 준비가 되다
be reluctant to부정사	~하기를 꺼리다
be scheduled[due] to부정사	~할 예정이다 **cf** be scheduled for + 시점 ~로 예정되어 있다
be sure[certain] to부정사	반드시 ~하다
be supposed to부정사	~하기로 예정되어 있다
be willing to부정사	기꺼이 ~하다
feel free to부정사	편하게[마음껏] ~하다

✅ **too / enough와 함께 쓰이는 to부정사**

too + 형용사/부사 + to부정사	너무 ~해서 …할 수 없다
형용사/부사 + enough + to부정사	~하기에 충분히 …하다

Practice

1. ------- moving expenses, you will need certain information on how to get packing boxes and cushioning materials to prevent breakage.

   (A) Reduces
   (B) To be reduced
   (C) To reduce
   (D) Has reduced

2. Anchor Apparel is offering 30 to 50 percent discounts on all winter clothing to ------- room for the new spring stock.

   (A) making
   (B) make
   (C) makes
   (D) be made

3. The Peachtree Community Center has an auditorium which is large enough ------- 200 people.

   (A) seat
   (B) to seat
   (C) seated
   (D) seating

4. Dongyang Bank is adopting a new online banking system ------- its customer satisfaction.

   (A) improve
   (B) will improve
   (C) is improving
   (D) to improve

5. The purpose of the board meeting ------- a successor to retiring president Rio Hong.

   (A) had chosen
   (B) is to choose
   (C) choosing
   (D) choose

6. 고난도 Once the employees have completed the company's largest project successfully, they will be offered an opportunity ------- for a promotion.

   (A) considering
   (B) to consider
   (C) to be considered
   (D) considers

7. In compliance with the new regulations, Web site administrators are unable ------- photos of members without their consent.

   (A) post
   (B) posted
   (C) posting
   (D) to post

8. 고난도 Walters Commercial Bank's security software has been updated ------- address security concerns.

   (A) when
   (B) in order to
   (C) during
   (D) in front of

9. ------- better serve our customers, Bali Cleaning Service will relocate to a larger retail space.

   (A) In order to
   (B) Due to
   (C) With regard to
   (D) Owing to

10. 고난도 In order ------- the motor to function properly, all settings must be reset after a loss of power.

    (A) to
    (B) of
    (C) with
    (D) for

11. The ferry service in Bangkok is a convenient way for people ------- since the city experiences serious traffic congestion.

(A) commute
(B) commuted
(C) to commute
(D) commutes

12. Proceeds will help finance the construction of the new library, which is scheduled ------- on April 28.

(A) beginning
(B) to begin
(C) begin
(D) begun

13. Ashwood Hotel invites everyone who has joined the fitness center ------- tomorrow's new-member orientation.

(A) to attend
(B) attended
(C) to be attended
(D) be attending

14. Technicians are advised ------- with all of the laboratory's safety regulations.

(A) compliances
(B) complies
(C) to comply
(D) complying

15. Many economists predict that Free Trade Agreements will help Korean automakers ------- their market share in Europe and America.

(A) expand
(B) expanded
(C) expands
(D) expansion

16. Mr. Hansen said he was about ------- when his friend telephoned him.

(A) to leave
(B) leaving
(C) leave
(D) left

17. Even though all drivers are ------- to obey the rules of the road, many drivers ignore them and cause accidents.

(A) obligated
(B) insisted
(C) provided
(D) allowed

18. 고난도 Tenants who ------- to vacate the property before the lease expires must provide written notification of their plans.

(A) consider
(B) suggest
(C) plan
(D) preview

19. 고난도 ------- change your mailing address, click the personal information button at the top of the screen.

(A) For
(B) Across
(C) With
(D) To

20. 고난도 ------- awareness of environmental issues, Jack Milton is leading a nationwide campaign.

(A) To promote
(B) For the promotion
(C) By promoting
(D) As a promotion

분사

분사에는 「동사 + -ing」 형태의 현재분사와 「동사 + -ed」 형태의 과거분사가 있다. 분사는 동사를 형용사로 변형시킨 것으로, 형용사와 마찬가지로 명사를 수식하거나 주어나 목적어를 보충 설명하는 보어 역할을 한다.

> **Tip!** 명사를 수식하는 분사는 명사의 앞뒤에 모두 올 수 있어. 분사가 수식하는 명사를 정확히 파악해서 해석을 통해 정답을 고르는 것이 좋아.

🗨 기본 개념 이해하기

1. 분사의 형태: 현재분사와 과거분사

	형태	의미
현재분사 (V-ing)	동사 + -ing	능동: '~하는', '~하고 있는'
과거분사 (p.p.)	동사 + -ed	수동: '~된', '~되는'

• 「동사 + -ing」 형태의 현재분사는 '~하는 것'이란 의미를 갖는 동명사와 형태가 동일하다.

2. 감정을 나타내는 동사의 분사

감정 동사의 현재분사 '(사람을) ~하게 만드는'	amazing news boring movie exciting game embarrassing result	놀라게 만드는 소식 지루하게 만드는 영화 흥미로운 경기 당황스러운 결과
감정 동사의 과거분사 '~하게 된(사람들)'	amazed woman bored student excited spectator embarrassed counselor	놀란 여성 지루해진 학생 흥분한 관객 당황한 상담사

3. 분사구문

능동 분사구문	Missing her flight, she went to the ticketing counter to rebook it. 비행기를 놓치자, 그녀는 다시 예약하러 발권 카운터로 갔다.
수동 분사구문	Submitted too late, the proposal could not be accepted. 너무 늦게 제출된 탓에, 그 제안은 받아들여질 수 없었다.

• 「접속사 + 주어 + 동사」 형태의 부사절에서, 「접속사 + 주어」를 생략한 후 동사를 분사로 전환하여 간결하게 표현한 것을 분사구문이라 한다. 이때 현재분사는 능동·진행의 의미를, 과거분사는 수동의 의미를 갖는다.

명사의 앞이나 뒤에서 명사를 수식하는 형용사 자리에 알맞은 분사의 형태를 선택하는 문제의 출제 비중이 가장 높다. 난이도가 높은 문장 전체를 수식하는 분사구문은 상대적으로 출제 비중이 떨어지므로 기본적인 형태에 집중한다.

해설서 p.32

1. 분사의 종류와 역할

Q1 명사 앞에서 수식하는 분사: 관사/소유격 + [현재분사 vs. 과거분사] + 명사

Please submit a **[revising / revised]** copy of the report by tomorrow. [1]

명사 뒤에서 수식하는 분사: 명사 + [현재분사 vs. 과거분사]

A consumer survey **[performing / performed]** by Best Reviews shows that customers care about energy efficiency when they choose home appliances. [2]

Please submit documentation **[verifies / verifying]** your eligibility for the position. [3]

>> **출제 포인트** ❶ **분사의 종류와 구별:** 동사-ing(현재분사)와 동사-ed(과거분사)가 분사의 기본 형태이다. 분사와 수식받는 명사의 의미상 관계가 능동이나 진행('~하는')의 의미이면 현재분사를, 수동이나 완료('~된')의 의미이면 과거분사를 쓴다.

❷ **분사의 역할:** 형용사 역할을 하는 분사는 명사의 앞뒤에서 명사를 수식하거나, 주격/목적격 보어로 쓰인다.

+ check

1. Every summer, Roller Air sells travel packages at **[reduce / reduced]** rates.

2. Both firms must approve all **[proposing / proposed]** changes to the merger agreement.

3. Paylessforit.co.uk, a renowned Web site **[helping / helped]** people make hotel reservations, has attracted more than two million members.

4. All employees must attend the seminar **[scheduling / scheduled]** for March 1.

Q2 주격 보어로 쓰이는 분사: 주어 + 2형식 동사 + [현재분사 vs. 과거분사]

The proposal to renovate the cafeteria remains **[unchanging / unchanged]**. [1]

목적격 보어로 쓰이는 분사: 5형식 동사 + 목적어 + [현재분사 vs. 과거분사]

We need to keep our customers **[informing / informed]** of new products. [2]

>> 출제 포인트 분사는 주어나 목적어로 쓰인 명사를 서술하는 주격/목적격 보어로 쓰인다.

❶ **주격 보어로 쓰이는 분사:** 주어와 주격 보어의 의미상 관계가 능동이면 현재분사, 수동이면 과거분사를 쓴다.

> 주어 + 2형식 동사 [be, become, remain, seem, appear, prove] + -ing('~하는')/p.p.('~된')

❷ **목적격 보어로 쓰이는 분사:** 목적어와 목적격 보어의 의미상 관계가 능동이면 현재분사, 수동이면 과거분사를 쓴다.

> 주어 + 5형식 동사 [keep, make, find, leave] + 목적어 + -ing('~하는')/p.p.('~된')

2. 유의해야 할 분사

Q3 특정 형태의 분사형 형용사

Due to the **[grown / growing]** concerns about financial difficulties in Europe, the Dow Jones Index fell 300 points yesterday. [1]

We need to recruit more **[experiencing / experienced]** employees for this project. [2]

>> 출제 포인트 분사와 수식받는 명사의 의미상 관계에 따라 현재분사와 과거분사를 구별해야 하나, 현재분사나 과거분사 중 하나의 형태만을 취하여 형용사로 굳어진 특정 분사형 형용사들에 유의해야 한다.

❶ 현재분사형 형용사

challenging task	힘든 과제
promising candidate	유망한 후보자
demanding supervisor / test	까다로운 상사 / 부담이 큰[힘든] 시험
leading supplier	선도적인 납품 업체
lasting impression	지속되는 인상
missing luggage	분실된 짐
existing facility	기존 시설
opposing point of view	대립되는 견해
remaining paperwork	남아 있는 서류 작업
growing[increasing] demand	증가하는 수요
outstanding medical professional	뛰어난 의학 전문가
mounting pressure	증가하는 압력
rewarding career	보람 있는 직업
preceding / following year	지난 / 다음 해
upcoming merger	다가오는[곧 있을] 합병
surrounding area	주변 지역
ongoing maintenance	진행 중인 유지 보수
on a rotating basis	돌아가며
opening remarks	개회사
presiding officer	사회자
closing speech	폐회사
entertaining film	재미있는 영화

❷ 과거분사형 형용사

qualified / motivated / skilled / talented / experienced / dedicated[devoted] employee	자격을 갖춘 / 동기가 부여된 / 숙련된 / 재능이 있는 / 경험이 있는 / 헌신적인 직원
accomplished / renowned / distinguished sculptor	기량이 뛰어난 / 유명한 / 저명한 조각가
complicated instructions	복잡한 설명서
sophisticated new equipment	정교한[세련된] 새로운 장비
detailed information	상세한 정보
customized program	맞춤형 프로그램
preferred means	선호되는 수단
limited period	제한된 기간
enclosed brochure	동봉된 안내 책자
attached document	첨부된 문서
written permission / consent	서면 허가 / 동의
completed form	작성된 양식
damaged goods	파손된 제품
informed decision	심사숙고한[현명한] 결정
authorized service provider	인증[허가]받은 서비스 제공업체

1. Customers have said that our user manuals are overly **[complicating / complicated]**.

2. Although this year's sales at Best Choice have decreased dramatically, it is still a **[leading / led]** company in the industry.

3. Employees complained that the current workload is too **[demanding / demanded]** for them.

4. The employees at Mason, Inc. are asked to organize staff meetings on a **[rotating / rotated]** basis.

5. The gallery will feature paintings by the **[accomplishing / accomplished]** artist, Olivia Chang.

Q4 감정 동사의 [현재분사 vs. 과거분사]

Based on the **[overwhelming / overwhelmed]** number of early registrations, we anticipate a record number of conference attendees. [1]

The CEO found the presentation rather **[disappointing / disappointed]**, contrary to expectations. [2]

>> 출제 포인트   감정을 유발하는 의미를 가진 타동사가 형용사로 전환되어 분사로 쓰일 경우, 감정을 일으키는 원인 (주로 사물 명사)을 수식하면 현재분사를, 감정을 경험하고 느끼는 대상(주로 사람 명사)을 수식하면 과 거분사를 쓴다.

✔ 감정 유발 타동사

interest	흥미를 끌다	excite	흥미진진하게 만들다
thrill	열광시키다	please	기쁘게 하다
fascinate	매혹시키다	attract	매료시키다
impress	깊은 인상을 주다	satisfy	만족시키다
overwhelm	압도하다	encourage	격려하다
exhaust, tire	지치게 하다	distract	산만하게 하다
disappoint	실망시키다	annoy	짜증나게 하다
worry	걱정시키다	disturb	불안하게 하다
alarm, amaze, surprise	놀라게 하다	frustrate, discourage, depress	좌절시키다
embarrass, bewilder, confuse	당황하게 하다		

1. After 10 years as a market researcher at Vectra Motorcycles, Ms. Seiko will be leaving her position to pursue an **[exciting / excited]** career in consulting.

2. The members of the Marketing Department were **[disappointing / disappointed]** with the first-quarter sales.

3. 분사구문

Q5 [현재분사 vs. 과거분사], S + V

[Preferring / Preferred] by young customers, our products have considerable market share. [1]

[Considered / Having considered] every proposal, the CEO decided to hire Arch-Shoes. [2]

S + V, [현재분사 vs. 과거분사]

Bexter, Inc. announced that it would acquire Max Co. next year, **[confirming / confirmed]** rumors of its overseas expansion plans. [3]

>> **출제 포인트**

❶ **분사구문의 개념:** 「접속사 + 주어 + 동사」로 되어 있는 부사절을 「접속사 + 주어(주절의 주어와 같을 경우)」를 생략한 후, 동사를 분사로 전환하여 간결하게 표현한 것을 분사구문이라 한다. 분사구문은 주절의 앞 또는 뒤에 위치한다.

❷ **분사구문의 태:** 분사구문에서 분사는 주절의 주어와 의미상 관계가 능동이면 현재분사를, 수동이면 과거분사를 쓴다.

❸ **분사구문의 시제:** 주절의 시제보다 분사구문의 내용이 먼저 일어난 경우, 능동은 「having p.p.」 수동은 「having been p.p.」를 쓴다.

☑ **분사구문의 형태**

V-ing ~	주절의 주어와 능동 관계: '~하는' 주어	
p.p. ~	주절의 주어와 수동 관계: '~된' 주어	
Having p.p. ~	주절의 주어와 능동 관계이며 주절의 시제보다 먼저 일어난 경우: '~하고 난 후에'	, S + V
Having been p.p. ~	주절의 주어와 수동 관계이며 주절의 시제보다 먼저 일어난 경우: '~된 후에'	

❹ 주절 뒤에 분사구문이 위치하는 경우, 주절의 주어와 의미상 능동관계인 현재분사 형태의 분사구문이 일반적이며 이때 현재분사는 '그래서 ~하다, ~하면서'로 해석한다.

S + V ~, V-ing	그래서 ~하다, ~하면서

+check

1. **[Employing / Employed]** more than 3,000 people worldwide, Clarina, Inc. is a leader in the cosmetics industry.

2. We now offer more options, **[allowing / allowed]** users to customize their phone plans.

Practice

1. ------- most Latin American regions, Suncor Natural Gas announced on Wednesday that it had sold some of its northern branches.

(A) Serving
(B) Will be serving
(C) May have serving
(D) Serves

2. The mobile phone is the ------- means of communication for sales representatives who travel extensively.

(A) prefer
(B) preference
(C) preferred
(D) preferring

3. The enclosed brochure specifies the services ------- by Rapid Shipping, and I have highlighted in green those which you inquired about.

(A) provide
(B) providing
(C) provided
(D) are provided

4. In his keynote speech, Mr. Bernson described his ------- path to becoming a scholar.

(A) challenges
(B) challenging
(C) challenge
(D) challenger

5. The magazine's editor in chief, Mr. Barnett, regularly meets with writers to provide ------- feedback on their articles.

(A) detailed
(B) detail
(C) to detail
(D) details

6. In a ------- interview, renowned violinist Hanna Jang spoke about her musical training during her childhood.

(A) fascinating
(B) fascinate
(C) fascination
(D) fascinated

7. Anyone ------- to volunteer to give rides to coworkers will be reimbursed for overtime and fuel expenses.

(A) wishes
(B) wishing
(C) wished
(D) wish

8. ------- in the early 19th century, the old warehouses were converted into apartment buildings when the port closed.

(A) Built
(B) Building
(C) Been built
(D) Having built

9. The airport's food court is open around the clock, ------- that travelers have the dining service no matter when their flight arrives.

(A) ensure
(B) ensuring
(C) ensured
(D) was ensured

10. Information about mandatory employee training sessions is located on page three of the ------- contract.

(A) enclose
(B) enclosing
(C) enclosed
(D) encloses

11. Mike Ritter has starred in several of the most ------- adventure films of the past twenty years.

(A) thrilling
(B) thrilled
(C) thrill
(D) thriller

12. SF University is granting an ------- deadline to those applicants experiencing technical difficulties with the online application system.

(A) extend
(B) extends
(C) extensive
(D) extended

13. Parking spaces ------- with yellow crosses
고난도 are reserved for patients who are visiting the clinic.

(A) marking
(B) marked
(C) that mark
(D) are marked

14. The Ferguson Health Foundation
고난도 yesterday celebrated its 25th anniversary with a ceremony ------- its founder, Jeremy Ferguson.

(A) honor
(B) honors
(C) honored
(D) honoring

15. The board of directors approved the revised plans, ------- the first of three construction phases for the sports complex to begin in August.

(A) allowing
(B) allow
(C) were allowed
(D) allowed

16. The Human Resources Department of Intec Combo has interviewed more than 100 applicants ------- in the advertised position.

(A) interested
(B) interest
(C) interesting
(D) interests

17. Zhang Education Group, an ------- Taiwan-based company, provides its foreign employees with housing assistance.

(A) establishes
(B) establish
(C) establishing
(D) established

18. The Mino Corporation's finance committee
고난도 has released a formal memo ------- its goals for the next fiscal year.

(A) outline
(B) outlines
(C) outlining
(D) outlined

19. ------- the company's yearly goals for
고난도 productivity, all employees in Hasian Corporation's manufacturing division received a bonus.

(A) Having exceeded
(B) To exceed
(C) Exceeded
(D) Being exceeded

20. A common problem local inhabitants face
고난도 is that the amount of unwanted mail they receive has become -------.

(A) overwhelmingly
(B) overwhelming
(C) overwhelmed
(D) overwhelms

REVIEW TEST 03

1. The initiative ------- by the community organization to reduce public transportation fees was rejected after a lengthy debate.

(A) suggest
(B) suggests
(C) suggested
(D) suggesting

2. According to the article ------- in *Trendy Car Magazine*, Harold Motors is going to discontinue producing its biggest sport utility vehicle.

(A) publishing
(B) publish
(C) published
(D) to publish

3. Thank you for giving your presentation to our personnel, and I look forward to ------- from you again.

(A) hearing
(B) hear
(C) heard
(D) hears

4. Since revising its vacation policy, Veltro Tech has been getting ------- fewer complaints from its employees.

(A) significant
(B) signifying
(C) significantly
(D) signified

5. In ------- of the spring season, Maiko's Sushi will be offering an outdoor dining option beginning on May 28.

(A) considering
(B) considered
(C) consideration
(D) considerable

6. *The Consumer Today Guide* can help you sort through the ------- options and make well-founded purchasing decisions.

(A) bewilderment
(B) bewildering
(C) bewilders
(D) bewildered

7. The New York Dairy was forced to discard 65 percent of its yogurt because it failed ------- quality standards.

(A) had met
(B) to meet
(C) meets
(D) meet

8. After consulting the editor, Ms. Trinh was finally able ------- the news article.

(A) completing
(B) to complete
(C) being complete
(D) completed

9. The ------- of the Harbin facility has had a significant impact on Feilin Furniture's delivery services.

(A) expanding
(B) expanded
(C) expand
(D) expansion

10. Risk management strategies can enable small business owners to survive and succeed ------- economic challenges.

(A) prior to
(B) however
(C) in spite of
(D) yet

11. Instead of being transferred to an overseas branch, Mr. Shah chose ------- the job offer at C&C.com's headquarters in New York.

(A) accept
(B) to accept
(C) accepting
(D) accepted

12. The CEO of Newyen Industries is confident that the new strategy director will contribute ------- to the growth of the company.

(A) substantive
(B) substantially
(C) substantial
(D) substantiate

13. ------- be eligible for a refund, you must present the original receipt to a store employee.
고난도

(A) Even as
(B) In order to
(C) Since
(D) Unless

14. Recently, $70 million in funds derived from oil industry operations have been set aside to ------- in social infrastructure.

(A) having invested
(B) be invested
(C) invests
(D) being invested

15. The fund balance of Barrington City may fall below the ------- $10 million level since the Silco Lake Cleanup Project took a lot longer than planned.

(A) desire
(B) desires
(C) desired
(D) desiring

16. My manager strongly encouraged us to attend a lecture on public speaking because it will help ------- sales performance.
고난도

(A) improves
(B) improved
(C) improving
(D) improve

17. ------- launching his trademark cookware line, Mr. Pers worked for over 25 years in various restaurants.
고난도

(A) Prior to
(B) In order to
(C) So that
(D) Provided that

18. The planning ------- at each step of creating a business plan will have a direct impact on the chances of acquiring funding.
고난도

(A) invest
(B) invested
(C) investor
(D) investing

19. In a depressed economy, small business owners may consider ------- some of their contracts.

(A) renegotiation
(B) to renegotiate
(C) renegotiating
(D) renegotiated

20. Xiandai Department Store released a popular skincare product ------- the soothing scents of lavender and vanilla.
고난도

(A) combined
(B) combining
(C) combines
(D) combine

부사절 접속사

두 개의 단어, 구, 절을 연결해주는 역할을 하는 품사를 접속사라 한다. 접속사의 종류에는 등위접속사, 상관접속사, 부사절 접속사, 명사절 접속사, 형용사절 접속사(관계사)가 있다.

Tip!
토익에서 가장 많이 출제되는 접속사는 양보를 의미하는 although, even though, even if야. 하지만 다양한 의미의 접속사가 골고루 출제되니 교재에 정리된 여러 접속사의 의미를 꼼꼼히 암기하자! 최근에는 접속사 as soon as가 새롭게 부각되고 있고 「unless / otherwise / p.p.」 표현이 2회 연속 출제되기도 했으니 잘 알아둬~

 기본 개념 이해하기

1. 등위접속사

종류	의미	예문
and	그리고	Lunch will be catered by Alameda Cafe **and** Star Kitchen. 점심은 Alameda Cafe와 Star Kitchen에 의해 제공될 것이다.
but	그러나	Our official check-in time is 3:00 P.M., **but** Mr. Fisher's room will be ready when he arrives from the airport. 공식 체크인 시간은 오후 3시이지만, Mr. Fisher가 공항으로부터 도착하셨을 때쯤이면 방이 준비될 겁니다.
or	또는	For more information on this event **or** the center, please feel free to visit www.laneway.com. 이 행사나 센터에 대한 추가 정보를 원하시면 www.laneway.com을 참조하십시오.

• 같은 표현 요소(단어, 구, 절)를 이어주어 병렬 구조를 만드는 접속사를 등위접속사라 한다.

2. 상관접속사

종류	의미	예문
both A and B	A와 B 둘 다	Mr. Cruise will provide support to **both** the Marketing Department **and** the Accounting Department. Mr. Cruise는 마케팅 부서와 회계 부서 모두를 지원하게 될 것이다.
either A or B	A와 B 둘 중 하나	Please contact the customer service center at this e-mail address **either** to request a replacement **or** to confirm your order cancellation. 교환을 요청하거나 주문 취소를 확정하려면 이 이메일 주소로 고객 서비스 센터에 연락하십시오.
neither A nor B	A와 B 둘 다 아닌	**Neither** refunds **nor** exchanges will be granted after opening the packages. 포장 상자를 연 후에는 환불이나 교환이 불가능해질 것이다.
not only A but (also) B = B as well as A	A뿐만 아니라 B도	The workshop is intended **not only** for hotel employees **but also** for those who wish to renew their food and beverage licenses. 이 워크숍은 호텔 직원뿐만 아니라 식음료 면허를 갱신하고자 하는 직원들을 위한 것이기도 하다.

• 두 단어가 짝을 이루어 쓰이는 접속사를 상관접속사라 한다.

3. 부사절 접속사

종류	의미	접속사	예문
양보	비록 ~일지라도	though, although, even though, even if	**Even though** Ms. Chow is not here to help with the task right now, she will be able to assist us next week. 비록 Ms. Chow가 지금 당장 일을 돕기 위해 여기 와 있지는 않지만, 다음 주에 우리를 도울 수 있을 것이다.
이유	때문에	because, now that, since	**Because** some features did not meet his needs, the customer asked for a refund. 일부 기능이 만족스럽지 못했기 때문에, 그 고객은 환불을 요청했다.
시간	~할 때	when	**When** museum members make a purchase at the gift shop, they are offered a discount. 박물관 회원이 선물가게에서 물건을 구매했을 경우 할인 혜택이 주어진다.
	~하자마자	as soon as	
	~하는 동안에	while	**While** the systems are being installed, the manufacturing operations will be shut down. 시스템을 설치하는 동안 제조 작업이 중단될 것이다.
	~하기 전에/후에	before/after	
	~할 때까지	until	All products must be inspected by a trained safety technician **before** we package them. 모든 제품은 포장되기 전에 숙련된 안전 기술자로부터 검사를 받아야 한다.
	~이래	since	
조건	만약 ~라면	if, provided that	**If** any information is omitted, the delivery date will be changed. 누락된 정보가 있으면 배송 날짜가 변경될 것이다.
	만약 ~하지 않는다면	unless	**Unless** measures are devised, the current drop in sales will continue. 대책이 마련되지 않는 이상, 지금의 매출 하락은 계속될 것이다.
	일단 ~하면	once	
목적	~하기 위해서	so that, in order that	Please check a few details **so that** our hotel can finalize the renovations. 저희 호텔이 보수공사를 마무리할 수 있도록 몇 가지 세부 사항을 확인해 주십시오.

- 부사절은 「부사절 접속사 + 주어 + 동사」 형태의 완전한 문장의 형태를 취한다는 점에서 「전치사 + 명사」 형태의 부사구와 구별된다.
- 문장에서 부사 역할을 하는 부사절은 주절 앞이나 뒤에 위치하며, 생략되어도 전체 문장에 영향을 주지 않는다.

문법적으로 접속사, 전치사, 접속부사의 자리를 구분한 후, 해석상 알맞은 부사절 접속사를 선택하는 문제의 출제 비중이 가장 높다. 부사절의 축약 구조와 관련된 고난도 문제도 최근에 자주 출제된다.

해설서 p.37

1. 부사절 접속사의 종류와 의미

Q1 양보·이유 부사절 접속사

[Even though / Because] his crew's work is behind schedule, the supervisor of the project is confident that it will be completed on time. [1]

[While / Now that] Mr. Won appreciated the promotion opportunity, he chose to take another job. [2]

William Smith was hired as assistant manager **[although / because]** he proved himself to be the most qualified candidate. [3]

>> 출제 포인트   부사절은 「부사절 접속사 + 주어 + 동사」 형태로 양보, 이유, 시간, 조건 등을 의미한다. 부사절은 주절의 앞이나 뒤에 위치할 수 있으며, 생략되어도 전체 문장에 영향을 주지 않는다.

✓ 양보·이유를 나타내는 부사절 접속사

양보	although, though, even though, even if	비록 ~일지라도
	while, whereas	~인 반면에
이유	because, now that, since, as	~때문에

Q2 시간·조건·목적 부사절 접속사

Construction will start **[while / as soon as]** the building permit is secured. [1]

Use the stairs **[while / as soon as]** the elevator is being fixed. [2]

[Once / Whereas] Mr. Hidings has organized a special task force team, the deadline for the Altoona project will be decided. [3]

[Unless / Because] our supplier can provide flour to us at a discount, we should raise the price of our baked goods. [4]

Jennifer Chang has been appointed senior engineer **[so that / if]** she can concentrate on the development of new products. [5]

>> 출제 포인트　☑ 시간·조건·목적 등을 나타내는 부사절 접속사

시간	while	~하는 동안
	as soon as	~하자마자
	before	~전에
	until	~할 때까지
	when, as	~할 때
	by the time	~할 때쯤에
	after	~이후에
	since	~한 이래로
조건	if, provided (that), providing (that)	만약 ~라면
	once	일단~하면(한 후에)
	as long as	~하기만 한다면, ~이기만 하다면
	only if	~하는 경우에만
	assuming (that), supposing (that)	~라고 가정하면
	in case (that), in the event (that)	~할 경우에 대비하여
	unless	~하지 않는다면
기타	so (that), in order that	~하기 위해서 [목적]
	so ~ that, such ~ that	너무 ~해서 …하다 [결과]
	as if, as though	마치 ~인 것 처럼
	given that, considering (that)	~라는 점을 고려했을 때
	whether ~or (not)	~이든 아니든

2. 부사절 접속사와 구별해야 하는 전치사와 접속부사

Q3 **[부사절 접속사 vs. 전치사]**

[Although / Despite] the NRT laptop is expensive, it is the fastest model available. [1]

[Even though / Notwithstanding] the tax auditor requested information about Georgetown Finance Accounting a month ago, it still has not arrived. [2]

[While / During] the security system is being upgraded, please check in at the front desk. [3]

[Given that / Owing to] Mauer Consulting has recently secured a lot more orders compared to last year, it needs to hire more research assistants. [4]

>> 출제 포인트 접속사 뒤에는 「주어 + 동사」가 포함된 절이 오고, 전치사 뒤에는 명사(구)가 와야 한다. 특히, 동일한 의미를 갖는 접속사, 전치사, (접속)부사가 보기에 함께 제시되는 문제가 많이 출제되므로, 다음에 정리된 어구의 품사와 의미를 정확히 학습해 두어야 한다.

	부사절 접속사 + 주어 + 동사		전치사 + 명사(구)	
양보	although, though, even though, even if	비록 ~일지라도	despite, in spite of, notwithstanding	~에도 불구하고
이유	because, now that, since	~때문에	because of, due to, owing to, on account of, thanks to	~때문에[덕분에]
시간	while	~동안에	during	~동안에
조건	in case (that), in the event (that)	~할 경우에 대비하여	in case of, in the event of	~할 경우에 대비하여
	unless	~하지 않는다면	without	~없이
목적	so that, in order that	~하기 위해서	for the purpose of cf so as to + 동사원형 in order to + 동사원형	~의 목적으로 ~하기 위해서
기타	except that/when	~라는 점/~할 때를 제외하고	except (for), excluding, barring	~을 제외하고
	as if, as though assuming that, supposing that	마치~인 것 처럼 ~라고 가정하면	in addition to, plus, besides instead of regardless of unlike ahead of	~외에도 ~대신에 ~와 관계없이 ~와 달리 ~보다 앞서

Q4 **[부사절 접속사 vs. 전치사 vs. 접속부사]**

[If / In spite of / Therefore] visitors to Sonna Graphics do not have a valid pass, they should present a form of photo identification at the security office. [1]

[Except that / Furthermore / In addition to] commission, sales associates will receive quarterly bonuses. [2]

[While / Regardless of / Instead] Mr. Tal was giving the demonstration, Ms. Locke distributed the product flyers. [3]

We will purchase new equipment **[once / thanks to / afterwards]** the director approves the order. [4]

>> **출제 포인트**

접속부사는 마침표로 끝난 앞 문장의 내용을 부가 설명하는 부사로, 한 문장 안에서 두 문장을 하나로 연결할 수 없다. 따라서, 두 문장을 연결할 때는 접속사 and나 세미콜론(;)과 함께 쓰인다. 이러한 접속부사의 문법적 특성을 묻는 문제는 Part 5에 출제되며, 문맥에 알맞은 접속부사를 선택하는 문제는 Part 6에서 출제된다.

however	그러나	nevertheless, nonetheless	그럼에도 불구하고
as a result, consequently	결과적으로	therefore, thus	그러므로
moreover, furthermore, besides, in addition, also	게다가	likewise	마찬가지로
if so	만약 그렇다면	otherwise	그렇지 않다면
then, thereafter	그리고 나서	afterward(s)	이후에
meantime, meanwhile	반면에, 동시에	rather	오히려
instead	대신에	on the contrary	대조적으로

> **cf** 접속사 and와 함께 자주 쓰이는 접속부사: and then '그리고 나서' | and therefore '그러므로' | and also '또한'
> - otherwise는 '그와 달리'라는 의미의 일반부사로도 쓰인다.
>   Unless **otherwise** noted, all daytime workshops for new employees last five hours.
>   별다른 공지가 없는 한 신입직원들을 위한 모든 주간 워크숍은 5시간 동안 진행한다.
> - however는 뒤에 형용사/부사를 수반하는 경우, '아무리 ~할지라도'라는 의미를 갖는 접속사로도 쓰인다.
>   **However** proficient they are in English, candidates are required to take a language exam when applying for the position.
>   지원자들은 아무리 영어에 능통하다 해도 그 직책에 지원할 때 어학 시험을 치러야 한다.

Q5 접속사와 전치사로 쓰이는 어구

Those who want to rent an apartment in a foreign country should review the contract carefully **[before / prior to]** they sign it. [1]

[With / Until] this scanner is repaired, use the photocopier on the third floor. [2]

Payroll systems will be offline from 6 A.M. to 7 A.M. next Thursday **[due to / since]** routine maintenance. [3]

>> 출제 포인트 ❶ 접속사와 전치사로 둘 다 쓰이는 어구들 중에, since와 as는 접속사로 쓰일 때와 전치사로 쓰일 때 의미가 달라진다는 점에 유의해야 한다.

✓ **접속사와 전치사 둘 다 쓰이는 어구**

부사절 접속사 + 주어 + 동사		전치사 + 명사(구)	
before	~전에	before, prior to	~전에
after	~후에	after, following	~후에
until	~까지	until	~까지
considering (that)	~라는 점을 고려했을 때	considering	~라는 점을 고려했을 때
since	~이래로, ~때문에	since	~이래로
as	~때문에, ~할 때, ~대로	as	~로서(자격)

❷ 의미에 따른 since의 품사

(1) 이유 ('~때문에'): since가 이유나 원인을 의미할 때는 부사절 접속사로만 쓰인다. 따라서, 전치사나 부사로 쓰인 since는 이유가 아닌 시간의 의미만을 갖는다는 점에 유의해야 한다.
The prices on the list may not be accurate **since** manufacturers often change their prices. [부사절 접속사]
제조업체들이 자주 가격을 변경하기 때문에 목록에 나와있는 가격은 정확하지 않을 수도 있습니다

(2) 시간 ('~한 이래로'): since가 과거의 특정 시점부터 현재까지를 의미할 때는 부사절 접속사와 전치사 둘 다 쓰인다. 이 때, since 뒤에는 과거 시점이 오고, 주절에는 현재 완료 시제가 함께 한다는 점에 유의해야 한다. 또한, since는 '그때 이후로'의 의미를 갖는 부사로도 쓰인다.
William's grades **have been** showing signs of improvement **since** he **began** taking private lessons. [부사절 접속사]
William의 점수는 개인 수업을 받기 시작한 이후 향상될 기미를 보여왔다.

Our operating expenses **have declined** by 10 percent **since last year**. [전치사]
운영 비용은 작년 이후 10퍼센트 감소했다.

3. 부사절 축약

Q6

when + [동사 vs. 분사]

When **[making / make]** a purchase online, be sure to use a secure network. [1]

[while vs. during] + V-ing

Technicians are required to adhere to all safety guidelines **[while / during]** working in the lab. [2]

>> **출제 포인트** ❶ 시간을 나타내는 부사절 접속사 when, while, before, after는 주절과 동일한 주어를 생략하고 동사를 분사로 바꿔 축약 형태로 쓸 수 있다. 이때 분사는 주절의 주어와 의미상 능동관계이면 현재분사(V-ing)를, 수동관계이면 과거분사(p.p.)를 쓴다. 따라서, 부사절 접속사 뒤에 주어가 없고 빈칸이 나올 경우, 동사의 능동/수동을 확인하여, 능동이면 현재분사를, 수동이면 과거분사를 정답으로 선택한다.

❷ 축약구조와 연계하여 동일한 의미의 while과 during을 구별하는 문제가 출제된다. 접속사 while은 축약 구조로 뒤에 분사나 전치사구가 바로 올 수 있으나, 전치사 during은 분사나 전치사구를 뒤에 바로 취하지 못한다. during은 뒤에 목적어로 동명사도 올 수 없고, 오로지 명사만을 목적으로 취한다.

while + 주어 + 동사	while[~~during~~] the concert is in progress 콘서트가 진행되는 동안에
during + 명사	during[~~while~~] the concert 콘서트 동안에
while + V-ing / p.p. / 전치사구	while[~~during~~] staying at the hotel 호텔에 머무르는 동안에 while[~~during~~] on duty 근무하는 동안에 while[~~during~~] in a foreign country 해외에 있는 동안에

Q7

as + [동사 vs. 과거분사]

Despite mechanical issues, the train departed as originally **[has scheduled / scheduled]**. [1]

unless + otherwise + [현재분사 vs. 과거분사]

All ingredients in our products are organic unless otherwise **[specifying / specified]**. [2]

>> **출제 포인트** 접속사 as나 unless는 뒤에 과거분사만 올 수 있고, 관용적인 표현으로 많이 출제된다.

as **discussed**	논의되었듯이	as **noted**	언급되어 있듯이
as **indicated**	표시되어 있듯이	as **mentioned**	언급되어 있듯이
as **detailed**	설명되어 있듯이	as **stated**	명시되어 있듯이
as **projected**	예상되었듯이		

✓ unless otherwise p.p. / unless p.p. otherwise 관용 표현

unless otherwise noted	달리 언급되어 있지 않으면
unless otherwise instructed	달리 지시받지 않는다면
unless otherwise indicated	달리 표시되어 있지 않으면

4. 등위접속사와 상관접속사

Q8 [등위접속사 vs. 부사절 접속사] + 주어 + 동사, 주어 + 동사

[**But / Although**] Ms. Sherman is on vacation, she can respond to important e-mails. [1]

[**Either vs. Neither**] A or B

[**Either / Neither**] complete an application online or submit one in person. [2]

>> 출제 포인트 ❶ 등위접속사는 같은 품사나 구조를 연결하여, 병렬구조를 이룬다. 등위 접속사가 두 문장을 연결할 때, 두 문장의 가운데에 위치하며, 첫 번째 문장의 앞에 쓰일 수 없다.

| and | 그리고 | but, yet | 그러나 | or | 또는 | so | 그래서 |

┌→ 명사구   ┌→ 명사구
Please turn off your phone **and** other electronic devices.
고객님의 전화기와 그 밖의 다른 전자 기기를 꺼 주시기 바랍니다.

┌→ But ⋯→ 등위접속사는 문장 맨 앞에 올 수 없다.
Although gas prices have risen, KM Logistics did not increase its delivery fees.
연료비가 오르긴 했지만, KM 택배는 배송비를 올리지 않았다.

❷ 상관 접속사는 두 단어 이상이 짝을 이루어 쓰인다.

both A and B	A와 B 둘 다
either A or B	A와 B 둘 중 하나
neither A nor B	A와 B 둘 다 아닌
not only A but (also) B	A뿐만 아니라 B도 (= B as well as A)
not A but B	A가 아니라 B (= B, but not A)

After discussing the new benefits package, **both** management **and** employees reached an agreement.
새 복리후생제도에 대해 논의하고 나서, 경영진과 직원들 모두 합의를 보았다.

5. 복합관계부사

Q9 [복합관계부사 vs. 복합관계대명사] + 완전한 문장

Please call us **[whatever / whenever]** you have a technical issue. [1]

[however vs. whenever] + 형용사/부사 + 주어 + 동사

[However / Whenever] often public speakers may stand in front of large audiences, most of them still experience some stage fright. [2]

no matter how + [형용사 vs. to부정사]

All employees should report any incident, no matter how **[trivial / to trivialize]** it is. [3]

>> 출제 포인트　**❶**「관계부사 + -ever」형태의 복합관계부사 wherever, whenever, however는 양보(~든지)의 의미로, 각각 no matter where, no matter when, no matter how로 바꿔 쓸 수 있다.

❷ 복합관계부사는 관계부사와 마찬가지로 완전한 구조의 문장과 함께하며, 부사절 접속사 역할을 한다.

❸ 복합관계부사 however (= no matter how)는 바로 뒤에 형용사나 부사가 온다는 점에 유의한다.

복합관계부사	의미	이어지는 구조
wherever	어디에서든지 (= no matter where)	+ 완전한 문장
whenever	언제든지 (= no matter when = every time)	+ 완전한 문장
however	아무리 ~할지라도 (= no matter how)	+ 형용사/부사 + 주어 + 동사

Practice

1. ------- their previous model was quite popular among teens, few expect the next one to be as attractive.

(A) In spite of
(B) Even though
(C) Regardless of
(D) But

2. ------- Mr. Hong has received excellent performance appraisals for three consecutive years, he will certainly be promoted this spring.

(A) So that
(B) As
(C) Although
(D) As a result of

3. Some employees still tend to keep a daily work log ------- there is no longer a mandated requirement.

(A) as if
(B) so that
(C) in case
(D) although

4. ------- the delayed arrival of his flight, Mr. James made it on time to the conference.

(A) Otherwise
(B) While
(C) Despite
(D) In spite

5. Client requests for DNA tests cannot proceed ------- a deposit of $100 is received.

(A) despite
(B) even
(C) until
(D) prior to

6. ------- the marketing staff has completed the three-week intensive training, the manager will ask them to submit a report.

(A) Once
(B) Next
(C) Afterwards
(D) Then

7. Novizan Publishing installed new illustration software on its computers ------- book cover designers could work more effectively.

(A) so that
(B) as if
(C) so as
(D) due to

8. Greenychi Safety Shipping assures you that all shipments will be delivered on time ------- remote their destinations might be.

(A) no matter how
(B) insofar as
(C) nevertheless
(D) in order that

9. Parking in the building's basement garage will be prohibited this weekend ------- emergency repairs to the electrical system.

(A) so that
(B) as a result
(C) in order to
(D) because of

10. Lexington Museum is seeking a new curator not only to organize new exhibits ------- to give tours on special occasions.

(A) but also
(B) only if
(C) or
(D) and

11. Please review the article thoroughly ------- it has been received from the writer.

(A) then
(B) while
(C) despite
(D) as soon as

12. ------- Novana Industry's overall revenue has decreased for the last two years, some departments have seen slight increases in sales.

(A) While
(B) Since
(C) Instead
(D) However

13. 고난도 Alsacienne's restaurant has seen a dramatic increase in sales ------- it relocated to the downtown area.

(A) when
(B) after
(C) whereas
(D) since

14. Ms. Norman, the accounting manager of the company, wishes to review the fourth-quarter revenue ------- the annual financial report is compiled.

(A) prior
(B) ahead
(C) before
(D) earlier

15. ------- more people are connected through social media, it has become much easier for consumers to share product reviews.

(A) Instead of
(B) Now that
(C) Because of
(D) As if

16. 고난도 ------- signing the contract, Samwha Biotech agreed to start a collaborative research project with Midward Pharmaceutical Company.

(A) During
(B) To
(C) When
(D) Since

17. 고난도 The former CEO, Kate Hatfield, had no choice but to resign when ------- with stiff resistance from both inside and outside the company.

(A) face
(B) faced
(C) facing
(D) faces

18. 고난도 ------- the January company newsletter is published, the final decision on the outsourcing contract will have been made.

(A) By the time
(B) In order to
(C) Following
(D) Now that

19. Over 2,000 people attended last Sunday's International Food Fair, ------- the heavy rains that swamped parts of the area.

(A) while
(B) whereas
(C) notwithstanding
(D) moreover

20. 고난도 ------- the budget allocated for this project is strictly limited, it is important to consider cost-efficiency at each phase of the project.

(A) Even if
(B) Because of
(C) Unless
(D) Given

UNIT 13 명사절 접속사

what(~것), that(~것), whether/if(~인지 아닌지), 의문사 등이 이끄는 명사절은 문장에서 주어, 목적어, 보어 역할을 한다.

 Tip! 명사절 접속사 whether와 다양한 의문사의 쓰임에 유의해야 해. 복합관계사 중에서는 선행사 없이 뒤에 동사가 바로 오는 whoever가 가장 많이 출제돼.

기본 개념 이해하기

1. that, whether/if, what 절

that	~것	It is certain **that** he will come. ⋯▶ 진주어 역할 그가 올 것이 확실하다. I think **(that)** she is smart. ⋯▶ 목적어 역할 나는 그녀가 똑똑하다고 생각한다. The reason is **that** he can't speak at all. ⋯▶ 보어 역할 그 이유는 그가 말을 전혀 못하기 때문이다.
if/whether	~인지 아닌지	**Whether** she comes or not is unimportant to me. ⋯▶ 주어 그녀가 오든 안 오든 나에게는 중요하지 않다. I don't care **whether[if]** your car broke down or not. ⋯▶ 목적어 당신 차가 고장 났든 말든 저와는 상관없습니다. The problem is **whether** the machine is cheap. ⋯▶ 보어 문제는 그 기계가 저렴하냐는 것이다.
what	~것	The workshop will explain **what** new employees should do. ⋯▶ 목적어 워크숍에서 신입 사원들이 해야 하는 일에 대해 설명할 것이다.

2. 명사절을 이끄는 의문사

의문대명사 who, what, which	He couldn't guess **what** was inside the box. 그는 상자 안에 무엇이 있는지 추측할 수 없었다.
의문형용사 which, whose, what	Ken is choosing **which** fabric he wants for the sofa. Ken은 소파에 놓을 천을 고르고 있다.
의문부사 when, where, how, why	These are the instructions on **how** we can use the equipment. 이것은 장비를 어떻게 사용할 수 있는지에 대한 지침이다.

3. 명사절을 이끄는 복합관계대명사

Whoever	~하는 사람은 누구나	**Whoever** the manager hires will start on Monday. 지배인이 고용하는 사람이 누구든 월요일부터 일을 시작할 것이다.
Whatever	~하는 것은 무엇이나	The President emphasized the ability to cope with **whatever** happens. 대통령은 무슨 일이 있어도 대처할 수 있는 능력을 강조했다.
Whichever	~하는 것은 어느 것이나	You can buy **whichever** you want. 원하는 것은 무엇이든지 살 수 있다.

문법적으로 명사절 접속사, 관계대명사, 부사절 접속사의 자리를 구분한 후, 해석상 알맞은 명사절 접속사를 선택하는 복합적인 문제가 출제되므로 고득점 학생들도 어렵게 느끼는 부분이다. 명사절 접속사가 위치하는 자리를 파악하기 위한 전체 문장의 구조 분석 연습과 더불어 that, whether, 의문사, 복합관계대명사의 정확한 의미에 유의하며 학습해야 한다.

해설서 p.40

1. 명사절 접속사 that

Q1 **명사절 접속사 [that vs. what] + 완전한 문장**

Our annual financial report indicates **[that / what]** we should reduce the overall operating costs. [1]

명사절 접속사 [that vs. what] + 불완전한 문장

[That / What] Mr. Wyatt proposed at the meeting impressed the board of directors. [2]

>> 출제 포인트

❶ 「접속사 + 주어 + 동사」의 명사절은 명사처럼 주어, 목적어, 보어 역할을 한다. 명사절은 명사 역할을 하므로, 부사 역할을 하는 부사절이나 명사를 뒤에서 꾸며주는 형용사 역할의 관계절과 구별된다.

주어	Whether the company will open a branch office will be discussed during the meeting. 회사가 지사를 열 것인지는 회의 동안 논의될 것이다.
목적어	The participants reported that the seminar had been a huge success. 참가자들은 세미나가 큰 성공을 거두었다고 알려왔다.
보어	The belief of the chairman of the board is that more foreign investment is needed. 이사회 의장의 믿음은 더 많은 해외투자가 필요하다는 것이다.

❷ 명사절 접속사 that 뒤에는 완전한 구조의 절이, 명사절 접속사 what 뒤에는 불완전한 구조의 절이 온다.

The record shows **that** Mr. Scott paid an additional fee for express shipping.
주어와 타동사 pay의 목적어가 모두 있는 완전한 구조
기록에 따르면 Mr. Scott은 빠른 배송을 위해 추가요금을 지불했다.

The business section is **what** most readers of the daily newspaper read first.
주어는 있으나 타동사 read의 목적어가 없는 불완전한 구조
비즈니스 섹션은 대부분의 일간지 독자들이 가장 먼저 읽는 부분이다.

❸ 선행 명사를 뒤에서 수식하는 관계대명사 that은 뒤에 불완전한 구조의 절이 온다는 점에서 명사절 접속사 that과 구분된다.

┌ 타동사 + 명사절 접속사('~것')　　　　┌ 선행사(명사) + 관계대명사('~한')
The company insists **that** they use only ingredients **that** have been classified as environmentally safe.
회사는 환경적으로 안전하다고 분류된 재료만을 쓴다고 주장한다.

1. It is crucial for marketers to understand **[that / what]** potential clients need.

2. Both CEOs announced **[that / what]** the new management would expect employees to work cooperatively after the upcoming merger.

Q2 **명사절 접속사 that과 함께 쓰이는 표현**

Please be aware **[that / what]** the changed regulations for vehicle inspection will take effect on December 1. **¹**

It is important **[that / what]** employees regularly attend safety workshops. **²**

>> 출제 포인트 ❶ 특정 형용사 뒤에 that 명사절이 와서 하나의 관용 표현으로 쓰인다.

「be + 형용사 + that 절」	
be aware[conscious] that	~인 것을 인식하다
be certain[sure, confident] that	~인 것을 확신하다
be concerned[worried] afraid that	~인 것을 걱정[우려]하다
be pleased[happy, glad] that	~인 것에 대해 기뻐하다
be disappointed that	~인 것에 대해 실망하다
be sorry that	~인 것에 대해 유감스러워하다

❷ 명사절 접속사 that이 이끄는 절이 주어일 경우, 그 자리에 가주어 it을 쓰고 that절을 뒤로 보내는 「가주어 it ~ 진주어 that」 구문으로 흔히 쓴다.

☑ **It(가주어) is + 형용사 + that 절(진주어)**

It is +	likely ~일 것 같다 ∣ impossible ~인 것은 불가능하다 ∣ important ~인 것은 중요하다 ∣ necessary[essential] ~인 것은 필수다	+ that ~

2. 명사절 접속사 whether

Q3 **whether vs. if**

We have not determined **[whether / if]** the annual company picnic will be on company grounds or in Jackson Park. [1]

The office manager will decide **[whether / if]** to order paper from Light-Office or Gartol. [2]

The company will hire employees regardless of **[whether / if]** applicants have university diplomas. [3]

>> **출제 포인트** ❶ 명사절 접속사 whether와 if는 둘 다 '～인지 아닌지'라는 의미이며, 결정이나 불확실성을 나타내는 표현과 함께 쓰인다.

주어 +	determine ～인지 아닌지 결정하다	decide 결심하다	choose 선택하다	ask 묻다	inquire 문의하다	consider 고려하다	wonder 궁금해 하다	doubt 의심하다	be not sure ～ 확실하지 않다	+ whether / if ～

❷ 명사절 접속사 whether와 if의 차이

(1) 명사절 접속사 whether는 주어, 동사나 전치사의 목적어, 보어 등 명사 역할을 하는 자리에 모두 쓰일 수 있으나, 명사절 접속사 if는 타동사의 목적어로만 쓰인다.

(2) 명사절 접속사 if는 or not과 함께 쓰이지 못하나, 명사절 접속사 whether는 다양한 형태로 쓸 수 있다.

whether (or not) + 완전문장 | whether + 완전문장 + (or not)	～인지 아닌지
whether A or B	A든지 B든지
whether to 동사원형	～할지 말지

(3) 명사절 접속사 if는 전치사 뒤에 올 수 없으나 명사절 접속사 whether는 전치사 뒤에 올 수 있다.

+ check

1. Canterra employees can choose **[whether / if]** to work from home or at the office.

2. Mr. Romano called to ask **[if / that]** the upcoming seminar on September 10 could be postponed until next week.

3. 명사절 접속사로 쓰이는 의문사

Q4 명사절을 이끄는 의문사

The ongoing legal dispute has delayed the launching of Home Skin Care because it was unclear **[who / which]** had invented it. [1]

Before making a decision, we will review **[how / whose]** idea is the most creative. [2]

The event organizer has decided **[where / what]** to hold the party. [3]

>> 출제 포인트 ❶ 의문사는 명사절을 이끌며, 토익에 출제되는 명사절을 이끄는 의문사의 선택 문제는 대부분 해석을 통해 문맥에 적합한 것을 고르는 유형이다.

❷ why를 제외하고 의문사가 명사절을 이끄는 접속사로 쓰이는 경우, 뒤에 문장뿐만 아니라 「의문사 + to부정사」 형태로도 쓸 수 있다. which와 whose는 to부정사가 바로 올 수 없고 「which / whose + 명사 + to부정사」 형태로 쓸 수 있다.

✓ **명사절을 이끄는 의문사**

의문대명사	who	누가 ~하는지
	what	무엇이(을) ~하는지
	which	어떤 것이(을) ~하는지
의문형용사 + 명사	which + 명사	어떤 + 명사
	whose + 명사	누구의 + 명사
	what + 명사	무슨 + 명사
의문부사 + 완전한 구조의 절	when	언제 ~하는지
	where	어디서 ~하는지
	how	어떻게 ~하는지
	why	왜 ~하는지

4. 복합관계대명사

Q5 [복합관계대명사 vs. 대명사] + 동사 + 동사

[Whoever / Anyone] is interested in reserving an exhibition booth should fill out the enclosed registration form. [1]

[복합관계대명사 vs. 복합관계부사] + 불완전한 문장

You can bring **[whatever / wherever]** you need for the vacation in this suitcase. [2]

[복합관계대명사 vs. 의문사]

[Whoever / Who] gets the best evaluation will be promoted to Branch Manager. [3]

>> 출제 포인트 ❶ 「관계대명사 + -ever」의 형태의 복합관계대명사 who(m)ever, whatever, whichever는 '~든지'의 의미로 명사절(주어와 목적어 자리에서)과 부사절을 모두 이끌 수 있다.

❷ 복합관계대명사는 「선행사 + 관계대명사」로 자체에 선행사를 포함하고 있기 때문에, 관계대명사와 달리 그 앞에 선행사가 필요 없으나, 관계대명사와 마찬가지로 불완전 구조의 문장을 동반한다. 하지만, 복합관계부사 wherever, whenever, however는 관계부사와 마찬가지로 완전한 구조의 문장을 이끈다.

❸ 복합관계대명사와 의문사의 구분은 해석을 통해 문맥에 따라 결정한다.

복합관계대명사	명사절	부사절
whoever	~하는 사람은 누구든지 = anyone who	누가 ~하든지 = no matter who
whatever	~하는 것은 무엇이든지 = anything that	무엇을 ~하든지 = no matter what
whichever	~하는 것은 어느 것이든지 = anything that	어떤 것을 ~하든지 = no matter which

Practice

1. ------- manager you should report to depends on the project that you are assigned.

(A) Which
(B) Each
(C) Either
(D) Something

2. 고난도 The city council considered ------- the citizens suggested at the public hearing about the subway expansion project.

(A) what
(B) that
(C) about
(D) after

3. The talk by Laura Stevenson on her latest book, *Why I Sing*, is open to ------- is interested.

(A) whoever
(B) wherever
(C) whatever
(D) however

4. 고난도 The Fabolia Dance School will hold an information session on April 7 for ------- interested in signing up for summer classes.

(A) whoever
(B) they
(C) anyone
(D) them

5. It is necessary ------- managers give their staff equal opportunities to prove themselves capable of their responsibilities.

(A) should
(B) that
(C) upon
(D) to

6. Visitors invited to tour Lowell Auto can see ------- our products are made from the design room to the assembly line.

(A) during
(B) about
(C) how
(D) while

7. Please contact Gina before 5 P.M. on November 10 to let her know ------- you will be attending or not.

(A) unless
(B) whether
(C) whenever
(D) as if

8. ------- needs an income verification form should ask Ms. Roh in the Accounting Department.

(A) Some
(B) Who
(C) Whoever
(D) Anyone

9. The survey indicated ------- almost all of the product reviewers found Everyday Bath shampoo's scent appealing.

(A) that
(B) what
(C) those
(D) even if

10. The board of directors is meeting this afternoon to decide ------- research projects to fund.

(A) which
(B) who
(C) where
(D) when

11. The board of directors has to decide ------- will be appointed as Vice President at next Monday's meeting.

(A) that
(B) whatever
(C) who
(D) when

12. Supervisors ------- have technical difficulties with the online employee evaluation form should contact the Tech Team for assistance.

(A) who
(B) when
(C) what
(D) whose

13. Participants are allowed to ask about ------- they would like to know during the question and answer session.

(A) wherever
(B) however
(C) anyone
(D) whatever

14 Ms. Hwang must decide ------- to submit the proposal to the city council by the end of the week.

(A) whether
(B) whereas
(C) if
(D) unless

15. We need to learn ------- to overcome the 고난도 financial crisis or at least minimize its effects on our business.

(A) next
(B) whether
(C) how
(D) as

16. ------- I need you to understand is that we must complete the Epsontech project within a limited time and budget.

(A) That
(B) What
(C) Whether
(D) Which

17. ------- the year-end profit shares will be 고난도 half of last year's is disappointing news to the entire staff.

(A) What
(B) Although
(C) That
(D) Because

18. As soon as the management of Extell 고난도 Trading has reviewed the documents, they will determine ------- proposal will be chosen.

(A) who
(B) whom
(C) whoever
(D) whose

19. The budget committee is still having a discussion about ------- it is necessary to allocate funds for monthly staff training.

(A) which
(B) whether
(C) what
(D) while

20. Due to the availability of online video streaming services, it is not common for people nowadays to just watch ------- appears on television.

(A) anyone
(B) whatever
(C) unless
(D) however

형용사절 접속사

관계사가 「접속사 + 대명사」의 역할을 하면 '관계대명사'이고, 「접속사 + 부사」의 역할을 하면 '관계부사'라 부른다.

> **Tip!**
> 토익에서 가장 많이 출제되는 관계대명사는 주격 *who*와 소유격 *whose*야.
> 관계부사 *where*가 보기에 있으면 뒤에 완전한 문장이 온다는 점을 잊지 말자!

🗣 기본 개념 이해하기

1. 관계대명사절

선행사	격	관계대명사 = 「접속사 + 선행사」를 받아주는 대명사	
사람	주격 [+ 동사]	who[that]	The chef **who[that] won the contest** studied in Paris. 그 대회에서 우승한 요리사는 파리에서 공부했다.
사물		which[that]	I can see the cat **which[that] is lying on the chair**. 의자에 누워있는 고양이가 보인다.
사람	목적격 [+ 주어 + 동사]	whom[that]	Is that the man **whom[that] you invited**? 저 남자가 당신이 초대한 사람인가요?
사물		which[that]	The shirt **which[that] you bought me** fits well. 당신이 제게 사준 셔츠가 잘 맞아요.
사람	소유격 [+ 명사]	whose	The man **whose leg was broken** is my uncle. 다리가 부러진 그 남자는 우리 삼촌이다.
사물		whose	She bought a book **whose price is amazing**. 그녀는 가격이 놀라운 책을 샀다.

- 관계사는 문장을 연결하는 접속사 기능을 하므로 그 뒤에 동사를 추가로 하나 더 가진다.
- **관계대명사의 계속적 용법:** 관계대명사 앞에 쉼표(,)가 있으며 앞 내용을 추가적으로 설명해준다. 관계대명사 that은 계속적 용법으로 쓰일 수 없다.

  ┌ that
  There are parking lots, **which** are only for bank customers. 주차장이 있는데, 은행 고객들 전용이다.

2. 관계부사절

선행사		관계부사 = 「접속사 + 부사」 = 「전치사 + 관계대명사」
시간 (time)	when	The time **when[at which]** the fire truck came was 9 P.M. 소방차가 온 시간은 오후 9시였다.
장소 (place)	where	I know the hotel **where[at which]** he's staying. 나는 그가 묵고 있는 호텔을 안다.
이유 (the reason)	why	The reason **why** he didn't come is unknown. 그가 오지 않은 이유는 알려지지 않았다.
방법 (the way)	how	This is **how** I memorized a lot of English words. 이것이 내가 많은 영어 단어를 외운 방법이다.

- 방법을 나타낼 때는 관계부사 how나 선행사 the way 중 하나만 써야 한다.
- 관계대명사와 마찬가지로 관계부사는 뒤에 쉼표(,)를 써서 계속적 용법으로 쓰일 수 있다.

  I went to Texas, **where** I stayed for a week. 나는 텍사스에 가서 한 주 동안 있었다.

선행사와 격에 따른 알맞은 관계대명사 선택, 관계대명사와 관계부사의 구분, 관계사와 다른 접속사와의 구분 문제가 주로 출제 된다. 관계대명사 중에 주격의 출제 비중이 가장 높으나, 소유격과 전치사 뒤의 목적격을 묻는 문제가 최근에 증가하고 있으며, 관계사 생략구조가 고난도 문제로 출제된다.

해설서 p.43

1. 관계대명사의 종류와 선택

Q1 사물 선행사 + [who vs. which] + 동사 (주어가 없는 불완전한 문장)

There has been unusually heavy snow, **[who / which]** has caused many flight cancelations. [1]

사람 선행사 + [who vs. which] + 동사 (주어가 없는 불완전한 문장)

The manager **[who / which]** is currently in charge of the project will resign next month. [2]

>> 출제 포인트

① 접속사와 대명사의 역할을 겸하여, 앞의 명사를 수식하는 관계대명사와 달리 대명사는 문장과 문장을 연결하지 못하며, 앞의 명사를 수식하지 못한다.

② 선행사의 종류와 관계대명사 뒤에 빠진 문장 성분에 따라 관계대명사의 격이 결정된다.

선행사	주격 [+ 동사]	소유격 [+ 무관사 명사]	목적격 [+ 주어 + 동사]
사람 명사	who/that	whose	whom/that
사물 명사	which/that	whose	which/that
선행사 없음	what		what

③ 관계대명사 자리 뒤에 주어가 없고 동사가 바로 오면, 관계사절에서 주어 역할을 하는 주격 관계대명사 를 쓴다. 주격 관계대명사 뒤에 오는 동사의 수와 태는 선행사에 따라 결정된다.

주격 관계대명사 + 주어가 없는 불완전한 문장: 선행사 + 주격 관계대명사(who/which/that) + 동사

④ 주격 및 목적격 관계대명사를 대신할 수 있는 관계대명사 that은, 콤마 뒤나 전치사 뒤에 쓰일 수 없다.

┌ that
As a further token of our appreciation, please accept a full season pass, **which** will allow you and one guest to enter at no charge.
감사의 표시로, 귀하와 동반 1인이 무료 입장할 수 있는 자유 이용권을 받아 주시기 바랍니다.

Q2 선행사 + [which vs. whose] + 관사나 소유격 없는 명사 주어 + 동사 (완전한 문장)

The famous author is scheduled to give a speech at the conference **[which / whose]** attendees are mostly college students. [1]

>> 출제 포인트 관계대명사 자리 뒤에 관사나 소유격이 없는 명사가 오면, 관계사절에서 소유격 역할을 하는 소유격 관계대명사를 쓴다. 해석은 두 명사를 연결하는 소유격 의미를 살려 '(선행사)의 (명사)' 라고 한다.

> **관계대명사 + 완전한 문장**: 선행사 + 소유격 관계대명사(whose) + 관사[소유격] 없는 명사

Q3 선행사 + [which vs. whose] + 주어 + 타동사 (목적어가 없는 불완전한 문장)

The sports festival **[which / whose]** the HR team has organized will take place on Saturday. [1]

>> 출제 포인트 관계대명사 자리 뒤에 목적어가 없는 「주어 + 타동사」의 불완전한 문장이 오면, 관계사절에서 목적어 역할을 하는 목적격 관계대명사를 쓴다. 목적격 관계대명사는 생략이 가능하다.

> **관계대명사 + 목적어가 없는 불완전한 문장**
> : 선행사 + (목적격 관계대명사(whom / which / that)) + 주어 + 타동사[자동사 + 전치사]

Q4 [관계대명사 what vs. 접속사 that] + 불완전한 문장

[That / What] is important to us is that customers are satisfied with our services. [1]

>> 출제 포인트 ❶ '~하는 것(=the thing which)'이라는 의미의 관계대명사 what은 스스로 선행사를 포함하고 있기 때문에 형용사절을 이끄는 다른 관계대명사들과 달리 선행사 없이 명사절을 이끈다. 주격이나 목적격 관계대명사로 쓰이는 관계대명사 what은 뒤에 주어나 목적어가 없는 불완전한 문장이 온다.

❷ 관계대명사 who, which를 대신하여 선행사를 수식하는 관계대명사 that은 뒤에 불완전한 문장이 오고, 명사절을 이끄는 접속사 that(~하는 것) 뒤에는 완전한 문장이 온다.

☑ 관계대명사 what, 관계대명사 that, 명사절 접속사 that의 비교

The instructions show **what** passengers should do in case of an emergency landing.
설명서에는 승객들이 비상착륙 시 해야 하는 일이 나와 있다.

⋯ 선행 명사 없이 앞에 타동사(show)가 있고 뒤에 타동사 do의 목적어가 없는 불완전한 문장이 오므로 what은 목적격 관계대명사

The director reviewed the proposal **that** Mr. Leighton submitted.
이사는 Mr. Leighton이 제출한 기획안을 검토했다.

⋯ 선행 명사(proposal)가 있고 뒤에 타동사 submit의 목적어가 없는 불완전한 문장이 오므로 that은 목적격 관계대명사

The company is conducting a study **that** assesses the effectiveness of last year's advertising campaign. 회사는 작년도 광고 캠페인의 효과를 평가하는 연구를 실시하고 있다.

⋯ 선행 명사(study)가 있고 뒤에 동사(assess)의 주어가 없는 불완전한 문장이 오므로 that은 주격 관계대명사

West Airlines announced **that** it will increase its nonstop flights to Los Angeles.
West 항공은 로스앤젤레스로 가는 직항 노선을 증편할 것이라고 발표했다.

⋯ 선행 명사 없이 앞에 타동사(announce)가 있고 뒤에 완전한 문장이 오므로 that은 명사절 접속사

2. 관계부사

Q5 선행사 + [which vs. where] + 완전한 문장

The company **[which / where]** she is currently conducting an investigation has been blamed for causing air pollution. [1]

>> **출제 포인트** ❶ 「접속사 + 부사」 역할을 하는 관계부사는 「전치사 + 관계대명사」로 바꿔 쓸 수 있다.

선행사	관계부사		전치사 + 관계대명사
장소 (the place, the company 등)	where	~하는 장소	장소 전치사(in, on, at, to 등) + which
시간 (the time, the period 등)	when	~하는 때	시간 전치사(in, on, at, during 등) + which
이유 (the reason)	why	~하는 이유	for which
방법 (the way)	how	~하는 방법	in which

❷ 관계부사는 뒤에 완전한 문장이 온다.

❸ 선행사 the way와 관계부사 how는 함께 쓰이지 못하므로, 둘 중 하나만 써야 한다.

The substantial organizational restructuring has resulted in a number of adjustments to how we work. 대대적인 구조조정은 우리가 일하는 방식에 많은 조정을 야기했다.
└ the way how

3. 전치사와 관계대명사

Q6 전치사 + [관계대명사 vs. 관계부사] + 완전한 문장

The community center offers a facility in **[which / where]** residents can enjoy fitness activities. [1]

선행사 + [전치사] + 목적격 관계대명사

The city will provide the land **[on / from]** which the theater is to be built. [2]

사물 선행사, + 부정대명사 + of + [whom vs. which]

E-logics, Inc. carries a wide range of computer accessories, all of **[whom / which]** can be purchased online. [3]

>> 출제 포인트

❶ 전치사 뒤에는 관계부사가 올 수 없고, 전치사 앞의 선행사에 따른 목적격 관계대명사를 쓴다. 목적격 관계대명사 앞에 전치사가 있다면 완전한 문장이 온다.

> 선행사(사람/사물) + 전치사 + 목적격 관계대명사(whom/which) + 완전한 문장

❷ 목적격 관계대명사 앞에 오는 전치사는 관계대명사 절의 동사나 선행사에 의해 결정된다.

The date **from** which members may purchase tickets for the new exhibition has been pushed back. 회원들이 새 전시회 입장권의 구매를 시작할 수 있는 날짜가 미루어졌다.

⋯→ which는 the date를 받아주는 대명사이므로 which 대신 the date를 넣고 문맥에 맞는 전치사를 선택한다. '입장권은 그 날짜부터 구매할 수 있다'는 의미가 되므로 전치사 from이 쓰였다.

❸ 선행사의 일부나 전체를 나타낼 때는 「선행사, + 수량 표현 + of + 목적격 대명사」 형태로 쓴다.

> 선행사(사람), + [all/many/most/several/some/both/half/none] + of + whom
> 선행사(사물), + [all/many/most/several/some/both/half/none] + of + which

There is a $5 admission fee to the seminar, **half of which** goes to the guest authors.
~~whom~~
세미나에는 5달러의 입장료가 있으며, 그 중 절반은 초청 저자들에게 주어진다.

Blimp Co. sells various office supplies, **all of which** can be delivered anywhere in the country within five business days for a small fee.
~~whom them~~
Blimp 사는 다양한 사무용품들을 판매하며, 그 모든 제품들은 국내 전 지역에 소정의 비용으로 5일 내에 배송될 수 있다.

4. 관계대명사의 생략

Q7 **주격 관계대명사의 생략**

Employees **[interest / interested]** in attending the workshop should contact Ms. Lim. [1]

To be reimbursed for used ink cartridges, take them to any store **[sell / selling]** our Clean Ink products. [2]

>> 출제 포인트 ❶ 주격 관계대명사 뒤에 be동사가 오는 경우 「주격 관계대명사 + be동사」를 함께 생략할 수 있다. 생략된 뒤에는 분사가 선행사인 명사를 뒤에서 수식하는 구조가 된다.

> 선행사 + who/which + be동사 + V-ing/p.p. ⋯▸ 선행사 + **V-ing/p.p.**

❷ 관계대명사 뒤에 일반동사가 오는 경우는 주격 관계대명사를 생략하고 일반동사를 분사(V-ing/p.p.)로 전환한다.

> 선행사 + who/which + 일반동사 ⋯▸ 선행사 + **일반동사의 -ing/p.p.**

Q8 **목적격 관계대명사의 생략**

Please use the copier sparingly, since the toner cartridges it requires **[are / being]** temporarily unavailable. [1]

I will put into practice all I **[have learned / was learned]** under Dr. Wayne's guidance. [2]

>> 출제 포인트 전치사 뒤에 위치한 목적격 관계대명사를 제외하고, 목적격 관계대명사 whom, which, that은 생략 가능하다. 따라서, 「명사 + 주어 + 동사」 형태로 관계대명사 없이 명사를 뒤에서 수식할 수 있다.

> 선행사 + [whom/which/that] + 주어 + 동사 ⋯▸ 선행사 + 주어 + 동사

The cafeteria **(which)** Max Ltd. has been renovating will open to employees next week.
Max 사가 개조 중인 구내식당은 다음 주에 직원들에게 개방된다.
⋯▸ renovate의 목적어 역할을 하는 목적격 관계대명사 which는 생략 가능

Many of the customers have praised the superior quality of the beef **(that)** Lazy Ranch produces. 고객들 중 상당수가 Lazy 농장이 생산하는 소고기의 우수한 품질을 칭찬했다.
⋯▸ produce의 목적어 역할을 하는 목적격 관계대명사 that은 생략 가능

Applicants are required to provide the date on **which** they are available.
지원자들은 시간이 있는 날짜를 알려주셔야 합니다.
⋯▸ 전치사 뒤의 목적격 관계대명사는 생략 불가

Practice

해설서 p.44 / 제한 시간 6분

1. Employees ------- have problems with their computers should call the company's IT support team during regular working hours.
   (A) those
   (B) who
   (C) they
   (D) some

2. Royal Tableware, Inc., ------- specializes in traditional dish making techniques, expanded its market into Latin America last year.
   (A) what
   (B) which
   (C) that
   (D) where

3. A free copy of Mr. Murphy's latest book will be given to someone that ------- in the contest.
   (A) participating
   (B) participates
   (C) will be participated
   (D) participation

4. Carol MacMillan, a world-famous author, ------- work has been translated into many languages, used to be an English teacher.
   (A) who
   (B) her
   (C) whose
   (D) that

5. Hamasaki Autos has just announced the merger with Liberty Motors, ------- will make the company the third largest vehicle manufacturer in the world.
   (A) which
   (B) what
   (C) who
   (D) whose

6. The recent increase in electricity prices has affected businesses ------- energy consumption is usually high.
   (A) whose
   (B) which
   (C) who
   (D) their

7. Please refer to the purchase order sheet, ------- you can find in the envelope, to learn when you can expect to receive your order.
   (A) whose
   (B) where
   (C) that
   (D) which

8. Every spring semester, the university holds a job fair ------- local companies interview students for job openings.
   (A) where
   (B) there
   (C) it
   (D) which

9. To visit the headquarters of Harington Corporation, please take Highway 11 south to Exit 3, ------- is next to the Eliot Building.
   (A) which
   (B) where
   (C) that
   (D) who

10. The internationally renowned architect ------- designed the Sydney Art Center will be the team leader of the project.
    (A) who
    (B) which
    (C) she
    (D) what

11. A professor of philosophy, ------- latest book was published last month, will hold a book signing event at Alpha bookstore.

(A) what
(B) his
(C) whoever
(D) whose

12. The Hill Bank offers all loan applicants one-on-one consultations during ------- details of each applicant's financial history are discussed.

(A) which
(B) where
(C) while
(D) whose

13. The Center One Building, ------- which DGN Industries has resided since it was founded, needs a lot of updating and repair.

(A) in
(B) from
(C) until
(D) down

14. Thomas Wyatt's sculptures are purchased by customers ------- tastes in art are sophisticated.

(A) who
(B) each
(C) whose
(D) what

15. Authorities will reward local manufacturers ------- decrease carbon emissions.

(A) will
(B) when
(C) that
(D) if

16. Groove Construction won this year's Building Award for its environmentally-friendly project that ------- by Ms. Schmidt.

(A) is overseeing
(B) has overseen
(C) was overseen
(D) overseen

17. The PR manager could not start the presentation because the reference material ------- requested was not ready.

(A) she
(B) that
(C) was
(D) whose

18. The Community Heritage Pride Award honors residents ------- volunteer their time to assist in restoring Grant City's historic buildings.

(A) for
(B) whose
(C) as
(D) who

19. Many customers participated in the product survey conducted by Hrudy Furniture, ------- advertisements appear in magazines and newspapers.

(A) whose
(B) its
(C) which
(D) what

20. Miles Shipping first began using larger trucks for prompt delivery, all of ------- were imprinted with the company's unique logo.

(A) them
(B) it
(C) whom
(D) which

REVIEW TEST 04

1. As neither the auditorium ------- the conference room will be available due to the renovations, regular staff meetings will not be held this month.

   (A) nor
   (B) but
   (C) or
   (D) both

2. Michelle Park not only contributes frequently to *Women's Quarterly Magazine*, but ------- articles also appear regularly in other similar publications.

   (A) whose
   (B) herself
   (C) her
   (D) whom

3. ------- other engineers at Gekko Software, Inc., Marco Shaw has extensive experience in computer programming.

   (A) Altogether
   (B) Similarly
   (C) For example
   (D) Like

4. Customers can buy the dress with 고난도 matching accessories or -------.

   (A) separating
   (B) separately
   (C) separation
   (D) to separate

5. Employees at Player-tech Company will not get paid for overtime work ------- a supervisor's approval is given in advance.

   (A) despite
   (B) without
   (C) against
   (D) unless

6. The graph shows the sales figures for Pumar Motors's top-selling automobiles ------- the past three years.

   (A) while
   (B) between
   (C) over
   (D) toward

7. Many of the bigger stores in Edinburgh are now carrying postal supplies, including ------- stamps.

   (A) commemorates
   (B) commemorate
   (C) commemorations
   (D) commemorative

8. Route 33 will be closed until the afternoon 고난도 of Saturday, September 6, ------- necessary road repairs.

   (A) instead of
   (B) due to
   (C) even though
   (D) now that

9. This exclusive range of fashion accessories will add style and ------- to any formal outfit.

   (A) sophisticate
   (B) sophistication
   (C) sophisticated
   (D) sophisticatedly

10. ------- consumer prices have been rising dramatically over the last few years, average salaries of office workers remain almost the same.

    (A) While
    (B) Since
    (C) When
    (D) However

11. ------- involved in the project needs to focus on the expected benefits and define the critical factors that will make the project successful.

(A) Who
(B) Some
(C) Everyone
(D) These

12. Baliville's newly promoted councilor is taking a ------- unique approach to improving the city's transportation network.

(A) deciding
(B) decided
(C) decidedly
(D) decision

13. The shipment from Indonesia was supposed to arrive in Chicago last Friday, ------- it has not yet left due to the unexpected adverse weather.

(A) because
(B) but
(C) unless
(D) nor

14. The building's market value has increased ------- it was acquired three years ago.

(A) when
(B) how
(C) since
(D) if

15. During the hiring season, Lea Yim will largely be responsible for one task, ------- is to arrange interviews.

(A) what
(B) that
(C) which
(D) whose

16. ------- the improving economy, job opportunities in the Larma region are increasing.

(A) In order that
(B) As a result of
(C) On behalf of
(D) Providing that

17. ------- there were some disputes about vacation days, the employees and management were able to reach an agreement.

(A) Anyone
(B) Something
(C) Although
(D) Wherever

18. ------- you do not set up a Web site immediately, be sure to select a domain name and reserve it by registering your site.

고난도

(A) Considering
(B) Even if
(C) In
(D) Yet

19. If any major defects in the home's physical structure are reported, sellers should have them repaired ------- marketing their property to prospective buyers.

고난도

(A) next
(B) before
(C) whereas
(D) finally

20. ------- difficult they may be, all tasks must be well documented and prioritized for future implementation.

고난도

(A) Almost
(B) Yet
(C) Seldom
(D) However

비교·가정법·도치

비교 구문은 형용사나 부사의 형태를 변화시켜 둘 이상의 대상을 비교할 때 사용되며, 원급, 비교급, 최상급 형태로 나타낼 수 있다. 특수 구문으로는 가정법과 도치 구문이 주로 출제된다. 실제로 일어나지 않은 상황을 가정할 때 쓰는 가정법은 if절의 동사 시제와 주절의 동사 시제에 근거하여 가정법 기본 형태를 학습한다. 가정법에서 if를 생략하거나 강조하고 싶은 내용을 문장 앞에 내보내는 경우 주어와 동사의 순서를 바꿔 도치 구문을 형성한다.

Tip! 비교급과 최상급의 단서를 파악하는 것이 포인트야. 가정법은 출제 비중이 줄긴 했지만 가정법 과거 완료와 미래에 신경 쓰자.

기본 개념 이해하기

1. 원급, 비교급, 최상급의 형태

❶ 규칙 변화

	원급	비교급	최상급
2음절 이하의 형용사	strong	stronger (원급 + er)	strongest (원급 + est)
3음절 이상의 형용사	important	more important (more + 원급)	most important (most + 원급)
부사	efficiently	more efficiently (more + 원급)	most efficiently (most + 원급)

❷ 불규칙 변화

원급	비교급	최상급
good / well	better	best
bad / ill	worse	worst
many / much	more	most
little	less	least
late	later 더 늦은 / latter 후자	latest 최근의 / last 마지막의
far	farther 더 먼 / further 추가의, 더	farthest 가장 먼 (거리) / furthest 가장 먼 (정도)

2. 비교

원급 비교	as + 원급 + as	~만큼 …한
	not + as / so + 원급 + as	~만큼 …하지 않은
비교급 비교	2음절 이하 형용사 + er + than	~보다 더 …한
	more + 3음절 이상 형용사 / 부사 + than	~보다 더 …한 / 하게
	less + 형용사 / 부사 + than	~보다 덜 …한 / 하게
	참고 비교급 강조: even, much, still, a lot, far, significantly + 비교급	
최상급 비교	the / 소유격 + 2음절 이하 형용사 + -est	가장 ~한
	the / 소유격 + most + 3음절 이상 형용사 / 부사	가장 ~한 / 하게
	the / 소유격 + least + 형용사 / 부사	가장 ~하지 않은 / 않게
	참고 최상급 강조: the + single + 최상급 ǀ even, simply, by far + the 최상급	

3. 가정법

가정법 현재 [단순 사실 · 예측]	If + 주어 + 동사(현재), 주어 + 조동사 현재형 [will / can / may] + 동사원형 　　　　　　앞으로 ~라면,　　…할 것이다 If it rains tonight, the game will be canceled. 만약 오늘밤 비가 오면, 경기는 취소될 것이다.
가정법 과거 [현재의 반대를 가정]	If + 주어 + 동사(과거), 주어 + 조동사 과거형 [would / could / might] + 동사원형 　　　　　　지금 ~라면,　　…할 텐데 If I were a millionaire, I would buy an island. 만약 내가 백만장자였다면, 섬을 샀을 텐데. ⋯▸ I am not a millionaire, so I can't buy an island. 나는 백만장자가 아니므로 섬을 살 수 없다.
가정법 과거 완료 [과거의 반대를 가정]	If + 주어 + 동사(과거 완료), 주어 + 조동사 과거형 [would / could / might] + have + p.p. 　　　　　　그때 ~했다면,　　…했을 텐데 If I'd had my cell phone yesterday, I could have contacted you. 어제 내가 휴대폰을 가지고 있었다면, 당신에게 연락할 수 있었을 텐데요. ⋯▸ I didn't have my cell phone yesterday, so I could not contact you. 어제 휴대폰이 없어서 당신에게 연락할 수 없었습니다.
혼합 가정법 [과거의 반대 + 현재의 반대]	If + 주어 + 동사(과거 완료), 주어 + 조동사 과거형 [would / could / might] + 동사원형 　　　　　　그때 ~했다면,　　지금 …할 텐데 If she had not saved my life then, I would not be alive today. 만약 그녀가 그때 내 목숨을 구하지 않았다면, 나는 오늘날 살아있지 못했을 것이다. ⋯▸ As she saved my life then, I am alive today. 그녀가 내 목숨을 구했기 때문에, 나는 오늘날 살아 있다.

비교급과 최상급의 선택 문제나 도치가 일어나는 경우와 관련된 문제가 가장 많은 출제 비중을 차지한다. 가정법 과거완료와 미래의 도치가 고난도 문제로 출제된다.

해설서 p.48

1. 비교

> **Q1** 원급 비교: as + [원급 vs. 비교급] + as
>
> Fortunately, the trip to Beijing was as **[fascinating / more fascinating]** as I expected. [1]
>
> Our firm aims to provide as much information **[as / than]** possible on environmental issues. [2]

>> **출제 포인트** 두 비교 대상이 정도 차이가 없이 동등할 때 원급 비교를 쓴다.

❶ **as + 형용사/부사의 원급 + as** '~만큼 …한/하게'

원급 비교 구문인 as ~ as 사이에 형용사나 부사의 원급이 들어가며 비교급과 최상급은 들어갈 수 없다. 원급의 품사는 as ~ as를 제외하고 문장 구조를 파악하여 결정한다.

The advertising campaign for the new computer should be changed **as dramatically as** possible to attract customer attention.
고객들의 관심을 끌려면 새 컴퓨터의 광고 캠페인이 가능한 한 크게 변경되어야 한다.

❷ **as + many/much/few/little + 명사 + as** '~만큼이나 많은/적은 …'

원급 비교 구문에서 as ~ as 사이에 가산 명사 복수를 쓰는 경우, 그 앞에 many나 few의 수식을 받고, 불가산 명사를 쓰는 경우 much나 little의 수식을 받아 함께 쓰인다.

The manager should collect **as many opinions as** possible to make an effective decision.
매니저는 효과적인 결정을 내리기 위해 되도록 많은 의견을 수집해야 한다.

Q2 비교급 비교: [비교급 vs. 최상급] + than

Our store guarantees that we offer **[cheaper / cheapest]** products than our competitors. [1]

Because the investment was much more profitable **[than / as]** he expected, Mr. Cruze decided to give a bonus to the analyst. [2]

Now that Mr. Karmer's restaurant is **[so / even]** more profitable than last year, he is planning to open another one in the downtown area. [3]

Since Ben became Head Chef, the restaurant's dishes have become **[chiefly / markedly]** better. [4]

>> **출제 포인트** 정도 차이가 있는 두 대상을 비교할 때 비교급 비교를 쓴다.

❶ **비교급 비교 형태**

1 음절 단어+ -er + than	~보다 더 …한/하게
more + 2음절 이상 단어 + than	~보다 더 …한/하게
less + 형용사/부사 + than	~보다 덜 …한/하게

❷ **비교급 강조 부사**: even, much, still, a lot, far, significantly, considerably, noticeably, markedly는 '훨씬'이라는 의미로 형용사나 부사의 비교급을 강조한다. very, so, quite, too는 '매우'라는 의미로 형용사나 부사의 원급을 강조하고, 비교급 앞에는 쓸 수 없다.

❸ '~보다'라는 의미의 than은 문맥상 비교 대상인 A와 B가 명확할 경우 than이 없이도 비교급을 쓸 수 있다.

Payment problems have become **much more manageable** since a new computer system was installed. 새 컴퓨터 시스템이 설치된 이후 대금지불 문제의 취급이 훨씬 더 쉬워졌다.

⤍ 새로운 시스템이 설치된 이래로 설치되기 이전보다 납부 관련 문제들이 처리되기 쉬워졌다는 내용으로 비교 대상을 명확히 알 수 있어 than 이하를 생략한 문장이다. much는 비교급을 강조하는 부사이다.

❹ **-or 형 비교급**은 비교 대상 앞에 than 대신 to를 쓴다.

prior to (= earlier than, ahead of)	~보다 먼저, ~이전에
superior to	~보다 우수한
inferior to	~보다 열등한

The recently released version of the software is far **superior to** last year's version.
최근에 출시된 버전의 소프트웨어가 작년 버전보다 훨씬 더 훌륭하다.

Q3 최상급 비교: the/소유격 + [비교급 vs. 최상급]

The ZPX Pro is currently regarded as the **[more speed / speediest]** tablet PC on the market. [1]

Updating the customer database is one of your **[more important / most important]** duties. [2]

The ratings received by the television news program were the **[high / highest]** of all local news shows. [3]

>> **출제 포인트** 셋 이상의 비교 대상 중 하나가 우월함을 나타낼 때 최상급 비교를 쓴다.

❶ 최상급 형태: 최상급은 그 앞에 특정 대상을 보여주는 정관사 the나 소유격이 있어야 한다.

the/소유격 + 1음절 단어 + -est	가장 ~한
the/소유격 + most + 2음절 이상 단어	가장 ~한
the/소유격 + least + 형용사/부사	가장 덜 ~한/하게

The washing machine was **the most energy efficient** model we have ever tested.
그 세탁기는 우리가 테스트해본 것들 중 에너지 효율성이 가장 높은 모델이었다.

Mr. Lesley**'s latest** novel will be on sale in bookstores in March.
Mr. Lesley의 최신 소설은 3월에 서점에서 판매될 것이다.

❷ 최상급 단서

☑ **최상급과 함께 쓰이는 표현**

the + 최상급 + 명사 + **of[among]** + 전체 명사	~중에서 가장 …한
the + 최상급 + 명사 + **in** + 장소 명사	~에서 가장 …한
the + 최상급 + 명사 + 주어 + **have (ever) p.p.**	지금까지 ~한 것 중 가장 …한
one of[among] + the + 최상급 + 복수 명사	가장 ~한 것들 중 하나
the + **서수** + 최상급 + 명사	~번째로 …한
the + **single** + 최상급 + 명사	단연 가장 ~한
the + 최상급 + 명사 + **available[possible]**	이용 가능한 것 중 가장 …한

Martha's Inn is now **the most popular** choice among Delaware's bed and breakfasts.
Martha 호텔은 현재 델라웨어에서 아침식사를 제공하는 숙박시설 중 가장 인기 있는 선택이다.

Advertising on TV is one of **the most effective** means to attract prospective customers.
TV 광고는 잠재적 고객들을 이끄는데 가장 효과적인 수단 중 하나이다.

Port Durban is **the second largest** port in Africa.
Port Durban은 아프리카에서 두 번째로 큰 항구이다.

Rinnest Labs continually updates its equipment to make **the most accurate** reports available to its technicians.
Rinnest 연구소는 기술자들이 가장 정확한 보고서를 이용할 수 있도록 지속적으로 장비를 업데이트한다.

❸ 최상급 강조 부사: even, by far, simply, single, ever

The results of these tests are **the single most important** factor in determining each year's new product line.

이러한 테스트의 결과가 매년 신제품군을 결정하는 데 있어 가장 중요한 요인이다.

❹ 최상급 뒤에 오는 명사의 의미가 명백할 때 명사는 생략 가능하다.

The expandable dinner table remains among **the most popular** (dinner tables).

확장식 식탁은 가장 인기 있는 식탁 중 하나이다.

The painting, *The Boy with the Blue Feather*, is **the most valuable** (painting) in the museum's collection.

회화작품 〈The Boy with the Blue Feather〉는 미술관의 소장품 중에서 가장 가치 있는 것이다.

Q4 비교급 앞에 **the**를 쓰는 경우

The more information we gather from customers, **[more / the more]** accurate our research findings will be. [1]

The government decided to give support and subsidies to the **[small / smaller]** of the two companies. [2]

>> 출제 포인트   비교급 앞에는 the를 쓰지 않지만, 예외적으로 반드시 the를 써야 하는 비교급 표현들이 있다.

the + 비교급 ~, the + 비교급	~하면 할수록, 더욱 …하다
the + 비교급 + of the two ~	둘 중에서 더 ~한 것

Q5 관용 표현

Please submit the application form no **[longer / later]** than June 20. [1]

Mr. Iwata's flight was delayed for **[more / rather]** than five hours, so he couldn't make it to the client meeting. [2]

The sales event is most **[probably / probable]** the reason for the increase in customers. [3]

>> 출제 포인트　✓ 비교 관용 표현

the same(+ 명사) as	~와 같은
no later than, by	늦어도 ~까지
no longer, not any longer	더 이상 ~하지 않다
rather than	~보다는
other than	~이외에
more than	~이상
less than	~미만
at least	적어도, 최소한
비교급 + than any other 단수 명사	다른 어떤 ~보다 더 …하다
more than doubled / tripled	두 배/세 배 이상
비교급 + than ever	그 어느 때보다 더 ~한
비교급 than expected / planned	예상/계획했던 것보다 더 ~한
most probably[likely] the + 명사	아마도(가장 가능성이 큰)

2. 가정법

Q6 **가정법의 형태**

If he had received the building design earlier, Mr. Hoffman **[had been beginning / could have begun]** the project before the end of March. [1]

Barton, Inc. warned that it **[will / would]** reevaluate its business relations with its distributors if they did not abide by the terms and conditions. [2]

If you **[had / should have]** any questions, please feel free to call our customer center. [3]

>> 출제 포인트   if절과 주절의 동사 시제를 짝지어, 가정법 형태를 암기해야 한다.

가정법 과거 (현재의 사실과 반대되는 가정)

If 주어 + 과거 동사, 주어+ <u>would/should/could/might</u> + 동사원형
  (지금) 만약 ~한다면,   …일 텐데

가정법 과거 완료 (과거의 사실과 반대되는 가정)

If 주어 + 과거 완료 동사(had p.p.), 주어 + <u>would/should/could/might</u> + have + p.p.
  (과거에) 만약 ~했다면,   …했을 텐데

가정법 미래 (미래에 실현 가능성이 적은 가정이나 매우 공손한 표현)

If + 주어 + <u>should</u> 동사원형, ┌ <u>명령문</u>
  (미래에) 혹시 ~하면,   └ …해라
                    └ 주어 + <u>will/can/would/could</u> + 동사원형
                           …할 것이다

가정법 현재 (미래에 실현 가능성이 있는 단순 가정)

If + 주어 + <u>현재 동사</u>, 주어 + <u>will/can</u> + 동사원형
  만약 ~하면,   …할 것이다

3. 도치 구문

Q7 if가 생략된 가정법 과거 완료

[Had / Have] the technicians complied with all safety measures, an accident would not have occurred. [1]

if가 생략된 가정법 미래

Poznaski Renovation will charge more than the initial estimate [when / should] additional working days be required to meet the deadline. [2]

>> 출제 포인트   가정법에서 if가 생략되면 (조)동사가 주어 앞으로 이동하는 도치가 일어난다. 토익에서는 가정법 과거 완료와 가정법 미래의 도치 구문이 주로 출제된다.

가정법 과거 완료

If + 주어 + had p.p., 주어 + would/could/might + have + p.p.

··· **Had + 주어 + p.p.**, 주어 + would/could/might + have + p.p.

가정법 미래

If + 주어 + should + 동사원형, 명령문/주어 + will[would] + 동사원형

··· **Should + 주어 + 동사원형**, 명령문/주어 + will[would] + 동사원형

Q8 부정어 도치: Never + [주어 + 동사 vs. 동사 + 주어]

Never **[we have / have we]** experienced such outstanding service anywhere. [1]

Be동사 보어 도치: [Enclosure vs. Enclosed] + Be동사 + 주어

[Enclosure / Enclosed] are the materials requested for the training session. [2]

긍정의 연속: 긍정문, and so + [주어 + 동사 vs. 동사 + 주어]

The rent should be paid by the 10th of every month, and so **[utility bills should / should utility bills]**. [3]

>> **출제 포인트**

도치는 의미 강조를 목적으로 주어와 (조)동사의 위치를 바꿔 표현하는 것을 말하며, 다음의 경우 도치 형태로 쓰인다.

❶ 부정어나 only가 문장의 맨 앞에 오는 경우

Never/Hardly/Seldom/Little + 동사 + 주어	거의 ~않다
Only + 부사(구/절) + 동사 + 주어	~만 …하다

Only with this receipt **can customers get** a fuel discount.
이 영수증이 있어야만 고객들이 주유비 할인을 받을 수 있습니다.

❷ be동사의 보어가 문장의 맨 앞에 오는 경우

Enclosed/Attached/Included + is(are) + 주어	주어가 동봉/첨부/포함되다

Attached **is a copy** of the lease agreement.
임대계약서 사본을 첨부했습니다.

❸ so, neither가 문장의 맨 앞에 오는 경우

긍정문, and so/as + 동사 + 주어	~도 그렇다
부정문, and neither/nor + 동사 + 주어	~도 그렇지 않다

The ones in the office were not working, and neither **were the outside surveillance cameras.** 사무실 내부의 감시카메라가 작동하지 않았으며 외부도 마찬가지였다.

Mr. Madden will not attend the marketing workshop nor **will Mr. Wareham.**
Mr. Madden은 마케팅 워크숍에 참석하지 않을 것이며 Mr. Wareham도 마찬가지다.

> **cf** neither는 부사이므로 접속사와 연결되고, nor는 접속사이므로 다른 접속사 없이 바로 절을 연결한다.
> 즉, and neither = nor의 관계가 성립된다. 마찬가지로 and so = as이다.

Practice

1. Ever since the stock market collapsed, consumers have been asked to sell stock as ------- as possible.

(A) cautious
(B) cautiously
(C) more cautious
(D) more cautiously

2. The results of the questionnaire showed that consumers responded even ------- to the new features of the APX Orange smart phone than expected.

(A) more favorable
(B) favorably
(C) most favorably
(D) more favorably

3. Had we been aware of the guests' complaints during their stay at our hotel, we ------- to move them to another room.

(A) would have offered
(B) has offered
(C) is being offered
(D) would have been offered

4. ------- are the descriptions of currently available positions that need to be posted in the next few days.

(A) Attach
(B) Attachment
(C) Attaching
(D) Attached

5. Few of the air purifiers tested for their capacity turned out to be as effective ------- their manufacturers claimed.

(A) either
(B) like
(C) as
(D) of

6. Because business language can be more technical and formal ------- conversational speech, decide whether or not you need an interpreter.

(A) than
(B) within
(C) as
(D) less

7. With the help of state-of-the-art equipment, the manager is expecting the workers to work much -------.

(A) more efficient
(B) most efficiently
(C) efficient
(D) more efficiently

8. ------- should any confidential document be distributed by interoffice correspondence such as a messenger, a text message, or an e-mail.

(A) Never
(B) Appropriately
(C) Although
(D) Ever

9. ------- all the applicants for the regional manager position, Jennifer Lee is obviously the most qualified for the job.

(A) In
(B) Of
(C) At
(D) Out

10. Of the 10 members of the Marketing
고난도 Department, Mr. Watters is the ------- about the target market.

(A) knowledgeable
(B) knowledge
(C) more knowledgeable
(D) most knowledgeable

11. ------- you have any further questions regarding our affiliate program, please do not hesitate to ask me after I have finished my presentation.

(A) Whether
(B) Should
(C) Throughout
(D) Although

12. If workers had followed the safety precautions more carefully, accidents ------- so frequently.

(A) will not happen
(B) didn't happen
(C) had not been happening
(D) would not have happened

13. Since her promotion last fall, Ms. Anderson has quickly become one of the company's ------- division supervisors.

(A) competently
(B) more competent
(C) most competent
(D) competency

14. The advertising director cannot participate in the board meeting on Thursday, and ------- can the marketing director.

(A) neither
(B) however
(C) so
(D) also

15. Given the steady decline in its sales, Pure Skin is ------- the primary cosmetics provider in the market.

(A) another
(B) no longer
(C) anymore
(D) not enough

16. Only recently have the company's architects ------- the proposed support beam modifications for the new factory.

(A) assessing
(B) assessed
(C) will assess
(D) assesses

17. The shipbuilding industry is the ------- largest business in this part of the country, which has created more than 20,000 jobs.

(A) single
(B) singles
(C) singly
(D) singled

18. Among the nine candidates Ms. Brook has interviewed, Mr. Sanders is the ------- highly qualified.

(A) much
(B) such
(C) so
(D) most

19. Ms. Williams ------- her position as Vice President of Wyn Motors had the merger with Damaso Automobile Company succeeded.

(A) is being relinquished
(B) would have relinquished
(C) has been relinquishing
(D) will be relinquished

20. Only after the quality standards were met did the electronics company ------- to mass produce its new products.

(A) began
(B) begin
(C) beginning
(D) begun

REVIEW TEST 05

해설서 p.50 / ⏱ 제한 시간 10분

1. We aim to offer you the ------- selection of chocolates in the country.

(A) wider
(B) widest
(C) more widely
(D) most widely

2. The Mandalu area's average temperatures have not been ------- high in almost a decade.

(A) much
(B) this
(C) how
(D) more

3. IPA is considering expanding and will look for an additional ------- that has stores in Florida.

(A) retails
(B) retailing
(C) retailed
(D) retailer

4. Janti's Diner conducts inspections on a regular basis to make sure it meets ------- food safety standards.

(A) rigorously
(B) rigors
(C) rigor
(D) rigorous

5. We proudly introduce our new product, which is much more cost-effective than ------- other merchandise on the market.

(A) each
(B) any
(C) one
(D) many

6. ------- the hospital's most experienced physicians are required to attend medical conferences every year.

(A) Nearly
(B) Even
(C) Although
(D) Such

7. While most customers will find the GXT 2000 model easy to use, those ------- familiar with smartphones should read the manual carefully first.

고난도

(A) little
(B) none
(C) less
(D) fewer

8. Moa Cosmetics strives to make high-quality and affordable skincare products more ------- available to consumers.

(A) ready
(B) readied
(C) readier
(D) readily

9. Comfort Electronics is going through more changes ------- what the management had previously expected.

(A) where
(B) that
(C) which
(D) than

10. If you are not satisfied with any product that we sell, we will promptly replace it with ------- one or refund your money.

(A) another
(B) each other
(C) all
(D) other

11. When applying to GXT Mart, you have the option of ------- visiting the office and applying in person, or submitting a job application online.

(A) not only
(B) neither
(C) either
(D) both

12. The head chef at the Burmese Catering Firm indicated that ------- the highest-quality ingredients would be used for the banquet at the Imperial Hotel.

(A) once
(B) only
(C) ever
(D) when

13. The most ------- of Criogenic's many 고난도 domestic subsidiaries is the Chicagobased Virtel Corporation.

(A) profits
(B) profit
(C) profitable
(D) profitably

14. Candidates were asked to talk about the project on which they worked the ------- and a project that they look forward to starting.

(A) hard
(B) harder
(C) hardest
(D) hardly

15. The career of actress Wilma Bernhoff started ------- her appearance on a local television show in Germany.

(A) regarding
(B) toward
(C) with
(D) over

16. The Meteorological Department forecasts that there will be ------- two inches of rain between tonight and Sunday morning.

(A) approximate
(B) approximately
(C) approximation
(D) approximated

17. The software developers recently created 고난도 a program that is ------- too complex for the majority of users.

(A) well
(B) pretty
(C) quite
(D) far

18. As our aging population continues to grow, 고난도 ------- the demand for both healthcare workers and residential care facilities.

(A) so does
(B) as long as
(C) whereas
(D) as to

19. Our company has ------- been stronger or better positioned for sustained growth than it is now.

(A) none
(B) anytime
(C) never
(D) quite

20. No sooner had they released their new 고난도 products ------- their sales more than doubled.

(A) while
(B) but
(C) than
(D) and

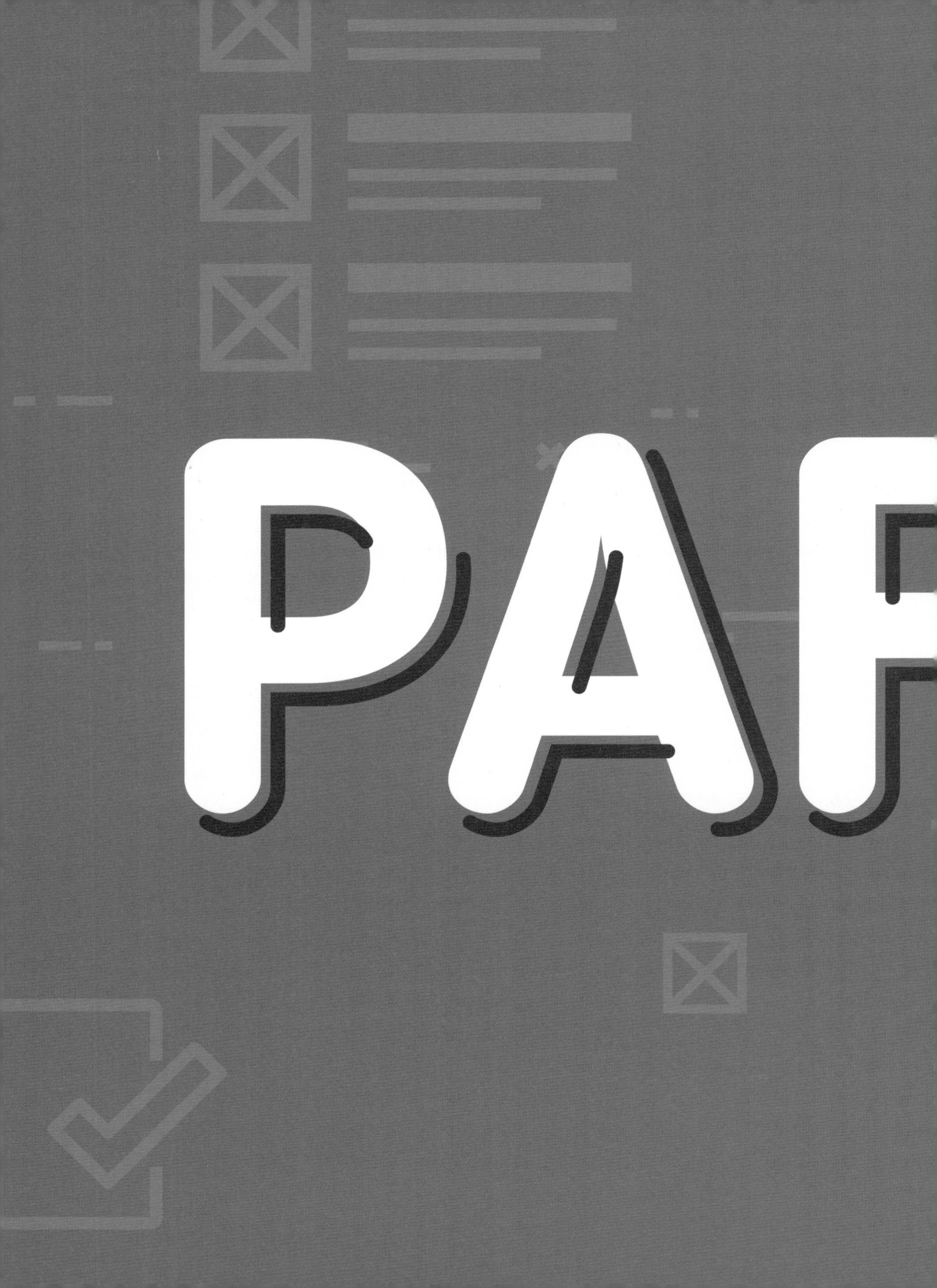

VOCA

RT5

단문 빈칸
채우기

동사

어휘 유형 확인하기

해설서 p.53

Q1 특정 전치사를 단서로 접근하는 자동사 어휘 문제

Employees who work in the Design Department should contact Kent Abone to **[attend / register]** for the workshop. [1]

Attorneys for the Local Business Association will **[respond / review]** to any questions concerning the recently revised contracts. [2]

>> **출제 포인트** 빈칸 뒤에 **전치사가 위치한 동사 어휘 문제는 자동사를 묻는 문제**이므로 자주 출제되는 자동사와 타동사를 정확히 구분하며 암기해야 한다.

✓ 시험에 자주 출제되는 「자동사 + 전치사」

to	adhere to	~을 준수하다
	respond[reply] to	~에 응답하다
	react to	~에 반응하다
	talk[speak] to	~에게 말하다
from	refrain from	~을 삼가다
	differ from / in	~와 / ~에서 다르다
	benefit from	~로부터 이익을 얻다
with	comply with	~을 준수하다
	deal with	~을 다루다
	experiment with	~을 가지고 실험하다
	interfere with	~을 방해하다
	compete with[against]	~와 경쟁하다
on	depend[rely] on	~에 의존하다
	concentrate[focus] on	~에 집중하다
	collaborate on / with	~에 관해 / ~와 함께 협력하다
	agree (up)on	~에 관하여 동의하다
	comment on	~에 대해 논평하다
of	dispose of	~을 폐기하다
	consist of	~으로 구성되어 있다
in	enroll in	~에 등록하다
	specialize in	~을 전문으로 하다
	participate in	~에 참여하다
for	look[search] for	~을 찾다
	apply for	~에 지원하다
	account for	~을 설명하다
	register[sign up] for	~에 신청하다

Q2 목적어를 단서로 접근하는 타동사 어휘 문제

The decision to **[extend / promote]** the deadline was made after a thorough examination of company priorities. [1]

The property developer is currently collecting the documents that are required to **[inform / obtain]** a permit for construction. [2]

Mr. Hahn, the senior engineer at Helicon Tech, **[invented / exceeded]** several groundbreaking communication devices. [3]

>> 출제 포인트

타동사 어휘 문제의 경우 뒤에 위치한 **목적어**를 가장 중요한 단서로 파악하여 문제를 해결한다. 특히, inform, remind, notify, advise가 어휘 문제로 제시된 경우에는 뒤에 대상(~에게)에 해당하는 목적어가 위치할 경우에만 정답이 될 수 있음에 주의한다.

> inform / remind / notify / advise + 사람 / 회사 등의 대상 + of 명사 / that 주어 + 동사

☑ 시험에 자주 출제되는 「타동사 + 목적어」

address the issue	문제를 처리하다	meet the needs	요구를 충족시키다
conduct a survey	(설문) 조사를 실시하다	obtain a permit / pass	허가증 / 출입증을 얻다
express concern	우려를 표하다	reach a conclusion	결론에 도달하다
implement the plan	계획을 시행하다	renew an agreement	계약을 갱신하다
invent medical devices	의료장치들을 발명하다	reserve a seat	좌석을 예약하다
issue a statement	성명서를 발표하다	streamline the production process	생산 과정을 능률적으로 만들다
make a decision	결정을 내리다		

Q3 수동태 문장에서 주어를 목적어로 파악하여 접근하는 동사 어휘 문제

A customer survey will be **[conducted / predicted]** to determine what changes to make to our advertising campaign. [1]

All of the Freshwater Hotel's conference rooms have been **[reserved / conducted]** for this weekend, so we need to find another venue for our company's banquet. [2]

>> 출제 포인트

be동사 뒤 과거분사 자리의 동사 어휘 문제는 **수동태 구조의 주어가 능동태 구조에서 목적어**임을 활용하여 문제를 푼다.

빈출 어휘	의미	기출 표현
1 **accommodate**	수용하다	accommodate a tour group ⋯ 단체 여행객을 수용하다
2 **acknowledge**	(받았음을) 알리다, 인정하다	acknowledge receipt of ⋯ ~의 수령을 알리다
3 **acquire**	취득하다, 인수하다	acquire the property ⋯ 부동산을 취득하다
4 **address**	(일, 문제 등을) 다루다, 연설하다	address concerns/complaints ⋯ 우려/불평을 다루다
5 **afford**	~할 여유가 있다 (+ to 동사원형)	can't afford to replace ⋯ 대체할 여력이 없다
6 **allocate**	할당하다	allocate limited resources ⋯ 제한된 자원을 할당하다
7 **analyze**	분석하다	analyze the market situation ⋯ 시장 상황을 분석하다
8 **appreciate**	감사하다, 진가를 알다	appreciate your contribution ⋯ 귀하의 기여에 감사 드린다
9 **appoint**	임명하다, 정하다	appoint a new President ⋯ 신임 대표를 임명하다
10 **arrange**	(일정, 약속 등을) 처리[주선]하다 준비하다	arrange interviews for potential employees ⋯ 구직자들을 위한 면접을 잡다 arrange for all letters of recommendation to be sent ⋯ 모든 추천서가 발송되도록 준비해 두다
11 **assemble**	조립하다	assemble the product ⋯ 제품을 조립하다
12 **assume**	(직책, 책임을) 떠맡다, 추정하다	assume responsibility ⋯ 책임을 떠맡다
13 **attend**	참석하다	attend a conference/seminar ⋯ 회의/세미나에 참석하다
14 **attract**	유치하다, 끌어모으다	attract new customers ⋯ 신규 고객들을 유치하다
15 **attribute**	A를 B 덕택으로 생각하다 (A to B)	attribute the company's success to its employees ⋯ 그 회사의 성공을 직원들 덕택이라고 생각하다
16 **collaborate**	협력하다 (with/on)	collaborate closely with the university on this project ⋯ 그 대학과 이 프로젝트에 대해 긴밀히 협력하다
17 **certify**	인증하다	certify a product ⋯ 제품을 인증하다
18 **clarify**	명확히 하다	clarify schedule changes ⋯ 일정 변경들을 명확히 하다
19 **coincide**	(두 가지 일이) 동시에 일어나다, 일치하다 (with)	coincide with the opening ceremony ⋯ 개막식과 동시에 일어나다
20 **complete**	완료하다	complete a survey form ⋯ 설문 양식을 완료하다

빈출 어휘	의미	기출 표현
21 **commute**	통근하다	commute to work by bus ⋯ 버스로 통근하다
22 **conduct**	수행하다, 실시하다	conduct a survey / an inspection / research ⋯ 설문 / 검사 / 연구를 실시하다
23 **confirm**	확인하다	confirm an appointment ⋯ 약속을 확인하다
24 **conform**	(규칙, 법 등을) 따르다 (to)	conform to safety regulations ⋯ 안전 규정을 따르다
25 **conserve**	절약하다, 보존하다	conserve energy / resources ⋯ 에너지 / 자원을 절약하다
26 **decline**	감소하다	have declined substantially ⋯ 상당히 감소했다
	거절하다	decline the invitation ⋯ 초대를 거절하다
27 **demonstrate**	보여주다, 입증하다	demonstrate capabilities of the new software ⋯ 새로운 소프트웨어의 성능을 보여주다
28 **designate**	지정하다, 임명하다	be specially designated for library employees only ⋯ 도서관 직원들만을 위해 특별히 지정되다
29 **determine**	결정하다, 알아내다	determine the location ⋯ 장소를 결정하다
30 **diagnose**	진단하다	diagnose a disease ⋯ 병을 진단하다
31 **dispose**	~을 처리하다(없애다) (of)	dispose of waste products appropriately ⋯ 산업 폐기물을 올바르게 처리하다
32 **disregard**	무시하다	disregard the previous bills ⋯ 이전의 청구서들을 무시하다
33 **distinguish**	구별하다 (A from B)	distinguish fact from opinion ⋯ 사실과 의견을 구별하다
34 **distribute**	배포하다, 유통시키다 (A to B / A among B)	distribute a memo to employees ⋯ 직원들에게 회람을 배포하다
35 **endorse**	(광고 등에서 상품을) 보증하다	endorse the new product ⋯ 신제품을 홍보하다
36 **enhance**	향상시키다	enhance the efficiency / capacity ⋯ 효율성 / 용량을 향상시키다
37 **exceed**	초과하다	exceed expectations ⋯ 예상을 초과하다
38 **expand**	확대하다	expand presence ⋯ (시장에서) 입지를 확대하다
39 **expire**	(기한이) 만료되다	The warranty / contract is due to expire. ⋯ 보증 / 계약이 만료될 예정이다.
40 **enroll**	등록하다 (in)	enroll in an advanced course ⋯ 고급 과정에 등록하다

빈출 어휘	의미	기출 표현
41 **extend**	연장하다	extend the deadline ⋯› 마감일을 연장하다
42 **entitle**	~ 할 자격[권한]을 주다 (to 명사/동사원형)	be entitled to a full refund / paid vacation ⋯› 전액 환불 / 유급 휴가의 권한이 주어지다
43 **ensure**	확실히 하다 (that 절)	ensure that the fire equipment operates properly ⋯› 화재 장비가 올바르게 작동하는지 확실히 하다
44 **evaluate**	평가하다	evaluate the employee's performance ⋯› 직원들의 업무 성과를 평가하다
45 **generate**	발생시키다, 초래하다	generate revenue ⋯› 수익을 발생시키다
46 **handle**	처리하다, 다루다	handle urgent requests ⋯› 긴급한 요청들을 처리하다
47 **hesitate**	주저하다 (to 동사원형)	Do not hesitate to ask for assistance. ⋯› 도움을 요청하는 것을 주저하지 마세요.
48 **illustrate**	설명하다, 예시하다	illustrate an abstract concept ⋯› 추상적인 개념을 설명하다
49 **implement**	실행하다, 시행하다	implement a strategy / policy ⋯› 전략 / 정책을 실행하다
50 **institute**	(제도, 규정 등을) 마련하다, 실시하다	institute a new benefits package ⋯› 새로운 복리후생 제도를 마련하다
51 **intend**	의도하다 (to 동사원형)	intend to promote the weekend activities ⋯› 주말 활동을 홍보하고자 의도하다
52 **interfere**	지장을 주다 (with)	interfere with the legislative process ⋯› 입법 과정에 지장을 주다
53 **lower**	(정도, 양, 가격 등을) 낮추다	lower overhead costs ⋯› 간접비를 낮추다
54 **locate**	위치하다 ~의 위치를 찾아내다	be conveniently / centrally located ⋯› 편리하게 / 중앙에 위치하다 locate nearby libraries ⋯› 가까운 도서관들을 찾다
55 **modify**	(부분적으로) 변경하다, 수정하다	modify the terms of a contract ⋯› 계약 조건들을 변경하다
56 **observe**	준수하다, 관찰하다	observe safety regulations / guidelines ⋯› 안전 규정 / 지침들을 준수하다
57 **obtain**	얻다, 획득하다	obtain consent / a permit / a pass ⋯› 허가 / 허가증 / 통행증을 얻다
58 **participate**	참석하다 (in)	participate in the seminar ⋯› 세미나에 참석하다
59 **postpone**	연기하다	postpone the fundraising event ⋯› 기금 모금 행사를 연기하다
60 **proceed**	진행하다 (with) ~로 나아가다 (to)	proceed with negotiations ⋯› 협상을 진행하다 proceed to the baggage counter ⋯› 수하물 카운터로 가다

	빈출 어휘	의미	기출 표현
☐ 61	**prohibit**	금지하다	prohibit the use of electronics ⋯→ 전자기기 사용을 금지하다
☐ 62	**promote**	홍보하다, 촉진시키다 승진시키다	promote a tourist destination ⋯→ 여행 목적지를 홍보하다 be promoted to Vice President ⋯→ 부사장으로 승진되다
☐ 63	**qualify**	~에 대한 자격을 갖추다 (for)	qualify for reimbursement ⋯→ 환급에 대한 자격을 갖추다
☐ 64	**recognize**	(공로를) 인정[표창]하다, 인식하다	be recognized for good customer service ⋯→ 좋은 고객 서비스에 대해 인정받다
☐ 65	**refrain**	삼가다, 자제하다 (from)	refrain from bringing beverages ⋯→ 음료수를 가지고 오는 것을 삼가다
☐ 66	**release**	공개하다, 출시하다	release further information ⋯→ 추가 정보를 공개하다
☐ 67	**renew**	갱신하다	renew membership/subscription/contract ⋯→ 회원 자격/구독/계약을 갱신하다
☐ 68	**reserve**	예약하다 (권리를) 가지다	reserve a venue ⋯→ 장소를 예약하다 reserve the right ⋯→ 권리를 가지다
☐ 69	**respond**	응답하다, 대응하다 (to)	respond to inquiries ⋯→ 문의에 응답하다
☐ 70	**retain**	보유하다, 유지하다	retain all receipts ⋯→ 모든 영수증을 보유하다
☐ 71	**reveal**	보여주다, 밝히다 (that 절)	a recent report/study/analysis revealed that ~ ⋯→ 최근의 보고서/연구/분석은 ~하다는 내용을 보여줬다
☐ 72	**secure**	확보하다, ~을 고정시키다 [형] 안전한	secure a parking place 주차공간을 확보하다
☐ 73	**simplify**	간소화하다	simplify application procedures ⋯→ 지원 절차들을 간소화하다
☐ 74	**specialize**	~을 전문으로 하다 (in)	specialize in computer repairs ⋯→ 컴퓨터 수리를 전문으로 하다
☐ 75	**specify**	(구체적으로) 명시하다	specify a desired salary figure ⋯→ 희망 연봉을 명시하다 as specified ⋯→ 명시된 대로 [cf] as + p.p. ~한대로
☐ 76	**sustain**	지속시키다, 유지하다	sustain revenue growth ⋯→ 수익 성장을 지속시키다
☐ 77	**undergo**	(변화·일 등을) 겪다(받다), 경험하다	undergo extensive renovations ⋯→ 대규모 수리를 받다
☐ 78	**urge**	권고하다 (A + to 동사원형)	strongly urge employees to attend the seminar ⋯→ 직원들이 세미나에 참석하도록 강력히 권고하다
☐ 79	**verify**	확인하다, 입증하다	verify plants' compliance with local health laws ⋯→ 공장들의 지역 보건법 준수를 확인하다
☐ 80	**waive**	(요금을) 면제해 주다	waive a delivery/entry fees ⋯→ 배송비/입장료를 면제해 주다

Practice

해설서 p.53 / ⏱ 제한 시간 6분

1. Mr. Fujimori has decided to ------- the sales meeting because of a scheduling conflict

(A) evaluate
(B) postpone
(C) identify
(D) promote

2. Please ------- from feeding animals while visiting the National Zoo.

고난도

(A) refrain
(B) emerge
(C) prohibit
(D) differ

3. Due to the ongoing repairs in the laboratory, please do not enter the facility until you are ------- otherwise.

고난도

(A) realized
(B) searched
(C) notified
(D) achieved

4. Professor Harrison's achievement is impressive, considering how hastily he had to ------- the project to meet the deadline.

(A) qualify
(B) entitle
(C) complete
(D) attend

5. A new regulation, which ------- all residents in the apartment complex from smoking, has just been passed unanimously.

(A) holds
(B) alienates
(C) turns
(D) prohibits

6. The estimate we requested yesterday has already been received, so we can ------- to the next step more quickly.

(A) proceed
(B) impress
(C) depend
(D) support

7. To ------- the increasing demand for environmentally-friendly products, McKane, Inc. is developing an eco-friendly laundry detergent.

(A) exchange
(B) predict
(C) accommodate
(D) justify

8. It is better for the team to ------- the roles and responsibilities of each team member before starting the new project.

(A) conduct
(B) respond
(C) clarify
(D) conform

9. All of the employees at Borrester Marketing and their family members are invited to ------- the Borrester Movie Night, which takes place once a month.

(A) specialize
(B) admit
(C) attend
(D) participate

10. Managers at Kerry's Megamart are expected to ------- any employee issues that may arise.

(A) set
(B) have
(C) resolve
(D) wonder

11. Peter Simpson, the renowned fashion designer, recently ------- with Eder Electronics in order to design a new refrigerator.

(A) employed
(B) collaborated
(C) offered
(D) retired

12. The HR director will review the designs for the expanded break room and ------- one to submit to the CEO.

(A) agree
(B) operate
(C) apply
(D) choose

13. Over the last decade, Ms. Sharma has been ------- as an exceptionally valuable member of the sales team by her colleagues.

(A) recognized
(B) accustomed
(C) resigned
(D) implemented

14. Xia Motors ------- its increased market 고난도 share to the acquisition of GX Motors.

(A) randomizes
(B) accounts
(C) assumes
(D) attributes

15. The committee voted to ------- a tentative 고난도 agreement with the developer that wants to construct a fairly large stadium next to the city's convention center.

(A) justify
(B) elevate
(C) endorse
(D) obtain

16. The phone reservation system has been discontinued as of today, so all patients must ------- appointments via e-mail.

(A) arrange
(B) convince
(C) instruct
(D) say

17. The management at Prix, Inc. wants to ------- employees' stress by promoting more flexible work schedules.

(A) enhance
(B) lower
(C) dedicate
(D) refrain

18. At the 35th anniversary ceremony, Ms. Moon was honored for having ------- dedication over 20 years of service to the company.

(A) demonstrated
(B) collaborated
(C) granted
(D) explained

19. A representative from the Human 고난도 Resources Department is scheduled to meet with employees to ------- any concerns relating to performance appraisals.

(A) comment
(B) address
(C) enhance
(D) observe

20. Once their application documents have been reviewed, selected candidates will be ------- for interviews.

(A) stated
(B) signaled
(C) produced
(D) invited

UNIT 02 명사

🔍 어휘 유형 확인하기

해설서 p.55

Q1 전치사를 단서로 접근하는 명사 어휘 문제

Office Supplies sells computer desks in a **[connection / variety]** of styles and sizes to suit your needs. [1]

Random inspections are conducted to verify plants' **[compliance / access]** with the safety regulations. [2]

>> 출제 포인트 **특정 전치사**와 함께 쓰이는 명사 표현에 유의하여 명사 어휘 문제를 푼다.

to	access to	~에 대한 접근
	admission to	~에 입장
	contribution to	~에 대한 기여
	answer to	~에 대한 답변
	alternative to	~의 대안
	commitment[dedication] to	~에 대한 전념
	solution to	~에 대한 해결책
	reaction to	~에 대한 반응
in	a decrease[decline, reduction] in	~에서의 감소
	a rise[increase] in	~에서의 증가
	a change[shift] in	~에서의 변화
	advances in	~의 진보
	investment in	~에 대한 투자
	interest in	~에 대한 관심
for	demand for	~에 대한 수요
	request for	~에 대한 요구
	preference for	~에 대한 선호
	reason for	~에 대한 이유
with	compliance with	~에 대한 준수
	problem[matter] with	~의 문제
	agreement with	~와의 합의
on	information on	~에 관한 정보
	effect[influence, impact] on	~에 대한 영향
	emphasis on	~에 대한 강조
of	a variety/a number/an amount of	다양한/많은 수의/많은 양의
	lack[a shortage] of	~의 부족

in accordance with	~와 일치하여	in writing	서면으로
in advance	미리, 사전에	on behalf of	~을 대신하여
in transit	이동 중에	at one's convenience	~가 편리한 때에
in terms of	~라는 점에서	until further notice	추후 통보가 있을 때까지

Q2 주어나 주격 보어를 단서로 접근하는 명사 어휘 문제

Travel costs and conference fees will be paid by the advertising company, but dining expenses are the participants' **[requirement / responsibility]**. [1]

Even though some experts are concerned about unemployment, the general **[consensus / completion]** seems to be that the economy will improve this year. [2]

When inside the building, please make sure your **[decision / identification]** is visible at all times. [3]

>> 출제 포인트　주어나 주격 보어 자리에 적합한 명사 어휘를 묻는 문제의 경우, 의미상 **주어를 보완해주는 주격 보어**의 속성을 중요 단서로 접근한다.

Q3 타동사를 단서로 접근하는 명사 어휘 문제

Please reply to this e-mail to acknowledge **[receipt / support]** of payment in full on this account. [1]

The Alfine Technology Group strives to enhance the **[efficiency / dispute]** of its client's marketing activities. [2]

>> 출제 포인트　타동사를 주요 단서로 보고 그 **타동사와 의미상 적합한 명사**를 선택한다.

Q4 명사 뒤의 수식어구를 단서로 접근하는 명사 어휘 문제

In an **[effort / account]** to conserve paper, please make double-sided copies on photocopy machines whenever possible. [1]

All employees of Preenz Industries are welcome to use company **[guidelines / facilities]** such as the fitness center at no charge. [2]

>> 출제 포인트　명사를 뒤에서 수식해주는 **수식어구와 의미상 연관성**을 단서로 적절한 명사를 선택한다. 특히, to부정사의 수식을 받는 특정 명사에 유의한다.

opportunity	기회	effort	노력	
right	권리	authority	권한	+ to부정사
ability	능력	decision	결정	

	빈출 어휘	의미	기출 표현
1	**access**	접근, 이용 권한 (to) 图 접속하다, 이용하다	gain temporary access to the confidential documents ⋯ 기밀 문서들에 임시적인 접근 권한을 얻다
2	**admission**	입장(료) (to)	free admission to the event ⋯ 그 행사의 무료 입장
3	**advance**	진보, 발전 (in) 图 발전하다	rapid advances in medical technology ⋯ 의학 기술에 있어서의 급속한 진보
4	**affiliation**	제휴, 가맹	form affiliations with several organizations ⋯ 여러 단체들과 제휴하다
5	**agreement**	합의, 계약(서)	reach a tentative agreement ⋯ 잠정적인 합의에 이르다
6	**alternative**	대안, 대체품 (to)	seek an alternative to online banking ⋯ 온라인 은행 업무에 대한 대안을 찾다
7	**appraisal**	평가, 감정	carry out[conduct] performance appraisals ⋯ 업무 평가를 실행[실시]하다
8	**asset**	자산, 귀중한 존재 (to)	become an asset to the firm ⋯ 회사에 귀중한 존재가 되다
9	**authority**	권위(권한), (영향력이 있는) 권위자 (on), 정부 기관	an authority on fundraising for non-profit groups ⋯ 비영리 기구를 위한 기금 모금에 대한 권위자
10	**authorization**	허가(증)	obtain proper authorization ⋯ 적절한 허가를 얻다
11	**budget**	예산(안)	approve the revised budget ⋯ 수정된 예산을 승인하다
12	**capacity**	수용량 능력	increase/improve the seating capacity ⋯ 좌석 수용 인원을 늘리다/개선하다 at full capacity ⋯ 전면[최대한] 가동해서
13	**claim**	청구, 주장 图 요구하다, 주장하다	file a claim for lost baggage ⋯ 분실된 짐에 대해 배상을 청구하다
14	**closure**	폐쇄, 종료	the bridge/factory closure ⋯ 교량/공장 폐쇄
15	**compensation**	보상(금), 배상 (for)	receive/claim additional compensation for unemployment ⋯ 실직에 대한 추가적인 보상을 받다/청구하다
16	**complaint**	불평, 항의	file/address complaints about the new policies ⋯ 새로운 정책들에 대한 불평들을 제기하다/처리하다
17	**compliance**	준수 (with)	ensure compliance with the safety regulations ⋯ 안전 규정 준수를 확실히 하다
18	**concentration**	집중, 밀집, 농도	the highest concentration of population ⋯ 가장 높은 인구 집중
19	**concern**	관심, 걱정, 우려 (over/ about)	voice/raise concerns about the proposal ⋯ 제안서에 대한 우려를 표하다/제기하다
20	**conflict**	충돌, 갈등	due to a scheduling conflict ⋯ 일정이 겹치기 때문에

빈출 어휘	의미	기출 표현
21 **congestion**	(교통) 혼잡	relieve[ease/reduce] traffic congestion ⋯▸ 교통 혼잡을 완화하다
22 **consent**	동의 ⑧ 동의하다 (to)	without the consumer's prior written consent ⋯▸ 소비자의 사전 서면 동의 없이
23 **contingency**	(뜻밖의) 사건, (만약의) 사태	come up with contingency plans/measures ⋯▸ 만약의 일을 대비한 계획/대책을 제시하다
24 **contract**	계약(서) ⑧ 계약하다	secure/renew a contract ⋯▸ 계약을 따내다/갱신하다
25 **contribution**	기여, 기부(금) (to)	make significant contribution to the success of ~ ⋯▸ ~의 성공에 상당한 기여를 하다
26 **demand**	수요, 요구 (for) ⑧ 요구하다	the growing/declining demand for our new products ⋯▸ 우리의 신제품에 대한 증가하는/감소하는 수요
27 **division**	부서 분할, 나눔	expand the accounting division ⋯▸ 회계 부서를 확장하다 the division of language into grammar and vocabulary ⋯▸ 언어를 문법과 어휘로 나눔
28 **duration**	지속, (지속되는) 기간	for the duration of the performance ⋯▸ 공연이 진행되는 동안
29 **emphasis**	강조 (on)	place[put] an emphasis on customer service ⋯▸ 고객 서비스에 대해 강조하다
30 **establishment**	시설(물), 기관, 설립	fine dining establishments ⋯▸ 고급 식당들
31 **estimate**	견적(서) ⑧ 견적을 내다	a free estimate for the new contract ⋯▸ 신규 계약에 대한 무료 견적
32 **exhibition**	전시(회)	attend an art exhibition ⋯▸ 예술 전시회에 참석하다
33 **expenditure**	지출, 경비	reduce expenditures for raw materials ⋯▸ 원자재들에 대한 지출을 줄이다
34 **expertise**	전문 지식(기술)	expertise in interior design ⋯▸ 실내 디자인에 대한 전문 지식
35 **facility**	시설, 기관	the expansion of the fitness/parking facilities ⋯▸ 운동/주차 시설의 확장
36 **fluctuation**	(가격, 수치의) 변동, 불안정 (in)	fluctuations in exchange rates ⋯▸ 환율의 변동
37 **gain**	이익, 증가(분) ⑧ 얻다	significant gains in revenue ⋯▸ 상당한 수익 증가
38 **improvement**	개선, 향상	make improvement to the facility ⋯▸ 시설을 개선하다
39 **indicator**	지표, 지수	an important economic indicator of ⋯▸ ~의 중요한 경제 지표
40 **initiative**	진취성, 주도(권), (새로운) 계획	take the initiative ⋯▸ 주도권을 가지다, 솔선수범하다

	빈출 어휘	의미	기출 표현
41	inquiry	문의	make/respond to an inquiry ⋯ 문의하다/~에 응답하다
42	inspection	검사, 점검, 검열	carry out[conduct] the annual safety inspection ⋯ 연례 안전 점검을 실시하다
43	interruption	중단, 방해	a brief interruption in our services ⋯ 서비스의 일시 중단
44	itinerary	여행 일정(표)	change the itinerary for the upcoming excursion ⋯ 다가오는 여행에 대한 일정을 바꾸다
45	maintenance	유지, 보수	conduct routine maintenance of the system ⋯ 시스템에 대한 정기 보수를 실시하다
46	malfunction	오작동, 고장	the equipment/system malfunction ⋯ 기기/시스템 오작동
47	management	경영(진)	under new management ⋯ 새로운 경영진 하에
48	market	(소비처로서의) 시장 (for)	emerging/international market for cosmetics ⋯ 화장품에 대한 신흥/해외 시장
49	morale	사기, 의욕	boost morale among staff ⋯ 직원들 사이에 사기를 진작시키다
50	negligence	부주의, 업무 태만	damage caused by consumer negligence ⋯ 고객 부주의에 의해 초래된 손상
51	negotiation	협상	proceed with contract negotiations ⋯ 계약 협상을 진행하다
52	notice	공지, 통지 동 알아차리다	until further notice ⋯ 추후 공지가 있을 때까지
53	passion	열정 (for)	have a passion for serving customers ⋯ 고객 응대에 대한 열정을 가지다
54	performance	업무(수행), 성과, 공연	conduct a thorough assessment of the division's performance ⋯ 부서의 업무 실적에 대한 철저한 평가를 실시하다
55	phase	양상, 단계 (of)	the second phase of construction/development ⋯ 건설/개발의 제2단계
56	policy	정책	the policy regarding the exchange of online purchases ⋯ 온라인 구매품 교환에 관한 정책
57	preference	선호(도), 우선권 (for)	consumer's preference for online shopping ⋯ 온라인 쇼핑에 대한 소비자의 선호
58	preparation	준비, 대비	in preparation for the upcoming inspection ⋯ 다가오는 점검에 대비하여
59	presence	(회사의) 입지(존재감), 참석	establish/expand the company's presence in the market ⋯ 시장에서 그 회사의 입지를 확립하다/확장하다
60	pressure	압박, 부담감	under considerable pressure ⋯ 상당한 부담감을 느끼는

	빈출 어휘	의미	기출 표현
☐ 61	**priority**	우선 사항, 우선순위	a high/top priority ··· 우선순위가 높은/최우선 사항
☐ 62	**procedure**	절차, 방법	the revised procedures for handling customer service inquiries ··· 고객 서비스 문의 처리를 위해 수정된 절차들
☐ 63	**progress**	진전, 진척 图 진행하다	monitor the progress of the advertising campaign ··· 광고 캠페인의 진척을 감독하다
☐ 64	**proximity**	가까움, 근접 (to)	proximity to public transportation ··· 대중 교통에 근접함
☐ 65	**purchase**	구입(품) 图 구입하다	keep the receipt as a proof of purchase ··· 구매 증명으로 영수증을 간직하다
☐ 66	**receipt**	수령, 영수증	acknowledge receipt of the order ··· 주문 수령을 알리다
☐ 67	**reference**	참고, 추천서	a manual for future reference ··· 추후 참고를 위한 안내서
☐ 68	**regulation**	규정, 규제	comply with safety regulations ··· 안전 규정을 준수하다
☐ 69	**reimbursement**	상환, 정산	requests for reimbursement of travel expenses ··· 출장 비용에 대한 상환 요청
☐ 70	**relocation**	이전, 재배치	review expenses related to upcoming relocation ··· 다가올 이전과 관련된 비용들을 검토하다
☐ 71	**remainder**	나머지, 잔여분	continue for the remainder of this year ··· 올해 남은 기간 동안 지속되다
☐ 72	**reminder**	(통지문, 메모, 독촉장 등) 상기시키는 것	a reminder about the new insurance policy ··· 새로운 보험 증권에 대해 알려 주는 통지문
☐ 73	**replacement**	교체(품), 후임자	provide replacements for the defective items ··· 결함이 있는 제품의 교체품을 제공하다
☐ 74	**reputation**	명성, 평판 (for)	gain a good reputation for exceptional service ··· 뛰어난 서비스에 대한 좋은 명성을 얻다
☐ 75	**revenue**	이익, 수익	a sharp increase in sales revenues ··· 영업 이익의 급격한 증가
☐ 76	**shift**	변화 (in)	an abrupt shift in ··· ~에서의 갑작스러운 변화
☐ 77	**shortage**	부족, 결핍 (of)	a local shortage of raw materials ··· 지역의 원자재 부족
☐ 78	**statement**	성명(서), (청구)명세서	issue a statement ··· 성명서를 발표하다
☐ 79	**transaction**	거래	bank/real estate transactions ··· 은행/부동산 거래
☐ 80	**transfer**	이체, 양도, 전근, 환승 图 송금하다, 이동하다, 갈아타다	electronic money transfer ··· 온라인 송금

Practice

1. ------- to the music festival is free for family members of all volunteer workers.

(A) Preparation
(B) Insertion
(C) Admission
(D) Imposition

2. Members of the graphic design team are encouraged to attend the upcoming -------.

(A) subject
(B) division
(C) workshop
(D) plan

3. Inquiries about these paintings should be forwarded to Ms. Kapoor, the museum's leading ------- on 18th century art.

(A) example
(B) station
(C) advantage
(D) authority

4. The main building's second floor cafeteria will be closed for renovation, so please use the one on the 5th floor until further -------.

(A) attention
(B) notice
(C) post
(D) response

5. PACT Manufacturing Company will review its accounting process to ensure ------- with revised accounting standards.

(A) probability
(B) precaution
(C) compliance
(D) indication

6. Landmark Corporation has recently developed a new process for assessing the ------- of job candidates.

(A) feature
(B) fact
(C) resource
(D) suitability

7. Mr. Miwanda is unable to accept the invitation to the president's dinner party because of a scheduling -------.

(A) indicator
(B) inception
(C) conflict
(D) date

8. 고난도 In an important ------- in its strategy, LB Machinery has decided to provide extensive training to each sales staff member.

(A) shortage
(B) loss
(C) shift
(D) prediction

9. Professor Victoria Cohen could not continue her project because of a ------- of research funds.

(A) supply
(B) direction
(C) program
(D) shortage

10. The city's safety officers conduct thorough ------- at various manufacturing facilities on a regular basis.

(A) operations
(B) inspections
(C) institutions
(D) modifications

11. No confidential documents should be released to employees without ------- from the company's Legal Department.

(A) justification
(B) qualification
(C) authorization
(D) transition

12. Continuing the company's steady growth requires honest and open communication between ------- and employees.

(A) panel
(B) procedures
(C) benefits
(D) management

13. The repairperson warned about the ------- of not cleaning the dishwasher, including the build-up of bacteria and mold.

고난도

(A) consequences
(B) solutions
(C) actions
(D) appearances

14. In her presentation, Ms. Martinez will talk about the ------- that the new law will have on the nation's use of energy.

고난도

(A) development
(B) requirements
(C) impact
(D) transfer

15. All Payroll Department employees are required to follow the company's new accounting -------, which were updated last month.

(A) procedures
(B) conduct
(C) consequences
(D) actions

16. Food processing factories in the Portland region are working at full ------- to handle soaring demand for their corn products.

(A) capacity
(B) deadline
(C) cost
(D) budget

17. Improving customer satisfaction while reducing operational costs will take ------- over all other goals this year.

(A) force
(B) direction
(C) priority
(D) advantage

18. The ------- of the Marketing and Sales Departments into two separate teams will enable a more efficient distribution of tasks.

(A) accuracy
(B) authority
(C) division
(D) oversight

19. Anyone doing business internationally should prepare for possible ------- since the world economic condition has changed dramatically in recent years.

고난도

(A) contingencies
(B) extensions
(C) requirements
(D) circumstances

20. All employees are expected to familiarize themselves with revisions to the company's ------- materials by attending next week's seminar.

고난도

(A) reference
(B) convenience
(C) improvement
(D) suspension

형용사

해설서 p.57

Q1 직접 수식하는 명사를 단서로 접근하는 형용사 어휘 문제

A **[consenting / valid]** company identification card is mandatory to access restricted areas of the solar power facility. [1]

In his capacity as Human Resources Director, Mr. Smith has been particularly competent at handling **[sensitive / adequate]** personnel issues. [2]

>> 출제 포인트 명사 앞에서 직접 수식하는 한정적 용법의 형용사 어휘 문제는 그 형용사가 **수식하는 명사**를 주요 단서로 접근한다.

Q2 주어로 쓰이는 명사를 단서로 접근하는 형용사 어휘 문제

All audiovisual materials listed in this catalog index are **[available / reachable]** for short-term loan. [1]

Any researcher who has worked here for five years or more is **[possible / eligible]** to apply for a branch transfer. [2]

>> 출제 포인트 be동사 뒤의 보어 자리에 쓰인 서술적 용법의 형용사는 **주어 자리에 쓰인 명사**를 주요 단서로 접근한다. 특히, possible은 사람이 아닌 프로젝트 등의 실현 가능한 대상의 명사와 쓰이는 형용사임에 유의한다.

Q3 특정 전치사를 단서로 접근하는 형용사 어휘 문제

Mr. Sanchez will be **[capable / responsible]** for presenting the weekly reports while the President is away on a business trip. [1]

When surveyed, it was found that most customers were **[distant / unfamiliar]** with the new line of eco-friendly hybrid cars. [2]

>> 출제 포인트 **특정 전치사**와 함께 쓰이는 형용사 표현에 유의하여 형용사 어휘 문제를 푼다.

be responsible for	~에 대해 책임이 있다
be eligible for	~에 대한 자격이 있다
be famous[noted, known, renowned] for	~로 유명하다
be attentive to	~에 주의를 기울이다
be devoted[committed] to	~에 헌신하다
be exposed to	~에 노출되다
be responsive to	~에 대응하다
be relevant to	~에 관련[연관]되다
be associated with	~와 관련되다
be compatible with	~와 호환되다
be consistent with	~와 일치하다[일관되다]
be faced[confronted] with	~에 직면하다
be familiar/unfamiliar with	~을 잘 알다/모르다, ~에 익숙하다/익숙하지 않다
be concerned about	~에 대해 걱정하다
be enthusiastic about	~에 대해 열정적이다
be optimistic/pessimistic about	~에 관해 낙관/비관하다
be capable/incapable of	~할 수 있다/없다
be aware[conscious] of	~을 인식하다
be indicative of	~을 나타내다
be appreciative of	~에 감사하다
be exempt from	~로부터 면제되다
be representative of	~을 대표하다, ~을 나타내다

Q4 문법적 특성을 고려해야 하는 형용사 어휘 문제

Many participants at the corporate workshop indicated that Dr. Becks gave an **[impressed / informative]** presentation on time management skills. [1]

HKV Corporation is proud to provide its employees with **[satisfied / competitive]** salary packages in addition to outstanding opportunities for professional development. [2]

Team leaders must ensure that **[every / all]** interns have completed an orientation workshop. [3]

In spite of the complicated registration process, most customers are satisfied with our credit cards due to their **[numerous / rigorous]** benefits. [4]

>> 출제 포인트 ❶ 감정 동사의 과거분사형 형용사(impressed '인상 깊은', satisfied/pleased '만족한', disappointed '실망한', interested '관심 있는' 등)가 형용사 어휘 문제의 보기에 제시된 경우 **사람 명사**만을 수식할 수 있다는 문법적 특성에 유의해야 한다.

❷ 수량형용사가 형용사 어휘 문제의 보기로 제시된 경우, **뒤에 이어지는 명사의 단수/복수**에 유의해야 한다.

- every 모든 | each 각각의 | another 다른 하나의 + 가산 명사 단수
- various 다양한 | numerous 수많은 | several 여럿의 | multiple 많은 + 가산 명사 복수

빈출 어휘	의미	기출 표현
1 **abundant**	충분한, 풍부한	abundant harvest/rainfall … 충분한 수확/강수량
2 **additional**	추가적인	at no additional charge[fee] … 추가적인 비용 없이
3 **adequate**	충분한, 적절한	adequate training/seating … 충분한 훈련/좌석
4 **affordable**	(가격이) 적정한, 알맞은	at affordable rates[prices] … 적정한 가격에
5 **applicable**	적용 가능한, 관련 있는, 해당되는	at least five years of applicable experience … 적어도 5년의 관련된 경험
6 **appropriate**	적절한	appropriate responses/strategies … 적절한 반응들/전략들
7 **attentive**	주의를 기울이는 (to)	be very attentive to patients' needs … 환자들의 요구에 매우 주의를 기울이다
8 **authentic**	진짜인, 진품인	a wide selection of authentic pottery … 다양한 진품 도자기
9 **authorized**	(정식으로) 권한을 부여 받은, 공인된	be distributed to authorized personnel … 승인을 받은 직원에게 배포되다
10 **available**	(사물이) 이용 가능한, (사람이) 시간이 있는	be available exclusively to members … 회원들만 이용 가능하다
11 **beneficial**	유익한	be mutually beneficial to parents and local schools … 부모와 지역 학교들 상호 간에 유익하다
12 **cautious**	주의하는, 조심하는	be extremely cautious about investments … 투자에 극도로 주의를 기울이다
13 **challenging**	도전적인, 힘든	one of the most challenging research projects … 가장 힘든 연구 프로젝트들 중 하나
14 **comparable**	비슷한, 필적하는 (to/with)	be comparable to[with] … ~와 비슷하다
15 **compatible**	호환이 되는, 양립될 수 있는 (with)	be compatible with the existing system … 기존 시스템과 호환이 되다
16 **competitive**	경쟁력이 있는, 경쟁이 치열한	competitive salaries/rates … 경쟁력 있는 급여/요금
17 **complete**	완전한, 완벽한 완료된, 전체의	a complete schedule of events … 행사들의 전체 일정 until the renovation of its production facility is complete … 생산 시설의 수리가 완료될 때까지
18 **complimentary**	무료의, 칭찬하는	a complimentary beverage/brochure … 무료 음료/안내 책자
19 **comprehensive**	종합적인, 포괄적인	a comprehensive inspection/health care plan … 종합적인 점검/의료 제도
20 **confidential**	기밀의	confidential information/documents … 기밀 정보/문서

빈출 어휘	의미	기출 표현
21 **consecutive**	연속적인	for four consecutive years ⋯ 4년 연속하여
22 **contrary**	반대되는, 대조적인 (to)	be contrary to expectations/what analysts predicted ⋯ 예상/분석가들이 예측했던 것과 반대되다
23 **critical**	중대한 비판적인	a critical factor/issue ⋯ 중대한 요소/사안 be highly critical of the analysis ⋯ 분석에 대해 매우 비판적이다
24 **defective**	결함이 있는	defective products/merchandise ⋯ 결함이 있는 제품/상품
25 **demanding**	(일, 사람이) 까다로운, 다루기 힘든	a demanding task/customer ⋯ 까다로운 업무/고객
26 **detailed**	상세한	detailed descriptions/reports ⋯ 상세한 설명/보고서
27 **effective**	효과적인 효력이 발생하는	an effective method/measure ⋯ 효과적인 방법/조치 effective on January 1 ⋯ 1월 1일부터 효력이 발생하는
28 **efficient**	효율적인, 유능한	more efficient devices/strategies ⋯ 더 효율적인 장비들/전략들
29 **eligible**	자격이 있는	be eligible for promotion/paid holidays ⋯ 승진/유급 휴가에 자격이 있다
30 **enclosed**	동봉된, 벽으로 둘러싸인	the enclosed contract ⋯ 동봉된 계약서
31 **enthusiastic**	열광적인, 열심인	be enthusiastic about the release ⋯ 출시에 대해 열광적이다
32 **essential**	필수적인, 중대한, 본질적인	essential ingredients/equipment ⋯ 필수적인 요소들/장비
33 **exceptional**	뛰어난, 예외적인	exceptional job performance/customer service ⋯ 뛰어난 업무 수행/고객 서비스
34 **experienced**	경험이 풍부한, 숙련된	seek highly experienced editors ⋯ 매우 경험이 풍부한 편집자들을 구하다
35 **exempt**	면제되는 (from)	be exempt from paying delivery fees ⋯ 배송료를 지불하는 것이 면제되다
36 **familiar**	익숙한, 잘 알고 있는 (with)	be familiar with the policies/rules ⋯ 정책들/규칙들에 익숙하다
37 **flexible**	융통성 있는, 유연한	flexible work schedules ⋯ 융통성 있는 업무 일정
38 **fragile**	깨지기 쉬운	fragile goods[merchandise] ⋯ 깨지기 쉬운 제품
39 **generous**	후한, 관대한, 넉넉한	generous bonus/donation ⋯ 후한 보너스/기부
40 **impending**	임박한, 곧 있을	impending merger/issues ⋯ 임박한 합병/문제들

	빈출 어휘	의미	기출 표현
41	**improper**	부당한, 부적절한	improper transaction/use ···› 부당한 거래/사용
42	**informative**	유익한	an informative lecture/seminar ···› 유익한 강의/세미나
43	**innovative**	혁신적인	innovative management/marketing strategies ···› 혁신적인 경영/마케팅 전략
44	**knowledgeable**	학식이 풍부한, 많이 아는 (about)	be knowledgeable about every phase of construction ···› 건설 전 과정에 대해 학식이 풍부하다
45	**leading**	주요한, 선도하는	among the country's leading suppliers[providers] ···› 그 나라의 주요 공급 업체들 중 하나
46	**limited**	제한된, 한정된	limited selection/parking space ···› 제한된 선택/주차 공간
47	**lucrative**	수익성이 높은	a lucrative contract/industry ···› 수익성이 높은 계약/산업
48	**nearby**	근처의, 인접한	a nearby dining establishment ···› 근처의 식당
49	**official**	공식적인	official opening/announcement ···› 공식 개관/발표
50	**operational**	작동[가동] 준비가 된, 운영상의	become fully operational ···› 완전히 작동 준비가 되다
51	**outstanding**	뛰어난 미지불된	outstanding service/skills ···› 뛰어난 서비스/기술 an outstanding balance ···› 미지불된 잔액
52	**overwhelming**	압도적인, 엄청난	an overwhelming demand/volume ···› 압도적인 수요/양
53	**perishable**	상하기 쉬운	perishable items such as meat and dairy ···› 고기와 유제품과 같이 상하기 쉬운 제품들
54	**potential**	가능성이 있는, 잠재력이 있는	potential clients/employees ···› 잠재적인 고객들/직원들
55	**preliminary**	예비의	preliminary interviews/studies ···› 예비 면접/연구
56	**productive**	생산적인	a highly productive partnership ···› 매우 생산적인 제휴 관계
57	**punctual**	시간을 엄수하는	punctual delivery/payment ···› 시간을 엄수하는 배송/납부
58	**reasonable**	가격이 합리적인, 적당한	at reasonable prices ···› 합리적인 가격에
59	**reliable**	신뢰할 만한	reliable transportation/employees ···› 믿을 만한 교통수단/직원들
60	**responsible**	책임지고 있는 (for)	be responsible for damages ···› 파손을 책임지다

빈출 어휘	의미	기출 표현
61 **rewarding**	보람찬, 가치가 있는	a rewarding occupation ⋯ 보람찬 직업
62 **rigorous**	엄격한, 철저한	rigorous training program/standards ⋯ 엄격한 훈련 프로그램/기준
63 **sensitive**	민감한	sensitive client information/issues ⋯ 민감한 고객 정보/사안들
64 **significant**	중요한, 의미 있는	a significant contribution to ⋯ ~에 중대한 기여
65 **spacious**	(공간이) 넓은	a spacious meeting room ⋯ 넓은 회의실
66 **strategic**	전략적인	a strategic decision/approach ⋯ 전략적 결정/접근
67 **stringent**	엄격한	a stringent inspection process 엄격한 검사 과정
68 **sufficient**	충분한	sufficient inventory/resources ⋯ 충분한 재고/자원
69 **temporary**	임시의, 일시적인	a temporary discount/position ⋯ 임시 할인/직
70 **tentative**	잠정적인	a tentative suggestion/agreement ⋯ 잠정적인 제안/합의
71 **unanimous**	만장일치의	unanimous support ⋯ 만장일치의 지지
72 **unique**	독특한	a unique style/process ⋯ 독특한 스타일/과정
73 **unprecedented**	전례 없는	unprecedented growth/revenue ⋯ 전례가 없는 성장/수익
74 **urgent**	긴급한	an urgent request ⋯ 긴급한 요청
75 **vacant**	비어 있는	vacant positions/properties ⋯ 비어 있는 직책들/건물들
76 **valid**	유효한, 타당한	a valid photo identification card ⋯ 유효한 사진이 부착된 신분증
77 **valuable**	귀중한	valuable experience/asset ⋯ 귀중한 경험/자산
78 **versatile**	다재다능한, 다용도의	a versatile performer ⋯ 다재다능한 연주자
79 **vulnerable**	취약한 (to)	be vulnerable to changes in a financial policy ⋯ 재정 정책의 변화에 취약하다
80 **willing**	기꺼이 하는 (to 동사원형)	be willing to assist ⋯ 기꺼이 돕다

Practice

1. Over the past 30 years, Axterp Construction Company has offered ------- services, with the up-to-date technology for constructing buildings.

(A) apparent
(B) comprehensive
(C) upcoming
(D) reluctant

2. Friday's lecture will start promptly at 10:00 A.M., so attendees are encouraged to be -------.

(A) instant
(B) advanced
(C) sudden
(D) punctual

3. The new Auto Organizer software is ------- with any Jet operating system, version 10.0 or higher.

(A) reportable
(B) reflective
(C) compatible
(D) conclusive

4. Marley Automobile's sales increased in February to 150,000 units as compared to 145,000 units sold in the ------- month the previous year.

(A) same
(B) found
(C) later
(D) open

5. It is ------- that you consult investment professionals before investing in newly emerging markets.

(A) conclusive
(B) essential
(C) entire
(D) negligible

6. The popularity of the Nouta software system can be attributed to its ------- price.

(A) exclusive
(B) affordable
(C) extensive
(D) accountable

7. All of the candidates were fully qualified, but Ms. Norman's interview was especially -------.

(A) incorporated
(B) impressive
(C) confidential
(D) eventual

8. 고난도 Applicants for Exia Travel should have a minimum of two years of experience in the travel industry and should be ------- about travel.

(A) honest
(B) definite
(C) fluent
(D) enthusiastic

9. Pinksea Advertising has been developing a ------- marketing plan for its new products for the last three months.

(A) punctual
(B) detailed
(C) vague
(D) relative

10. Yomaha Wellbeing Food expects its organic suppliers to deliver fresh ingredients in a consistently ------- manner.

(A) extensive
(B) demanding
(C) approximate
(D) efficient

11. Our recent marketing research has shown celebrity endorsements are significantly ------- in boosting sales.
(A) effective
(B) specific
(C) lengthy
(D) partial

12. To eliminate the costs of watering and caring for the natural plants in our office, we're going to replace them with ------- ones.
(A) domestic
(B) finite
(C) fragile
(D) artificial

13. Due to the ------- rainfall this summer, water usage restrictions have been temporarily relaxed.
(A) abundant
(B) accidental
(C) common
(D) occasional

14. Although heavily discounted prices are appealing, customers must keep in mind that outlet stores may sometimes sell ------- products.
(A) apparent
(B) comprehensive
(C) upcoming
(D) defective

15. Mr. Zako's presentation was so ------- that 고난도 the overseas clients decided to invest in the product's development.
(A) verified
(B) convincing
(C) probable
(D) gratified

16. Bandelectro's new line of air conditioners 고난도 is ------- in price to its previous line, although the new designs are more attractive.
(A) benevolent
(B) comparable
(C) authorized
(D) abundant

17. Olivera, Inc.'s new line of office furniture has helped to boost the company's ------- performance this month.
(A) interested
(B) financial
(C) available
(D) believable

18. With our 20 years in the business, Country 고난도 Shipping Service provides specialized delivery services for handling ------- goods.
(A) spacious
(B) cautious
(C) apparent
(D) fragile

19. A recent study revealed that manufacturing 고난도 workers tend to be least ------- to their jobs during overtime shifts.
(A) attentive
(B) informative
(C) advisory
(D) knowledgeable

20. Although management calls her plan ------- , Ms. Macondo doesn't think it will be difficult to implement.
(A) impractical
(B) unavoidable
(C) indifferent
(D) spotless

부사

해설서 p.59

Q1 동사를 단서로 접근하는 부사 어휘 문제

Petroleum prices rose **[highly / slightly]** again last week, but many industry experts predict a significant decrease next week. ¹

Sales associates should read the employee manual **[thoroughly / considerably]** in order to understand how to handle customer complaints. ²

Mr. Foucault is not here today, but he **[previously / typically]** attends every university faculty meeting. ³

>> 출제 포인트   동사를 수식하는 부사 어휘 문제는 그 **부사가 수식하는 동사**를 단서로 접근하며, 아래에 정리된 자주 출제되는 부사들에 유의한다.

❶ **증가**(increase, rise, grow), **감소**(decrease, fall, decline, reduce), **확장**(expand), **향상** (improve), **변화**(change)를 의미하는 동사와 함께 쓰이는 부사들

considerably, significantly, substantially	상당히
dramatically, sharply, markedly, drastically, rapidly	급격히
abruptly, suddenly	갑자기
gradually, steadily, incrementally	점진적으로
slightly, modestly, moderately, somewhat, marginally	약간, 조금

❷ **검토** 의미의 동사(review, check, examine, inspect)와 함께 쓰이는 부사들

thoroughly, closely	철저히
carefully	주의 깊게
periodically, regularly, routinely	주기적으로

❸ 형용사와 부사를 수식하지만 **동사를 수식할 수 없는** 부사들

so, very, fairly, quite	꽤
extremely, excessively, overly, highly, exceptionally	극도로

❹ 특정 시제와 함께 쓰이는 부사들

과거	previously, formerly	이전에
과거나 현재완료	lately, recently	최근에
현재	usually	보통
	periodically	주기적으로
현재(진행)	currently	현재
미래 시제	soon, shortly	곧

Q2 형용사나 부사를 단서로 접근하는 부사 어휘 문제

Interest rate levels are expected to remain [**relatively / exactly**] low. [1]

Sales of the newest book in the *Dark Monday* mystery series have recently boosted Darwin Publisher's profits by [**more / nearly**] 20 percent. [2]

>> 출제 포인트

형용사나 부사 앞의 부사 어휘 선택 문제는 그 **부사가 수식하는 형용사나 부사**를 핵심 단서로 접근한다. 특히, **수량형용사를 수식**하는 다음의 부사에 유의한다.

☑ 수량형용사나 수사와 함께 쓰이는 부사

approximately, about, around, roughly	대략
nearly, almost	거의
exactly	정확히
just, only	단지
more than, over	~보다 많은
less than, under	~미만
up to	최대한
at least	최소한, 적어도

핵심 어휘

	빈출 어휘	의미	기출 표현
1	accordingly	그에 따라, 따라서	alter the reservation accordingly ⋯ 그에 따라 예약을 변경하다
2	adversely	부정적으로, 불리하게	adversely affect ⋯ 불리하게 영향을 미치다
3	approximately	대략	approximately a week/3,000 people ⋯ 대략 일주일/3,000명
4	arguably	(주로 최상급 형용사 앞에서) 거의 틀림없이	arguably the most valuable invention ⋯ 틀림없이 가장 귀중한 발명품
5	briefly	잠시, 간결하게	briefly visited a fabric supplier ⋯ 직물 공급업체를 잠시 방문했다
6	closely	면밀히	closely examine/monitor ⋯ 면밀히 조사하다/감시하다
7	consistently	일관되게, 지속적으로	consistently positive reviews ⋯ 일관되게 긍정적인 평가들
8	conveniently	편리하게	conveniently located[situated] ⋯ 편리하게 위치한
9	currently	현재	be currently out of stock/inaccessible ⋯ 현재 재고가 없다/접속이 불가하다
10	definitely	반드시, 확실히	definitely reach the sales goal ⋯ 반드시 영업 목표에 도달하다
11	directly	직접, 곧바로	be shipped directly from the manufacturer ⋯ 제조 업체로부터 직접 보내지다 report directly to the manager ⋯ 매니저에게 직접 보고하다
12	discreetly	신중하게, 조심스레	deal with customer information discreetly ⋯ 고객 정보를 신중히 다루다
13	dramatically	상당히, 극적으로	dramatically grow/increase[rise] ⋯ 상당히 성장하다/증가하다
14	eagerly	간절히	eagerly await/anticipate ⋯ 간절히 기다리다/기대하다
15	effortlessly	손쉽게, 어려움 없이	adapt effortlessly[easily] to new surroundings ⋯ 새로운 환경에 어려움 없이 적응하다
16	exclusively	독점적으로, 오로지	available exclusively to current customers ⋯ 오로지 기존 고객들만이 이용 가능한
17	finally	마침내	finally approve/announce ⋯ 마침내 승인하다/발표하다
18	formerly	이전에	was formerly a residential area/Vice President ⋯ 예전에 거주 지역/부사장이었다
19	frequently	자주, 빈번히	frequently change/visit ⋯ 자주 바꾸다/방문하다
20	gradually	점차, 서서히	be gradually replacing traditional shopping methods ⋯ 전통적인 쇼핑 방식들을 점차 대체하고 있다

빈출 어휘	의미	기출 표현
21 **highly**	매우, 대단히	highly recommended / rated ⋯ 매우 추천되는 / 높은 등급을 받은
22 **immediately**	즉시, 즉각적으로	immediately following / after the presentation ⋯ 발표 바로 뒤이어 / 직후에
23 **inadvertently**	부주의하게, 우연히	inadvertently omit / leak ⋯ 부주의하게 빠뜨리다 / (비밀을) 누설하다
24 **individually**	개별적으로, 따로	be individually wrapped / purchased ⋯ 개별적으로 포장되다 / 구입되다
25 **moderately**	적당히, 알맞게	stock prices rose moderately ⋯ 주가가 적당히 올랐다
26 **mutually**	상호간에	mutually beneficial / acceptable ⋯ 상호간에 이로운 / 받아들일 수 있는
27 **nearly**	거의	nearly complete / a week ⋯ 거의 끝난 / 일주일
28 **originally**	본래, 원래	was originally scheduled for August 1 ⋯ 원래 8월 1일로 예정되어 있었다
29 **otherwise**	그와 달리, 그렇지 않으면	unless otherwise stated / instructed ⋯ 그와 달리 언급되지 / 지시되지 않으면
30 **periodically**	주기적으로	periodically check the equipment ⋯ 주기적으로 장비를 점검하다
31 **previously**	이전에	more productive than previously thought / expected ⋯ 이전에 생각 / 예상했던 것보다 더 생산적인
32 **primarily**	주로, 무엇보다도 먼저	primarily[mainly] due to weak sales ⋯ 주로 낮은 판매 때문에
33 **promptly**	즉시, 정시에	respond / report promptly ⋯ 즉시 답하다 / 보고하다
34 **publicly**	공개적으로, 대중 앞에서	publicly[openly] apologize for the accident ⋯ 그 사건에 대해 공개적으로 사과하다
35 **rapidly**	빠르게, 신속하게	grow / expand rapidly ⋯ 빠르게 성장하다 / 확장하다
36 **regularly**	정기적으로	regularly check / adjust ⋯ 정기적으로 점검하다 / 조절하다
37 **relatively**	상대적으로, 비교적	relatively new / low ⋯ 상대적으로 신생의 / 낮은
38 **shortly**	곧, 바로	will be distributed / completed shortly ⋯ 곧 배포 / 완성될 것이다
38 **slightly**	약간, 조금	rise / differ slightly ⋯ 약간 오르다 / 다르다
40 **thoroughly**	철저히, 완전히	thoroughly inspect / review ⋯ 철저히 검사하다 / 검토하다

1. Building safety inspectors should not make any assumptions before they ------- check everything on their checklist.

(A) thoroughly
(B) formerly
(C) inadvertently
(D) approximately

2. Design555 is ------- new in the field, but the firm has quickly become a threat to its competitors.

(A) closely
(B) relatively
(C) normally
(D) collectively

3. 고난도 If the customer meeting shifts to next week, we will have to postpone our panel discussion -------.

(A) lately
(B) accordingly
(C) namely
(D) particularly

4. When driving on a slippery road, turn the steering wheel slowly and ------- in the direction that you want to go.

(A) finely
(B) timely
(C) gently
(D) openly

5. Mayoral candidate Amin Fahlan spoke ------- yesterday regarding his position on current environmental laws.

(A) previously
(B) publicly
(C) expensively
(D) periodically

6. According to the report, Normanti Ltd.'s earnings grew ------- at the end of the last quarter after falling for three years.

(A) overly
(B) rapidly
(C) preferably
(D) meticulously

7. Potential buyers of the newly built apartment complex were informed of how ------- it is located.

(A) consistently
(B) reliably
(C) periodically
(D) conveniently

8. The presentation lasted ------- three hours, but most of the attendees were so interested in the topic that they did not mind it.

(A) impressively
(B) necessarily
(C) nearly
(D) originally

9. Keep in mind that the terms of housing loans are subject to change ------- as updates take effect.

(A) overly
(B) quarterly
(C) formerly
(D) nearly

10. Gardening sessions at Bloomings Flower Shop ------- last about 50 minutes.

(A) lightly
(B) typically
(C) patiently
(D) doubly

11. The Skin Market's new eye cream is ------- ready for the market after numerous customer surveys were conducted.

(A) accidentally
(B) repeatedly
(C) finally
(D) exclusively

12. We at Sound Track are pleased to inform you that the TX301 speakers will be arriving -------.

(A) shortly
(B) barely
(C) faintly
(D) intermittently

13. The drought ------- affected this year's harvest, resulting in higher prices for wheat and rice.

고난도

(A) exactly
(B) valuably
(C) adversely
(D) strenuously

14. All furniture made by Morrison Interior can be taken apart ------- for easy transportation.

고난도

(A) vitally
(B) attentively
(C) effortlessly
(D) accurately

15. Mr. Kim called the owner of the restaurant to set up a ------- agreeable time to discuss the renovation work.

(A) commonly
(B) separately
(C) definitely
(D) mutually

16. Most shareholders of D&U Chemical are satisfied because the firm ------- makes huge annual profits.

(A) readily
(B) consistently
(C) impulsively
(D) vaguely

17. The manager of the General Affairs Department reminded the employees to return defective office equipment ------- to the manufacturer.

(A) extensively
(B) miraculously
(C) directly
(D) modestly

18. Cams Sports Goods attributes its recent success ------- to its new line of baseball gear.

(A) importantly
(B) primarily
(C) tightly
(D) extremely

19. Mr. Parr correctly predicted that stock value would increase ------- as the demand for the firm's new line of computers continues to grow.

고난도

(A) arguably
(B) reportedly
(C) productively
(D) incrementally

20. When demonstrating a new product to customers, employees should avoid using ------- technical terms.

고난도

(A) frequently
(B) highly
(C) distantly
(D) readily

REVIEW TEST

해설서 p.62 / ⏱ 제한 시간 10분

1. The owner of the restaurant hopes to ------- more diners by closing later on weekends.

   (A) attract
   (B) relocate
   (C) remind
   (D) launch

2. Ms. Trang is not going to be in the office -------, so contact her via e-mail.

   (A) scarcely
   (B) frequently
   (C) closely
   (D) lately

3. Applicants interested in the open position should possess ------- experience in international trade.

   (A) arrogant
   (B) extensive
   (C) central
   (D) possible

4. If you must answer a phone call during the performance, please do so as ------- as possible.

   (A) greatly
   (B) weakly
   (C) quietly
   (D) lightly

5. 고난도 Mr. Renner loves sharing with young journalists the experience he has ------- over the decades.

   (A) completed
   (B) cautioned
   (C) gained
   (D) performed

6. 고난도 Please have the serial number of your laptop ------- when contacting the technical support center.

   (A) refurbished
   (B) available
   (C) operational
   (D) useful

7. Tetsudo Restaurant issued a ------- to all customers letting them know about the closure of the patio area.

   (A) bill
   (B) tag
   (C) notice
   (D) guide

8. Ms. Phan, who ------- heads HCMC Securities' marketing division, will be promoted to Vice President early next month.

   (A) currently
   (B) precisely
   (C) finally
   (D) soon

9. Those applicants who meet every ------- listed in the online job posting will be contacted.

   (A) audition
   (B) award
   (C) step
   (D) qualification

10. The maintenance crew is working ------- to repair the damage caused by the storm as fast as possible.

    (A) variably
    (B) diligently
    (C) longingly
    (D) vastly

11. *Sports Review's* ------- of episodes featuring famous athletes has proven to be quite popular.

(A) process
(B) course
(C) series
(D) activity

12. There is an increasing demand ------- experienced medical professionals in the Downing area.

(A) behind
(B) into
(C) for
(D) also

13. Cooking demonstrations by renowned chefs are one of the events that will be ------- during the Daoust Cultural Festival Week.

고난도

(A) setting
(B) remaining
(C) happening
(D) offering

14. An ------- in ancient Greek history, Ms. Ichihara regularly gives guest lectures at local universities.

고난도

(A) authorization
(B) authoritative
(C) authorize
(D) authority

15. The IT Department will inspect all computers in the company to ------- antivirus programs are up-to-date.

(A) measure
(B) install
(C) ensure
(D) adjust

16. To start the staff replacement process, ------- a team and write job descriptions to post.

(A) achieve
(B) decide
(C) assemble
(D) compromise

17. Bookings need to be made online to qualify ------- the special summer discount at Swansea Resort.

(A) ahead
(B) close
(C) while
(D) for

18. Econnewsfront.net is an ------- source of financial information for small business owners.

고난도

(A) aware
(B) accurate
(C) attentive
(D) acquainted

19. As renovation work is being done in the lobby, ------- to the main entrance of the building is temporarily blocked.

(A) diagnosis
(B) access
(C) position
(D) direction

20. Those who ------- the construction on Garner Street should sign the petition now.

(A) secure
(B) dedicate
(C) oppose
(D) attain

RT6

장문 빈칸
채우기

OVERVIEW

Part 6은 4문항의 문제가 있는 4개의 지문이 나와 총 16문항이 출제된다.
각각의 빈칸에 가장 적절한 단어나 구, 그리고 문장을 고르는 문제는
Part 5와 Part 7을 접목한 형태로 볼 수 있다.

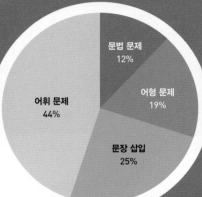

문법 문제
12%

어형 문제
19%

어휘 문제
44%

문장 삽입
25%

문제 유형

어형 문제 | 빈칸의 자리를 파악하여 선택지 중 알맞은 품사나 형태를 고르는 문제
어휘 문제 | 같은 품사의 네 개 어휘 중 정확한 용례를 파악하여 알맞은 단어를 고르는 문제
문법 문제 | 문장의 구조를 파악하여 구와 절을 구분하여 접속사나 전치사, 부사를 고르는 문제
문장 삽입 | 앞뒤 문맥을 파악하여 네 개의 문장 중에 알맞은 문장을 고르는 문제

지문 유형

편지·이메일 / 기사 / 공지 / 지시문 / 광고 / 회람 / 설명서 / 발표문 / 정보문 등

출제 포인트

• 앞뒤 문맥을 통해 시제를 결정하는 문제의 출제 비중이 높다. 시제를 묻는 문제는 Part 5에서는
  시간 부사구로 결정하지만, Part 6에서는 맥락으로 파악해야 한다.
• 두 문장을 자연스럽게 이어주는 접속부사를 선택하는 문제가 많이 출제된다.
• 맥락상으로 파악해야 하는 대명사의 인칭 일치 문제, 수 일치 문제가 출제된다.
• 어휘는 그 문장만 보고는 문제를 풀 수 없고 앞뒤 문맥을 파악하여 고르는 문제가 출제된다.

PART 6 이렇게 대비하자!

• Part 5처럼 단순히 문장 구조나 문법을 묻는 문제도 출제되지만, 전체적인 내용이나 앞뒤 문장
  내용과 연결되는 어휘나 시제, 접속부사를 묻는 문제들이 주로 출제된다는 것에 유의한다.
• 문장 삽입 문제는 빈칸 앞뒤 문장의 대명사나 연결어 등을 확인하고 상관관계를 파악한다.
• 지문의 길이가 짧기 때문에 전체 내용을 파악하는 데 많은 시간이 걸리지 않으므로 정독해서
  읽으면 오히려 더 쉽게 해결할 수 있다.

PART 6 문제 유형별 문제 풀이 접근법

Questions 143-146 refer to the following article.

Jakarta, INDONESIA (5 June) — An Indonesian steelmaker, Irwan Steel Company, announced that it had named Maghfirah Baldraf its new Chief Operating Officer of the Java Division effective 1 September. His 30 years of experience in the ------- made him the obvious choice for the position.
143.
Baldraf majored in metal engineering at the National University of Indonesia. After graduation, he then ------- his career in the quality control department at Putirai Metal. 15 years ago, he joined
144.
Irwan Steel Company. -------. Baldraf will go to Java to oversee the daily operations of Irwan Steel
145.
Company ------- its inauguration on September 1.
146.

1. 어휘 문제

Part 5 어휘 문제와는 달리 그 한 문장만 봐서는 여러 개가 답이 될 수 있을 것 같은 선택지들이 나온다. 따라서 Part 6의 어휘 문제는 앞뒤 문맥을 정확히 파악하여 답을 골라야 한다.

| 143. | (A) license | (B) industry | (C) outset | (D) program |

이 문제에서는 '그 산업 분야에서의 30년 경력 때문에 그가 그 자리에 확실한 선택이었다'라는 의미를 파악해서 (B)를 골라야 한다.

2. 어형 문제

한 단어의 네 가지 형태가 나오는 문제를 어형 문제 또는 자리 찾기 문제라고 한다. Part 5와 마찬가지 방법으로 풀면 되지만, 동사 시제 문제는 문맥을 파악하는 까다로운 문제로 출제된다.

| 144. | (A) started | (B) had started | (C) was starting | (D) will start |

이 문제는 동사의 시제를 고르는 문제로 문맥상 이 사람이 처음으로 직장 생활을 시작한 것을 이야기하고 있으므로 과거 시제인 (A)가 답이 되며, then도 힌트가 될 수 있다.

3. 문장 삽입 문제

Part 6에서 가장 어려운 문제로 전체적인 문맥을 파악하고, 접속부사나, 시제 등을 종합적으로 봐야 답을 고를 수 있다.

145.	(A) The company also has a division in Singapore.
	(B) He has been interested in engineering since he was young.
	(C) Most recently, he has served as Vice President of Development of Irwan Steel Company.
	(D) As soon as Baldraf is appointed, the company will go through a major restructuring.

이 문제에서는 대학교 졸업 후부터 이 사람의 경력을 시간 순서로 나열하고 있으므로 (C)가 답이 된다.

4. 문법 문제

문법 문제는 보통 문장의 구조를 파악하여 구와 절을 구분하는 문제이다.

| 143. | (A) by the time | (B) as soon as | (C) when | (D) after |

이 문제에서는 빈칸 뒤에 명사구가 있으므로 명사를 목적어로 취하는 전치사가 답이 되어야 하는데 보기 중에 전치사로 쓰일 수 있는 것이 (D)뿐이다.

PART 6 유형 분석

핵심 문제 유형

1. 문맥에 맞는 문장 선택 유형

▶ 지문의 흐름에 맞는 문맥상 알맞은 문장을 선택하는 유형으로 각 지문당 한 문항씩 출제된다. 빈칸은 지문의 앞부분 – 중간 부분 – 마지막 부분 모두에 위치한다.

》 출제 포인트 빈칸 앞 부분을 단서로 활용하는 문제

빈칸 앞 부분에 정답의 결정적인 단서가 제시되는 경우가 많으므로, 앞 부분에 언급된 핵심 내용을 정확히 파악하여 연관성이 없는 보기들을 오답으로 소거한 후, 남은 보기를 빈칸에 넣어 뒷문장과 흐름이 자연스러운지 확인한다. 빈칸 앞 부분에서 언급되지 않은 소재나 반대되는 내용들이 주로 오답으로 제시된다.

The Revon Central **Library has the most extensive collection** of local history **materials**. -------. With prior reservations, library members can also access several hundred rare manuscripts, which are located in specially designated areas. Members interested in viewing these materials must fill out a form stating a valid purpose for doing so. In addition, they must hand in their library cards and photo IDs to a Revon employee before accessing the documents. The form can be picked up at the front desk.

---

1. (A) The book must be returned within one week of being checked out.
   (B) Library members can pay late fees through our online system.
   (C) The archive contains thousands of articles and photos that are available to library members.
   (D) Library employees organize all of the books at the end of each day.

정답 (C)

해석 Revon 중앙 도서관은 가장 폭넓은 지역 역사 자료를 소장하고 있습니다. **기록 보관소는 도서관 회원들이 이용 가능한 수천 종의 기사와 사진을 보유하고 있습니다.** 사전 예약으로, 도서관 회원들은 특별히 지정된 구역에 위치한 수백 가지의 희귀한 사본들에 접근할 수 있습니다. 이러한 자료를 보는데 관심이 있는 회원들은 거기에 대한 타당한 목적을 밝히는 서류를 작성해야 합니다. 덧붙여, 문서에 접근하기 전에 반드시 Revon 직원에게 도서관 카드와 사진이 부착된 신분증을 제출해야 합니다. 서류는 안내 데스크에서 받을 수 있습니다.

(A) 책은 대출 일주일 안에 반납되어야 합니다.
(B) 도서관 회원들은 연체료를 저희 온라인 시스템을 통해 낼 수 있습니다.
(C) 기록 보관소는 도서관 회원들이 이용 가능한 수천 종의 기사와 사진을 보유하고 있습니다.
(D) 도서관 직원들은 매일 마지막에 모든 책들을 정리합니다.

Telecompu staff members with at least two years of full-time working experience here are eligible to apply for promotions and internal transfers. -------. We will consider those interested alongside external candidates. Workers with relevant skills will be given preference unless the company believes that outside hiring is the better option.

2. (A) We are delighted to welcome new employees to Telecompu.
   (B) As a matter of fact, staff members need to log their working hours every day.
   (C) Only full-time employees will receive a comprehensive benefits package.
   (D) Workers who want to apply must talk to their supervisors first.

정답 (D)

해석 이곳에서 최소 2년 이상 정직원으로서 근무한 Telecompu 직원들은 승진과 내부 이동에 지원할 자격이 됩니다. **지원을 원하는 직원들은 먼저 반드시 자신의 상사에게 이야기해야 합니다.** 회사에서는 관심이 있는 직원들을 외부 후보자들과 함께 고려할 것입니다. 관련 기술을 가진 직원들은 회사측에서 외부 고용이 더 나은 선택이라고 생각하지 않는 한 우선권이 주어질 것입니다.

(A) 우리는 Telecompu에 새 직원들을 환영하게 되어 기쁩니다.
(B) 사실, 직원들은 매일 근무 시간을 기록할 필요가 있습니다.
(C) 정직원들만 종합적인 복지 혜택을 받을 것입니다.
(D) 지원을 원하는 직원들은 먼저 반드시 자신의 상사에게 이야기해야 합니다.

>> **출제 포인트 지시어나 연결어를 단서로 활용하는 문제**

보기나 빈칸 바로 뒷문장에 지시어(it, them, these, those, such 등)나 연결어(however, in addition 등)가 있는 경우 중요한 단서로 활용한다.

Residents of Glenn Harbor are encouraged to enjoy the camping facilities at any of our city's parks, but a permit must be obtained first. No special permission is required for daytime visits. However, for overnight stays, a permit that costs $5 is required.

Many visitors misunderstand the rules and think they can simply claim a camp site by arriving early, with no reservation. -------. A reservation must be obtained by a group representative beforehand. If a Parks Department employee finds unauthorized campers at a site, the group will be asked to leave and may have to pay a fine.

1. (A) This is actually not the case.
   (B) Those without permits must wait.
   (C) Extra space will be available.
   (D) Many campers are local residents.

정답 (A)

해석 Glenn Harbor의 주민들은 우리 도시의 모든 공원에 있는 캠핑 시설을 즐기도록 권장되지만, 먼저 허가증을 취득해야 합니다. 낮 동안의 방문에는 어떤 특별 허가도 필요하지 않습니다. 그러나 숙박을 하기 위해서는 5달러의 허가증이 요구됩니다.
많은 방문객들은 규칙을 잘못 이해하고 예약 없이 캠프장에 일찍 도착해서 자리를 잡기만 하면 되는 것으로 생각합니다. **이것은 사실 그렇지가 않습니다.** 사전에 단체 대표에 의해 예약이 되어야 합니다. 만약 공원 관리직원이 캠프장에서 허가 받지 않은 캠퍼들을 발견하면, 그 단체는 떠나도록 요청받을 것이고 벌금을 내야 할 수도 있습니다.

(A) 이것은 사실 그렇지가 않습니다.   (B) 허가증이 없는 사람들은 기다려야 합니다.
(C) 여분의 공간이 이용 가능할 것입니다.   (D) 많은 캠퍼들이 지역 주민들입니다.

August 10 — The Carlsbad Town Council **announced its decision to sign a contract with Badmaev Construction for a new project**. According to the terms, Badmaev will upgrade the 300-yard stretch of beach north of Highway 78. The town's mayor, Miguel Cervantes, anticipates that the recreational activities offered at **the renovated facilities** will make it popular with families. "Children need a place where they can learn to swim, surf, and enjoy the water safely," Mr. Cervantes said. "This is exactly what our community needs." -------. Badmaev spokesperson Joe Marsh notes that **this area will have a medical clinic and professional lifeguards**, but also points out that it's **impossible to prevent every accident**. "Naturally, we will give our best effort, but there is simply no way to eliminate all potential dangers from the beach."

2.   (A) On the other hand, the city has yet to make a decision on a construction company.
    (B) Recently, many residents have made complaints about the waste at the beach.
    (C) However, even with a more secure environment, activities near the ocean can never be completely risk-free.
    (D) For the time being, the project cannot be approved because of budget limitations.

정답 (C)

해석 8월 10일 – Carlsbad 시의회는 새 프로젝트를 위하여 Badmaev 건설과 계약을 맺기로 한 결정을 발표했다. 약정에 따라 Badmaev 사는 78번 고속도로 북쪽에 있는 300야드의 해변 구간을 개조할 것이다. 시장 Miguel Cervantes는 개조된 시설에서 제공되는 여가 활동이 이곳을 가족들에게 인기 있는 곳으로 만들어줄 것이라고 기대한다. "아이들은 수영과 서핑을 배우고, 안전하게 물을 즐길 수 있는 곳이 필요하죠." Cervantes가 말했다. "이것이 바로 우리 지역 공동체가 필요로 하는 것입니다." **그러나 더 안전한 환경이라 할지라도 바다 근처에서의 활동에 위험이 전혀 없을 수는 없다.** Badmaev 사 대변인 Joe Marsh는 이 구역에 진료소와 전문 인명구조원이 있을 것이라고 강조하기도 하지만 모든 사고를 예방하는 것은 불가능하다는 점도 지적한다. "당연히 저희는 모든 노력을 다 하겠지만, 해변의 모든 잠재적인 위험을 제거할 방법은 없습니다."

(A) 반면에, 시는 아직 건설사를 결정하지 않았다.
(B) 최근에, 많은 주민들이 해변 쓰레기에 대해 불평을 했다.
(C) 그러나 더 안전한 환경이라 할지라도 바다 근처에서의 활동에 위험이 전혀 없을 수는 없다.
(D) 당분간 예산 제한 때문에 그 프로젝트는 승인되지 못한다.

2. 문맥에 맞는 어휘 선택 유형

▶ 지문의 흐름에 맞는 문맥상 알맞은 어휘를 선택하는 유형으로 각 지문당 1~2문항씩 출제된다. 다양한 품사의 어휘 문제가 출제되며, 연결어 출제 비중이 가장 높다.

>> **출제 포인트 어휘 문제**
빈칸 앞뒤 부분에서 정답의 단서를 찾아야 한다.

This e-mail is regarding your recent online purchase of our Signature X3 stereo system. We received your message stating that the item you received does not work properly. We'd like to express our sincere apologies and want to rectify the situation promptly. To avoid spending unnecessary time and money sending the ------- product back to us, just take it to your nearest retail dealer that carries our products. They will then replace the item for you with a new one. Make sure to take the original receipt with you. We hope that you will be pleased with the solution we have offered.

---

1. (A) additional
(B) defective
(C) missing
(D) confidential

정답 (B)

해석 이 이메일은 귀하가 최근 저희의 Signature X3 스테레오 시스템을 온라인으로 구매하신 것과 관련된 것입니다. 저희는 귀하가 받은 제품이 제대로 작동하지 않는다고 언급하신 메시지를 받았습니다. 정말 죄송하다는 말씀을 드리며 상황을 즉시 바로잡으려 합니다. **결함이 있는** 제품을 보내는데 불필요한 시간과 돈을 쓰시는 것을 피하기 위해, 저희 제품을 취급하는 가까운 소매점으로 상품을 가져가시기만 하면 됩니다. 그쪽에서 새 상품으로 교환해 드릴 것입니다. 영수증 원본을 꼭 지참하시기 바랍니다. 저희가 제공하는 해결책에 만족하시길 바랍니다.

(A) 추가적인 | (B) 결함이 있는 | (C) 잃어버린 | (D) 기밀의

Upper management has recently made the decision to ------ the dress code policy. All employees will now be required to wear the blue shirts displaying the company logo and name.

---

2. (A) discuss
(B) abolish
(C) survey
(D) revise

정답 (D)

해석 고위 경영진이 최근 복장 규정 방침을 **수정하는** 결정을 내렸습니다. 모든 임직원들은 이제 회사 로고와 이름이 표기된 푸른색 셔츠를 입어야 할 것입니다.

(A) 토론하다 | (B) 폐지하다 | (C) 조사하다 | (D) 수정하다

>> 출제 포인트 연결어 문제

앞뒤 문장의 의미상 관계를 묻는 연결어 선택 유형은 출제 비중이 높다.

✓ Part 6에 자주 출제되는 연결어

역접·대조	however on the contrary in contrast	그러나 그와는 반대로 그에 반해서	otherwise on the other hand even so	그렇지 않으면 반면에 그렇다 하더라도
	nevertheless, nonetheless			그럼에도 불구하고
인과	therefore, thus	그러므로	accordingly	그에 따라서
	as a result, consequently			결과적으로
순서	previously	이전에	since then	그때 이래로
	afterwards	나중에	finally	마침내
추가	in addition, additionally, moreover, furthermore, besides, also			게다가, 또한
대안	instead	대신에	alternatively	대안으로
강조	in particular	특히	actually	실제로
예시	for example, for instance			예를 들어
기타	likewise, similarly	마찬가지로	if so	만일 그렇다면
	in short	요컨대	unfortunately	유감스럽게도
	rather	오히려, 더 정확히 말하면	in other words, that is	즉, 다시 말해서

This is to remind everyone that our building will be undergoing major construction work starting next week. **Three new elevators will replace the current single elevator**, which is extremely slow and old. -------, all of the stairwells will be renovated, and a new heating system will be installed. We apologize to all employees for any disturbance that this work may cause.

1. (A) Instead
(B) Likewise
(C) Consequently
(D) In addition

정답 (D)

해석 이것은 다음 주부터 우리 건물이 주요 공사 작업에 들어간다는 것을 여러분에게 상기시키기 위한 것입니다. 세 대의 새로운 엘리베이터가 현재 한 대 있는 매우 느리고 오래된 엘리베이터를 대체할 것입니다. **덧붙여**, 모든 계단이 개조될 것이고, 새로운 난방 시스템이 설치될 것입니다. 이 작업으로 야기될 수 있는 방해에 대해 모든 임직원들에게 사과 드립니다.

(A) 대신에 | (B) 마찬가지로 | (C) 결과적으로 | (D) 덧붙여

After thoroughly reviewing all your information, I am delighted to inform you that **your application for a personal loan has been approved**. -------, the amount of $20,000 will be deposited into **your bank** account by 4:00 P.M. next Thursday.

2. (A) Accordingly
(B) Otherwise
(C) Similarly
(D) Nevertheless

해석 당신의 모든 정보를 철저히 검토한 결과, 개인 대출 신청이 승인되었음을 알려드리게 되어 기쁩니다. **그에 따라서,** 2만 달러가 다음 주 목요일 오후 4시까지 당신의 은행 계좌로 입금될 것입니다.

(A) 그에 따라서 | (B) 그렇지 않으면 | (C) 유사하게 | (D) 그럼에도 불구하고

3. 문법 유형

▶ Part 5 문법 문제와 동일한 유형으로, 각 지문당 1~2 문항씩 출제된다. 앞뒤 문장의 문맥을 고려해야 하는 동사 시제와 대명사의 출제 비중이 높다.

≫ 출제 포인트 **동사 문제**

Part 5 동사 문제와 마찬가지로 동사 자리인지 확인 후, 「수 일치 → 태 → 시제」 순서로 풀이한다. 다만 Part 6에서는 앞뒤 문장에 제시된 정보들을 단서로 사건의 진행 순서를 파악하여 시제를 결정해야 한다는 점에 유의한다.

✅ Part 6에 자주 출제되는 시제 형태

「would / should + 동사원형」: 앞으로 일어날 미래 내용

I **would be** happy to help you with any questions about our product.
저희 제품에 대한 귀하의 어떤 질문에도 기쁜 마음으로 귀하를 도와드릴 것입니다.

⋯→ would + 동사원형: ~일 것이다 (will보다 약한 의미)

To secure a seat at the upcoming finance convention, interested managers **should register** online by the end of next week. 다가오는 금융 회의에 좌석을 확보하기 위해, 관심 있는 매니저들은 다음 주 말까지 온라인으로 등록해야 한다.

⋯→ should + 동사원형: ~해야 한다

「would / should / could + have p.p.」: 과거에 실제로 일어나지 않은 과거 내용

The merger, which **would have united** the two clothing manufacturers, was reconsidered in light of new market research. 신규 시장 조사에 비추어, 이전에 두 의류 제조 업체를 합치기로 했던 합병이 재고되었다.

⋯→ would + have p.p.: ~했을 텐데

The sales clerk **should have included** a brochure that explains how to recharge the batteries.
그 판매원은 배터리를 재충전하는 방법을 설명하는 안내 책자를 포함했어야 했다.

⋯→ should + have p.p.: ~했어야만 했는데

「will have p.p.」: 과거에 시작된 일이 계속되어 미래의 특정 시점에 완료되는 내용

The headquarters will **have completed** the renovation of its meeting rooms when the budget is approved.
예산이 승인될 즈음, 본사는 회의실들의 신축 공사를 마무리할 예정이다.

⋯→ will have p.p.: (과거에 시작된 일이) ~일 예정이다

I am writing regarding the opening for the sales representative position posted in the *Boston Weekly Paper* last Wednesday. Actually, I already ------- a couple of e-mails after seeing the job posting last week, but I have yet to receive a reply from you.

1. (A) was sent
(B) will send
(C) sent
(D) would send

정답 (C)

해석 지난 수요일 〈Boston Weekly Paper〉에 공지된 영업 담당자 공석에 관해 편지를 씁니다. 사실 저는 지난주에 구인 공고를 본 이후 벌써 이메일 몇 통을 **보냈습니다**만 아직 답장을 받지 못했습니다.

After a number of delays, the construction of SM Energy's new building in Poca was finally finished this week. All workers from our seven branches in various locations ------- into our new headquarters. The move dates of all employees are listed on our corporate homepage. The transition is set to begin next month, and everyone should be settled into their new offices by the end of August.

2. (A) had moved
(B) will have moved
(C) to move
(D) will be moving

정답 (D)

해석 수차례의 지연 후, Poca에 위치한 SM 에너지 신사옥의 건설이 이번 주 마침내 완공되었습니다. 각 지역에 있는 일곱 개 지점의 모든 직원들은 우리의 새로운 본사로 **이동하게 될 것입니다.** 모든 직원들의 이전일은 회사 홈페이지에 열거되어 있습니다. 이동은 다음달에 시작되는 것으로 정해져 있으며, 전 직원은 8월 말까지 각자의 새 사무실에 자리를 잡게 될 것입니다.

앞 문장을 단서로 접근하는 유형으로, 문맥상 앞 문장의 어떤 명사를 대신하는지를 파악한다.

Developer Jody Cooling has announced that her newest venture, Star Complex, is scheduled to open next summer in Chicago, IL. Currently in the final stages of construction, the project has **a movie theater and a hotel**. ------- will be located on Rosewood Avenue.

1. (A) Several
   (B) Both
   (C) Some
   (D) Few

정답 (B)

해석 개발업자 Jody Cooling은 자신의 새로운 사업체인 Star Complex가 일리노이 주 시카고에서 내년 여름 개관할 것이라고 발표했습니다. 현재 공사의 막바지에 있는 이 프로젝트는 영화관과 호텔을 포함합니다. **둘 다** Rosewood 가에 위치할 것입니다.

This message is in response to your October 6 e-mail. According to our database, **two of our workers** were scheduled to visit you on October 5 to set up **your WasteClean unit** (order #1022934F), which you ordered on October 2. I was surprised to learn that you have not yet seen -------. Installation normally occurs within three days of the purchase date.

2. (A) it
   (B) one
   (C) some
   (D) them

정답 (D)

해석 이 메시지는 귀하의 10월 6일 이메일에 대한 답변입니다. 저희 데이터베이스에 따르면, 저희 직원 중 두 명이 10월 5일 귀하께서 10월 2일 주문하신 WasteClean을 설치하기 위해 방문할 예정이었습니다. 귀하가 아직도 **그들을** 보지 못하셨다는 사실을 알고 놀랐습니다. 설치는 보통 구매일로부터 3일 이내에 이루어집니다.

Questions 1-4 refer to the following e-mail.

To: Paddy Murphy <PMurphy@paone.com>
From: John Kohl <JKohl@minami.com>
Date: December 15
Subject: Follow-up

Dear Mr. Murphy,

Thank you for your interest in working at Minami Sushi as a chef. The ------- is still open. -------.
   1.   **2.**

I ------- that you worked in a Korean seafood restaurant for several years. So, you should be
   3.

familiar with some of the dishes here. -------, there are also significant differences between the
                                       4.

two countries' cooking styles, so you will have to undergo some training.

We were thinking of arranging your demonstration for this Friday at 10 A.M. To confirm the on-

site interview, please give me a call at (858) 555-1212 at your convenience. I hope to hear from

you soon.

Best regards,

John Kohl, Manager
Minami Sushi

---

1. (A) restaurant
(B) conversation
(C) position
(D) room

2. (A) Specifically, are you familiar with
       fishes native to Japan?
(B) If you are interested, you would have
       to come in and demonstrate your
       skills.
(C) The complete layout of our business
       is available on our home page.
(D) Our normal hours of operation are
       11 A.M. to 11 P.M.

3. (A) have been noticed
(B) will notice
(C) would notice
(D) noticed

4. (A) However
(B) Therefore
(C) Furthermore
(D) Likewise

Questions 5-8 refer to the following Web page.

The Wingfried Excellence in Education Award

Great high schools help shape the future of the country. It is no secret that ------- success lies in
                                                                                        5.

having a faculty full of passionate instructors. Caring teachers have a strong impact on students'

academic achievements. -------. The Wingfried Excellence in Education Award was ------- two
                            6.   **7.**

decades ago to honor public and private schools that recruit instructors who truly enjoy teaching.

-------, hundreds of schools across the United States have been selected as winners. To read
  8.

about past winners, check out the Winners section on this Web site.

---

5. (A) whose
   (B) their
   (C) its
   (D) our

6. (A) Recipients from other countries were
      selected this time.
   (B) This can be seen in excellent test
      scores and grades.
   (C) By doing so, they can receive more
      funding.
   (D) Public schools only can apply for the
      award.

7. 고난도 (A) researched
   (B) created
   (C) postponed
   (D) recognized

8. (A) Finally
   (B) Since then
   (C) Even so
   (D) In the same way

Questions 9-12 refer to the following article.

Desert Business Times

Palm Desert (April 25) — Janell Cantu has been selected as the new CEO of Forrest Financial Services. The board of directors ------- the appointment yesterday. -------. As CEO, Ms. Cantu
         9.   10.
will be responsible for creating a new business model to adapt to the challenge of low-cost alternatives. -------, she will be in charge of Forrest's newly-designed internet banking services.
                 11.
Her former employer is the company ------- the online financial services currently rated highest in
                                    12.
consumer surveys.

9.
(A) postponed
(B) confirmed
(C) reversed
(D) considered

10. 고난도
(A) The company will continue to look for a new CEO.
(B) Forrest Financial Services will continue with its current successful strategy.
(C) Ms. Cantu previously led the Marketing Department at Forrest's largest competitor.
(D) *Desert Business Times* has just launched its newly designed online edition.

11.
(A) Nonetheless
(B) Consequently
(C) Otherwise
(D) Furthermore

12.
(A) that developed
(B) which will develop
(C) develops
(D) whose development

Questions 13-16 refer to the following e-mail.

To: Masha@mauvais.com
From: Ashraf@crazycloud.pk
Date: May 22
Subject: Product inquiry
Attachment: cc.doc

Dear Masha,

I am pleased to hear of your interest in our CrazyCloud software. This unique program allows remote storage of data, ------- efficiency and productivity. Please ------- the brochure attached to
                                    13.   **14.**
this e-mail.

It contains CrazyCloud user testimonials. You will see that all of them particularly enjoyed the ability to easily back up files. -------, the program can store and save an important video you
                                                 15.
recorded as long as you have an internet connection. Also, CrazyCloud offers a large amount of file space, so users do not have to worry about storing big files. -------.
                                                                                16.

Please contact me with any other questions you might have.

Ashraf Kodur
CrazyCloud Sales Director

---

13. (A) enhancing
(B) enhancement
(C) enhances
(D) enhanced

14. (A) submit
고난도 (B) copy
(C) review
(D) discard

15. (A) Even so
(B) As long as
(C) Previously
(D) For example

16. (A) Security is a very important
고난도   consideration for many users.
(B) Additional data storage options can be
     purchased for a fee.
(C) Only some of our videos can be
     downloaded.
(D) The server problem will be fixed within
     the week.

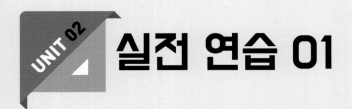

실전 연습 01

Questions 1-4 refer to the following memo. 해설서 p.66 / 제한 시간 10분

To: Zenetech employees
From: The security team
Date: September 12
Subject: New system

All employees should be aware of a change to the security policy regarding entry to the office. -------, your ID badges allowed access to our building. However, starting September 20, fingerprint scanners ------- at every entrance. Therefore, staff members will no longer be able to use their badges to enter the building. Next week, you will be asked to come to the security office to get your fingerprints scanned. Once the department managers have sent their staff's available hours, a ------- of the scheduled times will be sent to employees. -------. If you have any questions regarding the policy, please call one of our security officers.

1.
1.
2.
2.
3.
3.
4.
4.

---

1. (A) Finally
(B) Accordingly
(C) Previously
(D) Consequently

2. (A) installed
(B) will be installed
(C) installs
(D) have been installed

3. (A) notify
(B) notification
(C) notified
(D) notifying

4. (A) There is a fee to replace your ID badges.
(B) This project must still be approved by the board.
(C) The scanning process should not take more than five minutes.
(D) This maintenance work is performed once a week.

Questions 5-8 refer to the following e-mail.

From: bradhouser@ellieassociates.com
To: s_davis@tcshsecurity.com
Date: April 27
Subject: Appreciation

Dear Ms. Davis,

I am writing to thank you for ------- our office on Tuesday. Your security presentation -------.
                              5.   6.
Our management, in particular, appreciated the time you took to carefully explain how the new

servers work and how to keep our network safe.

In July, some employees from another branch will be relocating here. Would ------- be open to
                                                                            7.
returning to give another demonstration then? -------. I look forward to hearing from you soon.
                                               8.

Best regards,

Brad Houser

---

5. (A) calling
   (B) moving
   (C) opening
   (D) visiting

6. (A) informs
   (B) will be informative
   (C) had informed
   (D) was informative

7. (A) theirs
   (B) you
   (C) they
   (D) yours

8. 고난도 (A) Your feedback in the recent survey was much appreciated.
   (B) We invite all managers to attend the opening of the new branch.
   (C) The staff here follows all security rules strictly.
   (D) Our new members would definitely find it useful.

Questions 9-12 refer to the following letter.

Ms. Stephanie Marx
Washington Industries
598 Central Avenue NW
Montreal, QC H3Z 2Y1

Dear Ms. Marx,

We are happy to hear of your interest in Fast Step Flooring. Our flooring products are simply the best, and we are certain you will be pleased with what we have to offer.

In busy offices such as yours, floors take a beating. Given such ------- abuse, your flooring has
                                                                    9.
to be tough enough to last for several years and still look good.

To ------- these needs, Fast Step Flooring has created our patented Ten-Year line of flooring. In
      10.
fact, the Ten-Year line is built to be the strongest flooring possible. And as the name tells you,

this line ------- to last at least 10 years and still look as good as it did on day one. -------.
          11.   **12.**

To obtain a free estimate, call us today at 514-639-1000!

Sincerely,

Stanley Friedman
Fast Step Flooring

---

9. (A) constant
        (B) constantly
        (C) constable
        (D) constancy

10. (A) prevent
        (B) address
        (C) improve
        (D) research

11. (A) will be guaranteeing
        (B) will guarantee
        (C) is guaranteed
        (D) was guaranteed

12. (A) This flooring will easily last half a
            decade or more.
        (B) Let us send someone to look at your
            home for a small fee.
        (C) Thank you for installing our special line
            of flooring in your kitchen.
        (D) If you're unsatisfied for any reason,
            we'll refund your money.

Questions 13-16 refer to the following article.

Manufacturers' Conference, November 11 — This year's World Manufacturers' Conference was held in Miami this past week. -------. Just like last year, U.S. and Canadian corporations were
                                                      13.
------- represented. -------, participants noticed that there were a significant number of European
 14.   15.
attendees this time. Noticeable was the fact that food packaging plants had a stronger presence
at the ------- this year.
        16.

13. (A) A similar convention also took place a
고난도   week before.
      (B) Miami residents helped coordinate
          the tours.
      (C) The conference invited companies
          from across the globe to attend.
      (D) Registration fees were waived for
          those who volunteered.

14. (A) heavy
      (B) heavily
      (C) heavier
      (D) heaviness

15. (A) Moreover
      (B) Therefore
      (C) Instead
      (D) Rather

16. (A) luncheon
      (B) demonstration
      (C) event
      (D) class

실전 연습 02

Questions 1-4 refer to the following advertisement.

해설서 p.68 / ⏱ 제한 시간 10분

Do you work at night and sleep during the day? Then visit AdenaPoly's Web site today.

This December, AdenaPoly is conducting a special study on behalf of HN Pharmaceutical. That is why we are ------- late-night workers between the ages of 18 and 45. Participants must have
1.
worked a full-time night shift for at least one year ------- the start of the experiment. -------.
2. **3.**

Those who would like more information are asked to fill out some questions on our Web site.

To show our thanks, all participants ------- $75 for taking part in the study.
4.

---

1. (A) promoting
(B) seeking
(C) informing
(D) insuring

2. (A) except for
고난도 (B) due to
(C) at
(D) as

3. (A) We ask that you provide contact
고난도 information for your current workplace.
(B) We think that the cost of the program is
worth it.
(C) We will send you an information packet
about how to apply for a job here.
(D) We want our patients to know about
the changes to the original schedule.

4. (A) will receive
(B) had received
(C) to receive
(D) to be received

Questions 5-8 refer to the following e-mail.

To: Matthew Lee <mlee@datazerox.net>
From: Hollis Anderson <hollisa2@gu.edu>
Subject: Parking permit
Date: January 21

We appreciate you contacting us about your ------- parking permit for Lot 49. Your license plate
5.
is still in our system, and you will not receive any additional tickets for parking there for the next

week. Your current fine comes to $22.50.

I contacted the parking lot attendant to see if anyone had found and ------- the permit. -------.
6. 7.
If you cannot locate your permit by next week, go on our Web site, where you can ------- a new
8.
one. Please note that the replacement permit will cost $15.

Sincerely,

Hollis Anderson
Gervano University Parking Services

5. (A) missing
(B) misses
(C) to miss
(D) missed

6. (A) return
(B) are returning
(C) returned
(D) will return

7. 고난도
(A) A new ticket will be issued next week.
(B) As of yet, no one has come forward.
(C) Also, parking hours will be extended.
(D) Parking permits should be hung in a
visible location.

8. (A) approve
(B) design
(C) order
(D) remove

Questions 9-12 refer to the following article.

Oakdale Daily Gazette

(March 12) Earlier this week, Superintendent Wendy Biggs revealed the board of education's plan to begin a new community outreach program to train future educators. During a television interview, Ms. Biggs mentioned the increased ------- for middle and high school instructors.
9.
-------, she emphasized the effects of the recent retirement of many math and science teachers.
10.
Her statement ------- with great excitement by community leaders. John Tuft, a long-time city
11.
council member, however, did not agree. -------.
12.

---

9. (A) settlement
(B) demand
(C) resolution
(D) entertainment

10. (A) Despite this
(B) Otherwise
(C) Alternatively
(D) In particular

11. (A) had been receiving
고난도 (B) was received
(C) to receive
(D) will be received

12. (A) He believes it is better to hire
experienced instructors.
(B) He thinks the science program
deserves additional funding.
(C) He anticipates that many teachers will
attend the training session.
(D) He projects that there will be more
students interested in math.

Questions 13-16 refer to the following information.

Congratulations on your purchase of a Hybridoma appliance. We are confident you will enjoy using this product. However, if for any reason you are not ------- , you can exchange or return
13.
the item for a full refund within two months as long as it is unused. In order to do so, simply complete the return label that came in the package and send the appliance back. Your product
------- in the box it came in. ------- . Refunds will be issued by cash or credit. We appreciate your
14.   15.
business and sincerely hope you continue to ------- with us.
16.

13. (A) satisfy
(B) satisfied
(C) satisfaction
(D) satisfying

14. (A) will mail
(B) should be mailed
(C) is mailing
(D) has been mailed

15. (A) We assure you that this problem will never occur again.
(B) We pride ourselves in the high-quality of our merchandise.
(C) Processing will take three to four weeks.
(D) It should be kept out of the reach of young children.

16. (A) meet
(B) dine
(C) learn
(D) shop

실전 연습 03

Questions 1-4 refer to the following notice.

해설서 p.70 / 제한 시간 10분

To Sales Employees,

In the office, we try to maintain the maximum possible security for our electronic files. The same should be true when you travel to meet clients. It is ------- that you keep all work-related files 1. on your notebook computers protected. If you are transporting files on a memory stick, keep it in your possession at all times to protect the data on it. -------. Lastly, when you are having 2. business discussions over the phone, avoid discussing detailed information about our company as much as possible. By ------- these simple rules, you can help ------- our security even when 3. 4. outside the office. Thank you.

Nikita Bayul
Director of Information Technology

1.
(A) probable
(B) essential
(C) traditional
(D) conclusive

2. 고난도
(A) It would be best if you encrypted the files as well.
(B) Be careful not to talk about business on the phone, either.
(C) Employees are not allowed to copy any files at the office.
(D) Do not remove any work-related files from office computers.

3.
(A) observed
(B) observation
(C) to observe
(D) observing

4.
(A) ensuring
(B) ensured
(C) ensure
(D) is ensured

Questions 5-8 refer to the following e-mail.

To: Hugh Grant <hgrant@andefitnesscenter.ca>
From: Mark Dion <mdion@andefitnesscenter.ca>
Re: Exceptional Reviews
Date: October 3

Dear Hugh,

All of the managers were delighted about the excellent reviews of our fitness center in the recent

issues of *Zoom Health Magazine* and *Exercise Weekly*. Your contributions to the A and E Fitness

Center have been -------. For that reason, we are pleased ------- you a bonus with your paycheck
                        5.   6.

on October 10. -------, we are giving you a salary raise starting next month. Since you became a
                   7.

personal trainer here at the beginning of the year, membership at our fitness center has increased

by more than 50 percent. -------. Such positive trends are largely due to your performance.
                            8.

We'd like to extend a sincere thank you from the management team.

Mark

---

5. (A) withdrawn
   (B) equaled
   (C) outstanding
   (D) affordable

6. (A) an award
   (B) to award
   (C) which awards
   (D) it awarded

7. (A) On the other hand
   (B) Even so
   (C) For example
   (D) In addition

8. 고난도 (A) We will be extending our fitness
       center's business hours soon.
   (B) Our fitness center's ratings in other
       similar publications have also risen.
   (C) A new manager will oversee the
       operations of our fitness center.
   (D) This is the most popular event that
       takes place at our fitness center.

Questions 9-12 refer to the following article.

BOSTON (January 10) — Fizz Pop Company has announced that it will be selling its soft drinks in limited-edition containers for six months. The soft drinks will be sold in the same classic bottles used over half a century ago, when the company ------- became popular. Fizz Pop will also be
9.
releasing two new soft drinks, ------- the number of its flavors; this new line will complement the
10.
traditional bottles in a novel way.

Cindy Grover, Fizz Pop's CEO, says the promotion will honor the founding of the company.
-------. The company believes this will bridge the gap between their existing consumers and a
11.
new generation. Fizz Pop's limited-edition bottles will become available starting next Monday,
while its new ------- will debut in March.
12.

9.
(A) every
(B) yet
(C) it
(D) first

10.
(A) had tripled
(B) will triple
(C) triples
(D) tripling

11.
(A) Recent market trends show that consumers prefer these flavors.
(B) This is the reason Fizz Pop became well-known.
(C) Soft drinks have been losing popularity since last year.
(D) It will also attract customers who want to remember the old days.

12. 고난도
(A) services
(B) methods
(C) varieties
(D) devices

Questions 13-16 refer to the following press release.

Dr. Bill Sumpter, president of Willsbourough University, has announced that the main library ------- to accommodate more students. Over the last several years, enrollment at the university
13.
has nearly doubled. This is likely due to the increasing number of reputable professors joining the university's faculty. The construction project is expected to take two years. -------. Library
14.
materials can be accessed in the basement of the building ------- the expansion of the first and
15.
second floors. This may result in some inconvenience as the space in the basement is smaller than the other floors. "However, ------- this project is completed, students will have a lot more
16.
room to study," said Dr. Sumpter.

13. (A) will renovate
(B) will be renovated
(C) has renovated
(D) has been renovating

14. (A) Dr. Sumpter is very proud of the
고난도   achievements of the faculty.
(B) This is the result of an increase in
student tuition fees.
(C) The initial timeline of sixteen months
had to be revised after further review.
(D) The university is currently seeking
funding from various companies.

15. (A) even
(B) while
(C) in order to
(D) during

16. (A) whether
(B) since
(C) unless
(D) once

REVIEW TEST

해설서 p.72 / ⏱ 제한 시간 10분

Questions 1-4 refer to the following e-mail.

To: Harriet Watkins <hwatkins@mymail.co.ca>
From: Customer Inquiries <inquiries@lextech.com>
Date: Monday 5, May 3:41 P.M.
Subject: Information requested

We appreciate the time you took to contact us regarding the user guide for your Sonic Q tablet PC. We agree with you ------- the steps showing how to connect to a wireless network are a

1.

bit complex. -------. Our technical team has ------- simplified those instructions so that they are

2. **3.**

much more easy to follow. The ------- guide can be found by visiting our Web site and clicking

4.

on the Online Manuals tab. To thank you for your input, we will mail a discount coupon for 10 percent off your next LexTech purchase.

1.
(A) regarding
(B) that
(C) what
(D) for

2.
고난도
(A) We hope you take a few minutes to fill out the survey.
(B) The Sonic Q tablet PC is our most popular product.
(C) Our helpful staff is always ready to hear from you.
(D) Other users have brought up the same issues.

3.
(A) similarly
(B) nonetheless
(C) instead
(D) therefore

4.
(A) rough
(B) original
(C) updated
(D) detailed

Questions 5-8 refer to the following article.

PINEWOOD (November 1) — Today marks the groundbreaking on the new Harvest Square Mall, which is being supported through several corporate donations. As a result of this -------, 5. construction of the main buildings, as well as an inventory storage area, is expected to progress rapidly. City leaders believe that the town will greatly benefit from the new mall. -------. Residents 6. are also excited about the mall. Kira Siebrand, ------- lives close to the newly planned complex, 7. states, "I'm really looking forward to getting my shopping done in such a convenient location. I've had to deal with the increasing traffic ------- some time now, crossing town to the old Fairland 8. Mall. I know I'll be a regular visitor at Harvest Square."

5. (A) design
(B) funding
(C) sale
(D) policy

6.
고난도
(A) Several corporations will attend the grand opening.
(B) The center will support the creation of 250 full-time jobs.
(C) Residences near the area will have to get used to the additional noise.
(D) The mall may cause traffic problems during the holiday season.

7. (A) who
(B) where
(C) likewise
(D) one

8. (A) about
(B) with
(C) along
(D) for

Questions 9-12 refer to the following e-mail.

To: annad@mcclellancomp.com
From: ericd@mcclellancomp.com
Date: July 31
Subject: Store Manager Promotions

Dear Ms. Dietrich,

We had our first round of interviews for promotions last week. Next Monday, we will start the

second phase of interviews with candidates who are the most ------- for store manager positions.
                                                                    9.
As you are a long-time manager, we believe you know which ------- our company is looking for.
                                                            10.
Would you be able to create a brief exam for the next interview? -------, could you send it to me
                                                                  11.
by this Friday? The test would ideally have candidates give solutions to difficult store scenarios.

-------.
12.

Thank you,

Eric Davis
Human Resources Director
McClellan Computers

9. (A) suits
   (B) suiting
   (C) suitable
   (D) suitably

10. (A) locations
    (B) performances
    (C) agreements
    (D) qualities

11. (A) If so
    (B) Even so
    (C) Instead
    (D) For example

12. (A) We plan on implementing your
        solutions soon.
    (B) I hope to hear from you shortly.
    (C) When you arrive, we will discuss the
        available position.
    (D) I look forward to interviewing you next
        week.

Questions 13-16 refer to the following press release.

Terracotta Hi-Tech, Miami's best-known electronics supplier, says it ------- $15,000 to Camten
13.

University's campus expansion project. The money was raised during a charity banquet last

week at the company's -------. Terracotta CEO Alan Leno will meet with the university's dean this
14.

Friday afternoon to hand over the check in person. ------- the last decade, Terracotta Hi-Tech
15.

has hosted multiple fundraisers for various schools and educational programs. -------.
16.

13. (A) may award
고난도 (B) award
(C) will award
(D) awarding

14. (A) store
(B) resort
(C) library
(D) school

15. (A) Among
(B) Behind
(C) Although
(D) Over

16. (A) Last week's event was by far the most
고난도   successful.
(B) Mr. Leno will arrive at approximately
2 P.M.
(C) The company is going to open another
location in Florida next month.
(D) The university decided to accept more
students this year.

PAF

RT7

독해

OVERVIEW

지문을 읽고 그에 해당하는 질문에 알맞은 답을 고르는 문제이다. 지문은 문자 메시지와 온라인 채팅과 같은 문자 대화문부터 신문 기사나 웹사이트 페이지까지 그 종류가 다양하며, 그 형태도 1개의 지문으로 된 단일 지문, 2개의 지문으로 된 이중 지문, 3개의 지문으로 이루어진 삼중 지문 문제로 구분할 수 있다. 단일 지문 29문항, 이중 지문 10문항, 삼중 지문 15문항씩 총 54문항이 출제된다.

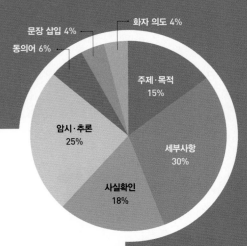

문제 유형

단일 지문(10개) | 이메일, 편지, 문자 메시지, 온라인 채팅, 광고, 기사, 양식, 회람, 공지, 웹페이지 등

이중 지문(2개) | 이메일−이메일, 기사−이메일, 웹페이지−이메일, 웹페이지(광고)−웹페이지(사용 후기)

삼중 지문(3개) | 다양한 세 지문들의 조합

출제 포인트

- 지문과 문제의 길이가 점점 길어지고 있다. 지문과 선택지를 일일이 대조할 필요가 있는 사실확인 문제 유형의 비중을 늘려서 난이도를 조절하기도 한다.

- 암시·추론 문제의 비중이 증가하고 있다. 지문에 나와 있는 정보를 토대로 알 수 있는 사실확인 및 암시·추론 문제가 많이 등장하고 있다.

- 동의어 문제가 매회 1~4문제의 출제 비율을 유지하고 있다.

PART 7 이렇게 대비하자!

- Part 7은 글의 흐름 파악이 중요하기 때문에 빠르고 정확한 독해력이 필요하다. 어휘력을 쌓고 문장의 구조를 파악하는 훈련을 통해 독해력을 뒷받침하는 기본기를 다져야 한다.

- 문자 메시지나 온라인 채팅은 난이도가 비교적 높지 않다. 그러나 구어체적 표현이 많이 나오고 문자 그대로의 사전적인 의미가 아닌 문맥상 그 안에 담겨 있는 숨은 뜻을 찾는 화자 의도 파악 문제가 꼭 출제되기 때문에 평소 구어체 표현을 숙지하고 대화의 흐름을 파악하는 연습을 한다.

- 질문의 키워드를 찾고 질문이 요구하는 핵심 정보를 본문에서 신속하게 찾아내는 연습이 필요하다.

- 본문에서 찾아낸 정답 정보는 선택지에서 다른 표현으로 제시되므로 같은 의미를 여러 가지 다른 표현들(paraphrased expressions)로 전달하는 패러프레이징 찾기 연습이 필요하다.

PART 7 문제 풀이 접근법

1. 지문 순서대로 풀지 말자.

Part 7은 처음부터 또는 마지막부터 순서대로 풀지 않아도 된다. 15개의 지문 중에서 당연히 가장 쉬워 보이는 것부터 먼저 풀고 어려운 문제는 시간이 남으면 푼다는 마음으로 풀어야 한다. 다음과 같은 순서로 문제를 풀어 보도록 한다.

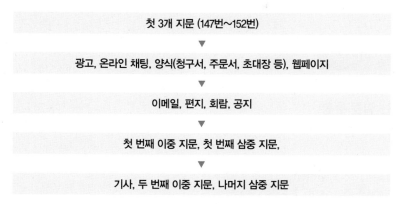

첫 3개 지문 (147번~152번)

▼

광고, 온라인 채팅, 양식(청구서, 주문서, 초대장 등), 웹페이지

▼

이메일, 편지, 회람, 공지

▼

첫 번째 이중 지문, 첫 번째 삼중 지문,

▼

기사, 두 번째 이중 지문, 나머지 삼중 지문

2. 패러프레이징(Paraphrasing)된 정답을 찾는 것이 핵심이다.

같은 표현은 절대 반복되지 않는다. 정답은 지문에 나온 표현을 다른 말로 바꿔 나온다.

> • **지문에서 나오는 표현** National Museum is <u>located just minutes from Oxford Street Station</u> in Richmont's shopping district. 국립 박물관은 Richmont의 쇼핑가에 있는 Oxford Street 역에서 단 몇 분 거리에 있다.
>
> • **문제** What is suggested about the Morlen Museum? 국립 박물관에 관하여 암시되는 것은?
>
> • **정답** It is <u>conveniently located</u>. 편리한 곳에 위치해 있다.

3. 지문 내용에 기반하여 정답을 찾는다.

정답은 반드시 지문 내용에 기반하여 사실인 것만 고른다. 절대 '그럴 것 같다, 그렇겠지'라고 상상하여 답을 고르면 안 된다. Part 7 문제 유형 중에는 추론해야 하는 문제들이 많이 나오기는 하지만 아무리 추론 문제이더라도 지문에 있는 근거 문장을 패러프레이징한 보기를 찾는 문제일 뿐이다. 추론 이상의 상상은 금물이다.

4. 문제를 먼저 읽고 키워드를 파악하자!

지문 유형 확인 ▶ 문제의 핵심어 확인 ▶ 지문 읽기 ▶ 문제 풀이

- 주제나 목적, 대상을 묻는 문제는 대개 지문의 첫머리에 단서가 제시되므로 도입부 내용을 잘 확인하여 이 내용을 포괄할 수 있는 선택지를 고른다.

- 세부사항, 사실확인 문제의 경우 핵심 단어 및 표현에 집중하여 질문에서 키워드를 파악하고 관련 내용이 언급된 부분을 지문에서 찾아 문제를 해결한다.

- 동의어 문제에서는 해당 단어의 대표적인 의미를 무작정 선택하는 것이 아니라 반드시 문맥상 어떤 의미로 쓰였는지 확인하여 정답을 찾는다.

주제·목적

단일 지문의 경우에는 첫 번째 문제로 출제되며, 첫 번째 문제가 주제·목적 문제가 아니라면 그 지문에서 주제·목적 문제는 출제되지 않은 것이다. 이중이나 삼중 지문에서는 단일 지문처럼 첫 번째 문제로만 출제되지 않고 첫 번째와 네 번째 문제 사이에서 주제·목적 문제가 출제될 수 있다.

🔍 질문 유형 확인하기

1. 잘 나오는 질문 유형

목적

What is the purpose of this letter? 이 편지의 목적은 무엇인가?
Why was this notice **written**? 이 공지는 왜 쓰였는가?
Why was the e-mail **sent**? 왜 이메일이 보내졌는가?

주제

What is the topic of the article? 이 기사의 주제는 무엇인가?
What is the announcement **mainly about**? 공지는 주로 무엇에 관한 것인가?
What is mainly discussed in the advertisement? 광고에서는 무엇을 주로 논의하는가?

2. 독해 전략

▶ 주로 지문의 앞부분에서 글의 주제나 목적이 드러나지만, 최근에는 전체적인 내용과 흐름을 파악한 뒤에 글의 주제나 목적을 찾을 수 있는 문제의 출제 빈도가 높아지고 있는 추세이다.

▶ 지문을 처음부터 빠르게 읽어내려가며 풀거나, 다른 문제들을 먼저 푼 뒤에 지문의 내용이 전체적으로 파악되면 마지막에 풀도록 한다.

주제·목적 문제 풀이 써머리

STEP 1 단서는 주로 지문의 앞부분에 등장하며, 지문 전체를 토대로 주제를 파악해야 할 경우 앞부분부터 읽어 내려가면서 보기와 매칭시킨다.

STEP 2 주제 문장을 패러프레이징(paraphrasing)하거나, 지문 전체의 내용을 요약한 보기를 선택한다.

Question 1 refers to the following letter.

Hello,

STEP 1 첫 번째 단락 읽기

❶ I'm contacting you in order to tell you about a special feature on *Advantage Journal*'s Web site. Starting today, you'll be able to enjoy *Advantage Journal* TV on our site.

···▸ a new service

You can now view video clips of our writers and resident tennis pros reviewing various sports equipment, discussing the latest sports news, and presenting techniques to help improve your game. You can also watch highlights of major matches along with commentary from our experts.

This service is only available to our magazine subscribers, so you will be asked for your subscriber number and password when you visit this section. Please visit advantagejournal.com/TV today to experience these exciting, new features.

Best,

Mark Rogers

• ▪ 글의 주제 · 목적
Advantage Journal의 새로운 특징(Advantage Journal TV)을 소개

• ▪ Advantage Journal TV를 통해 고객들이 받는 혜택

• ▪ 혜택 받는 대상 및 이용 방법 안내

1. What is the purpose of the letter?

(A) To offer professional lessons
(B) To advertise job openings
(C) To announce a new service ···▸ STEP 2 주제 문장을 바꿔 쓴 보기 선택
(D) To request feedback from subscribers

해석 및 해설

1. 편지의 목적은 무엇인가?

(A) 전문가 수업을 제안하기 위해
(B) 직원 모집을 광고하기 위해
(C) 새로운 서비스를 안내하기 위해
(D) 구독자들에게 피드백을 요청하기 위해

해설 첫 번째 단락에서 웹사이트의 특징에 관하여 알려주기 위해 연락한다고 하면서 〈Advantage Journal TV〉를 웹사이트상에서 즐길 수 있게 되었다고 했으므로 새로운 서비스를 알리기 위해 편지를 쓴 것임을 알 수 있다. 따라서 (C) To announce a new service가 정답이다.

Questions 1-2 refer to the following text message.

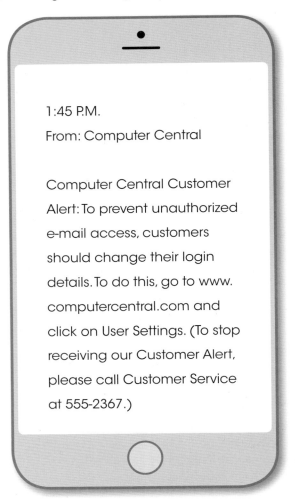

1:45 P.M.

From: Computer Central

Computer Central Customer Alert: To prevent unauthorized e-mail access, customers should change their login details. To do this, go to www.computercentral.com and click on User Settings. (To stop receiving our Customer Alert, please call Customer Service at 555-2367.)

1. What is the purpose of the text message?

(A) To suggest modifying some credentials
(B) To verify a recent login
(C) To request feedback on an e-mail program
(D) To announce a system update

2. According to the text message, how can customers stop receiving similar messages?

(A) By replying to an electronic message
(B) By going to a Web site
(C) By updating some computer settings
(D) By contacting Customer Service

Questions 3-4 refer to the following Web page.

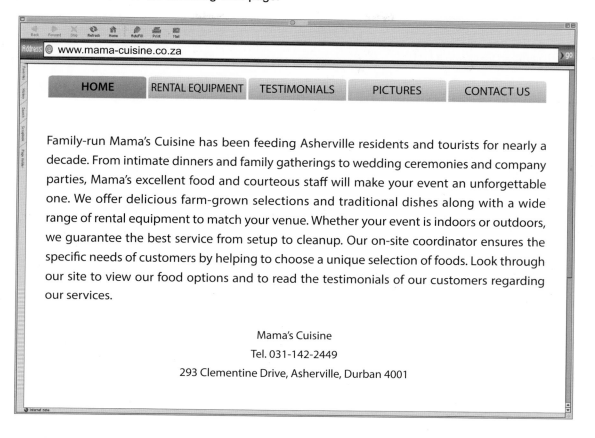

Family-run Mama's Cuisine has been feeding Asherville residents and tourists for nearly a decade. From intimate dinners and family gatherings to wedding ceremonies and company parties, Mama's excellent food and courteous staff will make your event an unforgettable one. We offer delicious farm-grown selections and traditional dishes along with a wide range of rental equipment to match your venue. Whether your event is indoors or outdoors, we guarantee the best service from setup to cleanup. Our on-site coordinator ensures the specific needs of customers by helping to choose a unique selection of foods. Look through our site to view our food options and to read the testimonials of our customers regarding our services.

Mama's Cuisine
Tel. 031-142-2449
293 Clementine Drive, Asherville, Durban 4001

3. What is advertised?

(A) A grocery store
(B) A catering service
(C) A local farm
(D) A kitchen appliance service

4. What is indicated about Mama's Cuisine?

(A) It sells unique silverware.
(B) It is closed on holidays.
(C) It is a new business.
(D) It conforms to customers' needs.

Questions 5-7 refer to the following letter.

Benita's Dance Academy
Award-winning dance instruction for people of all ages
2125 West Windy Road
Houston, Texas 77001

May 10

Ms. Jocelyn Montoya
218 Amarilly Lane
Houston, Texas 77002

Dear Ms. Montoya,

I enjoyed speaking to you during your recent interview for an instructor position at Benita's Dance Academy. We would like you to come to work full-time for us, starting in September. Right now, we offer classes in jazz, ballet, and tap-dancing. Since your specialty is ballroom dancing, we want to feature some new ballroom classes taught by you in the autumn.

I would also like to ask you whether you would be interested in a substitute teaching position to fill in for our ballet instructor who is scheduled to be on vacation in August. This will help you familiarize yourself with our school before your sessions begin in September.

I am looking forward to working with you. We feel that your decades of teaching experience will be a valuable asset to our school. Please contact me at 555-0150 by the end of July so that we can set up an appointment to finalize your paperwork and schedule autumn classes.

Sincerely,

Benita Juarez

Benita Juarez
Director

---

5. What is the purpose of the letter?

(A) To announce the opening of a new school
(B) To schedule a job interview
(C) To advertise dance classes
(D) To make an offer of employment

6. According to the letter, what is true about Ms. Montoya?

(A) She has won awards for dance.
(B) She is currently a substitute teacher.
(C) She will be on vacation in August.
(D) She has a lot of teaching experience.

7. What dance classes are NOT currently offered at Benita's Dance Academy?

(A) Ballroom
(B) Jazz
(C) Ballet
(D) Tap

Questions 8-11 refer to the following letter.

May 26

Marie Dupont
300 Boulevard Haussmann
75008 Paris, France

Dear Ms. Dupont,

Congratulations! We are delighted to inform you that you have been selected as one of eight finalists in the seventh annual French Haute Cuisine Cooking Competition. Your recipe for Niçoise Salad Quiche was selected from over 200 entries as a fine example for delicate use of authentic French ingredients. As a finalist, you will receive a $150 gift certificate to the award-winning Fruits de Terre Restaurant, which has kindly sponsored the competition.

We would also like you to prepare your dish for a panel of judges during the city's annual French Food Festival. This year's festival will be held on Friday, June 29, through Sunday, July 1. Finalists will begin cooking at 1:00 P.M. on Sunday in a camping area just outside the Fruits de Terre Restaurant. Judging will begin at 4:30 P.M., and the award ceremony will take place immediately afterwards. The first prize will be a top cuisine course taught by our renowned head chef and TV personality, Louis Lebrun. Mr. Lebrun will provide private one-on-one cooking classes to the winner for one week.

Upon notifying us that you intend to enter the final round, you will be required to complete and return a printed form to secure your place in the competition. Please confirm by calling our office at 01 83 46 94 72 no later than Tuesday, June 5.

We look forward to your response!

Sincerely,

Pierre Beaufort
French Haute Cuisine Event Coordinator

---

8. Why did Mr. Beaufort write to Ms. Dupont?

(A) To identify her as an award recipient
(B) To confirm receipt of her application
(C) To recruit her as a cooking teacher
(D) To ask her to judge a competition

9. When must competitors be available?

고난도
(A) On May 28
(B) On June 5
(C) On June 29
(D) On July 1

10. What is the prize for winning the French Haute Cuisine Cooking Competition?

(A) A certificate of completion
(B) An invitation to appear on a TV show
(C) A job as a chef
(D) A series of cooking lessons

11. What is Ms. Dupont asked to confirm?

(A) A convenient time for an interview
(B) Her participation in an event
(C) Her contact details
(D) A reservation at a restaurant

상세정보

Part 7에서 여전히 가장 많은 출제 비중을 갖는 유형이다. 지문에 대한 종합적인 내용이나 추론 포인트를 묻기보다는 특정 위치에 있는 구체적인 키워드나 정보를 묻는 유형이므로 비교적 빨리 풀 수 있는 문제이다. 의문사와 키워드에 따라 빠르게 문제의 단서가 있는 부분을 찾고, 패러프레이징이 되어 있는 보기를 찾으면 된다.

Tip! Part 7에서 가장 많이 출제되는 유형이야!

🔍 질문 유형 확인하기

1. 잘 나오는 질문 유형

의문사 what, which, who, when, where, how, why 등이 이끄는 세부 정보에 관한 문제

Where should the applicants send the résumés? 지원자들은 이력서를 어디로 보내야 하는가?

Who will be the keynote speaker for the opening ceremony? 누가 개회식의 기조 연설자가 될 것인가?

What is Mr. Murdock asked to do? Mr. Murdock은 무엇을 하도록 요청받는가?

Why did TM Motors hire more workers? TM 자동차는 왜 더 많은 근로자들을 고용했는가?

How much should Mr. Kim pay for the late fee? Mr. Kim은 연체료로 얼마나 내야 하는가?

When did the representative contact the customer? 언제 직원이 고객에게 연락을 취했는가?

2. 독해 전략

▶ 의문사와 키워드에 표시를 하고 지문에서 해당 키워드와 겹치거나 패러프레이징이 되어 있는 부분을 빠르게 훑어 가며 찾는다.

▶ 보통 세부사항을 묻는 문제는 비교적 쉽게 풀 수 있는 문제이므로 본문에서 질문의 키워드가 언급된 부분을 빠르게 찾는 연습을 해두도록 한다.

상세정보 문제 풀이 써머리

STEP 1 질문에 쓰인 의문사와 키워드를 확인한다.

STEP 2 지문에서 질문의 키워드와 관련된 내용을 포착한다.

STEP 3 질문의 단서를 그대로 언급하거나 패러프레이징한 보기를 선택한다.

Question **1** refers to the following advertisement.

SUMMIT HOTELS
● 구인 광고 회사 이름

Date Posted: September 14
Type of Position: Head of Housekeeping
Contact: Caitlyn Tam, HR Director
Location: Montpelier, Vermont, USA

Employer
Founded on this location over a century ago, Summit Hotels is a national
chain with over 100 franchises employing upwards of 15,000 employees.
Our hotels are typically located near ski resorts, and in Vermont alone,
there are 12 locations. Our company consistently ranks among the top ten
hotel chains for excellence in customer service. Our employees enjoy great
benefits and a competitive salary. There are also ample opportunities for
career development.

● 구인 광고 회사 정보

Responsibilities and Requirements
The head of housekeeping is responsible for overseeing and training all of
the hotel staff in cleaning guest suites, doing laundry, and monitoring the
sanitation system. This position's responsibilities also include checking
inventory and ordering cleaning supplies. To obtain this position, the
successful candidate must demonstrate superb communication and
organization skills, as well as thorough knowledge of current health and
safety and sanitation guidelines.

● 지원 자격

STEP 2 질문의 키워드와 관련된 내용 포착
① To apply for this position, please send a short cover letter and a copy
of your résumé to Ms. Caitlyn Tam at catetam@summithrmail.com by
October 31. Qualified applicants will be contacted to interview between
November 13 and 17.

● 지원 방법과 지원 기간

---

1. When is the deadline for application? ⋯ STEP 1 질문의 의문사와 키워드 확인 → 지원서 마감일

(A) September 14
(B) October 31 ⋯ STEP 3 질문의 단서를 언급한 보기 선택
(C) November 13
(D) November 17

해석 및 해설

1. 지원서 마감일은 언제인가?
(A) 9월 14일
(B) 10월 31일
(C) 11월 13일
(D) 11월 17일

해설 질문의 deadline, application을 키워드로 삼아 단서를 찾으면 마지막 단락에서 자기소개서와 이력서를 10월 31일까지 이메일로 보내달라고 했
으므로 (B)가 정답임을 알 수 있다.

Questions 1-2 refer to the following letter.

21 January

Elene Labeire
23 Rue Majeure Street
Lyon, France 3232

Dear Ms. Labiere,

Congratulations! You have been chosen to receive *Computer Today* for six months absolutely free.

Inside each issue of this award-winning publication, you can find articles by notable writers and information about a broad range of computer products, helpful Web sites, and maintenance advice.

To receive these six issues, simply mail the enclosed prepaid reply card back to us. Once your complimentary six-month period is over, we hope that you will consider signing up for a yearly subscription at our low introductory price of €25.99.

Sincerely,

Marissa Jeune
Marissa Jeune
Sales Department

ENCLOSURE

1. What is being advertised?

(A) A renowned magazine
(B) A book club membership
(C) A discounted repair service
(D) An electronics company

2. What is Ms. Labiere asked to do?

(A) Choose a payment option
(B) Access a Web site
(C) Send in a reply card
(D) Write an article

Pressman Rugs

85 Hougang Avenue
04-32 Hougang Shopping Center
Singapore, 548756
www.pressmanrugs.co.sg

Special Event on Sunday, June 3!

As one of our most loyal patrons, we invite you to an exclusive event where we will introduce our new line of Easiwipe rugs manufactured from an innovative new rug fiber. We have found from recent product tests that Easiwipe rugs attract 30 percent less dust and have greater durability than similarly priced rugs. Also, if you decide to buy an Easiwipe rug at our store on June 3, you can receive a discount of up to 50 percent off the normal price. Just bring this notice with you to our store on June 3 and present it to a store staff member to gain entrance to the Easiwipe showroom. We hope to see you there!

3. What is indicated about Easiwipe rugs?

(A) They are 50 percent more durable than other rugs.
(B) They are delivered free of charge.
(C) They are sold in a variety of colors.
(D) They are manufactured with a unique new material.

4. How can a customer be eligible for a discount on an Easiwipe rug?

(A) By attending a store event
(B) By completing a computer survey
(C) By ordering the rug online
(D) By introducing a friend to Pressman Rugs

Questions 5-9 refer to the following article and e-mail.

May 30 – Works by impressionist artist Sam Gibbins will be on display in the lobby of the Pendulum Hotel in Downtown Culver throughout June and July. As a long-time supporter of local artists, Wayne Bond, the hotel's owner, has utilized the hotel's lobby to display their works. He presents a new exhibit about every two months. This hotel has previously featured works of other local artists such as sculptor Jamie Wu and cubist painter Jasmine Tom.

"My hotel has plenty of space. What better way to use it than to showcase works of talented artists from the Culver area?" Mr. Bond said, welcoming the public to drop by and peruse the artwork. "People can also diversify their cultural experience by dining at La Cantina, our famous four-star Spanish bistro."

To	Idina Cusack <icusack@mic.com>
From	Wayne Bond <wbond@pendulumhotel.com>
Date	July 15
Subject	Upcoming exhibit

Dear Ms. Cusack,

We are pleased to display all eight of your paintings at the Pendulum Hotel next month. Your show at the convention center was quite impressive, and I am positive that your work will get the recognition it deserves at our hotel.

Please send me the dimensions of each piece in order to arrange their respective placements. I would appreciate it if you would provide me with this information by the end of next week.

Sincerely,

Wayne Bond
CEO, Pendulum Hotel

5. What does the article discuss?

(A) A change in hotel management
(B) How a hotel's lobby is used
(C) The rise of one local artist
(D) A new art gallery

6. What is mentioned about Mr. Bond?

고난도

(A) He showcases his artwork as well.
(B) He will open an art museum.
(C) He promotes local artists.
(D) He teaches art classes.

7. What does Mr. Bond invite visitors to do at the hotel?

(A) Enjoy free beverages in the lobby
(B) Drop by the newly renovated gift shop
(C) Eat at the hotel's restaurant
(D) Attend an art lecture by Mr. Gibbins

8. What is implied about Ms. Cusack?

고난도

(A) She lives in the Culver area.
(B) She is a portrait painter.
(C) She has a reservation at La Cantina.
(D) She was recommended by Jamie Wu.

9. According to the e-mail, what does Mr. Bond need to know about the paintings?

(A) Their prices
(B) Their sizes
(C) Their dates
(D) Their colors

사실확인

Part 7에서 상세정보를 묻는 문제와 함께 가장 빈번히 출제되는 유형이다. TRUE 또는 NOT TRUE를 묻는 사실확인 문제는 지문의 내용과 문제의 선택지를 꼼꼼히 비교·대조하여 일치하거나 일치하지 않는 정보를 찾아야 하므로, 정답을 찾는 데 많은 시간이 소요되는 유형이기도 하다.

🔍 질문 유형 확인하기

1. 잘 나오는 질문 유형

TRUE ▷ What is true / stated / mentioned / indicated ~? 형태의 질문

What is true about the report? 보고서에 대해 사실인 것은 무엇인가?
What is stated about the meeting? 회의에 대해 언급된 것은 무엇인가?
What is mentioned in the announcement? 공지에 대해 언급된 것은 무엇인가?
What is indicated about the plan? 계획에 대해 나타난 것은 무엇인가?

NOT TRUE ▷ NOT이 대문자로 크게 쓰여져 있는 질문

What is **NOT** true about the article? 기사에 대해 사실이 아닌 것은?
What is **NOT** stated in the letter? 편지에 언급되지 않은 것은?
What is **NOT** offered at the conference? 회의에서 제공되지 않는 것은?
What is **NOT** included in the workshop? 워크숍에 포함되지 않은 것은?

2. 독해 전략

▶ 각 보기에서 가장 특이한 키워드를 체크한 후, 지문으로 가서 해당 정보가 사실로 성립하는지를 찾아본다. 예를 들어, 보기가 '(A) The headquarters is located in Boston.'이라면 지문을 훑어 내려가다가 headquarters, head office, 혹은 Boston 등이 나올 때 사실 여부를 확인한다. 이와 같은 식으로 모든 보기를 대조해보면 된다.

▶ TRUE 문제는 네 개의 보기 중 단 하나만이 지문에 언급되어 있으므로 보기를 하나씩 지문과 대조해서 찾아보다가 해당 보기가 지문에 나와있는 경우, 다른 보기를 더 보지 않고도 문제를 풀 수 있다.

▶ NOT TRUE 문제는 네 개의 보기 중 지문에 나와있는 세 개의 보기를 소거하고 남은 하나가 정답이 된다. 보기에서 한 번에 아닌 것을 찾아낼 수 있기보다는 먼저 제시되어 있는 것 세 개를 찾아내야 문제가 풀리는 유형이 증가하고 있다는 점에 유의한다.

사실확인 문제 풀이 써머리

STEP 1 질문에 쓰인 의문사와 키워드를 확인한다.
STEP 2 지문에서 질문의 키워드와 관련된 내용을 포착한다.
STEP 3 각 보기와 지문 내용을 대조해가며 정·오답을 가린다.

해설서 p.80

Question 1 refers to the following news.

Weekend News

The city of Franconia will be holding its annual autumn fireworks display next week at Saunders Park on October 4. Everyone is welcome, so come see this outstanding display. Saunders Park is located on Telegraph Road, ❶ (C) just five minutes from the city's downtown area. ❶ (D) Please be informed that there will be very little space for parking on this day, so we suggest that you use public transportation. ❶ (A) The Franconia city bus will be running from downtown Franconia to the park every 10 minutes. Come enjoy the festivities!

→ near

- Franconia 시내 중심가에서 5분 거리이다. → Franconia 시에서 가깝다.

- 행사 당일에 주차 공간이 매우 적을 것이다. → 모든 방문자들에게 충분한 주차 공간이 제공되지 않을 것이다.

- Franconia 시내 버스는 시내 중심가에서 공원까지 10분 간격으로 운행될 것이다. → 시내 버스로 도달할 수 있다.

STEP 2 + **3** 질문의 키워드와 관련된 내용 포착 및 정답 판별

1. What is NOT stated about the park? ⋯→ **STEP 1** 질문에 쓰인 의문사와 키워드 확인 → 공원에 관하여 언급되지 않은 것

(A) It can be reached by the city bus.
(B) It is open on most days of the week.
(C) It is near downtown Franconia.
(D) It has limited parking space.

해석 및 해설

1. 공원에 관해 언급되지 않은 것은?
(A) 시내 버스로 갈 수 있다.
(B) 주중 대부분 문을 연다.
(C) Franconia 시내 근처에 있다.
(D) 주차 공간이 제한되어 있다.

해설 park를 키워드로 삼아 언급된 특징들을 보기와 매칭시키면 (A) → The Franconia city bus will be running from downtown Franconia to the park every 10 minutes, (C) → just five minutes from the city's downtown area, (D) → Please be informed that there will be very little space for parking on this day에 해당하며, (B)는 언급된 바 없다.

해설서 p.80 / ⏱ 제한 시간 11분

Questions 1-2 refer to the following flyer.

Beckington Railway
Special Promotions

Passengers who plan to travel in groups of more than 15 can save 20 percent on the regular train fare. Families traveling in groups of more than 5 are eligible for a 15 percent discount. These offers are only valid during the months of May and June.

Discounts are available for trips taken on both weekdays and weekends to any destination. However, please book early as it is not possible to obtain these special discounts on the day of travel at the station ticket office. Passengers who qualify for the discounts may order their tickets through our Web site at www.btrail.net/tickets at least seven working days prior to traveling. Further travel information and details, including baggage restrictions, may also be found on our Web site.

---

1. What is indicated about Beckington Railway?

(A) It offers reduced prices for families.
(B) It often waives baggage fees.
(C) It will have fewer trains running in June.
(D) It provides travel to over 15 destinations.

2. What are the passengers advised to do?

(A) Travel on working days
(B) Pay by credit card
(C) Request discounted tickets at the ticket office
(D) Purchase tickets before the day of travel

Questions 3-4 refer to the following advertisement.

Shenzen Apartments

New Horizon Construction is happy to announce that the 50-unit complex Shenzen Apartments in North Shanghai is nearing completion. The units should be ready for tenants to move in by October 31. The first-floor units have three bedrooms and two bathrooms, and the second-floor units have two bedrooms, one full and one 1/2 bathrooms, and a balcony facing the river. All of these wonderful, low-maintenance apartments come with a climate control system, a refrigerator, a gas range, and a dishwasher. The complex is located within walking distance of Red Cliff Subway Station and is adjacent to Sunzu Park. Tenants will also enjoy easy access to shopping, restaurants, health care facilities, and schools. Model units are currently open for viewing, but half of the units have already been leased. Contact the Shenzen Apartment Office to arrange a guided tour. The office can be reached at 555-9423 or realestateoffice@shenzenmail.com.

3. What is stated about the apartments?

고난도
(A) Construction has been completed.
(B) Kitchen appliances are included.
(C) The living rooms are spacious.
(D) Laundry facilities are available.

4. What information is NOT included in the advertisement?

(A) The features of the apartments
(B) The number of units being built
(C) The expected price for the units
(D) The location of the complex

Read and Save
2389 Fort Street
San Juan, Puerto Rico 00907

Join Read and Save to receive outstanding deals on your favorite literary genres. We carry all types of fiction, from mystery to fantasy to romance, and you can choose which types of new books you prefer to read. Members of our club enjoy the following benefits:

- Access to our members-only Web site
- Up to 60 percent off the publisher's recommended sale price
- Hundreds of titles across 10 genres to choose from
- Free access to our monthly e-mail newsletter containing a list of newly-released books as well as reviews from our own editors

Members must order at least one title per month as a condition of membership. Visit our Web site www.readandsave.com to register.

5. What is NOT a benefit of membership?

(A) Free overnight shipping
(B) Discounted prices
(C) Access to various works
(D) A complimentary subscription

6. What does Read and Save sell?

(A) Magazines
(B) Textbooks
(C) Newspapers
(D) Novels

7. According to the information, how can people join the club?

(A) By sending an e-mail
(B) By visiting a Web site
(C) By mailing a form
(D) By calling customer service

Questions 8-11 refer to the following e-mail.

From	Colin Moore
To	Gilderoy's Bookstore staff
Date	July 15
Subject	Paddy O'Reilly

It is my pleasure to inform you all about an upcoming book signing and lecture with local entrepreneur Paddy O'Reilly.

As you may remember, Mr. O'Reilly was a part-time worker at Gilderoy's Bookstore for six years while working hard to establish his own landscape gardening business. His company is now flourishing, and Mr. O'Reilly has published a new book, *Business Success*. Already popular for his series of landscape gardening books, Mr. O'Reilly has broadened his range of subject matter with a book that provides very useful information to those starting their own business.

Mr. O'Reilly will be giving his talk at 1:00 P.M. on August 5 at the Micklesfield Center. He has allocated enough free tickets so that every Gilderoy's Bookstore employee can attend. Also, additional tickets are on sale for your friends and family members at the low price of $3 each. If you plan on attending, please email Susan Bateman (s.bateman@gilderoybooks.com) and also indicate how many extra tickets you need.

Sincerely,

Colin Moore
Senior Manager

8. Why was the e-mail sent?

(A) To notify staff about an event
(B) To advertise a new business
(C) To request information about an author
(D) To arrange a book signing

9. The word "establish" in paragraph 2, line 2, is closest in meaning to

(A) relocate
(B) decorate
(C) make straight
(D) set up

10. What is NOT stated about Mr. O'Reilly?

(A) He helped design the Micklesfield Center.
(B) He used to work at Gilderoy's Bookstore.
(C) He is a landscape gardener.
(D) He has published several books.

11. What is offered free of charge to Gilderoy's Bookstore staff members?

(A) A book written by Mr. O'Reilly
(B) A ticket to an upcoming lecture
(C) An individual consultation with Mr. O'Reilly
(D) A tour of a landscape garden

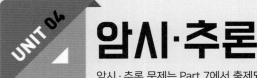

암시·추론

암시·추론 문제는 Part 7에서 출제되는 유형 중에서 가장 까다로운 유형에 속하며, 최근 들어 그 출제 비중이 커지고 있다. 보기에 나오는 표현이 그대로 지문에 나오지 않는 점이 특징이며 정답을 암시 또는 추론하는 내용을 주어진 지문에서 찾아야 한다.

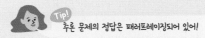

질문 유형 확인하기

1. 잘 나오는 질문 유형

What is implied ~?   What is implied in the e-mail? 이메일에서 암시된 것은 무엇인가?

What is suggested ~?   What is suggested about Mr. Kim? Mr. Kim에 관하여 알 수 있는 것은?

What can be inferred ~?   What can be inferred about this article? 이 기사에서 무엇을 추론할 수 있는가?

~ suggest ~?   What does the article suggest? 이 기사는 무엇을 암시하고 있는가?

~ most likely ~?   Where would this memo most likely be found?
이 공지는 어디에서 볼 수 있겠는가?

                  Who most likely is Ms. Chan? Ms. Chan은 누구이겠는가?

What can be ~?   What can be learned from this announcement?
이 공지에서 무엇을 알 수 있는가?

2. 독해 전략

▶ 암시·추론 문제는 보통 지문을 전체적으로 이해해야 풀 수 있는 문제가 대다수이므로, 지문 전체를 읽지 않고 문제의 정답을 찾는 방향으로 풀어서는 오답을 피하기 힘들 것이다.

▶ 만약 선택한 정답에 대해 확신이 없다면 같은 지문의 다른 문제를 먼저 해결한 후에 푸는 것이 좋다. 다른 세부사항 문제들을 푸는 동안 지문의 전체적인 내용이 종합적으로 파악되기 때문이다.

▶ 암시·추론 문제의 정답은 항상 선택지에 그대로 주어지지 않고 패러프레이징되어 있다는 것을 기억하자!

암시·추론 문제 풀이 써머리

STEP 1 질문의 키워드를 확인하고, 키워드가 없는 전체 추론 문제인 경우에는 보기들을 먼저 확인해둔다.

STEP 2 지문에서 질문의 키워드와 관련된 내용을 포착한다.

STEP 3 지문의 단서를 토대로 추론할 수 있는 내용의 보기를 선택한다.

Question 1 refers to the following news.

Local Business Wins Award

By Abigail Milton

Logan Manufacturing, Inc. recently received an award from the National Ecological Association (NEA) for their Smart Commute Program (SCP). The Award for Corporate Preservation Efforts was presented to company CEO Alicia Sanchez at the NEA's branch office in St. Louis. NEA council member Sean O'Reilly praised the company's program, which provided employees with fuel-efficient hybrid company cars and enforced carpooling among employees who live in the same areas.

Employees were given incentives to prevent them from driving their own vehicles to work, such as free public transportation vouchers. ❶ Through nationwide enforcement of these new policies, it is estimated that the SCP has reduced company fuel consumption by approximately 800,000 liters since last year. Due to an increase in physical activity caused by using public transportation, many employees also reported feeling better physically.

Smart Commute
Program의 성과
작년 약 80만 리터의
에너지 소비 절약
대중 교통 활용 증가로 인
한 신체 활동 증가와 건강
증진

STEP 2 보기의 키워드와 관련된 내용 포착

1. What can be inferred from this passage? ⋯ STEP 1 키워드가 없는 전체 추론 문제이므로 보기 확인

(A) Alicia Sanchez is Ms. Milton's colleague.
(B) The SCP has been successful.
(C) Many companies have implemented the SCP.
(D) The NEA award ceremony is held annually.

STEP 3 지문의 단서를 토대로 추론 가능한 보기 선택

해석 및 해설

1. 이 지문에서 유추할 수 있는 것은?
(A) Alicia Sanchez는 Ms. Milton의 동료이다.
(B) SCP는 성공적이었다.
(C) 많은 업체들이 SCP를 시행했다.
(D) NEA 시상식은 매년 개최된다.

해설 두 번째 단락에서 SCP의 시행을 통해 에너지 소비를 줄이고, 대중 교통을 이용하게 하여 몸이 더 좋아졌다는 보고를 토대로 Smart Commute Program(SCP)이 성공적이라는 사실을 유추할 수 있다. 따라서 정답은 (B)이다.

해설서 p.83 / ⏱ 제한 시간 17분

Questions 1-2 refer to the following information.

The following pages will explain how to use your Pantek 900 digital camera as well as how to transfer captured images to your personal computer. If the steps are not clear to you, please contact a Pantek representative during normal business hours. Please refer to page 7 to find your local support center and its contact details.

1. Where would the information most likely appear?

(A) In a product advertisement
(B) In an owner's manual
(C) In an electronics magazine
(D) In a company pamphlet

2. According to the information, how can a Pantek representative help?

(A) By processing a refund
(B) By providing purchase options
(C) By clarifying instructions
(D) By scheduling an appointment

Questions 3-4 refer to the following e-mail.

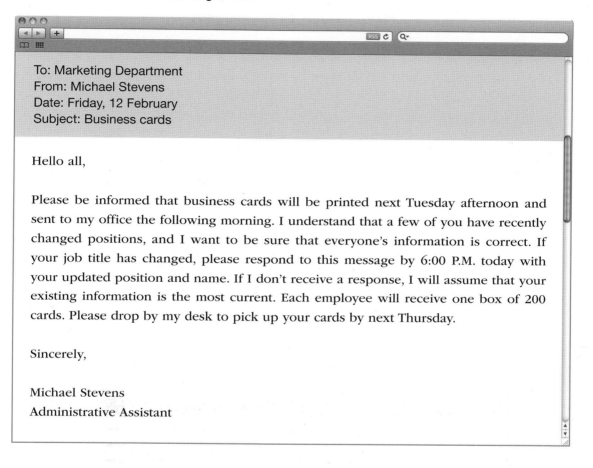

To: Marketing Department
From: Michael Stevens
Date: Friday, 12 February
Subject: Business cards

Hello all,

Please be informed that business cards will be printed next Tuesday afternoon and sent to my office the following morning. I understand that a few of you have recently changed positions, and I want to be sure that everyone's information is correct. If your job title has changed, please respond to this message by 6:00 P.M. today with your updated position and name. If I don't receive a response, I will assume that your existing information is the most current. Each employee will receive one box of 200 cards. Please drop by my desk to pick up your cards by next Thursday.

Sincerely,

Michael Stevens
Administrative Assistant

3. When will the new business cards most likely arrive in Mr. Stevens' office?

(A) On Tuesday
(B) On Wednesday
(C) On Thursday
(D) On Friday

4. Who is asked to reply to the e-mail?

(A) Employees who have recently been hired by the company
(B) Employees who have moved to a new building
(C) Employees who have changed jobs
(D) Employees who have less than 200 business cards

Questions 5-9 refer to the following notice and calendar.

Marreton Small Business Brunch

During the August 7 meeting, members of the Marreton Chamber of Commerce (MCC) voted unanimously to start the Small Business Brunch at the MCC Banquet Hall. It will be held every Thursday from 10:30 A.M. to 1 P.M. and will go throughout the year. Local business owners are invited to join by signing up in the MCC lobby or online. Formal attire is encouraged, though not mandatory—and be sure to bring many business cards! Please check the online calendar for news and information related to this and many other business opportunities around Marreton. If you require assistance, please call our scheduling manager, Benjamin Crane, at 404-555-2983.

Marreton Chamber of Commerce Weekly Schedule for November

On Monday
11 A.M.   Business Leaders' Roundtable (2nd and 4th weeks) - MCC Conference Room 102
6 P.M.   Professional Networking Hour - Marquis Hotel

On Tuesday
1 P.M.   Business Analysis and Advice - City Hall, B302
2:30 P.M.   School-to-Trade Council - Marreton Unified District Building

On Wednesday
6 P.M.   Human Resources Best Practices - MCC Conference Room 103

On Thursday
10:30 A.M. Small Business Brunch (1st and 3rd weeks) - MCC Banquet Hall, $7 per person
4:30 P.M.   Marreton Community Outreach - Marreton Community Center

On Friday
9 A.M.   Tech Support for Start-up Companies (North Tech Center) $10 per person, proceeds go to charity

On Saturday
Noon   Community Luncheon—open to the public! - MCC Banquet Hall, $15, $10 for senior members
3 P.M.   MCC Board Meeting (last Friday of the month) - MCC Conference Room 101

To receive the calendar via e-mail or for further information about any scheduled function, please contact Member Support at members@marretoncc.org or by phone at 404-555-9471.

5. Why was the notice posted?

(A) To inform MCC members of a new event
(B) To announce the expansion of the Marquis Hotel
(C) To hire temporary workers for the North Tech Center
(D) To provide directions to an upcoming MCC meeting

6. In the notice, the word "go" in paragraph 1, line 3, is closest in meaning to

(A) advance
(B) pass
(C) happen
(D) travel

7. What is implied about the Small Business Brunch in November?

(A) It provides complimentary meals.
(B) It occurs less often than originally scheduled.
(C) It was moved to a larger venue.
(D) It has limited space.

8. Which activity takes place only once in November?

(A) The Professional Networking Hour
(B) The Marreton Community Outreach
(C) The Community Luncheon
(D) The MCC Board Meeting

9. What is mentioned about the MCC?

(A) It has several conference rooms.
(B) It is next to the community center.
(C) It is looking for a new scheduling manager.
(D) It holds events only for business owners.

Questions 10-14 refer to the following article, Web page, and form.

Big Changes at Lion Airways

February 14 — Lion Airways will soon begin hiring for their new headquarters at Charleston International Airport. Lion looked at several regional airports, but Charleston International Airport representatives closed the deal by emphasizing the unique advantages of this area.

"After looking at a number of cities, we came to the conclusion that Charleston would best fit the company and its hiring needs," explained Daniel Harris, CEO of Lion Airways. He said that the city's excellent universities help produce a highly qualified workforce. Construction of Lion's new headquarters was completed in January. Interviews will start March 1.

Lion Airways is also currently building smaller facilities in Los Angeles and New York, which are expected to open before the summer travel season begins. Lion Airways plans to have all three locations fully staffed by the end of May.

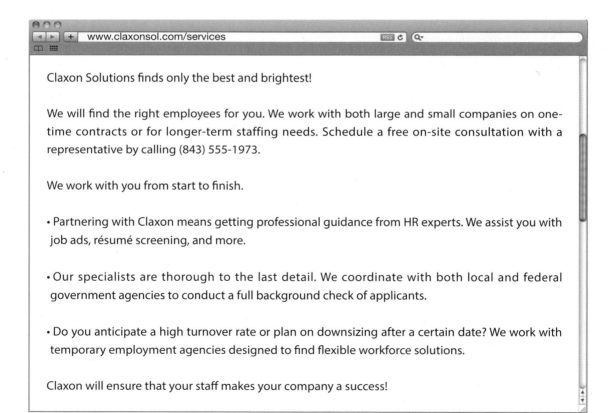

www.claxonsol.com/services

Claxon Solutions finds only the best and brightest!

We will find the right employees for you. We work with both large and small companies on one-time contracts or for longer-term staffing needs. Schedule a free on-site consultation with a representative by calling (843) 555-1973.

We work with you from start to finish.

• Partnering with Claxon means getting professional guidance from HR experts. We assist you with job ads, résumé screening, and more.

• Our specialists are thorough to the last detail. We coordinate with both local and federal government agencies to conduct a full background check of applicants.

• Do you anticipate a high turnover rate or plan on downsizing after a certain date? We work with temporary employment agencies designed to find flexible workforce solutions.

Claxon will ensure that your staff makes your company a success!

Claxon Solutions

Fill out the form below to schedule a meeting with one of our professional consultants.

Company: Lion Airways
Company Representative: Louis Hermann
Phone: (843) 555-0045
E-mail: lhermann@lionairways.com
Address: 8843 Aviation Ave., Charleston, SC
Desired Consultation Date: February 24
Availability: ☑ Morning ☐ Afternoon

We will call you to finalize a meeting time that works with your schedule.

10. In the article, paragraph 1, line 6, the word "closed" is the closest in meaning to

(A) blocked
(B) finalized
(C) silenced
(D) canceled

11. What is implied about Lion Airways?

(A) Its current CEO was appointed in February.
(B) It will finish hiring new workers by May.
(C) It has partnerships with some universities.
(D) Its headquarters was originally in New York.

12. What service does Claxon Solutions offer?

(A) Training for temporary workers
(B) Writing résumés for employees
(C) Investigating job applicants
(D) Enrolling students in college

13. What is suggested about the Aviation Avenue location?

(A) It was built recently.
(B) It is next to a Claxon Solutions office.
(C) It requires additional repairs.
(D) It has staff who attended prestigious schools.

14. What will probably happen on February 24?

(A) Mr. Hermann will hold a department meeting.
(B) A Claxon Solutions representative will go to Aviation Avenue.
(C) A welcoming ceremony will be held.
(D) Job interviews will take place.

문장 삽입

제시된 문장이 지문의 흐름상 어느 곳에 들어가야 적절한지를 찾는 유형으로써 단일 지문 중 보통 기사나 이메일에서 한 회에 두 문제가 출제된다. 이중 지문과 삼중 지문에서는 출제되지 않는다.

Tip!

단일 지문에만 등장하는 문장 삽입 유형은 문장을 넣어서 앞뒤 내용
뿐만 아니라 지문의 전체적인 흐름에도 자연스러운지 확인해야 해~

🔍 질문 유형 확인하기

1. 잘 나오는 질문 유형

문장 삽입 문제는 다음과 같은 한 가지 유형으로만 나온다.

In which of the positions marked [1], [2], [3], and [4] does the following sentence best belong?

"This has simultaneously resulted in our profits declining severely."

[1], [2], [3], [4]로 표시된 곳 중에서 다음 문장이 들어가기에 가장 적절한 곳은 어디인가?

"이것은 동시에 우리 수익의 막대한 감소를 야기했습니다."

2. 독해 전략

▶ 전체 지문에서 한 문장이 삽입될 곳을 찾는 유형이니만큼, 전체적인 문맥 파악이 중요하다. 항상 단일 지문의 마지막 문제로만 출제되는데, 다른 문제들을 먼저 풀면서 전체 문맥을 좀 더 종합한 후에 풀도록 하자.

▶ 지시어(this, each, he, she, it, they 등의 대명사)와 연결어구(also, additionally, specifically, therefore, however 등의 접속부사)를 단서로 삼아 연결해본다. 이런 단어들은 앞뒤 문장과 밀접한 관계를 갖기 때문에 중요한 키워드가 된다.

▶ 삽입 문장 바로 앞뒤 문장에서 접속부사나 대명사와의 연결이 잘 드러나지 않는 경우에는 전체 지문 해석과 삽입 문장의 해석을 연결해서 풀어볼 수 밖에 없다. 이 경우에는 흐름상 적절하지 않은 것들 위주로 소거해나가다 보면 좀 더 쉽게 접근할 수 있다. 전체적인 흐름이 중요하지만 보통 바로 앞뒤에 있는 문장이 중요한 단서가 된다는 점을 기억해 두자.

문장 삽입 문제 풀이 써머리

STEP 1 주어진 문장을 읽고, 키워드를 확인한다.

STEP 2 지문에서 키워드와 관련된 내용을 포착하여 주어진 문장을 넣어서 문맥을 살펴본다.

STEP 3 주어진 문장을 넣었을 때 문맥상 가장 어울리는 위치를 정답으로 선택한다.

Question 1 refers to the following article.

STEP 3 문맥상 가장 어울리는 위치 [1]을 정답으로 선택

The Petros Group announced that Janet Thompson has been hired as
its newest vice president of product manufacturing. — [1] —. **1** Her
primary role is to see that the company's fortunes, which have plummeted
lately, turn around and improve. Ms. Thompson has been involved in the
manufacturing industry for 22 years and is expected to help Petros turn a
profit for the first time in six years. — [2] —.

STEP 2 키워드와 관련된 내용 포착 후 주어진 문장을 넣어서 문맥 확인

Prior to joining Petros, Ms. Thompson worked for the Daley Corporation,
where she held the same position. — [3] —. She was widely liked there
and was especially popular with assembly line workers. This should come
as no surprise because that was the job she had when she started her career.
During her time at Daley, the company reported record-high earnings.
— [4] —. Ms. Thompson has also worked at Riley Manufacturing, where
she served as a special assistant to the CEO.

• 기사의 주제

• Petros에서의
Ms. Thompson의 역할
설명을 통해 최근 회사
재산이 급감한 사실 확인

• Ms. Thompson이 맡았던
직책

1. In which of the positions marked [1], [2], [3], and [4] does the following
sentence best belong?

"The company's latest toy line did not sell well, causing it to lose
millions of dollars." ⋯ STEP 1 주어진 문장에서 키워드 확인 → 장난감 판매 저조로 손실을 봄

(A) [1]
(B) [2]
(C) [3]
(D) [4]

해석 및 해설

1. [1], [2], [3], [4]로 표시된 곳 중에서 다음 문장이 들어가기에 가장 적절한 곳은 어디인가?

"해당 회사는 최근 장난감 라인의 판매 저조로 수백만 달러의 손실을 보았다."

(A) [1]
(B) [2]
(C) [3]
(D) [4]

해설 지문 첫 두 문장에서 Janet Thompson이란 사람의 고용을 밝히면서, 그녀의 주된 역할이 회사의 수익을 끌어올리는 데 있다고 했으므로 그 두
문장 사이에 회사가 손실을 보았다는 문장이 들어가야 자연스럽게 연결된다. 따라서 (A)가 정답이다.

해설서 p.86 / ⏱ 제한 시간 13분

Questions 1-3 refer to the following press release.

Lakeshore Park Announcements

April 28 – The Ashville Parks and Recreation Department is pleased to announce that the progress on Lakeshore Park is going well and that the park is expected to open on schedule on May 15. — [1] —.

Lakeshore Park, which will be alongside the eastern shore of Bear Lake, will be the city's newest and largest park. — [2] —. Covering more than 40 acres, it will feature a soccer field, a baseball diamond, an extensive picnic area, and numerous trails for hiking and cycling. — [3] —.

There will also be facilities catering to boaters and people interested in outdoor sports. — [4] —. For a complete description of these facilities, visit the city's Web site at www. ashville.org/lakeshorepark. The park will be open every day of the week from 5 A.M. to 10 P.M.

---

1. What is the main topic of the press release?

(A) An expansion of a lake
(B) Renovations on a city facility
(C) The construction of a park
(D) An upcoming outdoor event

2. What is NOT mentioned as a feature of the park?

(A) Sports facilities
(B) Walking trails
(C) A dining area
(D) A bicycle rental shop

3. In which of the positions marked [1], [2], [3], and [4] does the following sentence best belong?

"These include boat ramps and rentals of waterskiing equipment and life vests."

(A) [1]
(B) [2]
(C) [3]
(D) [4]

Questions 4-6 refer to the following article.

New Plaza

By Stephanie Cruz, Editor of *Sage City Reporter*

October 27 — On the northeast corner of Anderson Street and Creosote Avenue, Sage City officials broke ground on the new commercial center, Cactus Wren Plaza. Sage City Mayor Al Bryce cut the ribbon in the empty lot, located across the street from the public library. — [1] —.

The construction of the plaza is largely being funded by Sage Investment Group (SIG), a local organization that helps businesses fund beneficial projects. Its final design will have space for over 200 stores in four single-story buildings. — [2] —.

SIG plans to operate the plaza under a contract with Sage City for the next 10 years. "Before, most of our residents had to drive to nearby Shellyville." Mr. Bryce said. "But we are now getting a lot of requests from businesses to open in the new plaza. — [3] —. Our current downtown renovations are helping a little bit, but a larger space is clearly needed."

Over 60 businesses, including a sporting goods store and several restaurant chains, have stated that they are interested in renting out spaces in Cactus Wren Plaza. — [4] —. SIG's marketing manager, Maya Vasquez, is currently in talks with a well-known computer retail chain regarding opening a new location. The plaza is scheduled to open at the beginning of next year.

---

4. Who is Mr. Bryce?

(A) A construction worker
(B) A government official
(C) A store manager
(D) A computer programmer

5. What type of business does SIG want to attract to Cactus Wren Plaza?

(A) A supermarket
(B) A fashion retailer
(C) An electronics store
(D) A recreation center

6. In which of the positions marked [1], [2], [3], and [4] does the following sentence best belong?

"Each one will have an underground parking lot, and bus 724 will also stop nearby to reduce traffic."

(A) [1]
(B) [2]
(C) [3]
(D) [4]

Questions 7-9 refer to the following information.

Feelway, Inc. is sorry to see Ms. Bianca Carrera leave us on September 30 after 16 years of dedicated service to the company. The process of finding a replacement to take Ms. Carrera's position as the head of public relations in our Chicago headquarters will begin next week. — [1] —.

Ms. Carrera worked directly underneath the managing director of marketing and sales, communicating with local divisions globally. — [2] —. The challenges that go along with this position aren't small: candidates will need experience organizing public events in multiple languages, finalizing press releases, and travel frequently.

"It's a position that not many can fill," Carl Kline, the managing director of marketing and sales said. "We need someone who has a solid background in international media management."

The recruiting process will close just three weeks into October. — [3] —. Ms. Carrera has promised to provide help for training purposes, with the new head assuming full duties sometime in early December. — [4] —.

7. What is suggested about Ms. Carrera?

(A) Her position will be open in December.
(B) She relocated to Chicago 16 years ago.
(C) Her supervisor is Mr. Kline.
(D) She will manage the company's media strategies.

8. According to Mr. Kline, what is an important requirement to be a candidate?

(A) Considerable experience doing similar work
(B) A graduate degree in marketing and sales
(C) The willingness to appear on TV
(D) The flexibility to work on weekends

9. In which of the positions marked [1], [2], [3], and [4] does the following sentence best belong?

"That means that any applicants applying later than October 22 will not be considered for the job."

(A) [1]
(B) [2]
(C) [3]
(D) [4]

Questions 10-13 refer to the following article.

County Fair to Be Held in Jacksonville

Jacksonville – This year's Jefferson County Fair will be held in Jacksonville. This will be the first time the town has had the privilege of hosting the annual event, which is scheduled for July 8 and 9. — [1] —. The fair is one of the most popular events in the county, and more than 10,000 people are expected to attend each day of it.

Every year, the county fair features numerous events including various games, rides, shows, and farmers' markets. This year's event will also have something new: a handicrafts section for local artists and artisans to show off and sell their wares. — [2] —.

"Jacksonville has a thriving handicrafts community," said Jacksonville Mayor Jeff Randall. "Since we're hosting the fair, we decided to publicize the work our local residents do by letting them participate in the event. — [3] —. We hope visitors stop by, check out the works our residents have created, and maybe buy a piece or two for their homes."

Mayor Randall further commented that preparations for the fair are going well. He said that while the town doesn't have enough parking to accommodate all the expected visitors, it's working on creating some temporary parking lots. — [4] —. He added that the town might use shuttle buses to transport fairgoers from their vehicles to the fairgrounds.

The Jefferson County Fair will be held in Jasmine Park. The hours are from 9 A.M. to 7 P.M., and entrance is free.

---

10. In which section of the newspaper does this article most likely appear?

(A) Lifestyle and culture
(B) Sports
(C) Business and technology
(D) Classified ads

11. What is implied about Jacksonville?

(A) It is unprepared to hold the event.
(B) It is located in Jefferson County.
(C) It has many local art galleries.
(D) It recently opened a new park.

12. What is mentioned about Mr. Randall?

(A) He was elected as mayor last year.
(B) He will be giving a welcome speech.
(C) He is trying to support some Jacksonville residents.
(D) He was born in Jacksonville.

13. In which of the positions marked [1], [2], [3], and [4] does the following sentence best belong?

"That should enable other people to become familiar with what they do."

(A) [1]
(B) [2]
(C) [3]
(D) [4]

동의어

동의어 문제는 Part 7에서 2~4문제 정도 출제되고 있다. 단어 고유의 의미와 더불어 문맥적 의미를 파악하여 바꿔 쓸 수 있는 단어를 선택하는 문제이며 이중이나 삼중 지문에서 많이 출제되었으나, 최근에는 단일 지문에서도 종종 등장하는 추세이다.

🔍 질문 유형 확인하기

1. 잘 나오는 질문 유형

동의어 찾기 문제는 한 가지 유형으로만 나온다. 질문에서 몇 번째 단락, 몇 번째 줄인지를 명시해주며, 이중 지문이나 삼중 지문에서는 어느 지문인지도 함께 알려준다.

단일 지문의 경우:

The word "explain" in paragraph 3, line 7, is closest in meaning to

세 번째 단락, 일곱 번째 줄의 단어 "explain"과 의미상 가장 가까운 것은

이중/삼중 지문의 경우:

In the e-mail, the word "assure" in paragraph 2, line 5, is closest in meaning to

이메일에서, 두 번째 단락, 다섯 번째 줄의 단어 "assure"와 의미상 가장 가까운 것은

2. 독해 전략

▶ 질문에서 묻는 단어의 일반적이거나 대표적인 의미만 생각하지 말고, 해당 단어가 문맥상 어떤 뜻으로 쓰였는지를 파악하여, 해당 문맥에서 대체어로 쓰일 수 있는 어휘를 고르도록 한다.

▶ 동의어 찾기 문제에 대비하여 토익에서 자주 출제되는 단어들을 중심으로 어휘력을 강화하도록 하자.

동의어 문제 풀이 써머리

STEP 1 질문에 제시된 단어와 그 위치를 확인한다.

STEP 2 해당 문장을 해석하여 제시된 단어의 문맥상 의미를 파악한다.

STEP 3 보기 중 제시된 단어와 바꿔 써도 의미가 통하는 보기를 선택한다.

Question 1 refers to the following announcement.

Instructions

In order to improve security, we have recently replaced the old, outdated
security system with something more modern.

To gain access to the office during the day, each employee will be issued
a security card. Whenever you want to get in, simply place your card over
the card reader ❶ located to the right of the door. When you receive your
personalized card, you will be asked to sign for it.

STEP 1 + ❷ 질문에 제시된 단어의 위치와 문맥상 의미 확인

Should you lose the card, please report it immediately to the security guard,
who will then cancel that card and make sure that you are issued another as
soon as possible.

● **글의 목적**
보안 시스템 변경 안내

● **세부 사항**
시스템 사용 방법

● **세부 사항**
분실 시 이용 안내

---

1. The word "located" in paragraph 2, line 3, is closest in meaning to

(A) situated ⋯ **STEP 3** located와 바꿔 써도 의미가 통하는 situated 선택
(B) pressed
(C) released
(D) closed

해석 및 해설

1. 두 번째 단락 세 번째 줄의 단어 "located"와 가장 의미가 가까운 것은
   (A) 위치한
   (B) 눌린
   (C) 배포된
   (D) 닫힌

해설 해당 문장에서 located는 '~에 위치한'의 의미로 쓰여 '문 오른쪽에 위치한 카드 인식기'라는 의미를 완성한다. 따라서 이와 같은 의미를 갖는 (A)
가 정답이다.

Questions 1-4 refer to the following letter.

Owen and Williams Partners in Accounting
6 Pennance Road
Cardiff CF1
Wales

25 March

Jenny Poulter, Owner
Gwendoline's of Cardiff
110-121 City Road
Cardiff CF1
Wales

Dear Ms. Poulter,

I am writing with regard to the staff retirement party which you hosted for our company on 21 March.

Although it was my first visit to your establishment, we were referred to you by our former senior partner, Vanita Shah, who was honored by our firm that evening. I enjoyed the food so much that I have already booked a table to bring a party of friends for dinner next week.

What especially impressed me was the degree of professionalism demonstrated by your staff members. The waiters were efficient and friendly, and they were able to respond to any questions we had concerning the menu.

Many thanks for this enjoyable experience! We hope to make holding parties at Gwendoline's of Cardiff a new Owen and Williams' tradition.

Yours sincerely,

David Owen

David Owen, Senior Partner

---

1. What is Gwendoline's of Cardiff?

   (A) An accounting firm
   (B) A restaurant
   (C) An appliance store
   (D) A supermarket

2. Why was Ms. Shah honored in March?

   (A) She retired from Owen and Williams.
   (B) She was promoted to senior partner.
   (C) She started a new company.
   (D) She graduated from business school.

3. The word "degree" in paragraph 3, line 1, is closest meaning to

   (A) position
   (B) level
   (C) summary
   (D) qualification

4. What does Mr. Owen imply in the letter?

   (A) He will do business with Gwendoline's of Cardiff again.
   (B) He is expecting to hear further news from Ms. Poulter.
   (C) He is currently recruiting new employees for his company.
   (D) He first learned about Gwendoline's of Cardiff from a friend.

Questions 5-8 refer to the following information.

Alpina Resort
Locarno, Switzerland

Food and Dining Information

Not only does Alpina Resort offer some of the best skiing and accommodations in the region, but it also features a five-star restaurant. Located to the left of the reception area, Ristorante Alpina is a relaxing place to enjoy your morning coffee as the sun rises over the mountains. Our experienced chefs prepare an impressive range of dishes including regional favorites. Breakfast is served daily from 6:30 A.M. to 9:30 A.M. and lunch from 11 A.M. to 3 P.M. Dinner is served every day from 4 P.M. to 11 P.M., except on Sundays when the kitchen closes at 9 P.M.

Our pastry chefs prepare fresh breads and cakes every morning for our guests to indulge in. Guests may select from among our warm or cold breakfast dishes, fresh fruit (when in season), milk, espresso, tea, and various juices. For lunch or dinner, you may select from a menu featuring Italian, German, and French favorites, as well as a variety of international dishes.

We offer room service 24 hours a day, although breakfast items are only available between 5 A.M. and 10 A.M. We have a certified dietician on staff, which enables our chefs to meet any guest's particular dietary needs. Please refer to the room service menu for selections and prices. A 10 percent service charge is added to all room service orders. To place an order, call the restaurant kitchen at extension 556.

5. For whom is the information most likely intended?

(A) Alpina Resort managers
(B) Housekeeping staff
(C) Guests of Alpina Resort
(D) Servers at Ristorante Alpina

6. According to the information, what happens every day?

(A) Tours are given.
(B) Pastries are baked.
(C) Health seminars are held.
(D) Performances take place.

7. What is stated about Ristorante Alpina?

(A) It closes earlier on Sundays.
(B) It employs famous chefs.
(C) It is offering a special promotion.
(D) It has recently been remodeled.

8. The word "meet" in paragraph 3, line 2, is closest in meaning to

(A) allow
(B) introduce
(C) assemble
(D) fulfill

20 February
Susan Romano
44 West Street
London W14 3DY

Dear Ms. Romano,

Thank you for committing to writing a 3,000-word critique on shifting trends in international markets for our April issue. Please find enclosed our revised writers' manual as promised. The manual will replace the guidelines currently posted on our Web site. Could you please submit your piece by March 15, though we can allow a short extension if necessary? If you do need more time, please call me as soon as possible. We now offer writers who adhere to their original deadlines four free e-books from our online economics publications catalogue.

As discussed, payment will be £600.00 upon acceptance of your manuscript. This amount includes the time spent on revision and checking of facts requested by our editors. When completed, please email your piece to me at rforest@femarkets.co.uk.

Sincerely,

Ryan Forest

Ryan Forest
Managing Editor, *Financial and Economic Markets*

ENCLOSURE

To	Ryan Forest (rforest@femarkets.co.uk)
From	Susan Romano (sromano@edmail.net)
Date	May 1
Subject	My article

Dear Mr. Forest,

I was delighted to see my article published on the first page of your April issue. I'm so glad that the suggested revisions I was asked to provide following the first editorial comments on the article gave the angle you were looking for. I'd like you to pass on my appreciation for the well-presented graphics and tables your design team supplied. I now have an idea to write a similar story in the field of international finance. I look forward to discussing this on the phone with you next week.

Just to let you know, I took your editor's advice and completed the online survey for potential book reviewers. I must also thank you for the free e-books. I am very impressed by your range of titles.

Sincerely,

Susan Romano

9. What is the purpose of the letter?

(A) To ask for additional information
(B) To offer the opportunity of a full-time position
(C) To confirm the details of an assignment
(D) To suggest an idea for an article

10. What is suggested about *Financial and Economic Markets*?

(A) It publishes only articles about British financial markets.
(B) It publishes both books and magazines.
(C) It has recently updated its Web site.
(D) It accepts only short articles of 600 words.

11. What does Mr. Forest ask Ms. Romano to send by e-mail?

(A) Her completed manuscript
(B) A request for a deadline extension
(C) Feedback on writer's guidelines
(D) Future article ideas

12. In the e-mail, the word "tables" in paragraph 1, line 4, is the closet meaning to

(A) data listings
(B) instructions
(C) pieces of furniture
(D) groups of people

13. What is NOT suggested about Ms. 고난도 Romano?

(A) She submitted her article on time.
(B) She is interested in reviewing books.
(C) She has visited the publisher's art department.
(D) She had to revise her article.

Questions 14-18 refer to the following e-mails and report.

From	jlandry@sparklemo.uk
To	bcabbot@sparklemo.us
Subject	Meeting
Date	March 4

Dear Mr. Cabott,

My flight from England landed a while ago, but I am writing this e-mail from the terminal. I'm sorry to have to tell you this, but my luggage was sent to the wrong city, possibly creating issues for our meeting with the retailers tomorrow. Fortunately, I still have my presentation slides on the laptop in my carry-on, but dozens of our new products are in my lost suitcase. The airline told me that my bag should arrive in three days, so I won't have it before tomorrow afternoon's meeting. Would it be possible to postpone tomorrow's product demos until my suitcase is returned? I look forward to hearing from you.

Sincerely,

Jane Landry

Claim for Misplaced Items

We regret that you are temporarily unable to claim your property. With the information below, our agents will trace your possessions as soon as possible. For faster results, please include as many details as you can.

- Claim No. 34210002111
- Full Name: Jane Landry
- E-mail: jlandry@sparklemo.uk
- Permanent residence: 532 Hoovershire Pl., Dartford WC1H 2AH, UK
- Temporary residence: Zanza Hotel, 1543 W. Ashford Road, Orlando, FL 32806

Luggage Description: Dark purple, wheeled, steel-sided Travelancer suitcase

Description of luggage contents:

Items	Quantity
Bracelets, necklaces, rings, earrings, etc.	48
Mixed nuts, dried fruits, assorted hard candies, etc.	7
Dress pants, blouses, sweaters, scarf, etc.	9
Printed documents, notepad, pens, and pencils	6

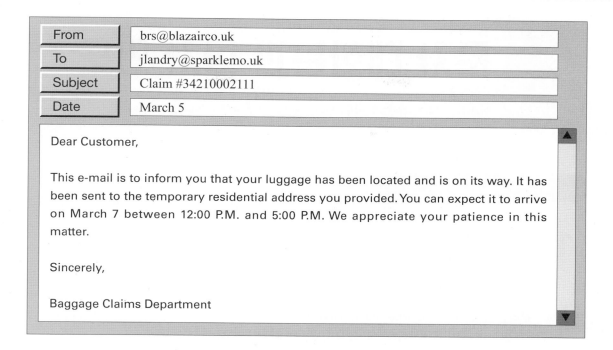

From	brs@blazairco.uk
To	jlandry@sparklemo.uk
Subject	Claim #34210002111
Date	March 5

Dear Customer,

This e-mail is to inform you that your luggage has been located and is on its way. It has been sent to the temporary residential address you provided. You can expect it to arrive on March 7 between 12:00 P.M. and 5:00 P.M. We appreciate your patience in this matter.

Sincerely,

Baggage Claims Department

14. What does Ms. Landry indicate about her slides?

(A) They will be emailed to Mr. Cabott.
(B) They are missing.
(C) They are not complete.
(D) They are ready for display.

15. What does Ms. Landry ask Mr. Cabott to do?

(A) Organize some new products
(B) Move an appointment time
(C) Upgrade her hotel room
(D) Arrange an airport shuttle service

16. What does Ms. Landry want to present?

(A) Clothing
(B) Snacks
(C) Paperwork
(D) Jewelry

17. In the report, the word "trace" in paragraph 1, line 2, is closest in meaning to?

(A) mark
(B) find
(C) return
(D) follow

18. Where will the delivery be sent?

(A) To London
(B) To Orlando
(C) To Washington
(D) To Dartford

문자 대화문과 화자 의도

보통 2~4인이 서로 몇 마디씩 문자나 메신저로 대화를 주고 받는 형식의 지문이다. 문자나 채팅답게 간결하고 쉬운 말투로 대화가 진행된다. Part 7에서 총 2지문이 출제된다.

🔍 지문·질문 유형 확인하기

1. 잘 나오는 지문 유형

문자 대화문 (Text message chain)
▶ 두 명이 실시간으로 문자를 주고 받는 내용, 업무 관련 도움 요청 등

온라인 채팅 대화문 (Online chat discussion)
▶ 두 명 이상이 실시간으로 이야기를 나누는 내용, 업무 보고나 서로 의견을 주고 받는 내용

2. 잘 나오는 질문 유형

▶ 문자 대화에 나오는 인물의 정보를 묻는 질문
▶ 대화에서 언급된 내용의 세부사항을 묻는 질문
▶ 문자 대화에서 특정 인물이 언급한 말의 의도를 묻는 질문

3. 독해 전략

▶ 3인 이상 대화하는 문자나 채팅 지문에서는 특히 사람 이름을 잘 파악해야 한다.
▶ 대화를 주고 받는 내용이므로 특정 내용보다는 처음부터 끝까지 흐름을 잘 따라가며 읽어야 한다.
▶ 짧고 간결한 구어체 위주로 대화를 주고 받기 때문에 문자 메시지와 온라인 채팅 상의 구어 표현을 익혀두어야 한다.
▶ 보통 문자 대화 내용은 '용건 → 구체적인 질문 및 요청 사항 → 마무리' 순으로 전개되므로, 전체적인 흐름을 파악한 뒤 문제를 하나씩 풀어나가면 된다.

화자 의도 파악 문제 풀이 써머리

STEP 1 질문에 등장한 인용 문장과 그 위치를 확인한다.
STEP 2 지문에서 인용 문장의 주변 대화 내용을 확인하여, 그 문맥상의 의미를 파악한다.
STEP 3 인용 문장의 의도를 가장 잘 나타낸 보기를 선택한다.

Questions 1-2 refer to the following text message chain.

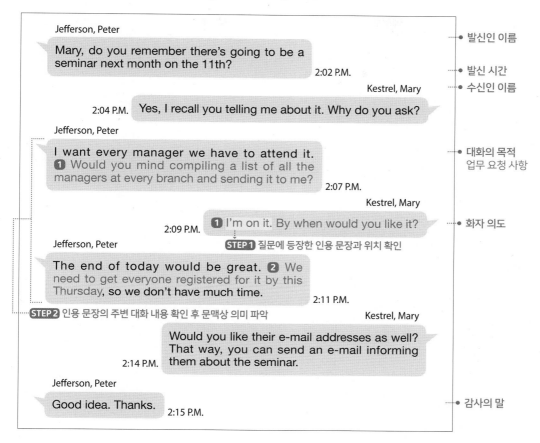

Jefferson, Peter

Mary, do you remember there's going to be a seminar next month on the 11th?
2:02 P.M.

발신인 이름

발신 시간

Kestrel, Mary

수신인 이름

2:04 P.M. Yes, I recall you telling me about it. Why do you ask?

Jefferson, Peter

I want every manager we have to attend it. ❶ Would you mind compiling a list of all the managers at every branch and sending it to me?
2:07 P.M.

대화의 목적
업무 요청 사항

Kestrel, Mary

2:09 P.M. ❶ I'm on it. By when would you like it?

화자 의도

STEP 1 질문에 등장한 인용 문장과 위치 확인

Jefferson, Peter

The end of today would be great. ❷ We need to get everyone registered for it by this Thursday, so we don't have much time.
2:11 P.M.

STEP 2 인용 문장의 주변 대화 내용 확인 후 문맥상 의미 파악

Kestrel, Mary

Would you like their e-mail addresses as well? That way, you can send an e-mail informing them about the seminar.
2:14 P.M.

Jefferson, Peter

Good idea. Thanks.
2:15 P.M.

감사의 말

1. At 2:09 P.M., what does Ms. Kestrel mean when she writes, "I'm on it"?

(A) She will carry out a task.
(B) She has already completed her work.
(C) She is going to apply for a new position.
(D) She will give a presentation.

STEP 3 인용 문장의 의도를 가장 잘 나타낸 보기 선택

2. What is suggested about the seminar?

(A) It runs until 6 P.M.
(B) Mr. Jefferson is the key note speaker.
(C) The registration deadline is Thursday.
(D) It requires a fee.

해석 및 해설

1. 오후 2시 9분에, Ms. Kestrel이 "그렇게 할게요."라고 할 때 그녀가 의미한 것은?

(A) 일을 처리할 것이다.
(B) 이미 자신의 일을 완료했다.
(C) 새로운 직책에 지원할 것이다.
(D) 발표를 할 것이다.

해설 먼저 Jefferson이 매니저들 목록을 편집해서 보내달라고 요청했고, Kestrel이 "I'm on it."이라고 하면서 언제까지 받길 원하는지 물었으므로 해당 표현은 자신이 그 일을 하겠다는 의미이다. 따라서 (A)가 정답이다.

2. 세미나에 관하여 알 수 있는 것은?

(A) 오후 6시까지 운영된다.
(B) Mr. Jefferson이 기조 연설자이다.
(C) 등록 마감일은 목요일이다.
(D) 회비가 요구된다.

해설 Jefferson이 이번 주 목요일까지는 모든 사람들이 등록되어야 한다고 했으므로 세미나의 등록 마감일이 목요일임을 유추할 수 있다. 따라서 (C)가 정답이다.

Questions 1-2 refer to the following text message chain.

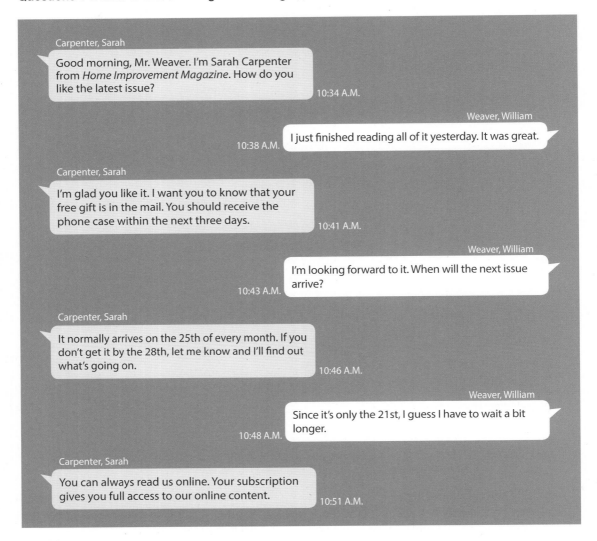

Carpenter, Sarah

Good morning, Mr. Weaver. I'm Sarah Carpenter from *Home Improvement Magazine*. How do you like the latest issue?
10:34 A.M.

Weaver, William

10:38 A.M.
I just finished reading all of it yesterday. It was great.

Carpenter, Sarah

I'm glad you like it. I want you to know that your free gift is in the mail. You should receive the phone case within the next three days.
10:41 A.M.

Weaver, William

10:43 A.M.
I'm looking forward to it. When will the next issue arrive?

Carpenter, Sarah

It normally arrives on the 25th of every month. If you don't get it by the 28th, let me know and I'll find out what's going on.
10:46 A.M.

Weaver, William

10:48 A.M.
Since it's only the 21st, I guess I have to wait a bit longer.

Carpenter, Sarah

You can always read us online. Your subscription gives you full access to our online content.
10:51 A.M.

1. Why does Ms. Carpenter write to Mr. Weaver?

   (A) To check if he is satisfied with a service
   (B) To explain an increase in fees
   (C) To introduce a new membership feature
   (D) To thank him for his article

2. At 10:43 A.M., what does Mr. Weaver mean when he writes, "I'm looking forward to it"?

   (A) He is waiting for a phone call.
   (B) He has not received his magazine yet.
   (C) He is eager to get his complimentary item.
   (D) He is excited to meet Ms. Carpenter.

Questions 3-4 refer to the following text message chain.

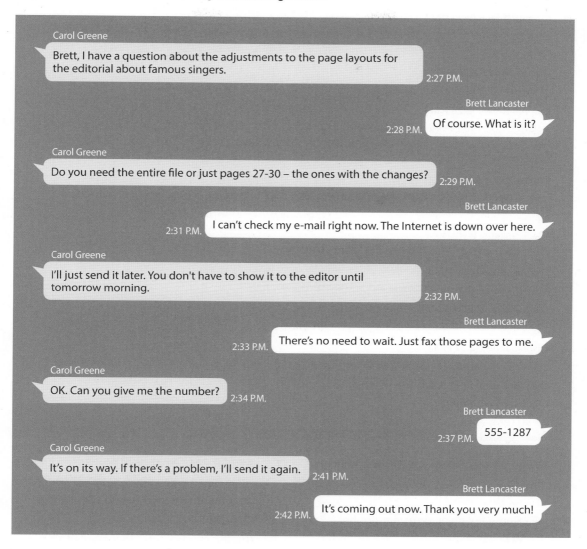

Carol Greene

Brett, I have a question about the adjustments to the page layouts for the editorial about famous singers.

2:27 P.M.

Brett Lancaster

2:28 P.M.

Of course. What is it?

Carol Greene

Do you need the entire file or just pages 27-30 – the ones with the changes?

2:29 P.M.

Brett Lancaster

2:31 P.M.

I can't check my e-mail right now. The Internet is down over here.

Carol Greene

I'll just send it later. You don't have to show it to the editor until tomorrow morning.

2:32 P.M.

Brett Lancaster

2:33 P.M.

There's no need to wait. Just fax those pages to me.

Carol Greene

OK. Can you give me the number?

2:34 P.M.

Brett Lancaster

2:37 P.M.

555-1287

Carol Greene

It's on its way. If there's a problem, I'll send it again.

2:41 P.M.

Brett Lancaster

2:42 P.M.

It's coming out now. Thank you very much!

3. Who most likely is Ms. Greene?

(A) A concert organizer
(B) A computer programmer
(C) A real estate agent
(D) A graphic designer

4. At 2:33 P.M., what does Mr. Lancaster mean when he writes, "There's no need to wait"?

(A) He prefers not to postpone a meeting.
(B) He does not want to wait for a phone call.
(C) He would like to get a document right away.
(D) He wants to know about a schedule change.

Questions 5-8 refer to the following online chat discussion.

Cynthia Brown [2:23 P.M.]
Do you have a minute, Dianna? I can't seem to find the expense report forms for this month. Can you locate them?

Dianna Jones [2:25 P.M.]
They're not showing up on my computer, either. When did you notice this?

Cynthia Brown [2:26 P.M.]
I just got off the phone with Alice who was trying to log receipts for the promotional posters her team purchased last week. She saw that they weren't there. Can you message tech support?

Dianna Jones [2:27 P.M.]
Hey Clark, I think some of our accounting files might have been deleted. Can you check it out?

Clark Williams [2:29 P.M.]
How odd. I remember them being there yesterday.

Dianna Jones [2:30 P.M.]
Those documents are also saved somewhere else, right?

Clark Williams [2:31 P.M.]
We back them up daily. I'll put them up right now.

Dianna Jones [2:32 P.M.]
Thanks. We should email all the departments to let them know the issue has been resolved.

Cynthia Brown [2:33 P.M.]
I can do that right now.

---

5. What problem does Ms. Brown mention?

   (A) An expense report was not submitted on time.
   (B) Some financial forms cannot be accessed.
   (C) A computer is not turning on.
   (D) Some receipts are missing.

6. From which department did Ms. Brown most likely learn about the issue?

   (A) Human Resources
   (B) Accounting
   (C) Technical Support
   (D) Advertising

7. At 2:30 P.M., what does Ms. Jones most likely mean when she writes, "Those documents are also saved somewhere else, right"?

   (A) She wants some documents to be uploaded again.
   (B) She is worried about a travel budget.
   (C) She asks that an employee order some supplies.
   (D) She would like access to the company system.

8. What will Ms. Brown most likely do next?

   (A) Install a program
   (B) Call technical support
   (C) Send an e-mail
   (D) Hold a department meeting

Questions 9-12 refer to the following online chat discussion.

Huey Jackson [3:09 P.M.]
Malina, are you free? I need to ask you something about our warehouse facility.

Malina Chavez [3:10 P.M.]
Sure.

Huey Jackson [3:12 P.M.]
I'm looking at our inventory logs right now, and they say there are only 20 Woodwin cabinets left. We've been selling a lot of those recently. Should I place a new order?

Malina Chavez [3:14 P.M.]
That won't be necessary. Woodwin has raised its prices, so we've decided to go with a more affordable brand. When you were on vacation last week, I ordered 200 Marydale cabinets. They will come in tomorrow.

Huey Jackson [3:15 P.M.]
That sounds great.

Malina Chavez [3:16 P.M.]
On Tuesday, I informed all the retail shops that order from our catalog. They have all agreed to the change.

Huey Jackson [3:17 P.M.]
Fantastic! Thank you.

SEND

9. At 3:10 P.M., what does Ms. Chavez most likely mean when she writes, "Sure"?

(A) She completed what Mr. Jackson assigned.
(B) She is available to address Mr. Jackson's question.
(C) She has approved Mr. Jackson's project request.
(D) She is confirming a time to call Mr. Jackson.

10. What is mentioned about Mr. Jackson?

고난도 (A) He ordered more supplies last week.
(B) He just fixed an inventory file.
(C) He took time off recently.
(D) He will update a catalog tomorrow.

11. What type of business do Ms. Chavez and Mr. Jackson work for?

(A) A furniture supplier
(B) A wood manufacturer
(C) A home improvement store
(D) An interior designing firm

12. What did Ms. Chavez do earlier in the week?

(A) She led a staff education workshop.
(B) She organized a large sale.
(C) She helped Mr. Jackson check the inventory.
(D) She notified clients of a new product.

편지·이메일

Part 7에서 가장 많이 출제되는 편지와 이메일은 회사와 고객, 회사와 회사 간의 비즈니스 상황에서 발생할 수 있는 다양한 주제로 출제된다. 일반적으로 일정한 패턴(인사말 - 목적 - 세부 사항 - 요청 - 끝인사)에 따라 전개된다는 점에 유의한다.

🔍 지문·질문 유형 확인하기

1. 잘 나오는 지문 유형

고객 대 회사 편지
▶ 제품·서비스·요금 등에 대한 (불)만족, 제품 할인 구매 기회 안내, 거래 중단·연장, 물품 주문 및 배송 관련 문의, 거래 내역 확인, 제품 및 서비스에 대한 설문 조사

회사 대 회사 편지
▶ 행사(세미나, 총회 등) 안내, 사업 제안, 회사와 거래처의 업무 내용, 오류 정정

구직·구인 관련 편지
▶ 일자리 제의, 구직 지원, (불)합격 통보

2. 잘 나오는 질문 유형

▶ 글을 쓴 목적을 묻는 질문

▶ 수신/발신인과 관련된 정보를 묻는 질문

▶ 동봉된 또는 첨부된 내용을 묻는 질문

▶ 요청 사항, 연락 방법 등과 관련된 세부사항을 묻는 질문

3. 독해 전략

▶ 목적이나 이유를 묻는 질문은 글의 도입부에서 답을 찾는다. 특히 이메일의 경우 본문과 문제를 읽기 전에 반드시 제목(Subject[주제]나 Re[~에 관하여] 다음 부분)을 확인한다.

▶ 편지·이메일의 수신자와 발신자 정보(직책 등) 및 두 사람의 관계를 파악한다. 특히 문제에 이름이 언급된 경우 그 사람이 누구인지를 지문에서 정확히 파악한다.

▶ 첨부 사항이나 요청(당부, 부탁, 제안) 사항은 주로 글의 중반 이후에 주목한다.

▶ 질문의 키워드를 기억하여 본문에서 그 키워드에 대응하는 패러프레이징 표현을 찾는다.

▶ 질문 유형별 단서가 나오는 지문의 표현을 기억해둔다.

❶ 편지와 이메일의 주제나 목적을 묻는 유형 'Why was the letter written?'의 빈출 단서:

I'm very sorry to tell[inform] you that ~. ~를 알려드리게 되어 죄송합니다.
I want to extend our gratitude ~. ~에 대해 감사드리려 합니다.
I am pleased to announce that ~. ~를 알리게 되어 기쁩니다.
I would like to inform you that ~. ~라는 것을 알려드리고자 합니다.
however/unfortunately ~. 하지만/불행히도~
RE: ~, Subject: ~ [이메일의 경우]

❷ 요청 및 요구를 묻는 유형 'What is/are ~ requested/required/advised/encouraged/urged to do?'의 빈출 단서:

(Please) 동사원형 ~. ~해 주세요.
Can[Could] 주어 + ~? ~해 주실 수 있을까요?
I would appreciate if you ~. ~해 주시면 감사하겠습니다.
I wonder if you could send us ~. ~를 저희에게 보내 주실 수 있을지 궁금합니다.
Do not hesitate to ~. = Feel free to ~. 망설이지 마시고 ~하세요. = 얼마든지[편하게] ~하세요.

Questions 1-3 refer to the following letter.

Medical Labs of Australia
39 Main Street
Melbourne, VIC 2930
Australia

⋯⋯• 발신자(회사) 정보

Ms. Janet Fernandez
452 Hill Side Road
Sydney, NSW 2000
Australia

⋯⋯• 수신자(회사) 정보

August 27

Dear Ms. Fernandez,

Thank you very much for your interest in Medical Labs of Australia. We have received and reviewed your application for the public relations position that we had advertised earlier this month in *The Melbourne Daily News*. ❶ Unfortunately, the position has already been filled. However, there is no need to be discouraged as we anticipate that a similar position will open up in October.

⋯⋯• 글의 목적과 주제

We think that you are well qualified for that position, and we will keep your application paperwork, including your cover letter and résumé, on file. ❷ The position will also be for the headquarters of our company in Melbourne. However, the job will require some travel to our branch offices in Canberra, Brisbane, as well as several cities in Europe.

⋯⋯• 구체적 세부 사항

❸ Please keep watching for this opening on our Web site, and contact us when it is posted.

⋯⋯• 요청/부탁

We look forward to discussing career opportunities for you at Medical Labs of Australia in greater detail soon.

⋯⋯• 맺음말

Sincerely,

Marshall Baxter
Director of Personnel

⋯⋯• 발신자(회사) 정보

1. What is the main purpose of the letter?

(A) To inform Ms. Fernandez about a new magazine
(B) To announce that a job is no longer available
(C) To set up a time for an interview
(D) To request that Ms. Fernandez provide additional information

2. Where is Medical Labs of Australia's main office located?

(A) In Brisbane
(B) In Canberra
(C) In Melbourne
(D) In Sydney

3. What is Ms. Fernandez encouraged to do?

(A) Submit an application next winter
(B) Renew a subscription
(C) Check a Web site regularly
(D) Book a flight ticket

해석 및 해설

1. 편지의 주된 목적은 무엇인가?
(A) Ms. Fernandez에게 새로운 잡지에 관하여 알리기 위해
(B) 어떤 일자리가 더 이상 없다는 것을 알리기 위해
(C) 면접 시간을 정하기 위해
(D) Ms. Fernandez에게 추가 정보 제공을 요청하기 위해

해설 Marshall Baxter가 Janet Fernandez에게 쓴 편지로 서두에서 지원에 감사 드린다고 하면서, 아쉽게도 그 자리가 이미 충원되었다고 했으므로 (B)가 정답이다.

2. Medical Labs of Australia의 본사는 어디에 위치해 있는가?
(A) 브리즈번에
(B) 캔버라에
(C) 멜버른에
(D) 시드니에

해설 두 번째 단락에서 Janet Fernandez가 처음에 지원한 부문과 비슷한 자리에 대해 이야기하면서, 그 자리가 멜버른에 소재한 회사 본사에 있다고 했으므로 (C)가 정답이다.

3. Ms. Fernandez는 무엇을 하라고 권유받는가?
(A) 내년 겨울에 지원서를 제출한다
(B) 구독을 갱신한다
(C) 웹사이트를 정기적으로 확인한다
(D) 비행기 표를 예약한다

해설 세 번째 단락에서 해당 공석을 웹사이트상에서 계속 지켜보다가 게시가 되면 연락을 달라고 했으므로 (C)가 정답이다.

해설서 p.97 / 제한 시간 11분

Questions 1-2 refer to the following e-mail.

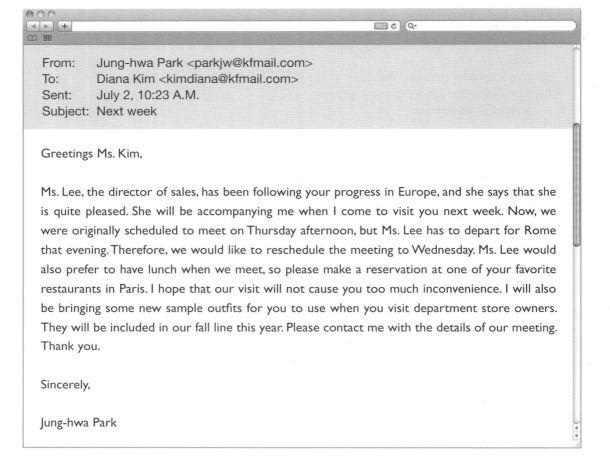

From: Jung-hwa Park <parkjw@kfmail.com>
To: Diana Kim <kimdiana@kfmail.com>
Sent: July 2, 10:23 A.M.
Subject: Next week

Greetings Ms. Kim,

Ms. Lee, the director of sales, has been following your progress in Europe, and she says that she is quite pleased. She will be accompanying me when I come to visit you next week. Now, we were originally scheduled to meet on Thursday afternoon, but Ms. Lee has to depart for Rome that evening. Therefore, we would like to reschedule the meeting to Wednesday. Ms. Lee would also prefer to have lunch when we meet, so please make a reservation at one of your favorite restaurants in Paris. I hope that our visit will not cause you too much inconvenience. I will also be bringing some new sample outfits for you to use when you visit department store owners. They will be included in our fall line this year. Please contact me with the details of our meeting. Thank you.

Sincerely,

Jung-hwa Park

1. According to the e-mail, what does Ms. Park want to do?

(A) Request a special meal
(B) Change an appointment
(C) Purchase plane tickets to Rome
(D) Visit department stores in Paris

2. When will Ms. Lee leave Paris?

(A) On Tuesday
(B) On Wednesday
(C) On Thursday
(D) On Friday

June 28

John Mansfield
Greenway Marching Band
3143 Witmer Road
Brooklyn, New York 11201

Dear Mr. Mansfield,

Congratulations! The Organizing Committee has selected your marching band to perform in the Brooklyn Winter Parade. The festivities will start at 3:00 P.M. on Sunday, January 13. Please inform your musicians to come to the convention center by 2:00 P.M. Performers will first meet near the north entrance of the convention center and then proceed east on Main Street, past City Square, and toward the Jonas Bridge. The celebrations will conclude at Norwood Park, where there will be a shuttle service available to go back to the convention center.

We are all excited to see you perform at the parade!

Sincerely,

Joe Simmons
Joe Simmons
Event Coordinator

3. Who most likely is Mr. Mansfield?

(A) A shuttle bus driver
(B) A parade organizer
(C) A band leader
(D) A convention center worker

4. Where will the parade begin?

(A) At the convention center
(B) In Norwood Park
(C) At the City Square
(D) Under the Jonas Bridge

Questions 5-7 refer to the following e-mail.

To	Nora McNeal <nmcneal@atlantadeco.com>
From	Ken Nikki <knikki@apexwarehouse.com>
Date	September 21
Subject	RE: Atlanta Deco Henes

Dear Ms. McNeal,

I'm writing concerning one of the bed frame models manufactured by your company, Atlanta Deco Henes. A number of our customers who bought the frame have informed us that the bolts needed to put it together were missing. Luckily, we had some similar-sized bolts in stock and were able to replace the missing parts.

However, there are still several customers who need them, so I would be grateful if you could send us three packets of the bolts that are supposed to come with the bed frame.

Due to the concern regarding the missing bolts, we will not be placing any more orders for the bed frame for the time being. Let us know when this problem has been taken care of, and we would be glad to resume our business with you.

Thank you for your help in this matter.

Sincerely,

Ken Nikki, Manager
Apex Warehouse

5. Why did Mr. Nikki write the e-mail?

(A) To answer a question
(B) To promote a product
(C) To inquire about a policy
(D) To address a problem

6. What does Mr. Nikki ask Ms. McNeal to do?

(A) Supply some items
(B) Attract more local customers
(C) Provide a refund
(D) Explain how to construct a frame

7. What decision has Apex Warehouse made?

(A) It will charge customers for certain parts.
(B) It will return some defective merchandise.
(C) It will carry a wide choice of bed models.
(D) It will suspend orders for a specific product.

Questions 8-11 refer to the following e-mail.

From	Martin Dekker <martind@bre.org>
To	Pin Tran Hyun <pintranh@ausmail.com>
Sent	April 11
Subject	Exhibition

Dear Mr. Hyun,

The next Barrier Reef Exhibition for Local Artists will be held from July 10 through August 20. We understand that you declined to attend last year's exhibition due to a family event overseas. We completely understood your situation, but we want you to know that you were greatly missed, particularly by the guests. — [1] —. Your works are very popular here in Australia, and we would be honored if you would rejoin us this year.

In addition to the items you sell at your booth, you would be required to submit three works to be included in an auction on the final night of the event. — [2] —. We will use this information on our Web site to advertise the auction. We will also be including a new lecture series as a part of the exhibition. — [3] —. We plan to have 10 artists give lectures in the afternoons during the event. Those who do will be exempt from the normal $300 participant fee.

— [4] —. If you would like to reserve a booth for this event, please contact me via e-mail at your earliest convenience. Thank you.

Sincerely,

Martin Dekker
Executive Director
Barrier Reef Artisans' Association

8. What is the main purpose of this e-mail?

(A) To advertise an upcoming event
(B) To extend an invitation
(C) To explain recent changes
(D) To place an order

9. What is indicated about Mr. Hyun?
고난도
(A) He is a local artist.
(B) He was invited to participate last year.
(C) He will be overseas during the event.
(D) He currently has works displayed in Australia.

10. The word "exempt" in paragraph 2, line 5
고난도 is closest in meaning to

(A) excused
(B) expected
(C) extended
(D) exceeded

11. In which of the positions marked [1], [2], [3], and [4] does the following sentence best belong?

"Once you have selected the pieces you wish to include, please send us photographs with a short description of each item."

(A) [1]
(B) [2]
(C) [3]
(D) [4]

광고

편지·이메일 지문만큼 빈번하게 출제되는 광고 지문은 소비자 또는 광고 대상자에게 광고 내용을 명확히 알려주며 내용이 추상적이지 않기 때문에 문제가 까다롭지 않다. 대체로 핵심 문구나 제목이 상단에 크게 제시되므로, 제목이나 글의 도입부에서 먼저 광고하는 내용이 무엇인지 파악한 후 질문에 따른 세부적인 사항을 정확히 파악하는 것이 중요하다.

🔍 지문·질문 유형 확인하기

1. 잘 나오는 지문 유형

▶ 임시직, 경력직, 매니저, 연구원, 교수 등의 구인 광고

▶ 호텔이나 레스토랑의 할인, 여행사 패키지 투어의 조기 예약 할인 홍보

▶ 비즈니스 오너나 신입 사원을 대상으로 하는 세미나 또는 직무 연수 공지

▶ 온라인 신규 서비스 및 회원 가입 혜택 공지

▶ 부동산 매매 및 임대 광고

2. 잘 나오는 질문 유형

▶ 구인 광고의 경우 지원 자격, 담당 업무, 지원 방법을 묻는 질문

▶ 광고 목적과 대상을 묻는 질문

▶ 상품이나 서비스 등의 장점, 혜택, 특징을 묻는 질문

3. 독해 전략

▶ 업무 소개 – 지원 자격 – 급여 및 복리 혜택 – 지원 방법 – 연락처 순서로 전개되는 일반적인 구인 광고의 구조를 활용하여 문제에 대한 단서를 지문에서 빠르게 찾는다.

▶ 광고의 제목과 도입부에서 광고 목적, 대상, 업종 등과 관련된 광고의 기본적인 정보를 먼저 파악한다.

▶ 제품 및 서비스의 특징(feature)과 장점(advantage)에 대한 NOT / TRUE 유형의 문제가 많이 나오므로, 광고 중반부에서 해당 키워드를 확인하여 정확히 지문의 내용을 파악한다.

▶ 질문의 키워드를 기억하여 본문에서 그 키워드를 패러프레이징한 표현을 찾는다.

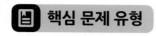
핵심 문제 유형

해설서 p.99

Questions 1-3 refer to the following advertisement.

Daniel & Johnson, Inc.

Positions are for the day shift (8:00 A.M. to 5:00 P.M.) unless otherwise indicated.

Warehouse Manager
Must have a university degree, strong knowledge of inventory procedures, and experience in a retail environment. **1** Must also possess basic knowledge of computers and finance. Previous management experience is desirable but not necessary.

Inventory Control Technician
Must have a high school diploma and at least one year of experience of heavy-volume inventory work. Must also be able to operate heavy lifting equipment. **2** (D) Night work is required.

Data Entry Assistant
Must have a high school diploma, excellent typing skills and experience in a retail environment. **2** (A) Some night work is required.

Circulation Specialists and Stock Clerks
Must be hardworking and reliable. **2** (C) Some night work is required for the stock clerk positions.

3 Please send résumé to:　Human Resources, Daniel & Johnson, Inc.
Distribution Center, 104 E. Riverside Drive
Twin Pines, NC 50964

No phone calls or e-mails please.

구인 광고 회사 이름

모집 부문
창고 매니저

모집 부문
재고 관리 기술자

모집 부문
데이터 입력 보조원

모집 부문
유통 전문가 / 창고 담당자

지원 방법 - 우편
지원 서류 - 이력서

주의 사항
전화, 이메일 받지 않음

---

1. What is a requirement for the warehouse manager position?

(A) Some knowledge of finance
(B) A degree in computer science
(C) Willingness to work at night
(D) Previous management experience

2. What position does NOT involve night shifts?

(A) Data entry assistant
(B) Circulation specialist
(C) Stock clerk
(D) Inventory control technician

3. How can candidates apply for the positions?

(A) By telephone
(B) By mail
(C) In person
(D) Online

---

2. 야간 근무와 관련 없는 자리는 무엇인가?
(A) 데이터 입력 보조원
(B) 유통 전문가
(C) 창고 담당자
(D) 재고 관리 기술자

해설 Circulation Specialist에는 야간 근무에 대한 언급이 없으므로 (B)가 정답이다.

해석 및 해설

1. 창고 관리직의 요건은 무엇인가?
(A) 재무 지식
(B) 컴퓨터 공학 학위
(C) 야간 근무 용의
(D) 이전 관리 경력

해설 학사 학위, 재고 절차 지식, 소매업 분야 경력이 필수라고 하면서, 컴퓨터와 재무에 대한 기본 지식도 요구하고 있으므로 (A)가 정답이다.

3. 지원자들은 어떻게 지원할 수 있는가?
(A) 전화로
(B) 우편으로
(C) 직접
(D) 온라인으로

해설 지문 하단부에 주소가 기재되어 있고, 이곳으로 이력서를 보내달라고 했으므로 (B)가 정답이다.

해설서 p.100 / ⏱ 제한 시간 10분

Questions 1-2 refer to the following advertisement.

HELP WANTED

Oscar Pharmaceutical has an urgent opening for a research director at our North View location. The director must oversee the use of all the laboratory equipment as well as ensure that the research materials comply with current regulations.

A degree in chemistry or medical technology with at least three years experience in a research facility are required. The successful candidate should already be licensed by the National Association of Medical Researchers.

Interested applicants should email a cover letter and résumé to Tricia Thornton at thornton.t@oscarpharmaceutical.com.

1. What is suggested about Oscar Pharmaceutical?

(A) It has been operating for three years.
(B) It is looking for a temporary worker.
(C) It is expanding its research facility.
(D) It needs to quickly fill a position.

2. According to the job posting, what is a duty of the research director?

(A) Enforcing laboratory rules
(B) Submitting medical reports
(C) Hiring research assistants
(D) Contacting patients

If you haven't read *Individual Homes Weekly* (*IHW*) recently, you're missing out on the latest designs in home décor. The new *IHW* brings you more features, such as interviews with established professionals and new designers. In addition, you'll still get the same great coverage of the newest home interior designs from across the world that you've come to look forward to with *IHW*, but now with more images. We've also included a Q&A section with our chief editor, and we will award a special prize each week to the reader who offers the best design advice to our popular My Home Needs Help! section. Go to our award-winning Web site, ihw.com, to renew or begin your subscription today!

3. What is mentioned about the magazine?

(A) It hired a new chief editor.
(B) It shows interior designs from all over the world.
(C) Its subscription costs will increase.
(D) Its publication had temporarily halted.

4. What is suggested about the Web site?

(A) It allows access to past issues of *Individual Homes Weekly*.
(B) It features discount vouchers for home furniture.
(C) It provides a way to renew a subscription to the magazine.
(D) It describes a complimentary gift that will be sent to new subscribers.

Questions 5-7 refer to the following advertisement.

For Sale
Silver Tepco Pride Van

Fuel economy: 9 litres/100km on the highway. 15 litres/100 km in city streets. 30 percent more efficient than its market competitors, according to www.yearlycarsummary.co.uk. 35,000 kilometers (mostly highway)

Features: Built-in surround sound speakers, remote entry system, GPS navigation, power windows, tire pressure indicator, accident avoidance system, convertible roof, and heated seats.

Ask price: £13,000 or best offer

Other details: 1 year left on the manufacturer's warranty. Went through regular maintenance at a local auto shop. Has always been owned by the same person. Used regularly as a taxi. Must be sold within this month due to owner's move abroad.

If you are interested in seeing or test driving the van, please email Ronald Floyd at ronfloyd@vizmail.co.uk to arrange a meeting.

5. What is indicated about the Tepco Pride Van?

(A) It uses more fuel than its competition.
(B) It is the fastest of its kind.
(C) Its price is negotiable.
(D) Its warranty is no longer valid.

6. Which is NOT mentioned as a feature of the Tepco Pride Van?

(A) A signal that monitors tire pressure
(B) A system that warms seats
(C) A rearview camera
(D) An audio system

7. What is true about Mr. Floyd?

고난도

(A) He has only used the van as a personal vehicle.
(B) He works as an auto-mechanic.
(C) He will be out of the country until this month.
(D) He purchased his van new.

Questions 8-10 refer to the following advertisement.

Brickett's Chocolates
15 High Street in Maplebury
645-132-5631

Once you sample our Brickett's Chocolates, you'll find yourself coming back again and again. Brickett's is conveniently located in the local shopping district, and is the only chocolate store in town that has a private party room.

We offer:
· 20 different types of chocolates, produced here in our store using only the best ingredients
· A wide variety of milk flavors
· Customized chocolate cakes
· Free wireless internet access in our event rooms

Hours: Monday through Saturday, 10 A.M. to 7 P.M.
Winter (December through February): Open until 9 P.M.
Every Thursday is Children's Day - Kids under the age of 12 can receive a bag of selected chocolates at 45 percent off.

---

8. What is mentioned about Brickett's Chocolates?

(A) Its products are available in grocery stores.
(B) It is a family-run business.
(C) Its chocolates are made in the store.
(D) It has created a Web site.

9. According to the advertisement, what happens in December?

(A) The store recruits more workers.
(B) The menu is updated.
(C) The business hours change.
(D) The event room is closed.

10. What is indicated about the discount?

(A) It ends in February.
(B) It is offered just once a week.
(C) It is valid for any type of chocolate.
(D) It applies only to milk chocolates.

공지·회람

공지는 특정 다수의 사람들을 대상으로 새로이 시행되는 방침이나 변경된 규정 또는 행사 등을 전달하는 글이며, 회람은 회사나 단체 내에서 전달 사항이 있을 때 이메일 형식으로 신속히 전달될 수 있도록 간단히 작성하는 글이다. 두 지문 모두 전달하는 내용이 모호하지 않기 때문에 비교적 쉽게 답을 찾을 수 있으며, 기본적인 구성에 따라 작성되므로 도입부에서 전달 내용과 목적을 먼저 확인한 후, 문제에 제시된 키워드를 파악하여 그에 따른 세부 사항들을 빠르게 찾아낸다.

🔍 지문·질문 유형 확인하기

1. 잘 나오는 지문 유형

- ▶ 사내 주차장 공사, 내부 수리, 보수 공사, 시스템 점검 알림
- ▶ 유급 휴가, 출장 비용 등 경비 관련 사내 규정
- ▶ 퇴임, 인사 이동, 시상식 등 인사 관련 알림
- ▶ 공연, 세미나, 대회 등의 일정 및 신청 방법
- ▶ 문화 및 스포츠 시설 등의 일시적 휴관과 개관, 이용 방법

2. 잘 나오는 질문 유형

- ▶ 주제·목적, 출처, 발신/수신인을 묻는 질문
- ▶ 전달 사항과 관련된 세부 정보를 묻는 질문
- ▶ 추가적인 요청, 주의, 당부, 제안 사항을 묻는 질문

3. 독해 전략

- ▶ 공지와 회람의 일반적인 구조(글의 목적 → 세부 사항 → 요청이나 제안 사항)에 따라, 글의 도입부에서 주제나 목적, 수신/발신처와 관련된 문제의 답을 찾고, 요청이나 제안 사항은 지문 중반 이후에서 답을 찾는다.
- ▶ 구체적인 사실이나 내용 등 세부 정보 관련 문제가 많이 출제되므로, 질문의 키워드를 기억하여 본문에서 그 키워드에 대응하는 패러프레이징 표현을 찾는다. 특히 문제에서 제시되는 고유명사나 특정 요일과 날짜는 문제 풀이에 중요한 단서가 되므로 꼼꼼히 체크한다.

Questions 1-3 refer to the following notice.

Fairview Construction
New Regional Coordinator

❶ We are happy to announce the appointment of Linda Edwards to the position of ❷ Regional Coordinator for Latin America. She will be responsible for overseeing the smooth running of regional affairs. Linda comes to us with 15 years' experience in the housing sector at SMD Construction, where she was the development manager. She received her degree in management from the University of Lupton.

As you all know, the previous year has been very challenging for Fairview. ❸ We have undergone many changes in management following the corporate takeover in May. There has also been substantial organizational restructuring, and this has resulted in a number of adjustments to the way we work.

Overseas, Linda is looking forward to getting our Latin American operations back on track.

• 회사 이름
  공지의 제목

• 공지의 주제, 목적
  라틴 아메리카 지역 담당
  코디네이터 임명
• Linda Edwards의
  이력 사항

• 세부 정보
  회사 인수 합병으로 인한
  구조 조정과 그로 인한
  변경 사항

• 바람
  회사를 정상화시키고 싶어
  하는 Linda의 바람

---

1. What is the purpose of the notice?

(A) To announce a new appointment
(B) To show appreciation to local residents
(C) To discuss the opening of a position
(D) To talk about an environmental program

2. Who is Linda Edwards?

(A) The head of a company
(B) A development manager
(C) A new coordinator
(D) A university official

3. What is stated about Fairview?

(A) It recently expanded to Latin America.
(B) It is under new management.
(C) It was established 15 years ago.
(D) It will move its headquarters in May.

---

2. Linda Edwards는 누구인가?

(A) 회사 대표
(B) 개발 매니저
(C) 새 코디네이터
(D) 대학 관계자

해설 Linda Edwards가 키워드이며, 1번 문제와 동일한 단서에서 Linda Edwards를 남미 지역 코디네이터에 임명한다고 했으므로 (C)가 정답이다.

해석 및 해설

1. 공지의 목적은 무엇인가?
(A) 새로운 임명을 발표하기 위해
(B) 지역 주민들에게 감사를 전하기 위해
(C) 한 직책의 공석에 대해 논의하기 위해
(D) 환경 프로그램에 관해 이야기하기 위해

해설 서두에서 Linda Edwards를 남미 지역 코디네이터에 임명하게 되어 기쁘다고 했으므로 (A)가 정답이다.

3. Fairview에 관하여 언급된 것은 무엇인가?
(A) 최근에 남미로 확장했다.
(B) 새 경영 방침 하에 놓여 있다.
(C) 15년 전에 설립되었다.
(D) 5월에 본사를 옮길 것이다.

해설 작년 Fairview에 많은 변화들이 있었다고 하면서, 5월 기업 인수 후에 경영상에 많은 변화를 겪었다고 했으므로 (B)가 정답이다.

해설서 p.102 / ⏱ 제한 시간 12분

Questions 1-2 refer to the following memo.

From: Anne Jones, Personnel Director
To: Finance Department & Sales Department staff
Subject: Notice of transfer
Date: Tuesday, February 11, 5:20 P.M.

I would like to inform you that Wayne Clarke has accepted the decision to transfer from the Finance Department to the Sales Department. Wayne will start training with Alvez Vasquez this week and will assume the role of administrative manager in the Sales Department when Mr. Vasquez retires at the beginning of next month.

Russell Green, my assistant in the Personnel Department, will post the job opening for the administrative manager position in the Finance Department tomorrow. We expect to fill this position by the beginning of next month.

Please congratulate Mr. Vasquez on his retirement after almost 20 years with this company and wish Mr. Clarke good luck as he moves on to a new team.

---

1. Who is leaving the company?

(A) Anne Jones
(B) Wayne Clarke
(C) Alvez Vasquez
(D) Russell Green

2. What is expected to happen at the beginning of next month?

(A) Someone in the Personnel Department will be promoted.
(B) The company CEO will retire.
(C) A job opening will be posted.
(D) An office will have a new administrative manager.

Questions 3-5 refer to the following notice.

Blenhaim Bus Company
February 1

To all passengers:

Due to growing operating costs, Blenhaim Bus Company will increase passenger fares starting on May 1. The cost of a ride for adults, seniors, and university students will increase by 10 percent. The fare will continue to be free for children under the age of eight.

We apologize to our passengers for any inconvenience this may cause. We would also like to draw attention to the fact that this is our first fare increase in five years. Revenue from the fares is used for general vehicle maintenance and employee salaries.

We will continue providing you with the high level of service that you have come to expect from us.

Thank you for choosing Blenhaim Bus Company.

---

3. What is indicated about Blenhaim Bus Company?

(A) It is introducing new routes.
(B) It responded to customer complaints.
(C) It raised its fares five years ago.
(D) It is experiencing a decline in passenger numbers.

4. What is suggested about university students?

(A) Their fares will increase by the same percentage as the fare for seniors.
(B) They are able to purchase discounted monthly bus passes.
(C) Their school identification card must be renewed by May 1.
(D) They ride on Blenhaim Buses for free.

5. According to the notice, what is one way that revenue collected from fares is spent?

(A) To increase advertising
(B) To expand bus routes
(C) To renovate stations
(D) To pay employees

Questions 6-9 refer to the following notice.

Buena Vista Community Library Welcomes Maria Moreno

Maria Moreno is a well-known author and the current president of Arena Communications. On 9 February, Ms. Moreno will speak at the Buena Vista Community Library about her approach to business management; she will be in the South Room afterward signing copies of her volumes. Although admission is free, you still have to register by 18 January due to limited space. Please email our library's event coordinator, Ana Gonzalez (agonzalez@ buenavistalibrary.org.ar), with any inquiries or to register.

Ms. Moreno first started working as an office assistant at Rodriguez and Company and quickly worked her way up. After being at Rodriguez for 10 years, Ms. Moreno left to start up her own company and has enjoyed great success. Her insights into media communications and strategies are often cited in both printed and online materials, and her most recent book, *Communicate and Collaborate*, will be available in bookstores starting 17 October.

6. What event is being advertised?

(A) An awards presentation
(B) A business talk
(C) A library grand opening
(D) A job fair

7. What is suggested about Ms. Moreno?

(A) She has donated funds to the library.
(B) She has written more than one book.
(C) She runs a well-known Web site.
(D) She plans to open a new business.

8. What are the attendees asked to do prior to the event?

(A) Visit the South Room
(B) Contact Ms. Gonzalez
(C) Purchase a ticket
(D) Send Ms. Moreno an e-mail

9. What will happen on October 17?

(A) A book will be available for purchase.
(B) Ms. Moreno will sign autographs at a bookstore.
(C) A new president will take over a company.
(D) Ms. Moreno will find a new venue.

May Pannara Novelty Contest

Do you have a great idea to improve everyday life? If so, enter them into the May Pannara Novelty Contest.

What is the May Pannara Novelty Contest?

The contest was started by Thai inventor May Pannara, who also founded the Bangkok Center for Research and Development (BCRD). The aim of the contest is to find solutions to everyday problems. The winner will receive 10,000 baht to implement their solutions. Last year's winner designed a universal remote compatible with most electronic entertainment devices. The winner will be announced October 30 during a ceremony in the Bhumibol Auditorium at Trang University.

Am I eligible?

This contest is open to people of all ages, professions, and interests. Experts, amateurs, and students are encouraged to enter. Entries submitted to previous contests are not permitted.

How do I apply?

Entries must be received by June 20 through either postal mail or e-mail. To download application forms and other documents, please visit our Web site at www.bcrd.co.th/mpnc/entries. For inquiries regarding contest rules, please contact Pat Wattana at (02)-555-4354. Those who are interested in being a part of the judging should contact our evaluations supervisor, Robin Montri, at (02)-555-4359.

10. What is the purpose of the notice?

(A) To outline guidelines for a university course
(B) To attract sponsors for an event
(C) To announce a competition
(D) To promote a business conference

11. What is stated about the BCRD?

(A) It was started by May Pannara.
(B) It has an office on Trang University's campus.
(C) It produces electronic devices.
(D) It owns the Bhumibol Auditorium.

12. According to the notice, why would an individual contact Mr. Montri?

(A) To confirm eligibility of students
(B) To extend a deadline for a project
(C) To inquire about implementing a new policy
(D) To volunteer to help determine a contest winner

기사

보통 4~7문제가 출제되며, 단일 지문 중 마지막 부분에 배치되는 기사는 지문 길이가 길고 난이도 있는 어휘들이 많이 나오기 때문에 Part 7에서 어렵게 느껴지는 지문 중 하나이다. 하지만 지문이 까다로울수록 문제는 단순하게 출제되는 경향이 있으므로, 모르는 단어, 복잡한 문장, 세부적인 사항에 연연해하지 말고, 질문의 핵심어를 단서로 빠르게 전체 문맥을 파악하는 속독 연습을 해야 한다. 또한 다양한 질문이 골고루 출제되며 다른 지문에 비해 상대적으로 길고 어려우므로 시간 조절에 특히 유의해야 한다.

🔍 지문·질문 유형 확인하기

1. 잘 나오는 지문 유형

경제 관련 기사
▶ 국가 경제, 시장 상황, 물가 인상/인하 정보, 산업 전망, 첨단 기술을 이용한 신제품 개발 및 소개

기업 관련 기사
▶ 기업의 인수 합병, 구조 조정, 공장 설립, 이전 확장, 성장 기업 설립자 인터뷰

사회 관련 기사
▶ 환경 문제, 실업 문제, 특정 국가 및 지역 관련 기사

비평
▶ 영화·공연·문화 비평, 도서 비평, 레스토랑 소개, 여행 정보, 조리법 소개

2. 잘 나오는 질문 유형

▶ 기사의 주제 및 의도를 묻는 질문

▶ 기사의 출처와 예상 독자를 묻는 질문

▶ 특정한 일과 관련된 사실 여부를 묻는 질문

▶ 미래 상황에 대한 전망이나 계획 및 제안에 관한 질문

3. 독해 전략

▶ 기사의 주제나 목적은 일반적으로 도입부에 제시되나, 글 전반에 걸쳐 주제가 제시되는 경우도 있으므로 다른 문제부터 해결하고 마지막에 답을 확정하는 것이 효율적이다.

▶ 특히 문제수가 3문제 이상인 기사 지문은 먼저 대략적으로 빠르게 읽어 전체적인 내용을 파악한 후, 고유 명사나 수치 같은 질문의 키워드에 따라 정답의 단서 부분을 체크해 두고 답을 찾는 것이 효율적이다.

▶ 미래에 대한 전망, 제안과 관련된 질문의 단서는 주로 지문의 후반부에서 제시되는데, 미래 의미를 갖는 동사 표현(be planning / scheduled / expected to 동사원형)에 유의해야 한다.

Questions 1-4 refer to the following article.

Saville Concert Hall
Highlights
Week of 30 March
By Krista Martinez, music critic

Silent Masquerade
Oberon Opera Company, 676 Cather Road

Despite being founded only a year ago, the Oberon Opera Company has revolutionized the classical music scene in Saville and performed three of the most wonderful performances in recent history. The opera from last summer, *Blooming Spring*, received the Mannlich Award for Best Tenor, and ❶ the fall performance of *Sweet Serenity* sold more concert tickets than any other show last year. Two days ago, Oberon had its premiere of what is probably its best performance to date: *Silent Masquerade*, written by Saville resident Pedro Inez.

❷ Mr. Inez's musical abilities, demonstrated in his previous works, *Moonlight Fiona* and *An Endless Journey*, have once again been displayed in this latest masterpiece. Although not much happens in the actual plot, ❸ the way the male actors and female actresses interact with each other through music in the performance is quite amazing. It may very well be nominated for this year's Mannlich Awards.

If you have to choose to see one concert this year, make it this one. *Silent Masquerade* will be performed every night at 7:30 P.M. throughout the month of April. As with all Oberon performances, ❹ a portion of the ticket sales will be given to the Trent Fund, which supports emerging artists in Spain.

● 기사 제목

● Oberon 오페라단의 업적 과 개막 공연 소개

● Mr. Inez 씨의 작품 <Moonlight Fiona>, <An Endless Journey> 및 배우들의 공연 특징

● <Silent Masquerade> 공연 안내

1. According to the article, what performance was the most popular in Saville last year?

(A) *Silent Masquerade*
(B) *An Endless Journey*
(C) *Blooming Spring*
(D) *Sweet Serenity*

2. What is mentioned about Mr. Inez?

(A) He plays numerous instruments.
(B) He has received a Mannlich Award.
(C) He has written more than one piece of music.
(D) He is an actor as well as a composer.

3. Why does the critic particularly like *Silent Masquerade*?

(A) Its plot is particularly exciting.
(B) It makes use of a small stage.
(C) It uses music in an impressive way.
(D) Its cast includes a tenor who received an award last year.

4. What is suggested about the Oberon Opera Company?

(A) It designates some of its earnings to be donated to an organization.
(B) It has a schedule that offers both afternoon and evening performances.
(C) It recently relocated to Saville from another city.
(D) It must expand its facilities to accommodate its growing audiences.

해석 및 해설

1. 기사에 따르면, Saville에서 지난해 가장 인기 있었던 공연은 무엇인가?
(A) 〈Silent Masquerade〉
(B) 〈An Endless Journey〉
(C) 〈Blooming Spring〉
(D) 〈Sweet Serenity〉

해설 첫 번째 단락에서 작년에 가장 많은 표를 팔았던 공연은 Sweet Serenity임을 알 수 있다. 따라서 정답은 (D) Sweet Serenity이다.

2. Mr. Inez에 관하여 언급된 것은?
(A) 다양한 악기를 연주한다.
(B) Mannlich 상을 받았다.
(C) 하나 이상의 음악 작품을 썼다.
(D) 작곡가이면서 연기자이다.

해설 Mr. Inez에 대하여 언급이 된 문장을 찾는다. 지문의 두 번째 단락에서 그의 이전 작품들이 언급되는 것으로 보아 다른 여러 작품들을 썼음을 알 수 있다. 그러므로 정답은 (C) He has written more than one piece of music.임을 유추할 수 있다.

3. 평론가는 왜 특히 〈Silent Masquerade〉를 마음에 들어하는가?
(A) 줄거리가 특히 흥미롭다.
(B) 작은 무대를 활용한다.
(C) 음악을 인상적인 방식으로 사용한다.
(D) 출연진에 작년에 수상했던 테너가 포함되어 있다.

해설 평론가가 남녀 배우들 간의 음악을 통한 상호작용이 인상적이라고 언급하고 있으므로 정답은 (C) It uses music in an impressive way.이다.

4. Oberon 오페라단에 관하여 알 수 있는 것은?
(A) 수익의 일부가 한 단체에 기부되도록 지정한다.
(B) 오후와 저녁 공연을 둘 다 제공하는 일정이 있다.
(C) 최근 다른 도시에서 Saville로 이전했다.
(D) 증가하는 관객들을 수용하기 위해 시설을 확장해야 한다.

해설 지문의 마지막 줄에서 스페인의 떠오르는 예술가를 지원하는 공연 관련 단체 Trend 기금에 수익의 일부를 보낸다는 것을 확인할 수 있으므로 정답은 (A) It designates some of its earnings to be donated to an organization.이다.

해설서 p.105 / 제한 시간 14분

Questions 1-2 refer to the following article.

Karmel Science Journal
Conference Information

On October 25 and 26, the International Organization of Medical Research (IOMR) will host its bi-annual conference at the recently renovated Kenyatta International Conference Center in Nairobi, Kenya.

This year's conference will feature speakers Julia Fox, Professor of Physics at Kingley University, and Mohammed Kahn, President of the IOMR. Furthermore, eight plenary meetings will be chaired by frontrunners in the medical science field.

Online registration for the conference is now open at www.iomr.org/kenyatta. A list of nearby hotels can also be found on the IOMR Web site.

---

1. What is mentioned about the conference?

(A) It will be held for two days.
(B) It is being put together by Julia Fox.
(C) It is free of charge for IOMR members.
(D) It will provide accommodation for attendees.

2. What information is the organization providing online?

(A) Names of places to stay
(B) Descriptions of tourist attractions
(C) A map to the conference center
(D) A list of restaurants near the conference center

Euston, London (July 28) – Milway Pharmaceuticals will move its headquarters from the current Oxford Street site to a 1,500-square meter office space in the Prader Building on September 3, the company announced this morning.

"This is good news for Euston," said Will Matthews, the director of Bentley Loans, an organization that offers low-interest start-up loans to new companies. "Milway Pharmaceuticals has 120 employees who will become valuable patrons of local businesses and support the local community in many different ways." Mr. Matthews noted that the loan company assisted Milway Pharmaceuticals in covering the cost of the relocation.

Milway Pharmaceuticals, which develops and markets medicines, recently acquired several new clients and intends to employ additional pharmacists, explained Ella Milway, a senior partner of Milway Pharmaceuticals. "We needed extra room, and we were attracted by the excellent rental terms offered by the Prader Building," she said. "The financial assistance from Bentley Loans was another big motivation."

The Prader Building, which is on the east side of Euston, was developed by Comcord Real Estate. Among its tenants are the Smith Legal Society, CRI Accountants, Lullington Table Tennis Club, and Pulford's Sporting Goods. Now that Milway Pharmaceuticals will move in, the building is fully occupied.

---

3. Why was the article written?

(A) To announce a company's move to a new location
(B) To notify of salary increases in a company
(C) To give information about updates to a business' services
(D) To describe renovations done to a building

4. What is NOT suggested about Milway Pharmaceuticals?

(A) The number of employees
(B) The size of an office
(C) The expected salary range
(D) The company's new location

5. The word "terms" in paragraph 3, line 4, is closest in meaning to

(A) expansions
(B) directions
(C) conditions
(D) expressions

6. What type of business does NOT occupy 고난도 space in the Prader Building?

(A) A financial services company
(B) A property management firm
(C) A retail store
(D) A sports club

Questions 7-10 refer to the following article.

Daily Market Herald

On Wednesday, Spangler Market announced that it will acquire five Bargain Buy grocery stores. Three of the stores are in Cardiff, and the other two are in Portas. Their sales prices will not be disclosed.

For now, the acquired stores are still being run under Bargain Buy's name. It is not yet known when they will transition to the new name.

In a press release, Spangler's CEO Jacob Bitzer said, "I'm very excited about adding these locations to our business. I eagerly anticipate becoming the main grocery store for the Cardiff and Portas communities. We intend to provide them with the finest selection of top quality foods." Mr. Jacob Bitzer confirmed that there are no planned changes to personnel.

Spangler Market was founded in Manchester 95 years ago by Mr. Bitzer's great-grandfather. Mr. Bitzer became the CEO after his father retired 8 years ago. There are now Spangler Market locations all across the UK.

---

7. What is the purpose of the article?

(A) To report on the purchase of some stores
(B) To describe a company's move
(C) To promote some new items
(D) To announce a new opening

8. According to the article, what has NOT been decided yet?

(A) Who will head the transition team
(B) How much a transaction will cost
(C) When a name change will occur
(D) Where the company headquarters will be located

9. 고난도 What does Mr. Bitzer suggest about employment at the Cardiff and Portas stores?

(A) He plans to introduce performance-based bonuses.
(B) He intends to retain the current staff.
(C) He hopes to hire workers from the local community.
(D) He wants to implement some new sales strategies.

10. What is indicated about Spangler Market?

(A) It will soon open branches in Manchester.
(B) It provides many discounts.
(C) It is a family-run business.
(D) It is a recently opened business.

After receiving many letters from citizens upset about recent trends in the real estate market, the Dartmouth City Council carried out a study to assess the situation. They released their findings today, and they will meet tomorrow to decide what measures should be taken, if any.

— [1] —. At even a cursory glance, it is apparent that there has been a marked increase in the rent for residential apartments across the board. While occupancy rates across the city rose by about 0.6 percent, slightly less than last year's 0.71 percent, rents climbed an average 4.6 percent to an average of $823 per month. — [2] —. It should be stressed that these are average amounts, and that the increases in some neighborhoods were far more significant. The Riverside area, which was once an important business district, has seen an explosion in apartment construction. The old factories and warehouses have been torn down, and developers are taking advantage of the opportunity to build luxury apartments. The two major complexes, Dartmouth Rapids and Streamside Apartments, average about $1,457 per month, or $634 above the regional average.

— [3] —. This has resulted in the construction of an additional station in the Bamoral Heights area, which has raised the average rent there to $982 per month.

— [4] —. A few areas, however, have actually seen a decrease in value. Elsey Ridge, which is the farthest-outlying area of the city, saw an average decrease of 1.5 percent, making the average monthly rent there just $635 per month.

11. What is the main purpose of this article?

(A) To analyze past occupancy rates
(B) To announce public transportation projects
(C) To summarize real estate trends in the city
(D) To describe population growth in different areas

12. According to the article, why are 고난도 developers interested in Riverside?

(A) It is a popular tourist destination.
(B) Higher rents can be charged there.
(C) The area has many important factories.
(D) It is conveniently located near a shopping center.

13. What is indicated about the Dartmouth 고난도 Rapids and Streamside Apartments?

(A) They have attracted many potential tenants already.
(B) They are the first luxury apartments to be constructed in Dartmouth.
(C) They are situated far from the city center.
(D) They were built in place of old manufacturing plants.

14. In which of the positions marked [1], [2], [3], and [4] does the following sentence best belong?

"One other development project that has had a significant impact is the extension of Subway Line 3 to Deerfallow Station."

(A) [1]
(B) [2]
(C) [3]
(D) [4]

양식

양식은 다른 종류의 지문에 비해 내용이 적고 비교적 간단하기 때문에 어렵지는 않지만, 양식의 구성을 모르면 이를 파악하는 데 시간을 낭비할 수 있다. 따라서 평소 토익에 자주 등장하는 비즈니스 양식들을 유형별로 잘 정리해 두면, 지문을 전부 읽지 않고도 문제에서 요구하는 정보가 제시된 부분을 바로 찾아내어 시간을 절약할 수 있다.

🔍 지문·질문 유형 확인하기

1. 잘 나오는 지문 유형

송장 (Invoice)
▶ 배송 제품 내역, 수량, 단가, 세금, 총액

일정 (Schedule, Itinerary)
▶ 여행 일정표, 숙박 장소, 항공편, 워크숍 장소 및 세부 일정

설문지 (Survey)
▶ 제품 구매자나 호텔 및 식당 이용 고객 만족도 조사

신청서 (Application)
▶ 입사·입학·가입·지원·잡지 구독 신청 및 신청 시 받는 혜택, 조건

기타 양식
▶ 초대장(invitation), 청구서(bill), 구매 영수증(receipt), 할인 쿠폰(coupon), 보증서(warranty), 계약서(contract)

2. 잘 나오는 질문 유형

▶ 목적 또는 수신/발신인 등의 출처를 묻는 질문

▶ 일정, 날짜, 단가, 총액, 수량, 지급 시점 등의 구체적인 내용을 묻는 질문

▶ 예외·부가 사항이나 제안에 관한 질문

3. 독해 전략

▶ 각종 양식의 경우 특히 일정, 날짜, 금액, 수량 등의 구체적인 수치와 관련된 질문은 질문의 키워드를 바탕으로 내용의 전개상 지문의 어느 부분에 단서가 나올지를 예측해 빨리 답을 찾는다.

▶ 양식을 작성한 목적, 용도, 수신자와 발신자 관련 질문은 주로 지문의 제목 부분이나 글의 초반부에서 답을 찾는다.

▶ Note, Remarks, *표시가 붙은 부분에 제시되는 주의 사항이나 예외 사항이 자주 출제되므로 독해 시 그 부분에 특히 유의한다.

▶ 다양한 양식에서 공통적으로 앞으로 일어날 내용이 자주 출제되므로, 미래의 의미를 갖는 동사 표현(be planning/scheduled/expected to 동사원형)에 유의한다.

Questions 1-2 refer to the following invoice.

CBI Electronics Warehouse
2250 Beacon Highway, Manchester, NH 03101
604-987-0097
Delivery Invoice

Order Date: March 3
2 Shipment Date: March 4
Estimated Delivery Date: March 6
Invoice No: 45003
Purchased by: **1** Ray Escobar
Delivery Address: Rafagalbra 540, Nashua, NH 03060

Electra Chrome Computer Desk / Workstation	$149.95
Comfortmax Swivel Chair	$99.95
PCI 21-inch Monitor	$249.99
PCI Computer (Model #: a150)	$ 999.99
Subtotal	$1,499.88
1 Frequent Shopper Discount	- $150.00
Shipping charge	0
Tax	$ 80.99
Total	$1,430.87

---

* No shipping fee is charged to order above $ 1,000.00.
2 You will not be charged until the date of shipment.
Any replacement is carried out within 30 days of order shipment.

Thank you for shopping at CBI Warehouse.

회사 이름
회사 주소, 전화번호

주문일
송장 번호
구매인
배송 주소

청구 금액

단골 고객 할인
구매자 Ray Escobar가
단골 고객임을 말해준다.

---

1. What is suggested about Mr. Escobar?

(A) He will purchase a new computer next month.
(B) He works for a delivery company.
(C) He has a new mailing address.
(D) He is a regular customer.

2. When most likely will Mr. Escobar pay for his order?

(A) On March 3
(B) On March 4
(C) On March 6
(D) On March 7

해석 및 해설

1. Mr. Escobar에 관하여 알 수 있는 것은?
(A) 다음 달에 새 컴퓨터를 구매할 것이다.
(B) 배송 회사에서 근무한다.
(C) 새 우편물 주소가 있다.
(D) 단골 고객이다.

해설 Ray Escobar는 구매자이며, 청구액 목록에서 단골 할인 정보를 토대로 Ray Escobar가 이 업체와 계속 거래하는 고객임을 알 수 있다. 따라서 frequent shopper를 regular customer로 바꿔 표현한 (D)가 정답이다.

2. Mr. Escobar는 그의 주문품에 대해 언제 지불을 하겠는가?
(A) 3월 3일
(B) 3월 4일
(C) 3월 6일
(D) 3월 7일

해설 배송일이 3월 4일이라고 나와 있으며 지문 하단에서 배송일까지는 청구되지 않는다고 했으므로 Mr. Escobar의 대금 결제일은 3월 4일임을 유추할 수 있다. 따라서 (B) On March 4가 정답이다.

Practice

해설서 p.108 / ⏱ 제한 시간 10분

Questions 1-2 refer to the following Web page.

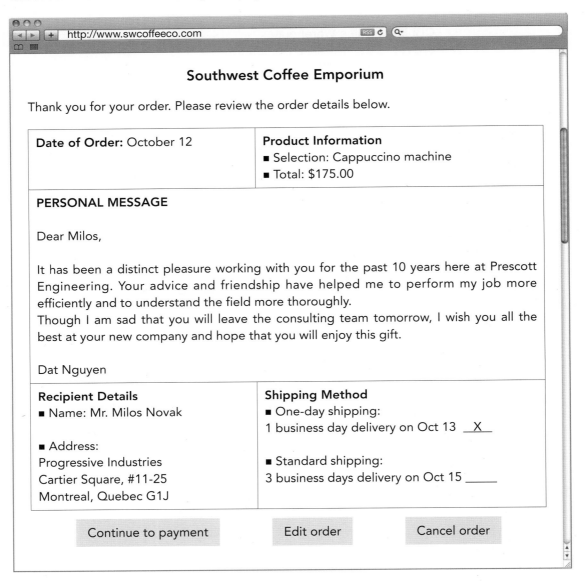

http://www.swcoffeeco.com

Southwest Coffee Emporium

Thank you for your order. Please review the order details below.

Date of Order: October 12	**Product Information** ■ Selection: Cappuccino machine ■ Total: $175.00

PERSONAL MESSAGE

Dear Milos,

It has been a distinct pleasure working with you for the past 10 years here at Prescott Engineering. Your advice and friendship have helped me to perform my job more efficiently and to understand the field more thoroughly.
Though I am sad that you will leave the consulting team tomorrow, I wish you all the best at your new company and hope that you will enjoy this gift.

Dat Nguyen

Recipient Details ■ Name: Mr. Milos Novak ■ Address: Progressive Industries Cartier Square, #11-25 Montreal, Quebec G1J	**Shipping Method** ■ One-day shipping: 1 business day delivery on Oct 13 ___X___ ■ Standard shipping: 3 business days delivery on Oct 15 _____

Continue to payment	Edit order	Cancel order

---

1. What is indicated about the company Mr. Nguyen works for?

(A) It has employed him for at least 12 years.
(B) It manufactures baskets.
(C) It will move to a new location soon.
(D) It has its own consulting team.

2. 고난도 What will most likely happen on October 13?

(A) Mr. Nguyen will make a payment for a gift.
(B) Mr. Novak will leave Southwest Coffee Emporium.
(C) Mr. Nguyen will cancel an order.
(D) Mr. Novak will receive a package.

Questions 3-4 refer to the following invoice.

Sternberg Manufacturing
273 Georgetown Street, Washington, D.C. 20007
(202) 555-9213
www.sternberg-mfg.com

Order Number: 582714
Date: April 18
Customer: Jennie Hills
1321 Pennsylvania Avenue
Washington, D.C. 20460
(202) 555-2192

Item	Number	Quantity	Price
Executive office chair, brown leather	53912	1	$101.99
Computer corner desk, fine oak	31614	1	$87.99
4-shelf file cabinet, metal	49321	1	$72.99
		Subtotal	$262.97
		Tax	$23.30
		Delivery	$35.00
		Deposit	$150.00
		Total Amount	$171.27

Sternberg Manufacturing will refund or exchange items up to 30 days following delivery of items.

3. What does Sternberg Manufacturing sell?

(A) Business cards
(B) Computer hardware
(C) Leather bags
(D) Office furniture

4. What is indicated about Ms. Hills?

(A) Her order did not include shipping charges.
(B) Her items will be delivered by April 18.
(C) She had made a partial payment.
(D) She returned one of her items.

Subscription Form

Name   Steve Parker
Mailing Address   325 Niles Drive, Cork 3
E-mail Address   sparker@ifax.com

Please mail this form to *Organic Botanics* Magazine, 840 Harlington Ave. Cork 2. Your bill will be sent later.

Your Subscription

Type of Subscription	Price	New/Renewing
X 1 year (10 issues)	€30.00	New
___ 2 years (20 issues)	€48.00	

Subscription Gift

On top of your own subscription, send a subscription gift to someone for 50 percent off the original price!

Name of Recipient Brenda Jules
Mailing Address   92 Suttlecreek Lane, Cork 3
Attached Message   Happy birthday to an amazing cousin!

Type of Subscription	Price
X 1 year (10 issues)	€15.00
___ 2 years (20 issues)	€24.00

5. What is indicated about Mr. Parker?

(A) He wants to receive *Organic Botanics* for two years.
(B) He is receiving a subscription as a gift.
(C) He is subscribing to *Organic Botanics* for the first time.
(D) He is paying by credit card.

6. Who is Ms. Jules?

(A) A relative of Mr. Parker
(B) A customer service representative
(C) A magazine writer
(D) A coworker of Mr. Parker

Questions 7-10 refer to the following form.

GIOVANNI LEATHER

Giovanni Leather fully guarantees the quality of every product it manufactures. As such, we provide an unconditional guarantee against any product defects for up to one year of use. If you encounter any defects within this period, you may receive a full refund or exchange the defective item for one of equal or lesser value.

You can activate your guarantee by registering your product. Just fill out this pre-paid postage card and mail it back to us.

Name: <u>Kevin Troust</u>
E-mail: <u>ktroust@zotmail.com</u>
Address: <u>100 Windsor Ave, Jamestown, VA 10923</u>
Product Number: <u>BF302ZXU992</u>
Product Description: <u>Brown document case with combination lock</u>
How many Giovanni Leather products do you own? <u>1</u>
Was this product a gift? <u>No</u>
What other makes of leather products do you own? <u>Good Old Texan, Westwing, Falco</u>
Please provide us with any comments regarding Giovanni Leather:
<u>Your Web site was convenient to navigate and I easily found the product I was looking for. I am very satisfied with my purchase and the only suggestion I have is it would be great if you had a larger selection of men's items to choose from (such as pants and boots). It seems like Giovanni mainly carries women's accessories, like wallets and purses.</u>

---

7. Why did Mr. Troust fill out the form?

(A) To complain about an item with a defect
(B) To apply for a program that provides discounts to members
(C) To allow himself to return a product in the future
(D) To request a set of instructions from a store

8. What did Mr. Troust buy?

(A) A bag for papers
(B) A purse
(C) A pair of boots
(D) A wallet

9. What is indicated about Mr. Troust?

(A) He received a Giovanni Leather product as a gift.
(B) He owns many Giovanni Leather products.
(C) He shops exclusively at Giovanni Leather.
(D) He purchased a Giovanni Leather product online.

10. In Mr. Troust's opinion, how could Giovanni Leather improve?

(A) By offering more types of products
(B) By extending its product guarantee period
(C) By offering more product discounts
(D) By selling better quality products

이중 지문

이중 지문은 서로 관련된 두 개의 지문이 한 세트를 이루며, 각 세트당 5문항씩 구성되어 출제된다. 이중 지문은 지문 자체의 난이도는 높은 편이 아니나, 읽어야 되는 양이 많고 두 지문을 연계시켜 추론하는 문제 (5문제 중 1~2문제)의 경우 두 지문을 번갈아 봐야 하므로 미리 전략을 세워 시간 관리에 신경을 써야 한 다.

Tip! 이중 지문에서는 두 지문을 연계해서 푸는 문제가 1~2문제씩 등장해.

🔍 지문·질문 유형 확인하기

1. 잘 나오는 지문 유형

E-mail / Letter + E-mail / Letter
- ▶ 호텔에서 고객 만족도를 묻는 이메일과 고객의 답장 이메일
- ▶ 인터넷 접속 오류 관련 2개의 이메일
- ▶ 회의 장소 예약이나 일정 변경 관련 2개의 이메일

Advertisement + E-mail / Letter, Itinerary, Invitation, Article, Report, Résumé, etc.
- ▶ 구인 광고 + 구직 지원용 이메일
- ▶ 제품 광고 + 제품 문의, 주문, 배송 지연 관련 이메일
- ▶ 호텔 서비스에 대한 광고 + 호텔 서비스에 대한 항의나 환불 요청 이메일

Notice + E-mail / Letter
- ▶ 행사 개최 또는 변경 사항 공지 + 그에 대한 추가 정보 문의 이메일
- ▶ 행사 참여 권고 공지 + 행사 참여자의 문의 이메일
- ▶ 사내 정책 변경 공지 + 공지 내용이나 후속 대책 문의 이메일

Article + E-mail / Letter
- ▶ 지역 건설 계획 관련 기사 + 그 기사에 대한 이메일
- ▶ 인물, 회사 영업 실적, 경제, 제품 등에 대한 기사 + 그에 대한 문의나 오류 정정 요구 이메일
- ▶ 식생활, 운동 등 건강 정보 기사 + 그 기사에 대한 추가 정보 요청 이메일

Form(Invoice, Invitation, Survey, Itinerary, Text message, etc.) + E-mail / Letter
- ▶ 송장 + 이의 제기 이메일
- ▶ 초청장 + 그에 대한 의사 표시 및 감사 이메일
- ▶ 식당, 호텔 서비스에 대한 의견 요청 이메일 + 고객 만족도를 나타내는 설문지
- ▶ 여행 일정 및 숙박 시설에 대한 표 + 회의 참석을 위한 비행 및 숙박 예약 관련 이메일
- ▶ 부재중 전화 메모 + 메모 관련 내용을 담은 이메일

2. 잘 나오는 질문 유형

▶ 이메일/편지의 목적이나 주제, 지문에 언급된 내용이나 사실 관계를 확인하는 NOT/TRUE 문제 등 전반적인 내용을 묻는 질문

▶ 가격, 할인율, 변동 사항, 요청 및 요구 사항, 동봉 자료나 첨부 자료 등에 언급된 구체적인 내용을 묻는 질문

▶ 동의어를 묻는 질문

▶ 두 개의 지문 연계를 통해 특정 내용을 추론하는 질문

3. 독해 전략

▶ 먼저 지문 앞에 나오는 지시문(Questions 181–185 refer ...... 부분)을 통해 두 지문의 관계를 파악한 후, 문제부터 읽어 키워드를 확인하고 지문에서 해당 키워드가 언급된 부분의 앞뒤를 살펴보며 답을 찾는다.

▶ 시간을 절약하기 위해 5문제가 두 지문 중 어느 지문과 관련되었는지를 파악하는 것이 좋다. 일반적으로 5개의 문제 중 앞의 2~3개 문제가 첫 번째 지문과 관련되어 있으므로, 앞의 3개 문제를 먼저 읽고 첫 번째 지문에서 답을 찾은 뒤 나머지 문제의 답을 두 번째 지문에서 찾는다.

▶ 문제의 순서와 내용의 순서가 다를 수도 있지만, 일반적으로 지문의 전개 순서와 문제의 순서가 동일하게 제시되므로 문제 순서에 따라 본문에서 답을 찾아나간다.

▶ 두 지문 중 한 지문이 편지나 이메일인 경우 수신자와 발신자의 신원과 두 사람의 관계를 파악하는 문제가 자주 출제되므로, 누가 누구에게 쓴 글인지 정확히 체크해야 한다.

▶ 두 지문을 연계하여 이끌어낸 정보를 통해 정답을 고르는 이중 지문 연계 문제가 5문제 중 1–2문제 출제된다. 시간이 많이 걸리는 이 유형은 질문 속의 키워드가 있는 문장을 읽고, 그 키워드와 밀접한 관련이 있는 핵심 단서를 다른 지문에서 찾아내는 것이 관건이다.

복수 지문 연계 문제 풀이 써머리

STEP 1 질문의 키워드를 확인하여 먼저 봐야 할 지문을 결정한다.

STEP 2 먼저 봐야 할 지문에서 첫 번째 단서를 포착한 후, 연관성을 고려하여 추가로 필요한 두 번째 단서를 다른 지문에서 찾는다.

STEP 3 둘 이상의 단서를 종합하여 보기와 매칭시킨다.

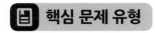
Questions 1-5 refer to the following article and e-mail.

A Birmingham Company Becomes a Leader in Educational Films

Birmingham, 4 September – Joseph Ford established Ford Productions 50 years ago, and ❶ the company quickly rose to become a leader in the field of educational films. The business is family-run, and today, Joseph Ford's son, Martin Ford, is the current CEO of the company. Although the company has undergone many changes since its establishment, its core aim to educate people in the areas of literature, science, history, and mathematics still remains strong.

> **STEP 2-2** 두 번째 단서 포착 → Mr. Ford가 버밍엄에서 회사 설립

❹ When Joseph Ford started his company in Birmingham, he focused mainly on producing and distributing films for local high schools. Over the years, the company has expanded its customer base and constantly upgraded its technology to keep up with the times. The first major upgrade involved releasing all the films on DVDs. Then, just last year, ❷ the company decided to stop manufacturing DVDs altogether and moved on to streaming their films online. Joseph Ford's granddaughter, Alicia Ford, graduated with degrees in digital media and multimedia technology. She was the mastermind behind the move, ❶ which led to an even larger growth of Ford Productions' customer base and product lines.

At 87, Joseph Ford is still actively involved in his company. He believes that people are always looking for innovative methods of education and that this business should strive to meet these needs. "Education is always evolving and as a company dedicated in providing instructional productions, we must constantly evolve as well," he says.

- Ford 프로덕션의 설립 역사와 사명
- Ford 프로덕션의 발전 과정과 변화
- Joseph Ford의 견해

To: Martin Ford <mford@fordproductions.com>
From: Lee Akman <l_akman@ksmedia.com>
Subject: Conference
Date: 23 October

> **STEP 2-1** Mr. Akman이 Mr. Ford에게 보낸 이메일에서 첫 번째 단서 포착
> → 과거 Ford 프로덕션에서 마케팅 보조로 근무

Dear Martin,

It was a pleasure seeing you at the conference last week in Telford. Although it took a while to ❸ adjust, I am now enjoying life in a larger city. I would love to show you around if you are ever in town again. ❹ I find it hard to believe that it has been almost two decades since I was a marketing assistant at your company. So much has happened since then! ❺ I have some amazing pictures of you giving your keynote speech at the conference, so I'll email them to you tomorrow. Let me know the next time you visit Telford so that we can get dinner together.

Lee Akman   **STEP 3** 두 단서를 종합하여 정답 선택

- 수신인
- 발신인
- 제목
- 날짜
- Lee Akman이 Ford 프로덕션에서 근무했을 당시의 일 회상과 Martin Ford 초대 권유

1. What is the purpose of the article?

   (A) To recommend the service of a company
   (B) To discuss the growth of a business
   (C) To introduce a new executive board
   (D) To report on a recent merger

2. What major change did Ford Productions recently make?

   (A) It put all its contents online.
   (B) It moved its main office.
   (C) It hired new workers.
   (D) It appointed Alicia Ford as CEO.

3. In the e-mail, the word "adjust" in paragraph 1, line 2, is closest in meaning to

   (A) correct
   (B) adapt
   (C) relate
   (D) achieve

4. 고난도 What is indicated about Mr. Akman?

   (A) He plans on attending a conference.
   (B) He hired a marketing assistant.
   (C) He used to work in Birmingham.
   (D) He runs his own business.

5. What does Mr. Akman say he will do?

   (A) Visit Ford Productions
   (B) Call Martin Ford
   (C) Produce an educational video
   (D) Send some photographs

---

3. 이메일에서 첫 번째 단락, 두 번째 줄의 "adjust"와 의미상 가장 가까운 것은

   (A) 바로잡다
   (B) 적응하다
   (C) 관련시키다
   (D) 달성하다

   해설 이메일 내용을 보면 적응하기는 시간이 오래 걸리긴 했으나, 더 큰 도시에서의 삶을 즐기고 있다는 내용이므로 문맥에 알맞은 어휘로는 (B) adapt가 적합하다.

해석 및 해설

1. 기사의 목적은 무엇인가?
   (A) 회사의 서비스를 추천하기 위해
   (B) 기업의 성장을 논의하기 위해
   (C) 새 이사회를 소개하기 위해
   (D) 최근의 합병을 보고하기 위해

   해설 기사 첫머리의 교육 영상물 분야에서 주도적인 기업으로 성장했다는 내용, 그리고 두 번째 단락의 고객층과 제품 라인을 한층 더 성장시키는 결과를 가져왔다는 내용을 통해 회사의 성장에 대해 이야기하고 있음을 알 수 있다. 따라서 (B) To discuss the growth of a business가 정답이다.

2. Ford 프로덕션에 최근 일어난 변화는 무엇인가?
   (A) 모든 콘텐츠를 온라인으로 전환했다.
   (B) 본점을 이전했다.
   (C) 신입 직원들을 채용했다.
   (D) Alicia Ford를 최고경영자로 임명했다.

   해설 기사 두 번째 단락에서 Ford Productions가 DVD 사업을 그만두고 온라인 미디어로 변경했다는 것을 확인할 수 있으므로 정답은 (A) It put all its contents online이다.

4. 고난도 Mr. Akman에 관하여 언급된 것은?
   (A) 회의에 참석할 계획이다.
   (B) 마케팅 보조원을 고용했다.
   (C) 버밍엄에서 일했었다.
   (D) 개인 사업을 운영한다.

   해설 이메일 지문에서 Mr. Akman은 이메일 발신자이고 이메일 수신자는 Mr. Ford이다. 이메일에서 Mr. Akman이 과거에 Ford Productions에서 마케팅 보조로 일했음을 확인할 수 있고, 기사에서 Ford Productions이 버밍엄에서 사업을 시작하였고, 본사가 계속 그 자리에 있음을 파악할 수 있다. 따라서 Mr. Akman이 버밍엄에서 일했음을 유추할 수 있으므로 정답은 (C) He used to work in Birmingham이다.

5. Mr. Akman은 다음에 무엇을 하겠다고 하는가?
   (A) Ford 프로덕션을 방문한다
   (B) Martin Ford에게 전화한다
   (C) 교육용 영상을 제작한다
   (D) 몇 장의 사진을 보낸다

   해설 이메일에서 Mr. Akman이 몇 장의 멋진 사진을 보낸다고 했으므로 정답은 (D) Send some photographs이다.

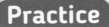

해설서 p.111 / ⏱ 제한 시간 18분

Questions 1-5 refer to the following e-mail and schedule.

To	Song Myung <msong@himail.co.uk>
From	Peter Barlow <pbarlow@harzok.co.uk>
Date	20 February
Subject	Open house
Attachment	schedule.doc

Good morning Mr. Myung,

I received your e-mail about next month's recruitment session. The registration, which is done through our Web site, unfortunately closed on 10 February. However, when I emailed the schedule to the registered participants last week, one of them replied saying that he would not be able to attend. This means that I can add you to our list of participants.

Please find attached the schedule for Thursday. You stated in your e-mail that you cannot arrive until 9:30 A.M. That should be fine. I will leave your visitor badge at the reception desk, along with a meal voucher for lunch. After picking them up, please go to room 221.

You indicated that you already have experience in Harzok's line of work, which is great. Please confirm your attendance by replying to this e-mail. Thank you.

Regards,

Peter Barlow
Director of Human Resources

Recruitment Information Session
Harzok Medical Insurance Headquarters
2244 Blackdown Road, London
8:30 A.M. - 11:30 A.M., Thursday, 1 March

8:30-9:30 A.M. (Room 212)
Introduction to Harzok - First, there will be a short presentation about our company, and you will learn about the various career opportunities we offer. Then, we will give you a tour of the headquarters' offices so that you get an idea of the work environment here.

9:30-10:30 A.M. (Room 221)
Meet the Team - Talk to members of the Harzok family in a casual, relaxed setting. Experienced staff including senior management will be available to address any questions or comments you may have.

10:30-11:30 A.M. (Room 222)
Application Process – If you think Harzok is a good match for you, complete an application form. Should there be a suitable position, we will contact you within one week to arrange a face-to-face interview with the director of human resources.

1. What is indicated about the people who received the schedule last week?

   (A) They plan to arrive at 9:30 A.M.
   (B) They registered for the event online.
   (C) They all made errors on their applications.
   (D) They are staff members of Harzok.

2. What does Mr. Barlow plan to do?

   (A) Book a flight
   (B) Welcome visitors at the reception desk
   (C) Arrange entry authorization for Mr. Myung
   (D) Add information to a Web site

3. In the e-mail, the word "fine" in paragraph 2, line 2, is closest in meaning to

   (A) delicate
   (B) overdue
   (C) acceptable
   (D) correct

4. In what field does Mr. Myung most likely work?
   고난도

   (A) Health insurance
   (B) Online marketing
   (C) International relations
   (D) Human resources

5. What part of the open house will Mr. Myung miss?

   (A) Lunch with other attendees
   (B) The meeting with senior managers
   (C) The office building tour
   (D) Individual interviews

Questions 6-10 refer to the following information and form.

HOLDING EVENTS AT KINGSTON LIBRARY

The Jefferson Room at the Kingston Library is mainly used for library programs, but it may also be used for private meetings and company events on any day with the exception of Sundays. Please complete a request form in order to reserve the room.

Overview of Fees for Using the Jefferson Room
The fees below are determined by the user type and the number of expected attendees.

	1-40 Attendees	41-80 Attendees	81-120 Attendees
Library card holders (private meetings and social gatherings)	$20 per individual	$40 per individual	$80 per individual
Nonmembers (private meetings and social gatherings)	$40 per individual	$80 per individual	$160 per individual
Company groups	$80 per individual	$120 per individual	$240 per individual

Important Details
• Selling or advertising products is not allowed in the Jefferson Room.
• The library is open daily from 8 A.M. to 6 P.M. Events held after hours require a security guard to be on site. This arrangement can be made through the library for an extra fee. Alternatively, individuals are also welcome to hire a security guard on their own.

KINGSTON LIBRARY

Reservation Request Form for the Jefferson Room

Individual/Group name: Hermes Architecture Firm
Contact representative: Penelope Sack
Phone: 555-4930
E-mail: p_sack@hermesarchitect.com

Event description: Our architecture firm is in the process of making preliminary plans for a new shopping mall that will be constructed in the city of Kingston. Before finalizing the designs, we would like to show our plans to the residents of Kingston and receive their input. Participants will consist of the design team, our client, and Kingston residents who want to attend.
Expected number of attendees: 120
Do you own a library card? No
Date and time of event: Friday, April 20, 6:30 P.M. – 8:30 P.M.

I have read and consent to all room policies. I understand that it is my responsibility to leave the room in its original state and to return all extra chairs and folding tables to the storage closet.

Signature: _Penelope Sack_   **Date:** March 25

6. What does the information indicate about Kingston Library?

(A) The library closes earlier on weekends.
(B) The library allows events to take place after its business hours.
(C) A fee is charged for all library programs.
(D) Discounts are provided to Kingston residents for library room rentals.

7. Why will Penelope Sack hold a meeting?

(A) To plan a fundraiser for a project
(B) To celebrate the opening of a building
(C) To get feedback from people in the community
(D) To nominate individuals for an award

8. How much will Hermes Architecture be charged per person if Ms. Sack's request is approved?

(A) $80
(B) $120
(C) $160
(D) $240

9. What is implied about the Jefferson Room?

(A) It can be reserved for any day of the week.
(B) Additional furniture can be set up to accommodate large parties.
(C) It is open only to companies on Wednesdays.
(D) Library card holders may use the room free of charge.

10. What would Ms. Sack be required to do before her event?

(A) Arrange for a security guard to be present
(B) Get permission from city officials
(C) Extend her library membership period
(D) Send a list of attendees

Questions 11-15 refer to the following information and e-mail.

Associated Flight Corporation (AFC)
Intern Program

AFC offers internships throughout the year. Currently, AFC's IT and Communications Departments are seeking new interns.

To qualify for an intern position, applicants must:
- be finishing up their last year of university study;
- fill out an application form;
- submit a résumé and a recommendation letter from a university professor

Interns will contribute to current projects along with AFC professionals. Interns are also expected to meet deadlines, successfully work with their department members, and work independently.

Visit www.afc.au/applications to download the application form. Mail the completed application and required documents to Mr. Neil Devinish, Human Resources Director, AFC, 9 Dunbar Road, Melbourne 3004, Australia.

Note: The selection process can take up to six weeks, as all submitted applications are carefully examined by the Hiring Committee. Applications are kept in the AFC database for two years from the date it was received.

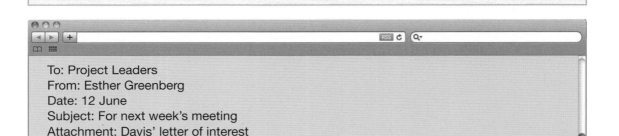

To: Project Leaders
From: Esther Greenberg
Date: 12 June
Subject: For next week's meeting
Attachment: Davis' letter of interest

Dear all,

Beginning 23 August, Vanessa Davis will be joining our team as an intern. Vanessa, who possesses a good command over the German language, will be involved in interpretation work as well as undertaking other assignments for our department.

I am attaching Vanessa's letter of interest that she sent with her application form. Please read it over, and for our June 19 meeting, be prepared to discuss how we can effectively use Vanessa's skills during the six months she will work with us. After the meeting, I plan on informing Vanessa of the types of projects she will be working on.

Thank you,

Esther Greenberg
Director of Communications

11. According to the information, what must interns be able to do?

(A) Work as part of a team
(B) Plan a work schedule .
(C) Write reports in German
(D) Use IT software programs

12. What is indicated about the internship
고난도 applications?

(A) They must have applicants' work samples attached.
(B) They are retained in a database for up to six weeks.
(C) They are read by a panel of AFC staff members.
(D) They must be uploaded to the AFC Web site.

13. What is the purpose of the e-mail?
고난도
(A) To ask for assistance in designating work to a temporary employee
(B) To request managers to send proposals to Ms. Davis
(C) To announce changes in Ms. Greenberg's working hours
(D) To notify supervisors that a meeting time has been changed

14. In the e-mail, the word "command" in paragraph 1, line 2, is closest in meaning to

(A) instruction
(B) appreciation
(C) respect
(D) mastery

15. What is suggested about Ms. Davis?
고난도
(A) She has been asked to resubmit her application package.
(B) She has applied to work in the IT Department.
(C) She is set to work at AFC for a year.
(D) She is currently a university student.

삼중 지문

서로 연계되어 있는 지문 3개를 활용해 5문제가 출제된다. 각 지문에 대한 문제를 묻기도 하지만 지문 2개 나 3개를 함께 봐야 정답을 찾을 수 있는 연계 문제도 보통 2문제씩 출제된다.

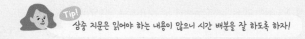

Tip!
삼중 지문은 읽어야 하는 내용이 많으니 시간 배분을 잘 하도록 하자!

🔍 지문·질문 유형 확인하기

1. 잘 나오는 지문 조합

Web page + E-mail + Notice
▶ 특정 정보 웹페이지 + 문의 이메일 + 공고문

E-mail + Letter + Schedule
▶ 업무 요청 이메일 + 이메일에 대한 답변 + 일정표

Notice + E-mail + Form (Invoice, Invitation, Survey, Itinerary, etc.)
▶ 공고문 + 문의 이메일 + 송장

Article + Review + Letter
▶ 특정 주제 기사 + 해당 주제에 대한 평론 + 문의 편지

Information / Advertisement + Online review + E-mail / Letter
▶ 식당, 영화, 여행 등의 정보/광고 + 해당 정보에 관한 온라인 평 + 문의 이메일/편지

2. 잘 나오는 질문 유형

▶ 각 지문의 주제나 목적 또는 지문에서 언급되는 인물 등 전반적인 정보 관련 질문

▶ 사실 정보를 확인하는 NOT/TRUE 문제 등의 세부 정보 질문

▶ 지문 2개나 3개를 연계하여 특정 내용을 추론하는 질문

▶ 동의어를 묻는 질문

3. 독해 전략

▶ 보통 1번과 2번 문제는 첫 번째 지문과 두 번째 지문에 대해 묻는 유형이므로 두 지문을 읽고 1번과 2번까지 푼다.

▶ 3번부터 5번까지는 연계 질문이 보통 1~2 문제 분포되어 있는 구간이므로, 세 번째 지문을 1번과 2번 문제를 푼 시점에 읽고 3번, 4번, 5번의 순으로 문제를 푼다.

▶ 연계형 문제를 풀기 위해서는 전체적으로 지문이 어떤 흐름을 가지고 연결되어 있는지를 볼 필요가 있으며, 두 개 이상의 지문에서 고유명사나 사람, 날짜, 요일 따위가 겹치는 경우에는 특히 신경 써서 봐야 한다.

▶ 전체적인 내용이 종합되어야 풀 수 있는 추론형 문제가 많으므로, 독해를 모두 할 생각으로 접근하는 것이 바람직하다.

▶ 종합하자면 지문 1, 지문 2 → 1번, 2번 문제 → 지문 3 → 3번, 4번, 5번 문제 순으로 접근하는 것이 가장 좋다.

Questions 1-5 refer to the following Web page, order form, and e-mail.

http://www.metropolitancleaners.com

| Home | Services | Receive a Quote | Contact Us |

• 웹사이트 서비스 탭

Make Your Home Like New Again!

• 청소 팀 특징

Our team of professional cleaners has over 20 years of experience. Our staff is fast, efficient, and thorough; we can ❶ assure that our work is top-notch. From condos to office buildings, we can make any space seem new again!

Our basic rates* are:
2 cleaners = $60; 3 cleaners = $110; 4 cleaners = $150; ❸ 5 cleaners = $170
*Note: A one-hour minimum is required

• 청소 요금 안내

Every residence and office is different, so rates are subject to change depending on the amount of work needed. For more detailed pricing information, just fill out the work request form as completely as possible.

• 주의사항 및 요청

Spring Cleaning Event: ❹ Arrange a time Monday to Friday to get a coupon good for 10 percent off your next purchase at Smithy's Grocery Store.

Metropolitan Cleaners Work Request Form	
Request date	Tuesday, April 17
Full Name	Gary Daniels
E-mail	g_daniels@softcreek.ca
Phone Number	(414) – 555 – 4547
Business Name (If applicable)	Softcreek Rental Cabins
Address to be cleaned	604 E. Moonside Ln., Appleton, WI 54911
Appointment	May 7
Work Request	2 lakeside cabins: one is 500 square feet and one story, and one is 1,800 square feet and two stories.
Comments	I'm preparing my rental cabins for the summer season. ❷ Both contain a lot of glasses and dinnerware, so please be very careful. I've also contacted several other cleaning agencies to get the best deal. Although I indicated May 7 as the day of the cleaning, ❹ I'd prefer that you come sooner—so long as I still get the voucher mentioned on your home page.

• 요청서 (요청일, 이름, 연락처, 사업체명, 주소, 요청사항 등)

To: Gary Daniels
From: Nadia Baxter
Date: April 18
Subject: Your appointment
Attachment: Estimate for #302445-TLM33.rtf

• 수신인
• 발신인
• 날짜
• 제목
• 첨부파일

Thank you for contacting Metropolitan Cleaners. Based on our experience cleaning homes of similar size to your cabins, two workers would be unable to finish in a day, even for the smaller cabin. Attached is the itemized estimate ❸ for five cleaners, cleaning supplies and equipment, and a fixed transportation fee. Please be aware that the pricing does not include any outdoor cleaning. Also, ❺ we have an opening in our schedule eight days before your requested cleaning date. This would still qualify you for our promotional event. If you have any questions about the estimate, please call our office at 414-555-1824. Once you have approved the pricing, we will confirm a date and details of the cleaning.

• 요청서에 대한 답장 (고지사항 안내)

Sincerely,

Nadia Baxter
Metropolitan Cleaners

1. On the Web page, the word "assure" in paragraph 1, line 2, is closest in meaning to

(A) convince
(B) secure
(C) promote
(D) promise

2. What does Mr. Daniels mention about his cabins?

(A) They are closed during spring.
(B) They have fragile items.
(C) They are all rented out.
(D) They have been renovated recently.

3. If Mr. Daniels uses Metropolitan Cleaners, what is the basic hourly payment he will most likely pay?

고난도

(A) $60
(B) $110
(C) $150
(D) $170

4. What is suggested about Mr. Daniels?

(A) He is planning to travel during the summer.
(B) He wants to hire an experienced landscaping company.
(C) He will construct more cabins in Appleton.
(D) He would like a weekday cleaning scheduled.

5. According to Ms. Baxter, what can her company do?

(A) Clean earlier than anticipated
(B) Lower the cost of a service
(C) Offer a list of customer testimonials
(D) Take some measurements

해석 및 해설

1. 웹페이지의 첫 번째 단락, 두 번째 줄의 "assure"와 의미상 가장 가까운 것은
(A) 설득하다
(B) 확보하다
(C) 홍보하다
(D) 약속하다

해설 '우리 회사의 작업이 일류라고 장담할 수 있다'는 확신의 의미를 가지고 있으므로 (D) promise와 바꿔 쓰기에 가장 적절하다.

2. Mr. Daniels는 오두막들에 대해 뭐라고 언급하는가?
(A) 봄에는 폐쇄한다.
(B) 깨지기 쉬운 물건들이 있다.
(C) 모두 이미 임대되었다.
(D) 최근 보수했다.

해설 작업 요청서에서 유리들과 식기류들을 많이 가지고 있기 때문에 특별히 조심해 달라고 당부를 하고 있다. 따라서 (B)가 정답이다.

3. 만약 Mr. Daniels가 Metropolitan 청소 회사를 이용한다면 지불하게 될 시간당 기본 요금은 어떻게 되는가?
고난도
(A) 60달러
(B) 110달러
(C) 150달러
(D) 170달러

해설 이메일에서 2명의 직원으로는 하루에 마칠 수 없기 때문에 5명의 직원을 고용할 것을 권장하고 있고 웹페이지에서 5명의 청소부 고용은 170달러이므로 정답은 (D)이다.

4. Mr. Daniels에 대해 무엇을 알 수 있는가?
(A) 여름에 여행을 할 계획이다.
(B) 경험 많은 조경 회사를 고용하고 싶어한다.
(C) Appleton에 더 많은 오두막을 지을 것이다.
(D) 주중에 청소 스케줄을 잡기 원한다.

해설 웹페이지 마지막 단락에서 월~금 중에 청소를 예약하면 Smithy's 식료품점에서 쓸 수 있는 10% 할인 쿠폰을 받을 수 있음을 알 수 있고, 주문 양식에서 Mr. Daniels는 할인 쿠폰을 받을 수 있도록 주중 청소 스케줄을 원하는 것을 유추할 수 있다. 따라서 정답은 (D)이다.

5. Mr. Baxter에 의하면, 그녀의 회사는 무엇을 할 수 있는가?
(A) 예상보다 더 일찍 청소를 시작한다
(B) 서비스 비용을 깎아준다
(C) 고객들의 후기 목록을 제공한다
(D) 치수를 측정한다

해설 이메일에서 Mr. Daniels가 요청한 날짜보다 8일 빠른 날에 청소를 진행할 수 있다고 하고 있고, 그 다음 내용에서 여전히 할인 쿠폰을 받을 수 있다고 하고 있으므로 정답은 (A)이다.

Questions 1-5 refer to the following advertisement, e-mail, and article.

Bayside Tower

Construction on Bayside Tower is nearing completion.
There are still residential, business, and commercial spaces available for purchase or rent.
Bayside Tower is expected to open its doors on May 1.

Bayside Tower will be the city of Piedmont's biggest building upon opening. Located downtown on the waterfront and across from the Westside Mall, Bayside Tower is ideally located for your business and personal needs.

Apartments (Floors 10-25) Residences have one, two, or three bedrooms, each of which comes with a kitchen, a living room, and one or two bathrooms. Furnished and unfurnished apartments are available.

Offices (Floors 2-9, Floors 26-40) Office spaces for small, medium, and large companies. A wide variety of layouts are available.

Retail Stores (Floor 1) Spaces for several small and medium shops. Some spots are available for restaurants.

Call 508-4444 for more information. Prices available upon request.

To	Jacob Nelson <jnelson@wilmington.com>
From	Karen Hester <karenh@baysideproperties.com>
Subject	Bayside Tower
Date	April 18

Dear Mr. Nelson,

Thank you for your inquiry regarding the apartments available at Bayside Tower. We still have several units available that would be perfect for you and your family. You indicated you are interested in a three-bedroom apartment since you and your wife have two children. The price to purchase one of these apartments is $350,000 while you can rent one for $2,500 a month. Should you decide to rent, you must sign a contract for a minimum of two years.

Since you work at the Westside Mall, it should be easy to meet for us to take a tour of an apartment. Just let me know when you have time to visit Bayside Tower, and I can meet you at the front entrance. My office is in Bayside Tower, so I am available all throughout the day. Feel free to call me at 481-0498 during regular business hours.

Sincerely,

Karen Hester
Bayside Properties

Piedmont (May 2) – The long-awaited opening of Bayside Tower happened yesterday on May 1. There were a large number of festivities, including a ribbon-cutting ceremony attended by Mayor Chip Taylor and other prominent individuals.

Construction on Bayside Tower took more than five years. Many in the community believed it would never be completed due to a variety of issues concerning the tower. Its original owner, Marge Hamel, had to sell the property due to financial difficulties. Then, there were several construction accidents during which the building was repeatedly damaged. The bad luck continued even on the opening day, when a water pipe burst at one of the building's restaurants.

Nevertheless, the building is now complete and open for business. More than 95 percent of its apartments have been sold or rented, and 99 percent of its office space is occupied. This means more than 2,000 individuals either live or work in the tower, which makes it one of the busiest buildings in the city.

1. What is indicated about Bayside Tower?

(A) It has 25 floors.
(B) It has three floors of retail stores.
(C) It is near a shopping center.
(D) It has its own security team.

2. According to the advertisement, what is NOT available for rent?

(A) Space for a restaurant
(B) Office space
(C) Residential space
(D) Space for a school

3. Why did Ms. Hester write to Mr. Nelson?

(A) To explain how to rent an office in Bayside Tower
(B) To confirm an appointment to see an apartment
(C) To ask about signing a contract for a lease
(D) To respond to a customer's question

4. What is suggested about Mr. Nelson's workplace?

(A) It is located in Bayside Tower.
(B) It is in a suburb of Piedmont.
(C) It is across the street from Bayside Tower.
(D) It has recently moved to Piedmont.

5. According to the article, which floor encountered a problem?

(A) The basement floor
(B) The first floor
(C) The second floor
(D) The tenth floor

Questions 6-10 refer to the following Web pages.

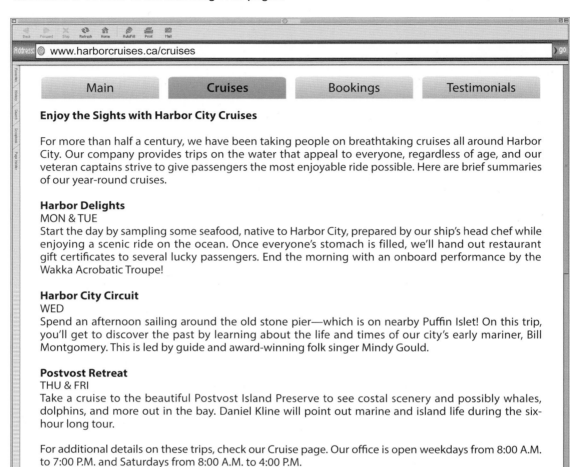

www.harborcruises.ca/cruises

| Main | Cruises | Bookings | Testimonials |

Enjoy the Sights with Harbor City Cruises

For more than half a century, we have been taking people on breathtaking cruises all around Harbor City. Our company provides trips on the water that appeal to everyone, regardless of age, and our veteran captains strive to give passengers the most enjoyable ride possible. Here are brief summaries of our year-round cruises.

Harbor Delights
MON & TUE
Start the day by sampling some seafood, native to Harbor City, prepared by our ship's head chef while enjoying a scenic ride on the ocean. Once everyone's stomach is filled, we'll hand out restaurant gift certificates to several lucky passengers. End the morning with an onboard performance by the Wakka Acrobatic Troupe!

Harbor City Circuit
WED
Spend an afternoon sailing around the old stone pier—which is on nearby Puffin Islet! On this trip, you'll get to discover the past by learning about the life and times of our city's early mariner, Bill Montgomery. This is led by guide and award-winning folk singer Mindy Gould.

Postvost Retreat
THU & FRI
Take a cruise to the beautiful Postvost Island Preserve to see costal scenery and possibly whales, dolphins, and more out in the bay. Daniel Kline will point out marine and island life during the six-hour long tour.

For additional details on these trips, check our Cruise page. Our office is open weekdays from 8:00 A.M. to 7:00 P.M. and Saturdays from 8:00 A.M. to 4:00 P.M.

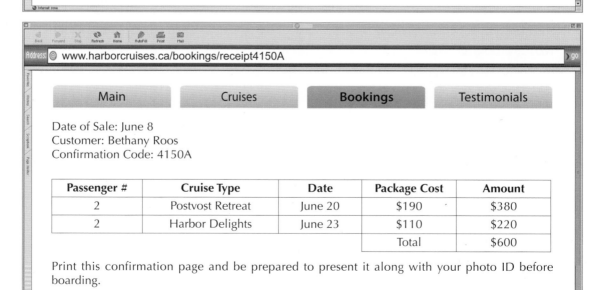

www.harborcruises.ca/bookings/receipt4150A

| Main | Cruises | Bookings | Testimonials |

Date of Sale: June 8
Customer: Bethany Roos
Confirmation Code: 4150A

Passenger #	Cruise Type	Date	Package Cost	Amount
2	Postvost Retreat	June 20	$190	$380
2	Harbor Delights	June 23	$110	$220
			Total	$600

Print this confirmation page and be prepared to present it along with your photo ID before boarding.

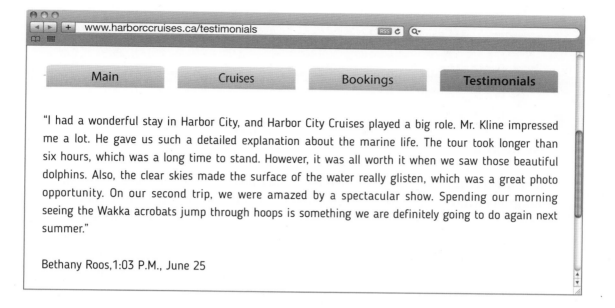

"I had a wonderful stay in Harbor City, and Harbor City Cruises played a big role. Mr. Kline impressed me a lot. He gave us such a detailed explanation about the marine life. The tour took longer than six hours, which was a long time to stand. However, it was all worth it when we saw those beautiful dolphins. Also, the clear skies made the surface of the water really glisten, which was a great photo opportunity. On our second trip, we were amazed by a spectacular show. Spending our morning seeing the Wakka acrobats jump through hoops is something we are definitely going to do again next summer."

Bethany Roos,1:03 P.M., June 25

6. What is NOT implied about Harbor City Cruises?

 고난도

(A) It has been operating for over five decades.
(B) It employs experienced guides.
(C) Senior citizens are welcome to join its activities.
(D) It is an award-winning company.

7. When can passengers learn about local history?

(A) On Mondays and Tuesdays
(B) On Wednesdays
(C) On Thursdays and Fridays
(D) On Saturdays

8. What was part of Ms. Roos' June 23 trip?

고난도

(A) Seeing a concert
(B) Going to a farm
(C) Completing a customer survey
(D) Trying local dishes

9. What does Ms. Roos imply in the testimonial?

고난도

(A) The Postvost Retreat cruise had no photo opportunities.
(B) The Harbor Delights cruise carried many passengers.
(C) The Postvost Retreat cruise ended late.
(D) The Harbor Delights cruise had a knowledgeable guide.

10. According to the testimonial, what will Ms. Roos most likely do next year?

(A) Enroll in a cooking class
(B) Visit an aquarium
(C) Tour an island preserve
(D) Watch a performance

Questions 11-15 refer to the following e-mail, review, and article.

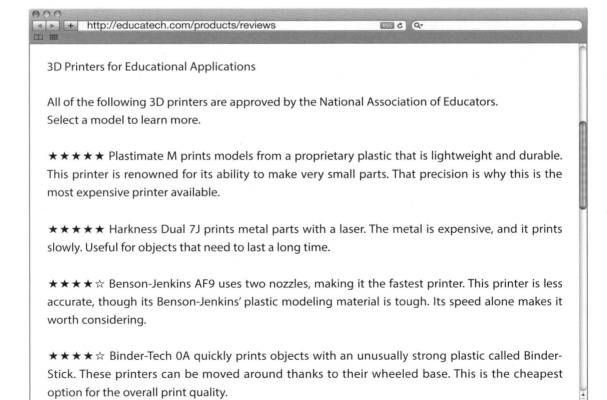

To	Roberta Moss
From	Jared Smith
Date	Monday, April 5
Subject	New Machine

Dear Roberta,

There are a couple of things we need to consider before we buy a machine for our startup company. Our business plan involves supplying 3D printed materials to classrooms without requiring minimum orders. We're going to need an affordable printer that can easily travel with us when we give demo presentations to show potential clients how our technology works. Check out the reviews on educatech.com to see if you can find a product that meets our needs. Let me know what you learn, and we can work it into our budget.

Jared

---

http://educatech.com/products/reviews

3D Printers for Educational Applications

All of the following 3D printers are approved by the National Association of Educators. Select a model to learn more.

★★★★★ Plastimate M prints models from a proprietary plastic that is lightweight and durable. This printer is renowned for its ability to make very small parts. That precision is why this is the most expensive printer available.

★★★★★ Harkness Dual 7J prints metal parts with a laser. The metal is expensive, and it prints slowly. Useful for objects that need to last a long time.

★★★★☆ Benson-Jenkins AF9 uses two nozzles, making it the fastest printer. This printer is less accurate, though its Benson-Jenkins' plastic modeling material is tough. Its speed alone makes it worth considering.

★★★★☆ Binder-Tech 0A quickly prints objects with an unusually strong plastic called Binder-Stick. These printers can be moved around thanks to their wheeled base. This is the cheapest option for the overall print quality.

Educational Startup "Hand Outs"

By Carol Hernandez

November 2 — Scan any recent educational catalog, and you'll see them: companies advertising educational materials made with 3D printers. These businesses transform classrooms into miniature factories. They allow students to dream up, design, and deliver (the 3 "D"s) their projects. Educational projects and lesson plans themselves are usually provided for free; however, companies then charge for special parts and 3D printer usage. Some, like ProEd 3D focus on large deals, often with entire school districts, of more than 150 kits per order. Another is Grab-itate, which makes high-end supplies in batches of as few as 10. Finally, Fun-D-Mental and Beta-ED, which have been around for seven months and three years respectively, will make classroom materials for even one student if need be.

---

11. What is mentioned about the Plastimate M?

(A) It is capable of creating fine details.
(B) It is popular for its classic design.
(C) It is smaller than most printers.
(D) It is made of many complicated parts.

12. What do all of the printers listed on the Web page have in common?
고난도

(A) They can be easily carried.
(B) They are very fast.
(C) They produce durable items.
(D) They are quite affordable.

13. What 3D printer did Ms. Moss most likely recommend to Mr. Smith?
고난도

(A) The Plastimate M
(B) The Harkness Dual 7J
(C) The Benson-Jenkins AF9
(D) The Binder-Tech 0A

14. In the article, the word "scan" in paragraph 1, line 1, is closest in meaning to

(A) browse
(B) mark
(C) focus on
(D) pass over

15. What business do Ms. Moss and Mr. Smith most likely work for?
고난도

(A) ProEd 3D
(B) Grab-itate
(C) Fun-D-Mental
(D) Beta-ED

REVIEW TEST

Questions 1-2 refer to the following receipt.

Petty Cash Receipt	
Date: 7 August	
Name (please print): Hannah Gould	
DESCRIPTION	**AMOUNT**
This is to provide for food, transportation, and lodging for the 9-11 August Medical Expo in Brussels where I will present our latest research.	£1,150
I acknowledge the receipt of the amount above.	
Signature: *Hannah Gould*	

1. What will Ms. Gould do in Brussels in August?

(A) Promote a product
(B) Tour a research facility
(C) Give a lecture
(D) Negotiate a contract

2. What does Ms. Gould acknowledge?

(A) Paying a registration fee
(B) Buying health insurance
(C) Receiving an allowance
(D) Making a donation

Questions 3-4 refer to the following text message chain.

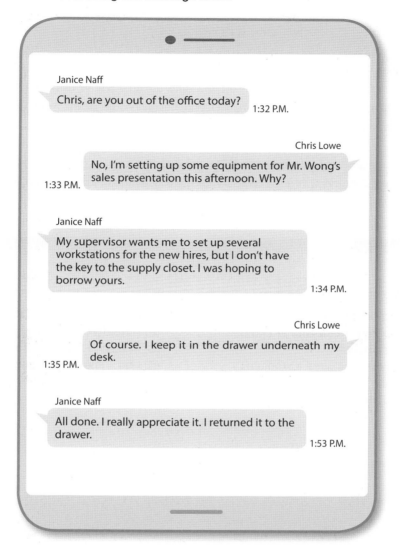

Janice Naff

Chris, are you out of the office today?

1:32 P.M.

Chris Lowe

No, I'm setting up some equipment for Mr. Wong's sales presentation this afternoon. Why?

1:33 P.M.

Janice Naff

My supervisor wants me to set up several workstations for the new hires, but I don't have the key to the supply closet. I was hoping to borrow yours.

1:34 P.M.

Chris Lowe

Of course. I keep it in the drawer underneath my desk.

1:35 P.M.

Janice Naff

All done. I really appreciate it. I returned it to the drawer.

1:53 P.M.

3. What department does Mr. Lowe probably work in?

(A) Sales
(B) Maintenance
(C) Personnel
(D) Accounting

4. At 1:35 P.M., what does Mr. Lowe mean when he writes, "Of course"?

(A) He approves of an office layout.
(B) He will review a presentation for Mr. Naff.
(C) He thinks a schedule is feasible.
(D) He will permit Ms. Naff to take his key.

Public Alert:

Renovation work will begin at Chisholm Stadium on December 6 and finish on December 22. While the stadium itself will host several events during this time, all parking areas will be unavailable. Visitor entry will be restricted to the South Gate, as the North Gate will be closed for repairs.

Next year, extra concession areas will be installed. The second and third levels will be closed from February 2 through February 10. The concession area work is the final phase of the planned upgrades to the stadium.

5. What is the purpose of the notice?

(A) To describe changes to a stadium
(B) To encourage readers to attend a sports competition
(C) To notify the public of a stadium reopening
(D) To announce an increase in parking fees

6. What are visitors asked to do?

(A) Use public transportation
(B) Attend a community meeting
(C) Purchase tickets in advance
(D) Use a specific entrance

Questions 7-8 refer to the following Web page.

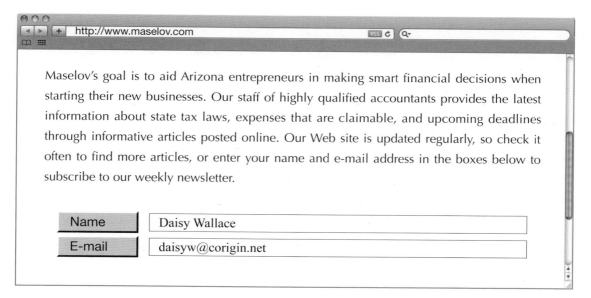

7. For whom is the Web page mainly intended?

(A) New business owners
(B) Tax experts
(C) Financial advisors
(D) Corporate lawyers

8. What is implied about Ms. Wallace?

(A) She will be sent a publication.
(B) Her paperwork needs to be revised.
(C) She works for Maselov.
(D) Her name will be added to a directory.

The Livingston Talent Agency, with seven locations throughout metro Los Angeles, is proud to represent people of all ages and is committed to training and promoting artistically-gifted community members. Created by a group of agents with a mission to discover and foster the next generation of actors and musicians, the Livingston Talent Agency is committed to building the best career for every one of its aspiring performers. —[1]—. All of our 74 staff members live and work in this area. —[2]—. Also, more than 90 percent of our work assignments are located right here in Los Angeles, thanks to the strong reputation of our training process. —[3]—. With the Livingston Talent Agency, your future is in the hands of an agency that has been in the business for half a century. —[4]—.

9. Where would the information most likely appear?

(A) In a local business directory
(B) In a company training manual
(C) In a pamphlet for potential clients
(D) In a handbook for talent agents

10. How long has the agency been in operation?

(A) For 7 years
(B) For 50 years
(C) For 74 years
(D) For 90 years

11. In which of the positions marked [1], [2], [3], and [4] does the following sentence best belong?

"Many of them are involved in a variety of performing arts education programs at our local schools."

(A) [1]
(B) [2]
(C) [3]
(D) [4]

Questions 12-14 refer to the following letter.

August 6

Ms. Julia Norell, Branch Manager
Hotshots Coffee Shops
841 2nd Avenue
Woods Cross, UT 84010

Dear Ms. Norell,

This fall, Hotshots will produce a series of advertisements for its brand new seasonal beverages and merchandise. The campaign kicks off September 1 and continues through November 1. The ads will appear in the *Salado Tribune* and the *Lago Gazette* newspapers, as well as on their Web sites.

At first, we thought about creating a radio ad, but decided to forego that option because of the tight deadline. However, we are going to create a video commercial for online audiences later in October.

Included are store leaflets and posters for your reference. If you have any comments or feedback, you can get in touch with me at any time.

James McAllister, VP Sales
Hotshots Coffee Shops

Enclosures

12. When will Hotshots Coffee Shops begin to advertise the new products?

(A) In August
(B) In September
(C) In October
(D) In November

13. According to the letter, what kind of advertisements will Hotshots Coffee Shops do without?

(A) Newspaper
(B) Radio
(C) Online
(D) Print

14. What has Mr. McAllister sent with the letter?

(A) Promotional materials
(B) Item samples
(C) An original receipt
(D) A survey

Questions 15-17 refer to the following e-mail.

To: staff@frostybeachcafé.com
From: Guy Kojiki
Date: May 2
Subject: Summer drinks

Hello all,

With spring ending, the upcoming summer months will give us more opportunities to increase our sales figures. To get off to a good start, we will hold our very first frozen drink competition. Workers will be invited to invent fun and unique recipes to be sold by Frosty Beach Café from June to August. The top three winners will get two free tickets to a concert of their choice at the newly renovated Sandy Performance Center, just a five-minute walk away.

Fill out an entry form and put it in the submission box in the break room. Recipes will be evaluated based on how they taste, the low price of ingredients, and how easy they are to make.

I look forward to your ideas!

15. What is the purpose of the e-mail?

(A) To discuss recent sales
(B) To promote a new drink brand
(C) To thank employees for their hard work
(D) To announce a contest

16. What is indicated about the Sandy Performance Center?

(A) It provides seasonal discounts.
(B) It changed ownership in the spring.
(C) It is close to the café.
(D) It features famous artists.

17. What is NOT mentioned as a requirement for a good product?

(A) Having a nice flavor
(B) Being simple to prepare
(C) Being a certain color
(D) Having affordable ingredients

3 April

Ravi Patel
206 Argos Circle
Cape Town, South Africa 7974

Mr. Patel,

It is a pleasure to inform you that you have been accepted to Detrich-Barnes Law Firm's 3-month internship program. —[1]—. We plan to have you begin on Wednesday, June 1. However, if you have other obligations, we are able to be somewhat flexible regarding the exact starting day. As the time draws closer, let's revisit this since it may be difficult for you to predict your exact schedule at this point. —[2]—.

We have assigned you to work under the management of Lisa Truman, Senior Director of the International Law Department, to aid in developing approaches to pursue matters related to medical insurance. Ms. Truman recently told me that she noticed your story in the *Journal of Medical Ethics* and that she found it very informative. —[3]—.

We would appreciate it if you could look over the enclosed contract and send it back, signed and dated, by 19 April. After we receive it, Janet Foss in Personnel will contact you to provide further information about transportation and lodging for the summer, as well as getting an official e-mail account. —[4]—.

Sincerely,

José Luciano
Personnel Manager
Detrich-Barnes Law Firm

Enclosure

18. What aspect of Mr. Patel's internship is NOT mentioned?

(A) The project he will be assigned to
(B) His work period
(C) His manager's name
(D) The pay he will receive

19. What does the letter indicate about Ms. Truman?

(A) She conducted Mr. Patel's interview.
(B) She read Mr. Patel's article.
(C) She supervises Mr. Luciano's staff.
(D) She is a well-known attorney.

20. What will Mr. Patel probably do next?

(A) Discuss a starting date
(B) Set up a time to meet with Ms. Truman
(C) Log on to an e-mail account
(D) Return some paperwork to Mr. Luciano

21. In which of the positions marked [1], [2], [3], and [4] does the following sentence best belong?

"I am sure that you will be a great asset to her team."

(A) [1]
(B) [2]
(C) [3]
(D) [4]

Questions 22-25 refer to the following e-mail.

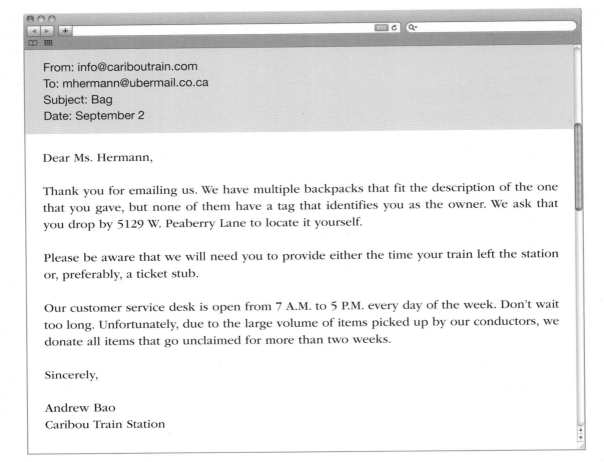

From: info@cariboutrain.com
To: mhermann@ubermail.co.ca
Subject: Bag
Date: September 2

Dear Ms. Hermann,

Thank you for emailing us. We have multiple backpacks that fit the description of the one that you gave, but none of them have a tag that identifies you as the owner. We ask that you drop by 5129 W. Peaberry Lane to locate it yourself.

Please be aware that we will need you to provide either the time your train left the station or, preferably, a ticket stub.

Our customer service desk is open from 7 A.M. to 5 P.M. every day of the week. Don't wait too long. Unfortunately, due to the large volume of items picked up by our conductors, we donate all items that go unclaimed for more than two weeks.

Sincerely,

Andrew Bao
Caribou Train Station

22. Where does Mr. Bao work?

(A) In a post office
(B) At a travel agency
(C) At a bag shop
(D) In a transportation center

23. What did Ms. Hermann most likely inquire about?

(A) Booking options
(B) Missing belongings
(C) Trip arrangements
(D) Discounted tickets

24. What will Ms. Hermann need to provide?

(A) Her home address
(B) Her departure information
(C) Her original destination
(D) Her full name

25. What is Ms. Hermann urged to do?

(A) Review a billing statement
(B) Check a Web site
(C) Sign a form
(D) Stop by an office soon

Questions 26-29 refer to the following online chat discussion.

Miles Higginson [8:42 A.M.]	Fellow travel reporters, can you help me? I'm getting sent on assignment to Clipper Island to check out Palm Town, Golden Point, and Tin Ridge.
Evan Paulson [8:52 A.M.]	My cousin recently visited Clipper Island. She said that the beaches were really spectacular.
Miles Higginson [8:54 A.M.]	That's what everybody says. I've heard that it's really easy to get around since it's so small. Do you think I can just use a bicycle? Or should I drive a rental car while I'm there?
Lexi Sardi [9:07 A.M.]	I rode a bicycle and saved a lot on gas when I was there. Every street has bike lanes, and bicycles are provided by the government free of charge.
Miles Higginson [9:13 A.M.]	Lexi, are the bicycles in Clipper Island easy to find?
Evan Paulson [9:26 A.M.]	Renting a car may be useful if you decide to visit the more remote side of the island, though.
Lexi Sardi [9:31 A.M.]	They're everywhere. Bicycle stations are located every 700m on most large streets.
Naomi Christensen [9:35 A.M.]	But if you're carrying around a lot of reporting gear, riding a bike can be a real challenge.
Miles Higginson [9:37 A.M.]	That's really convenient. Our city planners could learn a few things from their Clipper Island counterparts. Oh, and Naomi, I'm glad you pointed that out. That settles it; I'll rent.
Naomi Christensen [9:59 A.M.]	There are a few companies with kiosks at the airport that offer deals you can't get in the city. Be sure to check with them first.
Miles Higginson [10:06 A.M.]	I appreciate everyone's advice.

SEND

---

26. With whom has Mr. Higginson most likely been chatting?

(A) People who will give him a tour
(B) People who work at a rental agency
(C) People who reside in Clipper Island
(D) People who travel for work

27. Why has Mr. Higginson decided to rent a car?

(A) Because he will have a lot of equipment
(B) Because he does not know how to ride a bicycle
(C) Because there are no bicycle lanes at his destinations
(D) Because public transportation is unreliable

28. At 9:37 A.M., what does Mr. Higginson most likely mean when he writes, "Our city planners could learn a few things from their Clipper Island counterparts"?

(A) The bicycle rentals in his town are expensive.
(B) The bicycle lanes in his town are poorly designed.
(C) The bicycles stations in his town are located too far apart.
(D) The bicycles in his town are old.

29. What does Ms. Christensen indicate about the airport?

(A) It provides a cheap shuttle service to the city.
(B) Visitors can learn about special promotions there.
(C) It has information kiosks for tourists near the exit.
(D) Cars can only be rented there.

Questions 30-34 refer to the following e-mail and advertisement.

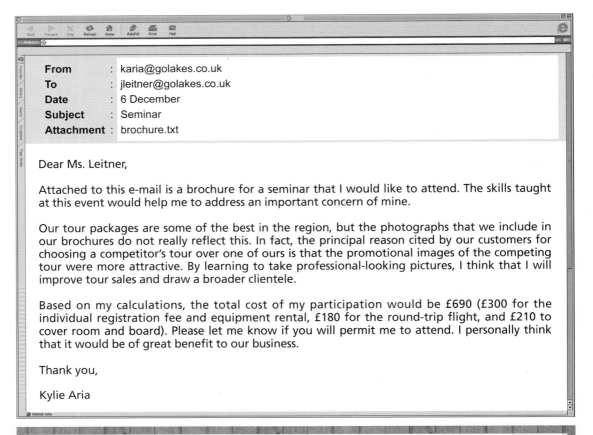

Dear Ms. Leitner,

Attached to this e-mail is a brochure for a seminar that I would like to attend. The skills taught at this event would help me to address an important concern of mine.

Our tour packages are some of the best in the region, but the photographs that we include in our brochures do not really reflect this. In fact, the principal reason cited by our customers for choosing a competitor's tour over one of ours is that the promotional images of the competing tour were more attractive. By learning to take professional-looking pictures, I think that I will improve tour sales and draw a broader clientele.

Based on my calculations, the total cost of my participation would be £690 (£300 for the individual registration fee and equipment rental, £180 for the round-trip flight, and £210 to cover room and board). Please let me know if you will permit me to attend. I personally think that it would be of great benefit to our business.

Thank you,

Kylie Aria

Skills Course: Guide to Being a Great Photographer

Wood Green Studio
79 Morlee St.
Wood Green, London

31 January -2 February
10 A.M. - 5 P.M.

This seminar is intended to instruct participants in beginner—and intermediate—level photography skills in a fun, supportive classroom environment. Whether you want to learn photography skills to improve your business's existing image portfolio or simply to become a better photographer, this seminar will prove useful.

This course will be led by Lyle Pershings, a professional with over 15 years' experience in landscape and studio photography. He has taken portraits of celebrities, done work with major advertisers, and even had a Westshore Gallery show here in London.

At Wood Green Studio, every participant in our courses receives personal guidance and feedback from our qualified instructors, high-quality textbooks, and additional exercises which may be completed at any time online.

A fee of £370 for registration and the necessary supplies will be charged for an individual applicant. Groups of more than three, however, are eligible for a £35-per-person discount. Visit www.woodgreenstudio.co.uk for more information.

30. What is the purpose of the e-mail?

(A) To promote a class
(B) To address a travel problem
(C) To ask for funding
(D) To suggest a new service

31. In the e-mail, the word "principal" in paragraph 2, line 2, is closest in meaning to

(A) basic
(B) top
(C) initial
(D) necessary

32. What is indicated about Ms. Aria?

(A) She would like to visit London.
(B) She recently designed a brochure.
(C) She will lead a tour in December.
(D) She teaches courses at a university.

33. What has Ms. Aria misunderstood about the course?

(A) The venue
(B) The topic
(C) The time
(D) The cost

34. What is suggested about Mr. Pershings?

(A) He teaches seminar attendees.
(B) He owns Wood Green Studio.
(C) He provides images to travel agencies.
(D) He currently works at Westshore Gallery.

To: Alan Turner <aturner@variant.com>
From: Juliet Miao <julietm@variant.com>
Date: May 17
Subject: Brief note

Dear Mr. Turner,

I am pleased that you selected me to participate in this summer's leadership training retreat for management positions at Variant Electric. Working as an on-site engineer has been a fantastic experience, and I hope that I will be chosen for a management role when the training is complete.

However, I do have one issue: I am taking a five-week evening class entitled *Organizational Responsibility through Teamwork*, which concludes on Tuesday, June 21. Since the retreat begins on Monday, June 20, I would have to miss the first two days. Is it okay for me to arrive at the retreat on Wednesday morning? I feel that this class will help me become a more effective manager, and I sincerely hope that I can still take part in the training.

Thank you for your time.

Sincerely,

Juliet Miao

To: Juliet Miao <julietm@variant.com>
From: Alan Turner <aturner@variant.com>
Date: May 17
Subject: Re: Brief Note

Dear Ms. Miao,

I appreciate you reaching out to me. Your class certainly sounds like it will be helpful in upper-level positions. I'm happy to report that due to our current staffing needs, Human Resources has scheduled two week-long training sessions instead of just one. The June 21 training will be followed by one beginning June 28. This should resolve any scheduling issue you might have had.

Once both training retreats have concluded, we will determine which candidates will move forward into the formal interview stage for leadership positions. Those decisions will be made by July 31 and selected candidates will be promoted on August 15.

Please contact my assistant at extension 512 to finalize your schedule.

Sincerely,

Alan Turner

35. What is a purpose of the first e-mail?

(A) To announce the completion of a management class
(B) To ask for scheduling flexibility from a university
(C) To accept an invitation for a training session
(D) To confirm that a certification has been received

36. What is indicated about the *Organizational Responsibility through Teamwork* class?

(A) It is related to the job of a manager.
(B) It is offered online for full-time employees.
(C) It is instructed by Mr. Turner.
(D) It is required for obtaining a diploma.

37. How long is a single training period?

(A) One week
(B) Two weeks
(C) One month
(D) Two months

38. When will Ms. Miao most likely participate in a Variant Electric gathering?

(A) On June 20
(B) On June 21
(C) On June 28
(D) On July 31

39. According to the second e-mail, what will happen on August 15?

(A) Some employees will have new roles.
(B) Managers will attend a business conference.
(C) A new leadership class will begin.
(D) A training workshop will end.

Questions 40-44 refer to the following Web page, e-mail, and survey.

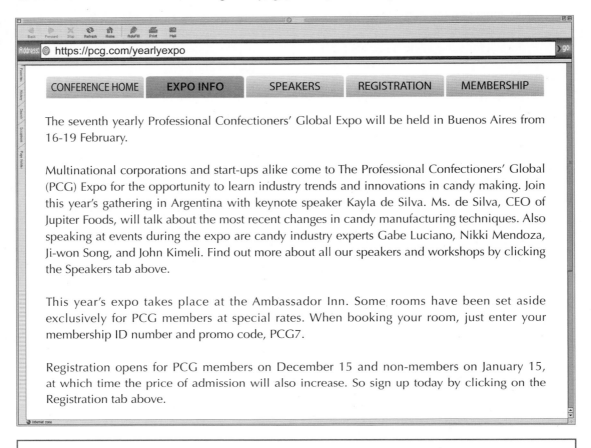

To: Nikki Mendoza <nmendoza@prochocolatier.co.ca>
From: Milo d'Antoni <mdantoni@pcg.com>
Subject: Info
Date: 22 Feb
Attachment: Response.doc

_____

Dear Ms. Mendoza,

Thank you for flying all the way to Argentina to present at the PCG Expo. It was an honor to meet you in person, and I would like to thank you again for your wonderful presentation on making hard candies. Everyone in attendance left with an appreciation for how easy it can be to make new and interesting tastes. Included with this e-mail is a response form given by Mr. Randy Fischer, and is representative of the attendees' reviews of your session.

Regards,

Milo d'Antoni
Chair, PCG Event Committee

Professional Confectioners' Global Expo Participant Survey

	★★★★	★★★	★★	★
Presentations	X			
Organization			X	
Location	X			
Meals	X			

Other comments:

Getting to the expo was quite hectic. Although I registered in early December, I received my travel information at the last minute, causing confusion about how to get from the airport to the venue. I was unable to attend the first morning's keynote speech and events because of this. However, the other presentations I was able to see were excellent. In particular, I liked the presentation given by the owner of Tutti's Hard Candy. I plan to use the techniques I learned in my own store.

Randy Fischer

40. What is indicated about the expo?

(A) Some participants will pay a reduced rate for accommodations.
(B) PCG members must register before January 15.
(C) It is only open to candy manufacturers.
(D) It has been held in Buenos Aires before.

41. What is the purpose of the e-mail?

(A) To submit a presentation proposal
(B) To inquire about a venue's location
(C) To give input on a session
(D) To request survey responses

42. In the e-mail, paragraph 1, line 3, the word "appreciation" is the closest in meaning to

(A) sympathy
(B) increase
(C) gratitude
(D) understanding

43. What is suggested about Mr. Fischer?

(A) He thought that the hotel was expensive.
(B) He was unable to attend the afternoon events.
(C) He could not listen to Ms. de Silva's talk.
(D) He did not complete his registration in time.

44. Which speaker did Mr. Fischer particularly like?

(A) Gabe Luciano
(B) Nikki Mendoza
(C) Ji-won Song
(D) John Kimeli

Alphalumen Star Computer Projector: Model LU-X

Stop wasting money buying a new projector every one to two years! Our top-selling model, the LU-X, is built with long-lasting aluminum and easy-to-clean glass.

Advantages: The powerful lamp and high-quality lens make this a state-of-the-art piece of equipment, perfect for demonstrations in all types of sales situations.

Warranty: Included is a five-year money-back guarantee on every projector we sell. That's our promise to you that this projector is built to operate for many years.

Retail price: £1,999.00
AL-S Member price: £1,499.00

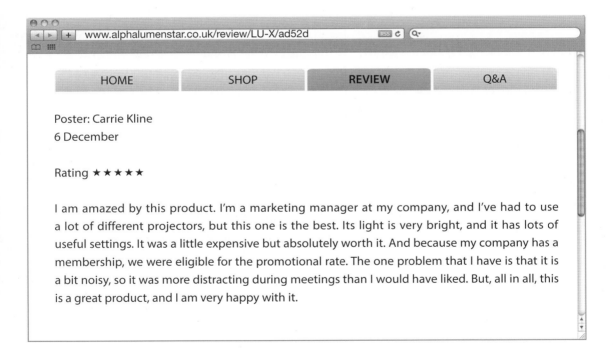

www.alphalumenstar.co.uk/review/LU-X/ad52d

| HOME | SHOP | REVIEW | Q&A |

Poster: Carrie Kline
6 December

Rating ★ ★ ★ ★ ★

I am amazed by this product. I'm a marketing manager at my company, and I've had to use a lot of different projectors, but this one is the best. Its light is very bright, and it has lots of useful settings. It was a little expensive but absolutely worth it. And because my company has a membership, we were eligible for the promotional rate. The one problem that I have is that it is a bit noisy, so it was more distracting during meetings than I would have liked. But, all in all, this is a great product, and I am very happy with it.

| HOME | SHOP | REVIEW | Q&A |

Poster: Alphalumen Star Customer Relations
7 December

We were pleased to see your positive review of the LU-X projector. User satisfaction is very important to us. Concerning the issue you are experiencing, we have a suggestion. Our LU-E model may suit your quiet office environment better. The LU-E is just as bright as the LU-X, but is built with a much smaller fan inside. This model's price, however, is slightly higher than that of the LU-X. Learn more about it by visiting www.alphalumenstar.co.uk/shop/lu-e.

45. What is NOT stated in the product description as a feature of the LU-X projector?

(A) It is popular.
(B) It is ideal for business presentations.
(C) It is long-lasting.
(D) It is brighter than other brands.

46. What is indicated in the customer review?

(A) Ms. Kline is satisfied with a purchase.
(B) Owners feel the LU-X is too heavy.
(C) Alphalumen Star's online store is easy to navigate.
(D) The LU-X's user guide is very helpful.

47. What is suggested about Ms. Kline?

(A) She presented at an expo on December 6.
(B) She has not tried using a projector before.
(C) She was charged £1,499 for the projector.
(D) She bought additional parts for the projector.

48. Why would the LU-E projector most likely be recommended as more suitable for Ms. Kline?

(A) It is cheap.
(B) It is portable.
(C) It is quiet.
(D) It is easy to update.

49. In the online response, the word "Concerning" in paragraph 1, line 2, is closest in meaning to

(A) Worrying
(B) Involving
(C) Regarding
(D) Comparing

Teich Arena to Hold Final CSF Event

Teich Arena has been closed for remodeling, but it will be done in time to hold the final round of the CSF Hockey Championship in Wien this December. While this renovation has been planned for several years, the chance to bring the championship here was a big motivation for finally getting it underway. Government officials confirm that construction is going according to plan, and they anticipate everything will be done well before the championship event.

Although Teich Arena is a regional landmark, it has never hosted a CSF event before and the arena's directors are pleased to host the final competition this year. The momentous event will be the public's first chance to see the completed renovations. Planners anticipate that the event will pull in thousands of hockey fans, and that Teich Arena will meet everybody's expectations. Teich Arena will comfortably hold 23,500 people, three times as many as before.

CSF Hockey Championship Quarterfinal Rounds			
England vs. Germany 4 December, 5 P.M., Toplitzbach Stadium, Salzburg	Austria vs. Italy 4 December, 8:30 P.M., Kulm Center, Graz	Sweden vs. France 5 December, 5 P.M., Haslach Center, Linz	Netherlands vs. Spain 5 December, 8:30 P.M., Oberalm Stadium, Wien
CSF Hockey Championship Semifinal Rounds			
Winning teams of 4 December games 8 December, 5:00 P.M., Kulm Center, Graz		Winning teams of December 5 games 8 December, 8:30 P.M., Haslach Center, Linz	

Final Round
Winning teams from 8 December
11 December, 5:30 P.M., Teich Arena, Wien
IMPORTANT: Be aware that seats for the final round will sell out quickly, so reserve yours before the semifinal rounds are decided. Only ticketholders will be permitted entry. No refunds.

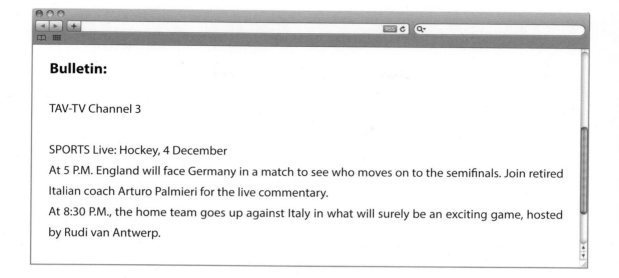

Bulletin:

TAV-TV Channel 3

SPORTS Live: Hockey, 4 December
At 5 P.M. England will face Germany in a match to see who moves on to the semifinals. Join retired Italian coach Arturo Palmieri for the live commentary.
At 8:30 P.M., the home team goes up against Italy in what will surely be an exciting game, hosted by Rudi van Antwerp.

50. In the article, the word "meet" in paragraph 2, line 10, is closest in meaning to

(A) contact
(B) greet
(C) satisfy
(D) join

51. What will be changed about Teich Arena?

(A) The seating capacity
(B) The parking availability
(C) The directors
(D) The admission fees

52. When will the first game be held at a new host venue?

(A) On December 4
(B) On December 5
(C) On December 8
(D) On December11

53. In the schedule, what are people advised to do?

(A) Arrive at a venue early
(B) Reserve seats right after the semifinal rounds end
(C) Ask for a refund before an event
(D) Purchase seats for a certain game as early as possible

54. Where will Mr. Palmieri report from?

(A) Salzburg
(B) Graz
(C) Linz
(D) Wien

HALF
TEST

HALF TEST 01

해설서 p.134 / 제한 시간 35분

1. A team manager was supposed to make sure that ------- of the employees received basic computer training.

(A) every
(B) either
(C) each
(D) much

2. The Board of Directors ------- the staff bonus after the company accounts are signed off on.

(A) will announce
(B) was announcing
(C) announced
(D) has announced

3. Many game developers ------- withdrawing their apps from Europe.

(A) have considered
(B) are considered
(C) will be considered
(D) considering

4. Our book is popular with readers ------- we give unbiased opinions of tourist attractions, restaurants, and hotels we visit.

(A) until
(B) because
(C) not only
(D) so that

5. The Hargrove Group routinely provides financial support to local nonprofit organizations that are ------- new buildings.

(A) investing
(B) centering
(C) constructing
(D) addressing

6. The company's forest managers are ------- to take courses on wildlife biology to get certification.

(A) trustworthy
(B) obliged
(C) promised
(D) engaged

7. Before he came to Paris, Mr. Bach had worked ------- a researcher in the Sydney Art Museum.

(A) over
(B) to
(C) on
(D) as

8. Tomorrow's seminar begins at 9:00 A.M. sharp, so attendees should try to be -------.

(A) punctual
(B) advanced
(C) instant
(D) sudden

9. The firm's CEO spoke only ------- at the anniversary celebration before departing for a business trip.

(A) briefly
(B) frequently
(C) usually
(D) constantly

10. All mail or packages that are ------- ten days after delivery may be returned to senders at the discretion of Postal Services.

(A) neglected
(B) unclaimed
(C) deleted
(D) rejected

11. Blackbird Media specializes in ------- managed live webinars, on-demand learning, and continuing education.

(A) professional
(B) professionals
(C) professionalism
(D) professionally

12. Customers who would like to offer comments or suggestions are welcome to do so ------- completing the feedback form.

(A) into
(B) over
(C) by
(D) from

13. A midsize design -------, Hawkeye & Horns specializes in making Web sites for local companies.

(A) firm
(B) program
(C) piece
(D) industry

14. If you are not entirely satisfied with your purchase, you ------- the unused item in its original packaging within 60 days.

(A) should be returned
(B) to be returned
(C) may return
(D) returning

15. ------- the occasional hot weather in summer, the climate in Tessa City is generally temperate.

(A) Even though
(B) Unless
(C) Opposing
(D) Except for

16. The company provides quality services and has won ------- a reputation as one of the best Asian food suppliers in the country.

(A) some
(B) theirs
(C) them
(D) itself

17. The Local Finance Board voted yesterday to approve the funding, most of ------- will be used to improve the city's aging water system.

(A) whom
(B) those
(C) that
(D) which

18. There are many factors to consider when determining whether to stay in your current office space or -------.

(A) transmit
(B) relocate
(C) deliver
(D) refer

19. Email Broadcast offers an immediate response, and you will see ------- links in your e-mails are getting the most clicks.

(A) who
(B) that
(C) when
(D) which

20. ------- aids should support the theme of the presentation without detracting by being too complicated or entertaining.

(A) Substantial
(B) Legal
(C) Financial
(D) Visual

International Association of Accountancy Professionals
254 Antilles Avenue
New York, NY 10013

Dear Ms. Mumtaz,

Thank you for your 15 July letter ------- about membership in the International Association of
                              21.
Accountancy Professionals. -------. So I am enclosing an application form for you.
                      22.

As you may know, we will hold our Annual North American Conference on 28 August in Palm

Springs, CA. If you decide to join the association this month, you will ------- for a special 20%
                                                    23.
reduction on the attendance fee for the conference.

If you wish to take advantage of this special offer, please inform the association ------- two
                                                                        24.
weeks prior to the conference.

Please do not hesitate to contact me if you have any questions.

Sincerely,

Herbert Groell
Herbert Groell
President, IAAP

---

21. (A) inquires
    (B) inquiring
    (C) inquired
    (D) to have inquired

22. (A) Our membership is full, so we cannot
        take any new members.
    (B) The application form should have
        arrived a few days ago.
    (C) I'm pleased to inform you that we are
        accepting new applications.
    (D) We are pleased to welcome you as
        our newest member.

23. (A) compete
    (B) reflect
    (C) serve
    (D) qualify

24. (A) so that
    (B) only if
    (C) in spite of
    (D) at least

Questions 25-28 refer to the following memo.

Date: Feb 12
To: All staff

Please assist us in reducing energy costs by cutting the unnecessary use of electricity in our offices. As you all know, the cost of electric power has increased significantly this year, so we all need to make an effort to cut costs. -------.
25.

Please switch off lights when not in -------. At the end of the working day, the last staff member
26.
to leave the office should check each room to ensure that all lights and all pieces of electronic equipment are turned off. It is also the responsibility of all staff members to switch off their computers ------- any personal electrical appliances such as humidifiers and under-desk heaters
27.
before leaving the office.

As ever, it is also ------- that photocopiers are turned off at the end of the day as these can be
28.
a fire hazard if left unattended overnight. The last person to leave the office is responsible for checking that copiers are switched off.

Sincerely,

Yuki Sakamoto
Manager, Facilities Management

25. (A) This can be done in a variety of ways.
    (B) There will be no electricity in the office tomorrow.
    (C) Our electric bills have decreased steadily.
    (D) We need ideas regarding what to do.

26. (A) usage
    (B) use
    (C) used
    (D) using

27. (A) and
    (B) despite
    (C) too
    (D) in addition

28. (A) timely
    (B) inefficient
    (C) productive
    (D) essential

Questions 29-30 refer to the following e-mail.

To	Sam Kravitz, Director of Marketing
From	Stephanie Fordham, Director of Customer Operations
Date	July 1
Subject	Milly Levy

Dear Sam,

I heard that your department has recently acquired a number of new clients and that you need to hire extra staff. I urge you to consider Milly Levy for a marketing assistant position on your social media team. She has been working as an intern in my department since last July, and has proven to be very competent. She is excellent at following instructions and has shown that she can work both independently and in a team. There has been very positive feedback on her work.

Ms. Levy received her degree in management just last month, and I know that she wishes to pursue a career in marketing here at the Creighton Group. Becoming a member of your team would certainly be ideal for her.

I would be more than happy to provide you with more information, so please feel free to email me with any questions.

Sincerely,

Stephanie Fordham
Director of Customer Operations
Creighton Group

29. What is the purpose of the e-mail?

(A) To announce a change in hiring policies
(B) To ask for an updated client list
(C) To propose a new project
(D) To make a recommendation

30. What does the e-mail indicate about Ms. Fordham?

(A) She has known Ms. Levy for one year.
(B) She has applied for a new job.
(C) She recently put together a team.
(D) She is a new client of Mr. Kravitz.

LFT Losing Customers

By Owen Nordman

Holland, 11 June — Results from a recent survey submitted by customers showed that LFT Rail is one of the least customer-friendly transport companies, with just 61 percent of travelers claiming they were satisfied with its service. The study, carried out by the ENC Research Group in May, reveals that LFT is still ahead of its main regional rival, Andros Rail, but compared to last year when LFT was rated number two, its position has dropped significantly.

"Although we have fallen behind some of our competitors, we are dedicated to dealing with our customers' concerns," commented LFT spokesperson Julius de Haan. "Starting next month, we plan on implementing certain procedural changes to ensure all our trains run according to schedule. Additionally, we are improving our customer service by introducing 25 new staff members who will be placed in various stations beginning in February next year."

The effectiveness of these measures to regain the confidence of consumers remains to be seen.

31. When did LFT conduct the customer survey?

(A) In February
(B) In March
(C) In May
(D) In July

32. What did the passengers most likely say about LFT?

(A) Its trains are overcrowded.
(B) Its ticket prices are too expensive.
(C) Its employees are not friendly.
(D) Its trains sometimes don't arrive on time.

33. What will LFT do next year?

(A) It will introduce new trains.
(B) It will add new train routes.
(C) It will hire more workers.
(D) It will merge with another company.

Questions 34-36 refer to the following job advertisement.

Independent Mining Company of Brazil (IMCB)
37 Riviera House · Sao Paulo · Brazil
www.imcb.br

VACANCY ANNOUNCEMENT

For 40 years, IMCB has been advising landowners in the use of proper mining methods. Our aim is to improve yields without compromising the mine workers' health or endangering the environment. We are a private organization headquartered in Sao Paulo, with additional branches in the Brazilian cities of Rio de Janeiro, Salvador, and Fortaleza.

We are currently seeking applications for the associate research director position. The successful candidate, who will be stationed in Rio de Janeiro, must demonstrate leadership and serve as a liaison between our managers of the Research Division and the Safety Department. He or she should have a background in health and safety, preferably in mining, and have at least three years' professional management experience.

If you are interested, please submit your cover letter and résumé by mail, in person, or through our Web site at www.imcb.br/careers. The application deadline is November 2. The successful candidate will be expected to start work on December 14.

---

34. What is indicated about IMCB?

(A) It is committed to the well-being of workers.
(B) It receives financial support from the government.
(C) It manufactures mining equipment.
(D) It is updating its corporate policies.

35. Where does IMCB have an open position?

(A) In Rio de Janeiro
(B) In Sao Paulo
(C) In Salvador
(D) In Fortaleza

36. What is NOT suggested about the position?

(A) It involves collaboration between departments.
(B) It requires managerial experience.
(C) It will be filled by the end of the year.
(D) It is limited to Brazilian nationals.

Questions 37-40 refer to the following online chat discussion.

Valarie Thayer [9:12 A.M.]
I want to discuss which computer monitor brand we should get. There are two choices: Avonetics and Procomp. I'd like to get everyone's input.

Jesse Hollis [9:13 A.M.]
Procomp is the company that makes those smart monitors, right?

Valarie Thayer [9:15 A.M.]
That's correct. But they're famous for their high-definition screens, which are ideal for when we make graphics and logos.

Jesse Hollis [9:16 A.M.]
Andrea, don't you have a Procomp monitor at home?

Andrea Garcia [9:19 A.M.]
I do, and I love it. It has such high resolution that it's easy to see fine details in pictures. I'm sure that it will help us produce better quality work for our clients.

Valarie Thayer [9:20 A.M.]
OK. Then I'm going to call their vendor this afternoon and place the order. We still have some funds left in the budget. Is there anything else we need?

Andrea Garcia [9:21 A.M.]
Our printer is running low on color ink right now. Usually, we order from Harnet, but they recently raised their prices. What do you think about asking Procomp to include some cartridges with the purchase?

Jesse Hollis [9:22 A.M.]
Well, with such a large order, I'm sure that Procomp would be willing to include some ink cartridges for free. I don't think it would be too much to ask.

Valarie Thayer [9:24 A.M.]
That's a good point. I will see what I can do when I call them. Right now, Andrea, could you finalize the order list and send it to me?

Andrea Garcia [9:25 A.M.]
I'll get on it.

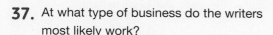
SEND

37. At what type of business do the writers most likely work?

(A) A software company
(B) An electronics store
(C) A design company
(D) An office supply store

38. What is mentioned about Procomp monitors?

(A) They can only be purchased online.
(B) They are affordable.
(C) They can display clear images.
(D) They are environmentally friendly.

39. What is suggested about Harnet?

(A) Ms. Garcia used to work there.
(B) It sells printer cartridges.
(C) Most of its employees use Procomp monitors.
(D) It has acquired a computer manufacturer.

40. At 9:25 A.M., what does Ms. Garcia mean when she writes, "I'll get on it"?

(A) She will update a Web site.
(B) She will carry out a request.
(C) She will contact a vendor.
(D) She will join a membership program.

Questions 41-45 refer to the following form and e-mail.

SECURITY ACCESS CODE (SAC) APPLICATION FORM

Send the completed form to Ms. Andrea Delgadillo, fax number 555-1924, or email a_delgadillo@ntel.gov.

SAC Recipient's Information:

Name: _Victoria Sherman_   **Department:** _Accounting_   **Employee ID Number:** _7745_

__ **Daily Access:** Monday through Friday, 7:00 A.M. – 7:00 P.M.

_X_ **Extended Access:** Monday through Friday, 7:00 A.M. – 10:00 P.M.

_X_ **Special Access** (Please fill in relevant days and time): _Saturdays, 10:00 A.M. – 7:00 P.M._

Building(s): __ Newport   _X_ Danes

Start Date: _October 7_   **End Date:** _November 2_

Requestor's Information (requestor must be either a manager or director of the recipient's department):

Name: _Christopher Rosovich_   **E-mail:** _c_rosovich@ntel.gov_

Signature and Date: _Christopher Rosovich_ / _September 29_

Note:

Once we receive your SAC request, it will take approximately three working days to process. When access has been granted, an e-mail containing a 6-digit SAC will be sent to the recipient.

To	Victoria Sherman <v_sherman@ntel.gov>
From	Andrea Delgadillo <a_delgadillo@ntel.gov>
Date	October 2
Subject	SAC

Dear Ms. Sherman,

Your request for special and extended access to the Danes Building and its facilities has been approved. To gain entry, you must use the provided security access code (SAC) along with your company employee card. Your SAC is 938233. In order to access the building after normal business hours, please follow these steps:

• Place your card close to the card reader. An orange light on the reader will begin to flash.
• Next, enter your SAC on the number pad.
• The flashing orange light will then turn green, allowing you to enter the building.

If you input your SAC incorrectly, the light will turn red, and you will hear a loud beep for five seconds. Afterwards, you will have three more chances to input the correct code before you are completely locked out. Please go to the security management office and present your employee card if you wish to reset your code.

If you have any concerns or issues while you are here in the building, please call the phone number on the back of your card. Finally, please note that your SAC will expire at 10:00 P.M. on the final day of your particular project. Your employee card will still work during normal office hours until December 31.

Sincerely,

Andrea Delgadillo, Security Management

41. What is suggested about Mr. Rosovich?

(A) He has a leadership role in the
Accounting Department.
(B) He submitted the application form in
October.
(C) He works in a different office than Ms.
Sherman.
(D) He will have a meeting with Ms.
Sherman regarding her project.

42. What is true about the SAC application
form?

(A) It must be submitted in person to the
security management office.
(B) It must provide a reason for the access
request.
(C) It must include a copy of the
employee's card.
(D) It must be filed at least three days in
advance of the code being used.

43. How will Ms. Sherman know that the SAC
she enters is valid?

(A) The color of a light will change.
(B) A sound will ring for five seconds.
(C) A light will repeatedly flash.
(D) The volume of a sound will increase.

44. What is NOT indicated about the security
management office?

(A) It has a fax machine.
(B) It provides after-hours access.
(C) It issues access codes to employees.
(D) It has introduced new security policies.

45. When is Ms. Sherman expected to
complete her project?

(A) On September 29
(B) On October 7
(C) On November 2
(D) On December 31

Questions 46-50 refer to the following notice and e-mails.

Senbay Park Stadium proudly announces:

A Look Back
by Bailey Itani
June-August

Bailey Itani is the director of the Museum of Sports History in Springfield.

In collaboration with the Massachusetts Sports Administration, Bailey Itani has selected works of art depicting various sporting events at the stadium over its 120 year history. Ms. Itani showcases competitions that have been overlooked throughout time.

After passing through the stadium's main entrance, visitors will be surrounded by sights from the stadium just as it was at the turn of the century. By following the exhibit numbers, they will be led on a journey through time, getting the best feel for the stadium's development and the people and events it has hosted over the years. Along the way, they'll view never-before-seen photographs, news clippings, and video footage.

Tickets:
Free to the public weekdays 9 A.M. to 2 P.M.; other dates/times subject to event prices.

Ms. Itani will give a talk about this project at Senbay Public Library on Saturday, June 7, at 10:00 A.M. Tickets are $5 and can be purchased online at https://Senbayevents.org.

From: m.tomasi@meyer.edu
To: itani@mmh.org
Date: June 17
Subject: Documentary film

Dear Ms. Itani,

I wanted to let you know that I was quite impressed with your lecture last week.

I am planning to make a documentary about a favorite topic of mine: past and present baseball players in New England, and I am looking for someone to help write the script. This project was commissioned by the American History Center, and I have authorization to hire one research associate at an attractive rate of compensation. After hearing you speak, I am confident that we would work together well.

Please consider my proposal and get in touch with me soon. I will be in New York this week, but I could visit Springfield to meet you any time after June 24. You can contact me at this e-mail address at your convenience.

Marla Tomasi

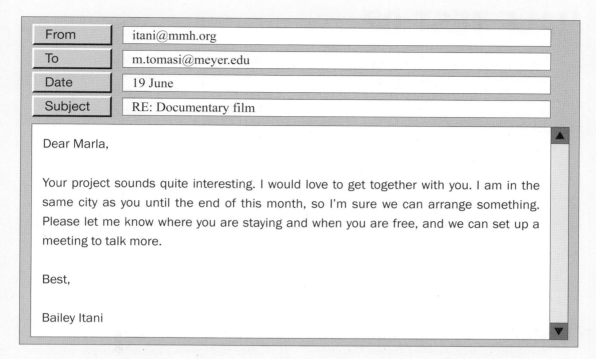

From	itani@mmh.org
To	m.tomasi@meyer.edu
Date	19 June
Subject	RE: Documentary film

Dear Marla,

Your project sounds quite interesting. I would love to get together with you. I am in the same city as you until the end of this month, so I'm sure we can arrange something. Please let me know where you are staying and when you are free, and we can set up a meeting to talk more.

Best,

Bailey Itani

46. What does the notice suggest about the exhibit?

(A) It will be the main topic of a documentary.
(B) It includes well-known athletes from Springfield.
(C) It was sponsored by the American History Center.
(D) It focuses on less famous events.

47. What is implied in the notice?

(A) The stadium exhibit will start with a discussion.
(B) Visitors should look at the display in a specific sequence.
(C) Ms. Itani urges residents to go watch sports competitions.
(D) The exhibit's gift shop is open every day of the week.

48. Where most likely did Ms. Tomasi hear Ms. Itani speak?

(A) At the Museum of Sports History
(B) At the Senbay Public Library
(C) At the Massachusetts Sports Administration
(D) At the American History Center

49. What is suggested about Ms. Itani?

(A) She will pay Ms. Tomasi well.
(B) She is selling some sports memorabilia.
(C) She will meet Ms. Tomasi in New York.
(D) She will be back in Springfield on June 24.

50. In what field do Ms. Tomasi and Ms. Itani share knowledge?

(A) Filmmaking
(B) Sports history
(C) Modern art
(D) Journalism

HALF TEST 02

1. The workers from the manufacturing department can sign up for vacations ------- the quota is reached.

(A) promptly
(B) as soon as
(C) in time for
(D) right away

2. The retrospective of Steve Miller's films ------- in the National Modern Art Center.

(A) holds
(B) has held
(C) is holding
(D) is being held

3. The Chairman of Biz Core moved to New York City, ------- he founded a financial services company called Avalon Research.

(A) what
(B) where
(C) which
(D) while

4. We Care is a free fundraising Web site created for individuals wanting ------- funds for helping people in need.

(A) raised
(B) raises
(C) is raising
(D) to raise

5. Should the event be fully reserved, a waiting list will be kept and places offered if there are -------.

(A) cancels
(B) cancelled
(C) cancellations
(D) canceling

6. Although the performances are free to watch, people are required to reserve a ticket ------- admittance to the event.

(A) for
(B) between
(C) near
(D) from

7. Survey results indicate that the number of Astro Sports Network's viewers is currently ------- to that of ANP Sport, its main competitor.

(A) equality
(B) equal
(C) equally
(D) equals

8. We look forward to sending you what we proudly believe is the best magazine of ------- kind on the market today.

(A) it
(B) its
(C) they
(D) them

9. Employers use probationary employment periods to ascertain ------- new workers will be able to handle their duties.

(A) while
(B) whenever
(C) whereas
(D) whether

10. A renowned journalist, Maria Gray announced her ------- to compile a book regarding her days as a correspondent in India.

(A) explanation
(B) intent
(C) construction
(D) ideal

11. Koma Construction ------- invites academics and other experts to train employees in the latest industry practices.

(A) regularly
(B) evenly
(C) exactly
(D) timely

12. Part-time employees typically work fewer hours ------- a work week than full-time employees.

(A) between
(B) among
(C) during
(D) above

13. ------- economic growth to gain acceleration, it is important to invest in education, which is the most important component of human capital.

(A) When
(B) For
(C) Which
(D) In addition to

14. Establishing shipping ------- is problematic because rates vary depending on weight and distance.

(A) fares
(B) charges
(C) values
(D) figures

15. The more ------- managers treat their employees, the more effective they will be with their clients.

(A) repeatedly
(B) recently
(C) relatively
(D) respectfully

16. The company CEO ------- Ms. Frances for winning the contract with High Tech Corp.

(A) demonstrated
(B) entrusted
(C) agreed
(D) congratulated

17. The branch manager emphasized that to deliver the product orders on time, ------- must work overtime.

(A) no one
(B) nobody
(C) one another
(D) everyone

18. The development of the Universe Smart Phone will ------- people to work outdoors without renting an office.

(A) avoid
(B) provide
(C) show
(D) allow

19. All passengers are asked to check the overhead compartments for their belongings when ------- an airplane.

(A) exit
(B) exits
(C) exited
(D) exiting

20. The *Dawlish Gazette* advertises its other online publications ------- links to affiliated Web sites.

(A) towards
(B) past
(C) with
(D) up

Questions 21-24 refer to the following instructions.

If your luggage has been lost, please submit a claim by filling out this form. Please ensure that you clearly ------- all items contained in the missing luggage.
21.

When you have completed the form, please hand it to a staff member at the lost luggage desk in the arrivals hall.

Our staff will use our computerized system ------- your luggage, and can usually recover your
22.
luggage within 48 hours. -------.
23.

We apologize for the inconvenience caused due to your lost luggage, and you can rest assured that we will do everything we can to reunite you with your ------- as soon as possible.
24.

21. (A) locate
(B) list
(C) prevent
(D) find

22. (A) being traced
(B) is tracing
(C) to trace
(D) has traced

23. (A) Afterward, you can pay for the extra service we provide.
(B) Thankfully, everyone got the bags they had lost.
(C) As a result, we almost never lose any passengers' bags.
(D) Then, your luggage will be personally delivered to you.

24. (A) invoices
(B) documents
(C) recordings
(D) belongings

Questions 25-28 refer to the following letter.

Dear Private Banking Customer,

At Jessop Bank, we take our private banking customers' security extremely seriously. That's why we will never request that you confirm your Internet banking log-in information or ------- security
25.
information by e-mail or telephone.

We will always treat your personal information with complete confidentiality. We also recommend that customers take the ------- measures outlined below to protect their personal information.
26.
Always choose a password that nobody would be able to guess. Also, ensure that you change your password often.

Never reply to e-mails that ask for your personal information, account numbers, etc. These e-mails will not be from us.

Finally, if you ever suspect that an e-mail is fraudulent, contact our fraud prevention team at 1-800-999-7261. -------.
27.

Thank you in advance for your ------- in protecting the confidentiality of your information.
28.

Sincerely,

Justin Charles
Head of Fraud Protection

25. (A) any other
(B) one another
(C) each other
(D) another

26. (A) relative
(B) extra
(C) excess
(D) extreme

27. (A) It will be necessary to provide your password.
(B) They will look into the matter immediately.
(C) This will cause you to lose confidentiality.
(D) You will be charged with fraud for doing so.

28. (A) view
(B) support
(C) proposal
(D) suggestion

Questions 29-30 refer to the following text message chain.

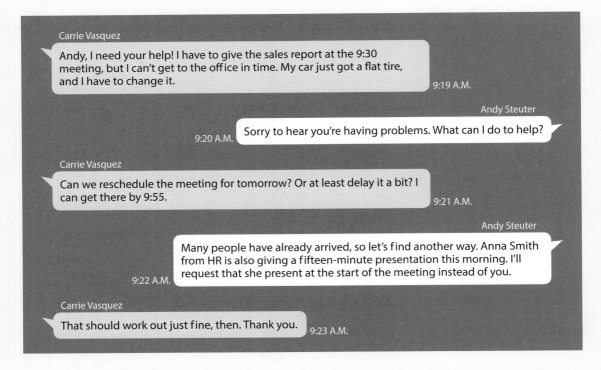

Carrie Vasquez

Andy, I need your help! I have to give the sales report at the 9:30 meeting, but I can't get to the office in time. My car just got a flat tire, and I have to change it.

9:19 A.M.

Andy Steuter

9:20 A.M.

Sorry to hear you're having problems. What can I do to help?

Carrie Vasquez

Can we reschedule the meeting for tomorrow? Or at least delay it a bit? I can get there by 9:55.

9:21 A.M.

Andy Steuter

Many people have already arrived, so let's find another way. Anna Smith from HR is also giving a fifteen-minute presentation this morning. I'll request that she present at the start of the meeting instead of you.

9:22 A.M.

Carrie Vasquez

That should work out just fine, then. Thank you.

9:23 A.M.

29. What does Mr. Steuter indicate he will do?

(A) Book a conference room
(B) Give Ms. Vasquez a ride
(C) Switch presentation times
(D) Delay a meeting

30. At 9:23 A.M., what does Ms. Vasquez most likely mean when she writes, "That should work out just fine, then"?

(A) She is fine with being the first speaker.
(B) She thanks Mr. Steuter for calling a technician.
(C) She agrees to Mr. Steuter's solution.
(D) She is okay with rescheduling her job interview.

Questions 31-33 refer to the following section of a brochure.

Cameron Klein Interior Design Center

Welcome to the Cameron Klein Interior Design Center. This brochure is designed to help you as you take a self-guided tour through this impressive indoor area.

Most of the designs you see here were made by Mr. Klein during his 25-year career. Other designs were made by interior designers who studied under Mr. Klein and whose works embody his style. During this tour, please help yourself to some of the pamphlets in the box near the front entrance. They are complimentary and include a brief biography of Mr. Klein, as well as a list of links to online articles for further reading. The décor and furniture in the design center were donated by members of the Berkeley Architectural Society.

The group's headquarters is located opposite the main exit of the center and is open from 9:00 A.M. to 5:00 P.M. Monday through Saturday. Visitors to the interior design center are invited to drop by between those hours to discover more about the center's collection of interior decorations.

31. Where would the brochure most likely be found?

(A) At a history library
(B) At a bookstore
(C) At an exhibit
(D) At an art school

32. What is mentioned as being available at no cost to visitors?

(A) Reading materials
(B) Introductory architecture courses
(C) Sample decorations
(D) Tours led by interior designers

33. What is indicated about the Berkeley Architectural Society?

(A) Its headquarters is open four days a week.
(B) It was established 25 years ago.
(C) Its members have designed many decorations.
(D) It contributed by providing furniture.

Questions 34-36 refer to the following information on a Web site.

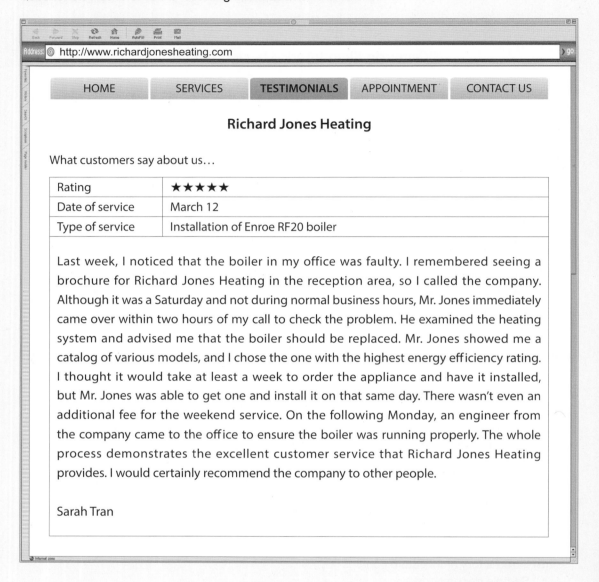

| HOME | SERVICES | **TESTIMONIALS** | APPOINTMENT | CONTACT US |

Richard Jones Heating

What customers say about us…

Rating	★★★★★
Date of service	March 12
Type of service	Installation of Enroe RF20 boiler

Last week, I noticed that the boiler in my office was faulty. I remembered seeing a brochure for Richard Jones Heating in the reception area, so I called the company. Although it was a Saturday and not during normal business hours, Mr. Jones immediately came over within two hours of my call to check the problem. He examined the heating system and advised me that the boiler should be replaced. Mr. Jones showed me a catalog of various models, and I chose the one with the highest energy efficiency rating. I thought it would take at least a week to order the appliance and have it installed, but Mr. Jones was able to get one and install it on that same day. There wasn't even an additional fee for the weekend service. On the following Monday, an engineer from the company came to the office to ensure the boiler was running properly. The whole process demonstrates the excellent customer service that Richard Jones Heating provides. I would certainly recommend the company to other people.

Sarah Tran

34. Why has the information most likely been included on the Web site?

(A) To explain company regulations
(B) To outline an installation process
(C) To promote new merchandise
(D) To attract potential customers

35. What is indicated about Mr. Jones?

(A) He advertises his services in a magazine that Ms. Tran subscribes to.
(B) He completed work for Ms. Tran on the same day she requested it.
(C) He charged an additional fee for working during the weekend.
(D) He fixed a broken boiler on March 12.

36. What is a stated feature of the Enroe RF20 boiler?

(A) It is easy to install.
(B) It is reasonably priced.
(C) It is available in various colors.
(D) It is energy efficient.

Creekberry Home Appliances
1029 E. Dorsette Ave.
Salt Lake City, UT 84111
www.creekberryhome.com

June 12

Ms. Amanda Rucker
KPHV Channel 10
44983 W. Chaparral Rd.
Sun City, AZ 85351

Dear Ms. Rucker,

Thank you for contacting Creekberry Home Appliances; I could not be happier to hear from KPHV and the *Community Business Spotlight* team. As CEO of Creekberry Home Appliances, I would be pleased to visit your studio for an interview and demonstrate our redesigned dehumidifier. — [1] —. Two years ago, after our vacuum was featured on your program, we saw a noticeable rise in sales, as well as many more telephone and e-mail inquiries than usual. Our new product is specially designed to be easy to clean and almost impossible to break. Its efficiency is 75 percent better, meaning that it can remove 170 pints of water from the air every day. — [2] —. At its core, however, the new Creekberry dehumidifier does what it has always done — make the most comfortable household environment around.

Enclosed with this letter is a brochure detailing the specifications of the Creekberry dehumidifier. Please read through it and contact us by e-mail or phone at your earliest convenience. Also, if you would like additional promotional materials, we can send some over at any time. — [3] —.

I look forward to promoting my company's brand on *Community Business Spotlight*, or any other station programming that you feel would help us reach our audience. — [4] —. I appreciate you reaching out to us to present our product to the KPHV audience.

Please let me know if you have any questions or if there is anything that I can do to help.

Most Sincerely,

Dagny Leitner
Dagny Leitner
CEO, Creekberry Home Appliances

Enclosure

37. Why did Ms. Leitner write a letter to Ms. Rucker?

(A) To request details of an appliance
(B) To ask for recent sales figures
(C) To accept an invitation to a show
(D) To find out about a new program

38. What did Ms. Leitner include in her letter?

(A) A promotional poster
(B) A list of product features
(C) An agreement form
(D) A map to a store

39. The phrase, "reaching out to" in paragraph 3, line 3, is closest in meaning to

(A) holding on to
(B) grabbing at
(C) communicating with
(D) looking carefully at

40. In which of the positions marked [1], [2], [3], and [4] does the following sentence best belong?

"It's also fully digitized, with options for different levels of energy use."

(A) [1]
(B) [2]
(C) [3]
(D) [4]

Questions 41-45 refer to the following e-mail and survey.

To	r_sanger@mbwhiteinsurance.com
From	orders@stewartstationerysupplies.com
Date	November 5, 9:12 A.M.
Subject	Your order number 21987QT2

Dear Mr. Sanger,

Thank you for ordering from Stewart Stationery Supplies' online store. Your order has just been processed and will ship from our Billington warehouse today at 2:00 P.M.

Qty	Product	Cost
1	Large brown envelopes (3,000 pieces per box)	$60.00
1	Stewart T2 white mailing labels (6,000 pieces per box)	$20.50
1	Stewart S1 printing paper (6,000 sheets per box) FINAL SALE	$95.50
1	Fine Print 13B color ink printer cartridge (4 packs per box)	$270.00
3-Day Shipping		$20.00
Total paid by Stewart gift card TR541G		$466.00
Amount remaining on gift card TR541G		$10.50

Please be advised that used or opened products marked 'FINAL SALE' cannot be returned. To view our full return policy, visit http://www.stewartstationerysupplies.com/returns.

To ensure that we always provide you with the best customer service and highest quality products, please complete our online customer satisfaction survey at http://www. stewartstationerysupplies.com/survey. If you fill out the survey by November 20, we will send you a thank-you gift!

Stewart Stationery Supplies Customer Support Team
Tel: (800) 555-2135, 9 A.M. - 9 P.M., Monday-Friday

Customer Satisfaction Survey

Once you have completed this survey, we will email you a printable voucher for 15 percent off your next purchase. Please include your e-mail address:

Part 1
How did you find out about Stewart Stationery Supplies?
☐ A newspaper ad   ☐ A flyer sent out by mail   ☐ Other magazine advertisement

Part 2
If you purchased items at one of our store branches, please indicate the location. (If you ordered online, please leave this part blank.)
☐ Romford City   ☐ Mountfield   ☐ Ashridge

How would you rate our services?
☐ Excellent   ☐ Average   ☐ Unsatisfactory

Part 3
If you purchased items at our Web site, was it easy for you to navigate?
(If you purchased your item at a retail store, please leave this part blank.)
☐ Yes   ☐ Somewhat   ☐ No

If you required technical assistance with our Web site, how was the level of service?
☐ Excellent   ☐ Good   ☐ Unsatisfactory

Part 4
Please rate the quality of the items you bought from us.
☐ Excellent   ☐ Good   ☐ Unsatisfactory

---

41. What product has Mr. Sanger ordered that cannot be returned?

(A) Printer cartridges
(B) Printing paper
(C) Mailing labels
(D) Envelopes

42. What is indicated about the order that Mr. Sanger placed?

(A) He has requested a change in quantities.
(B) It has been scheduled for delivery on November 5.
(C) It will be shipped to his office in Billington.
(D) He used a gift card for payment.

43. What benefit is being offered to customers who complete the survey?

(A) Packs of free ink cartridges
(B) An invitation to a sales event on November 20
(C) Free shipping on a future order
(D) A reduction in price on their next purchase

44. What part of the survey should Mr. Sanger NOT complete?

(A) Part 1
(B) Part 2
(C) Part 3
(D) Part 4

45. What is suggested on the survey about Stewart Stationery Supplies?

(A) It has 24-hour customer support available.
(B) It advertises its products through television.
(C) It has at least three retail stores.
(D) It recently updated its Web site.

From the Garden to Your Table

If you don't have the time to shop for and prepare three meals a day, you aren't alone. Even if you make it as far as the store, how do you know which fruits, vegetables, and meats are healthy? The Beech Creek Gardeners' Market has a solution for Riverdale Metro residents to help them fit a nutritious diet into their busy schedules. The market has set up BeechCreekGardens.net which lets customers order healthy meals containing all the right ingredients! "Delivering wholesome foods to our customers can help them eat better," said Erin Woods, a Beech Creek representative. "That's why Beech Creek promises to use only fresh produce for its meals. Hopefully, this will help people improve their diets."

Ted Gilbert for *Riverdale Tribune*

New Series to Explore National Food Trends

Shrink-wrapped Nation, a new VesterMedia series by the creator of *Takeout Mania*, Cy Leuck, dives into the world of prepackaged meals by documenting the deceptive ingredients and nutritional claims their manufacturers make. Many aspects of our nation's diet get put under the microscope, and the show's dedication to scientific truth is what makes this series so interesting to watch. Episodes involve producers touring factories and interviewing the people who trick the public into believing that frozen, dried, and microwave-ready meals are safe. The series really sheds light on some of the foods we choose to eat. When asked about their plans going forward, the creators said that their next project, *Garden Fresh*, will begin production within the year. Cy Leuck looks forward to seeing audiences' reactions to the first episode of *Shrink-wrapped Nation*, which airs right after *Restaurant City*, next Monday, September 18.

September 19

Cy Leuck
VesterMedia
197 N. Mission Ave.
Oceanside, CA 92054

Dear Mr. Leuck,

I watched the premiere of *Shrink-wrapped Nation* immediately after my favorite program last night. I represent the Beech Creek Gardeners' Market, and I think our Web site may interest you. We try to make garden-fresh food as conveniently available as the unhealthy frozen food shown on your program. We'd love to talk to you about our approach and the success we've had, if you can make it to Beech Creek's offline store for a show. If you can, please contact me at (661) 555-7783 or at erinwoods@beechcreekgardens.net.

Sincerely,

Erin Woods
Erin Woods

46. What is the main purpose of the article?

(A) To describe a creative recipe
(B) To explain an ordering process
(C) To introduce a new type of business
(D) To advertise the opening of a restaurant

47. In the review, the word "claims" in paragraph 1, line 3, is closest in meaning to

(A) requests
(B) possessions
(C) statements
(D) rewards

48. According to the review, what is suggested about *Shrink-wrapped Nation*?

(A) It has been aired worldwide.
(B) It shows viewers how to grow their own gardens.
(C) It is broadcast once a week.
(D) It presents prepackaged meals in a negative way.

49. What is most likely Ms. Woods' favorite show?

(A) *Shrink-wrapped Nation*
(B) *Takeout Mania*
(C) *Garden Fresh*
(D) *Restaurant City*

50. What does Ms. Woods imply in her letter?

(A) She believes Mr. Leuck may be interested in joining her market.
(B) She thinks that recent health measures have not been successful.
(C) She suggests that Beech Creek has many happy customers.
(D) She agrees that frozen foods can be dangerous.

HALF TEST 03

1. Mr. Peterson in the lost and found office is satisfied with his job helping people ------- their lost possessions.

   (A) assist
   (B) remind
   (C) locate
   (D) conduct

2. Angels' Support Group is committed to providing food and places for homeless people ------- no cost.

   (A) on
   (B) after
   (C) at
   (D) in

3. All the information in this set of records is up-to-date as of July 1, 2017 ------- otherwise indicated.

   (A) thus
   (B) unless
   (C) besides
   (D) despite

4. Mr. Chan's outstanding presentation ------- convinced the board of the need for more diverse employee training programs.

   (A) easiest
   (B) easy
   (C) easier
   (D) easily

5. An attractive office and ------- support staff can go a long way toward attracting an outside purchaser.

   (A) attentive
   (B) attentively
   (C) attention
   (D) attentiveness

6. The 25% discounted price for English classes ------- only to those who enroll early.

   (A) apply
   (B) applying
   (C) applies
   (D) application

7. Orange Mac places an ------- on the customer service culture and the shopping experience.

   (A) emphasized
   (B) emphasis
   (D) emphasizing
   (D) emphatically

8. The promotion plan for our newly released line of televisions is by Michael Choi, an ------- marketing director.

   (A) impress
   (B) impresses
   (C) impressively
   (D) impressive

9. The yogurt company Twinkle Berry is managing to grow by keeping capacity in line ------- demand through infrastructure investments.

   (A) to
   (B) with
   (C) on
   (D) for

10. The CEO of Bare Foot, Inc. is seeking a transaction that ------- and enhance the company's market position.

    (A) will maintain
    (B) maintained
    (C) to maintain
    (D) maintain

11. Only customers with store memberships are ------- for the special discount prices mentioned in the online advertisement.

(A) relevant
(B) eligible
(C) lucrative
(D) considerate

12. The data can reveal the root cause of business problems when subjected ------- further analysis.

(A) to
(B) through
(C) while
(D) during

13. Public transportation was delayed due to the inclement weather, so Ms. Javier did not ------- on time for her client meeting.

(A) arrive
(B) arrival
(C) arrives
(D) arriving

14. Mr. Kim finally took over as director of advertising in an ------- to earn more market share.

(A) item
(B) issue
(C) advice
(D) effort

15. This checklist is intended to help employers implement the best practices for employees ------- alone at hazardous jobs.

(A) worked
(B) working
(C) have worked
(D) are working

16. The date of manufacture should be printed on the side of the package or ------- on the bottom of the can containing the seafood.

(A) directly
(B) nearly
(C) busily
(D) questionably

17. Ms. Hwang has spent the last six months doing research for her ------- presentation.

(A) inward
(B) recurrent
(C) upcoming
(D) estimated

18. The school administrator plans to ------- a program that integrates regular classroom activities and practical career experience.

(A) reconnect
(B) institute
(C) exceed
(D) balance

19. The staff of the Palm Tree Resort will do ------- they can to make your stay as comfortable as possible.

(A) some
(B) whatever
(C) above
(D) each

20. According to a consumer survey conducted last month, a great ------- of people prefer to buy items online rather than off-line.

(A) major
(B) majority
(C) majored
(D) majors

Questions 21-24 refer to the following instructions.

Recycling Printer Toner Cartridges

Extec Printer Supplies is fully committed to protecting the environment. Thus, we encourage all our customers to recycle their used printer toner cartridges ------- possible.
21.

Recycling your printer toner cartridges is simple. Just take your used cartridges to any retailer that sells Extec products, where you will find an Extec recycling container. -------. Our retail
22.
partners ------- the deposited cartridges to us on a regular basis for recycling.
23.

In addition, returning your used cartridges entitles you to reduced prices on your future purchases. For further ------- on this, please see our Web site.
24.

21. (A) someday
(B) whenever
(C) all in all
(D) rather

22. (A) An employee can show you how to install them.
(B) Then, deposit the cartridges in the receptacle.
(C) You can purchase new toner cartridges there.
(D) It may take a while for the cartridges to be recycled.

23. (A) are sent
(B) have sent
(C) send
(D) were sending

24. (A) opinions
(B) restrictions
(C) information
(D) problems

Questions 25-28 refer to the following advertisement.

Over 30 miles of forest, countless lakes, and a wide variety of birds and other wildlife ------- for

25.

you at Zorilla nature reserve. You'll find Zorilla just 10 miles north of Priestfield, right off the Great

Northern Highway at Exit 3. The reserve's closeness to the city means that it is the perfect -------

26.

for a day trip or a weekend getaway.

If you decide to stay for the night, there are a number of great hotels and guest houses to

choose from, all in a wonderful rural setting. To find out more about Zorilla, email us at www.

zorillareserve.com. In reply, we'll send you a brochure, a map, and lots of information on things

to do at the reserve, so you can get planning your trip -------. -------.

27.   28.

25. (A) await
(B) waited
(C) are waiting
(D) has been waiting

26. (A) exhibit
(B) choice
(C) contest
(D) nature

27. (A) right above
(B) straight away
(C) up until
(D) as follows

28. (A) Our doors will be opening soon.
(B) Thank you for visiting us recently.
(C) Look for us in the center of the city.
(D) We look forward to seeing you soon.

Welcome to Mandy's Dry Cleaning and Tailoring

Open Tuesday through Saturday
7:00 A.M. to 7:00 P.M.

Customer: Ruth Madeiros
Order: #75432246
Tuesday, June 15, 9:37 A.M.

Item	Service	Pick-up date / time	Cost
Cardigan	Sleeve stitching	Tue, June 15 / 4 P.M.	$5.00
Jacket	Dry cleaning	Fri, June 18 / 4:30 P.M.	$12.00
Pants	Repair	Mon, June 21 / 10 A.M.	$18.00
Blazer	Button fastening	Mon, June 21 / 10 A.M.	$7.00

Total cost: $42.00
Amount paid: $42.00
Balance due: $0.00

Thank you for choosing Mandy's
Ask about our Wednesday Specials

29. For what item did Ms. Madeiros receive same-day service?

(A) The cardigan
(B) The jacket
(C) The pants
(D) The blazer

30. What is indicated about Ms. Madeiros' order?

(A) It was paid in full.
(B) It contained several jackets.
(C) It was delivered on June 18.
(D) It included a discount.

Questions 31-33 refer to the following notice.

Ferry Transport Notice

Due to maintenance being done on the docks, regular ferry service from the Triangle Port will experience periodic interruptions from Friday, 20 March to Monday, 23 March. Although most ferries will run during regular hours, some routes will be temporarily suspended. Please refer to the schedule below for detailed information. Passengers should arrive early, as there may not be enough space on the remaining ferries to accommodate all passengers. Copies of the temporary ferry schedule can be picked up at the ticketing booth.

Date	Triangle Port Departing Times			
Friday, 20 March	8 A.M.	10 A.M.	2 P.M.	Not in service
Saturday, 21 March	Not in service	10 A.M.	Not in service	5 P.M.
Sunday, 22 March	8 A.M.	10 A.M.	2 P.M.	5 P.M.
Monday, 23 March	Not in service	10 A.M.	2 P.M.	5 P.M.

31. What is being announced?

(A) The suspension of a service
(B) Delays in boat departures
(C) The remodeling of a ticketing booth
(D) Longer business hours

32. Why are the passengers asked to come early?

(A) To choose the best boat for their needs
(B) To ensure that they secure a place on a boat
(C) To avoid waiting in a long line
(D) To make sure the ferry leaves on schedule

33. When will the ferry service NOT be affected by the maintenance?

(A) March 20
(B) March 21
(C) March 22
(D) March 23

To	Frederik Clayton <fclayton@lamousse.nl>
To	Frederik Clayton <fclayton@lamousse.nl>
From	Arthur Mosley <amosley@ngualodge.ng>
Date	16 May
Subject	Reservation

Dear Mr. Clayton,

Thank you for recently booking the Wildlife Sanctuary Safari Package at the Ngua Lodge for the second time this year. We are delighted to have you back. Your package includes three nights in our modern lodge with a free continental breakfast every morning and three days of safari excursions with an experienced local guide from the Humaba National Park. A wildlife description book of endangered species in the area and a coupon worth 20 percent off selected purchases at our lodge's gift shop are also part of the package.

You can dine at Safari Bistro, which, as you might recall, is inside the Ngua Lodge. Chef Sammi Dwani's innovative dishes have recently received excellent reviews in *National Nigerian Monthly* magazine, which can be read by clicking the link below. www.nigerianmonthly.co.ng/ngualodge

We are looking forward to seeing you at the Ngua Lodge on 22 May.

Warm Regards,

Arthur Mosley
Ngua Lodge, Manager of Guest Services

34. What is indicated about Mr. Clayton?

(A) He made several inquiries about his reservation.
(B) He plans to attend an animal conservation fundraiser.
(C) He lives near Humaba National Park.
(D) He has made a previous visit to the Ngua Lodge.

35. Why does Mr. Mosley include a link in the e-mail?

(A) To share information about a restaurant
(B) To provide wildlife tour schedules
(C) To advertise a local guide's services
(D) To offer directions to the Ngua Lodge

36. What is NOT included in the package?

(A) A morning meal
(B) A gift shop voucher
(C) A book for wildlife enthusiasts
(D) A map of a safari park

Questions 37-40 refer to the following instructions.

Waver Electronics Quick-Start Guide

For product VG4193:

1. Insert the red end of the black power cable into the blue port on the side of the scanner. Plug the opposite end of the black cable into an electrical socket. (We advise that you use a surge protector.)
2. Connect the scanner to your computer using the yellow data cable.
3. Insert the accompanying CD into your disc drive to install the scanner's software. You will need the software's password, found on the cover of the CD in order to finish the installation process.
4. Once you have installed the software, eject the CD and reboot your computer.
5. To register your scanner, go to www.waverelectronics.com/registration and log in with the serial number located on the back of the scanner. After registration, you will be issued a product identification number, which can be used to access various services such as repair requests and software updates.

Installation problems:

If you experience problems setting up your scanner, first read the troubleshooting section found on the Frequently Asked Questions page in the instruction manual. If you can't find the information you need there, visit our Web site. Please use your product identification number to access our online technical support page, which includes a forum where users are able to ask questions and share common issues. If you continue to have difficulties, call us at 1-800-555-0184 to talk to a technical support specialist.

---

37. What are the instructions for?

(A) Activating an online account
(B) Setting up a scanner
(C) Ordering an item
(D) Installing a video program

38. What are users instructed to do first?

(A) Insert a CD
(B) Attach a power cable
(C) Register a product
(D) Turn on a computer

39. What is required to update the software?

(A) An identification number
(B) A customized password
(C) A blank CD
(D) An electronic invoice

40. What strategy is NOT recommended to solve technical problems?

(A) Contacting Waver Electronics
(B) Reviewing the instruction manual
(C) Visiting the online discussion forum
(D) Rebooting the computer

Questions 41-45 refer to the following e-mail and schedule.

To	Mia Kaverin <mkaverin@arpex.ni>
From	Sergei Gusev <sgusev@rci.org>
Re	RCI Conference
Date	21 June
Attachment	Workshop schedule (updated 19 June)

Dear Ms. Kaverin,

Thank you for expressing interest in the 10th Annual Conference of the Russian Construction Industry. Unfortunately, since your registration two months ago, there have been some changes to the program. As a result, we require further information from you by 30 June.

First, Vladimir Solomin's workshop, "Disposing Toxic Waste", which you registered for, has been canceled. Instead, a presentation on "Hazardous Substance Removal" will be given by Boris Garin. Please let us know if you would like to attend the new session.

Also, Igor Burkov's talk has been moved from Monday morning to Monday afternoon. Consequently, his session will run concurrently with Arthur Gansk's. Since you're registered for both, you have to decide which one you will attend. Lastly, please indicate which Monday morning workshop you would like to attend.

The conference management team offers our deepest apologies for any inconvenience these changes may cause you. Rest assured that all other speakers have promised to honor their speaking commitments. Therefore, barring any unexpected circumstances, I fully expect the workshops by Luis Cameron and Alex Vasin, in which you had also expressed interest, to proceed as scheduled.

Sincerely,

Sergei Gusev, Seminar Coordinator

Russian Construction Industry (RCI)
10th Annual Seminar • 4-5 July • Moscow, Russia

Monday Workshops

Time	Workshop Title	Presenter
8:00-9:45	Relationships between Exports and Imports	Olav Dansk, business owner
	Selecting the Right Supplier	Andrew Smithson, management consultant
10:00-11:45	Building in the 21st Century	Luis Cameron, senior architect
	Funding for Large Projects	Simone Balashov, financial expert
(Lunch from 12:00-1:00)		
1:15-3:00	The State of Steel	Arthur Gansk, senior engineer
	Designing an Effective Web Site	Igor Burkov, web designer

Tuesday Workshops

Time	Workshop Title	Presenter
8:00-11:00	Construction Worldwide	Anton Ivanovic, Professor of Architecture
	Attracting Foreign Clients	Alex Vasin, marketing director
(Lunch from 11:30-12:30)		
1:00-4:00	Hazardous Substance Removal	Boris Garin, waste specialist
	Online Marketing Survey: What I learned from it	Benjamin Kleinfield, business journalist

41. What is the purpose of the e-mail?

(A) To announce some schedule adjustments
(B) To promote an upcoming conference
(C) To invite new members to join a committee
(D) To confirm a seminar registration

42. What is indicated about Mr. Garin?

(A) He was selected as a replacement for Mr. Solomin.
(B) He was scheduled to give a presentation with Mr. Solomin.
(C) He will hold his workshop on Monday morning.
(D) He had requested a different date and time for his talk.

43. In the e-mail, the word "honor" in paragraph 4, line 2, is closest in meaning to

(A) fulfill
(B) limit
(C) announce
(D) celebrate

44. What session was originally scheduled for Tuesday?

(A) Designing an Effective Web Site
(B) The State of Steel
(C) Disposing Toxic Waste
(D) Building in the 21st Century

45. According to the schedule, who will talk about conducting marketing research through the Internet?

(A) A financial expert
(B) A university professor
(C) A reporter
(D) An engineer

Documentary Films of the Year Awards

The Distant Pebble
Is there a way to save the Earth? Daniel Sankh tracks the progress of wildlife conservationists for a decade looking for clues in the data.

The Longest Way
Helen Linden captures the amazing story of Susan Peters, a biology graduate student, at her home in Whitehorse, Canada. Covering the 25 months after beginning school together, the film shows the real story of how Ms. Peters made a revolutionary discovery.

A Day for Ben Markette
A film following the two-year-long campaign trail of a local professor who became a governor to save the environment. Ben Markette narrates his experiences on the road to becoming head of his state.

The Mystery at Carob Creek
Filmmakers Theresa Meyer and Mary Naff capture a series of strange summers, while trying to protect the forests.

---

http://www.lesdocsfestival.org

Awards Schedule
Main Event Speakers
Sarkowitz Hall, April 7

9:00 — Opening and Keynote Lecture
Speaker and award winner Daniel Sankh talks about a recent documentary; its styles, themes, and how it influenced his own work. He will interview its director Helen Linden about the film, as she is here to get an award for it.

10:30 — The Documentary Awards Ceremony
Host Bryan Forrest presents this year's Documentary Film Awards after playing a short interview with Matt MacKenzie, a contestant who sadly cannot attend the event. Theresa Meyer will join Mr. Forrest in presenting this year's awards.

1:30 — Beyond Documentaries
Theresa Meyer presents a panel discussion with this year's winners focused on film funding. They will talk about ways to get funding and how they paid for their own films.

To	feedback@adconference.com
From	kelly.jensen@milkywaygames.com
Date	April 8
Subject	New Event

I have been a true supporter at the LesDocs Awards Festival ever since it began and always look forward to the keynote speaker. Every year, they have been entertaining, educational, and inspiring. This year's inclusion of a new presentation was most welcome. Every filmmaker has been wonderful to listen to, and the audience always has excellent questions, but this year's guest was a particular treat.

I knew Ms. Meyer when she was at Maryglen University, and remember her focus and determination to succeed at every project. I worked with her friend, Ms. Naff, after we graduated. I was surprised to learn that she has begun her own production company and look forward to seeing what she creates.

Thank you for hosting such a valuable event.

Kelly Jensen

46. What is one common feature in all of the documentaries?

(A) They are dedicated to famous conservationists.
(B) They took several years to make.
(C) They concentrate on wild animals.
(D) They were filmed in Canadian cities.

47. What documentary did Daniel Sankh discuss during his speech?

(A) *The Distant Pebble*
(B) *The Longest Way*
(C) *A Day for Ben Markette*
(D) *The Mystery at Carob Creek*

48. What is indicated about Beyond Documentaries?

(A) It was moved to a different time slot.
(B) It used to be hosted by Helen Linden.
(C) It was just added to an event schedule.
(D) It originally was presented at 10:30.

49. In the e-mail, the word "true" in paragraph 1, line 1, is closest in meaning to

(A) loyal
(B) correct
(C) accurate
(D) honest

50. What is probably true of Kelly Jensen?

(A) She has presented a keynote speech.
(B) She organized an awards ceremony.
(C) She has worked in the film industry.
(D) She was a speaker at Beyond Documentaries.

HALF TEST 04

해설서 p.159 / ⏱ 제한 시간 35분

1. Luxurious rooms, a world-class spa, and polished service make this hotel excellent ------- for the money.

   (A) value
   (B) cost
   (C) discount
   (D) price

2. By the end of the month, Mr. Henderson will ------- for this firm for a year.

   (A) work
   (B) working
   (C) has worked
   (D) have been working

3. The Epic Web browser is currently the most ------- used browser in the world.

   (A) wide
   (B) wider
   (C) widest
   (D) widely

4. Mr. Fitzpatrick requested that the contract ------- to him immediately because he needed to make changes.

   (A) be sent
   (B) were sent
   (C) to send
   (D) will send

5. Research shows that ------- working more than 40 hours a week makes you unproductive and very tired.

   (A) broadly
   (B) formerly
   (C) consistently
   (D) repetitiously

6. Workers must adhere to safety guidelines when handling ------- products at the packaging stations.

   (A) defective
   (B) defectively
   (C) defects
   (D) defect

7. The efforts to monitor and reduce expenditure can be ------- to a single individual or department.

   (A) limited
   (B) remained
   (C) assorted
   (D) started

8. The manager simply asks that team members provide their ------- about how they perceive him in certain situations.

   (A) observing
   (B) observes
   (C) observations
   (D) observantly

9. Since the CEO trusts the managers ------- place, they should be able to assist him in hiring the rest of the staff.

   (A) for
   (B) in
   (C) at
   (D) on

10. You can deduct the cost of car travel, lodging and meals ------- the trip was undertaken primarily for business purposes.

    (A) as long as
    (B) for the period of
    (C) in the time of
    (D) at which time

11. Uni Rise is committed to ------- the highest levels of consumer service and is dedicated to its philosophy of social and environmental responsibility.

(A) providing
(B) provision
(C) provided
(D) provide

12. Although ------- of the concert organizers agreed to feature Rizelle as a special guest, the plan has been rejected due to a lack of funds.

(A) anybody
(B) both
(C) each other
(D) those

13. Patients prefer doctors ------- in formal attire and a white coat to images of doctors in informal clothes.

(A) photograph
(B) photographs
(C) photographed
(D) photography

14. ------- is especially different about Mega Supermarket is its well-systemized delivery service.

(A) Which
(B) That
(C) Why
(D) What

15. ------- the economic recession, computer companies focused on developing low-priced computers in new markets.

(A) Of
(B) Even
(C) When
(D) During

16. Without the ------- of the song writer, this piece of music may not be remade by any other musicians.

(A) identification
(B) permission
(C) reluctance
(D) association

17. The department to which the new employee, Mr. Hwang, will be assigned is ------- to be determined.

(A) yet
(B) beyond
(C) rarely
(D) permanently

18. Glide Shipping will not send out shipments made after 5:00 P.M. until the ------- business day.

(A) latest
(B) following
(C) recent
(D) leading

19. The Grand Hotel is ------- offering a weekend spa package for couples needing to get away from the fast-paced life of the city.

(A) partially
(B) rarely
(C) currently
(D) desirably

20. It is necessary ------- all staff members to register their cars with the security department prior to using the building's parking lot.

(A) so
(B) for
(C) that
(D) because

Dear Ms. Roberts,

Many thanks for choosing Radcliffe & Arnold as your security system provider for your home. We assure you that you have made a wise decision in relying on us to ------- your house.
21.

For the last 20 years, we have been the country's number one choice for home security, and we also provide security for some of the biggest companies nationwide. -------. We are always
22.
improving our systems and services ------- that you can enjoy the highest possible levels of
23.
safety.

If you have any questions about anything related to your security system or our services, please get in touch with us. We take pride in making sure that all our customers are completely -------
24.
with our performance and products.

Yours sincerely,

John Tucker
John Tucker
Customer Relations Director

21. (A) purchase
(B) modernize
(C) improve
(D) safeguard

22. (A) Nobody looks after clients as well as us.
(B) Several break-ins occurred in the past month.
(C) Our system has remained the same for years.
(D) Please send the check for our services as soon as you can.

23. (A) ensure
(B) to ensure
(C) have ensured
(D) will have ensured

24. (A) pleased
(B) pleasing
(C) pleasure
(D) pleasingly

Questions 25-28 refer to the following letter.

Dear Sir,

I write with reference to your article on August 10 entitled "Local Business Thrives in Southeast Asian Markets." The writer of the article included an ------- in the piece when stating that
25.
Wireless Tech, Inc. has become the market leader in the Cambodian market. While it is indeed true that Wireless Tech has greatly increased its market share in Cambodia, it is still ------- the
26.
market leader. I should know, as I am Country Manager at the market leader, Vox Comm, Inc.

For the purpose of accuracy, I would like to request that you ask the writer to correct the version of his article that ------- on your Web site. It would also be good if you could print a correction in
27.
the daily edition of your newspaper. -------.
28.

Kind regards,

Samuel Nhek
Samuel Nhek

---

25. (A) indulgence
(B) ineptitude
(C) importance
(D) inaccuracy

26. (A) further to that
(B) in the case of
(C) by no means
(D) far and away

27. (A) appear
(B) appears
(C) appearing
(D) was appeared

28. (A) Your reporter wrote an outstanding, mistake-free article.
(B) I look forward to your response regarding this error.
(C) Thank you for making the changes that we requested.
(D) If you want an interview with us, please call me anytime.

Apply Today for the Planex Air Frequent Flyers Card.
Frequent Flyer members get extra privileges!

■ **Priority Boarding and Seating**
Make use of your membership card and be one of the first to choose your seat and board your flight.

■ **Somewhere to Relax**
While waiting to board, enjoy all the comforts of our Planex Flyers Lounge, available only to cardholders.

■ **Accumulate More Miles**
Earn triple mileage points on any flight traveling Sunday through Thursday.

■ **Free Checked Baggage**
When you earn 40,000 points or more, you can check in all your bags for free on two Planex Air operated flights.

■ **Additional Carry-on Luggage**
When you earn 80,000 points or more, you can bring one additional piece of carry-on baggage on three Planex Air operated flights. Overweight fees will be applied to bags that are over 18 kilograms. For further information regarding our baggage policy, please visit www.planexair.com.

29. How can triple points be earned?

(A) By purchasing group tickets
(B) By booking two flights in one month
(C) By referring a friend
(D) By flying on certain days of the week

30. What is NOT mentioned as a benefit of the card?

(A) Access to an exclusive lounge
(B) The chance to board flights before others
(C) A fee waiver for luggage weighing over 18 kilograms
(D) The opportunity to reserve a specific seat

Questions 31-33 refer to the following Web page.

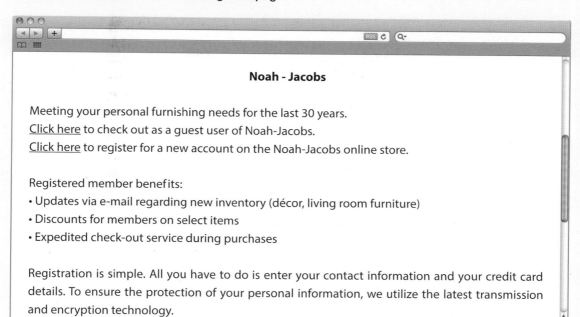

Noah - Jacobs

Meeting your personal furnishing needs for the last 30 years.
Click here to check out as a guest user of Noah-Jacobs.
Click here to register for a new account on the Noah-Jacobs online store.

Registered member benefits:
• Updates via e-mail regarding new inventory (décor, living room furniture)
• Discounts for members on select items
• Expedited check-out service during purchases

Registration is simple. All you have to do is enter your contact information and your credit card details. To ensure the protection of your personal information, we utilize the latest transmission and encryption technology.

31. What is the purpose of the Web page?

(A) To confirm the details of an online order
(B) To encourage customers to sign up for membership
(C) To advertise new home furnishing products
(D) To announce an anniversary event

32. What is NOT mentioned as a benefit?

(A) Discounted shipping fees
(B) A faster check-out process
(C) Reduced prices on certain products
(D) Messages about new items

33. What is indicated about Noah-Jacobs?

(A) It was recently featured in a magazine.
(B) It is a new company.
(C) It uses current security technology.
(D) It has multiple branches in the country.

An End to Free City Parking
June 18
By Tara Shepherd

In an attempt to reduce congestion in Downtown Albury, city council members are proposing changes to parking regulations. "The evening traffic on our roads is often the busiest," said Gillian Sampson, a representative for the Albury City Council. "That's because both residents and tourists come to the downtown district to enjoy our restaurants, theaters, and music venues. Visitors try to avoid the parking lots as they have to pay a fee. So, they drive around searching for free parking on the street, and this increases congestion."

Currently, street parking is charged only from 7:30 A.M. to 5:30 P.M., and parking is free at night. "This has to change," Ms. Sampson said. "In other cities, parking payments are required 24 hours, every day of the week, so we'd like to do the same."

If this proposed change takes place, it is going to be the second one this year. In April, the city installed new parking meters that take both credit cards and coins, as well as Albury's own parking cards. These cards were introduced in May and can be purchased at any convenience store.

34. What is suggested about Albury?

(A) It has a traffic problem.
(B) Its roads need to be repaired.
(C) Its parking lots are free to residents.
(D) It holds an annual festival.

35. What is the city council considering?

(A) Increasing hourly parking rates
(B) Introducing evening parking fees
(C) Adding more parking spaces
(D) Hiring additional parking attendants

36. What has recently happened in Albury?

(A) Some parking meters were fixed.
(B) New payment options for parking were introduced.
(C) Some downtown parking lots were closed.
(D) City officials acquired more land for parking.

Questions 37-40 refer to the following page from a Web site.

The publishing industry has been greatly affected by the Internet. To keep up with the changing times, Thoth Solutions is assisting small and medium bookstores with setting up an online presence with easy-to-use content and management tools. — [1] —. In today's competitive market, attracting customers and earning loyalty requires the latest technologies. Our online retail package has just been upgraded for mobile and tablet devices, complete with a tap-to-purchase system for e-books, a feature proven to increase customer sales and satisfaction.

Thoth Solutions also provides inventory tracking services for both small businesses and those looking to franchise. — [2] —. If you're struggling to expand your operations, let us help double or even triple your sales. We can improve your shipment tracking capabilities, create print ads, and help with inventory services so that you can spend less time and money on supply management and more time bringing in new customers. — [3] —. Keep and create new readers of all ages that look to your bookstore first for the latest bestsellers!

In addition, Thoth Solutions provides monthly Internet training sessions, individually tailored consulting, and has recently begun free clinics on hot topics like brand management, partnerships with international online retailers, and making memorable ads. — [4] —. Contact Thoth Solutions at thothsolutionsnow.com and register for a free phone consultation today.

37. What section of the Web site most likely is shown?

(A) Company Services
(B) Customer Reviews
(C) Product Listings
(D) Employment Opportunities

38. What kind of clients do Thoth Solutions most likely help?

(A) Large franchises
(B) Independent shop owners
(C) Telecommunication providers
(D) Software developers

39. What change did Thoth Solutions recently make?

(A) It moved its headquarters.
(B) It acquired a bookstore chain.
(C) It upgraded an application.
(D) It put all its items online.

40. In which of the positions marked [1], [2], [3], and [4] does the following sentence best belong?

"After all, it's their loyalty that matters the most."

(A) [1]
(B) [2]
(C) [3]
(D) [4]

Questions 41-45 refer to the following e-mail and information.

From	Joo Wan Lee <jlee@tgcommunications.com>
To	Min Seo Park <mpark@elormetals.com>
Date	September 15
Subject	Confirmation of Your Order

Dear Ms. Park,

Thank you for deciding to open a business account with TG Communications. We are happy to confirm the following purchase of mobile phones and plans:

Phone Model	Quantity	Plan
Danbi	10	Local Plus
Simban	18	Basic Line
Sum Bi	9	Blue Light
Renji	5	Universal

Your devices will be shipped from our Min Ju warehouse within three days. Once the phones are delivered, please activate them. You can do so by simply dialing (+82) 02 4675-3354 from your device.

As requested, your Elor Metals credit card will be automatically charged for regular payments. For prepaid service phones, users will receive a text message whenever their account falls below 10 USD. Users may purchase additional credit via text message, phone call, our Web site, or through third-party providers such as local convenience stores. Any minutes or data that are purchased directly through us will be billed to your TG Communications' account.

We appreciate your patronage and look forward to doing business with you again.

Sincerely,

Joo Wan Lee
TG Communications

Below is a list of mobile phone plans for TG Communications' business customers. Additional data and minutes are available with both prepaid and monthly payment plans. Free weekend international calling minutes is available to users who are on the plan with unlimited domestic minutes and unlimited data.

Plan Details

Plan	Voice Plan Options		Data Plan Options	Monthly Fee
	Domestic	International		
Universal	Unlimited minutes	400 minutes	Unlimited	80 USD
Local Plus	Unlimited minutes	200 minutes	5GB	40 USD
Basic Line	300 min	0 min	10GB	30 USD
Blue Light (prepaid)	0 min	0 min	0GB	0 USD

Overuse Costs (determined by the amount of the usage over the monthly rate)

Additional International Minutes	Additional Data	Additional Domestic Minutes
0.20 USD/min	6.00 USD/GB	0.05 USD/min

41. How is Ms. Park instructed to activate the phones?

(A) By sending a text message
(B) By accessing a Web page
(C) By calling a specific phone number
(D) By visiting a store

42. What is suggested about credit bought in stores?

(A) It will not be charged to a customer's TG Communications' account.
(B) It is available in units of 10 USD.
(C) It can be only applied to text messages.
(D) It is offered at a cheaper rate.

43. What does the information provide?

(A) Shipping options
(B) Contact information
(C) Product features
(D) Service rates

44. What plan allows customers to make free international calls on weekends?

(A) Universal
(B) Local Plus
(C) Basic Line
(D) Blue Light

45. Who will automatically receive text messages with account information?

(A) Users of the Sum Bi phone
(B) Users of the Renji phone
(C) Users of the Danbi phone
(D) Users of the Simban phone

Questions 46-50 refer to the following notice, e-mail, and comment form.

Turningpages Bookstore, Indianapolis
Weekly events for the month of July
All events start at 5:00 P.M. at the information table by the front entrance.

Event and Coordinator	Description
Meet the Author Tuesdays Hosted by Erma Nguyen	Every week, a different author visits our bookstore to talk about their work and answer your questions. Free, but donations on behalf of the Marion County Reading Initiative will be accepted throughout the evening.
Community Music Night Wednesdays Hosted by Aaron Thomas	Come enjoy live music in our lounge. $5 at the door to cover musician and catering costs. (Vegetarian option available.)
Bookcraft Thursdays Hosted by Alana Carver	Join our team of volunteer "book doctors" who repair used books for resale. Supplies will be provided at no additional cost. Optionally, you may bring your own damaged books.
Rare Book Collectors Meeting Hosted by Dean Fernandez	Come get advice on how to find old and valuable books. A one-time fee of $10 required for all new club members.

To register, drop by our information table.

To	Undisclosed recipients
From	Jerry Walker <j.walker@turningpagesind.com>
Date	July 2
Subject	Notice

To all staff:

This is to inform everyone of a couple of changes to this month's event calendar. Aaron and Dean will be out from July 17-23, so I will host Aaron's event. Erma cover for Dean. Also, don't forget that July 4 is a holiday.

Thanks for all your hard work.

Jerry Walker
Turningpages General Manager

https://www.turningpagesind.com/feedback/

Customer: The Fussels
Posted: July 25
Event Date(s): 18-22
Rate Us! ★★★★★

Comments:

My family and I had a great time participating in your store's evening activities. It truly was like a home away from home. Getting a chance to see the area's best musicians live was an unexpected high point of our visit. The host made us laugh out loud, and the band was excellent. Although I couldn't fit Ms. Carver's presentation into my schedule, my son attended and said it was great. We're back on the road again this weekend, heading to Mexico. My wife will put Ms. Nguyen's advice to good use there. She'll be on the lookout for first editions at every opportunity! Thank you again for such a wonderful week.

46. Which event includes a fundraiser?

(A) Tuesday's event
(B) Wednesday's event
(C) Thursday's event
(D) Saturday's event

47. Why did Mr. Walker send the e-mail?

(A) To remind staff of a workshop
(B) To announce changes in schedule
(C) To reply to a customer inquiry
(D) To set up a meeting

48. In the comment form, the word "fit" in paragraph 1, line 4, is closest in meaning to

(A) adapt to
(B) equip with
(C) match
(D) include

49. Who hosted the band that the customers watched?

(A) Ms. Nguyen
(B) Mr. Walker
(C) Ms. Carver
(D) Mr. Fernandez

50. What is Ms. Fussel planning to do in Mexico?

(A) Attend a Mexican music festival
(B) Locate some rare items
(C) Sell some used books
(D) Meet a Mexican author

HALF TEST 05

해설서 p.167 / ⏱ 제한 시간 35분

1. Insurance companies found that it made good business ------- for them to promote industrial safety programs and research industrial safety issues.

   (A) to sense
   (B) sensing
   (C) sensation
   (D) sense

2. Once the ------- upgrade has been installed, your computer should operate more quickly.

   (A) suggest
   (B) suggested
   (C) suggesting
   (D) suggests

3. It's easy to find inexpensive or even free budget templates to ------- to your needs.

   (A) customarily
   (B) customization
   (C) customize
   (D) custom

4. The automobile company ran dozens of tests to discover the optimum working hours for worker -------.

   (A) produce
   (B) product
   (C) productive
   (D) productivity

5. It is required that all trainees attend the company outing ------- for June 13 at Teton National Park.

   (A) scheduled
   (B) schedules
   (C) will schedule
   (D) has been scheduled

6. When a customer contacts them with a problem, the salespeople get right on it and work on the issues ------- the problem is resolved.

   (A) during
   (B) until
   (C) while
   (D) by

7. Regarding offers of free products or services, gifts can be offered only ------- there are no strings attached.

   (A) to
   (B) though
   (C) by
   (D) if

8. The Reward Plus Program allows customers to ------- double points on certain purchases and apply those points to future discounts.

   (A) earn
   (B) win
   (C) create
   (D) catch

9. The information you enter into this database is strictly ------- and will not be shared with other business entities.

   (A) concentrated
   (B) potential
   (C) confidential
   (D) dedicated

10. Ms. Riku is having dinner with one of our clients, but did not mention ------- one.

   (A) whose
   (B) which
   (C) each
   (D) neither

11. The customer service team is ------- to do whatever it takes to answer a patient's question.
    (A) extended
    (B) expected
    (C) exposed
    (D) expelled

12. FX Techno has been ------- its employees to obtain the recommended qualifications for each department.
    (A) encourage
    (B) encouraged
    (C) encouraging
    (D) encouragement

13. Prisco, Inc. offers products and services directly through ------- resellers and thousands of retail outlets worldwide.
    (A) authorized
    (B) precious
    (C) limited
    (D) sufficient

14. The advertising budget for the product will most likely ------- since audiences are already aware of the product.
    (A) shrink
    (B) heighten
    (C) reduce
    (D) lessen

15. Once management has decided that it is ------- that the project go ahead, a feasibility study will be needed.
    (A) desire
    (B) desirably
    (C) desiring
    (D) desirable

16. In order to maximize profits from the theater, we are discussing plans to increase the seating -------.
    (A) aptitude
    (B) intensity
    (C) preparation
    (D) capacity

17. The seafood restaurant receives daily ------- from diners on the establishment's numerous aquariums.
    (A) compliment
    (B) compliments
    (C) complimented
    (D) complimentary

18. Hornsfeld Appliances' downtown branch is ------- qualified and educated salespersons to start training next month.
    (A) looking
    (B) entering
    (C) seeking
    (D) inquiring

19. A team ------- of engineers and architects will go to the site to discuss strategies for expanding the factory.
    (A) consists
    (B) will consist
    (C) consisting
    (D) to be consisted

20. A ------- of experts from the National Health Institute was in Delhi to give talks at the Global Sanitation Forum.
    (A) revision
    (B) nomination
    (C) description
    (D) delegation

Questions 21-24 refer to the following e-mail.

To: All members, Association of Entrepreneurs
From: Jenny Deng, CEO
Date: May 9
Subject: Professional Development Seminars
Attachment: Seminar program and registration form

Dear all,

It was great to see you all at our third annual conference last month. Thank you for coming along

and ------- your knowledge, skills, and expertise with the rest of the organization.
    21.

I am writing to you now to let you know about the first in our series of professional development

seminars. As requested by members at the conference, all seminars will deal with practical -------
    22.

of direct relevance to our everyday working lives. I hope you'll agree that the first seminar, which

is on contract negotiations, fits this bill. The session will give attendees ------- tips on all stages
    23.

of the contract negotiation process from initial discussions to agreeing on the final contract.

-------.
 24.

For more details and to sign up, please see the attached document.

Best regards,

Jenny Deng
CEO, Association of Entrepreneurs

---

21. (A) share
(B) sharing
(C) to share
(D) would have shared

22. (A) conclusions
(B) subjects
(C) professions
(D) resources

23. (A) invaluable
(B) valuation
(C) value
(D) valuing

24. (A) Even those with years of experience should find it educational.
(B) Simply sign the contract and return it to me by the end of May.
(C) You can learn more by calling me at 490-5405 during regular business hours.
(D) Your feedback regarding this session is eagerly requested.

To: Veronica Lara
From: Tatsuya Abe
Subject: Mailing Issue
Date: August 18

Dear Veronica,

I just wanted to inform you of a complaint that ------- in to us by Mr. Fujimori. He ordered the
25.
home furnishings catalog last week from our Web site and was expecting delivery on Tuesday of

this week. However, it did not arrive. I apologized and dispatched a catalog to him right away by

express mail.

I'm afraid to say that this is the fifth time this month that this issue has occurred. I think we need

to look into what is going wrong with our online catalog request form. I suggest that we -------
26.
someone in our technology department to investigate this as a matter of urgency. -------. Please
27.
let me know your ------- on this idea.
28.

Best regards,

Tatsuya

25. (A) sends
(B) sent
(C) had sent
(D) has been sent

26. (A) assign
(B) contain
(C) explain
(D) understand

27. (A) Have someone there speak with
Mr. Fujimori about his order.
(B) This problem cannot be allowed to
continue any longer.
(C) We must learn where all of the missing
catalogs have gone.
(D) Talk to Jeb Wilkins for more information
on the security breach.

28. (A) orders
(B) thoughts
(C) collections
(D) developments

Watch out for *Get Busy Living*, a passionate and moving drama, starring Golden Award winner Paul Livingston as Jamie Brooks, a troubled, but talented musician who dreams of becoming a famous pianist. Directed by Shawn Jordan, this film is sure to stir up high emotions and top the box office. Be sure to check it out in theaters on Friday, June 30.

29. Who is Paul Livingston?

(A) A movie producer
(B) An actor
(C) A musician
(D) A theater manager

30. According to the article, what will happen on June 30?

(A) A movie will be released.
(B) An award will be given.
(C) An audition will start.
(D) A review will be published.

Questions 31-33 refer to the following e-mail.

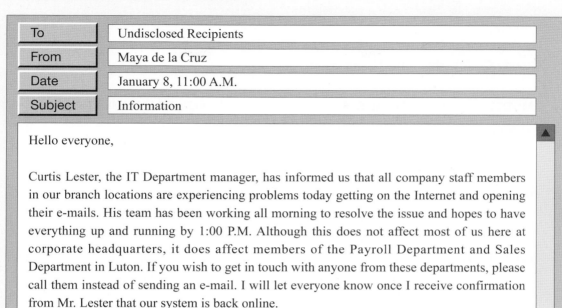

To	Undisclosed Recipients
From	Maya de la Cruz
Date	January 8, 11:00 A.M.
Subject	Information

Hello everyone,

Curtis Lester, the IT Department manager, has informed us that all company staff members in our branch locations are experiencing problems today getting on the Internet and opening their e-mails. His team has been working all morning to resolve the issue and hopes to have everything up and running by 1:00 P.M. Although this does not affect most of us here at corporate headquarters, it does affect members of the Payroll Department and Sales Department in Luton. If you wish to get in touch with anyone from these departments, please call them instead of sending an e-mail. I will let everyone know once I receive confirmation from Mr. Lester that our system is back online.

Best wishes,

Maya de la Cruz
Executive Assistant

31. Who most likely received the e-mail?

(A) Staff members in Payroll
(B) Sales team in Luton
(C) Employees at corporate headquarters
(D) Managers of branch offices

32. According to the e-mail, what is Mr. Lester's staff trying to do?

(A) Update a contact list
(B) Make a marketing decision
(C) Restore Internet access
(D) Organize IT files

33. What are recipients of the e-mail advised to do?

(A) Use an alternative method of communication
(B) Report technical issues to Mr. Lester
(C) Collect their paychecks at 1:00 P.M.
(D) Work at another computer station

http://www.coffeemakers.com

Quality Coffee Machines Under $400

MODEL	DETAILS	REVIEWER COMMENTS
Janko Instant	Weight: 2 kgs Capacity: 30 cups Suggested Retail Price: $199	Available online only Low noise level during operation
Pinto Expresso Maker	Weight: 1.5 kgs Capacity: 40 cups Suggested Retail Price: $249	Hard to follow set-up instructions Complex control system
Elite Cafetiere	Weight: 3 kgs Capacity: 60 cups Suggested Retail Price: $399	Five-year warranty on parts Fast brewing process
Maxwell 300	Weight: 3.5 kgs Capacity: 120 cups Suggested Retail Price: $399	Large capacity Needs less frequent refilling

34. Why would someone most likely refer to the chart?

(A) To learn about coffee machines in a certain price range
(B) To find the replacement part numbers for each coffee machine
(C) To determine how many coffee machines are purchased annually
(D) To compare the warranty periods of coffee machines

35. What is a stated advantage of the Janko Instant?

(A) It can be ordered from any store.
(B) It is easy to set up.
(C) It runs quietly.
(D) It has a long warranty.

36. How are the Elite Cafetiere and Maxwell 300 similar?

(A) They cost the same amount.
(B) They both brew coffee quickly.
(C) They are the same weight.
(D) They both received negative reviews.

Questions 37-40 refer to the following online chat discussion.

Melinda Kennedy [10:07 A.M.]
Good morning, I want updates from everyone about the schedule for the Lemore Supermarket project. Jose, have you spoken to the factory about mixing the ingredients?

Jose Cruz [10:08 A.M.]
Yes, they called on Monday. Unfortunately, one of their machines is broken. Candice is calling them for an update to find out when they can begin making our order.

Melinda Kennedy [10:09 A.M.]
The empty boxes and cartons arrive tomorrow. Can we delay that shipment?

Jose Cruz [10:10 A.M.]
I'm not sure. I haven't talked to the packaging company about this problem yet. I was waiting to hear from Candice about the revised date for the factory delivery. Candice, have you called them?

Candice Kagan [10:15 A.M.]
I just talked to Stuart Bryce, the factory's production manager. He said that they can start making our chocolate on Wednesday and that our order will be shipped out on Saturday.

Jose Cruz [10:16 A.M.]
That's great! I'll tell them to postpone the packaging delivery until then.

Candice Kagan [10:17 A.M.]
Don't forget that the stickers need to get placed on the boxes before the products are shipped out. And make sure that they are stored in a cool area.

Melinda Kennedy [10:18 A.M.]
So all of the Lemore's order will be delivered on time?

Candice Kagan [10:19 A.M.]
That's right. They should get it Sunday morning. Luckily, we're still on schedule, even with the factory problem.

Melinda Kennedy [10:21 A.M.]
Wonderful. I'm confident projects like this will lead to great success for us. Going forward let's keep at it, and continue to look for opportunities to manufacture other limited edition flavors.

SEND

---

37. What type of business does Ms. Kagan most likely work at?

(A) A supermarket chain
(B) A dessert manufacturer
(C) A shipping company
(D) An advertising agency

38. When will Lemore's order arrive?

(A) On Monday
(B) On Wednesday
(C) On Saturday
(D) On Sunday

39. What will Mr. Cruz most likely do next?

(A) Move some boxes to a cool area
(B) Ship out some merchandise
(C) Contact a business
(D) Cancel an order

40. At 10:21 A.M., what does Ms. Kennedy mean when she writes, "Going forward let's keep at it"?

(A) She is happy that the project was completed earlier.
(B) She thinks that customers will enjoy a service.
(C) She believes her company should do similar projects in the future.
(D) She hopes that a product receives good reviews.

Questions 41-45 refer to the following e-mail and online article.

To	Melanie McKenna <mmckenna@artdesigns.com>
From	Harry Keen <hkeen@ascentpublishing.com>
Subject	Emmanuel's Book
Date	August 12, 2:32 P.M.
Attachment	Israel Cover

Hi Melanie,

This morning, I received an e-mail from Emmanuel Chung regarding the front cover for *Architecture in Ancient Greece*, his latest book in what is going to become a three-volume series on ancient world architecture. He does not want to go with the bright colors that we chose and prefers that the cover design resemble that of the second book in this series, *City Designs in Israel*. So I would like to ask you to create some more preliminary sketches by the end of this week so that I can forward them to Mr. Chung. For your reference, I have attached a scanned image of *City Designs in Israel*'s cover.

Mr. Chung also brought up some other issues regarding the book design in the e-mail he sent me. Instead of me relaying them to you, I think it would be better if everyone involved with the project could hear his views directly. Therefore, he will be video-conferencing with us on Thursday at 7:00 P.M. from his office at Fasselheim University. I will be sending a link for the video conference on that day. Please inform the rest of the team members about this.

Harry

Address: www.theworcesternews.com/book-review go

Wednesday, December 22

The Year in Book Design

The Worcester News annually invites professionals in cover art and book design to present the best book covers to our readers. Mark Varga, who lectures in fine art at the Grandia School of Design in Hungary, reveals his choice for this year.

Mark Varga: I am intrigued by book cover designs that show very little information about the contents of the book and yet are interesting enough to make me want to pick up the book and skim through it. So, when I came upon a copy of *Architecture in Ancient Greece*, written by Emmanuel Chung of Fasselheim University and published by Ascent Publishing, I was fascinated by its cover, which bears neither the book's title nor the writer's name. Instead, the cover contains an image of pale, gray ruins covered with thick, dark brown foliage. This cover design is very similar to that of the second book in what is to be a three-book series by Mr. Emmanuel Chung; the second book's cover similarly features architecture with plants but has ancient stone temples in the background and less detail in general. Melanie McKenna, the artist responsible for the cover of *Architecture in Ancient Greece*, is truly an expert in using colors and intricate structures to draw in readers to a book. I commend her beautiful minimalism.

41. What is one purpose of the e-mail?

(A) To set a deadline for more work to be done on a project
(B) To notify a staff member about a meeting cancellation
(C) To remind a colleague to return a borrowed book
(D) To announce the press launch of an author's latest book

42. What is implied about Harry Keen?

(A) He invited Emmanuel Chung to participate in a meeting.
(B) He is an expert on ancient architecture.
(C) He will visit Fasselheim University next week.
(D) He is the author of three books.

43. What is indicated about the cover of *City Designs in Israel*?

(A) Mark Varga designed it.
(B) It includes images of temples.
(C) Emmanuel Chung was displeased with it.
(D) It has bright colors.

44. In the online article, the word "bears" in paragraph 2, line 5, is closest in meaning to

(A) displays
(B) accepts
(C) requires
(D) fits

45. What is NOT suggested about Melanie McKenna?

(A) An expert selected her work as his favorite design of the year.
(B) A design school in Hungary will exhibit her work.
(C) She makes effective use of color in her work.
(D) Her work was featured in a book published by Ascent Publishing.

Questions 46-50 refer to the following advertisement, online shopping cart, and e-mail.

Clifton's Art Wholesaler

Liven up the walls of your home or office with a painting from Clifton's Art Wholesaler. Clifton's employs professional artists in our studios to suit every taste. Just visit our Web site, www.cliftonarts.com. to find thumbnail samples of current artwork for sale. There, you can search for paintings by artist, color, or size. Whether you're shopping for a picture to match your office furniture or for a piece to brighten up your living room, we make it easy. When you've chosen the perfect pieces, use our simple online ordering system, and we'll have your merchandise delivered within four to six business days. You can also receive it the following day by paying an extra delivery fee.

*If you are unsatisfied with your purchase, you may exchange or return it. Having trouble deciding? Then we encourage you to contact one of our design specialists to help choose the perfect painting for you!

---

https://www.cliftonarts.com/checkout

Order Summary #42	Customer: ESV Dentistry	
Item	**Size**	**Price**
Abstract Sunshine S2039	11 × 14	$90.00
Still Life with Gentleman G3821	16 × 20	$70.00
Country Estate E2390	20 × 24	$100.00
Cornfield Bloom B3312	24 × 36	$80.00
Sub Total		$340.00
Tax (10%)		$34.00
Express shipping		$30.00
Total		$404.00

From	allie.kim@esvdentistry.com
To	orders@cliftonsart.com
Date	November 11
Subject	Order #42

Thank you for the prompt delivery of my order (#42). Our maintenance team hung the paintings in the lobby over the weekend. However, instead of *Abstract Sunshine*, I received *Abstract Moonlight*. As the names of the paintings are similar, I think your staff got them mixed up. Could you please locate and deliver the missing piece? In addition, a lot of our patients have praised the painting with the farm scenery (B3312). I was wondering if you could make another piece similar to this one. Please let me know.

Sincerely,

Allie Kim
Office Manager
ESV Dentistry

46. In the advertisement, the word "taste" in paragraph 1, line 2, is closest in meaning to

(A) flavor
(B) sample
(C) preference
(D) sense

47. What are Clifton's Art Wholesaler customers urged to do?

(A) Test out a product
(B) Drop by a studio
(C) Consult with an expert
(D) Attend a gallery showing

48. What is most likely true about order #42?

(A) It included complimentary artwork.
(B) It includes discounted items.
(C) It was paid for in October.
(D) It arrived in one day.

49. Which painting do ESV Dentistry patients indicate that they like?

(A) *Abstract Sunshine*
(B) *Still Life with Gentleman*
(C) *Country Estate*
(D) *Cornfield Bloom*

50. What problem did Ms. Kim mention in her e-mail?

(A) Some merchandise was damaged.
(B) Her credit card was charged the wrong amount.
(C) An incorrect item was delivered.
(D) She cannot find her tracking number.

ACTUAL TEST

ACTUAL TEST

해설서 p.175

READING TEST

In the Reading test, you will read a variety of texts and answer several different types of reading comprehension questions. The entire Reading test will last 75 minutes. There are three parts, and directions are given for each part. You are encouraged to answer as many questions as possible within the time allowed.

You must mark your answers on the separate answer sheet. Do not write your answers in the test book.

PART 5

Directions: A word or phrase is missing in each of the sentences below. Four answer choices are given below each sentence. Select the best answer to complete the sentence. Then mark the letter (A), (B), (C), or (D) on your answer sheet.

---

101. All team members are expected to get to the gate two hours before ------- scheduled flight.

(A) their
(B) them
(C) they
(D) themselves

102. The ------- draft of the marketing report needs to be received by this Friday.

(A) final
(B) blank
(C) various
(D) certain

103. Mr. Lee offers patients ------- health consultations and insurance claim assistance.

(A) neither
(B) if only
(C) not just
(D) both

104. Jeremy Struker ------- by the board of directors to lead the new advertising campaign.

(A) selecting
(B) was selecting
(C) selected
(D) was selected

105. Cornwall Music Ltd. is hiring skilled artisans to address the present ------- for handcrafted instruments.

(A) demand
(B) denial
(C) measure
(D) claim

106. Vonex Apparel has seen an increase in sales ------- they introduced their new coat line last month.

(A) over
(B) although
(C) besides
(D) since

107. Since the supplies have been delivered ahead of schedule, the product will be produced ------- than originally projected.

(A) earliest
(B) earliness
(C) early
(D) earlier

108. Based on the updated timetable, the training workshop is going to start at 4:00 P.M. ------- 3:00 P.M.

(A) after
(B) instead of
(C) while
(D) so that

109. Since renovation work is being done at the station, this train is going to proceed ------- Topeka without making any stops.

(A) through
(B) direct
(C) aboard
(D) swiftly

110. Meteorologists International, a non-profit organization, will collect air samples in the deserts ------- Riyadh.

(A) to
(B) around
(C) under
(D) about

111. Candidates will be contacted ------- a final decision has been made on their application.

(A) despite
(B) like
(C) once
(D) unless

112. Assured that Ms. Suarez was ------- more experienced than other employees, Nitussa Automotive's executive board promoted her to General Manager.

(A) beside
(B) much
(C) so
(D) barely

113. At Clint's Photography, we are proud to offer only ------- processed images.

(A) professions
(B) profession
(C) professionally
(D) professional

114. All of Art Three Medias' ------- have worked in the graphic arts industry for at least five years.

(A) design
(B) designers
(C) designs
(D) designing

115. The music reviewer at the *Tampa Daily News* ------- the songs on Rod Oliver's new album as unoriginal.

(A) listened
(B) acquired
(C) received
(D) described

116. The construction of the performing arts theater went well over the initial budget, but the result was well worth the -------.

(A) expense
(B) tariff
(C) fare
(D) quantity

117. Wakano Electronics has finalized its purchase of the Bergo Tech store chain in order to expand ------- North and South America.

(A) there
(B) now
(C) every
(D) into

118. The use of high-quality yet ------- building materials led to a decrease in costs for Takata Construction Co.

(A) inexpensive
(B) unhappy
(C) incomplete
(D) undecided

GO ON TO THE NEXT PAGE

119. A veteran golfer -------, Ms. Mayweather was also a mentor to Bishop Duarte, the nation's top-earning golfer.

(A) hers
(B) she
(C) herself
(D) her

120. The Orion Homeowners' Association is the group that is ------- the speed limit increase for vehicles in residential areas.

(A) opposing
(B) opposed
(C) opposes
(D) oppose

121. An intriguing ------- in yesterday's *Dallas Metro Times* argued that increasing competition in the job market will affect real estate prices.

(A) book
(B) listing
(C) index
(D) editorial

122. Since he came to the company 15 years ago, Mr. Pelt has been the lead ------- of labor contracts and disputes.

(A) negotiates
(B) negotiating
(C) negotiation
(D) negotiator

123. Ware Hardware was ------- the businesses affected during the great storm last month.

(A) among
(B) down
(C) within
(D) for

124. For any inquiries regarding salary employees should contact ------- or Ms. Singh directly.

(A) me
(B) my
(C) I
(D) mine

125. While the director ------- projected this quarter's revenue to be high, he later reported that the outlook was not so great.

(A) very
(B) eventually
(C) initially
(D) greatly

126. Tusco has been listed as the top steel manufacturer due to their recent sales ------- and production increases.

(A) growth
(B) grower
(C) growing
(D) grew

127. Due to ------- concerning its operating hours, Mavin Apparel, Co. has decided to stay open until 10 P.M.

(A) products
(B) resources
(C) complaints
(D) challengers

128. Please be sure to carefully look over your office supply request form because you cannot make any revisions ------- the order is placed.

(A) once
(B) next
(C) resulting
(D) immediately

129. The academy gave away gift packages throughout August ------- an assortment of items and vouchers that students can use.

(A) contain
(B) contains
(C) containing
(D) contained

130. ------- delays to the novel's publication, Stephen Brodard will begin his country-wide tour as scheduled and attend all book signing events.

(A) Accordingly
(B) In addition to
(C) Consequently
(D) Regardless of

PART 6

Directions: Read the texts that follow. A word, phrase, or sentence is missing in some of the sentences. Four answer choices are given below each of these sentences. Select the best answer to complete the text. Then mark the letter (A), (B), (C), or (D) on your answer sheet.

Questions 131-134 refer to the following letter.

Dear Ms. Morimoto,

I am writing to ------- you that you have reached the third and final stage of interviews to
          131.
become a flight attendant. Your interview is scheduled for 11:15 on Monday, May 18. -------
                                                                                        132.
that date, I recommend that you practice speaking English. Two of the airline representatives

at the interview will be from our corporate headquarters in Canada. They will not ask you

any questions in Japanese, nor can you answer them in it. -------. We already ------- that
                                                            133.   **134.**
you are qualified for the position, so now your main focus should be on impressing them.

Good luck.

Sincerely,

Robin Turner
Recruiter
Canadian Airlines

---

131. (A) present
(B) announce
(C) admit
(D) notify

132. (A) Since
(B) Before
(C) Onto
(D) Over

133. (A) Instead, you need to speak to them in the language they use with you.
(B) As a result, you will be tested on your knowledge of French and English.
(C) Therefore, you have successfully passed the Japanese part of the exam.
(D) Meanwhile, you need to improve the language skills you use on the job.

134. (A) was learned
(B) have learned
(C) will learn
(D) learning

GO ON TO THE NEXT PAGE

Questions 135–138 refer to the following article.

Summer Music Series Returns

The Turlington College symphony orchestra has officially announced that they will perform

a second series of summer concerts. ------- the incredible response to last year's inaugural
                                      135.

event, the performances will be taking place in the Caner Theater. The smaller Grimm

Theater proved too small to accommodate the number of people who wanted tickets last

year.

The program itself has also been ------- to encompass 10 weekends instead of 8. -------.
                                   136.   **137.**

They will perform pieces that require vocalists, so the Turlington College Choir -------
                                                                                  138.

joining them on stage as well.

If this year is as successful as they expect it to be, they plan to make the Summer Music

Series an annual event.

---

135. (A) So that
(B) Because of
(C) Moreover
(D) Therefore

136. (A) expanded
(B) expand
(C) expansion
(D) expanse

137. (A) They apologized for having to shorten the schedule in this manner.
(B) All these performances will take place in the Grimm Theater at 9 P.M.
(C) Every performance will only include music played by the orchestra.
(D) This will permit the orchestra to play even more pieces than before.

138. (A) were
(B) to be
(C) was
(D) will be

Office Organizers cleaning service will ------- its fifth office in Brisbane on November 2
139.

of this year. -------, we are looking for 10 experienced cleaners to manage teams of 15
140.

to 20 individuals. Executives and companies contract our teams to clean their offices on

a regular basis.

As a team manager, your ------- will include ordering supplies, managing your cleaning
141.

staff, and interacting with our clients on a personal basis. Applicants should have

at least two years' janitorial experience, and a knowledge of heavy-duty cleaning

machinery.

To apply, please send your résumé with a cover letter to Jacqueline Carter at

Jacqicarter@oohrmail.com. -------.
142.

139. (A) expand
(B) open
(C) visit
(D) inspect

140. (A) Consequently
(B) Consequent to
(C) Consequence of
(D) The consequences

141. (A) businesses
(B) descriptions
(C) examples
(D) responsibilities

142. (A) There is no need to submit any
paperwork when you apply.
(B) If you are qualified, she will contact
you to set up an interview.
(C) How your clients feel about your work
will determine if you are rehired.
(D) Ms. Carter is willing to work hard for
you and your company.

GO ON TO THE NEXT PAGE

Questions 143-146 refer to the following notice.

The Montressor Transit Authority announced today that construction of the new Yellow Line, Subway Line 5, is nearing completion. Locations ------- by this line include the Montressor
143.
Art Museum, Smith College and Merrick Park. -------. Once the line begins -------,
144. **145.**
congestion in many neighborhoods along the route is expected to decrease. Passengers will

be able to use their old transit cards, but they will have to pass through ticket gates when

they transfer at some stations. -------, there will be no extra fee charged for transferring.
146.
Line 5 is scheduled to open on October 17. There will be a ribbon cutting ceremony at

Merrick Park Station before the first train departs. The mayor plans to give a speech at the

ceremony.

143. (A) servicing
(B) to be serviced
(C) will service
(D) are being serviced

144. (A) These are the only three spots where passengers can get on and off.
(B) The line will start at Hazel Park and end in the Westborough neighborhood.
(C) The subway should be completed sometime in the month of November.
(D) More passengers than expected have been taking the new line recently.

145. (A) proposing
(B) modifying
(C) operating
(D) collecting

146. (A) However
(B) Likewise
(C) Indeed
(D) Since

PART 7

Directions: In this part you will read a selection of texts, such as magazine and newspaper articles, letters, and instant messages. Each text or set of texts is followed by several questions. Select the best answer for each question and mark the letter (A), (B), (C), or (D) on your answer sheet.

Questions 147-148 refer to the following invitation.

La Fayette Apartment Complex
Grand Opening on Minton Road

Wednesday, June 10
West Side Real Estate of Mavon City,
University Ave, Suite 200
Toronto, ONM5G,

Courteously welcomes you to see our FANTASTIC properties
available for immediate rent!

Tours from 3 P.M. to 7 P.M.
Food and drinks will be served.

Contact J. M. Stanton at (416) 555-1245
for leasing contracts and rental rates.

---

147. Why is an event being held?

(A) To arrange employment interviews at a company
(B) To display new housing in the area
(C) To announce a building plan to the residents
(D) To celebrate a remodeled head office

148. What most likely is J. M. Stanton's profession?

(A) Interior decorator
(B) Catering manager
(C) City tour guide
(D) Sales agent

GO ON TO THE NEXT PAGE

Questions 149–150 refer to the following text message.

From: Maria Bertoni

To: Rosaria Ducia

My lunch appointment with our client is taking longer than expected, so go ahead and start the meeting without me. Start with last quarter's sales report and then go on to the predictions for next quarter. I should get there in 30 minutes.

149. Why was the message sent?

(A) To ask for help
(B) To provide instructions
(C) To verify some information
(D) To arrange a lunch meeting

150. What is indicated by Ms. Bertoni?

(A) She will arrive late to the sales meeting.
(B) She wants to start a new project.
(C) She expects sales to decrease.
(D) She has acquired a new client.

To: Jan Ling
From: Elias Namora
Date: September 12
Subject: Slater request

Good morning Jan,

A patron, Carrie Slater, came by earlier today inquiring about the renovation projects in the Avonlea Business District. She wanted to see if we had any relevant newspaper articles that were published this year. Since she had another appointment, she told me she would come back later today for the articles. I found a number of articles in our library's archives, which I printed out and left at the front desk with Ms. Slater's name on them. When you are working your shift later, do you mind searching the archives from this year and printing out any other articles you find? Ms. Slater said she would return later tonight to pick up whatever we found.

Thank you,

Elias Namora

151. Who most likely is Mr. Namora?

(A) A newspaper editor
(B) A researcher
(C) A construction worker
(D) A librarian

152. What does Mr. Namora ask Ms. Ling to do?

(A) Email some files
(B) Add names to a database
(C) Locate some information
(D) Look over an article

GO ON TO THE NEXT PAGE

Questions 153–154 refer to the following text message chain.

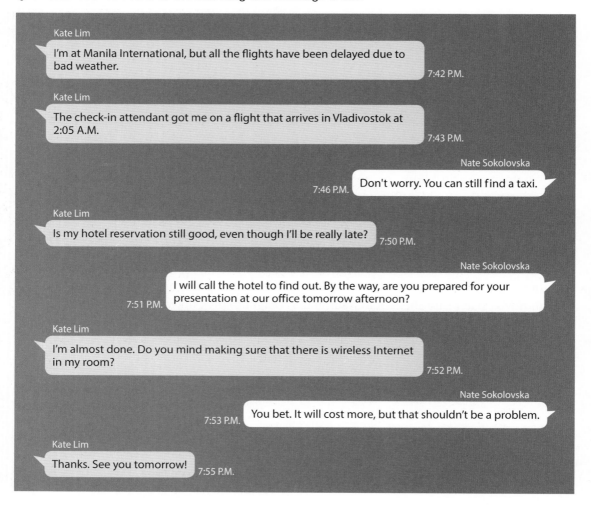

Kate Lim

I'm at Manila International, but all the flights have been delayed due to bad weather.

7:42 P.M.

Kate Lim

The check-in attendant got me on a flight that arrives in Vladivostok at 2:05 A.M.

7:43 P.M.

Nate Sokolovska

7:46 P.M.

Don't worry. You can still find a taxi.

Kate Lim

Is my hotel reservation still good, even though I'll be really late?

7:50 P.M.

Nate Sokolovska

7:51 P.M.

I will call the hotel to find out. By the way, are you prepared for your presentation at our office tomorrow afternoon?

Kate Lim

I'm almost done. Do you mind making sure that there is wireless Internet in my room?

7:52 P.M.

Nate Sokolovska

7:53 P.M.

You bet. It will cost more, but that shouldn't be a problem.

Kate Lim

Thanks. See you tomorrow!

7:55 P.M.

153. What is suggested about Ms. Lim?

(A) She has visited Manila before.
(B) She works in Vladivostok.
(C) She is traveling for business.
(D) She is a check-in attendant.

154. At 7:53 P.M., what does Mr. Sokolovska mean when he writes, "You bet"?

(A) He will confirm Ms. Lim's flight schedule.
(B) He will ensure a room has Internet service.
(C) He will pick Ms. Lim up from the airport.
(D) He will arrange a taxi service.

Questions 155–157 refer to the following letter.

Ellis Dentistry
High Beach Shopping Center
5830 Round Street, Miami 33195
(305) 555-3758
www.ellisdentistry.com

June 3

Mr. Chuck Lom
21 Ranch Road,
Miami 33195

Dear Mr. Lom,

According to our records, you are due for your annual check-up. As you are aware, regular check-ups are necessary to maintain good dental hygiene, so please contact us to arrange a visit at your convenience.

We recently moved from the Coastal Mall location to a new spot in Downtown Miami. To celebrate this opening, we are offering 30 percent off any teeth whitening treatment until June 26. Please see the enclosed promotional flyer for more details.

Our operating hours will remain the same.
Monday to Friday, 9:00 A.M. to 6:00 P.M.
Saturday, 9:00 A.M. to 3:00 P.M.

We look forward to seeing you soon.

Manny Buck

Manny Buck
Office Manager
Enclosure

155. Why has Mr. Buck written to Mr. Lom?

(A) To confirm the receipt of an order
(B) To ask him to send a payment
(C) To report the results of his check-up
(D) To remind him to schedule an appointment

156. What has been sent with the letter?

(A) A discount offer
(B) A list of health insurance providers
(C) A catalog of dental products
(D) A billing statement

157. According to the letter, what has Ellis Dentistry changed?

(A) Its Web site layout
(B) Its business hours
(C) Its payment options
(D) Its office location

GO ON TO THE NEXT PAGE

Endura's Batteries Make Their Mark

By Jared Mendoza

NEW YORK (13 January) — Endura, the battery manufacturer, announced its record-breaking third quarter profits to a standing ovation from shareholders. Barely known just a year ago, Endura's most recent product lineup uses its new DENSE technology. — [1] —. All this publicity is sending Endura's stock prices sky high.

Hundreds of companies are interested in using Endura's products. — [2] —. In everything from phones to electric vehicles, Endura batteries last hundreds of times longer than competing brands, leaving key industry players, such as Vexon, scrambling to catch up. Analysts expect Endura's technology to be in most electronic devices in the future.

"Endura's products will allow companies to revolutionize their products over a very short term," said Dr. Vera Lincoln, Professor of Chemical Engineering at Hildreth University. — [3] —. "Endura's DENSE technology increases the energy output of its batteries, which results in smaller models for existing products." — [4] —.

After announcing its quarterly earnings this morning, the company's spokesperson announced that, based on the demand that they have seen so far, there will be many profitable quarters ahead.

---

158. What is indicated about Endura?

(A) It has been profitable for three quarters straight.
(B) It will sign a contract with Vexon.
(C) It was established one year ago.
(D) It is attracting many investors.

159. What is reported about Endura's batteries?

(A) They are found in most electronic devices.
(B) They are smaller than any other competitor brands.
(C) They produce energy for a long time.
(D) They were developed by Dr. Vera Lincoln.

160. In which of the positions marked [1], [2], [3], and [4] does the following sentence best belong?

"Endura's new batteries are being described as unbelievable by various news outlets."

(A) [1]
(B) [2]
(C) [3]
(D) [4]

Questions 161-163 refer to the following table of contents of a magazine.

CONTENTS
Issue 421 June

10 Natural Health

Mary Southwood gives some tips for cultivating edible flowers.

19 Delicious Trees

Our writers offer some insight on choosing different types of fruit trees.

22 Tips

Alana Han explains the advantages of rich soil.

26 Essentials

Dominic Levin discusses ways to keep your lawn beautiful.

32 Reflections

Maya Sandifer shares photos of glass greenhouses from her recent overseas trip.

36 Chef Katie Simmons

The owner of Katie's Bistro describes how to prepare a delicious salad using homegrown vegetables.

38 Working on a Budget

Paul Mason shows us how to design affordable and attractive patios.

44 Next Issue

Preview of the July issue

---

161. What is the focus of the magazine?

(A) Travel
(B) Restaurants
(C) Gardening
(D) Fitness

162. Based on the table of contents, who recently traveled abroad?

(A) Ms. Sandifer
(B) Mr. Levin
(C) Ms. Southwood
(D) Ms. Han

163. Where in the magazine would a recipe most likely be found?

(A) On page 10
(B) On page 22
(C) On page 36
(D) On page 44

GO ON TO THE NEXT PAGE

Questions 164-167 refer to the following online chat discussion.

Izumi Lane [10:05 A.M.]: Good morning, everyone. I need some feedback. Betsy Allen just got off the phone with Carrie Moss from Hardigan Transport, and they want us to double the quantities of everything for this weekend's party. Is this possible?

Marie Schupe [10:06 A.M.]: If the staff works overtime, we can prepare that much food in two days.

Lynn Kim [10:08 A.M.]: We don't have enough people, but if you give me a day, I can recruit some temporary workers.

Andy Jansen [10:09 A.M.]: Before any of that happens, we'll need to set the menu. I'll make sure my crew does that before noon today.

Izumi Lane [10:12 A.M.]: It looks like this might work. By the end of the day on Thursday, everything will be prepared, and we'll have enough employees for the event. But what about delivery?

Marie Schupe [10:13 A.M.]: I can rent two additional trucks with your approval.

Izumi Lane [10:14 A.M.]: OK. I can sign off on that. Gavin, how long will it take you to print all the place cards for the tables?

Gavin Wong [10:16 A.M.]: I can have that done by the end of the day on Friday.

Izumi Lane [10:17 A.M.]: That's wonderful. I'll tell Betsy to call the client back with the news.

164. At 10:05 A.M., what does Ms. Lane mean when she writes, "I need some feedback"?

(A) She is requesting approval.
(B) She wants to invite additional guests.
(C) She is asking for some opinions.
(D) She would like to discuss a new product.

165. For what kind of business does Ms. Lane most likely work?

(A) An auto center
(B) A catering company
(C) A printing center
(D) A shipping company

166. According to the discussion, which team must complete their work before the others?

(A) Ms. Schupe's team
(B) Ms. Kim's team
(C) Mr. Wong's team
(D) Mr. Jansen's team

167. What will Ms. Allen most likely tell Ms. Moss?

(A) That the costs for an event will be reduced
(B) That she can increase an order
(C) That a delivery will be made on Wednesday
(D) That she will visit Ms. Moss on Thursday

To	wso@ganttech.com
From	xhuang@XPSenterprises.com
Date	August 29
Subject	Your inquiry

Dear Mr. So,

Thank you for contacting XPS Enterprises. I am delighted to hear that you are considering our services to help your company, Gant Tech, promote its products online.

XPS Enterprises has been in business for over 15 years. We have served as marketing consultants for various major organizations, both domestically and abroad. Some of our clients include CFC Manufacturing of Manila, Frasier Corporation of New York, and UK Automakers of London. By working with us, organizations are able to benefit from increased global exposure on the Internet.

Should you decide to work with XPS Enterprises, we assure you that you won't be disappointed. XPS Enterprises has an outstanding reputation for finishing projects in a timely manner and within budget. We are certain that you will be satisfied with the results.

If you wish to arrange a meeting to talk about your needs in more detail, please contact me directly at 864-555-5142. I hope to hear from you soon.

Sincerely,

Xiao Huang
Customer Relations Manager, XPS Enterprises

---

168. Why did Ms. Huang send the e-mail?

(A) To confirm a future meeting at Gant Tech
(B) To describe how to design a Web site
(C) To provide information about the start date of a new project
(D) To encourage a company to pursue a business relationship

169. What does Gant Tech most likely want to do?

(A) Advertise its products on the Internet
(B) Build a new facility
(C) Raise the prices of its services
(D) Increase employee numbers

170. What is mentioned about XPS Enterprises?

(A) It has recently hired new staff members.
(B) Its fees are more affordable than those of other consulting firms.
(C) It does business in more than one country.
(D) Its headquarters are in Manila.

171. The word "assure" in paragraph 3, line 1, is closest in meaning to

(A) convince
(B) secure
(C) promote
(D) promise

GO ON TO THE NEXT PAGE →

Community Bulletin Advertising Space Available

Carvier University invites students to post ads on its large bulletin kiosks, on the west side of Alumni Square, north of the recreation center. Room on the kiosks is limited to save space for campus news, so notices may only stay up for a week.

All material must be emailed to the Carvier Communications Office for review at communications@carvier.edu. Any content that does not adhere to the University's regulations and standards will be rejected. Please make sure that the ad is suitable for A3 or A4 paper-sized prints. — [1] —. In your e-mail, indicate the exact dates during which you want your ad to run. — [2] —. Please also include your phone number and a convenient time to reach you. — [3] —.

Upon approval, a payment of $70 must be made in person at the University Registrar's Office located in the Memorial Union. Students may pay with cash or credit card. — [4] —. It typically takes one to three business days for an ad to be approved.

Carvier University Communications Office
www.carvier.edu

172. What is indicated about an advertisement on the Carvier University bulletin kiosk?

(A) It must be printed in color.
(B) It costs $70 per week.
(C) Its content must be delivered in person.
(D) It can only be posted for three days.

173. What is NOT mentioned as a requirement for an advertisement to be posted on the kiosk?

(A) It should be approved in advance.
(B) It should be a certain size.
(C) It should include a mailing address.
(D) It should comply with university rules.

174. Where does the payment have to be made?

(A) At the Memorial Union
(B) In the Communications Office
(C) At Alumni Square
(D) In the Recreation Center

175. In which of the positions marked [1], [2], [3], and [4] does the following sentence best belong?

"Alternatively, wire transfers to Carvier University are also accepted."

(A) [1]
(B) [2]
(C) [3]
(D) [4]

GO ON TO THE NEXT PAGE

Questions 176–180 refer to the following advertisement and Web page.

La Roche Orchard
Your number one source for fresh fruits!

Bring your family and pick any fruit you want from our 100-acre orchard. Come for just a few hours or for the entire day. Large groups are welcome. We provide baskets for your convenience and also offer free on-site parking. Small buses will take you from the parking lot to the orchard.

General harvest seasons (all fruits are sold by weight):
June - July
Pears, cherries, blueberries, and grapes
August - October
Apples (three kinds), pumpkins, and pineapples

Browse our farm's store, where you can buy locally grown fruits and vegetables as well as homemade jams and pies.

Experience our local wildlife and plants by going on the La Roche Trailblazer Walk. The four-kilometer trail is open to any visitors from June to October.

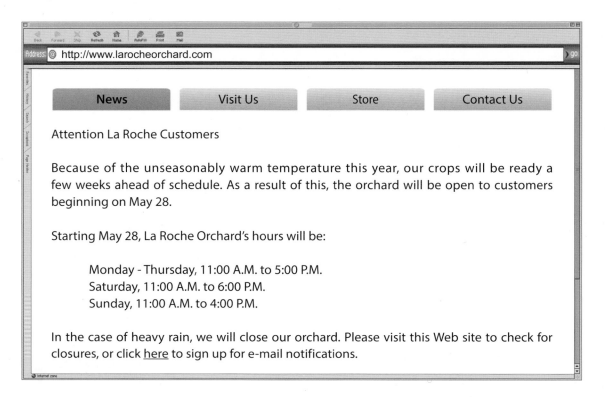

http://www.larocheorchard.com

| News | Visit Us | Store | Contact Us |

Attention La Roche Customers

Because of the unseasonably warm temperature this year, our crops will be ready a few weeks ahead of schedule. As a result of this, the orchard will be open to customers beginning on May 28.

Starting May 28, La Roche Orchard's hours will be:

> Monday - Thursday, 11:00 A.M. to 5:00 P.M.
> Saturday, 11:00 A.M. to 6:00 P.M.
> Sunday, 11:00 A.M. to 4:00 P.M.

In the case of heavy rain, we will close our orchard. Please visit this Web site to check for closures, or click <u>here</u> to sign up for e-mail notifications.

176. What does the advertisement NOT mention about La Roche Orchard?

(A) Sales of local products
(B) Transportation to the orchard
(C) Complimentary parking
(D) Picnic areas

177. What is suggested about the trail?

(A) It will be extended in the winter.
(B) It is a popular attraction at La Roche Orchard.
(C) It is for only for experienced hikers.
(D) It will be closed on Fridays.

178. What does the Web page indicate about La Roche Orchard?

(A) It has had an unusual growing season.
(B) Its operating hours have been shortened.
(C) Its harvest has created more employment opportunities.
(D) It is a family-run business.

179. In what month will berries most likely first become available for picking this season?

(A) In May
(B) In June
(C) In July
(D) In September

180. According to the Web page, what can customers register to receive?

(A) Passes for the bus rides
(B) Recipes for jams and pies
(C) Invitations to the May 28 opening
(D) Announcements of the orchard closing

GO ON TO THE NEXT PAGE

Questions 181-185 refer to the following Web site posts.

Landon Computers Community Forum

Landon FN2 Slimline cannot maintain wireless connectivity
Post by Daniel Palmer
Aug 10, 10:32 A.M.

After using the Landon FNT model for nearly four years, I decided to buy the new Landon FN2 Slimline laptop three days ago. Overall, I am very happy with this new model, but I keep having trouble staying connected to my wireless Internet network at home. The laptop initially connects to the network, but gets disconnected after ten minutes. I have tried several solutions, including restarting my FN2 Slimline laptop and reconnecting to my home network. Nothing seems to work.

Has anyone else encountered this problem? I'm not sure whether this problem occurs with all FN2 laptops or just with mine. I am quite certain that my network is okay. My roommates, who use different brands of laptops, have no problems with their Internet connections.

Landon Computers Community Forum

Re: Landon FN2 Slimline cannot maintain wireless connectivity
Post by Amira Mirelli
Aug 10, 12:17 P.M.

Hi Daniel,

I recently purchased the same laptop as you from Landon Computers, and a few coworkers and I experienced a similar problem. I tried resetting my network box, rebooting my laptop as well as checking and reinserting the power cables, but without any success. I then decided to call the Landon Computers' support center. A technician immediately helped me resolve the issue. She sent me a direct link to a software update that fixed the problem right away. Simply download and install the update (it should only take about five minutes). The software update can be found in the Downloads section of the Landon Computers Web site. Once the update is installed, you should not have any more problems staying connected.

181. What is the subject of the first post?

(A) A technical problem with a new laptop
(B) Errors in a laptop user guide
(C) A delayed repair service
(D) Broken links on a Web site

182. What is suggested about Mr. Palmer's wireless network?

(A) It needs to be replaced.
(B) It was configured by a roommate.
(C) It is functioning properly.
(D) It is seldom used.

183. How did both Mr. Palmer and Ms. Mirelli try to correct the problem?

(A) By adjusting the Internet settings
(B) By replacing a damaged part
(C) By inspecting power cables
(D) By restarting the laptop

184. What is indicated about Ms. Mirelli?

(A) She is a long-time customer of Landon Computers.
(B) She emailed Mr. Palmer previously.
(C) She works at Landon Computers.
(D) She contacted a Landon Computers' representative.

185. What does Ms. Mirelli recommend?

(A) Returning a product to Landon Computers
(B) Installing a software update
(C) Arranging a meeting with a technician
(D) Obtaining an instruction booklet

GO ON TO THE NEXT PAGE

Questions 186-190 refer to the following product information, online review, and response.

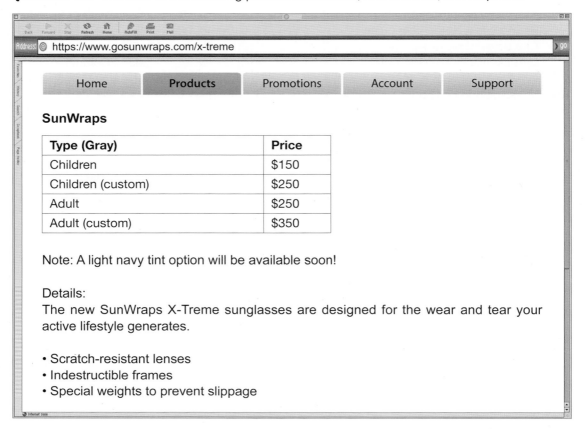

SunWraps

Type (Gray)	Price
Children	$150
Children (custom)	$250
Adult	$250
Adult (custom)	$350

Note: A light navy tint option will be available soon!

Details:
The new SunWraps X-Treme sunglasses are designed for the wear and tear your active lifestyle generates.

• Scratch-resistant lenses
• Indestructible frames
• Special weights to prevent slippage

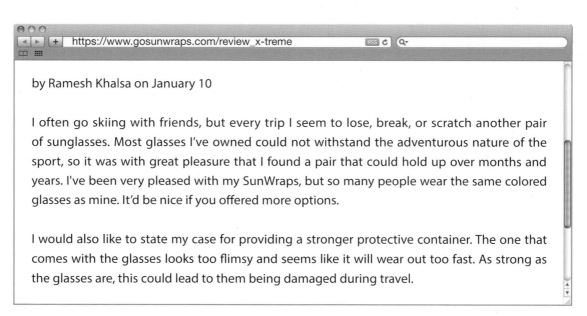

by Ramesh Khalsa on January 10

I often go skiing with friends, but every trip I seem to lose, break, or scratch another pair of sunglasses. Most glasses I've owned could not withstand the adventurous nature of the sport, so it was with great pleasure that I found a pair that could hold up over months and years. I've been very pleased with my SunWraps, but so many people wear the same colored glasses as mine. It'd be nice if you offered more options.

I would also like to state my case for providing a stronger protective container. The one that comes with the glasses looks too flimsy and seems like it will wear out too fast. As strong as the glasses are, this could lead to them being damaged during travel.

Dear Mr. Khalsa,

I'm pleased to hear that you enjoy our sunglasses. And I've got great news for you: because of your request and many like it, we will make our product available in two types. Please email b.herman@gosunwraps to get a complimentary pair of standard X-Treme glasses in our beautiful new color. Before we mail this gift to you, you must first forward the confirmation e-mail you received after making your post.

We also understand that you have some worries about the durability of the case. I'd like to reassure you that, though it is slim, the state-of-the-art materials we use can easily withstand the stress of being tossed around in a suitcase or sat on. We had it lab-tested thoroughly, and the slim version proved to be exceptionally sturdy and long-lasting.

Bob Herman
General Manager, SunWraps

186. What does Mr. Khalsa write about his sunglasses?

(A) He would like a different size for his current frames.
(B) The lenses are too thick.
(C) They do not get damaged during recreational activities.
(D) He purchased them recently.

187. In the review, the word, "case" in paragraph 2, line 1, is closest in meaning to

(A) inventory
(B) appearance
(C) position
(D) container

188. What does Mr. Herman offer to Mr. Khalsa?

(A) Standard gray sunglasses
(B) Standard navy sunglasses
(C) Custom gray sunglasses
(D) Custom navy sunglasses

189. What must Mr. Khalsa do to receive a gift from SunWraps?

(A) Fill out a brief questionnaire about a new item
(B) Remove negative comments written on a Web site
(C) Return some glasses that are defective
(D) Send a document proving he wrote a review

190. What does Mr. Herman indicate about the protective case?

(A) It underwent rigorous tests.
(B) It is more flimsy than the previous version.
(C) It weighs less than other types.
(D) It was made to be more flexible.

GO ON TO THE NEXT PAGE

Questions 191-195 refer to the following notice, e-mail, and article.

Alert: Pack Up Your Desk on Friday

As you may be aware, Agro-Gene's staff will be relocating to its brand-new research building across from Sonoma Plaza over the weekend. The moving company has agreed to work late Friday to take everything to the new building and will begin at 5:00 P.M. sharp.

It is important that you secure your laboratories by locking important documents in drawers and putting away all research equipment 30 minutes before quitting time.

We look forward to seeing everyone on Monday in our new building, and we hope that your weekend is a pleasant one.

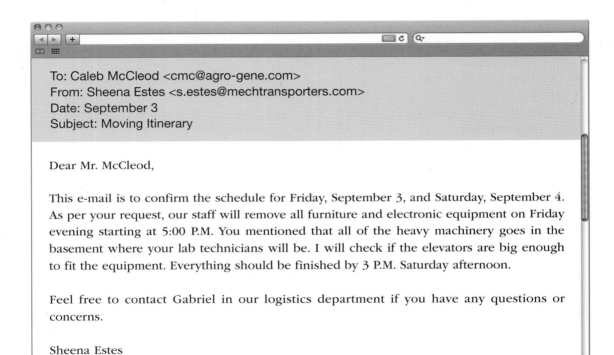

To: Caleb McCleod <cmc@agro-gene.com>
From: Sheena Estes <s.estes@mechtransporters.com>
Date: September 3
Subject: Moving Itinerary

Dear Mr. McCleod,

This e-mail is to confirm the schedule for Friday, September 3, and Saturday, September 4. As per your request, our staff will remove all furniture and electronic equipment on Friday evening starting at 5:00 P.M. You mentioned that all of the heavy machinery goes in the basement where your lab technicians will be. I will check if the elevators are big enough to fit the equipment. Everything should be finished by 3 P.M. Saturday afternoon.

Feel free to contact Gabriel in our logistics department if you have any questions or concerns.

Sheena Estes
Mech Transporters

Agro-Gene Relocates Headquarters
By Jennifer D'Amato

You wouldn't know it by looking at the outside, but the old Tempero Tower got quite a makeover. "While the building maintains its historic façade, many changes happened to its first floor and its basement, the new locations of Argo-Gene's headquarters" says Caleb McCleod, President of Agro-Gene.

The startup has been pioneering research into grapes and grape vines. In particular, it is working to make the vines require less water. Lead scientist Kim Scotts explains, "Temperature changes are causing traditional wine regions to see less annual rainfall, so we're making vines that thrive in drier conditions."

A recent press tour of the new facilities allowed reporters to peek into Agro-Gene's advanced labs. "This new space ensures that no dangerous chemicals are leaked into the atmosphere," stated Howard Ruiz, a spokesperson for Agro-Gene.

Agro-Gene also offers public seminars on the state of genetically engineered foods on the first and third Saturdays of the month. The sessions are meant to inform and dispel myths surrounding the risks of modified foods. All are welcome to attend.

---

191. Who most likely wrote the notice?

(A) Mr. Ruiz
(B) Mr. McCleod
(C) Ms. Scotts
(D) Ms. Estes

192. What are staff members instructed to do on September 3?

(A) Organize a workspace
(B) Make a password for their computers
(C) Meet at Sonoma Plaza
(D) Review a budget for a project

193. What is indicated about the lab technicians?

(A) They will stay until 5 P.M. on Friday.
(B) They research animals.
(C) They will work underground.
(D) They will study desert environments.

194. What is true about Agro-Gene?

(A) It recently appointed a new president.
(B) It is closed on Saturdays.
(C) It manufactures various wines.
(D) It develops new kinds of plants.

195. What does Mr. Ruiz say about the new facilities?

(A) They protect the environment from harmful elements.
(B) The cost of rent is very affordable.
(C) They do not allow outside visitors.
(D) There is more room to conduct experiments.

GO ON TO THE NEXT PAGE

Questions 196–200 refer to the following notice, review, and article.

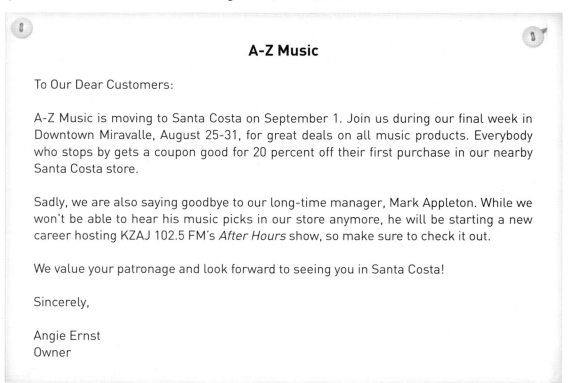

A-Z Music

To Our Dear Customers:

A-Z Music is moving to Santa Costa on September 1. Join us during our final week in Downtown Miravalle, August 25-31, for great deals on all music products. Everybody who stops by gets a coupon good for 20 percent off their first purchase in our nearby Santa Costa store.

Sadly, we are also saying goodbye to our long-time manager, Mark Appleton. While we won't be able to hear his music picks in our store anymore, he will be starting a new career hosting KZAJ 102.5 FM's *After Hours* show, so make sure to check it out.

We value your patronage and look forward to seeing you in Santa Costa!

Sincerely,

Angie Ernst
Owner

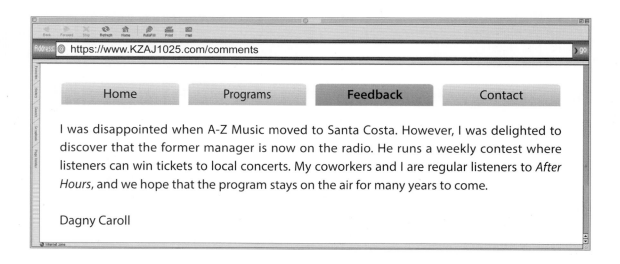

Address: https://www.KZAJ1025.com/comments

| Home | Programs | Feedback | Contact |

I was disappointed when A-Z Music moved to Santa Costa. However, I was delighted to discover that the former manager is now on the radio. He runs a weekly contest where listeners can win tickets to local concerts. My coworkers and I are regular listeners to *After Hours*, and we hope that the program stays on the air for many years to come.

Dagny Caroll

Revitalizing the City Center

The Miravalle city council announced that the second phase of the downtown renovation is nearly complete. All of the oldest buildings have undergone major restoration. While the construction has forced some existing shops to relocate, Mayor Nevardo Flores believes that the changes will attract more tourists, which would definitely benefit the town. Financial analysts who have reviewed the plans agree with Mr. Flores' views on this matter.

While many welcome the change in the downtown's image, some longtime local businesses are leaving for neighboring towns. Residents will certainly miss old favorites such as Hermosa Flowers, Gabby's Fashions, and A-Z Music—each has relocated, citing the city's plan to increase rents by up to 40 percent.

However, Jeff Gary, a city official, says that once the downtown renovation is complete, the effect on the town will be positive. "It's unfortunate that some businesses like Gabby's Fashions have to relocate during this time," said the councilman. "But we are optimistic that changing in this way will bring more profitable businesses and create more jobs for our residents."

196. Why most likely is Ms. Ernst moving her store?

(A) Because property prices are too high
(B) Because she is changing careers
(C) Because she needs more space for her store
(D) Because she found a more convenient location

197. What is indicated about Mr. Appleton's program?

(A) It gives out prizes.
(B) It used to be hosted by Ms. Ernst.
(C) It has been on the air for many years.
(D) It provides discounts to local businesses.

198. In the review, the word "runs" in paragraph 1, line 2, is closest in meaning to

(A) drives
(B) powers
(C) races
(D) organizes

199. What is suggested about Downtown Miravalle?

(A) It includes several historic sites.
(B) The city council building will be moved there.
(C) It will probably draw more visitors.
(D) Mr. Gary's office is located there.

200. According to the article, why does Mr. Gary have a positive view of the renovation project?

(A) Because it will result in more public transportation
(B) Because it will increase employment
(C) Because it will create a fashion district
(D) Because it will be finished early

ANSWER SHEET

파고다 토익 실력 완성 RC - ACTUAL TEST

READING (Part Ⅴ-Ⅶ)

NO.	ANSWER A B C D	NO.	ANSWER A B C D	NO.	ANSWER A B C D	NO.	ANSWER A B C D	NO.	ANSWER A B C D
101	Ⓐ Ⓑ Ⓒ Ⓓ	121	Ⓐ Ⓑ Ⓒ Ⓓ	141	Ⓐ Ⓑ Ⓒ Ⓓ	161	Ⓐ Ⓑ Ⓒ Ⓓ	181	Ⓐ Ⓑ Ⓒ Ⓓ
102	Ⓐ Ⓑ Ⓒ Ⓓ	122	Ⓐ Ⓑ Ⓒ Ⓓ	142	Ⓐ Ⓑ Ⓒ Ⓓ	162	Ⓐ Ⓑ Ⓒ Ⓓ	182	Ⓐ Ⓑ Ⓒ Ⓓ
103	Ⓐ Ⓑ Ⓒ Ⓓ	123	Ⓐ Ⓑ Ⓒ Ⓓ	143	Ⓐ Ⓑ Ⓒ Ⓓ	163	Ⓐ Ⓑ Ⓒ Ⓓ	183	Ⓐ Ⓑ Ⓒ Ⓓ
104	Ⓐ Ⓑ Ⓒ Ⓓ	124	Ⓐ Ⓑ Ⓒ Ⓓ	144	Ⓐ Ⓑ Ⓒ Ⓓ	164	Ⓐ Ⓑ Ⓒ Ⓓ	184	Ⓐ Ⓑ Ⓒ Ⓓ
105	Ⓐ Ⓑ Ⓒ Ⓓ	125	Ⓐ Ⓑ Ⓒ Ⓓ	145	Ⓐ Ⓑ Ⓒ Ⓓ	165	Ⓐ Ⓑ Ⓒ Ⓓ	185	Ⓐ Ⓑ Ⓒ Ⓓ
106	Ⓐ Ⓑ Ⓒ Ⓓ	126	Ⓐ Ⓑ Ⓒ Ⓓ	146	Ⓐ Ⓑ Ⓒ Ⓓ	166	Ⓐ Ⓑ Ⓒ Ⓓ	186	Ⓐ Ⓑ Ⓒ Ⓓ
107	Ⓐ Ⓑ Ⓒ Ⓓ	127	Ⓐ Ⓑ Ⓒ Ⓓ	147	Ⓐ Ⓑ Ⓒ Ⓓ	167	Ⓐ Ⓑ Ⓒ Ⓓ	187	Ⓐ Ⓑ Ⓒ Ⓓ
108	Ⓐ Ⓑ Ⓒ Ⓓ	128	Ⓐ Ⓑ Ⓒ Ⓓ	148	Ⓐ Ⓑ Ⓒ Ⓓ	168	Ⓐ Ⓑ Ⓒ Ⓓ	188	Ⓐ Ⓑ Ⓒ Ⓓ
109	Ⓐ Ⓑ Ⓒ Ⓓ	129	Ⓐ Ⓑ Ⓒ Ⓓ	149	Ⓐ Ⓑ Ⓒ Ⓓ	169	Ⓐ Ⓑ Ⓒ Ⓓ	189	Ⓐ Ⓑ Ⓒ Ⓓ
110	Ⓐ Ⓑ Ⓒ Ⓓ	130	Ⓐ Ⓑ Ⓒ Ⓓ	150	Ⓐ Ⓑ Ⓒ Ⓓ	170	Ⓐ Ⓑ Ⓒ Ⓓ	190	Ⓐ Ⓑ Ⓒ Ⓓ
111	Ⓐ Ⓑ Ⓒ Ⓓ	131	Ⓐ Ⓑ Ⓒ Ⓓ	151	Ⓐ Ⓑ Ⓒ Ⓓ	171	Ⓐ Ⓑ Ⓒ Ⓓ	191	Ⓐ Ⓑ Ⓒ Ⓓ
112	Ⓐ Ⓑ Ⓒ Ⓓ	132	Ⓐ Ⓑ Ⓒ Ⓓ	152	Ⓐ Ⓑ Ⓒ Ⓓ	172	Ⓐ Ⓑ Ⓒ Ⓓ	192	Ⓐ Ⓑ Ⓒ Ⓓ
113	Ⓐ Ⓑ Ⓒ Ⓓ	133	Ⓐ Ⓑ Ⓒ Ⓓ	153	Ⓐ Ⓑ Ⓒ Ⓓ	173	Ⓐ Ⓑ Ⓒ Ⓓ	193	Ⓐ Ⓑ Ⓒ Ⓓ
114	Ⓐ Ⓑ Ⓒ Ⓓ	134	Ⓐ Ⓑ Ⓒ Ⓓ	154	Ⓐ Ⓑ Ⓒ Ⓓ	174	Ⓐ Ⓑ Ⓒ Ⓓ	194	Ⓐ Ⓑ Ⓒ Ⓓ
115	Ⓐ Ⓑ Ⓒ Ⓓ	135	Ⓐ Ⓑ Ⓒ Ⓓ	155	Ⓐ Ⓑ Ⓒ Ⓓ	175	Ⓐ Ⓑ Ⓒ Ⓓ	195	Ⓐ Ⓑ Ⓒ Ⓓ
116	Ⓐ Ⓑ Ⓒ Ⓓ	136	Ⓐ Ⓑ Ⓒ Ⓓ	156	Ⓐ Ⓑ Ⓒ Ⓓ	176	Ⓐ Ⓑ Ⓒ Ⓓ	196	Ⓐ Ⓑ Ⓒ Ⓓ
117	Ⓐ Ⓑ Ⓒ Ⓓ	137	Ⓐ Ⓑ Ⓒ Ⓓ	157	Ⓐ Ⓑ Ⓒ Ⓓ	177	Ⓐ Ⓑ Ⓒ Ⓓ	197	Ⓐ Ⓑ Ⓒ Ⓓ
118	Ⓐ Ⓑ Ⓒ Ⓓ	138	Ⓐ Ⓑ Ⓒ Ⓓ	158	Ⓐ Ⓑ Ⓒ Ⓓ	178	Ⓐ Ⓑ Ⓒ Ⓓ	198	Ⓐ Ⓑ Ⓒ Ⓓ
119	Ⓐ Ⓑ Ⓒ Ⓓ	139	Ⓐ Ⓑ Ⓒ Ⓓ	159	Ⓐ Ⓑ Ⓒ Ⓓ	179	Ⓐ Ⓑ Ⓒ Ⓓ	199	Ⓐ Ⓑ Ⓒ Ⓓ
120	Ⓐ Ⓑ Ⓒ Ⓓ	140	Ⓐ Ⓑ Ⓒ Ⓓ	160	Ⓐ Ⓑ Ⓒ Ⓓ	180	Ⓐ Ⓑ Ⓒ Ⓓ	200	Ⓐ Ⓑ Ⓒ Ⓓ

ANSWER SHEET

3rd Edition

해설서

벽돌영문법

토익 개념&실전 종합서

실력완성

RC

파고다교육그룹 언어교육연구소, 정진영, 정성배 | 저

PAGODA Books

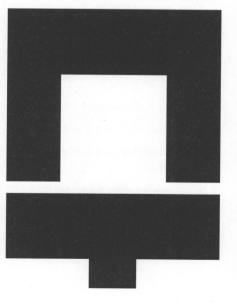

3rd Edition

토익 개념&실전 종합서

실력 완성

RC

PART 5 – GRAMMAR

UNIT 01. 명사

본서 p.21

Q1 1. commitment 2. initiative

1. BRT 사는 회사의 제품 품질에 확고한 헌신을 보였다.
해설 부정관사 뒤의 명사

2. Hex-Corp의 높은 매출은 고객 서비스를 개선하려는 최근의 계획에서 나온 결과이다.
해설 형용사 뒤 '-ive'형 명사

+ check 1. proposal 2. understanding

1. Mr. Yang은 결정을 내리기 전 내 제안서를 주의 깊게 검토할 것이다.

2. 저희는 공사 동안 보여주신 귀하의 이해에 대해 감사를 표현하고자 합니다.

Q2 1. positive 2. thoroughly

1. Blue Oak 레스토랑의 소유주는 지역 신문에서 긍정적인 리뷰를 받게 되어 만족했다.
해설 명사로 쓰인 reviews 수식 형용사

2. 물품 재고 목록을 당신이 자세히 확인하도록 하세요.
해설 동사로 쓰인 check 수식 부사

Q3 1. Entries 2. operation

1. 미술 경연대회 출품작들은 이번 달 말까지 제출되어야 한다.
해설 주어 역할의 명사

2. 공장의 조립 기계 운영을 설명하는 안내 매뉴얼이 있다.
해설 정관사 the와 전치사 of 사이 명사

+ check 1. Construction 2. response 3. emphasis

1. 새 Pinewood 기차역 공사가 12월 초에 시작된다.

2. 귀하의 금전 출납 창구 직원 공고에 대한 응답으로 HR에 이력서를 보냈습니다.

3. Poco는 빠른 배달에 큰 중점을 두어 업계의 선두주자가 되었다.

Q4 1. increase 2. Applicants

1. Redmond 화학의 경영진은 생산성의 20퍼센트 증가를 새로 설치된 장비 때문으로 여겼다.
해설 부정관사 a/an 뒤의 단수 명사

2. 연구원 직책 지원자들은 직접 지원해야 한다.
해설 가산 명사는 관사와 함께 쓰거나 복수 형태로 써야 하며 한정사 없이 단수 형태로 쓸 수 없음

+ check 1. Refunds 2. information

1. 하자가 있는 제품의 환불은 3 영업일 안으로 처리될 것이다.

2. 면접관들은 당신이 직책을 맡을 자격이 되는지 보기 위하여 경력 정보를 요청할 것이다.

Q5 1. applicant 2. employment

1. 지난주 Mr. Hopkins가 면접 본 12명의 후보자들 중, Julia Sarawati가 영업 관리직에 가장 적격인 지원자이다.
해설 형용사 qualified의 꾸밈을 받기에 의미상 적합한 사람 명사 자리

2. 연례 취업 박람회는 일자리를 찾고 있는 사람들에게 많은 자원을 제공할 것이다.
해설 employee는 가산 명사이므로 한정사 없이 단독 사용 불가

+ check 1. supervisors 2. accounting

1. 직원들은 업무를 끝마친 뒤 직속 상사에게 보고해야 한다.

2. 우리 회사의 모든 세무 전문가들은 회계학 대학원 학위를 소지하고 있다.

Q6 1. plan

1. CEO는 무료 전문 개발 코스를 제공하겠다는 계획을 승인했다.
해설 planning은 불가산 명사이므로 부정관사와 사용 불가

+ check 1. Access 2. survey 3. marketing 4. certificate

1. 인가받은 출입증을 소지하고 있지 않으면 이 시설의 출입이 허용되지 않는다.

2. 최근의 한 설문조사에 따르면 지난 6개월에 걸쳐 회사 헬스클럽을 이용하는 직원의 수가 상당히 감소했다.

3. 광고 컨퍼런스는 마케팅과 디자인에서 혁신을 보여준 이들의 공로를 인정할 것이다.

4. 용접공이 되기 위한 자격증을 따는 것에 관한 질문은 Cindy Wong에게 보내야 한다.

Q7 **1. productivity**

1. 새 매니저가 근무를 시작한 이후 직원 생산성이 크게 향상되었다.

해설 복합 명사 employee productivity (직원 생산성)

+ check **1. training** **2. service**

1. 교육 시간에 관한 정보를 전부 보시려면 저희 웹사이트를 확인하십시오.

2. 고객 서비스에 관한 설문지를 작성하시고 무료 선물을 받으세요.

Practice

본서 p.30

1. (D)	**2.** (C)	**3.** (C)	**4.** (D)	**5.** (C)
6. (C)	**7.** (D)	**8.** (C)	**9.** (D)	**10.** (C)
11. (A)	**12.** (D)	**13.** (D)	**14.** (D)	**15.** (D)
16. (A)	**17.** (C)	**18.** (D)	**19.** (C)	**20.** (D)

1. 고객 설문 자료의 면밀한 평가는 고객들이 최근 경제 위기 이후로 지출을 줄이고 있다는 것을 시사한다.

해설 부정관사와 형용사 뒤에는 명사를 써야 하므로 '평가'라는 의미의 명사 (D) evaluation이 정답이다.

어휘 suggest ~을 시사하다 | reduce 줄이다 | crisis 위기 | evaluative 평가하는 | evaluate ~을 평가하다 | evaluation 평가, 분석

2. 인사부의 우선 사항에는 신입직원들을 모집하는 것과 기관의 목표를 전달하는 것이 포함된다.

해설 빈칸은 문장의 주어 역할을 하는 명사 자리이므로 (A)와 (C) 중 선택해야 한다. 문장의 동사가 include이므로 복수 명사 (C) Priorities가 정답이다.

어휘 priority 우선 사항 | recruit 모집하다, 뽑다 | communicate 전달하다

3. 파손된 제품을 받은 고객들은 제품 교환이나 환불을 받기 위해 곧바로 제조사에 연락해야 한다.

해설 관사 뒤나 타동사 contact 뒤 명사 자리를 묻는 문제이다. 동사, 명사가 모두 되는 manufacture(제조)와 manufacturer(제조사) 중 문맥상 적합한 (C) manufacturer가 정답이다.

어휘 damaged 손상된 | replacement 교체, 대체, 교환

4. 참가자들은 대회 일정과 식권 2장을 받을 것이다.

해설 빈칸은 주어 자리이므로 명사가 와야 한다. 문맥상 받는 주체는 사람 명사이며, 사람 명사는 가산 명사이므로 반드시 관사와 함께 쓰거나 복수형으로 써야 한다. 따라서, 사람 명사의 복수형인 (D)가 정답이다.

어휘 meal voucher 식권 | participant 참가자 | participation 참가 | participate 참가하다

5. Roseville 공항에서 입국과 출국 비행편들은 활주로가 혼잡한 결과로 종종 지연된다.

해설 전치사의 목적어 자리에는 명사를 써야 하므로 '혼잡'이라는 의미의 명사 (C) congestion이 정답이다.

어휘 inbound 입국하는 | outbound 출국하는 | as a result of ~의 결과로 | runway 활주로 | congest 정체시키다 | congested 혼잡해진 | congestion 혼잡 | congestive 충혈성의

6. 지원서를 보낼 때 상세한 자기소개서와 두 통의 추천서를 동봉해야 한다.

해설 부정관사 뒤의 명사 자리인데 보기에 명사가 두 개 있으므로 해석을 통해 정답을 찾는다. 문맥상 '지원서'라는 의미의 명사 (C) application이 정답이다.

어휘 enclose 동봉하다 | detailed 상세한 | letter of reference 추천서 | applicant 지원자 | application 지원서

7. 개발 중인 새로운 차 모델의 디자인은 기밀을 보장하기 위해서 Verman 자동차의 몇 중역들에게만 공개되었다.

해설 타동사 ensure에서 만들어진 to ensure도 목적어로 명사를 취해야 하므로 '기밀'이라는 의미의 명사 (D) confidentiality가 정답이다.

어휘 under development 개발 중인 | in order to 부정사 ~하기 위해서 | ensure ~을 보장하다 | confide (비밀을) 털어 놓다 | confident 자신감 있는 | confidential 기밀의 | confidentiality 기밀

8. 해당 분야에서의 광범위한 연구에 대한 인정을 받아, Dr. Henry Park은 유전 공학 분야에서 세계 최고의 권위자이다.

해설 소유격과 형용사 뒤에 명사를 써야 할 자리이므로 (A) '인가'와 (C) '권한, 권위자' 중에서 문맥에 적절한 답을 골라야 한다. Henry Park 박사에 관해서 이야기하고 있으므로 문맥상 (C) authority가 정답이다.

어휘 recognized for ~에 대해서 인정받은 | extensive 광범위한 | leading 선도적인 | genetic engineering 유전 공학 | authorize ~을 인가하다 | authoritatively 권위적으로

9. Marlinson 솔루션은 온라인 시장에서 상당한 성장을 하고 있어서, 이 분야에서 추가적인 도움을 구하고 있다.

고난도

해설 타동사 'seek(~을 찾다)'의 목적어 역할을 하면서 형용사 'additional(추가적인)'의 수식을 받을 성분이 필요하므로 명사인 (A)와 (D) 중에 해석을 통해 정답을 찾아야 하나, 해석상으로도 두 명사가 모두 가능하므로 명사의 종류를 생각해 본다. (A)는 가산 명사로 an assistant나 assistants로 써야 하고 (D)는 불가산 명사이므로 복수형이나 부정관사와 함께 쓰지 않는데, 빈칸 앞에는 부정관사도 없고 단수형으로 써야 하므로 (D) assistance가 정답이다.

어휘 considerable 상당한 | growth 성장 | seek ~을 구하다 | additional 추가적인 | assistant 조수 | assist ~을 돕다 | assistance 도움

10. 새로운 정책에 따르면, 모든 사무실 간의 서신은 각각의 직원 대신 각 부서의 우편함에 배달될 것이다.

해설 문장의 주어 자리에 쓰일 명사가 필요하므로 (A) '통신원'과 (C) '서신'

중에서 해석을 통하여 답을 골라야 하며, 배달이 되는 것은 서신일 것이므로 문맥상 (C) correspondence가 정답이다.

어휘 according to ~에 따르면 | interoffice 사무실 간의 | A rather than B B보다는[대신에] A | correspondent 통신원 | correspond 서신을 주고받다 | correspondence 서신

11. Tyler 의료 장비의 영업직원들은 새로운 의료 기구들에 대한 지식을 갖추기 위해서 많은 의학 잡지들을 구독하도록 권장받는다.

해설 'subscribe to (구독하다)'의 목적어 역할을 하는 명사가 필요한 자리이므로 (A) '잡지들', (B) '신문 잡지업', (C) '언론인' 중에서 문맥상 (A) journals가 가장 적절하다.

어휘 sales representative 영업직원 | subscribe to ~을 구독하다 | multiple 많은 | clinical 의학의 | be knowledgeable about ~에 대해서 잘 알다

12. 6세 미만의 어린이들이 있는 부모들은 아이들이 TV를 보도록 허락할 때 조심하도록 권고받는다.
고난도

해설 타동사 use에서 만들어진 to use도 목적어로 명사를 취해야 하므로 (D) caution이 정답이다.

어휘 be advised to부정사 ~하도록 권고받다 | allow A to부정사 A가 ~하도록 허락하다 | cautious 조심스러운 | cautiously 조심스럽게 | caution 조심

13. 영업부는 Enco 프로젝트와 관련된 미지불된 비용들이 있고 그 프로젝트의 이윤은 계속해서 감소하고 있다.

해설 수량 표시어 several과 형용사 outstanding 뒤에는 명사를 써야 하는데, expense는 가산 명사이며 앞에 한정사가 없으므로 복수 명사 (D) expenses가 정답이다.

어휘 outstanding 결제가 되지 않은, 미지불된 | consistently 꾸준하게 | expend ~을 쓰다 | expense 비용

14. South Port에 신규 공항의 공식 개장식이 시장의 참석하에 열릴 것이다.

해설 정관사 the와 형용사 official 뒤의 명사 자리를 묻는 문제이다. open, openness, opening 모두 명사로 쓰이나 공식 개막이라는 의미에 적합한 (D) opening이 정답이다.

어휘 official 공식적인 | take place 개최되다 | open 야외; 열린; 열다 | openness 솔직함 | opening 개장, 개막, 공석

15. Colonial 가의 2차선에서 4차선으로의 확장은 6개월이 걸릴 것이다.
고난도

해설 정관사 The 뒤의 주어(명사) 자리이다. 명사인 (A) width와 (D) widening 중 문맥을 통해 정답을 선택해야 하는데, width는 '폭, 너비'라는 뜻이고, widening은 '확장'이라는 뜻이므로 문맥상 (D) widening이 정답이다.

어휘 lane 차선, 길 | width 폭, 너비 | wide 넓은 | widening 확장

16. 허가증이나 면허증을 신청하기 전에 요구사항들을 확인하기 위해서 교통부 웹사이트를 방문하십시오.

해설 빈칸 앞에 부정관사 a가 있기 때문에 가산 명사인 (A) permit이 정답이다. (B)는 불가산 명사로 부정관사 a(n)와 쓰일 수 없다.

어휘 apply for ~을 신청하다 | permit 허가증 | license 면허증

17. 사업 확장 전략의 일환으로, ST 의류는 남성 및 여성 정장 의류를 판매하기 시작할 것이다.

해설 빈칸은 전치사 as part of 의 목적어 자리로, 빈칸 앞의 명사들과 복합명사를 이루는 명사 (C) strategy가 정답이다.

어휘 as part of ~의 일환으로 | business expansion strategy 사업 확장 전략 | strategize 전략을 짜다 | strategic 전략적인 | strategy 전략 | strategically 전략적으로

18. 우리 판매 사원의 부적절한 행동에 대한 불만 사항이 있다는 것은 매우 유감스러운 일이다.
고난도

해설 there be 뒤의 주어 자리에 명사가 와야 하며 복수 동사 have를 통하여 복수 명사 (D) complaints가 정답임을 알 수 있다.

어휘 inappropriate 부적절한, 부당한 | behavior 행동

19. 상자가 이미 개봉되었거나 운송사에 의해 파손되었다면 상자의 수령을 거부하세요. 그러면 그 물품은 교환을 위해 돌려보내질 것입니다.

해설 타동사의 목적어 자리이면서 뒤에 of가 이끄는 전치사구의 수식을 받는 명사가 와야 하며, 명사 (C)와 (D) 중에 문맥상 적절한 (C) receipt이 정답이다.

어휘 package 상자, 포장 | carrier 운송회사, 수송회사 | receipt 수령, 인수 | recipient 수령인

20. 새 지점을 방문하는 모든 신규 고객에게 10퍼센트까지의 할인을 제공하는 것은 우리 회사의 정책이다.
고난도

해설 타동사의 목적어 자리에 명사가 와야 하며, 문맥상 적합한 명사 discount는 가산 명사로, 부정관사 a가 없으므로 복수 형태로 쓰여야 하기 때문에 (D) discounts가 정답이다.

어휘 policy 정책

UNIT 02. 대명사
본서 p.33

Q1 1. she 2. his 3. his 4. his

1. Ms. Lane은 Mr. Kim의 항공편을 예매한 뒤 여행 일정표를 그에게 보냈다.
해설 동사 앞의 주어 자리

2. James Lennon은 자신의 다음 소설을 위해 유명 작가와 협력하기 위하여 유럽에 머무르기로 결정했다.
해설 명사 앞의 소유격 자리

3. Jason은 이탈리아 식당에서의 20년간의 경력을 바탕으로 마침내 자신의 식당을 열었다.
해설 소유격을 강조하는 own 앞 자리

4. Mr. Lin은 그 디자인이 그의 검토를 위해 언제 준비가 될지 물었다.
해설 명사로 쓰인 review 앞의 소유격 자리

Q2 1. us 2. them 3. hers

1. 주문하신 물품에 결함이 있을 경우 수령 후 일주일 이내에 저희에게 제품을 보내시면 됩니다.
해설 문맥상 '우리에게 ~을 보내라'의 의미이므로 목적격 자리

2. Ms. Schmitt와 동료들은 마감기한 연장을 요청했지만 매니저는 우선 그들과 이야기를 나누고 싶어한다.
해설 전치사의 목적어 자리

3. Ben이 Jane보다 기획안을 훨씬 늦게 제출했음에도 불구하고 매니저는 Jane의 것 대신 Ben의 아이디어를 채택했다.
해설 뒤에 명사가 없고 '~의 것'이란 의미를 갖는 소유대명사 자리

Q3 1. himself 2. himself 3. herself

1. 발표를 하면서, Mr. Brown은 자기 자신이 박식하다는 것을 증명했다.
해설 주어와 동일한 대상의 목적어 자리

2. 건축가는 건물의 공사를 반드시 7월 말까지 완료하기 위하여 직접 감독했다.
해설 절 끝의 부사 자리에 쓰이는 강조 용법의 재귀대명사

3. Ms. Anais는 Mr. Conrad가 현재 휴가 중이기 때문에 고급 간부 워크샵에 혼자 참석할 것이다.
해설 '혼자서'의 의미를 갖는 관용적 표현

Q4 1. those 2. those

1. TPR, Inc.의 현재 매출액은 작년의 그것과 무척이나 비슷하다.
해설 복수 명사 sales figures를 대신 받는 복수 대명사 those 자리

2. 모든 지원서가 검토되면 자격이 되는 사람들은 면접과 관련해 연락을 받게 될 것이다.
해설 관계절의 복수 동사 are qualified와 수 일치되는 복수 대명사 those 자리

+ check 1. their 2. themselves 3. them 4. herself

1. 저희 Istanbul Dissiz 병원은 예약된 시간에 환자들을 만나기 위해 최선을 다합니다.

2. 도서관 회원은 자료를 직접 선반에 꽂으면 안 된다.

3. 예술가들에게 연락을 하고, 작품을 기부 받는 일에 대해 도움이 필요합니다.

4. Ms. Park은 그녀 자신이 R&D팀의 충실하고 혁신적인 구성원이라는 것을 증명했다.

Q5 1. Many 2. neither 3. few 4. none

1. 매니저들 중 다수가 당신의 제안이 매우 유용하다고 여겼으며 다음 달에 그것을 시행하기로 결정했습니다.
해설 부정대명사 자리에 Every 사용 불가

2. 안타깝게도 두 행사장 전부 창립 파티를 개최할 정도의 수용 능력을 갖고 있지 않다.
해설 neither of 복수 명사 + 단수 동사(has)

3. 여름 동안 근무한 인턴 사원들 중에는 회계부서의 Mr. Lee보다 더 좋은 평가를 받은 사람이 거의 없다.
해설 앞에 있는 복수 명사(interns)를 받으므로 복수 부정대명사

4. 지역 공급업체에 딸기 재고 물량이 아예 없어서 딸기를 더 주문할 수 없다.
해설 문맥상 '재고가 없다'는 부정의 의미를 전달할 수 있는 부정대명사 none 자리

Q6 1. the others 2. one another

1. 학회 참석자들 중 일부는 오전 수업을 선호했지만, 나머지는 모두 저녁 수업을 선호했다.
해설 주어 자리에 들어갈 부정대명사

2. 직원들은 사무실에서 서로 함께 힘을 합쳐 일해야 한다.
해설 목적어 자리에 들어갈 부정대명사

Practice

본서 p.38

1. (B)	2. (A)	3. (B)	4. (C)	5. (C)
6. (A)	7. (D)	8. (D)	9. (D)	10. (B)
11. (A)	12. (A)	13. (A)	14. (B)	15. (C)
16. (B)	17. (C)	18. (D)	19. (A)	20. (D)

1. Langan's는 최고의 남미 레스토랑으로 뽑혔고 그 요리사는 그의 독특한 요리법들 때문에 칭송받아 왔다.
해설 전치사 for의 목적어로 쓰인 명사 'unique recipes(독특한 요리법들)' 앞에서 명사를 수식할 소유대명사가 필요하므로 (B) his가 정답이다.
어휘 praise ~을 칭찬하다 I unique 독특한 I recipe 요리법

2. 생화학 연구에 참여하는 데 관심이 있는 사람들은 Glen 병원의 Ms. Hall에게 이메일을 보내야 한다.
해설 관계대명사 who의 수식을 받는 대명사는 (A) Anyone과 (D) Those

인데 who 뒤에 동사가 단수이므로 (A)가 정답이다.

어휘 　biochemistry 생화학

3. 고속도로를 타기 전에, 승객들 모두가 안전벨트를 매었는지 확인하십시오.

해설 　빈칸 뒤에 「of the 복수 명사 + 복수 동사」를 썼고 복수 동사 fasten
과 수가 일치해야 하므로 주어 자리에는 복수 취급을 받는 부정대명사
(B) all이 알맞다. every는 단독으로 부정대명사로 쓸 수 없고, 「each
of the 복수 명사」는 단수 동사를 취한다.

어휘 　fasten one's seatbelt 안전벨트를 매다

4. Mr. Marshall이 다음 주에 연간 수익 보고서를 완성한 후에, 그것은
회의를 위해 Mr. Byeon에게 보내질 것이다.

해설 　동사 앞에 빈칸이 있으므로 주어 역할의 대명사를 쓸 자리이며, 단수
명사인 연간 수익 보고서를 지칭해야 하므로 (C) it이 정답이다. (B)는
복수 명사 또는 불가산 명사와 쓰는 형용사이므로 단독으로 대명사 역
할을 할 수 없고, (A)는 주어 자리에 못 오며 (D)는 목적격으로 쓰는 대
명사이다.

어휘 　annual 연간의 | earnings 수익

5. 비자 신청자들은 이 일을 행하기 위해서 여행사 직원들이나 다른 사람
들에게 의존하지 않고도 혼자서 양식을 작성할 수 있다.

해설 　전치사 by 뒤에는 (B)와 (C)를 쓸 수 있는데, (B)는 '그들에 의해서',
(C)는 '혼자서'라고 해석되므로 해석상 자연스러운 (C) themselves가
정답이다.

어휘 　complete (서식을 빠짐없이) 작성하다 | form 양식 | depend on
~에 의존하다 | travel agent 여행사 직원 | perform ~을 행하다 |
task 임무

6. 왜 극장 도시로써 런던의 명성이 세계적으로 알려져 있는지 당신이 직
접 알아 보십시오.

해설 　재귀대명사는 동작의 주체와 반드시 일치해야 한다. 주어진 문장은 행
위자 you가 생략된 명령문이므로 (A) yourself가 정답이다

어휘 　reputation 명성

7. 새로운 회계 프로그램은 당신이 급여 지급 명부를 훨씬 더 빠르고 효
율적으로 처리하게 해줄 것이다.

해설 　타동사의 목적어 자리에는 소유대명사나 목적격을 쓸 수 있는 데, '당
신의 것이(yours) 처리할 수 있게 해준다'와 '당신이(you) 처리할 수
있게 해준다'라는 해석 중 후자가 자연스러우므로 목적격 (D) you가
정답이다.

어휘 　accounting 회계 | process ~을 처리하다 | payroll 급여 지급
명부 | efficiently 효율적으로

8. 국제 무역 부서에서 5년 이상 일한 사람들은 해외의 직책들에 지원할
자격이 된다.

해설 　관계대명사 who의 수식을 받는 대명사는 (A) Anyone과 (D) Those
인데 who 뒤에 동사가 복수이므로 정답은 (D) Those이다.

어휘 　be eligible for ~에 대한 자격이 있다 | abroad 해외에서

9. Hasselhoff Point에 오는 많은 관광객들이 안내원과 함께 마을 투어
를 하지만 일부는 그저 해변에서 쉬고 싶어한다.

해설 　빈칸은 동사 앞의 주어 자리이므로 형용사인 (C)는 오답이며, (A)
another와 (B) anyone은 단수 취급하므로 문장의 동사 want와 수
의 일치를 이루지 못한다. 따라서, '일부, 몇몇'의 의미인 (D) some이
정답이다.

어휘 　guided tour 안내원이 딸린 여행 | relax 휴식을 취하다

10. 신입 직원들은 자신의 회사 편람을 참조하여 회사 규정을 익히도록 요
청받는다.

해설 　전치사 to의 목적어인 명사 company manuals(회사 편람) 앞에서
명사를 수식해줄 소유격 대명사가 필요하므로 (B) their가 정답이다.

어휘 　refer to ~을 참조하다 | company manual 회사 편람 |
regulation 규정

11. 한 명의 관리자가 비용과 관하여 우려를 표명하긴 했지만, 대부분의
선임 관리자들은 본사 이전에 대한 계획에 찬성했다.

해설 　주어 자리에 쓰이는 부정대명사 (A) one이 정답이다. (B), (C)는 주어
자리에 쓰이지 못하며, (D) other는 형용사이므로 명사 없이 단독으로
주어 자리에 쓸 수 없다.

어휘 　approve of ~에 찬성하다 | head office 본사 | relocation 이
전 | express concern 우려를 표하다

12. 만약 귀하가 이 직책에 관심이 있다면 저희의 편리하게 위치한 사무실
로 오는 길 안내를 받을 수 있도록 저희에게 전화 주십시오.

해설 　전치사 to의 목적어는 'conveniently located office(편리하게 위치
한 사무실)'이고 그 앞에 '우리의'라고 수식해줄 대명사가 필요하므
로 소유격 (A) our가 정답이다.

어휘 　be interested in ~에 관심이 있다 | directions to ~로의 길 안
내 | conveniently located 편리하게 위치한

13. Klamore 전자 직원들은 장비 창고에서 그들이 직접 물건을 꺼내기보
다 유지보수 관리자에게 도움을 구해야 한다.

해설 　빈칸은 '타동사(remove) + 목적어(items)' 뒤의 부사 자리이므로, 문
장 끝에 위치하여 강조 용법으로 쓰이는 재귀대명사 (A)가 정답이다.

어휘 　seek 구하다, 찾다 | assistance 지원, 도움 | maintenance 유지
보수 | instead of ~대신에 | closet 벽장

14. Gallagher 자동차의 인수 이후로, Mando 자동차는 세계에서 가장
큰 자동차 부품 제조업체 중 하나가 되었다.

해설 　가장 큰 자동차 부품 제조업체들 중에 하나가 되었다는 해석이 자연스
러우므로 「one of the (최상급) 복수 명사」의 형태를 만드는 (B) one
이 정답이다.

어휘 　acquisition 인수 | auto-component 자동차 부품 |
manufacturer 제조업체

15. 연구에 대한 그의 노력과 헌신을 통하여, Mr. Trilby는 스스로가 SLS
고난도 Biotex에 귀중한 자산임을 입증했다.

해설 　타동사 show의 목적어 자리에는 (B), (C)가 모두 가능하지만, 열심히

노력해서 스스로가 중요한 자산임을 입증했다는 해석이 가장 자연스러우므로 재귀대명사인 (C) himself가 정답이다. 주어와 목적어가 일치할 때 재귀대명사를 사용한다.

어휘 through ~을 통해서 | dedication to ~에 대한 헌신 | valuable 귀중한 | asset 자산

16. 기금 모금 파티의 초대장이 20명의 시 위원회 위원들 모두에게 보내졌지만, 참석할 수 있는 사람들이 거의 없을 것이다.
고난도

해설 주어 역할을 할 수 있는 품사가 필요한 자리이므로 부정대명사 (A)나 (B) 중에 답을 골라야 한다. 이때 빈칸에 들어가는 부정대명사는 가산 복수 명사인 시 위원회 위원들을 지칭하는 것으로 가산 명사에 쓰는 부정대명사 (B) few가 정답이다.

어휘 invitation 초대장 | fundraising party 기금 모금 파티 | attend 참가하다

17. 모든 인턴들의 수행 평가를 검토한 후에, 각 부서의 매니저들은 누구에게 그 정규직 자리를 제안할 것인지를 결정할 것이다.

해설 동사 review 앞에는 주어가 필요하므로 주격대명사 (C) they가 정답이다. review는 명사와 동사 모두 쓰이지만 이 문제에서는 뒤에 쓰인 목적어로 보아 '~을 검토하다'라는 뜻의 타동사로 쓰였음을 파악해야 답을 고를 수 있다.

어휘 review ~을 검토하다 | performance 수행 | permanent 정규직의, 상근직의

18. 지붕에 태양열 판을 설치하는데 들어가는 초기 비용은 높지만, 그것들은 이미 제값을 한 셈이다.
고난도

해설 빈칸 뒤에 명사가 없으므로 소유격인 (A), (C)는 답이 될 수 없다. 주어인 복수 명사 solar panels와 수 일치된 재귀대명사 (D) themselves가 정답이다.

어휘 initial cost 초기 비용 | install ~을 설치하다 | pay for oneself 제값을 하다

19. 식단에 제한이 있는 사람들을 위해서, Aringston 항공사는 미리 요청하는 경우에 특별 기내식을 제공한다.
고난도

해설 빈칸 뒤에 동사가 있는 절이 아니라 전치사구만 동반하고 있으므로 대명사인 (A)와 (B) 중에 답을 골라야 하며, 특정한 그들을 지칭하는 것이 아니라 막연하게 '~하는 사람들'이라는 뜻으로 해석되므로 (A) those가 정답이다.

어휘 dietary 식단의 | restriction 제한 | in-flight meal 기내식 | in advance 미리

20. 회의 참석자들 각각은 각 발표의 일정과 요약본들을 제공하는 자료 묶음을 받았다.
고난도

해설 문장의 주어 자리에 빈칸이 있고 'of the 복수 명사' 뒤에 단수 동사가 쓰였으므로 단수 취급을 하는 부정대명사 (D) Each가 정답이다. (A)와 (B)는 of the 뒤에 쓰인 명사가 복수 명사이면 복수 취급을 하는 부정대명사이므로 동사와 수가 맞지 않는다. (C)는 부정대명사로 쓸 수 없으므로 답이 될 수 없다.

어휘 participant 참가자 | information packet 자료 묶음 | summary 요약

UNIT 03. 형용사

Q1 1. exceptional　2. recent　3. timely
4. responsible

1. 이 상의 의도는 고객들에게 특출한 서비스를 제공하는 직원들의 공로를 인정하는 것입니다.
해설 명사 수식 형용사

2. Tersla의 최근 발표에 따르면 이 회사는 새 제품을 출시할 것이라고 한다.
해설 명사 수식 형용사

3. 이 안내 책자는 신입 직원들이 시기적절하게 기술적인 문제를 해결하도록 돕기 위해 쓰여졌다.
해설 명사 수식 '-ly'형 형용사

4. Ms. Leman은 회사 서버를 업그레이드하는 책임을 맡은 기술자이다.
해설 명사 수식 '-able'형 형용사

Q2 1. competitive　2. beneficial

1. 얇은 노트북 시장은 최근 아주 경쟁이 치열해졌다.
해설 2형식 동사 become 뒤의 주격 보어 자리에 들어갈 형용사

2. 많은 사용자들이 새 소프트웨어가 상당히 유익하다고 생각했다.
해설 5형식 동사 find 뒤의 목적격 보어 자리에 들어갈 형용사

+ check 1. available　2. comfortable

1. 그 전시회는 8월 15일에 일반 대중에게 이용 가능하게 될 것이다.

2. 이 창틀은 실내 온도를 편안하게 유지하도록 고안되었다.

Q3 1. every　2. investments　3. much　4. other
5. Other

1. 한 달에 한 번 모든 지점의 매니저들이 본사에서 만난다.
해설 every + 단수 명사(branch)

2. 위험을 최소화하려면, 투자자들은 다양한 분야의 투자 상품에 돈을 투입함으로써 다양한 포트폴리오를 유지해야 한다.
해설 various + 가산 명사 복수(investments)

3. 연료 소비를 줄이기 위한 캠페인은 대중에게 많은 영향을 끼치지 못했다.
해설 much + 불가산 명사(impact)

4. Cape 자동차의 훌륭한 서비스는 회사를 다른 경쟁업체들과 차별화해준다.
해설 other + 복수 명사(competitors)

PART 5　UNIT 03

5. 매장으로 운전해 오시는 길을 포함한 다른 정보는 온라인에서 보실 수 있습니다.

해설 불가산 명사와 쓰이는 other

Q4 **1. all**   **2. any**

1. 더 많은 문제를 피하기 위해 우리는 고객 피드백을 모든 판매 직원들에게 정기적으로 알릴 필요가 있다.

해설 the와 같은 한정사 앞에 위치할 수 있는 all

2. 이 품질 보증서는 제조사가 손상이 있는 어떤 제품이라도 수리해줄 것이라고 말하고 있다.

해설 불특정 가산 명사 단수를 동반할 수 있는 any

+ check **1. departments**   **2. All**

1. 그 위원회는 회사의 다양한 부서에서 온 직원들로 구성되어 있다.

2. 모든 비즈니스 스위트룸은 가구가 모두 갖춰져 있고, 무선인터넷이 연결되어 있다.

Q5 **1. considerate**   **2. confidential**

1. 타인을 배려하셔서 모든 쓰레기는 별도 표시가 있는 쓰레기통에 버려주시기 바랍니다.

해설 be considerate of는 '~에게 사려 깊게 행동하다'라는 의미

2. 우리 고객의 개인 정보는 엄격히 기밀로 유지되고 있다.

해설 be동사의 보어 자리이므로 주어(고객 개인 정보)를 수식하기에 의미상 적절한 형용사

+ check **1. successful**   **2. reliable**

1. 식당이 얼마나 성공을 거두게 될지는 아무도 예측할 수 없다.

2. 이 직책의 합격자들에게는 확실한 교통 수단과 운전 면허가 있어야 한다.

Practice
본서 p.46

1. (A)	2. (B)	3. (A)	4. (A)	5. (A)
6. (B)	7. (C)	8. (C)	9. (A)	10. (D)
11. (D)	12. (A)	13. (A)	14. (C)	15. (A)
16. (C)	17. (A)	18. (D)	19. (B)	20. (C)

1. 다음 달, Ms. Reston은 직원 생산성에 관한 그녀의 연구의 첫 결과를 발표할 것이다.

해설 관사와 명사 사이의 형용사 자리이므로 (A) initial이 정답이다.

어휘 release 발표하다, 공개하다 I finding 연구 결과 I employee productivity 직원 생산성 I initial 처음의, 초기의; 첫 글자 I

---

initiative (특정한 목적을 달성하기 위한) 새로운 계획 I initiate 착수시키다

2. 모든 참가자는 이틀간의 워크샵이 몹시 바쁜 일정에도 불구하고 매우 유익하다는 것을 알게 되었다.

해설 뒤에 단수 가산 명사가 왔기 때문에 (B) Every가 정답이다. (A), (D) 뒤에는 복수 명사가 와야 하며, (C) Single은 앞에 반드시 한정사가 있어야 하므로 오답이다.

어휘 informative 유익한 I hectic 몹시 바쁜

3. 시설물의 공사가 시작되려면 그전에 관련 허가 신청서들이 승인되어야 한다.

해설 빈칸은 복합 명사 permit applications 앞의 형용사 자리이므로 (A) relevant가 정답이다.

어휘 facility 시설(물) I permit application 허가 신청서 I approve 승인하다 I relevant 관련된 I relevantly 관련되어, 관련성 있게 I relevance 관련성

4. 많은 항공사들이 15퍼센트까지 운임을 올릴 계획을 하고 있기 때문에 해외 여행은 더 비싸질 것 같다.

해설 빈칸 앞에 to become more가 있으므로 빈칸에 들어갈 품사는 형용사인 (A) expensive이다.

어휘 be likely to ~일 것 같다 I airline 항공사 I increase 증가시키다 I fare 운임 I by up to (숫자) ~까지 I expensive 비싼 I expense 비용 I expensively 비싸게

5. Barkin Brands의 분기 회의는 관련된 다양한 부서의 협력 덕택에 매끄럽게 진행되었다.

해설 departments를 수식하는 형용사 자리이므로 (A)와 (D) 중 '다양한'을 뜻하는 (A) various가 정답이다. variable은 '변동이 심한'이라는 뜻이므로 해석상 오답이다.

어휘 collaboration 공동 협력 I variation 변화(량)

6. 사장은 Sargon 자동차의 XW2000 모델의 엔진 결함으로 인한 긴급 리콜 필요성에 대해 논의하기 위해서 특별 회의를 소집했다.
고난도

해설 소유격 Sargon Motors와 명사 사이에 빈칸이 쓰였으므로 (A)를 써서 복합 명사를 만들 것인지 (B)를 써서 수식할 것인지를 결정해야 하는데, '긴급한 필요'라고 명사를 수식하는 해석이 자연스러우므로 (B) urgent가 정답이다.

어휘 call a special meeting 특별 회의를 소집하다 I defect 결함 I urgency 긴급함 I urgent 긴급한 I urgently 긴급하게

7. 할인 받은 물건들은 어떤 상황에서도 환불될 수 없음을 유념해주세요.

해설 be동사 뒤의 주격 보어 자리에 적합한 품사를 묻는 문제이다. 주격 보어로 명사, 형용사, 분사가 모두 올 수 있기 때문에, 해석을 통해 적절한 품사를 선택해야 한다. 명사 (A), (D)는 주어인 discounted items와 동일한 것이 아니므로 오답이며, 주어인 discounted items는 환불의 대상으로 수동의 의미가 되어야 하므로, 능동의 의미를 갖는 현재분사 (B)도 오답이 된다. 따라서, 형용사 (C) refundable이 정답이다.

어휘 keep in mind ~을 명심하다 | under any circumstances 어떤 일이 있더라도

8. 모든 팀원들은 3주마다 그들의 업무 진척도에 대해서 상관에게 간단하게 보고를 하도록 요구받는다.

해설 빈칸 뒤에 three weeks가 쓰였으므로 (C) every를 써서 '3주마다'라는 뜻의 관용구를 만든다.

어휘 brief A on B A에게 B에 대해서 간단히 보고하다 | progress 진척

9. Grandview의 호텔들은 반드시 모든 지역 보건 지침을 따라야 한다.

해설 빈칸은 복합 명사 health guidelines 앞의 형용사 자리이므로, (A) local이 정답이다.

어휘 abide by ~을 따르다[준수하다] | health guideline 보건 지침 | local (특정) 지역의; (특정) 지역 주민

10. 청중들은 중간 휴식 시간에 휴식을 취하고 나서 질서 정연하게 그들의 자리로 돌아왔다.

해설 명사 앞의 형용사 자리를 묻는 문제이다. 따라서 정답은 (D) orderly이다.

어휘 intermission 중간 휴식 시간 | orderly 정돈된, 정연한

11. 인사부는 최근 채용된 직원들에게 특히 유용한, 개정된 직원 편람을 제공할 계획이다.

해설 빈칸 앞에 「be + 부사」가 있으므로 빈칸에 들어갈 단어는 부사의 수식을 받는 형용사이다. 따라서 정답은 (D) useful이다. be동사 뒤에 현재분사 (A)도 올 수 있으나 직원 안내서와 의미상 수동 관계(사용되는)이므로 능동을 나타내는 현재분사 (A)는 오답이다.

어휘 human resources 인사부 | revised 개정된 | employee handbook 직원 편람 | especially 특히 | user 사용자 | useful 유용한

12. 공연 동안, 청중들은 그 어떤 전자 녹화 장비도 사용하는 것이 허용되지 않습니다.

해설 빈칸 뒤에 불가산 명사(equipment)가 왔으므로 뒤의 명사의 수와 무관하게 쓸 수 있는 (A) any가 정답이다. (B) another와 (C) one 뒤에는 단수 가산 명사가 와야 하고 (D) many 뒤에는 복수 가산 명사가 와야 하므로 오답이다.

어휘 performance 공연, 연주회 | recording 녹음, 녹화 | equipment 장비, 기구

13. 모든 면접 대상자들 중에서, Mr. Hernandez가 전자 통신 사업 운영에서 가장 인상적인 배경을 가지고 있다.

해설 사물 명사 background를 수식하는 형용사 자리이므로, '인상적인 배경'으로 해석되는 형용사 (A) impressive가 정답이다. (B) impressed는 사람 명사를 수식하는 형용사이므로 오답이다.

어휘 telecommunications business 전자 통신 사업 | operation 운영 | impressive 인상적인 | impressed 감명 받은 | impress ~에게 감동을 주다 | impressively 인상적으로

14. Mr. Jacob은 결항으로 내일 아침 관리자 회의에 참석할 수 없을 것이다.
고난도

해설 '결항으로 회의에 참석할 수 없다'라는 의미가 되는 (C) unable이 정답이다. (B) impossible은 실현 가능성을 논할 수 있는 대상과 쓰이기 때문에 사람 주어(Mr. Jacob)와 쓰이지 못한다.

어휘 be unable to ~할 수 없다

15. 최근 실행된 소프트웨어는 비교적 짧은 시간에 많은 양의 고객정보를 처리하는 일을 가능하게 했다.

해설 5형식 동사 「make + 목적어 + 형용사」 구조의 문장이므로 정답은 (A) possible이다.

어휘 make it possible to부정사~ (it: 가목적어, to부정사: 진목적어) ~하는 것을 가능하게 하다 | implement 실행하다 | process 처리하다 | relatively 비교적 | possible 가능한 | possibility 가능성 | possibly 아마

16. 사무실에서 야근하는 직원은 누구든지 퇴근 전에 문을 잠가야 한다는 것을 기억하세요.
고난도

해설 빈칸은 명사를 수식하는 형용사 자리이므로 대명사인 (B)는 오답이다. 명사 employee는 가산 명사의 단수형이므로 뒤에 오는 명사의 수와 무관하게 쓸 수 있는 (C) Any가 정답이다. 수량형용사가 보기에 제시되어 있으므로 뒤에 있는 명사의 수를 파악해야 한다.

어휘 work late 늦게까지 일하다

17. 편집장은 그 표현이 너무 반복적이었기 때문에 기사를 수정했다.

해설 빈칸은 be동사의 보어 자리로 형용사인 (A)와 현재분사인 (B)가 모두 올 수 있다. 하지만, 주어인 the language는 반복되어지는 대상이므로 수동태 형태가 되어야 한다. 따라서 be동사 뒤에 수동 의미의 과거분사가 와야 하므로 현재분사인 (B)는 오답이며, 정답은 (A) repetitive이다.

어휘 editor-in-chief 편집장 | language 표현, 언어 | repetitive 반복적인

18. 광고 컨설턴트는 현지 유명 인사들을 고용할 것을 제안했는데 왜냐하면 그것이 효과적인 마케팅 전략으로 밝혀졌기 때문이다.

해설 명사 marketing 앞의 형용사 자리이므로 '효과적인'을 뜻하는 (D) effective가 정답이다.

어휘 celebrity 유명인사 | turn out to be ~인 것으로 밝혀지다 | effect 효과; 어떤 결과를 가져오다

19. 브레인스토밍 회의 중에 어떤 아이디어가 있다면 아무리 그 아이디어가 말도 안 되는 것 같아도 큰 소리로 말하는 것을 두려워하지 마십시오.
고난도

해설 'no matter how[however] + 형용사/부사 + 주어 + 동사'를 묻는 문제이다. 이때, 형용사와 부사의 구분은 뒤에 오는 문장 구조에 의해 결정되는데, 뒤에 온 동사 seem은 형용사를 보어로 취하는 동사이므로 빈칸에 형용사 (B) ridiculous가 와야 한다.

어휘 brainstorming 브레인스토밍(무엇에 대해 여러 사람들이 동시에 자유롭게 자기 생각을 제시하는 방법) | shout 큰 소리로 말하다 | ridiculous 말도 안 되는

20. South Palm 병원에는 자원봉사자들이 자신의 기술과 근무 시간을
고난도 맞출 수 있는 광범위한 분야의 직종들이 있다.

해설 형용사 several, various는 복수 명사와 함께하므로 단수 range라는
명사와는 쓰일 수 없으므로 '다양한'의 의미를 갖는 (C) wide가 정답
이다.

어휘 range 범위 | prolonged 장기적인

UNIT 04. 부사

본서 p.49

Q1 1. directly 2. slowly 3. aggressively
4. carefully 5. shortly

1. 모든 후보들은 hr@elvira.com에 직접 지원서를 이메일로 보내야
한다.
해설 타동사에 수반된 목적어 뒤의 부사 자리

2. 이 프린트 일은 기술적 문제 때문에 느리게 진행되었다.
해설 자동사 뒤의 부사 자리

3. Bex 건설은 Herman 건축을 공격적으로 매입하려 하고 있다.
해설 be동사와 현재분사 사이의 부사 자리

4. 예산 제안서는 승인되기 전 아주 주의 깊게 검토되어야 한다.
해설 be동사와 과거분사 뒤의 부사 자리

5. 인턴 사원들은 업무 수행 평가에 근거하여 적절한 자리에 곧 배정될
것이다.
해설 조동사와 동사원형 사이의 부사 자리

+ check 1. adversely 2. significantly 3. nationally

1. Hankens 정유회사는 높은 원유 가격이 어떤 경우에라도 회사의 순
이익에 나쁘게 영향을 미치지 않을 것이라고 확신한다.

2. Hidy Norman이 CEO로 임명된 이후에, Cordin 제조사의 생산
성은 상당히 좋아졌다.

3. 농구 챔피언십 경기는 전국적으로 방송될 것이다.

Q2 1. efficiently 2. thoroughly

1. 경영진은 업무량을 효율적으로 재편성함으로써 생산성을 늘릴 필요
성에 관해 강조했다.
해설 동명사를 수식하는 부사 자리

2. 계약서에 서명하기 전 모든 계약 조건을 꼼꼼하게 검토하는 것이 중
요하다.
해설 to부정사구에서 동사원형을 수식하는 부사 자리

+ check 1. politely 2. efficiently

1. 고객 주최 행사에 참가할 수 없다면 미리 그 초청을 공손히 거절하도
록 하십시오.

2. 그 회사는 직원들을 효율적으로 관리함으로써 생산성을 증가시키는
데 성공했다.

Q3 1. nationally 2. exclusively 3. Unfortunately

1. Mr. Kong은 회계사로 일을 시작했으나 이제는 전국적으로 유명한
금융 분석가이다.
해설 형용사를 수식하는 부사 자리

2. 오늘부터 음악 스트리밍 서비스는 우리 회사의 구독자들에게만 무료
로 제공됩니다.
해설 전치사구를 수식하는 부사 자리

3. 안타깝게도 마케팅 이사가 일정에 차질이 생겨서 회의에 참석할 수
없게 되었다.
해설 문장 전체를 수식하는 부사 자리

Q4 1. hard 2. approximately 3. formerly
4. still 5. otherwise 6. still

1. 엄청나게 열심히 일했음에도 불구하고 그 분석가의 급여 인상 신청
은 승인되지 않았다.
해설 hard는 '열심히', hardly는 '거의 ~ 않는'의 의미

2. 주문하실 물품을 받으시는 데는 대략 5 영업일이 걸립니다.
해설 숫자 앞에서 '대략'의 의미를 갖는 approximately가 정답

3. 다섯 개의 사무실 단지가 이전에 주거 구역이었던 Greenwood 지
역에 최근 문을 열었다.
해설 형용사 former는 관사 앞에 올 수 없음

4. 업무 요청을 보냈지만 유지 보수 쪽에서는 여전히 답을 하지 않았다.
해설 yet은 not 뒤나 문장 끝에 올 수 있음

5. 달리 언급되지 않는 한, 이 웹사이트의 모든 내용은 Nomukon 제
약회사의 독점 재산이다.
해설 'unless otherwise: 달리 ~하지 않으면' 표현을 완성하는
otherwise가 정답

6. 비록 그 영화가 교육적이긴 하지만, 감독은 관람객들이 그것을 여전
히 재미있어 할 거라고 생각한다.
해설 해석상으로는 still과 quite가 모두 가능해 보이지만, quite는 동사
를 수식할 수 없고 주로 형용사나 다른 부사를 수식하는 부사이므로
still이 정답

Practice

본서 p.54

1. (D)	2. (D)	3. (D)	4. (D)	5. (B)
6. (B)	7. (D)	8. (D)	9. (D)	10. (A)
11. (A)	12. (A)	13. (A)	14. (B)	15. (C)
16. (D)	17. (D)	18. (A)	19. (C)	20. (D)

1. 새로운 제품 라인을 개발하는 데 많은 시간과 노력을 기울여서, 회사는 그것이 다음 달에 성공적으로 출시되기를 기대한다.

해설 「be동사 + 과거분사」 뒤의 부사 자리를 묻는 문제이므로 정답은 (D) successfully이다.

어휘 launch 출시하다, 시작하다 I succession 연속, 잇따름 I succeed 성공하다 I successful 성공적인 I successfully 성공적으로

2. 세계 경제가 2008년의 금융 위기로부터 회복하기 시작하긴 했어도, 주택 시장은 아직 회복하지 못했다.

해설 have와 to부정사 사이에 쓸 수 있는 부사가 필요한 자리이며 해석상 부정의 의미를 만들어야 하므로 (D) yet이 정답이다.

어휘 recover from ~에서 회복되다 I financial 금융의 I housing market 주택 시장 I have yet to부정사 아직 ~하지 않았다 I afterwards 이후에

3. 우리 컨설턴트 몇 명이 다른 긴급한 일을 처리해야 했기 때문에 월요일 고객과의 회의가 갑자기 취소되었다.

해설 be동사와 과거분사 사이에 부사를 써야 하므로 (D) abruptly가 정답이다.

어휘 client 고객 I deal with ~을 처리하다 I urgent 긴급한 I abrupt 갑작스런 I abruptness 갑작스러움 I abruption 중단, 종결 I abruptly 갑자기

4. 새로운 시스템으로의 순조로운 이행을 확실히 하기 위해 모든 부서 관리자들은 그 업무에 협력하여 일하도록 요청받았다.

해설 자동사와 전치사구 사이에 올 수 있는 품사는 부사이므로 정답은 부사인 (D) collaboratively이다.

어휘 task 업무 I smooth 순조로운 I transition 이행 I collaboration 협력 I collaborate 협력하다 I collaborative 협력하는 I collaboratively 협력적으로

5. 회사 저녁 만찬에 얼마나 많은 직원들이 참석할 것인지 확인한 후, 행사 책임자는 그에 따라 메뉴를 결정할 것이다.

해설 '타동사(determine) + 목적어(the menu)' 뒤에 쓰이는 부사 자리이므로 (B) accordingly가 정답이다.

어휘 determine ~을 결정하다 I accordance 일치 I accordingly 그에 따라서 I according 일치하는 I accord 합의

6. 최근 한 뉴스 보도가 그와 다르게 시사했음에도 불구하고, 많은 소비자들이 새 하이브리드 전기 자동차가 곧 출시될 것으로 기대하고 있다.

해설 빈칸은 앞의 동사 indicate를 수식하는 부사 자리로 문맥상 '(앞에 언급된 것과) 다르게'를 의미하는 (B) otherwise가 정답이다. (D) else는 '(앞에 언급된 것에 덧붙여) 그 밖의 다른'의 의미이므로 오답이다.

어휘 indicate 나타내다, 시사하다 I somehow 어떻게든 I otherwise (앞에 나온 내용과) 다르게, 그와 달리

7. 영업 부장은 지난 분기 수익이 원래 예상보다 상당히 더 높아서 매우 기뻐했다.

해설 be동사와 비교급 형용사 사이에 부사가 필요하므로 정답은 (D) significantly이다.

어휘 profit 수익 I forecast 예상 I significance 중요성 I significant 중요한 I significantly 상당히

8. _{고난도} Newport 전자의 직원들은 압도적으로 새로운 휴가 정책에 찬성하고 있다.

해설 be동사 뒤이므로 동사 형태인 (B)와 (C)는 오답이다. be동사 뒤에 현재분사나 과거분사가 오기에 (A)를 정답으로 오인할 수 있으나 주어인 직원들은 감정을 느끼는 대상이므로 현재분사 (A)는 올 수 없다. 또한 뒤에 온 in favor of(~을 찬성하는)가 형용사 의미의 전치사구이므로 그것을 수식하는 부사 (D) overwhelmingly가 정답이다.

어휘 in favor of ~에 찬성하는 I overwhelm ~을 압도하다 I overwhelmingly 압도적으로

9. 고객 서비스 부서는 매달 대략 60통의 항의 서한을 받았었지만, 그 숫자가 줄어들고 있다.

해설 뒤에 오는 명사구를 수식하는 부사 자리이므로 정답은 (D) roughly이다.

어휘 complaint 불평(항의) I decrease 줄어들다 I roughness 거침 I rough 거친 I roughen 거칠어지게 만들다 I roughly 대략

10. 판매원들은 제품 카탈로그에 대한 공급사로부터의 요청에 즉시 응답하도록 요구된다.

해설 자동사 respond와 전치사 to 사이의 부사 자리를 묻는 문제이므로 (A) promptly가 정답이다.

어휘 respond to ~에 응답하다 I vendor 공급사 I promptly 즉시 I prompt 즉각적인

11. Everyday 여행사는 성수기가 아닌 때에 Woodstock에서의 관광을 홍보하기 위해서 경쟁력 있게 가격이 매겨진 관광 패키지들을 소개했다.

해설 타동사의 목적어인 tour packages 앞에 명사를 수식하는 형용사 역할을 하는 과거분사 priced가 쓰였고 '경쟁력 있게 가격이 매겨진'이라고 이 형용사를 수식할 요소가 필요하므로 빈칸에는 부사인 (A) competitively를 쓴다.

어휘 priced 가격이 매겨진 I promote ~을 홍보하다 I beyond (특정 시간을) 지나 I competitively 경쟁력 있게 I competitive 경쟁력 있는 I competition 경쟁

12. 원래 50년 전 작은 지역 극장으로 문을 열었던 Tretiak 홀은 현재 세계적으로 유명한 공연 예술 센터이다.

해설 빈칸은 과거분사로 시작하는 분사 구문을 수식하는 자리이며, 빈칸이 없어도 문장에 영향을 주지 않는 부사 자리이므로 (A) Originally가 정답이다.

어휘 performing arts 공연·무대 예술

13. 지원자들은 그들의 컴퓨터 과학 기술에 대한 기본 지식을 평가하는 짧은 시험 바로 후에 면접을 보게 될 것이다.

해설 '~후에'라는 의미의 following과 after로 시작하는 부사구 앞에 부사를 써서 '바로 ~후에'라고 해석하므로 (A) immediately가 정답이다. immediately after/following은 어휘 시험에서도 자주 출제된다.

어휘 following ~후에 | assess ~을 평가하다 | immediately 즉시 | immediate 즉각적인 | immediateness 직접적임 | immediacy 직접성

14. 항공 승객들은 무게로 엄격하게 수하물을 제한하는 규정을 준수해야 한다.

해설 동사 앞에서 동사를 수식하는 부사를 묻는 문제이므로 정답은 (B) strictly이다.

어휘 observe 준수하다 | regulation 규정 | limit 제한하다 | baggage 수하물 | strictness 엄격함 | strictly 엄격하게 | stricter 더 엄격한 | strict 엄격한

15. 상급 회계사 자리에 대한 모든 지원자들은 인터뷰에 대한 지침을 꼼꼼히 읽도록 지시 받았다.

해설 '타동사(read) + 목적어(the guidelines)' 뒤에 있는 부사 자리이므로 정답은 (C) meticulously이다.

어휘 senior accountant 상급 회계사 | guideline 지침 | meticulousness 꼼꼼함 | meticulous 꼼꼼한 | meticulously 꼼꼼히 | meticulosity 소심함

16. 귀하가 주문하기를 원하시는 유기농 채소는 일시적으로 품절 상태이지만, 물건이 새로 수송되는 대로 귀하께 알려 드리겠습니다.
(고난도)

해설 형용사 의미를 갖는 out of stock(품절 상태인)을 수식하므로 정답은 부사 (D) temporarily이다.

어휘 organic vegetable 유기농 채소 | out of stock 품절인 | notify 알리다, 통지하다 | shipment 수송품 | temporary 일시적인 | temporize 미루다, 시간을 끌다 | temporal 일시적인 | temporarily 일시적으로

17. 소비자들이 우리 제품의 포장에 불만스러워한다는 소식은 분명히 연구의 가장 가치 있는 결과이다.
(고난도)

해설 빈칸을 명사를 수식하는 형용사 자리로 생각할 수 있으나, 형용사는 the와 명사 사이에 위치해야 하므로 빈칸은 형용사 자리가 아니다. 또한, 빈칸을 be동사 뒤의 보어 자리에 오는 형용사 자리로 생각할 수 있으나, 형용사 뒤에 바로 'a/the + 명사'가 올 수 없다. 「a/the + 명사」 형태의 명사구 앞에 와서 명사구 전체를 수식하는 부사인 (D) arguably가 정답이다.

어휘 dissatisfied 불만스러워하는 | packaging 포장재 | finding (조사·연구 등의) 결과, 결론 | arguably 분명히, 거의 틀림없이

18. 회사들은 그들의 월간 공과금을 그들의 법인 계좌에 직접 청구되게 할 수 있다.

해설 빈칸은 목적보어 자리에 쓰인 과거분사 charged를 수식하는 자리로, 부사 (A) automatically가 정답이다.

어휘 monthly 매월의 | utility bill 공과금 | charge 청구하다 | directly 직접 | corporate account 법인 계좌

19. 고객들은 그 소프트웨어가 그들이 필요로 하는 모든 정보를 얼마나 손쉽게 찾고 저장하도록 해 주는지에 대해 놀라워했다.
(고난도)

해설 의문사 how 뒤에 형용사나 부사가 올 수 있는데, 문맥상 '손쉽게 찾고 저장하다'의 의미가 되어야 하므로 정답은 부사인 (C) effortlessly 이다.

어휘 effortful 노력한 | effortless 손쉬운 | effortlessly 손쉽게 | effort 노력

20. Mr. Tal은 10년 전 연구개발팀에서 근무를 시작했으며 그 후 매니저가 되었다.
(고난도)

해설 빈칸은 「have + p.p.」 사이의 부사 자리로, 문맥에 알맞은 부사를 선택하는 문제이다. Mr. Tal이 10년 전에 근무를 시작했고, 그 후 어느 시점에 매니저가 되었다는 의미를 나타내므로 현재완료 has become과 함께 쓰여 '그 후(어느 시점에)'를 의미하는 부사 (D) since가 정답이다. 부사 since는 과거에 있었던 일들을 이야기할 때, 과거 이후 어느 시점에 또 다른 일이 생겼을 때 현재완료와 함께 쓰인다. since가 부사뿐 아니라 '~한 이래로'의 의미의 전치사나 접속사로 쓰이는 경우에도 현재완료 시제와 함께 쓰인다는 점에 유의한다.

어휘 since [부사] 그 후(어느 시점에); [전치사/접속사] ~한 이래로; [접속사] ~때문에

UNIT 05. 전치사

본서 p.57

 1. on

1. 회의에 참석하실 분들은 토요일 저녁 장소에 일찍 도착하도록 권고됩니다.

해설 요일에 쓰이는 시간 전치사

Q2 **1. by** **2. since** **3. prior to**

1. 본사 건물의 공사는 올해 말까지 완료될 예정이다.

해설 동작 완료 의미의 동사와 함께하는 시점 전치사

2. Mr. Kensmore는 대학 졸업 이후로 해외에서 근무해왔다.

해설 현재완료 + since + 시점: ～이후로 …해왔다

3. Cristal Sky 항공은 승객 여러분이 예정되어 있는 출발시간 최소 한 시간 전에 공항에 도착하실 것을 권장합니다.

해설 prior to + 시점: ～전에

Q3 1. during 2. for 3. within 4. throughout

1. Mr. Lane은 평소 업무 시간에 다시 전화하라는 요청을 받았다.

해설 during + 특정 사건이 일어나는 기간: ～하는 동안

2. Lukas 사의 경영진은 지난 10년 동안 직원 생산성의 향상에 대한 헌신적인 태도를 보여왔다.

해설 for + 특정 (숫자) 기간: ～동안

3. 귀하의 주문을 구매일 3일 내에 배달할 것입니다.

해설 within + 특정 (숫자) 기간: ～이내에

4. 한 번의 작은 퇴보를 제외하면 매출은 올해 내내 지속적으로 증가했다.

해설 throughout + 기간: ～내내

Q4 1. along 2. throughout 3. past

1. 시에서는 Ran 강을 따라 가는 경치 좋은 보트 타기를 제공한다.

해설 along + 장소: ～을 따라

2. 우리는 수년 간의 연구 끝에 마침내 새로운 혁신적인 제품을 개발했고 전 세계적으로 인기를 얻고 있다.

해설 throughout + 장소: ～ 전역에 걸쳐

3. 시민회관은 West 가에 있는 영화관을 약간 지나서 위치해 있다.

해설 past: ～을 지나서

+ check 1. between 2. in 3. within 4. through

1. 관광객들은 오전 9시에서 오후 6시 사이에 가이드가 딸린 투어에 참여할 수 있다.

2. 편의를 위해 반신용 봉투에 신청서를 동봉해드립니다.

3. Ms. Park은 사무실에서 걸어올 수 있는 거리 안에 살지만 회의에 자주 지각한다.

4. Kenneth 자동차 시장조사팀은 인터뷰와 설문지를 통해 신모델에 관한 고객만족도 설문조사를 실시했다.

Q5 1. due to 2. regarding 3. Instead of 4. for 5. along with

1. Ashai Kitchen은 뛰어난 고객 서비스로 5년 연속 보스턴에서 최고의 식당으로 뽑혔다.

해설 최고 식당으로 선정된 이유를 나타내는 전치사

---

2. 귀하의 소프트웨어 프로그램에 관하여 어떤 문제라도 발생할 경우 기술 지원팀에 연락하시기 바랍니다.

해설 명사구를 이끄는 전치사 자리

3. 외부 지원자들을 택하는 대신 CEO는 Mr. Roman을 운영 이사에 임명했다.

해설 instead of: ～대신에 / except for: ～을 제외하고

4. 환불을 위해서는 주문일 30일 내로 고객 지원센터에 연락하십시오.

해설 고객들이 고객 지원센터에 연락하는 목적을 나타내는 전치사

5. 결함이 있는 제품과 함께 영수증 원본을 보내주셔야 한다는 점을 기억하시기 바랍니다.

해설 문맥상 '결함 있는 제품과 원본 영수증을 보내야 한다'라는 의미를 완성하는 '～와 함께'라는 의미 전치사. 둘의 관계를 나타내는 between은 「between + 복수 명사」, 「between A and B」 형태로 쓰임

+ check 1. in spite of 2. In addition to 3. such as 4. regardless of 5. without

1. WRB 공업은 최근의 수익 감소에도 불구하고 인센티브 프로그램을 유지했다.

2. 편집자 직책에는 좋은 글쓰기 실력에 더해 유창한 한국어 실력이 요구된다.

3. Garrix 금융은 보너스와 더 긴 휴가 등의 더 많은 혜택을 제공할 것이다.

4. 우리 회사는 교육 배경과는 관계 없이 지원자들을 면접에 선정한다.

5. 그들은 어제 정리해고 없이 회사를 재편하기 위한 모든 노력을 다 하겠다고 발표했다.

Q6 1. with 2. in 3. from

1. 새 안전 규정을 준수하기 위해 회사에서는 일부 오래된 장비를 교체할 것이다.

해설 '준수하다'의 의미로 동사 comply와 함께하는 전치사

2. 그 직책은 학사 학위와 소매업 환경에서의 경험을 요구한다.

해설 '～에 대한 경험'의 의미로 명사 experience와 함께하는 전치사

3. 그 부매니저는 어제 회의에 불참했다.

해설 '～불참하다'의 의미로 형용사 absent와 함께하는 전치사

Practice

본서 p.64

1. (D)	**2.** (B)	**3.** (B)	**4.** (D)	**5.** (A)
6. (B)	**7.** (B)	**8.** (D)	**9.** (A)	**10.** (D)
11. (D)	**12.** (D)	**13.** (D)	**14.** (D)	**15.** (D)
16. (A)	**17.** (C)	**18.** (B)	**19.** (C)	**20.** (C)

1. 프로젝트 기간 내내 여분의 장비가 Hung 자동차 상하이 공장의 개발 팀에게 제공될 것이다.

해설 빈칸 뒤에 기간 명사 the duration of the project가 온 점에 유의하여 정답을 선택한다. 장비는 프로젝트가 시작된 시점부터 끝나는 시점까지 계속 필요할 것이므로 '내내'라는 의미의 (D) throughout이 정답이다.

어휘 extra 여분의 I plant 공장 I upon ~하자마자

2. 경쟁사들의 대부분의 다른 비슷한 시스템들과는 달리 Hisakawa의 녹음 시스템은 쉽게 설치될 수 있다.

해설 빈칸 뒤에 명사가 온 구조이므로, 전치사 인 (A) ,(B) 중 문맥에 맞는 것을 선택해야 한다. 다른 경쟁업체 제품과 차별화된 Hisakawa 녹음 시스템의 장점을 나타내는 문장으로, 문맥상 '~와 다르게' 를 의미하는 (B) Unlike 가 정답이다. (C)는 접속부사, (D)는 접속사이므로 전치사 자리인 빈칸에 적합하지 않다.

어휘 comparable 비슷한 I easily 쉽게 I install ~을 설치하다

3. Kitt 국립공원은 경치 좋은 도시의 해안가를 따라 매일 연락선 투어를 제공한다.

해설 빈칸 뒤의 장소 명사 waterfront와 함께 쓰여 '해안가를 따라'라는 의미의 (B) along이 정답이다.

어휘 ferry (사람·차량 등을 운반하는) 연락선 I scenic 경치가 좋은 I waterfront 해안가

4. 개인 정보는 고객들의 승인 없이 공유되어서는 안 된다.

해설 보기가 모두 전치사 이므로, 해석을 통해 적절한 전치사를 선택하는 문제이다. 문맥상 '고객들의 승인 없이'라는 의미에 적합한 (D) without 이 정답이다.

어휘 share 공유하다 I approval 승인

5. 광고에 나간 상품에 대한 이 판촉 할인을 반드시 받으시려면 24시간 이내에 주문하시기 바랍니다.

해설 빈칸 뒤의 기간 명사 24 hours와 함께 쓰여 '24시간 이내에'라는 의미의 (A) within이 정답이다. '~이내에'라는 의미인 (B) into는 기간 명사와 쓰이지 못하며, (C) since는 과거 시점과 쓰이므로 오답이다.

어휘 promotional 홍보, 판촉의 I place an order 주문하다

6. Walmont 고용 센터의 설문을 작성했던 참가자들 대다수가 은퇴 연령이 지난 후에도 계속해서 일할 계획이라고 진술했다.

해설 빈칸 뒤에 명사가 온 구조이므로, 전치사인 (B), (C) 중 문맥에 맞는 것을 선택해야 한다. '은퇴 연령이 지난 후에도 계속해서 일할 계획이다'

라는 문맥에 따라, (B) past가 정답이다. 전치사 past는 시점 및 장소 명사와 쓰여 '(시점이나 위치상으로) 지나서' 라는 의미를 갖는다. 전치사인 (C)는 문맥상 적합하지 않으며, (A), (D)는 부사로 전치사 자리인 빈칸에 적합하지 않다.

어휘 the majority of ~의 대다수 I questionnaire 설문(지) I state 진술하다 I retirement age 은퇴 연령 I past (전)지나서, (형) 지난

7. Rojanho 프로젝트 팀원들은 그들의 성공을 축하하기 위한 9월 10일 회사 사장과의 저녁 식사에 초대 받았다.

해설 빈칸 뒤 명사 the company president와 의미상 연결되는 전치사는 (B) with이다.

어휘 celebrate ~을 축하하다 I success 성공 I off 떨어져서 I throughout 도처에 I among 사이에서

8. 사장님이 현재 싱가포르에서 국제 경영 회의에 참석하고 있기 때문에, 목요일까지 사무실에 안 계실 겁니다.

해설 빈칸 뒤의 시점 명사 Thursday에 유의하여 정답을 선택한다. 대표가 자리를 계속 비울 것이라는 문맥에 따라 지속의 의미를 나타내는 (D) until이 정답이다. (A)는 과거 시점의 명사 앞에 와서 '~한 이래로'의 의미로 현재 완료와 쓰이므로 오답이다.

어휘 out of office 사무실 자리를 비운 I currently 현재

9. 1년의 근무 완료 후에, Finnerman 전자의 직원들은 일주일 유급 휴가를 갈 자격이 있다.

해설 보기에 품사가 섞여 있으므로 먼저, 빈칸에 알맞은 품사가 무엇인지 선택해야 한다. 빈칸 뒤에 명사가 온 구조이므로, 전치사 자리이다. (B)는 접속사, (C)는 접속 부사로 문법상 오답이며, 전치사인 (A) '후에', (D) '제외하고' 중 문맥상 적합한 (A) Following이 정답이다.

어휘 completion 완성, 완료 I employment 고용 I be eligible for ~에 대한 자격이 있다 I paid vacation 유급 휴가

10. 신규 고객들의 자료를 입력하는 직원들은 추가 지시 사항에 대해서 고객 서비스 부서의 Ms. Ahn에게 연락해야 한다.

해설 문맥상 연락의 목적을 나타내는 (D) for가 정답이다.

어휘 enter data 자료를 입력하다 I further 추가의 I instruction 지시 사항들

11. KD 음료 회사는 음료수 재료에 관련한 우려에 대처하기 위해 성명을 발표했다.

해설 '~에 관한 우려'의 의미에 적합한 (D) regarding이 정답이다.

어휘 issue 발표[공표]하다 I statement 성명, 진술 I address (일·문제 따위에) 본격적으로 착수하다, 대처하다 I concerns regarding [over] ~에 관한 우려

12.
고난도 급여에 관한 질문들은 급여 업무들을 담당하는 회계부서의 Ms. Avilia에게 보내져야 한다.

해설 '~에 관한'의 의미를 갖는 표현 중 to와 함께 하는 (D) pertaining이 정답이다. (A)는 의미상으로 적합하나 뒤에 전치사 to와 쓰이지 못하므로 오답이다.

14

어휘 paycheck 급료, 봉급 | accounting department 회계부 |
payroll 급여 대상자 명단, 급여 지불 총액

13. 모든 것이 계획에 따라 진행되면 접수처의 리모델링이 목요일까지 완료될 것이다.

해설 문맥상 '~에 따라' 를 의미하는 (D) according to 가 정답이다.

어휘 remodeling 리모델링, 수리 | reception area 로비, 안내실

14.
고난도 Volgasy 솔루션과 Xerman 화학에서 온 대표들은 서로 함께 일하기로 합의했다.

해설 빈칸 뒤에 쓰인 부정대명사 one another를 목적어로 취할 수 있는 전치사가 필요한 자리이므로 (D) alongside가 정답이다. (A)와 (C)는 부사로 대명사 목적어를 취할 수 없고 (B)는 자동사에서 만들어진 현재분사로 역시 대명사 목적어를 취할 수 없다.

어휘 representative 대표자, 대리인 | one another (셋 이상이) 서로 | jointly 공동으로 | collaborating 협력하는 | alongside ~과 함께

15. Walton Technologies는 중국과 베트남에 10개 이상의 생산 공장을 가진 아시아에서 선두적인 자동차 시트 제조업체 중 한 곳이다.

해설 여러 선두업체 중의 하나라는 문맥에 적합한 (D) among이 정답이다.

어휘 manufacturer 제조업체 | more than ~이상

16.
고난도 지원자들은 늦어도 이번 주 금요일까지는 Ms. Lynn에게 추천서와 함께 이력서를 제출해야 한다.

해설 빈칸 뒤에 명사가 왔으므로 부사 (C)는 오답이다. '추천서와 함께 이력서를 제출해야 한다'는 문맥에 따라 (A) along with가 정답이다.

어휘 applicant 지원자 | letter of recommendation 추천서 | no later than 늦어도 ~까지는

17. Bektal 건설사는 아시아 태평양 지역을 넘어서 시장을 확장하려는 노력으로 유럽에 지사들을 열 계획을 세우고 있다.

해설 '~지역을 넘어서 시장을 확대하다'라는 문맥이므로 (C) beyond가 정답이다.

어휘 branch office 지사 | in an effort to ~하려는 노력으로 | broaden ~을 넓히다 | region 지역

18. Alma Roberto의 새 책 여기저기에 실린 많은 사진들은 독자들이 패션 경향의 변화를 이해하는 데 도움이 된다.

해설 빈칸 뒤에 온 명사 new book과 문맥상 이어지는 (B) throughout이 정답이다. throughout은 기간을 말할 때는 '내내'라고 해석되고, 장소를 말할 때는 '도처에, 여기저기에'라고 해석된다.

어휘 photograph 사진 | trend 경향 | among ~사이에 | during ~동안 | toward ~을 향해

19.
고난도 관광 업계에서 25년 된(역사를 가진) Always Loving 여행사는 이 업계에서는 선도적인 회사로서 널리 인정받고 있다.

해설 선도적인 기업으로 널리 인정받고 있는 Always Loving 여행사가 25년 된(역사를 가진) 기업이라는 문맥에 따라, (C) With가 정답이다. (D) Past는 문맥상으로 적절하지 못할 뿐 아니라, 전치사로 쓰일 때,

시점을 나타내는 명사와 쓰이기 때문에 기간명사 '25 years'와 쓰일 수 없다. (A), (B)는 문맥상 부적절하므로 오답이다.

어휘 widely 널리 | be recognized as ~로 인정받다 | leading 선도적인 | ahead of ~에 앞서 | until now 지금까지 | past [전] (시점, 위치상으로) ~을 지나서, [형] 지난

20.
고난도 연례 음악축제의 인기를 고려해 볼 때 참석에 관심이 있는 사람들은 사전에 입장권을 구매해야 한다.

해설 문맥상 '인기를 고려해 볼 때'가 적합하므로 (C) Given이 정답이다. since가 '~때문에'라는 의미일 때는 접속사로만 쓰인다는 점에 유의해야 한다. 이 문제에서는 빈칸 뒤에 명사가 온 구조이므로, 전치사 자리이다. 따라서, since는 '~한 이래로'의 의미로 오답이다.

어휘 well in advance 사전에 | since [전치사, 접속사] ~한 이래로; [접속사] ~때문에

REVIEW TEST 01

본서 p.66

1. (D)	2. (C)	3. (B)	4. (B)	5. (C)
6. (D)	7. (C)	8. (D)	9. (B)	10. (C)
11. (A)	12. (C)	13. (D)	14. (D)	15. (D)
16. (C)	17. (B)	18. (D)	19. (A)	20. (D)

1. John Burnett 법률 회사에 전화하셔서 무료 상담 예약을 하세요.

해설 관사와 형용사 뒤 빈칸이므로 명사를 쓸 자리인데, 문맥상 '무료 상담'이 자연스러우므로 (D) consultation이 정답이다.

어휘 schedule 일정을 잡다 | consult 상담하다 | consultant 상담원 | consultation 상담

2. Otteron 다리는 Hanso 강의 범람 때문에 일시적으로 폐쇄되었다.

해설 빈칸 뒤에 명사구가 연결되어 있으므로 빈칸은 전치사 자리이다. 문맥상 Hanso 강의 범람 때문에, Otteron 다리가 일시적으로 폐쇄되었다는 의미이므로 이유를 나타내는 전치사 (C) owing to가 정답이다.

어휘 temporarily 일시적으로 | flooding 홍수, 범람

3. 관리자들은 정기적으로 그들의 부서에 있는 직원들의 성과를 평가해야 한다.

해설 빈칸은 명사 앞자리이므로 소유격 대명사 (B) their가 정답이다.

어휘 assess 평가하다 | performance 성과, 실적 | department 부서 | on a regular basis 정기적으로

4. Vandenberg 전자는 모든 직원들에게 컴퓨터 교육 워크숍을 제공하며, 대부분은 그 시간에 많은 혜택을 받았다.

해설 빈칸은 주어 자리로, 동사가 복수(have)이므로, 보기 중 복수 취급하는 부정대명사 (B) most가 정답이다. 이때 most는 'employees'를 지칭하는 대명사이다. 나머지 보기인 대명사 (A), (C), (D)가 주어로 쓰이면 단수동사를 취해야 한다.

어휘 benefit from ~로부터 혜택을 받다

5. 다음 주 마케팅 세미나를 위한 일정표가 오후에 참석자 전원에게 이메일로 보내질 것이다.

해설 다음 주 마케팅 세미나를 위한 일정표란 의미로 목적을 나타내는 전치사 (C) for가 정답이다.

어휘 participant 참석자, 참가자

6.
고난도
해설 빈칸은 정관사 the 뒤의 명사 자리인데, 보기가 모두 동일 어근의 명사들이므로 명사의 단수/복수 관련 문법과 해석을 통해 정답을 골라야 한다. 빈칸 앞의 'upon their arrival'에서 복수의 사람들(their)이 도착하자마자, 그들이 기자회견을 할 것임을 파악할 수 있으므로, 주어 자리에는 복수 명사가 와야 한다. 따라서, (D) delegates가 정답이다.

컨벤션 센터에 도착하자마자, 대표자들은 기자 회견을 열었다.

어휘 upon ~하자마자 | press conference 기자 회견

7. 새롭게 문을 연 Watson Valley 리조트에는 멋진 식사 장소와 더불어 스포츠와 오락을 위한 훌륭한 시설이 있다.

해설 빈칸 뒤에 명사를 목적어로 취할 성분을 쓸 자리이므로 전치사인 (C) in addition to가 정답이다.

어휘 fabulous 멋진, 훌륭한

8. 동기 부여 연설가들은 의도적으로 청중들로부터 감정적인 반응을 유도한다.

해설 빈칸은 동사 수식 부사 자리이므로 (D) intentionally가 정답이다.

어휘 motivational 동기 부여의 | induce 설득하다, 유도하다 | emotional 감정적인

9. 환경을 보호하려는 세계적인 노력에도 불구하고, Greener Earth 대변인은 지구의 평균 온도가 점차 상승하고 있다고 말했다.

해설 콤마 앞 뒤의 내용이 대조를 이루고 있으며, 빈칸 뒤에 명사만 쓰였으므로 (B) Despite가 정답이다.

어휘 gradually 점차로

10. 회사들은 점점 더 직원들에게 자기평가 과정의 일환으로 업무와 관련된 성과를 서면으로 요약해서 제공하라고 요구한다.

해설 소유격과 형용사 뒤에는 명사를 써야 하므로 (C) accomplishments가 정답이다.

어휘 accomplished 기량이 뛰어난

11. Namyang 출판사는 대다수의 독자들이 Murasaki Hitori의 신간 소설인 〈The Road to End〉에 우호적으로 반응했다고 보도했다.

해설 자동사와 전치사 사이에는 자동사를 수식하는 부사를 써야 하므로 (A) favorably가 정답이다.

어휘 majority 대다수의 | favorably 우호적으로

12. 생산 일정이 매우 뒤처졌기 때문에 교대근무가 사전 공지 없이 변경될 수 있음을 이해하여 주십시오.

해설 빈칸 뒤에 명사가 연결되어 있으므로 전치사를 써야 하고, 사전 공지 '없이'라는 의미가 자연스러우므로 (C) without이 정답이다.

어휘 behind schedule 일정이 늦은 | prior notice 사전 공지

13. Sherwin 사가 제조한 페인트 제품들은 주거용으로만 만들어졌다.

해설 전치사 for 뒤의 use는 동사가 아닌 명사로 쓰였으므로 그 앞의 빈칸에는 형용사가 위치해야 한다. 따라서, (D) residential (거주의)이 정답이다.

어휘 be intended for ~을 위해 계획되다

14. Ms. Miller가 시장이 된 이후로, 증가하는 교통혼잡을 완화시키는 것이 그녀가 처리해야 할 가장 시급한 문제 중 하나가 되었다.

해설 명사를 수식하는 형용사 앞에 들어갈 알맞은 대명사는 소유격이므로, (D) her가 정답이다.

어휘 alleviate 경감시키다, 완화시키다 | urgent 긴급한 | address 처리하다, 해결하다

15. 고객의 전화가 기술 지원 부서로 연결되기 전에 잘못해서 끊겼다.

해설 빈칸은 동사 was disconnected를 수식하는 부사 자리이므로 (D) accidentally가 정답이다.

어휘 disconnect (연결·접속을) 끊다 | transfer 옮기다, 이동하다

16.
고난도 Jensen 전자의 최신 모델인 XP 336 노트북 컴퓨터는 업계의 다른 어떤 모델의 사양도 뛰어넘는 사양으로 설계되었다.

해설 빈칸이 전치사의 목적어 자리에 위치해 있으므로 명사를 써야 하고, 다른 모델들의 사양들과 신제품의 사양들을 비교하고 있으므로 복수 명사인 (C) capabilities가 정답이다.

어휘 design 설계하다, 고안하다 | capability 역량

17.
고난도 비록 모두가 어제 학회에서 말할 기회를 얻은 건 아니지만, 참가자들은 온라인 토론 포럼장에 그들의 논평을 게시할 수 있었다.

해설 (B) everyone은 전체, 즉 복수를 지칭하나 문법적으로는 단수 취급하는 대명사로 복수명사인 participants를 대신 할 수 있으며, 또한 'not everyone'의 형태로 자주 쓰인다. 따라서 (B) everyone이 정답이다. 보기 (C) much는 양을 나타내는 개념으로 사람을 대신할 수 없기 때문에 오답이며, 보기 (D) each는 대명사로 단독으로 쓰일 수 있으나, 명확한 대상의 단수를 의미하므로 전체 문맥과 어울리지 않아 오답이다. 이처럼 문법적으로 가능한 보기가 두 개 이상 제시된 경우 해석을 통해 문맥상 적절한 보기를 최종 정답으로 선택하는 것이 실전 문제 풀이의 중요한 원칙이다.

어휘 opportunity 기회 | conference 회의, 학회 | post 게시하다 | comment 논평, 언급 | forum 포럼(장), 토론회

18.
고난도 Mr. Dreyfus가 우리 프린터의 신제품에 관심을 보였지만, 회사용으로 주문할지에 대해서는 확정을 하지 않았다.

해설 빈칸은 동사 expressed의 목적어 자리로 명사가 필요한데, 명사 interest는 가산 명사일 때와 불가산 명사일 때의 의미 차이가 있다. '관심사' 또는 '이익, 이해관계'의 의미일 때는 가산 명사로 쓰이므로 복수형이 가능하다. 하지만, '관심, 흥미' 또는 '이자'를 의미할 때는 불가산 명사로 항상 단수 형태를 취해야 한다. '새로 나온 프린터에 관심을 보였다'는 문맥에 따라, interest가 불가산명사로 쓰였기 때문에 (D) interest가 정답이다.

어휘 **express** 표현하다, 나타내다 | **line** (상품의) 종류, (공장의) 작업라인 | **confirm** 확정하다, 승인해주다 | **order** 주문하다

19. 귀하의 지불액을 수령하자마자 24시간 이내로 상품을 발송할 것입니다.

해설 '지불액을 수령하자마자 24시간 이내로 상품 발송을 할 것'이라는 문맥에 따라, '~하자마자'의 의미를 지닌 'upon + 명사'를 묻는 문제이다. 따라서, 전치사 (A) upon이 정답이다.

어휘 **ship out** 발송하다, ~을 보내다 | **upon** + 명사 ~하자 마자 | **receipt** 수령, 영수증 | **payment** 지불(금)

20. Charlin Residence는 저희가 보유한 가장 넓은 빌라이며, 온 가족
고난도 이 즐거운 시간을 보낼 수 있는 확실한 최고의 선택입니다.

해설 빈칸에는 and 뒤의 명사구 the best choice for the whole family to have a great time을 수식하는 '분명히, 확실히'라는 의미의 부사 (D) definitely가 정답이다. 형용사인 보기 (A) (B) (C)가 명사를 수식한다고 생각하여 오답으로 선택할 수 있으나, 형용사가 명사를 수식하는 경우 정관사 the와 명사 사이에 위치 해야 하므로, the 앞의 빈칸에는 정답이 될 수 없다. 이 유형은 고난도 문제로 최근에 자주 출제되고 있으며, 명사구를 수식하는 대표적인 부사인 'formerly, previously 이전에 | originally 원래 | arguably 아마도, 거의 틀림없이 | once 한때 | largely, mainly 주로'를 참고로 알아두자.

어휘 **residence** 주택, 거주지 | **spacious** 공간이 넓은 | **choice** 선택

UNIT 06. 동사의 형태와 수 일치 본서 p.69

Q1 1. welcome 2. boost 3. be

1. Ms. Goro의 마케팅팀 합류를 환영해주십시오.
해설 please로 시작하는 명령문의 동사원형 자리

2. Gloria Claughton의 설문조사에 따르면 텔레비전 광고가 반드시 매출을 증진시켜주는 것은 아니다.
해설 조동사 뒤의 동사원형 자리

3. 이사회는 금요일까지 예산 제안서를 제출하라고 요청했다.
해설 요청 동사 ask 뒤 should가 생략된 동사원형 자리

+ check 1. contact 2. arrive 3. examine

1. 검토해보시고, 추가적인 질문이 있으면 상급자에게 연락하세요.

2. 안내서 한 부가 이번 주에 우편으로 도착할 것이다.

3. 매니저는 Mr. Kim이 도쿄 시설의 비용을 줄일 수 있는 모든 가능한 방법들을 조사해야 한다고 요청했다.

Q2 1. required 2. promised

1. 모든 직원은 출장에서 돌아온 직후 출장비 보고서를 작성해야 합니다.
해설 be동사 뒤의 분사 자리

2. 회장은 회사 구내 식당을 업그레이드하겠다고 약속했다.
해설 have 동사 뒤의 분사 자리

Q3 1. is 2. is 3. reside 4. were

1. Cal 가전은 낮은 가격에 질 좋은 물건을 제공하는 데 전념한다.
해설 회사명 등의 고유명사는 어미의 형태(-(e)s)와 관계 없이 단수 취급

2. 회사의 이익을 극대화하는 가장 좋은 방법은 미리 사고를 예방하는 것이다.
해설 동명사가 주어인 경우 단수 취급

3. 이 가구 라인은 작은 주택에 거주하는 고객들을 위해 디자인되었다.
해설 관계대명사 who 앞의 선행사인 복수 명사 customers에 동사의 수 일치

4. Brooks 자동차는 결함이 있는 브레이크로 인해 여러 건의 사고가 있었기 때문에 TX301 모델을 리콜하고 있다.
해설 「there + be동사」 구문에서는 be동사 뒤의 명사에 수 일치

+ check 1. possess 2. requires 3. are

1. 기술적 지식을 갖춘 편집자들에 대한 증가하는 요구가 있어 왔다.

2. Sencomp 전자는 새로운 신원 확인 시스템의 사용을 요구하고 있다.

3. 안타깝게도 문의하신 Toronto 세션에는 남는 좌석이 없습니다.

Q4 1. is 2. are 3. is

1. 각 신입사원은 근무 시작 전 교육 과정을 이수해야 합니다.
해설 each of the + 복수 명사(employees) + 단수 동사

2. 많은 안전 검열관들이 다음 주에 회사의 안전규정 준수를 확인하기 위해 올 것이다.
해설 a number of + 복수 명사(inspectors) + 복수 동사

3. 저희 제품에 관한 대부분의 정보는 웹사이트에서 이용하실 수 있습니다.
해설 most of the + 불가산 명사(information) + 단수 동사

+ check 1. is 2. has 3. were

1. 우리 회사의 문제점들 중 하나는 자금 부족이다.

2. 대중교통을 이용하는 사람들의 수가 유가 상승으로 급격하게 증가했다.

3. 지원자들 대부분이 그 직책을 위한 자격이 충분했다.

Q5 **1.** are **2.** are **3.** was

1. 회사의 임원들이 중요한 발표를 할 것으로 예상된다.
해설 수식어인 전치사구 앞의 주어 Executives와 수 일치

2. 분석가들의 제안사항들은 회사 회보에 요약되어 있다.
해설 수식어인 과거분사 made 앞의 주어 suggestions와 수 일치

3. Ms. Borgen이 기획회의에 제출한 기획안이 흥미로웠다.
해설 수식어인 목적격 관계대명사 that 앞의 주어 proposal과 수 일치

+ check **1.** were **2.** need **3.** orders

1. 회계 관리자에 의해 아직 승인되지 않은 일부 영수증들이 카운터에 남아 있었다.

2. 매장 고객카드를 신청하실 고객들께서는 온라인 신청서를 작성하셔야 합니다.

3. 프론트 데스크 지원 직원 Ms. Yoo는 매주 금요일 사무용품을 주문한다.

Practice
본서 p.74

1. (D)	**2.** (D)	**3.** (A)	**4.** (C)	**5.** (D)
6. (D)	**7.** (B)	**8.** (C)	**9.** (A)	**10.** (B)
11. (D)	**12.** (B)	**13.** (C)	**14.** (B)	**15.** (D)
16. (A)	**17.** (A)	**18.** (B)	**19.** (D)	**20.** (A)

1. Dr. Johnson과 다른 유명한 교수들이 나오는 세미나들이 토요일 저녁 7시 30분 Maylor 강당에서 예정되어 있다.
해설 문장의 동사 자리이며 현재분사 featuring의 수식을 받은 복수 명사 seminars가 문장의 주어이므로 복수 동사 (D) are가 정답이다.
어휘 feature 특별히 포함하다, 특징으로 삼다 ǀ distinguished 유명한, 성공한 ǀ auditorium 강당

2. 유명인이 광고에 등장한다는 사실이 제품의 성공을 보장하지는 않는다.
고난도
해설 동격의 that절의 수식을 받는 주어 The fact 뒤의 동사 자리를 묻는 문제이다. (C)는 동사가 아니므로 오답이며, 「do(does/did) not + 동사원형」 형태로 부정문을 만드는 조동사 (D) does가 정답이다. have 뒤의 동사는 과거분사형이 와야 하나 동사원형 guarantee가 있으므로 (B)도 오답이다.
어휘 celebrity 유명인 ǀ appear 등장하다 ǀ advertisement 광고 ǀ guarantee ~을 보장하다

3. Lindsey 공원에 있는 시립 박물관의 입장료는 6세 이하의 어린이에게 무료이다.
해설 빈칸은 주어 자리이며 단수 동사 is와 수의 일치를 고려하여 단수 명사 (A) Admission이 정답이다.
어휘 municipal 시의, 지방 자치의 ǀ admission 입장, 입장료

4. 저희 책의 늦은 반납에 대한 추가 요금을 이미 지불했을 경우 이 편지를 무시하셔도 됩니다.
해설 Please 뒤의 주어가 생략된 명령문에서는 동사원형을 써야 하므로 (C) disregard가 정답이다.
어휘 additional 추가적인 ǀ charge 요금 ǀ disregard 무시하다

5. 그 카페가 메뉴에 추가한 디저트들에 고객들이 열광적으로 반응했다.
해설 한 문장에는 하나의 동사가 존재해야 하나, 이 문제의 문장에 동사가 없기 때문에 빈칸은 동사 자리이다. 따라서, (D) responded가 정답이다.
어휘 enthusiastically 열광적으로 ǀ add 추가하다

6. Chaikrabi Skin Care의 모든 상품 배송은 3일에서 5일을 잡으세요.
해설 동사 자리이며 주어가 생략된 명령문 구조이므로 동사원형 (D) Allow가 정답이다.
어휘 allow (특정한 목적을 위해 계산하여) 잡다

7. Queen's 전자는 TV와 냉장고 같은 다양한 가전제품들을 생산한다.
해설 회사명 Queen's Electronics는 단수 취급을 해야 하며, 동사가 필요한 자리이므로 (B) produces가 정답이다.
어휘 a variety of 다양한 ǀ electronic home appliance 가전제품 ǀ such as ~와 같은

8. Maria Nguyen은 주간 온라인 기사 〈Eastern Exchange〉에서 아시아의 주식 시장 동향을 분석한다.
해설 보기가 동사, 명사, 준동사로 구성되어 있기 때문에 빈칸이 동사 자리인지 아닌지부터 확인을 해야 한다. 하나의 문장에는 하나의 동사가 반드시 존재해야 하나, 문장에 동사가 없으므로 빈칸은 동사 자리이며 단수 명사와 수 일치된 단수 동사 (C) analyzes가 정답이다.
어휘 stock market 주식 시장 ǀ trend 동향, 추세

9. Greensville 사의 대략 절반의 직원들이 자가용으로 혼자 출퇴근을 한다.
해설 half of 뒤의 명사[employees]에 동사의 수를 일치시켜야 하므로 복수 동사 (A) commute가 정답이다.
어휘 commute 통근하다

10. 〈Current Business Journal〉은 지난 5년간 제약 업계에서 인수 합병 거래의 수가 일정하게 유지되고 있다고 보도했다.
고난도
해설 주어가 「the number of + 복수 명사」 형태인 경우 단수 명사 the number에 수의 일치를 이루어 단수 동사가 와야 하므로 정답은 (B) has remained이다.
어휘 merger and acquisition 인수 합병(M&A) ǀ pharmaceutical 제약의 ǀ deal 거래

11. Goodwill 금융 은행을 위한 개정된 제안서는 그 은행이 지역의 다른 은행들이 그랬던 것처럼 이자율을 올려야 한다고 제안한다.
해설 문장의 주어는 단수 명사 A revised proposal이고 동사가 필요한 자리이므로 (D) suggests가 정답이다.

어휘 revised 개정된 I interest rate 이자율 I suggest ~을 제안하다 I suggestion 제안

12. Degas' Island 레스토랑은 테이블 예약은 적어도 일주일 전에 되어야 한다고 요청한다.
고난도

해설 주장, 요구, 제안 등을 의미하는 타동사 request의 목적어로 쓰인 that절에는 동사원형을 써야 하며 '예약이 되다'라는 수동의 의미이므로 정답은 (B) be made이다.

어휘 request ~을 요청하다 I reservation 예약 I in advance 미리

13. 토론토는 대부분의 주요한 건물들을 연결하는 잘 발달된 지하철 시스템을 가지고 있다.

해설 빈칸은 주격 관계대명사 that 뒤의 동사 자리이다. 따라서 선행사 a well-developed underground system과 수를 일치시켜야 하므로 정답은 (C) connects이다.

어휘 underground 지하철 I major 주요한 I connection 연결 I connect ~을 연결하다

14. Orlando 대학교의 예술 센터가 될 그 인상적인 건축물은 유명한 건축가 Carmen Olsen에 의해 디자인되었다.

해설 빈칸은 주격 관계대명사 that 앞의 선행사에 해당하는 명사 자리이며, 주절의 동사가 단수 동사 was이므로 단수 명사 (B) structure가 정답이다.

어휘 renowned 유명한 I architect 건축가 I structure 건축물

15. 다가오는 연구 프로젝트의 모든 지원자들은 허용 자질 수준에 부합하기 위해서 지원 지침을 준수해야 한다.

해설 빈칸은 문장의 주어에 해당하는 명사 자리이며, all of 뒤의 명사에 동사의 수를 맞추어야 하므로 주절의 복수 동사 have와 수의 일치를 이루는 복수 명사 (D) applicants가 정답이다.

어휘 upcoming 다가오는, 곧 있을 I observe 준수하다, 지키다 I guideline 가이드라인(지침)

16. 인기를 얻고 있는 Rubber Lovers의 장화 판매량은 그 회사의 2분기 수익을 극적으로 증가시킬 것으로 예상된다.

해설 수식어인 전치사구(of ~) 앞의 Sales가 문장의 주어이며 문장의 서술어인 동사 자리를 묻는 문제이므로 동사가 아닌 (B), (C)는 오답이다. 복수 명사 Sales가 주어이므로 단수 동사 (D)는 오답이다. 만약 (D)가 have로 제시되었다면 수의 일치는 충족시키나 '예상된다'라는 수동형은 아니므로 오답이 된다. 수의 일치와 수동 모두를 충족시키는 (A) are가 정답이다.

어휘 dramatically 극적으로 I be expected to~ 예상되다 I profit 이익, 수익

17. 저희는 고객 각각이 저희의 서비스에 완전히 만족하는 것을 보장하는고난도 데 책임질 준비가 되어 있습니다.

해설 ensuring 뒤에 명사절을 이끄는 접속사 that이 생략된 구조로 빈칸에는 동사를 써야 하며, 문장의 주어가 단수 취급을 받는 each이므로 (A) is가 정답이다.

어휘 be ready to ~할 준비가 되다 I take responsibility for ~에 대한 책임을 지다 I ensure (that) 주어 + 동사 ~을 보장하다 I be completely satisfied with ~에 완전히 만족하다

18. 시간과 비용을 절감하기 위해, RTA 사는 출장 가는 직원 어느 누구나 그들이 가져가는 수하물의 양을 최소화하도록 권고한다.

해설 제안, 요청 동사 뒤에 오는 that절에는 'should+ 동사원형'이나 '동사원형'을 쓴다. 따라서, 빈칸은 recommend 뒤에 이어지는 that 절의 동사에 해당하므로, 정답은 동사원형 (B) minimize 이다.

어휘 associate (직장) 동료 I luggage 수하물 I minimize 최소화 하다

19. 영업 부서가 요청했던 제품 안내책자가 어제 속달 우편으로 도착했다.
고난도

해설 명사 뒤에 「주어 + 동사」가 바로 올 경우 목적격 관계대명사 that이 생략되어 명사를 수식하는 구조임을 파악해야 풀 수 있는 문제이다. 즉, the Sales Department had asked for가 명사 the product manual을 수식하는 구조로 주어 the product manual에 이어지는 동사가 빈칸에 와야 하므로 (A)와 (B)는 오답이고, 주어인 the product manual이 단수이므로 (C)도 오답이다. 수식하는 절의 동사가 과거완료이므로 과거 동사 (D) arrived가 정답이다.

어휘 manual 안내책자 I express mail 속달 우편

20. 측량 기사들은 지면의 구성 성분들을 분석하고 공사를 위한 적합성을 평가한다.

해설 문제에 제시된 동사가 복수 동사 형태인 analyze이므로, 그 동사의 주어가 복수명사임을 알 수 있다. 따라서, 빈칸은 (A) technicians가 정답이다. 특히, 빈칸을 동사 analyze 앞의 부사 자리라고 생각하여 (B) technically를 선택할 수 있으나, 그 경우 복수 동사 analyze의 주어가 단수명사 survey가 되는 구조가 되므로, 문법적으로 올바르지 않다.

어휘 composition 구성 요소 I ground 지면, 땅 I evaluate 평가하다 I suitability 적합성 I technician 기사, 기술자 I technicality 전문적 성질

UNIT 07. 능동태와 수동태
본서 p.77

Q1 **1. approved**

1. 귀하의 대출 신청이 매니저에 의해 승인되자마자 은행에서 서면으로 연락드릴 것입니다.

해설 주어(대출 신청)가 동사 approve의 대상이며 '대출 신청이 승인되다'라는 의미이므로 수동태

Q2 **1. has conducted** **2. will be revised**

1. 마케팅 부서는 새 마케팅 전략을 짜기 위해 철저한 조사를 실시했다.

해설 타동사 conduct 뒤에 목적어 a thorough survey가 있으므로 능동

2. 조사에 대응하여 조립 라인의 안전 규정이 수정될 것이다.

해설 타동사 revise 뒤에 목적어가 아닌 전치사구가 있으므로 수동

 check   1. provides   2. made

1. Tripfolio는 모든 회사 차량 경비를 기록할 수 있는 쉬운 방식을 제공한다.

2. 저희 구독 가격에 대한 변경은 내년부터 있을 것입니다.

Q3   1. be given

1. 영업 경력이 있는 지원자들은 그 자리에 면접을 볼 기회를 받게 될 것이다.

해설 지원자들은 인터뷰 기회를 주는 주체가 아닌 받는 대상이므로 수동

Q4   1. been named   2. clear   3. advised

1. 의료 컨설팅 업체인 Wheelers 사는 경영 연구기관 Best Biz가 뽑은 보스턴 지역 최고의 직장으로 거명되었다.

해설 주어가 최고의 직장으로 선정된 대상이므로 수동

2. 화재 비상구는 건물 각 층에 위치해 있으며 어떠한 장애물도 없는 상태로 유지되어야 한다.

해설 빈칸은 앞에 있는 5형식 동사 keep의 목적격 보어 자리로 형용사 자리. 수동태가 되면서 목적어가 주어가 되어 앞으로 나가고, 뒤에는 형용사 목적격 보어가 남아 있는 형태

3. 통근자들은 오늘 대중교통을 이용할 것을 강하게 권유받았다.

해설 주어가 대중교통 이용을 권장받는 대상이므로 수동이며 5형식 동사 뒤에 to부정사가 바로 위치해 있다는 점도 수동태의 단서

 check   1. confidential   2. expected

1. 귀하의 개인정보는 Farisys 사에 의해 기밀로 유지됩니다.

2. 모든 직원들은 고객들과 소통할 때 적절한 수준의 전문성을 유지할 것으로 기대된다.

Q5   1. take place

1. Ms. Kovac은 목요일에 있을 지역 회의에 당신의 참석을 요청하셨습니다.

해설 take place는 항상 능동형으로 쓰임

 check   1. shipped   2. will expire

1. 온라인으로 넣어진 주문은 48시간 이내에 우리 부산 창고에서 출하될 것이다.

2. 당신의 Terryvale 어린이 동물원 회원권이 7월 31일에 만료된다는 것을 기억해 주세요.

Q6   1. with

1. 매장 매니저는 세일 행사에 관한 긍정적 반응에 만족했다.

해설 please는 주어가 사람인 경우 수동으로 쓰며, 뒤에 by가 아닌 전치사 with를 수반

Practice
본서 p.82

1. (C)	**2.** (B)	**3.** (D)	**4.** (A)	**5.** (B)
6. (D)	**7.** (D)	**8.** (B)	**9.** (C)	**10.** (B)
11. (D)	**12.** (D)	**13.** (A)	**14.** (B)	**15.** (B)
16. (B)	**17.** (D)	**18.** (C)	**19.** (D)	**20.** (B)

1. 변제에 대한 모든 요청들은 이번 주말 전에 승인을 위해서 부서장에게 제출되어야 한다.

해설 보기가 모두 동사이므로 수의 일치를 먼저 파악해야 한다. 문장의 주어 All requests가 복수 명사이므로 단수 동사인 (B)는 오답이다. 주어인 '모든 요청들'이 '제출되다'라는 수동으로 해석되며, 뒤에 목적어가 없기 때문에 수동태인 (C) should be submitted가 정답이다.

어휘 **request for** ~에 대한 요청 **l reimbursement** 변제 **l approval** 승인

2. 강이 내려다보이는 전망을 갖춘 고급스러운 스위트룸은 이사회 회의를 위해 이번 주말에 예약되었다.

해설 주어진 문장에 동사가 없기 때문에 빈칸은 동사 자리이므로 (A)는 오답이다. 동사와 관련된 문제는 먼저 주어와 수의 일치 여부를 체크해야 하는데 주어 A luxury suite가 단수이므로 (D)는 오답이다. 주어 A luxury suite가 예약하는 주체가 아닌 예약되는 대상이며 뒤에 목적어가 아닌 전치사가 왔으므로 능동형인 (C)는 오답이며 수동형인 (B) has been reserved가 정답이다.

어휘 **view** 전망 **l overlook** ~을 내려다보다

3. 다음 주에 새 잉크 카트리지가 설치될 때까지 구석에 있는 다른 복사기를 쓰십시오.

해설 문장의 주어는 단수이므로 (B)와 (D) 중에 답을 골라야 한다. 새 잉크 카트리지는 '설치된다'라고 수동으로 해석되고 뒤에 목적어가 없기 때문에 수동태인 (D) has been installed가 정답이다. 시간의 부사절에서는 현재 완료가 미래 완료를 대신한다는 점에 주의한다. (A)는 과거 진행, (B)는 미래 진행, (C)는 현재 완료로 모두 능동태이다.

어휘 **photocopier** 복사기 **l install** ~을 설치하다

4. 캠퍼스 외부 조명에 대한 정기 점검은 일주일 단위로 유지 관리 직원에 의해서 시행된다.

해설 be동사 뒤에 빈칸이 왔으므로 동사 (D)는 오답이며, 문맥상 명사 (B)도 오답이다. 정기 점검이 '시행된다'라고 수동으로 해석되며 뒤에 목적어가 없이 전치사가 왔으므로 과거분사인 (A) conducted가 정답이다.

어휘　routine check 정기 점검 I maintenance (유지, 보수) 관리

5. 일단 새로운 영업 직원들을 고용하는 것에 대한 결정이 승인되면, 인사부는 광고를 낼 것이다.

해설　주어가 단수(decision)이므로 (A)는 오답이다. 결정은 '승인된다'는 수동의 해석이 적절하며, 빈칸 뒤에 목적어가 없으므로 현재 완료 수동태인 (B) has been approved가 정답이다.

어휘　representative 직원 I place an advertisement 광고를 내다

6. Bowson 전자의 예산 흑자에서 나온 기금들은 주로 회사 웹사이트를 개선하고 사무 기기들을 갱신하기 위해 할당된다.

해설　동사가 필요한 자리이므로 명사 (C)는 오답이며 (B)는 주어가 복수(funds)이므로 오답이다. 기금들은 '할당된다'고 수동으로 해석되며, 빈칸 뒤에 목적어가 없기 때문에 수동태인 (D) are allocated가 정답이다. (A)는 능동태이므로 오답이다.

어휘　fund 기금 I budget surplus 예산 흑자 I primarily 주로 I office equipment 사무 용품 I allocate ~을 할당하다 I allocation 할당

7. 부동산 소유권에 대한 법원 심리가 당사자들 간에 합의되어 취소될 것이다.

해설　접속사 now that이 있기 때문에 빈칸은 동사자리이므로, to부정사 (A)는 오답이며, 주어 The court hearing이 단수명사이므로 (B) cancel은 수 일치에 적합하지 않다. 해석상 주어가 취소되는 대상에 해당하며, 문법적으로 타동사 cancel 뒤에 목적어가 없는 구조이므로, 수동태 (D) will be canceled가 정답이다. now that이 이끄는 절은 부사절이므로 타동사 cancel의 목적어가 될 수 없다.

어휘　court hearing 법원 심리 I ownership 소유권 I property 부동산 I now that ~때문에 I party 관계 당사자 I reach a settlement 합의에 이르다, 타결하다

8. WTX 스마트폰의 처리 속도는 같은 가격 대에 있는 어떤 모바일 기기의 속도와도 견줄만하다.

해설　빈칸은 be 동사 뒤의 주격보어 자리로, 동사 (A)를 제외한 형용사 (B), 명사 (C), 현재분사 (D)가 올 수 있으나, 문맥상 '~와 비슷하다'라는 의미를 지닌 형용사 (B) comparable이 정답이다. 명사 (C)가 주격보어가 되기 위해서는 '주어 = 명사'의 의미가 되어야 하나, 문맥상 적절하지 못하다. 또한, 주어가 비교하는 행위의 주체가 아닌 비교되는 대상에 해당하므로, 수동태가 되어야 한다. 따라서, 그 앞의 be동사와 쓰여 능동태를 이루는 현재분사 (D)는 오답이다.

어휘　processing 처리; 가공 I device 기기, 장치 I price range 가격대 I be comparable to ~와 비슷하다

9. 오늘 워크숍에서, Dr. Ikeda는 특정한 마케팅 목표들을 달성하는 방법들을 다룰 것이다.

해설　조동사 뒤에 동사원형을 써야 하므로 (B)와 (C) 중 답을 골라야 하며, Ikeda 박사가 방법들을 '다룰 것이다'라는 능동으로 해석되며 빈칸 뒤에 목적어인 ways가 쓰였기 때문에 능동인 (C) address가 정답이다.

어휘　achieve ~을 달성하다 I particular 특정한 I objective 목표 I address (문제나 상황 등에 대해) 다루다

10. 제안된 수도 요금 인상에 대해 걱정하는 모든 주민들은 다음 달에 공개 청문회에 초대 받을 것이다.

해설　사람의 감정은 수동태로 표현하며 be concerned about은 '~에 관해 걱정하다'라는 뜻의 관용구이므로 정답은 (B) concerned이다.

어휘　resident 거주자 I be concerned about ~에 대해 걱정하다 I proposed 제안된 I hearing 청문회

11. 지구 온난화의 영향에 관한 심포지움에 신청한 모든 사람들은 일정에 관한 편지를 받았다.
고난도

해설　신청한 사람들이 일정을 보내는 주체가 아니라 받는 대상이 되므로 정답은 수동인 (D) was sent이다. 타동사 send는 '~에게 …을 보내다'라는 뜻의 4형식 동사로 쓰여 목적어를 두 개 취할 수도 있어서 목적어의 유무만으로 태를 구별할 수 없으므로 해석에 의해 정답을 찾아야 한다.

어휘　sign up for ~을 신청하다 I regarding ~에 관해

12. 내일 Lygon 호텔에서의 마케팅 세미나에 참석하는 모든 사람들은 접수처에서 이름을 기록하도록 권고(요청)된다.

해설　해석상으로 마케팅 세미나에 참석하는 모든 사람들이 권고(요청)받는 대상이므로 수동태 (D) is invited가 정답이다. 권고를 나타내는 5형식 동사 invite 뒤에 to부정사가 바로 온 수동태 구조에 유의한다.

어휘　sign in ~의 이름을 기록하다 I invite (정식으로) 요청하다

13. 일자리를 찾는 사람들은 취업 박람회에 적어도 10장의 이력서를 가져오고 간단한 면접을 준비해 오도록 권고받는다.

해설　해석상 (A) advised가 정답이며, 5형식 동사의 수동태 관용구인 「be advised to부정사(~하라고 권고받는다)」에 유의한다.

어휘　those who ~하는 사람들 I look for ~을 찾다 I at least 적어도 I job fair 취업 박람회 I criticize 비난하다 I monitor 감시하다 I excuse 용서하다

14. 출장비 청구 절차는 많은 직원들이 서류작업이 너무 복잡하다고 불평했기 때문에 간소화되었다.

해설　빈칸은 동사 자리이므로 준동사인 (A), (D)는 오답이다. 주어인 '절차들은 '간소화되다'라는 수동으로 해석되며, 뒤에 목적어가 없기 때문에 수동태인 (B) have been streamlined가 정답이다.

어휘　claim 청구[신청]하다 I business travel expense 출장비 I streamline 간소화[능률화]하다

15. Jefferson 사는 오늘 회사의 연간 운영 비용이 작년의 것과 비교해볼 때 고정적인 상태를 유지했다고 발표했다.
고난도

해설　announced의 목적어에 해당하는 명사절(that절)의 동사가 필요한 자리이므로 (C)는 오답이다. 복수 명사인 expenses가 주어이므로 (A)는 오답이며, remain은 '~한 상태로 남아 있다'라는 뜻의 2형식 자동사이기 때문에 수동태를 쓸 수 없으므로 능동태 (B) have remained가 정답이다.

annual 연간의 I operating expense 운영비용 I steady 변동 없는, 고정적인 I compare ～을 비교하다 I remain ～한 상태로 남아 있다

16. 그 행사에 등록한 사람들의 수는 200명이 넘을 것으로 추정된다.

해설 주어진 문장에 관계대명사 who가 있으므로 have registered 외에 하나의 동사가 더 필요하다. 동사 자리의 경우 주어와 수의 일치를 먼저 따져야 하는데 주어 the number는 단수이므로 복수 동사 (D)는 오답이며 주어 the number가 추정하는 주체가 아닌 추정되는 대상이므로 수동 (B) is estimated가 정답이다. (C), (D)는 능동형이므로 오답이다.

어휘 register for 등록하다 I estimate 추정하다, 어림잡다

17. 지난밤의 퇴직 기념 파티에서, Charles Choi는 그의 30년 동안의 노고와 회사에 대한 헌신에 대해서 상을 받았다.

해설 문장의 동사가 필요하며 문장의 주어인 Charles Choi는 상을 '받았다'라는 수동의 해석이 되며, 빈칸 뒤에 목적어가 없기 때문에 정답은 (D) was honored이다. 보기 (A), (B)는 능동태이므로 오답이다.

어휘 retirement party 퇴직 기념 파티 I dedication to ～에 대한 헌신 I be honored for ～으로 상을 받다

18. 최근의 가격 인상 탓에, 없어도 되는 연구실 장비 구매는 추후 공지가
고난도 있을 때까지 미뤄질 것이다.

해설 동사와 관련된 문제는 수의 일치를 먼저 파악해야 하는데, 단수 명사 purchase가 문장의 주어이므로 복수 동사 (D)는 오답이다. 장비 구입이 '미뤄지다'는 수동의 해석이 적절하며, 빈칸 뒤에 목적어가 없으므로 수동태 (C) will be deferred가 정답이다.

어휘 nonessential 없어도 되는, 불필요한 I defer 연기하다 (= postpone)

19. 단골 고객들을 많이 확보하고 있기 때문에, Cotter's Market은 그
고난도 지역 신생 슈퍼마켓들로부터의 치열한 경쟁을 견뎌왔다.

해설 접속사 since가 있기 때문에 동사가 두 개 존재해야 한다. 따라서 동사가 아닌 보기 (A), (C)는 오답이며, Cotter's Market이 치열한 경쟁을 이겨내는 주체로 능동 해석이 적합하므로 (D) has withstood가 정답이다. 또한, 타동사 withstand(견뎌내다, 이겨내다) 뒤에 목적어인 명사가 바로 오므로 능동태가 정답이다.

어휘 faithful 충실한 I fierce 치열한, 격렬한, 사나운 I withstand 견뎌내다, 이겨내다

20. Bridgeport-Tech 사는 매우 경쟁력 있는 가격으로 입찰에 응하여 2
고난도 년짜리 계약을 따냈다.

해설 빈칸은 동사 자리이므로 (D)는 오답이며, 해석상 Bridgeport-Tech 사가 입찰에 경쟁력 있는 가격을 제안했으므로 계약을 주는 주체가 아닌 계약에 대한 대상이므로 수동태 (B) has been awarded가 정답이다. 수여동사 award의 경우 수동태가 되어도 뒤에 명사가 남을 수 있으므로, 동사의 태를 구분할 때는 뒤에 목적어의 유무보다는 해석을 우선하여 정답을 선택해야 한다.

어휘 competitive 경쟁력 있는 I bid 입찰, 응찰 I award 수여하다

UNIT 08. 시제
본서 p.86

Q1 1. implemented   2. holds   3. will attend   4. normally

1. 경영진은 어제 에너지 절약을 위한 규정을 시행했다.
해설 yesterday는 과거 시제임을 표시하는 단서

2. 매니저는 매주 금요일 아침 정기 직원회의를 연다.
해설 every Friday morning은 현재 시제임을 표시하는 단서

3. 재무 이사는 다음 주 런던에서 회의에 참석할 것이다.
해설 Next week는 미래 시제임을 표시하는 단서

4. 제조 시설의 안전 검사는 보통 시 공무원들이 행한다.
해설 현재 시제와 어울리는 부사는 normally

Q2 1. has expanded   2. has improved

1. 회사는 지난 2년간 사업을 확장해왔다.
해설 '2년 전부터 지금까지 확장하고 있다'는 문맥을 통해 과거부터 지금까지 지속되고 있는 일을 나타내는 현재 완료

2. 작년에 공장이 몇 가지 새 장비를 구입한 이후 직원 생산성이 상당히 개선되었다.
해설 '구입한 과거 시점 이래로 지금까지 향상되었다'는 문맥을 통해 과거부터 지금까지 지속되고 있는 일을 나타내는 현재 완료

Q3 1. had conducted   2. had approved   3. had suffered

1. Lucky Mart는 또 다른 지점을 열기로 결정하기 전 설문 조사를 진행했다.
해설 시간 접속사 before에 의해 두 개의 절이 연결된 문장에서 시제를 묻는 문제. 문제에서 제시된 기준 시제가 과거(decided)이며 그 결정이 있기 전에 설문을 시행했다는 내용이므로 과거 완료 시제

2. 임상 실험의 결과는 연구소장이 발표를 승인한 후 공개되었다.
해설 시간 접속사 after에 의해 두 개의 절이 연결된 문장에서 시제를 묻는 문제. '발표를 승인한 후에 대중에게 공개가 이루어졌다'는 문맥에 따라, 기준 시점인 과거(were made public) 전에 공개를 승인했다는 내용이므로 과거 완료 시제

3. 합병이 발표되었을 때쯤 Roxy 사는 장기간 수익 감소를 겪고 있었다.
해설 시간 접속사 by the time에 의해 두 개의 절이 연결된 문장에서 시제를 묻는 문제. 기준 시점인 과거(was announced) 전에 손실을 겪었다는 내용이므로 과거 완료 시제

Q4   **1.** are   **2.** will help   **3.** will be

1. 모든 이력서들이 검토된 후, 2단계의 면접 절차가 시작될 것입니다.

해설   시간 부사절에서는 현재 시제가 미래 시제를 대신함

2. 당신이 채용된다면 제가 마케팅 캠페인을 개발하는 것을 돕게 될 거예요.

해설   조건 부사절에는 현재 시제를, 주절에는 미래 시제를 씀

3. 연설이 끝나는 대로, 손님들은 로비에서 간식을 즐길 수 있을 것이다.

해설   시간 부사절은 현재 시제가 미래 시제를 대신하며, 주절에는 미래 시제를 씀

Practice

본서 p.90

1. (C)	**2.** (A)	**3.** (C)	**4.** (D)	**5.** (B)
6. (D)	**7.** (D)	**8.** (C)	**9.** (A)	**10.** (B)
11. (B)	**12.** (A)	**13.** (D)	**14.** (D)	**15.** (B)
16. (B)	**17.** (D)	**18.** (B)	**19.** (C)	**20.** (B)

1. 다음 해 GKM 자동차의 최대 판매 자동차 모델의 개선된 버전이 봄 광고 캠페인에서 소개될 것이다.

해설   자동차가 소개되므로 능동형인 보기 (A), (D)는 오답이며, 시제를 나타내는 next year가 있으므로 미래 (C) will be introduced가 정답이다.

어휘   **refined** 정제된, 세련된, 개선된

2. 안전 점검이 진행되는 동안에 Nelson 제조사의 생산이 중지되었다.

해설   빈칸이 동사 자리이므로 (B)는 오답이며, 주어인 안전 점검은 실행의 대상이므로 수동인 (A), (C) 중에 답을 찾아야 한다. 생산이 중단된 시점이 과거이므로, 문맥상 그 과거 시간 동안 안전 점검이 이루어졌다는 의미가 되도록 과거시제 (A) were being conducted가 적절하다. 또한, 시간 접속사 while에 의해 연결된 두 문장의 동사는 시제 일치를 이루므로, 주절의 was suspended 와 시제 일치된 과거동사 (A)를 정답으로 선택할 수 있다.

어휘   **production** 생산 | **suspend** ~을 중지하다 | **safety inspection** 안전 점검

3. 작년에, Harington 컴퓨터의 품질 관리부는 생산 효율성을 향상시키기 위해서 몇 가지 새로운 정책들을 실행했다.

해설   동사가 필요한 자리이므로 (B)와 (C) 중에 답을 골라야 하며, 과거 시점을 표시하는 last year가 쓰였으므로 (C) implemented가 정답이다.

어휘   **quality control department** 품질 관리부 | **improve** ~을 향상시키다 | **production efficiency** 생산 효율성 | **implementation** 실행 | **implement** ~을 실행하다

4. 공사 책임자가 건축 계획들을 승인하면, 신축 도서관에 대한 공사가 다음 주에 시작될 것이다.

해설   조건의 부사절에서는 미래 시제를 대신하여 현재 시제가 쓰이므로 주어와 수의 일치를 이룬 (D) approves가 정답이다.

어휘   **construction** 공사, 건축 | **approve** 승인하다

5. Cherub 은행은 경쟁사와 공식적으로 합병을 한 후에도 현재의 이름을 유지하게 될 것이다.

해설   시간을 나타내는 접속사가 두 절을 연결하는 경우 하나의 동사를 단서로 시제를 파악한다. 주절의 시제가 미래이므로 시간 접속사 after가 이끄는 절도 미래 내용임을 알 수 있으나, 시간이나 조건의 부사절에서는 미래대신 현재를 쓰므로 수의 일치를 만족시키는 현재 동사 (B) merges가 정답이다.

어휘   **retain** 유지하다, 보유하다 | **merge** 합병하다

6. 저희가 귀하 계약서의 세부사항들을 검토한 후에, 회의를 잡기 위해 귀하께 연락드릴 것입니다.

고난도

해설   해석상 세부사항들을 검토한 후(현재 완료 시제)에 연락할 것이므로 미래 시제인 (D) will contact가 정답이다. 또한, 주절과 부사절의 시제 일치에서 시간이나 조건의 부사절에 현재나 현재 완료를 쓰면 주절은 미래 시제를 써야 하므로 (D)가 정답이다.

어휘   **review** ~을 검토하다 | **arrange a meeting** 회의를 잡다

7. Luky Star 사는 가전 제품 업계에서 최고의 소기업들 중 하나로 지명되기 전까지 사업을 확장하는 것에 대해 고려하지 않았었다.

해설   동사 관련 문제는 '수의 일치 → 태 → 시제' 순으로 접근해야 한다. 선택지 모두가 수의 일치에 적합하므로, 태를 살펴보면 Luky Star 사가 운영 확장을 고려하는 주체이므로 능동태가 되어야 하므로, 수동태인 (B)는 오답이다. 다음으로 before가 이끄는 부사절과 주절의 시제 일치를 파악해야 한다. Luky Star 사가 지명된 것은 과거인데, 고려를 하지 않은 것은 그 전의 사실이므로 대과거인 (D) had not considered가 정답이다. 또한 시간의 접속사에 의한 시제 일치를 적용하여 과거에 해당하는 (B), (D) 중 능동에 해당하는 (D)를 정답으로 고를 수 있다.

어휘   **expand** ~을 확장하다 | **operation** 사업 | **home appliance** 가전 제품

8. 우리는 다음 주에 있을 Beuve의 신형 TXL 430 모델의 시험 주행은 당신의 기대를 넘어설 것이라고 확신합니다.

해설   접속사 that이 있으므로 동사 are 외에 하나의 동사가 더 존재해야 하므로 동사가 아닌 (B)는 오답이다. 나머지 보기 (A), (C), (D)는 모두 능동이므로 시제를 따져야 하는데 미래 시점을 표시하는 next week와 어울리는 미래 시제인 (C) will exceed가 정답이다.

어휘   **confident** 확신하는 | **test drive** 시험 주행 | **exceed one's expectations** ~의 기대를 넘어서다

9. Timberlake Golf Club은 지난 5년 동안 뉴질랜드에서 최고의 골프 클럽들 가운데 하나로 평가된다.

해설   'over the last five years(지난 5년 동안)'는 현재 완료 시제의 단서이므로 (A) has ranked가 정답이다.

어휘   **rank** (등급, 순위를) 차지하다

10. 저희 고객 서비스 정책에 따라, 회사는 추가적인 비용 없이 1년 동안 무상 수리 서비스를 제공합니다.

해설 문장의 동사가 필요한 자리이며, 1년간 무상 서비스를 제공한다는 회사의 정책은 반복적으로 행해지는 습관적인 사실이므로 현재 시제 (B) provides가 정답이다.

어휘 according to ~에 따르면 | policy 정책 | at no additional cost 추가적인 비용 없이

11. Gonyang 아파트 건설 현장에서의 사고들은 개정된 안전 규정 절차들이 시행된 이래로 상당히 줄었다.
고난도

해설 since(~이래로 계속)가 있는 문장에서 주절에는 현재 완료를 쓰고 since절의 동사는 과거를 쓰므로 (B) were implemented가 정답이다.

어휘 construction site 건설 현장 | substantially 상당히 | reduce ~을 줄이다 | procedure 절차 | implement ~을 시행하다

12. Mega 건설은 관례적으로 상업용 개조 프로젝트에 대해 무료 견적을 내준다.

해설 시제와 연계되는 부사 어휘를 묻는 문제이다. 문장의 동사가 현재 동사이므로 일반적인 사실이나 반복되는 상황을 나타내는 현재 시제와 함께 쓰이는 부사인 (A) routinely가 정답이다. '정기적으로'의 의미를 갖는 regularly, periodically, consistently도 현재 시제와 쓰이며, (B), (D)는 과거 시제와 (C)는 현재 완료나 과거 시제와 함께 주로 쓰인다는 점에 유의한다.

어휘 estimate 견적서 | commercial 상업의 | routinely 정기적으로, 관례적으로

13. 시인 Hakim Gomez는 〈The Bostonian Review〉의 지난달 판에 그의 새로운 시를 발표했다.

해설 보기가 모두 동사이므로 먼저 수의 일치를 파악한다. 주어 poet이 단수이므로 (B)는 오답이며 시인이 시를 발표하므로 능동형이 되어야 한다. 따라서 (A)는 오답이다. 마지막으로 시제를 파악해야 하는데 last month라는 과거 시점 표시가 있으므로 과거 동사인 (D) presented가 정답이다.

어휘 edition 판 | present 제출하다, 주다

14. 구매부가 다른 주문을 할 준비가 될 무렵에 Startrack 사무용품점은 새로운 가격표를 발행할 것이다.

해설 by the time(~할 즈음에)이 이끄는 부사절에 현재 시제를 쓰는 경우, 주절은 미래 완료 시제를 쓰기 때문에 정답은 (D) will have published이다.

어휘 by the time ~할 즈음에 | purchasing department 구매 부서 | be ready to부정사 ~할 준비가 되다 | place an order 주문하다 | price list 가격표

15. 모든 후보자들은 면접 전에 그들이 어떤 면허들을 소지하고 있는지를 명시하라는 요청을 받았다.
고난도

해설 빈칸이 동사 자리이므로 (C)는 오답이며, 선택지들이 수의 일치를 모두 충족하고 모두 능동태이므로 알맞은 시제를 파악해야 한다. 일반적인 사실에 해당하는 내용[현재 그들이 소지하고 있는 면허증이 무엇인지]을 나타내므로 현재 시제 (B) possess가 정답이다.

어휘 candidate 후보 | be asked to ~하도록 요청받다 | indicate ~을 보여 주다, ~을 명시하다 | license 면허 | possess ~을 소유하다

16. 이것은 모든 사람에게 우리 건물이 다음 주부터 주요 건설 공사가 있을 것임을 상기시켜 드리는 것입니다.

해설 접속사 that에 의해 연결된 문장이므로 빈칸에는 동사가 필요하다. 동사가 아닌 (A), (C)는 오답이며 미래 시제를 나타내는 next week를 단서로 (B) will be undergoing이 정답임을 알 수 있다. (D)는 실제로 일어나지 않은 과거 사실을 나타내므로 오답이다.

어휘 undergo 겪다. 경험하다 | major 주요한 | starting ~부터

17. 부사장은 일정이 겹치지 않았다면 지난주 목요일 기자 회견에 참석했을 것이다.

해설 과거(last Thursday)에 일어난 일이므로 (A)와 (C)는 오답이다. 뒷부분에 일정이 겹쳤다는 문맥에 따라 참석하지 않은 내용을 나타내므로 (D) would have attended가 정답이다. 「must have p.p.」는 '~했음에 틀림없다'라는 의미로 오답이며, 「would have p.p.」는 '~였을 텐데(그러나 그러지 못했다)'라는 의미로 과거에 일어나지 않은 일을 의미한다.

어휘 press conference 기자 회견 | scheduling conflict 일정의 겹침

18. Davies 실험실 연구원들은 유럽에서 가장 잘 팔리는 브랜드와 질적인 면에서 비슷한 의료 석고를 최근에 개발했다.

해설 현재 완료 시제와 함께하는 부사를 묻는 문제이므로 (B) recently가 정답이다.

어휘 researcher 연구원 | medicine plaster 의료 석고 | in quality 질적인 면에서 | comparable 비슷한, 비교할 만한

19. Shanghai International 항공은 경영진이 홍콩 항공사와 합병을 할지에 대해 결정을 하게 되면 기자 회견을 열 것이다.
고난도

해설 해석상 합병 여부를 결정하면 기자 회견을 개최할 것이므로 미래 시제 (C) will hold가 정답이다. 또한, 주절과 부사절의 시제 일치에서 시간이나 조건의 부사절에 현재나 현재완료를 쓰면 주절은 미래 시제를 써야 하므로 (C)가 정답이다.

어휘 hold a press conference 기자 회견을 열다

20. 회사는 지난 4월 새로운 모델 출시 이래로 매출이 상당히 증가했음을 알리게 되어 매우 기쁩니다.
고난도

해설 빈칸 뒤에 과거 시점 명사[지난 4월 새로운 모델 출시]가 나오고 주절에 현재완료 시제가 온 구문이므로 전치사 (B) since가 정답이다.

어휘 be pleased to ~하게 되어 기쁘다 | significantly 상당히 | launch 출시

REVIEW TEST 02

본서 p.92

1. (A)	**2.** (C)	**3.** (D)	**4.** (B)	**5.** (D)
6. (A)	**7.** (A)	**8.** (B)	**9.** (B)	**10.** (B)
11. (D)	**12.** (C)	**13.** (A)	**14.** (B)	**15.** (B)
16. (D)	**17.** (C)	**18.** (B)	**19.** (B)	**20.** (A)

1. 재무 분석가들은, 이자율이 줄어든 후에는 주택시장이 개선되기 시작할 것이라고 예측한다.

해설 명사절 접속사 that이 있으므로 주절의 동사가 필요하다. 따라서 동사인 (A) predict가 정답이다.

어휘 analyst 분석가 | housing market 주택시장 | interest rate 이자율 | cut 줄이다, 삭감하다

2. 전국 시장에 서비스를 제공하는 운송 회사들은 전국 어디든 언제든 물품을 가지러 가고 배송할 준비가 되어 있어야 한다.

해설 빈칸 앞에 조동사 must가 있으므로 동사원형이 와야 하며 운송 회사들은 '준비가 되어 있어야' 한다는 의미가 적절하므로 수동태인 (C) be prepared가 정답이다.

어휘 freight 화물, 화물운송 | pick up ~을 가지러 가다 | deliver 배달하다, 배송하다

3. 그 음악가의 세계 순회공연은 제작상의 지체로 인해 사흘간 보류되었다.

해설 순회공연은 '보류되는' 것이므로 수동형의 동사가 적절하며, 기간의 전치사구 for three days와 함께 쓰일 수 있는 현재 완료 시제가 필요하므로 (D) has been put이 정답이다.

어휘 musician 음악가 | tour (여러 곳을 방문하는) 여행, 순회 | put on hold ~을 보류하다, 연기하다 | due to ~로 인해, ~때문에 | delay 지연, 지체

4. Katarina Volgaskaya가 영화 〈In Sight〉에서 그녀의 역에 대해 최근 호평을 받았다.

해설 주어가 긍정적인 평가를 받는 주체에 해당하므로, 능동태 동사가 와야 한다. 따라서, 수동태 (C)는 오답이며, 과거나 현재완료와 함께 쓰이는 부사 recently를 단서로 과거시제 (B) received가 정답이다.

어휘 positive 긍정적인 | review 평가 | role 역할 | film 영화

5. 남미 주식 시장의 갑작스러운 감소가 대부분의 투자사들을 놀라게 했다.

해설 하나의 문장에는 하나의 동사가 존재해야 하므로, 빈칸은 동사자리이다. (A)는 동사형태가 아니므로 오답이며, 나머지 보기 중 주어가 3인칭 단수(decline)와 수의 일치를 이룬 단수동사 (D) has surprised가 정답이다.

어휘 decline 하락 | stock market 주식시장; 증권거래소 | investment firm 투자회사

6. 주말 동안 로스앤젤레스에서 출발하는 항공기들은 활주로가 점검을 확인받는 동안 오후 10시부터 오전 6시 사이에 운행이 중단될 것이다.

해설 문장의 동사를 쓸 자리이며, 부사절에 현재 진행형이 미래 사실을 말하고 것으로 보아 주절에는 미래 시제를 써야 하므로 (A) will be suspended가 정답이다.

어휘 depart 출발하다 | suspend 보류하다, 중지하다

7. Lafayette 미술 협회는 시 의회 의원들이 공공 박물관 폐쇄를 재고하도록 요구했다.

해설 주장, 명령, 요청, 제안의 동사(ask, suggest, recommend, demand등)이 이끄는 that절의 동사는 'should + 동사원형' 또는 '동사원형' 형태이다. 따라서, should를 생략한 동사원형 (A) reconsider가 정답이다.

어휘 city council 시의회 | closing 폐쇄, 마감 | public museum 공공 박물관

8. SG는 자사의 전자책 단말기와 스마트폰 제품들의 생산을 중단할 것이며 PC 부서를 구조조정할 수 있다고 발표했다.

해설 빈칸은 동사 자리이므로 (A), (C)는 오답이며 수 일치상 (D)도 답이 될 수 없다. 문맥상 앞으로의 회사 계획을 발표하는 것이므로 미래 시제인 (B) will discontinue가 정답이다.

어휘 announce 발표하다, 공고하다 | discontinue (생산을) 중단하다 | restructure 구조조정하다 | division 분과, 부

9. 지역 사업주들은 지난 몇 년에 걸친 꾸준한 매출 성장률에 만족해 왔다.

해설 정관사 the와 명사 rate 사이는 복합 명사를 이루는 명사 또는 명사를 수식하는 형용사 자리인데, '꾸준한 성장률'의 의미가 자연스러우므로 형용사 (B) steady가 정답이다.

어휘 owner 주인, 소유주 | be satisfied with ~에 만족하다 | growth 성장

10. 컨퍼런스 요금은 다양한 강연과 모임들의 입장을 포함한다.

해설 동사가 존재하지 않으므로 빈칸은 동사 자리이며, '수 일치 → 태 → 시제' 순서로 접근한다. (D)는 동사가 아니므로 오답이며, 주어인 The conference fee가 단수 명사이므로 복수동사 (A)도 오답이다. 타동사 include가 목적어 admittance를 수반하고 있고, '회의 비용이 ~로의 입장을 포함한다'는 문맥에 따라 능동태 (B) includes가 정답이다.

어휘 admittance (~로의) 입장 | networking event (사교 활동을 위한) 모임

11. Boden Carpeting은 사업 20주년을 기념하기 위해 다음 달 특별 할인을 시행할 것이다.
고난도

해설 동사 관련 문법 문제이므로 '수 일치 → 태 → 시제' 순서로 접근한다. 고유명사는 단수 취급해야 하므로 복수동사 (B)는 오답이다. 주어가 특별 할인 판매를 실시하는 주체에 해당하므로 수동태 (A)는 오답이다. 마지막으로, next month를 단서로 미래 시제인 (D) will be running이 정답이다.

어휘 run ~을 운영하다, 관리하다 | special sale 특별 할인 | celebrate 기념하다, 축하하다

12. 지명된 후보자들은 선거에 나가기를 희망하지 않는 경우, 9월 25일 이전에 위원회에 알려야 한다.

해설 현재 시점에서 지명이 완료된 상태이고 후보자(candidate)들은 지명(nominate)이 '되는 것'이므로 현재완료 수동형이 와야 한다. 따라서 (C) have been nominated가 정답이다.

어휘 candidate 후보자 | nominate 지명하다, 추천하다 | inform 알리다 | committee 위원회 | run for election 선거에 입후보하다

13. 헌신적인 사회복지사 Ms. Annan은 다양한 연령층의 자원봉사자들과 함께 일해 왔다.

해설 빈칸 뒤에 사람 명사(volunteers)를 취하여 '~와 함께 일하다'는 의미를 완성하는 전치사 (A) with가 정답이다.

어휘 dedicated 헌신적인 | social worker 사회복지사 | a variety of 다양한

14. 그저 동봉된 양식과 함께 하자품을 반납하면, 교환품이 당신의 집 주소로 배송될 것입니다.
고난도

해설 빈칸 뒤는 주어가 생략된 명령문으로 빈칸은 동사 수식 부사 자리에 해당하며, '하자품을 반납하기만 하라'는 의미가 자연스러우므로 강조 부사 (B) Just가 정답이다. (D) Quite는 부사로 쓰일 경우, 동사를 수식하지 않고, 주로 형용사나 부사를 수식한다는 것을 알아두자.

어휘 return 반납하다, 반환하다 | defective 결함이 있는 | enclose 동봉하다 | replacement 교체, 대체(품)

15. 기후 변화에 대한 축적된 증거에도 불구하고 환경 친화적 개발과 관련한 그 권고사항은 하나도 시행되지 않았다.

해설 빈칸 뒤에 of the recommendations라는 '전체'가 명시되어 있으므로 이 집합의 일부를 나타내는 부정대명사가 올 자리임을 알 수 있다. '아무것도' 시행되지 않았다는 의미가 적절하므로 (B) none이 정답이다.

어휘 accumulated 축적된, 누적된 | evidence 증거 | recommendation 권고, 추천 | sustainable development 지속 가능한 발전, 환경친화적 개발 | implement 시행하다

16. Ms. Martin은 자신이 최상위급 지도자가 갖추어야 할 기술들을 모두 통달했다고 강하게 믿는 관리자와 함께 일했다.

해설 관리자가 자신이 기술을 마스터했다고 하는 것은 그렇게 믿었다(believed)는 과거 시점 이전에 일어나야 하므로 과거 완료 (D) had mastered가 정답이다.

어휘 strongly 강력하게 | require 필요로 하다

17. 컴퓨터 비밀번호가 기밀로 유지되어야 하는 것은 필수다.
고난도

해설 빈칸의 주어인 컴퓨터 비밀번호는 유지되어야 하는 대상에 해당하므로 빈칸의 동사는 수동태가 되어야 한다. 따라서, 능동태인 (A)와 (D)는 오답이다. 가주어 it으로 시작하는 구문에서 이성적 판단을 나타내는 imperative, necessary, essential, important 등의 형용사가 나올 때, 〈진주어 + that 절〉의 동사는 'should + 동사원형'이나 '동사원형'을 취하므로 should가 생략된 동사원형 (C) be kept가 정답이다.

어휘 imperative 필수적인 | confidential 기밀의

18. Maria Fuentes는 다음 달 Gerald Monard가 은퇴한 후에 고객서비스 책임자로 업무를 인계 받을 것이다.
고난도

해설 빈칸 뒤에 '주어+동사' 구조의 절이 왔으므로 빈칸은 접속사 자리이며, 문맥상 'Gerald Monard가 은퇴한 후에 Maria Fuentes가 인계 받을 것이다' 라는 의미가 적절하므로 시간 부사절을 이끄는 접속사 (B) after가 정답이다. 빈칸에 after를 쓰면, 주절 동사의 시제가 미래일 경우 after가 이끄는 시간 부사절 동사는 미래대신 현재를 써야 한다는 문법에도 정확히 일치하게 된다. '~까지'의 의미를 지닌 시간부사절 접속사 (C) until은 주절의 동사로 stay나 open 등 상태의 지속을 나타내는 동사를 취하며, '인계 받다'는 의미와 같은 1회성 완료 동사를 취하지 않으므로 오답이다. 부사인 (A)는 접속기능이 없기 때문에 오답이며, '~하기 보다는'의 의미를 가진 (D) rather than은 문맥상 적절하지 못하다.

어휘 take over 인계 받다, (일을) 떠 맡다 | retire 은퇴하다 | rather than ~하기 보다는

19. 지역의 많은 사람들은 최근의 할인들이 소규모 회사의 폐업을 야기하는 가격 인하 파동을 일으킬 수 있다고 우려하고 있다.

해설 빈칸 앞에는 형용사(recent), 뒤에는 동사(could cause)가 있으므로 빈칸에는 형용사의 수식을 받으면서 that절의 주어가 될 수 있는 명사가 필요하다. 일회성이 아닌, 최근에 있었던 일련의 '할인들'이라는 의미의 복수 명사가 문맥상 적절하므로 (B) discounts가 정답이다.

어휘 sector 지역, 지구, 분야 | cause 야기하다 | go out of business 폐업하다

20. 많은 직원들은 공사의 소음이 업무에 지장을 주었다고 불평했다.
고난도

해설 문법상 be동사 뒤의 빈칸에는 형용사 (A)와 과거분사 (D)가 올 수 있기 때문에 해석을 통해 정답을 가려야 한다. 주어인 '소음이 업무에 지장을 주었다'는 문맥에 따라, (A) disruptive가 정답이다. '방해 받은, 지장을 받은'을 의미하는 과거분사 (D) disrupted는 수동의 의미를 나타내어, 주어인 공사의 소음이 방해 받았다, 지장을 받았다'로 해석이 되기 때문에, 문맥상 적절하지 않다.

어휘 disrupt 지장을 주다, 혼란 시키다 | complain 불평하다

UNIT 09. 동명사
본서 p.95

Q1   1. Assisting   2. enhancing   3. reducing   4. improving

1. 고객들을 즉시 돕는 것이 우리가 그들의 만족을 유지하는 방법입니다.

해설 is의 주어 자리이므로 명사 역할을 하는 동명사 자리

2. 영업팀은 더 많은 고객을 끌기 위해 서비스 품질을 개선할 것을 권한다.

해설 타동사 recommends의 목적어 자리이므로 명사 역할을 하는 동명사 자리

3. 시에서는 실업자 주민들의 수를 줄이는 것을 목표로 잡았다.

해설 전치사 of의 목적어 자리이므로 명사 역할을 하는 동명사 자리

4. 추가 휴가일을 제공하는 목적은 스트레스를 감소하는 한편 생산성을 증대하는 것이다.

해설 주어와 내용이 동일한 경우 명사가 be동사의 보어로 쓰이므로 명사 역할을 하는 동명사 자리

Q2 **1. Your informing**

1. 제휴사에게 귀하의 호텔 경험에 관해 알려주시는 것은 저희 서비스를 향상하는 데 도움이 될 것입니다.

해설 동사 will help의 주어 자리로 동명사 informing 앞에 의미상 주어를 소유격으로 표시한 형태

Q3 **1. having sold**

1. Mr. Walker는 일주일 만에 열 대의 차를 판매한 뒤 보너스를 받았다.

해설 전치사 뒤의 동명사 자리. 동명사의 의미상의 주어에 해당하는 Mr. Walker가 자동차를 판매하는 동작의 주체로 동명사와 능동관계이며, 본동사(was given)보다 먼저 일어난 동작이므로 완료 동명사 having sold

---

Q4 **1. establishing** **2. demand**

1. 보안 부서는 새로운 사무실 안전 지침을 마련하는 중이다.

해설 전치사 뒤에 명사나 동명사 모두 쓰일 수 있으나, 그 뒤에 목적어인 a new set of safety guidelines가 있으므로 목적어를 취할 수 있는 타동사 출신의 동명사 establishing

2. 최근의 보고에 따르면 휴대용 선풍기 수요가 올해 50퍼센트 늘었다고 한다.

해설 주어 자리에는 명사나 동명사가 모두 가능하지만, 뒤에 목적어가 아닌 전치사 for가 왔으므로 명사 demand가 정답. 만약, 타동사 출신의 동명사 demanding이 정답이려면 뒤에 목적어가 필요함 (demand for ~: ~에 대한 수요)

+ check **1. renewing** **2. access**

1. 멤버십을 1년 더 연장해주셔서 감사합니다.

2. 귀하의 계좌 정보에 접속하기 위해서는 개인 식별 번호가 필요합니다.

Q5 **1. carefully** **2. adequate** **3. approval**

1. 지시 사항을 주의 깊게 살펴본 뒤 프로그램을 설치하십시오.

해설 전치사 after 뒤의 동명사 reviewing을 수식하는 부사 자리

---

2. 모든 직원들은 정교한 장비를 사용하는 데 있어 적절한 교육을 받아야 한다.

해설 명사로 굳어진 -ing형태의 training을 수식하는 형용사 자리

3. 계약은 CEO의 최종 승인 없이는 체결되지 않을 것이다.

해설 관사 the와 형용사 final의 수식을 받는 명사 자리

+ check **1. unanimous** **2. careful**

1. 입법자들은 새 정책에 대해 만장일치로 동의에 이를 수 있었다.

2. 세심한 기획 덕분에 건설 프로젝트는 예산보다 적은 비용으로 완공될 것이다.

Q6 **1. honoring** **2. confirming**

1. 일부 이사회 임원들은 연례 연회에서 회사 창업주를 기리자고 제안했다.

해설 suggest는 동명사를 목적어로 취하는 동사

2. 약사의 의무는 의사와 환자의 처방전을 확인하는 것을 포함한다.

해설 a patient's prescription을 목적어로 취하면서 타동사 include의 목적어 역할을 할 수 있는 동명사 자리

Q7 **1. lowering** **2. hiring** **3. attending**

1. Nex Innovation은 귀하의 월별 공과금을 낮추는 것에 헌신하고 있습니다.

해설 be committed to(~에 헌신하다)의 to는 전치사이므로 동명사 자리

2. 회사는 경험이 많은 회계사들을 채용하는 것을 기대하고 있다.

해설 look forward to(~을 고대하다)의 to는 전치사이므로 동명사 자리

3. 손님들은 강의에 참석하기 전 프론트 데스크에 등록해야 한다.

해설 prior to는 '~이전에'라는 뜻의 전치사이므로 동명사 자리

Q8 **1. attracting** **2. designing** **3. receiving**

1. 회사는 해외 고객을 끌어들이는 일에 어려움을 겪고 있다.

해설 have difficulty 뒤의 동명사 자리

2. 건설 매니저는 건물 수리 계획을 디자인하며 몇 주를 보냈다.

해설 spend 뒤의 동명사 자리

3. 구매물품을 받으신 후 어떤 문제를 겪으신다면 저희 고객서비스 센터 555-3000로 전화 주시기 바랍니다.

해설 upon 뒤의 동명사 자리

Practice

본서 p.100

1. (C)	**2.** (D)	**3.** (A)	**4.** (D)	**5.** (B)
6. (C)	**7.** (C)	**8.** (C)	**9.** (D)	**10.** (A)
11. (A)	**12.** (B)	**13.** (C)	**14.** (A)	**15.** (C)
16. (C)	**17.** (C)	**18.** (C)	**19.** (B)	**20.** (D)

1. 예상된 비용이 적당했기 때문에 그 부서는 새 프린터를 구매하는 대신에 수리를 맡기기로 결정했다.

해설 전치사의 목적어 자리이며, 빈칸 뒤에 명사를 목적어로 취했으므로 동명사 (C) purchasing이 정답이다.

어휘 estimate 예상하다 I reasonable (가격이) 적당한 I instead of ~ 대신에

2. 우리 사장은 다음 달에 은퇴하는 Mr. Jason의 뒤를 이을 편집장으로 Ms. Myer를 임명하는 것을 고심했다.

해설 '~을 고려하다'라는 의미의 타동사 consider는 동명사를 목적어로 취하므로 (D) appointing이 정답이다.

어휘 chief editor 편집장 I succeed ~의 뒤를 잇다 I retire 은퇴하다 I appoint A (as) B A를 B로 임명하다

3. 직원들은 휴가 신청양식을 제출해서 휴가에 대한 공식 승인을 받아야 한다.

해설 타동사 receive의 목적어 자리로 명사인 (A)와 동명사인 (D)가 모두 가능하나, 형용사(official)의 수식을 받는 자리이므로 (A) approval이 정답이다.

어휘 official 공식적인 I approval 승인 I time off (활동의) 일시적 중단, 휴식, 휴가

4. 현대적인 배경에서 문화적 유물들을 획기적으로 전시함으로써, Lenningrad 박물관의 전시 책임자는 특별한 전시회를 만들었다.

해설 「by -ing (~함으로써)」 구조에서 동명사를 수식하는 품사는 부사이므로 (D) innovatively가 정답이다. 해석 또한 '혁신적으로 전시함으로써'이므로 부사가 정답이다.

어휘 artifact 인공 유물 I curator 큐레이터, (미술관, 박물관 등의) 전시 책임자

5. 직원들의 근무 시간대를 조정하는 것이 매니저의 가장 중요한 임무들 중에 하나이다.

해설 목적어를 동반하고 단수 동사 is의 주어 역할을 하는 동명사 (B) Arranging이 정답이다. 명사 (C)도 주어 자리에 올 수 있으나 목적어를 취할 수 없으므로 오답이다.

어휘 shift 교대 근무 (시간)

6. Stylish 제화는 운동화 생산을 중단하고 대신 등산화에 중점을 두는 것이 더 나을 듯하다.

해설 '~을 그만두다'라는 뜻의 타동사 discontinue는 동명사를 목적어로 취하므로 (C) producing이 정답이다.

어휘 discontinue ~을 그만두다 I focus on ~에 중점을 두다

7. Extreme 스포츠 의류의 연구개발 팀은 극심한 온도를 견딜 수 있는 새로운 직물을 개발하는 일을 진행해 왔다.

해설 전치사의 목적어 자리이며, 빈칸 뒤에 명사를 목적어로 취하고 있으므로 동명사인 (C) developing이 정답이다. (B) 명사를 수식하는 과거분사라고 보면 '개발된 새로운 직물에 대해 작업했다'로 해석되어 어색하므로 답이 될 수 없다.

어휘 fabric 직물 I withstand ~을 견디다 I extreme 극심한

8. High Point 연락선 경영진은 승객에게 사전 통보 없이 출발 시간을 변경할 수 있는 법적인 권리를 보유하고 있다.

해설 전치사 without 뒤에 동명사 (C)와 명사 (D)가 모두 가능한데, 바로 뒤에 목적어 passengers가 오기 때문에 정답은 (C) notifying이다.

어휘 reserve the legal right 법적 권리를 보유하다 I in advance 미리, 사전에

9. 마닐라에서 가장 큰 버스 회사가 고객들을 유치할 방법으로 요금을 내리기로 결정했다.

해설 전치사의 목적어 자리이며, 빈칸 뒤에 명사를 목적어로 취하고 있으므로 동명사인 (D) attracting이 정답이다. 전치사의 목적어 자리에는 명사를 쓸 수 있지만, 명사는 목적어를 취할 수 없으므로 (B)는 오답이며, 명사 앞에 형용사가 올 수 있으나 문맥상 적합하지 않아 (A)도 오답이다.

어휘 fare 요금 I as a way of ~의 방법으로 I attraction 매력 I attractive 매력적인 I attract ~을 끌다

10. Daily 증권 거래 방송은 정확한 투자 정보를 제공하는 데 전념한다.

해설 be dedicated to의 to는 전치사 to이다. 전치사 to 뒤에 동명사인 (A)와 명사인 (D)가 모두 가능한데, 바로 뒤에 목적어 accurate investment information이 오기 때문에 (A) providing이 정답이다.

어휘 accurate 정확한 I investment 투자 I dedicated 전념하는

11. 모든 야외 활동들은 고지 없이 취소될 수 있음을 유념하기 바랍니다.

고난도

해설 be subject to의 to는 전치사이다. 전치사 to 뒤에 동명사 (B)와 명사 (A) 모두 가능한데 타동사 출신의 동명사 canceling이 정답이 되기 위해서는 바로 뒤에 목적어가 와야 하나, 대신 전치사구가 왔기 때문에 명사 (A) cancellation이 정답이다.

어휘 keep in mind that ~ ~를 명심(유념)하다

12. Indigo 전자는 조직의 효율성을 극대화할 수 있는 혁신적인 소프트웨어를 제공합니다.

해설 문맥상 '~할 수 있다'라는 의미의 「be capable of -ing」를 묻는 문제이므로 정답은 (B) capable이다. 동일한 의미의 (A) able은 뒤에 to부정사와 함께 쓰이므로 오답이다.

어휘 maximize 극대화하다, 최대한 활용하다 I efficiency 효율성

13. Daubert 센터는 지하철 5호선을 이용함으로써 가장 빨리 도달할 수 있다.

해설 문맥상 '～함으로써'의 의미를 갖는 「by -ing」를 묻는 문제이므로 (C) by가 정답이다.

어휘 by ～ing ～함으로써 | reach ～에 이르다/닿다/도달하다

14. 노트북을 점검하자마자 전문가는 보호용 봉인이 파손되었다는 것을 알게 되었다.

해설 전치사 upon 다음에 빈칸이 있고, 빈칸 뒤에는 목적어인 명사가 오므로 정답은 (A) examining이다.

어휘 examine 검사하다 | expert 전문가 | protective 보호용의 | seal 밀봉 부분 | broken 고장난, 파손된

15. 회사 정책들을 갱신하는 것이 지난 두 달간 법무팀의 주요 업무였다.

해설 빈칸은 문장의 주어 자리이며 뒤에 목적어 company policies가 오기 때문에 동명사인 (C) Updating이 정답이다. company policies를 수식하는 과거분사 (B)가 올 수 있으나, 이 경우 주어가 policies가 되므로 단수 동사 has와 쓰일 수 없기 때문에 오답이다.

어휘 update ～을 최신식으로 하다, 갱신하다

16. Speed Lending Services는 이 귀하의 대출 신청을 조건부로 승인했지만, 저희는 이 문서에 열거된 항목들의 수령을 기다리고 있습니다.

해설 타동사 뒤에 목적어로 명사나 준동사가 올 수 있는데 빈칸 뒤에 전치사가 있으므로 즉, 타동사 receive의 목적어가 바로 온 구조가 아니다. 따라서 타동사 출신의 준동사 (A)나 (B)는 오답이며 명사 (C), (D) 중에 선택해야 하는데 문맥상 제품들의 수령을 기다리는 것이므로 정답은 (C) receipt이다.

어휘 provisionally 조건부로 (= conditionally, temporarily)

17. Greenbaum 종합병원의 직원들은 환자들의 요구사항을 만족시키는데 전념한다.

해설 be committed to -ing는 '～에 전념하다'라는 뜻의 동명사 관용구로 (C) committed가 정답이다.

어휘 satisfy ～을 만족시키다 | express ～을 표현하다 | be scheduled to ～하기로 일정이 잡혀 있다 | be designed to ～하기 위해 고안되다

18. 그 컨설턴트는 사무실에 변화를 성공적으로 도입하기 위한 몇 가지 제안들을 했다.

해설 빈칸을 전치사 for의 목적어 자리로 생각하여 동명사를 선택할 수 있으나, 빈칸 뒤에 전치사 for의 목적어에 해당하는 동명사가 존재하므로 동명사(A)는 오답이다. 빈칸은 전치사 for의 목적어에 해당하는 동명사 introducing 을 수식하는 자리이므로, 동명사를 수식하는 부사 (C) successfully가 정답이다.

어휘 introduce 도입하다, 소개하다

19. Jane's 서점은 고객들을 배려하는 것으로 좋은 평판을 받고 있어서, 보스턴에서 최고의 서점으로 이름나 있다.

해설 보어를 동반하는 be동사(～이다, ～하다)에서 만들어진 동명사 being

과 함께 쓸 보어를 묻는 문제이다. (A)는 '배려', (B)는 '배려하는', (D)는 '조심성'이라고 해석되므로, 이중 해석상 가장 자연스러운 (B) attentive가 정답이다.

어휘 have a good reputation for ～해서 평판이 좋다 | attention 배려, 주의 | attentive 배려하는, 주의하는 | attentively 배려해서, 조심스럽게 | attentiveness 조심성

20. Greenville에 있는 아파트를 임대하기로 결정하기 전에, Mr. Weber 는 그의 동료들에게 그 지역에 대해서 문의했다.

해설 전치사 다음에 빈칸이 쓰였고, 빈칸 뒤에는 decide의 목적어인 to부정사가 쓰였으므로 (D) deciding이 정답이다.

어휘 coworker 직장 동료

UNIT 10. to부정사

본서 p.103

Q1 1. competitive 2. confidentiality

1. Mr. McConnell은 경쟁력을 유지하기 위해 추가적인 제품 개발에 집중하자고 제안했다.

해설 형용사를 주격 보어로 취하는 자동사 remain과 to remain 뒤에 오는 구조는 동일하므로 형용사 자리

2. 새 노트북 시제품은 기밀을 보장하기 위해 고위 경영진에게만 보여졌다.

해설 명사를 목적어로 취하는 타동사 ensure와 to ensure 뒤에 오는 구조는 동일하므로 명사 자리

Q2 1. for

1. 직원들이 고객의 불만에 즉시 대응하는 것이 중요하다.

해설 to부정사 앞에서 그 동작의 주체를 의미하는 의미상 주어를 표시하는 전치사 for

Q3 1. to be reviewed 2. be installed

1. 잡지 기사들은 금요일까지 검토되어야 한다.

해설 의미상 주어 articles와 to부정사 to review의 의미상 관계를 파악해야 하는 문제. 기사들은 검토의 대상으로 수동관계이므로 수동 형태의 to부정사 자리

2. 새 바닥재가 설치되기 위해 사무실은 화요일에 문을 닫을 것이다.

해설 의미상 주어 the new flooring과 to부정사 to install의 의미상 관계를 파악해야 하는 문제. 새 바닥재는 설치의 대상으로 수동관계이므로 수동 형태의 to부정사 자리

Q4   1. To submit   2. It

1.   내일까지 마케팅 제안서를 제출하는 것은 불가능하다.
해설   동사 is의 주어 자리이므로 명사 역할을 하는 to부정사 자리

2.   생산성을 증대하기 위해 동료 직원들과 협력하여 일하는 것은 중요하다.
해설   진주어 to work ~ 부분이 문장 뒤로 이동한 구조로 가주어 it이 필요

Q5   1. to resolve

1.   고객서비스 부서의 목표는 고객의 모든 불만사항을 시기 적절하게 해결하는 것이다.
해설   be동사 뒤에 주어 goal의 구체적인 내용을 나타내는 주격 보어로 쓰인 to부정사. be동사 뒤에 과거분사가 올 수 있으나 문맥상 적절하지 않아 오답

Q6   1. to revise   2. refused

1.   고객께서 주문을 변경하고자 하신다면 오늘 영업시간 종료 전에 알려주시기 바랍니다.
해설   목적어로 to부정사를 취하는 타동사 wish

2.   디자인 팀은 상사가 마감기한 연장을 거절했기 때문에 야근을 해오고 있다.
해설   목적어로 to부정사를 취하는 동사 refuse

Q7   1. attend   2. to turn off   3. strengthen

1.   긴급한 프로젝트 마감 기한은 Ms. Liou가 학회에 참석할 수 없게 할 것이다.
해설   5형식 동사 allow의 목적격 보어 자리에 쓰이는 to부정사

2.   직원들은 사무실을 떠나기 전 데스크톱 컴퓨터를 꺼야 합니다.
해설   목적격 보어로 to부정사를 취하는 5형식 동사 remind의 수동태

3.   회사 워크숍은 직원들이 업무 관계를 강화하는 것을 돕는다.
해설   help의 목적격 보어 자리에 쓰이는 to를 생략한 원형부정사

+ check   1. to withdraw   2. to type   3. to take

1.   정부는 전국 복권단체에 과장된 광고를 내리라고 촉구했다.

2.   Mr. Park은 조수에게 회의록을 타자로 치라고 요청했다.

3.   조립 구역에서 일하는 모든 직원은 기계 작동에 관한 수업을 듣도록 요구받을 것이다.

Q8   1. to refuse   2. to respond

1.   Pinnacle 항공은 유효한 신분증을 소지하지 않은 고객의 탑승을 거부할 권리를 가진다.
해설   right은 to부정사의 수식을 받는 명사

2.   판매 직원들은 24시간 이내에 고객의 문의에 답하기 위해 노력할 것이다.
해설   effort는 to부정사의 수식을 받는 명사

Q9   1. accommodate   2. To   3. To be

1.   폭넓은 일정을 수용하기 위해 워크숍의 날짜와 시간을 다양하게 제공합니다.
해설   「To + 동사원형 ~, 주어 + 동사」 ~하기 위해

2.   귀하의 연락 정보를 업데이트하시려면 계정에 로그인하십시오.
해설   문장 앞에서 목적을 나타내는 to부정사 자리

3.   영업 매니저 직책 요건에 부합하려면 지원자들은 마케팅 학사 학위가 있어야 합니다.
해설   being으로 시작하는 분사구문과 to be로 시작하는 목적의 to부정사 모두 문장 앞에 위치할 수 있으므로 문맥을 통해 결정해야 한다. '영업 관리자 직에 대한 자격을 갖기 위해, 지원자들은 마케팅 학위가 있어야 한다'는 문맥에 따라 목적을 나타내는 to부정사 자리

+ check   1. To apply   2. In order to   3. for   4. Being

1.   이 공석에 지원하려면, 지원자는 3년 이상의 경력이 있어야 합니다.

2.   프로젝트 책임자는 새 쇼핑센터의 공사를 제때 완료하기 위하여 10명의 직원을 추가로 고용하기로 결정했다.

3.   자선행사의 수익금은 모두 지역 의료센터의 개조에 사용될 것이다.

4.   Mr. Simpson은 지사장이기 때문에 전반적인 지사 운영을 담당한다.

Q10   1. to announce   2. likely   3. to store   4. enough

1.   Leisure 식당은 새 지점의 개점을 발표하게 되어서 기쁩니다.
해설   감정을 나타내는 형용사 뒤에서 감정의 원인을 나타내는 부사 역할의 to부정사

2.   교육부 대표단은 시카고 투어 기간 동안 시에서 유명한 교육센터들을 방문할 가능성이 크다.
해설   '~할 것 같다'는 의미의 「be likely to부정사」 표현

3.   건물 창고에 오래된 파일들을 보관하는 것은 너무 많은 비용이 든다. (비용이 너무 많이 들어서 오래된 파일들은 건물 창고에 보관할 수 없다.)
해설   too + 형용사 + to부정사 (너무 ~해서 ...할 수 없다) 관용표현

4. 새 등산화는 가혹한 기상 조건을 견디기에 내구성이 충분히 강하다.

해설 형용사 + enough + to부정사 (~하기에 충분히 ...하다) 관용표현

1. 이사 비용을 줄이기 위하여, 포장 상자 및 파손 방지 완충재를 어떻게 구하는지에 대한 특정 정보가 필요할 것이다.

해설 목적을 나타내는 to부정사를 묻는 문제이다. '이사 비용을 줄이기 위하여'라는 능동의 의미이며, 뒤에 목적어를 수반했으므로 능동형 to부정사인 (C) To reduce가 정답이다.

어휘 cushioning material 완충재 | breakage 파손

2. Anchor 의류는 봄 신상품들을 위한 공간을 만들기 위해서 모든 겨울 의류에 대해 30~50%의 할인을 제공하고 있다.

해설 목적을 나타내는 to부정사 자리이므로 to 뒤에 동사원형이 와야 하며, 문맥상 '공간을 만들기 위해서'라는 능동이 적합하므로 정답은 (B) make이다. (D)는 수동 형태이므로 오답이다.

어휘 discount on ~에 대한 할인 | clothing 의류 | room 공간

3. Peachtree 주민회관은 200명의 사람들을 앉게 할 충분히 큰 강당을 가지고 있다.

해설 '~하기에 충분히 ...하다'라는 의미의 「형용사/부사 + enough + to부정사」 구조를 묻는 문제이므로 (B) to seat이 정답이다.

어휘 auditorium 강당 | seat 앉히다, 좌석이 있다

4. Dongyang 은행은 고객 만족도를 향상시키기 위하여 새로운 온라인 뱅킹 시스템을 채택하고 있다.

해설 동사 is adopting이 존재하므로, 빈칸은 동사 자리가 아니며 '고객 만족을 향상시키기 위하여'라는 능동의 의미이며 뒤에 목적어를 수반했으므로 능동 부사인 (D) to improve가 정답이다.

어휘 adopt ~을 채택하다 | customer satisfaction 고객 만족

5. 이사회 회의의 목적은 은퇴하는 사장 Rio Hong의 후임자를 선정하는 것이다.

해설 「the purpose is to 동사원형 (목적은 ~이다)」 구문을 묻는 문제이므로 (B) is to choose가 정답이다.

어휘 purpose 목적 | successor 후임자 | retiring 은퇴하는

6. 직원들이 회사의 가장 큰 프로젝트를 성공적으로 완료한다면, 승진을 위해 고려될 기회를 제공 받을 것이다.
고난도

해설 빈칸은 opportunity를 수식하는 to부정사 자리이며, '승진을 위해 고려되어지는 기회'라는 수동의 의미이며 뒤에 목적어가 없으므로 수동

형태 to부정사 (C) to be considered가 정답이다.

어휘 complete 끝내다, 완료하다 | promotion 승진

7. 새로운 규정에 따라서, 웹사이트 관리자들은 회원들의 동의가 없으면 그들의 사진을 게시할 수 없다.

해설 「be unable to부정사」는 '~할 수 없다'라는 뜻의 to부정사 관용구이므로 (D) to post가 정답이다.

어휘 in compliance with ~에 따라서 | regulation 규제 | administrator 관리자 | post ~을 게시하다 | consent 동의

8. Walters 상업 은행의 보안 소프트웨어는 보안 문제를 처리하기 위해서 업데이트되었다.
고난도

해설 빈칸 뒤에 동사원형과 어울리는 보기는 '~하기 위해'로 해석되는 (B) in order to이다. (A)는 「주어 + 동사」의 절이나 분사와 함께 쓰이고, (C)와 (D)는 전치사이므로 동사원형을 바로 취할 수 없으므로 오답이다.

어휘 address (문제 등을) 다루다, 처리하다

9. 고객들에게 더 나은 서비스를 하기 위해, Bali Cleaning Service는 더 큰 소매점으로 이전할 것이다.

해설 빈칸 뒤의 serve는 동사원형이므로, 목적을 나타내는 to부정사 (A) In order to가 정답이다. 보기 (B), (C), (D)의 to는 전치사로, 뒤에 명사나 동명사를 수반해야 하기 때문에 오답이다.

어휘 serve (서비스를) 제공하다 | relocate 이전하다 | retail space 소매점

10. 모터가 제대로 작동하기 위해서는 전력이 나간 후에 모든 설정이 다시 맞춰져야 한다.
고난도

해설 앞에 in order를 보고 to를 고르지 않아야 한다. 만약 빈칸에 동사원형이 있으면 「in order to부정사」가 될 수 있으나 빈칸 뒤에 명사가 오고 그 뒤에 to 동사원형이 있으므로 to부정사의 의미상의 주어를 묻는 문제이다. 정답은 (D) for이다.

어휘 function 기능하다 | loss 상실

11. 방콕이 심각한 교통 혼잡을 겪고 있기 때문에 그곳의 연락선 서비스는 사람들이 통근하는 편리한 방법이다.

해설 빈칸은 명사 way를 수식하는 to부정사 자리를 묻는 문제이므로 정답은 (C) to commute이며, 빈칸 앞에 쓰인 「for + 명사」는 to부정사의 의미상의 주어이다.

어휘 convenient 편리한 | traffic congestion 교통 혼잡 | commute 통근하다

12. 수익금은 4월 28일에 시작할 예정인 신규 도서관의 건설 자금을 대는 데 도움이 될 것이다.

해설 '~하기로 예정되어 있다'라는 의미의 「be scheduled to부정사」 표현을 묻는 문제이므로 (B) to begin이 정답이다.

어휘 proceeds (물건 판매 · 행사 등을 통해 얻은) 수익금 | finance 자금을 대다

13. Ashwood 호텔은 피트니스 센터에 가입한 모든 분들을 내일 신규 회원 오리엔테이션에 참석하도록 초청한다.

해설 동사 invite는 목적 보어로 to부정사를 취하여 「invite + 목적어 + to 부정사(~를(가) ~하도록 초대(초청)하다)」 형태로 쓰이므로 정답은 (A) to attend이다.

어휘 invite 초대하다

14. 기술자들은 실험실의 모든 안전 규정들을 따르도록 권고된다.

해설 to 부정사를 목적보어로 취하는 5형식 동사 advise의 수동태 구문인 'be advised to 동사원형'을 묻는 문제이다. 따라서, (C) to comply 가 정답이다.

어휘 technician 기술자 | advise 권고하다 | comply with ~을 따르다[준수하다] | safety regulation 안전규정

15. 많은 경제학자들은 자유 무역 협정은 한국 자동차 회사들이 유럽과 미국에서 그들의 시장 점유율을 늘리는 것을 도울 것이라고 예측한다.

해설 help는 목적어 뒤에 목적 보어로 동사원형이나 to부정사를 취하여 「help + 목적어 + (to) 동사원형」 형태로 쓰이므로 (A) expand가 정답이다.

어휘 economist 경제학자 | predict ~을 예측하다 | market share 시장 점유율 | expand ~을 확장하다 | expansion 확장

16. Mr. Hansen은 친구가 전화했을 때 막 나가려던 참이었다고 말했다.

해설 '막 ~하려고 하다' 라는 의미의 「be about to + 동사원형」 표현을 묻는 문제이므로 (A) to leave가 정답이다.

어휘 be about to부정사 ~하려던 참이다

17. 모든 운전자들이 도로 규칙을 준수할 의무가 있음에도 불구하고, 많은 운전자들이 그것들을 무시하고 사고를 일으킨다.

해설 해석상 빈칸 뒤 to obey the rules of the road(도로 규칙을 준수할 ~)에 어울리는 동사는 '의무를 지우다'라는 의미의 동사 obligate이므로, 정답은 (A) obligated이다. 수동형 뒤에 to부정사를 취하는 패턴으로 쓰이는 'be obligated to 동사원형 (~해야 한다)', 「be allowed to 동사원형 (~하도록 허락되다)」라는 표현에 유의해야 한다.

어휘 obey 따르다 | ignore 무시하다

18. 임대 계약이 만료되기 전에 건물을 비우려는 세입자들은 그들의 계획에 대해 서면 통지를 제공해야 한다.
고난도

해설 해석을 통해 알맞은 어휘를 고르는 문제이나 빈칸 뒤에 to 동사원형이 온 점에 유의하면 to부정사를 목적어로 취하는 타동사 (C) plan이 정답임을 알 수 있다.

어휘 tenant 세입자 | vacate 비우다 | property 부동산, 건물 | lease 임대 계약 | notification 통지

19. 우편 주소를 변경하기 위하여, 스크린 윗부분의 개인정보 버튼을 클릭하세요.
고난도

해설 문장의 앞쪽에 위치하여, '~하기 위하여'라는 목적을 나타내는 문장을 완성하는 문제이다. 목적은 「to + 동사원형」과 「for + 명사」 형태로 나타낼 수 있으며, 위 문장에서 change는 뒤에 목적어 your mailing

address를 취한 동사로 쓰였기 때문에 「to + 동사원형」 구조로 쓰여야 하므로 (D) To가 정답이다

어휘 personal 개인의

20. 환경 문제에 대한 의식을 고취하기 위해서, Jack Milton은 전국적으로 캠페인을 이끌고 있다.
고난도

해설 「-------, 주어 + 동사」 구조에서 빈칸은 부사에 해당하므로, 부사적 용법의 to부정사 (A)뿐만 아니라 전치사를 포함한 부사구 형태인 (B), (C), (D)도 문법적으로 가능하다. 이처럼 문법적으로 가능한 보기가 두 가지 이상일 경우에는, 해석을 통해 문맥상 알맞은 것을 최종 정답으로 선택해야 한다. 환경 문제에 대한 인식을 촉진시키고자 하는 목적으로 전국적인 홍보를 진행하고 있다는 문맥에 따라, 빈칸에는 캠페인 진행의 목적을 의미하는 부사 (A) to promote가 정답이다.

어휘 awareness of ~에 대한 의식 | environmental 환경의 | lead ~을 이끌다 | promote ~을 고취하다, ~을 홍보하다

UNIT 11. 분사

본서 p.113

Q1 1. revised   2. performed   3. verifying

1. 수정된 보고서 복사본을 내일까지 제출하세요.
해설 '수정된 보고서 복사본'이라는 의미에 따라 수동 의미의 과거분사

2. Best Reviews에 의해 시행된 고객 설문조사는 고객들이 가전을 선택할 때 에너지 효율에 신경 쓴다는 점을 보여준다.
해설 'Best Reviews에 의해서 시행되어진 소비자 설문'이라는 의미에 따라 수동 의미의 과거분사

3. 이 직책에 대한 귀하의 자격을 증명하는 서류를 제출하십시오.
해설 '그 직책에 대한 적격성을 입증해주는 서류'라는 의미에 따라 능동 의미의 현재분사

+ check 1. reduced   2. proposed   3. helping
4. scheduled

1. 매년 여름 Roller 항공은 할인된 가격으로 여행 패키지를 판매한다.

2. 두 회사 모두 합병 합의서의 제안된 수정 내용을 승인해야 한다.

3. 호텔 예약을 도와주는 유명 웹사이트 Paylessforit.co.uk는 2백만 명 이상의 회원을 유치했다.

4. 모든 직원들은 3월 1일 진행될 예정인 세미나에 참석해야 한다.

Q2 1. unchanged　2. informed

1. 구내 식당을 수리하는 데 대한 제안서는 바뀌지 않은 채 남아 있다.
해설 remain 뒤의 주격 보어 자리에 알맞은 분사 선택 문제. 주어인 제안서는 변경의 대상이므로 수동 의미의 과거분사

2. 우리는 고객이 새 제품을 계속 알도록 해야 한다.
해설 keep 뒤의 목적격 보어 자리에 알맞은 분사 선택 문제. 목적어인 고객들은 제품에 대한 통지의 대상이므로 수동 의미의 과거분사

Q3 1. growing　2. experienced

1. 유럽의 재정적 어려움에 관해 늘어나는 우려 때문에 다우존스 지수는 어제 300포인트가 하락했다.
해설 명사 앞에서 항상 현재분사형인 형용사 growing이 명사 concern을 수식하는 구조

2. 이 프로젝트를 위해 경험이 많은 직원들을 더 채용해야 한다.
해설 명사 앞에서 항상 과거분사형인 형용사 experienced가 명사 employees를 수식하는 구조

+ check 1. complicated　2. leading　3. demanding
4. rotating　5. accomplished

1. 고객들은 우리 회사의 사용자 매뉴얼이 너무 복잡하다고 말했다.

2. Best Choice는 올해 판매량이 급격히 감소했음에도 불구하고 여전히 업계를 선도하는 기업이다.

3. 직원들은 현재의 업무량이 너무 부담이 크다고 불평했다.

4. Mason 사 직원들은 돌아가면서 직원 회의를 준비하도록 요구된다.

5. 화랑은 기량이 뛰어난 예술가인 Olivia Chang의 그림을 전시할 것이다.

Q4 1. overwhelming　2. disappointing

1. 압도적인 조기 등록 수를 기반으로, 우리는 기록적인 학회 참석자 수를 예상한다.
해설 감정동사 overwhelm이 명사 number 앞에서 수식하는 구조. 수식받는 명사 number는 감정을 일으키는 원인에 해당하므로 감정동사 overwhelm의 현재분사

2. CEO는 기대와 달리 그 발표가 실망스럽다고 느꼈다.
해설 감정동사 disappoint가 find의 목적격 보어자리에 쓰이므로 목적어와 의미상 관계를 파악해야 한다. 목적어인 presentation은 감정을 느끼는 대상이 아닌 감정을 일으키는 원인에 해당하므로 감정동사 disappoint의 현재분사

+ check 1. exciting　2. disappointed

1. Vectra 오토바이에서 시장 연구원으로 10년을 보낸 Ms. Seiko는 컨설팅 분야에서 흥미 있는 일을 해 나가기 위해 자리에서 물러날 것이다.

2. 마케팅 부서의 직원들은 1분기 매출에 실망했다.

Q5 1. Preferred　2. Having considered
3. confirming

1. 우리 제품들은 젊은 고객들에 의해 선호되어 상당한 시장 점유율을 차지하고 있다.
해설 주절의 주어인 우리 제품들(our products)은 선호의 대상이므로 수동 의미의 과거분사

2. 모든 제안을 고려한 뒤 CEO는 Arch-Shoes를 고용하기로 결정했다.
해설 주절의 주어인 CEO가 제안을 고려했던 주체이므로 능동 의미의 현재분사. 또한, having considered는 완료형 분사구문으로 주절 동사의 시제(decided) 보다 앞서 일어난 일임을 나타냄

3. Bexter 사는 내년 Max 사를 인수할 것이라고 발표하여 해외 확장 계획에 대한 소문이 사실임을 보여주었다.
해설 완전한 문장 뒤의 현재분사로 시작하는 분사구문. '그래서 소문이 사실임을 확인해주었다'라는 능동 의미로 해석

+ check 1. Employing　2. allowing

1. 세계적으로 3,000명 이상의 사람들을 고용하고 있는 Clarina 사는 화장품 업계의 선두주자이다.

2. 저희는 이제 사용자들이 휴대폰 요금제를 개인 맞춤으로 구성할 수 있게 하여 더 많은 옵션을 제공합니다.

Practice
본서 p.118

1. (A)	2. (C)	3. (C)	4. (B)	5. (A)
6. (A)	7. (B)	8. (A)	9. (B)	10. (C)
11. (A)	12. (D)	13. (B)	14. (D)	15. (A)
16. (A)	17. (D)	18. (C)	19. (A)	20. (B)

1. 라틴 아메리카 대부분의 지역에 서비스를 제공하는 Suncor 천연가스는 수요일에 북부 지사들 중 일부를 매각했다고 발표했다.
해설 접속사나 관계사가 없고, 동사 announced가 있기 때문에, 빈칸은 동사 자리가 아니다. 따라서, 동사인 (B), (C), (D)는 오답이며, 주절의 주어를 수식하는 분사구문의 현재분사 (A) Serving이 정답이다.
어휘 region 지역 | serve (상품·서비스를) 제공하다

2. 휴대전화는 여러 곳으로 이동하는 영업 직원들에게 선호되는 연락 수단이다.

해설 관사와 명사 사이의 형용사 자리이므로 동사 prefer를 분사로 전환해야 한다. 수식받는 명사인 수단은 '선호되는' 것이므로 수동의 상태를 표시하는 과거분사 (C) preferred가 정답이다.

어휘 mobile phone 휴대전화 I means 수단 I communicate 연락하다 I extensively 널리 I prefer ~을 선호하다

3. 동봉된 책자는 Rapid 해운에 의해서 제공되는 서비스들을 명시하고 있으며, 저는 귀하께서 문의하신 것들을 녹색으로 표시해놨습니다.

해설 동사 specifies가 있으므로 빈칸은 동사 자리가 아니고, 명사 the services를 수식하는 분사 자리이다. 수식받는 명사인 서비스가 '제공된다'는 수동 의미가 되므로 과거분사 (C) provided가 정답이다.

어휘 brochure 책자 I specify ~을 명시하다 I highlight ~을 강조하다 I in + 색 ~색으로 I inquire about ~에 대해서 문의하다

4. 기조 연설에서, Mr. Bernson은 학자가 되기 위해 걸어온 자신의 힘든 여정을 설명했다.

해설 소유격과 명사 사이의 형용사 자리를 묻는 문제이다. 항상 현재분사 형태로 쓰이는 형용사 (B) challenging이 정답이다.

어휘 path 길 I describe (~이 어떠한지를) 말하다 / 서술하다

5. 잡지의 편집장인 Mr. Barnett은 기사에 대한 상세한 피드백을 제공하기 위하여 저자들을 정기적으로 만난다.

해설 동사 provide의 목적어로 쓰인 명사 feedback을 수식하는 형용사 자리를 묻는 문제이다. 항상 과거분사 형태로 쓰이는 형용사 (A) detailed가 정답이다.

어휘 editor-in-chief 편집장 I regularly 정기적으로 I article 기사

6. 대단히 흥미로운 인터뷰에서 유명한 바이올린 연주자인 Hanna Jang은 어린 시절의 음악 훈련에 대해서 이야기했다.

해설 관사와 명사 사이의 형용사 자리이므로 감정 동사 fascinate을 분사로 전환해야 한다. 감정 동사가 사물 명사를 수식하는 경우 현재분사 형태를 취하며, 수식받는 명사인 인터뷰가 '흥미를 일으키는' 것이므로, 능동의 상태를 표현한 현재분사 (A) fascinating이 정답이다.

어휘 renowned 유명한 I training 훈련 I childhood 어린 시절

7. 회사 동료들에게 차편 제공을 자원하고자 하는 사람은 누구나 초과 근무수당과 유류비를 변제받게 된다.

해설 동사 will be reimbursed가 있으며 접속사나 관계사가 문장에 없기 때문에 빈칸은 동사 자리가 아니고, 명사 Anyone을 수식하는 분사 자리이다. 수식 받는 명사 Anyone은 희망하는 주체이므로 능동 의미의 현재분사 (B) wishing이 정답이다.

어휘 coworker 회사동료 I reimburse 변제하다, 지급하다 I fuel expense 유류비

8. 19세기 초에 지어진 오래된 창고들은 항구가 폐쇄되자 아파트 건물로 개조되었다.

해설 분사구문의 태를 선택하는 문제는 주절의 주어와 의미상 관계를 파악해야 한다. 주절의 주어 the old warehouses는 지어지는 대상으로 수동 분사구문의 과거분사 (A) Built가 정답이다. (B), (D)는 능동의 분사구문이므로 오답이며, (C)의 「been + p.p.」 구조는 존재하지 않는다.

어휘 convert 전환시키다, 개조하다 I port 항구

9. 공항 푸드코트는 24시간 내내 영업해서 여행객들이 비행편이 언제 도착하더라도 식사 서비스를 받도록 보장해준다.

해설 동사 is가 존재하며 접속사나 관계사가 없으므로 동사인 (A), (D)는 오답이다. 푸드코트가 24시간 영업되어 여행객들이 식사할 수 있도록 보장해준다는 문맥에 따라 능동의 현재분사 (B) ensuring이 정답이다. 완전한 문장 뒤에 분사구문이 오는 경우 현재분사로 시작하는 경우가 대부분인 점에 유의한다.

어휘 around the clock 24시간 내내 I dining 식사 I no matter when 언제 ~일지라도

10. 의무 직원교육에 관한 정보는 동봉된 계약서 3페이지에 있습니다.

해설 관사와 명사 사이의 형용사 자리이므로 동사인 enclose를 분사로 전환해야 한다. 수식받는 명사인 계약서는 '동봉되는' 것이므로, 수동을 의미하는 과거분사인 (C) enclosed가 정답이다.

어휘 mandatory 의무적인 I locate (특정 위치에) 두다

11. Mike Ritter는 지난 20년 동안의 가장 스릴 넘치는 모험 영화 여러 편에서 주역을 맡았다.

해설 빈칸은 관사와 명사 사이의 형용사 자리이므로 감정동사 thrill을 분사로 전환해야 한다. 해석상 수식을 받는 명사인 모험 영화들이 감정을 일으키는 주체이므로 능동의 의미를 가지는 현재분사 (A) thrilling이 정답이다.

어휘 star (영화·연극 등에서) 주연[주역]을 맡다 I thrill 열광시키다, 스릴 넘치다

12. SF 대학은 온라인 지원 시스템에 대한 기술적 어려움을 겪은 지원자들에게 연장된 마감 시한을 승낙(허가)해 주고 있다.

해설 관사와 명사 사이의 형용사 자리를 묻는 문제이다. 선택지에 형용사와 함께 형용사로 쓰이는 과거분사가 함께 있기 때문에 해석을 통해서 정답을 선택해야 한다. extensive는 '(범위가) 광범위한'의 의미로 마감일과는 의미상 적합하지 않다. 따라서 연장된 마감일이라는 의미에 적합한 (D) extended가 정답이다.

어휘 grant (요구, 탄원 따위를) 승낙(허가)하다

13. 노란색 X표로 표시된 주차 공간들은 병원을 방문하는 환자들을 위해 예약되어 있다.
고난도

해설 본동사 are가 있고, 그 앞에 문장을 연결해주는 접속사나 관계사가 없기 때문에, 빈칸은 동사 자리가 아니다. 따라서, 동사 (D)는 오답이며, 빈칸 앞의 명사 parking spaces를 수식해주는 분사자리임을 알 수 있다. 수식 받는 명사인 '주차 공간들'이 '표시된다'는 수동의 의미가 되므로 과거분사 (B) marked가 정답이다. (C)는 관계대명사 that이 있기 때문에 동사 mark를 쓸 수 있지만, 선행사 parking spaces와 동사 mark는 의미상 수동 관계이므로 'be + p.p'의 수동태가 되어야 한다. 따라서, 능동형의 (C) that mark는 오답이다.

어휘   **mark** 표시하다, 나타내다 (= indicate) | **cross** X표, 십자 | **reserve** 예약하다 | **patient** 환자 | **clinic** 병원, 진료소

14. Ferguson Health 재단은 어제 설립자인 Jeremy Ferguson에게
고난도 경의를 표하는 의례로 그것의 25주년 기념일을 축하했다.

해설   문맥상 명사 ceremony를 수식할 성분이 필요하므로 분사 (C)와 (D) 중에서 답을 골라야 하며, 그것의 설립자를 '기념하는' 행사를 한 것이므로 능동의 현재분사 (D) honoring이 정답이다.

어휘   **celebrate** ~을 축하하다 | **anniversary** 기념일 | **ceremony** 식, 의례 | **founder** 설립자 | **honor** 예우하다

15. 이사회가 수정된 계획안들을 승인했으며, 이는 종합 운동장 건설 세 단계 중 첫 번째 단계가 8월에 시작될 수 있도록 했다.

해설   동사 approved가 존재하며 접속사나 관계사가 없으므로 동사인 (B), (C)는 오답이다. 이사회가 수정 계획들을 승인했고 그래서 건설 계획이 시작될 수 있게 되었다는 능동 의미의 현재분사로 시작하는 분사구문이므로 (A) allowing이 정답이다.

어휘   **approve** 승인하다 | **phase** 단계, 국면

16. Intec Combo의 인사부는 그 광고된 자리에 관심이 있는 100명 이상의 지원자들을 면접했다.

해설   빈칸은 관사와 명사 사이의 형용사 자리이므로 감정동사 interest를 분사로 전환해야 한다. 해석상 수식을 받는 명사인 지원자들 (applicants)이 감정을 느끼는 대상이므로 수동의 의미를 가지는 과 거분사 (A) interested가 정답이다.

어휘   **applicant** 지원자 | **position** 일자리

17. 대만에 본사를 둔 (자리를 잡은) 기업 Zhang 교육그룹은 외국인 직원들에게 주거지원을 제공한다.

해설   관사와 명사 사이의 형용사 자리이므로, '확실히 자리를 잡은'의 의미인 과거 분사형 형용사 (D) established가 정답이다.

어휘   **established** 확실히 자리를 잡은, 인정받는 | **based** (~에) 근거지(본사)를 둔 | **housing assistance** 주거지원

18. Mino 사의 재무 위원회는 내년 회계 연도에 대한 기업 목표를 요약 기술한 공식 메모를 공개했다.
고난도

해설   has released라는 동사가 있기 때문에, 빈칸은 동사 자리가 아니므로 동사 (A), (B)는 오답이며, 명사 memo를 수식하는 분사의 알맞은 형태를 찾는 문제이다. 그 기업의 목표를 기술해주는 메모이므로 능동 의미의 (C) outlining이 정답이다.

어휘   **release** ~을 발표[공개]하다 | **outline** ~의 개요(요약)를 기술하다

19. 회사의 연례 생산 목표량을 초과 달성했던 Hasian 사 생산부서의 모든 직원들은 보너스를 받았다.
고난도

해설   문장 맨 앞에 올 수 있는 대표적인 구조가 분사구문과 목적을 나타내는 to부정사이다. '목표량을 초과 달성했기 때문에 직원들이 보너스를 받았다'는 문맥에 따라 목적(~하기 위하여)을 나타내는 (B)는 오답이다. 분사구문의 태를 선택하는 문제는 주절의 주어와 의미상 관계를 파악해야 하는데, 주절의 주어 all employees는 목표량을 달성하는

주체로 능동 분사구문의 (A) Having exceeded가 정답이다. (C) p.p. 나 (D) being p.p.는 수동 분사구문 형태이므로 오답이다.

어휘   **exceed** 넘다, 초과하다 | **productivity** 생산성 | **division** (조직의) 부, 국

20. 지역 주민들이 직면하는 흔한 문제는 그들이 받은 원치 않는 우편물의
고난도 양이 엄청나다는 것이다.

해설   동사 become 뒤에 감정동사 overwhelm의 알맞은 형태를 고르는 문제이다. 이 문장의 구조는 unwanted letters 뒤에 목적격 관계대명사 that이 생략된 구조로 they receive가 선행사 letters를 수식하고 있으며 become의 주어는 the amount가 된다. 따라서 현재분사 (B) overwhelming이 정답이다.

어휘   **overwhelm** (대응할 수 없을 정도의 어떤 것으로) 당황하게[난처하게] 하다, 압도[제압]하다

REVIEW TEST 03   본서 p.120

1. (C)	2. (C)	3. (A)	4. (C)	5. (C)
6. (B)	7. (B)	8. (B)	9. (D)	10. (C)
11. (B)	12. (B)	13. (B)	14. (B)	15. (C)
16. (D)	17. (A)	18. (B)	19. (B)	20. (B)

1. 대중 교통 요금을 줄이기 위해 지역 사회 단체에 의해 제안된 발의안이 긴 논의 끝에 기각되었다.

해설   주어진 문장에는 문장을 연결하는 접속사나 관계사가 없으므로 하나의 동사(was rejected)만 필요하다. 따라서, 빈칸은 동사자리가 아니고, 앞의 명사 the initiative를 수식하는 분사자리가 된다. initiative는 제안되는 대상에 해당하므로 수동의미를 지닌 과거분사 (C) suggested가 정답이다.

어휘   **initiative** 발의안, 계획 | **reject** 기각하다, 거부하다

2. 〈Trendy Car Magazine〉에 나온 기사에 따르면, Harold 자동차는 가장 큰 SUV 생산을 중단할 것이다.

해설   빈칸은 전치사의 목적어인 명사 뒷자리이므로 명사를 수식할 수 있는 준동사를 써야 하고, 기사는 '출간되는' 것이므로 수동의 의미를 갖는 과거분사 (C) published가 정답이다.

어휘   **discontinue** 중단하다

3. 저희 직원들에게 발표를 해주셔서 감사드리며, 다시 연락을 받기를 고대합니다.

해설   '~을 고대하다'를 의미하는 look forward to의 to는 전치사로 뒤에 명사나 동명사가 와야 한다. 따라서, 동명사인 (A) hearing이 정답이다.

어휘   **give a presentation** 발표하다 | **personnel** 직원들 | **look forward to ~ing** ~하기를 고대하다 | **hear from** ~으로부터 (편지, 이메일, 전화 등의) 연락을 받다

4. 휴가 규정을 개정한 이후로, Veltro 전자는 직원들로부터 받는 불만이 상당히 줄어들었다.

해설 명사 complaints를 수식하는 형용사 또는 형용사의 비교급 fewer를 수식하는 부사 자리이다. 상당히 더 적은 불만들을 받았다는 의미로 (C) significantly가 정답이다.

어휘 revise 개정하다, 수정하다 | complaint 불만

5. 봄 시즌을 고려하여, Maiko's Sushi는 5월 28일부터 야외 식사 옵션을 제공할 것이다.

해설 '~을 고려하여' 라는 의미의 관용표현인 in consideration of를 묻는 문제로, 전치사와 전치사 사이는 명사자리이므로 '고려, 염두'라는 의미를 지닌 (C) consideration이 정답이다.

어휘 outdoor 야외의, 옥외의 | dining 식사 | beginning on ~부터

6. 〈Consumer Today Guide〉는 혼란스럽게 하는 선택 사항들을 잘 살펴보고 충분히 근거 있는 구매 결정을 내리도록 도울 수 있다.

해설 빈칸은 명사 options를 수식하는 감정동사 bewilder의 분사 자리이다. 문맥상 선택 사항들이 (소비자들을) 혼란스럽게 만드는 것이므로 능동의 현재분사 (B) bewildering이 정답이다. 이처럼, 감정동사가 사물 명사를 수식하는 경우에는 현재 분사를 쓴다.

어휘 sort through 자세히 살펴보다 | well-founded 충분히 근거 있는, 기초가 튼튼한

7. New York 유업은 품질 기준을 충족하지 못한 65퍼센트의 요거트를 폐기해야 했다.

해설 동사 fail은 to부정사를 목적어로 취하여 '~하는 데 실패하다'를 의미하므로 (B) to meet이 정답이다.

어휘 be forced to 어쩔 수 없이 ~하다 | discard 버리다, 폐기하다 | quality standard 품질 기준

8. 편집자와 상의한 후에, Ms. Trinh은 마침내 뉴스 기사를 작성할 수 있었다.

해설 '~할 수 있다' 라는 의미를 갖는 'be able to 동사원형' 구문을 완성하는 문제이다. 따라서, 빈칸 앞의 able을 단서로, 형용사 able과 함께 쓰이는 to 부정사인 (B) to complete가 정답이다.

어휘 consult 상의하다, 상담하다 | editor 편집자 | finally 마침내, 결국 | complete 완결하다, 마무리짓다

9. Harbin 시설의 확장이 Feilin 가구의 배송 서비스에 중대한 영향을 끼쳤다.

해설 빈칸은 정관사 the와 전치사 of 앞의 명사자리이므로, 명사인 (D) expansion이 정답이다. 타동사 expand의 동명사 형태인 (A)는 뒤에 of 없이 목적어를 취하며, 정관사 the와 쓰일 수 없으므로 오답이다.

어휘 expansion 확장 | have a significant impact on ~에 중대한 영향을 끼치다

10. 위기관리 전략은 경제적 어려움에도 불구하고 소규모 자영업자들이 생존하고 성공할 수 있도록 해 준다.

해설 빈칸은 명사 economic challenges를 목적어로 하는 전치사 자리이

다. '경제적 어려움에도 불구하고'라는 의미가 적절하므로 (C) in spite of가 정답이다.

어휘 risk management 위기관리 | strategy 전략 | enable ~을 가능하게 하다 | economic challenge 경제적 어려움

11. 해외 지사로 옮기는 대신 Mr. Shah는 뉴욕에 있는 C&C.com 본사의 일자리 제의를 받아들이기로 결정했다.

해설 동사 choose는 to부정사를 목적어로 취해서 '~을 결정하다'는 의미를 가지므로 (B) to accept가 정답이다.

어휘 transfer 전근가다 | headquarters 본사

12. Newyen 산업의 CEO는 새로운 전략 책임자가 회사의 성장에 상당히 기여할 것을 확신한다.

해설 빈칸은 동사 contribute를 수식하는 부사 자리로 (B) substantially가 정답이다.

어휘 CEO(=Chief Executive Officer) 최고경영자 | confident 확신하는; 자신감 있는 | contribute to ~에 기여하다

13. 환불을 받을 수 있으려면, 상점 직원에게 원본 영수증을 보여줘야만
고난도 한다.

해설 빈칸 뒤의 동사원형과 문맥상 '환불을 받기 위해서'를 단서로, 목적을 의미하는 부정사를 만드는 (B) in order to가 정답이다. 전치사나 접속사로 쓰이는 (A) Even as 와 (C) Since, 접속사인 (D) Unless 는 뒤에 동사원형을 바로 취하지 못하므로 오답이다.

어휘 refund 환불 | present 보여주다, 제시하다 | be eligible for ~의 자격이 있다

14. 최근에 석유산업 영업에서 얻은 7천만 달러의 기금이 사회기반시설에 투자되도록 확보되었다.

해설 빈칸 앞의 to는 목적을 나타내는 to부정사이므로 뒤에 동사원형이 와야 한다. 문맥상 7천만 달러의 기금($70 million in funds)은 투자되는 (be invested) 것이므로 수동태인 (B) be invested가 정답이다.

어휘 recently 최근 들어 | derive from ~에서 유래하다, 파생하다, 나오다 | industry 산업 | set aside 곁에 두다, 확보하다, 챙겨두다 | social infrastructure 사회기반시설

15. Silco 호수 정화 프로젝트가 계획했던 것보다 훨씬 더 오래 걸렸기 때문에 Barrington 시의 자금 잔고가 바랐던 천만 달러 수준 밑으로 떨어질 수도 있다.

해설 명사 level을 수식하는 형용사 자리이므로 '바랐던'을 뜻하는 (C) desired가 정답이다. desire는 want와 같이 '바라다'라는 의미의 상태 동사여서 진행형을 쓰지 않으므로 (D) desiring은 답이 될 수 없다.

어휘 fund 자금 | balance 잔고, 잔액 | fall below ~이하가 되다 | since ~때문에 | plan 계획하다; 계획

16. 우리 매니저는 공개 연설에 대한 강연이 영업 실적을 개선하는 데 도
고난도 움이 될 것이기 때문에 그 수업에 참석할 것을 적극 권장했다.

해설 타동사 help는 목적어로 'to 동사원형'이나 '동사 원형'을 취하여 '~하는 데 도움이 되다'라는 의미를 갖는다. 따라서, 동사원형 (D) improve가 정답이다.

어휘 public speaking 대중 연설 | help + (to) 동사원형 ~하는 데 도움이 되다 | sales performance 영업 실적

17. 트레이드마크인 조리도구 라인을 출시하기 전에, Mr. Pers는 25년
고난도 넘게 여러 식당에서 일해왔다.

해설 빈칸은 동명사 launching 앞의 전치사 자리이므로, 전치사인 (A) Prior to 가 정답이다. 목적을 나타내는 to 부정사 (B) In order to뒤에는 동사원형이 와야 하고, 접속사인 (C), (D) 뒤에는 '주어+동사' 구조의 절이 와야 하기 때문에 동명사가 이어진 빈칸에는 적합하지 않다.

어휘 launch 출시하다 | trademark 트레이드마크 (어떤 사람의 특징이 되는 것), (등록) 상표 | cookware 조리도구

18. 사업 계획을 짜는 데 각 단계마다 투여된 계획 수립이 자금 조달을 받
고난도 을 가능성에 직접적인 영향을 미칠 것이다.

해설 문장을 연결해주는 접속사 없이 동사 will have가 존재하므로 빈칸은 동사자리가 아니며, 의미상 빈칸 앞의 명사를 수식하는 분사자리이다. '각 단계마다 투여되는 계획 수립'이라는 문맥에 따라, 수동을 나타내는 과거분사 (B) invested 가 정답이다.

어휘 invest (노력, 시간 등을) 투여하다, 쏟다, 쓰다 | impact 영향

19. 불황에는 소규모 사업주들이 계약의 일부를 재조정하는 것을 고려할
수 있다.

해설 빈칸은 consider의 목적어 자리로 명사 (A)와 동명사 (C)가 올 수 있으나, 빈칸 뒤에 동사 renegotiate의 목적어에 해당하는 명사구 some of their contracts가 바로 연결되어 있기 때문에, 동명사 (C) renegotiating이 정답이다. 타동사 consider는 to 부정사를 목적어로 취하지 않기 때문에 (B)는 오답이다.

어휘 depressed economy 불경기 | renegotiate 재조정하다, 재협상하다 | contract 계약

20. Xiandai 백화점은 라벤더와 바닐라의 진정 기능의 향기를 결합한 인
고난도 기 피부관리 제품을 공개했다.

해설 빈칸 뒤의 명사구 the soothing scents of lavender and vanilla를 목적어로 취하면서 빈칸 앞의 명사 skincare product를 수식하는 기능을 해야 하므로 현재분사 (B) combining이 정답이다.

어휘 release 공개하다, 발표하다 | skincare 피부관리 | soothing 완화하는, 진정하는 | scent 향기, 냄새

UNIT 12. 부사절 접속사
본서 p.124

Q1 **1.** Even though **2.** While **3.** because

1. 팀원들의 업무가 일정에 뒤처져 있어도 프로젝트 관리자는 프로젝트
가 제 시간에 완료될 것이라고 자신하고 있다.

해설 팀원들의 업무가 일정상 뒤처져 있다는 문장과 프로젝트를 제때 완료할 거라는 문장은 문맥상 상반되므로 양보를 나타내는 부사절 접속사 자리

2. Mr. Won이 그 승진 기회를 감사히 여기긴 했지만, 그는 다른 일을
하기로 결정했다.

해설 승진 기회를 감사히 여겼다는 문장과 다른 일을 하기로 했다는 문장은 문맥상 상반되므로 양보를 나타내는 부사절 접속사 자리

3. William Smith는 자신이 가장 자격을 갖춘 후보라는 것을 증명했
기 때문에 부매니저로 채용되었다.

해설 William Smith가 부매니저로 채용되었다는 문장과 자신을 가장 자격 있는 후보로 증명했다는 문장은 인과 관계가 성립하므로 이유를 나타내는 부사절 접속사 자리

Q2 **1.** as soon as **2.** while **3.** Once
4. Unless **5.** so that

1. 건축 허가를 받는 대로 공사가 시작될 것이다.

해설 건축 허가를 받는 대로 공사가 시작될 거라는 문맥이므로 '~하자마자'라는 뜻의 부사절 접속사 자리

2. 엘리베이터가 수리되는 동안 계단을 이용하십시오.

해설 엘리베이터가 수리되는 기간 동안 계단을 이용하라는 문맥이므로 '~하는 동안'이라는 뜻의 부사절 접속사 자리

3. Mr. Hidings가 특별 업무팀을 조직하고 나면 Altoona 프로젝트의
마감 기한이 결정될 것이다.

해설 Mr. Hidings가 특별 팀을 조직하고 나면 마감 기한이 결정될 거라는 문맥이므로 '일단 ~하면'이라는 뜻의 부사절 접속사 자리

4. 공급사가 할인된 가격에 밀가루를 공급해주지 않는 한 우리는 제빵
제품의 가격을 올려야 한다.

해설 공급사가 밀가루를 할인가로 제공할 수 없다면 빵 가격을 올려야 한다는 문맥이므로 '~하지 않는다면'이라는 뜻의 부사절 접속사 자리

5. Jennifer Chang은 새 제품 개발에 집중할 수 있도록 선임 엔지니
어로 임명되었다.

해설 Jennifer Chang이 신제품 개발에 집중할 수 있도록 하기 위해 선임 엔지니어로 임명했다는 문맥이므로 '~하기 위해'라는 뜻의 부사절 접속사 자리

Q3 1. Although 2. Even though 3. While 4. Given that

1. NRT 노트북이 비싸기는 해도 구매 가능한 것들 중 가장 빠른 모델이다.
해설 「------ + 주어 + 동사, 주어 + 동사」 구조이므로 부사절 접속사가 들어가야 할 자리

2. 세무 감사가 Georgetown 재무 회계의 정보를 한 달 전 요청했지만 자료는 아직도 도착하지 않았다.
해설 「------ + 주어 + 동사, 주어 + 동사」 구조이므로 부사절 접속사가 들어가야 할 자리

3. 보안 시스템이 업그레이드되는 동안 프론트 데스크에서 체크인 하십시오.
해설 「------ + 주어 + 동사, 명령문」 구조이므로 부사절 접속사가 들어가야 할 자리

4. Mauer 컨설팅이 작년에 비해 최근 훨씬 더 많은 주문을 확보했다는 점을 고려했을 때 회사는 더 많은 연구 조교를 고용해야 한다.
해설 「------ + 주어 + 동사, 주어 + 동사」 구조이므로 부사절 접속사가 들어가야 할 자리

Q4 1. If 2. In addition to 3. While 4. once

1. 만약 Sonna Graphics의 방문객들이 유효한 패스를 소지하지 않았다면 보안 사무실에서 사진이 있는 신분증을 보여야 한다.
해설 「------ + 주어 + 동사, 주어 + 동사」 구조이므로 부사절 접속사가 들어가야 할 자리

2. 커미션뿐만 아니라 판매원들은 분기별 보너스를 받게 될 것이다.
해설 「------ + 명사, 주어 + 동사」 구조이므로 전치사가 들어가야 할 자리

3. Mr. Tal이 시연을 하는 동안 Ms. Locke는 제품 전단지를 배포했다.
해설 「------ + 주어 + 동사, 주어 + 동사」 구조이므로 부사절 접속사가 들어가야 할 자리

4. 우리는 책임자가 주문을 승인하는 즉시 새 장비를 구매할 것이다.
해설 「주어 + 동사 + ------ + 주어 + 동사」 구조이므로 부사절 접속사가 들어가야 할 자리

Q5 1. before 2. Until 3. due to

1. 외국에서 아파트를 빌리고 싶은 사람들은 계약을 하기 전 계약서를 주의 깊게 검토해야 한다.
해설 「주어 + 동사 ------ 주어 + 동사」 구조이므로 부사절 접속사가 들어가야 할 자리

2. 이 스캐너가 수리되기 전까지 3층에 있는 복사기를 이용하세요.
해설 「------ + 주어 + 동사, 명령문」 구조이므로 부사절 접속사가 들어가야 할 자리

3. 급여 시스템은 정기 보수 작업 때문에 다음 주 목요일 오전 6시에서 7시까지 오프라인 상태가 될 것이다.
해설 「주어 + 동사 ------ + 명사구」 구조이므로 전치사가 들어가야 할 자리이며, 정기 보수 작업 때문에 시스템이 오프라인 상태일 거라는 문맥이므로 '~때문에'라는 뜻의 이유를 나타내는 전치사 자리

Q6 1. making 2. while

1. 온라인에서 구매할 때는 안전한 네트워크를 사용하십시오.
해설 부사절 접속사(When)와 명사구(a purchase) 사이에 주어 없이 동사를 써야 할 때는 주어가 생략된 분사구문으로 판단하고 목적어로 명사구가 있으므로 능동의 현재분사를 쓸 자리

2. 기술자들은 연구실에서 일하는 동안 모든 안전 규정을 준수해야 한다.
해설 전치사 during 뒤에는 특정 기간을 나타내는 명사나 명사 상당어구가 오며, 'working in the lab'과 같은 형태를 취하지 않으므로 주어(Technicians)가 생략된 분사구문으로 접속사를 쓸 자리로 판단

Q7 1. scheduled 2. specified

1. 기술적 문제에도 불구하고 기차는 원래 일정대로 출발했다.
해설 수동 축약구조 「as + p.p. (~된 대로)」

2. 저희 제품의 모든 재료는 다르게 명시되지 않은 한 모두 유기농입니다.
해설 수동 축약구조 「unless otherwise + p.p. (그와 다르게 ~되지 않는다면)」

Q8 1. Although 2. Either

1. Ms. Sherman이 휴가 중이긴 하지만, 그녀는 중요한 이메일들에 답변을 줄 수 있다.
해설 「------ + 주어 + 동사, 주어 + 동사」 구조이므로 부사절 접속사 자리이며, 등위접속사 But은 항상 두 문장 사이에 위치해야 하므로 오답

2. 신청서를 온라인으로 작성하시거나 직접 제출하시면 됩니다.
해설 「------ + A or B」 구조의, 상관 접속사 either 자리

Q9 1. whenever 2. However 3. trivial

1. 기술적 문제가 있을 때는 저희에게 전화 주십시오.
해설 '기술적 문제가 있을 때는 언제든지'라는 해석뿐만 아니라 뒤에 「주어 + 동사 + 목적어」의 완전한 구조의 절이 왔으므로 복합관계부사 자리

2. 대부분의 대중 연설자들은 많은 청중 앞에 서는 일이 아무리 자주 있다 하더라도 여전히 약간의 무대 공포증을 경험한다.

해설 뒤에 형용사나 부사를 수반하는 복합관계부사 however

3. 모든 직원들은 아무리 사소한 것이라 할지라도 어떤 사고든 보고해야 한다.

해설 복합관계부사 however는 no matter how로 쓸 수 있으며 뒤에 형용사나 부사가 와야 한다.

Practice

본서 p.132

1. (B)	**2.** (B)	**3.** (D)	**4.** (C)	**5.** (C)
6. (A)	**7.** (A)	**8.** (A)	**9.** (D)	**10.** (A)
11. (D)	**12.** (A)	**13.** (D)	**14.** (C)	**15.** (B)
16. (C)	**17.** (B)	**18.** (A)	**19.** (C)	**20.** (D)

1. 그들의 이전 모델이 10대들 사이에서 상당히 인기가 있었다 하더라도, 다음 모델도 매력적일 것이라고 기대하는 사람은 거의 없다.

해설 빈칸 뒤에 「주어 + 동사」의 절의 구조가 왔으므로 접속사 (B) Even though가 정답이다. 해석상 (A) in spite of도 가능하나 전치사구이므로 오답이다.

어휘 previous 이전에 ‖ quite 상당히 ‖ popular 인기 있는 ‖ attractive 매력적인

2. Mr. Hong이 3년 연속으로 뛰어난 업적 평가를 받았기 때문에, 그는 올 봄에 분명히 승진할 것이다.

해설 빈칸 뒤에 「주어 + 동사」의 절의 구조가 왔으므로 접속사 (A) ‘~하기 위해’, (B) ‘~때문에’, (C) ‘~이긴 하지만’ 중에 승진할 것이라고 말하는 이유를 나타내는 접속사 (B) As가 정답이다.

어휘 appraisal 평가 ‖ consecutive 연이은 ‖ promote 승진시키다

3. 일부 직원들은 법에 규정된 요구사항이 더 이상 없음에도 불구하고 여전히 업무 일지를 작성하는 경향이 있다.

해설 보기가 모두 접속사이므로 해석을 통하여 문맥상 적합한 접속사를 묻는 문제이다. 규정된 요구사항이 없지만 업무일지를 작성한다는 해석에 적합한 양보의 접속사인 (D) although가 정답이다.

어휘 tend to (~하는) 경향이 있다 ‖ keep a daily work log 업무 일지를 작성하다 ‖ mandated 법에 규정된

4. 비행기의 연착에도 불구하고, Mr. James는 제시간에 회의에 도착했다.

해설 빈칸 뒤에 명사구가 왔으므로 전치사인 (C) Despite가 정답이다.

어휘 delay 지연시키다 ‖ on time 정각에, 제시간에

5. 고객들의 DNA 테스트 요청은 100달러의 보증금이 지급되기 전까지는 진행될 수 없다.

해설 두 절을 연결하는 접속사가 들어갈 자리이므로 (C) until이 정답이다. 전치사 (A), (D)나 부사 (B)는 절을 연결하는 역할을 할 수 없으므로 오답이다.

어휘 request for ~에 대한 요청 ‖ proceed 진척되다

6. 마케팅 직원들이 3주짜리 집중 교육을 이수하면, 매니저가 그들에게 보고서를 제출하라고 요청할 것이다.

해설 빈칸 뒤에 「주어 + 동사」의 절의 구조가 왔으므로 접속사인 (A) Once가 정답이다.

어휘 intensive 집중적인 ‖ training 교육, 훈련

7. Novizan 출판사는 책 표지 디자이너들이 좀 더 효과적으로 일할 수 있도록, 컴퓨터에 새로운 삽화 소프트웨어를 설치했다.

해설 빈칸 뒤에 「주어 + 동사」의 절의 구조가 왔으므로 접속사인 (A) ‘~하기 위해서’, (B) ‘마치~인 것처럼’ 중에서 해석상 자연스러운 (A) so that이 정답이다. (C) so as는 존재하지 않는 표현으로 오답 보기로 자주 제시되는데 뒤에 to부정사가 연결되어야 한다.

어휘 install ~을 설치하다 ‖ illustration 삽화 ‖ effectively 효과적으로

8. Greenychi Safety 해운은 모든 수송품이 목적지가 아무리 멀지라도 제때에 배달될 것임을 귀하께 보장합니다.

해설 문법적으로 빈칸 뒤에 형용사가 오고 「주어 + 동사」의 구조가 왔으므로 복합관계부사 (A) no matter how(= however)가 정답이다. 해석상으로도 ‘no matter how remote’가 ‘아무리 멀지라도’라고 해석되어 문맥상 적당하다.

어휘 assure A that A에게 ~을 보장하다 ‖ shipment 수송품 ‖ on time 제때에 ‖ remote 먼 ‖ destination 목적지

9. 이번 주말 건물 지하 주차장에서는 전기 시스템의 응급수리로 인해 주차가 금지됩니다.

해설 빈칸 뒤에 명사구의 구조가 왔으므로, 전치사인 (D) because of가 정답이다. 접속사 (A)는 뒤에 「주어 + 동사」의 절이 와야 하고, 접속부사 (B)는 명사구 앞에 못 오며, (C) in order to 뒤에는 동사원형이 와야 하므로 오답이다.

어휘 basement garage 지하 주차장 ‖ prohibit 금하다 ‖ emergency repair 응급수리 ‖ electrical system 전기 시스템

10. Lexington 박물관은 새 전시품들을 준비할 뿐만 아니라 특별 행사들에 투어를 시켜 줄 새 큐레이터를 구하고 있다.

해설 ‘A 뿐만 아니라 B도’의 의미를 갖는 상관접속사 ‘not only A but also B’를 묻는 문제이므로 (A) but also가 정답이다.

어휘 seek 구하다, 찾다 ‖ organize 조직하다, 계획하다 ‖ exhibit 전시품 ‖ occasion 행사; 경우

11. 작가에게서 기사를 받는 대로 꼼꼼하게 검토해주세요.

해설 빈칸 뒤에 「주어 + 동사」의 절의 구조가 왔으므로, 접속사인 (B) ‘~동안에’ 와 (D) ‘~하자 마자’ 중에서 문맥상 적절한 (D) as soon as 가 정답이다. (B) while이 시간의 의미를 나타낼 때는, 주로 진행형과 함께 진행중인 동작을 나타내기 때문에 오답이다. 빈칸은 접속사 자리이므로, 부사 (A)와 전치사 (C)는 오답이다.

어휘 review 검토하다 ‖ thoroughly 철저히, 완전히

12. Novana 공업의 전체 수익은 지난 2년 동안 감소했지만, 어떤 부서들은 매출은 약간 증가했다.

해설 빈칸 뒤에 「주어 + 동사」의 절이 왔으므로, 접속사 (A) '반면에'와 (B) '때문에' 중 문맥상 적절한 대조의 접속사 (A) While이 정답이다.

어휘 overall 전체의, 종합적인 | revenue 수입 | decrease 감소하다

13. Alsacienne's 레스토랑은 도심 지역으로 이전한 이래로 엄청난 매출 증가를 경험했다.
고난도

해설 빈칸 앞 현재 완료 시제와 연결해서 '~이래로 계속'이라는 의미의 (D) since가 정답이다. 접속사 since가 '~이래로 계속'의 의미를 갖는 경우 「주어 + 현재 완료 시제 ~ since + 주어 + 과거 시제」로 쓰인다는 점에 유의한다.

어휘 dramatic 극적인 | increase 증가 | relocate to ~로 이전하다

14. 회사의 경리 부장인 Ms. Norman은 연례 재무 보고서가 작성되기 전에 4분기 수익을 검토하고 싶어 한다.

해설 빈칸 뒤에 「주어 + 동사」의 절이 왔으므로, 접속사 역할을 하는 (C) before가 정답이다. (A)는 '이전에'라는 의미의 형용사, (B)는 부사, (D)는 형용사와 부사 모두로 쓰인다.

어휘 accounting manager 경리 부장 | revenue 수익 | compile 작성하다, 엮다, 편집하다

15. 점점 더 많은 사람들이 소셜미디어를 통해 연결되고 있기 때문에, 소비자들이 상품평을 공유하는 일이 훨씬 더 쉬워졌다.

해설 「------- 주어 + 동사, 주어 + 동사」 구조로 빈칸은 두 절을 이어줄 수 있는 부사절 접속사가 필요한 자리이므로 전치사인 (A)와 (C)를 소거한 후, Now that과 As if 중에서 답을 골라야 한다. 소셜미디어를 통해 많은 사람들이 연결된 것이 상품평 공유가 더 쉬워진 이유가 되므로 '~이기 때문에'를 뜻하는 (B) Now that이 정답이다.

어휘 consumer 소비자 | share 공유하다 | product review 상품평 | instead of ~대신에 | now that ~이기 때문에 | because of ~ 때문에 | as if 마치 ~인 것처럼

16. 계약서에 서명할 때, Samwha 생명공학은 Midward 제약사와 공동 연구 프로젝트를 시작하기로 합의했다.
고난도

해설 접속사 when 뒤에 주어를 생략하고 동사가 분사 형태로 올 수 있으므로 (C) When이 정답이다. 해석상 (A)도 적절하나 전치사 during 뒤에 바로 -ing가 올 수 없다는 점에 유의한다.

어휘 sign the contract 계약서에 서명하다 | collaborative 공동의, 협력적인

17. 전 대표이사 Kate Hatfield는 회사의 내외부로부터 강한 저항에 직면했을 때 사직하지 않을 수 없었다.
고난도

해설 접속사 when 뒤에 「주어 + 동사」의 절이 오지 않은 경우, 「주어 + be 동사」가 생략된 것이다. 해석상으로 전직 대표이사가 강한 저항에 직면되므로 「when + 주어 + be faced with~」 구조이며 여기에서 「주어 + be동사」가 생략된 구조로 정답은 (B) faced이다.

어휘 have no choice but ~하지 않을 수 없다 | resign 사직하다 | stiff 심한, 힘든

18. 1월 사내 소식지가 출간될 때 즈음에, 외주 계약에 관한 최종 결정이 날 것이다.
고난도

해설 빈칸 뒤에 「주어 + 동사」의 절의 구조가 왔으므로 접속사인 (A) '~할 즈음에'와 (D) '~이기 때문에' 중에서 해석이 자연스러운 (A) By the time이 정답이다. (B) In order to를 쓰려면 빈칸 뒤에 동사원형이 와야 하므로 오답이다.

어휘 newsletter 소식지 | outsourcing contract 외주 계약

19. 일부 지역을 물에 잠기게 한 폭우에도 불구하고 2,000명 이상의 사람들이 지난 일요일의 국제 식품 박람회에 참석했다.

해설 빈칸 뒤에 명사구의 구조가 왔으므로, 전치사인 (C) notwithstanding이 정답이다.

어휘 fair 박람회 | notwithstanding ~에도 불구하고 | swamp ~을 물에 잠기게 하다

20. 이 프로젝트에 할당된 예산이 매우 한정되어 있다는 점을 고려해 볼때, 그 프로젝트의 각 단계마다 비용 효율성을 고려하는 것이 중요하다.
고난도

해설 빈칸 뒤에 「주어 + 동사」의 절이 왔으므로 접속사 자리이며, 예산이 제한된 점을 고려할 때 비용 효율성을 고려해야 한다는 문맥에 적절한 (D) Given이 정답이다.

어휘 allocate 할당하다 | limited 제한된 | cost-efficiency 비용 효율성 | given (that) 고려하면, 고려할 때

UNIT 13. 명사절 접속사
본서 p.135

Q1 **1. that** **2. What**

1. 연간 재무 보고서는 우리가 전체적인 운영비를 절감해야 한다는 것을 보여준다.

해설 뒤에 주어와 타동사의 목적어가 올바르게 있는 완전한 구조의 절이 오므로 명사절 접속사 that

2. Mr. Wyatt이 회의에서 제안한 것은 이사회에게 깊은 인상을 남겼다.

해설 뒤에 타동사 proposed의 목적어가 없는 불완전한 구조의 절이 오므로 명사절 접속사 what

+ check **1. what** **2. that**

1. 잠재 고객이 필요로 하는 것을 이해하는 일은 마케터들에게 아주 중요하다.

2. 양측 CEO들은 새 경영진이 다가오는 합병 후에 직원들이 협력적으로 일하기를 기대한다고 밝혔다.

Q2 1. that 2. that

1. 변경된 차량 점검 규정은 12월 1일부터 효력이 발생한다는 점을 알고 계시기 바랍니다.

해설 문장 구조상 완전한 구조의 절이 오며, 알고 있는(aware)과 함께 쓰이는 명사절 접속사 that

2. 직원들이 정기적으로 안전 워크숍에 참석하는 것이 중요하다.

해설 문장 구조상 완전한 구조의 절이 오며, 가주어 it 뒤의 진주어에 해당하는 명사절을 이끄는 접속사 that

Q3 1. whether 2. whether 3. whether

1. 우리는 연례 회사 야유회를 회사 마당에서 할지 Jackson 공원에서 할지 결정하지 못했다.

해설 「whether A or B」 A인지, B인지

2. 사무실 매니저는 종이를 Light-Office에서 주문할지 Gartol에서 주문할지 결정할 것이다.

해설 「whether + to부정사」 ~인지 아닌지

3. 회사는 지원자들의 대학 졸업장 소지 여부에 관계 없이 직원을 채용할 것이다.

해설 명사절 접속사 if는 타동사의 목적어로만 사용 가능

+ check 1. whether 2. if

1. Canterra의 직원들은 집에서 일할지 사무실에서 일할지 선택할 수 있다.

2. Mr. Romano가 전화해서 다가오는 9월 10일 세미나가 다음 주로 연기될 수 있는지 물었다.

Q4 1. who 2. whose 3. where

1. 진행 중인 법률 분쟁으로 인해 Home Skin Care의 출시가 지연되었는데, 이것은 누가 그것을 발명했는지 불분명했기 때문이다.

해설 '누가 그 제품을 발명했는지 명확하지 않았다'는 문맥에 맞는 의문대명사 who

2. 결정을 하기 전 우리는 누구의 아이디어가 가장 독창적인지 검토할 것이다.

해설 '누구의 아이디어가 가장 독창적일지 검토할 것이다'는 문맥에 맞는 의문형용사 whose

3. 행사 조직자는 파티를 열 장소를 결정했다.

해설 '어디에서 파티를 열 것인지를 결정했다'는 문맥에 맞는 의문부사 where

Q5 1. Whoever 2. whatever 3. Whoever

1. 전시 부스 예약에 관심이 있는 분은 누구든지 동봉된 등록 양식을 작성해야 합니다.

해설 뒤에 동사가 둘(is, should fill out)이므로 두 개의 문장을 연결하는 접속사 기능을 가진 복합관계대명사 자리

2. 이 여행 가방에 휴가에 필요한 것은 무엇이든 가져오실 수 있습니다.

해설 뒤에 타동사 need의 목적어가 없는 불완전 구조의 절이 오므로 복합관계대명사 자리

3. 가장 좋은 평가를 받는 사람은 누구든지 지점 매니저로 승진할 것이다.

해설 둘 다 명사절을 이끄는 역할을 할 수 있으므로 해석을 통해 문맥에 맞는 것을 선택해야 한다. '최고의 평가를 받는 사람은 어느 누구나 매니저 자리를 얻을 수 있다'는 문맥에 따라 복합관계대명사 whoever

Practice
본서 p.140

1. (A)	2. (A)	3. (A)	4. (C)	5. (B)
6. (C)	7. (B)	8. (C)	9. (A)	10. (A)
11. (C)	12. (A)	13. (D)	14. (A)	15. (C)
16. (B)	17. (C)	18. (D)	19. (B)	20. (B)

1. 어느 매니저에게 보고해야 하는지는 배정받는 프로젝트에 의해 결정된다.

해설 두 개의 동사(should report, depends)가 존재해 두 개의 절을 연결할 수 있는 접속사가 필요한 자리이므로 명사절을 이끄는 의문 형용사 (A) Which가 정답이다. 부정형용사인 (B), (C)나 부정대명사인 (D)는 접속기능이 없기 때문에 오답이다.

어휘 report to ~에게 업무 보고를 하다 | assign 맡기다, 배정하다, 부과하다

2. 시 위원회는 시민들이 지하철 확장 프로젝트에 대해서 공개 청문회에서 제안한 것을 고려했다.
고난도

해설 타동사 consider의 목적어 역할을 하는 명사절을 이끌면서 동시에 빈칸 뒤 명사절의 동사 suggested의 목적어가 없는 불완전 구조의 절을 이끌어야 하므로 (A) what이 정답이다. 전치사인 (C)는 명사절을 이끌지 못하며, 부사절을 이끄는 부사절 접속사인 (D)는 타동사의 목적어 자리에서 명사절을 이끌 수 없으므로 오답이다.

어휘 city council 시 위원회 | suggest ~을 제안하다 | public hearing 공개 청문회 | expansion 확장

3. Laura Stevenson의 최신 서적인 〈Why I sing〉에 관한 그녀의 강연은 관심 있는 누구에게나 열려 있다.

해설 전치사 뒤의 명사절을 이끄는 복합관계대명사를 선택하는 문제이다. '~한 사람은 누구나'라는 의미뿐만 아니라 빈칸은 is의 주어 자리이므로 복합관계대명사 주격인 (A) whoever가 정답이다.

어휘 talk (~의 스스름 없는) 연설, 강연, 대화

4.
고난도 Fabolia 무용 학원은 여름 강좌 등록에 관심 있는 사람들을 위하여 4월 7일에 정보 안내 시간을 마련할 것입니다.

해설 (A) whoever는 anyone who의 개념으로 분사(interested in)의 수식을 받을 수 없다. 또한 인칭대명사 (B) they, (D) them도 과거분사의 수식을 받을 수 없으므로 오답이다. 따라서 정답은 (C) anyone이다.

어휘 sign up for 등록하다 (= register for)

5. 매니저들은 직원들에게 그들 스스로 업무를 할 수 있는 능력이 있음을 증명할 공평한 기회를 주는 것이 필요하다.

해설 빈칸 뒤에「주어 + 동사」구조의 절이 왔으므로 접속사 (B) that이 정답이며,「가주어 it ~ that 명사절 ~」의 구조이다.

어휘 equal 공평한 I prove A 형용사 A가 ~한 것을 증명하다 I capable of ~을 할 수 있는

6. Lowell 자동차를 견학하도록 초대 받은 방문객들은 디자인실에서 조립 라인까지 우리 제품들이 어떻게 만들어지는지를 볼 수 있습니다.

해설 타동사 see의 목적어 역할을 하는 명사절을 이끄는 의문사가 필요하므로 (C) how가 정답이다. (D)는 부사절을 이끄는 접속사로 동사의 목적어 역할을 하는 명사절을 이끌 수 없다.

어휘 tour ~을 견학하다 I assembly line 조립 라인

7. 11월 10일 오후 5시 전에 Gina에게 연락하셔서 참석 여부에 대해서 알려 주십시오.

해설 타동사 know의 목적어 역할을 하는 명사절을 이끄는 접속사가 필요한데 문장 끝에 or not이 쓰였으므로 (B) whether가 정답이다.

어휘 attend 참석하다

8. 소득 증명서가 필요한 사람은 누구나 회계부의 Ms. Roh에게 요청해야 한다.

해설 빈칸 뒤에 '동사 + 동사' 구조이므로, 두 개의 문장을 연결해 줄 수 있는 접속 기능을 가진 의문사 (B) '누구'와 복합관계대명사 (C) '~한 사람은 누구나' 중에 해석을 통해 정답을 선택하면 (C) Whoever가 정답이다.

어휘 income verification form 소득 증명서

9. 조사는 거의 모든 제품 평가단들이 Everyday Bath 샴푸의 향기가 아주 매력적이라고 생각한다는 것을 보여 주었다.

해설 타동사 indicated 뒤에 목적어 역할을 하는 명사절 접속사 자리를 묻는 문제이다. 빈칸 뒤에 절이 완전한 구조의 절이므로 (A) that이 정답이다.

어휘 find + 목적어 + 형용사 ~가 ~하다고 생각하다 I scent 향기 I appealing 매력적인

10. 이사회는 어느 연구 프로젝트에 자금을 제공할지 결정하기 위해 오늘 오후에 만날 것이다.

해설 타동사 decide의 목적어 자리에서 명사절을 이끄는 의문사를 선택하는 문제이다. '어떤 연구 프로젝트에 자금을 제공할지'라는 문맥에 따라 의문형용사인 (A) which가 정답이다. 해석을 통해 명사절을 이끄

는 의문사를 선택한다는 점에 유의한다.

어휘 board of directors 이사회 I fund 자금(기금)을 제공하다

11. 이사회는 다음 주 월요일 회의에서 누가 새로운 부사장으로 임명될 것인지를 결정해야 한다.

해설 타동사 decide의 목적어 역할을 하는 명사절 접속사 자리를 묻는 문제이다. 해석상 '누가'라는 의미가 적합하며, 빈칸 뒤에 주어가 없는 불완전 구조의 절이 왔기 때문에 (C) who가 정답이다.

어휘 be appointed as ~으로 임명되다

12. 온라인 직원 평가서를 작성하는 데 기술적인 어려움이 있는 관리자들은 기술지원팀에 연락해서 도움을 받아야 합니다.

해설 빈칸은 사람 선행사 supervisors를 수식해주는 형용사절을 이끄는 관계대명사 자리이며, 빈칸 뒤에 주어가 빠진 불완전 구조이므로 주격 관계대명사인 (A) who가 정답이다. 11번의 who는 타동사의 목적어 자리에서 명사절을 이끄는 의문사이나, 이 문제의 경우 who는 사람 선행사 뒤에서 선행사를 수식하는 형용사절을 이끄는 관계대명사인 점에 유의한다.

어휘 supervisor 감독관, 관리자 I evaluation 평가, 사정

13. 참가자들은 질의응답 시간 동안에 그들이 알고 싶은 것이 무엇이든지 질문하는 게 허용된다.

해설 두 개의 동사(are, would like)가 존재해 두 개의 절을 연결할 수 있는 접속사가 필요한 자리이므로 대명사 (C)는 오답이다. 빈칸 뒤 절에 to know의 목적어가 없는 불완전 구조인 점과 해석을 고려할 때 (D) whatever가 정답이다. 복합관계부사 (A)와 (B) 뒤에는 완전한 구조의 절이 와야 하므로 오답이다.

어휘 participant 참석자 I question and answer session 질의응답 시간

14. Ms. Hwang은 이번 주말까지 제안서를 시 위원회에 제출할지를 결정해야 한다.

해설 타동사 decide의 목적어 자리에서 to부정사와 함께 쓰여 목적어 역할을 할 수 있는 보기는 (A) whether이다. 명사절 접속사 whether는 'whether 절'이나 'whether to부정사' 형태로 쓰인다.

어휘 submit ~을 제출하다

15.
고난도 우리는 재정 위기를 극복하거나 적어도 그것이 우리 사업에 미치는 영향을 최소화하는 방법을 배울 필요가 있다.

해설 명사절 접속사인 의문사와 whether는 to부정사와 함께 쓸 수 있다. 따라서, to learn의 목적어 자리에서 빈칸 뒤에 to부정사가 쓰였으므로, to부정사와 함께 쓰여 목적어 역할을 할 수 있는 (B)와 (C) 중에 해석상 적합한 (C) how가 정답이다.

어휘 overcome ~을 극복하다 I crisis 위기 I minimize ~을 최소화하다 I effect on ~에 미치는 영향

16. 제가 귀하가 이해하셨으면 하는 것은 저희가 제한된 시간과 예산 내에서 Epsontech 프로젝트를 완수해야 한다는 것입니다.

해설 빈칸 뒤에「주어 + 동사 + 동사」가 쓰였으므로 빈칸부터 understand

까지가 문장 전체의 주어 역할을 하도록 만들어 주는 명사절 접속사를 선택하는 문제이다. to understand의 목적어가 없는 불완전 구조인 점과 해석을 고려할 때 (B) What이 정답이다.

어휘 within ~이내에 I limited 제한된

17. 연말 수익 배분이 지난해의 반밖에 되지 않을 것이라는 것은 전체 직
고난도 원들에게 실망스러운 소식이다.

해설 빈칸 뒤에 「주어 + 동사 + 동사」가 쓰였으므로 빈칸부터 두 번째 동사 앞인 the year's까지 문장 전체의 주어 역할을 하도록 만들어 주는 (A)나 (C)를 써야 하며, 명사절의 구조가 완전 구조이므로 (C) That을 쓴다.

어휘 year-end 연말 I profit share 이윤 배분 I entire 전체의

18. Extell 상사의 경영진이 서류들을 검토하자마자, 누구의 제안서가 선
고난도 택될 것인지를 결정할 것이다.

해설 빈칸은 완전한 절을 이끌어 타동사 determine의 목적어 역할을 할 명사절 접속사가 필요하므로 명사 앞에 써서 '누구의'로 해석되는 의문형용사 (D) whose가 정답이다. (A)와 (C)는 주어가 없는 불완전 구조의 절을 이끌고, (B)는 목적어가 없는 불완전 구조의 절을 이끈다.

어휘 review ~을 검토하다 I determine ~을 결정하다

19. 예산 위원회는 월례 직원 교육을 위해서 기금을 할당할 필요가 있는지에 대해서 여전히 논의 중이다.

해설 전치사의 목적어 역할을 하는 완전 구조의 명사절을 이끌 접속사가 필요하므로 (B) whether가 정답이다. (A)와 (C)는 불완전 구조의 명사절을 이끌므로 답이 될 수 없으며 (D)는 부사절을 이끄는 부사절 접속사이므로 전치사의 목적어 자리에 올 수 없다.

어휘 allocate ~을 할당하다 I funds 기금 I monthly 매달의

20. 온라인 비디오 스트리밍 서비스의 이용 용의성으로 인해, 사람들이 요즘에는 텔레비전에 나오는 것은 무엇이든 시청하는 일이 흔하지 않다.

해설 빈칸은 앞뒤의 두 개의 동사를 연결하는 접속사 자리이므로 대명사 (A)는 올 수 없다. 빈칸 뒤는 주어 없이 동사가 바로 온 불완전한 문장이므로, 불완전한 구조의 절을 이끄는 복합관계대명사 (B) whatever가 정답이다. 부사절 접속사 (C)와 복합관계부사 (D)는 완전한 문장을 이끌기 때문에 오답이다.

어휘 availability 유용성, 유효성 I video streaming 영상 데이터 연속 전송 I nowadays 요즘에는

UNIT 14. 형용사절 접속사

본서 p.143

Q1 1. which   2. who

1. 이례적인 폭설이 내렸고 이는 다수의 항공기 결항으로 이어졌다.
해설 사물이 선행사이며 뒤에 주어가 빠진 불완전한 문장이 왔으므로 주격 관계대명사 which

2. 현재 프로젝트를 담당하고 있는 매니저는 다음 달에 사임한다.
해설 사람이 선행사이며 뒤에 주어가 빠진 불완전한 문장이 왔으므로 주격 관계대명사 who

Q2 1. whose

1. 그 유명 저자는 참석자들이 대부분 대학생인 학회에서 연설을 할 예정이다.
해설 완전한 문장이 뒤에 이어지므로 소유격 관계대명사 자리. which 뒤에는 불완전한 문장이 와야 하므로 오답

Q3 1. which

1. HR 팀이 조직한 스포츠 축제가 토요일에 열릴 것이다.
해설 타동사 organized의 목적어가 없는 불완전한 문장이 뒤에 오므로 관계절에서 목적어 역할을 하는 목적격 관계대명사 자리. 소유격 관계대명사 뒤의 명사는 관사나 소유격이 없는 명사가 오므로 오답

Q4 1. What

1. 우리에게 중요한 것은 고객들이 우리 서비스에 만족하는 것이다.
해설 뒤에 주어 없이 동사가 바로 위치한 불완전한 문장이 오므로 선행사 없이 쓰이는 관계대명사 what

Q5 1. where

1. 현재 그녀가 조사를 진행하고 있는 회사는 대기 오염을 유발하는 것으로 비난받아왔다.
해설 뒤에 완전한 문장이 오므로 관계부사 자리. 관계대명사 which 뒤에는 주어나 목적어가 빠진 불완전한 문장이 와야 하므로 오답

Q6 1. which   2. on   3. which

1. 주민 센터는 주민들이 체력 단련 활동을 즐길 수 있는 시설을 제공한다.
해설 전치사 뒤의 목적어 자리이므로 목적격 관계대명사 자리

2. 시에서 극장이 지어질 땅을 제공할 것이다.

해설 which는 the land를 받아주는 대명사이므로 which 대신 the land를 넣어보고 문맥에 맞는 전치사를 선택한다. 생산 시설들은 땅 위에 지어지는 것이므로 전치사 on

3. E-logics 사는 다양한 컴퓨터용 소모품을 취급하며, 이 모든 것들은 온라인으로 구매할 수 있습니다.

해설 전치사 of 뒤의 목적격 관계대명사 자리이며 선행사 accessories가 사물이므로 which

Q7 **1.** interested **2.** selling

1. 워크숍 참석에 관심이 있는 직원들은 Ms. Lim에게 연락해야 한다.

해설 주어진 문장에는 동사(should contact)가 존재하나 접속사나 관계사가 없기 때문에 동사가 아닌 과거분사가 정답. 또한, '참석에 관심 있는 직원들'이란 문맥에 따라, 'employees who are interested in~'에서 '주격 관계대명사 who와 be동사'를 생략하여 과거분사 interested가 명사 employees를 뒤에서 수식하는 구조

2. 다 쓴 잉크 카트리지에 대한 보상을 받으시려면 저희 Clean Ink 제품을 판매하는 매장으로 가져오시면 됩니다.

해설 주어진 문장에는 동사(take)가 존재하나 접속사나 관계사가 없기 때문에 동사가 아닌 현재분사가 정답. 또한, '제품을 파는 가게'란 문맥에 따라, 'any store which is selling ~'에서 주격 관계대명사 which와 be동사를 생략하여 현재분사 selling이 명사 store를 뒤에서 수식하는 구조

Q8 **1.** are **2.** have learned

1. 복사기에 필요한 토너 카트리지가 임시 품절 상태이므로 복사기를 아껴 써주시기 바랍니다.

해설 선행사 the toner cartridges와 it requires 사이에 목적격 관계대명사 which가 생략된 구조이므로 동사가 하나 더 필요함

2. Dr. Wayne의 지도 아래 내가 배운 모든 것을 실행할 것이다.

해설 선행사 all 뒤에 목적격 관계대명사 which가 생략된 구조로 '내가 배워 온 모든 것'이란 능동 의미에 맞는 능동태

Practice

1. (B)	2. (B)	3. (B)	4. (C)	5. (A)
6. (A)	7. (D)	8. (A)	9. (A)	10. (A)
11. (D)	12. (A)	13. (A)	14. (C)	15. (C)
16. (C)	17. (A)	18. (D)	19. (A)	20. (D)

1. 컴퓨터에 문제가 있는 직원들은 정규 업무 시간 동안 회사의 IT 지원 팀에 전화를 해야 한다.

해설 두 개의 동사(have, should call)를 연결해주는 접속사나 관계사가 필요하기 때문에 대명사인 (A), (C), (D)는 오답이다. 사람 선행사 뒤에

주어가 없는 불완전 구조의 절이 쓰였으므로 주격 관계대명사인 (B) who가 정답이다.

어휘 regular working hours 정규 업무 시간

2. 전통 접시를 만드는 기술을 전문으로 하는 Royal Tableware 사는, 작년에 남미로 시장을 확장했다.

해설 사물 선행사 뒤에 주어가 없는 불완전 구조의 절이 쓰였으므로, (B) which가 정답이다.

어휘 specialize in ~을 전문으로 하다 | expand ~을 확장하다

3. Mr. Murphy의 최신작 한 권이 대회에 참가한 우승자에게 무료로 주어질 것이다.

해설 주격 관계대명사 that 뒤이므로 동사 자리이며, 그 동사는 선행사에 수나 태를 맞춰야 하므로 (B) participates가 정답이다.

어휘 copy 사본 | participate (in) (~에) 참가하다

4. 전 세계적으로 유명한 작가인 Carol MacMillan의 작품이 여러 언어로 번역되었는데, 그녀는 예전에 영어 선생님이었다.

해설 명사 앞의 소유격 관계대명사 자리이므로 (C) whose가 정답이다. (A)와 (D)는 주어가 없는 불완전 구조가 와야 하며, (B)는 두 개의 동사를 연결하는 접속사 역할을 하지 못하므로 오답이다.

어휘 world-famous 세계적으로 유명한 | author 작가 | translate ~을 번역하다 | used to 동사원형 (과거에) ~했다, ~였다

5. Hamasaki 자동차는 그 회사를 세계에서 세 번째로 큰 자동차 생산업체로 만들어 줄 Liberty 자동차와의 합병을 막 발표했다.

해설 사물 선행사 뒤에 주어가 없는 불완전 구조의 절이 쓰였으므로, (A) which가 정답이다. (B)는 그 앞에 선행사를 취하지 않으며, (C)는 사람 선행사와 쓰이며, (D)는 뒤에 명사가 와야하는 소유격 관계대명사이므로 오답이다.

어휘 merger 합병 | manufacturer 생산자

6. 최근의 전기요금 인상은 평소 에너지 소비량이 많은 사업체들에게 영향을 미쳤다.

해설 명사 energy 앞의 소유격 관계대명사 자리이므로 (A) whose가 정답이다. 관계 대명사 (B) which는 뒤에 주어나 목적어가 빠진 불완전 구조가 와야 하며, 주격 관계대명사 (C) who는 그 앞에 사람 선행사와 뒤에 주어가 빠진 불완전 구조가 와야 하며, 명사인 (D)는 두 개의 동사(has affected, is)를 연결하는 접속사 역할을 할 수 없으므로 오답이다.

어휘 electricity price 전기요금 | affect ~에 영향을 미치다 | consumption 소비, 소모(량)

7. 귀하가 주문한 물건을 언제 받을 수 있을지를 알기 위해서는 봉투 안에 있는 주문서를 참조하십시오.

해설 사물 선행사 뒤에 목적어가 없는 불완전 구조의 절이 쓰였으므로 (D) which가 정답이다. 소유격 관계대명사 (A)나 관계부사 (B)는 완전 구조의 절을 이끌어야 하며, (C)는 콤마 뒤의 계속적 용법으로 쓰일 수 없으므로 오답이다.

어휘 refer to ~을 참조하다 | purchase order sheet 주문서 | envelope 봉투

8. 그 대학은 매년 봄 학기에 그 지역의 기업들이 일자리에 대해 학생들을 인터뷰하는 취업 박람회를 개최한다.

해설 장소를 선행사로 뒤에 완전한 문장이 왔으므로 관계부사 (A) where가 정답이다. 관계대명사 (D) which 뒤에는 주어나 목적어가 빠진 불완전한 구조가 와야하므로 오답이며, 부사 (B)와 대명사 (C)는 접속사 역할을 하지 못하므로 쓰일 수 없다.

어휘 semester 학기 | job fair 취업 박람회

9. Harington 사의 본사를 방문하기 위해 남방향 11번 고속도로를 타고 3번 출구까지 오시면, Eliot Building 옆에 있습니다.

해설 사물 선행사 뒤에 주어가 없는 불완전 구조의 절이 쓰였으므로, (A) which가 정답이다. (B)는 주어가 있는 완전 구조의 절을 이끌어야 하고, (C)는 콤마 뒤에 쓸 수 없으며, (D)는 선행사가 사람 명사이어야 하므로 오답이다.

어휘 headquarters 본사 | next to ~의 옆에

10. Sydney 미술관을 설계한 국제적으로 유명한 건축가가 프로젝트의 팀장이 될 것이다.

해설 사람 선행사 뒤에 주어가 없는 불완전 구조의 절이 쓰였으므로, (A) who가 정답이다. (B)는 사물 선행사와 쓰여야 하며, 대명사인 (C)는 두 개의 동사(designed, will be)를 연결하는 접속사 역할을 하지 못하며, (D)는 선행사를 취하지 못하므로 오답이다.

어휘 renowned 유명한 | architect 건축가

11. 지난달에 신간을 출간한 철학 교수가 Alpha 서점에서 책 사인회를 열 것이다.

해설 명사 앞의 소유격 관계대명사 자리이므로 (D) whose가 정답이다. (B)는 두 개의 동사(was published, will hold)를 연결하는 접속사 역할을 할 수 없고, (A)는 선행사를 취하지 못하며, 복합 관계대명사인 (C)는 뒤에 동사가 오고, 선행사를 취하지 못하므로 오답이다.

어휘 publish ~을 출판하다 | hold ~을 개최하다

12. Hill 은행은 모든 대출 신청자들에게 각 신청자의 재무기록에 대한 세부사항들이 논의 되어지는 1대 1 상담을 제공한다.

해설 사물 선행사와 쓰이며 전치사 during 뒤에 오는 목적격 관계대명사인 (A) which가 정답이다. 전치사 뒤의 목적어 자리에는 관계부사인 (B), 부사절접속사인 (C), 소유격 관계대명사인 (D)는 쓰일 수 없다.

어휘 one-on-one 1대 1의 | consultation 상담

13. DGN 산업이 설립 이래로 주재하고 있는 Center One 빌딩은 많은 개선과 수리를 필요로 한다.
고난도

해설 관계대명사 목적격 앞의 전치사를 묻는 문제이다. 빈칸 뒤의 동사 reside와 선행사 building을 연결해보면 그 건물 안에 거주한다는 의미가 되어야하므로 (A) in이 정답이다.

어휘 reside 거주하다, 주재하다 | updating 개선, 개정

14. Thomas Wyatt의 조각작품은 미술에 있어서 세련된 기호가 있는 고객들이 구매한다.

해설 명사 tastes 앞의 소유격 관계대명사 자리이므로 (C) whose가 정답이다. 대명사인 (B)는 두 개의 동사(are, are)를 연결하는 접속사 역할을 할 수 없으므로 오답이다.

어휘 taste 기호, 취향 | sophisticated 세련된

15. 당국은 탄소 배출을 줄이는 지역 제조업체들에 포상할 것이다.

해설 두 개의 동사(reward, decrease)를 연결하는 접속사 역할을 하며, 주어가 빠진 불완전 구조를 이끄는 주격 관계대명사 (C) that이 정답이다. 조동사 (A) will은 문장을 연결하는 접속사 역할을 못하며, 「주어 + 동사」의 완전한 문장을 이끄는 부사절 접속사 (B), (D)는 빈칸 뒤에 주어 없이 동사가 왔기 때문에 쓰일 수 없다.

어휘 authority 당국 | reward (일, 공적 등에 대해) 포상하다 | decrease 감소시키다 | carbon 탄소 | emission 배출

16. Groove 건설사는 Ms. Schmidt가 감독한 환경 친화적인 프로젝트로 올해의 건축상을 탔다.

해설 주격 관계대명사 that 뒤의 동사는 선행사에 수나 태를 맞춰야 한다. 선행사로 쓰인 project는 '감독되는' 것이므로 수동태 (C) was overseen이 정답이다.

어휘 environmentally-friendly 환경 친화적인 | oversee ~을 감독하다

17. 홍보 담당자는 요청한 참고 자료가 준비되지 않아 발표를 시작할 수 없었다.
고난도

해설 「선행사 + 목적격 관계대명사 + 주어 + 동사」의 구조를 묻는 문제이다. 이때 목적격 관계대명사는 생략 가능하므로 주어에 해당하는 (A) she가 정답이다. 만약 주격 관계대명사인 (B)가 정답이라면 선행사(참고자료)와 그 뒤에 오는 동사가 수의 일치와 태가 올바르게 되어야 하는데 참고 자료가 요청되는 대상이므로 수동의 형태(was requested)가 되어야 한다. 하지만 문제 속의 동사는 능동형(requested)이므로 주격 관계대명사는 정답이 될 수 없다. 소유격 관계대명사인 (D)는 뒤에 완전 구조가 와야 하므로 주어가 없는 불완전 구조에 쓰일 수 없다.

어휘 PR 홍보 | reference material 참고 자료

18. Community Heritage Pride 상은 Grant 시의 역사적인 건물들을 복원하는 것을 돕는데 시간을 자원하여 내준 주민들에게 영예를 준다.

해설 선행사로 사람명사가 오고 빈칸 뒤에 주어가 빠진 불완전 문장이 왔으므로 주격 관계대명사인 (D) who가 정답이다. 빈칸 뒤의 volunteer는 뒤에 their time을 목적어로 가진 타동사이므로 뒤에 명사를 취하는 전치사인 (A), (C), 소유격 관계대명사인 (B)는 오답이다.

어휘 honor ~에게 영예(명예)를 주다 | volunteer 자진(자원)하여 제공하다 | restore 복원/복구하다

19. 많은 고객들이 잡지와 신문에 광고가 나가는 Hrudy 가구에 의해 실시되는 제품 설문조사에 참여했다.
고난도

해설 명사 앞의 소유격 관계대명사 자리이므로 (A) whose가 정답이다. 대명사인 (B)는 두 개의 동사(participated, apper)를 연결하는 접속사

역할을 못하며, (C)는 주어나 목적어가 빠진 불완전 문장이 와야 하므로 오답이며, (D)는 선행사를 취하지 못한다.

어휘 appear 나오다, 발간되다

20. Miles 해운은 신속한 배송을 위해 먼저 더 큰 트럭을 사용하기 시작
고난도 했는데, 그것들 모두에는 회사 고유의 로고가 새겨져 있다.

해설 두 개의 동사를 연결해주는 접속사 기능을 가진 관계대명사 (C)와 (D) 중 사물 선행사와 쓰이며 전치사(of) 뒤에 오는 목적격 관계대명사에 해당하는 (D) which가 정답이다. 대명사 (A), (B)는 두 개의 동사를 연결해주는 접속사 역할을 못하며, (C)는 사람 선행사와 쓰여야 하므로 오답이다.

어휘 prompt 신속한 | delivery 배송 | unique 고유의 | imprint 새기다

REVIEW TEST 04   본서 p.150

1. (A)	2. (C)	3. (D)	4. (B)	5. (D)
6. (C)	7. (D)	8. (B)	9. (B)	10. (A)
11. (C)	12. (C)	13. (B)	14. (C)	15. (C)
16. (B)	17. (C)	18. (B)	19. (B)	20. (D)

1. 강당과 회의실 둘 다 수리 때문에 이용할 수 없을 것이므로, 정기 직원 회의가 이 달에는 열리지 않을 것이다.

해설 상관접속사 「neither A nor B」 'A, B 둘 다 아닌' 구문으로 빈칸 앞에 neither와 짝을 이루는 (A) nor가 정답이다.

어휘 auditorium 강당

2. Michelle Park는 〈Women's Quarterly Magazine〉에 자주 기고할 뿐만 아니라 그녀의 기사들은 다른 유사 출간물에서도 정기적으로 나온다.

해설 등위접속사(but) 앞뒤로 절이 연결된 형태로 articles가 주어이므로 이를 수식해 주는 소유격 대명사 (C) her가 정답이다.

어휘 contribute 기고하다; 기여하다 | appear 나오다, 발간되다 | publication 출판(물), 발행(물)

3. Gekko 소프트웨어의 다른 엔지니어들과 마찬가지로, Marco Shaw는 컴퓨터 프로그래밍에 폭넓은 경험을 가지고 있다.

해설 빈칸 뒤에 명사구가 연결되어 있고, 콤마 뒤로 절이 이어져 있으므로 빈칸은 이 둘을 연결시켜 줄 수 있는 전치사 자리이다. 보기 중 전치사는 (D) Like 뿐이다.

어휘 extensive 아주 많은; 폭넓은, 광범위한

4. 손님들은 옷과 그에 어울리는 액세서리를 같이 또는 따로 구입할 수
고난도 있다.

해설 등위접속사가 같은 문장 성분을 연결한다는 점을 알고 있다면 쉽게 풀 수 있는 문제이다. 등위접속사 or 앞에 전명구(부사구)가 연결되어 있으므로 or 뒤에도 부사가 연결되어야 하므로 (B) separately가 정답이다. or 앞의 matching accessories만 보고 빈칸 뒤의 품사를 명사로 착각하여 separation을 선택하지 않도록 주의하자.

어휘 matching 어울리는 | separately 각각, 따로

5. Player-tech 사 직원들은 관리자의 승인을 미리 받지 않으면, 초과 근무 수당을 받지 못할 것이다.

해설 빈칸 앞뒤로 절이 연결되어 있으므로 빈칸은 접속사 자리이며, 보기 중 접속사는 (D) unless 뿐이다.

어휘 overtime work 초과 근무 | supervisor 관리자 | approval 승인 | in advance 미리

6. 그래프는 지난 3년 동안 Pumar 자동차에서 가장 잘 팔린 자동차들의 매출액을 보여 준다.

해설 빈칸 뒤 기간 명사구(the past three years)가 결정적 힌트가 되며, 그래프가 이 기간 동안의 매출액을 보여 준다는 의미이므로 '~동안에'의 의미를 갖는 전치사 (C) over가 정답이다.

어휘 sales figure 매출액 | top-selling 가장 많이 팔리는 | automobile 자동차

7. 에든버러에 있는 많은 대형 상점들은 이제 기념 우표를 포함해 우편 물품을 취급한다.

해설 빈칸은 명사 stamps와 복합 명사를 이루는 명사 자리 또는 명사를 수식하는 형용사 자리로 '기념 우표'라는 의미를 완성하는 형용사 (D) commemorative가 정답이다.

어휘 postal 우편의 | supplies 용품 | stamp 우표 | commemorative 기념하는, 기념으로 발행된

8. 필요한 도로 공사 때문에, 33번 노선은 9월 6일 토요일 오후까지 폐쇄
고난도 될 것이다.

해설 빈칸 뒤에 명사구가 왔기 때문에 빈칸은 전치사자리이다. 전치사 (A), (B) 중에 '필요한 고속도로 보수공사 때문에, 길이 폐쇄될 것'이라는 문맥에 맞는 이유를 나타내는 전치사 (B) due to가 정답이다. 접속사인 (C) even though와 (D) now that 뒤에는 '주어+동사' 형태의 절이 와야 하므로 오답이다.

어휘 route 노선, 길 | repair 수리, 수선

9. 이곳에서만 접할 수 있는 다양한 패션 액세서리들은 어느 정장 의복에나 스타일과 세련미를 더해줄 것입니다.

해설 빈칸은 명사 style과 and로 연결되어 병렬 구조를 이루고 있는 명사 자리이므로 '교양, 세련'이라는 의미의 (B) sophistication이 정답이다. (A) '세련된 사람'이라는 의미의 명사, (C) '세련된, 교양 있는'이라는 의미의 형용사, (D) '세련되게'라는 의미의 부사이므로 오답이다.

어휘 exclusive 독점적인, 배타적인 | formal outfit 정장 의복

10. 소비자 물가는 지난 몇 년간 급격히 오른 반면, 사무직 종사자들의 평균 급여는 거의 똑같다.

해설 빈칸 뒤에 콤마로 두 개의 절이 연결되어 있으므로 부사절 접속사를 쓸 자리이며, 소비자 물가가 올랐다는 내용과 평균 급여가 그대로라는 대조의 내용을 연결해야 하므로 '반면에'라는 의미의 (A) While이 정답이다.

어휘 rise dramatically 급격하게 오르다

11. 그 프로젝트에 개입하고 있는 모든 사람들은 기대되는 이득에 중점을 두고 프로젝트를 성공으로 이끌 핵심 요인을 분명히 밝혀야 한다.

해설 문맥상 적절한 부정대명사를 선택하는 문제이다. 빈칸은 '(who is) involved in the project'의 수식을 받는 명사 자리로서 전체 문장의 주어가 필요하다. '그 프로젝트에 개입하고 있는 사람이라면 모두'라는 문맥이 적절하므로 (C) Everyone이 정답이다. 문장의 동사 needs가 단수동사이므로 복수대명사인 (B), (D)는 문법상 오답이다.

어휘 be involved in ~에 관련되다, 개입하다 I focus on ~에 주력하다, 중점을 두다 I expected 예상되는, 기대되는 I critical factor 핵심 요인 I successful 성공적인

12. Baliville의 새로 승진한 의원은 그 도시의 운송망을 개선하기 위해 확실히 독특한 접근법을 사용하고 있다.

해설 빈칸은 형용사 unique를 수식하는 부사 자리이므로 (C) decidedly가 정답이다.

어휘 promote 승진시키다 I councilor 의원 I approach 접근법, 처리 방법 I transportation 운송, 수송

13. 인도네시아에서 출발한 선적물이 지난주 금요일 시카고에 도착할 예정이었지만, 예기치 못한 악천후 때문에 아직 출발하지도 못했다.

해설 두 개의 대조되는 의미의 문장을 연결하는 자리이므로 '역접'의 등위접속사 (B) but이 정답이다.

어휘 adverse weather 악천후

14. 그 건물의 시장가치는 3년 전 그 건물이 취득된 이래로 계속 상승해 왔다.

해설 빈칸 뒤의 과거 특정시점(3 years ago)부터 건물의 시장 가치가 올랐다는 문맥에 따라, 접속사 (C) since가 정답이다. 접속사 since가 '~한 이래로'의 의미로 쓰이는 경우 since 뒤에는 과거 시제가 오고 주절에는 현재완료 시제가 쓰인다. 이 문제의 경우에도 since 뒤의 동사는 과거시제(was acquired)이고, 주절의 동사는 현재완료시제(has increased)이다.

어휘 market value 시장가치 I increase 증가하다, 인상되다 I acquire 획득하다, 취득하다

15. 채용 시즌 동안, Lea Yim은 면접 일정을 짜는 한 가지 일을 주로 담당하게 될 것이다.

해설 선행사인 task를 꾸미는 관계 대명사를 찾는 문제로, 선행사가 사물이며 뒤에 동사(is)가 나오므로 사물 주격 관계대명사인 (C) which가 정답이다.

어휘 largely 주로, 대개 I be responsible for ~을 맡다, 책임지다 I arrange 일정을 마련하다

16. 경제 발전의 결과로, Larma 지역의 취업 기회가 늘어나고 있다.

해설 빈칸 뒤에 명사가 온 구조로, 전치사 (B), (D) 중 문맥상 적합한 것을 선택해야 한다. '경제 발전의 결과로 취업 기회가 늘어나고 있다'는 의미가 적절하므로 '결과'의 의미를 지닌 전치사구 (B) As a result of가 정답이다.

어휘 improve 개선되다, 나아지다 I job opportunity 취업 기회 I

region 지역 increase 증가하다

17. 휴가 일수에 대해 약간의 논쟁이 있기는 했지만 직원들과 경영진은 합의에 이를 수 있었다.

해설 두 개의 절을 연결할 접속사를 쓸 자리이며, 논쟁이 '있기는 했지만'이라는 양보의 해석이 자연스러우므로 (C) Although가 정답이다.

어휘 dispute 논쟁

18. 당장 웹사이트를 개설하지 않는다고 하더라도 도메인 이름을 고르고 사이트 등록을 해서 이름을 보유해 놓도록 하세요.

고난도

해설 'do not set up'과 'be'라는 두 개의 동사가 존재하므로, 빈칸은 두 문장을 연결해주는 접속사 자리이다. '즉시 웹사이트 개설을 하지 않는다'는 내용과 '도메인 이름을 골라 사이트 등록을 한다'는 내용은 문맥상 반대되는 내용으로, 양보의 접속사 (B) Even if가 정답이다. 접속사와 전치사로 쓰이는 (A)는 문맥상 적절하지 못하며, 전치사 (C)는 문장을 연결하는 역할을 하지 못한다. 접속사 (D) Yet은 문장의 맨 앞에서 부사절을 이끌지 못하므로 오답이다.

어휘 set up 건립하다, 설립하다 I immediately 즉시, 곧바로 I reserve 보유하다; 예약하다 I register 등록하다

19. 만약 집의 물리적인 구조에 중대한 결함이 보고된다면 판매자는 잠재 구매자들에게 그들의 주택을 광고하기 전에 결함들을 수리해야 한다.

고난도

해설 빈칸 뒤에 동명사가 위치해 있고, '결함을 파악하면, 주택을 판매하기 전에 수리를 해야 한다'는 문맥이 적합하므로, 전치사 (B) before가 정답이다.

어휘 defect 결함 I physical structure 물리구조 I repair 수리하다, 보수하다 I market 상품을 내놓다, 광고하다 I property 주택, 부동산 I prospective 장래의, 유망한, 잠재적인

20. 그것이 얼마나 어렵든지 간에 모든 임무들은 미래의 실행을 위해 잘 기록되고 우선순위가 매겨져야 한다.

고난도

해설 '얼마나 어렵든지 간에'라는 의미가 되어야 하므로 빈칸에는 difficult they may be라는 절을 이끄는 양보의 부사절 접속사 (D) However가 와야 한다. however는 no matter how로 바꿔 쓸 수 있다는 점을 참고해두자.

어휘 document 기록하다 I prioritize 우선 순위를 매기다 I implementation 이행, 실행

UNIT 15. 비교·가정법·도치

본서 p.154

Q1 **1. fascinating**　**2. as**

1. 다행히도 베이징 여행은 내가 예상했던 만큼 훌륭했다.
해설 as ~ as 사이에 형용사나 부사의 원급 자리

2. 우리 회사는 환경 문제에 관해 가능한 많은 정보를 제공하려고 한다.
해설 동급 비교 as ~ as 사이에 much와 함께 불가산 명사가 온 구조

Q2 **1. cheaper**　**2. than**　**3. even**　**4. markedly**

1. 우리 매장은 경쟁 회사들보다 더 값싼 제품을 제공하는 것을 보증한다.
해설 뒤에 than이 있으므로 비교급 자리

2. 투자가 예상보다 훨씬 더 수익성이 있었기 때문에 Mr. Cruze는 분석가에게 보너스를 주기로 결정했다.
해설 앞에 비교급이 위치하므로 than

3. Mr. Karmer는 식당이 작년보다 훨씬 더 많은 수익을 남겼기 때문에 시내에 한 군데를 더 개업하려고 계획 중이다.
해설 뒤에 위치한 비교급을 강조하는 부사는 even. so는 원급을 강조하는 부사

4. Ben이 수석 요리사가 된 이후 레스토랑 메뉴는 현저히 더 나아졌다.
해설 '눈에 띄게 더 좋아지다'란 의미를 완성하는 markedly가 정답

Q3 **1. speediest**　**2. most important**　**3. highest**

1. ZPX Pro는 현재 시장에서 가장 빠른 태블릿 PC로 여겨지고 있다.
해설 앞에 최상급과 함께하는 정관사가 있고 뒤에 최상급과 함께 쓰이는 표현(available in the market)이 있기 때문에 최상급 자리

2. 고객 데이터베이스 업데이트는 당신의 가장 중요한 직무 중 하나입니다.
해설 「one of + the/소유격 + 최상급 복수 명사」와 함께 하는 최상급

3. 그 텔레비전 뉴스 프로그램의 시청률이 지역의 모든 뉴스 쇼 중 가장 높았다.
해설 최상급 뒤에 오는 명사는 의미가 명백할 때 생략이 가능. 따라서, the 뒤에 명사가 없는 경우는 최상급 표현이 쓰여 생략됨

Q4 **1. the more**　**2. smaller**

1. 고객들로부터 더 많은 정보를 모을수록 연구 결과는 더 정확해질 것이다.
해설 「the 비교급, the 비교급('~하면 할수록 더 …하다')」 구문

2. 정부는 두 회사 중 더 작은 쪽에 지원과 보조금을 지급하기로 결정했다.
해설 뒤에 '둘 중에서'라는 의미의 'of the two'가 있기 때문에 the 뒤에 비교급이 옴

Q5 **1. later**　**2. more**　**3. probably**

1. 이 지원서를 6월 20일 전까지 제출하십시오.
해설 날짜 앞에 '늦어도 ~까지'의 의미를 갖는 no later than

2. Mr. Iwata는 비행편이 다섯 시간 이상 연착했기 때문에 고객 회의에 참석할 수 없었다.
해설 숫자 앞에 '~이상'의 의미를 갖는 more than

3. 그 할인 행사는 아마 고객이 증가한 가장 큰 이유일 것이다.
해설 be동사(is)를 꾸며줄 수 있는 부사 자리. most probably 아마도(확실성이 강할 때)

Q6 **1. could have begun**　**2. would**
　　3. should have

1. Mr. Hoffman이 건물의 설계도를 더 일찍 받았더라면 프로젝트를 3월 말 전에 시작할 수 있었을 것이다.
해설 if가 포함된 조건절의 동사 시제가 과거완료이므로, 가정법 과거완료의 주절 동사시제인 「조동사 과거 + have + p.p.」 자리

2. Barton 사는 대리점들이 약관을 준수하지 않는다면 사업 관계를 재평가하겠다고 경고했다.
해설 if가 포함된 조건절의 동사 시제가 과거이므로, 가정법 과거의 주절 동사 시제인 「조동사 과거형 + 동사원형」 자리

3. 문의사항이 있으실 때는 언제든 고객서비스 센터에 전화하시기 바랍니다.
해설 주절이 명령문이므로, 가정법 미래의 조건절 동사시제인 「should + 동사원형」 자리

Q7 **1. Had**　**2. should**

1. 기술자들이 모든 안전 대책을 준수했더라면 사고가 일어나지 않았을 것이다.
해설 주절의 동사가 would have p.p.이므로 가정법 과거완료. 가정법 과거완료의 조건절 「if + 주어 + had p.p.」가 있어야 하나, if가 없으므로 주어와 동사가 도치된 구조

2. Poznaski Renovation은 마감기한을 맞추기 위해 추가적인 작업 일수가 필요할 경우 초기 견적가보다 더 많은 비용을 청구할 것이다.
해설 가정법 미래 「if + 주어 + should 동사원형」에서 if가 생략되어 「should + 주어 + 동사원형」으로 도치된 문장. 접속사 when 뒤에는 「주어 + 동사」가 와야 하는데 시제 반영이 안된 동사원형 be가 있기 때문에 오답

Q8   **1. have we**   **2. Enclosed**   **3. should utility bills**

1. 이렇게 훌륭한 서비스는 어디에서도 경험해본 적 없습니다.

해설 부정어 never가 문두에 위치한 도치 구문

2. 교육을 위해 요청하신 자료가 동봉되어 있습니다.

해설 are의 보어가 문두에 온 도치 구문. be동사 앞 명사를 주어로 혼동할 수 있으나 해석을 통해 오답임을 파악할 수 있음

3. 임대료는 매월 10일까지 지불되어야 하며 공과금도 마찬가지다.

해설 긍정문 뒤에 so가 문두에 위치한 도치 구문

Practice

본서 p.162

1. (B)	**2.** (D)	**3.** (A)	**4.** (D)	**5.** (C)
6. (A)	**7.** (D)	**8.** (A)	**9.** (B)	**10.** (D)
11. (B)	**12.** (D)	**13.** (C)	**14.** (A)	**15.** (B)
16. (B)	**17.** (A)	**18.** (D)	**19.** (B)	**20.** (B)

1. 주식 시장이 붕괴한 이래로 소비자들은 가능한 한 신중하게 주식을 매각하도록 요청받았다.

해설 as와 as 사이이므로 형용사의 원급 (A)와 부사의 원급 (B) 중에 알맞은 품사를 선택해야 한다. '주식을 신중하게 매각하다'의 해석에 따라 부사 (B) cautiously가 정답이다.

어휘 collapse 붕괴하다 | cautious 신중한, 주의하는

2. 설문조사 결과에 따르면 소비자들은 APX Orange 스마트폰의 새 기능에 대하여 예상보다 훨씬 더 호의적인 반응을 보였다.

해설 빈칸은 「자동사 + 전치사」 사이의 부사 자리이며, 뒤에 than이 있으므로 부사의 비교급인 (D) more favorably가 정답이다.

어휘 questionnaire 설문지 | favorable 호의적인 | feature 특색, 특징, 특성

3. 우리 호텔 투숙 기간 동안에 손님들의 불만사항들을 알았더라면, 우리는 다른 방으로 옮겨주겠다는 제안을 했을 것이다.

해설 Had we been ~ 은 「had + 주어 + p.p.」 형태의 가정법 과거완료 도치구문이므로, 주절에는 「would have p.p.」 형태가 와야 하며, 호텔은 제안을 하는 주체이므로 능동의 (A) would have offered가 정답이다.

어휘 be aware of ~을 알다

4. 향후 며칠 후에 공지되어야 하는 현재 가능한 일자리들에 대한 설명들이 첨부되어 있다.

해설 「Attached/Enclosed/Included + is[are] + 주어」 (주어가 첨부/동봉/포함되다) 구문을 묻는 문제이므로 (D) Attached가 정답이다.

어휘 description 기술, 설명, (말에 의한) 묘사

5. 성능에 대해 실험된 공기 청정기들 중에서 그 제품들의 제조업체가 주장했던 것만큼 효과적이라 판명된 것은 거의 없었다.

해설 빈칸 앞에 'as 형용사'가 쓰인 것으로 봐서 'as~as 비교급」이므로 동급 비교를 만드는 (C) as가 정답이다.

어휘 air purifier 공기 청정기 | capacity 성능, 기능 | turn out to부정사 ~한 것으로 판명되다 | claim ~을 주장하다

6. 비즈니스 언어는 일상 대화에서 쓰이는 말보다 더 기술적이며 형식적이기 때문에, 통역자가 필요한지 아닌지를 결정하세요.

해설 빈칸 앞에 「more + 형용사」의 비교급이 쓰였으므로 비교하는 대상 앞에 쓰는 (A) than이 정답이다.

어휘 formal 형식에 얽매인, 공식의 | interpreter 통역자

7. 최첨단 장비의 도움으로, 매니저는 직원들이 훨씬 더 효율적으로 일할 것으로 기대하고 있다.

해설 빈칸 앞에 비교급을 수식하는 부사 much가 쓰였으므로 (D) more efficiently를 쓴다.

어휘 with the help of ~의 도움으로 | state-of-the-art 최첨단의 | equipment 장비

8. 어떠한 기밀서류도 메신저, 문자 메시지 그리고 이메일과 같은 회사 내 연락망에 의해 절대 배포되어서는 안 된다.

해설 부정의 부사가 문장의 맨 앞에 오는 경우 주어 동사의 어순이 바뀌는 도치구문이 가능하기 때문에 부정의 부사 (A) Never가 정답이다.

어휘 interoffice correspondence 사내 연락망

9. 지역 매니저 직책의 모든 지원자들 중에서, Jennifer Lee가 분명히 그 자리에 가장 자격이 있다.

해설 빈칸 뒤에 복수 명사가 쓰였고, 문장에 최상급이 쓰였으므로 '~중에서'라는 의미의 (B) Of가 정답이다.

어휘 regional manager 지역 매니저 | obviously 분명히 | qualified for ~에 대한 자격이 갖춰진

10. 마케팅 부서의 열 명의 직원 중 Mr. Watters가 표적 시장에 대해 가장 잘 알고 있다.
고난도

해설 '~중에서'의 의미를 갖는 전치사 of를 보고 the 뒤에 최상급을 생각한다면 쉽게 문제를 해결할 수 있다. 다만, the 뒤에 명사가 정답이라고 생각하여 보기 (B)를 정답으로 할 수 있는데, the 뒤에 형용사의 최상급이 올 때 그 뒤의 명사는 생략될 수 있다는 점에 유의하여 문맥에 적합한 형용사의 최상급 (D) most knowledgeable을 정답으로 해야 한다.

어휘 knowledgeable 아는 것이 많은, 잘 아는

11. 제휴 프로그램에 관하여 추가 질문이 있으시다면 발표가 끝난 후 주저말고 물어봐 주세요.
고난도

해설 추가질문이 있으면 질문하라는 문맥에 따라, 가정법 미래 도치구문인 「should + 주어 + 동사원형」 구조를 묻는 문제이다. 따라서 정답은 (B) Should이다. 전치사인 (C)는 뒤에 「주어 + 동사」의 절을 이끌 수 없으며, 접속사인 (A), (D)는 뒤에 '주어 + 동사'의 절을 이끌 수 있으

나, 문맥상 적합하지 않아 오답이다.

어휘 **affiliate** 계열사, 제휴

12. 직원들이 안전 예방 조치들을 좀 더 신중하게 따랐더라면, 사고들이 그렇게 자주 발생하지 않았을 것이다.

해설 if와 had followed로 봐서 가정법 과거완료의 문장이므로, 주절에는 「조동사의 과거형 + have + 과거분사」의 형태인 (D) would not have happened가 정답이다.

어휘 **follow** ~을 따르다 **| safety precaution** 안전 예방 조치 **| frequently** 자주

13. Ms. Anderson은 지난 가을 승진 이후 빠르게 회사의 가장 유능한 부서 관리자들 중 한 명이 되었다.

해설 빈칸은 명사 'division supervisors'를 수식하는 형용사이며, '가장 유능한 관리자 중 하나'라는 의미에 따라 최상급인 (C) most competent가 정답이다.

어휘 **competent** 유능한

14. 광고 이사는 목요일에 이사회에 참석할 수 없는데, 마케팅 담당 이사도 역시 참석할 수 없다.

해설 부정문이 나온 뒤에 부정어 neither가 나오면 그 뒤에 주어와 (조)동사의 어순이 바뀌는 도치가 발생하므로 정답은 (A) neither이다. neither는 부사로 두 문장을 연결하는 접속사 기능이 없기 때문에, 두 문장을 연결하는 접속사 and와 함께 쓰였다.

어휘 **participate in** ~에 참석하다 **| board meeting** 이사회

15. 지속적인 매출 하락을 고려해 볼 때, Pure Skin은 시장에서 더 이상 주요한 화장품 공급업체가 아니다.

해설 비교의 관용 표현 중 'no longer (더 이상~아니다)'를 묻는 문제로 정답은 (B)이다. 문장에 부정어가 있다면 (C) anymore도 정답일 수 있으나 부정어가 없기 때문에 오답이다.

어휘 **decline** 하락, 감소 **| primary** 주된, 주요한

16. 최근에야 비로소 그 회사의 건축가들은 신규 공장에 대해 제안된 서포트 빔 변경사항들을 검토 평가했다.

해설 「Only + 부사(구)」가 문두에 나오는 경우 뒷부분이 도치되어야 하며, 도치되는 문장의 동사가 「have + p.p.」 형인 경우 「have + 주어 + p.p.」 형태가 되므로 (B) assessed가 정답이다.

어휘 **assess** 평가하다 **| modification** 변경, 수정

17. 조선업이 이 지역에서는 가장 큰 사업이며, 그것은 2만 개 이상의 일자리를 창출했다.

해설 the와 최상급 사이에서 최상급을 강조하는 (A) single이 정답이다.

어휘 **shipbuilding industry** 조선업

18. Ms. Brook이 면접했던 아홉 명의 지원자들 중에서, Mr. Sanders가 가장 자질이 뛰어나다.
고난도

해설 the 뒤에 명사가 없으므로 그 앞에 최상급이 오고 명사가 생략된 구조임을 파악해야 한다. 최상급과 함께 오는 among도 단서가 된다. 따라

서 부사 highly의 최상급이 되려면 필요한 (D) most가 정답이다.

어휘 **candidate** 지원자 **| qualified** 자질 있는

19. Damaso 자동차 회사와의 합병이 성공을 거두었더라면 Ms.
고난도 Williams는 Wyn 자동차 부사장 자리에서 사퇴했을 것이다.

해설 had the merger with Damaso Automobile Company succeeded는 「had + 주어 + p.p.」 형태의 가정법 과거 완료 도치구문으로, 주절에는 would have p.p.형태가 와야 하므로, (B) would have relinquished가 정답이다. 해석과 함께 보기가 모두 동사이고, 뒷문장에 had가 있어 동사가 둘이나, 접속사나 관계사 없다는 점에서 가정법 if가 생략된 구조임을 추론하는 문제이다. 이처럼 가정법 과거 완료 도치구문이 문장의 뒤에 위치하는 경우는 매우 어려운 난이도 문제에 속한다.

어휘 **relinquish** (지위·직 따위를) 사퇴하다

20. 품질 기준이 충족된 후에야 비로소 그 전자회사는 신상품을 대량생산
고난도 하기 시작했다.

해설 Only after ~가 문두에 나오는 경우 뒷부분이 도치되어야 하며, 도치되는 문장의 동사가 일반 동사인 경우 「do[does, did] + 주어 + 동사원형」 형태가 되므로 (B) begin이 정답이다.

어휘 **quality standard** 품질 기준 **| mass produce** 대량생산하다

REVIEW TEST 05 본서 p.164

1. (B)	2. (B)	3. (D)	4. (D)	5. (B)
6. (B)	7. (C)	8. (D)	9. (D)	10. (A)
11. (C)	12. (B)	13. (C)	14. (C)	15. (C)
16. (B)	17. (D)	18. (A)	19. (C)	20. (C)

1. 우리는 당신에게 국내에서 가장 선택의 폭이 넓은 초콜릿을 제공하는 것을 목표로 합니다.

해설 빈칸 앞의 the와 범위를 한정하는 전치사구 in the country를 힌트로 빈칸에는 형용사의 최상급 형태가 적절하다는 사실을 알 수 있다. 따라서 (B) widest가 정답이다.

어휘 **aim to** ~하는 것을 목표로 하다 **| selection** 엄선된 것, 선정

2. Mandalu 지역의 평균 기온은 거의 10년 동안 이 정도로 높지는 않았다.

해설 빈칸은 원급 형용사 high 앞에 오는 부사 자리이다. this/that은 대명사, 형용사, 부사로 쓰이며, this가 부사일 때 'this + 형용사' 형태로 '이 정도로 ~한'의 의미를 지닌다. (A) much는 원급이 아닌 비교급 앞에 위치하여 비교급 강조 역할을 하므로, 원급 형용사 high앞에 쓰일 수 없고(much higher ⭕, much high ❌), (D) more는 2음절 이상의 긴 형용사를 비교급으로 만드는 기능을 하므로, 형용사 high 앞에 쓸 수 없다 (more expensive ⭕, more high ❌). (C) how는 'how + 형용사/부사' 형태의 의문사로 쓰일 경우 뒤에 '주어 + 동사' 구조를 수반하므로 오답이다. 따라서 정답은 (B) this이다.

어휘 **decade** 10년

3. IPA는 확장하는 것을 고려하고 있으며 플로리다에 상점을 가지고 있는 추가 소매업자를 찾을 것이다.

해설 빈칸은 형용사 additional의 수식을 받는 명사 자리이므로 '소매업자'를 뜻하는 (D) retailer가 정답이다.

어휘 expand 확대하다, 확장하다 | look for 찾다 | additional 추가의 | retailer 소매업자

4. Janti's 식당은 엄격한 식품 안전 기준을 충족하기 위해 정기적으로 점검을 실시한다.

해설 빈칸은 복합명사로 쓰인 food safety standards를 수식하는 형용사 자리이므로 (D) rigorous가 정답이다.

어휘 conduct (특정한 활동을) 하다 | inspection 점검, 조사 | on a regular basis 정기적으로 | make sure 반드시 ~하다 | meet 충족시키다 | food safety standard 식품 안전 기준

5. 저희는 시판되는 다른 어떤 제품보다 훨씬 더 비용 효율적인 저희의 신제품을 자랑스럽게 소개합니다.

해설 빈칸 뒤에 other과 어울리는 수량 표시어를 쓸 자리로 (B) any가 정답이다. 「비교급 + than any other」(그 밖의 다른 어떤 ~보다 더 …하다) 패턴을 기억해두자.

어휘 proudly 자랑스럽게 | merchandise 상품

6. 병원에서 가장 경험이 많은 의사들조차 매년 의학 학회에 참석하도록 요구된다.

해설 경험 많은 의사들조차 학회에 매년 참석을 요구 받는다는 문맥이 적절하므로 (B) Even이 정답이다. (C) Although는 종속절을 이끄는 접속사로 빈칸 뒤에 주어, 동사가 연결되어 있다 하더라도, 그 뒤에 주절이 있어야 한다.

어휘 physician (내과)의사 | require 요구하다, 필요로 하다 | attend 참석하다 | medical 의학의

7. 대부분의 소비자들은 GXT 2000 모델이 사용하기 쉽다는 것을 알겠지만, 스마트폰에 덜 친숙한 사람들은 사용 설명서를 먼저 주의 깊게 읽어야 한다.
고난도

해설 비교급 대명사를 뒤에서 수식하는 형용사 familiar를 수식할 부사가 필요한 자리로 GXT 2000을 사용하기 쉽다고 생각하는 소비자들보다 스마트폰을 잘 모르는 사람들은 사용서 설명서를 잘 읽어야 한다는 의미가 자연스러우므로 '덜'이라는 의미의 little의 비교급 (C) less가 정답이다.

어휘 familiar with …에 친숙한 | manual 설명서

8. Moa 화장품은 고품질의 저렴한 피부 관리 제품들을 소비자들이 더 손쉽게 이용할 수 있도록 노력을 한다.

해설 동사 make가 목적어와 목적보어를 이끄는 5형식 문장으로 빈칸은 형용사 available을 수식하는 부사 (D) readily가 정답이다.

어휘 strive to 노력하다, 힘쓰다 | high-quality 고품질의

9. Comfort 전자는 경영진이 전에 예상했던 것보다 더 많은 변화들을 겪고 있다.

해설 비교급 기본 형태 빈칸 앞에 more와 짝을 이뤄 비교급을 만들 (D) than이 정답이다.

어휘 go through 겪다

10. 저희가 판매하는 상품에 만족하지 못하신다면 즉시 다른 것으로 교체하거나 돈을 환불해 드리겠습니다.

해설 '구매한 상품을 다른 상품으로 바꾸다'라는 문맥이다. one은 product을 대신하는 명사이며 '또 다른 하나의'라는 의미의 한정사 another가 수식하는 것이 적합하므로 (A) another가 정답이다.

어휘 be satisfied with ~에 만족하다 | promptly 즉시 | replace A with B A를 B로 대체하다, 교체하다 | refund 환불하다

11. GTX Mart에 지원하실 때, 여러분은 직접 사무실로 방문하여 지원하시거나 온라인 상으로 입사 지원서를 제출하시는 선택권이 있습니다.

해설 상관접속사의 경우 두 개의 접속사가 한 문장에서 함께 사용되는 경우이므로 빈칸 이외의 문장에서 사용된 접속사를 찾으면 정답을 쉽게 선택할 수 있다. 빈칸 뒤에 전치사 or가 있으므로 'visiting the office and applying in person' 또는 'submitting a job application online' 둘 중에 한 가지 방법을 선택해서 지원할 수 있다라는 내용임을 알 수 있다. 따라서 정답은 (C) either이다.

어휘 apply to 신청하다, 지원하다 | have the option of ~의 선택권이 있다 | either A or B A 또는 B | in person 직접, 본인 스스로 | not only A but (also) B A뿐만 아니라 B도 | neither A nor B A도 B도 아닌 | both A and B A와 B 둘 다

12. Burmese 출장연회 회사의 수석 주방장은 가장 품질이 우수한 재료들만이 Imperial 호텔의 연회에 사용될 것임을 시사했다.

해설 명사구 'the highest-quality ingredients'를 수식하여 '가장 품질이 우수한 재료들만이'란 의미를 완성하는 강조부사 (B) only가 정답이다.

어휘 indicate 보여주다 | ingredient 재료 | banquet 연회

13. Criogenic의 많은 국내 산하 회사들 중 가장 수익성 있는 곳은 시카고에 본사를 둔 Virtel 사이다.
고난도

해설 빈칸을 정관사 the 뒤의 명사 자리로 판단하여, 명사 (A) profits나 (B) profit를 선택할 수 있는데, 이 보기들이 정답일 경우 '이득=시카고 기반의 Virtel 회사'라는 의미가 되어 문맥상 적절하지 못하다. 빈칸은 관사 뒤의 명사 자리이기도 하지만, 최상급 뒤의 명사는 생략 가능하다는 문법에 기초하여 빈칸을 최상급의 형용사 자리로 파악할 수 있어야 한다. 즉, 빈칸에 형용사 profitable을 넣어 최상급 the most profitable이 되면 이 문장 내에서 의미가 명확한 명사인 subsidiary를 생략할 수 있게 된다. 이 경우 '가장 수익성 있는 (자회사는)'이란 의미가 되어 문맥상으로 적합하다. 따라서, 정답은 형용사 (C) profitable이다.

어휘 domestic 국내의 | subsidiary 산하 회사, 자회사 | profitable 수익성 있는, 이윤을 창출하는

14. 지원자들은 자신들이 가장 열심히 일했던 프로젝트와 시작하기를 고대하는 프로젝트에 대해 말하도록 요구 받았다.

해설 빈칸은 동사 worked를 수식하는 부사 자리인데, 빈칸 앞에 the가 있으므로 이와 함께 동사를 수식하는 최상급 표현이 필요하다는 사실을 알 수 있다. 최상급인 hardest가 와서 '가장 열심히 일한 프로젝트'라는 의미가 적절하므로 (C) hardest가 정답이다.

어휘 candidate 지원자, 응시자 | look forward to ~ing ~하기를 고대하다 | hardly 거의 ~하지 않는

15. 여배우 Wilma Bernhoff의 경력은 독일의 한 지역 텔레비전 쇼 출연과 함께 시작되었다.

해설 여배우 Wilma Bernhoff의 경력이 어떤 쇼의 출현과 '함께' 시작되었다는 내용이므로 전치사 (C) with가 정답이다.

어휘 career 경력 | actress 여배우 | appearance 출현, 출연, 등장

16. 기상청은 오늘밤과 일요일 아침 사이에 거의 2인치 가량의 비가 내릴 것으로 예측하고 있다.

해설 빈칸을 제외한 문장은 어법상 하자가 없는 완벽한 문장이고, 빈칸 뒤에는 '수량을 나타내는 표현' two inches of rain이 있으므로 빈칸에는 이를 수식하는 부사가 필요하다는 사실을 알 수 있다. 문맥상 '거의 2인치에 달하는' 비가 온다는 내용이므로 '대략'을 뜻하는 부사 (B) approximately가 정답이다.

어휘 meteorological department 기상청 | forecast 예보하다, 예측하다 | approximately 대략, 거의(nearly) | between A and B A와 B 사이에 | approximate 대략의, 거의 정확한, 근사치인 | approximation 근사치

17. 그 소프트웨어 개발자들은 최근에 대다수의 사용자들에게 너무 복잡한 프로그램을 만들었다.
고난도

해설 빈칸은 「부사 + 형용사」인 too complex를 수식하는 부사 자리이다. '훨씬'이라는 의미의 부사로 too를 수식하므로 (D) far가 정답이다. too를 수식하는 부사에는 far, much, simply 등이 있다.

어휘 developer 개발자 | create 만들다, 창조하다 | complex 복잡한 | majority 대다수의

18. 노령화 인구가 지속적으로 증가함과 더불어 보건 전문가와 재택 간호 시설에 대한 수요도 증가한다.
고난도

해설 콤마 뒤의 절에 동사가 보이지 않으므로 동사가 주어 앞으로 도치된 구문임을 알 수 있다. 문맥상 앞 절의 동사 continues to grow를 받아서 '~또한 증가한다'라는 의미가 되어야 하므로 (A) so does가 정답이다.

어휘 aging population 노령화 인구 | demand 수요 | healthcare worker 보건 전문가 | residential care 재택 간호 | facility 시설, 기관

19. 우리 회사는 지속적인 성장을 위해 지금보다 더 강력하고 목적에 맞게 배치된 적이 없었다.

해설 문맥상 동사의 현재완료형 has been의 부정형을 만드는 부사가 필요하다. '한번도 ~않다'라는 의미의 부정문을 만드는 부사 (C) never가 정답이다.

어휘 position (특정 위치에) 배치하다, (특정 목적을 위해) 시장에 내놓다 | sustained 지속된, 한결같은 | growth 성장

20. 그들이 신제품을 출시하자마자 매출이 두 배 이상 증가했다.
고난도

해설 문두에 쓰인 비교급 No sooner와 짝을 이루는 (C) than이 정답이다. 「no sooner than + 동사 + 주어」 패턴과 같이 부정의 부사구가 문두에 쓰이면 주어와 동사가 도치되는 구조를 기억해 두자.

어휘 release 출시하다

PART 5 – VOCA

UNIT 01. 동사

본서 p.168

Q1 1. register   2. respond

1. 디자인 부서에서 근무하는 직원들은 워크숍에 등록하기 위해 Kent Abone에게 연락해야 한다.

2. Local Business Association의 변호사들은 최근에 수정된 계약서에 관한 모든 질문들에 답할 것이다.

Q2 1. extend   2. obtain   3. invented

1. 마감일을 연장하는 결정은 기업 우선순위를 면밀히 조사하고 나서 내려졌다.

2. 공사 허가를 얻는데 필요한 서류들을 부동산 개발업자가 현재 모으고 있다.

3. Helicon 전자의 선임 엔지니어인 Mr. Hahn은 여러 획기적인 커뮤니케이션 기구들을 발명했다.

Q3 1. conducted   2. reserved

1. 우리 광고 캠페인에 어떤 변화를 줄지 결정하기 위한 고객 설문조사가 행해질 것이다.

2. Freshwater 호텔의 모든 회의실이 이번 주말에 예약되어서 우리 회사 연회를 위해 다른 장소를 찾아야 한다.

Practice

본서 p.174

1. (B)	2. (A)	3. (C)	4. (C)	5. (D)
6. (A)	7. (C)	8. (C)	9. (D)	10. (C)
11. (B)	12. (D)	13. (A)	14. (C)	15. (C)
16. (A)	17. (B)	18. (A)	19. (B)	20. (D)

1. Mr. Fujimori는 일정이 맞지 않아 영업 회의를 연기하기로 결정했다.

해설 the sales meeting을 목적어로 취하는 타동사 중, '일정이 맞지 않음'을 의미하는 a scheduling conflict 와 어울리는 동사는 (B) postpone이다.

어휘 sales meeting 영업회의 I conflict 충돌 I evaluate 평가하다 I postpone 연기하다 I identify 분간(식별)하다 I promote (판매를) 촉진시키다, 홍보하다

2. 국립 동물원 방문 중 동물들에게 먹이 주는 것을 자제해 주십시오.
고난도
해설 빈칸 뒤 전치사 from을 수반하면서 '동물에게 먹이 주는 것을 ------

'주십시오'에 어울리는 동사는 (A) refrain(삼가다)이다.

어휘 refrain from -ing ~하는 것을 삼가다 I feed ~에게 음식을 주다 I emerge 나타나다 I prohibit A from B A가 B하는 것을 금지하다 I differ from ~와 다르다

3. 진행 중인 실험실 수리 작업으로 인해, 별도로 통보될 때까지 해당 시
고난도 설물에 들어가지 마시기 바랍니다.

해설 문맥상 '별도로 -------될 때까지'에 어울리는 동사는 (C) notified이다. 또한 이 문제는 be동사 뒤의 과거분사 자리에 알맞은 동사 어휘를 선택하는 유형이므로, 수동태의 주어가 능동태에서 타동사의 목적어임을 단서로 능동태로 전환하여 해석하면 명확하게 정답을 선택할 수 있다. '~을 깨닫다'의 의미를 지닌 (A) realized, '~을 찾다'의 의미를 지닌 (B) searched, '~을 성취하다'의 의미를 지닌 (D) achieved가 능동태 동사일 때 수동태 주어인 you를 목적어로 취한다면, 의미상 적절하지 못하므로 오답이다. 하지만, 통보의 대상을 목적어로 취하는 타동사 (C) notified는, 수동태 주어인 you를 목적어로 취해 '당신에게 통보하다'라는 적절한 의미를 나타내므로 정답이다.

어휘 ongoing 진행 중인 I repair 수리 작업 I laboratory 실험실 I facility 시설

4. 마감 기한을 맞추기 위해 얼마나 급히 프로젝트를 완성해야만 했는지를 고려한다면 Harrison 교수님의 업적은 인상적이다.

해설 '마감 기한을 맞추기 위해 얼마나 급히 프로젝트를 ------- 했는지를 고려한다면'에 어울리는 단어는 (C) complete(완성하다)이다.

어휘 impressive 인상적인 I hastily 급히, 서둘러서 I meet the deadline 마감 기한을 맞추다 I qualify 자격을 갖추다 I entitle 자격을 주다 I complete 완성하다 I attend 참석하다

5. 아파트 단지 내 모든 주민들에게 흡연을 금지하는 새로운 규정이 이제 막 만장일치로 통과되었다.

해설 '아파트 단지 내 모든 주민들에게 흡연을 -------하는'에 어울리는 동사는 (D) prohibits(금지하다)이다.

어휘 regulation 규정 I resident 주민 I apartment complex 아파트 단지 I pass 통과시키다 I unanimously 만장일치로 I alienate 소원하게 만들다 I prohibit A from B A가 B하는 것을 금지하다

6. 우리가 어제 요청했던 견적서를 이미 받아서, 우리는 다음 단계로 좀 더 빠르게 진척할 수 있다.

해설 '우리가 어제 요청했던 견적서를 이미 받아서, 우리는 다음 단계로 좀 더 빠르게 -------할 수 있다'에 어울리는 어휘는 (A) proceed(진척하다)이다.

어휘 estimate 견적서 I request ~을 요청하다 I proceed 진척하다 I impress 감명시키다 I depend ~에 달려 있다. 의존하다 I support 지원[지지]하다

7. 환경친화적인 제품들에 대한 증가하는 수요를 충족시키기 위해 McKane 사는 환경친화적인 세탁 세제를 개발하고 있다.

해설 환경친화적인 세탁 세제를 개발하는 이유가 들어가야 하는 문맥이므로 '수요를 충족시키기 위해'라는 의미를 만들어 주는 (C) accommodate(수용하다)가 정답이다.

어휘 **demand for** ~에 대한 수요 l **environmentally-friendly** 환경친화적인 l **eco-friendly** 환경친화적인 l **laundry detergent** 세탁 세제 l **exchange** 교환하다 l **predict** 예측하다 l **accommodate** 수용하다, 부응하다 l **justify** 정당화하다

8. 새로운 프로젝트를 시작하기 전에 각 팀원의 역할과 책임을 명확히 하는 것이 팀을 위해 좋다.

해설 '새로운 프로젝트를 시작하기 전에 팀원의 역할과 책임을 ------ 것이 좋다'에 어울리는 어휘는 '~를 명확하게 하다'를 뜻하는 (C) clarify이다.

어휘 **role** 역할 l **responsibility** 책임 l **conduct** 수행하다 l **respond** 반응하다, 응답하다 l **clarify** 명확하게 하다 l **conform** 순응하다

9. Borrester 마케팅사의 모든 직원들과 그들의 가족들은 한 달에 한 번 열리는 Borrester 영화의 밤에 초대된다.

해설 '무비 나잇에 참석하다'에 어울리는 어휘는 (C) attend와 (D) participate이다. Participate는 in과 함께 쓰여 '~에 참석하다'로 쓰이므로 정답은 타동사로 쓰이는 (C) attend이다.

어휘 **family member** 가족 구성원 l **take place** 발생하다, 일어나다 l **specialize** 전문으로 하다 l **admit** 시인하다 l **attend** 참석하다 l **participate** 참석하다

10. Kerry's Megamart의 관리자들은 발생할 수 있는 그 어떠한 직원 문제도 해결할 것으로 기대된다.

해설 '관리자들이 직원 문제들을 ------ 것으로 기대된다'에 어울리는 동사는 (C) resolve(해결하다)가 적절하다.

어휘 **expect** 기대하다, 예상하다 l **issue** 문제 l **arise** 발생하다, 생기다 l **set** 정하다; 맞추다 l **resolve** 해결하다; 다짐하다 l **wonder** 궁금하다

11. 저명한 패션 디자이너 Peter Simpson은 최근 새로운 냉장고를 고안하기 위해 Eder 가전과 협력했다.

해설 빈칸 뒤에 있는 전치사 with와 함께 쓰이는 자동사를 찾아야 한다. with를 수반하여 '~와 협력하다'로 쓰이는 (B) collaborated가 정답이다.

어휘 **renowned** 유명한, 명성이 있는 l **recently** 최근에 l **refrigerator** 냉장고 l **employ** 고용하다 l **collaborate** 협력하다 l **offer** 제공하다 l **retire** 은퇴하다

12. 인사 책임자가 확장된 휴게실 디자인들을 검토하고 CEO에게 제출할 디자인을 선택할 것이다.

해설 빈칸 뒤의 목적어 one은 앞에 나온 디자인들 중 하나를 의미하므로, '~에 제출할 디자인을 ------할 것이다'라는 해석에 어울리는 동사는, 선택의 의미를 지닌 (D) choose이다. (A) agree는 뒤에 목적어를 취할 때 전치사를 취해야 하는 자동사이므로 오답이다.

어휘 **review** 검토하다 l **break room** 휴게실 l **submit** 제출하다 l **operate** 운영하다 l **apply** 지원하다

13. 지난 10년 넘게, Ms. Sharma는 동료들에게 판매팀 중에서도 특히 소중한 구성원으로 인정받아 왔다.

해설 Ms. Sharma는 동료들에게 판매팀 중에서도 특히 소중한 구성원으로 ------해왔다'에 어울리는 어휘는 (A) recognized(인정받는)이다.

어휘 **recognized** 인정받는 l **exceptionally** 특별히 l **valuable** 소중한, 가치 있는 l **sales team** 판매팀 l **colleague** 동료 l **be accustomed to** ~에 익숙해지다 l **resign** 사임하다 l **implemented** 시행된

14. Xia 자동차는 시장점유율 증가를 GX 자동차의 인수 덕분으로 생각한다.
고난도

해설 빈칸 뒤가 A to B의 구조로 되어 있으며 의미상으로도 원인을 나타내는 표현이 나와야 자연스러우므로 (D) attributes A to B(A를 B의 덕분으로 보다)가 정답이다.

어휘 **market share** 시장 점유율 l **acquisition** 인수 l **randomize** 무작위로 순서를 정하다 l **account** 설명하다 l **assume** 가정하다, 추측하다 l **attribute A to B** A를 B의 덕분으로 보다

15. 위원회는 도시 컨벤션 센터 옆에 상당히 큰 경기장을 건설하기를 원하고난도 는 개발업자와 맺은 잠정적인 합의를 지지하기 위해 투표했다.

해설 '개발업자와 맺은 잠정적인 합의를 ~하기 위해 투표했다'라고 했으므로 빈칸에 들어갈 가장 어울리는 동사는 (C) endorse(지지하다)이다.

어휘 **committee** 위원회 l **tentative agreement** 잠정적인 합의 l **developer** 개발업자 l **fairly** 상당히, 꽤 l **justify** 정당화하다 l **elevate** 올리다 l **endorse** 지지하다 l **obtain** 얻다

16. 전화 예약 시스템이 오늘 부로 중단되어서 모든 환자들은 이메일을 통해 예약을 잡아야 한다.

해설 '전화 예약 시스템이 오늘 부로 중단되어서 모든 환자들은 이메일을 통해 예약을 ------ 해야 한다'에 해석상 어울리는 동사는 (A) arrange(약속 등을 주선하다)이다.

어휘 **discontinue** 중단하다 l **as of** ~시점 부로 l **patient** 환자 l **appointment** 예약 l **via** ~를 통해 l **arrange** (일정, 약속 등) 처리하다, 마련하다 l **convince** 확신시키다 l **instruct** ~에게 지시하다

17. Prix 사의 경영진은 더 탄력적인 근무 스케줄을 장려함으로써 직원들의 스트레스를 낮추기를 원한다.

해설 'Prix 사의 경영진은 더 탄력적인 근무 스케줄을 장려함으로써 직원들의 스트레스를 ------ 하기를 원한다'에 어울리는 어휘는 (B) lower(낮추다)이다. 참고로 refrain은 from과 함께 쓰이는 자동사이다.

어휘 **enhance** (좋은 점, 가치, 지위를) 높이다 l **lower** 낮추다 l **dedicate** 전념하다, 헌신하다 l **refrain from** ~를 삼가다

18. 35주년 기념 시상식에서 Ms. Moon은 20년 넘게 회사에 헌신을 보여준 것에 대해서 예우되었다.

해설 목적어 dedication과 어울리면서 전체 해석에도 맞는 어휘를 골라 줘야 한다. '20년 넘게 회사에 헌신을 ------ 것에 대해서 예우되었다'에 어울리는 어휘는 (A) demonstrated(보여주었다)이다.

어휘 **anniversary** 기념일 l **ceremony** 시상식, 수여식 l **dedication** 헌신 l **demonstrate** 보여주다 l **collaborate** 협력하다 l **grant** 허가하다 l **explain** 설명하다

19. 인사과 대표자는 업무 수행 평가에 대한 우려 사항을 다루기 위해 직
고난도 원들과 만나기로 예정되어 있다.

해설 빈칸 뒤의 목적어 concerns와 어울려 '우려 사항을 다루다, 해결하다'
라고 해야 문맥상 적절하므로, (B) address가 정답이다.

어휘 representative 대표자, 직원 | human resources
department 인사과 | be scheduled to ~할 예정이다 |
employee 직원 | concerns 우려 사항 | relating to ~와 관련된 |
performance appraisals 업무 수행 평가 | comment 논평하
다, 견해를 밝히다 | address (문제, 상황 등에 대해) 다루다, 해결하다 |
enhance 향상시키다 | observe 관찰하다, 준수하다

20. 선발된 지원자들의 지원 서류들이 검토되고 나면, 그들은 면접에 초대
될 것이다.

해설 문맥상 '선발된 지원자들이 면접에 ------- 될 것이다'에 어울리는 동
사는 (D) invited이다. 만약 나머지 보기와 정답의 구분이, 위와 같은
해석으로 명확하지 않는다면, 수동태의 주어가 능동태에서 타동사의
목적어임을 활용하면 보다 정확한 정답을 선택할 수 있다. 즉, 위 빈칸
부분을 능동태로 바꿔 '면접을 위해 선발된 지원자들을 -------할 것이
다'로 해석하면, 보다 정확하게 타동사 invite를 고를 수 있다. 이 문제
에서처럼 be동사 뒤의 과거분사 자리에 알맞은 동사 어휘를 선택하는
유형은, 능동태로 전환하여 해석하면 명확하게 정답을 선택할 수 있다.

어휘 review 검토하다 | selected 선발된 | candidate 지원자 | state 진
술하다 | signal 신호를 알리다

UNIT 02. 명사

본서 p.176

Q1 1. variety 2. compliance

1. Office Supplies는 여러분의 필요에 맞는 다양한 스타일과 크기의
컴퓨터 책상을 판매합니다.

2. 공장들의 안전 규정 준수 확인을 위해 무작위 검사가 시행된다.

Q2 1. responsibility 2. consensus 3. identification

1. 여행 비용과 컨퍼런스 비용은 광고사가 지불할 것이지만, 식대는 참
가자 부담입니다.

2. 몇몇 전문가들이 실업에 대해 우려하지만 일반적인 의견은 올해 경
제가 개선될 것으로 보는 듯하다.

3. 건물 내에 있을 때, 당신의 신분증이 항상 잘 보이도록 해 주십시오.

Q3 1. receipt 2. efficiency

1. 이 계좌로 전액 지불 수취를 확인하는 이 이메일에 답장해주세요.

2. Alfine Technology Group은 고객 마케팅 활동의 효율성을 강화
하기 위해 노력한다.

Q4 1. effort 2. facilities

1. 종이를 아끼기 위한 노력의 일환으로 가능할 때마다 양면 복사를 해
주세요.

2. Preenz 산업의 모든 직원들은 헬스클럽과 같은 회사 시설을 무료로
사용할 수 있습니다.

Practice

본서 p.182

1. (C)	2. (C)	3. (D)	4. (B)	5. (C)
6. (D)	7. (C)	8. (C)	9. (D)	10. (B)
11. (C)	12. (D)	13. (A)	14. (C)	15. (A)
16. (A)	17. (C)	18. (C)	19. (A)	20. (A)

1. 모든 자원 근로자 가족들에게는 음악 축제 입장료가 무료이다.

해설 빈칸 뒤의 전치사 to 와 함께 하며, 문맥상 '피트니스 센터에 -------
입장이 무료다'에 어울리는 명사는 (C) Admission이다.

어휘 free 무료의 | volunteer 자원 봉사자; 자원하다 | preparation 준
비 | insertion 삽입 | admission (to) ~에 입장 | imposition
(세금, 의무 등을) 부과, 과하기

2. 그래픽 디자인 팀원들은 곧 있을 워크숍 참석이 권장된다.

해설 타동사 attend 를 단서로 문맥상 '다가오는 -------에 참석하도록'에
어울리는 명사는 (C) workshop이다.

어휘 encourage 권장하다, 장려하다 | upcoming 곧 있을, 다가오는 |
subject 주제, 교과 | division 분할, 부서

3. 이 그림들에 관한 문의 사항들은 그 박물관에서 18세기 미술의 선두적
인 권위자인 Ms. Kapoor에게 전달되어야 한다.

해설 빈칸은 Ms. Kapoor와 동격에 해당하므로, 사람을 나타내는 명사가
와야 한다. (D) authority는 '권위, 권한'이란 뜻으로 자주 사용되지만,
'권위자, 대가'라는 의미로 사람을 나타내기도 하므로 정답이다. (B)와
(C)는 사람을 의미하기에 부적합하며, '모범, 예' 라는 뜻으로 사람을
설명할 때도 사용 될 수 있는 (A) example을 넣으면, '19세기 미술의
예시' 라는 의미로, 이 문제에선 사람보다는 특정 예술 작품을 의미하
게 되므로 오답이다.

어휘 inquiry 문의 | forward 전달하다 | leading 선두적인, 가장 중요한

4. 본관 2층 카페테리아는 개조 공사로 인해 폐쇄될 예정이므로, 추후 공
지가 있을 때까지 5층에 있는 곳을 이용하세요.

해설 further notice(추후 공지)라는 표현을 알고 있다면 정답을 빨리 찾을
수 있다. 문장에서 '추후 -------까지 5층에 있는 카페테리아를 이용하
세요'라고 했으므로 빈칸에는 (B) notice(공지)가 가장 적절하다.

어휘 renovation 개조[보수] 공사 | further notice 추후 공지 |
attention 관심 | post 우편 | response 응답

5. PACT 제조사는 수정된 회계 기준을 준수했는지를 확실히 하기 위해 회사의 회계 절차를 검토할 것이다.

해설 전치사 with와 함께 사용되며 목적어 revised accounting standards(수정된 회계 기준)와 어울리는 명사를 찾는다. compliance with는 '~을 준수'라는 의미이므로 (C) compliance가 정답이다.

어휘 probability 개연성, 확률 I precaution 예방책 I compliance 준수 I indication 지시, 암시

6. Landmark 사는 최근에 입사 지원자들의 적정성을 평가하기 위한 새로운 절차를 개발했다.

해설 평가(assessing)의 대상으로 적절한 것은 입사 지원자들의 적정성이므로 (D) suitability(적정성)가 정답이다.

어휘 process 절차, 과정 I assess 평가하다 I job candidate 입사 지원자 I feature 특징 I fact 사실 I resource 자원 I suitability 적정성

7. Mr. Miwanda는 일정이 겹쳐서 사장의 저녁 파티 초대를 수락할 수 없다.

해설 빈칸 앞에 있는 scheduling과 결합하여 '일정상의 충돌'이라는 의미로 scheduling conflict가 되는 것이 자연스러우므로 정답은 (C) conflict이다.

어휘 be unable to ~할 수 없다 I accept 수락하다 I invitation 초대 I scheduling conflict 일정상의 충돌 I indicator 지표 I inception (단체, 기관 등의) 시작, 개시 I date 날짜

8. 전략상의 중요한 변화로 LB 기계는 각각의 영업 직원에게 폭넓은 교육을 제공하기로 결정했다.
고난도

해설 LB Machinery 이하의 주절에서 이 회사가 영업 직원에게 교육을 제공하기로 결정한 사항은 이 회사의 전략상 중요한 변화라고 할 수 있으므로 (C) shift(변화)가 정답이다.

어휘 strategy 전략 I extensive 광범위한, 대규모의 I shortage 부족 I loss 손실 I shift (위치, 방향, 입장의) 변화; 교대 근무, 교대조 I prediction 예측, 예견

9. Victoria Cohen 교수는 연구 자금의 부족으로 그녀의 프로젝트를 계속할 수 없었다.

해설 빈칸 뒤의 전치사 of 를 동반하며, 문맥에 어울리는 (D) shortage가 정답이다.

어휘 research 연구(조사) I funds 자금, 기금 I supply 공급 I direction 방향, 지시

10. 그 도시의 안전 공무원들은 정기적으로 다양한 제조 시설들을 대상으로 철저한 검사를 실시한다.

해설 '그 도시의 안전 공무원들은 철저한 ------을 실시한다'에서 주어가 '안전 공무원들'이며, 앞에 온 동사가 conduct(실시[시행]하다)임을 감안하면 conduct의 목적어로 가장 어울리는 것이 (B) inspections(검사)임을 알 수 있다.

어휘 safety officer 안전 공무원 I conduct an inspection 검사를 실시하다 I thorough 철저한 I on a regular basis 정기적으로 I operation 작동 I institution 기관 I modification 수정

11. 어떤 기밀 문서도 회사 법무 부서의 승인 없이 직원들에게 유출되어서는 안 된다.

해설 '어떤 기밀 문서도 회사 법무 부서의 ------ 없이 직원들에게 유출되어서는 안 된다'에 어울리는 어휘는 (C) authorization(승인, 허가)이다.

어휘 confidential 기밀의 I release ~를 풀어주다, 공개하다 I legal department 법무 부서 I justification 정당화 I qualification 자격 요건 I authorization 승인, 허가 I transition 이행

12. 회사의 꾸준한 성장을 지속하려면 경영진과 직원들 사이에 정직하고 공개적인 의사소통이 필요하다.

해설 '꾸준한 성장을 지속하려면 ------과 직원들 사이의 의사소통이 필요하다'는 문장이므로 직원들과 의사소통을 할 만한 대상은 (D) management(경영진)뿐이다.

어휘 steady 꾸준한 I growth 성장 I panel (특정한 문제에 대해 견해를 제공하는 전문가) 집단 I procedure 절차 I benefit 혜택 I management 경영진

13. 수리공은 박테리아와 곰팡이의 증가를 포함해, 식기세척기를 청소하지 않았을 때의 결과에 대해 경고하였다.
고난도

해설 박테리아와 곰팡이의 증가를 포함해, 식기세척기를 청소하지 않은 결과를 경고했다는 의미가 문맥상 적절하므로 (A) consequences(결과)가 정답이다.

어휘 repairperson 수리공, 수선공 I warn 경고하다 I dishwasher 식기세척기 I build-up 증가 I mold 곰팡이 I consequence 결과 I solution 해결책 I action 조치, 활동 I appearance 외양

14. 그녀의 발표에서, Ms. Martinez는 새로운 법이 국가의 에너지 사용에 미칠 영향에 대해 이야기할 것이다.
고난도

해설 새로운 법이 미칠 영향이라는 의미가 자연스러우므로 (C) impact(영향)가 정답이다. have an impact on은 '~에 영향을 미치다'라는 의미이다.

어휘 presentation 발표 I law 법 I nation 국가 I use 사용 I requirement 요건 I impact 영향 I transfer 이전, 이동

15. 모든 급여 지급 부서 직원들은 지난달 갱신된 회사의 새로운 회계 절차를 따르도록 요구된다.

해설 '모든 급여 지급 부서 직원들은 회사의 새로운 회계 ------를 따르도록 요구된다'에 어울리는 어휘는 (A) procedures(절차)이다.

어휘 payroll department 급여 지급 부서, 경리부 I be required to ~하도록 요구 받다 I procedure 절차 I conduct 수행 I consequence 결과

16. 포틀랜드 지역에 있는 식품 가공 공장들은 그들의 옥수수 제품들에 대한 치솟는 수요를 처리하기 위해 전면 가동해서 작업하고 있다.

해설 옥수수 제품들에 대한 수요가 치솟고 있는 상황에 대처해야 하는 문맥을 고려했을 때 '전면 가동해서'라는 표현인 at full capacity가 되어야 가장 적절하다. 따라서 (A) capacity가 정답이다.

어휘 food processing 식품 가공 I region 지역 I at full capacity

전면 가동해서 | **soaring** 치솟는 | **demand for** ~에 대한 수요 | **deadline** 마감 기한 | **cost** 비용 | **budget** 예산

17. 올해 다른 목표들보다 운영 비용을 줄이면서 고객 만족을 향상시키는 것이 우선 순위를 차지할 것이다.

해설 빈칸 뒤의 전치사 over와 함께, '올해 다른 목표들보다 고객 만족을 향상시키는 것이 ------를 차지할 것이다'에 어울리는 명사 어휘는 '우선 순위'를 뜻하는 (C) priority이다. 명사 priority는 전치사 over와 함께 쓰여 '~보다 우선 순위'를 뜻하며, 형용사 high, top이 명사 priority와 함께 자주 쓰인다.

어휘 **improve** 개선시키다 | **customer satisfaction** 고객 만족 | **operational cost** 운영[업무] 비용 | **advantage** 혜택, 이익 | **priority** 우선순위 | **take priority over** ~보다 우선하다

18. 마케팅부와 영업부를 두 개의 별도의 팀으로 분할하는 것은 더 효율적인 업무 배분을 가능하게 할 것이다.

해설 into two separate teams를 단서로, 문맥상 '마케팅 부와 영업부를 두 개의 별도의 팀으로 ------'에 어울리는 '분할, 분리'를 뜻하는 (C) division이 정답이다.

어휘 **separate** 별도의 | **accuracy** 정확(성) | **enable** ~을 가능하게 하다 | **distribution** 배분 | **task** 업무 | **authority** 권위(자) | **division** 분할, 분리 | **oversight** 간과, 누락

19. 최근 몇 년 동안 세계 경제 상황이 급격히 변하고 있기 때문에 국제적으로 사업을 하는 사람이면 누구든 가능한 만일의 사태에 대비해야만 한다.
고난도

해설 '최근 몇 년 동안 경제 상황이 급격히 변하고 있기 때문에 국제적으로 사업을 하는 사람이면 누구든 가능한 ------에 대비해야만 한다'에 어울리는 어휘는 '만일의 사태'라는 의미의 명사 (A) contingencies이다.

어휘 **internationally** 국제적으로 | **possible** 가능한 | **economic condition** 경제 상황 | **dramatically** 급격히 | **contingency** 만일의 사태 | **extension** 연장 | **requirement** 요구 사항 | **circumstance** 상황, 정황

20. 모든 직원들은 다음 주 세미나에 참석하여 회사의 참고 자료에 수정된 사항을 숙지하도록 해야 한다.
고난도

해설 빈칸 뒤 명사 materials(자료)와 가장 잘 어울리는 명사는 선택지 중에서 (A) reference밖에 없다.

어휘 **familiarize** 익숙해지게 하다 | **revision** 수정 | **reference** 참고 | **convenience** 편리 | **improvement** 향상 | **suspension** 중단, 연기

Q1 1. valid   2. sensitive

1. 태양열 발전 시설의 규제된 구역들에 들어가기 위해서는 유효한 사원증이 의무적이다.

2. 인사부장으로서 Mr. Smith의 기량은 민감한 인사 사항들을 처리하는 데 특히 능숙했다.

Q2 1. available   2. eligible

1. 이 카탈로그 색인에 나열되어 있는 모든 시청각 자료들은 단기 대여가 가능하다.

2. 5년 이상 이곳에서 근무한 연구원은 누구든 지점 이동에 지원할 자격이 있다.

Q3 1. responsible   2. unfamiliar

1. Mr. Sanchez는 사장님이 출장을 가 계신 동안 주간 보고를 발표하는 책임을 질 것이다.

2. 조사했을 때, 대부분의 소비자들이 새로운 라인의 친환경 하이브리드 자동차에 생소해 하는 것이 밝혀졌다.

Q4 1. informative   2. competitive   3. all
4. numerous

1. 회사 워크숍의 많은 참가자들은 Dr. Becks가 시간 운용 기술에 대해 유익한 발표를 했다고 나타냈다.

2. HKV 기업은 직원들에게 전문성 개발을 위한 눈에 띄는 기회와 더불어 경쟁력 있는 연봉을 제공하는 데 자부심이 있다.

3. 팀 리더들은 모든 인턴들이 오리엔테이션 워크숍을 이수했는지 꼭 확인해야 한다.

4. 복잡한 등록 절차에도 불구하고, 그것들이 지닌 수많은 혜택 때문에 대부분의 고객들은 우리 신용카드에 만족했다.

Practice

본서 p.190

1. (B)	2. (D)	3. (C)	4. (A)	5. (B)
6. (B)	7. (B)	8. (D)	9. (B)	10. (D)
11. (A)	12. (D)	13. (A)	14. (D)	15. (B)
16. (B)	17. (B)	18. (D)	19. (A)	20. (A)

1. 지난 30년간, Axterp 건설사는 빌딩을 건설하는 데 최첨단 기술과 함께 포괄적인 서비스를 제공했다.

해설 빈칸 뒤 명사 service를 가장 잘 수식하면서 문맥상 어울리는 형용사는 (B) comprehensive(포괄적인)이다.

어휘 construction 건설 | offer 제공하다 | up-to-date 첨단의 | technology 기술 | apparent 분명한 | comprehensive 포괄적인 | upcoming 다가오는, 곧 있을 | reluctant 주저하는

2. 금요일의 강의는 오전 10시 정각에 시작할 것이므로, 참석자들은 시간을 엄수할 것이 권장된다.

해설 회의가 오전 10시 정각에 시작하니 참석자들은 시간을 엄수해 달라는 문맥이므로 (D) punctual(시간을 엄수하는)이 정답이다.

어휘 lecture 강의 | promptly 지체 없이, 정확히 | attendee 참석자 | instant 즉각의 | advanced 선진의; 고급의 | sudden 갑작스러운 | punctual 시간을 엄수하는

3. 새로운 Auto Organizer 소프트웨어는 버전 10.0 이상의 어떤 Jet 운영 시스템과도 호환된다.

해설 보기 중 compatible이 전치사 with를 동반한다는 사실을 알고 있다면 쉽게 풀 수 있는 문제이다. 새로운 소프트웨어가 버전 10.0 이상의 운영 시스템과 호환된다는 의미가 적절하므로 (C) compatible(호환이 되는)이 정답이다.

어휘 operating system 운영 시스템 | reportable 보고할 수 있는; 보고할 가치가 있는 | reflective (of) 빛을 반사하는; ~을 반영하는 | compatible (with) 호환이 되는 | conclusive 결정적인, 확실한

4. Marley 자동차의 매출은 작년 같은 달에 팔린 14만 5천 대와 비교하여 2월에 15만 대로 늘었다.

해설 명사 month를 수식하기에 적절한 형용사를 고르는 문제이다. 앞에서 자동차 회사의 2월 판매량을 언급하면서, 작년 같은 달의 판매량과 비교하여 더 늘었다는 문맥이 적절하므로 (A) same(같은)이 정답이다.

어휘 sales 매출액, 판매량 | unit (상품의) 한 개[단위] | as compared to[with] ~와 비교해서 | previous 이전의 | same 같은, 동일한 | found 발견된 | later ~보다 뒤의/나중의 | open 열려 있는, 개방된

5. 신흥 시장에 투자하기 전에 투자 전문가들과 상담하는 것이 필수적이다.

해설 보통 가주어(It)와 진주어 사이에 많이 쓰이면서, '신흥 시장에 투자하기 전에 전문가들과 상담하는 것은 필수적이다'라는 문장이 자연스러우므로 (B) essential이 정답이다.

어휘 consult ~와 상담하다 | invest in ~에 투자하다 | emerging market 신흥 시장 | conclusive 결정적인 | essential 필수적인 | entire 전체의 | negligible 무시해도 될 정도의

6. Nouta 소프트웨어 시스템의 인기는 그것의 저렴한 가격 덕분이다.

해설 price를 수식하기에 알맞은 형용사를 고르는 문제로 소프트웨어 시스템의 인기가 저렴한 가격에 기인한다는 문맥이 자연스러우므로 (B) affordable이 정답이다.

어휘 popularity 인기 | be attributed to ~에 기인하다 | exclusive 독점적인 | affordable (가격이) 알맞은 | extensive 광범위한 | accountable 책임이 있는

7. 모든 후보자들의 자격이 완벽했지만, Ms. Norman의 인터뷰는 특히 인상적이었다.

해설 '모든 후보자들의 자격이 완벽했지만, Ms. Norman의 인터뷰는 특히 -------이었다'에 어울리는 형용사는 (B) impressive(인상적인, 감명 깊은)이다.

어휘 candidate 후보자 | qualified 자격을 갖춘 | especially 특히나 | incorporated 통합된 | impressive 인상적인 | confidential 기밀의 | eventual 궁극적인, 최종적인

8. Exia 여행사 지원자들은 여행 업계에서 최소 2년의 경력이 있어야 하며 여행에 대해 열정적이어야 한다.

고난도

해설 여행사의 입사 지원자들이 갖춰야 하는 자격 요건으로 어울리는 것은 여행에 대해 (D) enthusiastic(열정적인)해야 한다는 것이다.

어휘 travel industry 여행 업계 | honest 정직한 | definite 확실한 | fluent (말 따위가) 유창한 | enthusiastic 열정적인

9. Pinksea 광고회사는 지난 세 달 동안 신제품을 위한 세부 마케팅 계획안을 개발해오고 있다.

해설 '지난 세 달 동안 신제품을 위한 ------- 마케팅 계획안을 개발해오고 있다'라는 문맥과 어울리는 형용사는 (B) detailed(세부적인)밖에 없다.

어휘 punctual 시간을 지키는 | detailed 세부적인, 자세한 | vague 모호한 | relative 비교적인, 상대적인

10. Yomaha Wellbeing 식품은 그 유기농 공급 업자들이 계속해서 효율적인 방식으로 신선한 재료들을 배달하기를 기대한다.

해설 '------- 방식으로 신선한 재료들을 배달하는 것'에 어울리는 어휘가 들어가야 하므로 '효율적인'을 뜻하는 (D) efficient가 정답이다.

어휘 supplier 공급 업자 | ingredient 재료 | consistently 지속적으로 | extensive 광범위한 | demanding 힘든, 까다로운 | approximate 거의 정확한, 근사치인 | efficient 효율적인

11. 우리의 최근 마케팅 조사는 유명 인사의 추천이 판매를 신장시키는 데 있어 상당히 효과적이라는 것을 보여주었다.

해설 '유명 인사의 추천이 판매를 신장시키는 데 있어 ------- 하다'와 어울리는 형용사는 (A) effective(효과적인)이다.

어휘 celebrity 유명 인사 | endorsement 지지 | significantly 상당히 | boost 신장시키다 | effective 효과적인 | specific 구체적인 | lengthy 너무 긴, 장황한 | partial 부분적인, 불완전한

12. 우리 사무실에 있는 천연 식물들에 물을 주고 보살피는 데 드는 비용을 없애기 위해, 우리는 그것들을 조화로 대체할 예정이다.

해설 천연 식물들을 키우는 데 들어가는 비용을 없애기 위해 이들을 인공 식물 즉, 조화로 대체할 것이라는 문맥이 적절하므로 (D) artificial(인공의)이 정답이다.

어휘 water 물을 주다 | care for ~을 보살피다 | eliminate 제거하다 | natural plant 천연 식물 | domestic 국내의 | finite 한정된, 유한

한 | **fragile** 부서지기 쉬운 | **artificial** 인공의; 인위적인

13. 올 여름 풍부한 강수량으로 인해, 물 사용 규제가 일시적으로 완화되었다.

해설 빈칸 뒤의 명사 rainfall을 수식하여 문맥상 '풍부한 강수량'의 의미를 완성하는 (A) abundant가 정답이다.

어휘 **rainfall** 강수(량) | **water usage** 물 사용 | **restriction** 규제 | **temporarily** 일시적으로 | **relax** 완화하다 | **abundant** 풍부한, 넘칠 정도로 많은 | **accidental** 우연한, 우발적인 | **common** 흔한 | **occasional** 간혹, 이따금

14. 심하게 할인된 가격이 매력적일지라도, 아울렛 매장들이 때때로 결함 있는 상품들을 판매한다는 사실을 소비자들은 명심해야 한다.

해설 문장이 Although(~임에도 불구하고)로 이끌어졌기 때문에 주절에는 상반된 내용이 나오는 것이 맥락상 어울린다. 따라서 해석상 '가격이 매력적임에도 불구하고, 때때로 defective(결함이 있는) 제품들을 판매한다'가 어울린다. 따라서 (D) defective가 정답이다.

어휘 **heavily** 심하게, 아주 많이 | **discounted** 할인된 | **outlet** 아울렛 | **keep in mind** 명심하다 | **apparent** 분명한 | **comprehensive** 포괄적인 | **upcoming** 다가오는, 곧 있을 | **defective** 결함이 있는

15. Mr. Zako의 발표는 너무 설득력이 있어서 해외 고객들은 제품 개발에 투자하기로 결정했다.

해설 「so ~ that … 구문(너무 ~해서 …하다)」의 형용사 자리로 that 이하의 '해외 고객들이 제품 개발에 투자하기로 결정했다'의 결과와 자연스럽게 연결될 수 있는 것은 (B) convincing(설득력 있는) 뿐이다.

어휘 **decide** 결정하다 | **invest** 투자하다 | **development** 개발, 발달, 성장 | **verified** 검증된, 확인된 | **convincing** 설득력 있는 | **probable** 있을 것 같은, 개연성 있는 | **gratified** 만족한, 기뻐하는

16. Bandelectro의 새로운 에어컨 제품 라인은 비록 새 디자인이 더 매력적이긴 해도 그것의 기존 라인과 가격 면에서 비슷하다.

해설 although 앞 절은 although 절과 상반된 내용을 담고 있어야 한다. '디자인은 더 매력적이지만, 기존의 라인과 가격 면에서는 -------하다'가 되어야 자연스러우므로 (B) comparable(비슷한)이 정답이다.

어휘 **air conditioner** 에어컨 | **previous** 이전의 | **attractive** 매력적인 | **benevolent** 자애로운, 자비로운 | **comparable** 비슷한, 비교할 만한 | **authorized** 인정받은, 공인된 | **abundant** 풍부한, 풍족한

17. Olivera 사의 새 사무용 가구 라인이 회사의 이번 달 재무 성과를 끌어올리는 데 도움을 주었다.

해설 빈칸 뒤의 명사 performance를 수식하여 전체 문맥상 '회사의 재무 성과'의 의미를 만드는 (B) financial이 정답이다. 감정동사의 과거 분사형인 (A) interested는 사람명사를 수식하므로 문법적으로 적합하지 않아 오답이다.

어휘 **boost** 끌어올리다, 신장시키다 | **performance** 성과, 실적 | **interested** 관심이 있는 | **financial** 재무의, 재정의 | **available** 이용 가능한, 구입 가능한 | **believable** 믿을 수 있는

18. 20년 동안의 사업 경력으로 Country 해운 서비스사는 부서지기 쉬운 제품을 취급하는 전문화된 배송 서비스를 제공한다.
고난도

해설 '~한 제품을 취급하는 특별 배송 서비스'에 가장 어울리는 형용사는 (D) fragile(부서지기 쉬운)이다.

어휘 **specialized** 전문화된 | **handle** 취급하다 | **spacious** 넓은 | **cautious** 조심스러운 | **apparent** 분명한 | **fragile** 부서지기 쉬운

19. 최근의 한 연구는 제조업 근로자들이 초과 근무 시간 동안 일에 가장 덜 주의를 기울이는 경향이 있다고 밝혔다.
고난도

해설 '초과 근무 시간 동안 근로자들이 가장 덜 ------- 하다'에 어울리는 단어는 (A) attentive(주의를 기울이는)이다.

어휘 **recent** 최근의 | **study** 연구 | **reveal** 밝히다 | **manufacturing** 제조업 | **tend to** ~하기 쉬운 경향이 있다 | **overtime shift** 초과 근무 조 | **attentive** 주의를 기울이는 | **informative** 유익한 | **advisory** 자문의, 고문의 | **knowledgeable** 박식한, 아는 것이 많은

20. 경영진은 그녀의 계획을 비현실적인 것으로 여기지만, Ms. Macondo는 그것이 실행하기 어려울 것이라고 생각하지 않는다.

해설 동사 call이 '부르다, 전화 걸다'의 의미 외에 '~로 여기다'의 의미로 쓰일 수 있는데, 이때는 「call + 목적어 + 목적보어」의 패턴을 취한다. 목적어(her plan) 뒤에 의미상 알맞은 형용사를 넣어야 하는 문제로 call의 또 다른 의미와 사용 패턴을 알고 있어야 하는 문제이다. 양보 절을 이끄는 접속사 Although가 쓰였으므로 두 문장이 서로 대비되어야 하는데, 경영진은 그녀의 계획이 비현실적이라고 여기지만, 그녀는 그렇게 생각하지 않는다는 문맥이 적절하므로 (A) impractical(비현실적인)이 정답이다.

어휘 **management** 경영진; 관리, 경영 | **call** ~라고 여기다 | **implement** 시행하다 | **impractical** 터무니 없는, 비현실적인 | **unavoidable** 불가피한, 어쩔 수 없는 | **indifferent** 무관심한 | **spotless** 티끌 하나 없는

UNIT 04. 부사

본서 p.192

Q1 1. slightly 2. thoroughly 3. typically

1. 유가가 지난주에 다시 약간 올랐지만 많은 산업 전문가들은 다음 주에 상당한 하락을 예상한다.

2. 판매원들은 고객 항의를 처리하는 법을 이해하기 위해서 직원 매뉴얼을 철저하게 읽어야 한다.

3. Mr. Foucault는 오늘은 이곳에 없지만, 그는 보통 모든 대학 교직원 회의에 참석한다.

1. 이자율 수준이 상대적으로 낮을 것으로 예상된다.

2. 〈Dark Monday〉 미스터리 시리즈의 최신작 매출은 최근에 Darwin 출판사의 수익을 거의 20%까지 신장시켰다.

Practice

본서 p.196

1. (A)	2. (B)	3. (B)	4. (C)	5. (B)
6. (B)	7. (D)	8. (C)	9. (B)	10. (B)
11. (C)	12. (A)	13. (C)	14. (C)	15. (D)
16. (B)	17. (C)	18. (B)	19. (D)	20. (B)

1. 건물 안전 검사원들은 그들이 안전 점검 목록에 모든 사항들을 철저히 검토하기 전에 추측해서는 안 된다.

해설 '모든 사항들을 '철저히' 검토하기 전에 추측해서는 안 된다'가 자연스러우므로 부사 (A) thoroughly(철저히)가 정답이다.

어휘 inspector 검사원 | assumption 추측 | check ~을 검토하다 | safety inspection 안전 검사 | checklist 점검 목록 | thoroughly 철저히 | formerly 이전에 | inadvertently 무심코, 부주의로 | approximately 대략

2. Design555는 그 분야에서 상대적으로 신참이지만, 그 경쟁사들에게 빠르게 위협이 되어 왔다.

해설 문장 전체를 해석하면 'Design555는 그 분야에서 -------하게 신참이지만, 경쟁사들에게 빠르게 위협이 되어 왔다'라고 했으므로 빈칸에 가장 적절한 부사는 '상대적으로'라는 의미의 단어 (B) relatively이다.

어휘 threat 위협 | competitor 경쟁자 | closely 밀접하게, 친밀히 | relatively 상대적으로 | normally 보통은 | collectively 집합적으로

3. 고객과의 회의가 다음 주로 이동한다면, 우리는 그에 맞춰 공개 토론
고난도 회를 연기해야만 할 것이다.

해설 '고객 회의가 다음 주로 이동한다면 그에 맞춰[그에 상응하여] 공개 토론회를 연기해야 한다'는 것이 의미상 자연스러우므로 (B) accordingly(그에 맞춰)가 정답이다.

어휘 shift 이동하다, 옮기다 | postpone 연기하다 | panel discussion 공개 토론회 | lately 최근에 | accordingly 그에 맞춰, ~에 부응해서 | namely 즉, 다시 말해 | particularly 특히

4. 미끄러운 도로에서 운전할 때, 핸들을 가고자 하는 방향으로 천천히 부드럽게 돌리시오.

해설 동사 turn을 수식하는 부사 자리로 A and B(slowly and -------)의 구조를 취하므로 '-ly'형 형용사 timely는 소거한다. 자동차의 핸들을 천천히 부드럽게 돌리라는 의미가 적절하므로 (C) gently(부드럽게)가 정답이다.

어휘 slippery 미끄러운, 미끈거리는 | steering wheel (자동차의) 핸들

direction 방향; 위치 | finely 잘게; 멋있게 | timely 시기 적절한 | gently 부드럽게, 다정하게 | openly 터 놓고, 솔직하게

5. 시장 후보자인 Amin Fahlan이 현재 환경법에 대한 그의 입장에 관하여 어제 공개적으로 말했다.

해설 동사 spoke 를 수식하여 '여러 사람들 앞에서 공개적으로 말했다' 라는 내용을 완성하는 (B) publicly가 정답이다. '이전에'를 의미하는 (A) previously와 '정기적으로'를 의미하는 (D) periodically는 빈칸 뒤의 yesterday와 의미상 어울리지 않아 오답이다.

어휘 mayoral 시장의 | candidate 후보자, 지원자 | regarding ~에 관하여 | position 입장; 위치 | current 현재의 | environmental law 환경법 | previously 이전에 | publicly 공개적으로 | expensively 비싸게 | periodically 정기적으로

6. 보고서에 따르면, Normanti 사의 수입이 3년간의 추락 이후 지난 분기 말에 급속히 증가했다.

해설 '3년간 떨어진 후에 지난 분기 말에 ------- 증가했다'에 어울리는 어휘는 (B) rapidly(급속히)뿐이다.

어휘 according to ~에 따르면 | earnings 수입 | quarter 분기 | overly 지나치게 | rapidly 급속히, 빠르게 | preferably 가급적이면 | meticulously 꼼꼼하게, 좀스럽게

7. 새로 지은 아파트의 잠재 구매자들은 그것이 얼마나 편리하게 위치해 있는지에 대해 들었다.

해설 '새로 지은 아파트가 얼마나 ------- 위치해 있는지'에 어울리는 어휘는 (D) conveniently(편리하게)이다.

어휘 newly 새롭게 | inform 알리다 | located 위치한 | consistently 지속적으로 | reliably 믿을 수 있게, 확실히 | periodically 주기적으로 | conveniently 편리하게

8. 발표는 거의 3시간 동안 지속되었으나, 대부분의 참석자들은 그 주제에 너무 관심이 많아서 그것을 개의치 않았다.

해설 '발표가 ------- 3시간 동안 지속되었으나, 대부분의 참석자들은 그 주제에 너무 관심이 많아서 그것을 개의치 않았다'에 어울리는 어휘는 (C) nearly(거의)이다.

어휘 presentation 발표 | last 지속되다 | interested 관심이 있는 | impressively 인상 깊게 | necessarily 어쩔 수 없이, 필연적으로 | nearly 거의 | originally 원래

9. 최신 개정 사항들이 발효되면서 주택 자금 대출의 계약 조건이 분기별로 변경될 수 있음을 유념해주세요.

해설 빈칸은 be subject to change를 수식하는 부사 자리로, 문맥상 '분기마다 변경될 수 있다'는 의미가 적절하므로 (B) quarterly가 정답이다. 나머지 보기는 문맥상 적절하지 못하며, 특히, (A) overly는 동사를 수식하지 못하고, (C) formerly는 과거 시제를 나타낸다는 문법 사항도 함께 정리해 두어야 한다.

어휘 terms (계약) 조건 | housing loan 주택 자금 대출 | be subject to ~의 대상이 되다, ~될 수 있다 | update 최신 정보 | take effect 발효되다, 효력을 발생하다

10. Bloomings 꽃집의 정원 가꾸기 수업은 보통 약 50분간 지속된다.

해설 동사 last를 수식하기에 적절한 부사를 고르는 문제이다. 수업이 보통 50분 지속된다는 의미가 적절하므로 (B) typically(보통)가 정답이다.

어휘 gardening 정원 손질 | session (활동) 시간[기간] | last 지속되다 | lightly 가볍게, 약간 | typically 보통, 일반적으로 | patiently 끈기 있게, 참을성 있게 | doubly 두 배로

11. Skin Market의 새로운 아이 크림이 수많은 고객 설문 조사가 행해진 후에 마침내 시판 준비가 되었다.

해설 '수 많은 고객 설문 조사가 행해진 후에 아이 크림이 ------- 시판 준비가 되었다'에서 빈칸에 어울리는 어휘는 (C) finally(마침내)뿐이다.

어휘 numerous 수많은 | survey 설문 조사 | conduct 행하다 | accidentally 우연히, 실수로 | repeatedly 반복적으로 | finally 마침내 | exclusively 독점적으로

12. 저희 Sound Track은 TX301 스피커가 곧 도착할 예정임을 귀하께 알리게 되어 기쁩니다.

해설 'TX301 스피커가 ------- 도착할 것을 알려 드리게 되어 기쁘다'에 어울리는 어휘는 (A) shortly(곧)이다.

어휘 be pleased + to부정사 ~하게 되어 기쁘다 | inform A that A에게 ~을 알리다 | shortly 곧 | barely 거의 ~하지 않다 | faintly 희미하게 | intermittently 간헐적으로

13. 가뭄은 밀과 쌀의 더 높은 가격을 야기하며 올해 수확에 불리하게 영향을 미쳤다.
고난도

해설 빈칸 뒤 '밀과 쌀의 가격을 더 상승시키는 결과를 가져왔다'의 내용과 잘 어울리는 부사를 찾는다. 따라서 정답은 '불리하게'라는 의미의 부사인 (C) adversely이다.

어휘 drought 가뭄 | affect 영향을 주다 | harvest 수확 | result in ~한 결과를 야기하다 | wheat 밀 | exactly 정확히 | valuably 값비싸게, 고가로 | adversely 불리하게 | strenuously 활기차게, 열심히

14. Morrison 인테리어가 만든 모든 가구는 용이한 수송을 위해 쉽게 분리될 수 있다.
고난도

해설 용이한 배송을 위해 가구가 쉽게 분리될 수 있다는 의미가 적절하므로 (C) effortlessly(쉽게)가 정답이다.

어휘 take ~ apart ~을 분리하다 | transportation 운송, 수송 | vitally 사실상, 실질적으로는 | attentively 조심스럽게, 신경 써서 | effortlessly 노력하지 않고, 쉽게 | accurately 정확히

15. Mr. Kim은 보수 공사에 대한 논의를 위해 상호간에 동의할 만한 시간을 정하기 위해 식당 소유주에게 전화를 걸었다.

해설 빈칸 뒤에 '보수 공사에 대한 논의를 위해 ------- 동의할 만한 시간'에 어울리는 부사를 찾는다. 따라서 '상호간에'를 뜻하는 부사 (D) mutually가 정답이다.

어휘 agreeable 동의할 만한 | discuss 논의하다 | renovation 개조, 보수 | commonly 일반적으로 | separately 별도로 | definitely 분명히 | mutually 상호간에

16. 회사가 지속적으로 막대한 연간 수익을 얻고 있기 때문에 D&U 화학의 대다수의 주주들은 만족스러워 한다.

해설 주절 문장에서 'D&U Chemical의 대부분의 주주들은 만족한다'라고 했으므로 빈칸에는 이와 어울리는 의미의 부사가 필요하다. 따라서 정답은 (B) consistently(지속적으로)이다.

어휘 shareholder 주주 | satisfied 만족하는 | annual profit 연간 수익 | readily 손쉽게, 순조롭게 | consistently 지속적으로, 일관적으로 | impulsively 충동적으로 | vaguely 애매하게

17. 총무 부장은 직원들에게 결함이 있는 사무 장비를 제조 업체에 직접 반품할 것을 상기시켰다.

해설 '직원들에게 결함이 있는 사무 장비를 제조 업체에 ------- 반품할 것을 상기시켰다'에 어울리는 부사는 (C) directly(직접)이다.

어휘 general affairs department 총무부 | remind 상기시키다 | defective 결함이 있는 | office equipment 사무 장비 | manufacturer 제조 업체 | extensively 광범위하게 | miraculously 기적적으로 | directly 직접 | modestly 겸손하게

18. Cams 스포츠용품은 최근의 성공을 주로 새로운 야구 장비 때문으로 본다.

해설 동사 attributes를 수식하기에 적절한 부사를 고르는 문제이다. attribute A to B는 'A를 B 때문으로 여기다'란 뜻으로 그 최근 성공을 주로 새 야구 장비 때문으로 여긴다는 의미가 적절하므로 (B) primarily(주로)가 정답이다.

어휘 gear 장비 | importantly 중요하게 | primarily 주로 | tightly 단단히, 꽉 | extremely 극도로, 극히

19. Mr. Parr는 회사의 새 컴퓨터 라인의 수요가 계속 성장하면서, 주가가 점진적으로 성장할 것임을 정확하게 예측했다.
고난도

해설 빈칸 앞의 increase와 같은 증가, 감소 등의 변화를 의미하는 동사와 함께 쓰이는 특정 부사를 선택하는 문제이다. 따라서, 증감 동사를 수식하며, 전체적인 문맥에 적합한 (D) incrementally 가 정답이다. has predicted 와 함께한 correctly[정확하게] 는 that절 뒤에 보다 구체적이고 확정적인 예측내용을 수반함을 나타낸다. 따라서, '거의 틀림없이'의 의미를 지닌 (A) arguably 와 '소문에 의하면' 을 의미하는 (B) reportedly는 보다 구체적이며 확정적인 예측내용과 거리가 있으므로, 문맥상 적절하지 못하다. 또한 (A) arguably는 'the 최상급 + 명사' 형태의 명사구 앞에 위치하여 명사구를 수식하는 부사로 주로 쓰인다. 위와 같은 혼동을 줄이기 위해 증가, 감소의 의미를 나타내는 동사와 함께 하는 부사를 완벽히 학습해두어야 한다.

어휘 correctly 정확하게, 올바르게 | predict 예측하다 | stock value 주가 | demand 수요 | arguably 아마도 | reportedly 소문에 의하면 | productively 생산적으로 | incrementally 점진적으로

20. 새로운 상품을 고객들에게 시연할 때, 직원들은 높은 수준의 전문 용어들의 사용을 피해야 한다.
고난도

해설 '-------한 전문 용어들의 사용을 피해야 한다'는 문맥이므로 '매우, 높은 수준의'를 뜻하는 부사 (B) highly(매우, 높은 수준의)가 정답이다.

어휘 demonstrate 보여주다 | technical term 전문 용어 |

frequently 자주 I highly 매우, 높은 수준의 I distantly 멀리, 떨어져서 I readily 기꺼이, 당장

본서 p.198

REVIEW TEST

1. (A)	2. (B)	3. (B)	4. (C)	5. (C)
6. (B)	7. (C)	8. (A)	9. (D)	10. (B)
11. (C)	12. (C)	13. (C)	14. (D)	15. (C)
16. (C)	17. (D)	18. (B)	19. (B)	20. (C)

1. 레스토랑 사장은 주말에 문을 늦게 닫음으로써 더 많은 손님들을 끌어들이기를 바란다.

해설 문맥상 '늦게 문을 닫아서 더 많은 손님들을 끌어들이기를 바란다'는 내용이 적합하므로 (A) attract(끌어들이다)가 정답이다.

어휘 diner 식사하는 사람, 손님

2. Ms. Trang은 자주 사무실을 비우게 될 것이므로 이메일로 연락하십시오.

해설 접속사 so로 연결된 두 문장의 의미 관계를 고려하면, '사무실을 자주 비우게 될 것이니 이메일로 연락하라'는 내용이 자연스러우므로 (B) frequently(자주)가 정답이다.

어휘 contact 연락하다 I via ~을 통해서

3. 공석이 난 직책에 관심이 있는 지원자들은 국제 무역에서 폭넓은 경험을 가지고 있어야 한다.

해설 문맥상 '국제 무역 분야에 폭넓은 경험이 있어야 한다'는 내용이 적합하므로 (B) extensive(폭넓은)이 정답이다.

어휘 applicant 지원자 I possess 소유하다. 가지고 있다 I experience 경험 I international trade 국제 무역

4. 공연 중 전화를 받아야만 하신다면, 가능한 조용히 해주시기 바랍니다.

해설 if절과 주절의 의미를 고려할 때, '전화를 받아야만 한다면 가능한 한 조용히 해달라'는 내용이 적합하므로 (C) quietly(조용히)가 정답이다.

어휘 performance 공연 I as ~ as possible 가능한 ~한

5. Mr. Renner는 지난 수십 년 동안 쌓아온 경험들을 젊은 기자들과 나누는 것을 매우 좋아한다.
고난도

해설 빈칸은 명사 experience를 선행사로 하는 관계절 내 동사 자리로, 문맥상 '그가 수십 년간 쌓아온 경험들'이라는 의미가 적합하므로 (C) gained(쌓다)가 정답이다.

어휘 share 나누다. 공유하다 I journalist 기자 I experience 경험 decade 10년

6. 기술 지원 센터에 연락하실 때는 고객님의 노트북 일련번호를 준비하십시오.
고난도

해설 빈칸은 사역동사 have의 목적보어 자리. 목적어 serial number의 상태를 설명하는 자리이므로, 종속절과 주절 간 문맥을 고려할 때, '일

련번호를 이용할 수 있는 상태로 해달라'는 내용이 되어야 하므로 (B) available(이용 가능한)이 정답이다.

어휘 contact 연락하다 I technical support 기술 지원

7. Tetsudo 레스토랑은 파티오 구역 폐쇄에 대해 알리는 공지를 모든 고객들에게 발표했다.

해설 고객들에게 특정 구역의 폐쇄에 관한 공지를 발표했다는 의미가 적합하므로 (C) notice(공지)가 정답이다.

어휘 issue 발표하다. 공표하다 I closure 폐쇄 I patio 파티오 (집 뒤쪽에 만드는 테라스)

8. 현재 HCMC 보안 회사의 마케팅 부서를 이끄는 Ms. Phan은 다음 달 초에 부사장으로 승진할 것이다.

해설 부서를 이끄는(heads) 시점이 현재 시제로 쓰여, 현재 시제와 어울리는 부사가 들어가야 하며, 현재 마케팅 부서를 이끄는 Ms. Phan이 다음 달 승진할 거란 의미가 적합하므로 (A) currently(현재)가 정답이다.

어휘 head 이끌다. 책임지다 I division (조직의) 부. 국 I promote 승진시키다 I vice president 부사장

9. 온라인 구인 광고에 열거된 모든 자격 조건에 부합하는 지원자들은 연락을 받게 될 것이다.

해설 명사 applicants를 수식하는 형용사절(who meet every ~ job posting)의 목적어 자리로, '모든 자격 조건에 부합하는 지원자들'이란 의미가 적합하므로 (D) qualification(자격 조건)이 정답이다.

어휘 applicant 지원자 I job posting 구인 광고

10. 유지 보수 작업반은 폭풍이 야기한 피해를 가능한 빨리 보수하기 위해 부지런히 일하고 있다.

해설 동사 is working을 수식하는 부사 자리로, '유지보수반이 보수를 위해 부지런히 일하고 있다'는 의미가 적합하므로 (B) diligently(부지런히)가 정답이다.

어휘 maintenance 유지보수 I crew 작업반 I repair 수리하다 I damage 손상. 피해

11. 〈Sports Review〉에서 유명 운동선수들을 다룬 에피소드 시리즈는 상당히 인기가 많은 것으로 증명되었다.

해설 '유명 운동선수들을 다루는 에피소드 시리즈'라는 의미가 적합하므로 (C) series(시리즈)가 정답이다.

어휘 feature ~를 싣다. 특징으로 하다 I athlete 운동 선수

12. Downing 지역에서 경험 많은 의학 전문가에 대한 수요가 높아지고 있다.

해설 '수요'를 뜻하는 명사 demand는 전치사 for를 동반하므로 (C) for가 정답이다.

어휘 demand 수요 I experienced I 경험이 많은 I professional 전문가

13. 저명한 요리사들의 요리 시연은 Daoust 문화 축제 주간 동안 일어날 행사들 중 하나이다.
고난도

해설 명사 events를 수식하는 형용사절(that will ～ Week)의 보어 자리로, '그 주간 동안 일어날 행사들'이란 의미가 적합하므로 (C) happening(일어나다, 발생하다)이 정답이다.

어휘 demonstration 시연 I renowned 저명한 I cultural 문화의

14. 고대 그리스 역사의 권위자인 Ms. Ichihara는 지역 대학들에서 정기적으로 초청 강연을 한다.
고난도

해설 빈칸은 관사 뒤 명사 자리로, 보기 중 명사는 '허가'를 뜻하는 (A) authorization과, '권위자; 당국; 권한'을 뜻하는 (D) authority 두 개이며, (A)는 불가산명사로서 부정관사(An)를 취할 수 없을 뿐만 아니라 문맥상 '고대 그리스 역사의 권위자인 Ms. Ichihara'가 적합하므로 (D) authority(권위자)가 정답이다.

어휘 authority n. 권위자 I regularly 정기적으로 I local 지역의

15. IT 부서에서는 백신 프로그램이 최신인지 확실히 하기 위해, 회사 내의 모든 컴퓨터를 조사할 것이다.

해설 문맥상 백신 프로그램이 최신 버전인지 확실히 하기 위해 모든 컴퓨터들을 점검할 거란 의미가 적합하므로 (C) ensure(확실히 하다)가 정답이다.

어휘 inspect 조사하다 I antivirus 백신 I up-to-date 최신의

16. 직원 대체 절차를 시작하기 위해 팀을 모으고, 게시할 직무 기술서를 작성하시오.

해설 목적어로 team을 취하기에 적합한 동사를 고르는 문제로, 팀을 모아서 직무 기술서를 작성하라는 의미가 자연스러우므로 (C) assemble(모으다)이 정답이다.

어휘 replacement 대체, 교체 I job description 직무 기술, 설명 I post 게시하다

17. Swansea 리조트에서 특별 여름 할인의 자격을 얻으려면 온라인으로 예약해야 한다.

해설 '자격을 갖추다'를 뜻하는 동사 qualify는 전치사 for를 동반하므로 (D) for가 정답이다.

어휘 booking 예매 I qualify (자격을) 얻다, 획득하다 I discount 할인

18. Econnewsfront.net은 소기업 소유주들을 위한 정확한 재정 정보 출처이다.
고난도

해설 명사 source를 수식하기에 적합한 형용사를 고르는 문제로, '정확한 정보 출처'라는 의미가 자연스러우므로 (B) accurate가 정답이다.

어휘 independently 독립적으로 I source 출처 I financial 재정의 I aware 알고 있는 I attentive 주의를 기울이는 I acquainted 알고 있는

19. 로비에서 보수 작업이 진행 중이기 때문에, 건물 정문을 통한 입장은 당분간 차단됩니다.

해설 전치사 to를 동반하여 건물 정문으로의 입장이 차단된다는 의미가 적합하므로 (B) access(입장, 접근)가 정답이다.

어휘 temporarily 일시적으로

20. Garner 가 공사에 반대하는 사람들은 지금 탄원서에 서명해야 한다.

해설 'Those who(～하는 사람들)'의 형용사절의 동사 자리로, '공사에 반대하는 사람들'이라는 의미가 자연스러우므로 (C) oppose(반대하다)가 정답이다.

어휘 petition 탄원서

PART 6

UNIT 01. PART 6 유형 분석

Practice

본서 p.212

1. (C)	**2.** (B)	**3.** (D)	**4.** (A)	**5.** (B)
6. (B)	**7.** (B)	**8.** (B)	**9.** (B)	**10.** (C)
11. (D)	**12.** (A)	**13.** (A)	**14.** (C)	**15.** (D)
16. (B)				

[1-4] 다음 이메일에 관한 문제입니다.

수신: Paddy Murphy 〈PMurphy@paone.com〉
발신: John Kohl 〈JKohl@minami.com〉
날짜: 12월 15일
제목: 후속 조치

Mr. Murphy께,

Minami 스시에서 요리사로 일하는 데 관심을 가져주셔서 감사합니다. 그 **1** 자리는 아직 비어 있습니다. **2** 관심 있으시다면, 오셔서 당신의 기량을 선보여 주십시오. 저는 당신이 수년 동안 한국 해산물 식당에서 일해온 점에 **3** 주목했습니다. 그런 까닭에 당신은 이곳 음식들 몇 가지에 친숙할 것입니다. **4** 하지만, 두 나라의 요리 스타일 간에는 상당한 차이점이 있기도 해서, 어느 정도 훈련을 받으셔야 할 것입니다.
저희는 당신의 시범 일정을 이번 주 금요일 오전 10시로 정하려고 생각하고 있었습니다. 현장 인터뷰를 확정하시려면, 편한 시간에 제게 (858) 555-1212로 전화주세요. 곧 당신에게서 연락받기를 바랍니다.

안부 전하며,

John Kohl, 매니저
Minami Sushi

어휘 chef 요리사, 주방장 ǀ seafood 해산물, 수산식품 ǀ be familiar with ~에 친숙하다 ǀ significant 중요한 ǀ undergo 겪다 ǀ demonstration 시연, 시범 ǀ confirm 확정하다 ǀ on-site 현장의 ǀ at one's convenience 편한 때에

1. **해설** 빈칸 앞에서 요리사로 일하는데 관심을 가져줘서 감사하다고 했고, 빈칸 뒷부분에 그 일자리와 관련된 정보와 채용을 위한 현장 인터뷰 일정이 나오므로, 아직 요리사를 고용하지 않았음을 알 수 있다. 따라서, 빈칸은 Mr. Murphy가 관심을 보인 요리사 일자리이므로 (C) position이 정답이다. (A) restaurant '식당', (B) conversation '대화', (D) room '공간, 방'

2. (A) 특히, 당신은 일본산 수산물에 익숙한가요?
(B) 관심 있으시다면, 오셔서 당신의 기량을 선보여 주십시오.
(C) 저희 사업장의 전체 배치도는 홈페이지에 있습니다.
(D) 저희 일반 영업시간은 오전 11시부터 오후 11시입니다.

해설 빈칸 앞부분에 요리사 일자리가 공석이라 했고, 빈칸 뒷부분에 일자리에 대한 정보와 시연을 선위한 현장 인터뷰 일정이 나오기 때문에, 관심이 있다면 기량을 선보여야 한다는 (B) If you are interested, you would have to come in and demonstrate your skills.가 흐름상 적절하다.

3. **해설** 보기가 모두 동사이므로 「수 일치 → 태 → 시제」의 순서로 정답을 확인한다. 매니저가 that절의 내용을 인지한 주체이므로 수동형인 (A)는 오답이다. 이 이메일은 Mr. Murphy의 요리사 직책 관심에 대한 답장으로, 매니저인 John Kohl은 이미 Mr. Murphy의 근무 경력을 알고 있었음을 알 수 있다. 따라서, 과거 시제인 (D) noticed가 정답이다.

4. **해설** 보기가 모두 접속부사이므로 빈칸 앞, 뒤 문장의 의미 관계를 파악하여 정답을 선택해야 한다. should는 '~해야 한다'는 의무와 더불어 '당연히 ~하다'라는 당위를 함께 의미하는데, 빈칸 앞 문장은 '한국 식당에서 일한 경험을 통해 우리 식당 음식들도 익숙할 것이다'라는 당위적 의미이며, 빈칸 뒷문장은 '큰 차이가 있으니 훈련을 해야 한다'라는 의미이므로, 풍부한 경험에도 불구하고 훈련이 필요하다는 문맥을 완성한다. 따라서, 반대되는 내용을 연결하는 접속부사 (A) However가 정답이다. (B) Therefore '그러므로', (C) Furthermore '더욱이', (D) Likewise '마찬가지로'

[5-8] 다음 웹페이지에 관한 문제입니다.

Wingfried 교육 최우수상

훌륭한 고등학교는 국가의 미래를 설계하는 데 도움을 줍니다. **5** 학교의 성공은 열정적인 교사들로 가득한 교수진을 갖는 것에 있다는 것은 누구나 알고 있는 사실입니다. 학생들을 잘 보살피는 교사는 학업 성취에 강력한 영향을 미칩니다. **6** 이것은 뛰어난 시험 점수와 학점에서 드러납니다. Wingfried 교육 최우수상은 20년 전 진심으로 가르치기를 즐기는 교사를 모집하는 공립 및 사립 학교들에게 영예를 주기 위하여 **7** 만들어졌습니다. **8** 그 후로 지금까지 미국 전역의 수백 개의 학교들이 수상기관으로 선정되었습니다. 과거 수상기관들에 관한 글을 읽어보시려면 이 웹사이트의 '수상기관' 부분을 확인하시기 바랍니다.

어휘 shape 형성하다 ǀ lie 있다, 발견되다 ǀ faculty 교수진 ǀ passionate 열정적인 ǀ caring 배려하는, 보살피는 ǀ academic achievement 학습 성취 ǀ honor 영예[명예]를 주다 ǀ recruit 모집하다 ǀ grade 성적, 학점

5. **해설** 두 개의 동사(is, lies)를 연결하는 접속사 that이 있으므로 접속사 역할을 하는 소유격 관계 대명사 (A)는 오답이다. 빈칸 앞의 high schools를 의미상으로 받아주는 대명사 (B) their가 정답이다

6. (A) 이번에는 다른 국가에서 수상 기관들이 선발되었습니다.
(B) 이것은 뛰어난 시험 점수와 학점에서 드러납니다.
(C) 이렇게 함으로써 그들은 더 많은 기금을 받을 수 있습니다.
(D) 공립학교만이 상에 지원할 수 있습니다.

해설 빈칸 앞부분의 학생들을 잘 보살피는 교사가 학업 성취에 강력

64

한 영향을 준다는 내용과 연관성이 있는 보기를 선택해야 한다. (B)의 지시대명사 this는 빈칸 앞 문장 내용인 선생님이 학업 성취에 영향을 미친다는 것을 가리키며, 그 구체적 사례로 뛰어난 시험 점수와 학점이 언급되었으므로 흐름상 적절하다. (C) '선생님들이 학업 성취에 강력한 영향을 줌으로써 자금 지원을 더 받을 수 있다'는 의미는 자금 지원을 목적으로 선생님들이 학업 성취에 영향을 주고 있다는 의미가 되므로 글의 흐름에 적절하지 않고, (A)는 빈칸 뒷부분에 미국 전역의 학교들이 수상기관으로 선정되었다는 내용과 일치하지 않으며, (D)는 빈칸 뒷부분에 그 상이 공립 및 사립 학교들에게 영예를 주기 위해 만들어졌다는 내용과 일치하지 않는다.

7.
고난도
해설 빈칸 뒤에 미국 전역 수백 개의 학교들이 Wingfried 교육 최우수상의 과거 수상기관이었다고 했으므로, 20년 전에 그 상이 만들어졌다는 의미가 적절하다. 따라서 (B) created가 정답이다. (A) researched '조사했다', (C) postponed '연기했다', (D) recognized '인정했다'

---

8. **해설** 보기가 모두 접속부사이므로 빈칸 앞뒤 문장의 관계를 파악하여 정답을 선택해야 한다. 빈칸 앞 문장은 20년 전에 상이 만들어졌다는 내용이고 빈칸 뒤 문장은 미국 전역의 수백 개 학교들이 수상했다는 내용이므로, 두 문장이 사건의 순서에 따라 연결되어 있다. 즉, 앞 문장이 먼저 일어난 일이고, 뒷문장이 그 이후에 일어난 일이기 때문에, '그때 이래로, 그 후에'의 의미를 가지며 사건의 순서를 나타내는 (B) Since then이 정답이다. (A) Finally '마침내', (C) Even so '그렇다 하더라도', (D) In the same way '같은 방법으로'

[9-12] 다음 기사에 관한 문제입니다.

Desert Business Times

Palm Desert (4월 25일) – Janell Cantu가 Forrest 금융 서비스의 새 CEO로 선정되었다. 이사회는 어제 그 임명을 **9** 확정했다. **10** Ms. Cantu는 이전에 Forrest의 가장 큰 경쟁사의 마케팅 부서를 이끌었다. CEO로서, Ms. Cantu는 저비용 대안들의 도전에 적응하기 위한 새로운 비즈니스 모델을 만드는 일을 담당할 것이다. **11** 더욱이, 그녀는 Forrest의 새롭게 디자인된 인터넷 금융 서비스를 책임질 것이다. 그녀의 전 고용 업체는 현재 소비자 설문조사에서 가장 높은 등급을 받은 온라인 금융 서비스를 **12** 개발했던 회사이다.

어휘 select 선정하다, 선택하다 | board of directors 이사회 | appointment 임명 | be responsible for 책임지다, 담당하다 | adapt 적응하다 | alternatives 대안 | in charge of ~을 담당하는 | former 이전의 | rate 등급을 매기다, 평가하다

---

9. **해설** 빈칸 뒷부분에 Ms. Cantu가 CEO로서 앞으로 하게 될 업무들이 나오므로, 이사회가 Ms. Cantu의 임명을 확정했다는 내용의 (B) confirmed가 정답이다. (A) postponed '연기했다', (C) reversed '뒤바꿨다', (D) considered '고려했다'

10.
고난도
(A) 기업은 새 CEO를 계속해서 찾아볼 것이다.

(B) Forrest 금융 서비스는 성공적인 현재 전략을 지속할 것이다.

(C) Ms. Cantu는 이전에 Forrest의 가장 큰 경쟁사의 마케팅 부서를 이끌었다.

(D) 〈Desert Business Times〉는 새롭게 디자인한 온라인 판을 이제 막 출시했다.

해설 빈칸 앞 부분에 Ms. Cantu의 신임 CEO 임명에 관련된 내용이 나오고, 빈칸 뒤에 Ms. Cantu가 신임 CEO로서 하게 될 업무에 대한 내용이 나오므로 이전에 Ms. Cantu가 경쟁사의 마케팅 부서를 이끌었다는 (C) Ms. Cantu previously led the Marketing Department at Forrest's largest competitor.가 흐름상 적절하다. 신임 CEO를 계속 찾을 거라는 (A)는 Ms. Cantu가 신임 CEO로 임명되었다는 앞 내용과 일치하지 않고, Forrest 금융 서비스가 현재의 전략을 유지할 것이라는 (B)와 〈Desert Business Times〉의 온라인 판을 출시했다는 (D)는 빈칸 앞, 뒤의 내용과 연관성이 없으므로 오답이다.

---

11. **해설** 빈칸 앞뒤 문장 모두 CEO의 신규 업무에 관한 내용들로 앞 문장은 신임 CEO로서 새로운 비즈니스 모델을 만드는 일을 책임질 것이고, 뒷문장은 인터넷 금융 서비스를 책임질 것이라는 내용이다. 따라서, 앞 문장의 신규 업무에 또 다른 업무가 뒤에 추가되는 것이기 때문에 추가, 부연을 나타내는 (D) Furthermore가 정답이다. (A) Nonetheless '그럼에도 불구하고', (B) Consequently '결과적으로', (C) Otherwise '그렇지 않으면'

---

12. **해설** 빈칸 앞의 사물 선행사 the company를 수식하는 주격 관계대명사절인 (A), (B) 중에 정답을 선택해야 한다. (A)와 (B)의 가장 큰 차이점은 동사의 시제이다. 관계대명사의 수식을 받는 the company는 Ms. Cantu를 이전에 고용했던 업체이므로 온라인 금융 서비스를 개발한 것은 과거에 해당한다. 따라서, 과거 시제 동사가 포함된 (A) that developed가 정답이다.

[13-16] 다음 이메일에 관한 문제입니다.

수신: Masha@mauvais.com
발신: Ashraf@crazycloud.pk
날짜: 5월 22일
제목: 제품 문의
첨부파일: cc.doc

Masha께,

저희 CrazyCloud 소프트웨어에 대해 당신이 관심이 있다는 걸 듣게 되어 기쁩니다. 이 특별한 프로그램은 원격 데이터 저장을 가능하게 해주어 효율성과 생산성을 **13** 강화시킵니다. 이 이메일에 첨부된 책자를 **14** 검토해 주세요.
거기에는 CrazyCloud 사용자 추천글이 포함되어 있습니다. 그들 모두가 특히 파일을 쉽게 백업하는 기능을 좋아했다는 것을 알게 될 것입니다. **15** 예를 들어, 이 프로그램은 인터넷 연결만 되어 있으면 당신이 기록했던 중요한 비디오를 보관 및 저장할 수 있습니다. 또한, CrazyCloud는 많은 양의 파일 저장 공간을 제공하여, 사용자들이 대용량 파일들을 저장하는 것에 대해 걱정할 필요가 없습니다. **16** 추가적인 데이터 저장 옵션이 유료로 구매 가능합니다.

그 밖에 다른 어떤 질문이라도 생기면 제게 연락주세요.

Ashraf Kodur
CrazyCloud 영업 책임자

어휘 unique (아주) 특별한 I remote 먼, 원격의 I storage 저장 I
efficiency 효율성 I productivity 생산성 I attached 첨부
된 I testimonial 추천의 글

13. 해설 동사 allows가 빈칸 앞에 존재하며, 보기의 동사 enhance를
연결해주는 접속사나 관계사가 빈칸 앞에 없으므로, 동사인 (C), (D)
는 오답이다. 특별 프로그램이 원격 데이터 저장을 가능하게 해주어,
효율성과 생산성을 강화시킨다는 문맥에 따라 능동의 현재 분사인 (A)
enhancing이 정답이다. 완전한 문장 뒤에 분사구문이 오는 경우 현
재분사로 시작하는 경우가 대부분인 점에 유의한다.

14.
고난도 해설 빈칸 뒷부분에서 첨부된 책자에 담긴 CrazyCloud 제품 사용
자 추천글을 통해 사용자들이 파일을 쉽게 백업하는 기능을 좋아했다
는 점을 고객이 알게 될 것이라는 내용이 나온다. 따라서, 제품 문의한
고객이 이메일에 첨부된 책자를 꼼꼼히 살펴봐야 그 내용을 알게 될
것이므로, 문맥상 (C) review가 정답이다. (A) submit '제출하다', (B)
copy '복사하다', (D) discard '버리다'

15. 해설 빈칸 앞 문장에서 기존 사용자들이 파일 백업 기능을 좋아했다
고 하면서 뒷문장에서는 기존 사용자들이 좋아했던 백업 기능의 구체
적인 예에 해당하는 인터넷 연결을 통한 비디오 보관 및 저장에 관한
내용이 나오므로 (D) For example이 정답이다. (A) Even so '그렇다
하더라도', (B) As long as '~하는 한', (C) Previously '이전에'

16.
고난도 (A) 많은 사용자들에게 보안은 매우 중요한 고려사항이다.
(B) 추가적인 데이터 저장 옵션이 유료로 구매 가능합니다.
(C) 저희 비디오의 몇 개만 다운로드 가능합니다.
(D) 서버 문제점이 이번 주 안에 고쳐질 것입니다.

해설 빈칸 앞 부분에 CrazyCloud사가 많은 양의 파일 공간을 제공
하므로, 사용자는 대용량 파일 저장에 대한 걱정을 할 필요가 없다는
내용이 나왔기 때문에, 빈칸에는 파일 저장 관련 내용이 오는 것이 흐
름상 적절하다. 따라서, 데이터 추가 옵션을 유료로 구입할 수 있다는
(B) Additional data storage options can be purchased for a
fee.가 정답이다. 사용자들의 보안이 가장 중요한 고려사항이라는 (A),
일부 비디오만 다운로드 가능하다는 (C), 일주일 내로 서버 문제가 고
쳐질 것이라는 (D)는 빈칸 앞 부분의 핵심 내용인 '대용량 파일 저장'과
연관성이 없으므로 오답이다.

UNIT 02. 실전연습 01

본서 p.216

1. (C)	**2.** (B)	**3.** (B)	**4.** (C)	**5.** (D)
6. (D)	**7.** (B)	**8.** (D)	**9.** (A)	**10.** (B)
11. (C)	**12.** (D)	**13.** (C)	**14.** (B)	**15.** (A)
16. (C)				

[1-4] 다음 메모에 관한 문제입니다.

수신: Zenetech 직원들
발신: 보안팀
날짜: 9월 12일
제목: 신규 시스템

전 직원들은 사무실 출입에 관한 보안 정책 변경 사항을 알고 있어
야 합니다. **1** 이전에, 여러분의 신분증 배지로 건물 출입이 가능했
습니다만, 9월 20일부터, 지문 인식 스캐너가 모든 출입구에 **2** 설
치될 것입니다. 따라서, 직원들은 더 이상 건물 출입을 위해 배지를
이용할 수 없습니다. 다음 주, 여러분은 지문을 스캔하러 경비실로
올 것을 요청받게 될 것입니다. 부서 매니저가 직원들이 올 수 있는
시간들을 보내오는 대로, 직원들에게 예정 시간대가 **3** 고지될 것입
니다. **4** 스캐닝 절차는 5분도 채 걸리지 않을 것입니다. 정책에 관
한 질문이 있으면, 보안 직원들 중 한 명에게 연락 바랍니다.

어휘 aware of ~을 알고 있는 I security policy 보안 정책 I
regarding ~에 관하여 I entry 출입 I access to ~로의
접근[접속] I fingerprint 지문 I no longer 더 이상 ~않는 I
security office 경비실 I scan (스캐너로) 스캔하다

1. 해설 빈칸 뒤에는 새로운 보안 정책 이전에 활용되어진 신분증 사용
방식이 나오므로 (C) Previously가 정답이다. (A) Finally '마침내', (B)
Accordingly '따라서', (D) Consequently '결과적으로'

2. 해설 보기가 모두 동사로 구성되어 있기 때문에, 「수 일치 → 태
→ 시제」 순서로 정답을 확인한다. (C)는 복수 주어 fingerprint
scanners와 수 일치가 안되므로 오답이며, 스캐너들은 설치되는 것
이므로 능동형인 (A) 역시 오답이다. 보내는 날짜(September 12)
이후인 September 20일부터 시행되므로 미래 시제인 (B) will be
installed가 정답이다.

3. 해설 빈칸은 관사와 전치사 사이의 명사 자리이므로 명사인 (B)
notification이 정답이다.

4. (A) 신분증 배지를 교체하는데 비용이 있습니다.
(B) 이 프로젝트는 아직 이사회에서 승인되어야 합니다.
(C) 스캐닝 절차는 5분도 채 걸리지 않을 것입니다.
(D) 이 유지 작업은 일주일에 한 번 실행됩니다.

해설 빈칸 앞부분에서 직원들의 지문 스캔을 위한 예정 시간대가 고지될 거라 했기 때문에 빈칸에는 이와 관련된 내용이 언급되는 것이 자연스럽다. 따라서, 보기 중 스캐닝 과정을 나타낸 (C) The scanning process should not take more than five minutes.가 정답이다.

[5-8] 다음 이메일에 관한 문제입니다.

발신: bradhouser@ellieassociates.com
수신: s_davis@tcshsecurity.com
날짜: 4월 27일
제목: 감사

Ms. Davis께,

화요일에 저희 사무실을 **5** 방문하신 데 대해 감사드리기 위해 이메일 드립니다. 귀하의 보안 관련 발표는 **6** 유익했습니다. 특히, 저희 경영진은 새로운 서버들이 어떻게 작동하고 어떻게 우리의 네트워크가 안전하게 유지될 수 있는지를 시간을 들여 정성껏 설명해주신 데 대해 고마워했습니다.

7월에, 다른 지점에 있는 일부 직원들이 이곳으로 이동하게 됩니다. 그때 **7** 귀하께서는 한 번 더 시연을 하러 다시 오실 의향이 있으신가요? **8** 저희 새 직원들이 분명 그것이 유용하다는 것을 알게 될 것입니다. 곧 답변 듣기를 고대합니다.

안부 전하며,

Brad Houser

어휘 security 보안 | presentation 발표 | appreciate 고마워하다, 환영하다 | carefully 정성을 다해, 주의 깊게 | relocate 이전하다 | return to ~로 돌아오다 | demonstration 시연, 시범 | look forward to ~ing ~하기를 고대하다

5. **해설** 빈칸 뒤의 서버와 관련된 발표가 유익했다는 내용에 근거하여 사무실 방문에 감사드린다는 의미의 (D) visiting이 정답이다. (A) calling '전화하는 것', (B) moving '이동하는 것', (C) opening '여는 것'

6. **해설** 보기가 모두 동사로 구성되어 있기 때문에 「수의 일치 → 태 → 시제」 순서로 정답을 확인한다. 수의 일치에 어긋나는 보기는 없고, 주어인 your ~ presentation은 알리는(inform) 주체가 아니라 대상이므로 능동형인 (A), (C)는 오답이다. 빈칸 뒷문장에서 시간을 들여 설명해 준 데 대해 감사하다고 했으므로, 과거 시제인 (D) was informative가 정답이다.

7. **해설** 빈칸은 유익한 발표를 해준 상대편에게 다른 시연을 해줄 의향이 있는지를 묻는 문장의 주어이므로 (B) you가 정답이다.

8. (A) 최근 설문조사에 남겨주신 피드백에 매우 감사드립니다.
고난도 (B) 저희는 새 지점 개장식에 모든 매니저들이 참석하도록 초대합니다.
(C) 이곳의 직원은 모든 보안규칙을 엄격하게 따릅니다.
(D) 저희 새 직원들이 분명 그것이 유용하다는 것을 알게 될 것입니다.

해설 앞에서 유익한 발표에 대해 고마워하며 시연을 요청한다고 했으므로 그 시연과 관련된 내용인 (D) Our new members would definitely find it useful.이 정답이다. (D)의 지시대명사 it은 정답의 주요 단서로 빈칸 앞의 another demonstration를 나타낸다. (A)의 설문에서의 의견, (B)의 신규지점 개장식 참여 권유, (C)의 보안규칙 준수는 빈칸 앞 부분의 핵심 내용인 시연 요청과 연관되지 않으므로 오답이다.

[9-12] 다음 편지에 관한 문제입니다.

Ms. Stephanie Marx
Washington 공업
Central 가 589번지 NW
몬트리올, 퀘백 H3Z 2Y1

Ms. Marx께,

고객님께서 Fast Step 바닥재에 보여주시는 관심에 대해 듣게 되어 기쁩니다. 저희 회사의 바닥재 상품은 그야말로 최고이며, 저희 회사가 제공하는 제품에 대해 고객님이 만족해하실 것을 확신합니다.
고객님의 사무실과 같은 바쁜 장소에서 사무실 바닥은 많은 손상을 입습니다. 그러한 **9** 지속적인 혹사를 고려할 때, 바닥재는 수년을 견디면서 좋은 외관을 유지할 정도로 충분히 견고해야 합니다.
이와 같은 필요에 **10** 부응하여, Fast Step 바닥재는 특허를 획득한 Ten-Year 라인 바닥재를 만들었습니다. 사실, Ten-Year 라인 바닥재는 가능한 한 가장 튼튼한 바닥재로 제작된 것입니다. 이름이 말해주듯이, 이 라인은 최소 10년간은 구매 첫날과 같은 외관이 지속될 것을 **11** 보장합니다. **12** 어떠한 이유로라도 귀하가 불만족스럽다면, 저희는 환불해 드릴 것입니다.
무료 견적을 받길 원하시면, 오늘 514-639-1000으로 전화하세요!

진심으로,

Stanley Friedman
Fast Step 바닥재

어휘 flooring 바닥, 바닥재 | simply 그야말로, 간단히 | be pleased with ~에 만족하다 | take a beating 손상을 입다, 대패하다 | abuse 혹사, 남용, 혹사시키다. 남용하다 | tough 강한, 거친 | last 지속하다 | needs 필요성 | patented 특허를 받은 | at least 최소한, 적어도 | estimate 견적서, 평가서 | constant 지속적인 | prevent 방지하다 | address 해결하다, 부응하다 | improve 향상시키다 | research 연구 조사하다, 연구 조사 | guarantee 보증하다

9. **해설** 빈칸 뒤의 abuse는 동사와 명사 둘 다로 쓰이기 때문에 이 문제에서 어떤 품사로 쓰였는지를 판단하는 것이 중요하다. abuse는 타동사이기 때문에 그 뒤에 목적어가 수반되어야 하나, 여기에서는 뒤에 목적어가 없기 때문에 명사로 쓰였다. 따라서, 빈칸은 명사를 꾸며주는 형용사 자리이므로 (A) constant가 정답이다. (C) constable은 순경을 의미하는 명사이므로 오답이다.

10.
고난도

해설 빈칸 뒤의 these needs는 앞 문장의 바닥재 상품이 견고해야 한다는 내용을 받아준다. 문맥상 이러한 요구 사항들에 부응하기 위해 특허 획득 바닥재를 만들었다는 내용이 알맞으므로 '부응하다, 해결하다'의 뜻을 가진 (B) address가 정답이다. (A) prevent '예방하다', (C) improve '향상시키다', (D) research '조사하다'

11.
고난도

해설 수의 일치에 어긋나는 보기는 없고, 바닥재 제품은 보장되는 것이므로 능동형인 (A), (B)는 오답이다. 이미 정해놓은 일이 미래까지 일정기간 지속되는 공연 일정, 대중교통 시간표, 계약서, 품질 보증 등은 현재 시제를 사용하므로 (C) is guaranteed가 정답이다.

12. (A) 이 바닥재는 5년 이상 쉽게 지속됩니다.
(B) 작은 비용으로 저희가 사람을 보내 귀하의 집을 살펴보게 해주십시오.
(C) 귀하의 부엌에 저희 특별 제품 바닥재를 설치해주셔서 감사합니다.
(D) 어떠한 이유로라도 귀하가 불만족스럽다면, 저희는 환불해 드릴 것입니다.

해설 빈칸 앞 부분에 제품의 품질이 뛰어나 최소 10년간 보장한다고 했기 때문에 품질에 대한 확신을 추가적으로 나타낸 (D) If you're unsatisfied for any reason, we'll refund your money.가 흐름상 자연스럽다. (A)는 앞에서 적어도 10년간 보장된다는 내용이 제시되었으므로 연결이 자연스럽지 못하다. 사무실 바닥재 관련(In busy offices such as yours) 글이므로 집을 살펴보기 위해 사람을 보내겠다는 (B)도 본문의 내용과 일치하지 않으며, 제품 설치에 관심 있는 고객에게 제품을 소개하므로 이미 설치한 것에 대해 감사한다는 (C)도 오답이다.

[13-16] 다음 기사에 관한 문제입니다.

제조업 학회, 11월 11일 – 올해의 세계 제조업 학회가 지난주 마이애미에서 열렸다. **13** 학회는 전 세계의 업체들이 참석하도록 초대했다. 지난해와 마찬가지로, 미국과 캐나다 기업들이 **14** 크게 두각을 나타냈다. **15** 더욱이, 참가자들은 이번에 상당히 많은 유럽 참석자들이 있었다는 데 주목했다. 눈에 띈 점은 음식 포장 공장들이 올해의 **16** 행사에서 더 큰 존재감을 보여줬다는 사실이었다.

어휘 corporation 기업, 회사 | represent 대표하다, 나타내다 | notice 주목하다, 알아차리다 | significant 상당한 | attendee 참석자 | noticeable 뚜렷한 | packaging 포장 | plant 공장 | presence 입지, 존재감

13.
고난도
(A) 비슷한 학회가 한 주 전에 열렸다.
(B) 마이애미 주민들이 여행을 조직하는데 도움을 주었다.
(C) 학회는 전 세계의 업체들이 참석하도록 초대했다.
(D) 자원 봉사를 했던 이들에게는 등록비가 면제되었다.

해설 빈칸 앞부분에서 학회가 지난주에 개최되었다고 했고 뒷부분에서는 참석한 여러 국가 기업들 중 미국과 캐나다 기업들이 두각을 나타냈다고 했으므로 빈칸에는 지난주 학회에 참석했던 대상과 관련된 내용이 흐름상 자연스럽다. 따라서, 그 학회가 전 세계 기업들에게 참석하도록 했다는 (C) The conference invited companies from across the globe to attend.가 정답이다. (A)의 유사한 회의, (B)의

여행, (D)의 봉사자에게 면제된 등록비는 앞뒤 문장의 핵심 내용의 조합인 '지난주 개최된 학회 + 참석 기업들'과 연결고리가 없기 때문에 오답이다. 이처럼, 문장 선택 문제는 추상적으로 연결 내용을 생각해서 정답을 선택하지 말고, 빈칸 앞, 뒤의 핵심 내용을 정확히 파악하여 그 범위를 좁혀 흐름과 어울리는 문장을 선택해야 한다는 점에 유의한다.

14. **해설** 빈칸은 「be + 과거분사」 사이의 부사 자리이므로 정답은 (B) heavily이다.

15. **해설** 미국과 캐나다 기업뿐만 아니라 유럽 참석자들도 많았다는 내용이므로 동일한 내용의 추가, 부연을 의미하는 (A) Moreover가 정답이다. (B) Therefore '그러므로', (C) Instead '대신에', (D) Rather '오히려'

16. **해설** 이번 학회에서 더 큰 존재감을 보였다는 의미이므로 World Manufacturers' Conference를 의미하는 (C) event가 정답이다. (A) luncheon '오찬', (B) demonstration '시연', (D) class '수업'

UNIT 03. 실전연습 02
본서 p.220

1. (B)	2. (C)	3. (A)	4. (A)	5. (A)
6. (C)	7. (B)	8. (C)	9. (B)	10. (D)
11. (B)	12. (A)	13. (B)	14. (B)	15. (C)
16. (D)				

[1-4] 다음 광고에 관한 문제입니다.

여러분은 밤에 일하고 낮에 잠을 청하시나요? 그렇다면 AdenaPoly 웹사이트를 오늘 방문하세요.
올해 12월, AdenaPoly는 HN 제약을 대신하여 특별 연구를 수행할 것입니다. 이것이 우리가 18~45세 사이의 야간 근로자들을 **1** 구하고 있는 이유입니다. 참가자들은 실험이 시작될 **2** 시점에 반드시 야간 정규 근무를 적어도 일 년은 해왔어야 합니다. **3** 저희는 여러분의 현 직장의 연락처를 제공할 것을 요청합니다.
더 많은 정보를 원하는 분들께서는 저희 웹사이트에서 몇 가지 질문에 대한 답변을 작성하셔야 합니다.
감사를 전하기 위해, 모든 참가자들은 연구 참가에 대한 대가로 75달러를 **4** 받을 것입니다.

어휘 conduct 수행하다 | on behalf of ~을 대신하여 | participant 참가자 | full-time 전일직의, 정규직의 | night shift 밤 교대 | experiment 실험 | fill out 작성하다 | take part in 참가하다

1. **해설** 빈칸 뒤에 특별 연구 참가자들의 자격조건이 나오므로 문맥상 참가자들을 구하고 있다는 의미가 되는 (B) seeking이 정답이다. (A) promoting '홍보하는', (C) informing '알리는', (D) insuring '보험에 드는'

2. **고난도** **해설** '시작할 시점(초반)에'의 의미를 갖는 at the start[beginning] of를 묻는 문제이므로 (C) at이 정답이다. (A) except for '~을 제외하고', (B) due to '~때문에', (D) as '~할 때'

3. **고난도** (A) 저희는 여러분의 현 직장의 연락처를 제공할 것을 요청합니다.
(B) 저희는 프로그램의 비용이 가치가 있다고 생각합니다.
(C) 이곳 일자리에 지원하는 방법에 관한 정보지를 보내드리겠습니다.
(D) 저희는 원래 일정의 변경에 대해 저희 환자들이 알기를 바랍니다.

해설 빈칸 앞부분에서 적어도 일 년간 야간 정규 근무를 했어야 한다고 했으므로 이 자격 조건을 확인하기 위한 직장 연락처를 요청하는 내용인 (A) We ask that you provide contact information for your current workplace.가 정답이다. (B)의 프로그램 비용, (D)의 환자들 일정 변경은 빈칸 앞부분의 실험 참가자들의 자격과 연관되지 않으므로 오답이다. (C)의 지원 방식 관련 정보 책자를 발송할 것이라는 내용은 빈칸 뒷부분에 더 많은 정보를 얻고자 하는 사람들은 웹사이트에서 질문을 작성해야 한다는 내용보다 앞에 위치하기에 흐름상 적절하지 않으므로 오답이다.

4. **해설** 문장에 동사가 없기 때문에 준동사인 (C), (D)는 오답이다. 특별 연구는 앞으로 시행할 예정이기 때문에 그 연구에 참가한 사람들이 75달러를 받는 시점도 미래다. 따라서, 미래 시제인 (A) will receive가 정답이다.

[5-8] 다음 이메일에 관한 문제입니다.

수신: Matthew Lee 〈mlee@datazerox.net〉
발신: Hollis Anderson 〈hollisa2@gu.edu〉
제목: 주차 허가증
날짜: 1월 21일

5 분실된 49번 주차장 주차 허가증에 관련하여 저희에게 연락 주셔서 고맙습니다. 고객님의 차량 번호가 여전히 저희 시스템에 있으며 다음 주 동안은 그곳에서 추가로 주차위반 딱지를 받지는 않으실 겁니다. 현재 벌금은 총 22.50달러입니다.
주차장 안내원에게 연락해서 혹시 주차허가증을 발견해서 **6** 가져다 준 사람이 있는지 알아봤습니다. **7** 아직까지는 아무도 오지 않았다는군요.
다음 주까지 허가증을 찾지 못하실 경우 저희 웹사이트에 가시면 새 것을 **8** 주문하실 수 있습니다. 허가증 교체발급 비용은 15달러라는 점 알려드립니다.

진심을 담아,

Hollis Anderson
Gervano 대학교 주차 서비스

어휘 parking permit 주차 허가증 | lot 지역, 부지 | license plate (자동차) 번호판 | attendant 종업원, 안내원 | as of yet 아직[그때](까지) | come forward (도움 등을 주겠다고) 나서다

5. **해설** 빈칸은 소유격과 명사 사이의 형용사 자리이므로 현재 분사형 형용사인 (A) missing이 정답이다.

6. **해설** 빈칸은 had found와 and에 의해 병렬 구조를 이루는 동사 자리이므로 (C) returned가 정답이다.

7. **고난도** (A) 다음 주에 새 딱지가 발급될 겁니다.
(B) 아직까지는 아무도 오지 않았다는군요.
(C) 또한, 주차 시간이 연장될 것입니다.
(D) 주차 허가증은 보이는 곳에 달려있어야 합니다.

해설 빈칸 앞부분에는 주차 허가증을 발견해서 가져다 준 사람이 있는지 알아보기 위해 연락했다는 내용이고 뒷부분에는 다음 주까지 못 찾으면 웹사이트에서 주문하라는 내용이므로 분실된 주차 허가증을 다시 찾았는지 여부와 관련된 내용인 (B) As of yet, no one has come forward.가 흐름상 가장 잘 어울린다. (A)는 글의 앞부분에서 다음 주 동안에 추가 주차 위반 딱지를 받지 않을 것이라는 내용과 일치하지 않으므로 오답이다. (C)의 주차 시간, (D)의 주차 허가증을 부착하는 위치는 빈칸 앞뒤의 핵심 내용인 분실된 주차 허가증을 찾았는지 여부와 연관되지 않으므로 오답이다.

8. **해설** 빈칸 앞에 주차 허가증을 찾지 못한다는 전제 조건이 나오고 뒤에 교체 발급 비용을 알려주고 있으므로 새로운 주차 허가증을 주문한다는 의미의 (C) order가 정답이다. (A) approve '승인하다', (B) design '설계하다', (D) remove '제거하다'

[9-12] 다음 기사에 관한 문제입니다.

Oakdale Daily Gazette
(3월 12일) 이번 주 초 Wendy Biggs 위원장은 앞으로 교육자가 될 사람들을 육성하기 위한 새로운 지역 복지 프로그램을 시작하겠다는 교육 위원회의 계획을 밝혔다. Ms. Biggs는 한 텔레비전 인터뷰에서 중고등학교 교사에 대한 증가된 **9** 수요를 언급했다. **10** 특히, 그녀는 최근 많은 수학, 과학 교사들의 은퇴로 인한 영향을 강조했다. 그녀의 말(진술)은 지역 지도층의 매우 열렬한 반응을 **11** 얻었다. 그러나 시의회 원로 의원 John Tuft는 동의하지 않았다. **12** 그는 경험이 많은 교육자를 임용하는 것이 더 낫다고 생각한다.

어휘 gazette 신문 | superintendent 관리자, 감독관 | board 위원회 | outreach 봉사[복지, 구제] 활동 | statement 말, 진술, 성명

9. **해설** 빈칸 뒤에 최근 많은 수학, 과학 교사들이 은퇴했다는 내용을 단서로 중고등학교 교사들에 대한 수요가 증가했음을 알 수 있다. 따라서 정답은 (B) demand이다. (A) settlement '합의', (C) resolution '해결', (D) entertainment '연예, 오락'

10. **해설** 빈칸 뒤 문장은 앞 문장의 구체적이며 특정한 내용이므로 정답은 (D) In particular이다. (A) Despite this '이것에도 불구하고', (B) Otherwise '그렇지 않으면', (C) Alternatively '그 대신'

11.
고난도 **해설** 문장에 동사가 없기 때문에 준동사인 (C)는 오답이다. Ms. Biggs의 말(진술)은 열렬한 반응을 받는 대상이므로 능동형인 (A)는 오답이며, 과거에 이루어진 일이므로 과거 시제 수동형인 (B) was received가 정답이다.

12. **(A) 그는 경험이 많은 교육자를 임용하는 것이 더 낫다고 생각한다.**
(B) 그는 과학 프로그램이 추가 기금을 받을만하다고 생각한다.
(C) 그는 많은 교사들이 연수에 참여할 것이라고 예상한다.
(D) 그는 수학에 관심 있는 학생들이 더 많을 것이라 생각한다.

해설 빈칸 앞부분에 John Tuft는 Ms. Biggs가 밝힌 앞으로 교육자가 될 사람들을 양성하는 프로그램에 대해 동의하지 않았다는 내용이 나오므로, Ms. Biggs의 프로그램과 반대되는 그의 생각(신규 교육자 양성보다는 경험이 풍부한 교육자들을 고용하는 것이 좋다)을 나타낸 (A) He believes it is better to hire experienced instructors.가 정답이다.

[13-16] 다음 정보에 관한 문제입니다.

Hybridoma 가전제품의 구매를 축하합니다. 이 제품의 사용이 즐거우실 것이라고 확신합니다. 그러나 어떤 이유로든 **13** 만족하지 않는다면, 물건을 사용하지 않았다는 가정 하에 두 달 이내에 교환을 받으시거나 반품하시고 전액 환불을 받으실 수 있습니다. 그렇게 하시려면 포장 상자에 들어 있던 반송 라벨을 작성하셔서 제품을 돌려보내주시기만 하면 됩니다. 제품은 받으신 상자에 넣어서 **14** 보내져야 합니다. **15** 처리하는 데는 3, 4주가 소요될 것입니다. 환불은 현금 지급이나 계좌 입금으로 이행됩니다. 구입에 감사드리며 계속해서 저희 제품을 **16** 주문해주시길 진심으로 바랍니다.

어휘 appliance (가정용) 기기 | process 처리하다 | issue 발부 [지급, 교부]하다 | credit (계좌에 넣는) 입금

13. **해설** 감정을 느끼는 대상인 사람 명사가 주어이므로 감정동사 satisfy의 과거분사인 (B) satisfied가 정답이다.

14. **해설** 문장의 주어인 제품(your product)은 우편으로 발송되는 대상이므로 능동형인 (A), (C)는 오답이다. 만약 만족하지 못하면 반송하여 환불 받으라는 내용이므로 과거부터 현재까지 일어난 일을 나타내는 현재 완료 (D)는 오답이다. 따라서 정답은 (B) should be mailed이다.

15. (A) 이와 같은 문제가 다시는 발생하지 않을 것임을 장담합니다.
(B) 저희는 고품질인 저희 제품에 대해 자부심을 느낍니다.
(C) 처리하는 데는 3, 4주가 소요될 것입니다.
(D) 그것은 어린이들의 손이 닿지 않는 곳에 보관되어야 합니다.

해설 빈칸 앞부분은 제품에 만족하지 않는 경우 반송하는 방식에 대한 내용이고 뒷부분은 환불 방식에 대한 내용이므로 반송을 보낸 후 환불 전까지 처리되는 기간과 관련된 내용인 (C) Processing will take three to four weeks.가 흐름상 가장 잘 어울린다. (A)는 이 문제점(this problem)이 지시하는 내용이 앞 문장에 존재하지 않아 오답이고, (B)의 자사 제품의 고품질에 대한 자부심. (D)의 어린이 손이 닿지 않은 곳에 제품을 두라는 내용은 빈칸 앞뒤의 핵심 내용인 반품과 환불 처리 방식과 연관되지 않으므로 오답이다.

16. **해설** 이 글은 제조사가 가전 제품을 구입한 고객에게 불만족시 환불해주겠다는 고객 서비스 관련 내용으로, 추후에도 고객들에게 자사의 제품을 계속 구입해 달라는 의미가 문맥상 적절하므로 (D) shop이 정답이다. (A) meet '만나다', (B) dine '식사하다', (C) learn '배우다'

UNIT 04. 실전연습 03
본서 p.224

1. (B)	**2.** (A)	**3.** (D)	**4.** (C)	**5.** (C)
6. (B)	**7.** (D)	**8.** (B)	**9.** (D)	**10.** (D)
11. (D)	**12.** (C)	**13.** (B)	**14.** (C)	**15.** (D)
16. (D)				

[1-4] 다음 공지에 관한 문제입니다.

영업 직원들에게,

사무실 내에서 저희는 전자 파일에 대한 가능한 최대한의 보안을 유지하기 위해 노력합니다. 여러분이 고객들을 만나기 위해서 이동을 할 때도 같아야 할 것입니다. 여러분의 노트북에 있는 모든 업무 관련된 파일들을 보호하는 것은 **1** 매우 중요합니다. 만약 여러분이 파일들을 USB에 옮긴다면, USB에 있는 자료들을 보호하기 위해서 USB를 항상 소지하십시오. **2** 파일을 암호화하는 것 또한 아주 좋을 것입니다. 마지막으로, 전화로 업무를 논의할 때는, 가능한 회사에 관한 자세한 정보에 대해서 논의하는 것을 피하십시오. 이러한 간단한 규칙들을 **3** 준수함으로써, 여러분은 사무실 바깥에 있을 때도 보안을 **4** 확실히 하는 것을 도울 수 있습니다. 감사합니다.

Nikita Bagul
정보기술부장

어휘 maintain ~을 유지하다 | maximum 최대한의 | security 보안 | related 관련된 | protect ~을 보호하다 | transport ~을 옮기다 | possession 소유 | at all times 항상 | lastly 마지막으로 | over the phone 전화로 | avoid ~을 피하다 | discuss ~에 대해서 논의하다 | detailed 자세한 | observe ~을 지키다 | ensure ~을 확실히 하다, 보장하다

1. **해설** 빈칸 앞에 고객들을 만날 때 전자 파일에 대한 보안을 유지해야 한다는 내용을 단서로, 노트북에 있는 업무 관련 파일들을 보호하는 것은 매우 중요하다는 의미가 문맥상 적절하므로 (B) essential이 정답이다. (A) probable '있음직한', (C) traditional '전통의', (D) conclusive '결정적인'

2. 고난도

(A) 파일을 암호화하는 것 또한 아주 좋을 것입니다.

(B) 전화로 사업에 대해 이야기하지 않도록 또한 조심하십시오.

(C) 직원들은 사무실에서 어떠한 파일도 복사하는 것이 허락되지 않습니다.

(D) 사무실 컴퓨터에서 일과 관련된 파일들을 삭제하지 마십시오.

해설 빈칸 앞부분에 고객을 만나러 나갈 때 보안을 유지하기 위해서 전자 파일들을 USB로 이동시키는 경우 USB를 지참하라는 내용이 나오므로 파일과 관련된 또 다른 보안 유지법인 (A)가 흐름상 가장 잘 어울린다. (A)의 as well(또한)은 파일들의 보안 관련 추가 내용을 나타내므로 앞 문장과 흐름이 자연스럽다. 빈칸 뒷부분에 사업 논의를 하되 세부 정보를 논의하지 말라 했으므로 전화상으로 사업 논의를 하지 말라는 (B)는 본문의 내용과 일치하지 않으며, (C)의 사무실에서 복사 금지, (D)의 사무실 컴퓨터에서 업무 관련 파일들 삭제 금지는 사무실 내에서 이루어지는 내용으로 고객을 만날 때와 같은 사무실 밖 보안 유지를 위한 규칙들에 대한 빈칸 앞뒤의 내용과 연관되지 않으므로 오답이다.

3. 해설 전치사 by 뒤에 명사와 동명사 모두 올 수 있으나 빈칸 뒤에 목적어 these simple rules가 있으므로 동명사인 (D) observing이 정답이다.

4. 해설 help 뒤에 동사가 오는 경우 '(to) 동사원형' 형태이어야 하므로 to가 생략된 (C) ensure가 정답이다.

[5-8] 다음 이메일에 관한 문제입니다.

수신: Hugh Grant ⟨hgrant@andefitnesscenter.ca⟩
발신: Mark Dion ⟨mdion@andefitnesscenter.ca⟩
제목: 훌륭한 후기
날짜: 10월 3일

Hugh에게,

매니저들은 모두 ⟨Zoom Health Magazine⟩과 ⟨Exercise Weekly⟩ 최신호에 실린 우리 헬스클럽에 관한 훌륭한 후기를 보고 기뻤습니다. A and E 헬스클럽에 대한 당신의 기여가 **5** 훌륭했어요. 이러한 이유로 기꺼이 10월 10일 급여와 함께 보너스를 **6** 지급하겠습니다. **7** 또한 다음 달부터는 급여도 인상해드리겠습니다. 당신이 올 초 이곳의 개인 트레이너가 된 이후 우리 헬스클럽의 회원 수가 50퍼센트 이상 증가했습니다. **8** 다른 유사한 간행물에 나온 우리 헬스클럽에 관한 평가 또한 높아졌습니다. 이러한 긍정적인 흐름은 대부분 당신의 성과 덕분입니다. 경영진으로부터의 진심 어린 감사를 전합니다.

Mark

어휘 review 논평, 비평 | issue (잡지·신문 같은 정기 간행물의) 호 | paycheck 급료 | rating 순위, 평가 | performance 실적, 성과 | extend 주다, 베풀다 | management 경영[운영, 관리]진 | award 수여하다 | publication 출판물

5. 해설 빈칸 앞부분에 매니저들이 Hugh의 후기에 기뻐했고 빈칸 뒷부분에 Hugh에게 보너스와 급여 인상을 제공한다는 내용을 근거로 그의 기여가 뛰어났다는 의미인 (C) outstanding이 정답이다. (A) withdrawn '철회하는', (B) equaled '동등한', (D) affordable '알맞은'

6. 해설 'be pleased to 동사원형'을 묻는 문제이므로 (B) to award가 정답이다.

7. 해설 뛰어난 기여에 대한 보상으로 앞 문장에 보너스 지급이 나오고 뒤에 추가적으로 급여 인상을 제공한다는 내용이 이어지므로 (D) In addition이 정답이다. (A) On the other hand '한편', (B) Even so '그렇기는 하나', (C) For example '예를 들어'

8. 고난도

(A) 저희는 곧 헬스클럽 영업 시간을 연장할 것입니다.

(B) 다른 유사한 간행물에 나온 우리 헬스클럽에 관한 평가 또한 높아졌습니다.

(C) 새로운 관리자가 헬스클럽의 운영을 감독할 것입니다.

(D) 이것은 저희 헬스클럽에서 열리는 가장 인기 있는 행사입니다.

해설 빈칸 앞부분에 Hugh의 뛰어난 기여 덕분에 헬스클럽의 회원수가 증가했다는 내용이 나왔고, 빈칸 뒷문장이 such positive trends로 시작하므로 빈칸에는 헬스클럽의 긍정적인 흐름과 관련된 내용이 적합하다. 따라서, 다른 출판물에서도 그 헬스클럽의 평가가 높아졌다는 (B) Our fitness center's ratings in other similar publications have also risen.이 정답이다. (A)의 운영시간 연장, (C)의 헬스클럽 운영을 감독하는 관리자, (D)의 가장 인기 있는 행사는 빈칸 앞뒤의 핵심 내용인 Hugh의 뛰어난 기여에 따른 헬스클럽의 긍정적인 흐름과 관련성이 없으므로 오답이다.

[9-12] 다음 기사에 관한 문제입니다.

보스턴 (1월 10일) – Fizz Pop 사는 6개월간 청량음료를 한정판 용기에 담아 판매하겠다고 발표했다. 음료수는 회사가 **9** 처음 인기를 얻기 시작했던 50여 년 전에 사용했던 고전적인 스타일의 병과 같은 것에 담겨 판매될 것이다. Fizz Pop은 또한 두 가지 새로운 청량음료를 출시하여, 현재 제공하고 있는 맛의 종류를 **10** 세 배로 늘릴 것이다. 이것들은 새로운 방식으로 전통적인 병 마케팅을 보충할 것이다.

Fizz Pop의 CEO Cindy Grover는 이 판촉행사는 회사의 창립을 기념하는 것이라고 말한다. **11** 또한 옛 시절을 기억하고자 하는 고객들을 유치하게 될 것이다. 회사는 이것이 기존 소비자들과 신세대 사이의 간극을 줄여줄 것이라고 생각한다. Fizz Pop의 한정판 음료는 다음 주 월요일부터 이용할 수 있으며 새로운 맛 **12** 음료들은 3월에 출시된다.

어휘 soft drink 청량음료 | container 그릇, 용기 | classic 고전적인 | release 공개[발표]하다 | flavor 풍미, 향미, 맛 | complement 보완하다 | novel 새로운 | honor 명예를 주다 | founding 설립 | bridge the gap 간극을 메우다 | existing 기존의 | triple 세 배로 만들다 | attract 끌어들이다, 끌어 모으다

9. **해설** 빈칸은 주어와 동사 사이의 부사 자리이며, 앞에 나온 50년 전의 의미를 뒷받침해주는 부분임을 고려할 때 문맥상 (D) first가 적절하다.

10. **해설** 동사 will be가 존재하며 동사 triple을 연결해주는 접속사나 관계사가 없으므로 동사인 (A), (B), (C)는 오답이다. 두 가지 새로운 청량음료를 출시하여, 현재 제공하고 있는 맛의 종류를 세 배로 늘린다는 문맥에 따라 능동의 현재분사인 (D) tripling이 정답이다. 완전한 문장 뒤에 분사구문이 오는 경우 현재분사로 시작하는 경우가 대부분인 점에 유의한다.

11. (A) 최근 시장 동향은 소비자들이 이 맛들을 선호한다는 것을 보여준다.
(B) 이것이 Fizz Pop이 유명해진 이유이다.
(C) 작년부터 청량음료가 인기를 잃어가고 있다.
(D) 또한 옛 시절을 기억하고자 하는 고객들을 유치하게 될 것이다.

해설 빈칸 앞부분과 뒷부분이 전통적인 병을 활용하는 홍보가 주는 긍정적인 효과들과 관련된 내용이므로, 이 홍보가 옛 시절을 기억하고자 하는 고객들을 유치할 것이라는 내용의 (D) It will also attract customers who want to remember the old days.가 흐름상 알맞다. (D)의 it과 빈칸 뒷문장의 this는 모두 the promotion을 받는 대명사인 점도 정답임을 보여주는 중요한 단서가 된다.

12. **해설** 글의 앞 부분에서 이 회사가 전통적인 병과 새로운 두 가
고난도 지 맛 음료들을 출시할 것이라 했으므로, 새로운 두 가지 맛 음료들을 의미하는 (C) varieties가 정답이다. (A) services '서비스들', (B) methods '방법들', (D) devices '장치들'

[13-16] 다음 보도자료에 관한 문제입니다.

Willsbourough 대학 총장 Dr. Bill Sumpter는 더 많은 학생을 수용하도록 중앙 도서관이 **13** 새롭게 단장될 것이라고 발표했다. 지난 몇 년 동안 이 대학교의 등록자 수는 거의 두 배가 되었다. 이것은 점점 더 많은 수의 평판이 좋은 교수들이 교수진에 합류하고 있기 때문인 것으로 보인다. 공사 프로젝트는 2년이 걸릴 것으로 예상된다. **14** 초기에 잡았던 16개월의 추진일정은 추가 검토 후 변경되어야만 했다. 1층과 2층을 확장하는 **15** 동안은 도서관 자료는 건물 지하에서 이용할 수 있다. 지하는 다른 층보다 공간이 더 적기 때문에 이것이 약간의 불편을 초래할 수 있다. Sumpter 박사는 "그러나 **16** 일단 이 프로젝트가 완료되면 학생들은 공부할 공간을 훨씬 더 많이 갖게 될 것입니다."라고 말했다.

어휘 **president** 총장 | **accommodate** 수용하다 | **enrollment** 등록[재적]자 수 | **reputable** 평판이 좋은 | **faculty** 교수진 | **material** 자료 | **access** 이용하다 | **basement** 지하층 | **initial** 처음의, 초기의 | **timeline** 추진일정

13. **해설** 도서관은 새롭게 단장되는 대상이므로 능동형인 (A), (D)는 오답이며, 빈칸 뒤에 공사가 2년 소요될 거라 예상된다 했으므로, 미래시제인 (B) will be renovated가 정답이다.

14. (A) Dr. Sumpter는 교수진의 업적이 매우 자랑스럽다.
고난도 (B) 이것이 학생 등록금 인상의 결과이다.
(C) 초기에 잡았던 16개월의 추진일정은 추가 검토 후 변경되어야만 했다.
(D) 대학은 현재 여러 기업들로부터 자금 지원을 구하고 있다.

해설 빈칸 앞에 대학의 도서관 공사 기간을 2년으로 예상한다는 내용이 나왔기 때문에 공사 추진 기간과 관련된 내용인 (C) The initial timeline of sixteen months had to be revised after further review.가 흐름상 적절하다. (A)의 교수 업적에 대한 Dr. Sumpter의 자부심, (D)의 기업으로부터 자금 지원을 구하고 있다는 내용은 빈칸 앞의 도서관 공사 예상 기간과 연관성이 없으므로 오답이다. 또한, (B)는 대명사 this가 지시하는 내용이 빈칸 앞에 없기 때문에 오답이다.

15. **해설** 빈칸 뒤에 명사구가 있으므로 전치사인 (D) during이 정답이다. (A) even '심지어', (B) while '~동안', (C) in order to '~하기 위해서'

16. **해설** 빈칸 뒤의 this project는 앞으로 있을 대학 도서관 공사를 의미하므로 일단 이 공사가 완료되면(완료될 때), 학생들이 학습할 더 많은 공간을 가지게 된다는 의미에 적합한 (D) once가 정답이다. (A)의 whether가 '~이든 아니든 관계없이'의 부사절 접속사로 쓰이는 경우 whether A or B/whether ~ or not 형태로 쓰이므로 오답이다. (B) since '~이래로', (C) unless '~하지 않는다면'

REVIEW TEST
본서 p.228

1. (B)	**2.** (D)	**3.** (D)	**4.** (C)	**5.** (B)
6. (B)	**7.** (A)	**8.** (D)	**9.** (C)	**10.** (D)
11. (A)	**12.** (B)	**13.** (C)	**14.** (A)	**15.** (D)
16. (A)				

[1-4] 다음 이메일에 관한 문제입니다.

수신: Harriet Watkins 〈hwatkins@mymail.co.ca〉
발신: Customer Inquiries 〈inquiries@lextech.com〉
날짜: 5월 5일 월요일 오후 3:41
제목: 요청하신 정보

고객님의 Sonic Q 태블릿 PC의 사용자 설명서와 관련하여 시간을 내서 연락 주셔서 고맙습니다. 무선 네트워크에 연결하는 방법을 보여주는 단계별 설명이 다소 복잡하다는 **1** 점에 대하여 동의합니다. **2** 다른 사용자들도 같은 문제를 제기하셨습니다. **3** 따라서 저희 기술팀은 그 설명들을 이해하기 훨씬 더 쉽도록 간결하게 만들었습니다. **4** 갱신된 설명서는 웹사이트를 방문하셔서 '온라인 매뉴얼' 메뉴를 클릭하시면 찾으실 수 있습니다. 조언에 대한 감사의 표시로 다음 번 LexTech 제품을 구입하실 때 10퍼센트 할인받으실 수 있는 쿠폰을 보내드리겠습니다.

어휘 **bring up** (화제를) 꺼내다 | **input** 조언

1. **해설** 빈칸은 두 개의 동사(agree, are)를 연결하는 접속사 자리이므로 전치사 (A), (D)는 오답이다. 타동사 agree의 목적어 자리의 명사절을 이끄는 접속사를 선택하는 문제로 빈칸 뒤에 완전한 구조의 문장이 왔으므로 (B) that이 정답이다.

---

2. (A) 이 설문지를 작성하기 위해 잠시만 시간을 내어주시길 바랍니다.
고난도
(B) Sonic Q 태블릿 PC는 저희의 가장 인기 있는 제품입니다.

(C) 저희의 적극적으로 돕는 직원들은 항상 들을 준비가 되어있습니다.

(D) 다른 사용자들도 같은 문제를 제기하셨습니다.

해설 빈칸 앞에 제품 설명서에 나온 무선 네트워크를 연결하는 단계들이 복잡하다는 문제점에 동의한다는 내용이 나오고, 그 후속 조치로 기술팀에서 간결하게 만들었다는 내용이 뒤따르므로, 다른 사용자들도 제품 설명서가 복잡하다는 동일한 문제를 제기했다는 (D) Other users have brought up the same issues.가 흐름상 알맞다.

---

3. **해설** 빈칸 앞 문제점 관련 내용이 원인이고, 뒤에 설명들을 간결하게 만들었다는 것이 결과이므로 인과관계를 나타내는 (D) therefore가 정답이다. (A) similarly '유사하게', (B) nonetheless '그럼에도 불구하고', (C) instead '대신에'

---

4. **해설** 복잡하다는 문제점에 따라 설명들을 간결하게 만들었다고 했으므로 기존 문제점을 반영하여 갱신된 사용자 설명서란 의미의 (C) updated가 정답이다. (A) rough '대략', (B) original '원래의', (D) detailed '자세한'

[5-8] 다음 기사에 관한 문제입니다.

PINEWOOD (11월 1일) — 오늘 몇몇 기업들의 기부로 후원을 받는 새 Harvest Square 쇼핑몰의 기공식이 있다. 이번 **5** 자금 지원의 결과로 본관뿐만 아니라 재고 보관구역의 공사까지 신속히 진행될 것으로 예상된다. 시 당국자들은 도시가 새 쇼핑몰로부터 크게 이익을 누릴 것이라고 생각한다. **6** 이 쇼핑몰은 250개의 정규직 일자리 창출을 지원할 것이다. 주민들 또한 쇼핑몰에 관하여 흥분된 반응을 보이고 있다. 새로 계획된 복합단지 인근에 살고 있는 **7** Kira Siebrand는 "이렇게 편리한 곳에서 쇼핑을 하는 게 정말 기대돼요. 지금까지 오랜 시간 **8** 동안 교통체증과 씨름하며, 오래된 Fairland 쇼핑몰까지 동네를 건너 다녔어요. Harvest Square의 단골이 될 것 같습니다."라고 말한다.

어휘 mark 기념[축하]하다 | groundbreaking 기공(起工)(식) | inventory 재고(품) | benefit from ～로부터 이익을 얻다 | complex (건물) 단지 | funding 자금 제공

---

5. **해설** 빈칸 앞에 여러 기업들의 기부로 후원을 받은 쇼핑몰 기공식이라 했으므로, donations를 바꿔 쓴 (B) funding이 정답이다. (A) design '설계', (C) sale '판매', (D) policy '정책'

---

6. (A) 여러 기업들이 개장식에 참석할 것이다.
고난도
(B) 이 쇼핑몰은 250개의 정규직 일자리 창출을 지원할 것이다.

(C) 지역 주변 거주자들은 더해지는 소음에 익숙해져야 할 것이다.

(D) 연휴기간 동안 쇼핑몰은 교통 문제를 야기할지도 모른다.

해설 빈칸 앞에서 그 시가 신규 쇼핑몰로부터 크게 혜택을 얻을 거라 했으므로, 그 혜택에 대한 일자리 창출 관련 내용인 (B) The center will support the creation of 250 full-time jobs.가 정답이다. 빈칸 뒤에 주민들 또한 신규 쇼핑몰을 통한 편리한 쇼핑을 기대하고 있다고 했으므로, 신규 쇼핑몰의 긍정적 효과를 언급한 (B)가 흐름상 적절하다. (A)의 쇼핑몰 개장 참석 예정이나, (C), (D)의 신규 쇼핑몰이 초래할 부정적인 내용들은 신규 쇼핑몰의 혜택과 흐름상 관련이 없기 때문에 오답이다.

---

7. **해설** 두 개의 동사(lives, states)를 연결하는 접속 기능을 해야 하므로 부사인 (C)와 대명사인 (D)는 오답이다. 빈칸 앞에 사람 선행사가 오고 빈칸 뒤에 주어가 빠진 불완전 구조이므로 주격 관계대명사인 (A) who가 정답이다. 관계부사인 (B)는 뒤에 주어가 있는 완전 구조의 문장이 와야 하므로 오답이다.

---

8. **해설** '지금까지 꽤 오랫동안'이란 의미의 'for some time now'를 묻는 문제이므로 (D) for가 정답이다. (A) about '～에 대해', (B) with '～와 함께', (C) along '～를 따라서'

[9-12] 다음 이메일에 관한 문제입니다.

수신: annad@mcclellancomp.com
발신: ericd@mcclellancomp.com
날짜: 7월 31일
제목: 점장 승진 건

Ms. Dietrich께,

지난주에 1차 승진 면접이 있었습니다. 다음 주 월요일에는 점장 자리에 가장 **9** 적임인 후보자들을 대상으로 2차 면접을 시작할 것입니다. 당신은 오랜 기간 점장이셨기 때문에 회사가 어떤 **10** 자질을 찾고 있는지 알고 계실 것이라고 믿습니다. 다음 면접에 사용할 간단한 시험문제를 만들어주실 수 있겠습니까? **11** 만일 그렇다면, 이번 주 금요일까지 저에게 보내주실 수 있을까요? 그 시험은 후보자들이 (예상되어지는) 어려운 매장 상황들에 대한 해결책들을 제시하도록 하는 것이 좋겠습니다. **12** 신속한 답장 기다리겠습니다.

고맙습니다.

Eric Davis
인사부 부장
McClellan 컴퓨터

어휘 round 한 차례 | phase 단계 | fit 맞는 것 | quality 자질 | ideally 이상적으로 말하면 | shortly 곧

9. 해설 the 뒤에 오는 빈칸이므로 (A)를 명사로 보고 정답으로 할 수 있으나, 그 경우 '지원자들 = 양복 한 벌'의 의미가 되므로 문맥상 적절하지 않다. the 뒤에 최상급이 온 경우에, 문맥이 명확한 명사는 생략할 수 있다는 점에 유의하여 형용사 최상급을 정답으로 해야 한다. 따라서 (C) suitable이 정답이다.

10. 해설 빈칸 앞에 점장 선발을 위한 2차 면접을 실시한다 했고, 빈칸 뒤에 면접을 위한 문제를 의뢰하는 내용이 나오므로, 오랫동안 점장을 지낸 Ms. Dietrich은 이 회사가 찾는 지원자들의 자질을 잘 알고 있다는 의미가 문맥상 적합하다. 따라서, 정답은 (D) qualities이다. (A) locations '위치, 장소', (B) performances '수행', (C) agreements '합의'

11. 해설 빈칸 앞 문장은 면접 문제 개발이 가능한지 문의하는 내용이고, 빈칸 뒤는 금요일까지 그 문제를 보내주겠냐는 내용이다. 글의 흐름상 문제 개발에 동의를 해야 금요일까지 그 문제를 보내줄 수 있기 때문에, '앞 문장에 대한 동의를 한다면'의 의미인 (A) If so가 문맥상 적합하다. (B) Even so '그렇다 하더라도', (C) Instead '대신에', (D) For example '예를 들어'

12. (A) 저희는 당신의 해결책을 곧 시행할 계획입니다.
(B) 신속한 답장 기다리겠습니다.
(C) 도착하시면, 가능한 직책에 관해 논의할 것입니다.
(D) 다음 주에 인터뷰하길 고대합니다.

해설 빈칸 앞 부분이 2차 면접에 필요한 면접 문제 관련하여 Ms. Dietrich에게 문의한 내용이므로 그 문의 내용에 대한 신속한 답변을 기다리겠다는 (B) I hope to hear from you shortly.가 흐름상 적절하다.

[13-16] 다음 보도자료에 관한 문제입니다.

마이애미의 가장 유명한 전자제품 공급 업체 Terracotta Hi-Tech는 Camten 대학교 캠퍼스 확장 프로젝트에 15,000달러를 🔞 내놓겠다고 밝혔다. 이 돈은 지난주 회사 🔞 매장에서 있었던 자선 연회에서 모금되었다. Terracotta의 CEO Alan Leno는 이번 주 금요일 오후 대학 학장을 만나 직접 수표를 전달할 것이다. Terracotta Hi-Tech는 🔞 지난 10년 동안 다양한 학교들과 교육 프로그램들을 위한 여러 번의 모금 행사를 주최해왔다. 🔞 지난주 행사는 단연코 가장 성공적인 것이었다.

어휘 electronics 전자 장치 | supplier 공급 업체 | award 수여하다 | raise (자금·사람 등을) 모으다 | charity banquet 자선 연회 | dean 학장 | fundraiser 모금 행사 | by far 단연코

13. 해설 지문 중간에 'CEO, Alan Leno가 그 돈을 직접 전달한다'는
고난도 부분을 단서로, 'Camten 대학 캠퍼스 확장 프로젝트에 15,000달러를 내놓을 것이다'라는 문맥이 적합하다. 따라서, 미래에 발생할 일을 나타내는 미래시제 (C) will award가 정답이다. 빈칸은 동사 자리이므로 (D)는 적절하지 않으며, (B)는 수 일치가 되지 않으므로 오답이다. (A)의 조동사 may는 (C)의 조동사 will보다 실현 가능성이 낮은 상황을 나타내기 때문에, '직접 전달할 것'이라는 본문의 단서에 비춰봤을

때 부적절하다. (A) may award '금액을 전달할지도 모른다' (C) will award '금액을 전달할 것이다'

14. 해설 지문 맨 앞에서 이 회사의 업종이 전자제품 공급 업체임을 밝히고 있으므로 자선 연회가 열린 장소는 전자제품을 취급하는 '매장'으로 유추하는 것이 바람직하다. 따라서 (A) store가 정답이다. (B) resort '리조트', (C) library '도서관', (D) school '학교'

15. 해설 빈칸 뒤의 구조가 「------- + 명사구(the last decade), 절」이므로 명사구를 이끄는 전치사가 필요하며 기간을 나타내는 명사구가 위치해 있으므로 '~동안에'를 뜻하는 (D) Over가 정답이다. (A) Among '~중에', (B) Behind '~뒤에', (C) Although '~에도 불구하고'

16. (A) 지난주 행사는 단연 가장 성공적인 것이었다.
고난도 (B) Mr. Leno는 약 오후 두 시에 도착할 것이다.
(C) 회사는 또 다른 지점을 다음 달 플로리다에 열 것이다.
(D) 대학은 올해 더 많은 학생들을 받기로 결정했다.

해설 앞에서 지난주에 자선 연회를 열었다고 했으며, 이 업체가 지난 10년 동안 여러 차례의 모금 행사를 주최했다고 했으므로 그 뒤에는 이 행사들의 성과 등이 언급되는 것이 문맥상 적절하다. 따라서 '지난주 행사가 단연코 가장 성공적이었다'는 (A) Last week's event was by far the most successful.이 정답이다.

PART 7

UNIT 01. 주제·목적

핵심 문제 유형

본서 p.237

1. (C)

---

[1] 다음 편지에 관한 문제입니다.

안녕하세요,

1 여러분께 〈Advantage Journal〉 웹사이트의 특징에 관하여 말씀드리기 위해 연락드립니다. 오늘부터, 여러분은 〈Advantage Journal TV〉를 저희 사이트에서 즐기실 수 있습니다.

여러분은 다양한 스포츠 장비들을 평가하고, 최신 스포츠 뉴스를 논의하며, 여러분의 경기를 향상할 수 있도록 도와주는 기법들을 보여주는 작가와 저희 상임 테니스 프로 선수의 테니스 프로그램 비디오 클립을 보실 수 있습니다. 여러분은 또한 전문가들의 해설과 함께 주요 경기들의 하이라이트를 시청하실 수 있습니다.

이 서비스는 오직 저희 잡지 구독자 분들만이 이용 가능해서 이 섹션을 방문하실 때 구독자 번호와 비밀 번호가 요구될 것입니다. 오늘 advantagejournal.com/TV에 방문하셔서 신나는 새 특징들을 경험하시기 바랍니다.

어휘   resident 주민 | match 경기 | along with ~와 함께 | commentary 실황 방송, 해설 | subscriber 구독자 | experience 겪다, 경험하다

Practice

본서 p.238

1. (A)	2. (D)	3. (B)	4. (D)	5. (D)
6. (D)	7. (A)	8. (A)	9. (D)	10. (D)
11. (B)				

[1-2] 다음 문자 메시지에 관한 문제입니다.

오후 1시 45분
발신: Computer Central
Computer Central 고객들을 위한 알림: **1** 승인되지 않은 이메일의 접속을 차단하기 위해, 고객 여러분께서는 로그인 정보를 변경해 주셔야 합니다. 그렇게 하시려면 www.computercentral.com으로 접속하셔서 '사용자 설정'을 클릭하세요. (**2** 고객들을 위한 알림을 더 이상 받지 않으려면, 고객 서비스 센터 555-2367로 전화 주세요.)

어휘   alert 알림, 경보 | prevent 막다, 차단하다 | unauthorized 공인되지 않은, 승인되지 않은 | access 접근 | setting 설정

---

1. 문자 메시지의 목적은 무엇인가?
(A) **인증 정보 수정을 제안하기 위해**
(B) 최근 로그인을 확인해 주기 위해
(C) 이메일 프로그램에 대한 피드백을 요청하기 위해
(D) 시스템 업데이트를 알리기 위해

해설   문자 메시지의 첫머리에 승인되지 않은 접속을 피하기 위해 로그인 정보를 변경하라는 내용이 주제/목적으로 제시되어 있다. 따라서 (A) To suggest modifying some credentials가 정답이다.

---

2. 문자 메시지에 따르면, 고객들은 어떻게 유사한 메시지를 받는 것을 그만둘 수 있는가?
(A) 전자 메시지에 답변함으로써
(B) 웹사이트를 방문함으로써
(C) 컴퓨터의 설정을 업데이트함으로써
(D) **고객 서비스 센터에 연락함으로써**

해설   유사한 메시지를 받지 않는 법을 묻고 있는 세부사항 문제이다. 메시지를 받지 않는 방법으로 고객 서비스 센터에 전화하라는 내용이 있으므로 (D) By contacting customer service가 정답이다.

[3-4] 다음 웹페이지에 관한 문제입니다.

www.mama-cuisine.co.za

홈	장비 대여	추천의 글	사진	연락 정보

가족 경영 기업인 Mama's Cuisine은 10년 가까이 Asherville 주민들과 관광객들에게 음식을 제공해 왔습니다. **4** 분위기 있는 저녁 식사와 가족 모임에서부터 결혼식과 회사 파티에 이르기까지, Mama's의 훌륭한 음식과 정중한 직원들은 당신의 행사를 잊지 못할 일로 만들어 드릴 것입니다. **3** 저희는 귀하의 장소에 어울리는 폭넓은 종류의 대여 장비들과 함께, 농장에서 길러진 엄선된 농작물과 전통적인 요리들을 제공해 드립니다. 귀하의 행사가 실내에서 진행되든 야외에서 진행되든, 저희는 설치부터 뒷정리에 이르기까지 최고의 서비스를 보장합니다. **4** 저희의 현지 담당자가 특별히 엄선된 음식들을 선택할 수 있도록 도움으로써 고객들의 구체적인 요구를 만족시켜 드립니다. 저희 사이트를 둘러보시며 메뉴들을 살펴보시고, 저희 서비스에 대한 고객 분들의 추천의 글을 읽어 보십시오.

Mama's Cuisine
전화번호 031-142-2449
293 Clementine 로, Asherville, 더반 4001

어휘   family-run 가족 경영의 | decade 10년 | intimate 분위기 있는 | gathering 모임 | courteous 정중한, 공손한 | a wide range of 폭넓은 | rental 임대, 임차, 대여 | venue 장소 | guarantee 보장하다 | specific 구체적인, 명확한, 특정한 | unique 독특한 | view 보다 | testimonial 추천의 글

3. 무엇이 광고되는가?
(A) 식료품점
(B) **출장 요리 서비스**
(C) 지역 농장
(D) 주방 가전제품 서비스

해설   Mama's Cuisine이라는 상호명에서 식당 또는 요식업이라는 것을

알 수 있으며, 업체가 제공하는 서비스가 행사에 필요한 음식 전반과 필요 장비를 마련해주는 것임을 알 수 있으므로 (B) A catering service가 정답이다.

---

4. Mama's Cuisine에 관하여 언급된 것은 무엇인가?
(A) 독특한 은식기류를 판매한다.
(B) 휴일에는 영업하지 않는다.
(C) 신생 업체이다.
(D) 고객의 필요에 따른다.

해설 (A)는 독특한 음식들을(A unique selection of foods)이라고 했으나 은식기류에 대한 언급은 없기 때문에 오답이며 (B)는 영업시간이 나와 있지 않으므로 확인할 수 없다. (C)는 10년 가까이 영업을 해왔다는 점에서 성립될 수 없다. (D)는 현지 담당자가 고객의 필요에 맞추어 서비스를 제공한다는 내용에서 정답임을 알 수 있다.

[5-7] 다음 편지에 관한 문제입니다.

Benita's 무용 학원
수상 경력에 빛나는 모든 연령대를 위한 무용 지도
2125 West Windy 가
휴스턴, 텍사스 77001

5월 10일

Jocelyn Montoya
218 Amarilly 가
휴스턴, 텍사스 77002

Ms. Montoya 귀하,

저는 최근에 있었던 Benita's 무용 학원의 강사직을 위한 귀하와의 면접이 즐거웠습니다. **5** 귀하께서 9월부터 전임으로 일할 수 있다면 좋겠습니다. **7** 지금 현재 저희는 재즈, 발레, 탭 댄스 수업을 하고 있습니다. 귀하의 전공이 사교 댄스이므로, 저희는 귀하가 가르치는 새로운 사교 댄스 수업을 가을에 개설하려 합니다.

6 또한 8월에 휴가가 예정되어 있는 발레 강사를 대신할 대리 강사직에 관심이 있으신지도 묻고 싶습니다. 그러면 9월에 수업을 시작하기에 앞서 저희 학원에 익숙해지시는 데 도움이 될 것입니다.

저는 귀하와 함께 일할 것을 고대하고 있습니다. **6** 저희는 귀하의 10년 이상의 교육 경험들이 저희 학원에 귀중한 자산이 될 것이라는 느낌이 듭니다. 7월 말까지 555-0150으로 제게 연락 주시면, 시간 약속을 정해 귀하의 서류 작업을 마무리 짓고 가을 수업 일정을 짤 수 있을 것입니다.

진심으로,

Benita Juarez
Benita Juarez
감독

어휘 award-winning 수상 경력에 빛나는 | instruction 지도, 가르침 | instructor position 강사직 | full-time 정규직의, 전임의 | specialty 전공 | ballroom dancing 사교 댄스 | feature 포함하다 | whether ~인지 아닌지 | substitute-teaching position 대리 교사[강사]직 | fill in

채우다, 대신하다 | be scheduled to ~할 예정이다 | familiarize 익숙하게 하다 | look forward to ~하기를 고대하다 | valuable 소중한 | set up an appointment 시간 약속을 정하다 | finalize 마무리 짓다 | job interview 채용 면접 | make an offer 제안을 하다 | employment 채용 | currently 현재 | substitute teacher 대리 교사[강사]

5. 이 편지의 목적은 무엇인가?
(A) 새로운 학원의 개원을 알리기 위해
(B) 취업 면접 일정을 잡기 위해
(C) 댄스 수업들을 광고하기 위해
(D) 채용을 제안하기 위해

해설 지문의 첫단락에서 이미 Benita's 무용 학원의 강사 직위에 관한 인터뷰를 진행하였고, 9월부터 근무를 시작하기를 바란다는 이야기를 한 것을 보아서 편지의 목적은 (D) To make an offer of employment 임을 확인할 수 있다.

---

6. 이 편지에 따르면, Ms. Montoya에 관해서 옳은 것은 무엇인가?
(A) 무용 대회 수상을 했다.
(B) 현재 대리 강사이다.
(C) 8월에 휴가를 갈 것이다.
(D) 많은 강의 경험이 있다.

해설 (A)는 언급되지 않은 내용이며 (B)와 (C)는 휴가를 갈 사람은 다른 강사이고, Ms. Montoya가 관심 있을 시에 대리 강사를 하는 것이므로, 현재 대리 강사가 아님을 알 수 있다. 세 번째 단락에서 Ms. Montoya의 강의 경력이 최소 10년 이상임을 알 수 있으므로 정답은 (D) She has a lot of teaching experience.이다.

---

7. 현재 Benita's 무용 학원에서 제공되지 않는 무용 강좌는 무엇인가?
(A) 사교 댄스
(B) 재즈
(C) 발레
(D) 탭 댄스

해설 지문 첫 번째 단락에서 현재 제공하고 있는 강의는 jazz, ballet, tap-dancing인 것을 확인할 수 있다. Ballroom은 앞으로 강의할 내용으로 현재 제공하는 강의가 아니므로 정답은 (A) Ballroom이다.

[8-11] 다음 편지에 관한 문제입니다.

5월 26일

Marie Dupont
300 Haussmann 대로
75008 파리, 프랑스

Ms. Dupont께,

축하합니다! **8** 귀하께서 제7회 연례 프랑스 고급 요리 경연대회에서 여덟 명의 결승 진출자 중 한 명으로 뽑히셨음을 알려드리게 되어 매우 기쁩니다. 200개가 넘는 출품작들 중, 진짜 프랑스 재료들의 섬세한 활용을 잘 보여주는 적절한 예로 귀하의 니스와즈 샐러드 키시 레시피가 선정되었습니다. 귀하는 결승 진출자이기에, 이 대회에 아낌없는 후원을 하고 있으며 수상 경력이 있는 **8** Fruits de Terre 식당의 150달러 상품권을 받을 것입니다.

또한, 시의 연례 프랑스 음식 축제 기간 동안 판정단을 위해 귀하의 요리를 준비해 주시기 바랍니다. **9** 올해 축제는 6월 29일 금요일부터 7월 1일 일요일까지 열릴 것입니다. 결승 진출자들은 일요일 오후 1시에 Fruits de Terre 식당 밖에 있는 캠핑 구역에서 요리를 시작할 것입니다. 심사는 오후 4시 30분에 시작되며, 시상식은 그 후에 바로 진행될 것입니다. **10** 1등상은 저명한 수석 요리사이자 텔레비전 유명인사인 Louis Lebrun이 가르치는 최고의 요리 강좌를 받게 될 것입니다. Mr. Lebrun은 우승자에게 일주일 동안 일대일 개인 요리 강습을 해주실 예정입니다.

11 이 경연의 결승에 참여하실 의향이 있음을 알려주시고, 대회에서 귀하의 자리를 확보하시기 위해 출력된 양식을 작성하셔서 제출하셔야 합니다. 저희 사무실 01 83 46 94 72로 전화하셔서 늦어도 6월 5일 화요일까지는 알려주시기 바랍니다.

답변 기다리겠습니다!

진심으로,

Pierre Beaufort
프랑스 고급 요리 행사 진행자

어휘　select 선택하다 | finalist 결승 진출자 | competition 경연 | recipe 요리법, 레시피 | entry 출품작 | delicate 섬세한, 우아한 | authentic 진짜인, 정확한 | ingredient 재료 | sponsor 후원하다 | panel 패널(전문가 집단) | judging 심사 | immediately 즉시 | renowned 잘 알려진, 유명한 | head chef 총괄 요리사, 수석 요리사 | personality 인물, 유명인 | notify 알리다, 통지하다 | intend to ~하려고 하다 | secure 확보하다 | confirm 확인하다 | no later than 늦어도 ~까지는

8. Mr. Beaufort는 Ms. Dupont에게 왜 편지를 썼는가?
(A) 상품 수령자임을 확인시켜 주기 위해
(B) 지원서의 수령을 확인해 주기 위해
(C) 요리 강사로 채용하기 위해
(D) 대회의 심사를 부탁하기 위해

해설　편지 첫머리에서 경연대회의 결승 진출 소식을 전하며 상품권을 받게 될 것이라고 말하고 있으므로 (A) To identify her as an award recipient가 정답이다.

9. 경연 참가자들은 언제 시간을 내야 하는가?
고난도　(A) 5월 28일에
(B) 6월 5일에
(C) 6월 29일에
(D) 7월 1일에

해설　축제는 6월 29일 금요일부터 7월 1일 일요일까지이며, 결승 진출자들은 일요일 오후 1시에 요리를 시작한다고 했으므로 축제 기간 중 경연 참가자들이 결승을 벌이는 것은 일요일인 (D) On July 10다.

10. 프랑스 고급 요리 경연대회 수상자의 상품은 무엇인가?
(A) 수료증
(B) 텔레비전 쇼 출연 초청
(C) 요리사 일자리
(D) 일련의 요리 강좌들

해설　Ms. Dupont이 받는 상품이 아닌, 경연대회의 최종 우승자가 받는 상품을 묻는 문제이다. 1등상은 일주일간 진행되는 유명 요리사의 요리 강좌라는 점을 알 수 있으므로 정답은 (D) A series of cooking lessons이다.

11. Ms. Dupont은 무엇에 관하여 확인 요청을 받는가?
(A) 인터뷰 가능 시간
(B) 행사 참석 여부
(C) 연락처 세부 사항
(D) 식당 예약

해설　편지의 마지막 단락에서 경연 참가 여부를 알리며 자리 확보를 위해 양식을 보낼 것을 요청하고 있다. 즉, 참가 여부를 확인하는 것이므로 정답은 (B) Her participation in an event이다.

UNIT 02. 상세정보

핵심 문제 유형　　　본서 p.243

1. (B)

[1] 다음 광고에 관한 문제입니다.

SUMMIT 호텔

게시일: 9월 14일
직책 유형: 시설 관리 책임자
연락처: Caitlyn Tam, 인사 책임자
위치: 몬트필리어, 버몬트, USA

고용 업체
1세기 전에 이 지역에 설립된 Summit 호텔은 15,000명 이상의 직원들을 둔 100여 개의 프랜차이즈를 가진 전국 체인입니다. 저희 호텔은 일반적으로 스키 리조트 인근에 위치해 있으며, 버몬트 한 곳에만 12개의 지점이 있습니다. 저희 회사는 고객 서비스의 탁월함 면에서 한결같이 최고 열 개의 호텔 체인에 순위를 올리고 있습니다. 저희 직원들은 큰 혜택과 경쟁력 있는 급여를 누리고 있습니다. 또한 경력 개발을 위한 충분한 기회도 있습니다.

책무와 요구 조건

시설 관리 책임자는 객실 청소와 세탁, 위생 시스템 감시에 있어서 호텔 직원들 전체를 감독하고 교육할 책임이 있습니다. 이 직책의 책무는 재고 확인과 청소용품 주문도 포함됩니다. 이 직책을 얻기 위해, 합격자는 반드시 훌륭한 의사소통 능력과 조직력 및 현행 보건, 안전, 위생 지침에 대한 완벽한 지식을 입증해야 합니다.

1 이 직책에 지원하시려면, 10월 31일까지 짧은 자기소개서와 이력서 사본을 Ms. Caitlyn Tam에게 catetam@summithrmail.com으로 보내주세요. 자격을 갖춘 지원자 분들은 면접을 위해 11월 13~17일 사이에 연락을 받을 것입니다.

어휘 found 설립하다 | typically 보통, 일반적으로 | consistently 한결같이, 일관되게 | rank (순위를) 차지하다 | competitive 경쟁력 있는 | ample 충분한 | career development 경력 개발 | laundry 세탁(물) | inventory 재고 | cleaning supplies 청소용품 | successful candidate 합격자 | demonstrate 입증하다, 보여주다 | superb 최상의, 대단히 훌륭한 | thorough 완전한, 철저한 | sanitation 위생 | qualified 자격이 있는

Practice

1. (A)	**2.** (C)	**3.** (D)	**4.** (A)	**5.** (B)
6. (C)	**7.** (C)	**8.** (A)	**9.** (B)	

[1-2] 다음 편지에 관한 문제입니다.

1월 21일

Elene Labeire
23 Majeure 가
리옹, 프랑스 3232

Ms. Labiere께,

축하드립니다! **1** 귀하께서는 6개월간 완전 무료로 〈Computer Today〉를 받아 보실 수 있도록 선정되셨습니다. **1** 상을 받은 이 출간물의 각 호에서, 귀하는 유명한 작가들이 쓴 기사와 컴퓨터 제품에 대한 광범위한 정보, 유익한 웹사이트, 유지에 관한 조언들을 찾으실 수 있습니다. **2** 이 여섯 권을 받으시려면, 동봉된 선지불 답장 카드를 저희에게 보내주시기만 하면 됩니다. 6개월 무료 이용 기간 만료 시, 귀하께서 25.99유로라는 저렴한 입회 가격으로 연간 구독권 등록을 고려해 보시기를 희망합니다.

진심으로,

Marissa Jeune
Marissa Jeune
영업부

동봉물 재중

어휘 issue (잡지, 신문의) 호, 발행(물) | award-winning 상을 받은, 수상한 | publication 출판(물), 발행 | notable 눈에 띄는, 주목할 만한 | a broad range of 범위가 다양한, 폭이 넓은 | maintenance 유지, 지속 | prepaid 선불[선납]된 | complimentary 무료의 | subscription 구독 | introductory 서두의; 소개(용)의, 입회의

1. 무엇이 광고되고 있는가?

(A) 유명 잡지
(B) 북 클럽 회원권
(C) 할인된 수리 서비스
(D) 전자 회사

해설 편지 첫머리에서 〈Computer Today〉를 받도록 선정되었다는 것을 알 수 있고, 다음 문장에서 〈Computer Today〉는 수상 경력이 있는 출간물 임을 알 수 있으므로, 광고되고 있는 것은 (A) A renowned magazine이다.

---

2. Ms. Labiere는 무엇을 하라고 요청받는가?
(A) 결제 옵션을 선택하라고
(B) 웹사이트에 접속하라고
(C) 답장 카드를 발송하라고
(D) 기사를 작성하라고

해설 밑에서 세 번째 줄에서 무료 출간물을 받으려면 동봉된 선지불 카드를 보내달라고 요청하고 있으므로 정답은 (C) Send in a reply card이다.

[3-4] 다음 공지에 관한 문제입니다.

Pressman 양탄자
85 Hougang 로
04-32 Hougang 쇼핑 센터
싱가포르, 548756
www.pressmanrugs.co.sg

6월 3일 일요일, 특별 행사!

저희의 단골 고객 중 한 분으로서, **3** 획기적이고 새로운 양탄자 섬유로 제작된 저희 Easiwipe 양탄자의 새 라인을 소개하는 단독 행사에 당신을 초대합니다. 저희는 최근 제품 실험을 통해 Easiwipe 양탄자가 비슷한 가격대의 다른 양탄자들보다 먼지를 30퍼센트 더 적게 들러붙게 하며, 더 강한 내구성을 가지고 있음을 발견했습니다. 또한, **4** 여러분이 6월 3일에 저희 가게에서 Easiwipe 양탄자를 구입하시면, 정상 가격에서 최대 50퍼센트까지 할인을 받으실 수 있습니다. 6월 3일 Easiwipe 전시실에 입장하시려면 이 공지문을 저희 가게로 가져오셔서, 직원들에게 제시만 해주시면 됩니다. 그곳에서 귀하를 만나 뵙기를 바랍니다!

어휘 rug 깔개, 양탄자 | special 특별한, 독특한 | loyal patron 단골 손님 | exclusive 독점적인, 전용의 | manufacture 제작하다 | innovative 혁신적인 | fiber 섬유 | product test 제품 실험 | attract 끌다 | dust 먼지 | durability 내구성, 내구력 | similarly 비슷하게, 유사하게 | priced 가격이 매겨진 | up to ~까지 | present 제시하다, 보여주다 | entrance 문, 입장 | showroom 전시실

3. Easiwipe 양탄자에 관하여 언급된 것은 무엇인가?

(A) 다른 양탄자들보다 50퍼센트 이상 더 내구성이 뛰어나다.

(B) 무료로 배송된다.

(C) 다양한 색깔로 판매된다.

(D) 독특하고 새로운 재료로 제작된다.

해설 (A)는 다른 양탄자들보다 내구성이 더 있으나 구체적으로 수치가 언급되지 않았기 때문에 오답이며 (B), (C)는 언급되지 않았다. 첫 번째 줄에서 양탄자가 새로운 섬유로 제작되었음을 확인할 수 있으므로 정답은 (D) They are manufactured with a unique new material.이다.

---

4. 고객은 어떻게 Easiwipe 양탄자의 할인을 받을 자격이 되는가?

(A) 매장 행사에 참석함으로써

(B) 고객 설문지를 작성함으로써

(C) 양탄자를 온라인으로 주문함으로써

(D) Pressman 양탄자를 친구에게 소개함으로써

해설 6월 3일에 Easiwipe 양탄자를 구입할 시에, 편지의 고객에게 일반 가격에서 최대 50%까지 할인을 해준다고 했으므로 양탄자를 구입하는 행사에 참여할 시에 할인을 받을 수 있다는 (A) By attending a store event가 정답이다.

[5-9] 다음 기사와 이메일에 관한 문제입니다.

5월 30일 – 인상주의 예술가 Sam Gibbins의 작품들이 Downtown Culver의 Pendulum 호텔 로비에서 6월과 7월에 걸쳐 전시될 예정이다. ⑥ 지역 예술가들의 오랜 후원자로서, ⑤ 호텔 소유주인 Wayne Bond는 그들의 작품 전시를 위해 호텔 로비를 활용해 왔다. 그는 두 달마다 새로운 전시를 선보인다. 이 호텔은 이전에는 조각가 Jamie Wu나 입체파 예술가 Jasmine Tom 같은 지역 예술가들의 작품을 특집으로 전시했었다. ⑤⑥⑧ "저희 호텔은 공간이 많습니다. 그것을 활용하는 방법으로 Culver 지역의 재능 있는 예술가들의 작품을 전시하는 것보다 더 좋은 것이 무엇이 있겠습니까?" Mr. Bond는 이렇게 말하면서, 대중들이 들러서 미술품들을 감상하는 것을 환영한다. ⑦ "사람들은 또한 저희의 유명한 별 네 개짜리 스페인 식당인 La Cantina에서 식사를 하면서 문화적 경험을 다양하게 할 수도 있습니다."

어휘 **impressionist** 인상주의자, 인상파 예술가 I **long-time** 장기간에 걸친 I **supporter** 지지자, 후원자 I **utilize** 활용하다 I **display** 전시하다 I **previously** 이전에 I **feature** 특집으로 하다 I **sculptor** 조각가 I **showcase** 전시하다 I **talented** 재능 있는 I **drop by** ~에 들르다 I **peruse** 숙독하다, 잘 살펴보다 I **diversify** 다양하게 하다

수신: Idina Cusack 〈icusack@mic.com〉

발신: Wayne Bond 〈wbond@pendulumhotel.com〉

날짜: 7월 15일

제목: 다가오는 전시회

Ms. Cusack께,

⑧ 다음 달 Pendulum 호텔에서 귀하의 그림 여덟 점 모두를 전시하게 되어 기쁩니다. 컨벤션 센터에서의 귀하의 전시회는 대단히 인

상적이었고, 저희 호텔 전시에서 귀하의 작품이 마땅히 인정을 받게 되리라 확신합니다. ⑨ 각 작품의 배치를 위한 치수를 저에게 보내 주시기 바랍니다. 다음 주말까지 이 정보를 제게 알려주시면 감사하겠습니다.

진심으로,

Wayne Bond

최고경영자, Pendulum 호텔

어휘 **upcoming** 다가오는, 곧 있을 I **recognition** 인정 I **deserve** ~을 해야 마땅하다, ~을 받을 자격이 있다 I **dimension** (높이·너비·길이의) 치수 I **respective** 각자의, 각각의 I **appreciate** 고마워하다

---

5. 기사는 무엇에 대한 내용인가?

(A) 호텔 경영의 변화

(B) 호텔 로비가 이용된 방법

(C) 한 지역 예술가의 부상

(D) 새로운 미술 전시관

해설 기사 첫머리에서 호텔 로비에서 전시회가 열린다는 것을 알 수 있고, 이후에 호텔 소유주인 Wayne Bond가 지역 예술가 작품 전시를 위해 호텔 로비를 활용해 왔다는 내용에서 전체적인 주제가 (B) How a hotel's lobby is used임을 알 수 있다.

---

6. Mr. Bond에 관하여 언급된 것은 무엇인가?

고난도 (A) 그의 작품도 전시한다.

(B) 미술 박물관을 열 것이다.

(C) 지역 예술가들을 홍보한다.

(D) 미술 강의를 한다.

해설 (A)는 Mr. Bond가 호텔 소유주이지만 지역 예술가는 아니므로 오답이다. (B)는 호텔 로비에 예술가들의 작품을 전시하는 것이지, 따로 미술 박물관을 연다는 내용은 언급되어 있지 않다. (D) 또한 지문에서 찾아볼 수 없으므로 오답이다. 기사 두 번째 문단에서 Mr. Bond가 Culver 지역 예술가들의 작품을 호텔에 전시함으로써 홍보 및 후원을 하고 있음을 알 수 있으므로 정답은 (C) He promotes local artists.이다.

---

7. Mr. Bond는 방문객들에게 호텔에서 무엇을 하라고 권하는가?

(A) 로비에서 무료 음료를 즐긴다

(B) 새로 개조된 선물 가게에 들른다

(C) 호텔의 식당에서 식사를 한다

(D) Mr. Gibbins의 미술 강의에 참석한다

해설 기사 마지막 줄에서 Mr. Bond가 식당에서 식사를 함으로써 문화적 경험을 다양하게 넓힐 것을 권하였으므로 가장 적절한 답은 (C) Eat at the hotel's restaurant이다.

---

8. Ms. Cusack에 관하여 알 수 있는 것은 무엇인가?

고난도 **(A) Culver 지역에 거주한다.**

(B) 초상화 화가이다.

(C) La Cantina에 예약했다.

(D) Jamie Wu에 의해 추천되었다.

해설 이메일에서 Mr. Bond가 Ms. Cusack에게 그녀의 그림이 호텔에서 전시될 예정이라고 했고, 기사에서 호텔 전시 그림들이 Culver 지역 예술가들의 작품임을 알 수 있다. 따라서, Ms. Cusack도 해당 지역의 예술가임을 유추할 수 있으므로 정답은 (A) She lives in the Culver area.이다.

---

9. 이메일에 따르면, Mr. Bond가 그림에 관하여 알아야 하는 것은 무엇인가?

(A) 가격

(B) 크기

(C) 날짜

(D) 색상

해설 이메일에서 Mr. Bond가 그림의 크기를 알려달라고 했으므로 정답은 (B) Their sizes이다.

UNIT 03. 사실 확인

핵심 문제 유형

본서 p.249

1. (B)

---

[1] 다음 뉴스에 관한 문제입니다.

주말 뉴스

Franconia 시는 다음 주인 10월 4일, Saunders 공원에서 연례 가을 불꽃놀이를 개최할 것입니다. 누구든 환영하므로 이 멋진 놀이를 보러 오세요. Saunders 공원은 **1** (C) 시내 중심가에서 불과 5분 밖에 걸리지 않는 Telegraph로에 위치해 있습니다. **1** (D) 당일에 주차를 위한 공간이 매우 부족할 것이니 대중 교통을 이용해주실 것을 권합니다. **1** (A) Franconia 시내 버스가 Franconia 시내에서 공원까지 10분마다 운영될 것입니다. 오셔서 축제 행사를 즐기세요!

어휘 fireworks display 불꽃놀이 | outstanding 돋보이는, 눈에 띄는 | public transportation 대중교통 | run 운영하다 | festivity 축제 행사

Practice

본서 p.250

| 1. (A) | 2. (D) | 3. (B) | 4. (C) | 5. (A) |
| 6. (D) | 7. (B) | 8. (A) | 9. (D) | 10. (A) |
| 11. (B) |

[1-2] 다음 전단에 관한 문제입니다.

Beckington 철도
특별 판촉

15명 이상의 단체 여행을 계획 중인 승객들은 일반 열차 요금의 20퍼센트를 절약하실 수 있습니다. **1** 5명 이상의 가족 단위 여행객들은 15퍼센트의 할인 혜택을 받으실 자격이 됩니다. 이 혜택은 오직 5월과 6월, 두 달간만 유효합니다.

주말과 평일 둘 다, 어느 목적지로 가든 할인이 적용될 수 있습니다. **2** 그러나 여행 당일 역 매표소에서는 이 특별 할인을 받기 어려우시니, 일찍 예약하세요. 할인 자격이 되시는 승객분들께서는 여행일로부터 영업일 기준 최소 7일 이전에 웹사이트 www.btrail.net/tickets를 통해 티켓을 예매하실 수 있습니다. 수하물 제한을 포함한 더 많은 여행 정보 및 세부 사항 또한 저희 웹사이트에서 찾아보실 수 있습니다.

어휘 promotion 홍보 (활동) | in groups of 그룹으로, 떼를 지어 | fare 요금 | eligible for ~에 뽑힐 자격이 있는, 자격 기준을 갖춘 | valid 유효한 | destination 목적지 | book 예약하다 | obtain 얻다 | prior to ~에 앞서, 먼저 | baggage restriction 수하물 제한

---

1. Beckington 철도에 관하여 언급된 것은 무엇인가?

(A) 가족을 위한 할인가를 제공한다.

(B) 종종 수하물 요금이 면제된다.

(C) 6월에 열차 운행이 줄어들 것이다.

(D) 15곳 이상의 목적지로 운행한다.

해설 두 번째 문장에서 5명 이상의 가족 단위 여행객에게 가격 할인을 해준다고 언급하고 있으므로 (A) It offers reduced prices for families.가 정답이다. (B), (C), (D)는 언급되지 않은 내용이다.

---

2. 승객들은 무엇을 하라는 권고를 받는가?

(A) 평일에 여행을 간다

(B) 신용카드로 결제한다

(C) 매표소에서 할인 티켓을 요청한다

(D) 여행일 전에 티켓을 구매한다

해설 두 번째 문단에서 당일 매표소에서 할인을 받기 어려우니 일찍 구매하라고 조언해주고 있으므로 (D) Purchase tickets before the day of travel이 정답이다.

[3-4] 다음 광고에 관한 문제입니다.

Shenzen 아파트

3 **4** New Horizon 건설은 상하이 북부의 Shenzen 아파트 50가구가 거의 완공되었다고 발표하게 되어 기쁩니다. 세입자들이 10월 31일까지 입주할 수 있도록 준비될 것입니다. 1층 가구에는 3개의 침실과 2개의 욕실이 있고, 2층 가구에는 2개의 침실과 1개의 완전한 욕실 및 1개의 화장실, 그리고 강을 마주보고 있는 발코니가 있습니다. **3** 이 훌륭하고 관리비가 저렴한 아파트는 모두 실내 온도 조절기, 냉장고, 가스 레인지 및 식기 세척기를 갖추고 있습니다. **4** 단지는 Red Cliff 지하철 역까지 걸어서 갈 수 있는 거리에 위치해 있

고 Sunzu 공원과도 가깝습니다. 세입자들은 또한 쇼핑, 레스토랑, 의료 시설 및 학교에도 쉽게 접근할 수 있습니다. 현재 모델 하우스들이 관람할 수 있게 오픈되어 있지만, 가구들의 절반은 이미 판매되었습니다. 안내를 받으며 둘러보시려면 Shenzen 아파트 사무실로 빨리 연락하십시오. 사무실은 555-9423 또는 realestateoffice@shenzenmail.com으로 연락하실 수 있습니다.

어휘 announce 발표하다 | completion 완공 | tenant 세입자, 임차인 | move in 이사를 들어가다, 입주하다 | unit 한 개, 한 가구 | 1/2 bathroom 변기와 세면대만 있는 욕실(화장실) | low-maintenance 손이 많이 안 가는, 유지 보수가 적은 | climate control 실내 온도 조절기 | complex (건물) 단지 | adjacent 인접한, 가까운 | access 입장, 접근

3. 아파트에 관해서 언급하고 있는 것은 무엇인가?
고난도
(A) 공사가 완료되었다.
(B) 주방 기기들도 포함되어 있다.
(C) 거실 공간이 넓다.
(D) 세탁 시설이 사용 가능하다.

해설 공사 진행 사항에 대해 거의 완공 상태(nearing completion)라고 했으므로 (A)는 정답이 아니다. 아파트에는 냉장고, 가스 레인지, 식기 세척기가 있다고 했으므로 (B) Kitchen appliances are included.가 정답이다. 반면에 (C)와 (D)는 언급되지 않은 내용이므로 오답이다.

4. 광고에 포함된 내용이 아닌 것은 무엇인가?
(A) 아파트의 특징
(B) 짓고 있는 아파트 가구의 수
(C) 아파트 가구의 예상 가격
(D) 아파트의 위치

해설 첫 번째 문장에서 50가구를 짓고 있다고 했으므로 (B)는 오답이다. 아파트는 대략적인 위치를 Sunzu 공원과 가깝고 Red Cliff 지하철 역에 걸어갈 수 있는 거리라고 설명하고 있으므로 (D)도 오답이다. 광고에서 아파트 가격에 대한 언급은 없었으므로 (C) The expected price for the units가 정답이다.

[5-7] 다음 안내문에 관한 문제입니다.

Read and Save
2389 Fort 가
산후안, 푸에르토리코 00907

Read and Save에 가입해 여러분이 가장 좋아하는 장르에 대한 탁월한 가격 조건을 제안받으십시오. 🙋‍♂️6 저희는 공포물에서부터 판타지, 로맨스에 이르는 모든 종류의 소설을 취급하고 있으며, 여러분이 선호할 만한 신규 서적들의 종류들도 선택할 수 있습니다. 저희 클럽의 회원들은 다음과 같은 혜택을 누릴 수 있습니다.

- 5 회원 전용 웹사이트 접속
- 출판사 권장 판매 가격의 60%까지 할인
- 10가지 장르에 걸쳐 수백 권의 책을 선택 가능
- 새로 출간된 서적들의 목록과 저희 편집자들의 서평이 포함된 월간 이메일 소식지 무료 이용

회원들은 회원 조건에 따라 매달 적어도 한 권의 책을 주문해야 합니다. 7 등록하기 위해서는 저희 웹사이트 www.readandsave.com을 방문해주십시오.

어휘 outstanding 뛰어난 | deal 거래, 취급 | genre 장르 | fiction 소설 | benefits 혜택 | publisher 출판사 | title 서적, 출판물 | registered 등록한 | monthly 매달의 | released 발표한, 출시된 | at least 최소한 | condition 조건

5. 회원의 혜택이 아닌 것은 무엇인가?
(A) 무료 익일 배송
(B) 할인된 가격
(C) 다양한 작품의 이용
(D) 무료 소식지

해설 회원이 받는 혜택으로 가격 할인, 수백 권의 책 선택, 월간 이메일 소식지 등이 언급되었으므로 (B), (C), (D)는 정답이 아니다. 지문에서 배송에 관한 혜택은 언급된 바 없으므로 (A) Free overnight shipping이 정답이다.

6. Read and Save는 무엇을 판매하는가?
(A) 잡지
(B) 교재
(C) 신문
(D) 소설

해설 두 번째 문장에서 모든 종류의 fiction, 즉 소설을 다룬다고 했으므로 (D) Novels가 정답이다.

7. 안내문에 따르면, 사람들은 어떻게 클럽에 가입할 수 있는가?
(A) 이메일을 보냄으로써
(B) 웹사이트에 방문함으로써
(C) 서적을 우편으로 보냄으로써
(D) 고객 서비스에 전화함으로써

해설 마지막 문장에서 등록하려면 웹사이트를 방문하면 된다고 했으므로 (B) By visiting a Web site가 정답이다.

[8-11] 다음 이메일에 관한 문제입니다.

발신: Colin Moore
수신: Gilderoy's 서점 직원들
날짜: 7월 15일
제목: Paddy O'Reilly

8 여러분 모두에게 지역 기업인 Paddy O'Reilly의 다가오는 책 사인회와 강의에 대해 알려드리게 되어 기쁩니다.

아시다시피, 10 Mr. O'Reilly는 자신만의 조경 사업체를 9 설립하기 위해 열심히 일하는 동안에도 Gilderoy's 서점에서 6년 동안 임시직 근로자로 일했습니다. 그의 사업은 현재 번창하고 있고, Mr. O'Reilly는 그의 새로운 책 〈Business Success〉를 발표하였습니다. 10 조경술에 관한 일련의 책들만으로도 이미 인기를 얻었지만, Mr. O'Reilly는 개인 사업을 시작하려는 사람들에게 매우 유익한 정보가 담긴 책들로 그의 주제를 넓혔습니다.

Mr. O'Reilly는 Micklesfield 센터에서 8월 5일 오후 1시에 강연을 할 것입니다. **11** 그는 모든 Gilderoy's 서점의 직원들이 참석할 수 있도록 무료 티켓을 충분히 할당해 주었습니다. 또한, 여러분의 친구들과 가족 구성원들을 위해 추가 티켓들도 장당 3달러의 저렴한 가격으로 판매 중입니다. 만약 참석할 계획이라면, Susan Bateman(s.bateman@gilderoybooks.com)에게 이메일을 보내서 추가 티켓이 몇 장이나 필요한지를 알려주세요.

진심으로,

Colin Moore
선임 관리자

어휘 inform 알리다, 통지하다 | upcoming 다가오는, 곧 있을 | entrepreneur 사업가, 기업가 | establish 설립하다, 수립하다 | flourish 번창하다 | broaden 확장하다, 넓히다 | allocate 할당하다 | indicate 나타내다, 가리키다 | senior 선배의, 고참의

8. 이메일은 왜 보내졌는가?
  (A) 직원들에게 행사에 대해 알리기 위해
  (B) 새로운 사업을 광고하기 위해
  (C) 작가에 대한 정보를 요청하기 위해
  (D) 책 사인회를 준비하기 위해

해설 첫 번째 문장에서 책 사인회와 강의에 대하여 알려준다는 것을 확인할 수 있다. 따라서 정답은 (A) To notify staff about an event이다.

9. 두 번째 단락, 두 번째 줄의 단어, "establish"와 의미상 가장 가까운 것은
  (A) 이전하다
  (B) 장식하다
  (C) 똑바르게 하다
  (D) 세우다

해설 자신만의 조경 사업을 '설립'하기 위해 열심히 일한다는 의미이므로 문맥상 '세우다'란 의미의 (D) set up과 바꿔 쓸 수 있다.

10. Mr. O'Reilly에 관하여 언급되지 않은 것은 무엇인가?
  (A) Micklesfield 센터를 설계하는데 도움을 주었다.
  (B) Gilderoy's 서점에서 일했었다.
  (C) 조경사이다.
  (D) 몇 권의 책을 출간했다.

해설 (B)와 (C)는 두 번째 문단에 Mr. O'Reilly가 조경 사업체를 설립하기 위해 일하는 동안에 Gilderoy's 서점에서 6년 동안 일했다고 언급되어 있다. (D) 또한 조경술에 관한 책 여러 권을 출간했음을 확인할 수 있다. (A)는 Micklesfield가 센터에서 연설을 한다고 했지, Micklesfield 센터의 설계에 도움을 주었다는 내용은 없으므로 정답이다.

11. Gilderoy's 서점의 직원들에게 무엇이 무료로 제공되는가?
  (A) Mr. O'Reilly가 쓴 책
  (B) 곧 있을 강연의 티켓
  (C) Mr. O'Reilly와 함께 하는 개인 상담
  (D) 자연식 정원 견학

해설 Mr. O'Reilly가 8월 5일에 강연을 할 것이고, 그가 서점 직원들에게 무료 티켓을 제공한다고 언급되어 있으므로 정답은 (B) A ticket to an upcoming lecture이다.

UNIT 04. 암시·추론

핵심 문제 유형

본서 p.255

1. (B)

[1] 다음 뉴스에 관한 문제입니다.

지역 업체가 상을 받다
Abigail Milton 글

Logan 제조사가 그들의 스마트 통근 프로그램(SCP)으로 최근에 국립 생태계 협회(NEA)로부터 상을 받았다. Corporate Preservation Efforts 상이 세인트루이스에 소재한 NEA 지점에서 회사 대표인 Alicia Sanchez에게 수여되었다. NEA 위원인 Sean O'Reilly는 직원들에게 연료 효율성이 높은 하이브리드 회사 차량을 제공하고, 같은 지역에 사는 직원들 간의 카풀을 시행한 회사 프로그램을 칭찬했다.

직원들은 자기 차량을 직장에 가져오지 않도록 하기 위해 무료 대중교통 탑승권과 같은 인센티브를 받았다. **1** 이러한 새로운 정책들의 전국적인 집행을 통해, SCP는 작년부터 회사의 연료 소비를 약 80만 리터 감소시킨 것으로 추정된다. 대중 교통을 이용함으로써 발생된 신체 활동의 증가로 인해, 많은 직원들은 또한 몸이 더 좋아지고 있다고 보고했다.

어휘 ecological 생태계의 | commute 통근(하다) | present 주다, 수여하다 | council 자문 위원회 | praise 칭찬하다 | fuel-efficient 연료 효율이 높은 | enforce 집행하다 | incentive 장려책, 인센티브 | public transportation 대중교통 | voucher 할인권, 상품권 | nationwide 전국적인 | enforcement 집행 | consumption 소비

Practice

본서 p.256

1. (B)	2. (C)	3. (B)	4. (C)	5. (A)
6. (C)	7. (B)	8. (D)	9. (A)	10. (B)
11. (B)	12. (C)	13. (A)	14. (B)	

[1-2] 다음 정보에 관한 문제입니다.

다음 페이지는 **1** Pantek 900 디지털 카메라 사용법과 카메라에 담은 이미지들을 개인 컴퓨터로 전송하는 방법을 설명해 드릴 것입니다. **2** 만약 당신에게 그 단계들이 명확하지 않다면, 정상 영업 시간에 Pantek 직원에게 연락하세요. 7페이지에 있는 지역별 지원 센터와 연락처를 참고하세요.

어휘 following 그 다음의, 다음에 나오는 I explain 설명하다 I transfer 옮기다, 이동하다 I capture (사진이나 글 등으로) 포착하다, 담아내다 I image 이미지, 그림 I clear 분명한, 확실한 I contact 연락하다 I representative 대리인, 직원 I business hours 업무 시간, 영업 시간

1. 이 정보는 어디서 볼 수 있겠는가?
(A) 제품 광고에서
(B) 사용자 안내서에서
(C) 전자 제품 잡지에서
(D) 회사 팸플릿에서

해설 카메라 사용법과 이미지 옮기는 법을 알려주고 있으므로 (B) In an owner's manual이 정답임을 유추할 수 있다.

---

2. 정보에 따르면, Pantek 직원은 어떻게 도와줄 수 있는가?
(A) 환불을 처리해줌으로써
(B) 구매 옵션을 제공해줌으로써
(C) 설명을 명확하게 해줌으로써
(D) 예약을 잡아줌으로써

해설 설명이 명확하지 않으면 Pantek 직원에게 연락하라고 하므로, 직원이 명확한 설명을 제공해줄 것임을 알 수 있다. 따라서 (C) By clarifying instructions가 정답이다.

[3-4] 다음 이메일에 관한 문제입니다.

수신: 마케팅 부서
발신: Michael Stevens
날짜: 2월 12일, 금요일
제목: 명함

모두들 안녕하세요.

3 명함들이 다음 주 화요일 오후에 인쇄되어서 그 다음날 오전에 제 사무실로 보내질 것임을 여러분께 알려드립니다. 여러분들 중 몇 분은 최근에 직책이 바뀐 걸로 아는데, 모든 분들의 정보가 맞는지 확인하고 싶습니다. **4** 만약 직책이 변경되었다면, 오늘 오후 6시까

지 이 메시지에 바뀐 직책과 이름을 함께 회신해주세요. 제가 회신 메일을 받지 못하면, 여러분의 기존 정보가 가장 최근 것이라고 생각하겠습니다. 전 직원이 200장의 1박스 명함을 받을 것입니다. 다음 주 목요일까지 제 자리에 오셔서 명함을 가져가세요.

진심으로,

Michael Stevens
행정실 비서

어휘 inform 알리다, 통지하다 I business card 명함 I following 그 다음의, 다음에 나오는 I job title 직위, 직책 I updated 최신의, 갱신된 I assume 추정하다 I drop by 잠깐 들르다 I pick up 얻다, ~을 찾아오다

3. 새 명함들이 언제 Mr. Stevens의 사무실에 도착하겠는가?
(A) 화요일에
(B) 수요일에
(C) 목요일에
(D) 금요일에

해설 명함의 인쇄는 화요일에 되고 사무실에 도착하는 날짜는 다음날인 수요일이므로 정답은 (B) On Wednesday이다.

---

4. 이메일에 회신하라고 누가 요청을 받았는가?
(A) 최근에 회사에 고용된 직원들
(B) 새로운 건물로 옮겨간 직원들
(C) 일이 바뀐 직원들
(D) 200장 미만의 명함을 가지고 있는 직원들

해설 지문의 세 번째 단락에서 직책이 변경된 사람은 변경된 직책과 이름을 회신해달라고 요청했음을 확인할 수 있다. 따라서 정답은 (C) Employees who have changed jobs이다.

[5-9] 다음 공지와 일정에 관한 문제입니다.

Marreton 소기업 브런치

8월 7일 회의에서 **5** Marreton 상공 회의소(MCC)의 멤버들이 MCC 연회장에서 소기업 브런치를 열자고 만장 일치로 투표했습니다. **7** 매주 목요일 오전 10시 30분부터 오후 1시까지 **6** 열리게 되며 올해 내내 진행될 것입니다. 지역 사업주 분들도 MCC 로비나 온라인에서 등록하신 뒤 참여하실 수 있습니다. 정장을 입으실 것을 장려하지만 의무는 아닙니다. 그리고 명함을 많이 가져오시기 바랍니다! 이 행사와 Marreton의 다른 많은 비즈니스 기회와 관련된 소식과 정보를 위해 온라인 일정을 참조하시기 바랍니다. 도움이 필요하시면 일정 관리 매니저인 Benjamin Crane에게 404-555-2983으로 전화주십시오.

어휘 small business 소기업 I Chamber of Commerce 상공 회의소 I vote 투표하다 I unanimously 만장일치로 I sign up 신청하다, 등록하다 I formal attire 정장 I encourage 장려하다 I mandatory 의무적인 I business card 명함 I opportunity 기회 I assistance 도움, 보조

Marreton 상공 회의소 11월 주간 일정

월요일

오전 11시: 비즈니스 리더 원탁 회의 (둘째 주와 넷째 주) – **9** MCC 회의실 102호

오후 6시: 전문 네트워킹 시간 – Marquis 호텔

화요일

오후 1시: 비즈니스 분석과 조언 – 시청, B302

오후 2:30: 산학 협력 의회 – Marreton Unified 지역 빌딩

수요일

오후 6시: 인적 자원 최고의 사례 – **9** MCC 회의실 103

7 목요일

오전 10:30: 소기업 브런치 (첫째 주와 셋째 주) – MCC 연회장, 인당 7달러

오후 4:30: Marreton 지역사회 봉사활동 – Marreton 시민회관

금요일

오전 9시: 창업 회사들을 위한 기술 지원 (North Tech 센터), 인당 10달러, 수익금은 자선 단체에 기부됩니다

토요일

정오: 지역사회 오찬 – 대중에게 개방합니다! – MCC 연회장, 인당 15달러, 경로자 10달러

8 오후 3시: MCC 이사회 회의 (달의 마지막 금요일) – **9** MCC 회의실 101호

일정을 이메일로 받고 싶으시거나, 일정에 있는 행사에 대해 더 많은 정보를 알고 싶으시면 members@marretoncc.org나 404-555-9471로 회원 지원부에 연락해 주십시오.

어휘 roundtable 원탁 회의 | networking 인적 네트워크 형성 | analysis 분석 | advice 조언 | trade 거래, 사업, 무역 | council 의회, 자문 위원회 | human resources 인적 자원 | practice 사례, 관행 | outreach 봉사활동 | community center 시민회관 | start-up company 창업 회사 | proceeds 수익금 | charity 자선 단체 | luncheon 오찬 | senior 노인, 경로자 | function 행사, 의식

---

5. 이 공지는 왜 게시되었는가?

(A) MCC 회원에게 새로운 행사를 알리기 위해

(B) Marquis 호텔 확장을 발표하기 위해

(C) North Tech 센터의 임시 직원들을 채용하기 위해

(D) 다가오는 MCC 회의에 찾아오는 길을 제공하기 위해

해설 공지에서 소기업 브런치를 MCC 연회장에서 열자고 만장일치로 투표하였고, 매주 목요일에 진행한다고 언급하였으므로 새로운 행사를 개최한다는 것을 알 수 있다. 따라서 정답은 (A) To inform MCC members of a new event이다.

---

6. 공지의 첫 번째 단락, 세 번째 줄의 "go"와 의미상 가장 가까운 것은

(A) 전진하다

(B) 지나가다

(C) 일어나다

(D) 여행하다

해설 행사가 매주 목요일 오전 10시 30분부터 오후 1시까지 열리고, 매년 진행된다는 맥락으로 보아야 하므로 가장 문맥상 비슷한 단어는 (C) happen(일어나다)이다.

---

7. 11월에 있는 소기업 브런치에 대해 무엇을 추론할 수 있는가?
고난도

(A) 무료 식사를 제공한다.

(B) 원래 예정했던 것보다 더 적은 횟수로 개최된다.

(C) 더 큰 행사장으로 옮겨졌다.

(D) 공간이 제한되어 있다.

해설 공지 첫 단락에서 소규모 브런치가 매주 목요일에 진행된다고 나와 있지만, 달력의 네 번째 단락을 보면 1, 3주에만 진행되는 것을 확인할 수 있다. 따라서 본래 계획보다 적게 개최됨을 알 수 있으므로 정답은 (B) It occurs less often than originally scheduled.이다.

---

8. 어떤 행사가 11월에 단 한 번만 열리는가?

(A) 전문 네트워킹 시간

(B) Marreton 지역사회 봉사활동

(C) 지역사회 오찬

(D) MCC 이사회 회의

해설 달력의 토요일 행사 항목을 보면 MCC 이사회 회의가 11월의 마지막 금요일에만 한 번 열림을 확인할 수 있다. 그러므로 (D) The MCC Board Meeting이 정답이다.

---

9. MCC에 대해 무엇이 언급되었는가?
고난도

(A) 여러 개의 회의실을 가지고 있다.

(B) 시민회관 옆에 있다.

(C) 새 일정 관리 매니저를 찾고 있다.

(D) 사업주들만을 위해 행사를 연다.

해설 달력의 월요일, 수요일, 토요일 부분을 확인하면, 월요일은 MCC Conference Room 102, 수요일은 MCC Conference Room 103, 토요일은 MCC Conference room 101로, MCC는 적어도 3개 이상의 회의실을 가지고 있음을 확인할 수 있다. 따라서 정답은 (A) It has several conference rooms.이다.

[10-14] 다음 기사, 웹페이지 그리고 서식에 관한 문제입니다.

Lion 항공의 대변화

2월 14일 – **11 13** Lion 항공은 곧 Charleston 국제 공항에 들어설 새 본사를 위해 채용을 시작할 것이다. Lion이 몇몇 지역 공항들을 검토했지만 Charleston 국제 공항 담당자들이 이 지역의 독특한 이점들을 강조하면서 거래가 **10** 마무리되었다.

"많은 도시들을 둘러본 후에, 우리는 Charleston이 회사 및 고용 수요에 가장 적합할 것이라고 결론을 내렸습니다."라고 Lion 항공의 대표인 Daniel Harris는 설명했다. 그는 그 도시의 훌륭한 대학들이 충분한 자격을 갖춘 노동력을 창출하는 데 도움을 줄 것이라고 말했다. **13** Lion의 새 본사 건설은 1월에 완공되었다. 면접은 3월 1일에 시작될 것이다.

Lion 항공은 또한 현재 로스앤젤레스와 뉴욕에 더 작은 시설들을 짓는 중이며, 이들은 여름 여행 시즌이 시작되기 전에 문을 열 것

으로 기대된다. **11** Lion 항공은 5월 말까지 세 지역 모두에 인력을 완벽히 구비할 계획이다.

어휘 hiring 고용 I headquarters 본사 I regional 지역의 I representative 담당자, 대표 I deal 거래 I emphasize 강조하다 I unique 독특한 I come to a conclusion 결론을 내리다 I fit 적합하다, 어울리다 I workforce 노동력 I staff 직원을 제공하다

---

www.claxonsol.com/services

Claxon 솔루션은 오직 최상의, 가장 눈부신 것만을 찾습니다!

저희는 여러분을 위해 알맞은 직원들을 찾아 드립니다. 단 한 번의 계약 또는 더 오랜 기간의 직원 제공 수요에 대해 크고 작은 회사들 모두와 일하고 있습니다. (843) 555–1973으로 전화하셔서 **14** 담당자와 무료 현장 상담을 예약하세요.

저희는 처음부터 끝까지 여러분과 함께 일할 것입니다.

• Claxon과 파트너가 되는 것은 HR 전문가들에게서 전문적인 안내를 받는 것을 의미합니다. 저희는 여러분께 구인 광고, 이력서 심사 등을 지원합니다.

• 저희 전문가들은 사소한 것 하나까지 철저합니다. **12** 저희는 지원자들의 완벽한 신원 확인을 위해 지역 및 연방 정부 기관 모두와 어울려 일합니다.

• 특정일 이후에 높은 이직률을 예상하거나 인원 삭감을 계획하시나요? 저희는 유연한 노동력 해결책을 찾고자 고안된 임시 직업 소개소들과 일합니다.

Claxon은 반드시 여러분의 직원이 회사를 성공시킬 수 있도록 해드리겠습니다!

어휘 bright 밝은, 눈부신 I contract 계약(서) I on-site 현장의, 현지의 I partner 파트너가 되다 I guidance 지도, 안내 I screening 심사 I thorough 철저한 I to the last detail 사소한 것 하나까지 I coordinate with ~와 잘 어울리다 I federal government agency 연방 정부 기관 I conduct 수행하다 I background 배경 I anticipate 예상하다, 기대하다 I turnover rate 이직률 I downsizing 인원 삭감, 기구 축소 I temporary 임시의, 일시적인 I flexible 유연한

Claxon 솔루션

저희 전문 컨설턴트와 약속 일정을 잡기 위해 아래의 서식을 작성하세요.

회사명: Lion 항공
회사 담당자: Louis Hermann
전화번호: (843) 555-0045
이메일: lhermann@lionairways.com
13 주소: 8843 Aviation 가, 찰스턴, 사우스캐롤라이나
14 희망 상담 날짜: 2월 24일

가능 시간대: ☑ 오전 ☐ 오후

고객님의 일정에 맞는 약속 시간을 확정하기 위해 전화 드리겠습니다.

어휘 availability 이용 가능성

---

10. 기사에서 첫 번째 단락, 여섯 번째 줄의 단어 "closed"와 의미상 가장 가까운 것은
(A) 막았다
(B) 마무리지었다
(C) 침묵시켰다
(D) 취소했다

해설 Lion 항공이 여러 지역들을 검토했다고 하면서, Charleston 국제 공항이 지역의 이점을 강조함으로써 거래를 끝냈다는 것으로 close가 '마무리짓다'는 의미로 쓰였으므로 '확정하다, 마무리짓다'란 의미의 (B) finalized가 정답이다.

---

11. Lion 항공에 관하여 암시되는 것은 무엇인가?
(A) 현 CEO가 2월에 임명되었다.
(B) 5월까지 신입 직원 고용을 끝마칠 것이다.
(C) 일부 대학들과 파트너 관계를 맺고 있다.
(D) 본사는 원래 뉴욕에 있었다.

해설 기사 첫 문장에서 Lion 항공이 본사에 필요한 직원 채용을 곧 시작할 거라고 했으며 마지막 문장에서 5월 말까지 직원 채용을 완료할 계획이라고 했으므로 (B) It will finish hiring new workers by May.가 정답이다.

---

12. Claxon 솔루션이 제공하는 서비스는 무엇인가?
(A) 임시 직원들을 위한 교육
(B) 직원용 이력서 작성
(C) 지원자 조사
(D) 대학에 학생 등록

해설 웹페이지에 Claxon Solutions의 업종과 하는 일이 기술되어 있으며, 지원자들의 신원 확인을 위해 지역 및 연방 정부와 함께 일한다고 했으므로 Claxon은 지원자들에 대한 조사 업무까지 수행한다는 것을 알 수 있다. 따라서 (C) Investigating job applicants가 정답이다.

---

13. Aviation 가 지점에 관하여 알 수 있는 것은 무엇인가?
(A) 최근에 지어졌다.
(B) Claxon 솔루션 사무소 옆에 있다.
(C) 추가적인 수리작업이 필요하다.
(D) 일류 학교를 다닌 직원들이 있다.

해설 Aviation 가가 키워드로 첫 번째 지문에서 Lion 항공이 Charleston 국제 공항에 본사를 둘 것이라는 사실과 함께 본사의 건설이 1월에 완공되었다는 정보를 알 수 있으며, 서식에 언급된 Aviation 가가 Lion 항공 본사가 위치한 곳임을 유추할 수 있으므로 (A) It was built recently.가 정답이다.

14. 2월 24일에 무슨 일이 있겠는가?

(A) Mr. Hermann이 부서 회의를 열 것이다.

(B) Claxon 솔루션 담당자가 Aviation 가로 갈 것이다.

(C) 환영식이 열릴 것이다.

(D) 직원 면접이 있을 것이다.

해설 질문의 키워드가 February 24로 해당 날짜가 서식에서 희망 상담일임을 알 수 있고 상담과 관련하여 웹페이지에서 담당자와 무료 현장 상담을 위해 예약하라고 한 사실을 토대로 Claxon Solutions 담당자가 상담을 신청 회사에 직접 찾아가서 한다는 것을 알 수 있다. 따라서 (B) A Claxon Solutions representative will go to Aviation Avenue가 정답이다.

UNIT 05. 문장 삽입

핵심 문제 유형

본서 p.263

1. (A)

[1] 다음 기사에 관한 문제입니다.

Petros 그룹은 Janet Thompson이 새로운 제품 제조 부사장으로 고용되었다고 발표했다. **1** 해당 회사는 최근 장난감 라인의 판매 저조로 수백만 달러의 손실을 보았다. 그녀의 주된 역할은 최근 곤두박질친 회사의 재정이 호전되어 개선되도록 돌보는 일이다. Ms. Thompson은 제조업계에 22년 간 몸담아 왔고, Petros가 6년 만에 처음으로 수익을 내도록 도울 것으로 기대된다.

Petros에 들어오기 전, Ms. Thompson은 Daley 사에서 같은 직책으로 일했다. 그녀는 그곳에서 폭넓게 사랑을 받았고 특히 조립 라인 직원들에게 인기가 많았다. 그 일은 그녀가 사회생활을 시작했을 때 했던 것이어서 놀라운 일은 아니었다. Daley에서의 시간 동안, 회사는 사상 최고의 수익을 기록했다. Ms. Thompson은 Riley 제조사에서도 근무했으며 거기서 CEO의 특별 보좌관 역을 맡았다.

어휘 hire 고용하다 | primary 주된, 주요한 | role 역할 | fortune 재산 | plummet 곤두박질치다 | lately 최근에 | turn around 호전되다 | be involved in ~에 개입하다/연루되다 | turn a profit 수익을 내다 | come as no surprise | 놀라운 일은 아니다 | career 직장생활 | record-high 사상 최고의 | earning 수입, 소득 | serve as ~의 역할을 하다

Practice

본서 p.264

1. (C)	**2.** (D)	**3.** (D)	**4.** (B)	**5.** (C)
6. (B)	**7.** (C)	**8.** (A)	**9.** (C)	**10.** (A)
11. (B)	**12.** (C)	**13.** (C)		

[1-3] 다음 보도 자료에 관한 문제입니다.

Lakeshore 공원 소식

4월 28일 – The Ashville Park and Recreation Department는 **1** Lakeshore 공원의 공사가 잘 진행되고 있으며, 예정대로 5월 15일에 문을 열 것으로 기대된다는 발표를 하게 되어 기쁩니다.

Bear 호수의 동쪽 기슭에 위치한 Lakeshore 공원은 시에서 가장 최근에 지어진 가장 큰 공원이 될 것입니다. 그리고 면적이 40에이커도 더 되어. **2** 그 공원에는 축구장, 야구장, 광대한 소풍 지역 그리고 하이킹과 사이클링을 위한 많은 코스들이 구비될 것입니다.

야외 스포츠에 관심 있는 사람들과 보트 타는 사람들을 위한 시설들도 있을 것입니다. **3** 이 시설들에는 선착장도 있고 수상 스키 장비와 구명조끼들도 대여될 것입니다. 이 시설들에 대해 자세히 알고 싶으시면, 시의 웹사이트 www.ashville.org/lakeshorepark를 방문하십시오. 공원은 매일 오전 5시부터 오후 10시까지 문을 열 것입니다.

어휘 progress 진보, 진행 | go well 잘 되어가다 | on schedule 예정된 시간에 | alongside ~와 나란히 | eastern 동쪽의 | shore 해안 | acre 에이커(토지 면적의 단위) | feature ~의 특징을 이루다 | baseball diamond 야구의 내야 | numerous 많은 | trail 코스, 경로 | facility 시설 | cater to ~에 부합하다, ~를 충족하다 | outdoor 실외

1. 보도 자료의 주제는 무엇인가?

(A) 호수 확장

(B) 시의 시설 보수

(C) 공원 건립

(D) 다가오는 야외 이벤트

해설 새로 건립되는 공원에 대해 말하고 있으므로 (C) The construction of a park가 정답이다.

2. 공원의 특징으로 언급되지 않은 것은 무엇인가?

(A) 스포츠 시설들

(B) 걷는 루트들

(C) 식사 장소들

(D) 자전거 대여점

해설 두 번째 단락 마지막 문장에서 공원에 여러 스포츠 시설들과 소풍 공간, 하이킹 코스 등이 갖춰질 것임을 알 수 있다. 따라서 정답은 (D) A bicycle rental shop이다.

3. [1], [2], [3], [4]로 표시된 곳 중에서 다음 문장이 들어가기에 가장 적절한 곳은 어디인가?

"이 시설들에는 선착장도 있고 수상 스키 장비와 구명조끼들도 대여될 것입니다."

(A) [1]
(B) [2]
(C) [3]
(D) [4]

해설 보트 타기와 수상 스키는 야외에서 하는 스포츠이기 때문에 [4]에 오는 것이 적절하다. 바로 앞의 문장에서 실외 스포츠에 관심이 있거나 보트를 타는 사람들을 위한 시설들도 있다고 했기 때문에 정답은 (D) [4]이다.

[4-6] 다음 기사에 관련된 문제입니다.

새로운 플라자
Stephanie Cruz, 〈Sage City Reporter〉 편집자 씀

10월 27일 – Anderson 가와 Creosote 로의 북동쪽 코너에 Sage City의 공무원들이 Cactus Wren 플라자라는 이름의 새 상업 중심지 공사를 시작했다. **4** Sage 시장인 Al Bryce는 공공 도서관 맞은편에 위치한 빈 부지에서 리본 커팅식을 했다.

이 플라자 공사는 Sage 투자그룹(SIG)에 의해 많은 부분에 있어 재정 지원을 받았는데, 이 그룹은 사업체들이 유익한 프로젝트를 재정 지원하는 것을 돕는 지역 단체이다. 플라자의 최종 디자인은 단층 건물 네 채이며, 200개가 넘는 가게들이 들어설 공간을 갖게 된다. **6** 각 건물에는 지하 주차장이 지어질 예정이며 724번 버스가 교통 체증 감소를 위해 근처에 설 것이다.

SIG는 향후 10년간 Sage 시와 계약을 맺고 플라자를 운영할 계획이다. "이전에는 우리 시의 주민들이 근처의 Shellyville까지 운전해서 가야 했죠." Mr. Bryce가 말했다. "하지만 이제 새로운 플라자에서 영업하게 해 달라는 많은 사업체들의 요청이 들어오고 있습니다. 현재 시내에서 진행 중인 공사도 약간은 도움이 되지만, 더 큰 공간이 확실히 필요했어요."

스포츠용품 가게와 몇몇 레스토랑 체인들을 포함한 60여 개가 넘는 사업체들이 Cactus Wren 플라자에 공간을 임대하는 데 관심이 있다고 말했다. **5** SIG의 마케팅 매니저인 Maya Vasquez는 잘 알려진 컴퓨터 소매상 체인점과 새로운 지점을 여는 것을 현재 논의 중이다. 이 플라자는 내년 초에 개점할 예정이다.

어휘 direct 직접적인 | connection 연결 | editor 편집자 | northeast 북동쪽의 | official 공무원 | commercial center 상업 중심지 | mayor 시장 | lot 지역, 부지 | construction 공사 | fund 재정 지원을 하다 | investment 투자 | organization 단체 | beneficial 이로운, 이점이 많은 | operate 운영하다 | contract 계약 | resident 거주자 | request 요청 | renovation 수리, 개조 | retail 소매의, 소매상의

4. Mr. Bryce는 누구인가?
(A) 건설 직원
(B) 정부 공무원
(C) 가게 매니저
(D) 컴퓨터 프로그래머

해설 지문 첫 번째 단락에서 Al Bryce가 시장, 즉 (B) A government official임을 알 수 있다.

5. SIG는 Cactus Wren 플라자에 어떤 종류의 사업체를 끌어들이고 싶어하는가?
(A) 슈퍼마켓
(B) 패션 소매업
(C) 전자 제품 가게
(D) 오락장

해설 지문 네 번째 단락에서 SIG는 컴퓨터 소매상 체인점의 새로운 지점을 여는 것을 논의 중이므로, 컴퓨터 소매상 체인점이 전자 제품 가게임을 알 수 있다. 따라서 정답은 (C) An electronics store이다.

6. [1], [2], [3], [4]로 표시된 곳 중에서 다음 문장이 들어가기에 가장 적절한 곳은 어디인가?

"각 건물에는 지하 주차장이 지어질 예정이며 724번 버스가 교통 체증 감소를 위해 근처에 설 것이다."

(A) [1]
(B) [2]
(C) [3]
(D) [4]

해설 [2]의 앞 문장에서 공간 활용에 대하여 설명하고 있고, 삽입 문장 또한 건물 활용에 대한 설명이므로 (B) [2]가 가장 적당한 위치임을 알 수 있다.

[7-9] 다음 정보에 관련된 문제입니다.

Feelway 사는 16년 동안 회사에서 헌신적으로 일했던 Ms. Bianca Carrera가 9월 30일자로 우리를 떠나는 것을 보게 되어 유감입니다. 우리 시카고 본부의 홍보 부서 부장이었던 Ms. Carrera의 직책에 대체자를 찾는 일은 다음 주에 시작될 것입니다.

7 Ms. Carrera는 마케팅 및 영업 상무이사 바로 밑에서 일해 왔으며 국제적으로 지역 부서들과 소통했습니다. 이 직책에 따르는 도전은 쉬운 것이 아닙니다. 후보자들은 다국어로 공개 행사를 조직해본 경험과 보도자료를 최종 확정해 본 경험이 있어야 하고, 출장을 자주 가게 될 것입니다.

"많은 사람들이 대신할 수 있는 직책은 아닙니다."라고 **7** 마케팅 및 영업 상무이사인 Carl Kline이 말했습니다. **8** "국제 미디어 관리에 있어 탄탄한 배경을 가진 사람이 필요합니다."

채용 절차는 10월에 3주 동안만 진행됩니다. **9** 그것은 10월 22일 이후로 지원하는 어떤 지원자도 그 일자리에 고려되지 않을 것이라는 의미입니다. Ms. Carrera는 새로운 부장이 12월 초에는 완전히 직무를 수행할 수 있도록 직무 훈련에 필요한 도움을 주겠다고 약속했습니다.

7. Ms. Carrera에 대해 무엇을 알 수 있는가?

(A) 그녀의 직책은 12월에 공석이 된다.

(B) 16년 전에 시카고로 이전했다.

(C) 그녀의 상사는 Mr. Kline이다.

(D) 회사의 미디어 전략을 관리할 것이다.

해설 Ms. Carrera와 Carl Kline을 주의해서 봐야 한다. 두 번째 문단에서 Ms. Carrera는 상무이사의 하급자임을 확인할 수 있고, 세 번째 문단에서 Carl Kline은 마케팅 & 세일즈의 상무이사이므로 Ms. Carrera가 Carl Kline의 하급자임을 유추할 수 있다. 따라서 정답은 (C) Her supervisor is Mr. Kline.이다.

---

8. Mr. Kline에 따르면, 후보자에게 있어 중요한 자격 조건은 무엇인가?

(A) 비슷한 일과 관련한 상당한 경험

(B) 마케팅 및 영업 대학원 학위

(C) TV에 출연하고자 하는 의지

(D) 주말에 일을 할 수 있는 유연성

해설 두 번째 단락에서 국제 미디어 관리에 있어서 배경을 가진 사람, 즉 이 분야들에 경험이 있는 사람들을 구한다고 했으므로 (A) Considerable experience doing similar work가 정답이다.

---

9. [1], [2], [3], [4]로 표시된 곳 중에서 다음 문장이 들어가기에 가장 적절한 곳은 어디인가?

"그것은 10월 22일 이후로 지원하는 어떤 지원자도 그 일자리에 고려되지 않을 것이라는 의미입니다."

(A) [1]

(B) [2]

(C) [3]

(D) [4]

해설 [3]의 앞 문장이 채용 절차가 10월 셋째 주까지만 진행된다는 내용이므로, 비슷한 맥락이기 때문에 [3]에 들어가는 것이 문맥상 자연스럽다. 또한 보통 22일 이후는 셋째 주가 넘어갈 수 있음을 유추할 수 있다.

[10-13] 다음 기사에 관한 문제입니다.

Jacksonville에서 열리는 카운티 장날

Jacksonville – **10** **11** 올해 Jefferson 카운티 장날은 Jacksonville에서 열릴 것이다. 해당 시에서 이 연례 행사를 주관하는 것은 이번이 처음으로, 행사는 7월 8일과 9일로 예정되어 있다. 이 장날은 전국에서 가장 인기 있는 장날 중 하나로, 만 명이 넘는 사람들이 매일 참여할 것으로 예상된다.

매년 카운티 장날에는 다양한 게임, 놀이기구, 쇼 그리고 농산물 직판장을 비롯한 여러 이벤트들이 열린다. 올해의 행사에는 뭔가 새로운 것도 있을 것이다: 바로 지역 예술가들과 장인들이 자신들의 작품을 보여주고 팔 수 있는 수공예품 섹션이다.

"Jacksonville은 번창하는 수공예품 지역입니다." Jacksonville 시장 Jeff Randall이 말했다. "우리가 행사를 주최하기 때문에, **12** 지역 주민들을 참여시킴으로써 그들이 하고 있는 일을 홍보하기로 했습니다. **13** 그 덕에 다른 사람들은 그들이 하고 있는 일에 친숙해질 수 있을 것입니다. 우리는 관광객들이 들러, 우리 주민들이 만든 작품들을 보고 한두 점씩 사서 집에 가져가기 바랍니다."

Randall 시장은 장날 준비는 잘 되어가고 있다고 한 마디 더했다. 그는 시에는 현재 예상되는 방문객들을 모두 수용할 만한 주차 공간이 없지만, 임시 주차장 몇 개를 만들고 있는 중이라고 했다. 또한 시에서는 셔틀 버스들을 이용해 장날 방문객들을 그들의 차에서부터 장터까지 이송할 것이라는 말도 덧붙였다.

Jefferson 카운티 장날은 Jasmine 공원에서 열린다. 시간은 오전 9시부터 오후 7시까지이며, 참가비는 무료이다.

10. 이 기사는 신문의 어떤 부분에 나올 법한가?

(A) 생활 양식과 문화

(B) 스포츠

(C) 비즈니스와 기술

(D) 안내광고

해설 이 기사는 Jacksonville 시에서 열리는 장날에 대한 것이므로 (A) Lifestyle and culture가 정답이다.

---

11. Jacksonville에 대해 알 수 있는 사실은 무엇인가?

(A) 행사를 주관할 준비가 되어있지 않다.

(B) Jefferson 카운티에 위치해 있다.

(C) 많은 지역 갤러리들이 있다.

(D) 최근에 새로운 공원을 개장했다.

해설 카운티는 '자치주'라는 의미이고, Jefferson County Fair을 Jacksonville에서 연다는 것은 Jefferson 자치주에 위치해 있다는 것이므로, (B) It is located in Jefferson County.가 정답이다

---

12. Mr. Randall에 대해 언급된 것은 무엇인가?

(A) 그는 작년에 시장으로 선출되었다.

(B) 그는 환영사를 할 예정이다.

(C) 그는 일부 Jacksonville 주민들을 지원하려고 하는 중이다.

(D) 그는 Jacksonville에서 태어났다.

해설 세 번째 단락에서 주민들을 행사에 참여시킴으로써 그들이 하고 있

는 일을 홍보하기로 했다고 했으므로 (C) He is trying to support some Jacksonville residents.가 정답이다.

---

13. [1], [2], [3], [4]로 표시된 곳 중에서 다음 문장이 들어가기에 가장 적절한 곳은 어디인가?

"그 덕에 다른 사람들은 그들이 하고 있는 일에 친숙해질 수 있을 것입니다."

(A) [1]
(B) [2]
(C) [3]
(D) [4]

해설 지역 주민이 하고 있는 일을 알려 광고 효과를 노리는 것이므로 [3]에 들어가는 것이 적절하다. 따라서 정답은 (C) [3]이다.

UNIT 06. 동의어

핵심 문제 유형

본서 p.269

1. (A)

---

[1] 다음 안내에 관한 문제입니다.

안내문

보안을 개선하기 위해, 우리는 최근 낡고 구식이 된 보안 시스템을 더 현대적인 것으로 교체했습니다.

주간에 사무실에 들어오기 위해, 각 직원들은 보안 카드를 발급받을 것입니다. 여러분이 들어오기를 원할 때는 언제든 카드를 문 오른쪽에 **1** 위치한 카드 인식기에 대기만 하면 됩니다. 여러분은 개별 카드를 받은 후 서명 요청을 받을 것입니다.

카드를 잃어버리게 되면, 카드를 취소해줄 보안 요원에게 즉시 알려주시고, 되도록 빨리 다른 카드를 꼭 발급받으세요.

어휘 security 보안 | replace 교체하다, 대체하다 | outdated 구식인 | gain access 들어가다; 접속하다 | issue 발급하다 | personalized 개인의 필요에 맞춘

Practice

본서 p.270

1. (B)	**2.** (A)	**3.** (B)	**4.** (A)	**5.** (C)
6. (B)	**7.** (A)	**8.** (D)	**9.** (C)	**10.** (B)
11. (A)	**12.** (A)	**13.** (C)	**14.** (D)	**15.** (B)
16. (D)	**17.** (B)	**18.** (B)		

[1-4] 다음 편지에 관한 문제입니다.

Owen and Williams Partners 회계 법인
6 Pennance 로
카디프 CF1
웨일스

3월 25일

Jenny Poulter, 사장
Gwendoline's of Cardiff
110-121 City 로
카디프 CF1
웨일스

Ms. Poulter께,

2 3월 21일 저희 회사를 위해 주최해 주셨던 직원 은퇴 기념 파티에 관해 편지를 드립니다.

당신의 시설에는 처음 방문하는 것이었으나, 우리는 **2** 전 선임 파트너 Vanita Shah로부터 당신을 추천받았고, 그날 저녁 우리 회사는 그분을 축하해 드렸습니다. **1** 제가 그곳의 음식을 너무나 맛있게 먹어서, **4** 다음 주 저녁식사에 제 친구들을 데려오기 위해 이미 자리도 예약해 놓았습니다.

특히나 감동을 받은 부분은 당신의 직원들이 보여준 전문성의 **3** 수준이었습니다. 웨이터들은 매우 효율적으로 일했고, 친절하기도 했으며, 메뉴에 관하여 우리가 한 모든 질문에 대답해 줄 수 있었습니다.

이 즐거운 경험에 대단히 감사드립니다! 저희는 Owen and Williams의 새로운 전통으로 **4** Gwendoline's of Cardiff에서 정기 모임들을 갖게 되기를 희망합니다.

진심으로,

David Owen
David Owen, 선임 파트너

어휘 with regard to ~에 관해 | retirement party 은퇴/퇴직 파티 | host 개최하다, 열다 | establishment 시설, 기관 | former 예전의 | impress 감명을 주다, 감동시키다 | degree 정도, 단계 | professionalism 전문성 | demonstrate 보여주다, 입증하다 | efficient 효율적인, 유능한 | friendly 친절한 | concerning ~에 관한, 관해서 | enjoyable 즐거운

---

1. Gwendoline's of Cardiff는 어떤 곳인가?
(A) 회계 법인
(B) 식당
(C) 가전매장
(D) 슈퍼마켓

해설 지문 세 번째 줄에 Mr. Owen이 Gwendoline's of Cardiff에서 식사를 맛있게 해서 다음 주에 테이블을 예약을 했음을 알 수 있고 이후에 waiters, menu 같은 표현으로 (B) A restaurant이 정답임을 알 수 있다.

---

2. 3월에 Ms. Shah는 왜 축하를 받았는가?

(A) Owen and Williams에서 은퇴했다.

(B) 선임 파트너로 승진되었다.

(C) 새 회사를 열었다.

(D) 경영 대학원을 졸업했다.

해설 3월 21일에 직원 은퇴 기념 파티를 했고, 축하받은 사람이 Vanita Shah임을 확인할 수 있다. 즉, 은퇴하는 사람이 Vanita Shah이므로 정답은 (A) She retired from Owen and Williams.이다.

3. 세 번째 단락, 첫 번째 줄의 단어 "degree"와 의미상 가장 가까운 것은

(A) 직위

(B) 정도

(C) 요약

(D) 자격

해설 문맥상 직원들이 보여준 전문성의 '정도'를 보고 특히 감동을 받았다는 의미이므로 문맥상 (B) level이 정답이다.

4. 편지에서 Mr. Owen이 암시하는 것은?

(A) Gwendoline's of Cardiff와 다시 거래를 할 것이다.

(B) Ms. Poulter로부터 소식을 더 듣기를 기대한다.

(C) 현재 그의 회사에 신규 직원을 채용 중이다.

(D) 친구로부터 Gwendoline's of Cardiff에 대해 처음 듣게 되었다.

해설 첫 번째 단락에서 일전에 음식을 너무 맛있게 먹어서 다음 주 저녁식사에 친구들을 데려올 것이라고 했고, 마지막 단락에서 정기적으로 이 식당을 계속 이용할 것임을 판단할 수 있다. 따라서 (A) He will do business with Gwendoline's of Cadiff again.이 정답이다.

[5-8] 다음 안내문에 관한 문제입니다.

Alpina 리조트
로카르노, 스위스

음식 및 식당 정보

5 Alpina 리조트는 이 지역에서 가장 좋은 스키 및 숙박 시설을 제공할 뿐 아니라 5성급 레스토랑도 갖추고 있습니다. 접수처 왼쪽에 위치한 Ristorante Alpina는 태양이 산 위로 떠오르는 것을 보면서 아침 커피를 즐길 수 있는 편안한 장소입니다. 경험 많은 저희 요리사들이 현지에서 즐겨 먹는 음식들을 비롯해 인상적일 정도로 다양한 요리들을 준비합니다. 아침 식사는 매일 오전 6시 30분부터 오전 9시 30분까지 제공되고 점심 식사는 오전 11시부터 오후 3시까지 제공됩니다. **7** 저녁 식사는 오후 9시에 주방이 문을 닫는 일요일을 제외하고, 매일 오후 4시부터 오후 11시까지 제공됩니다.

6 저희의 제빵사들은 투숙객들이 마음껏 즐길 수 있도록 매일 아침 신선한 빵과 케이크를 준비합니다. 투숙객들은 따뜻하거나 차가운 아침 식사와 (제철인 경우) 신선한 과일, 다양한 주스와 우유, 에스프레소 또는 차를 선택할 수 있습니다. 점심 또는 저녁 식사로는 이탈리아, 독일 및 프랑스 식 요리로 구성된 메뉴뿐만 아니라 다양한 세계 각국의 요리를 선택할 수 있습니다.

저희는 하루 24시간 룸 서비스를 제공합니다. 아침 식사 품목은 오전 5시에서 10시까지만 이용할 수 있습니다. 공인 영양사가 직원으로 있으며, 그래서 저희 요리사들은 어느 투숙객의 특정 식단 요구도 **8** 충족시켜 드릴 수 있습니다. 선택 가능한 메뉴와 가격은 룸 서비스 메뉴를 참조하십시오. 모든 룸 서비스 주문에는 10%의 봉사료가 붙습니다. 주문하시려면 구내 전화 556번으로 레스토랑 주방으로 전화 주세요.

어휘 **offer** 제공하다 | **accommodation** 숙소 | **feature** 특징으로 삼다 | **impressive** 인상적인 | **indulge in** 마음껏 하다, 탐닉하다

5. 이 안내문은 누구를 대상으로 한 것 같은가?

(A) Alpina 리조트 매니저들

(B) 객실 관리 직원들

(C) Alpina 리조트 투숙객들

(D) Ristorante Alpina에서 서빙하는 사람들

해설 안내문의 대상을 묻고 있는 문제로, 주로 글의 첫 문장에 나타나는 글의 목적과 연관지어 답을 찾는다. 첫 번째 문장에서 Alpina 리조트의 장점들을 설명하고 있으므로, 이 리조트에 온 투숙객들을 대상으로 안내문이 쓰여졌다고 유추할 수 있다. 그러므로 (C) Guests of Alpina Resort가 정답이다.

6. 지문에 따르면, 매일 있는 일은 무엇인가?

(A) 투어가 제공된다.

(B) 빵을 굽는다.

(C) 건강 세미나가 열린다.

(D) 공연이 진행된다.

해설 두 번째 문단에서 매일 아침마다 신선한 빵을 준비한다고 했으므로 (B) Pastries are baked.가 정답이다.

7. Ristorante Alpina에 관해서 언급하고 있는 것은 무엇인가?

(A) 일요일에 일찍 문을 닫는다.

(B) 유명한 주방장을 고용한다.

(C) 특별 판촉을 제공한다.

(D) 최근에 개축되었다.

해설 첫 번째 문단 마지막에 저녁식사는 매일 오후 4시부터 11시까지 제공되나 일요일에는 오후 9시에 문을 닫는다고 했으므로 정답은 (A) It closes earlier on Sundays.이다.

8. 세 번째 문단, 두 번째 줄의 단어 "meet"와 의미상 가장 가까운 것은

(A) 허락하다

(B) 소개하다

(C) 모으다

(D) 만족시키다

해설 지문에서 meet는 '필요, 요구 등을 충족시키다'의 의미를 가지므로, '만족시키다'라는 의미의 (D) fulfill이 의미상 가장 가깝다.

[9-13] 다음 편지와 이메일에 관한 문제입니다.

2월 20일
Susan Romano
44 West 가
런던 W14 3DY

Ms. Romano께,

9 10 저희 4월호에 국제 시장의 변화하는 트렌드에 관한 3,000단어 논평을 작성하기로 약속해 주셔서 고맙습니다. **9** 약속대로 동봉해 드리는 저자 지침 수정본을 확인해 주십시오. 이 지침이 현재 저희 웹사이트에 게시되어 있는 지침들을 대신할 것입니다. 필요한 경우 짧은 기한 연장을 좀 더 해 드릴 수는 있지만, 3월 15일까지 글을 제출해 주실 수 있으신지요? 정말로 시간이 더 필요하시다면 최대한 빨리 제게 전화를 주십시오. **10 13** 현재 저희는 원래의 마감일을 지켜 주시는 작가분들께 온라인에 있는 저희 경제학 출판물 카탈로그에서 네 권의 무료 e-book을 드리고 있습니다.

논의했던 것처럼, **9** 원고료는 귀하의 원고를 받아들이기로 승인되면, 600파운드가 지급될 것입니다. 이 금액은 저희 편집자들에 의해 요청되는 수정 및 사실 확인에 소요되는 시간을 감안한 것입니다. **11** 완성되면, 귀하의 글을 제 이메일 rforest@femarkets.co.uk로 보내 주십시오.

진심으로,

Ryan Forest
Ryan Forest
〈Financial and Economic Markets〉 편집장

동봉물 재중

어휘 **commit to** ~을 약속하다 | **critique** 평론 | **shifting** 바뀌는 | **issue** (간행물의) 호 | **revise** 개정하다 | **post** 게재하다 | **submit** 제출하다 | **extension** 연장 | **adhere to** ~을 고수하다 | **original** 원래의, 본래의 | **deadline** 기한, 마감 시간 | **publication** 출간물, 간행물 | **acceptance** 동의, 수락 | **manuscript** 원고

수신: Ryan Forest (rforest@femarkets.co.uk)
발신: Susan Romano (sromano@edmail.net)
날짜: 5월 1일
제목: 저의 글

Mr. Forest께,

저의 글이 귀사의 4월호 첫 페이지에 실린 것을 보게 되어 매우 기쁩니다. 제가 기사에 대한 첫 편집자 의견을 받은 후 작업을 **13** 요청받았던 제안 수정본이 귀하가 바라던 관점을 제시해 주었다니 매우 기쁩니다. 귀하의 디자인 팀이 작업한 잘 정리된 이미지들과 **12** 표들에 대해 감사하다는 말을 전해 드리고 싶습니다. 저는 지금 국제 금융 분야에서 유사한 이야기를 쓰기 위한 아이디어가 있습니다. 다음 주에 전화상으로 귀하와 이것에 대해 논의하고 싶습니다.

이것은 그저 알려 드리는 것인데, 저는 귀사 편집자의 조언에 따라, **13** 잠재적인 서적 평론가들을 위한 온라인 설문조사를 마쳤습니다. **13** 무료 e-book에 대해서도 감사를 드려야겠습니다. 귀사의 다양한 출판물에 매우 깊은 인상을 받았습니다.

진심으로,

Susan Romano

어휘 **suggest** 제안하다 | **editorial** 편집의, 편집과 관련된 | **angle** 시각, 관점 | **pass on** 전달하다 | **appreciation** 감사 | **well-presented** 잘 되어 있는 | **table** 표 | **supply** 공급하다 | **similar** 유사한 | **finance** 자금, 재정 | **potential** 잠재적인 | **impressed** 감동한, 깊은 인상을 받은 | **title** 서적, 출판물

9. 편지의 목적은 무엇인가?
(A) 추가 정보를 요청하기 위해
(B) 정규직 기회를 제공하기 위해
(C) 업무 관련 세부 사항을 확인해 주기 위해
(D) 기사를 위한 아이디어를 제안하기 위해

해설 편지 첫 단락에서 4월호에 경제 관련 주제에 관한 논평을 쓰기로 했고, 이에 대한 작가 지침 확인 요청을 하는 것을 알 수 있다. 또한 두 번째 단락에서 승인 시에 원고료 확인까지 해주고 있으므로 (C) To confirm the details of an assignment가 정답이다.

---

10. 〈Financial and Economic Markets〉에 관하여 제시된 것은 무엇인가?
(A) 영국의 금융 시장에 관한 기사들만을 출간한다.
(B) 책과 잡지를 모두 출간한다.
(C) 최근에 웹사이트를 업데이트하였다.
(D) 600단어로 된 짧은 기사만을 받는다.

해설 편지의 발신자인 Mr. Forest는 〈Financial and Economic Markets〉의 편집장이고 첫 번째 단락에서 4월호라고 언급하였기 때문에 잡지를 출간함을 알 수 있다. 또한 마감일을 지킬 시 e-book을 무료로 제공해주겠다고 하고 있으므로 전자책도 출간함을 확인할 수 있다. 따라서 정답은 (B) It publishes both books and magazines.이다.

---

11. Mr. Forest는 Ms. Romano에게 이메일로 무엇을 보내달라고 요청하는가?
(A) 그녀의 완성된 원고
(B) 마감일 연장에 대한 요청
(C) 작가 지침에 대한 피드백
(D) 미래의 기사에 대한 아이디어들

해설 편지 마지막에 원고가 완성되면 이메일로 보내달라고 했으므로 정답은 (A) Her completed manuscript이다.

---

12. 이메일에서 첫 번째 단락, 네 번째 줄의 "tables"와 의미상 가장 가까운 것은
(A) 정보 목록들
(B) 지시 사항들
(C) 가구들
(D) 사람 집단들

해설 전체적인 문맥을 살펴보면 잡지에 실린 것에 대한 이야기이므로, 잘

정리된 이미지들과 표들이라는 의미의 (A) data listings가 가장 문맥상 적절하다.

13.
Ms. Romano에 관하여 제시되지 않은 것은 무엇인가?
(A) 기사를 제때 제출했다.
(B) 책 평론에 관심이 있다.
(C) 출판사의 미술 부서를 방문했다.
(D) 본인이 쓴 기사를 수정해야 했다.

해설 (A)는 편지에서 마감일을 지켰을 시 무료 e-book을 제공한다고 했는데 이메일을 보면 무료 e-book을 받아 고맙다고 언급하고 있으므로 Ms. Romano가 기사를 제때 제출했음을 알 수 있다. (B)는 이메일에서 평론에 관한 관심을 드러내고 있고 (D)는 이메일에서 기사를 수정했음을 확인할 수 있다. Ms. Romano가 미술 부서를 방문했다는 언급은 없으므로 정답은 (C) She has visited the publisher's art department.이다.

[14-18] 다음 이메일들과 신고서에 관한 문제입니다.

발신: jlandry@sparklemo.uk
수신: bcabbot@sparklemo.us
제목: 회의
일자: 3월 4일

Mr. Cabott께,

영국에서 온 제 비행기가 방금 착륙했지만 저는 이 이메일을 공항 터미널에서 쓰고 있습니다. 이런 말씀을 드리게 되어 죄송하지만 제 짐이 엉뚱한 도시로 보내져서 내일 우리가 소매상들과 가지는 회의에 지장을 초래할 수도 있을 것 같습니다. **14** 다행히 제 비행기에 가지고 탔던 짐에 노트북이 있어 발표 자료는 가지고 있지만 많은 신제품들은 제 분실된 여행 가방 안에 들어 있습니다. 항공사에서는 제 짐이 3일 후에 도착할 것이라고 했으니 내일 오후 회의 전에는 받지 못할 것입니다. **15** 제 여행 가방이 다시 돌아올 때까지 내일 제 품 시연을 미룰 수 있을까요? 답변을 기다리겠습니다.

진심으로,

Jane Landry

어휘 **land** 착륙하다 | **retailer** 소매상 | **fortunately** 다행히도 | **presentation** 발표 | **carry-on** (비행기 내부로 반입 가능한) 작은 캐리어 가방 | **postpone** 미루다 | **demo** (demonstration) 시연

분실 수하물 신고

귀하의 소유물을 일시적으로 찾을 수 없게 되어 유감으로 생각합니다. 아래 정보로 저희 직원들이 귀하의 소유물을 가능한 한 빨리 **17** 추적할 것입니다. 더 빠른 결과를 위해 가능한 한 많은 세부 정보를 적어 주십시오.

- 청구 번호. 34210002111
- 성명: Jane Landry
- 이메일: jlandry@sparklemo.uk

- 원주지: 532 Hoovershire 가, 다트퍼드 WC1H 2AH, 영국
- **18** 기류지: Zanza 호텔, 1543 W. Ashford 가, 올랜도, 플로리다 32806

수하물 설명: 진보라색, 바퀴가 달렸음, 양 옆은 강철로 된 Travelancer 여행 가방

16 수하물 내용물 설명:

항목	수량
16 팔찌, 목걸이, 반지, 귀걸이 등	48
혼합 견과류, 건조 과일, 캔디 모둠 등	7
정장 바지, 블라우스, 스웨터, 스카프 등	9
프린트한 서류, 메모장, 펜, 연필	6

어휘 **misplaced** 잘못된 | **property** 소유, 재산 | **possession** 소유물 | **permanent** 영구적인 | **temporary** 임시의 | **description** 묘사, 설명 | **content** 내용물 | **bracelet** 팔찌 | **assorted** 모둠의, 여러 가지의 | **document** 서류

발신: brs@blazairco.uk
수신: jlandry@sparklemo.uk
제목: 요청사항 #34210002111
일자: 3월 5일

고객님께,

귀하의 수하물을 찾았으며 수하물이 목적지로 향하고 있다는 것을 알려 드리기 위한 이메일을 드립니다. **18** 귀하께서 적으셨던 기류지 주소로 짐이 보내졌습니다. 짐은 3월 7일 오후 12시와 5시 사이에 받으실 수 있습니다. 기다려 주셔서 감사합니다.

진심으로,

수하물 수취소 부서

어휘 **locate** 위치를 알아내다 | **patience** 참을성, 인내

14.
Ms. Landry는 그녀의 발표 자료에 대해 무엇을 밝히는가?
(A) Mr. Cabott에게 이메일로 보낼 것이다.
(B) 없어졌다.
(C) 완성되지 않았다.
(D) 시연할 준비가 됐다.

해설 우선 Ms. Landry의 이메일을 훑어보면서 문제의 키워드 slides를 찾아내야 한다. 발표 자료는 비행기에 가지고 탔던 노트북 컴퓨터에 들어있다는 내용에서 정답을 알아낼 수 있는데, 발표 자료는 잃어버리지 않고 컴퓨터 안에 있어서 당장 발표에서 사용할 수 있다는 의미이므로 (D) They are ready for display.가 정답이다.

15. Ms. Landry는 Mr. Cabott에게 무엇을 하도록 요청하는가?

    (A) 신제품들 몇 개를 준비한다

    (B) 약속된 시간을 옮긴다

    (C) 호텔 방을 업그레이드한다

    (D) 공항 셔틀 서비스를 예약한다

해설 Ms. Landry의 이메일을 훑어보면서 문제의 키워드 ask Mr. Cabott to do를 찾아내야 한다. 내일 있을 제품 시연회를 연기할 수 있을지 묻는 부분에서 약속된 일정을 다른 때로 옮기자고 요청하고 있으므로 (B) Move an appointment time이 정답이다.

---

16. Ms. Landry는 무엇을 발표하고자 하는가?

    (A) 의류

    (B) 스낵

    (C) 서류

    (D) 보석

해설 Ms. Landry의 이메일에서 잃어버린 여행 가방에 신제품이 들어 있기 때문에 제품 시연회를 연기하자고 요청하는 내용이 나오고 작성한 분실 수하물 신고서를 보면 가방의 내용물로 팔찌, 목걸이, 반지, 귀걸이 등과 같은 보석류가 48점이라고 적혀 있다. 여기서 시연회에서 선보이고자 했던 제품은 보석류라는 것을 알 수 있으므로 정답은 (D) Jewelry이다.

---

17. 신고서의 첫 번째 단락, 두 번째 줄의 단어 "trace"와 의미상 가장 가까운 것은

    (A) 표시하다

    (B) 찾다

    (C) 반환하다

    (D) 따라가다

해설 (D) follow도 사전적 의미상 trace의 동의어가 될 수 있지만, 주어진 단어가 들어있는 문장은 직원들이 되도록 빨리 물건을 추적하여 찾아낼 것이라는 의미이므로 (B) find가 정답이다.

---

18. 짐은 어디로 보내질 것인가?

    (A) 런던으로

    (B) 올랜도로

    (C) 워싱턴으로

    (D) 다트퍼드로

해설 짐을 Ms. Landry가 제공한 임시 거주지로 보냈다고 했고 분실 수하물 신고서에 기류지 주소로 올랜도에 있는 호텔 주소가 적혀 있으므로 정답은 (B) To Orlando이다.

UNIT 07. 문자 대화문과 화자 의도

핵심 문제 유형

본서 p.277

1. (A)   **2.** (C)

[1-2] 다음 문자 대화문에 관한 문제입니다.

> Jefferson, Peter
>
> Mary, 다음 달 11일에 세미나가 있는 거 기억해요?
> 오후 2:02
>
> Kestrel, Mary
>
> 네, 당신이 제게 그 얘길했던 게 기억나요. 왜 물어보시는데요?
> 오후 2:04
>
> Jefferson, Peter
>
> 모든 매니저가 거기에 참석하기를 바라거든요. **1** 매니저들 전체 목록을 편집해서 제게 보내주셔도 괜찮을까요?
> 오후 2:07
>
> Kestrel, Mary
>
> **1** 그렇게 할게요. 언제까지 받길 원하세요?
> 오후 2:09
>
> Jefferson, Peter
>
> 오늘까지 해주면 좋겠어요. **2** 이번 주 목요일까지 모두 등록되어야 해서 시간이 많질 않네요.
> 오후 2:11
>
> Kestrel, Mary
>
> 이메일 주소도 원하세요? 그렇게 하면, 그들에게 세미나에 관해 알려주는 이메일을 보낼 수 있죠.
> 오후 2:14
>
> Jefferson, Peter
>
> 좋은 생각이네요. 고마워요. 오후 2:15

어휘 recall 상기하다 | compile 편집하다

Practice

본서 p.278

1. (A)   **2.** (C)   **3.** (D)   **4.** (C)   **5.** (B)

6. (D)   **7.** (A)   **8.** (C)   **9.** (B)   **10.** (C)

11. (A)   **12.** (D)

[1-2] 다음 문자 대화문에 관한 문제입니다.

Carpenter, Sarah

Mr. Weaver, 좋은 아침입니다. 저는 〈Home Improvement Magazine〉의 Sarah Carpenter입니다. **1** 최신호는 어떠셨나요?　오전 10:34

Weaver, William

오전 10:38　어제 막 다 읽었어요. 아주 좋았어요.

Carpenter, Sarah

마음에 드신다니 기쁘네요. 우편물 안에 무료 선물이 있다는 것을 알려드리려고 합니다. **2** 전화 케이스를 다음 3일 내로 받으실 겁니다.　오전 10:41

Weaver, William

2 정말 고대하고 있습니다. 다음 잡지는 언제 도착하나요?
오전 10:43

Carpenter, Sarah

보통 매달 25일에 도착합니다. 만일 28일까지 못 받으시면 제게 알려주세요. 그러면 어떻게 되었는지 확인하겠습니다.　오전 10:46

Weaver, William

아직 21일 밖에 안돼서, 조금 더 기다려야 할 것 같아요.
오전 10:48

Carpenter, Sarah

언제든 온라인으로 보실 수도 있습니다. 현재 구독하시는 건 저희 온라인 콘텐츠에 대한 전체 이용을 제공하거든요.　오전 10:51

어휘　normally 보통 | find out 알아내다 | subscription 구독 | access 접근 권한

---

1. Ms. Carpenter는 왜 Mr. Weaver에게 메시지를 쓰고 있는가?
(A) 서비스에 만족하는지 확인하기 위해
(B) 비용 인상을 설명하기 위해
(C) 새 멤버십 특징을 설명하기 위해
(D) 그의 기사에 감사하기 위해

해설　오전 10시 34분에 Mr. Carpenter가 잡지가 어땠는지 묻고 있으므로 메시지의 목적은 고객이 만족했는지 알아보기 위한 것임을 알 수 있다. 따라서 정답은 (A) To check if he is satisfied with a service 이다.

2. 오전 10시 43분에 Mr. Weaver가 "정말 고대하고 있습니다"라고 쓴 것은 어떤 의미인가?
(A) 전화를 기다리고 있다.
(B) 아직 잡지를 받지 못했다.
(C) 무료 상품을 받고 싶어한다.
(D) Ms. Carpenter를 만나길 고대한다.

해설　무료 상품으로 전화 케이스를 3일 안에 받을 것이라고 하자 Mr. Weaver가 그것을 받길 고대하고 있다고 하고 있으므로 정답은 (C) He is eager to get his complimentary item.이다. (B)의 his magazine이 가리키는 것은 남자가 정기 구독해서 받는 잡지이다. 3일 내로 도착한다는 것은 잡지가 아닌 선물이므로 (B)는 오답이다.

[3-4] 다음 문자 대화문에 관한 문제입니다.

Carol Greene

3 Brett, 유명한 가수들에 대한 사설 페이지 레이아웃 수정에 대해 물어볼 게 있어요.　오후 2:27

Brett Lancaster

오후 2:28　물론이죠. 뭔가요?

Carol Greene

파일이 전부 다 필요한가요? 아니면 변경이 있었던 27-30페이지만 필요한가요?　오후 2:29

Brett Lancaster

지금 이메일 확인을 할 수가 없어요. 이곳 인터넷이 다운됐거든요.
오후 2:31

Carol Greene

나중에 보낼게요. 내일 아침까지는 편집자에게 보여주지 않아도 되니까요.　오후 2:32

Brett Lancaster

4 기다릴 필요 없어요. 그냥 팩스로 그 페이지들을 보내주세요.
오후 2:33

Carol Greene

알았어요. 번호 좀 주시겠어요?　오후 2:34

Brett Lancaster

오후 2:37　555-1287이에요.

Carol Greene

지금 가고 있어요. 문제가 있으면 다시 보낼게요.　오후 2:41

Brett Lancaster

오후 2:42　지금 나오고 있네요. 정말 고마워요!

어휘　adjustment 수정, 조정 | editorial 사설 | entire 전부의, 전체의 | editor 편집자 | fax 팩스를 보내다

---

3. Ms. Greene은 누구인가?
(A) 콘서트 기획자
(B) 컴퓨터 프로그래머
(C) 부동산 중개인
(D) 그래픽 디자이너

해설　2시 27분에 Ms. Green이 사설의 레이아웃, 즉 디자인 수정에 관한 문의를 하고 있다. 따라서 정답은 (D) A graphic designer이다.

4. 오후 2시 33분에 "기다릴 필요 없어요"라고 Mr. Lancaster가 쓴 것은 무슨 의미인가?

(A) 회의를 미루고 싶지 않다.

(B) 전화를 기다리고 싶지 않다.

(C) 서류를 당장 받고 싶어한다.

(D) 일정 변경에 대해 알고 싶어한다.

해설 "기다릴 필요 없어요."라는 언급 후, 그냥 팩스로 보내달라는 내용이 나오므로, 서류를 빨리 받고 싶다는 의미로 해석해야 한다. 따라서 정답은 (C) He would like to get a document right away. 이다.

[5-8] 다음 온라인 채팅 대화문에 관한 문제입니다.

Cynthia Brown [오후 2:23]
Dianna, 잠깐 시간 좀 있으세요? **5** 이번 달 경비 보고서 양식을 찾을 수가 없네요. 그것들을 찾을 수 있으세요?

Dianna Jones [오후 2:25]
제 컴퓨터에도 안 뜨네요. 언제 이 문제를 알아차리셨어요?

Cynthia Brown [오후 2:26]
6 방금 Alice와 통화를 했거든요. Alice는 지난주 그녀의 팀이 구매한 홍보용 포스터들 영수증을 기록하려고 했어요. 그런데 그것들이 없어졌다는 걸 알게 됐죠. 기술 지원팀에 연락해주시겠어요?

Dianna Jones [오후 2:27]
안녕하세요 Clark, 우리가 가진 몇몇 회계 자료들이 지워졌을지도 모르겠어요. 확인해주실 수 있으세요?

Clark Williams [오후 2:29]
정말 이상하네요. 어제도 올라와 있던 걸 기억하는데.

Dianna Jones [오후 2:30]
7 그 서류들 다른 곳에도 저장되어 있죠, 그렇죠?

Clark Williams [오후 2:31]
7 매일 자료를 백업하죠. 지금 바로 올릴게요.

Dianna Jones [오후 2:32]
8 고마워요. 모든 부서에 이메일을 보내서 문제가 해결됐다고 알려야겠어요.

Cynthia Brown [오후 2:33]
8 지금 바로 보낼 수 있어요.

어휘 expense report 경비 보고서 | notice 알아차리다 | log 일지에 기록하다 | receipt 영수증 | purchase 구매하다 | tech support 기술 지원 | accounting 회계 | delete 지우다 | odd 이상한 | department 부서 | resolve 해결하다

---

5. Ms. Brown은 어떤 문제를 언급하는가?

고난도

(A) 경비 보고서가 제시간에 제출되지 않았다.

(B) 어떤 재무 양식이 이용 불가능하다.

(C) 컴퓨터가 켜지지 않는다.

(D) 영수증 몇 개가 없어졌다.

해설 2시23분에 Ms. Brown이 현재 경비 보고서 양식, 즉 재무 관련 양식을 찾지 못한다고 언급하고 있으므로 정답은 (B) Some financial forms cannot be accessed.이다.

---

6. Ms. Brown은 어떤 부서에서 이 문제를 전해 듣게 되었겠는가?

고난도

(A) 인사팀

(B) 회계팀

(C) 기술지원팀

(D) 광고팀

해설 2시 26분에 Ms. Brown이 Alice와의 통화를 통해 문제가 있다는 것을 알았는데, Alice의 부서는 홍보용 포스터 구매를 담당한다고 했으므로 보기에 있는 부서들 중 이러한 업무를 담당하는 곳은 (D) Advertising임을 알 수 있다.

---

7. 오후 2시 30분에 Ms. Jones가 "그 서류들 다른 곳에도 저장되어 있죠, 그렇죠?"라고 쓴 건 무슨 의미이겠는가?

(A) 일부 서류들이 다시 업로드되기를 원한다.

(B) 여행 예산이 걱정된다.

(C) 직원에게 어떤 물품을 주문해달라고 요청한다.

(D) 회사 시스템을 이용하고 싶어한다.

해설 바로 뒤의 Clark Williams의 오후 2:31 채팅에서 백업한 자료를 바로 올린다는 것을 확인할 수 있으므로 정답은 (A) She wants some documents to be uploaded again.이다.

---

8. Ms. Brown이 다음에 할 행동으로 예상되는 것은 무엇인가?

(A) 프로그램을 설치한다

(B) 기술 지원팀에 전화한다

(C) 이메일을 송신한다

(D) 부서 회의를 주최한다

해설 2:32에 Ms. Jones가 문제가 해결됐음을 모든 부서에 알려야 한다고 이야기하고 있고, 이후에 바로 Ms. Brown이 본인이 그 일을 할 수 있음을 이야기하고 있으므로, 그녀가 모든 부서에게 문제가 해결됐음을 알리는 이메일을 보낼 것을 유추할 수 있다. 따라서 정답은 (C) Send an e-mail이다.

[9-12] 다음 온라인 채팅 대화문에 관한 문제입니다.

Huey Jackson [오후 3:09]
Malina, **9** 시간 괜찮으세요? 우리 창고 시설에 대해 여쭤볼 게 있는데요.

Malina Chavez [오후 3:10]
9 그럼요.

Huey Jackson [오후 3:12]
재고 일지를 지금 살펴보고 있는데 **11** Woodwin 수납장이 스무 개밖에 안 남았다고 나와 있거든요. 최근 이 수납장이 많이 팔렸잖아요. 새로 주문을 해야 할까요?

Malina Chavez [오후 3:14]
그럴 필요는 없어요. **12** Woodwin이 가격을 올려서 더 가격이 적당한 브랜드로 가기로 결정했거든요. **10** 당신이 지난주에 휴가를 갔을 때 제가 Marydale 수납장을 200개 주문했어요. 내일 도착할 거예요.

Huey Jackson [오후 3:15]
좋네요.

Malina Chavez [오후 3:16]
12 화요일에 우리 카탈로그에서 주문하는 모든 소매 상점들에게 알렸어요. 모두가 이 변화에 동의했고요.

Huey Jackson [오후 3:17]
잘됐네요! 고마워요.

어휘 **warehouse** 창고 | **inventory** 재고 | **log** 일지 | **recently** 최근에 | **affordable** 가격이 더 적당한, 더 싼 | **inform** 공지하다, 알리다 | **retail shop** 소매 상점 | **fantastic** 환상적인, 멋진

---

9. 오후 3시 10분에 Ms. Chavez가 "그럼요"라고 쓴 것은 무슨 의미인가?
(A) Mr. Jackson이 지시한 것을 완수했다.
(B) Mr. Jackson의 질문에 답할 수 있다.
(C) Mr. Jackson의 프로젝트 요청을 승인했다.
(D) Mr. Jackson에게 전화할 시간을 확정해줄 것이다.

해설 3:09에 Mr. Jackson이 시간 괜찮으면 창고 시설에 관한 질문을 하고 싶다고 했고, 이후에 바로 Ms. Chavez가 "Sure"라고 했기 때문에, Mr. Jackson의 질문에 답변을 할 수 있음을 확인할 수 있다. 따라서 정답은 (B) She is available to address Mr.Jackson's question. 이다.

---

10. Mr. Jackson에 대해 무엇이 언급되었는가?
고난도 (A) 지난주에 물건들을 더 주문했다.
(B) 재고 파일을 방금 수정했다.
(C) 최근 휴가를 갔다.
(D) 내일 카탈로그를 업데이트할 것이다.

해설 3:14에 Ms. Chavez가 '당신이 지난주에 휴가를 갔을 때'라는 언급에서 '당신'이 Mr. Jackson인 것을 알 수 있다. 따라서 정답은 (C) He took time off recently.이다.

---

11. Ms. Chavez와 Mr. Jackson은 어떤 사업을 하고 있는가?
(A) 가구 공급 회사
(B) 나무 생산 회사
(C) 주택 개조 가게
(D) 인테리어 디자인 회사

해설 3:12에 Mr. Jackson이 Woodwin 수납장이 많이 팔려서 20개밖에 남지 않았다고 하고 있으므로, 수납장을 판매하는 회사, 즉 가구를 판매하는 사업을 하는 것을 알 수 있다. 지문에서 나무를 이용하여 가구를 만든다는 내용이 없으므로 (B)를 정답으로 하지 않도록 주의해야 한다. 따라서 정답은 (A) A furniture supplier이다.

---

12. Ms. Chavez는 이번 주 초에 무엇을 했는가?
(A) 직원 교육 워크샵을 진행했다.
(B) 큰 할인행사를 기획했다.
(C) Mr. Jackson이 재고를 확인하는 것을 도왔다.
(D) 새 제품을 고객들에게 알렸다.

해설 오후 3:14에 Ms. Chavez가 Woodwin이 제품 가격을 올렸기 때문에 다른 브랜드를 이용하기로 했고, 오후 3:16에 소매 상점들에게 이 변화에 대해서 알렸고, 모두 동의했다고 했으므로 정답은 (D) She notified clients of a new product.이다.

UNIT 08. 편지·이메일

핵심 문제 유형
본서 p.284

1. (B) **2.** (C) **3.** (C)

[1-3] 다음 편지에 관한 문제입니다.

Medical Labs of Australia
39 Main 가
멜버른, VIC 2930
호주

Ms. Janet Fernandez
452 Hill Side 로
시드니, NSW 2000
호주

8월 27일

Ms. Fernandez께,

Medical Labs of Australia에 보여주신 관심에 대단히 감사드립니다. 저희는 이달 초, 〈The Melbourne Daily News〉에 광고를 냈던 홍보직에 대한 당신의 지원서를 받아서 검토했습니다. **1** 아쉽게도, 그 자리는 이미 충원되었습니다. 하지만, 비슷한 자리가 10월에 날 것으로 예상되기 때문에 낙담하실 필요는 없습니다.

저희는 당신이 그 자리에 자격이 충분하다고 생각해서, 자기소개서와 이력서를 포함한 당신의 지원 서류를 파일로 보관해두겠습니다. **2** 그 자리는 또한 멜버른 본사에 있을 것입니다만, 캔버라나 브리즈번 지사 및 유럽의 여러 도시들로의 출장이 필요할 것입니다.

3 웹사이트상에서 이 자리에 대한 공고를 계속 지켜봐 주시고, 게시되면 저희에게 연락 바랍니다.

당신의 Medical Labs of Australia 취업 기회에 대해 곧 더 자세히 얘기 나눌 수 있기를 고대합니다.

진심으로,

Marshall Baxter
인사 책임자

어휘 public relations 홍보 | discourage 낙담시키다 | anticipate 예상하다 | open up 이용할 수 있게 되다 | well qualified 자격이 충분한 | including ~을 포함하여 | keep ~ on file ~을 파일로 보관하다 | headquarters 본사 | post 게시하다 | look forward to ~ing ~하기를 고대하다 | career opportunity 취업 기회 | in greater detail 더 자세히

해설 네 번째 줄에서 회의를 수요일로 재조정했으면 한다고 하고 있으므로 정답은 (B) Change an appointment이다. (A)는 이메일에서 식당 예약을 요청하는 것이지 특별식을 요청하는 것이 아니므로 오답이며 (C)는 Ms. Lee가 로마로 가야 해서 회의 일정을 변경하길 원한 것이지 로마행 비행기 표 구매를 부탁하진 않았으므로 정답이 아니다. (D)는 백화점을 방문할 사람은 Ms. Kim이므로 역시 오답이다.

2. Ms. Lee는 언제 파리를 떠날 것인가?
(A) 화요일에
(B) 수요일에
(C) 목요일에
(D) 금요일에

해설 파리에서 목요일에 만나기로 했지만 그날 저녁에 Ms. Lee가 로마로 떠나야 한다고 했으므로 정답은 (C) On Thursday이다.

Practice

본서 p.286

1. (B) **2.** (C) **3.** (C) **4.** (A) **5.** (D)
6. (A) **7.** (D) **8.** (B) **9.** (B) **10.** (A)
11. (B)

[3-4] 다음 편지에 관한 문제입니다.

6월 28일

John Mansfield
Greenway 악단
3143 Witmer 로
브루클린, 뉴욕 11201

Mr. Mansfield께,

축하합니다! **3** 브루클린 겨울 퍼레이드 공연을 위해 조직 위원회는 당신의 악단을 선택했습니다. 축제 행사는 1월 13일, 일요일 오후 3시에 시작될 것입니다. **4** 연주자들에게 오후 2시까지 컨벤션 센터로 오라고 알려주세요. 연주자들은 컨벤션 센터의 북문 근처에서 먼저 만나고, Main 가의 동쪽으로 이동한 후, 시 광장을 지나, Jonas 다리로 향할 것입니다. 축하 공연은 Norwood 공원에서 끝날 예정이며, 그곳에서 다시 컨벤션 센터로 돌아오는 셔틀 버스 서비스를 이용하실 수 있습니다.

여러분이 퍼레이드에서 행군하는 모습을 볼 것에 저희는 매우 흥분해 있습니다!

진심으로,

Joe Simmons
Joe Simmons
행사 코디네이터

[1-2] 다음 이메일에 관한 문제입니다.

발신: Jung-hwa Park 〈parkjw@kfmail.com〉
수신: Diana Kim 〈kimdiane@kfmail.com〉
날짜: 7월 2일, 오전 10시 23분
제목: 다음 주

안녕하세요, Ms. Kim.

영업 이사인 Ms. Lee는 유럽에서의 당신의 진척 사항을 지켜봐왔고, 꽤 만족하고 있다고 말합니다. 제가 다음 주에 당신을 만나러 갈 때 그녀가 저와 동행할 것입니다. **2** 우리는 원래 목요일 오후에 만나기로 했지만, Ms. Lee가 그날 저녁에 로마로 가야 합니다. **1** 그래서 회의를 수요일로 조정했으면 합니다. Ms. Lee는 우리가 만날 때 점심을 같이 하는 걸 더 선호할 것이니, 당신이 좋아하는 파리의 음식점들 중 한 곳을 예약해 주십시오. 저는 저희의 방문이 당신에게 너무 많은 불편을 끼치지 않기를 바랍니다. 또한 저는 당신이 백화점 소유주들을 만나러 갈 때 사용할 새로운 샘플 옷들을 몇 벌 가져갈 것입니다. 그것들은 올 가을 상품들에 포함될 것입니다. 우리의 만남과 관련된 자세한 사항에 대해선 제게 연락 주십시오. 감사합니다.

진심으로,

Jung-hwa Park

어휘 progress 진전, 진척 | accompany 동행하다 | be scheduled to ~할 예정이다 | prefer 선호하다 | make a reservation 예약하다 | inconvenience 불편, 애로 | outfit 옷 | include 포함하다

어휘 organizing committee 조직 위원회 | marching band (행진하면서 연주하는) 악단 | perform 공연하다 | festivity 축제 행사 | entrance 출입구 | proceed 진행하다, 진행되다, 계속해서 ~을 하다, (특정 방향으로) 나아가다 | past 지나서, 통과해서 | toward 향하여 | conclude 마치다, 결론짓다

1. 이메일에 따르면, Ms. Park이 원하는 것은 무엇인가?
(A) 특별식을 요청한다
(B) 약속을 변경한다
(C) 로마행 비행기 표들을 구입한다
(D) 파리의 백화점들을 방문한다

3. Mr. Mansfield는 누구이겠는가?
(A) 셔틀 버스 운전기사
(B) 퍼레이드 기획자
(C) 악단 리더
(D) 컨벤션 센터 직원

해설 Mr. Mansfield의 악단이 퍼레이드에서 연주하기로 선택됐음을 your marching band를 통하여 유추할 수 있다. 따라서 정답은 (C) A band leader이다.

---

4. 퍼레이드는 어디에서 시작될 것인가?
(A) 컨벤션 센터에서
(B) Norwood 공원에서
(C) 시 광장에서
(D) Jonas 다리 아래에서

해설 퍼레이드가 끝나는 곳과 혼동하지 않도록 주의해야 한다. 연주자들은 컨벤션 센터에서 오후 2시까지 집결 후에 이동한다고 하므로, 퍼레이드가 컨벤션 센터에서 시작됨을 확인할 수 있다. 따라서 정답은 (A) At the convention center이다.

[5-7] 다음 이메일에 관한 문제입니다.

수신: Nora McNeal 〈nmcneal@atlantadeco.com〉
발신: Ken Nikki 〈knikki@apexwarehouse.com〉
날짜: 9월 21일
제목: 회신: Atlanta Deco Henes

Ms. McNeal께,

귀사에서 제조한 침대 프레임 모델 중 하나인 Atlanta Deco Henes에 관하여 편지를 드립니다. **5** 그 프레임을 사 가신 많은 고객들이 그것을 조립하는 데 필요한 볼트가 빠져 있다고 알려주었습니다. 다행히, 우리에게는 유사한 크기의 볼트가 재고에 있어서 빠진 부품을 교체해 드릴 수 있었습니다.

그러나, 여전히 그것들을 필요로 하시는 고객이 몇 분 계시므로, **6** 침대 프레임과 함께 오게 되어 있는 볼트를 세 상자 보내주실 수 있다면 감사하겠습니다.

7 빠진 볼트와 관련된 우려 때문에, 우리는 당분간은 그 침대 프레임을 더 이상 주문하지 않으려 합니다. 이 문제가 해결되고 나서 알려주시면, 우리는 기꺼이 귀사와 거래를 재개하도록 하겠습니다.
이 문제에 대한 도움에 감사 드립니다.

진심으로,

Ken Nikki, 관리자
Apex 창고

어휘 concerning ~에 관한 | manufacture 제조하다 | missing 사라진, 없는 | grateful 고마워하는, 감사하는 | for the time being 당분간 | resume 재개하다

---

5. Mr. Nikki는 왜 이메일을 썼는가?
(A) 문의에 답변하기 위해
(B) 상품을 홍보하기 위해
(C) 규정에 대해 문의하기 위해
(D) 문제를 처리하기 위해

해설 첫 번째 문단에서 침대 조립에 필요한 볼트가 빠졌고, 그에 대한 처리를 요구하고 있음을 확인할 수 있다. 따라서 정답은 (D) To address a problem이다.

---

6. Mr. Nikki는 Ms. McNeal에게 무엇을 해 달라고 요청하는가?
(A) 어떤 물품을 제공한다
(B) 더 많은 지역 손님들을 유치한다
(C) 환불을 한다
(D) 프레임 구축 방법을 설명한다

해설 두 번째 단락에서 침대 프레임에 딸려오는 볼트 세 상자를 보내달라고 요청하는 것을 알 수 있다. 따라서 정답은 (A) Supply some items이다.

---

7. Apex 창고는 어떤 결정을 내렸는가?
(A) 특정 부품에 대해 고객에게 청구할 예정이다.
(B) 몇몇 결함 있는 제품을 반환할 것이다.
(C) 다양한 침대 모델을 취급할 것이다.
(D) 특정 제품에 대한 주문을 중단할 것이다.

해설 세 번째 단락에서 볼트가 빠진 문제 때문에 해당 침대 프레임을 주문하지 않는다고 했으므로 정답은 (D) It will suspend orders for a specific product.이다.

[8-11] 다음 이메일에 관한 문제입니다.

발신: Martin Dekker 〈martind@bre.org〉
수신: Pin Tran Hyun 〈Pintranh@ausmail.com〉
날짜: 4월 11일
제목: 전시회

Mr. Hyun께,

다음번 지역 화가들을 위한 Barrier Reef 전시회가 7월 10일부터 8월 20일까지 열릴 예정입니다. **9** 저희는 귀하께서 해외에서의 가족 행사 때문에 작년의 전시회 참석을 거절하셨던 것으로 알고 있습니다. 저희는 귀하의 상황을 전적으로 이해했지만, 특히 관람객들은 귀하를 많이 그리워했었다는 걸 아셨으면 합니다. 귀하의 작품들은 여기 호주에서 매우 인기가 많으며, **8** 올해 다시 저희와 함께하신다면 영광이겠습니다.

귀하께서는 귀하의 전시 부스에서 판매하실 작품 외에 행사 마지막 날 밤 경매에 포함시킬 작품 세 점도 제출해주셔야 합니다. **11** 포함시킬 작품들을 선정하셨다면, 저희에게 각 작품의 짧은 설명과 함께 사진을 보내 주십시오. 저희는 이 정보를 저희 웹사이트에서 경매 홍보용으로 활용할 것입니다. 또한 전시회의 일부로 새로운 강의들도 포함시킬 것입니다. 저희는 전시회 기간 동안 매일 오후에 아티스트 열 명의 강의도 계획하고 있습니다. 강의하시는 분들께는 300달러의 참가자 비용을 **10** 면제해드릴 것입니다.

이번 행사의 전시 부스를 예약하고 싶으시면, 이메일로 되도록 일찍 제게 연락 주십시오. 감사합니다.

진심으로,

Martin Dekker
사무총장
Barrier Reef 화가 협회

어휘 exhibition 전시회, 전시 | decline 거절하다 | miss 그리워하다 | rejoin 재가입하다, 다시 참가하다 | auction 경매 | description 설명, 묘사 | lecture 강의 | exempt 면제된 | booth 부스, 점포

8. 이 이메일의 주요 목적은 무엇인가?

(A) 곧 있을 행사를 광고하려고

(B) 초대를 하려고

(C) 최근 변화를 설명하려고

(D) 주문하려고

해설 이메일의 목적을 묻는 문제이다. 지역 화가들을 위한 전시회를 열면서 Mr. Hyun에게 작년에는 가족 행사로 참여하지 못했지만 올해는 다시 참가해 줄 것을 요청하고 있으므로 정답은 (B) To extend an invitation이다. 포괄적 개념으로 행사 참석을 유도하기 위한 행사 홍보의 글로 보고 (A) 행사 광고를 정답으로 고를 수 있으나, 보기 중에 보다 구체적 내용에 해당하는 (B) 행사 참여에 대한 초대(권유)가 있기 때문에 (B)가 정답이다.

9.
고난도 Mr. Hyun에 관하여 언급된 것은 무엇인가?

(A) 지역 화가이다.

(B) 작년에 참가하도록 초대받았다.

(C) 행사 기간 동안 해외에 있을 것이다.

(D) 현재 호주에 전시된 작품이 있다.

해설 이메일 수신인인 Mr. Hyun의 정보를 문제 보기와 비교하며 정답을 찾는다. 가족 행사 때문에 작년 전시회 참석을 거절했다는 내용을 통해 Mr. Hyun이 작년 행사에 초대받았음을 알 수 있으므로 (B)가 정답이다. 이 전시회가 지역 예술가를 위한 것이라는 내용 때문에 대표적 오답으로 (A)를 선택하는데, 전시회에 참석한 사람들이 모두 다 지역 예술가라는 언급이 없으므로 Mr. Hyun을 지역 예술가라고 한 (A)는 오답이다. 예컨대, A대학 축제 초대 가수들이 전부 A대학 가수라고 할 수 없듯이, 지역 예술가들을 위한 전시회에 초대받은 Mr. Hyun을 지역 예술가라고 단정할 수 없다.

10.
고난도 두 번째 단락, 다섯 번째 줄의 단어 "exempt"와 의미상 가장 가까운 것은

(A) 면제되는

(B) 기대되는

(C) 연장한

(D) 초과하는

해설 주어진 단어 exempt는 '면제되는'이라는 의미의 형용사이다. 따라서 '용납되는, 면하는, 면제되는'이란 의미의 (A) excused가 의미상 가장 적절하다.

---

11. [1], [2], [3], [4]로 표시된 곳 중에서 다음 문장이 들어가기에 가장 적절한 곳은 어디인가?

"포함시킬 작품들을 선정하셨다면, 저희에게 각 작품의 짧은 설명과 함께 사진을 보내 주십시오."

(A) [1]

(B) [2]

(C) [3]

(D) [4]

해설 주어진 문장은 경매에 내놓을 작품들이 결정되면 그 정보를 보내달라는 의미로, 경매와 관련된 내용이다. 따라서 경매에 포함시킬 작품들에 대한 문장 뒤에 위치해야 하며, 특히 그 뒷문장의 this information이

'photographs with a short description of each item'을 받는다는 점을 단서로 문제를 해결한다. 따라서 정답은 (B) [2]이다.

UNIT 09. 광고

토익 핵심 문제 유형

본서 p.291

1. (A)   2. (B)   3. (B)

[1-3] 다음 광고에 관한 문제입니다.

Daniel & Johnson, Inc.

달리 언급된 사항이 없으면, 모집 부문들은 주간 교대 근무(오전 8시 ~ 오후 5시)를 대상으로 합니다.

창고 관리직

학사 학위와 재고 절차에 대한 지식 및 소매업 분야 경력이 필수입니다. **1** 또한 컴퓨터와 재무에 대한 기본 지식을 반드시 갖추고 있어야 합니다. 이전 관리 경력은 우대하지만, 필수는 아닙니다.

재고 관리 기술자

고교 졸업장과 최소 일 년간 다량의 재고 업무 경력이 있어야 합니다. 또한 리프팅 중장비를 다룰 줄 알아야 합니다. **2** 야간 근무가 요구됩니다.

데이터 입력 보조원

고교 졸업장과 탁월한 타이핑 기술 및 소매업 분야 경력이 있어야 합니다. **2** 일부 야간 근무가 요구됩니다.

유통 전문가와 창고 담당자

근면하고 신뢰할 수 있어야 합니다. **2** 창고 담당자들은 일부 야간 근무가 요구됩니다.

3 이력서를 다음 주소로 보내주세요:

인적 자원부, Daniel & Johnson 사
유통 센터 104 E. Riverside 로 Twin Pines, 노스캐롤라이나 50964

전화나 이메일은 받지 않습니다.

어휘 day shift 주간 교대 | unless otherwise 달리 ~하지 않는다면 | inventory 재고 | procedures 절차 | possess 소유하다 | desirable 바람직한, 호감이 가는 | diploma 졸업장 | heavy-volume 다량의 | stock clerk 창고 담당자 | hardworking 근면한, 부지런한 | reliable 신뢰할 수 있는

Practice

1. (D)	2. (A)	3. (B)	4. (C)	5. (C)
6. (C)	7. (D)	8. (C)	9. (C)	10. (B)

[1-2] 다음 광고에 관한 문제입니다.

사람을 구함

1 Oscar 제약회사에서는 North View 지역 연구 책임자 공석을 채울 사람을 급히 구하고 있습니다. **2** 책임자는 연구 자료들이 현재의 규정을 준수하는지 확인하는 것뿐만 아니라 모든 실험 장비의 사용도 감독해야 합니다.

화학이나 의료 공학 학위와 더불어 연구 기관에서 최소 3년의 경력이 필수입니다. 합격자는 국립 의료 연구자 협회의 허가를 이미 소지하고 있어야 합니다.

관심이 있으신 지원자들은 자기 소개서와 이력서를 Tricia Thornton에게 thornton.t@oscarpharmaceutical.com으로 보내 주십시오.

어휘 urgent 급한 | comply with ~에 순응하다, 지키다 | degree 학위 | chemistry 화학 | at least 최소한 | required 필수인 | candidate 입후보자, 출마자 | licensed 허가를 받은 | applicant 지원자 | cover letter 자기소개서 | résumé 이력서

1. Oscar 제약회사에 관하여 알 수 있는 것은 무엇인가?
(A) 3년간 운영되어 왔다.
(B) 임시 근로자를 찾고 있다.
(C) 연구 시설을 확충하고 있다.
(D) 빈 자리를 빨리 충원해야 한다.

해설 첫 번째 단락에서 Oscar Pharmaceutical이 연구 책임자를 긴급 채용하고 있다는 사실을 알 수 있으므로 정답은 (D) It needs to quickly fill a position.이다.

2. 구인 광고에 따르면, 연구 책임자의 직무는 무엇인가?
(A) 실험실 규칙을 시행하는 것
(B) 의료 보고서를 제출하는 것
(C) 연구 조교들을 고용하는 것
(D) 환자들에게 연락하는 것

해설 첫 번째 단락에서 책임자들은 연구 자료들이 현재의 규정을 준수하는지와 모든 연구실 장비들을 관리해야 한다고 명시하고 있다. 따라서 (A) Enforcing laboratory rules가 정답이다.

[3-4] 다음 광고에 관한 문제입니다.

최근에 〈Individual Homes Weekly〉 (IHW)를 읽지 못하셨다면, 여러분은 실내 장식의 최근 디자인을 놓치고 계신 것입니다. 새로운 IHW는 그 분야의 저명한 전문가들과 새로운 디자이너들의 인터뷰와 같이 더 많은 특집 기사들을 여러분께 전해 드립니다. 게다가, 여러분이 IHW에서 너무나 보고 싶어하셨던, **3** 전 세계적으로 가장 최신의 실내 장식 디자인에 관한 놀라운 보도를 이제 보다 많은 사진들을 통해 보실 수 있습니다. 저희 편집장과 함께하는 Q&A 섹션도 추가하였으며, 인기 있는 My Home Needs Help! 섹션에 가장 멋진 디자인 조언을 제시해 주시는 독자 분들께 매주 특별한 경품을 드릴 것입니다. **4** 구독을 갱신하시거나 신청하시려면, 상을 받은 저희 웹사이트인 ihw.com을 오늘 방문해 주세요!

어휘 latest 최근의, 최신의 | home décor 집 장식 | feature 특집 | established 인정받는, 저명한 | coverage (TV나 라디오의) 보도 | come to ~하게 되다 | section (신문의) 란, 구획 | chief editor 편집장 | award 수여하다, 지급하다 | award-winning 상을 받은 | renew 재개하다, 갱신하다 | subscription 구독

3. 광고에 관하여 언급된 것은 무엇인가?
(A) 새로운 편집장을 고용했다.
(B) 전 세계의 실내 디자인을 보여준다.
(C) 구독 비용이 오를 것이다.
(D) 출간이 일시적으로 중단되었다.

해설 구독자가 전 세계적으로 가장 최신의 실내 장식 디자인에 관한 보도를 얻을 수 있다고 하였으므로 (B) It shows interior designs from all over the world.가 정답이다.

4. 웹사이트에 관하여 알 수 있는 것은 무엇인가?
(A) 〈Individual Homes Weekly〉의 지난 호를 볼 수 있도록 해 준다.
(B) 가정용 가구의 할인권을 포함하고 있다.
(C) 잡지 구독권 갱신 방법을 제공한다.
(D) 신규 구독자들에게 주는 무료 선물에 대해 설명해 준다.

해설 지문 제일 마지막에서 웹사이트를 통하여 잡지 구독을 신청할 수 있음을 알 수 있으므로 정답은 (C) It provides a way to renew a subscription to the magazine.이다.

[5-7] 다음 광고에 관한 문제입니다.

판매
은색 Tepco Pride 밴

연비: 고속도로에서 100킬로미터당 9리터, 시내에서 100킬로미터당 15리터. www.yearlycarsummary.co.uk에 따르면 시장 내 경쟁업체들에 비해 30퍼센트 이상 더 효율적임. 35,000킬로미터 주행(대부분 고속도로)

특징: **6** 내장형 서라운드 사운드 스피커, 원격 입력 시스템, GPS 내비게이션, 파워 윈도우, **6** 타이어 공기압 표시계, 사고 예방 시스템, 개폐형 지붕, **6** 보온 좌석.

5 호가: 13,000파운드 또는 시가

다른 세부사항들: 제조사 보증 1년 남음. 지역 자동차 정비소에서 정기 유지 관리를 받음. **7** 줄곧 같은 사람이 소유해 왔음. 택시로 정기적으로 사용되었음. 소유주가 해외로 가기 때문에 이달 내로 판매되어야 함.

밴을 보고자 하시거나 시험 운전하시는 데 관심이 있으시다면, 만남 일정 정하기 위해 ronfloyd@vizmail.co.uk로 Ronald Floyd에게 이메일을 보내 주세요.

어휘 **fuel economy** 연료 소비율 ㅣ **efficient** 효율적인 ㅣ **built-in** 내장된 ㅣ **remote entry system** 원격 입력 시스템 ㅣ **indicator** 표시기, 계기 장치 ㅣ **convertible** 전환 가능한; 컨버터블(차량 지붕을 접었다 폈다 할 수 있는) ㅣ **warranty** 보증 ㅣ **own** 소유하다

---

5. Tepco Pride 밴에 관하여 언급된 것은 무엇인가?

(A) 경쟁업체보다 더 많은 연료를 소모한다.

(B) 해당 차종 중에서는 가장 빠르다.

(C) 가격은 협상 가능하다.

(D) 보증기간이 더 이상 유효하지 않다.

해설 세 번째 단락의 호가(ask price)나 시가(best offer)라는 표현을 통해 가격은 협상 가능함을 알 수 있다. 따라서 정답은 (C) Its price is negotiable.이다.

---

6. Tepco Pride 밴의 특징으로 언급되지 않은 것은 무엇인가?

(A) 타이어 공기압을 알려주는 표시

(B) 좌석을 데워주는 시스템

(C) 후방 주시 카메라

(D) 오디오 시스템

해설 (A)는 tire pressure indicator을 통해 확인할 수 있고, (B)는 heated seats을 통해 알 수 있다. (D) 또한 Built-in surround sound speakers에서 알 수 있다. 후방 주시 카메라에 대한 언급을 찾을 수 없으므로 정답은 (C) A rearview camera이다.

---

7. Mr. Floyd에 관하여 사실인 것은 무엇인가?

고난도 (A) 밴을 개인용 차량으로만 사용해왔다.

(B) 자동차 기계공으로 일한다.

(C) 이번 달까지 국외에 있을 것이다.

(D) 밴을 새차(인 상태로) 구입했다.

해설 Mr. Floyd가 자동차의 첫 구매자이자 계속 소유해 왔음을 확인할 수 있으므로 정답은 (D) He purchased his van new.이다. (A)는 택시로 이용이 되었던 것이지, 개인 차량으로 사용했던 것이 아니며 (C)는 해외로 가기 위해 팔아야 하는 것이므로 오답이다. Mr. Floyd는 밴의 소유주이므로 (B)는 오답이다.

[8-10] 다음 광고에 관한 문제입니다.

Brickett's 초콜릿
Maplebury의 15 High 가
645-132-5631

저희 Brickett's 초콜릿을 한 번 시식하시면 계속해서 다시 오시게 될 것입니다. Brickett's는 지역 쇼핑 지구에 편리하게 위치해 있고, 시내에서 유일하게 개인 파티용 방을 갖추고 있는 초콜릿 가게입니다.

저희는 다음을 제공합니다.

- **8** 최고급 재료를 사용해 이곳 저희 매장에서 생산된 20가지의 다양한 초콜릿
- 다양한 종류의 우유맛
- 주문 제작되는 초콜릿 케이크
- 행사실 내 무료 무선 인터넷 접속

영업 시간: 월요일부터 토요일, 오전 10시부터 오후 7시까지
9 동절기(12월부터 2월까지): 오후 9시까지 영업
10 매주 목요일은 어린이들의 날입니다. 12세 이하의 어린이들은 엄선된 초콜릿 한 봉지를 45% 할인받을 수 있습니다.

어휘 **sample** 시식·시음하다; 표본 조사를 하다 ㅣ **conveniently located** 편리한 곳에 위치한 ㅣ **shopping district** 쇼핑 지구 ㅣ **private** 사적인, 개인의 ㅣ **offer** 제공하다 ㅣ **produce** 생산하다 ㅣ **ingredient** 재료, 성분 ㅣ **customized** 개개인의 요구에 맞춘 ㅣ **wireless** 무선의 ㅣ **access** 접속

---

8. Bricket's 초콜릿에 관하여 언급된 것은 무엇인가?

(A) 식료품 가게에서 그 회사 제품을 이용할 수 있다.

(B) 가족 소유의 사업이다.

(C) 가게에서 초콜릿을 만든다.

(D) 웹사이트를 열었다.

해설 지문 두 번째 단락에서 초콜릿이 가게에서 자체적으로 최고급 재료를 사용해서 생산됨을 확인할 수 있으므로 정답은 (C) Its chocolates are made in store.이다.

---

9. 광고문에 따르면, 12월에는 어떤 일이 일어나는가?

(A) 가게가 추가 직원들을 고용한다.

(B) 메뉴가 업데이트된다.

(C) 영업 시간이 변경된다.

(D) 행사실이 문을 닫는다.

해설 일반적인 영업시간은 오전 10시부터 오후 7시까지지만, 겨울인 12월부터 2월까지는 오후 9시까지 영업 시간이 연장됨을 확인할 수 있으므로 정답은 (C) The business hours change.이다.

---

10. 할인에 관해 언급된 것은 무엇인가?

(A) 2월에 끝난다.

(B) 일주일에 한 번만 제공된다.

(C) 어떤 타입의 초콜릿이든지 유효하다.

(D) 오직 밀크 초콜릿에만 적용된다.

해설 지문 마지막 단락에서 매주 목요일에 12세 이하 어린이들에게만 초콜릿 한 봉지에 대하여 특별 할인 제공이 되는 것을 알 수 있다. 따라서 정답은 (B) It is offered just once a week.이다.

UNIT 10. 공지·회람

핵심 문제 유형

본서 p.297

1. (A) 2. (C) 3. (B)

[1-3] 다음 공지에 관한 문제입니다.

Fairway 건설
새 지역 코디네이터

1 우리는 **2** 남미 지역 코디네이터 자리에 Linda Edwards의 임명을 발표하게 되어 기쁩니다. 그녀는 지역 업무들에 대한 순조로운 운영을 감독하게 될 것입니다. Linda는 우리 회사와 함께하기 전 SMD 건설에서 15년의 주택 공급 부문 경력을 쌓았으며, 그곳에서 개발 매니저로 일했습니다. 그녀는 Lupton 대학교에서 경영학 학위를 받았습니다.

여러분 모두가 아시다시피, 지난해는 Fairview에게 매우 힘든 해였습니다. **3** 우리는 5월 기업 인수 이후 경영에 많은 변화들을 겪어왔습니다. 또한 상당한 조직 구조 조정이 있었고, 이로 인해 우리가 일하는 방식에 많은 조정이 있게 되었습니다.

해외에서 Linda는 남미 사업부가 다시 정상화되기를 고대하고 있습니다.

어휘 appointment 임명 | oversee 감독하다 | smooth 순조로운 | affair 일, 사건 | challenging 도전적인, 힘든 | undergo 겪다, 경험하다 | following ~ 이후에 | takeover 기업 인수 | substantial 상당한, 실질적인 | restructuring 구조조정 | result in ~에서 비롯되다 | back on track 다시 정상 궤도에 오른

Practice

본서 p.298

1. (C)	2. (D)	3. (C)	4. (A)	5. (D)
6. (B)	7. (B)	8. (B)	9. (A)	10. (C)
11. (A)	12. (D)			

[1-2] 다음 회람에 관한 문제입니다.

발신: Anne Jones, 인사부장
수신: 재무부와 영업부 직원들
제목: 이동에 관한 공지
날짜: 2월 11일, 화요일, 오후 5시 20분

여러분께 Wayne Clarke이 재무부에서 영업부로의 부서 이동 결정을 수락했음을 알려드리고자 합니다. Wayne은 이번 주 Alvez Vasquez와 교육을 시작할 것이며, **1** Mr. Vasquez가 다음 달 초 은퇴할 때 영업부의 행정 관리자로서의 역할을 맡게 될 것입니다. 인사부의 제 부하 직원인 Russell Green은 내일 재무부의 행정 관

리직 구인 공고를 게시할 것입니다. **2** 우리는 이 자리가 다음달 초까지 채워질 것으로 예상하고 있습니다.

우리 회사에서 20년 가까이 있었던 Mr. Vasquez의 은퇴를 축하해 주시고, Mr. Clarke가 새로운 팀으로 옮겨가니 행운을 빌어 주십시오.

어휘 personnel director 인사부장 | transfer 이동, 이적, 이동하다 | assume 책임을 맡다 | role 역할 | administrative 행정상의, 관리상의 | retire 은퇴하다 | post 게시하다 | job opening 공석, 빈 일자리 | retirement 은퇴

---

1. 누가 회사를 떠나는가?
(A) Anne Jones
(B) Wayne Clarke
(C) Alvez Vasquez
(D) Russell Green

해설 공지 첫 번째 단락 마지막줄에서 Wayne이 Vasquez가 다음달 초 은퇴할 때, 영업부의 관리자로서의 역할을 수행할 것이라고 하였으므로 정답은 (C) Alvez Vasquez이다.

---

2. 다음 달 초에 무엇이 일어날 것으로 예상되는가?
(A) 인사과에 있는 누군가가 승진할 것이다.
(B) 회사 대표가 은퇴할 것이다.
(C) 구인 공고가 게시될 것이다.
(D) 사무실에 새로운 행정 관리자가 올 것이다.

해설 공지 두 번째 단락에서 Anna Jones는 부하 직원인 Russell Green이 재무부의 행정 관리직 구인공고를 게시할 것이고, 이 자리가 다음 달 초까지 채워질 것이라고 예상을 하고 있으므로 정답은 (D) An office will have a new administrative manager.이다.

[3-5] 다음 공지에 관한 문제입니다.

Blenhaim 버스 회사
2월 1일

모든 승객분들께:
운영비 증가로 인해, Blenhaim 버스 회사는 5월 1일부터 승객 요금을 인상할 예정입니다. **4** 성인, 노인, 대학생들의 승차 요금이 10퍼센트 오를 것입니다. 8세 이하의 어린이들에게는 요금이 계속해서 무료일 예정입니다.

이것이 승객 여러분께 초래할 불편에 대해 사과를 드립니다. **3** 우리는 이것이 5년 만에 처음 있는 요금 인상이라는 사실도 상기시켜 드리고자 합니다. **5** 이 요금의 수익은 전반적인 차량 유지 및 직원 급여에 사용됩니다.

우리는 여러분들이 기대하셨던 높은 수준의 서비스를 계속해서 제공해 드릴 것을 약속합니다.

Blenhaim 버스 회사를 이용해 주셔서 감사합니다.

어휘 operating cost 운영비 | passenger 승객 | fare 요금 | adult 성인 | senior 연장자, 노인 | apologize 사과하다 | inconvenience 불편 | draw attention 주의를 끌다, 환기하다, 상기시키다 | revenue 수익, 수입 | maintenance 유지 | salary 급여, 봉급

3. Blenhaim 버스 회사에 관하여 언급되는 것은 무엇인가?
(A) 새로운 노선을 도입한다.
(B) 고객들의 불평에 응답했다.
(C) 5년 전에 요금을 올렸다.
(D) 승객 수 감소를 경험하고 있다.

해설 공지 두 번째 단락에서 5년 동안 한번도 요금을 올리지 않았음을 확인할 수 있으므로 정답은 (C) It raised its fares five years ago.이다.

4. 대학생들에 관하여 알 수 있는 것은 무엇인가?
(A) 요금이 노인 요금과 같은 비율로 인상될 것이다.
(B) 할인된 월간 버스 승차권을 구입할 수 있다.
(C) 학생증이 5월 1일까지 갱신되어야 한다.
(D) Blenhaim 버스를 무료로 탄다.

해설 공지 첫 번째 단락에서 성인, 노인, 대학생들의 요금은 전부 10퍼센트가 인상되는 것을 통해 버스요금 인상폭은 모두 같은 비율임을 유추할 수 있으므로 정답은 (A) Their fares will increase by the same percentage as the fare for seniors.이다.

5. 공지에 따르면, 요금에서 모인 수익이 사용되는 방법 중 하나는 무엇인가?
(A) 광고 증편을 위해
(B) 버스 노선 확장을 위해
(C) 정류장 개선을 위해
(D) 직원들 임금 지급을 위해

해설 지문 두 번째 단락 마지막 줄에서 수익이 차량 유지보수와 직원들의 급여로 사용된다고 했으므로 (D) To pay employees가 정답이다.

[6-9] 다음 공지에 관한 문제입니다.

Buena Vista 커뮤니티 도서관이 Maria Moreno를 환영합니다

Maria Moreno는 유명한 작가이자 현재는 Arena 커뮤니케이션의 회장입니다. 2월 9일에 Ms. Moreno는 Buena Vista 지역 도서관에서 **6** 경영 관리에 대한 그녀의 접근법에 관하여 강연을 할 것입니다. 그녀는 그 후에 South 실에서 **7** 그녀의 책들에 서명을 해줄 것입니다. 입장은 무료이지만, 제한된 좌석 때문에 1월 18일까지 등록하셔야 합니다. **8** 문의나 등록을 하시려면, 도서관 행사 담당자인 Ana Gonzalez(agonzalez@buenavistalibrary.org.ar)에게 이메일을 보내주세요.

Ms. Moreno는 Rodriguez and Company의 사무 보조원으로 일을 시작했고, 빠르게 승진했습니다. Rodriguez에서 10년을 일한 후, Ms. Moreno는 그녀의 회사를 차리기 위해 떠났고, 큰 성공을 이뤘습니다. 미디어 통신과 전략에 대한 그녀의 통찰력은 종종 출간물과 온라인 자료에서 자주 언급되며, **7** **9** 그녀의 최신 책인 〈Communicate and Collaborate〉은 10월 17일부터 서점에서 만나보실 수 있습니다.

어휘 author 작가 | approach 접근(법) | management 운영 | afterward 후에, 나중에 | volume (시리즈로 된 책의) 권 | admission 입장 | register 등록하다 | due to ~때문에 | limited 제한된 | coordinator 코디네이터, 진행자 | office assistant 사무 보조원 | work one's way up 승진하다 |

start up 시작되다. 시동을 걸다 | insight 영감 | media strategy 미디어 전략 | cite 언급하다

6. 어떤 행사가 홍보되고 있는가?
(A) 시상식
(B) 사업에 관한 이야기
(C) 도서관 개관
(D) 채용 박람회

해설 공지 첫 번째 단락 두 번째 줄에서 경영 관리에 대한 접근법에 관해 강연을 한다고 하였으므로 (B) A business talk이 정답이다.

7. Ms. Moreno에 관하여 알 수 있는 것은 무엇인가?
(A) 도서관에 기금을 기부했다.
(B) 한 권 이상의 책을 집필했다.
(C) 유명한 웹사이트를 운영한다.
(D) 새로운 사업을 시작할 계획이다.

해설 책들에 서명을 해줄 거라는 지문에서 그녀의 책이 적어도 한 권 이상임을 확인할 수 있다. 따라서 정답은 (B) She has written more than one book.이다.

8. 참석자들은 행사에 앞서 무엇을 하도록 요구되는가?
(A) South 실을 방문하도록
(B) Ms. Gonzalez에게 연락하도록
(C) 티켓을 구매하도록
(D) Ms. Moreno에게 이메일을 보내도록

해설 연락을 해야 하는 사람이 누군지 정확히 파악해야 한다. 문의나 등록에 관해 도서관 행사 담당자인 Ana Gonzalez에게 연락하라고 했으므로 (B) Contact Ms. Gonzalez가 정답이다. (D)는 이메일을 받는 주체가 다르므로 주의해야 한다.

9. 10월 17일에 무슨 일이 있을 것인가?
(A) 책을 구매할 수 있을 것이다.
(B) Ms. Moreno가 서점에서 서명을 할 것이다.
(C) 새로운 회장이 회사를 인수할 것이다.
(D) Ms. Moreno가 새로운 장소를 찾을 것이다.

해설 10월 17일에 관하여 언급이 된 문장을 찾는다. 지문의 마지막 줄에서 10월 17일에 Maria Moreno의 새 책이 서점에서 판매된다는 것을 확인할 수 있으므로 정답은 (A) A book will be available for purchase.이다.

[10-12] 다음 공지에 관한 문제입니다.

May Pannara 참신성 대회
매일의 삶을 향상시킬 좋은 아이디어가 있습니까? **10** 그러시다면, 그걸 May Pannara 참신성 대회에 내보세요.

10 May Pannara 참신성 대회란?
11 이 대회는 태국의 발명가 May Pannara에 의해 시작되었으며, 그녀는 또한 방콕 연구개발센터(BCRD)를 설립하였습니다. 대회의

목표는 일상의 문제들에 대한 해결책을 찾아내는 것입니다. 우승자는 자신들의 해결책을 실행하기 위한 1만 바트를 받게 됩니다. 작년의 우승자는 대부분의 전자오락기들에 호환 가능한 보편적인 원격제어기를 고안하였습니다. 우승자는 10월 30일 Trang 대학교의 Bhumibol 강당에서 시상식 중에 발표될 예정입니다.

⑩ 저도 참가 자격이 있나요?

이 대회는 모든 연령과 직업, 관심사를 가진 분들에게 열려 있습니다. 전문가, 아마추어, 그리고 학생들도 참가가 장려됩니다. 이전 대회에 제출된 출품작들은 허용되지 않습니다.

⑩ 어떻게 신청하나요?

출품작들은 우편이나 이메일로 6월 20일까지 접수되어야 합니다. 신청서와 다른 서류들을 다운로드받으시려면, 저희 웹사이트 www.bcrd.co.th/mpnc/entries를 방문해 주십시오. 대회 규칙에 대한 질문을 하시려면 Pat Wattana에게 (02) 555-4354로 연락 주십시오. ⑫ 심사단의 일원이 되시는 데 관심이 있는 분들께서는 저희의 심사 감독관인 Robin Montri에게 (02) 555-4359로 연락 주십시오.

어휘 novelty 새로움, 참신함 | found 설립하다 | solution 해결책 | baht 바트(태국의 화폐 단위) | implement 시행하다 | design 고안하다, 설계하다 | remote controller 원격제어기 | compatible 호환되는 | device 장치 | announce 발표하다 | ceremony 의식 | profession 직업 | submit 제출하다 | permit 허용하다 | inquiry 문의 사항 | rule 규칙 | judge 판단하다 | evaluation 평가

---

10. 공지의 목적은 무엇인가?
(A) 대학 과정 지침서에 대한 개요를 설명하기 위해
(B) 행사 스폰서를 유치하기 위해
(C) 대회 개최를 알리기 위해
(D) 사업 회의를 홍보하기 위해

해설 공지 첫 머리에서 대회 참여를 장려하고, 각 단락의 제목을 통해 대회 내용을 소개하고 참가 방법을 안내함을 확인할 수 있으므로 정답은 (C) To announce a competition이다.

---

11. BCRD에 관하여 언급된 것은 무엇인가?
(A) May Pannara에 의해 시작되었다.
(B) Trang 대학 캠퍼스에 사무실이 있다.
(C) 전자기기를 생산한다.
(D) Bhumibol 강당을 소유하고 있다.

해설 두 번째 단락 첫째 줄에서 BCRD는 태국의 발명가 May Pannara에 의하여 시작된 것을 확인할 수 있다. 따라서 정답은 (A) It was started by May Pannara.이다.

---

12. 공지에 따르면, 개인은 왜 Mr. Montri에게 연락하는가?
고난도 (A) 학생들의 자격을 확인하려고
(B) 프로젝트의 마감을 연장하려고
(C) 새로운 정책 시행에 대해 문의하려고
(D) 대회 우승자 결정에 도움을 주는 데 지원하려고

해설 제일 마지막 줄에서 심사단이 되는 것에 관심 있으면 Robin Montri에게 연락하라고 했다. 따라서 심사자가 되어서 우승자를 선출한다는 (D) To volunteer to help determine a contest winner가 정답이다.

UNIT 11. 기사

핵심 문제 유형   본서 p.304

1. (D)   2. (C)   3. (C)   4. (A)

[1-4] 다음 기사에 관한 문제입니다.

Saville 콘서트홀
하이라이트
3월 30일이 있는 주
음악 평론가 Krista Martinez 씀

〈Silent Masquerade〉
Oberon 오페라단, 676 Cather로

불과 1년 전에 설립되었음에도 불구하고, Oberon 오페라단은 Saville 고전 음악계에 대변혁을 일으키며 최근 역사상 가장 훌륭한 공연 작품 세 개를 공연했다. 지난 여름에 공연했던 오페라 〈Blooming Spring〉은 Mannlich 최우수 테너 상을 수상했고, ❶ 가을에 공연했던 〈Sweet Serenity〉는 지난해의 그 어느 공연 때보다도 더 많은 표를 팔았다. 이틀 전, Oberon은 Saville 주민인 Pedro Inez가 쓴, 지금껏 최고의 공연이 될 수도 있는 〈Silent Masquerade〉를 선보였다.

❷ 그의 이전 작품인 〈Moonlight Fiona〉와 〈An Endless Journey〉에서 입증된 Inez의 음악적 재능은 이 최근 걸작에서 다시 한 번 나타났다. 실제 줄거리 상 많은 사건이 발생하진 않지만, ❸ 남성과 여성 배우들이 공연 중 음악으로 소통하는 방식은 상당히 놀랍다. 이 작품은 올해의 Mannlich 시상식 후보로 지명될 것이 분명하다.

만약 올해 한 편의 연주회를 봐야 한다면, 이것으로 결정하라. 〈Silent Masquerade〉는 4월 한 달간 매일 밤 7시 30분에 공연이 있을 것이다. 모든 Oberon의 공연이 그런 것처럼, ❹ 티켓 판매의 일부는 스페인의 떠오르는 예술가들을 지원하는 Trent 기금에 기부될 것이다.

어휘 music critic 음악 평론가 | found 설립하다 | revolutionize 대변혁을 일으키다 | premiere 개봉, 초연 | to date 지금까지 | demonstrate 보여주다, 입증하다 | latest 최근의, 최신의 | masterpiece 걸작, 명작, 일품 | plot 줄거리 | interact 소통하다, 상호 작용하다 | amazing 놀라운 | nominate 지명하다 | portion 부분, 일부 | emerging 떠오르는, 최근 부상하는

Practice

본서 p.306

1. (A)	**2.** (A)	**3.** (A)	**4.** (C)	**5.** (C)
6. (B)	**7.** (A)	**8.** (C)	**9.** (B)	**10.** (C)
11. (C)	**12.** (B)	**13.** (D)	**14.** (C)	

[1-2] 다음 기사에 관한 문제입니다.

> **Karmel 과학 저널**
> **회의 정보**
>
> **1** 10월 25일과 26일, 국제 의료 연구 단체(IOMR)는 연 2회 열리는 회의를 케냐 나이로비에 최근 재단장한 Kenyatta 국제 회의 센터에서 개최할 예정이다.
> 올해의 회의는 Kingley 대학의 물리학 교수 Julia Fox와 IOMR 의장 Mohammed Kahn의 연설을 특별히 포함할 것이다. 또한, 여덟 번의 총회 미팅에는 의학 분야의 선두주자들이 참석할 것이다.
> 회의를 위한 온라인 등록은 현재 www.iomr.org/kenyatta에서 가능하다. **2** 인근 호텔 목록도 IOMR 웹사이트에서 찾아볼 수 있다.
>
> 어휘 host 열다, 개최하다 I bi-annual 연 2회의 I renovate 개조하다, 보수하다 I feature 특별히 포함하다, 특징으로 삼다 I furthermore 더욱이, 게다가 I plenary 총회의, 전원 출석의 I chair 의장을 맡다 I frontrunner 선두주자, 선구자 I medical science 의학 I registration 등록

1. 회의에 관하여 언급된 것은 무엇인가?
(A) 이틀간 개최될 것이다.
(B) Julia Fox에 의해 준비되고 있다.
(C) IOMR 회원들에게는 무료이다.
(D) 참가자들에게 숙소를 제공할 것이다.

해설 지문 첫 번째 단락에서 회의가 10월 25~26일 이틀간 개최되는 것을 확인할 수 있으므로 정답은 (A) It will be held for two days.이다.

2. 그 단체는 온라인으로 어떤 정보를 제공하는가?
(A) 숙박시설 이름
(B) 관광 명소 설명
(C) 회의장 오는 길 약도
(D) 회의장 근처의 식당들 목록

해설 online을 키워드로 삼아 해당 내용을 파악해야 한다. 지문 마지막에서 인근 호텔 목록을 IOMR 웹사이트에서 확인 가능하다는 것을 알 수 있으므로 정답은 (A) Names of places to stay이다.

[3-6] 다음 기사에 관한 문제입니다.

> Euston, 런던 (7월 28일) – 오늘 아침 **3 4** Milway 제약은 9월 3일 현재의 Oxford 가 부지에서 1,500 평방미터 넓이의 Prader 빌딩으로 본사를 이전할 것이라고 발표했다.
>
> "이는 Euston에 좋은 소식입니다." 신규 회사들에게 저금리 창업 대출을 제공하는 조직인 Bentley 대출의 이사인 Will Matthews는 말했다. "Milway 제약은 지역 사회의 귀중한 후원자가 될 **4** 직원

> 120명이 있어 다양한 방법으로 지역 사회를 지원하게 될 것입니다." Mr. Matthews는 대출 회사가 Milway 제약의 이전 비용을 대는 데 도움을 주었다고 밝혔다.
>
> 약을 개발하고 판매하는 회사인 Milway 제약은 최근 새로운 고객들을 여럿 확보해 추가 약사들을 고용할 계획이 있다고 Milway 제약의 사장인 Ella Milway가 설명했다. "우리는 추가적인 공간이 필요했고, Prader 빌딩이 제시한 뛰어난 임대 **5** 조건에 끌렸습니다." 라고 그녀가 말했다. "Bentley 대출로부터의 재정적 지원 또한 매우 매혹적인 요소였습니다."
>
> **4** Euston 동쪽에 위치한 Prader 빌딩은 Comcord 부동산에 의해 개발되었다. Smith 법률 협회, **6** CRI 회계, Lullington 탁구 클럽, 그리고 Pulford's 운동용품점이 빌딩의 세입자들이다. 이제 Milway 제약이 이전할 것이니 이 빌딩은 자리가 모두 찬 셈이다.
>
> 어휘 pharmaceutical 약학의, 제약I move 옮기다, 이전하다 I headquarters 본부 I announce 공지하다 I organization 기관 I low-interest 저금리의 I start-up loans 소규모 창업 대출 I valuable 귀중한, 소중한 I patron 고객; 후원자 I note ~에 주목하다 I assist 돕다 I cover the cost 요금을 충당하다 I market 상품을 광고하다 I intend to ~할 작정이다 I pharmacist 약사 I senior partner (조합 등의) 장, 사장 I terms (계약) 조건 I motivation 자극, 동기 부여 I tenant 세입자

3. 기사는 왜 쓰였는가?
(A) 회사가 새로운 장소로 이전하는 것을 알리기 위해
(B) 회사의 급여 인상을 공지하기 위해
(C) 업체들의 서비스 업데이트에 대한 정보를 주기 위해
(D) 한 건물에 대한 개조 공사를 설명하기 위해

해설 기사 첫머리에서 Milway 제약이 Prader Building으로 이전한다고 밝히며 회사 이전의 기대 효과, 배경, 빌딩 소개 등을 설명하고 있으므로 기사의 주요 화제는 Milway 제약의 이전임을 알 수 있다. 따라서 정답은 (A) To announce a company's move to a new location 이다.

4. Milway 제약에 관하여 암시되지 않은 것은 무엇인가?
(A) 직원 수
(B) 사무실의 크기
(C) 희망 급여 범위
(D) 회사의 새 위치

해설 (A)는 두 번째 단락에 직원 120명이 있다고 언급하고 있고 (B)는 첫 번째 단락에서 1,500 평방미터 넓이의 Prader 빌딩으로 이전한다고 되어있으며 Prader 빌딩이 Euston 동쪽에 위치해 있다는 정보를 토대로 (D) 역시 알 수 있는 사실이다. 급여의 범위에 대해 언급된 것은 없으므로 (C) The expected salary range가 정답이다.

5. 세 번째 단락, 네 번째 줄의 'terms'와 의미상 가장 가까운 것은
(A) 확장
(B) 방향
(C) 조건
(D) 표현

해설 Prader 빌딩이 제시한 '임차 조건에 끌렸다'라는 의미로 terms가 '조건'의 의미로 쓰였으므로, 이와 바꿔 쓸 수 있는 (C) conditions가 의미상 가장 적절하다.

---

6. Prader 빌딩에서 공간을 차지하고 있지 않은 업종은 무엇인가?
고난도

(A) 재무 서비스 회사

(B) 부동산 관리 업체

(C) 소매점

(D) 스포츠 클럽

해설 (A), (C), (D) 모두 마지막 단락의 'CRI Accountants, Lullington Table Tennis Club, Pulford's Sporting Goods'로 확인할 수 있으므로 (B) A property management firm이 정답이다. property는 재산의 가장 기본이 되는 단위인 주택, 상가, 호텔 등의 부동산 건물을 의미한다.

[7-10] 다음 기사에 관한 문제입니다.

Daily Market Herald

수요일에. **7** Spangler Market은 5개의 Bargain Buys 식료품점들을 인수할 계획이라고 밝혔다. 이 상점 중 세 곳은 Cardiff에 있고, 다른 상점 두 곳은 Portas에 있다. 그들의 판매 가격은 밝혀지지 않을 것이다.

현재로는, 인수된 상점들은 여전히 Bargain Buys의 이름으로 운영되는 중이다. **8** 언제 새로운 이름으로 변경될지는 아직 알려진 바가 없다.

언론 보도에서, Spangler의 최고경영자인 Jacob Bitzer는 이렇게 말했다. "이 지점들을 저희 사업에 포함시키게 되어 매우 흥분됩니다. 저는 Cardiff와 Portas 지역 사회의 주요 식료품점이 되기를 열렬히 기대하고 있습니다. 저희는 지역 사회에 엄선된 최고 품질의 음식을 제공하고자 합니다." Mr. Jacob Bitzer는 **9** 직원 변동 계획은 없다는 것을 확실히 하였다.

10 Spangler Market은 95년 전 Mr. Bitzer의 고조부에 의해 맨체스터에 설립되었다. 8년 전 그의 부친이 은퇴를 하면서 Mr. Bitzer가 대표이사가 되었다. Spangler Market 지점들은 이제 영국 전역에 있다.

어휘 acquire 인수하다 I sales price 판매 가격 I run 운영하다, 경영하다 I transition 이행, 과도 I press release 언론 보도 I eagerly 열심히, 간절히 I anticipate 예상하다 I intend to ~할 작정이다, ~하려고 생각하다 I selection 선별, 선택 I quality 품질 I confirm 확인하다 I personnel 직원들 I great-grandfather 고조부 I retire 은퇴하다 I all across 전역에

---

7. 기사의 목적은 무엇인가?

(A) 일부 상점들의 매입을 보고하기 위해

(B) 회사 이전을 설명하기 위해

(C) 몇 가지 새로운 상품을 홍보하기 위해

(D) 새로운 개점을 알리기 위해

해설 기사 첫머리에서 Spangler Market이 다섯 개의 식료품점들을 사들일 거라며, 향후 Spangler Market의 계획이 언급되어 있어, 상점 매입이 이슈임을 알 수 있으므로 정답은 (A) To report on the purchase of some stores이다.

---

8. 기사에 따르면, 아직 결정되지 않은 것은 무엇인가?

(A) 누가 인수팀을 이끌 것인지

(B) 거래에 얼마의 비용이 들 것인지

(C) 언제 상호명이 변경될 것인지

(D) 어디에 회사의 본사가 위치할 것인지

해설 아직 결정되지 않은 사항에 대한 언급을 찾는다. 지문 두 번째 단락에서 이름이 언제 바뀔지는 결정되지 않은 것을 알 수 있으므로 (C) When a name change will occur이 정답이다.

---

9. Mr. Bitzer가 Cardiff와 Portas 상점들의 직원 채용에 관하여 암시하고난도 는 것은 무엇인가?

(A) 성과급 보너스를 도입할 계획이다.

(B) 현 직원들을 유지하려고 한다.

(C) 지역사회로부터 직원들을 채용하고 싶어한다.

(D) 새로운 판매 전략을 시행하고 싶어한다.

해설 세 번째 단락에서 인사 변동 계획은 없다고 했으므로 정답은 (B) He intends to retain the current staff.이다.

---

10. Spangler Market에 관하여 언급되는 것은 무엇인가?

(A) 맨체스터에 곧 지점들을 개점할 것이다.

(B) 많은 할인을 제공한다.

(C) 가족 경영 사업이다.

(D) 최근 사업을 시작했다.

해설 지문 마지막 단락에서 현재 Spangler Market의 대표이사인 Jacob Bitzer의 고조부에 의해 회사가 설립되었고, Jacob Bitzer는 대를 이어 회사의 대표이사가 됐음을 확인할 수 있다. 즉, 대를 이어 내려오는 가족 경영 회사임을 알 수 있으므로 (C) It is a family-run business. 가 정답이다.

[11-14] 다음 기사에 관한 문제입니다.

---

11 부동산 시장의 최근 동향을 우려하는 시민들로부터 많은 편지를 받은 뒤 Dartmouth 시 의회는 상황을 평가해보는 조사를 실시했다. 그들은 오늘 조사 결과를 발표했고, 조치를 취해야 할 건지 그리고 취한다면 어떤 조치를 취해야 할 건지를 결정하기 위해 내일 모일 것이다.

대충 살펴보더라도 전반적으로 주거용 아파트 임대료가 눈에 띄게 오른 게 분명해졌다. 시 전체의 임대율이 작년의 0.71%보다 약간 적은 0.6% 정도 오른 데 반해, 임대료는 월 823달러로 평균 4.6%나 오른 것이다. 이것들은 평균치이며 **12** 일부 지역들에서는 그 상승세가 훨씬 더 크다는 점에 주목해야 할 것이다. 한때 중요한 상업 지역이었던 Riverside 지역에서는 아파트 건설이 폭발적으로 늘고 있다. **13** 오래된 공장과 창고들이 헐렸으며, **12** 개발자들은 그걸 고급 아파트들을 건설할 기회로 삼고 있다. **13** 두 주요 단지인 Dartmouth Rapids와 Streamside Apartments는 월 평균 1,457달러로 지역 평균보다 634달러 더 비싸다.

14 중대한 영향을 끼친 또 다른 개발 프로젝트는 Deerfallow 역까지의 지하철 3호선 연장이다. 이는 Bamoral Height 지역까지 지하철역의 추가 건설을 초래했으며, 그곳의 평균 임대료를 월 982달러까지 올렸다.

그러나 Elsey Ridge 같은 몇몇 지역들은 실제로 그 가치가 떨어졌음을 보여주었다. 시에서 가장 멀고 외진 지역인 Elsey Ridge는 평균 임대료가 약 월 635달러가 되어 1.5%의 평균 하락세를 보였다.

어휘 upset 속상한 | carry out ~을 수행하다 | assess 평가하다 | findings 조사 결과들 | measures 방법, 조치 | cursory 대략적인 | apparent 분명한 | residential 주거하기 좋은 | across the board 전반적으로 | occupancy (건물, 방의) 사용 | significant 중요한, 의미 있는 | explosion 폭발적인 증가 | warehouse 창고 | tear down 허물다 | take advantage of ~을 이용하다, ~을 기회로 활용하다 | complex 건물 단지 | average 평균 ~이 되다 | impact 영향 | extension 연장 | decrease 감소, 하락 | farthest 가장 먼 | outlying 외진

11. 이 기사의 주요 목적은 무엇인가?
(A) 과거의 임대율을 분석하기 위해
(B) 대중교통 프로젝트를 발표하기 위해
(C) 시의 부동산 동향을 요약하기 위해
(D) 다른 지역들의 인구 증가를 설명하기 위해

해설 첫 번째 문장에서 최근 부동산 동향에 대해 시 의회가 상황을 평가하는 조사를 실시했다고 했고 그 조사 내용을 종합해서 기술하고 있으므로 정답은 (C) To summarize real estate trends in the city이다. 두 번째 단락에서 과거의 임대율과 현재의 임대율 인상폭을 비교하고 있지만 이는 현 부동산 동향을 설명하기 위한 수치일 뿐 글의 목적이라고 볼 수 없다.

12.
고난도 이 기사에 따르면, 왜 개발업자들이 Riverside 지역에 관심을 갖고 있는가?
(A) 인기 있는 관광지이다.
(B) 그곳에서 더 높은 임대료를 부과할 수 있다.
(C) 그 지역에는 많은 중요한 공장들이 있다.
(D) 쇼핑 센터 근처에 편리하게 위치해 있다.

해설 개발업자들이 Riverside 지역에 관심을 갖는 이유가 직접 언급되어 있지 않으므로 관련 내용을 종합해 정답을 찾는다. 두 번째 단락에서 시의 몇몇 지역 임대료가 크게 오르고 있다고 했고 중요 상업 지역이었던 Riverside 지역에 고급 아파트를 짓게 되면서 개발자들은 높은 임대료를 받을 수 있을 것이라고 추론해 볼 수 있다. 따라서 정답은 (B) Higher rents can be charged there.이다.

13.
고난도 Dartmouth Rapids와 Streamside Apartments에 대해 나타난 것은 무엇인가?
(A) 이미 많은 잠재적 세입자들을 끌어들였다.
(B) Dartmouth에 건설될 첫 번째 아파트이다.
(C) 시의 중심에서 멀리 떨어진 곳에 있다.
(D) 오래된 제조 공장 자리에 세워졌다.

해설 두 번째 단락에서 Riverside 지역에 공장이 헐리고 그 자리에 고급 아파트가 들어섰는데 Dartmouth Rapids와 Streamside Apartments는 그 고급 아파트들의 두 주요 단지라고 언급하고 있으므로 Dartmouth Rapids와 Streamside Apartments가 건설

된 부지는 이전의 공장 자리였음을 추론할 수 있다. 따라서 정답은 (D) They were built in place of old manufacturing plants.이다.

14. [1], [2], [3], [4]로 표시된 곳 중에서 다음 문장이 들어가기에 가장 적절한 곳은 어디인가?

"중대한 영향을 끼친 또 다른 개발 프로젝트는 Deerfallow 역까지의 지하철 3호선 연장이다."

(A) [1]
(B) [2]
(C) [3]
(D) [4]

해설 주어진 문장은 임대료 상승에 영향을 끼친 요인으로 지하철 연장을 언급하고 있으므로, 이것이 Bamoral Height 지역까지 지하철역을 추가하게 됐다는 문장 앞에 와야 한다. 정답은 (C) [3]이다.

UNIT 12. 양식

핵심 문제 유형
본서 p.311

1. (D) 2. (B)

[1-2] 다음 송장에 관한 문제입니다.

CBI 전자 창고
2250 Beacon 고속도로,
맨체스터, 뉴햄프셔 03101
604-987-0097
배송장

주문일: 3월 3일
2 배송일: 3월 4일
배송 수령 예상일: 3월 6일
송장 번호: 45003
구매인: **1** Ray Escobar
배송 주소: Rafagalbra 540, 내슈아, 뉴햄프셔 03060

Electra Chrome 컴퓨터 책상/워크스테이션	149.95달러
Comfortmax 회전의자	99.95달러
PCI 21인치 모니터	249.99달러
PCI 컴퓨터 (모델 번호: a150)	999.99달러

소계	1,499.88달러
1 단골 고객 할인	-150.00달러
배송비	0

세금	80.99달러

총계   1,430.87달러

----

*1,000달러 이상 주문하시면 배송비가 부과되지 않습니다.
2 배송일 이후에 청구됩니다.
주문 배송일로부터 30일 이내에는 교체가 가능합니다.

CBI Warehouse에서 쇼핑해주셔서 감사합니다.

어휘   **estimated** 추정된 | **swivel chair** 회전의자 | **subtotal** 소계 | **frequent** 잦은, 빈번한 | **charge** 청구하다 | **replacement** 교체(품) | **carry out** 수행하다

Practice
본서 p.312

1. (D)	2. (D)	3. (D)	4. (C)	5. (C)
6. (A)	7. (C)	8. (A)	9. (D)	10. (A)

[1-2] 다음 웹페이지에 관한 문제입니다.

http://www.swcoffeeco.com

Southwest Coffee Emporium
주문해 주셔서 감사합니다. 아래의 주문 상세내역을 검토해 주십시오.

주문일:10월 12일	품목 정보 ■ 선택: 카푸치노 기기 ■ 총액: 175달러
개인 메시지 Milos 귀하, 지난 10년 동안 이곳 Prescott 공업에서 귀하와 함께 일했던 것은 큰 즐거움이었습니다. 귀하의 조언과 우정은 제 일을 보다 능률적으로 하면서 이 분야를 더욱 철저히 이해하는 데 도움을 주었습니다. **1** 내일 귀하께서 컨설팅 팀을 떠나시게 되어 슬프지만, 새로운 회사에서 행운이 있으시길 바라고, 이 선물이 맘에 드셨으면 좋겠습니다. Dat Nguyen	
수취인 세부정보 **2** ■ 이름: Mr. Milos Novak ■ 주소: Progressive 공업 Cartier Square, #11-25 몬트리올, 퀘벡 G1J	배송 방식 ■ 1일 배송: 영업일 1일 이내 – **2** 10월 13일 배송 X ■ 일반 배송: 영업일 3일 이내 – 10월 15일 배송 _____

결제 진행	주문 수정	주문 취소

어휘   **emporium** 상점 | **distinct** 뚜렷한 | **consulting** 자문의 | **recipient** 수령인

---

1. Mr. Nguyen이 근무하는 회사에 대해 언급된 것은 무엇인가?
(A) 최소 12년 동안 그를 고용했다.
(B) 바구니를 제조한다.
(C) 곧 새로운 장소로 이전할 것이다.
(D) 자체 컨설팅 팀이 있다.

해설   Mr. Milos Novak이 Prescott 공업의 컨설팅 팀을 떠날 것이라고 했으므로 (D) It has its own consulting team.이 정답이다.

---

2. 10월 13일에 무슨 일이 있을 것인가?
고난도   (A) Mr. Nguyen이 선물에 대해 결제를 할 것이다.
(B) Mr. Novak이 Southwest Coffee Emporium을 그만둘 것이다.
(C) Mr. Nguyen이 주문을 취소할 것이다.
(D) Mr. Novak이 소포를 받을 것이다.

해설   Recipient Name: Mr. Milos Novak과 Delivery on Oct 13의 두 가지 정보를 통해 (D) Mr. Novak will receive a package.가 정답임을 알 수 있다.

[3-4] 다음 송장에 관한 문제입니다.

Sternberg 제조사
273 Georgetown 가, 워싱턴, D.C. 20007
(202) 555-9213
www.sternberg-mfg.com

주문번호: 582714
날짜: 4월 18일
고객명: Jennie Hills
1321 Pennsylvania 로
워싱턴, D.C. 20460
(202) 555-2192

3 품목	번호	수량	가격
중역용 의자, 갈색 가죽	53912	1	101.99달러
컴퓨터 코너형 책상, 오크목	31614	1	87.99달러
선반 4개짜리 문서 보관함, 철제	49321	1	72.99달러
소계			262.97달러
세금			23.30달러
배송료			35.00달러
4 예치금			150.00달러
총 지불액			171.27달러

Sternberg 제조사는 상품이 배송된 후 최대 30일까지 환불 또는 교환을 해 드립니다.

어휘   **order number** 주문번호 | **customer** 고객 | **quantity** 수량 | **leather** 가죽 | **oak** 오크나무 | **file cabinet** 문서 보관함 | **refund** 환불하다 | **exchange** 교환하다 | **up to** (특정한 수, 정도 등) ~까지 | **following** (시간상으로) 그 다음의, 다음에 나오는 | **delivery** 배달, 배송(품)

3. Sternberg 제조사는 무엇을 판매하는가?
(A) 명함
(B) 컴퓨터 하드웨어
(C) 가죽 가방
(D) 사무용 가구

해설 품목의 Executive office chair, Computer corner desk, file cabinet을 통하여 Sternberg 제조사는 사무용 가구를 파는 회사임을 확인할 수 있으므로 정답은 (D) Office furniture이다.

----

4. Ms. Hills에 관하여 언급된 것은 무엇인가?
(A) 그녀의 주문에 배송료가 포함되지 않았다.
(B) 그녀의 제품이 4월 18일까지 배송될 것이다.
(C) 주문 금액의 일부를 결제했었다.
(D) 그녀의 주문품 중 하나를 반품했다.

해설 총금액 262.97달러 중에서 예치금으로 150달러가 지불되었음을 확인할 수 있다. 따라서 주문 금액의 일부를 지불했다는 (C) She had made a partial payment.가 정답이다.

[5-6] 다음 양식에 관한 문제입니다.

구독 양식

이름 **5** *Steve Parker*
배송 주소 *325 Niles 로 cork 3*
이메일 주소 *sparker@ifax.com*
이 양식을 840 Harlington 가 Cork 2에 있는 〈Organic Botanics〉에 우편으로 보내 주십시오. 청구서는 나중에 발송됩니다

귀하의 구독

구독 유형	가격	신규/갱신
✗ 1년 (10호)	30유로	**5** 신규
__ 2년 (20호)	48유로	

구독 선물
귀하의 구독 외에, 원래 가격에서 50퍼센트 할인된 구독권 선물을 다른 분께 보내세요!

수령인 이름 **6** *Brenda Jules*
배송 주소 *92 Suttlecreek 로 cork 3*
첨부 메시지 **6** *나의 멋진 사촌, 생일 축하해!*

구독 유형	가격
✗ 1년 (10호)	15유로
__ 2년 (20호)	24유로

어휘 subscription 구독 I renew 갱신하다 I on top of ~뿐만 아니라, ~ 외에 I original 원래의 I attached 첨부된

5. Mr. Parker에 관하여 언급된 것은 무엇인가?
(A) 〈Organic Botanics〉를 2년간 받아 보고 싶어 한다.
(B) 선물로 구독권을 받을 것이다.
(C) 〈Organic Botanics〉를 처음 구독하고 있다.
(D) 신용카드로 결제한다.

해설 Mr. Parker가 Subscription Form을 작성했으므로 구독자임을 확인할 수 있고, 구독 옵션에서 1년 신규 구독을 신청했음을 확인할 수 있다. 따라서 Mr. Parker가 〈Organic Botanics〉를 처음 구독한다는 (C) He is subscribing to *Organic Botanics* for the first time.이 정답이다.

----

6. Ms. Jules는 누구인가?
(A) Mr. Parker의 친척
(B) 고객 서비스 담당자
(C) 잡지 기고가
(D) Mr. Parker의 동료

해설 Subscription Gift 항목을 보면, Ms. Jules는 Mr. Parker가 구독권을 선물로 보내는 대상임을 확인할 수 있고, 서로 사촌지간임을 알 수 있다. 따라서 정답은 (A) A relative of Mr. Parker이다.

[7-10] 다음 양식에 관한 문제입니다.

GIOVANNI 피혁

Giovanni 피혁은 생산하는 전 제품에 대한 품질을 보증합니다. 다음과 같이, 저희는 일 년까지의 사용에 있어 어떤 제품 결함에 대해서도 무조건적인 보증을 제공합니다. **7** 만약 이 기간 내에 어떠한 결함을 찾으시게 된다면 전액 환불받거나 결함이 있는 제품과 동일한 가격 또는 더 저렴한 상품으로 교환하실 수 있습니다.
제품을 등록함으로써 고객님의 보증을 활성화하실 수 있습니다. 이 선불 우편 카드를 기입하시고 저희에게 다시 보내주세요.

- -

이름: *Kevin Troust*
이메일: *ktroust@zotmail.com*
주소: *100 Windsor 로, 제임스타운, 버지니아 10923*
제품 번호: *BF302ZXU992*
8 제품 설명: *번호 자물쇠가 있는 갈색 서류가방*
소유하고 있는 다른 Giovanni 피혁 제품 수는?: *1*
이 제품은 선물이었습니까? *아니오*
소유하고 있는 다른 가죽 제품들은 무엇입니까? *Good Old Texan, Westwing, Falco*
Giovanni 피혁에 대한 코멘트를 적어 주세요:
9 *귀사의 웹사이트는 둘러보기 편했으므로, 그래서 제가 찾고 있던 제품들을 쉽게 찾았습니다. 제 구매에 매우 만족하며, (바지나 벨트와 같은)* **10** *남성용 제품들의 폭이 더 넓었으면 좋겠다는 게 저의 유일한 제안입니다. Giovanni는 지갑, 핸드백 같은 여성용 액세서리를 주로 취급하는 것 같습니다.*

어휘 fully 완전히, 충분히 I guarantee 보증하다 I quality 질 I manufacture 제조하다, 생산하다 I provide 제공하다 I unconditional 무조건적인 I defect 결점 I up to ~까지 I encounter 맞닥뜨리다, 접하다 I refund 환불 I exchange 교환 I defective 결함이 있는 I activate 작동시키다, 활성화시키다 I register 등록하다 I fill out 기입하다 I pre-paid 선불된 I combination lock 번호 자물쇠 I regarding ~에 관해 I convenient 편리한, 간편한 I navigate (인터넷·웹사이트를) 돌아다니다 I easily 쉽게, 수월하게 I find 찾다 I look for ~을 찾다 I satisfy 만족하다 I suggestion 제안 I selection 선택 I seem ~인 것 같다 I carry 취급하다

7. Mr. Troust는 왜 양식을 기입했는가?

고난도
(A) 결함이 있는 제품에 대해 항의하기 위해

(B) 회원들에게 할인을 제공하는 프로그램을 신청하기 위해

(C) 미래에 제품을 반품할 수 있게 하기 위해

(D) 가게에 일련의 지침들을 요청하기 위해

해설 지문 첫 단락에서 제품 등록 시에 전액 환불이나, 제품과 동일한 가격 또는 더 저렴한 상품으로 교환할 수 있음을 알 수 있다. 따라서 정답은 (C) To allow himself to return a product in the future이다.

---

8. Mr. Troust는 무엇을 샀는가?

(A) 서류를 넣을 수 있는 가방

(B) 핸드백

(C) 부츠 한 켤레

(D) 지갑

해설 제품 등록 상세 정보에서 구매 제품이 서류 가방인 것을 알 수 있다. 따라서 정답은 (A) A bag for papers이다.

---

9. Mr. Troust에 관하여 언급된 것은 무엇인가?

(A) Giovanni 피혁 제품을 선물로 받았다.

(B) Giovanni 피혁 제품을 많이 소유하고 있다.

(C) Giovanni 피혁에서만 쇼핑한다.

(D) Giovanni 피혁 제품을 온라인으로 구매했다.

해설 Mr. Troust는 양식을 작성하는 고객임을 인지하여, 제품 등록 상세 정보 및 고객 코멘트 내용에 주목해야 한다. 코멘트 내용 중 웹페이지에서 찾던 것을 쉽게 찾았다고 기입했으므로, 웹페이지에서 제품을 주문했음을 알 수 있다. 따라서 정답은 (D) He purchased a Giovanni Leather product online.이다.

---

10. Mr. Troust의 의견에서, Giovanni 피혁은 어떻게 개선될 수 있는가?

(A) 더 많은 종류의 제품들을 제공함으로써

(B) 제품 보증 기간을 연장함으로써

(C) 제품 할인을 더 많이 해줌으로써

(D) 더 질이 높은 제품을 판매함으로써

해설 고객 코멘트 내용에서 Giovanni Leather에 대한 제안 또는 불만 사항에 주목해야 한다. 코멘트 내용 중에서 Mr. Troust는 남성용 제품의 폭을 늘리기를 희망하는 것을 확인할 수 있다. 따라서 정답은 (A) By offering more types of products이다.

UNIT 13. 이중 지문

핵심 문제 유형

1. (B) **2.** (A) **3.** (B) **4.** (C) **5.** (D)

[1-5] 다음 기사와 이메일에 관한 문제입니다.

버밍엄에 있는 회사가 교육용 영화의 선두주자가 되다

버밍엄, 9월 4일 – Joseph Ford는 50년 전에 Ford 프로덕션을 설립했고, **1** 그 회사는 곧 교육 영상물 분야에서 주도적인 기업으로 성장했다. 이 회사는 가족 경영을 하는 기업이고, Joseph Ford의 아들인 Martin이 현재 이 회사의 최고경영자이다. 회사는 설립 이래 많은 변화들을 겪어 왔지만, 문학, 과학, 역사와 수학 분야의 사람들을 교육하겠다는 회사의 핵심 목표는 여전히 굳건하게 남아 있다.

4 Joseph Ford가 버밍엄에서 자신의 회사를 시작했을 때, 그는 현지 고등학교를 위한 영상물을 제작하고 유통하는 것에 초점을 두었다. 지난 몇 년 간, 회사는 고객층을 넓혀 왔고, 지속적으로 시대에 맞춰오기 위해 기술을 발전시켜 왔다. 가장 큰 첫 업그레이드는 모든 영상물을 DVD로 출시하는 것이었다. 그리고 바로 지난 해에, **2** 회사는 DVD 제조를 모두 중단하기로 하고 그들의 영상물을 온라인으로 전환해 올렸다. Joseph Ford의 손녀인 Alicia Ford는 디지털 미디어와 다중 매체 기술 분야의 학위를 받고 졸업했다. 그녀는 이 같은 움직임의 주역이었으며, **1** 이는 Ford 프로덕션의 고객층과 제품 라인을 한층 더 성장시키는 결과를 가져왔다.

87세의 나이에도, Joseph Ford는 여전히 그의 사업에 적극적으로 참여하고 있다. 그는 사람들이 항상 혁신적인 학습 방법을 찾고 있는데, 이 사업이 그러한 필요를 충족시켜주어야 한다고 믿는다. "교육은 항상 진화하고, 교육용 제작물을 제공하는 데 헌신하는 회사로서 우리 또한 지속적으로 발전해야 합니다"라고 그는 말한다.

어휘 establish 설립하다 | leader 선두주자 | educational 교육의 | family-run 가족 경영의 | undergo (특히 변화·안 좋은 일 등을) 겪다 | establishment 설립 | core 핵심의 | literature 문학 | focus 초점을 맞추다, 집중하다 | distribute 유통하다 | expand 확장하다 | customer base 고객층 | constantly 지속적으로 | keep up with ~에 발맞추다 | major 주요한, 중대한 | involve (중요 요소로·필연적으로) 수반하다 | release 출시하다 | manufacturing 제조업 | stream 스트림 처리하다(데이터 전송을 연속적으로 이어서 하다) | graduate 졸업하다 | mastermind 지휘 / 조종하는 사람 | lead to ~로 이어지다 | product line 제품 라인 | innovative 혁신적인 | method 방법 | strive to ~하려 애쓰다 | meet the needs 필요에 응하다 | evolve 진화하다 | dedicate 헌신하다 | instructional 교육용의

수신: Martin Ford 〈mford@fordproductions.com〉
발신: Lee Akman 〈l_akman@ksmedia.com〉
주제: 컨퍼런스
날짜: 10월 23일

Martin에게,

지난주 텔퍼드에서 개최된 컨퍼런스에서 당신을 만날 수 있어서 매우 반가웠습니다. **3** 적응하는 데 꽤 오래 걸리긴 했지만, 현재 저는 더 큰 도시에서의 생활을 즐기고 있습니다. 당신이 혹시 이 지역에 다시 방문할 일이 있다면, 저는 당신에게 이곳을 구경시켜 드리고 싶네요. **4** 제가 당신 회사의 마케팅 보조였던 이후 거의 20년이나 지났다는 것이 믿기 어렵습니다. 그 때 이후로 정말 많은 일들이 있었어요! **5** 컨퍼런스에서 기조 연설을 하는 당신을 찍은 멋진 사진들을 제가 몇 장 가지고 있는데, 그것들을 당신에게 내일 이메일로 보내 드리도록 하겠습니다. 텔퍼드에 오실 일이 있으면, 같이 저녁식사라도 할 수 있게 제게 알려주세요.

Lee Akman

어휘　adjust 조정하다, 조절하다 I show someone around ~에게 둘러보도록 안내하다 I decade 10년 I marketing assistant 마케팅 보조 I keynote speech 기조 연설

Practice

본서 p.320

1. (B)	2. (C)	3. (C)	4. (A)	5. (C)
6. (B)	7. (C)	8. (D)	9. (B)	10. (A)
11. (A)	12. (C)	13. (A)	14. (D)	15. (D)

[1-5] 다음 이메일과 일정표에 관한 문제입니다.

수신: Song Myung 〈msong@himail.co.uk〉
발신: Peter Barlow 〈pbarlow@harzok.co.uk〉
날짜: 2월 20일
제목: 일반 공개
첨부: schedule.doc

안녕하세요 Mr. Myung,

저는 다음 달 채용 설명회에 관한 당신의 이메일을 받았습니다. **1** 우리 웹사이트를 통한 등록은 안타깝게도 2월 10일자로 마감되었습니다. 하지만 제가 지난주 **1** 등록한 참가자들에게 일정을 이메일로 보냈을 때, 그들 중 한 명이 참석할 수 없을 거라고 답변을 보내왔습니다. 이는 제가 참가자 명단에 귀하를 추가할 수 있다는 것을 의미합니다.

첨부되어 있는 목요일 일정을 봐주세요. **5** 당신은 이메일에서 오전 9시 30분까지는 올 수 없다고 말씀하셨는데, 그건 **3** 괜찮습니다. **2** 제가 당신의 방문객 배지를 점심 식권과 같이 접수처에 남겨두겠습니다. 그것들을 찾으신 후, 221호실로 가 주세요.

4 당신은 이미 Harzok 사의 업무 분야에 경험이 있다고 말씀해 주셨고, 그것은 참으로 반가운 일입니다. 당신의 참석 여부를 확인할 수 있게끔 이메일로 답변을 해주세요. 감사합니다.

안부를 전하며,

Peter Barlow
인력자원부 부장

어휘　recruitment 채용 I registration 등록 I unfortunately 안타깝게도, 불행히 I participant 참가자 I attached 첨부된 I badge 배지 I reception desk 접수처 I meal voucher 식권 I indicate 보여주다, 시사하다

채용 정보 설명회
4 Harzok 의료 보험 본부
2244 Blackdown 로, 런던
3월 1일 목요일, 오전 8시 30분 – 11시 30분

5 오전 8:30–9:30 (212호실)
Harzok 소개 – 처음에 저희 회사에 대한 짧은 발표가 있을 것이고, 여러분은 저희가 제공하는 다양한 진로 기회에 관하여 알게 될 것입니다. 그리고 나서 여러분들이 이곳 업무 환경이 어떠한지 알 수 있도록 여러분들께 **5** Harzok의 본사 구경을 시켜드릴 것입니다.

오전 9:30–10:30 (221호실)
팀원들 만나기 – 편하고, 여유로운 환경에서 Harzok 팀 직원들과 이야기하게 됩니다. 고위 관리직을 포함해 경험이 풍부한 직원들이 여러분들이 가진 어떠한 질문이나 평에도 응답해 줄 수 있을 것입니다.

오전 10:30–11:30 (222호실)
지원 절차 – 만약 Harzok이 여러분께 적합한 곳이라고 생각하신다면, 지원서 양식을 작성해주세요. 적합한 자리가 생기는 경우, 저희가 인사 부장님과의 1대 1 면접을 잡기 위해 여러분께 일주일 내로 연락을 드릴 것입니다.

어휘　casual 격식을 차리지 않는, 편한 I relaxed 느긋한, 여유 있는, 편안한 I experienced 숙련된 I suitable 적절한 I face-to-face 마주보는, 대면하는 I director 임원, 중역

1.　지난주 일정표를 받은 사람들에 관하여 언급된 것은 무엇인가?
　　(A) 오전 9시 30분에 도착할 계획이다.
　　(B) 온라인으로 행사에 등록했다.
　　(C) 모두가 지원서에 실수를 했다.
　　(D) Harzok의 직원들이다.

해설　이메일에서 등록은 웹사이트로 했음을 확인할 수 있고 등록한 사람들에게 채용 설명회에 관한 일정표를 줬음을 알 수 있다. 따라서, 일정표를 받은 사람들은 온라인으로 등록한 사람임을 알 수 있으므로 정답은 (B) They registered for the event online.이다.

2.　Mr. Barlow는 무엇을 할 계획인가?
　　(A) 비행편을 예약한다
　　(B) 접수처에서 방문객들을 환영한다
　　(C) Mr. Myung을 위해 출입증을 준비한다
　　(D) 웹사이트에 정보를 추가한다

해설　이메일에서 Mr. Barlow는 이메일 발신인이며, 9시 30분에 Mr. Myung이 도착하지 못한다고 하자 그를 위해 방문 출입증을 접수처

111

에 준비해두겠다고 했으므로 (C) Arrange entry authorization for Mr. Myung이 정답이다.

---

3. 이메일에서 두 번째 단락, 두 번째 줄의 단어 "fine"과 의미상 가장 가까운 것은
(A) 섬세한
(B) 기한이 지난
(C) 용인되는
(D) 옳은

해설 이메일 지문에서 제시간에 도착하지 못해도 '괜찮은'이라는 의미로 쓰였기 때문에 (C) acceptable이 가장 적합하다.

---

4. Mr. Myung은 주로 어떤 분야에서 일을 하겠는가?
고난도 **(A) 건강 보험**
(B) 온라인 마케팅
(C) 국제 관계
(D) 인적 자원

해설 이메일 지문에서 Myung 씨는 편지의 수신자이고, 이미 Harzok의 업무 분야에 관하여 경험이 있음을 알 수 있다. 일정표에서 Harzok Medical Insurance Headquarters에서 채용 설명회를 한다고 하고 있고, 결국 Harzok는 건강 보험 관련 회사임을 확인할 수 있다. 따라서 정답은 (A) Health insurance이다.

---

5. Mr. Myung은 일반 공개의 어떤 부분을 놓치겠는가?
(A) 다른 참석자들과의 점심
(B) 고위 간부들과의 만남
(C) 사무실 건물 구경
(D) 개인 면접

해설 이메일에서 Mr. Myung이 9시 30분까지는 도착하지 못함을 알 수 있고 일정표에서 해당 시간인 8:30 - 9:30 A.M.에는 본사 구경을 하는 것을 확인할 수 있으므로 정답은 (C) The office building tour이다.

[6-10] 다음 안내문과 양식에 관한 문제입니다.

KINGSTON 도서관에서의 행사 개최

Kingston 도서관의 Jefferson 실은 도서관 프로그램에 주로 이용되지만, 일요일을 제외한 날들에는 사적인 모임과 회사 행사를 위해 이용될 수도 있습니다. 방을 예약하려면 신청서를 작성해 주십시오.

Jefferson 실 이용 요금에 대한 개요
아래 요금은 이용자 유형과 예상 참석자 수에 따라 결정됩니다.

	참석자 1-40명	참석자 41-80명	참석자 81-120명
도서관 카드 소지자 (사적 모임 및 사교 모임)	인당 20달러	인당 40달러	인당 80달러
비회원 (사적 모임 및 사교 모임)	인당 40달러	인당 80달러	인당 160달러
8 회사 단체	인당 80달러	인당 120달러	**8** 인당 240달러

중요 세부사항
- Jefferson 실에서 제품 판매나 광고는 허용되지 않습니다.
- **6** **10** 도서관은 매일 오전 8시부터 오후 6시까지 개방됩니다. 이 시간 이후의 행사들은 보안 요원의 현장 파견을 필요로 합니다. 이 것은 도서관을 통해 추가 요금을 지불한 후에 마련될 수 있습니다. 또는 그 대신 개인들이 직접 전용 보안 요원을 고용하는 것도 환영합니다.

어휘 private 사적인, 사사로운 ǀ with the exception of ~은 제외하고 ǀ complete 완성하다, 빠짐없이 기입하다 ǀ reserve 예약하다 ǀ fee 요금 ǀ expect 기대하다, 예상하다 ǀ attendee 참가자, 참석자 ǀ individual 개인 ǀ social gathering 친목회, 사교 모임 ǀ security guard 보안 요원 ǀ arrangement 준비, 마련, 주선 ǀ extra fee 추가 요금 ǀ alternatively 그렇지 않으면, 그 대신 ǀ hire 고용하다

KINGSTON 도서관

Jefferson 실 예약 신청서
개인/단체명: **8** Hermes 건축 회사
연락 담당자: Penelope Sack
전화번호: 555-4930
이메일: p_sack@hermesarchitect.com

행사 설명: 우리 건축 회사는 Kingston 시내에 지어질 쇼핑몰의 예비 계획들을 세우는 단계에 있습니다. **7** 디자인을 마무리하기 전에, 우리는 우리 계획을 Kingston 주민들에게 보여주고 그들의 조언을 얻고자 합니다. 참석자들은 디자인 팀과 우리 고객, 그리고 참가를 원하시는 Kingston 주민들로 구성될 것입니다.
예상 참석자 수: **8** 120명
도서관 카드를 소지하고 계십니까? 아니요
행사 날짜 및 시간: **10** 4월 20일 금요일 오후 6:30 - 오후 8:30

9 저는 방 (대관) 정책을 모두 읽었으며 이에 동의합니다. 저는 방을 원래 상태로 남겨놓고 모든 의자들과 접이식 테이블 여분을 수납함에 되돌려놓는 것이 제 책임임을 이해하였습니다.

서명: *Penelope Sack* 날짜: 3월 25일

어휘 description 묘사, 설명 ǀ preliminary 예비의 ǀ finalize 마무리 짓다 ǀ input 조언(의 제공) ǀ consist of ~로 구성되다 ǀ resident 주민 ǀ consent to ~에 동의하다 ǀ policy 정책 ǀ responsibility 책임, 의무 ǀ folding table 접이식 테이블 ǀ storage 저장

---

6. 이 안내문이 Kingston 도서관에 관하여 언급하는 것은 무엇인가?
고난도 (A) 도서관은 주말에는 일찍 닫는다.
(B) 도서관은 영업 시간 이후 행사가 열리는 것을 허용한다.
(C) 요금은 모든 도서관 프로그램에 부과된다.
(D) Kingston 주민들의 도서관 열람실 대관에는 할인이 제공된다.

해설 안내문의 유의사항에서 영업 시간은 오전 8시부터 오후 6시까지이나 영업 시간 이후에도 보안 요원을 대동하면 행사 개최가 가능하다는 것을 알 수 있다. 따라서 정답은 (B) The library allows events to take place after its business hours.이다.

7. Penelope Sack은 왜 모임을 주최할 것인가?

(A) 프로젝트를 위한 모금 행사를 계획하기 위해

(B) 건물 개관을 축하하기 위해

(C) 지역 주민의 피드백을 받기 위해

(D) 사람들을 수상자로 지명하기 위해

해설　양식의 첫 번째 단락 Event description에서 Penelope Sack은 일에 대한 내용을 주민들에게 확인받기 위하여 모임을 주최하는 것을 알 수 있다. 따라서 정답은 (C) To get feedback from people in the community이다.

8.
고난도　Hermes 건축 회사는 Ms. Sack의 요청이 승인될 경우 인당 얼마를 부과 받을 것인가?

(A) 80달러

(B) 120달러

(C) 160달러

(D) 240달러

해설　신청서 양식 지문에서 Hermes 건축 회사는 기업으로 참석하는 것을 볼 수 있으며, 예상 참석자 수가 120명인 것을 알 수 있다. 안내문 지문에서 120명에 해당하는 요금 항목을 확인하면 인당 240달러이므로 정답이 (D) $240임을 알 수 있다.

---

9. Jefferson 실에 관하여 알 수 있는 것은 무엇인가?

(A) 일주일 중 어느 날에든 예약될 수 있다.

(B) 많은 인원을 수용하기 위해 추가 가구들이 놓일 수 있다.

(C) 수요일에는 회사에만 개방된다.

(D) 도서관 카드 소지자들은 무료로 이용할 수 있다.

해설　신청서 양식에서 Jefferson Room의 대관 옵션을 보면 방을 원래 상태로 남겨 두고 여분의 의자들과 접이식 테이블은 사용 후 수납함에 보관을 한다는 것을 확인할 수 있다. 즉 원래 있던 가구들에 추가 가구들을 배치할 수 있음을 유추할 수 있으므로 정답은 (B) Additional furniture can be set up to accommodate large parties.이다.

10.
고난도　Ms. Sack은 행사 전에 무엇을 할 것을 요청받겠는가?

(A) 보안 요원을 현장에 배치한다

(B) 시 공무원들에게서 허가를 받는다

(C) 그녀의 도서관 회원 기간을 연장한다

(D) 참석자들의 목록을 보낸다

해설　안내문의 유의사항 중 도서관의 영업 시간은 오전 8시부터 6시 30분까지이고, 그 이후는 보안 요원 대동 시에 행사 개최가 가능함을 확인할 수 있다. 신청서 양식 지문에서 Hermes Architecture은 영업시간 이후인 오후 여섯시 반 이후에 행사를 개최하므로 보안 요원이 필요함을 알 수 있다. 따라서 정답은 (A) Arrange for a security guard to be present이다.

[11-15] 다음의 안내문과 이메일에 관한 문제입니다.

Associated Flight 사 (AFC)
인턴 프로그램

AFC는 연중 인턴십을 제공합니다. 이번에 AFC의 정보 기술 및 통신 부서에서 신입 인턴사원을 모집합니다.

이 인턴직의 자격을 얻기 위해서, 지원자들은 반드시:

- **15** 현재 학부 마지막 해의 학생들이어야 합니다.
- 지원서를 작성해야 합니다.
- 이력서와 대학교 교수님께 받은 추천서를 제출해야 합니다.

인턴 사원들은 AFC의 전문가들과 함께 현재 프로젝트에 기여하게 됩니다. 인턴 사원들은 정해진 마감 기한을 준수하여, **11** 부서의 동료들과 함께 성공적으로 작업을 수행해 나가며, 주도적으로 작업을 진행할 것이 요구됩니다.

www.afc.au/applications에 방문하시면 지원서 양식을 다운로드받으실 수 있습니다. 완성된 지원서와 구비서류들을 AFC, 9 Dunbar 로, 멜버른 3004, 호주의 Mr. Neil Devinish 앞으로 보내주세요.

주의: **12** 고용 위원회에 의해 모든 지원서들이 신중하게 평가되므로, 선발 과정은 최대 6주까지 걸릴 수도 있습니다. 지원서들은 접수된 날로부터 2년 간 AFC 데이터베이스에 보관됩니다.

어휘　corporation 기업, 회사 | internship 인턴십 | seek 찾다, 구하다 | qualify 자격을 주다, 자격이 있다 | applicant 지원자 | fill out 작성하다 | application form 지원서 | submit 제출하다 | résumé 이력서 | recommendation letter 추천서 | contribute to ~에 기여하다 | along with ~와 함께 | professional 전문적인 | deadline 마감 기한 | independently 독립적으로 | selection 선발, 선정, 결정 | process 과정, 절차 | take up to ~까지 걸리다 | examine 조사하다, 검토하다 | hiring committee 고용 위원회

수신: 프로젝트 관리자들

발신: Esther Greenberg

날짜: 6월 12일

주제: 다음 주 회의

첨부: Davis의 참여 편지

모든 분들께,

8월 23일부터, **15** Vanessa Davis가 인턴으로 우리 팀에 합류하게 될 것입니다. 독일어 구사력이 **14** 출중한 Vanessa는 우리 부서의 다른 업무 뿐만 아니라 번역 일을 맡을 것입니다.

Vanessa가 보낸 지원서와 함께 참여 편지를 첨부합니다. 읽어보시고, 6월 19일 회의에서 어떻게 하면 우리가 6개월 동안 **13** Vanessa의 능력을 최대한 효율적으로 잘 활용할 수 있는지에 대해 논의할 준비를 해오시기 바랍니다. 회의 직후에, 저는 Vanessa에게 그녀가 하게 될 프로젝트의 종류를 알려줄 예정입니다.

감사합니다.

Esther Greenberg

커뮤니케이션 부장

어휘 **attachment** 첨부파일 I **letter of interest** 참여 편지 I **command** (언어) 능력, 구사력 I **interpretation** 해석, 설명 I **undertake** ~을 맡다 I **assignment** 임무, 할당 I **plan on** ~할 계획이다 I **work on** 착수하다

11. 안내문에 따르면, 인턴들은 무엇을 할 수 있어야 하는가?
(A) 팀의 일원으로 작업한다
(B) 업무 일정을 계획한다
(C) 독일어로 보고서를 작성한다
(D) IT 소프트웨어 프로그램을 사용한다

해설 안내문 지문에서 인턴 자격 조건 및 업무를 주목해야 한다. 지문 두 번째 단락에서 부서 동료들과 어울려 일할 수 있어야 한다는 것을 확인할 수 있으므로 정답은 (A) Work as part of a team이다.

12. 인턴십 지원서에 관하여 알 수 있는 것은 무엇인가?
고난도 (A) 지원자들의 작업 견본을 첨부해야 한다.
(B) 최대 6주 간 데이터베이스에 유지된다.
(C) AFC 직원들로 구성된 패널이 읽는다.
(D) AFC 웹사이트에 게시되어야 한다

해설 안내문의 주의 항목을 보면 모든 지원서는 고용 위원회에 의하여 자세히 검토되는 것을 확인할 수 있다. 따라서 정답은 (C) They are read by a panel of AFC staff members.이다.

13. 이메일의 목적은 무엇인가?
고난도 (A) 임시 직원에게 업무를 배정하는 데 있어서 도움을 요청하기 위해
(B) 관리자들이 Ms. Davis에게 제안서를 보내라고 요청하기 위해
(C) Ms. Greenberg의 근무시간 변경을 알리기 위해
(D) 관리자들에게 회의 시간이 변경되었다고 알리기 위해

해설 이메일 첫머리에서 Vanessa Davis의 팀 합류를 확인할 수 있고, 6개월 간의 임시 직원 Vanessa의 능력을 활용할 방안에 대해 논의할 준비를 해오라고 하고 있으므로, 임시 직원의 업무 배정에 대한 도움을 요청하는 것으로 볼 수 있다. 따라서 정답은 (A) To ask for assistance in designating work to a temporary employee이다.

14. 이메일에서, 첫 번째 단락, 두 번째 줄의 단어 "command"와 의미상 가장 가까운 것은
(A) 설명
(B) 감사
(C) 존중
(D) 통달

해설 이메일에서 '출중한 독일어 구사력을 지닌 Vanessa'라는 의미로 볼 수 있기 때문에, '숙달, 통달'의 의미를 갖는 mastery가 문맥상 가장 적절하다. 따라서 정답은 (D) mastery이다.

15. Ms. Davis에 관하여 알 수 있는 것은 무엇인가?
고난도 (A) 그녀의 지원서 패키지를 다시 제출하라는 요청을 받았다.
(B) 정보 기술 부서의 일자리에 지원했다.
(C) 일 년 동안 AFC에서 일하도록 예정되어 있다.
(D) 현재 대학에 재학 중이다.

해설 안내문의 자격 요건에서 지원자는 대학의 마지막 학년에 재학 중이어야 하는 것을 확인할 수 있고, 이메일에서 새로운 인턴으로 Vanessa Davis가 합류됨을 알 수 있다. 따라서 지원을 해서 인턴에 합격한 Ms. Davis는 현재 대학에 재학 중임을 유추할 수 있으므로 정답은 (D) She is currently a university student.이다.

UNIT 14. 삼중 지문

핵심 문제 유형
본서 p.328

1. (D)   2. (B)   3. (D)   4. (D)   5. (A)

[1-5] 다음 웹페이지, 주문 양식, 이메일에 관한 문제입니다.

http://www.metropolitancleaners.com

홈	서비스	견적 받기	연락

집을 다시 새것처럼 만드세요!

전문적인 저희 회사의 청소팀은 20년이 넘는 경험을 가지고 있습니다. 직원들은 빠르고, 효율적이며 빈틈이 없습니다. 저희 회사의 작업은 일류라고 **1** 장담할 수 있습니다. 콘도에서 사무실 건물까지 그 어떤 공간이라도 다시 새것처럼 보이게 할 수 있습니다!

기본 요금*은 다음과 같습니다:
청소부 2명 = 60달러, 3명 = 110달러, 4명 = 150달러, **3** 5명 = 170달러
*참고: 최소 한 시간은 소요되어야 합니다.

모든 주택과 사무실이 다르기에 요금 역시 필요한 작업량에 따라 달라질 수 있습니다. 더욱 자세한 비용 정보를 위해 작업 요청서를 가능한 한 전부 작성해 주십시오.

봄 청소 이벤트: **4 월요일에서 금요일 사이에 청소 예약하시고 Smithy's 식료품점에서 다음 구매 시 10% 할인받을 수 있는 쿠폰을 받으세요.

어휘 **cleaner** 청소부 I **efficient** 효율적인 I **thorough** 빈틈없는 I **assure** 장담하다, 확언하다 I **top-notch** 최고의, 일류의 I **minimum** 최소한 I **residence** 주택 I **rate** 요금 I **work request** 업무 요청 I **completely** 완전히

Metropolitan 청소 회사 작업 요청서	
요청일	4월 17일 화요일
성명	Gary Daniels
이메일	g_daniels@softcreek.ca
전화번호	(414)-555-4547
사업체 이름 (있을 경우)	Softcreek 임대 오두막
청소할 곳 주소	604 E. Moonside 가, 애플턴, 위스콘신 54911
예약	5월 7일
작업 요청	2채의 호수 옆 오두막: 하나는 500평방피트에 1층이며, 다른 하나는 1,800평방피트에 2층짜리입니다.
코멘트	제가 갖고 있는 임대 오두막들을 여름 동안 내놓을 준비를 하려고 합니다. **2** 두 오두막 모두 유리와 식기류를 많이 갖고 있으므로 특별히 조심해 주십시오. 가장 좋은 거래를 하기 위해 다른 청소 업체에게도 연락해 봤습니다. **4** 제가 청소일을 5월 7일로 잡아놓긴 했지만, 더 일찍 와주실 수 있다면 좋겠습니다. 귀하의 홈페이지에서 언급한 쿠폰을 받을 수 있는 한 빨리 오셨으면 합니다.

어휘 lakeside 호반, 호숫가 ┃ cabin 오두막집 ┃ story 층 ┃ rental 임대의 ┃ dinnerware 식기 ┃ voucher 바우처, 할인권, 쿠폰

수신: Gary Daniels
발신: Nadia Baxter
일자: 4월 18일
제목: 귀하의 예약
첨부: #302445-TLM33.rif 견적

Metropolitan 청소 회사에 연락 주셔서 감사합니다. 귀하의 오두막들 크기와 비슷한 집들을 청소해 본 경험에 비추어볼 때 하루에 두 명의 직원으로는 더 작은 오두막일지라도 하루에 마칠 수 없을 것 같습니다. 첨부한 파일은 **3** 청소부 다섯 명으로 해서 아이템 항목으로 나누어 정리한 파일입니다. 청소 도구와 장비, 그리고 고정 교통비 역시 나와 있습니다. 요금은 야외 청소 비용은 포함하지 않았다는 걸 명심하십시오. 그리고 귀하께서 **5** 요청하셨던 날보다 8일더 빨리 자리가 있습니다. 시간을 옮겨도 여전히 홍보 행사를 위한 자격이 되십니다. 견적에 대해 질문이 있으실 경우 414-555-1824로 저희 사무실에 전화 주십시오. 가격에 동의하시면 청소 일자와 세부 사항을 확인할 것입니다.

진심으로,

Nadia Baker
Metropolitan 청소 회사

어휘 estimate 견적, 추산 ┃ itemized 항목별로 구분한 ┃ equipment 장비 ┃ fixed 고정된, 변하지 않는 ┃ transportation fee 교통비 ┃ outdoor 야외의 ┃ opening 빈 자리, 공석 ┃ qualify 자격을 주다 ┃ promotional 홍보용의 ┃ approve 찬성하다, 승인하다 ┃ confirm 확정하다

Practice

1. (C)	2. (D)	3. (D)	4. (C)	5. (B)
6. (D)	7. (B)	8. (D)	9. (C)	10. (D)
11. (A)	12. (C)	13. (D)	14. (A)	15. (C)

[1-5] 다음 광고와 이메일, 기사에 관한 문제입니다.

Bayside Tower

Bayside Tower의 공사가 거의 완공 상태입니다.
여전히 임대나 구매 가능한 거주용, 사업용, 상업용 공간이 있습니다.
Bayside Tower는 5월 1일에 개장할 것으로 예상됩니다.

Bayside Tower는 개장하자마자 Piedmont 시의 가장 큰 건물이 될 것입니다. Bayside Tower는 여러분의 사업체와 개인적인 필요에 맞는 이상적인 위치에 자리잡고 있고, 해안가와 **1** **4** Westside 쇼핑몰의 건너편 시내에 위치해 있습니다.

2 아파트 (10-25층) 주거지에는 1개, 2개 아니면 3개의 침실이 있으며, 각각 부엌과 거실 그리고 1개나 2개의 욕실이 있습니다. 가구 비치가 된 아파트와 안 된 아파트 둘 다 가능합니다.

2 사무실 (2-9층, 26-40층) 작은 기업, 중간 규모의 기업, 대기업을 위한 사무실 공간이 있습니다. 다양한 형태의 공간 배치가 가능합니다.

2 **5** 소매점(1층) 여러 개의 작은 상점 및 중간 규모의 상점을 위한 공간이 있습니다. 몇 군데는 식당으로 사용 가능합니다.

더 많은 정보가 필요하시면 508-4444로 전화 주십시오. 가격은 요청하실 경우 알려드립니다

어휘 near ~에 근접하다, 다가오다 ┃ completion 완성 ┃ residential 주거의 ┃ commercial 상업의 ┃ available 이용 가능한 ┃ purchase 구매 ┃ rent 임대 ┃ downtown 도심지에 ┃ waterfront 해안지구 ┃ ideally 이상적으로 ┃ residence 주택 ┃ living room 거실 ┃ furnished 가구가 있는 ┃ unfurnished 가구가 없는 ┃ layout 배치 ┃ upon request 신청에 의해

수신: Jacob Nelson ⟨jnelson@wilmington.com⟩
발신: Karen Hester ⟨karenh@baysideproperties.com⟩
제목: Bayside Tower
날짜: 4월 18일

Mr. Nelson 귀하,

3 저희 Bayside Tower 아파트에 대해 문의해주셔서 감사합니다. 저희는 여전히 귀하와 귀하의 가족을 위해 완벽한 여러 채의 아파트 가구들을 보유하고 있습니다. 귀하께서는 내외분이 두 자녀를 두고 계셔 침실 3개짜리 아파트에 관심이 있다고 하셨습니다. 이 아파트들 중 하나의 구매가는 35만 달러이며 월 2,500달러로 임대하실 수도 있습니다. 만일 임차하기로 결정하신다면, 최소 2년 기간의 계약서에 서명하셔야 합니다.

PART 7 ┃ UNIT 14

4 귀하께서 Westside 쇼핑몰에서 일하시기 때문에, 저희를 만나 아파트를 둘러보시기가 편하실 것입니다. 귀하께서 언제 Bayside Tower를 방문하실 시간이 있으신지 알려주시면, 귀하를 정문에서 만나 뵐 수 있습니다. 제 사무실이 Bayside Tower 안에 있어서 저는 온종일 시간이 됩니다. 정규 근무 시간에 481-0498로 부담 없이 전화 주시기 바랍니다.

감사합니다.

Karen Hester
Bayside 부동산

어휘 inquiry 문의 | indicate 암시하다 | contract 계약서 | entrance 입구 | throughout ~동안 죽 | business hours 영업 시간, 근무 시간

Piedmont (5월 2일) – 오랫동안 기다려온 Bayside Tower가 어제 5월 1일에 개장했다. Chip Taylor 시장과 다른 유명인사들이 참석한 개관식을 비롯한 많은 행사가 있었다.

Bayside Tower 건설 공사는 5년 넘게 걸렸다. 많은 지역 주민들이 Bayside Tower가 산적한 관련 문제들 때문에 완공되지 못할 거라고 생각했었다. 건물의 원 소유자였던 Marge Hamel은 파산으로 자산을 매각해야 했다. 이후 건설 공사 중에 몇 차례의 건설 사고가 발생해 반복적으로 건물이 손상되었다. 그 불운은 개장일에도 계속되어, **5** 건물 식당들 중 하나에서 송수관이 터졌다.

그럼에도 불구하고 건물은 현재 완공되어 운영 중이다. 95% 이상의 아파트가 팔리거나 임대되었고, 99%의 사무실 공간이 입주가 끝났다. 그러니까 2,000명 이상의 사람들이 이 건물 안에서 거주하거나 일을 하고 있어, 이제 시에서 가장 분주한 건물들 중 하나가 되었다.

어휘 long-awaited 오래 기다려왔던 | opening 개회식 | festivity (축제의) 행사 | ribbon cutting ceremony 개관식 | attend 참석하다 | prominent 저명한 | concerning ~관련된 | original 원래의 | property 자산 | construction accident 건설 (공사) 사고 | nevertheless 그럼에도 불구하고 | occupy (시간, 장소 등을) 차지하다

1. Bayside Tower에 대하여 암시되고 있는 것은 무엇인가?
(A) 25층까지 있다.
(B) 3개 층이 소매 점포들이다.
(C) 쇼핑 센터 가까이에 있다.
(D) 자체 경비원들이 있다.

해설 광고를 보면 Bayside Tower는 총 40층짜리 건물이므로 (A)는 오답이다. 또한 소매 점포들은 1층에만 있으므로 (B) 또한 오답이다. 경비원에 대한 언급은 아예 없었으므로 (D)도 오답이다. 광고 첫 번째 문단에서 Westside Mall의 건너편에 위치한다고 묘사되어 있으므로 (C) It is near a shopping center.가 정답이다.

2. 광고에 의하면, 임대가 가능하지 않은 것은 무엇인가?
(A) 식당을 위한 공간
(B) 사무실 공간
(C) 거주 공간
(D) 학교를 위한 공간

해설 광고에서 1층 소매점, 10-25층 아파트, 2-9, 26-40층은 사무실이고 전부 구매 및 임대가 가능하다고 했으므로, 언급되지 않은 (D) Space for a school이 정답이다.

---

3. Ms. Hester는 왜 Mr. Nelson에게 글을 썼는가?
(A) Bayside Tower의 사무실 임대 방법을 설명하려고
(B) 아파트를 보기 위한 약속을 확인하려고
(C) 임대 계약서 서명과 관련해 물어보려고
(D) 고객 문의에 대해 답변하려고

해설 이메일의 전체 내용은 Bayside Tower의 아파트에 대해 문의한 Mr. Nelson에 대한 답장이므로 (D) To respond to a customer's question이 정답이다.

---

4. Mr. Nelson의 직장에 대해 암시되고 있는 것은 무엇인가?
(A) Bayside Tower 안에 위치해 있다.
(B) Piedmont 근교에 있다.
(C) Bayside Tower 길 건너편에 있다.
(D) 최근 Piedmont로 이전했다.

해설 이메일의 두 번째 문단 첫 번째 줄에서 Mr. Nelson의 직장이 Westside Mall에 있다는 걸 알 수 있고, 또 광고에서 Westside Mall은 Bayside Tower의 건너편에 있다고 되어 있다. 따라서 정답은 (C) It is across the street from Bayside Tower.이다.

---

5. 어느 층에서 문제가 발생했겠는가?
(A) 지하층
(B) 1층
(C) 2층
(D) 10층

해설 두 지문을 내용적으로 연계해서 풀어야 하는 문제이다. 기사에서 두 번째 문단 끝부분에 개장일에 식당들 중 하나에서 송수관이 터졌다고 했고, 광고에서 1층 몇 지점이 식당으로 사용 가능하다고 했으므로 (B) The first floor가 정답이다.

[6-10] 다음 웹페이지들에 관련된 문제입니다.

www.harborcruises.ca/cruises

홈	크루즈	예약	후기

Harbor City 크루즈와 함께 경관을 즐기세요

6 50년이 넘도록 우리 회사는 Harbor City 전역에서 사람들에게 아름다운 크루즈 여행을 제공해 왔습니다. 우리 회사는 **6** 나이에 상관없이 모두에게 매력적으로 느껴질 만한 수상 여행을 제공합니다. 그리고 **6** 베테랑 선장들이 승객들에게 가장 즐거운 여행이 될 수 있도록 노력하고 있습니다. 1년 내내 계속되는 우리 회사의 크루즈 여행에 대한 간략한 요약이 여기 있습니다.

Harbor Delights

월&화

바다에서 아름다운 경관을 즐기며 우리 크루즈의 수석 요리사가 준비한 **8** Harbor City가 원산지인 해산물 요리들을 시식하며 하루를 시작하세요. 모두 배가 부른 뒤에는 레스토랑 상품권을 행운의 승객 몇 분에게 증정할 예정입니다. Wakka 아크로바틱 공연단의 배 위에서 하는 공연을 보면서 아침을 마무리합니다.

Harbor City Circuit

수

Puffin 섬 근처에 있는 오래된 석조 부두 근처에서 항해하며 오후를 보내세요! 이 여행에서는 우리 **7** 도시의 초창기 선원이었던 Bill Montgomery의 삶과 여정에 대해 배우며 과거를 발견하실 수 있습니다. 이 여행은 가이드이자 수상 경력이 있는 포크 송 가수인 Mindy Gould가 이끕니다.

Postvost Retreat

목&금

아름다운 Postvost 섬 보호 구역으로 크루즈 여행을 떠나 해안 경치와 고래, 돌고래, 그리고 바닷가에 있는 다른 것들도 즐기세요. **9** 이 여섯 시간에 걸친 관광을 하는 동안 Daniel Kline이 바다와 섬의 삶에 대해 이야기해줄 것입니다.

이 여행들의 추가 세부 사항에 대해서는 저희 크루즈 페이지를 참고하십시오. 사무실은 주중에 오전 8시부터 오후 7시까지 운영하며 토요일에는 오전 8시부터 오후 4시까지 운영합니다.

어휘 sight 장면, 광경 | century 세기, 100년 | breathtaking 숨이 멎는 듯한 | appeal 관심을 끌다 | regardless of ~ 와 관계없이 | veteran 전문가, 베테랑 | captain 선장 | summary 요약 | year-round 연중 계속되는 | sample 시식하다, 시음하다 | gift certificate 상품권 | onboard 승선한 | pier 부두 | islet 작은 섬 | mariner 선원, 뱃사람 | preserve 보호 구역 | coastal 해안의 | scenery 경치, 풍경

---

www.harborcruises.ca/bookings/receipt4150A

홈	크루즈	예약	후기

판매일: 6월 8일

고객명: Bethany Roos

확인코드: 4150A

승객 수	크루즈 타입	일시	패키지 가격	금액
2	Postvost Retreat	6월 20일	$190	380달러
2	**8** Harbor Delights	**8** 6월 23일	$110	220달러
			총액	600달러

이 확인 페이지를 프린트하셔서 탑승 전 신분증과 함께 제시해 주십시오.

어휘 confirmation 확인, 확정 | present 제시하다, 제출하다 | board 승선하다

---

www.harborcruises.ca/testimonials

홈	크루즈	예약	후기

"저는 Harbor City에서 정말 즐겁게 머물렀고 Harbor City 크루즈가 큰 기여를 했습니다. Mr. Kline에게 정말 깊은 인상을 받았어요. 해양 생물에 대해 정말로 자세히 설명해 주셨습니다. **9** 투어는 여섯 시간보다 더 오래 걸려서 서 있기에는 긴 시간이긴 했습니다. 하지만 우리가 아름다운 돌고래들을 봤기에 그럴 만한 가치가 있었어요. 그리고 맑은 하늘이 수면을 반짝거리며 빛나게 해서 사진을 찍기에 아주 좋은 기회가 되었습니다. **10** 두 번째 여행에서는 정말로 멋진 쇼에 감탄했습니다. Wakka 아크로바틱 공연단이 후프를 넘어 점프하는 것을 보면서 아침을 보내는 일은 내년 여름에도 우리가 정말로 다시 하고 싶은 일입니다."

Bethany Roos, 6월 25일 오후 1:03

어휘 impress 깊은 인상을 주다 | glisten 반짝이다 | spectacular 장관을 이루는, 극적인 | hoop 고리, 굴렁쇠

---

6. Harbor City 크루즈에 대해 암시되지 않은 것은 무엇인가?

고난도

(A) 50년이 넘게 운영되고 있다.

(B) 경험이 많은 가이드를 데리고 있다.

(C) 나이 많은 사람들이 활동에 참여해도 좋다.

(D) 상을 받은 회사이다.

해설 첫 번째 지문에서 (A)는 반세기가 넘은 회사임을 확인할 수 있고 (B)와 (C)는 나이에 상관없이 누구나 매력을 느낄 수상 여행을 제공하고, 베테랑 선장이 즐거운 여행이 될 수 있도록 노력하고 있다고 하는 것을 확인할 수 있다. 수상 경력이 있는 건 Mindy Gould이지 Harbor City 크루즈가 아니므로 정답은 (D) it is an award-winning company.이다.

---

7. 승객들은 지역의 역사에 대해 언제 배울 수 있는가?

(A) 월요일과 화요일에

(B) 수요일에

(C) 목요일과 금요일에

(D) 토요일에

해설 첫 번째 지문의 수요일 항목에서 초창기 선원이었던 Bill Montgomery의 삶과 여정을 배움으로써 과거를 발견할 수 있다고 하였으므로 정답은 (B) On Wednesday이다.

---

8. Ms. Roos의 6월 23일 여행의 일부는 무엇이었는가?

고난도

(A) 콘서트를 관람하는 것

(B) 농장을 방문하는 것

(C) 고객 설문 조사를 작성하는 것

(D) 지역 음식을 시식하는 것

해설 두 번째 지문의 표에서 6월 23일의 예약 크루즈는 Harbor Delights임을 확인할 수 있고, 첫 번째 지문의 Harbor Delights 항목에서 Harbor City가 원산지인 해산물 요리를 시식하는 것을 확인할 수 있으므로 정답은 (D) Trying local dishes이다. 대표적인 오답이 (A)인데, Acrobatic Troupe의 performance이기 때문에 체조단의 점프 시범 등에 해당하므로 concert라고 할 수 없다.

9. Ms. Roos는 후기에서 무엇을 암시하는가?
고난도 (A) Postvost Retreat에서는 사진을 찍을 기회가 없었다.
(B) Harbor Delight 크루즈는 많은 승객을 실어 날랐다.
(C) Postvost Retreat이 늦게 끝났다.
(D) Harbor Delight 크루즈에는 지식이 풍부한 가이드가 있었다.

해설 세 번째 지문에서 6시간보다 오래 걸렸고, 서 있기에는 긴 시간이었지만 아름다운 돌고래들을 봤기 때문에 그럴만한 가치가 있다고 하였으므로, Ms. Roos가 체험한 것은 첫 번째 지문의 Postvost Retreat 임을 확인할 수 있다. Postvost Retreat의 원래 행사 시간은 6시간이었음을 알 수 있으므로 정답은 (C) The Postvost Retreat cruise ended late.임을 유추할 수 있다.

- -

10. 후기에 따르면, Ms. Roos는 내년에 무엇을 할 것인가?
(A) 요리 수업에 등록한다
(B) 수족관을 방문한다
(C) 보존 구역 섬 관광을 한다
(D) 공연을 관람한다

해설 세 번째 지문 마지막 단락에서 Bethany Roos는 두 번째 여행의 Wakka 아크로바틱 팀 공연에서 정말 감탄하였고, 내년 여름에도 다시 하고 싶다고 희망하였으므로 정답은 (D) Watch a performance 임을 유추할 수 있다.

[11-15] 다음 이메일, 후기, 기사에 관한 문제입니다

수신: Roberta Moss
발신: Jared Smith
날짜: **15** 4월 5일 월요일
제목: 새 기계

Roberta에게,

우리의 스타트업 회사를 위해 기계를 구매하기 전에 고려해야 할 것들이 몇 가지 있습니다. 비즈니스 계획에 최저 발주 없이 교실들에 3D로 프린트된 자료를 공급하는 일이 포함되어 있어요. **13** 우리가 잠재 고객들에게 우리의 기술이 어떠한지를 보여주는 데모 발표를 할 때 쉽게 가져갈 수 있는 저렴한 프린터기가 필요합니다. educatech.com에 올라온 후기들을 확인하시고 우리의 필요에 맞는 기계를 찾을 수 있을지 한 번 보세요. 무엇을 알게 되었는지 알려주시면 그걸 우리 예산에 포함시키도록 하겠습니다.

Jared

어휘 consider 고려하다, 숙고하다 | startup 창업 | minimum order 최저 발주 | demo 시범, 시연 | potential 잠재적인 | budget 예산

http://educatech.com/products/reviews
교육 적용을 위한 3D 프린터들

다음 3D 프린터들은 모두 전국 교육자 연합회에서 승인받은 것들입니다.
더 많은 정보를 보시려면 모델을 선택하세요.

★★★★★ **12** Plastimate M은 가볍고 내구성이 강한, 상표 등록된 플라스틱으로 모델을 프린트합니다. **11** 이 프린터는 아주 작은 부품을 프린트하는 기능으로 아주 잘 알려져 있습니다. 정밀함이야말로 이 제품이 현재 나온 제품들 중 가장 비싼 이유입니다.

★★★★★ Harkness Dual 7J는 레이저로 금속 부품을 프린트합니다. 금속은 가격이 비싸며 프린트할 때 느립니다. **12** 오랫동안 지속되어야 하는 물건을 프린트할 때 유용합니다.

★★★★☆ Benson-Jenkins AF9는 두 개의 분사구를 사용하기에 가장 빠른 프린터입니다. 이 프린터는 정확성이 떨어지지만 **12** Benson-Jenkins의 플라스틱 모델링 재료는 내구성이 강합니다. 속도 하나만으로도 가치가 있는 프린터입니다.

★★★★☆ **12** Binder-Tech 0A는 Binder-Stick이라고 불리는 극도로 강한 플라스틱으로 물건을 빠르게 프린트합니다. **13** 이 프린터들은 바닥에 바퀴가 달려 있는 덕분에 움직일 수 있습니다. 전반적인 프린트 질을 고려했을 때 가장 싼 옵션입니다.

어휘 association 협회 | educator 교육자 | proprietary 등록 상표가 붙은 | lightweight 가벼운 | durable 내구성이 있는, 오래가는 | renowned 유명한, 명성 있는 | precision 정확, 정밀 | laser 레이저 | last 지속되다 | nozzle 노즐, 분사구 | accurate 정확한 | unusually 대단히, 몹시 | wheeled 바퀴가 달린 | overall 전반적인

교육 스타트업의 '인쇄물들'
Carol Hernandez 씀

15 11월 2일 – 최근에 나온 어떤 교육용 카탈로그라도 한 번 **14** 들여다보면 찾아볼 수 있을 것이다: 3D 프린터로 만들어진 교육용 자료를 광고하는 회사들을. 이 사업체들은 교실을 작은 공장으로 변화시킨다. 그리고 학생들이 자신들의 프로젝트에 대한 꿈(dream)을 꾸고, 디자인(design)을 하고, 만들어낼(deliver) 수 있게 해준다(3 "D"). 교육 프로젝트와 수업 계획은 보통 무료로 제공된다. 그러나 회사들은 3D 프린터 사용과 특정 부분에 대해 비용을 받는다. ProEd 3D와 같은 몇몇 회사는 큰 거래에 집중하는데, 학군 전체나 주문 당 150키트가 넘어가는 거래를 자주 한다. 또 다른 회사는 Grab-itate인데 10개 정도의 작은 주문까지도 받을 수 있으며 고급 비품을 만든다. 마지막으로, **15** Fun-D-Mental과 Beta-ED는 각각 7개월과 3년이 된 회사인데 만약 필요할 경우 한 명의 학생을 위해서라도 수업 자료를 제작한다.

어휘 advertise 광고하다 | transform 바꾸다, 변화시키다 | miniature 미니어처, 소형 | factory 공장 | district 지구, 지역 | batch 한 회분, 집단 | respectively 각각

11. Plastimate M에 대해 무엇이 언급되었는가?

(A) 정밀한 세부 사항을 만들어낼 수 있는 능력이 있다.

(B) 클래식한 디자인으로 인기가 많다.

(C) 대부분 프린터보다 크기가 작다.

(D) 복잡한 부품을 많이 사용하여 만들어졌다.

해설 Plastimate M의 후기 중 프린터가 매우 작은 부품을 만드는 기능으로 유명하다고 언급되어 있으므로 정답은 (A) It is capable of creating fine details.이다.

---

12. 웹페이지에 나열된 프린터들은 모두 어떤 공통점을 갖고 있는가?

고난도 (A) 쉽게 운반 가능하다.

(B) 매우 빠르다.

(C) 내구성 있는 물건들을 만든다.

(D) 가격이 적당하다.

해설 Plastimate M 제품은 가볍고 내구성이 강한 플라스틱으로 모델을 프린트한다고 했고 Harkness Dual 7J은 오랫동안 지속되는 물품에 유용하다고 나와있고, Benson-Jenkins AF9는 정확성이 떨어지나 플라스틱 모델링 재료는 내구성이 강하다고 했다. Binder-Tech 0A 또한 Binder-Stick이라고 불리는 극도로 강한 플라스틱으로 물건을 빠르게 프린트한다고 했다. 그러므로 모든 제품들의 공통점은 내구성이 강한 물건들을 만든다는 점이다. 따라서 정답은 (C) They produce durable items.이다.

---

13. Ms. Moss가 Mr. Smith에게 추천할 것으로 보이는 3D 프린터는 무엇인가?

고난도 (A) Plastimate M

(B) Harkness Dual 7J

(C) Benson-Jenkins AF9

(D) Binder-Tech 0A

해설 이메일에서 화자는 쉽게 운반할 수 있는 저렴한 프린터기가 필요하다고 했다. 후기에서 The Binder-Tech 0A가 프린트 질을 고려했을 때 가장 싸고, 바퀴 때문에 움직일 수 있기 때문에, 모든 조건에 부합함을 확인할 수 있다. 따라서 정답은 (D) The Binder-Tech 0A이다.

---

14. 기사의 첫 번째 단락, 첫 번째 줄의 "scan"과 의미상 가장 가까운 것은

(A) 훑어보다

(B) 표시하다

(C) 집중하다

(D) 제외시키다

해설 최근에 나온 어떤 교육용 카탈로그라도 한 번 들여다보면 찾아볼 수 있을 것이다는 의미로 해석할 수 있으므로 scan과 바꿔서 쓸 수 있는 단어는 (A) browse가 가장 적당하다.

---

15. Ms. Moss와 Mr. Smith는 어느 회사에서 일하는 것으로 보이는가?

고난도 (A) ProEd 3D

(B) Grab-itate

(C) Fun-D-Mental

(D) Beta-ED

해설 이메일에서 Ms. Moss에게 Mr. Smith가 4월 5일에 이메일을 쓴 것을 확인할 수 있고, 문단의 첫머리를 보면 스타트업을 위한 기계 구매에 관하여 이야기한 것을 알 수 있다. 기사는 11월 2일에 작성이 되었고, 기사의 마지막에서 Fun-D-Mental과 Beta-ED는 각각 7개월과 3년이 된 회사임을 알 수 있다. 이메일에서는 4월에 창업 이야기를 했고, 기사에서는 11월 기준으로 Fun-D-Mental이 7개월 된 회사임을 유추할 수 있으므로 Ms. Moss와 Mr. Smith는 Fun-D-Mental 회사 소속임을 알 수 있다. 따라서 정답은 (C) Fun-D-Mental이다.

REVIEW TEST

1. (C)	**2.** (C)	**3.** (B)	**4.** (D)	**5.** (A)
6. (D)	**7.** (A)	**8.** (A)	**9.** (C)	**10.** (B)
11. (B)	**12.** (B)	**13.** (B)	**14.** (A)	**15.** (D)
16. (C)	**17.** (C)	**18.** (D)	**19.** (B)	**20.** (D)
21. (C)	**22.** (D)	**23.** (B)	**24.** (B)	**25.** (D)
26. (A)	**27.** (B)	**28.** (C)	**29.** (B)	**30.** (C)
31. (B)	**32.** (A)	**33.** (B)	**34.** (A)	**35.** (C)
36. (A)	**37.** (A)	**38.** (C)	**39.** (B)	**40.** (A)
41. (C)	**42.** (D)	**43.** (B)	**44.** (B)	**45.** (D)
46. (A)	**47.** (C)	**48.** (C)	**49.** (C)	**50.** (C)
51. (A)	**52.** (D)	**53.** (D)	**54.** (A)	

[1–2] 다음 영수증에 관한 문제입니다.

소액 현금 수령증	
일자: 8월 7일 이름 (정자로 써 주세요): Hannah Gould	
설명	**금액**
이것은 **1** 8월 9일부터 11일까지 저의 최근 연구를 발표할 곳인 브뤼셀에서 열리는 의학 박람회와 관련된 음식, 교통편과 숙박을 제공하기 위한 것입니다.	1,150파운드
위의 금액을 수령하였음을 알립니다.	
서명: **2** *Hannah Gould*	

어휘 petty cash 소액 현금 | receipt 수령[영수](증) | transportation 운송 | lodging 임시 숙소 | expo 박람회(=exposition) | present 소개하다 | promote 홍보하다; 승진시키다 | facility 시설(물) | lecture 강연 | negotiate 협상하다 | contract 계약(서) | acknowledge ~을 받았음을 알리다; 인정하다 | registration fee 등록비 | health insurance 건강보험 | allowance 수당; 허용량 | donation 기부(금)

PART 7 REVIEW TEST

1. Ms. Gould는 8월에 브뤼셀에서 무엇을 할 것인가?

(A) 제품을 홍보한다

(B) 연구시설을 견학한다

(C) 강연을 한다

(D) 계약을 협상한다

해설 DESCRIPTION 섹션에서 9-11 August Medical Expo in Brussels where I will present our latest research (8월 9일부터 11일까지 저의 최근 연구를 발표할 곳인 브뤼셀에서 열리는 의학 박람회)라고 했으므로 (C) Give a lecture가 정답이다.

Paraphrasing

present ~ research → Give a lecture

---

2. Mr. Gould는 무엇을 알리는가?

(A) 등록비용을 낸 것

(B) 건강보험을 든 것

(C) 수당을 받은 것

(D) 기부를 한 것

해설 영수증 하단 I acknowledge the receipt of the amount above. / Signature: Hannah Gould (위의 금액을 수령하였음을 알립니다. / 서명: Hannah Gould) 부분을 통해 Ms. Gould가 위 금액 (Amount: £1,150)을 영수했다고 밝히고 있으므로 (C) Receiving an allowance가 정답이다.

Paraphrasing

acknowledge the receipt of the amount → Receiving an allowance

---

[3-4] 다음 문자 메시지 대화에 관한 문제입니다.

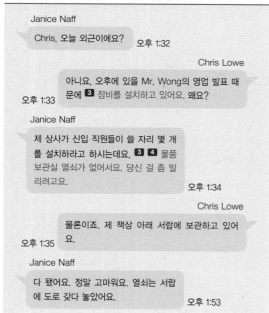

Janice Naff

Chris, 오늘 외근이에요? 오후 1:32

Chris Lowe

아니요, 오후에 있을 Mr. Wong의 영업 발표 때문에 **3** 장비를 설치하고 있어요. 왜요? 오후 1:33

Janice Naff

제 상사가 신입 직원들이 쓸 자리 몇 개를 설치하라고 하시는데요. **3** **4** 물품 보관실 열쇠가 없어서요. 당신 걸 좀 빌리려고요. 오후 1:34

Chris Lowe

물론이죠. 제 책상 아래 서랍에 보관하고 있어요. 오후 1:35

Janice Naff

다 됐어요. 정말 고마워요. 열쇠는 서랍에 도로 갖다 놓았어요. 오후 1:53

어휘 set up 설치하다 | equipment 장비 | supervisor 상사 | workstation (직원 1명이 일하기 위한) 자리 | hire 신입 직원 | supply closet 물품 보관실 | appreciate 고마워하다 | approve of ~을 승인하다 | layout 설계, 배치 | feasible 실현 가능한 | permit 허용하다

---

3. Mr. Lowe는 어느 부서에서 근무하겠는가?

(A) 영업

(B) 시설관리

(C) 인사

(D) 회계

해설 오후 1시 33분 ~ 1시 34분 대화에서 Chris Lowe가 I'm setting up some equipment (장비를 설치하고 있어요.)라고 하자, Janice Naff가 I don't have the key to the supply closet. I was hoping to borrow yours. (물품 보관실 열쇠가 없어서요. 당신 걸 좀 빌리려고요.)라고 말한 점에서 장비 설치 업무를 담당하고 있고, 물품 보관실 열쇠를 소지하고 있다는 점에서 근무 부서가 시설관리부일 것이라고 유추할 있으므로 (B) Maintenance가 정답이다.

---

4. Mr. Lowe는 오후 1시 35분에 "물론이죠"라고 쓸 때 무엇을 의미하는가?

(A) 사무실 배치를 승인한다.

(B) Ms. Naff 대신 발표를 검토할 것이다.

(C) 어떤 일정이 실현 가능하다고 생각한다.

(D) Ms. Naff가 자신의 열쇠를 가져가도록 허용할 것이다.

해설 오후 1시 34분 ~ 1시 35분 대화에서 Janice Naff가 I don't have the key to the supply closet. I was hoping to borrow yours. (물품 보관실 열쇠가 없어서요. 당신 걸 좀 빌리려고요.)라고 하자, Chris Lowe가 Of course (물론이죠.)라고 말한 것이므로 (D) He will permit Ms. Naff to take his key.가 정답이다.

[5-6] 다음 공지사항에 관한 문제입니다.

알림:

5 Chisholm 경기장 개조 작업이 12월 6일에 시작해서 12월 22일에 완료됩니다. 이 기간 동안 경기장 자체는 몇몇 행사를 주최하지만 모든 주차 구역은 이용하실 수 없습니다. 수리 작업으로 인해 북문이 폐쇄되기 때문에 **6** 방문객 입장은 남문으로 제한됩니다.

내년에는 구내 매점들이 추가로 설치됩니다. 2층과 3층이 2월 2일부터 2월 10일까지 폐쇄됩니다. 구내 매점 공사는 계획되어 있는 경기장 개선 작업의 최종 단계입니다.

어휘 alert 알림 | host 주최하다 | entry 입장 | restrict 제한하다 | concession 구내 매점 | phase 단계

---

5. 공지사항의 목적은 무엇인가?

(A) 경기장에 대한 변경 사항을 설명하는 것

(B) 독자들에게 스포츠 대회 참가를 장려하는 것

(C) 대중에게 경기장 재개를 알리는 것

(D) 주차 요금 인상을 발표하는 것

해설 첫 번째 단락에서 Renovation work will begin at Chisholm Stadium on December 6 and finish on December 22. (Chisholm 경기장 개조 작업이 12월 6일에 시작해서 12월 22일에 완료됩니다.)라며 공지를 시작하고 있으므로 (A) To describe changes to a stadium이 정답이다.

Paraphrasing
Renovation work → changes

----

6. 방문객들은 무엇을 하도록 요구받는가?
(A) 대중교통을 이용한다
(B) 주민 회의에 참석한다
(C) 사전에 티켓을 구매한다
(D) 특정 출입구를 이용한다

해설 첫 번째 단락에서 Visitor entry will be restricted to the South Gate (방문객 입장은 남문으로 제한됩니다.)라고 말했으므로 (D) Use a specific entrance가 정답이다.

Paraphrasing
South Gate → specific entrance

[7-8] 다음 웹페이지에 관한 문제입니다.

http://www.maselov.com

7 Maselov의 목표는 아리조나 지역의 기업가들이 새로운 사업들을 시작할 때 재무에 관한 현명한 결정을 내리도록 돕는 것입니다. 훌륭한 자질을 갖춘 회계사들인 저희 직원들이 온라인에 게재되는 유익한 기사를 통해 주 세법과 환급을 청구할 수 있는 비용, 다가오는 마감기한 등에 관한 최신 정보를 제공합니다. 저희 웹사이트는 정기적으로 갱신되므로 자주 확인하셔서 더 많은 기사를 찾아보시거나 **8** 아래 기입란에 이름과 이메일 주소를 입력하셔서 주간 소식지를 구독하시기 바랍니다.

이름: **8** Daisy Wallace
이메일: daisyw@corigin.net

어휘 aid 돕다 | entrepreneur 사업가 | accountant 회계사 | latest 최신의 | claimable 청구할 수 있는 | upcoming 다가오는 | informative 유익한 | post 게시[게재]하다 | update 갱신하다 | regularly 정기적으로 | newsletter 회보, 소식지 | directory 주소록

7. 웹페이지는 주로 누구를 대상으로 작성되었는가?
(A) 신규 사업 소유주들
(B) 세금 전문가들
(C) 재무 조언가들
(D) 법인 변호사들

해설 첫 번째 줄에서 Maselov's goal is to aid Arizona entrepreneurs in making smart financial decisions when starting their new businesses. (Maselov의 목표는 아리조나 지역의 기업가들이 새로운 사업들을 시작할 때 재무에 관한 현명한 결정을 내리도록 돕는 것입니다.)라고 말했으므로 (A) New business owners가 정답이다.

8. Ms. Wallace에 관하여 알 수 있는 것은 무엇인가?
(A) 간행물을 받을 것이다.
(B) 서류를 수정해야 한다.
(C) Maselov에서 근무한다.
(D) 주소록에 이름이 추가될 것이다.

해설 지문 하단에서 enter your name and e-mail address in the boxes below to subscribe to our weekly newsletter (아래 기입란에 이름과 이메일 주소를 입력하셔서 주간 소식지를 구독하시기 바랍니다)라고 했으며, Name: Daisy Wallace (이름: Daisy Wallace)로 적혀 있으므로 (A) She will be sent a publications.이 정답이다.

Paraphrasing
weekly newsletter → publication

[9-11] 다음 안내문에 관한 문제입니다.

로스앤젤레스 대도시권 도처에 7개의 지점을 가지고 있는 Livingston 연예기획사는 모든 연령대의 사람들을 자랑스럽게 대리하며 예술적으로 재능 있는 지역 출신인들을 교육하고 홍보하는 데 헌신합니다. 차세대 배우와 음악가들을 발굴 및 육성하는 사명을 지닌 한 에이전트 그룹에 의해 만들어진 Livingston 연예기획사는 각각의 연예인 지망생들이 최고의 경력을 쌓아가도록 할 것을 약속합니다. **10** 저희 74명의 직원 전원은 이 지역에 살며 근무합니다. 그 중 상당수가 지역의 학교들에서 다양한 공연예술 교육 프로그램에 참여하고 있습니다. **11** 또한 저희의 훈련 과정의 높은 명성 덕분에 90퍼센트 이상의 할당 업무가 바로 이곳 로스앤젤레스에서 이루어집니다. **9 10** Livingston 연예기획사와 함께하신다면 당신의 미래는 반 세기 동안 운영되어 온 기획사의 관리하에 있게 됩니다.

어휘 talent agency 연예기획사 | metro 대도시권의 | represent ~의 대리를 하다 | artistically-gifted 예술적 재능이 있는 | agent (예술, 연예, 스포츠 분야의) 에이전트 | foster 육성하다 | be committed to ~에 헌신하다 | career 경력 | aspiring 장차 ~이 되려는 | performer 연예인 | reputation 명성 | process 과정, 절차 | directory 주소록 | handbook 안내책자 | be involved in ~에 개입되다, 관계되다 | performing art 공연 예술

9. 어디에서 볼 수 있는 정보이겠는가?
(A) 지역 사업체 명부에서
(B) 회사 교육 매뉴얼에서
(C) 잠재 고객들을 위한 소책자에서
(D) 연예 에이전트들을 위한 안내책자에서

해설 지문 하단에서 With the Livingston Talent Agency, your future is in the hands of an agency that has been in the business for half a century. (Livingston 연예기획사와 함께 하신다면 당신의 미래는 반 세기 동안 운영되어 온 기획사의 관리하에 있게 됩니다.)라고 하여, Livingston 연예기획사의 훈련을 받고자 하는 연예인 지망생들을 대상으로 하는 글임을 알 수 있으므로 (C) In a pamphlet for potential clients가 정답이다.

----

10. 대행사는 얼마 동안 운영되어 왔는가?

(A) For 7 years
(B) For 50 years
(C) For 74 years
(D) For 90 years

해설 지문 하단에서 With the Livingston Talent Agency, your future is in the hands of an agency that has been in the business for half a century. (Livingston 연예기획사와 함께 하신다면 당신의 미래는 반 세기 동안 운영되어 온 기획사의 관리하에 있게 됩니다.)라고 했으므로 (B) For 50 years가 정답이다.

Paraphrasing

half a century → 50 years

---

11. [1], [2], [3], [4]로 표시된 곳 중에서 다음 문장이 들어가기에 가장 적절한 곳은 어디인가?

"그 중 상당수가 지역의 학교들에서 다양한 공연예술 교육 프로그램에 참여하고 있습니다."

(A) [1]
(B) [2]
(C) [3]
(D) [4]

해설 [2] 앞 문장의 All of our 74 staff members live and work in this area. (저희 74명의 직원 전원은 이 지역에 살며 근무합니다.)와 [2] 뒷 문장의 Also, more than 90 percent of our work assignments are located right here in Los Angeles, thanks to the strong reputation of our training process. (또한 저희 훈련 과정의 높은 명성 덕분에 90퍼센트 이상의 할당 업무가 바로 이곳 로스앤젤레스에서 이루어집니다.)의 내용을 토대로 대부분의 업무가 로스앤젤레스 지역 내에서 이루어지고 있음을 강조하고 있어 주어진 문장이 이 두 문장 사이에 들어가는 것이 자연스러우므로 (B) [2]가 정답이다.

[12-14] 다음 편지에 관한 문제입니다.

8월 6일

Ms. Julia Norell, 지점장
Hotshots 커피숍
841 2번가
Woods Cross, 유타 84010

Ms. Norell께,

12 올 가을 Hotshots는 새로운 계절 음료와 상품을 위한 일련의 광고를 제작할 것입니다. 캠페인은 9월 1일에 시작되며 11월 1일까지 계속됩니다. 광고는 〈Salado Tribune〉과 〈Lago Gazette〉 같은 신문뿐만 아니라 신문사 웹사이트에도 게재될 것입니다.

13 처음에는 라디오 광고 제작을 생각했으나 촉박한 마감일정 때문에 그 옵션은 포기하기로 했습니다. 그러나 10월 하순에는 웹 상의 청중들을 위한 동영상 광고를 만들 것입니다.

14 참고하시라고 매장 전단과 포스터를 포함했습니다. 지적 사항이나 의견이 있으시다면 언제든 저에게 연락 주세요.

James McAllister, 영업담당 부사장
Hotshots 커피숍

동봉물 재중

어휘 brand new 완전히 새로운 | kick off 시작되다 | forego 포기하다 | commercial 광고 | leaflet 광고 전단 | get in touch with ~와 연락하다 | enclosure 동봉된 것

---

12. Hotshots 커피숍은 언제 신제품 광고를 시작할 것인가?

(A) 8월
(B) 9월
(C) 10월
(D) 11월

해설 첫 번째 단락에서 This fall, Hotshots will produce a series of advertisements for its brand new seasonal beverages and merchandise. The campaign kicks off September 1 and continues through November 1. (올 가을 Hotshots는 새로운 계절 음료와 상품을 위한 일련의 광고를 제작할 것입니다. 캠페인은 9월 1일에 시작되며 11월 1일까지 계속됩니다.)라고 했으므로 (B) In September가 정답이다.

Paraphrasing

kicks off → begin

---

13. 광고에 따르면 Hotshots 커피숍은 어떤 종류의 광고 없이 영업할 것인가?

(A) 신문
(B) 라디오
(C) 온라인
(D) 인쇄물

해설 두 번째 단락에서 At first, we thought about creating a radio ad, but decided to forego that option because of the tight deadline. (처음에는 라디오 광고 제작을 생각했으나 촉박한 마감 일정 때문에 그 옵션은 포기하기로 했습니다.)라고 했으므로 (B) Radio가 정답이다.

Paraphrasing

forego → do without

---

14. Mr. McAllister는 편지와 함께 무엇을 보냈는가?

(A) 홍보자료
(B) 상품 견본
(C) 영수증 원본
(D) 설문조사지

해설 세 번째 단락에서 Included are store leaflets and posters for your reference. (참고하시라고 매장 전단과 포스터를 포함했습니다.)라고 했으므로 (A) Promotional materials가 정답이다.

Paraphrasing

Included → sent with the letter, store leaflets and posters → Promotional materials

[15-17] 다음 이메일에 관한 문제입니다.

발신: staff@frostybeachcafe.com
수신: Guy Kojiki
일자: 5월 2일
제목: 여름 음료들

모두 안녕하십니까.

봄이 끝나가면서, 다가오는 여름 달들은 우리의 매출액을 늘릴 수 있는 더 많은 기회를 제공할 것입니다. **15** 그 좋은 시작으로 우리 회사 최초로 냉동 음료 대회를 개최할 것입니다. **16** 직원들은 재미있고 독창적인 레시피를 개발하는 일에 참여하게 될 것이고 그렇게 개발된 것들은 Frosty Beach Café에서 6월부터 8월까지 판매될 것입니다. 상위 3명의 우승자들은 이곳에서 도보로 5분밖에 안 되는 거리에 있는, 새로 개조된 Sandy 공연 센터에서 열리는 무료 콘서트 티켓 두 장을 직접 골라서 받을 것입니다.

참가 양식을 작성하셔서 휴게실에 있는 제출용 상자에 넣어 주십시오. **17A** 레시피들은 맛, **17D** 재료들의 저렴한 가격, **17B** 그리고 얼마나 만들기 간편한가에 따라 평가될 것입니다.

여러분의 아이디어를 기다립니다!

어휘 upcoming 다가오는, 곧 있을 | sales figures 매출액 | get off 출발하다 | competition 대회, 경기 | invent 발명하다 | unique 독특한 | recipe 조리법 | of one's choice 직접 선택해서 | renovate 개조하다 | fill out 작성하다 | entry form 참가 양식 | submission form 제출용 상자 | break room 휴게실 | evaluate 평가하다 | based on ~을 기반으로[근거로] 하여 | ingredient 재료 | ownership 소유권 | flavor 맛

15. 이메일의 목적은 무엇인가?
(A) 최근의 매출액에 대해 논의하기 위해
(B) 새로운 음료 브랜드를 홍보하기 위해
(C) 직원들의 노고에 감사하기 위해서
(D) 경연대회를 알리기 위해서

해설 첫 번째 단락에서 To get off to a good start, we will hold our very first frozen drink competition. (그 좋은 시작으로 우리 회사 최초로 냉동 음료 대회를 개최할 것입니다)라고 했으므로 (D) To announce a contest가 정답이다.

Paraphrasing
competition → contest

16. Sandy 공연 센터에 관하여 알 수 있는 것은 무엇인가?
(A) 계절별 할인을 제공한다.
(B) 봄에 소유권이 바뀌었다.
(C) 카페 가까이 있다.
(D) 유명한 예술가들이 출연한다.

해설 첫 번째 단락의 Workers will be invited to invent fun and unique recipes to be sold by Frosty Beach Café from June to August. (직원들은 재미있고 독창적인 레시피를 개발하는 일에 참여하게 될 것이고 그렇게 개발된 것들은 Frosty Beach Café에서 6

월부터 8월까지 판매될 것입니다.)에서 카페 직원들을 대상으로 한 이메일임을 알 수 있고, The top three winners will get two free tickets to a concert of their choice at the newly renovated Sandy Performance Center, just a five-minute walk away. (상위 3명의 우승자들은 이곳에서 도보로 5분밖에 안 되는 거리에 있는, 새로 개조된 Sandy 공연 센터에서 열리는 무료 콘서트 티켓 두 장을 직접 골라서 받을 것입니다.)에서 Sandy 공연 센터가 카페와 가까운 곳에 있음을 알 수 있으므로 (C) It is close to the café.가 정답이다.

Paraphrasing
just a five-minute walk away → close to

17. 좋은 제품의 요건으로 언급되지 않은 것은 무엇인가?
(A) 맛이 좋을 것
(B) 준비하기 쉬울 것
(C) 특정한 색이 있을 것
(D) 저렴한 비용의 재료일 것

해설 지문의 단서와 보기를 매칭시키면 Recipes will be evaluated based on how they taste → (A) Having a nice flavor, the low price of ingredients → (D) Having affordable ingredients, and how easy they are to make → (B) Being simple to prepare와 일치하지만 특정 색상에 대해서는 언급된 바 없으므로 (C) Being a certain color가 정답이다.

[18-21] 다음 편지에 관한 문제입니다.

4월 3일

Ravi Patel
206 Argos Circle
케이프타운, 남아프리카 공화국 7974

Mr. Patel,

18B Detrich-Barnes 법률회사의 3개월 인턴 프로그램에 합격하셨음을 알려드리게 되어 기쁩니다. 근무는 6월 1일 수요일에 시작하시게 할 계획입니다. 그러나 다른 할 일이 있으시다면 정확한 근무 시작 날짜에 관해서는 어느 정도 융통성을 보여드릴 수 있습니다. 지금 이 시점에는 아마 일정을 정확히 예측하기 어려우실 테니 날짜가 가까워 오면 다시 이것을 논의하는 게 좋겠습니다.

18A **18C** 근무는 국제법무부 상임이사 Lisa Truman의 관리 하에 의료보험에 관련된 사안을 처리하기 위한 접근법 개발을 돕도록 배정해드렸습니다. **19** **21** Ms. Truman이 최근에 〈Journal of Medical Ethics〉에서 당신의 기사를 보셨는데 매우 유익하게 여긴다고 하시더군요. 당신은 그분의 팀에 큰 자산이 될 것이라고 확신합니다.

20 동봉해드린 계약서를 살펴보시고 서명과 날짜를 기입하셔서 4월 19일까지 보내주시면 고맙겠습니다. 저희가 그것을 받으면 인사부의 Janet Foss가 연락을 드려서 교통과 여름 동안의 임시 숙소뿐만 아니라 공식 이메일 계정 설정에 관한 추가 정보를 제공해드릴 것입니다.

진심을 담아,

123

José Luciano
인사부장
Detrich-Barnes 법률회사

동봉 문서 재중

어휘 **inform** 알리다 | **obligation** 의무, 책무 | **somewhat** 어느
정도 | **revisit** 다시 논의하다 | **assign** 배정하다 | **aid** 돕다 |
approach 접근법 | **pursue a matter** 어떤 사안을 처리하
다 | **informative** 유익한 | **look over** 살펴보다 | **enclose**
동봉하다 | **lodging** 임시 숙소 | **enclosure** 동봉된 것 | **set
up** (시간, 약속, 규칙 등을) 정하다 | **asset** 자산

---

18. Mr. Patel의 인턴 과정의 어떤 측면이 언급되지 않았는가?
(A) 배정될 프로젝트
(B) 근무 기간
(C) 매니저의 이름
(D) 받게 될 급여

해설 지문의 단서와 보기를 매칭시키면, you have been accepted to
Detrich-Barnes Law Firm's 3-month internship program.
(Detrich-Barnes 법률회사의 3개월 인턴 프로그램에 합격하셨습니
다.) → (B) His work period. We have assigned you to work
under the management of Lisa Truman (근무는 Lisa Truman
의 관리 하에 하도록 배정해드렸습니다) → (C) His manager's
name, to aid in developing approaches to pursue matters
related to medical insurance (의료보험에 관련된 사안을 처리
하기 위한 접근법 개발을 돕도록) → (A) The project he will be
assigned to와 일치하지만, 받게 될 급여에 대해서는 언급된 바 없으
므로 (D) The pay he will receive가 정답이다.

---

19. 편지는 Ms. Truman에 관하여 무엇을 보여주고 있는가?
(A) Mr. Patel의 면접을 실시했다.
(B) Mr. Patel의 기사를 읽었다.
(C) Mr. Luciano의 직원들을 감독한다.
(D) 잘 알려진 변호사이다.

해설 두 번째 단락에서 Ms. Truman recently told me that she
noticed your story in the *Journal of Medical Ethics* and that
she found it very informative. (Ms. Truman이 최근에 〈Journal
of Medical Ethics〉에서 당신의 기사를 보셨는데 매우 유익하게 여긴
다고 하시더군요.)라고 했으므로 (B) She read Mr. Patel's article.
이 정답이다.

Paraphrasing

noticed your story in the Journal → read Mr. Patel's article

---

20. Mr. Patel은 이후에 무엇을 하겠는가?
(A) 근무 시작 날짜를 논의한다
(B) Ms. Truman과 만날 시간을 정한다
(C) 어떤 이메일 계정에 로그온한다
(D) Mr. Luciano에게 서류를 돌려보낸다

해설 세 번째 단락에서 We would appreciate it if you could look

over the enclosed contract and send it back, signed and
dated, by 19 April. (동봉해드린 계약서를 살펴보시고 서명과 날짜
를 기입하셔서 4월 19일까지 보내주시면 고맙겠습니다.)라고 했으므로
(D) Return some paperwork to Mr. Luciano가 정답이다.

Paraphrasing

send back → Return, contract → paperwork

---

21. [1], [2], [3], [4]로 표시된 곳 중에서 다음 문장이 들어가기에 가장 적절
한 곳은 어디인가?

"당신은 그분의 팀에 큰 자산이 될 것이라고 확신합니다."

(A) [1]
(B) [2]
(C) [3]
(D) [4]

해설 두 번째 단락에서 Ms. Truman recently told me that she
noticed your story in the *Journal of Medical Ethics* and that
she found it very informative. (Ms. Truman이 최근에 〈Journal
of Medical Ethics〉에서 당신의 기사를 보셨는데 매우 유익하게 여
긴다고 하시더군요.)라고 하여, Mr. Patel을 칭찬하는 내용이어서 주
어진 문장이 이어지기에 자연스러우므로 (C) [3]이 정답이다.

[22-25] 다음 이메일에 관한 문제입니다.

발신: info@cariboutrain.com
수신: mhermann@ubermail.co.ca
제목: 가방
날짜: 9월 2일

Ms. Hermann께,

이메일 보내주셔서 고맙습니다. **23** 보내주신 백팩에 대한 설명과 맞
아 떨어지는 것이 다수 있지만 당신이 주인임을 식별시켜주는 꼬리
표가 있는 것은 없습니다. 5129 W. Peaberry 가에 들르셔서 직접
찾아보시기를 요청하는 바입니다.

24 탑승하셨던 기차가 역에서 출발한 시간 혹은 가급적이면 탑승권
의 승객 보관 부분을 제시해주셔야 한다는 점 유의하시기 바랍니다.

저희 고객 서비스 데스크는 휴무 없이 매일 오전 7부터 오후 5시까
지 근무합니다. **25** 너무 늦게 오지 않으시기 바랍니다. 안타깝지만
저희 승무원들이 수거해오는 물건의 양이 많기 때문에 2주 이상 주
인이 나타나지 않는 것들은 모두 기부합니다.

진심을 담아.

Andrew Bao
22 Caribou 역

어휘 **multiple** 다수의 | **fit** 맞다, 적합하다 | **description** 설명 |
tag 꼬리표 | **identify** ~의 신원을 확인하다 | **drop by** ~에
들르다 | **locate** ~의 정확한 위치를 찾아내다 | **aware** 알고 있
는 | **preferably** 가급적이면 | **ticket stub** 표의 승객 보관 부
분 | **volume** 양 | **conductor** 승무원 | **go unclaimed** 주
인이 나타나지 않다 | **urge** 권고하다 | **billing statement** 청
구 내역서

22. Mr. Bao는 어디에서 근무하는가?

    (A) 우체국에서

    (B) 여행사에서

    (C) 가방 가게에서

    (D) 교통 기관에서

해설　지문 하단의 발신자, Andrew Bao의 근무지가 Caribou Train Station (Caribou 역)으로 되어 있으므로 (D) In a transportation center가 정답이다.

Paraphrasing

train station → transportation center

··

23. Ms. Hermann은 무엇에 관하여 문의했겠는가?

    (A) 예약 선택사항

    (B) 분실된 소지품

    (C) 여행 준비

    (D) 할인권

해설　첫 번째 단락에서 We have multiple backpacks that fit the description of the one that you gave, but none of them have a tag that identifies you as the owner. (보내주신 백팩에 대한 설명과 맞아 떨어지는 것이 다수 있지만 당신이 주인임을 식별시켜주는 꼬리표가 있는 것은 없습니다.)라고 했으므로 (B) Missing belongings가 정답

Paraphrasing

backpack → belongings

··

24. Ms. Hermann은 무엇을 제시해야 하는가?

    (A) 집주소

    (B) 출발 정보

    (C) 당초 목적지

    (D) 성명

해설　두 번째 단락에서 we will need you to provide either the time your train left the station (탑승하셨던 기차가 역에서 출발한 시간을 알려주셔야 합니다)라고 했으므로 (B) Her departure information이 정답이다.

Paraphrasing

the time your train left the station → departure information

··

25. Ms. Hermann은 무엇을 하도록 권고받는가?

    (A) 청구 내역서를 검토한다

    (B) 웹사이트를 확인한다

    (C) 양식에 서명한다

    (D) 빨리 사무실에 들른다

해설　세 번째 단락에서 Don't wait too long. Unfortunately, due to the large volume of items picked up by our conductors, we donate all items that go unclaimed for more than two weeks. (너무 늦게 오지 않으시기 바랍니다. 안타깝지만 저희 승무원들이 수거해오는 물건의 양이 많기 때문에 2주 이상 주인이 나타나지 않는 것들은 모두 기부합니다.)라고 했으므로 (D) Stop by an office soon이 정답이다.

[26-29] 다음 온라인 채팅 대화문에 관한 문제입니다.

Miles Higginson [오전 8:42]
㉖ 동료 여행기자 여러분, 좀 도와주시겠어요? Clipper 섬에 출장을 가서 Palm Town과 Golden Point, Tin Ridge을 둘러보게 됐어요.

Evan Paulson [오전 8:52]
제 사촌이 최근에 Clipper 섬을 방문했어요. 해변이 정말 장관이라고 하던데요.

Miles Higginson [오전 8:54]
다들 그렇게 말하더라고요. 섬이 아주 작기 때문에 돌아다니기가 정말 쉽다는 말도 들었어요. 그냥 자전거를 이용하면 될까요? 아니면 거기 있는 동안 렌터카를 타고 다녀야 할까요?

Lexi Sardi [오전 9:07]
저는 거기 갔을 때 자전거를 타고 다녀서 연료비를 많이 절약했어요. 모든 길마다 자전거 도로가 있고요. 자전거는 정부에서 무료로 제공해줘요.

Miles Higginson [오전 9:13]
㉘ Lexi, Clipper 섬에서는 자전거를 찾기가 쉬운가요?

Evan Paulson [오전 9:26]
그래도 섬의 더 외진 지역까지 방문하기로 했다면 차를 렌트하는 게 유용할 거예요.

Lexi Sardi [오전 9:31]
㉘ 자전거는 어느 곳에나 있어요. 자전거 정류장은 대부분의 큰 도로에서 700미터마다 있고요.

Naomi Christensen [오전 9:35]
㉗ 하지만 보도 장비를 많이 가지고 다니실 거라면 자전거 타는 게 정말 힘들 수 있어요.

Miles Higginson [오전 9:37]
㉘ 그거 정말 편리하네요. 이곳 도시 계획가들은 Clipper 섬 도시 계획가들로부터 몇 가지는 좀 배웠으면 좋겠어요. ㉗ 아, 그리고 Naomi, 그 점 잘 지적해줬어요. 결정했어요; 차를 임대할래요.

Naomi Christensen [오전 9:59]
㉙ 공항에 안내소를 둔 회사들이 몇 군데 있는데, 거기서 시내에서는 받을 수 없는 혜택을 제공해요. 먼저 거기부터 꼭 확인해보세요.

Miles Higginson [오전 10:06]
모두들 조언 고마워요.

어휘　on assignment 임무를 맡아 | spectacular 장관을 이루는 | get around 돌아다니다 | free of charge 무료로 | remote 먼, 외진 | gear 장비 | city planner 도시 계획가 | counterpart (다른 곳에서 동일한 지위를 갖는) 상대 | settle 해결하다, 결정하다 | kiosk 간이 안내소, 매점 | deal 거래 조건 | rental agency 임대소 | reside 거주하다 | unreliable 신뢰할 수 없는 | information kiosk 간이 안내소

---

26. Mr. Higginson은 누구와 이야기를 나누고 있었겠는가?

    (A) 구경을 시켜줄 사람들

    (B) 임대업소에서 근무하는 사람들

    (C) Clipper 섬에 거주하는 사람들

    (D) 업무 차 여행을 다니는 사람들

오전 8시 42분, Miles Higginson의 메시지에서 Fellow travel reporters (동료 여행기자 여러분)이라고 했으므로 (D) People who travel for work가 정답이다.

Visitors can learn about special promotions there가 정답이다.

Paraphrasing

deals you can't get in the city → special promotions

---

27. Mr. Higginson는 왜 자동차를 임대하기로 결정했는가?

(A) 많은 장비를 가지고 다닐 것이기 때문에

(B) 자전거 타는 법을 모르기 때문에

(C) 여행지에 자전거 도로가 없기 때문에

(D) 대중교통을 신뢰할 수 없기 때문에

해설 오전 9시 35분 ~ 9시 37분 대화에서 Naomi Christensen이 But if you're carrying around a lot of reporting gear, riding a bike can be a real challenge. (하지만 보도 장비를 많이 가지고 다니실 거라면 자전거 타는 게 정말 힘들 수 있어요.)라고 하자, Miles Higginson이 Oh, and Naomi, I'm glad you pointed that out. That settles it; I'll rent. (아, 그리고 Naomi, 그 점 잘 지적해줬어요. 결정했어요; 차를 임대할래요.)라고 하여 Ms. Christensen의 제안을 듣고 결정한 것이므로 (A) Because he will have a lot of equipment가 정답이다.

Paraphrasing

reporting gear → equipment

---

28. 오전 9시 37분에 Mr. Higginson이 "이곳 도시 계획가들은 Clipper 섬 도시 계획가들로부터 몇 가지는 좀 배웠으면 좋겠어요."라고 할 때 그가 의미한 것은 무엇인가?

(A) 자신의 도시의 자전거 임대는 비싸다.

(B) 자신의 도시의 자전거 도로는 형편없이 설계되었다.

(C) 자신의 도시의 자전거 정류장들은 서로 너무 멀리 떨어진 곳에 위치해 있다.

(D) 자신의 도시의 자전거들은 낡았다.

해설 오전 9시 31분 ~ 9시 37분 대화에서 Lexi Sardi가 They're everywhere. Bicycle stations are located every 700m on most large streets. (자전거는 어느 곳에나 있어요. 자전거 정류장은 대부분의 큰 도로에서 700미터마다 있고요.)라고 한 말에 대해, Miles Higginson이 That's really convenient. Our city planners could learn a few things from their Clipper Island counterparts. (그거 정말 편리하네요. 이곳 도시 계획가들은 Clipper 섬 도시 계획가들로부터 몇 가지는 좀 배웠으면 좋겠어요.)라고 대답한 것이므로 (C) The bicycles stations in his town are located too far apart.가 정답이다.

---

29. Ms. Christensen이 공항에 관하여 시사한 것은 무엇인가?

(A) 시내까지 가는 값싼 셔틀버스를 제공한다.

(B) 방문객들이 특별 판촉행사에 관하여 알아볼 수 있다.

(C) 출구 근처에 관광객들을 위한 간이 안내소가 있다.

(D) 자동차를 임대할 수 있다.

해설 오전 9시 59분, Naomi Christensen의 메시지에서 There are a few companies with kiosks at the airport that offer deals you can't get in the city. (공항에 안내소를 둔 회사들이 몇 군데 있는데, 거기서 시내에서는 받을 수 없는 혜택을 제공해요.)라고 했으므로 (B)

[30-34] 다음 이메일과 광고에 관한 문제입니다.

발신: karia@golakes.co.uk
수신: jleitner@golakes.co.uk
날짜: 12월 6일
주제: 세미나
첨부파일: 안내책자.txt

Ms. Leitner께,

32 참가하고자 하는 세미나의 안내책자를 첨부했습니다. 이번 행사에서 배우게 될 기법들은 저의 중요한 고민거리들을 해결하는 데 도움을 줄 것입니다.

우리 회사의 관광 패키지 상품들은 지역 최고에 속하지만 안내책자에 포함되어 있는 사진들이 반드시 이러한 점을 보여주는 것 같지는 않습니다. **31** 사실 우리 고객들이 우리의 관광 상품보다 경쟁업체의 것을 선택하는 주된 이유로 든 것이 경쟁 관광 상품의 홍보용 이미지가 더 매력적이었다는 점입니다. **32** 제 생각에는 전문적으로 보이는 사진을 찍는 법을 배운다면 관광 상품 판매량을 개선하고 더 넓은 고객층을 끌어들이게 될 것입니다.

33 제 계산에 근거하여 저의 총 참가 비용은 690파운드(개인 등록비와 장비 임대료 300파운드 및 왕복 비행편 180파운드, 식사를 포함한 숙박 요금을 충당하기 위한 210파운드)입니다. **30** 참가를 허가해주실 것인지 알려주시기 바랍니다. 개인적으로 저희 사업에 큰 도움이 될 것이라고 생각합니다.

고맙습니다.

32 Kylie Aria

어휘 **address** (일, 문제 따위)에 본격적으로 착수하다, 대처하다 | **concern** 관심사 | **reflect** 반영하다 | **principal** 주요한 | **cite** (이유, 예를) 들다[끌어 대다] | **competitor** 경쟁업체 | **clientele** (어떤 기관, 상점 등의) 모든 의뢰인들[고객들] | **room and board** 식사를 포함한 숙박 요금 | **be of benefit to ~** 에게 도움이 되다, 유익하다

---

32 기술 강좌: 좋은 사진작가가 되기까지의 길잡이

Wood Green 스튜디오
79 Morlee 가
Wood Green, 런던

1월 31일 – 2월 2일
오전 10시 – 오후 5시

32 34 이번 세미나의 목표는 참가자들에게 초급과 중급 수준의 사진 기법을 재미있고 따뜻한 강의실 환경에서 알려주는 것입니다. 사진 기법을 배워 회사의 기존 이미지 포트폴리오를 향상시키고 싶어 하시든 단순히 더 좋은 사진작가가 되고 싶어 하시든 이 세미나는 유용할 것입니다.

이번 강좌는 15년 이상의 풍경 및 스튜디오 사진 경력의 프로 사진 작가 **34** Lyle Pershings가 지도합니다. 그는 유명인들의 인물 사진을 촬영해왔으며, 주요 광고주들과 함께 작업했고, 이곳 런던에서 Westshore 미술관 전시회도 열었습니다.

Wood Green 스튜디오에서는 모든 강좌 참가자가 자격이 있는 강사로부터의 개인 지도와 피드백 및 고품질의 교과서, 온라인으로 언제든 할 수 있는 추가 연습 기회를 받습니다.

33 개인 참가자에게는 등록과 필요 용품들의 비용으로 370파운드가 부과됩니다. 그러나 3인 이상의 단체는 1인당 35파운드의 할인을 받을 수 있습니다. 추가 정보를 원하신다면 www.woodgreenstudio. co.uk를 방문해 주세요.

어휘 instruct 가르치다 | intermediate 중급의 | supportive 따뜻하게 대하는 | existing 기존의 | landscape 풍경 | portrait 인물 사진 | guidance 지도[안내] | supplies 용품 | charge (요금을) 부과하다 | eligible 자격이 있는 | address (일, 문제 따위)에 본격적으로 착수하다, 대처하다 | funding 자금 제공, 재정 지원

30. 이메일의 목적은 무엇인가?
(A) 수업을 홍보하려고
(B) 출장의 문제를 처리하려고
(C) 자금 지원을 요구하려고
(D) 신규 서비스를 제안하려고

해설 Ms. Aria가 Ms. Leitner에게 보낸 첫 번째 지문(이메일), 세 번째 단락에서 Based on my calculations, the total cost of my participation would be £690 (£300 for the individual registration fee and equipment rental, £180 for the round-trip flight, and £210 to cover room and board). Please let me know if you will permit me to attend. I personally think that it would be of great benefit to our business. (제 계산에 근거하여 저의 총 참가 비용은 690파운드(개인 등록비와 장비 임대료 300파운드 및 왕복 비행편 180파운드, 식사를 포함한 숙박 요금을 충당하기 위한 210파운드)입니다. 참가를 허가해주실 것인지 알려주시기 바랍니다. 개인적으로 저희 사업에 큰 도움이 될 것이라고 생각합니다.)라고 했으므로 (C) To ask for funding이 정답이다.

31. 이메일 두 번째 단락, 두 번째 줄의 단어 "principal"과 의미상 가장 가까운 것은
(A) 기본적인
(B) 주요한
(C) 처음의
(D) 필요한

해설 Ms. Aria가 Ms. Leitner에게 보낸 첫 번째 지문(이메일), 두 번째 단락의 In fact, the principal reason cited by our customers for choosing a competitor's tour over one of ours is that the promotional images of the competing tour were more attractive. (사실 우리 고객들이 우리의 관광 상품보다 경쟁업체의 것을 선택하는 주된 이유로 든 것이 경쟁 관광 상품의 홍보용 이미지가

더 매력적이었다는 점입니다.)에서 principal은 주요한, 주된'이라는 의미로 쓰였으므로 비슷한 의미를 갖는 (B) top이 정답이다.

32. Ms. Aria에 관하여 알 수 있는 것은 무엇인가?
(A) 런던을 방문하고 싶어 한다.
(B) 최근에 안내책자를 디자인했다.
(C) 12월에 투어를 인솔할 것이다.
(D) 대학교에서 수업을 가르친다.

해설 Ms. Aria가 Ms. Leitner에게 보낸 첫 번째 지문(이메일), 첫 번째 단락에서 Attached to this e-mail is a brochure for a seminar that I would like to attend. (참가하고자 하는 세미나의 안내책자를 첨부했습니다.), 세 번째 단락에서 By learning to take professional-looking pictures, I think that I will improve tour sales and draw a broader clientele. (제 생각에는 전문적으로 보이는 사진을 찍는 법을 배운다면 관광 상품 판매량을 개선하고 더 넓은 고객층을 끌어들이게 될 것입니다.)라고 했는데, 두 번째 지문[광고]의 Skills Course: Guide to Being a Great Photographer/ Wood Green Studio/79 Morlee St., Wood Green, London (기술 강좌: 좋은 사진작가가 되기까지의 길잡이, Wood Green 스튜디오, 79 Morlee 가, Wood Green, 런던)과 This seminar is intended to instruct participants in beginner-and intermediate-level photography skills in a fun, supportive classroom environment. (이번 세미나의 목표는 참가자들에게 초급과 중급 수준의 사진 기법을 재미있고 따뜻한 강의실 환경에서 알려주는 것입니다.)라고 하여 강의 장소가 London임을 알 수 있으므로 (A) She would like to visit London.이 정답이다.

33. Ms. Aria가 수업에 관하여 오해한 것은 무엇인가?
(A) 장소
(B) 주제
(C) 시간
(D) 비용

해설 Ms. Aria가 Ms. Leitner에게 보낸 첫 번째 지문(이메일), 세 번째 단락에서 Based on my calculations, the total cost of my participation would be £690 (£300 for the individual registration fee and equipment rental, £180 for the round-trip flight, and £210 to cover room and board) (제 계산에 근거하여 저의 총 참가 비용은 690파운드(개인 등록비와 장비 임대료 300 파운드와 왕복 비행편 180파운드, 식사를 포함한 숙박 요금을 충당하기 위한 210파운드)입니다)라고 했는데, 두 번째 지문(광고)에서 A fee of £370 for registration and the necessary supplies will be charged for an individual applicant. (개인 참가자에게는 등록과 필요 용품들의 비용으로 370파운드가 부과됩니다.)라고 되어 있으므로 (D) The cost가 정답이다.

Paraphrasing
equipment rental → necessary supplies

34. Mr. Pershings에 관하여 알 수 있는 것은 무엇인가?

    (A) 세미나 참가자들을 가르친다.

    (B) Wood Green 스튜디오를 소유하고 있다.

    (C) 여행사들에게 이미지를 제공한다.

    (D) 현재 Westshore 미술관에서 근무한다.

해설 두 번째 지문(광고)에서 This seminar is intended to instruct participants in beginner-and intermediate-level photography skills in a fun, supportive classroom environment. (이번 세미나의 목표는 참가자들에게 초급과 중급 수준의 사진 기법을 재미있고 따뜻한 강의실 환경에서 알려주는 것입니다.), This course will be led by Lyle Pershings, (이번 강좌는 Lyle Pershings가 지도합니다.)라고 했으므로 (A) He teaches seminar attendees.가 정답이다.

[35-39] 다음 두 이메일에 관한 문제입니다.

수신: Alan Turner 〈aturner@variant.com〉
발신: Juliet Miao 〈julietm@variant.com〉
날짜: 5월 17일
제목: 잠깐만 읽어주세요

Mr. Turner께,

35 올 여름 Variant 전기 관리직을 위한 리더십 교육 수련회에 참가하도록 선발해주셔서 정말 기쁩니다. 현장 엔지니어로서의 근무는 멋진 경험이었으며 교육이 끝난 후에는 관리자로 채용되기를 바랍니다.

그러나 한 가지 문제가 있습니다. **36** **38** 〈팀워크를 통한 조직적 책임〉이라는 제목의 5주 과정의 야간 수업을 듣고 있는데 6월 21일 화요일에 종강합니다. 수련회는 6월 20일 월요일에 시작하기 때문에 첫 이틀은 결석해야 할 것 같습니다. 수련회에 수요일 오전에 도착해도 괜찮을까요? **36** 이번 수업이 제가 더 유능한 관리자가 되도록 도움을 줄 것이라고 생각하는데 교육에도 참가할 수 있기를 진심으로 바랍니다.

시간 내주셔서 고맙습니다.

진심을 담아,

Juliet Miao

어휘 note 주의, 주목 | retreat 수련회 | on-site 현장의 | issue 문제 | entitle 제목을 붙이다 | organizational 조직의 | conclude 끝나다 | sincerely 진심으로

수신: Juliet Miao 〈julietm@variant.com〉
발신: Alan Turner 〈aturner@variant.com〉
날짜: 5월 7일
제목: 회신: 잠깐만 읽어주세요

Ms. Miao께,

연락 주셔서 고맙습니다. **36** 당신의 수업은 확실히 상급직에서 유용할 것 같군요. **37** 기쁜 소식이 있는데, 현재 우리의 인력 수급의 필요 때문에 인사부가 일주일 과정의 교육 일정을 단 한번이 아닌 두 번 잡아 놓았습니다. **38** 6월 21일 교육 이후에 6월 28일에 시작하는 게 있습니다. 이것이 당신에게 있을 수도 있는 일정상의 문제를 해결해줄 겁니다.

39 두 번의 교육 수련회가 모두 끝나고 나면 어느 지원자가 관리직을 위한 정식 면접 단계에 진출할지 결정할 겁니다. 이 결정은 7월 31일까지 내려질 것이며 선발된 지원자는 8월 15일에 승진합니다.

내선 번호 512로 제 비서에게 연락해서 일정을 확정하세요.

진심을 담아,

Alan Turner

어휘 reach out to ~에게 연락하다 | staffing 직원 채용 | resolve 해결하다 | assistant 비서 | extension 내선 번호 | finalize 마무리하다 | flexibility 유연성, 융통성 | certification 증명서 | be related to ~와 관계가 있다 | instruct 가르치다 | obtain 획득하다 | diploma 졸업장, 수료증 | gathering 모임

---

35. 첫 이메일의 목적은 무엇인가?

    (A) 경영학 수업의 완료를 발표하는 것

    (B) 대학교에 일정상의 유연성을 요구하는 것

    (C) 교육 모임 초대를 수락하는 것

    (D) 증명서를 받았음을 확인시켜주는 것

해설 Ms. Miao가 Mr. Turner에게 쓴 첫 번째 지문(이메일), 첫 번째 단락에서 I am pleased that you selected me to participate in this summer's leadership training retreat for management positions at Variant Electric. (올 여름 Variant 전기 관리직을 위한 리더십 교육 수련회에 참가하도록 선발해주셔서 정말 기쁩니다.)라고 했으므로 (C) To accept an invitation for a training session이 정답이다.

---

36. 〈팀워크를 통한 조직적 책임〉 수업에 관하여 알 수 있는 것은 무엇인가?

    (A) 매니저 업무에 연관되어 있다.

    (B) 정규 직원들에게 온라인으로 제공된다.

    (C) Mr. Turner가 강사를 맡는다.

    (D) 수료증 취득에 필수이다.

해설 Ms. Miao가 Mr. Turner에게 쓴 첫 번째 지문(이메일), 두 번째 단락에서 I am taking a five-week evening class entitled Organizational Responsibility through Teamwork (〈팀워크를 통한 조직적 책임〉이라는 제목의 5주 과정의 야간 수업을 듣고 있

습니다). I feel that this class will help me become a more effective manager (이번 수업이 제가 더 유능한 관리자가 되도록 도움을 줄 것이라고 생각합니다)라고 했는데, Mr. Turner가 Ms. Miao에게 쓴 두 번째 지문(이메일), 첫 번째 단락에서 Your class certainly sounds like it will be helpful in upper-level positions. (당신의 수업은 확실히 상급직에서 유용할 것 같군요.)라고 하여 Ms. Miao가 듣고 있는 〈팀워크를 통한 조직적 책임〉이 매니저를 대상으로 한 수업임을 알 수 있으므로 (A) It is related to the job of a manager.가 정답이다.

37. 1회의 교육 기간은 얼마인가?
(A) 1주
(B) 2주
(C) 1개월
(D) 2개월

해설 Mr. Turner가 Ms. Miao에게 쓴 두 번째 지문(이메일), 첫 번째 단락에서 Human Resources has scheduled two week-long training sessions instead of just one. (인사부가 일주일 과정의 교육 일정을 단 한번이 아닌 두 번 잡아 놓았습니다.)라고 했으므로 (A) One week가 정답이다.

38. Ms. Miao는 Variant 전기의 모임에 언제 참여하겠는가?
(A) 6월 20일
(B) 6월 21일
(C) 6월 28일
(D) 7월 31일

해설 Ms. Miao가 Mr. Turner에게 쓴 첫 번째 지문(이메일), 두 번째 단락에서 I am taking a five-week evening class entitled Organizational Responsibility through Teamwork which concludes on Tuesday, June 21. Since the retreat begins on Monday, June 20, I would have to miss the first two days. (〈팀워크를 통한 조직적 책임〉이라는 제목의 5주 과정의 야간 수업을 듣고 있는데 6월 21일 화요일에 종강합니다. 수련회는 6월 20일 월요일에 시작하기 때문에 첫 이틀은 결석해야 할 것 같습니다.)라고 했는데, Mr. Turner가 Ms. Miao에게 쓴 두 번째 지문(이메일), 첫 번째 단락에서 The June 21 training will be followed by one beginning June 28. This should resolve any scheduling issue you might have had. (6월 21일 교육 이후에 6월 28일에 시작하는 게 있습니다. 이것이 당신에게 있을 수도 있는 일정상의 문제를 해결해줄 겁니다.)라고 했으므로 Ms. Miao가 참여할 날짜가 6월 28일임을 알 수 있으므로 (C) On June 28이 정답이다.

39. 두 번째 이메일에 따르면 8월 15일에는 무슨 일이 있을 것인가?
(A) 일부 직원들이 새 역할을 부여받는다.
(B) 매니저들이 사업상 회의에 참석한다.
(C) 새 리더십 수업이 시작된다.
(D) 교육 워크숍이 끝난다.

해설 Mr. Turner가 Ms. Miao에게 쓴 두 번째 지문(이메일), 두 번째 단락에서 Once both training retreats have concluded, ~ and selected candidates will be promoted on August 15. (두 번

의 교육 수련회가 모두 끝나고 나면 어느 지원자가 관리직을 위한 정식 면접 단계에 진출할지 결정할 겁니다. 이 결정은 7월 31일까지 내려질 것이며 선발된 지원자는 8월 15일에 승진합니다.)라고 했으므로 (A) Some employees will have new roles. 가 정답이다.

Paraphrasing

selected candidates will be promoted → Some employees will have new roles.

[40-44] 다음 웹사이트와 이메일, 설문지에 관한 문제입니다.

https://pcg.com/yearlyexpo

[학회 홈] [**박람회 안내**] [연사들] [등록] [회원]

제7회 연례 전문 제과업자 세계 박람회가 2월 16일부터 19일까지 부에노스아이레스에서 열릴 예정입니다.

다국적 기업이나 신생 기업이나 할 것 없이 사탕 제조 분야에서 업계 동향과 혁신적인 기술을 배울 기회를 갖기 위해 연례 전문 제과업자 세계 박람회(PCG)에 참여합니다. **43** 기조 연설자 Kayla de Silva와 함께 아르헨티나에서 열리는 올해의 모임에 참가하세요. Jupiter Foods CEO인 Ms. de Silva는 사탕 제조 기술의 가장 최신 변화에 대해 얘기할 것입니다. 또한 박람회 동안 행사에서 사탕 산업의 전문가들인 Gabe Luciano, Nikki Mendoza, Ji-won Song, 그리고 John Kimeli이 강연을 할 것입니다. 위의 '연사들' 탭을 클릭하여 모든 연설자들과 워크숍에 대해 자세히 알아보세요.

올해 박람회는 Ambassador Inn 에서 열립니다. **40** 일부 객실은 단독으로 PCG 회원만을 위해 특별 할인 요금으로 배정되었습니다. 방을 예약하실 때, 회원 아이디 번호와 프로모션 코드 PCG7를 입력하세요.

PCG 회원들 신청은 12월 15일부터 가능하고, 비회원의 신청이 가능한 시점인 1월 15일부터는 요금이 인상됩니다. 그러니 오늘 위의 등록 탭을 클릭하여 신청해주세요.

어휘 **yearly** 1년에 한 번씩 있는 | **professional** 전문적인 | **confectioner** 사탕이나 초콜릿을 만드는 사람, 제과업자 | **global** 세계적인 | **expo** 박람회 | **multinational** 다국적의 | **corporation** (큰 규모의) 기업 | **start-up** 스타트업 회사, 신생 벤처기업 | **alike** (서로) 유사하게, 마찬가지로 | **opportunity** 기회 | **industry** 산업 | **trend** 추세, 트렌드 | **innovation** 혁신 | **gathering** 모임 | **keynote speaker** 기조 연설자 | **manufacturing** 제조(업) | **technique** 기법, 공법 | **expert** 전문가 | **click** (마우스 등을) 클릭하다, 누르다 | **set aside** ~을 한쪽으로 치워 놓다, 챙겨 두다 | **exclusively** 독점적으로 | **rate** 요금, 요율 | **membership** 회원권, 회원 자격 | **promo** 홍보용의 | **registration** 등록 | **admission** 입장, 입학 | **sign up** 등록하다, 가입하다

수신: Nikki Mendoza 〈nmendoza@prochocolatier.co.ca〉
발신: Milo d'Antoni 〈mdantoni@pcg.com〉
제목: 정보
날짜: 2월 22일
첨부: 답변.doc

Ms. Mendoza께,

PCG 박람회에 참석하기 위해 멀리 아르헨티나까지 비행기를 타고 와주셔서 감사합니다. **44** 직접 만나 뵙게 되어 영광스럽게 생각하며, 하드캔디를 만드는 법에 관한 귀하의 멋진 발표에 다시 한번 감사드리고 싶습니다. **41** 참석자 모두가 새롭고 흥미로운 맛을 만들어 내는 것이 얼마나 쉬운지에 대해 잘 알게 되었습니다. 이 메일에는 Mr. Randy Fischer가 제공한 응답 양식이 포함되어 있으며, 귀하의 설명회에 대한 참석자들의 의견을 보여주고 있습니다.

안부를 전하며,

Milo d'Antoni
PCG 행사 위원회 의장

어휘 attachment 첨부(파일) | response 응답, 답변 | fly 비행하다 | present 발표하다 | honor 영광 | hard 단단한, 딱딱한 | in attendance 참석한 | appreciate 진가를 알게 되다 | representative of ~을 대표하는 | attendee 참석자 | review 평가, 검토 | session (미팅 등을 하기 위한) 시간[기간], 모임

전문 제과업자 세계 박람회 참가자 설문지

	★★★★	★★★	★★	★
발표	X			
구성			X	
장소	X			
식사	X			

기타 의견:
박람회에 찾아가는 것은 꽤 정신이 없었습니다. 비록 12월 초에 등록을 했지만, 제 여행 정보를 매우 늦게 받는 바람에 공항에 도착해서 행사장까지 가는 방법에 대해 혼란스러웠습니다. **43** 저는 이것 때문에 첫날 아침의 기조 연설과 행사들에 참석할 수 없었습니다. 그러나 제가 볼 수 있었던 다른 발표들은 훌륭했습니다. **44** 특히, 저는 Tutti's Hard Candy의 소유주가 한 발표가 좋았습니다. 저는 배운 그 기술들을 제 가게에서 사용할 계획입니다.

Randy Fischer

어휘 comment 언급, 의견, 논평 | get to ~에 도착하다 | hectic 정신 없이 바쁜 | at the last minute 임박해서 | confusion 혼란 | in particular 특히 | accommodation 숙박, 숙소 | register 등록하다 | be open to ~에게 개방[공개]되다 | venue 행사장 | input 의견, 조언, 입력 | in time 제시간에

---

40. 박람회에 관하여 알 수 있는 것은 무엇인가?
(A) 일부 참가자들은 할인된 요금으로 숙박비를 낼 것이다.
(B) PCG회원들은 1월 15일 전에 신청해야 한다.
(C) 사탕 제조업체들만 참가가 가능하다.
(D) 이전에 부에노스아이레스에서 개최된 적이 있다.

해설 첫 번째 지문(웹사이트), 세 번째 단락에서 Some rooms have been set aside exclusively for PCG members at special rates (일부 객실은 단독으로 PCG(= Professional Confectioners' Global Expo) 회원만을 위해 특별 할인 요금으로 배정되었습니다.)라고 했으므로 (A) Some participants will pay a reduced rate for accommodations. 가 정답이다.

Paraphrasing
special rate → reduced rate / rooms → accommodations

---

41. 이메일의 목적은 무엇인가?
(A) 발표 제안서를 제출하려고
(B) 행사장 장소에 대해 문의하려고
(C) 설명회에 대한 의견을 주려고
(D) 설문의 응답을 요청하려고

해설 Milo d'Antoni가 Ms. Mendoza에게 보낸 두 번째 지문(이메일), 세 번째 줄에서 Everyone in attendance left with an appreciation for how easy it can be to make new and interesting tastes. Included with this e-mail is a response form given by Mr. Randy Fischer, and is representative of the attendees' reviews of your session. (참석자 모두가 새롭고 흥미로운 맛을 만들어 내는 것이 얼마나 쉬운지에 대해 잘 알게 되었습니다. 이 메일에는 Mr. Randy Fischer가 제공한 응답 양식이 포함되어 있으며, 귀하의 설명회에 대한 참석자들의 의견을 보여주고 있습니다.)라고 했으므로 (C) To give input on a session가 정답이다.

Paraphrasing
response → input

---

42. 이메일에서, 첫 번째 단락, 세 번째 줄의 단어 "appreciation"과 의미상 가장 가까운 것은
(A) 동정
(B) 증가
(C) 감사
(D) 이해

해설 Milo d'Antoni가 Ms. Mendoza에게 보낸 두 번째 지문(이메일), 세 번째 줄의 Everyone in attendance left with an appreciation for how easy it can be to make new and interesting tastes. (참석자 모두가 새롭고 흥미로운 맛을 만들어 내는 것이 얼마나 쉬운지에 대해 잘 알게 되었습니다.)에서 'appreciation'은 '이해'의 의미로 쓰였으므로 보기 중 같은 의미를 갖는 (D) understanding이 정답이다.

---

43. Mr. Fischer에 관하여 알 수 있는 것은 무엇인가?
(A) 호텔이 비싸다고 생각했다.
(B) 오후 행사에 참석할 수 없었다.
(C) Ms. de Silva의 강연을 들을 수 없었다.

(D) 제시간에 신청을 완료하지 못했다.

해설 Mr. Fischer가 쓴 세 번째 지문(설문지)의 'Other comments'에서 I was unable to attend the first morning's keynote speech and events because of this. (저는 이것 때문에 첫날 아침의 기조 연설과 행사들에 참석할 수 없었습니다.)라고 했는데, keynote speech가 언급된 첫 번째 지문(웹사이트), 두 번째 단락에서 Join this year's gathering in Argentina with keynote speaker Kayla de Silva (기조 연설자 Kayla de Silva와 함께 아르헨티나에서 열리는 올해의 모임에 참가하세요.)라고 하여 기조 연설자(Ms. de Silva)의 이름을 확인했으므로 Mr. Fischer가 Ms. de Silva의 연설을 들을 수 없었다는 것을 유추할 수 있다. 따라서 (C) He could not listen to Ms. de Silva's talk. 가 정답이다.

---

44. Mr. Fischer는 특이 어떤 연사를 마음에 들어 했는가?

(A) Gabe Luciano

(B) Nikki Mendoza

(C) Ji-won Song

(D) John Kimeli

해설 Mr. Fischer가 쓴 세 번째 지문(설문지)의 'Other comments'에서 In particular, I liked the presentation given by the owner of Tutti's Hard Candy. (특히, 저는 Tutti's Hard Candy의 오너가 한 발표가 좋았습니다.)라고 했는데, hard candy가 언급된 Milo d'Antoni가 Ms. Mendoza에게 보낸 두 번째 지문(이메일), 두 번째 줄의 I would like to thank you again for your wonderful presentation on making hard candies. (직접 만나 뵙게 되어 영광스럽게 생각하며, 하드캔디를 만드는 법에 관한 귀하의 멋진 발표에 다시 한번 감사드리고 싶습니다.)와 이 글의 수신자, Ms. Mendoza가 Tutii's Hard Candy의 오너임을 알 수 있으므로 (B) Nikki Mendoza가 정답이다.

[45-49] 다음 제품 설명서와 고객의 평가, 온라인 응답에 관한 문제입니다.

Alphalumen Star 컴퓨터 프로젝터: 모델 LU-X

1. 2년마다 한 번씩 새 프로젝터를 사느라 돈을 낭비하는 일은 이제 그만하세요! **45A** 당사의 가장 잘 팔리는 모델 LU-X는 오래 가는 알루미늄과 닦기 쉬운 유리로 제작됩니다.

특장점: 강력한 램프와 고품질의 렌즈가 이 제품을 **45B** 모든 유형의 영업 상황에서 제품 시연에 완벽한 최첨단 장비로 만들어줍니다.

품질 보증: 판매되는 모든 프로젝터에는 5년 동안의 환불 보증이 포함됩니다. **45C** 이 프로젝터가 여러 해 동안 작동하도록 제작된다는 것은 고객에 대한 우리의 약속입니다.

소매가: 1,999.00파운드
47 AL-S 회원가: 1,499.00파운드

어휘 **projector** 영사기, 프로젝터 | **waste** 낭비하다 | **top-selling** 가장 잘 팔리는 | **long-lasting** 오래 가는 | **advantage** 이점, 장점 | **state-of-the-art** 최첨단의 | **demonstration** 제품 시연 | **warranty** 품질 보증 | **guarantee** 보장 | **operate** 작동하다 | **retail** 소매의

www.alphalumenstar.co.uk/review/LU-X/ad52d

홈페이지	구매	평가	Q&A

게시자: Carrie Kline
12월 6일

평점 ★★★★★

46 이 제품에 놀랐습니다. 회사에서 마케팅 매니저로 근무하고 있고 많은 다양한 프로젝터들을 사용해봤지만 이게 최고입니다. 빛이 매우 밝고 유용한 설정도 많습니다. 약간 비싸기는 했지만 틀림없이 그럴 만한 가치가 있습니다. **47** 그리고 저희 회사가 회원이기 때문에 판촉가를 이용할 수 있는 자격도 되었습니다. **48** 제가 겪고 있는 한 가지 문제점은 이게 조금 시끄러워서 회의 동안 제가 원했던 것보다 더 산만했다는 것입니다. 하지만 대체로 이것은 훌륭한 제품이며 저는 매우 만족하고 있습니다.

어휘 **poster** 게시자 | **rating** 평점 | **setting** 설정 | **eligible** 자격이 있는 | **promotional** 홍보의, 판촉의 | **rate** 가격, 요금 | **distracting** 산만하게 하는 | **all in all** 대체로

---

www.alphalumenstar.co.uk/review/LU-X/lrf69

홈페이지	구매	평가	Q&A

게시자: Alphalumen Star 고객 상담실
12월 7일

LU-X 프로젝터에 관한 고객님의 긍정적인 평가를 보고 기뻤습니다. 사용자의 만족은 저희에게 매우 중요합니다. **49** 현재 겪고 계신 문제와 관련하여 한 가지 제안해드리겠습니다. **48** 저희 LU-E 모델이 고객님의 조용한 사무실 환경에는 더 잘 맞을 것 같습니다. LU-E는 LU-X만큼 밝지만 내부에 훨씬 더 작은 팬을 사용하여 제작됩니다. 그러나 이 모델의 가격은 LU-X보다 약간 높습니다. www.alphalumenstar.co.uk/shop/lu-e를 방문하셔서 이 제품에 관하여 더 알아보시기 바랍니다.

어휘 **concerning** ~에 관하여 | **suit** ~에게 맞다 | **slightly** 약간 | **ideal** 이상적인 | **navigate** (웹사이트를) 돌아다니다 | **present** 발표하다 | **expo** 박람회 | **projector** 영사기, 프로젝터 | **charge** 요금을 부과하다 | **part** 부품

---

45. 제품 설명에서 LU-X projector의 특징으로 언급되지 않은 것은 무엇인가?

(A) 인기 있다.

(B) 비즈니스 발표에 알맞다.

(C) 오래 간다.

(D) 다른 브랜드보다 더 밝다.

해설 첫 번째 지문(제품 설명서)의 단서와 보기를 매칭시키면, Our top-selling model (당사의 가장 잘 팔리는 모델) → (A) It is popular./ perfect for demonstrations in all types of sales situations (모든 유형의 영업 상황에서 제품 시연에 완벽한) → (B) It is ideal for business presentations./built to operate for many years (여

러 해 동안 작동하도록 제작된다) → (C) It is long-lasting.과 일치하지 않지만 다른 브랜드들보다 더 밝다는 내용은 언급된 바 없으므로 (D) It is brighter than other brands. 가 정답이다.

....

46. 고객의 평가에서 알 수 있는 것은 무엇인가?

(A) **Ms. Kline이 구매한 물건에 만족하고 있다.**
(B) 소유자들은 LU–X가 너무 무겁다고 생각한다.
(C) Alphalumen Star의 온라인 매장은 물건을 찾기 쉽다.
(D) LU–X의 사용자 설명서는 매우 도움이 된다.

해설 Ms. Kline이 작성한 두 번째 지문(고객 평가), 첫 번째 줄에서 I am amazed by this product. I'm a marketing manager at my company, and I've had to use a lot of different projectors, but this one is the best. (저는 이 제품에 놀랐습니다. 회사에서 마케팅 매니저로 근무하고 있고 많은 다양한 프로젝터들을 사용해봤지만 이게 최고입니다.)라고 했으므로 (A) Ms. Kline is satisfied with a purchase. 가 정답이다.

....

47. Ms. Kline에 관하여 알 수 있는 것은 무엇인가?

(A) 12월 6일에 박람회에서 발표를 했다.
(B) 전에 프로젝터의 사용을 시도해본 적이 없다.
(C) **프로젝터의 가격으로 1,499파운드를 청구받았다.**
(D) 프로젝터의 추가 부품을 샀다.

해설 Ms. Kline이 작성한 두 번째 지문(고객 평가), 세 번째 줄에서 And because my company has a membership, we were eligible for the promotional rate. (그리고 저희 회사가 회원이기 때문에 판촉가를 이용할 수 있는 자격도 되었습니다.)라고 했으며, 첫 번째 지문(제품 설명서) 하단에서 AL-S Member price: £1,499.00 (AL-S 회원가: 1,499.00파운드) 정보를 확인할 수 있으므로 (C) She was charged £1,499 for the projector. 가 정답이다.

....

48. 왜 LU–E 프로젝터가 Ms. Kline에게 더 알맞은 것으로 권장되겠는가?

(A) 싸다.
(B) 휴대용이다.
(C) **조용하다.**
(D) 업데이트가 쉽다.

해설 Ms. Kline이 작성한 두 번째 지문(고객 평가), 네 번째 줄에서 The one problem that I have is that it is a bit noisy, so it was more distracting during meetings than I would have liked. (제가 겪고 있는 한 가지 문제점은 이게 조금 시끄러워서 회의 동안 제가 원했던 것보다 더 산만했다는 것입니다.)라고 했는데, Alphalumen Star 고객 상담실에서 답변한 세 번째 지문(온라인 답변)에서 Our LU–E model may suit your quiet office environment better. The LU–E is just as bright as the LU–X, but is built with a much smaller fan inside. (저희 LU–E 모델이 고객님의 조용한 사무실 환경에는 더 잘 맞을 것 같습니다. LU–E는 LU–X만큼 밝지만 내부에 훨씬 더 작은 팬을 사용하여 제작됩니다.)라고 했으므로 (C) It is quiet. 가 정답이다.

....

49. 온라인 응답에서 첫 번째 단락, 두 번째 줄의 단어 "Concerning"과 의미상 가장 가까운 것은

(A) 걱정스러운
(B) 수반하는
(C) **~에 관하여**
(D) 비교하는

해설 Alphalumen Star 고객 상담실에서 답변한 세 번째 지문(온라인 답변), 두 번째 줄의 Concerning the issue you are experiencing, we have a suggestion. (현재 겪고 계신 문제와 관련하여 한 가지 제안해드리겠습니다.)에서 'Concerning'은 '~에 관하여'라는 의미로 쓰였으므로 보기 중 같은 의미를 갖는 (C) Regarding이 정답이다.

[50-54] 다음 기사와 일정표, 최신 뉴스에 관한 문제입니다.

Teich 경기장, CSF 결승 개최

Teich 경기장은 개조를 위해 폐쇄되어 있지만, 올 12월 빈에서 있을 CSF 하키 선수권 대회의 결승전 개최에 맞춰 완공될 것이다. 이 개조공사가 여러 해 동안 진행되도록 계획되기는 했지만 선수권 대회를 이곳에 유치할 수 있는 기회는 마침내 일을 진행시키게 한 큰 동기부여가 되었다. 정부 관리들은 공사가 계획에 따라 진행 중임을 확인해줬으며 모든 것이 선수권 대회 훨씬 전에 완료될 것이라고 예상하고 있다.

52 Teich 경기장은 지역의 랜드마크임에도 불구하고 CSF 행사를 한 번도 주최한 적이 없기 때문에 경기장 책임자들은 올해의 결승 대회를 주최하게 된 것을 기쁘게 여기고 있다. 이 중대한 행사는 일반 대중이 완공된 개조물을 볼 수 있는 첫 기회가 될 것이다. **50** 주최측은 행사가 수천 명의 하키 팬들을 끌어 모을 것이며 Teich 경기장은 모든 이들의 기대를 충족시킬 것이라고 기대한다. **51** Teich 경기장은 전보다 세 배나 많은 23,500명을 넉넉하게 수용할 것이다.

어휘 arena 경기장 | hold 열다, 개최하다 | in time ~에 시간 맞춰 | final round 결승전 | motivation 동기부여 | underway 진행 중인 | official 공무원, 관리 | confirm 확인하다 | well before ~훨씬 전에 | landmark 명소 | director 책임자 | competition 대회 | momentous 중대한 | the public 일반인들 | meet expectations 기대를 충족시키다 | accommodate 수용하다 | comfortably 수월하게

CSF 하키 선수권 대회 8강			
54 잉글랜드vs. 독일 12월 4일 오후 5시., Toplitzbach 스타디움, 잘츠부르크	오스트리아vs. 이탈리아 12월 4일 오후 8시 30분, Kulm 센터, 그라츠	스웨덴vs. 프랑스 12월 5일 오후 5시, Haslach 센터, 린츠	네덜란드vs. 스페인 12월 5일 오후 8시 30분 Oberalm 스타디움, 빈

CSF 하키 선수권 대회 4강	
12월 4일 경기의 승리팀 12월 8일 오후 5시, Kulm 센터, 그라츠	12월 5일 경기의 승리팀 12월 8일 오후 8시 30분, Haslach 센터, 린츠
52 결승	

12월 8일 경기의 승리팀

52 12월 11일 오후 5시 30분, Teich 경기장, 빈

주의: **53** 결승전 좌석은 조기에 매진됨을 유의하시고 4강전 결과가 나오기 전에 예매하시기 바랍니다. 티켓 소지자만 입장이 허용됩니다. 환불 불가.

어휘 quarterfinal round 8강전 ∣ semifinal round 4강전 ∣ aware 알고 있는 ∣ sell out 매진되다

뉴스 단신:
TAV-TV 채널 3

54 스포츠 라이브: 하키, 12월 4일

오후 5시. 잉글랜드가 독일을 맞아 싸우는 경기에서 누가 4강에 진출하게 될지 지켜봅니다. 은퇴한 이탈리아 팀의 코치 Arturo Palmieri의 생중계 해설과 함께 하세요.

오후 8시 30분. 홈팀이 이탈리아를 맞아 싸우는 흥미진진할 것이 확실한 경기이며 Rudi van Antwerp가 진행합니다.

어휘 bulletin 뉴스 단신 ∣ face 맞닥뜨리다 ∣ commentary 해설 ∣ host 진행하다 ∣ venue 장소 ∣ semifinal round 4강전 ∣ certain 어떤

---

50. 기사에서 두 번째 단락, 열 번째 줄의 단어 "meet"과 의미상 가장 가까운 것은
(A) 연락하다
(B) 인사하다
(C) 만족시키다
(D) 합류하다

해설 첫 번째 지문(기사), 두 번째 단락의 Planners anticipate that the event will pull in thousands of hockey fans, and that Teich Arena will meet everybody's expectations. (주최측은 행사가 수천 명의 하키 팬들을 끌어 모을 것이며 Teich 경기장은 모든 이들의 기대를 충족시킬 것이라고 기대한다)에서 meet은 '~을 충족시키다'라는 의미로 쓰였으므로 보기 중 같은 의미를 갖는 (C) satisfy가 정답이다.

---

51. Teich 경기장에 관하여 무엇이 변경될 것인가?
(A) 수용 가능한 좌석 수
(B) 주차장 이용 가능 여부
(C) 책임자들
(D) 입장료

해설 첫 번째 지문(기사), 두 번째 단락에서 Teich Arena will comfortably hold 23,500 people, three times as many as before. (Teich 경기장은 전보다 세 배나 많은 23,500명을 넉넉하게 수용할 것이다.)라고 했으므로 (A) The seating capacity가 정답이다.

---

52. 새 개최지에서 첫 시합은 언제 있을 것인가?
(A) 12월 4일
(B) 12월 5일
(C) 12월 8일
(D) 12월 11일

해설 첫 번째 지문(기사), 두 번째 단락에서 Although Teich Arena is a regional landmark, it has never hosted a CSF event before, and the arena's directors are pleased to host the final competition this year. (Teich 경기장은 지역의 랜드마크임에도 불구하고 CSF 행사를 한 번도 주최한 적이 없기 때문에 경기장 책임자들은 올해의 결승 대회를 주최하게 된 것을 기쁘게 여기고 있다.)라고 했으며, 결승전 (Final competition)이 언급된 두 번째 지문(일정표)에서 Final Round, 11 December, 5:30 P.M., Teich Arena, Wien (12월 11일 오후 5시 30분, Teich 경기장, 빈)이라고 되어 있으므로 (D) On December 11이 정답이다.

---

53. 일정표에서는 사람들에게 무엇을 하라고 권하는가?
(A) 행사 장소에 일찍 도착한다
(B) 4강전이 끝난 직후에 좌석을 예약한다
(C) 행사 전에 환불을 요청한다
(D) 시합의 티켓을 되도록 빨리 구입한다

해설 두 번째 지문(일정표) 하단에서 Be aware that seats for the final round will sell out quickly, so reserve yours before the semifinal rounds are decided. (결승전 좌석은 조기에 매진됨을 유의하시고 4강전 결과가 나오기 전에 예매하시기 바랍니다.)라고 했으므로 (D) Purchase seats for a certain game as early as possible가 정답이다.

Paraphrasing
before the semifinal rounds are decided → as early as possible

---

54. Mr. Palmieri는 어디에서 보도할 것인가?
(A) 잘츠부르크
(B) 그라츠
(C) 린츠
(D) 빈

해설 Mr. Palmieri가 언급된 세 번째 지문(최신 뉴스)에서 SPORTS Live: Hockey, 4 December / At 5 P.M. England will face Germany in a match to see who moves on to the semifinals. Join retired Italian coach Arturo Palmieri for the live commentary. (스포츠 라이브: 하키, 12월 4일 / 오후 5시. 잉글랜드가 독일을 맞아 싸우는 경기에서 누가 4강에 진출하게 될지 지켜봅니다. 은퇴한 이탈리아 팀의 코치 Arturo Palmieri의 생중계 해설과 함께 하세요.)라고 했고, 두 번째 지문(일정표)에서 잉글랜드와 독일전을 확인하면 England vs. Germany / 4 December, 5 P.M., Toplitzbach Stadium, Salzburg (잉글랜드vs. 독일 / 12월 4일 오후 5시, Toplitzbach 스타디움, 잘츠부르크)로 되어 있으므로 (A) Salzburg가 정답이다.

PART 7 REVIEW TEST

HALF TEST

HALF TEST 01

본서 p.358

1. (C)	2. (A)	3. (A)	4. (B)	5. (C)
6. (B)	7. (D)	8. (A)	9. (A)	10. (B)
11. (D)	12. (C)	13. (A)	14. (C)	15. (D)
16. (D)	17. (D)	18. (B)	19. (D)	20. (D)
21. (B)	22. (C)	23. (D)	24. (D)	25. (A)
26. (B)	27. (D)	28. (D)	29. (D)	30. (A)
31. (C)	32. (D)	33. (C)	34. (A)	35. (A)
36. (D)	37. (C)	38. (D)	39. (B)	40. (B)
41. (A)	42. (D)	43. (D)	44. (D)	45. (C)
46. (D)	47. (B)	48. (B)	49. (C)	50. (B)

1. 팀 매니저는 각각의 직원들이 반드시 기초 컴퓨터 연수를 받도록 해야 했다.

해설 빈칸은 that절의 주어 자리로 대명사가 들어갈 자리이다. (A) every는 형용사이므로 주어 자리에 올 수 없다. (B) either는 전체가 둘인 경우에 쓸 수 있다. (D) much는 of the 뒤에 불가산 명사가 나와야 한다. 따라서 (C) each가 정답이다.

어휘 manager 매니저, 관리자 | be supposed to ~하기로 되어 있다 | make sure 반드시 ~하도록 하다, 확실히 하다 | computer training 컴퓨터 연수

2. 이사회는 회사 장부가 승인된 후에 직원 보너스를 발표할 것이다.

해설 '회사 장부에 대한 승인이 있은 후에 보너스를 지급할 것'이라는 문맥에 따라 주절 동사의 시제는 미래시제가 된다. 또한, 시간이나 조건 부사절에서는 미래시제 대신 현재시제를 사용해야 하므로, 시간이나 조건의 부사절의 현재시제 동사는 주절 동사의 시제가 미래시제임을 파악하는 단서가 된다. 따라서, 미래시제 (A) will announce가 정답이다.

어휘 Board of Directors 이사회 | staff 직원 | account (회계) 장부 | sign off on ~에 대해 승인하다 | announce 발표하다

3. 많은 게임 개발자들이 유럽 시장에서 그들의 애플리케이션 프로그램을 철수할 것을 고려했다.

해설 빈칸은 주어 game developers의 동사 자리이므로 (D)는 소거한다. 개발자들이 철수할 것을 고려하는 것이므로 consider가 능동태로 들어가야 한다. 따라서 수동태 (B) are considered, (C) will be considered도 소거시키면 능동태 현재완료 (A) have considered가 정답이다. 동사 문제는 항상 수 → 태 → 시제 순으로 접근해야 한다는 것을 기억한다.

어휘 developer 개발(업)자 | withdraw 철수하다, 물러나다 | app 애플리케이션, 응용프로그램(= application)

4. 우리 책은 직접 방문한 관광 명소, 레스토랑, 호텔에 대해 편견 없는 의견을 제시하기 때문에 독자들에게 인기가 많다.

해설 두 개의 절을 이어줄 접속사 자리이다. 독자들에게 인기가 있는 '이유'를 설명하고 있으므로 접속사들 중 (B) because가 정답이다.

어휘 popular 인기 있는 | unbiased 편견이 없는 | tourist attraction 관광 명소

5. Hargrove 그룹은 새 건물들을 건설하는 지역 비영리 기관들에 재정 지원을 일상적으로 제공한다.

해설 빈칸 뒤의 목적어 new buildings와 함께 쓰일 수 있는 문맥상 적절한 동사를 선택하는 어휘 문제이다. '신규 건물들을 건설하는 지역 비영리 기관'이란 문맥에 따라 '건설하다, 세우다'라는 의미의 (C) constructing이 정답이다.

어휘 financial support 재정 지원 | nonprofit organization 비영리 기관 | invest 투자하다 | center ~을 중심에 두다 | construct 건설하다 | address 연설하다; 처리하다

6. 그 회사의 산림 관리자들은 자격증을 취득하기 위해 야생생물 생물학 강의를 수강해야만 한다.

해설 '자격증 취득을 위해 수강을 해야 한다'는 문맥으로 빈칸에는 '(의무적으로) ~해야 하는'이라는 뜻의 형용사가 적절하므로 (B) obliged가 정답이다.

어휘 forest manager 산림 관리자 | take courses 수강하다 | trustworthy 신뢰할 수 있는 | obliged 의무적으로 해야 하는 | promised 약속이 된 | engaged 바쁜, 약혼한

7. 파리로 오기 전에, Mr. Bach는 시드니 미술관에서 연구원으로 일했다.

해설 '연구원으로서' 일했다는 것이 문맥상 가장 자연스러우므로 (D) as가 정답이다.

어휘 work for ~에서 일하다 | work as ~로 일하다

8. 내일 세미나는 오전 9시 정각에 시작되므로 참석자들은 시간을 엄수하도록 노력해야 한다.

해설 문맥상 '시간을 엄수하는'이라는 의미의 punctual이 자연스러우므로 (A) punctual이 정답이다.

어휘 attendee 참석자 | punctual 시간을 엄수하는 | advanced 진보된 | instant 즉각적인 | sudden 갑작스러운

9. 그 회사의 CEO는 출장을 떠나기 전에 기념식에서 간단하게만 얘기했다.

해설 빈칸 앞의 spoke only 와 함께 쓰일 수 있는 문맥상 적절한 부사를 선택해야 하는 어휘 문제이다. 문맥상 '~에서 짧게, 간단히 연설을 했다'는 문맥에 따라 '짧게, 간단히'라는 의미를 지닌 (A) briefly가 정답이다.

어휘 anniversary celebration 기념식 | depart 출발하다 | frequently 빈번하게 | usually 대개 | constantly 끊임없이

10. 배송된 후 열흘간 수취인이 나타나지 않는 모든 우편물이나 소포는 체신부의 재량에 따라 발송자에게 반송될 수 있다.

해설 문맥상 '배송 후 열흘 동안 수취인이 찾아가지 않는 우편물'이 가장 적절하므로 (B) unclaimed가 정답이다.

어휘 package 소포 | delivery 배송 | return 반송하다 | at the discretion of ~의 재량에 따라 | neglected 방치된, 도외시된 | unclaimed 수취인이 없는 | deleted 삭제된 | rejected 불합격된, 거부된

11. Blackbird Media는 전문적으로 운영되는 실시간 온라인 회의, 이용자 주문 방식의 학습, 평생 교육을 전문으로 한다.

해설 전치사 in의 목적어로 live webinars가 왔다. managed가 live webinars를 수식하고 있으므로 managed를 수식해 줄 부사가 와야 하는 자리이다. 따라서 명사, 형용사는 올 수 없고 부사 (D) professionally가 정답이다.

어휘 specialize in ~을 전문으로 하다 | webinar 온라인 회의 | on-demand 주문 방식의(이용자의 요구에 따라 네트워크를 통해 필요한 정보를 제공하는 방식) | continuing education 평생 교육 | professional 전문적인 | professionals 전문가들 | professionalism 전문성, 프로 근성 | professionally 전문적으로

12. 의견이나 제안을 하고 싶은 고객들은 피드백 양식을 작성함으로써 언제든 그렇게 할 수 있습니다.

해설 '피드백 양식을 작성함으로써 의견이나 제안을 할 수 있다'는 문맥에 따라 '~함으로써'를 의미하는 「by + V-ing」 구문을 묻는 문제이다. 따라서 (C) by가 정답이다.

어휘 comment 논평 | welcome to ~을 자유롭게 하다 | complete 작성하다

13. 작은 디자인 회사인 Hawkeye & Horns는 그 지역 회사들을 위해 웹사이트를 만드는 것을 전문으로 한다.

해설 문맥상 '작은 디자인 회사'가 적절하므로 (A) firm이 정답이다.

어휘 specialize in ~을 전문으로 하다 | local 지역의, 현지의 | firm 회사 | piece 한 부분 | industry 산업

14. 구매에 완전히 만족하지 못하신 경우 사용하지 않은 상품을 원래대로 포장해서 60일 이내에 반품하실 수 있습니다.

해설 빈칸은 동사 자리이므로 동사인 (A)와 (C) 중 정답을 선택한다. 주어 (you)가 동작(반품하다)을 행하는 주체에 해당하므로, 능동태 (C) may return이 정답이다. (B)와 (D)는 동사가 아니므로 오답이다.

어휘 entirely 완전히, 전적으로 | unused item 사용하지 않은 상품, 미개봉 상품 | original 원래의 | packaging 포장 | return 반품하다

15. 이따금씩 여름의 더운 날을 제외하고, Tessa 시의 기후는 일반적으로 온화했다.

해설 빈칸 뒤에 절이 아닌 명사(hot weather)가 왔기 때문에 접속사 (A) Even though, (B) Unless는 오답이며, 문맥상 '~을 제외하고'라는 의미의 전치사 (D) Except for가 정답이다.

어휘 occasional 이따금씩 | generally 일반적으로 | temperate 온화한 | even though 비록 ~이지만 | unless ~하지 않는 한, ~한 경우 외에는 | opposing 서로 대립되는 | except for ~을 제외하고

16. 그 회사는 양질의 서비스를 제공하며, 국내 최고의 아시아 식품 공급업체 중 하나로서 명성을 얻었다.

해설 (A) some, (B) theirs, (C) them은 복수형이므로 the company의 대명사가 될 수 없다. 동사 win은 「win + A + B」의 패턴을 취하여 '주어가 A에게 B를 얻게 하다'라는 뜻으로 쓰인다. 여기서 주어인 the company가 회사 스스로 최고의 아시아 식품 공급업체라는 명성을 얻은 것이므로, 목적어 자리에 그 회사 스스로를 언급하는 재귀대명사 (D) itself가 정답이다.

어휘 quality service 양질의 서비스 | reputation 평판, 명성 | Asian 아시아의; 아시아인 | food supplier 식품 공급업체

17. 지방 재정 이사회는 어제 자금을 승인하는 투표를 했으며, 이 자금의 대부분은 도시의 노후한 상수도 시설을 개선하는 데 사용될 것이다.

해설 동사가 두 개(voted, will be used)이므로 빈칸에는 두 문장을 연결해 줄 수 있는 관계사 (A), (C), (D)가 올 수 있다. 선행사가 사물(the funding)이므로 (D) which가 정답이다. 대명사 (B)는 두 문장을 연결해 줄 수 없으므로 오답이다. 관계사 (C)는 콤마(,) 뒤에 계속적 용법으로 쓸 수 없고, 관계사 (A)는 선행사가 사람일 때만 쓸 수 있으므로 오답이다.

어휘 vote 투표하다 | funding 자금 | aging 노화되고 있는, 노후한

18. 현재의 사무 공간에 머무를 것인지 다른 곳으로 이전할 것인지를 결정할 때는 고려해야 할 요소들이 많다.

해설 빈칸이 or로 연결되어 있으므로 문맥상 빈칸에는 '현재의 사무실에 머무르는 것'과 반대되는 내용의 동사가 와야 한다. 따라서 (B) relocate가 정답이다.

어휘 determine 결정하다 | transmit 전송하다 | relocate 이전하다 | deliver 배달하다 | refer 참조하게 하다

19. Email Broadcast는 즉각적인 반응을 제공하므로 당신은 당신의 이메일에서 어떤 링크가 가장 많은 조회수를 기록하는지 알 수 있게 됩니다.

해설 빈칸 앞에 타동사(see)가 왔기 때문에 보기에 제시된 who, which, that 등은 관계사가 아니라 명사절을 이끄는 접속사에 해당한다. '어떤 링크가 가장 많은 클릭을 받는지'라는 문맥에 따라 뒤에 오는 명사 links를 수식하는 의문 형용사 (D) which가 정답이다. 의문사 which가 「which + 명사」의 형태로 명사절을 이끄는 경우에는 선택을 의미하며, '어떤 ~'라고 해석한다.

어휘 offer 제공하다 | immediate 즉각적인 | response 반응, 응답

20. 시각 보조 자료들은 너무 복잡하거나 즐거움을 주는 데 치중하는 것 없이 발표의 주제를 뒷받침해야 한다.

해설 빈칸을 포함한 주어는 발표의 주제를 뒷받침하는 것이므로 '시각 자료'라는 의미가 되어야 한다. 따라서 (D) Visual이 정답이다.

어휘 visual aid 시각 보조 자료(그림, 비디오 등) | entertaining 재미 있는, 즐거움을 주는 | substantial 상당한 | legal 법률과 관련된 | financial 금융의, 재정의 | visual 시각의, 눈으로 보는

국제 회계전문가 협회
254 Antilles 가
뉴욕, 뉴욕 10013

Ms. Mumtaz께,

국제 회계전문가 협회 회원권과 관련하여 귀하께서 7월 15일에 주신 **㉑** 문의 편지에 감사드립니다. **㉒** 우리는 새로운 신청을 받게 됨을 알릴 수 있어서 기쁩니다. 귀하께 신청서 양식을 동봉하여 보내드립니다.

아시다시피, 저희는 8월 28일 캘리포니아 팜스프링스에서 연례 북미 회의를 개최할 예정입니다. 이번 달에 저희 협회 가입을 결정하시면, 회의 참가비의 20%를 특별 할인 받으실 **㉓** 자격을 가지게 되실 것입니다.

이 특가 제공 혜택을 받고자 하신다면, **㉔** 적어도 회의 2주 전에 협회에 알려 주시기 바랍니다.

질문이 있으시면, 망설이지 마시고 저에게 연락해 주십시오.

진심으로,

Herbert Groell
Herbert Groell
국제 회계전문가 협회 회장

어휘 accountancy 회계직, 회계 업무 | inquire 문의하다 | inform 알리다 | enclose 동봉하다 | application 신청(서) | hold 개최하다 | annual 연간의, 매년 열리는 | qualify for ~에 대해 자격을 갖추다 | compete 경쟁하다 | reflect 반영하다 | serve 제공하다, 도움이 되다 | reduction 할인, 축소 | attendance fee 참가비 | wish to ~하기를 희망하다 | take advantage of ~을 이용[활용]하다 | special offer 특가 제공 | retain 보유하다, 지참하다 | at least 최소한, 적어도 | prior to ~ 이전에 | only if 오직 ~하는 경우에만 | in spite of ~에도 불구하고 | hesitate to ~하기를 망설이다

21. **해설** letter까지 문장이 완벽하다. 따라서 빈칸에는 letter를 수식하면서 전치사구 about의 수식을 받을 수 있는 준동사가 와야 하므로 동사인 (A)를 소거시킨다. to부정사도 앞의 명사를 꾸며주는 기능이 있으나, to부정사의 경우에는 주로 앞으로 일어날 일을 나타낸다. 편지는 7월 15일에 이미 발송된 것이므로 (D)도 소거시킨다. 문맥상, 편지에서 Ms. Mumtaz가 회원권에 대해 '문의를 했다'이므로 능동의 의미가 적절하다. 따라서 수동의 의미로 앞의 말을 수식하는 과거분사 (C) inquired가 아닌 능동을 나타내는 현재분사 (B) inquiring이 정답이다.

22. (A) 저희 회원 수가 이미 만석이기 때문에 새로운 회원을 받을 수 없습니다.
(B) 지원 신청서는 며칠 전에는 도착했어야만 했습니다.
(C) 우리는 새로운 신청을 받게 됨을 알려 드리게 되어 기쁩니다.
(D) 귀하를 신규 회원으로 환영하게 되어 기쁩니다.

해설 앞 문장은 회계전문가 협회 회원권에 대한 문의 편지에 대해 감사를 표하고 있고, 다음 문장은 신청서 양식을 동봉한다는 내용이

므로, 문맥상 빈칸에 들어가기에 가장 적합한 문장은 (C)이다. 따라서 정답은 (C) I'm pleased to inform you that we are accepting new applications.이다. 아직 회원 가입을 하지 않은 상태이므로 (D)는 정답이 될 수 없고, 전체적인 편지 내용이 신청을 받는다는 의미이므로 거절의 의미인 (A) 또한 오답이다. 편지와 함께 신청서를 동봉한다고 했으므로 신청서가 이미 도착했어야 한다는 (B)도 적절하지 않다.

23. **해설** 이번 달에 협회 가입을 하면 참가비 20% 특별 할인 혜택을 받을 '자격이 주어진다'라는 의미가 가장 자연스럽다. 따라서 (D) qualify가 정답이다.

24. **해설** 빈칸 뒤에 명사 two weeks가 있기 때문에 접속사 (A)와 (B)는 소거시킨다. '적어도' 회의 2주 전에 알려 달라는 내용이 적합하므로 (D) at least가 정답이다.

날짜: 2월 12일
수신: 전 직원

우리 사무실의 불필요한 전기 사용을 줄여 에너지 비용을 감소시키는 것을 도와주십시오. 모두 아시다시피, 올해 전기료가 큰 폭으로 인상되었으므로, 우리 모두는 비용을 절감하기 위해 노력해야 합니다. **㉕** 여러 가지 방법으로 이 일을 할 수 있습니다.

㉖ 사용하지 않으실 때는 불을 꺼 주십시오. 근무가 끝나면, 마지막으로 퇴근하는 직원은 각 방의 모든 전등과 전자 장치가 꺼져 있는지 확인해야 합니다. 또한 퇴근하기 전에 컴퓨터 **㉗** 와 가습기 및 책상 아래 난방기와 같은 개인 전기 기구들을 끄는 것은 모든 직원들의 책임입니다.

또한 늘 그렇듯이, 복사기는 밤새 방치하면 화재의 위험이 있을 수 있으므로, 업무를 마치면 전원을 끄는 것이 **㉘** 필수적입니다. 마지막으로 퇴근하는 사람은 복사기들이 꺼져 있는지 확인할 책임이 있습니다.

진심으로,

Yuki Sakamoto
시설관리부장

어휘 staff 직원 | assist 돕다 | reduce 줄이다, 감소시키다 | unnecessary 불필요한 | electricity 전기 | electric power 전력 | significantly 상당히 | make an effort 노력하다 | cut costs 비용을 줄이다 | switch off lights 불을 끄다 | in use 사용되고 있는 | usage 용법 | ensure 반드시 ~하게 하다, 보장하다 | electronic equipment 전기 장치 | responsibility 책임 | despite ~에도 불구하고 | in addition 게다가 | personal 개인의 | electrical appliances 전기 기구 | humidifier 가습기 | timely 시기적절한 | inefficient 비효율적인 | productive 생산적인 | essential 필수적인 | (photo)copier 복사기 | fire hazard 화재 위험 | unattended 방치된 | overnight 밤사이에 | responsible for ~에 책임이 있는 | facility 시설 | management 관리

25. (A) 여러 가지 방법으로 이 일을 할 수 있습니다.

(B) 내일 사무실에 전력이 공급되지 않을 것입니다.

(C) 우리의 전기 요금이 꾸준하게 감소하고 있습니다.

(D) 우리는 어떻게 해야 할지에 대한 의견이 필요합니다.

해설 앞 문단의 내용은 전기료가 인상되었으므로 불필요한 전기 사용을 줄이자는 내용이고, 다음 문단의 내용은 에너지 절감을 위한 방법을 열거하는 것이므로, 정답인 (A) This can be done in a variety of ways가 문맥의 흐름상 가장 적합하다. 이미 다음 문단에서 에너지 절약에 대한 방법을 열거하고 있으므로 의견을 구하는 (D)는 적절하지 않다.

---

26. **해설** 문맥상 '사용하지 않을 때' 전등을 꺼 달라는 의미이고 빈칸은 전치사의 목적어 자리이므로 명사 (B) use가 정답이다.

---

27. **해설** 빈칸 뒤에 명사가 나오기 때문에, 부사 (C)와 연결부사 (D)는 소거시킨다. 문맥상 컴퓨터와 개인 전기 기구의 전원을 꺼 달라는 내용이므로 computers와 any personal electrical appliances 사이에는 등위접속사 and가 적절하므로 (A) and가 정답이다.

---

28. **해설** 'It ~ that' 가주어 진주어 구문이다. 화재 위험이 있으므로 복사기를 꼭 꺼 달라는 내용이므로 (D) essential이 정답이다.

[29-30] 다음 이메일에 관한 문제입니다.

수신: Sam Kravitz, 마케팅 책임자

발신: Stephanie Fordham, 고객 서비스 부장

날짜: 7월 1일

제목: Milly Levy

Sam에게,

당신의 부서가 최근 많은 신규 고객들을 확보했고, 그에 따라 추가 직원들을 고용할 필요가 있다고 들었습니다. **29** 당신의 소셜 미디어 팀 마케팅 보조직에 Milly Levy를 고려해 주시길 강력히 권고드립니다. **30** 그녀는 제 부서에서 작년 7월부터 인턴으로 일해 왔고 매우 유능하다는 것이 입증되었습니다. 그녀는 지시를 잘 따르고, 독립적으로나 또는 팀에 소속되어서나 업무를 잘 할 수 있다는 것을 보여주었습니다. 그녀의 업무는 매우 긍정적인 평가를 받아왔습니다.

Ms. Levy는 지난달에 막 경영학 학위를 취득했고, 이곳 Creighton 그룹의 마케팅 분야에서 이력을 쌓아 가길 원한다고 알고 있습니다. 당신의 팀원이 되는 것은 그녀에게 분명 이상적일 것입니다.

저는 당신에게 기꺼이 많은 정보를 제공해 드릴 것이므로, 어떤 문의든 제게 마음껏 이메일로 보내 주세요.

진심으로,

Stephanie Fordham

고객 서비스 부장

Creighton 그룹

어휘 Director of Customer Operations 고객 서비스 부장 ǀ acquire 습득하다, 인수하다 ǀ hire 고용하다 ǀ urge 강력히 권고하다 ǀ consider 고려하다 ǀ position 자리 ǀ competent 유능한, 능숙한 ǀ instruction 설명, 지시 ǀ independently 독립적으로, 자주적으로 ǀ positive feedback 긍정적인 응답 [평가] ǀ management 경영, 운영 ǀ career 직업, 이력, 경력 ǀ ideal 이상적인

---

29. 이메일의 목적은 무엇인가?

(A) 고용 정책의 변경 사항을 알리기 위해

(B) 갱신된 고객 명단을 요청하기 위해

(C) 새 프로젝트를 제안하기 위해

(D) 추천을 하기 위해

해설 이메일 첫머리에서 마케팅 보조직에 Milly Levy를 고려해 주길 강력히 권고드린다고 하므로 인력 충원에 따른 직원을 추천하기 위함임을 알 수 있다. 따라서 정답은 (D) To make a recommendation이다.

---

30. 이메일이 Ms. Fordham에 관하여 언급하는 것은 무엇인가?

(A) Ms. Levy를 1년 동안 알고 지냈다.

(B) 새로운 일자리에 지원했다.

(C) 최근 팀을 구성했다.

(D) Mr. Kravitz의 신규 고객이다.

해설 지문 마지막 부분에서 Ms. Fordham이 이메일의 발신인임을 확인할 수 있다. 따라서 지문에서 I, my, me에 관한 언급을 찾아야 한다. Ms. Levy가 지난 7월부터 현재까지 본인의 부서에서 인턴으로 일하고 있음을 확인할 수 있고, 편지가 쓰인 날짜가 7월 1일이므로 Ms. Fordham과 Ms. Levy는 1년간 함께 일했다는 것을 알 수 있다. 따라서 정답은 (A) She has known Ms. Levy for one year.이다.

[31-33] 다음 기사에 관한 문제입니다.

고객들을 잃고 있는 LFT
Owen Nordman 작성

네덜란드, 6월 11일 — 고객들에 의해 제출된 최근 설문 조사 결과는 LFT 철도가 가장 덜 고객 친화적인 운송회사 중 한 곳임을 보여주었고, 61퍼센트의 여행객들만이 그 서비스에 만족했다고 한다. **31** ENC Research Group에 의해 5월에 실시된 그 조사는 LFT가 여전히 지역의 경쟁 상대인 Andros 철도를 앞서고 있음을 보여주지만, LFT가 2위를 차지했던 작년에 비하면 그 위치가 눈에 띄게 추락했음을 알 수 있다.

"일부 경쟁업체들보다 뒤지기는 했지만, 우리는 고객들의 우려 사항들을 처리하는 데 전념하고 있습니다"라고 LFT의 대변인 Julius de Haan은 말했다. **32** "다음 달부터, 우리는 모든 기차들을 일정에 따라 운행하도록 하기 위해 특정 절차상의 변화들을 꾀할 계획입니다. 또한, **33** 우리는 내년 2월부터 여러 역에 배치될 25명의 신입 직원들을 고용하여 우리의 고객 서비스를 개선시킬 것입니다."

소비자 신뢰를 회복하기 위한 이 조치들의 효과는 두고 볼 필요가 있다.

어휘 | survey 설문 조사 | customer-friendly 고객 친화적인 | carry out 수행하다 | reveal 드러내다, 폭로하다 | ahead of ~ 앞의 | regional 지역의 | rival 경쟁 상대 | compare 비교하다 | drop 떨어지다 | significantly 눈에 띄게, 현저하게 | competitor 경쟁자 | be dedicated to ~에 헌신적이다 | procedural 절차의 | effectiveness 효과, 유효성 | measure 조치 | regain 되찾다, 회복하다 | confidence 신뢰 | consumer 소비자

31. LFT는 언제 고객 설문 조사를 했는가?
(A) 2월에
(B) 3월에
(C) 5월에
(D) 7월에

해설 지문에서 설문 조사와 실시 시기에 대해 언급된 내용을 찾으면 된다. 첫 번째 문단 여덟 번째 줄에서 설문 조사가 5월에 실시됐음을 확인할 수 있으므로 정답은 (C) In May이다.

32. 고객들은 LFT에 대해 무엇이라고 말했겠는가?
(A) 열차가 너무 붐빈다.
(B) 표 가격이 너무 비싸다.
(C) 직원들이 친절하지 않다.
(D) 열차가 때때로 제때 도착하지 않는다.

해설 두 번째 단락 두 번째 문장에서 고객들의 우려 사항들을 처리하는 데에 전념하고 있다고 하고 있고, 뒤이어서 다음 달부터 절차상의 변화를 주어 열차 운행이 일정에 맞게 이루어지도록 하겠다고 했으므로, 고객들이 열차의 운행 시간에 대해 불만을 가졌었음을 유추할 수 있다. 따라서 정답은 (D) Its trains sometimes don't arrive on time.이다.

33. LFT는 내년에 무엇을 할 것인가?
(A) 새로운 열차를 도입할 것이다.
(B) 새로운 열차 노선을 추가할 것이다.
(C) 더 많은 직원을 고용할 것이다.
(D) 다른 회사와 합병할 것이다.

해설 지문에서 next year를 키워드로 삼아 해당 내용을 찾아본다. 두 번째 문단에서 고객 서비스를 개선하기 위해 내년 2월부터 25명의 새 직원을 고용한다는 것을 확인할 수 있으므로 정답은 (C) It will hire more workers.이다.

[34-36] 다음 구인 광고에 관한 문제입니다.

브라질 독립 채굴 회사 (IMCB)
37 Riviera House · 상파울루 · 브라질
www.imcb.br

공석 발표

40년간 IMCB는 토지 소유주들에게 적절한 채굴 방법 이용에 관한 조언을 해 왔습니다. **34** 우리의 목표는 광산 노동자들의 건강이나 환경을 위태롭게 하는 일 없이 산출량을 늘리는 것입니다. 우리는 상파울루에 본사가 있는 민간조직이며, 리우데자네이루, 살바도르와 포르탈레자에 지사가 더 있습니다.

우리는 현재 동료 연구 책임자 직책에 지원자를 찾고 있습니다. **35** 합격자는 리우데자네이루로 배치될 것이며, 리더십을 증명하고 **36** 우리의 연구 부서와 안전 부서 운영자들 간의 연락 담당자로 활동해야 합니다. 보건과 안전 분야와 가능하면 채굴 분야에서의 이력이 있어야 하며, **36** 최소 3년간의 전문 관리 경력을 보유해야 합니다.

관심이 있으시면, 자기소개서와 이력서를 우편이나 직접, 또는 웹사이트 www.imcb.br/careers로 제출해 주세요. 지원서 마감일은 11월 2일입니다. **36** 합격자는 12월 14일에 일을 시작할 것으로 예상됩니다.

어휘 | landowner 지주, 토지 소유주 | proper 적절한 | method 방법 | aim 목표 | yield 산출량, 수확량 | compromise 타협하다; 위험에 처하게 하다 | endanger 위험에 빠뜨리다 | headquarter ~에 본부를 두다 | currently 현재 | application 신청서, 지원서 | successful candidate 합격자 | station 배치하다, 주둔시키다 | demonstrate 입증하다 | liaison 연락, 연락 담당자 | background 배경 | preferably 가급적 | professional 직업의, 전문적인 | submit 제출하다 | deadline 마감

34. IMCB에 관하여 언급된 것은 무엇인가?
(A) 근로자들의 복지에 기여한다.
(B) 정부로부터 재정 지원을 받는다.
(C) 채굴 장비를 제조한다.
(D) 회사 정책을 업데이트하고 있다.

해설 지문 첫 문단에서 IMCB는 광산 노동자들의 건강을 해치지 않으면서 생산량을 개선하는 것이 목표임을 확인할 수 있다. 여기서 광산 노동자들의 건강이 복지와 관련되어 있으므로 정답은 (A) It is committed to the well-being of workers.이다.

35. 어디에 IMCB의 공석이 있는가?
(A) 리우데자네이루에
(B) 상파울루에
(C) 살바도르에
(D) 포르탈레자에

해설 두 번째 단락에서 동료 연구 책임자 직책을 구하고 있고, 지원자가 리우데자네이루로 배치될 것이라고 언급하고 있다. 따라서 정답은 (A) In Rio de Janeiro이다.

36. 직책에 관하여 제시되지 않은 것은 무엇인가?

(A) 부서 간의 협업과 관련되어 있다.

(B) 관리 경력을 요구한다.

(C) 연말까지 채워질 것이다.

(D) 브라질 국적자로 제한되어 있다.

해설 직책에 관하여 알 수 없는 것을 확인하는 문제이므로, 알 수 있는 사항을 모두 확인해야 하는 문제이다. position과 관련된 내용을 보기와 대조해 본다. 두 번째 단락의 지원자 요건을 살펴보면, 우선 부서간 연락 업무를 해야 하므로 (A)가 언급되어 있음을 확인할 수 있고, 최소 3년의 관리 경력을 요구하므로 (B)도 관련 내용이 있음을 알 수 있다. 또한 합격자는 12월 4일에 일을 시작하게 되므로 연말까지 공석이 채워질 것이므로 (C) 또한 확인할 수 있다. 브라질 국적자만 가능하다는 내용은 없으므로 정답은 (D) It is limited to Brazilian nationals.이다.

[37-40] 다음 온라인 채팅 대화문에 관한 문제입니다.

Valarie Thayer [오전 9:12]
어느 브랜드의 컴퓨터 모니터를 살지 상의하고 싶어요. 두 가지 옵션이 있는데, Avonetics랑 Procomp예요. 모두의 의견이 필요합니다.

Jesse Hollis [오전 9:13]
Procomp가 스마트 모니터 만드는 회사죠?

Valarie Thayer [오전 9:15]
맞아요. ㊲ 근데 고화질 스크린으로 유명해서, 우리가 그래픽이나 로고 만들 때 이상적이에요.

Jesse Hollis [오전 9:16]
Andrea, 집에서 Procomp 모니터 쓰지 않아요?

Andrea Garcia [오전 9:19]
네, 아주 좋아요. ㊳ 정말 해상도가 높아서 사진에 있는 아주 작은 것들도 보기 쉬워요. 우리가 고객을 위해 더 나은 질의 작품을 생산해내는데 도움이 될 거라고 확신해요.

Valarie Thayer [오전 9:20]
그렇군요. 그럼 오늘 오후에 판매상에게 전화해서 주문해야겠어요. 아직 예산이 남았거든요. 또 다른 필요한 거 있나요?

Andrea Garcia [오전 9:21]
㊴ 프린터에 컬러 잉크가 부족해요. 보통 Harnet에서 주문하는데 최근에 가격을 올렸더라고요. Procomp에 구매할 때 카트리지 포함해 달라고 요청하는 게 어떨까요?

Jesse Hollis [오전 9:22]
음, 그렇게 구매액이 큰 주문이면, Procomp에서 기꺼이 잉크 카트리지를 공짜로 끼워줄 거예요. 너무 무리한 요구 같진 않은데요.

Valarie Thayer [오전 9:24]
좋은 지적이네요. 그럼 제가 전화할 때 알아볼게요. Andrea, ㊵ 지금 주문 리스트 확정해서 나에게 보내줄래요?

Andrea Garcia [오전 9:25]
㊵ 그렇게 할게요.

어휘 high-definition 고화질의 | fine 미세한 | vendor 판매상, 판매회사 | finalize 마무리 짓다, 완결하다

37. 글쓴이들이 종사하고 있는 회사로 가장 적절한 곳은 어디이겠는가?

(A) 소프트웨어 회사

(B) 전자제품 상점

(C) 디자인 회사

(D) 사무용품점

해설 지문에 등장하는 직업에 관련된 어휘를 통해 회사의 업종을 유추해야 한다. 9시 15분 Valarie Thayer의 말을 통해 이 회사는 그래픽과 로고를 만드는 곳이므로 (C) A design company가 정답임을 알 수 있다.

38. Procomp 모니터에 대해 언급된 것은 무엇인가?

(A) 온라인에서만 구매가 가능하다.

(B) 가격이 적당하다.

(C) 선명한 이미지를 보여준다.

(D) 환경 친화적이다.

해설 9시 19분 Andrea Garcia의 말에 의하면 해상도가 높고 사진 속 작은 것들도 보기 쉽다고 하므로 Procomp 모니터는 선명한 이미지를 보여준다는 것을 알 수 있다. 따라서 (C) They can display clear images.가 정답이다.

39. Harnet에 대해 알 수 있는 것은 무엇인가?

(A) Ms. Garcia가 그곳에서 근무했었다.

(B) 프린터 카트리지를 판매한다.

(C) 대부분의 직원들이 Procomp 모니터를 사용한다.

(D) 컴퓨터 제조업체를 인수했다.

해설 문제에 들어 있는 Harnet이라는 고유명사를 키워드로 잡고 지문에서 찾아내야 한다. 키워드가 발견되는 바로 앞 문장에서 프린터의 컬러 잉크가 다 떨어져간다고 했는데, 보통 이것을 Harnet에서 주문한다고 했으므로 Harnet이 프린터 카트리지를 판매하고 있음을 알 수 있다. 따라서 (B) It sells printer cartridges.가 정답이다.

40. 오전 9시 25분 Ms. Garcia가 "그렇게 할게요"라고 적은 의미는?

(A) 웹사이트를 업데이트할 것이다.

(B) 요청사항을 처리할 것이다.

(C) 판매업체에게 연락할 것이다.

(D) 멤버십 프로그램에 가입할 것이다.

해설 바로 앞 문장의 could you finalize the order list and send it to me?라는 부탁에 대한 대답으로 I'll get on it이라고 했으므로 요청사항을 수행하겠다는 의미이다. 그러므로 정답은 (B) She will carry out a request.이다.

보안 출입 암호 (SAC) 신청서

44 Ms. Andrea Delgadillo에게 팩스 번호 555-1924 또는 이메일 a_delgadillo@ntel.gov로 작성된 양식을 보내 주세요.

SAC 수령인 정보:

이름: Victoria Sherman　　　　부서: **41** 회계부

직원 ID 번호: 7745

＿ 매일 출입: 월요일부터 금요일, 오전 7시 – 오후 7시

✕ 연장 출입: 월요일부터 금요일, 오전 7시 – 오후 10시

✕ 특별 출입: (해당 날짜와 시간을 기재해 주세요.):

　　　　　토요일, 오전 10시 ~ 오후 7시

건물(들):　Newport　　✕ Danes

시작일: 10월 7일　　　　종료일: 11월 2일

신청자 정보 41 (신청자는 수령인 부서의 매니저나 책임자이어야 함):

이름: **41** christopher Rosovich

이메일: c_rosovich@ntel.gov

서명과 날짜: *Christopher Rosovich* / 9월 29일

주의:

42 우리가 귀하의 SAC 요청을 받으면, 이를 처리하는 데 영업일로 3일 정도가 걸릴 것입니다. **44** 출입이 허용되면, 6자리의 SAC가 담긴 이메일을 받으시게 될 것입니다.

어휘　security 보안, 경비 ǀ access 출입 ǀ completed 완성된 ǀ recipient 받는 사람, 수령인 ǀ extend 연장하다, 확장하다 ǀ relevant 관련 있는, 적절한 ǀ requestor 요청자 ǀ signature 서명 ǀ approximately 대략 ǀ grant (특히 공식적·법적으로) 승인하다 ǀ contain (무엇의 안에 또는 그 일부로) ~이 들어 있다

수신: Victoria Sherman ⟨v_sherman@ntel.gov⟩
발신: Andrea Delgadillo ⟨a_delgadillo@ntel.gov⟩
날짜: 10월 2일
제목: SAC

Ms. Sherman께,

44 Danes 건물과 시설물의 특별 및 연장 출입에 대한 귀하의 요청이 승인되었습니다. **44** 건물 출입 시 귀하께서는 회사 사원증과 함께 제공된 보안 출입 암호(SAC)를 사용해 주셔야 합니다. 귀하의 SAC는 938233입니다. 정상 근무 시간 이후에 건물에 출입하시려면 아래의 단계를 따라 주세요:

· 귀하의 카드를 카드 인식기 가까이에 대 주세요. 인식기의 오렌지색 불빛이 깜빡이기 시작할 것입니다.

· 다음에는, **43** 번호판에 귀하의 SAC를 입력하세요.

· **43** 깜빡이는 오렌지색 불빛이 그 다음에 초록색으로 변하면서, 건물 출입이 허락될 것입니다.

만약 귀하의 SAC를 잘못 입력하면, 불빛이 빨갛게 바뀌고, 큰 삐 소리를 5초간 듣게 됩니다. 그 뒤에, 문이 완전히 통제되기 전까지, 귀하에게는 올바른 암호를 입력할 기회가 세 번 더 주어집니다. 귀하의 암호를 재설정하고 싶으시면, 보안 관리 사무소로 가셔서 사원증을 보여 주세요.

건물 내에서 우려 사항 또는 문제가 생길 경우, 언제든 카드 뒷면에 있는 전화번호로 연락해 주세요. 마지막으로, 귀하의 SAC는 귀하의 특별 프로젝트 마지막 날 밤 10시에 만료된다는 것을 기억해 주십시오. 사원증은 12월 31일까지는 정상 근무 시간 동안 계속해서 작동할 것입니다.

진심으로,

Andrea Delgadillo, 보안 관리부

어휘　facility 시설, 기관 ǀ approve 승인하다 ǀ gain entry 입장하다 ǀ employee card 사원증 ǀ flash 비치다, 비추다 ǀ input 입력하다 ǀ afterwards 그 후에 ǀ completely 완전히 ǀ security management 보안 관리 ǀ present 제시하다 ǀ reset 재설정하다 ǀ issue 문제 ǀ expire 만기되다 ǀ office hours 영업[근무] 시간

41. Mr. Rosovich에 관하여 알 수 있는 것은 무엇인가?

(A) 회계 부서의 팀장 역할을 한다.

(B) 10월에 신청서를 제출했다.

(C) Ms. Sherman과는 다른 사무실에서 일한다.

(D) Ms. Sherman과 그녀의 프로젝트에 관하여 회의를 할 것이다.

해설　양식 지문에서 Mr. Rosovich에 관하여 암시되는 부분을 찾아야 한다. Requestor's Information(신청자 정보) 항목에서 Mr. Rosovich에 대하여 찾을 수 있고, 항목에 관한 설명을 통하여 수령인 부서의 매니저나 책임자만 신청할 수 있음을 알 수 있으므로 SAC의 수령인(recipient)은 Victoria Sherman, 수령인의 부서는 Accounting이며, SAC 신청자(requestor)인 Mr. Rosovich는 회계 부서(Accounting)의 책임자임을 알 수 있다. 따라서 정답은 (A) He has a leadership role in the Accounting Department.이다.

42. SAC 신청 양식에 관하여 사실인 것은 무엇인가?

(A) 보안 관리 사무실로 직접 제출되어야 한다.

(B) 출입 요청의 이유를 밝혀야 한다.

(C) 사원증 사본을 포함시켜야 한다.

(D) 암호를 사용하기 최소 3일 전에 제출되어야 한다.

해설　신청 양식 지문 하단의 Note에서 신청서가 접수되면 SAC 발급은 영업일로 3일 정도 걸린다는 것을 알 수 있으므로 정답은 (D) It must be filed at least three days in advance of the code being used.이다.

43. Ms. Sherman이 입력한 SAC가 유효하다는 것을 어떻게 알 수 있는가?

(A) 불빛의 색깔이 변할 것이다.

(B) 소리가 5초 동안 울릴 것이다.

(C) 불빛이 반복해서 깜빡일 것이다.

(D) 소리의 음량이 올라갈 것이다.

해설　이메일 지문에서 SAC 사용법에 대한 안내를 하는 부분을 참고해야 한다. 먼저 SAC를 입력하면 다음 절차로 오렌지색 불빛이 초록색으로 변하면서 출입이 승인되었음을 확인할 수 있다. 따라서 정답은 (A) The color of a light will change.이다.

44. 보안 관리 사무소에 관하여 언급되지 않은 것은 무엇인가?
(A) 팩스기가 있다.
(B) 근무 시간 이후의 출입을 허용한다.
(C) 직원들에게 출입 암호를 발부한다.
(D) 새로운 보안 정책을 도입했다.

해설 사실 확인 문제 유형이니 보기를 하나씩 지문과 대조해서 언급이나 명시가 되어 있는지의 여부를 확인해야 한다. 신청서 양식 지문 첫머리를 통하여 Andrea Delgadillo가 보안 관리 사무소의 담당자이고 팩스기가 있는 것을 확인할 수 있으므로 (A)는 정답이다. 이메일 지문의 첫 문장에서 특별 및 연장 출입 승인에 대하여 언급하므로 (B)도 정답임을 확인할 수 있다. 또한 이어지는 문장에서 건물 출입 시 출입 암호를 사용해야 한다고 말하며, 암호 신청서 하단의 Note에서 암호가 담긴 이메일을 발송한다고 언급하고 있으므로 (C)도 정답임을 알 수 있다. new security policies에 관한 내용은 언급된 바 없으므로 정답은 (D) It has introduced new security policies.이다.

---

45. Ms. Sherman은 프로젝트를 언제 완료할 것으로 예상되는가?
(A) 9월 29일에
(B) 10월 7일에
(C) 11월 2일에
(D) 12월 31일에

해설 이메일 지문의 유의 사항 관련 정보에서 프로젝트 완료일 저녁에 SAC 카드 만료가 되고, 신청서 양식 지문에서 Start Date: October 7이고 End Date: November 2를 통해 11월 2일이 프로젝트 종료일임을 확인할 수 있다. 따라서 정답은 (C) On November 2이다.

[46-50] 다음 공지사항과 이메일들에 관한 문제입니다.

Senbay 공원 경기장이 자랑스럽게 발표합니다.

A Look Back
작가 Bailey Itani
7월-8월

Bailey Itani는 Springfield에 있는 스포츠 역사 박물관입니다.

🔟 Bailey Itani는 매사추세츠 체육부와 협력하여 120년의 역사에 걸쳐 경기장에서 있었던 다양한 스포츠 행사를 묘사하는 미술작품들을 선택했습니다. 46 Ms. Itani는 오랜 세월동안 주목받지 못한 경기를 보여줍니다.

경기장 정문을 지나면 방문객들은 세기가 전환되던 시기 그대로의 경기장의 모습에 둘러싸이게 됩니다. 47 전시물 번호를 따라가다 보면 경기장의 개발과 여러 해에 걸쳐 진행된 행사와 거기에 모인 사람들의 생생한 모습을 보면서 시간 여행을 하게 됩니다. 도중에 한 번도 본 적이 없는 사진과 신문 스크랩, 비디오 영상 등을 보게 될 것입니다.

입장권:
주중 오전 9시부터 오후 2시까지 무료 공개; 기타 날짜와 시간에는 행사가 기준

48 Ms. Itani는 6월 7일 토요일 오전 10시 Senbay 공립 도서관에서 이 프로젝트에 관하여 강연을 합니다. 입장권은 5달러이며 https://Senbayevents.org에서 온라인 구매할 수 있습니다.

어휘 overlook 못 보고 넘어가다, 간과하다 | clipping (신문 따위의) 오려낸 것 | video footage 비디오 영상 | subject to ~의 권한 아래 있는

발신: m.tomasi@meyer.edu
수신: itani@mmh.org
날짜: 6월 17일
제목:회신: 다큐멘터리 영화

Ms. Itani께,

48 지난주 당신의 강연에 매우 감명받았다는 사실을 알려드리고 싶었습니다.

저는 제가 가장 좋아하는 주제, 뉴잉글랜드의 50 과거와 현재 야구 선수들에 관한 다큐멘터리를 만들려고 계획하고 있으며 대본 쓰는 것을 도와줄 누군가를 찾고 있습니다. 이 프로젝트는 아메리칸 역사 센터에서 위임받았으며 저에게는 매력적인 급여 조건으로 한 명의 연구원을 채용할 권한이 있습니다. 당신의 강연을 들은 후 우리가 함께 일을 잘 할 수 있다는 확신을 갖게 되었습니다.

제 제안을 고려해 보시고 조만간 연락 주시기 바랍니다. 49 제가 이번 주에는 뉴욕에 있는데 6월 24일 이후에는 아무 때나 Springfield를 방문해서 당신을 만날 수 있습니다. 편하실 때 이 이메일 주소로 연락하시면 됩니다.

Marla Tomasi

어휘 commission 의뢰[주문]하다 | authorization 허가, 인가 | associate 동료

발신: itani@mmh.org
수신: m.tomasi@meyer.edu
날짜: 6월 19일
제목: 회신: 다큐멘터리 영화

Marla에게,

당신의 프로젝트는 꽤 흥미롭게 들립니다. 꼭 당신과 함께 하고 싶군요. 49 저도 이달 말쯤이면 당신과 같은 도시에 있으니까 분명 어떤 자리를 마련할 수 있을 겁니다. 어디에 묵고 계신지와 언제 시간이 있으신지 말씀해 주시면 만날 약속을 잡아 얘기를 더 해보죠.

그럼 이만,

Bailey Itani

어휘 set up (어떤 일이 있도록) 마련하다

---

46. 공지사항은 전시회에 관하여 무엇을 시사하는가?
(A) 다큐멘터리의 주제가 될 것이다.
(B) Springfield 출신 유명 운동선수들이 포함된다.
(C) 아메리칸 역사 센터의 후원을 받았다.
(D) 덜 유명했던 행사에 초점을 맞춘다.

해설 오랜 세월 동안 사람들이 주목하지 않았던 경기를 보여준다는 문장이 패러프레이징되어 있는 (D) It focuses on less famous events.가 정답이다.

---

47. 공지사항에는 무엇이 암시되어 있는가?
(A) 경기장 전시회는 토론회로 시작될 것이다.
(B) 방문객들은 특정 순서로 전시물을 보아야 한다.
(C) Ms. Itani는 주민들에게 스포츠 경기를 보러 가라고 권한다.
(D) 전시회 선물가게는 주중 매일 문을 연다.

해설 공지사항 세 번째 단락에서 전시물 번호를 따라가다 보면 경기장 개발 과정의 생생한 모습을 보면서 시간 여행을 하게 된다고 했으므로, 번호 순서로 작품을 보도록 의도적으로 구성된 전시회라는 것을 알 수 있다. 그러므로 정답은 (B) Visitors should look at the display in a specific sequence.이다.

---

48. Ms. Tomasi는 Ms. Itani의 강연을 어디서 들었겠는가?
(A) 스포츠 역사 박물관에서
(B) Senbay 공립 도서관에서
(C) 매사추세츠 체육부에서
(D) 아메리칸 역사 센터에서

해설 공지사항을 보면 Ms. Itani가 Senbay 공립 도서관에서 이번 프로젝트에 관하여 강연회를 할 것이라는 내용이 있는데, Ms. Tomasi가 보낸 이메일이 Ms. Itani의 강연을 듣고 감명받았다는 문장으로 시작되고 있으므로 강연을 들은 장소는 (B) At the Senbay Public Library이다.

---

49. Ms. Itani에 관하여 시사되어 있는 점은 무엇인가?
(A) Ms. Tomasi에게 높은 급여를 줄 것이다.
(B) 스포츠 기념품 몇 점을 팔 것이다.
(C) 뉴욕에서 Ms. Tomasi와 만날 것이다.
(D) 6월 24일에 Springfield로 돌아올 것이다.

해설 Ms. Tomasi가 보낸 이메일에 이번 주에는 뉴욕에 있다고 하는데, Ms. Itani가 보낸 이메일에도 Ms. Tomasi와 같은 도시에 월말까지 있을 것이니 묵고 있는 장소와 편리한 시간을 알려주면 만날 수 있다는 내용이 나온다. 이 두 부분을 종합해보면 두 사람은 뉴욕에서 만날 것이라고 유추할 수 있으므로 정답은 (C) She will meet Ms. Tomasi in New York.이다. 자신에게는 매력적인 급여 조건으로 한 명의 연구원을 채용할 권한이 있다는 Ms. Tomasi의 글을 읽고 (A)를 정답으로 선택하지 않도록 주의해야 한다. 보수는 Ms. Tomasi가 Ms. Itani에게 제공하는 것이다.

---

50. Ms. Tomasi와 Ms. Itani는 어느 분야에서 지식을 공유하는가?
(A) 영화 제작
(B) 스포츠 역사
(C) 현대 미술
(D) 저널리즘

해설 공지사항에서 Ms. Itani의 전시회 주제가 12년에 걸친 다양한 스포츠 행사라고 나와 있는데, Ms. Tomasi가 보낸 이메일에서는 과거와 현재의 야구선수들에 관한 다큐멘터리를 만들겠다고 했으므로 두 사람이 공통으로 다루는 분야는 (B) Sports history이다.

HALF TEST 02

본서 p.370

1. (B)	2. (D)	3. (B)	4. (D)	5. (C)
6. (A)	7. (B)	8. (B)	9. (D)	10. (B)
11. (A)	12. (C)	13. (B)	14. (B)	15. (D)
16. (D)	17. (B)	18. (D)	19. (B)	20. (C)
21. (B)	22. (C)	23. (D)	24. (D)	25. (A)
26. (B)	27. (B)	28. (B)	29. (D)	30. (B)
31. (C)	32. (A)	33. (D)	34. (D)	35. (B)
36. (D)	37. (C)	38. (D)	39. (D)	40. (B)
41. (B)	42. (C)	43. (D)	44. (B)	45. (C)
46. (C)	47. (D)	48. (D)	49. (D)	50. (D)

---

1. 제조 부서의 근로자들은 할당량이 충족되는 대로 휴가 신청을 할 수 있다.

해설 이 문장의 동사가 2개(can sign up for, is reached)이므로 두 문장을 연결하는 접속사 (B) as soon as가 정답이다. 부사 (A)와 (D), 전치사 (C)는 문장을 연결하는 역할을 하지 못하므로 오답이다.

어휘 **manufacturing department** 제조 부서 | **sign up** 신청하다 | **quota** 할당량 | **reach** 도달하다 | **promptly** 즉시 | **right away** 곧, 지체하지 않고

---

2. Steve Miller의 영화 회고전이 국립현대미술관에서 열리고 있다.

해설 동사 문제는 수 일치 → 태 → 시제 순으로 접근하는데 이 문제는 태에서 정답이 나오는 문제이다. 선택지 중 (D)만 유일하게 수동태이다. 빈칸 뒤에 목적어가 없으며 주어인 회고전이 스스로 여는 것이 아니라 열리는 수동의 관계이기 때문에 수동태인 (D) is being held가 정답이다.

어휘 **retrospective** 회고전 | **hold** 개최하다

---

3. Biz Core의 회장은 뉴욕 시로 이전하여 Avalon Research라는 이름의 금융 서비스 회사를 설립했다.

해설 장소를 나타내는 선행사 New York City를 받아 주면서, 완전한 문장 구조를 이끄는 접속부사 (B) where가 정답이다. (D) while은 '~동안에'나 '~반면에'라는 뜻이므로 문맥상 적절하지 않고, 불완전 구조를 이끄는 관계사 (A) what, (C) which는 빈칸 뒤의 문장 구조가 완전하기 때문에 오답이다.

어휘 **found** 설립하다, 창립하다 | **financial services company** 금융 서비스 회사

---

4. We Care는 도움이 필요한 사람들을 위해 기금을 모으기를 원하는 개인들을 위해 개설된 무료 모금 활동 웹사이트입니다.

해설 준동사도 기본적으로는 동사의 성질을 가지고 있다. 따라서 현재분사 wanting은 동사 want와 마찬가지로 목적어로 to부정사를 취해야 하므로 (D) to raise가 정답이다.

어휘 **fundraising** 모금 활동 | **create** 만들다, 창조하다 | **people in need** 도움이 필요한 사람들

5. 행사 예약이 꽉 차는 경우, 대기자 명단을 작성하고 예약 취소가 발생하게 되면 장소가 제공될 것입니다.

해설 「there + be동사 + 주어」 구문을 묻는 문제로, there are 뒤의 빈칸은 주어에 해당한다. 동사가 복수동사인 are이므로 주어는 복수 명사가 되어야 한다. 따라서, (C) cancellations가 정답이다.

어휘 reserve 예약하다, 보유하다 ∣ waiting list 대기자 명단 ∣ cancel 취소하다 ∣ cancellation 취소

6. 비록 그 공연의 관람은 무료이지만, 사람들은 행사장 입장을 위해 표를 예약하도록 요구받는다.

해설 행사 입장을 위해 티켓 예약이 요구된다는 의미이므로 목적을 나타내는 전치사 (A) for가 정답이다.

어휘 performance 공연; 성과 ∣ admittance 입장, 들어감

7. 조사 결과는 Astro 스포츠 네트워크 시청자들의 수가 현재 주요 경쟁업체인 ANP 스포츠의 수와 동일하다는 것을 보여준다.

해설 빈칸은 be동사 뒤의 보어자리다. 'Astro 스포츠 네트워크 시청자 숫자가 ANP 스포츠의 시청자 숫자와 현재 동일하다'는 문맥에 따라 동일한 상태를 의미하는 형용사 (B) equal이 정답이다.

어휘 survey 설문(조사) ∣ indicate 나타내다, 보여주다 ∣ viewer (텔레비전) 시청자 ∣ currently 현재 ∣ competitor 경쟁자, 경쟁업체

8. 현재 시장에 나와 있는 동종업계 최고의 잡지로 자부하는 저희 잡지를 계속 보내드릴 수 있기를 고대합니다.

해설 뒤에 오는 명사를 '~의'라는 의미로 이어주는 형용사적 역할을 하는 소유격의 자리다. 따라서 (B) its가 정답이다.

어휘 look forward to V-ing ~하기를 고대하다 ∣ proudly 자신(감) 있게

9. 고용주들은 수습 채용 기간을 활용하여 신입 직원이 직무를 잘 수행할 수 있을지를 확인한다.

해설 빈칸 이하가 ascertain의 목적어가 되어야 하므로 명사절 접속사인 (D) whether가 정답이다.

어휘 probationary 시험 중인, 가채용의 ∣ ascertain 알아내다, 확인하다 ∣ handle 처리하다 ∣ duty 직무, 임무

10. 저명한 저널리스트 Maria Gray는 그녀의 인도 특파원 시절에 대한 책을 편찬하려는 계획을 발표했다.

해설 빈칸은 to부정사(to compile)의 수식을 받는 동시에 소유격 her의 수식을 받는 명사 자리임에 유의하여 전체 문맥을 파악해야 한다. '저명한 저널리스트가 인도 특파원 시절에 대한 책을 편찬하겠다는 계획을 발표했다'는 문맥에 따라 '~하려는 의지, 의향, 계획'을 의미하는 (B) intent가 정답이다.

어휘 renowned 저명한 ∣ compile 엮다, 편집하다 ∣ regarding ~에 대한 ∣ correspondent 기자, 특파원 ∣ explanation 설명 ∣ intent to + 동사원형 ~하려는 의지[의향, 계획] ∣ construction 건설 ∣ ideal 이상적인

11. Koma 건설은 교수들 및 그 외 전문가들을 정기적으로 초청하여 최신의 업계 관행에 대해 직원들을 훈련시킨다.

해설 문맥상 교수 및 전문가들을 정기적으로 초청한다는 의미로 '정기적으로'라는 의미의 부사가 와야 한다. 따라서 (A) regularly가 정답이다.

어휘 academic 교수 ∣ latest 최근의, 최신의 ∣ practice 관행, 관례 ∣ regularly 정기적으로 ∣ evenly 고르게, 균등하게 ∣ exactly 정확하게 ∣ timely 시기적절한

12. 파트타임 직원들은 일반적으로 평일 주당 근무 시간이 정규직 직원들보다 적다.

해설 between은 대상이 둘 있을 때 쓰이고, among은 대상이 셋 이상 있을 때 쓰이는데, 빈칸 뒤에 단수 명사가 있으므로 이 두 개의 선택지는 소거시킨다. above는 '~위에'라는 뜻이므로 적절하지 않으며, '일주일 동안의 근무 시간'과 어울려야 하므로 특정 기간을 나타내는 전치사 during이 적절하다. 따라서 (C) during이 정답이다.

어휘 employee 직원 ∣ typically 일반적으로, 전형적으로 ∣ fewer 더 적은 수의

13. 경제 성장이 가속도를 얻기 위해서는 인적 자본의 매우 중요한 요소인 교육에 투자하는 것이 중요하다.

해설 빈칸 뒤에 명사가 위치해 있으므로, 빈칸은 전치사 자리이다. '경제 성장이 가속도를 얻기 위해서'라는 의미가 적절하므로 to부정사(to grow)의 의미상 주어가 '------ economic growth '부분임을 알 수 있다. to부정사의 의미상의 주어는 「for + 명사」 형태로 나타내므로 (B) For가 정답이다. 빈칸 뒤에 동사가 수반되지 않았기 때문에, 문장을 연결하는 역할의 접속사 (A)나 관계사 (C)는 오답이며, 전치사 (C)는 문맥상 어울리지 않는다.

어휘 economic growth 경제 성장 ∣ acceleration 가속(도) ∣ invest in ~에 투자하다 ∣ component 요소 ∣ human capital 인적 자본

14. 배송비를 정하는 것은 문제가 되는데, 그 이유는 무게와 배송 거리에 따라 요금이 달라지기 때문이다.

해설 '상품의 배송 요금'을 뜻하는 복합명사 shipping charge를 묻는 문제이다. 따라서 (B) charges가 정답이다. 오답으로 자주 등장하는 (A) fare는 'a taxi/bus/air fare (택시/버스/항공 요금)'와 같이 교통수단의 요금을 의미할 때 쓴다.

어휘 problematic 문제가 있는 ∣ vary 상황에 따라 달라지다 ∣ depending on ~에 따라 ∣ fare 교통 요금 ∣ charge (상품이나 서비스에 대한) 요금 ∣ value 가치 ∣ figure 수치

15. 관리자들이 직원들을 존중하는 태도로 대하면 대할수록, 직원들은 더욱 효과적으로 고객들을 대하게 된다.

해설 'the 비교급, the 비교급' 구문으로, 'A할수록 더 B하게 된다'는 의미이다. 전후 의미 관계상 직원들을 '존중할수록' 직원들이 효과적으로 고객을 응대하게 된다는 문맥이 알맞다. 따라서 (D) respectfully가 정답이다.

어휘 treat 다루다, 취급하다 ∣ repeatedly 반복적으로, 되풀이하여 ∣ relatively 비교적 ∣ respectfully 존경심을 표하여

16. 회사 최고경영자는 Ms. Frances가 High Tech 사와의 계약을 따낸 일을 축하했다.

해설 해석만 따져서는 혼동되는 문제이다. 뒤에 전치사 for와 묶어서 쓰이는 표현이 congratulate A for B(A를 B에 대해서 축하해 주다)이므로 (D) congratulated가 정답이다. entrust는 entrust A to B나 entrust B with A로 쓰이며, agree는 자동사로서 전치사 with/on/upon/to 등과 함께 쓰인다.

어휘 win a contract 계약을 따내다 | demonstrate 입증하다 | entrust 맡기다 | agree 동의하다

17. 지점 관리자는 시간에 맞게 주문된 상품을 배송하기 위해서는 모든 사람이 초과 근무를 해야 한다고 강조했다.

해설 전체 문장의 의미를 파악하여 문맥상 가장 자연스러운 부정대명사를 선택하는 문제이다. 해석상 '모든 사람들'이 자연스러우므로 (D) everyone이 정답이다. no one이나 nobody는 문맥에 맞지 않으며, one another(서로)는 each other(서로)와 함께 주어로 쓰일 수 없는 대명사이다.

어휘 branch 지점 | emphasize 강조하다 | work overtime 초과 근무하다, 시간 외로 일하다

18. Universe 스마트폰의 개발은 사람들이 사무실을 임대할 필요 없이 실외에서 일하는 것을 가능하게 할 것이다.

해설 문맥상 빈칸에는 '~을 가능하게 하다' 또는 '~을 허락하다'라는 의미의 동사가 필요하다. 따라서 (D) allow가 정답이다. 또한, allow는 '목적어 + to부정사'를 취하는 5형식 동사이기 때문에 빈칸 뒤의 구조를 단서로 삼아 allow를 정답으로 선택할 수도 있다.

어휘 development 개발 | avoid 피하다 | provide 제공하다 | show 보여 주다 | allow 가능하게 하다

19. 모든 승객들은 비행기에서 나갈 때 본인의 소지품을 위해 짐칸을 확인하도록 요청받는다.

해설 「when + 주어 + be + V-ing/p.p.」 구조에서 「주어 + be동사」를 생략하여 「when + V-ing(능동)/when + p.p.(수동)」으로 쓰는 부사절 생략에 관한 문제이다. '탑승객들이 비행기에서 나갈 때'라는 문맥이므로 능동의 의미를 갖는 현재분사 (D) exiting이 정답이며, 'when they are exiting an airplane'에서 'they are'가 생략된 구조이다. 이 때 they는 주절의 주어인 passengers를 받는 대명사이다.

어휘 overhead compartment (비행기 내의 머리 위의) 짐칸 | belongings 소지품 | exit 퇴거하다, 나가다

20. 〈Dawlish Gazette〉는 제휴 웹사이트들과의 연결을 이용하여 자사의 다른 온라인 출판물들을 광고한다.

해설 보기 모두가 전치사이므로 문맥상 어울리는 전치사를 선택하는 문제이다. '제휴 웹사이트와의 연결을 이용해 온라인에서 광고를 한다'는 문맥에 따라, '~을 이용해, ~을 사용하여'를 뜻하는 (C) with가 정답이다.

어휘 gazette 관보, 신문, 가제트 | publication 출판물; 발행 | link 연결, 연계 | affiliated 제휴된; 연계된

[21-24] 다음 설명서에 관한 문제입니다.

고객님의 수하물이 분실되었다면, 이 서식을 작성하여 청구서를 제출해 주십시오. 분실된 수하물에 들어 있는 모든 품목을 명확하게 **21** 리스트로 작성해 주십시오.

서식을 다 작성하시면, 도착장에 있는 분실 수하물 데스크의 직원에게 서식을 건네 주십시오.

저희 직원들은 고객님의 수하물을 **22** 추적하기 위해 컴퓨터화된 시스템을 사용할 것이라서, 보통 48시간 안에 수하물을 되찾을 수 있습니다. **23** 그 다음에, 귀하의 수하물은 직접 귀하께 배송될 것입니다.

수하물 분실로 인해 불편을 끼쳐 드린 점을 사과드리며, 가능한 빨리 고객님의 **24** 소유물을 찾아드리기 위해 할 수 있는 모든 일을 다 할 것을 약속드립니다.

어휘 claim 청구, 신청, 주장 | fill out a form 서식을 작성하다 | ensure 반드시 ~하게 하다, 보장하다 | locate ~의 정확한 위치를 찾아내다 | list 리스트를 작성하다 | prevent 막다, 방지하다 | contain ~이 들어 있다 | computerized 컴퓨터화된 | trace 추적하다 | apologize for ~에 대해 사과하다 | inconvenience 불편 | due to ~로 인해 | rest assured ~임을 확신해도 된다 | reunite 재회하다 | invoice 청구서 | recording 녹음[녹화]된 것 | belongings [복수] 소유물 | as soon as possible 가능한 빨리

21. **해설** 문맥상 분실된 수하물에 들어 있는 모든 품목을 명확하게 목록을 작성해 달라는 의미가 자연스러우므로 빈칸에는 '리스트를 작성하다'라는 의미의 동사가 필요하므로 (B) list가 정답이다.

22. **해설** 빈칸 앞의 문장은 완성된 문장이므로 빈칸 뒷부분에는 앞 문장에 의미를 추가하는 부사적 역할을 하는 수식어구가 들어가야 한다. 해석상으로도 '직원들이 고객의 수하물을 추적하기 위해'이므로 '~하기 위해'라는 의미를 만들어 주는 to부정사가 들어갈 자리이다. 따라서 (C) to trace가 정답이다.

23. (A) 그 후에, 귀하께서는 저희가 제공하는 부가 서비스에 대해 비용을 지불하실 수 있습니다.
(B) 다행스럽게도, 모든 사람들이 잃어버렸던 가방들을 받았습니다.
(C) 결과적으로, 저희는 승객들의 어떤 가방이든 거의 잃어버리지 않습니다.
(D) 그 다음에, 귀하의 수하물은 직접 귀하께 배송될 것입니다.

해설 이전 문장이 수하물을 48시간 내에 되찾을 수 있다는 내용이므로 그 다음에 잃어버렸던 수하물이 어떻게 처리되는지 알려 주는 (D) Then, your luggage will be personally delivered to you.가 문맥상 가장 자연스럽다.

24. **해설** 문맥상 '가능한 빨리 고객님의 소유물을 찾아 드리기 위해'라는 의미가 되어야 하므로 빈칸에는 '소유물'이라는 뜻의 belongings가 필요하다. 따라서 (D) belongings가 정답이다.

[25-28] 다음 편지에 관한 문제입니다.

프라이빗 뱅킹 고객님께,

저희 Jessop 은행은 프라이빗 뱅킹 고객님들의 보안을 매우 진지하게 생각합니다. 그러므로 고객님의 인터넷 뱅킹 로그인 정보나 **25** 다른 어떤 보안 정보를 결코 이메일이나 전화로 요청하지 않을 것입니다.

저희는 항상 고객님의 개인 정보를 완전한 기밀로 다룰 것입니다. 또한 고객님들께서도 개인 정보 보호를 위해 아래 서술된 **26** 추가적 조치를 취해 주실 것을 권장합니다. 항상 아무도 짐작하지 못할 비밀번호를 선택하십시오. 또한 반드시 자주 비밀번호를 변경하십시오.

개인 정보, 계좌번호 등을 요청하는 이메일에 절대 회신하지 마십시오. 이러한 이메일들은 저희가 보낸 것이 아닐 것입니다.

마지막으로, 이메일이 사기성이 있는 것으로 의심된다면, 저희 사기 방지팀에 1-800-999-7261로 연락 주십시오. **27** 직원들이 그 문제를 즉각적으로 조사할 것입니다.

고객님 정보의 비밀 유지를 위해 **28** 협조해 주신 점 미리 감사드립니다.

진심으로,

Justin Charles 드림
사기 방지 팀장

어휘 **private banking** 프라이빗 뱅킹 | **take ~ seriously** ~을 진지[심각]하게 생각하다 | **personal information** 개인 정보 | **confidentiality** 비밀 | **recommend** 추천하다 | **outline** 개요를 서술하다 | **protect** 보호하다 | **ensure** 반드시 ~하게 하다 | **account number** 계좌번호 | **etc.** ~ 등 | **fraudulent** 사기를 치는 | **fraud** 사기 | **prevention** 예방 | **in advance** 미리

25. 해설 빈칸은 뒤에 있는 security information이라는 명사를 수식하는 한정사의 자리이다. (B) one another와 (C) each other는 명사 역할만 하므로 소거시킨다. 한정사로 쓰일 수 있는 건 any other와 another이다. another는 뒤에 가산 단수명사를 받아야 하는데 information은 불가산명사이므로 수식 관계가 성립되지 않는다. any other는 '(어떤 그 밖의) 다른'이라는 의미의 한정사로 쓰이는 표현이다. 따라서 (A) any other가 정답이다.

26. 해설 빈칸에는 뒤의 명사 measures를 수식하는 형용사가 와야 하고, 문맥상 고객들도 개인 정보 보호를 위해 아래 서술된 추가적 조치를 취해 달라는 의미가 되어야 하므로 '추가적'이라는 뜻의 형용사가 필요하다. 따라서 (B) extra가 정답이다. (A) relative는 '상대적인', (C) excess는 '지나침, 과잉', 그리고 (D) extreme은 '매우, 극단적인'이라는 의미이다.

27. (A) 고객님의 비밀번호를 제공하는 것이 반드시 필요합니다.
(B) 그들은 그 문제를 즉각적으로 조사할 것입니다.
(C) 이것은 고객님의 기밀을 잃게 할 것입니다.
(D) 고객님은 그렇게 하면 사기로 기소당할 것입니다.

해설 앞 문장에서 문제가 생기면 사기 방지팀으로 연락 달라고 했으므로, 문제에 대한 해결책을 제시하는 (B) They will look into the matter immediately.가 문맥의 흐름상 가장 적합하다. Jessop Bank는 절대 개인 정보에 대해서 물어보지 않으므로 (A)는 오답이다.

28. 해설 Thank you for 다음에는 고마워하는 이유에 해당하는 명사 또는 동명사가 와야 된다. 문맥상, 개인 정보 비밀 유지를 위해 협조해 주셔서 감사하다는 말이 되어야 자연스러우므로 (B) support가 정답이다.

[29-30] 다음 문자 메시지 대화에 관한 문제입니다.

Carrie Vasquez

Andy, 도움이 필요해요! 9시 30분 회의에서 영업보고서를 발표해야 하는데 사무실에 제시간에 못 가요. 내 차 타이어에 펑크가 나서 갈아 껴야 하거든요.
오전 9:19

Andy Steuter

오전 9:20 문제가 있다니 안됐어요. 어떻게 도와줄까요?

Carrie Vasquez

회의 일정을 내일로 다시 잡을 수 있을까요? 아니면 약간 연기라도 할 수 있을까요? 9시 55분까지는 갈 수 있을 것 같은데요.
오전 9:21

Andy Steuter

벌써 사람들이 많이 왔으니까 다른 방법을 찾아 봐요. 오늘 오전에 인사부의 Anna Smith도 15분짜리 발표를 하잖아요. **29 30** 그 사람에게 당신 대신 회의 첫머리에 발표해달라고 요청할게요.
오전 9:22

Carrie Vasquez

30 그럼 그렇게 하면 되겠네요. 고마워요.
오전 9:23

어휘 **get to** ~에 도착하다 | **flat tire** 바람 빠진 타이어 | **give a presentation** 보고하다 | **present** 발표하다 | **work out** 잘 풀리다

29. Mr. Steuter는 자신이 무엇을 할 것임을 언급하는가?
(A) 회의실을 예약한다
(B) Ms. Vasquez를 차에 태워준다
(C) 발표 시간대를 서로 바꾼다
(D) 회의를 연기한다

해설 Anna Smith와 Ms. Vasquez가 모두 발표를 해야 하는데, '그 사람에게 회의 첫머리에 당신 대신 발표해달라고 요청할게요'라고 말했으므로 두 사람의 발표 시간대를 서로 바꾸려고 시도할 것임을 알 수 있다. 따라서 (C) Switch presentation times가 정답이다.

30. 오전 9시 23분에 Ms. Vasquez가 "그럼 그렇게 하면 되겠네요"라고 썼을 때 무엇을 의미하는 것 같은가?

(A) 첫 발표자가 되는 것도 괜찮다.

(B) 기술자에게 전화해준 것에 대해 Mr. Steuter에게 고마워한다.

(C) Mr. Steuter의 해결책에 동의한다.

(D) 채용 면접의 일정을 다시 잡는 것도 괜찮다.

해설 주어진 문장은 앞 문장에서 Ms. Vasquez가 회의에 늦게 오는 상황에 대한 해결책으로 Ms. Steuter가 Anna Smith에게 회의 첫머리에 대신 먼저 발표해달라고 요청하겠다고 하자 그에 대한 응답으로 나온 말이다. '그럼 그렇게 하면 되겠네요'는 해결책에 대한 동의를 의미하므로 (C) She agrees to Mr. Steuter's solution.이 정답이다.

[31-33] 다음 안내책자의 한 섹션에 관한 문제입니다.

Cameron Klein 실내 디자인 센터

Cameron Klein 실내 디자인 센터에 오신 것을 환영합니다. **31** 이 안내책자는 이 멋진 실내를 혼자서 관람하시는 분을 돕도록 제작되었습니다.

귀하께서 여기에서 보시는 대부분의 디자인은 Mr. Klein이 25년의 경력 기간 동안 만든 것입니다. 다른 디자인들은 Mr. Klein 밑에서 공부하여, Mr. Klein의 스타일을 구현하는 실내 디자이너들에 의해 만들어졌습니다. 둘러보시는 동안, 현관 근처의 상자에 있는 팸플릿을 마음껏 이용하세요. **32** 이 무료 책자는 보다 많은 읽을거리를 위한 온라인 기사들의 링크 주소 목록뿐 아니라 Mr. Klein에 대한 짧은 전기를 담고 있습니다. **33** 디자인 센터 안의 장식 및 가구들은 Berkeley 건축협회의 회원들이 기증해주셨습니다.

이 단체의 본부는 센터의 중앙 출구 맞은편에 위치해 있고, 월요일부터 토요일 오전 9시부터 오후 5시까지 개방됩니다. 실내 디자인 센터 방문객들은 센터의 실내 장식들 모음을 더 보실 수 있도록 이 시간 동안에 들르시도록 초대합니다.

어휘 brochure 홍보[안내]책자 | be designed to ~하도록 제작되다 | self-guided 혼자[스스로] 하는 | impressive 인상적인 | embody 포함하다, 담다 | help yourself to 마음껏 ~하세요 | front entrance 현관 | complimentary 무료의, 칭찬하는 | include 포함하다 | brief 간략한 | biography 전기 | décor 장식 | headquarters 본사 | opposite 반대편의, 맞은편의 | drop by 잠시 들르다

---

31. 이 안내책자는 어디에서 찾을 수 있겠는가?

(A) 역사 도서관에서

(B) 서점에서

(C) 전시장에서

(D) 예술 학교에서

해설 지문에서 책자에 관한 언급을 찾아야 한다. 지문의 전체 내용은 Cameron Klein 실내 디자인 센터에 관한 글이고, 글 첫머리에 안내책자의 목적이 언급된 부분을 보면 이 책자는 혼자 디자인 센터 관람을 하는 사람에게 도움을 주기 위한 것임을 알 수 있으므로 정답은 (C) At an exhibit이다.

32. 방문객들이 무료로 이용 가능한 것으로 언급된 것은 무엇인가?

(A) 읽기 자료

(B) 기초 건축학 강좌

(C) 장식 견본

(D) 실내 디자이너가 인솔하는 관람

해설 지문 두 번째 단락을 통하여 현관 근처 상자에 있는 팸플릿을 보라고 했고, 그 팸플릿이 무료임을 확인할 수 있다. 따라서 정답은 (A) Reading materials이다.

33. Berkeley 건축협회에 관하여 언급된 것은 무엇인가?

(A) 본부는 일주일에 네 번 문을 연다.

(B) 25년 전에 설립되었다.

(C) 회원들이 많은 장식품을 디자인했다.

(D) 가구를 기증함으로써 공헌을 했다.

해설 지문 두 번째 단락을 통하여 Berkeley 건축협회가 장식과 가구를 기증했음을 알 수 있다. 그러므로 정답은 (D) It contributed by providing furniture.이다.

[34-36] 다음 웹사이트 정보에 관한 문제입니다.

---

http://www.richardjonesheating.com

홈	서비스	추천의 말	예약	연락처

Richard Jones 난방

34 고객의 말씀

34 점수 : ★★★★★

서비스 날짜: 3월 12일

서비스 종류: **36** Enroe RF20 보일러 설치

지난주에 저는 사무실의 보일러에 문제가 있는 것을 발견했습니다. 저는 접수처에서 Richard Jones 난방의 안내책자를 본 것을 기억해 내고 회사로 전화를 걸었습니다. 토요일이었고 정규 영업 시간이 아니었음에도, Mr. Jones는 전화를 건 지 두 시간 만에 즉시 문제를 점검하러 와 주셨습니다. 그분은 난방 시스템을 점검한 뒤 보일러가 교체되어야 한다고 제게 조언하셨습니다. Mr. Jones는 다양한 모델의 카탈로그를 제게 보여주셨고, **36** 저는 가장 에너지 효율 등급이 높은 모델을 골랐습니다. 저는 그 기기를 주문하고 설치하는 데 적어도 일주일은 걸릴 것이라 예상했습니다만, **35** Mr. Jones는 당일에 그것을 가져와서 설치해 주실 수 있었습니다. 주말 서비스에 대한 추가 요금조차도 없었습니다. 그 다음 월요일에, 회사의 기술자분이 보일러가 제대로 작동하는지 확인하러 사무실로 오셨습니다. 모든 과정이 Richard Jones 난방이 제공하는 뛰어난 고객 서비스를 보여주었습니다. 저는 다른 분들께 확실히 이 회사를 추천해 드리겠습니다.

Sarah Tran

어휘 | notice 알아차리다 | faulty 문제가 있는 | reception 접수처 | immediately 즉시 | examine 검사[점검]하다 | advise 조언하다 | replace 교체하다 | various 다양한 | appliance 기기 | install 설치하다 | additional 추가적인 | run 작동하다 | properly 적절히, 제대로 | whole 전체의 | process 과정, 절차 | demonstrate 나타내다 | recommend 추천하다

34. 이 정보가 왜 웹사이트에 포함되어 있겠는가?

(A) 회사 규정을 설명하기 위해

(B) 설치 과정에 대한 개요를 보여주기 위해

(C) 새로운 상품을 홍보하기 위해

(D) 잠재적 고객을 유치하기 위해

해설 글의 제목이 What customers say about us/Rating: ★★★★★ 이므로 고객이 회사의 서비스를 높이 평가한 것을 확인할 수 있다. 고객의 글을 웹사이트에 실음으로써 다른 고객들을 끌어들이기 위한 것이므로 정답은 (D) To attract potential customers이다. 글 전체 내용이 Richard Jones Heating의 뛰어난 고객 서비스에 대한 것이므로 (C)는 오답이다.

35. Mr. Jones에 관하여 언급된 것은 무엇인가?

(A) Ms. Tran이 구독하는 잡지에 그의 서비스를 광고했다.

(B) Ms. Tran이 요청한 날짜와 같은 날에 작업을 마쳤다.

(C) 주말 작업에 대한 추가 요금을 부과했다.

(D) 3월 12일에 고장 난 보일러를 수리했다.

해설 사실 확인 문제 유형이니 보기를 하나씩 지문과 대조해서 언급이나 명시가 되어 있는지의 여부를 확인해야 한다. Mr. Jones에 대한 언급을 지문에서 찾아야 한다. 지문의 중간 부분의 Mr. Jones was able to get one and install it on that same day를 통하여 Mr. Jones가 서비스 요청 당일에 보일러 설치를 해 준 것을 알 수 있으므로 정답은 (B) He completed work for Ms. Tran on the same day she requested it.이다.

36. Enroe RF20 보일러의 특징에 관하여 언급된 것은 무엇인가?

(A) 설치가 쉽다.

(B) 가격이 합리적이다.

(C) 다양한 색상으로 판매된다.

(D) 에너지 효율적이다.

해설 지문의 제목과 글에서 Enroe RF20 보일러는 서비스 평가를 쓴 Sarah Tran이 설치한 보일러임을 알 수 있고, 보일러 교체를 위해 에너지 효율이 가장 높은 모델을 선택했다는 언급을 통하여 이 모델이 에너지 효율성이 가장 높음을 확인할 수 있으므로 정답은 (D) It is energy efficient이다.

[37-40] 다음 편지에 관한 문제입니다.

Creekberry 가전
1029 E. Dorsette 가
솔트레이크 시티, 유타 84111
www.creekberryhome.com

6월 12일

Ms. Amanda Rucker
KPHV Channel 10
44983 W. Chaparral 로
선 시티, 아리조나 85351

Ms. Rucker께,

Creekberry 가전에 연락주셔서 고맙습니다. KPHV와 〈Community Business Spotlight〉 팀으로부터 소식을 듣고 더할 나위 없이 기뻤습니다. Creekberry 가전의 최고경영자로서 제가 🉗 기꺼이 스튜디오를 방문해서 인터뷰와 저희의 새로 디자인한 제습기의 시연회를 하겠습니다. 2년 전 저희 진공청소기가 당신의 프로그램에 나온 후 평소보다 훨씬 더 많은 전화와 이메일 문의가 있었을 뿐만 아니라 판매량도 눈에 띄게 늘었습니다. 이번 새 제품은 청소가 쉽고 고장이 거의 날 수 없도록 특별히 설계되었습니다. 효율성이 75퍼센트 향상되었는데, 이것은 매일 공기 중의 습기 170파인트를 제거할 수 있다는 것을 의미합니다. 🉐 또한 완전히 디지털화되었고, 다양한 에너지 사용량 옵션도 장착했습니다. 그러나 핵심은 새 Creekberry 제습기가 늘 해온 기능을 한다는 점, 즉 주변에 가장 편안한 가정 환경을 만들어준다는 점입니다.

🉘 Creekberry 제습기의 사양을 자세히 보여주는 안내책자를 이 편지에 동봉했습니다. 자세히 읽어보시고 편리하신 가장 빠른 시간에 이메일이나 전화로 연락해주시기 바랍니다. 추가적인 홍보 자료를 원하신다면 그것도 언제든지 몇 개 보내드릴 수 있습니다.

〈Community Business Spotlight〉 혹은 당신이 생각하기에 우리가 시청자들에게 다가가는 데 도움이 된다 싶은 다른 어떤 방송 프로그램에서든 저희 회사 브랜드를 홍보하게 되기를 기대합니다. KPHV 시청자들에게 제품을 선보일 수 있도록 저희에게 🉙 연락 주셔서 정말 고맙습니다.

질문이 있으시거나 무엇이든 도와드릴 일이 있다면 알려주십시오.

가장 큰 진심을 담아,

Dagny Leitner
Dagny Leitner
최고경영자, Creekberry 가전

동봉물 재중

어휘 | dehumidifier 제습기 | vacuum 진공청소기 | pint 파인트(계량) | at one's earliest convenience 가급적 빨리 | station 방송국 | programming 방송 프로그램 편성 | appreciate 고마워하다 | reach out to ~에게 연락하다, 관심을 보이다

37. Ms. Leitner는 왜 Ms. Rucker에게 편지를 썼는가?

    (A) 기기의 상세한 내용을 요청하려고

    (B) 최근 매출액을 요청하려고

    (C) 방송에 대한 초대를 수락하려고

    (D) 새 프로그램에 대해 알아보려고

해설 지문의 주제나 목적은 항상 도입부에서 알아낼 수 있다. 첫 문장의 연락 고맙다는 말에 이어서 다음 문장에서 인터뷰와 제품 시연회를 하겠다고 했으므로 방송 출연 요청을 수락하기 위한 편지라는 걸 알 수 있다. 따라서 정답은 (C) To accept an invitation to a show이다.

---

38. Ms. Leitner는 편지에 무엇을 포함하였는가?

    (A) 홍보 포스터

    (B) 제품 사양의 목록

    (C) 계약서

    (D) 매장까지 가는 지도

해설 문제의 키워드가 include in her letter인데, 동사 include는 거의 대부분 enclose(동봉하다)나 attach(첨부하다) 같은 동사로 바뀌어 지문에 등장한다. 두 번째 단락의 enclosed가 보이는 문장에서 정답을 알 수 있다. 제품의 사양(specifications)을 보여주는 안내책자를 동봉했다고 했으므로 specifications의 동의어 features가 들어 있는 (B) A list of product features가 정답이다.

---

39. 세 번째 단락, 세 번째 줄의 구문 "reaching out to"와 의미상 가장 가까운 것은

    (A) 붙잡고 있어서

    (B) 움켜쥐고 있어서

    (C) 연락해 주어서

    (D) 자세히 살펴보아서

해설 동사 reach는 연락하는 것을 의미하는데, 연락은 대화로 이루어지는 것이므로 역시 대화를 의미하는 communicating with와 의미상 가장 가깝다. 따라서 (C) communicating with가 정답이다.

---

40. [1], [2], [3], [4]로 표시된 곳 중에서 다음 문장이 들어가기에 가장 적절한 곳은 어디인가?

    "또한 완전히 디지털화되었고, 다양한 에너지 사용량 옵션도 장착했습니다."

    (A) [1]

    (B) [2]

    (C) [3]

    (D) [4]

해설 [2] 바로 앞 문장에서 청소의 용이함이나 내구성 향상, 효율성 향상과 같은 제품의 개선된 점을 설명하고 있으며, 뒤 문장에서는 모든 개선사항보다 강조하고 싶은 것은 가전제품 본연의 목적에 충실하다는 점이라고 말하고 있다. 여기에 주어진 문장을 삽입하면 제품의 개선 사항을 하나 더 나열해주는 것이므로 문맥이 자연스러워진다. 따라서 정답은 (B) [2]이다.

[41-45] 다음 이메일과 설문지에 관한 문제입니다.

수신: r_sanger@mbwhiteinsurance.com

발신: orders@stewartstationerysupplies.com

날짜: 11월 5일, 오전 9시 12분

제목: 귀하의 주문 번호 21987QT2

Mr. Sanger께,

🔢**44** Stewart 문구용품의 온라인 상점에서 주문해 주셔서 감사합니다. 귀하의 주문이 처리되었으며, 오늘 오후 2시에 Billington 창고에서 배송이 될 예정입니다.

수량	상품	비용
1	대형 갈색 봉투 (3,000장/박스)	60달러
1	Stewart T2 흰색 주소 라벨 (6,000장/박스)	20.50달러
1	Stewart S1 인쇄용지 (6,000장/박스) **41** 마지막 세일	95.50달러
1	Fine Print 13B 컬러 잉크 프린터 카트리지 (4팩/박스)	270달러
3일 내 배송		20달러
42 Stewart 기프트 카드 TR541G로 결제된 총액		466달러
기프트 카드 TR541G에 남아 있는 금액		10.50달러

41 '마지막 세일'이라고 표시된, 사용했거나 개봉된 제품은 반품될 수 없다는 것을 알아두세요. 전액 환불 보상 정책에 대해 알고 싶으시면 http://www.stewartstationerysupplies.com/returns를 방문해 주십시오.

저희가 고객 여러분께 항상 최상의 고객 서비스와 최고 품질의 제품을 제공해드릴 수 있도록, http://www.stewartstationerysupplies.com/survey에서 온라인 고객 만족도 설문 조사 양식을 작성해 주십시오. 11월 20일까지 이 설문 조사를 작성해 주시는 분들에게는 저희가 감사 선물을 보내드립니다!

Stewart 문구용품 고객 지원팀

전화번호: (800) 555-2135, 오전 9시-오후 9시, 월요일-금요일

어휘 order number 주문 번호 | process 처리하다 | ship 배송하다 | warehouse 창고 | envelope 봉투 | mailing label 수신인 주소 성명용 라벨 | cartridge 카트리지 | marked 표시된 | return policy 반품 정책 | ensure 반드시 ~하게 하다, 보장하다 | fill out 기입하다, 작성하다

---

http://www.stewartstationerysupplies.com/survey

고객 만족도 조사

43 설문지 작성을 마치시면, 저희가 다음 주문 시 사용하실 수 있는 출력 가능한 15퍼센트 할인 쿠폰을 이메일로 보내드릴 것입니다. 귀하의 이메일 주소를 포함하여 주십시오.

파트 1

Stewart 문구용품에 대해서 어떻게 알게 되셨습니까?

☐ 신문 광고   ☐ 우편으로 발송된 전단

☐ 기타 잡지 광고

파트 2

저희의 지점 중 한 곳에서 상품을 구매하셨다면, 지점을 표시해 주십시오. **(44)** 온라인으로 구매하셨다면, 이 부분은 빈칸으로 비워두세요.)

45 ☐ Romford City ☐ Mountfield ☐ Ashridge

저희의 서비스를 어떻게 평가하시겠습니까?

☐ 훌륭함 ☐ 보통 ☐ 불만족

파트 3

저희 웹사이트에서 상품을 구매하셨다면, 상품을 찾기 쉬우셨습니까? (소매점에서 구매하셨다면, 이 부분은 빈칸으로 비워두세요.)

☐ 그렇다 ☐ 다소 그런 편 ☐ 아니다

저희 웹사이트에 기술 지원이 필요하셨다면, 서비스의 수준은 어땠습니까?

☐ 훌륭함 ☐ 양호함 ☐ 열악함

파트 4

저희로부터 구매하신 상품의 품질에 대한 등급을 매겨 주십시오.

☐ 훌륭함 ☐ 양호함 ☐ 불만족

어휘 customer satisfaction survey 고객 만족 설문 조사 | printable 출력[인쇄]할 수 있는 | voucher 상품권, 할인권 | purchase 구매, 구입하다 | indicate 명시하다, 가리키다 | navigate 길을 찾다, (복잡한 상황을) 다루다 | retail store 소매점 | somewhat 다소 | technical assistance 기술 지원 | rate 평가하다

---

41. Mr. Sanger가 주문한 상품 중 반품될 수 없는 것은 무엇인가?

(A) 프린터 카트리지

(B) 인쇄용지

(C) 주소 라벨

(D) 봉투

해설 이메일 지문에서 '마지막 세일'이라고 표기되어 있는 제품들은 사용 또는 개봉이 되면 반품 불가함을 확인할 수 있고, 주문 품목에서 FINAL SALE이라고 표기된 것은 Stewart S1 인쇄용지이다. 따라서 정답은 (B) printing paper이다.

---

42. Mr. Sanger가 한 주문에 관하여 언급된 것은 무엇인가?

(A) 수량 변경을 요청했다.

(B) 배송일이 11월 5일로 잡혀 있다.

(C) Billington에 있는 그의 사무실로 배송될 것이다.

(D) 결제를 위해 기프트 카드를 사용했다.

해설 Mr. Sanger의 주문에 관한 사실을 확인해야 하는 문제다. 이메일 지문에서 Mr. Sanger가 주문한 품목들 또는 옵션을 확인하면 Total paid by Stewart gift card TR541G에서 기프트 카드로 결제를 했다는 것을 파악할 수 있다. 따라서 정답은 (D) He used a gift card for payment.이다. 이 문제의 경우, 이메일 작성일이 11월 5일이고 본문에 ~ will ship from our Billington warehouse today at 2:00 P.M.를 근거로 보기 (B)를 오답으로 많이 선택한다. 하지만, 본문의 주문내역서에서 3-day shipping: 20$ 부분에 집중하면, 고객이 제품 발송 후 수령하는 데 3일 소요되는 배송을 선택했음을 알 수 있다. 즉, 11월 5일에 상품을 발송해도 11월 5일 당일에 배송이 완료될 수 없기

때문에 11월 5일 배송 완료 예정이라는 보기 (B)는 오답이다. 이 문제와 같이 파트 7에서는 배송 기간에 따른 요금 차등과 배송 및 수령일 날짜와 관련된 유형이 자주 출제된다는 점에 유의해야 한다.

---

43. 설문 조사를 작성하는 고객들은 어떤 혜택을 받을 수 있는가?

(A) 무료 잉크 카트리지 팩

(B) 11월 20일에 있을 할인 판매 행사 초대

(C) 앞으로의 주문에 대한 무료 배송

(D) 다음 구매에 대한 가격 할인

해설 설문지 지문의 첫 단락에서 설문을 완료할 시에 다음 구매에 대한 할인권을 제공한다고 이야기하고 있으므로 정답은 (D) A reduction in price on their next purchase이다.

---

44. Mr. Sanger는 설문 조사의 어떤 부분을 작성하지 말아야 하는가?

(A) 파트 1

(B) 파트 2

(C) 파트 3

(D) 파트 4

해설 설문지 지문에서 생략해도·되는 부분에 대한 내용을 찾아야 한다. 이메일 지문의 첫 문장에서 Mr. Sanger는 온라인으로 물품들을 주문했음을 알 수 있고, 설문지의 Part 2 부분에서 온라인으로 구매했다면 이 부분을 비워두라고 하고 있다. 따라서 파트 2 부분은 공백으로 남겨두어야 하는 부분이다. 정답은 (B) Part 2이다.

---

45. Stewart 문구용품에 관한 설문 조사에서 알 수 있는 것은 무엇인가?

(A) 24시간 고객 지원이 가능하다.

(B) 텔레비전을 통해 제품을 광고한다.

(C) 적어도 세 곳의 소매점이 있다.

(D) 최근에 웹사이트를 업데이트했다.

해설 설문지 지문의 Part 2 부분에서 Romford City/Mountfield/Ashridge를 통하여 Stewart 문구용품은 최소한 세 곳의 지점이 있음을 유추할 수 있다. 따라서 정답은 (C) It has at least three retatil stores.임을 확인할 수 있다. (A), (B), (D)에 관한 내용은 지문에서 찾아볼 수 없다.

[46-50] 다음 기사와 논평, 편지에 관한 문제입니다.

정원에서 당신의 식탁까지

만약 하루 세끼를 위해 장을 보고 준비를 할 시간이 없다면, 당신만 그런 것이 아닙니다. 상점까지 간다 하더라도 어느 과일, 채소, 고기가 건강에 좋은지 어떻게 알겠습니까? **46** Beech Creek Gardeners' 시장은 Riverdale Metro 거주자 분들이 바쁜 일정에 영양가 높은 식단을 짜 넣을 수 있도록 해결책을 제시합니다. 그 시장은 손님들이 필요한 모든 성분들을 포함한 건강한 식사를 주문할 수 있는 BeechCreekGardens.net을 시작했습니다! "건강에 좋은 음식을 저희 손님들께 배달하여 그분들이 더 잘 먹을 수 있도록 도울 것입니다"라고 Beech Creek 대표인 Erin Woods가 말했습니다. "그것이 Beech Creek이 모든 식사에 오직 신선한 농산품만을 사용하겠다고 약속한 이유입니다. 바라건대, 이로 인해 사람들의 식단을 개선하는 데 도움이 되었으면 합니다. "

Ted Gilbert 글, 〈Riverdale Tribune〉

어휘 fit into ~에 맞게 하다[맞추다] | nutritious 영양가 높은 | set up 마련하다, 시작하다, 설립하다

전국 음식 동향을 알아볼 수 있는 새로운 시리즈

〈Takeout Mania〉의 제작자 Cy Leuck의 새로운 VesterMedia 시리즈인 **48** 〈Shrink-wrapped Nation〉은 선포장 식사의 기만적인 성분 및 그 제조업자들이 내세우는 영양학적 **47** 주장을 기록함으로써 선포장 식사 업계에 뛰어들었다. 우리나라 식단의 많은 면이 철저히 조사되었으며, 그 방송이 과학적 사실에 전념했다는 점이 이 시리즈를 흥미롭게 볼 수 있게 하였다. **50** 에피소드에서 피디들이 공장을 투어하며 대중들을 속여 냉동 건조된, 전자레인지에 돌려 먹기만 하면 되는 즉석 식품들이 안전하다고 믿도록 만드는 사람들을 인터뷰한다. 이 시리즈는 우리가 선택하여 먹는 음식들의 일부를 조명한다. 그들의 계획을 계속 진행할 것이냐고 묻는 질문에, 제작자들은 자신들의 다음 프로젝트인 〈Garden Fresh〉가 올해 안에 제작에 들어갈 것이라고 답했다. **49** Cy Leuck은 〈Restaurant City〉의 바로 다음인, 9월 18일 다음 주 월요일에 방영되는 〈Shrink-wrapped Nation〉의 첫 에피소드에 대한 관객들의 반응을 보기를 기대하고 있다.

어휘 shrink-wrapped 수축 포장된 | dive into ~로 뛰어들다, 돌입하다 | prepackage 미리 포장하다 | document 기록하다 | deceptive 기만적인, 현혹하는 | ingredient 재료 | put ~ under the microscope ~을 철저히 조사하다 | dedication 전념, 헌신 | shed light on ~을 비추다, 해명하다

9월 19일

Cy Leuck
VesterMedia
197 N. Mission 가
오션사이드, 캘리포니아 92054

Mr. Leuck께,

49 저는 어젯밤 제가 가장 좋아하는 프로그램 바로 직후에 〈Shrink-wrapped Nation〉의 첫 방송을 보았습니다. 저는 Beech Creek Gardeners' 시장을 대표하고 있으며, 저희 웹사이트가 당신에게 흥미롭게 느껴질 수 있을 것 같습니다. **50** 우리는 신선한 채소로 만든 음식을 당신의 프로그램에서 보여준 건강에 좋지 않은 냉동식품만큼이나 편리하게 이용할 수 있게 만들기 위해 노력하고 있습니다. 만약 당신이 방송을 위해서 저희 Beech Creek의 오프라인 상점에 오신다면, 저희의 접근법과 저희가 이룬 성공에 대해 당신과 얘기를 나눠보고 싶습니다. 가능하시다면, 저에게 (661) 555-7783 또는 erinwoods@beechcreekgardens.net으로 연락 주십시오.

진심으로,

Erin Woods
Erin Woods

어휘 premiere 초연 | garden-fresh 정원에서 갓 수확한 | approach 접근법, 처리 방법

---

46. 기사의 주요 목적은 무엇인가?
(A) 창의적인 요리법을 설명하기 위해
(B) 주문 절차를 설명하기 위해
(C) 새로운 유형의 사업을 소개하기 위해
(D) 식당 개업을 광고하기 위해

해설 기사의 목적은 초반부에서 정답을 알아낼 수 있다. 하루 세끼를 위해 장을 보거나 요리할 시간도 없고, 건강에 좋은 재료를 선택하기도 어려운 대중을 위해 이러한 어려움을 해결해주기 위한 온라인 매장을 열었다는 내용이므로 (C) To introduce a new type of business가 정답이다.

---

47. 논평에서 첫 번째 단락, 세 번째 줄의 단어 "claims"와 의미상 가장 가까운 것은
(A) 요청
(B) 소유물
(C) 진술
(D) 보상

해설 nutritional claims는 '영양학적 주장'이라는 의미이므로 (A), (B), (D)에 있는 '요청', '소유물', '보상'과는 동의어라고 볼 수 없다. 말로 하는 행위인 (C) statements가 의미상 가장 가깝다.

---

48. 논평에 따르면, 〈Shrink-wrapped Nation〉에 대해 알 수 있는 것은 무엇인가?
(A) 전 세계에 방영된다.
(B) 시청자들에게 정원을 가꾸는 방법을 보여준다.
(C) 일주일에 한 번 방송된다.
(D) 선포장 식품을 부정적으로 묘사한다.

해설 첫 문장에서 〈Shrink-wrapped Nation〉은 선포장 식품의 재료나 그 제조업체들의 영양학적 주장이 소비자를 기만하는 것이라는 내용의 다큐멘터리를 만든다고 했으므로 선포장 식품에 관해 부정적인 방식으로 묘사한다는 의미의 문장인 (D) It presents prepackaged meals in a negative way.가 정답이다.

---

49. Ms. Woods가 가장 좋아하는 방송은 무엇이겠는가?
(A) 〈Shrink-wrapped Nation〉
(B) 〈Takeout Mania〉
(C) 〈Garden Fresh〉
(D) 〈Restaurant City〉

해설 문제의 favorite show라는 키워드를 Ms. Woods가 보낸 편지에서 찾아내야 한다. 9월 19일에 보낸 편지에서 Ms. woods는 자신이 가장 좋아하는 프로그램 직후에 〈Shrink-wrapped Nation〉을 보았다고 했으므로 9월 18일 〈Shrink-wrapped Nation〉 바로 직전에 방영된 프로그램이 정답인데, 논평 마지막 문장을 보면 〈Restaurant City〉가 바로 그 프로그램임을 알 수 있다. 그러므로 정답은 (D) Restaurant City이다.

50. Ms. Woods가 편지에서 암시하는 것은 무엇인가?

(A) Mr. Leuck이 자신의 시장에 합류하는 것에 관심이 있을 수도 있다고 생각한다.

(B) 최근 보건 정책이 성공적이지 않다고 생각한다.

(C) Beech Creek에 만족하는 고객이 많다고 말한다.

(D) 냉동 식품이 위험할 수 있다는 것에 동의한다.

해설 논평 지문을 보면 전자레인지로 조리할 수 있는 냉동건조 식품이 안전하다고 믿도록 하는 것은 대중을 속이는 것이라고 했으므로 Cy Leuck는 냉동식품이 안전하지 않다고 믿고 있다. 그리고 편지의 '당신의 프로그램에서 보여준 건강에 좋지 않은 냉동식품만큼이나 편리하게 이용할 수 있게 만들기 위해 노력하고 있다' 부분에서 unhealthy frozen food라는 표현을 쓰고 있기 때문에 Ms. Woods도 이 견해에 동의한다는 것을 알 수 있다. 따라서 정답은 (D) She agrees that frozen foods can be dangerous.가 된다.

HALF TEST 03

본서 p.384

1. (C)	2. (C)	3. (B)	4. (D)	5. (A)
6. (C)	7. (B)	8. (D)	9. (B)	10. (A)
11. (B)	12. (A)	13. (A)	14. (D)	15. (B)
16. (A)	17. (B)	18. (B)	19. (B)	20. (B)
21. (B)	22. (B)	23. (C)	24. (C)	25. (C)
26. (B)	27. (B)	28. (D)	29. (A)	30. (A)
31. (A)	32. (B)	33. (C)	34. (D)	35. (C)
36. (D)	37. (B)	38. (B)	39. (A)	40. (D)
41. (A)	42. (A)	43. (A)	44. (C)	45. (C)
46. (B)	47. (B)	48. (C)	49. (A)	50. (C)

1. 분실물 사무소의 Mr. Peterson은 사람들이 잃어버린 소지품을 찾아주는 업무에 만족한다.

해설 Mr. Peterson이 the lost and found office(분실물 사무소) 소속이라고 했으므로 '~의 위치를 찾다'라는 의미의 locate가 의미상 가장 적절하다. 따라서 (C) locate가 정답이다.

어휘 lost and found office 분실물 사무소 | possessions [복수] 소유물, 소지품 | assist 원조하다 | remind 상기시키다 | locate ~의 위치를 찾다 | conduct 수행하다

2. Angels' Support Group은 노숙자들에게 음식과 장소를 무료로 제공하는 일에 헌신하고 있다.

해설 at no cost라는 표현을 묻는 문제이다. 따라서 (C) at이 정답이다.

어휘 support 후원, 원조 | be committed to ~에 전념하다 | homeless 집이 없는 | at no cost 비용 없이, 무료로

3. 이 일련의 기록에 있는 모든 정보는 달리 표시되어 있지 않는 한 2017년 7월 1일자로 최신 정보이다.

해설 빈칸 앞은 완전한 문장이다. 따라서 빈칸부터는 부사구/부사절이 돼야 한다. otherwise는 부사, indicated는 과거분사이므로 접속부사인 (A) thus, (C) besides는 들어가기에 적절하지 않다. 전치사 (D) despite도 뒤에 목적어가 없으므로 부적절하다. unless otherwise indicated는 '달리 표시되어 있지 않다면'이라는 의미로 자주 쓰이는 표현이다. unless (it is) otherwise indicated에서 주어와 동사가 생략된 분사구문으로 볼 수 있다. 따라서 (B) unless가 정답이다.

어휘 up-to-date 최신(최근)의 | as of ~일자로, ~현재 | otherwise 그렇지 않으면, 달리 | unless otherwise indicated 달리 표시되어 있지 않으면, 별도의 표시가 없으면 | thus 그래서 | unless 만약 ~가 아니라면 | besides 게다가 | despite ~에도 불구하고

4. Mr. Chan의 돋보이는 발표는 더욱 다양한 직원 교육 프로그램에 대한 필요성을 이사회에 쉽게 납득시켰다.

해설 빈칸은 동사를 수식하는 부사 자리이므로 (D) easily가 정답이다.

어휘 outstanding 뛰어난, 두드러진 | convince 납득시키다, 확신시키다 | diverse 다양한

5. 매력적인 사무실과 세심하게 배려하는 보조원들은 외부 구매자를 끌어들이는 데 큰 기여를 할 수 있다.

해설 빈칸은 명사 support staff를 수식하는 형용사 자리이다. 선택지 중 형용사는 attentive가 유일하므로 (A) attentive가 정답이다.

어휘 attractive 매력적인 | support staff 보조원 | go a long way toward ~에 크게 도움되다 | outside purchaser 외부 구매자 | attentive 배려하는, 신경을 쓰는 | attentively 조심스럽게 | attention 주의 | attentiveness 조심성

6. 영어 수업에 대한 25퍼센트 할인 가격은 미리 등록하는 사람들에게만 적용된다.

해설 두 문장을 연결하는 접속사 역할을 하는 관계대명사 who가 있기 때문에, 이 문장에는 두 개의 동사가 존재해야 한다. 하지만 동사 enroll 하나만 보이므로, 빈칸은 동사 자리이다. 동사와 관련된 문제는 주어와의 수 일치부터 확인해야 되는데, 이 문장의 주어인 The 25% discounted price가 단수명사이므로 단수동사 (C) applies가 정답이다.

어휘 enroll 등록하다 | apply 적용하다 | application 적용, 신청

7. Orange Mac은 고객 서비스 문화와 쇼핑 경험에 중점을 두고 있다.

해설 빈칸은 동사 places의 목적어 자리이며 관사 뒤이므로 명사 형태의 단어가 와야 된다. 문맥상 '~에 중점을 둔다'라는 의미가 되어야 하므로 (B) emphasis가 정답이다.

어휘 experience 경험 | place an emphasis on ~에 중점[역점]을 두다 | emphasize 강조하다 | emphasis 강조 | emphasizing 강조하는 | emphatically 강조하여, 힘차게

8. 새롭게 출시된 우리 텔레비전 라인에 대한 홍보 계획은 인상적인 마케팅 감독인 Michael Choi에 의해 이루어졌다.

해설 빈칸 앞에는 관사 an, 빈칸 뒤에는 복합명사 marketing director가 있으므로 빈칸에는 문법적으로 명사를 수식하는 형용사가 필요하다. 따라서 (D) impressive가 정답이다.

어휘 release 출시하다, 방출하다 | impress 감명을 주다 | impressively 인상적으로 | impressive 인상적인

9. 요거트 회사 Twinkle Berry는 기반 시설 투자를 통해 생산 능력을 수요에 맞춤으로써 성장하려 하고 있다.

해설 문맥상 '공급량을 수요에 맞추다'라는 뜻이 자연스러우므로 관용 표현인 in line with를 묻는 문제이다. 따라서 (B) with가 정답이다.

어휘 manage (어떻게든) 해내다, 처리하다 | capacity 생산 능력 | in line with ~ 와 함께, ~에 따라 | infrastructure 공공 기반 시설

10. Bare Foot 사의 최고경영자는 자사의 시장 지배력을 유지하고 향상시킬 거래를 물색하고 있다.

해설 빈칸은 주격 관계대명사 that 뒤의 동사 자리로, 수 일치 → 태 → 시제 순서로 접근한다. 먼저 수 일치를 파악하면, 동사 maintain의 주어가 관계대명사 that 앞의 선행사인 단수명사 a transaction이므로 (D)는 오답이다. 나머지 보기는 모두 능동이므로, 시제를 파악하여 정답을 선택해야 한다. '현재 거래를 찾고 있고, 그 거래가 앞으로 자사의 시장 지배력을 향상시킬 것이라 기대한다'는 문맥에 따라 미래시제 (A) will maintain이 정답이다.

어휘 transaction 거래, 매매 | enhance 높이다, 향상시키다 | market position 시장 지배력 | maintain 유지하다

11. 상점 회원권이 있는 고객들만 온라인 광고에 언급된 특별 할인가를 받을 자격이 있다.

해설 전체적인 문맥뿐 아니라 빈칸 뒤의 전치사 for를 단서로 볼 때 정답은 (B) eligible이다. 보기 (A) relevant는 전치사 to와 어울려 쓰이므로 오답이다.

어휘 membership 회원권 | relevant 관련된 | eligible 자격이 있는 | lucrative 유리한 | considerate 이해심이 있는

12. 그 데이터는 더 심도 있는 분석을 했을 때 사업상의 문제들에 대한 근본 원인을 밝혀낼 수 있다.

해설 '~의 대상이 되다'라는 의미의 be subjected to를 묻는 문제로 (A) to가 정답이다. when subjected는 부사절 접속사 when 뒤에 「주어 + be동사」가 생략된 구조이다.

어휘 reveal 드러내다 | root cause 근본 원인 | be subjected to 겪게 되다, ~을 당하다 | further 더 이상의 | analysis 분석

13. 혹독한 날씨 때문에 대중교통이 지연되어서, Ms. Javier는 고객 미팅에 제시간에 도착하지 못했다.

해설 빈칸 앞에 조동사 did not이 있다. 따라서 빈칸에는 동사원형이 필요하므로 (A) arrive가 정답이다.

어휘 public transportation 대중교통 | delay 지연시키다 | due to ~때문에 | inclement (날씨가) 혹독한, 춥고 사나운 | on time 제시간에

14. Mr. Kim은 더 큰 시장 점유율을 확보하려는 노력의 일환으로 마침내 광고 이사직을 맡았다.

해설 「in an effort to + 동사원형」은 '~을 해보려는 노력으로'라는 의미의 표현이다. 따라서 (D) effort가 정답이다.

어휘 take over as ~직(책)을 맡다 | in an effort to ~해보려는 노력으로 | market share 시장 점유율 | item 품목 | issue 사안, 문제 | advice 충고

15. 이 체크리스트는 위험한 업무를 혼자 하는 직원들을 위해 고용주들이 모범 경영을 시행하도록 돕기 위한 것입니다.

해설 문장을 연결해주는 접속사나 관계사가 없고, 동사 is intended가 존재하므로, 빈칸은 동사 자리가 아니다. 따라서, 빈칸은 명사 employees 를 수식하는 분사 자리이며, 동사인 (C), (D)는 오답 처리한다. '업무를 하는 직원들'이라는 해석에 따라, 능동을 의미하는 현재분사 (B) working이 정답이다.

어휘 be intended to ~하도록 의도되다 | employer 고용주 | implement 시행하다 | best practice 모범 경영 | hazardous 위험한

16. 제조일은 반드시 해산물을 담고 있는 포장의 측면이나 캔 바닥에 바로 인쇄되어 있어야 한다.

해설 동사 should be printed를 가장 적절하게 수식하는 부사이며 전치사의 목적어 the bottom과 문맥적으로 어울리는 부사가 필요하다. 따라서 '캔 바닥에 바로 인쇄된'이라는 의미를 가지는 (A) directly가 정답이다.

어휘 the date of manufacture 제조일자 | be printed on ~에 인쇄되어 있다 | containing ~을 담고 있는, ~을 포함하고 있는 | directly 바로, 직접적으로 | nearly 거의, 대략 | busily 바쁘게, 부지런히 | questionably 의심스럽게, 미심쩍게

17. Ms. Hwang은 곧 있을 발표에 대비해 지난 6개월을 연구하면서 보냈다.

해설 '앞으로 있을 발표에 대비해 지난 6개월간 연구를 했다'는 것이 가장 자연스러우므로 미래를 암시하는 형용사 upcoming이 와야 한다. 따라서 (C) upcoming이 정답이다.

어휘 inward 마음속의; 내부로 향한 | recurrent 반복되는, 재발되는 | upcoming 다가오는 | estimated 추산되는

18. 학교 행정관이 정규 수업 활동과 실제적인 업무 경력을 통합하는 프로그램을 도입할 계획이다.

해설 '새로운 프로그램을 도입하다'라는 문맥에 따라 '규칙, 시스템, 프로그램, 절차 등을 새롭게 도입[소개]하다'라는 의미를 지닌 (B) institute가 정답이다.

어휘 administrator 관리자, 행정관 | integrate 통합하다 | practical 실제적인, 현실적인 | career experience 업무 경력 | reconnect 다시 연결하다 | institute 도입하다 | exceed 초과하다 | balance 균형을 맞추다

19. Palm Tree 리조트의 직원들은 당신의 투숙을 가능한 한 편안하게 하기 위해 그들이 할 수 있는 모든 일을 할 것이다.

해설 이 문장의 동사가 두 개(will do, can)이므로 두 문장을 연결하는 접속사 역할을 하는 복합관계대명사 (B) whatever가 정답이다. 명사인 (A)와 (D), 전치사인 (C)는 문장을 연결하는 접속사 역할을 하지 못하므로 오답이다.

어휘 comfortable 편안한 | whatever ~하는 것은 무엇이나, ~는 무엇이든

20. 지난달 시행한 소비자 설문 조사에 따르면, 대다수의 사람들이 오프라인보다 온라인에서 물건을 구매하는 것을 선호한다.

해설 문맥상 '다수의'를 의미하는 a great majority of를 묻는 문제이다. 따라서 (B) majority가 정답이다.

어휘 according to ~에 따르면 | rather than ~보다는, ~대신에 | off-line 오프라인으로, 컴퓨터와 연결되지 않은 | a great majority of 대다수의 ~ | major 주요한

[21-24] 다음 설명서에 관한 문제입니다.

프린터 토너 카트리지 재활용

Extec 프린터 소모품점은 환경 보호를 위해 열심히 노력하고 있습니다. 따라서 모든 고객님들께 가능하면 **21** 언제나 사용하신 프린터 토너 카트리지를 재활용하실 것을 권장합니다.

프린터 토너 카트리지 재활용은 간단합니다. 사용하신 카트리지를 Extec 제품을 판매하는 아무 소매점에나 가져오시면, Extec 재활용 수거함을 발견하실 것입니다. **22** 그때, 카트리지를 수거함에 두세요. 저희 소매 협업업체들이 맡겨진 카트리지를 재활용을 위해 정기적으로 저희에게 **23** 보내줍니다.

게다가 사용하신 카트리지를 반납하시면 앞으로 구매하실 때 할인을 받으실 수 있습니다. 이에 대한 보다 상세한 **24** 정보는 저희 웹사이트를 참조해 주십시오.

어휘 toner cartridge (프린터) 토너 카트리지 | committed 헌신적인, 열성적인 | thus 그러므로 | whenever ~한 모든 경우에, 언제나, 언제든지 | all in all 대체로 | retailer 소매업체 | container 용기, 그릇 | install 설치하다 | deposit 두다 | receptacle 그릇, 용기 | on a regular basis 정기적으로 | entitle 자격을 주다 | reduced price 할인 가격 | purchase 구매

---

21. **해설** 문맥상 '가능한 언제나'라는 의미가 되어야 하므로 빈칸에는 '~한 모든 경우에, 언제나'라는 의미의 접속사가 필요하다. 따라서 (B) whenever가 정답이다.

22. (A) 직원이 토너 카트리지를 설치하는 방법을 보여줄 수 있습니다.
(B) 그때, 카트리지를 수거함에 두세요.
(C) 고객님들은 그곳에서 새 카트리지를 구입하실 수 있습니다.
(D) 카트리지들이 재활용되기까지는 시간이 좀 필요합니다.

해설 이전 문장에서 재활용 수거함을 발견할 수 있다고 언급하였고, 다음 문장에서 소매 협업업체들이 남겨진 카트리지들을 Extec

Printer Supplies에 보내준다고 하였으므로, 문맥의 흐름상 가장 적합한 보기는 (B) Then, deposit the cartridges in the receptacle. 이다.

23. **해설** 빈칸은 문장의 동사가 올 자리이다. 문맥상 소매 협업업체들이 맡겨진 카트리지를 재활용을 위해 정기적으로 보내준다는 의미로 규칙적으로 반복되는 사실을 말하고 있으므로 현재시제가 적절하다. 또한 빈칸 뒤에 목적어가 있으므로 능동태여야 한다. 따라서 (C) send 가 정답이다.

24. **해설** 빈칸은 앞에 있는 형용사 further의 수식을 받는 명사가 올 자리인데, 문맥상 '더 자세한 정보'라는 의미가 알맞으므로 '정보'라는 의미의 명사가 필요하다. 따라서 (C) information이 정답이다.

[25-28] 다음 광고에 관한 문제입니다.

30마일이 넘는 숲, 수많은 호수들, 다양한 종류의 새들과 야생동물들이 Zorilla 자연보호구역에서 여러분을 **25** 기다리고 있습니다. Zorilla는 Great Northern 고속도로에서 3번 출구로 나오시면 Priestfield에서 북북으로 10마일 떨어진 곳에 있습니다. 이 자연보호구역은 도시에서 가까우므로, 당일 여행이나 주말 휴가로 완벽한 **26** 선택이라 할 수 있습니다.

하룻밤 투숙하기로 결정하신 경우, 근사한 시골을 배경으로 한 다수의 훌륭한 호텔과 게스트하우스가 있습니다. Zorilla에 대해 더 알아보시려면, 저희에게 www.zorillareserve.com으로 이메일 주십시오. 여러분이 **27** 바로 여행을 계획하실 수 있도록 저희가 안내책자, 지도, 자연보호구역에서 할 것들에 대한 많은 정보를 회신으로 보내드릴 것입니다. **28** 곧 귀하를 뵙게 되길 고대합니다.

어휘 countless 수많은 | a wide variety of 매우 다양한 | wait for ~를 기다리다 | nature reserve 자연보호구역 | highway 고속도로 | exit 출구 | exhibit 전시 | contest 대회, 시합 | day trip 당일 여행 | getaway 휴가, 휴가지 | a number of 다수의 | guest house 게스트하우스 | rural 시골의 | setting 배경, 장소 | in reply 답장/회신으로 | right above 바로 위에 | straight away 바로, 즉시 | up until ~까지 | as follows 다음과 같이

---

25. **해설** 빈칸은 문장의 동사가 올 자리인데, 광고문이므로 문맥상 '30마일이 넘는 숲, 수많은 호수들, 다양한 종류의 새들과 야생동물들이 Zorilla 자연보호구역에서 여러분을 기다리고 있다'가 되는 것이 자연스럽다. 따라서 (C) are waiting이 정답이다. (D)는 주어가 복수이므로 문법상 맞지 않다.

26. **해설** 문맥상 '완벽한 선택'이라는 의미가 적절하다. 빈칸에는 '선택'이라는 뜻의 명사가 필요하므로 (B) choice가 정답이다.

27. **해설** 문맥상 '바로 여행을 계획할 수 있도록'이라는 의미가 적절하므로 빈칸에는 '바로, 즉시'라는 뜻의 어휘가 알맞다. 따라서 (B) straight away가 정답이다.

28. (A) 저희는 곧 개장할 것입니다.

(B) 최근에 저희를 방문해 주셔서 감사합니다.

(C) 도시의 중심에서 저희를 찾으세요.

(D) 곧 귀하를 뵙게 되길 고대합니다.

해설 광고문이므로 글의 제일 마지막에 들어갈 문장은 Zorilla 자연 보호구역 방문을 당부하는 (D) We look forward to seeing you soon.이 가장 적합하다.

[29-30] 다음 영수증에 관한 문제입니다.

Mandy's 드라이클리닝 및 수선소에 오신 것을 환영합니다.

화요일에서 토요일

오전 7시부터 오후 7시까지 영업합니다

고객: Ruth Madeiros

주문품: #75432246

㉙ 6월 15일, 화요일, 오전 9시 37분

품목	서비스	수거 날짜 / 시간	비용
㉙ 가디건	소매 박음질	6월 15일, 화요일 / 오후 4시	5달러
재킷	드라이클리닝	6월 18일, 금요일 / 오후 4시 30분	12달러
바지	수선	6월 21일, 월요일 / 오전 10시	18달러
블레이저	단추 고정	6월 21일, 월요일 / 오전 10시	7달러

총 비용: 42달러

지불액: 42달러

㉚ 잔금: 0달러

Mandy's를 선택해 주셔서 감사합니다

저희의 수요일 특가에 대해 문의하세요

어휘 dry cleaning 드라이클리닝 | tailoring 재봉, 양복 제조업 | pick-up 수거 | sleeve 소매 | stitching 바느질 | fasten 채우다, 잠그다 | amount paid 이미 지불한 금액 | balance due 잔금, 미불액

29. Ms. Madeiros가 당일 서비스를 받은 물품은 무엇인가?

(A) 가디건

(B) 재킷

(C) 바지

(D) 블레이저

해설 영수증 상단에서 서비스를 맡긴 날짜는 Tuesday, June 15, 9:37 A.M.인 것을 확인할 수 있다. 따라서 표에서 당일 서비스를 받은 물품은 수령 날짜가 Tue, June 15/4 P.M.인 Cardigan인 것을 확인할 수 있다. 따라서 정답은 (A) The cardigan이다.

---

30. Ms. Madeiros의 주문에 관하여 언급된 것은 무엇인가?

(A) 전액 지불되었다.

(B) 재킷 몇 벌을 포함했다.

(C) 6월 18일에 배송되었다.

(D) 할인이 포함되었다.

해설 지문의 마지막 부분에서 Total cost: $42.00에서 총 금액이 42달러인데 비하여 Balance due: $0.00로 잔금이 0달러인 것을 보아 전액 지불되었음을 알 수 있다. 따라서 정답은 (A) It was paid in full.이다.

[31-33] 다음 공지에 관한 문제입니다.

연락선 운행 공지

부두에서 이루어지고 있는 보수 작업 때문에, Triangle 항에서 출발하는 정기 ㉛ 연락선 서비스가 3월 20일 금요일부터 23일 월요일까지 주기적으로 중단될 것입니다. 대부분의 연락선들이 정규 시간에는 운행되겠지만, 몇몇 노선은 일시적으로 중단될 것입니다. 자세한 정보를 원하시면 아래 일정표를 참고하십시오. ㉜ 승객 분들께서는 일찍 도착하셔야 하는데, 이는 남아 있는 연락선에 모든 승객 분들을 수용할 공간이 충분치 않을 수도 있기 때문입니다. 임시 연락선 운행 스케줄은 매표소에서 가져가실 수 있습니다.

날짜	Triangle 항 출발 시간			
3월 20일 금요일	오전 8시	오전 10시	오후 2시	운행하지 않음
3월 21일 토요일	운행하지 않음	오전 10시	운행하지 않음	오후 5시
㉝ 3월 22일 일요일	오전 8시	오전 10시	오후 2시	오후 5시
3월 23일 월요일	운행하지 않음	오전 10시	오후 2시	오후 5시

어휘 transport 수송, 운송 | maintenance 유지, 보수 관리 | dock 부두, 선착장 | experience 겪다, 경험하다 | periodic 정기적인 | interruption 중단 | temporarily 당분간 | suspend 중단하다 | refer to ~을 참고하다 | accommodate 수용하다 | passenger 승객 | temporary 임시의, 단기의

31. 무엇이 공지되고 있는가?

(A) 서비스 중단

(B) 배 출항 연기

(C) 매표소 리모델링

(D) 영업 시간 연장

해설 공지 제목 Ferry Transport Notice를 통해 운행 관련 공지임을 확인할 수 있다. 또한 지문의 첫머리에 연락선 서비스가 3월 20일부터 3월 23일까지 보수 작업으로 인해 일시적 운행 서비스 중단을 한다는 것을 확인할 수 있으므로 정답은 (A) The suspension of a service이다.

---

32. 승객들은 왜 일찍 오라는 요청을 받는가?

(A) 그들의 요구에 가장 적합한 배를 선택하기 위해

(B) 배의 자리를 확보하기 위해

(C) 길게 줄을 서서 기다리는 것을 피하기 위해

(D) 연락선이 일정대로 출항하는 것을 확실히 하기 위해

해설 지문 다섯 번째 줄에서 배 안에 수용할 공간이 충분치 않기 때문에, 일찍 오라고 하고 있으므로 정답은 (B) To ensure that they secure a place on a boat이다.

---

33. 연락선 운행이 보수 작업에 의해 영향을 받지 않는 것은 언제이겠는가?

(A) 3월 20일

(B) 3월 21일

(C) 3월 22일

(D) 3월 23일

해설 지문에서 보수 작업은 20일부터 23일까지 진행되는 것을 확인할 수 있고 일정표 중 운행이 중단되지 않는 날은 Sunday, 22 March 밖에 없음을 알 수 있으므로 정답은 (C) March 22이다.

[34-36] 다음 이메일에 관한 문제입니다.

수신: Frederik Clayton ⟨fclayton@lamousse.nl⟩
발신: Arthur Mosley ⟨amosley@ngualodge.ng⟩
날짜: 5월 16일
제목: 예약

Mr. Clayton께,

34 최근 Ngua 산장의 Wildlife Sanctuary 사파리 패키지를 올해 들어 두 번째로 예약을 해 주셔서 감사합니다. 저희는 귀하를 다시 모시게 되어 매우 기쁩니다. 귀하의 패키지는 저희 현대식 산장에서의 매일 **36** 유럽식 무료 아침 식사와 Humaba 국립공원 출신의 숙련된 현지 가이드와 함께 하는 3일 간의 사파리 투어를 포함합니다. **36** 그 지역의 멸종 위기 동물에 대한 도감과 **36** 저희 산장 선물 가게의 선별된 구매품에 대한 20퍼센트 할인권 또한 패키지의 일부입니다.

귀하께서는 Safari 식당에서 식사를 하실 수 있고, 이곳은 귀하께서 기억하시겠지만 Ngua 산장 안쪽에 위치해 있습니다. 주방장 Sammi Dwani의 획기적인 메뉴가 ⟨National Nigerian Monthly⟩ 잡지에서 **35** 최근 매우 훌륭한 평가를 받았고, 이는 아래의 링크를 클릭하시면 읽어보실 수 있습니다.

www.nigerianmonthly.co.ng/ngualodge

5월 22일에 Ngua 산장에서 귀하를 뵐 수 있기를 고대합니다.

안부를 전하며,

Arthur Mosley
Ngua 산장, 고객 서비스 관리자

어휘 book 예약하다 | lodge 오두막집, 관광지의 여관 | modern 현대적인, 현대의 | continental breakfast 유럽식 아침 식사(보통 커피와, 버터와 잼을 바른 작은 빵) | excursion (짧은) 여행 | experienced 숙련된 | local guide 현지 가이드 | description 서술, 기술 | endangered species 멸종 위기에 처한 동식물의 종 | selected purchase 선별된[엄선된] 구매 물건 | dine 식사를 하다 | recall 회상하다 | innovative 획기적인 | review 논평, 비평

34. Mr. Clayton에 관하여 언급된 것은 무엇인가?

(A) 그의 예약에 대해 몇 가지 질문을 했다.

(B) 동물 보호 기금마련 행사에 참석할 계획이다.

(C) 그는 Humaba 국립공원 근처에 산다.

(D) Ngua 산장에 이전에 방문했었다.

해설 첫 단락의 첫 문장을 보면 Mr. Clayton은 산장 예약을 두 번째로 하는 것을 확인할 수 있으므로 정답은 (D) He has made a previous visit to the Ngua Lodge.이다.

35. Mr. Mosley는 왜 이메일에 링크를 포함시키는가?

(A) 식당에 대한 정보를 공유하려고

(B) 야생동물 관람 일정을 제공하려고

(C) 현지 안내인의 서비스들을 광고하려고

(D) Ngua 산장으로 가는 길을 알려주려고

해설 지문 두 번째 단락의 Sammi Dwani의 획기적인 메뉴가 ⟨National Nigerian Monthly⟩ 잡지에서 훌륭한 평가를 받았고 링크를 클릭하면 관련 내용을 확인할 수 있다고 한다. 따라서 정답은 (A) To share information about a restaurant이다.

36. 패키지에 포함되지 않은 것은 무엇인가?

(A) 아침 식사

(B) 선물 가게의 상품권

(C) 야생 동물 애호가들을 위한 서적

(D) 사파리 공원의 지도

해설 패키지에 포함된 것들을 먼저 다 찾아 본다. 보기와 지문을 대조하면 (A)는 a free continental breakfast every morning에서 찾을 수 있고, (B)는 a coupon worth 20 percent off selected purchases at our lodge's gift shop을 통하여 알 수 있다. (C) 또한 a wildlife description book으로 언급이 되어 있으나 지도에 관한 언급은 없었으므로 정답은 (D) A map of a safari park이다.

[37-40] 다음 설명서에 관한 문제입니다.

Waver 전자 빠른 시작 안내

상품 VG4193의 경우:

1. **38** 스캐너의 측면에 있는 파란 단자에 검정색 전원 케이블의 빨간 끝부분을 꽂아 주세요. 검은 케이블의 반대쪽 끝을 전기 소켓에 넣어주세요. (기기 보호 장치를 사용하시기를 추천합니다.)

2. 노란색 데이터 케이블을 사용하여 귀하의 컴퓨터에 **37** 스캐너를 연결시켜 주세요.

3. **37** 스캐너의 소프트웨어를 설치하기 위해 동봉된 CD를 디스크 드라이브에 넣으세요. 그 설치 과정을 끝내기 위해, CD의 겉면에 있는 소프트웨어의 암호가 필요할 것입니다.

4. 소프트웨어를 설치한 후, CD를 꺼내고 귀하의 컴퓨터를 다시 시작해 주세요.

5. 귀하의 스캐너를 등록하시려면 스캐너의 뒷면에 쓰여 있는 일련 번호를 사용하여 www.waverelectronics.com/registration에 로그인 해주십시오. **39** 등록 후 귀하께서는 제품 식별 번호를 받게 되실 것이고, 수리 요청과 소프트웨어 업데이트와 같은 다양한 서비스를 받기 위해 그것을 사용할 수 있을 것입니다.

설치 문제:

만약 귀하께서 스캐너를 설치하는 데 어려움을 겪고 있다면, **40** 먼저 취급설명서 FAQ 부분에서 찾을 수 있는 고장수리 섹션을 읽어보세요. 만약 필요하신 정보를 그곳에서 찾을 수 없다면, 저희 웹사이트를 방문하세요. 귀하의 제품 식별 번호를 사용하셔서 저희 온라인 기술 지원 웹페이지에 접속하실 수 있으며, **40** 이곳에는 사용자들이 질문을 하거나 유사한 문제에 대해서 공유하는 토론방이 포함되어 있습니다. 계속 문제를 겪고 있다면, **40** 기술 지원 전문가와 이야기하기 위해 1-800-555-0184로 전화 주세요.

37. 무엇을 위한 설명서인가?

(A) 온라인 계좌를 활성화시키는 것

(B) 스캐너를 설치하는 것

(C) 물품을 주문하는 것

(D) 동영상 프로그램을 설치하는 것

해설 설명서의 2번 항목에서 Connect the scanner와 3번 항목의 install the scanner's software를 통하여 스캐너의 설치임을 확인할 수 있다. 그러므로 정답은 (B) Setting up a scanner이다.

---

38. 사용자들은 먼저 무엇을 하도록 지시받는가?

(A) CD를 삽입한다

(B) 전원 케이블을 연결한다

(C) 상품을 등록한다

(D) 컴퓨터를 켠다

해설 가장 먼저 할 것을 찾아야 하므로 첫 번째 지시사항을 확인한다. 1번을 통해 전원 케이블을 연결하라는 것을 확인할 수 있다. 따라서 정답은 (B) Attach a power cable이다.

---

39. 소프트웨어 업데이트에 필요한 것은 무엇인가?

(A) 식별 번호

(B) 고객별 비밀번호

(C) 공 CD

(D) 전자 송장

해설 설명서의 지시사항 5번의 두 번째 문장에서 등록 후에 받는 제품 식별 번호는 수리 요청이나 소프트웨어 업데이트 등의 다양한 서비스에 사용될 수 있다고 하고 있으므로 정답은 (A) An identification number 이다.

---

40. 기술적 문제를 해결하기 위해 추천되는 방법이 아닌 것은 무엇인가?

(A) Waver 전자에 연락하는 것

(B) 취급설명서를 다시 보는 것

(C) 온라인 토론방에 방문하는 것

(D) 컴퓨터를 재부팅시키는 것

해설 사실 확인 문제 유형이므로 보기를 하나씩 지문과 대조해서 언급이나 명시가 되어있는지의 여부를 확인해야 한다. (A)는 '기술 전문가와 이야기하기 위해 1-800-555-0184로 전화 주세요'에서, (B)는 '먼저 취

급설명서 FAQ 부분에서 찾을 수 있는 고장수리 섹션을 읽어보세요' 로 알 수 있고, (C) 또한 '이곳에는 사용자들이 질문을 하거나 유사한 문제에 대해서 공유하는 토론방이 포함되어 있습니다'를 통하여 확인할 수 있지만 컴퓨터를 재부팅하라는 언급은 없으므로 정답은 (D) Rebooting the computer이다.

[41-45] 다음 이메일과 일정표에 관한 문제입니다.

수신: Mia Kaverin 〈mkaverin@arpex.ru〉

발신: Sergei Gusev 〈sgusev@rci.org〉

회신: RCI 컨퍼런스

날짜: 6월 21일

첨부: 워크숍 일정 (6월 19일에 업데이트됨)

Ms. Kaverin께,

열 번째 러시아 건설 산업 **41** 연례 컨퍼런스에 대한 관심을 보여주셔서 감사드립니다. 유감스럽게도, 두 달 전 귀하의 등록 이후로 프로그램에 일부 변동이 생겼습니다. 그 결과 저희는 6월 30일까지 귀하께 추가 정보를 요청합니다.

42 44 먼저, 귀하께서 신청하신 Vladimir Solomin의 워크숍, '유독성 폐기물 처분'은 취소되었습니다. 대신 Boris Garin이 '위험한 물질 제거'에 대한 발표를 할 것입니다. 귀하께서 이 새로운 세션에 참가를 원하시면 저희에게 알려주십시오.

또한, Igor Burkov의 담화는 월요일 오전에서 월요일 오후로 변경되었습니다. 결과적으로, 그의 세션은 Arthur Gansk의 세션과 동시에 진행될 것입니다. 귀하께서 두 가지 모두를 등록하셨으므로, 둘 중 어느 쪽에 참석하실 것인지 결정하셔야 합니다. 마지막으로, 월요일 오전 워크숍 중 어느 것에 참석하기를 원하시는지 표시해 주십시오.

컨퍼런스 관리팀은 이 변경으로 인한 모든 불편에 대해 깊은 사과를 드립니다. 모든 강연자들은 자신들의 강연에 대한 **43** 책임을 다할 것을 약속했으니 믿으셔도 됩니다. 따라서, 예기치 못한 상황을 제외하면, 귀하께서 관심을 표하셨던 Luis Cameron과 Alex Vasin의 워크숍은 틀림없이 예정된 대로 진행될 것이라 예상합니다.

진심으로,

Sergei Gusev, 세미나 진행 담당자

러시아 건설 산업 (RCI)

제 10회 연간 세미나 · 7월 4–5일 · 러시아 모스크바

월요일 워크숍

시간	워크숍 제목	발표자
8:00–9:45	수출과 수입의 관계	Olav Dansk, 사업주
	적절한 공급자 선택	Andrew Smithson, 경영 컨설턴트
10:00–11:45	21세기의 건축	Luis Cameron, 선임 설계자
	대형 프로젝트를 위한 기금 마련	Simone Balashov, 재정 전문가
(12시부터 1시까지 점심시간)		
1:15–3:00	강철의 상태	Arthur Gansk, 선임 기술자
	효율적인 웹사이트 디자인하기	Igor Burkov, 웹 디자이너

화요일 워크숍

시간	워크숍 제목	발표자
8:00–11:00	전세계의 건축	Anton Ivanovic, 건축학 교수
	해외 고객 유치	Alex Vasin, 마케팅 이사
(11:30분부터 12:30분까지 점심시간)		
1:00–4:00	위험한 물질 제거	**44** Boris Garin, 폐기물 전문가
	45 온라인 마케팅 설문 조사; 내가 거기서 알게 된 것	**45** Benjamin Kleinfield, 비즈니스 저널리스트

어휘 relationship 관계 | export 수출 | import 수입 | effective 효율적인 | hazardous 위험한 | substance 물질 | removal 제거

---

41. 이메일의 목적은 무엇인가?

(A) 일정 조정을 알리기 위해
(B) 다가오는 컨퍼런스를 홍보하기 위해
(C) 위원회에 새로운 멤버를 초대하기 위해
(D) 세미나 등록을 확인하기 위해

해설 첫 번째 지문 서두에서 컨퍼런스에 대한 관심을 보여줘서 감사하다고 하면서, 프로그램에 변동사항이 생겼다고 했으므로 (A) To announce some schedule adjustments가 정답이다.

---

42. Mr. Garin에 관하여 언급된 것은 무엇인가?

(A) Mr. Solomin을 대신할 사람으로 뽑혔다.
(B) Mr. Solomin과 함께 발표를 하기로 되어 있었다.
(C) 월요일 오전에 그의 워크숍을 열 것이다.
(D) 자신의 강연을 위해 다른 날짜와 시간을 요청했다.

해설 이메일에서 Solomin과 Garin에 관하여 언급된 부분에 주목하면, 강연 하나가 취소되고 Boris Garin이 대신 발표할 예정이라고 했으므로 (A) He was selected as a replacement for Mr. Solomin.이 정답이다

---

43. 이메일에서 네 번째 단락, 두 번째 줄의 단어 "honor"와 의미상 가장 가까운 것은

(A) 이행하다
(B) 제한하다
(C) 발표하다
(D) 축하하다

해설 강연자들이 책임을 다할 것을 약속했다는 내용이므로 문맥상 바꿔 쓸 수 있는 것은 '이행하다, 실행하다'는 의미의 (A) fulfill이 정답이다.

---

44. 화요일에는 원래 어떤 세션이 예정되어 있었는가?

(A) 효과적인 웹사이트 디자인
(B) 강철의 상태
(C) 유독성 폐기물 처리
(D) 21세기의 건축

해설 질문의 키워드가 was originally scheduled이므로, 수정된 일정표 상에는 반영되지 않았음에 주목한다. 이메일에서 Disposing Toxic Waste가 취소되고 Boris Garin의 Hazardous Substance Removal로 대체되었음을 알 수 있으며, 일정표 화요일 부분의 Boris Garin을 확인하면 (C) Disposing Toxic Waste가 정답임을 알 수 있다.

---

45. 일정표에 따르면, 누가 인터넷을 통한 마케팅 리서치 수행에 관하여 이야기할 것인가?

(A) 재정 전문가
(B) 대학 교수
(C) 기자
(D) 기술자

해설 특정 주제에 관해 이야기할 사람을 묻고 있다. 일정표 지문에서 '마케팅 리서치'와 관련된 주제를 찾으면 되는데, Online Marketing Survey에서 강연자는 Benjamin Kleinfield이고, 그의 직업은 business journalist로 확인되므로 journalist를 바꿔 표현한 (C) A reporter가 정답이다.

[46-50] 다음 목록과 일정표, 이메일에 관한 문제입니다.

올해의 다큐멘터리 영화상

〈The Distant Pebble〉

지구를 살릴 방법은 있는가? Daniel Sankh는 데이터에서 실마리를 찾고자 야생생물 보호활동가의 여정을 **46** 십 년 동안 추적한다.

47 〈The Longest Way〉

47 Helen Linden은 생물학을 전공하는 대학원생 Susan Peters가 캐나다 화이트호스에 있는 자신의 집에서 보여주는 놀라운 이야기를 담아낸다. 영화는 함께 학교를 시작한 후의 **46** 25개월을 취재하면서 Ms. Peters가 혁명적인 발견을 해내는 과정의 생생한 이야기를 보여준다.

〈A Day for Ben Markette〉

환경을 구하기 위해 주지사가 된 지역의 한 대학 교수의 **46** 2년에 걸친 캠페인의 여정을 따라가는 영화. Ben Markette가 주의 수장이 되는 과정에서의 경험을 들려준다.

157

HALF TEST 03

〈The Mystery at Carob Creek〉
영화감독인 Theresa Meyer와 ⁵⁰ Mary Naff는 숲을 보호하고자 고군분투하는 동안 ⁴⁶ 여러 해 연속으로 겪은 이상한 여름을 담아낸다.

어휘 track 추적하다 | conservationist 환경보호활동가 | clue 실마리 | revolutionary 혁명적인 | governor 주지사 | narrate 이야기를 들려주다

---

http://www.lesdocsfestival.org

시상식 일정
메인 이벤트 연설자
4월 7일 Sarkowitz 홀

9시 – 개막 및 기조 강의
연설자이자 수상자인 Daniel Sankh가 최근의 한 다큐멘터리와 관련하여 그것의 스타일과 주제, 그것이 자신의 작품에 끼친 영향 등을 논한다. ⁴⁷ 해당 작품으로 수상을 하기 위해 이곳에 온 감독 Helen Linden과는 영화에 대한 인터뷰를 진행한다.

10시 30분 – 다큐멘터리 시상식
진행자 Bryan Forrest가 안타깝게도 행사에 참석하지 못한 후보자 Matt MacKenzie와의 짧은 인터뷰 상영 후에 올해의 다큐멘터리 영화상을 수여한다. Theresa Meyer가 Mr. Forrest와 함께 올해의 상을 수여할 것이다.

1시 30분 – 다큐멘터리 너머로
⁴⁸ Theresa Meyer가 올해의 수상자들과 함께 영화제작 자금에 초점을 맞춘 공개토론회를 진행한다. 자금을 얻는 방식과 자신들의 영화의 비용은 어떻게 됐는지에 대해 이야기할 것이다.

어휘 influence 영향을 미치다 | contestant 참가자 | present (행사를) 진행하다

수신: feedback@adconference.com
발신: kelly.jensen@milkywaygames.com
날짜: 4월 8일
주제: 새로운 행사

저는 LesDocs 상 영화제가 시작된 이래 ⁴⁹ 진정한 지지자였고 항상 기조 연설자를 기대합니다. 매년 그들은 재미있으면서 교육적이고 고무적입니다. ⁴⁸ 올해는 새로운 순서가 포함된 것이 가장 환영될 일이었습니다. 모든 영화감독들의 말이 들을 만하게 멋졌고 청중들도 항상 좋은 질문을 했지만, 올해의 게스트는 특별했습니다.

⁴⁸ Ms. Meyer가 Maryglen 대학교에 있었을 때부터 알고 지냈는데, 모든 프로젝트를 성공시키기 위한 그녀의 집중력과 결심을 기억합니다. ⁵⁰ 졸업 후에는 그녀의 친구 Ms. Naff와 일하기도 했습니다. 그녀가 직접 제작사를 차렸다는 것을 알고 놀랐고 그녀가 만들어 낼 작품을 보는 게 기대됩니다.

이렇게 귀중한 행사를 주최해주셔서 고맙습니다.

Kelly Jensen

어휘 supporter 지지자 | look forward to ~을 고대하다 | inclusion 포함 | treat 특별한 것 | host 행사를 주최하다

---

46. 모든 다큐멘터리에서 한 가지 공통적인 특징은 무엇인가?
(A) 유명한 환경보호운동가에게 헌정되었다.
(B) 제작하는 데 몇 년이 걸렸다.
(C) 야생동물에 집중했다.
(D) 캐나다의 도시에서 촬영되었다.

해설 〈The Distant Pebble〉은 10년 동안의 야생생물 보호 활동을 추적했다고 소개했고, 〈The Longest Way〉는 Susan Peters가 학교를 시작한 후 25개월 동안의 연구를 다루었다. 또한 〈A Day for Ben Markette〉는 2년 동안의 캠페인을 다룬 영화이며, 〈The Mystery at Carob Creek〉은 여러 해 동안 여름마다 일어난 일들을 보여주는 작품이다. 이상의 사항들을 종합해보면 네 개의 작품이 모두 여러 해에 걸쳐 제작되었다는 것을 알 수 있다. 따라서 정답은 (B) They took several years to make.이다.

---

47. Daniel Sankh는 연설에서 어느 다큐멘터리에 대해 논하였는가?
(A) 〈The Distant Pebble〉
(B) 〈The Longest Way〉
(C) 〈A Day for Ben Markette〉
(D) 〈The Mystery at Carob Creek〉

해설 문제의 Daniel Sankh discuss가 키워드이므로 지문을 훑어서 이것을 찾아내야 하는데, 일정표의 9시 행사 설명에서 Daniel Sankh talks about을 발견할 수 있다. 최근의 한 다큐멘터리에 대해 논할 것인데, 작품의 감독이 Helen Linden이고 감독과의 인터뷰를 진행한다고 나와 있다. 다큐멘터리 영화를 소개하는 목록에서 Helen Linden이 감독인 작품은 〈The Longest Way〉이므로 (B) The Longest Way가 정답이다.

---

48. '다큐멘터리 너머로'에 대해 무엇이 나타나 있는가?
(A) 다른 시간대로 이동하였다.
(B) Helen Linden이 진행하곤 했다.
(C) 이제 막 행사 일정에 추가되었다.
(D) 원래 10시 30분에 방영되었다.

해설 일정표에서 이 순서에 해당하는 설명을 보면 Theresa Meyer가 공개토론회를 진행한다고 나와 있다. 그리고 이메일을 읽어보면 보낸 사람이 Ms. Meyer를 대학 시절부터 알고 지냈다고 말하고 있는데 Ms. Meyer는 앞 문장에서 말하는 올해의 초청 진행자이다. 이 부분 바로 앞 문장을 보면 초청 진행자 Ms. Meyer는 올해 신설된 순서를 진행한 사람임을 알 수 있는데 일정표에서 Ms. Meyer는 공개토론회를 진행한다고 했으므로 이메일에 나오는 new presentation은 일정표의 panel discussion을 가리킨다는 것을 알 수 있다. 두 지문의 내용을 종합해서 생각해보면 panel discussion은 올해 신설된 행사이므로 정답은 (C) It was just added to an event schedule.이다.

---

49. 이메일에서 첫 번째 단락, 첫 번째 줄의 단어 "true"와 의미상 가장 가까운 것은
(A) 충성된
(B) 옳은
(C) 정확한
(D) 정직한

해설   Kelly Jensen이 자신을 LesDocs Awards Festival의 진정한 지지자(true supporter)로 소개하고 있는데, 여기에는 오랫동안 이 영화제를 즐겨왔다는 의미가 내포되어 있으므로 의미상 가장 가까운 단어는 (A) loyal이라고 봐야 한다.

....

50. Kelly Jensen에 대해 가장 사실일 법한 것은 무엇인가?
(A) 기조 연설을 했다.
(B) 시상식을 준비했다.
(C) 영화업계에서 일해왔다.
(D) '다큐멘터리 너머로'의 연설자였다.

해설   이메일에서 Kelly Jensen은 자신이 Ms. Naff와 함께 일했다고 말하는데, 다큐멘터리 목록에서 Ms. Naff는 〈The Mystery at Carob Creek〉이라는 작품의 감독으로 소개되고 있다. Ms. Naff와 함께 일했다는 것은 영화업계에 종사한 적이 있다는 뜻이므로 (C) She has worked in the film industry.가 정답이다.

HALF TEST 04

본서 p.396

1. (A)	2. (D)	3. (D)	4. (A)	5. (C)
6. (A)	7. (A)	8. (C)	9. (B)	10. (A)
11. (A)	12. (B)	13. (C)	14. (D)	15. (D)
16. (B)	17. (A)	18. (B)	19. (C)	20. (B)
21. (D)	22. (A)	23. (A)	24. (A)	25. (D)
26. (C)	27. (B)	28. (B)	29. (D)	30. (C)
31. (B)	32. (B)	33. (C)	34. (A)	35. (B)
36. (B)	37. (B)	38. (B)	39. (B)	40. (C)
41. (C)	42. (A)	43. (D)	44. (A)	45. (A)
46. (A)	47. (B)	48. (D)	49. (B)	50. (B)

1. 호화로운 객실과 세계 최상급의 스파, 그리고 세련된 서비스는 이 호텔을 가격에 합당한 가치로 만들어 준다.

해설   for the money를 힌트로, 문맥상 호텔을 가격에 합당한 가치로 만들어 준다는 의미가 되어야 하므로 (A) value가 정답이다.

어휘   polished 세련된, 우아한 | value 가치 | cost 비용 | discount 할인 | price 가격

2. 이달 말이면 Mr. Henderson은 이 회사에 일 년째 재직하는 게 될 것이다.

해설   조동사 will 뒤에 동사원형이 와야 하므로, 미래시제 (A) will work와 미래완료 진행형 (D) will have been working이 정답 후보가 된다. 특정과거 시점부터 (현재에도 하고 있고) 미래까지 지속되는 동작을 나타내는 시제가 미래완료 진행형인데, '이달 말(by the end of the

month)이 되면 일년 동안(for a year) 재직하게 된다'는 문맥이므로 미래완료 진행형 (D) will have been working이 정답이다.

어휘   by the end of ~ 끝 무렵에 | firm 회사

3. Epic 웹 브라우저는 현재 전 세계에서 가장 널리 사용되는 브라우저이다.

해설   「The ~ 형용사 + 명사」의 구조이므로 빈칸은 형용사 used를 수식하는 부사 자리이다. 따라서 (D) widely가 정답이다.

어휘   web browser 웹 브라우저(웹 서버가 제공하는 자료들을 검색하는 프로그램) | wide 넓은 | widely 널리

4. Mr. Fitzpatrick은 계약서에 변경해야 할 사항이 있었으므로 그 계약서를 즉시 보내줄 것을 요청했다.

해설   '요구, 주장, 제안, 명령, 충고' 의미의 동사나 형용사 뒤에 이어지는 that절에는 '동사원형' 또는 'should + 동사원형' 형태의 동사가 쓰이므로 (A) be sent가 정답이다.

어휘   request 요청하다 | contract 계약서 | immediately 즉시 | make changes 변경하다

5. 연구 결과에 따르면 지속적으로 주 40시간 이상 일하는 것은 당신을 비생산적이고 매우 지치게 만든다.

해설   문맥상 지속적으로 주 40시간 이상 일하는 것이라는 뜻이 알맞으므로 '지속적으로'라는 의미의 부사가 필요하다. 따라서 (C) consistently가 정답이다.

어휘   unproductive 비생산적인 | broadly 대략적으로 | formerly 이전에, 예전에 | consistently 지속적으로 | repetitiously 자꾸 되풀이하여

6. 근로자들은 포장하는 곳에서 결함 있는 제품들을 다룰 때 반드시 안전 지침을 따라야 한다.

해설   빈칸은 명사 products를 수식하는 형용사 자리이므로, (A) defective가 정답이다.

어휘   adhere to ~을 고수하다 | safety guideline 안전 지침 | handle 다루다, 처리하다 | packaging 포장

7. 지출을 감시하고 줄이려는 노력은 한 개인이나 부서로 제한될 수 있다.

해설   문맥상 '어떤 범위 이내로 한정된다'는 의미를 나타내는 'be limited to(~로 제한되다)'가 적절하다. 따라서 (A) limited가 정답이다.

어휘   monitor 추적 관찰하다, 감시하다 | reduce 줄이다, 축소하다 | expenditure 지출, 비용, 경비 | limited 제한된 | assorted 여러 가지의

8. 그 관리자는 단순히 팀원들이 특정 상황에서 자신을 어떻게 인지하는지에 대해 의견을 제시해 줄 것을 요청한다.

해설   빈칸은 동사 provide의 목적어 자리이자 앞에 있는 소유격의 수식을 받는 자리이므로 명사가 와야 한다. 따라서 (C) observations가 정답이다.

어휘   simply 단순히, 단지 | perceive 인지하다, 여기다 | observe 관찰하다, 준수하다 | observation (관찰에 입각한) 의견

HALF

TEST 04

159

9. 그 최고경영자가 현재 직위에 있는 관리자들을 신뢰하기 때문에, 그들은 그를 도와 나머지 직원들을 고용하는 데 도움을 줄 수 있을 것이다.

해설 '제자리에 있는'이라는 뜻의 관용어구 in place를 아는지 묻는 문제이다. 여기서는 '현재 관리자 직위에 있는'의 의미로 쓰였다. 따라서 (B) in이 정답이다.

어휘 in place 제자리에 있는, 가동 중인 | assist 돕다 | hire 고용하다

10. 여행이 주로 업무를 목적으로 이뤄졌다면, 당신은 자동차 경비와 숙박비, 식대를 공제할 수 있다.

해설 빈칸은 두 문장을 이어주는 접속사 역할을 해야 하므로 문법상 접속사 (A) as long as (~하기만 하면)과 관계대명사 (D) at which time (그리고 그때에 (~하다))가 정답 후보가 된다. '업무 목적일 경우에만 여행 경비 공제가 가능하다'는 문맥에 따라, 조건을 의미하는 (A) as long as가 정답이다.

어휘 deduct 공제하다, 삭감하다 | lodging 숙박, 숙소 | undertaken 시행된, 착수된 | primarily 주로, 우선

11. Uni Rise는 최고 수준의 고객 서비스를 제공하는 데 전념하고 사회와 환경에 대한 책임이란 철학을 위해 헌신한다.

해설 'be committed to ~'에서 to는 전치사이므로 빈칸에는 전치사 to의 목적어에 해당하는 명사 (B)나 동명사 (A)가 올 수 있다. 명사와 동명사의 선택은 그 뒤에 목적어 수반 여부를 통해 파악할 수 있는데, 빈칸 뒤에 타동사 provide의 목적어에 해당하는 명사 the highest levels가 바로 연결되어 있으므로, 동명사 (A) providing이 정답이다.

어휘 be committed to ~에 헌신하다 | be dedicated to ~에 전념하다 | philosophy 철학 | environmental 환경적인 | responsibility 책임

12. 비록 두 명의 콘서트 기획자 모두가 Rizelle을 특별 게스트로 포함시키는 데 동의했지만, 자금 부족 때문에 그 계획은 거부되었다.

해설 문맥상 '둘 다 동의했다'라는 의미가 자연스러우므로 (B) both가 정답이다. (A) anybody는 수식어구를 동반하지 않으며, (C) each other는 주어 자리에 못 쓰이기 때문에 오답이다. (D) 부정대명사 those는 막연한 사람들을 지칭하기 때문에, 빈칸 뒤의 '콘서트 기획자들 중에'라는 특정한 범위를 의미하는 표현과 어울리지 않으므로 오답이다.

어휘 reject 거절하다

13. 환자들은 정장에 흰 가운을 입고 사진 찍은 의사들을 평상복 차림을 한 의사들 사진보다 선호한다.

해설 빈칸은 명사 doctors를 뒤에서 수식하는 분사 자리이다. 문맥상 '사진이 찍힌 의사들'이라는 의미가 되어야 하므로 doctors와 수동 관계인 과거분사가 필요하다. 따라서 (C) photographed가 정답이다.

어휘 prefer A to B B보다 A를 선호하다 | formal attire 정장 | informal clothes 평상복 | photograph 사진; ~의 사진을 찍다 | photography 사진술

14. Mega 슈퍼마켓이 특히 다른 점은 체계화된 배달 서비스이다.

해설 빈칸에는 '~ Mega Supermarket'을 전체 문장의 주어로 만들어 주는 명사절 접속사이면서, 동시에 명사절 내 주어 역할을 할 수 있는 단

어가 필요하다. 따라서 The thing which를 나타내는 (D) What이 정답이다.

어휘 different about ~에 대해 다른 | systemized 체계화된 | delivery service 배달 서비스

15. 경기 침체기 동안 컴퓨터 회사들은 새로운 시장에 내놓을 저가 컴퓨터를 개발하는 일에 집중했다.

해설 빈칸 뒤에 기간을 나타내는 명사구(the economic recession)가 왔으므로 빈칸에는 뒤에 절(주어+동사)이 따르는 접속사가 올 수 없다. 따라서 접속사인 (C) When은 정답에서 제외된다. 그리고 나머지 3개의 선택지 중 기간을 의미하는 명사 앞에 올 수 있는 것은 '~동안'을 의미하는 전치사인 during이므로 (D) During이 정답이다.

어휘 economic recession 경기 침체(기) | focus on ~에 집중하다 | low-priced 저가의, 낮은 가격의 | even 심지어, 더욱

16. 이 곡은 작곡가의 허락 없이 다른 음악가들에 의해 개작될 수 없다.

해설 의미상 '작곡가의 허락 없이'가 되는 것이 가장 적절하므로 (B) permission이 정답이다.

어휘 a piece of music 음악 한 곡 | remake 개작하다, 개조하다 | identification 신원 확인 | permission 허락, 허가 | reluctance 꺼림, 마음 내키지 않음 | association 협회, 연합

17. 새로운 직원인 Mr. Hwang이 배정될 부서는 아직 결정되지 않았다.

해설 「be yet + to부정사」 혹은 「have yet + to부정사」는 관용 표현으로서 '아직 ~하지 않고 있다'라는 의미이다. 따라서 (A) yet가 정답이다.

어휘 be yet to 아직 ~하지 않고 있다 | beyond ~을 넘어서는, ~을 능가하는 | rarely 좀처럼 ~하지 않는 | permanently 영구히

18. Glide 해운은 오후 5시 이후에 이루어진 선적은 다음 영업일까지 발송하지 않을 것이다.

해설 의미상 '다음 영업일'이 적절하므로 (B) following이 정답이다.

어휘 shipment 선적, 발송 | business day 영업일 | latest 최신의, 가장 늦은 | following 다음의 | recent 최근의 | leading 주요한, 선도하는

19. Grand 호텔은 빠르게 돌아가는 도시 생활에서 벗어날 필요가 있는 커플들을 위한 주말 온천 패키지 상품을 제공하고 있다.

해설 현재진행 시제(is offering)와 어울리고, 문맥상 '호텔은 ~ 주말 온천 패키지 상품을 제공하고 있다'는 문맥에 적합한 어휘는 currently(현재)이다. 따라서 (C) currently가 정답이다.

어휘 fast-paced life 빠르게 돌아가는 생활 | partially 부분적으로 | rarely 좀처럼 ~하지 않는 | currently 현재 | desirably 바람직하게

20. 모든 직원들은 건물의 주차장을 사용하기 전에 경비 부서에 자신의 차를 등록할 필요가 있다.

해설 빈칸은 to부정사 to register의 의미상 주어 자리에 해당하므로 (B) for가 정답이다. 가주어 it과 진주어 to부정사 구문에서 to부정사의 의미상의 주어는 「for + 명사」 형태로 나타낸다.

어휘 register 등록하다 | prior to ~이전에, ~을 하기에 앞서 | parking lot 주차장

[21-24] 다음 편지에 관한 문제입니다.

Ms. Roberts께,

고객님 주택의 보안 시스템 업체로 Radcliffe & Arnold를 선택해 주셔서 대단히 감사합니다. 고객님의 집을 **21** 보호하기 위해 저희에게 의지하시기로 한 것이 현명한 결정이었음을 확실히 보장합니다.

지난 20년간 저희는 주택 보안 분야에서 국내 1위 자리를 지켜왔으며, 전국적으로 일부 대기업들에도 보안 시스템을 제공합니다. **22** 저희만큼 고객님들을 잘 돌볼 수 있는 회사는 없습니다. 저희는 고객님께서 가능한 한 최고 수준의 안전을 누리실 수 있도록 **23** 보장하기 위해 항상 시스템과 서비스를 개선하고 있습니다.

보안 시스템 또는 저희 서비스에 대해 질문이 있으시면, 저희에게 연락 주십시오. 저희는 모든 고객님들이 저희 서비스 및 제품에 완전히 **24** 만족하시도록 보장하는 것을 자랑스럽게 생각합니다.

진심으로,

John Tucker 드림
고객관리 이사

어휘 provider 제공업체 I rely on ~에 의지하다 I modernize 현대화하다 I safeguard 보호하다 I nationwide 전국적인 I ensure 반드시 ~하게 하다 I safety 안전 I related to ~와 관련 있는 I get in touch with ~와 연락하다 I take pride in ~을 자랑하다

---

21. 해설 빈칸에는 뒤의 명사 your house를 목적어로 하는 동사가 와야 한다. 문맥상 '고객의 집을 보호하기 위해'라는 의미가 되어야 적절하므로 빈칸에는 '보호하다'라는 의미의 safeguard가 와야 한다. 따라서 (D) safeguard가 정답이다. (A) purchase는 '구매하다,' (B) modernize는 '현대화하다,' (C) improve는 '향상시키다'의 의미를 가진다.

---

22. (A) 저희만큼 고객님들을 잘 돌볼 수 있는 회사는 없습니다.
(B) 지난달에 몇 번의 침입 사건이 발생하였습니다.
(C) 저희 시스템은 몇 년 동안 항상 똑같이 유지되었습니다.
(D) 고객님께서는 가능한 빨리 저희 서비스에 대한 비용을 지불해주시기 바랍니다.

해설 20년 동안 명성을 쌓아온 Radcliffe & Arnold의 주택 보안 분야에서의 우수성을 앞 문장에서 설명하고 있기 때문에 (A) Nobody looks after clients as well as us.가 가장 어울리는 답이다. 다음 문장에서 항상 최고 수준의 안전을 위하여 서비스를 개선하고 있다고 하고 있기 때문에 (C)는 오답이다.

---

23. 해설 빈칸 앞의 문장은 '(저희는) 항상 시스템과 서비스를 개선하고 있다'는 의미로 주어와 동사가 있는 완전한 문장이다. 따라서 동사 ensure가 부사 역할을 해야 하므로 to부정사 형태의 (B) to ensure가 정답이다.

---

24. 해설 바로 앞에 be동사가 있으므로 빈칸은 보어가 올 자리이므로 형용사가 필요하다. 문맥상 모든 고객들이 (저희) 서비스 및 제품에 완전히 만족하도록 보장한다는 내용이 적절하므로 '기뻐하는, 만족해하는'이라는 의미의 형용사가 필요하다. 따라서 (A) pleased가 정답이다.

[25-28] 다음 편지에 관한 문제입니다.

담당자 분께,

저는 8월 10일자 '동남아 시장에서 지역의 사업체들이 선전하고 있다'라는 제목의 기사에 대하여 편지 드립니다. 이 기사의 작성자는 Wireless Tech 사가 캄보디아 시장에서 시장 선두기업이 되었다고 기술한 부분에서 **25** 부정확한 내용을 실었습니다. Wireless Tech가 캄보디아에서 시장 점유율을 크게 늘린 것은 사실이지만, 그래도 **26** 결코 시장 선두기업은 아닙니다. 저는 시장 선두기업인 Vox Comm 사의 해당 국가 담당 매니저이기 때문에 이 점을 알고 있습니다.

정확성을 위해 작성자 분께서 웹사이트에 **27** 있는 기사의 버전을 정정해 주길 요청해 주시기 바랍니다. 또한 귀하의 신문 일간판에 정정보도를 인쇄해 주시면 좋겠습니다. **28** 저는 이 부정확성에 대한 당신의 답신을 손꼽아 기다리고 있습니다.

안부를 전하며,

Samuel Nhek 드림

어휘 with reference to ~에 관련하여 I entitled ~라는 제목의 I indulgence 사치, 관용 I ineptitude 기량 부족 I piece (신문의) 기사, 글 I market leader 시장 주도기업 I increase 증가시키다 I market share 시장 점유율 I further 더 멀리에 I in the case of ~에 관하여는 I by no means 결코 ~이 아닌 I far and away 훨씬, 단연코 I for the purpose of ~의 목적으로, ~을 위해 I correction 정정, 수정 I daily edition 일간판

---

25. 해설 문맥상 기사에 부정확한 내용이 실렸다는 의미로 빈칸에는 '부정확'이라는 명사가 와야 한다. 따라서 (D) inaccuracy가 정답이다. (A) indulgence는 '사치, 관용,' (B) ineptitude는 '기량 부족,' (C) importance는 '중요성'이라는 의미이다.

---

26. 해설 문맥상 'Wireless Tech가 결코 시장 선두기업은 아니다'라는 의미로 부정어가 필요하다. 빈칸에는 '결코 ~이 아닌'이라는 의미의 숙어 by no means가 필요하므로 (C) by no means가 정답이다.

---

27. 해설 빈칸은 앞에 나오는 주격 관계대명사 that의 동사 자리로 선행사와 수 일치를 시켜야 하므로 the version of his article과 수 일치를 시켜보면 복수 동사인 (A) appear는 소거시킨다. 자동사인 appear는 수동태로 쓰이지 않으니 능동태인 (B) appears가 정답이다.

---

28. (A) 귀사의 기자가 아주 뛰어나고 실수 없는 기사를 작성하였습니다.
(B) 저는 이 오류에 대한 당신의 답신을 손꼽아 기다리고 있습니다.
(C) 저희가 요청한 대로 변경해 주셔서 감사합니다.
(D) 저희와 인터뷰를 원하시면, 언제든지 연락 주시기 바랍니다.

해설 기사에 실린 부정확한 부분에 대해 정정을 요구하는 글이므로 정반대의 내용인 (A)와 변경을 해줘서 감사하다는 (C)는 정답이 될 수 없다. 전체 글의 흐름이 정정을 요구하는 내용이므로 (B) I look forward to your response regarding this inaccuracy.가 문맥상 적합하다.

[29-30] 다음 광고에 관한 문제입니다.

> **Planex 항공 마일리지 카드를 오늘 신청하세요.**
> **자주 항공을 이용하시는 고객 여러분은 추가 특전을 받으세요!**
>
> ■ **탑승과 좌석의 우선권**
> ³⁰ 여러분의 회원 카드를 사용하셔서 가장 먼저 원하는 좌석을 선택하시고 비행기에 탑승하세요.
>
> ■ **느긋하게 쉴 곳**
> 탑승을 기다리시는 동안, ³⁰ 카드 소지자 분들만이 이용할 수 있는 저희 Planex 승객 라운지의 편안함을 만끽하세요.
>
> ■ **마일리지 더 쌓기**
> ²⁹ 일요일부터 목요일까지 여행하는 모든 항공편에 대해 마일리지 포인트를 세 배로 적립하세요.
>
> ■ **무료로 짐 부치기**
> 40,000점 이상을 모으신 고객께서는 Planex 항공의 항공편 이용 시 모든 짐을 두 번 무료로 부치실 수 있습니다.
>
> ■ **기내 반입 추가 수하물**
> 80,000점 이상을 모으신 고객께서는 세 번의 Planex 항공의 항공편 이용 시, 기내 반입 수하물을 추가로 하나 더 가져오실 수 있습니다. ³⁰ 중량 초과 비용은 18kg 이상인 수하물에 적용됩니다. 저희 수하물 규정에 관하여 더 알고 싶으시면, www.planexair.com을 방문해주시기 바랍니다.
>
> **어휘** frequent 빈번한, 잦은 | privilege 특권, 특전 | make use of ~을 이용하다, 활용하다 | board 탑승하다, 승차하다 | comfort 안락, 편안 | cardholder 카드 소지자 | accumulate 모으다, 축적하다 | triple 3배의, | check (비행기) 짐을 부치다 | carry-on baggage 기내 반입 가능한 수하물 | overweight 과체중의, 중량 초과의 | regarding ~에 관하여

29. 포인트를 세 배 적립할 수 있는 방법은 무엇인가?
(A) 단체 티켓을 구매함으로써
(B) 한 달에 항공권 2매를 예약함으로써
(C) 회원권을 친구에게 추천함으로써
(D) 일주일 중 특정한 요일들에 비행을 함으로써

해설 triple points가 키워드이다. '마일리지 더 쌓기'에서 일요일부터 목요일까지 여행 시에 세 배의 포인트가 적립되는 것을 알 수 있으므로 정답은 (D) By flying on certain days of the week이다.

---

30. 카드의 혜택으로 언급되지 않은 것은 무엇인가?
(A) 전용 라운지 출입
(B) 비행기 우선 탑승 기회
(C) 18kg이 넘는 수화물에 대한 비용 면제
(D) 특정 좌석 예약 기회

해설 비행 카드 소지자들에게 제공되는 혜택을 확인한다. (A)는 카드 소지자들이 이용할 수 있는 Planex 승객 라운지의 편안함을 만끽하라는 부분에서 확인할 수 있다. (B)와 (D)는 카드를 이용하여 비행기의 좌석을 먼저 선택해서 탑승한다는 것을 확인할 수 있다. (C)는 18kg 이상인 수하물에는 비용 면제가 아니라 초과 비용이 발생한다고 언급되어 있으므로 올바르지 않다. 따라서 (C) A fee waiver for luggage weighing over 18 kilograms가 정답이다.

[31-33] 다음 웹페이지에 관한 문제입니다.

> **Noah-Jacobs**
>
> 지난 30년간 고객님의 가구에 대한 요구를 충족시켜 왔습니다.
>
> Noah-Jacobs의 비회원으로 결제하시려면 <u>여기를 클릭하세요</u>. Noah-Jacobs의 온라인 가게에 새 계정을 등록하시려면 <u>여기를 클릭하세요</u>.
>
> ³¹ 등록 회원 혜택:
> • ³² 새 품목에 대한 이메일 업데이트 (장식, 거실 가구)
> • ³² 지정 상품에 대한 회원 할인
> • ³² 구매 시 신속한 결제 서비스
>
> 등록은 간단합니다. 연락처와 신용카드 정보를 입력하시기만 하면 됩니다. ³³ 고객님의 개인 정보 보호를 확실히 하기 위해, 저희는 최신 전송 및 암호화 기술을 사용합니다.
>
> **어휘** meet one's needs 요구에 응하다. 요구를 들어주다 | furnishing 가구, 비품 | last 마지막의 | check out 계산하다 | register 등록하다 | account 계정 | benefit 혜택 | regarding ~에 관해 | inventory 재고(품) | select 엄선된 | expedite 더 신속히 처리하다 | registration 등록 | contact information 연락처 | detail 세부 사항 | ensure 반드시 ~하게 하다, 보장하다 | protection 보호 | utilize 활용하다, 이용하다 | latest 최근의, 최신의 | transmission 전송, 송신 | encryption 암호화, 부호매김

31. 웹페이지의 목적은 무엇인가?
(A) 온라인 주문의 상세 정보를 확인하기 위해
(B) 고객들에게 회원 가입을 권장하기 위해
(C) 새로 나온 가정용 가구 제품을 광고하기 위해
(D) 기념일 행사를 알리기 위해

해설 지문의 전체적인 내용이 계정 등록에 관한 이야기이다. 결정적으로 'Registered member benefits'에 대한 자세한 설명이 기술되어 있으므로 정답은 (B) To encourage customers to sign up for membership이다.

---

32. 혜택으로 언급되지 않은 것은 무엇인가?
(A) 배송비 할인
(B) 더 빠른 결제 절차
(C) 특정 상품에 대한 할인가
(D) 신상품에 대한 메시지

해설 사실 확인 문제 유형이니 보기를 하나씩 지문과 대조해서 언급이나 명시가 되어 있는지의 여부를 확인하여 가입 고객 혜택에 관한 내용을 확인해야 한다. (B)는 Expedited check-out service during purchases을 통하여 확인이 가능하다. (C)는 Discounts for members on select items로 특정 상품에 관한 할인이 회원들에게 제공됨을 알 수 있다. (D) 또한 Updates via e-mail regarding new inventory를 통하여 확인할 수 있다. 배송비에 관한 언급은 따로 없었으므로 정답은 (A) Discounted shipping fees이다.

---

33. Noah-Jacobs에 관하여 언급된 것은 무엇인가?
(A) 최근 한 잡지에 소개되었다.
(B) 신생 회사이다.
(C) 최신 보안 기술을 사용한다.
(D) 국내에 다수의 지점들이 있다.

해설 Noah-Jacobs에 관하여 언급된 부분에 주목하여 문제를 풀이한다. 지문 마지막 부분에 보안을 위한 최신 전송 및 암호화 기술을 사용한다고 명시하고 있으므로 정답은 (C) It uses current security technology.이다.

[34-36] 다음 신문 기사에 관한 문제입니다.

시내 무료 주차 폐지
6월 18일
Tara Shepherd 작성

34 Downtown Albury의 교통 체증을 줄이기 위한 시도의 일환으로, 시 의회의 의원들은 주차 규정을 변경할 것을 제안하고 있다. "이 지역 도로의 저녁 시간 교통이 주로 가장 혼잡합니다."라고 Albury 시 의회의 대표인 Gillian Sampson이 말했다. "그 이유는 주민들과 방문객들 모두 식당과 극장, 그리고 음악 공연장을 즐기기 위해 도심가로 나오기 때문입니다. 방문객들은 비용을 지불해야 하기 때문에, 주차장을 피하려고 합니다. 그래서 그들은 도로에서 무료 주차 공간을 찾으면서 배회하고, 이것이 교통 체증을 증가시킵니다."

현재, 노상 주차는 오직 오전 7시 30분부터 오후 5시 30분까지만 요금이 부과되고, 밤에는 무료이다. "이것은 바뀌어야 합니다."라고 Ms. Sampson이 말했다. **35** "다른 도시에서는 일주일 내내 24시간 동안 주차 요금이 부과되고 있으므로, 우리도 똑같이 하려고 합니다."

만약 이 변경 안이 시행된다면, 올해 들어 두 번째가 될 것이다. **36** 4월에 시는 자체 주차 카드뿐만 아니라 신용카드와 동전 결제가 가능한 새로운 주차 요금 징수기를 설치했다. 이 카드는 5월에 도입되었고, 어느 편의점에서든 구매할 수 있다.

어휘 in an attempt 시도 중에 | reduce 줄이다 | congestion 혼잡, 정체 | city council 시 의회 | propose 제안하다 | regulation 규정 | representative 대표, 대리인 | resident 주민 | district 구역 | avoid 피하다 | pay a fee 요금을 지불하다 | search for ~을 찾다 | parking payment 주차료 | require 요구하다 | install 설치하다 | parking meter 주차 요금 징수기 | introduce 소개하다, 도입하다 | purchase 구매하다 | convenience store 편의점

---

34. Albury 시에 관하여 알 수 있는 것은 무엇인가?
(A) 교통 문제가 있다.
(B) 도로 보수가 필요하다.
(C) 주차장이 주민들에게는 무료이다.
(D) 연례 축제를 연다.

해설 Albury 시의 상황에 대해 언급된 부분에 주목을 해야 한다. 지문 첫 단락에서 현재 Albury 시에 교통 체증이 있음을 알 수 있으므로 정답은 (A) It has a traffic problem.이다.

---

35. 시 의회는 무엇을 고려하고 있는가?
(A) 시간당 주차 요금을 올리는 것
(B) 저녁 주차 요금을 도입하는 것
(C) 주차 공간을 더 추가하는 것
(D) 주차 보조원들을 추가로 고용하는 것

해설 Ms. Sampson의 발언에서 현재 저녁에는 주차 요금이 부과되지 않음을 알 수 있고, 다른 도시들은 24시간 내내 주차 요금을 부과하므로 Albury 시 또한 똑같이 할 것이라고 하고 있으므로 현재 고려 중인 사항은 (B) Introducing evening parking fees.이다.

---

36. Albury 시에서 최근에 어떤 일이 일어났는가?
(A) 일부 주차 요금 징수기들이 수리되었다.
(B) 새로운 주차 요금 지불 방식이 도입되었다.
(C) 몇몇 시내 주차장이 폐쇄되었다.
(D) 시 공무원들이 주차용 부지를 더 매입했다.

해설 최근에 Albury에 일어난 일에 대하여 주목해야 한다. 지문의 마지막 문단에서 새로운 주차 요금 징수기가 도입됐음을 알 수 있으므로 정답은 (B) New payment options for parking were introduced.이다.

[37-40] 다음 웹사이트의 페이지에 관한 문제입니다.

출판업이 인터넷에 큰 영향을 받고 있습니다. 시대의 흐름에 부응하기 위해, **37 38** Thoth 솔루션은 중소규모의 서점이 이용하기 쉬운 콘텐트와 관리 도구로 온라인에서 자리잡을 수 있도록 돕고 있습니다. 경쟁이 치열한 오늘날의 시장에서, 고객을 유치하고 충성을 얻는 것은 최신의 기술을 필요로 합니다. **39** 저희 온라인 소매 패키지는 고객 판매와 만족도를 늘리는 것으로 증명된 기능인, 터치만으로 e북을 구매할 수 있는 시스템이 완비된 모바일과 태블릿 기기용으로 이제 막 업그레이드를 마쳤습니다.

또한 저희 Thoth 솔루션은 소규모 사업체와 프랜차이즈를 고려 중인 사람들 모두에게 상품 재고 추적 서비스를 제공합니다. 만약 사업 영역을 확장하려고 하는 중이시라면, 저희가 귀하의 매출을 두 배, 세 배 늘릴 수 있도록 도와드리겠습니다. 귀하가 상품 공급 관리에 시간과 돈을 덜 들이고 새 고객을 유치하는 데 더 많은 시간을 할애할 수 있도록 저희가 배송 추적 능력을 향상시켜드리고, 인쇄 광고물을 만들어 드리며, 재고관리 서비스를 도와드릴 수 있습니다. **40** 결국, 가장 중요한 것은 바로 그들(새로운 고객들)의 충성도입니다. 최신 베스트셀러를 찾기 위해 귀하의 서점을 첫 번째로 찾는 모든 연령대의 새 독자들을 만들고 유지하십시오.

게다가, Thoth 솔루션은 매월 인터넷 교육 연수와 개인 맞춤 상담을 제공하며, 최근에는 브랜드 관리, 국제 온라인 소매상과의 제휴, 기

억에 남는 광고 제작과 같은 인기 있는 주제에 대한 무료 상담소를 시작했습니다. 오늘 thothsolutionsnow.com에서 Thoth 솔루션에 연락하셔서 무료 전화 상담을 신청하세요.

어휘 **set up** 건립하다, 설립하다 | **competitive** 경쟁이 심한 | **attract** 끌어 모으다 | **complete with** ~이 완비된 | **look to** ~을 생각해보다 | **operation** 사업, 영업 | **partnership** 동업 | **memorable** 기억에 남는, 기억할 만한 | **consultation** 협의, 상의

---

37. 웹사이트의 어떤 부분이 제시된 것인가?

(A) 회사 서비스
(B) 고객 후기
(C) 제품 목록
(D) 취업 기회

해설 첫 단락에서 중소 규모의 서점들이 온라인 상에 자리잡도록 도와주고, 최근에는 모바일이나 태블릿 기기에서도 사용할 수 있게 업그레이드된 서비스를 제공한다고 소개하고 있으므로 회사의 서비스를 소개하는 페이지이다. 그러므로 정답은 (A) Company Services이다.

---

38. Thoth 솔루션이 도움을 줄 수 있는 고객으로 가장 적절한 것은 무엇인가?

(A) 대형 프랜차이즈
(B) 독자적 상점 소유주
(C) 통신사
(D) 소프트웨어 개발자

해설 첫 단락에서 Thoth Solutions는 중소규모의 서점이 이용하기 쉬운 콘텐트와 관리 도구로 온라인에서 자리잡을 수 있도록 돕고 있다고 했으므로 Thoth Solutions의 고객은 중소규모의 서점 주인들, 즉 (B) Independent shop owners가 정답이다.

---

39. Thoth 솔루션이 최근 변화를 준 것은 무엇인가?

(A) 본사를 이동했다.
(B) 서점 체인을 인수했다.
(C) 앱(응용 프로그램)을 업그레이드했다.
(D) 모든 품목들을 온라인에 등록했다.

해설 문제의 change와 recently make를 키워드로 파악하고 지문을 훑어보면 첫 단락에서 has just been upgraded라는 동의 표현을 찾을 수 있다. 온라인 서비스 패키지 상품을 모바일이나 태블릿 기기에서 사용할 수 있도록 업그레이드했다는 문장이므로 (C) It upgraded an application.이 정답이다.

---

40. [1], [2], [3], [4]로 표시된 곳 중에서 다음 문장이 들어가기에 가장 적절한 곳은 어디인가?

"결국, 가장 중요한 것은 바로 그들의 충성도입니다."

(A) [1]
(B) [2]
(C) [3]
(D) [4]

해설 주어진 문장이 고객의 충성도를 강조하는 문장이므로 앞뒤에 이와 연관된 내용이 나오는 것이 적절하다. 앞 문장에 '귀하가 상품 공급 관리에 시간과 돈을 덜 들이고 새 고객을 유치하는 데 더 많은 시간을 할애할 수 있도록'과 뒤 문장에 '최신 베스트셀러를 찾기 위해 귀하의 서점을 첫 번째로 찾는 모든 연령대의 새 독자들을 만들고 유지하십시오'가 있는 [3]에 주어진 문장을 넣어야 문맥이 자연스러워진다. 따라서 정답은 (C) [3]이다.

[41-45] 다음 이메일과 안내문에 관한 문제입니다.

발신: Joo Wan Lee 〈jlee@tgcommunications.com〉
수신: Min Seo Park 〈mpark@elormetals.com〉
날짜: 9월 15일
제목: 귀하의 주문 확인

Ms. Park께,

TG 커뮤니케이션을 통해 사업용 계좌를 개설하기로 결정해 주셔서 감사합니다. 아래의 휴대전화와 요금제의 구매를 확인해 드리게 되어 기쁩니다.

전화 기종	수량	요금제
Danbi	10	Local Plus
Simban	18	Basic Line
45 Sum Bi	9	Blue Light
Renji	5	Universal

귀하의 기기들은 저희 Min Ju 창고에서 3일 내에 배송될 예정입니다. 일단 휴대전화들이 배송되면, 그것들을 활성화시켜 주십시오. **41** 간단히 귀하의 기기에서 (+82) 02 4675-3354로 전화하시기만 하면 됩니다.

요청하셨던 대로, 귀하의 Elor 금속 신용카드 계좌에서 정기 요금이 자동으로 차감될 것입니다. **45** 선불 서비스 전화를 이용하시는 고객님들은 잔액이 미화 10달러 이하로 떨어지게 되면 문자 한 통을 받게 될 것입니다. 이용자 분들은 문자 메시지, 전화, 또는 웹사이트를 통하거나 동네 편의점과 같은 제3 공급업체를 통해 추가 사용 금액을 구매하실 수 있습니다. **42** 저희에게 직접 구매하시는 모든 음성 사용량과 데이터는 TG 커뮤니케이션 계좌로 청구될 것입니다.

애용해 주셔서 감사 드리며, 앞으로도 귀하와 거래하기를 바랍니다.

진심으로,

Joo Wan Lee
TG 커뮤니케이션

어휘 **business account** 사업용 계좌 | **confirm** 확인하다 | **local** 지역의, 현지의 | **device** 기기, 기계 | **ship** 발송/배송하다 | **warehouse** 창고 | **activate** 작동시키다, 활성화시키다 | **automatically** 자동적으로 | **charge** 청구하다 | **third-party provider** 제3 공급자, 제3 공급업체 | **bill** 청구서를 보내다 | **appreciate** 감사하다 | **patronage** (고객의 특정 상점, 식당 등에 관한) 애용

164

43 아래는 TG 커뮤니케이션의 법인 고객들을 위한 휴대전화 요금제 목록입니다. 추가 데이터와 음성 사용량은 선불 요금제와 월별 결제 요금제에서 모두 이용 가능합니다. **44** 무료 주말 국제전화 통화는 무제한 국내 음성 요금제와 무제한 데이터 요금제 사용자 분께서 이용 가능합니다.

요금제 세부 내역

요금제	음성 요금제 옵션		데이터 요금제 옵션	월별 기본 요금
	국내	국제		
44 Universal	무제한	400분	무제한	80미국달러
Local Plus	무제한	200분	5GB	40미국달러
Basic Line	300분	0분	10GB	30미국달러
45 Blue Light (선불)	0분	0분	0GB	0미국달러

초과 이용 비용 (월별 요금제 한도 초과 사용량에 따라 결정됨)

추가 국제 음성	추가 데이터	추가 국내 음성
0.20미국달러 / 분	6.00미국달러 / GB	0.05미국달러 / 분

어휘 prepaid 선불된, 선납된 | international 국제적인 | unlimited 무제한의 | domestic 국내의 | data plan 데이터 요금제, 데이터 정액제 | overuse 초과 이용 | monthly rate 월 사용량

---

41. Ms. Park은 전화기를 활성화시키기 위해 어떻게 하라는 지시를 받는가?
(A) 문자 메시지를 보냄으로써
(B) 웹페이지에 접속함으로써
(C) 특정 번호로 전화함으로써
(D) 상점에 방문함으로써

해설 이메일 지문의 두 번째 단락에서 (+82) 02 4675-3354로 전화만 하면 전화기를 활성화할 수 있음을 확인할 수 있다. 그러므로 정답은 (C) By calling a specific phone number이다.

---

42. 상점에서 구매된 금액에 관하여 알 수 있는 것은 무엇인가?
(A) 고객의 TG 커뮤니케이션 계좌로 청구되지 않을 것이다.
(B) 미화 10달러 단위로 이용 가능하다.
(C) 문자 메시지로만 신청될 수 있다.
(D) 더 싼 가격에 제공된다.

해설 마지막 단락에서 추가 사용 금액은 문자 메시지, 전화, 웹사이트 혹은 동네 편의점과 같은 제3 공급업체를 통해 구매 가능하다는 것을 확인할 수 있고, 제3 공급업체가 아닌 TG Communication에서 직접 구매하는 것들만 TG Communications 계좌로 청구될 것이라 하였으니, 다른 방법으로 구매된 사용 금액은 TG Communications 계좌로 청구되지 않으리라는 것을 유추할 수 있다. 따라서 정답은 (A) It will not be charged to a customer's TG Communications' account.이다.

---

43. 안내문은 어떤 정보를 제공하는가?
(A) 배송 옵션
(B) 연락처
(C) 제품 특징
(D) 서비스 요금

해설 안내문 첫머리에서 TG Communications의 법인 고객들을 위한 휴대전화 요금제 목록이라고 하므로 안내문은 요금제에 관한 글임을 알 수 있다. 정답은 (D) Service rates이다.

---

44. 고객들이 주말에 무료 국제전화를 할 수 있도록 하는 요금제는 무엇인가?
(A) Universal
(B) Local Plus
(C) Basic Line
(D) Blue Light

해설 안내문 지문의 첫 번째 문단에서 주말 무료 국제전화 통화는 무제한 국내 음성 요금제와 무제한 데이터 요금제의 사용자에게만 해당됨을 알 수 있고, 표에서 해당하는 요금제는 Universal 밖에 없는 것을 알 수 있다. 그러므로 정답은 (A) Universal이다.

---

45. 계정 정보를 포함한 문자 메시지를 누가 자동으로 수신할 것인가?
(A) Sum Bi 단말기 이용자
(B) Renji 단말기 이용자
(C) Danbi 단말기 이용자
(D) Simban 단말기 이용자

해설 이메일 지문에서 선불 지불을 하는 고객 중 잔액이 10달러 이하로 떨어지는 사람이 문자 메시지를 받는다고 언급하고 있고, 안내문 지문에서 위에 해당하는 선불 요금제는 Blue Light 요금제 밖에 없다. 이메일 지문으로 다시 돌아와서 Blue Light 요금제를 쓰는 전화기 기종은 Sum Bi이다. 따라서 정답은 (A) Users of the Sum Bi phone이다.

[46-50] 다음 공지사항과 이메일, 참여후기 양식에 관한 문제입니다.

Turningpages 서점, 인디애나폴리스
7월 주간 행사
모든 행사는 정문 옆 안내데스크에서 오후 5시에 시작합니다.

행사와 진행자	설명
저자와의 만남 화요일 Erma Nguyen 진행	매주 다른 저자가 서점을 방문하여 자신의 작품에 관하여 이야기 나누고 여러분의 질문에 응답합니다. **46** 무료이지만 Marion County Reading Initiative를 대신하여 저녁 시간에 기부금을 받을 것입니다.
지역주민 음악의 밤 수요일 Aaron Thomas 진행	**49** 휴게실에 오셔서 라이브 음악을 즐기세요. 음악가의 출연료와 식사 비용 5달러를 입구에서 지불(채식주의 식단 이용 가능)
Bookcraft 목요일 Alana Carver 진행	중고서적을 수리해서 재판매하는 저희 자원봉사 '책 의사'단에 가입하세요. 용품은 무상 지급됩니다. 선택적으로, 여러분의 손상된 책을 가져오셔도 됩니다.
50 희귀 서적 수집가 모임 Dean Fernandez 진행	양질의 고서를 찾는 법에 대한 조언을 받으러 오세요. 모든 신입 회원에게 10달러의 회비를 1회 요청합니다.

등록하시려면 안내데스크를 방문해주세요.

| 어휘 | coordinator 진행자 \| host 진행하다 \| lounge 휴게실 \| cover (무엇을 하기에 충분한 돈을) 대다 \| catering 출장 요리 \| drop by (~에) 들르다 |

수신: 수신자 비공개
발신: Jerry Walker ‹j.walker@turningpagesind.com›
날짜: 7월 2일
제목: 공지

전 직원에게,

47 전 직원 여러분에게 이번 달 행사 일정의 몇 가지 변경사항을 알려드립니다. Aaron과 Dean이 7월 17-23일에 출장을 가기 때문에 **49** 제가 Aaron의 행사를 진행합니다. **50** Erma가 Dean을 대신합니다. 그리고 7월 4일은 휴일이라는 것 잊지 마세요.

여러분의 모든 노고에 감사 드립니다.

Jerry Walker
Turningpages 총괄 매니저

| 어휘 | undisclosed 밝혀지지 않은, 비밀에 붙여진 \| recipient 수신자 \| host 진행하다 \| cover for ~을 대신하다 |

https://www.turningpagesind.com/feedback/

고객: Fussels 가족
게시 날짜: 7월 25일
행사 날짜: 18-22
별점을 주세요! ★★★★★

참여후기:
저와 제 가족은 서점 저녁 활동에 참가하면서 정말 좋은 시간을 보냈습니다. 정말로 집 밖의 또 하나의 집 같았습니다. **49** 지역 최고의 음악가들을 라이브로 볼 기회를 갖는다는 것은 저희의 방문에서 예상치 못했던 가장 좋은 부분이었습니다. 진행자는 저희를 크게 웃게 만들었고 밴드는 훌륭했습니다. 비록 저는 스케줄에 Ms. Carver의 발표를 **48** 포함시키지 못했지만 제 아들이 다녀와서 좋았다고 하더군요. 저희는 이번 주말에 다시 멕시코로 돌아갑니다. 제 아내는 그곳에서 **50** Ms. Nguyen의 조언을 잘 활용할 것입니다. 기회 있을 때마다 초판을 찾기 위해 세심히 살펴보겠지요! 이렇게 멋진 한 주를 보내게 해주셔서 다시 한 번 고맙습니다.

| 어휘 | high point 가장 재미있는[좋은] 부분 \| host 진행자 \| put ~ to use ~을 사용하다, 이용하다 \| be on the lookout for (~이 있는지) 세심히 살피다 |

46. 기금마련 행사는 어느 이벤트에 포함되는가?
　　(A) 화요일 행사
　　(B) 수요일 행사
　　(C) 목요일 행사
　　(D) 토요일 행사

해설 문제의 키워드 fundraiser를 지문을 훑어보면서 찾아내야 하는데, donation이 보이는 문장 '무료이지만 Marion County Reading Initiative를 대신하여 저녁 시간에 기부금을 받을 것입니다.'에서 모금 활동이 포함되는 행사라는 점을 간파하고 이 행사가 있는 요일을 정답으로 선택해야 한다. 따라서 정답은 (A) Tuesday's event이다.

47. Mr. Walker는 왜 이메일을 보냈는가?
　　(A) 직원들에게 워크숍에 관하여 상기시키기 위해
　　(B) 일정 변경을 알리기 위해
　　(C) 고객의 문의 사항에 응답하기 위해
　　(D) 회의 일정을 잡기 위해

해설 지문의 주제나 목적은 거의 항상 도입부에서 파악할 수 있다. 이메일 첫 문장에서 직원들에게 이번 달 행사의 변경 사항을 알려주기 위한 이메일이라고 말하고 있으므로 (B) To announce changes in schedule이 정답이다.

48. 참여후기 양식에서 첫 번째 단락, 네 번째 줄의 단어 "fit"와 의미상 가장 가까운 것은
　　(A) ~에 적응하다
　　(B) ~을 갖추다
　　(C) (관련 있거나 비슷한 것을) 연결시키다
　　(D) 포함하다

해설 동사 fit의 사전적 의미를 봤을 때 보기에 있는 네 개의 동사가 문맥에 따라 모두 동의어가 될 수 있다. 여기서는 문장의 해석이 '저는 Ms. Carver의 발표를 제 일정에 포함시킬 수 없었음에도 불구하고'라고 되어야 자연스러우므로 fit와 의미상 가장 가까운 것은 (D) include라고 보아야 한다.

49. 이 고객들이 본 밴드의 행사를 주최한 사람은 누구인가?
　　(A) Ms. Nguyen
　　(B) Mr. Walker
　　(C) Ms. Carver
　　(D) Mr. Fernandez

해설 우선 참여후기에서 이 고객들이 라이브 음악 공연을 본 것이 가장 좋은 부분이었다고 했으므로 공지사항의 일정표에서 이러한 행사를 누가 진행했는지 파악해야 한다. 설명에서 Come enjoy live music(오셔서 라이브 음악을 즐기세요)이라는 문장이 보이는 행사는 원래 Aaron Thomas가 진행하기로 되어 있었다. 그런데 Jerry Walker가 직원들에게 보낸 이메일을 보면 Aaron의 행사는 자신이 맡겠다는 말이 있으므로 고객들이 즐긴 음악 공연의 진행자는 Mr. Walker이다. 따라서 정답은 (B) Mr. Walker이다.

50. Ms. Fussel은 멕시코에서 무엇을 할 계획인가?
　　(A) 멕시코 음악 축제에 참여한다
　　(B) 희귀 물품을 찾는다
　　(C) 중고 서적을 판매한다
　　(D) 어떤 멕시코인 저자를 만난다

해설 문제의 키워드는 Ms. Fussel planning to do인데, 참여후기에서 발견되는 My wife가 Ms. Fussel이므로 이 부분에서 정답을 찾아내야한다. 아내가 멕시코로 돌아가서 Ms. Nguyen의 조언을 받아들여 기회가 있을 때마다 초판을 찾으려는 노력을 할 것이라고 했으므로 공지사항과 Mr. Walker의 이메일을 통해 Ms. Nguyen이 진행한 행사를 찾아야 한다. 이메일의 Erma cover for Dean에서 Erma Nguyen이 Dean Fernandez의 행사를 대신 진행한다는 것을 알 수 있는데, 공지사항의 일정표를 보면 Dean Fernandez의 행사는 Rare Book Collectors Meeting이다. 행사 설명에 나오는 문장 Come get advice on how to find old and valuable books를 통해 참여후기의 first editions는 'old and valuable books'를 가리킨다는 것을 알 수 있고, 행사 이름 Rare Book Collectors Meeting까지 종합해서 생각해보면 이것은 Rare Book과도 동의 표현이다. 따라서 Ms. Fussel은 멕시코로 돌아가서 희귀 서적을 찾기 위한 노력을 할 것이라고 유추할 수 있다. 정답은 (B) Locate some rare items이다.

HALF TEST 05

본서 p.408

1. (D)	2. (B)	3. (C)	4. (D)	5. (A)
6. (B)	7. (D)	8. (A)	9. (C)	10. (B)
11. (B)	12. (C)	13. (A)	14. (A)	15. (D)
16. (D)	17. (B)	18. (C)	19. (C)	20. (D)
21. (B)	22. (B)	23. (A)	24. (A)	25. (D)
26. (A)	27. (B)	28. (B)	29. (B)	30. (A)
31. (C)	32. (B)	33. (A)	34. (B)	35. (C)
36. (B)	37. (B)	38. (D)	39. (C)	40. (C)
41. (A)	42. (A)	43. (B)	44. (A)	45. (B)
46. (C)	47. (C)	48. (D)	49. (D)	50. (C)

1. 보험회사들은 산업 안전 프로그램을 홍보하고 산업 안전 문제를 연구하는 것이 사업상 매우 타당성이 있다는 것을 발견했다.

해설 '이치에 맞다, 타당하다'라는 뜻의 표현인 make sense를 아는지 묻는 문제이다. 따라서 (D) sense가 정답이다.

어휘 insurance company 보험회사 | make sense 이치에 맞다. 타당하다 | industrial safety 산업 안전 | sense 지각, 일리; 감지하다 | sensation 느낌, 감각

2. 제안된 업그레이드가 설치되고 나면, 당신의 컴퓨터가 더 빨리 작동할 것이다.

해설 명사 upgrades를 수식하는 동사 suggest의 알맞은 분사를 선택하는 문제이다. '제안된 업그레이드'란 문맥에 따라 수동의 의미를 나타내는 과거분사 (B) suggested가 정답이다.

어휘 install 설치하다 | operate 작동하다, 운용하다

3. 자신의 필요에 맞추어 비싸지 않거나 심지어 무료인 예산 견본을 찾는 것은 쉽다.

해설 빈칸에 해당하는 to 이하가 명사 budget template을 수식해 주어야한다. to부정사는 형용사적 용법으로 명사를 뒤에서 수식할 수 있다. 따라서 (C) customize가 정답이다.

어휘 template 견본, 샘플 | customarily 관례적으로, 습관적으로 | customization 주문에 따라 만듦 | customize 원하는 대로 만들다. 주문 제작하다 | custom 관습, 풍습

4. 그 자동차 회사는 근로자들의 생산성을 위한 최적의 근무 시간을 알아내기 위해 수많은 테스트를 했다.

해설 빈칸은 전치사 for의 목적어 자리이므로 명사가 와야 한다. 문맥상 '근로자들의 생산성을 위한'이 가장 적절하므로 (D) productivity가 정답이다.

어휘 dozens of 수십의, 많은 | optimum 최적의, 최고의 | working hour 근무 시간 | produce 생산하다 | product 상품 | productive 생산적인 | productivity 생산성

5. 모든 훈련생들은 6월 13로 예정된 Teton 국립공원에서 있을 회사 야유회에 참석해야 한다.

해설 that절 이하에 주어(trainees), 동사(attend), 목적어(the company outing)를 갖춘 완전한 절이 왔으므로 빈칸 이하는 수식어로 보아야한다. 따라서 선택지 중 수식어가 될 수 있는 분사 (A) scheduled가 정답이다.

어휘 be required 요구되다 | attend 참석하다 | outing 소풍, 피크닉 | scheduled for ~로 예정된

6. 고객이 문제를 가지고 연락을 하면, 판매원들은 즉시 착수해서 그 문제가 해결될 때까지 해당 사안에 매달린다.

해설 두 문장을 연결할 접속사가 필요하다. 따라서 전치사 (A)와 (D)는 소거시킨다. 문맥상 '문제가 해결될 때까지 노력한다'는 의미가 적합하므로 (B) until이 정답이다.

어휘 get right on it 즉시 일에 착수하다 | work on ~에 노력을 들이다. 착수하다 | issue 문제 | resolve (문제 등을) 해결하다

7. 무상으로 제공하는 제품이나 서비스와 관련해서, 선물은 아무런 조건이 붙지 않는 경우에만 제공 가능하다.

해설 빈칸은 두 문장을 이어주는 접속사 자리이다. only if는 '~하는 경우에만'이라는 의미이므로 (D) if가 정답이다.

어휘 regarding ~에 관하여, ~에 대하여 | no strings attached 아무런 부대 조건 없이

8. Reward Plus 프로그램은 고객들이 특정 구매에 대해 두 배의 포인트를 얻고 이 포인트를 추후에 할인받을 때 쓸 수 있도록 허용한다.

해설 문맥상 '특정 상품을 구매하고 두 배의 포인트를 얻는다'는 의미가 적절하다. 따라서 (A) earn이 정답이다.

어휘 allow A to부정사 A가 ~할 수 있도록 허용하다 | certain 특정의 | apply A to B A를 B에 쓰다/적용하다 | earn 얻다, 돈을 벌다 | win 이기다, 쟁취하다 | create 창조하다 | catch 잡다

9. 당신이 이 데이터베이스에 입력하는 정보는 극비이며, 다른 기업들과 공유되지 않을 것이다.

해설 주어 information과 빈칸 뒤의 and 이하 부분을 단서로 문맥상 알맞은 형용사를 선택하는 어휘 문제이다. '정보가 기밀이기 때문에 공유되지 않을 것이다' 라는 문맥에 따라 '기밀의, 은밀한'의 의미를 지닌 (C) confidential이 정답이다.

어휘 strictly 엄격히 | share 공유하다 | business entity 기업, 기업 실체 | concentrated 응집된, 집중한 | potential 잠재적인 | dedicated 헌신적인

10. Ms. Riku는 우리 고객들 중 한 명과 저녁을 먹을 예정이나 어느 분인지는 언급하지 않았다.

해설 빈칸 앞 부분에 고객들 중 한 분과 식사를 했는데, 그 분들 중 누구와 식사했는지 언급하지 않았다는 문맥을 통해, 앞의 명사인 our clients 중 선택된 일인을 의미하는 (B) which가 정답이다. 의문형용사 which는 「which + 명사」의 형태로 타동사의 목적어 자리에서 명사절을 이끌며, 이때 which 뒤의 내용이 앞 문장과 중복되는 경우 뒤의 내용을 생략할 수 있다. 그러한 이유로 which one으로 끝나는 문장 구조를 이루며, 이 때의 one은 client를 의미한다.

어휘 client 고객 | mention 언급하다

11. 고객 서비스팀은 환자의 질문에 답변하기 위해 무엇이든 할 것으로 기대된다.

해설 문맥상 고객 서비스팀이 모든 방법을 동원해서 환자의 질문에 답변을 할 것으로 '기대된다, 예상된다'라는 의미가 적절하다. 따라서 (B) expected가 정답이다.

어휘 customer service 고객 서비스 | whatever it takes to ~하기 위한 것이라면 무엇이든지 | extend 연장하다, 넓히다 | expect 기대하다 | expose 드러내다 | expel 쫓아내다

12. FX Techno는 각 부서별로 직원들에게 권장되는 자격 요건을 갖추도록 장려해왔다.

해설 문장의 동사 has been이 이미 나왔고, 빈칸 뒤에 명사 employees가 있기 때문에 동사 (A), 명사 (D)를 소거시킨다. its employees는 의미상 has been의 보어가 될 수 없다. 따라서 빈칸은 its employees를 목적어로 취해야 하므로 능동이 와야 한다. 따라서 (C) encouraging이 정답이다.

어휘 recommended 권장된 | qualification 자격 요건

13. Prisco 사는 전 세계에 있는 공인된 재판매업자들과 수천 개의 소매점을 통해서 상품과 서비스를 직접 제공한다.

해설 문맥상 전 세계에 있는 '공인된 재판매업자들(resellers)과 수천 개의 소매점을 통해서'라는 의미가 적절하다. 따라서 (A) authorized가 정답이다.

어휘 reseller 재판매업자 | retail outlet 소매점 | worldwide 전 세계의 | authorized 공인된, 권한을 부여 받은 | precious 소중한, 귀중한 | limited 한정된 | sufficient 충분한

14. 이미 대중들이 그 상품을 알고 있기 때문에 그 상품의 광고 예산은 아마도 축소될 것이다.

해설 문맥을 고려할 때, 소비자가 이미 상품을 인지하고 있으므로 해당 상품에 대한 광고 예산이 '줄어들 것이다'라는 의미가 가장 적절하다. 빈칸 뒤에 목적어가 없으므로 '줄어들다'라는 의미를 가진 자동사가 들어가야 하는데, reduce는 주로 타동사로 쓰이며 lessen은 크기, 강도 등을 줄일 때 사용하는 동사이므로 적절하지 않다. 따라서 자동사로 쓰이는 (A) shrink가 정답이다.

어휘 advertising budget 광고 예산 | be aware of ~을 알고 있다, 인지하다 | shrink 줄어들다 | heighten 고조되다 | reduce 줄이다, 축소하다 | lessen (크기, 강도 등을) 줄이다

15. 일단 경영진이 프로젝트를 시작하는 것이 바람직하다는 결정을 하면, 타당성 조사가 필요할 것이다.

해설 빈칸은 be동사 is 뒤의 보어 자리로 be동사 뒤에 형용사와 분사가 모두 쓰일 수 있기 때문에, 보기에 형용사와 분사가 함께 제시된 경우에는 태를 고려해서 최종 정답을 선택해야 한다. 이 문장의 주어 it이 희망하는 주체가 될 수 없기 때문에, 능동의 현재분사 (D)는 오답이며, 형용사 (D) desirable이 정답이다.

어휘 management 경영(진) | go ahead 시작하다. 밀고 나가다 | feasibility study 타당성 조사

16. 극장의 이윤을 극대화하기 위해 우리는 좌석 수를 늘리는 계획을 논의하고 있는 중이다.

해설 '극장의 이윤을 극대화하기 위해 좌석의 ~을 늘리는 계획'이라는 문맥에 적합한 어휘는 (D) capacity이다.

어휘 maximize 극대화하다 | seating capacity 좌석 수 | aptitude 소질, 적성 | intensity 강도, 세기 | preparation 준비 | capacity 수용력, 역량

17. 그 해산물 식당은 그 식당의 수많은 수족관에 대해 손님들에게서 매일 찬사를 받는다.

해설 빈칸은 동사(receives)의 목적어 자리이므로 명사 자리이다. compliment(찬사)는 가산 명사인데 빈칸 앞에 관사가 없으므로, (A) compliment와 (B) compliments 중 빈칸에 올 수 있는 것은 복수명사인 compliments이다. 따라서 (B) compliments가 정답이다.

어휘 establishment 상점, 점포 | numerous 수많은 | compliment 찬사, 칭찬의 말; 칭찬하다 | complimentary 칭찬하는, 경의를 표하는

18. Hornsfeld 가전의 시내 지점은 다음 달부터 훈련을 시작할 자격을 갖추고 학력이 있는 판매 사원을 찾고 있다.

해설 다음 달에 훈련을 시작할 '판매 사원을 찾고 있다'는 문맥에 맞는 (C) seeking이 정답이다. (A) look이 '필요한 것을 찾고 있다'는 동사 seek과 동일한 의미를 갖기 위해서는 전치사 for와 함께 쓰여야 하므로 오답이다.

어휘 appliance (가정용) 기기 | branch 지점 | look 보다 | enter 들어가다 | seek 찾다, 구하다 | inquire 묻다

19. 기술자와 건축가로 구성된 팀이 공장 확장 전략을 논의하기 위해 현장에 갈 것이다.

해설 문장에 동사 will go가 있으므로 동사인 (A)와 (B)는 오답이며, 명사 A team을 뒤에서 수식해주는 현재분사 (C)와 부정사 (D) 중 정답을 선

택해야 한다. consist는 자동사로 항상 능동태로 쓰이기 때문에, 능동 의미를 지닌 현재분사 (C) consisting이 정답이며, to부정사의 수동 구조(to be + p.p.)인 (D)는 오답이다. '구성되다'의 해석으로 인해 consist의 수동태를 선택하기 쉬운 문제로, consist of는 항상 능동태로 쓰인다는 점에 유의해야 한다.

어휘 architect 건축가 ⎸ strategy 전략 ⎸ expand 확장하다 ⎸ consist of ~로 구성되다

20. 전국건강협회의 전문가 대표단은 국제 공중위생 회의에서 연설하기 위해 델리에 있었다.

해설 '전문가 ~은 연설하기 위해 델리에 있었다'는 문맥에 적합한 어휘는 delegation(대표단)이다. 따라서 (D) delegation이 정답이다.

어휘 sanitation 공중위생 ⎸ forum 회의, 공개토론 ⎸ revision 개정 ⎸ nomination 지명 ⎸ description 묘사 ⎸ delegation 대표단

[21-24] 다음 이메일에 관한 문제입니다.

수신: 기업가 협회의 모든 회원들
발신: Jenny Deng, 최고경영자
날짜: 5월 9일
제목: 전문성 개발 세미나들
첨부: 세미나 프로그램 및 등록 양식

회원님들께,

지난달 제3회 연례 컨퍼런스에서 여러분 모두를 보게 되어 반가웠습니다. 오셔서 여러분의 지식, 기술, 전문 지식을 협회의 다른 분들과 **21** 공유해 주셔서 감사합니다.

저희 전문성 개발 세미나 시리즈의 첫 번째 세미나에 대해 알려드리기 위해 편지 드립니다. 컨퍼런스에서 회원 분들께서 요청해 주셨듯이, 모든 세미나는 일상의 업무생활과 직접적으로 관련된 실질적인 **22** 주제들을 다룰 것입니다. 첫 번째 세미나는 계약 협상에 관한 것인데, 이 세미나가 여기에 꼭 들어맞는다는 데 동의하시기를 희망합니다. 이 세션은 참가자들에게 초기 논의부터 최종 계약에 합의하기까지 계약 협상 과정의 모든 단계에 대한 **23** 귀중한 조언을 제공할 것입니다. **24** 심지어 수년간의 경력이 있는 직원들조차도 이 세션이 교육적이라고 느낄 것입니다.

더 자세한 사항을 알아보고 신청하려면, 첨부된 문서를 참조해 주십시오.

감사합니다.

Jenny Deng 드림
기업가 협회 최고경영자

어휘 entrepreneur 사업가, 기업가 ⎸ expertise 전문 지식 ⎸ series 시리즈, 연속 ⎸ deal with ~을 다루다 ⎸ practical 실질적인 ⎸ conclusion 결론 ⎸ profession 직업 ⎸ resources 자원들 ⎸ relevance to ~와의 관련성 ⎸ contract 계약 ⎸ negotiation 협상 ⎸ fit the bill 꼭 들어맞다, 알맞다 ⎸ session 세션 ⎸ invaluable 귀중한 ⎸ valuation 평가, 가치액 ⎸ sign up 등록하다

21. **해설** 빈칸 앞의 coming along과 등위접속사 and로 연결되어야 하고, 빈칸도 전치사 for의 목적어가 되어야 한다. 따라서 coming과 동일하게 동명사가 되어야 하므로 (B) sharing이 정답이다.

22. **해설** 선택지는 모두 명사이다. 문맥상, 모든 세미나는 일상 업무생활과 직접적으로 관련된 실질적인 '주제들'을 다룰 것이라는 의미가 적절하므로 (B) subjects가 정답이다.

23. **해설** 문맥상, 이 세션은 참가자들에게 '귀중한' 조언을 제공할 것이라는 의미이므로 (A) invaluable이 정답이다.

24. (A) 심지어 수년간의 경력이 있는 직원들조차도 이 세션이 교육적이라고 느낄 것입니다.
(B) 5월 말까지 계약서에 서명하시고 그것을 저에게 보내시면 됩니다.
(C) 정규 근무시간 동안 490-5405로 전화 주시면 더 많은 정보를 얻으실 수 있습니다.
(D) 이 세션에 대한 피드백이 간절하게 요구됩니다.

해설 계약 협상 과정의 모든 단계에 대한 귀중한 조언이 경력 직원들에게도 도움이 될 것이라는 문장이 문맥상 적절하다. 따라서 정답은 (A) Even those with years of experience should find it educational.이다. 아직 세션이 열리지 않았으므로 (D)는 부적합하다. 또한 다음 문장에서 세부 정보를 얻으려면 첨부된 문서를 확인하라고 이미 언급되어 있으므로 (C)도 문맥상 어색하다. 특정 계약서에 대한 것이 아니라 일반적인 계약 과정에 대한 언급이 있었기 때문에 특정 계약서를 언급하는 (B)도 어색하다.

[25-28] 다음 이메일에 관한 문제입니다.

수신: Veronica Lara
발신: Tatsuya Abe
제목: 우편물 문제
날짜: 8월 18일

Veronica에게,

Mr. Fujimori가 우리에게 **25** 보낸 불만사항에 대해 당신에게 알려주고 싶었어요. 그분은 지난주 우리 웹사이트에서 가정용 가구류 카탈로그를 주문했고, 이번 주 화요일에 배송을 예상하고 있었습니다. 하지만 도착하지 않았어요. 제가 그분에게 사과하고 즉시 빠른 우편으로 카탈로그를 보냈습니다.

이달 들어 이 문제가 다섯 번째 발생했음을 말하게 되어 유감입니다. 우리 온라인 카탈로그 요청 서식에 무슨 문제가 있는 것인지 알아봐야 한다고 생각합니다. 기술부 직원에게 **26** 맡겨서 긴급 문제로 이 건을 조사할 것을 제안합니다. **27** 이 문제가 계속되는 것을 더 이상 허용할 수 없습니다. 이 아이디어에 대한 당신의 **28** 생각을 알려주세요.

감사합니다.

Tatsuya 드림

25. 해설 선행사 a complaint를 주격 관계대명사 that 이하가 수식해 준다. 관계대명사절에 동사가 없으므로 빈칸은 동사 자리이다. 문맥상 a complaint가 우리에게 '보내졌다'로 수동태가 와야 하므로 수동태인 (D) has been sent가 정답이다.

26. 해설 빈칸은 that절의 동사가 올 자리이다. 문맥상 기술부 직원에게 긴급하게 이 건을 조사하도록 '맡기는 것'을 제안한다고 하는 것이 적절하므로 (A) assign이 정답이다.

27. (A) 누군가를 시켜 Mr. Fujimori와 그의 주문에 대한 이야기를 나누게 하세요.
(B) 이 문제가 계속되는 것을 더 이상 허용할 수 없습니다.
(C) 우리는 사라진 카탈로그들이 어디로 갔는지 알아야 합니다.
(D) 보안 위반에 대한 더 많은 정보를 얻으려면 Jeb Wilkins와 이야기하세요.

해설 이미 다음 문장에 문제에 대한 Veronica Lara의 생각을 묻고 있으므로 중복되는 (D)는 적절하지 않다. Tatsuya Abe는 기술부의 누군가가 맡아서 조사해야 한다고 제안을 했기 때문에 문맥상 (A), (C)는 어색하다. 따라서 (B) This problem cannot be allowed to continue any longer.가 정답이다.

28. 해설 빈칸에는 소유격 your의 한정을 받는 명사가 온다. 문맥상 이 아이디어에 대한 당신의 '생각'이라는 의미가 자연스러우므로 (B) thoughts가 정답이다.

[29-30] 다음 기사에 관한 문제입니다.

유명한 피아니스트를 꿈꾸는, 문제가 많지만 재능 있는 음악가인 Jamie Brooks 역의 ²⁹ Golden 상 수상자 Paul Livingston이 주연하는 열정적이고 감동적인 드라마 〈Get Busy Living〉을 주목하세요. Shawn Jordan이 감독한 이 영화는 격한 감정을 불러일으킬 것이며 박스오피스 1위를 할 것입니다. ³⁰ 6월 30일 금요일에 극장에서 꼭 확인해 보세요.

29. Paul Livingston은 누구인가?
(A) 영화 제작자
(B) 배우
(C) 음악가
(D) 극장 관리자

해설 지문 첫 번째 문장에서 Golden 상 수상자인 Paul Livingston이 주인공 Jamie Brooks 역을 맡는다는 것을 확인할 수 있기 때문에 영화 배우임을 알 수 있다. 따라서 정답은 (B) An actor이다.

30. 기사에 의하면, 6월 30일에 어떤 일이 발생할 것인가?
(A) 영화가 개봉될 것이다.
(B) 상이 수여될 것이다.
(C) 오디션이 시작될 것이다.
(D) 논평이 게재될 것이다.

해설 6월 30일이 키워드이므로 지문에서 언급된 곳을 찾아 본다. 지문의 마지막 줄에 6월 30일에 극장에서 확인하라는 내용이 언급되었다. 지문 전체가 신작 영화에 대한 소개이므로 6월 30일에 개봉한다는 것을 알 수 있기 때문에 정답은 (A) A movie will be released이다.

[31-33] 다음 이메일에 관한 문제입니다.

수신: 밝혀지지 않은 수신인
발신: Maya de la Cruz
날짜: 1월 8일 오전 11시
제목: 정보

여러분 안녕하세요.

IT부서의 매니저인 Curtis Lester가 우리 지점들의 모든 회사 직원들이 오늘 인터넷에 접속하고 이메일을 열어보는 데 문제를 겪고 있다고 전해왔습니다. ³² 그의 팀은 아침 내내 이 문제를 해결하기 위해 작업을 하고 있으며, 오후 1시까지는 모든 것이 작동될 것으로 기대하고 있습니다. ³¹ 이곳 본사에 있는 우리들 중 대부분은 그 문제로 영향을 받지 않지만, Luton에 있는 급여 부서 직원들과 영업부 직원들에게는 여전히 영향을 주고 있습니다. ³³ 이 부서들의 직원들에게 연락하시려는 분들은 이메일을 보내는 대신 전화를 하시기 바랍니다. Mr. Lester로부터 우리 시스템이 다시 온라인 접속이 가능하다는 확인을 받는 즉시 여러분께 알려드리겠습니다.

행운을 빌며,

Maya de la Cruz
비서

31. 누가 이 이메일을 받았겠는가?

(A) 급여 부서 직원들

(B) Luton에 있는 영업팀

(C) 회사 본사에 있는 직원들

(D) 지사의 매니저들

해설 지문 네 번째 줄에서 본사에 있는 직원들은 인터넷 접속 불량에 대한 영향을 받지 않는다고 하였으므로, 이메일의 수신인들이 (C) Employees at corporate headquarters임을 확인할 수 있다.

---

32. 이메일에 따르면, Mr. Lester의 직원들은 무엇을 하기 위해 애쓰는가?

(A) 연락처를 업데이트한다

(B) 마케팅 의사 결정을 한다

(C) 인터넷 접속을 복구한다

(D) IT 파일을 정리한다

해설 이메일의 첫 번째 단락에서 'Curtis Lester, the IT Department manager'로 Curtis Lester는 IT부서의 매니저임을 확인할 수 있고, 그의 팀이 복구 작업을 하고 있는 것을 알 수 있다. 따라서 정답은 (C) Restore Internet access이다.

---

33. 이메일 수신자들은 무엇을 하도록 권고받는가?

(A) 다른 연락 방법을 이용한다

(B) 기술적 문제들을 Mr. Lester에게 보고한다

(C) 오후 1시에 그들의 급료를 수령해간다

(D) 다른 컴퓨터로 작업한다

해설 수신자들에게 요청하는 표현을 찾는 데에 중점을 둔다. 현재 특정 부서의 직원들이 인터넷에 접속할 수 없으므로, 이메일 대신 전화로 연락하라고 하는 것을 확인할 수 있다. 그러므로 정답은 (A) Use an alternative method of communication이다.

[34-36] 다음 차트에 관한 문제입니다.

http://www.coffeemakers.com

🔟34 **400달러 이하의 품질 좋은 커피 기기**

모델명	세부 정보	평가자 의견
Janko Instant	무게: 2킬로그램 용량: 30컵 희망 소매가: 199달러	온라인으로만 구매 가능 🔟35 작동 시 소음이 적음
Pinto Expresso Maker	무게: 1.5킬로그램 용량: 40컵 희망 소매가: 249달러	설치 지시사항을 따라하기가 어려움 복잡한 제어 시스템
Elite Cafetiere	무게: 3킬로그램 용량: 60컵 🔟36 희망 소매가: 399달러	부품 5년 보증 빠른 커피 제조 과정
Maxwell 300	무게: 3.5킬로그램 용량: 120컵 🔟36 희망 소매가: 399달러	풍부한 용량 채워넣기를 자주 하지 않아도 됨

171

어휘 capacity 용량, 용적 | suggested retail price 희망 소비자 가격 | available 이용 가능한 | instruction 지시사항 | warranty 보증 | brew (커피·차를) 끓이다, 제조하다 | frequent 잦은, 빈번한

34. 사람들이 왜 차트를 참고하겠는가?

(A) 특정 가격대의 커피 기기에 대해 알아보려고

(B) 각 커피 기기의 교체 부품 번호를 찾아보려고

(C) 연간 몇 대의 커피 기기가 구매되는지 확인하려고

(D) 커피 기기들의 보증 기간을 비교하려고

해설 카테고리의 제목이 Quality Coffee Machines Under $400인 것과 세부 정보, 의견 등이 언급되어 있는 것으로 보아, 400달러 이하의 커피 기기들에 대한 정보를 얻고자 하는 사람이 차트를 참고할 것으로 유추할 수 있다. 그러므로 정답은 (A) To learn about coffee machines in a certain price range이다.

---

35. Janko Instant의 장점으로 언급된 것은 무엇인가?

(A) 어느 상점에서나 주문이 가능하다.

(B) 설치하기 쉽다.

(C) 조용히 작동한다.

(D) 보증 기간이 길다.

해설 지문의 표에서 Janko Instant 항목에 주목한다. 평가자 의견의 Available online only와 Low noise level during operation을 통하여 소음이 적다는 것을 확인할 수 있다. 따라서 정답은 (C) It runs quietly.이다.

---

36. Elite Cafetiere와 Maxwell 300은 어떤 면에서 유사한가?

(A) 동일한 비용이 든다.

(B) 둘 다 커피를 빨리 끓인다.

(C) 무게가 같다.

(D) 둘 다 부정적인 평가를 받았다.

해설 지문의 표에서 Elite Cafetiere와 Maxwell 300의 공통점을 찾아야 한다. Suggested retail price: $399로 소매가가 동일함을 확인할 수 있으므로 정답은 (A) They cost the same amount.이다.

[37-40] 다음 온라인 채팅 대화문에 관한 문제입니다.

Melinda Kennedy [오전 10:07]

안녕하세요, Lemore 슈퍼마켓 프로젝트 일정과 관련해서 모두의 최신 진행 상황을 알아야겠어요. Jose, 재료 혼합에 대해 공장 측과 이야기를 해봤나요?

Jose Cruz [오전 10:08]

네, 월요일에 전화가 왔어요. 아쉽게도, 기계 중 하나가 고장이 났다고 합니다. Candice가 전화해서 우리 주문품의 제작을 언제 시작할 수 있는지 알아볼 거예요.

Melinda Kennedy [오전 10:09]

빈 상자들과 곽들이 내일 도착합니다. 이 배송을 연기할 수 있나요?

Jose Cruz [오전 10:10]
잘 모르겠어요. 이 문제에 대해서 포장재 회사와 아직 이야기를 안 했거든요. 공장 배송 관련해서 수정 일자를 알려고 Candice의 연락을 기다리고 있었어요. Candice, 연락해봤나요?

Candice Kagan [오전 10:15]
지금 막 공장 생산 담당 매니저인 Stuart Bryce와 통화했어요. 37 우리 초콜릿은 수요일에 만들기 시작할 수 있고, 토요일에 발송하겠다고 하던데요.

Jose Cruz [오전 10:16]
39 잘됐네요. 그때까지 포장재 배송은 연기하라고 할게요.

Candice Kagan [오전 10:17]
제품 발송하기 전에 박스에 스티커를 붙여야 한다는 거 잊지 마세요. 그리고 꼭 서늘한 곳에 보관하고요.

Melinda Kennedy [오전 10:18]
그래서 Lemore의 주문은 전부 제때 배송되는 거죠?

Candice Kagan [오전 10:19]
38 맞아요. 일요일 아침에 받을 수 있을 거예요. 다행히 공장 문제가 있는데도 일정을 맞출 수가 있네요.

Melinda Kennedy [오전 10:21]
좋아요. 이와 같은 프로젝트들이 우리에게 큰 성공을 이끌어줄 거라 확신해요. 40 앞으로 계속 진행하면서 다른 맛의 한정판을 찾을 기회를 만들어 봅시다.

어휘 carton 곽, 상자 | revise 수정된 | delivery 운송 | order 주문 | ship out 선적하다 | going forward 앞으로, 장차 | flavor 맛

37. Ms. Kagan은 어느 사업체에서 일하겠는가?
(A) 슈퍼마켓 체인
(B) 디저트 제조업체
(C) 운송회사
(D) 광고회사

해설 Ms. Kagan이 우리 초콜릿은 수요일에 만들기 시작할 수 있고, 토요일 오후에 발송하겠다고 말한 것으로 봐서 이 초콜릿을 만드는 회사, 즉 디저트 제조업체라고 생각해야 한다. 따라서 정답은 (B) A dessert manufacturer이다.

38. 언제 Lemore의 주문이 도착하겠는가?
(A) 월요일에
(B) 수요일에
(C) 토요일에
(D) 일요일에

해설 Ms. Kennedy가 Lemore의 주문은 전부 제때 배송되는 것인지 묻자 Ms. Kagan이 일요일 아침에 받을 수 있을 거라고 대답한 것을 보고 정답이 (D) On Sunday임을 쉽게 알 수 있다.

39. Mr. Cruz는 다음에 무엇을 하겠는가?
(A) 몇몇 박스를 서늘한 곳으로 옮긴다
(B) 몇몇 제품을 발송한다
(C) 어떤 사업체에 연락한다
(D) 주문을 취소한다

해설 10시 10분에 아직 포장재 회사와 얘기해보지 않았다고 말했는데, 10시 16분에 배달을 연기해달라고 말하겠다고 했고 이것이 Mr. Cruz의 마지막 대사이므로 이 화자가 뒤에 할 일은 포장재 제조업체에 연락하는 것이다. 그러므로 정답은 (C) Contact a business이다.

40. 오전 10시 21분에 Ms. Kennedy가 "앞으로 계속 진행하면서"라고 썼을 때 의미하고자 한 것은 무엇인가?
(A) 프로젝트가 더 일찍 완료되어 만족스럽다.
(B) 고객들이 서비스를 좋아할 것이라고 생각한다.
(C) 회사가 미래에도 비슷한 프로젝트를 해야 한다고 생각한다.
(D) 제품이 좋은 평가를 받기를 희망한다.

해설 Going forward let's keep at it이라고 말한 후에 이번 일이 잘되면 다른 맛의 한정판 제품도 찾아 보자고 했고 edition flavors는 다른 맛의 초콜릿을 가리키는 것이므로 장차 유사한 프로젝트를 진행할 수도 있다는 점을 시사하는 것이다. 따라서 정답은 (C) She believes her company should do similar projects in the future.이다.

[41-45] 다음 이메일과 온라인 기사에 관한 문제입니다.

수신: Melanie McKenna 〈mmckenna@artdesigns.com〉
발신: Harry Keen 〈hkeen@ascentpublishing.com〉
제목: Emmanuel의 책
날짜: 8월 12일, 오후 2시 32분
첨부: Israel 겉표지

안녕하세요 Melanie,

오늘 아침, 저는 Emmanuel Chung으로부터 고대 세계 건축학에 대한 세 편의 시리즈 중 그의 최신작인 〈Architecture in Ancient Greece〉의 앞표지에 관한 이메일을 받았습니다. 그는 우리가 선택했던 밝은 색상으로 하는 것보다는 43 이 시리즈의 두 번째 책인 〈City Designs in Israel〉의 표지 디자인과 유사했으면 좋겠다고 했습니다. 그래서 Mr. Chung에게 보낼 수 있도록 41 이번 주말까지 예비 도안을 좀 더 만들어 주실 것을 요청 드립니다. 참고하시라고 제가 스캔한 〈City Designs in Israel〉의 표지 이미지를 첨부합니다.

또한 Mr. Chung은 제게 보낸 이메일에서 책 디자인에 관한 몇 가지 다른 문제들을 제기하였습니다. 제가 당신께 그것들을 전달하는 대신, 이 프로젝트에 관련된 모든 분들이 그의 견해를 직접 듣는 것이 더 좋을 것이라고 생각합니다. 42 그러므로 그는 목요일 오후 7시에 Fasselheim 대학에 있는 그의 사무실에서 우리와 함께 화상회의를 할 것입니다. 제가 그날에 화상 회의를 위한 링크를 보내 드리겠습니다. 나머지 팀원들에게도 이것을 알려 주시기 바랍니다.

Harry

어휘 regarding ~에 관하여 | front cover 앞표지 | architecture 건축 | ancient 고대의 | latest 최신의 | bright 밝은 | choose 고르다 | prefer 선택하다 | resemble 닮다, 비슷하다 | create 창조하다, 만들다 | preliminary 예비의 | forward 보내다, 전달하다 | reference 참조 | attach 첨부하다 | image 그림 | bring up 제기하다 | issue 문제 | instead 대신에 | relay 전달하다 | involved 관련된 | view 견해, 관점 | directly 직접 | therefore 그러므로 | video-conference 화상 회의를 하다 | inform 알리다

---

ww.theworcesternews.com/book-review

12월 22일, 수요일

책 디자이너의 해

〈The Worcester News〉는 저희 독자들에게 최고의 책 표지들을 선사하기 위해 매년 표지 예술과 책 디자인의 전문가들을 초청합니다. 45 헝가리의 Grandia 디자인 학교에서 미술을 강의하는 Mark Varga가 올해 선정한 것을 공개합니다.

Mark Varga: 저는 책의 내용에 대해 매우 적은 정보만을 보여주지만 책을 집어 들고 훑어보고 싶게 만드는 책 표지 디자인에 대해 강한 호기심을 갖습니다. 그래서 저자가 Fasselheim 대학의 Emmanuel Chung이고, 45 Ascent 출판사에서 출간된 〈Architecture in Ancient Greece〉 한 권을 접했을 때, 저는 책의 제목도 작가의 이름도 44 보여주지 않는 그 표지에 매료되었습니다. 그 대신, 그 표지는 진한 갈색의 무성한 나뭇잎으로 덮인, 흐린 회색의 유적 이미지를 하나 보여주고 있습니다. 43 이 표지 디자인은 Emmanuel Chung의 세 편의 시리즈로 출간되는 책 중 두 번째 책과 매우 흡사합니다. 두 번째 책의 표지는 식물들과 건축물을 비슷하게 보여주고 있지만, 배경에 고대 석조 사원들이 있고 전체적으로 상세함이 덜했습니다. 〈Architecture in Ancient Greece〉의 책 표지를 담당한 예술가 45 Melanie McKenna는 독자들이 책에 빠져들도록 하는 색채와 정교한 구조를 사용하는 데 단연 전문가라고 할 수 있습니다. 저는 그녀의 아름다운 미니멀리즘을 높이 평가합니다.

어휘 annually 연례적으로 | cover art 표지 예술 | fine art 미술 | reveal 공개하다 | intrigue 강한 호기심을 불러 일으키다 | skim 훑어보다 | come upon ~을 우연히 만나다, 우연히 발견하다 | fascinate 마음을 사로잡다, 매혹하다 | bear 가지다 | pale 흐린 | ruin 폐허, 유적 | foliage 나뭇잎 | feature 특징을 갖다 | temple 사원 | in general 일반적으로 | responsible 담당하는, 책임감 있는 | truly 진정으로, 정말 | expert 전문가 | intricate 정교한 | structure 구조 | draw in 끌어당기다 | commend 칭찬하다 | minimalism 미니멀리즘, 최소 표현주의

---

41. 이메일의 한 가지 목적은 무엇인가?

(A) 프로젝트에 해야 할 추가 작업의 마감일을 정하기 위해

(B) 직원에게 회의 취소에 대해 알리기 위해

(C) 동료에게 빌린 책을 반납하도록 상기시키기 위해

(D) 작가의 최신 도서 출시를 언론에 발표하기 위해

해설 이메일의 첫 번째 문단에서 추가 도안을 이번 주말까지 보내달라는 것을 확인할 수 있다. 따라서 정답은 (A) To set a deadline for more work to be done on a project이다.

---

42. Harry Keen에 관하여 암시되어 있는 것은 무엇인가?

(A) Emmanuel Chung을 회의에 참석하도록 초대했다.

(B) 고대 건축 전문가이다.

(C) 다음 주에 Fasselheim 대학을 방문할 것이다.

(D) 세 권의 책을 쓴 작가이다.

해설 이메일 지문에서 발신인인 Harry Keen에 대해 언급된 부분에 주목해야 한다. Mr. Chung이 다른 문제들도 제기한 것을 확인할 수 있고, 모든 관계자들이 그의 의견을 직접 들을 수 있도록 Mr. Chung과 화상 회의를 가질 예정이라고 하고 있으므로, Emmanuel Chung을 화상 회의에 초대했음을 유추할 수 있다. 그러므로 정답은 (A) He invited Emmanuel Chung to participate in a meeting.이다.

---

43. 〈City Designs in Israel〉의 표지에 관하여 언급된 것은 무엇인가?

(A) Mark Varga가 디자인했다.

(B) 사원 이미지들을 포함하고 있다.

(C) Emmanuel Chung은 그것을 마음에 들어하지 않았다.

(D) 밝은 색상이다.

해설 이메일에서 Mr. Chung은 새 책의 표지에 밝은 색상을 사용하지 말고, 같은 시리즈의 두 번째 책 〈City Designs in Israel〉의 표지와 비슷하게 갔으면 좋겠다는 의사를 밝혔고, 두 번째 책 표지에 관한 정보는 두 번째 지문에서 시리즈의 두 번째 책 표지의 배경에 고대 석조 사원들이 있다고 언급하고 있으므로 〈City Designs in Israel〉의 표지에 사원 이미지들이 나와 있는 것을 확인할 수 있다. 따라서 정답은 (B) It includes images of temples.이다.

---

44. 온라인 기사에서 두 번째 단락, 다섯 번째 줄의 단어 "bears"와 의미상 가장 가까운 것은

(A) 보여주다

(B) 받아들이다

(C) 필요로 하다

(D) 맞다

해설 온라인 기사 지문에서 책의 제목도, 작가의 이름도 없는 그 책의 표지에 매력을 느꼈다는 내용이므로, 이 문장에서의 bear는 '갖다, 지니다'의 의미로 쓰였으므로 문맥상 '보여주다'의 의미인 displays가 가장 적절하다. 따라서 정답은 (A) displays이다.

---

45. Melanie McKenna에 관하여 알 수 없는 것은 무엇인가?

(A) 전문가가 그녀의 작품을 올해의 가장 마음에 드는 디자인으로 선택했다.

(B) 헝가리의 디자인 학교가 그녀의 작품을 전시할 것이다.

(C) 그녀는 그녀의 작품에서 색을 효과적으로 사용한다.

(D) 그녀의 작품은 Ascent 출판사에서 출간한 책에 특별히 포함되었다.

해설 사실 확인 문제 유형이니 보기를 하나씩 지문과 대조해서 언급이나 명시가 되어 있는지의 여부를 확인해야 한다. 온라인 기사 지문에서 '헝가리 Grandia 디자인 학교에서 미술을 강의하는 Mark Varga가 올해 선정한 것을 공개했다'라는 부분을 통해 (A)를 알 수 있다. (C)는 Melanie McKenna는 〈Architecture in Ancient Greece〉의 표지를 책임진 사람인데 색채 사용의 전문가라는 언급을 통하여 확인할 수 있고, (D) 또한 〈Architecture in Ancient Greece〉가 Ascent 출판사를 통해 출간되었음을 알 수 있다. 헝가리에 있는 디자인 학교는 작품을 선발한 전문가가 강연하는 곳으로 언급되었지, 그녀의 작품이 전시된다고 언급되지는 않았으므로 정답은 (B) A design school in Hungary will exhibit her work.이다.

[46-50] 다음 광고와 온라인 쇼핑 장바구니, 이메일에 관한 문제입니다.

Clifton's 미술품 도매상

당신의 가정이나 사무실의 벽에 Clifton's 미술품 도매상의 그림으로 활기를 더해 보세요. 저희 Clifton's는 모든 **46** 취향에 맞춰 드리기 위해 작업실에 전문 아티스트들을 고용하고 있습니다. 저희 웹사이트 www.cliftonarts.com에 방문하셔서 현재 판매용으로 나온 작품의 섬네일 샘플을 확인해 보세요. 그곳에서, 아티스트 별, 색상 별, 크기 별로 그림을 검색하실 수 있습니다. 당신이 사무실 가구에 맞출 그림을 구입하시려거나, 거실을 밝게 해줄 작품을 고르려 할 때, 저희가 쉽게 하도록 도와드리겠습니다. 완벽한 작품을 선택하시고, 저희의 간편한 온라인 주문 시스템을 사용하시면, 구입하신 물품을 영업일 기준으로 4-6일 내로 배송해 드립니다. **48** 추가 배송료를 지불하시면 바로 다음 날에도 받아보실 수 있습니다.

*구입하신 물건이 마음에 안 드실 때는 교환이나 환불이 가능합니다. 결정하기 힘드신가요? 그렇다면 **47** 당신에게 딱 맞는 그림을 선택하는 걸 도와드릴 수 있도록 저희 디자인 전문가들에게 연락해 주시기 바랍니다.

어휘 liven up 활기를 띠게 만들다 | suit ~에 맞다 | taste 기호, 취향 | thumbnail 섬네일(페이지 전체의 레이아웃을 검토할 수 있게 페이지 전체를 작게 줄여 화면에 띄운 것), 미리 보기 | merchandise 물품, 상품 | unsatisfied 처리되지 않는, 불만스러운

---

https://www.cliftonarts.com/checkout

주문 개요 #42	고객: ESV 치과	
품목	크기	가격
〈Abstract Sunshine〉 S2039	11 x 14	90.00달러
〈Still Life with Gentleman〉 G3821	16 x 20	70.00달러
〈Country Estate〉 E2390	20 x 24	100.00달러
49 〈Cornfield Bloom〉 B3312	24 x 36	80.00달러
소계		340.00달러
세금 (10%)		34.00달러
48 빠른 배송		30.00달러
합계		404.00달러

어휘 abstract 추상적인 | cornfield 옥수수 밭 | bloom 꽃

발신: allie.kim@esvdentistry.com
수신: orders@cliftonarts.com
날짜: 11월 11일
제목: 주문번호 42번

제가 주문한 물건(42번)을 신속하게 배송해 주셔서 감사합니다. 저희 관리팀이 주말 동안 로비에 그림들을 걸어두었습니다. **50** 하지만, 〈Abstract Sunshine〉이 아니라, 〈Abstract Moonlight〉을 받았습니다. 그림의 이름이 비슷하다 보니, 그쪽 직원들이 혼동했던 게 아닌가 싶습니다. 빠진 작품을 찾아서 배송해 주시겠습니까? 그리고 **49** 저희 환자 중 많은 분들께서 농장 풍경이 있는 그림을 칭찬해 주고 계십니다(B3312). 이 작품과 비슷한 다른 작품을 제작해 주실 수 있는지 궁금합니다. 연락 주십시오.

진심으로,

Allie Kim
사무실 관리자
ESV 치과

어휘 prompt 즉각적인, 지체 없는 | maintenance 유지 | mix up 혼동하다 | locate ~의 위치를 찾아내다 | praise 칭찬하다

---

46. 광고에서 첫 번째 단락, 두 번째 줄의 단어 "taste"와 의미상 가장 가까운 것은

(A) 맛

(B) 표본

(C) 선호

(D) 감각

해설 문맥상 '모든 취향에 맞춰 드리기 위해'라는 뜻이므로 여기서 taste는 미술품에 대한 '취향'을 나타내므로 '선호'라는 의미의 (C) preference가 동의어이다.

47. Clifton's 미술품 도매상의 고객은 무엇을 하도록 권고받는가?

(A) 제품을 시험 사용한다

(B) 작업실을 방문한다

(C) 전문가와 상의한다

(D) 갤러리 전시에 참석한다

해설 문제의 키워드 customers urged to do를 광고 지문에서 찾아보면 동사 urge를 encourage로 바꿔 놓은 마지막 문장 Then we encourage you to contact one of our design specialists to help choose the perfect painting for you!를 발견할 수 있다. 이 문장의 contact one of our design specialists를 paraphrasing 한 (C) Consult with an expert가 정답이다.

---

48. 주문번호 42번에 대해 사실인 것은 무엇인가?

(A) 무료 작품이 포함되었다.

(B) 할인된 물건들을 포함한다.

(C) 10월에 결제되었다.

(D) 하루 만에 도착했다.

해설 온라인 쇼핑 장바구니 지문의 42번 주문표 하단에 Express shipping: $30.00라고 나와 있으므로 빠른 배송을 통해 물건을 받았음을 알 수 있다. 광고 지문을 보면 추가 배송료를 냄으로써 물건이 다음 날(following day) 받을 수 있다고 했으므로 정답은 (D) It arrived in one day.이다.

---

49. ESV 치과 환자들은 어떤 그림을 좋아한다고 명시하고 있는가?

(A) 〈Abstract Sunshine〉

(B) 〈Still Life with Gentleman〉

(C) 〈Country Estate〉

(D) 〈Cornfield Bloom〉

해설 문제의 키워드가 patients indicate that they like이므로 지문을 훑어서 이 부분을 찾아내야 한다. 이메일에서 이 키워드가 patients have praised로 바뀌어 있다는 것을 간파하면 문제를 해결할 수 있다. 환자들이 B3312 그림을 칭찬했다고 했는데, 온라인 쇼핑 장바구니의 표를 보면 이 그림의 제목은 〈Cornfield Bloom〉이다. 그러므로 정답은 (D) Cornfield Bloom이다.

---

50. Ms. Kim이 이메일에 언급한 문제는 무엇인가?

(A) 구매품 중 일부가 손상되었다.

(B) 신용카드에 잘못된 금액이 청구되었다.

(C) 잘못된 물품이 도착했다.

(D) 배송 추적 번호를 확인할 수 없다.

해설 이메일 서두에서 주문한 그림 대신 다른 것이 배송되었음을 알 수 있다. 그러므로 정답은 (C) An incorrect item was delivered이다.

ACTUAL TEST

101. (A)	102. (A)	103. (D)	104. (D)	105. (A)
106. (D)	107. (D)	108. (B)	109. (A)	110. (B)
111. (C)	112. (B)	113. (C)	114. (B)	115. (D)
116. (A)	117. (D)	118. (A)	119. (C)	120. (A)
121. (D)	122. (B)	123. (C)	124. (D)	125. (C)
126. (A)	127. (C)	128. (C)	129. (C)	130. (D)
131. (D)	132. (B)	133. (A)	134. (B)	135. (B)
136. (B)	137. (D)	138. (D)	139. (B)	140. (A)
141. (D)	142. (B)	143. (B)	144. (B)	145. (C)
146. (A)	147. (B)	148. (B)	149. (D)	150. (A)
151. (B)	152. (C)	153. (C)	154. (B)	155. (D)
156. (A)	157. (D)	158. (C)	159. (C)	160. (A)
161. (C)	162. (A)	163. (C)	164. (B)	165. (B)
166. (D)	167. (B)	168. (C)	169. (A)	170. (D)
171. (D)	172. (B)	173. (C)	174. (B)	175. (D)
176. (D)	177. (D)	178. (A)	179. (A)	180. (D)
181. (A)	182. (C)	183. (D)	184. (D)	185. (B)
186. (C)	187. (B)	188. (B)	189. (D)	190. (A)
191. (B)	192. (A)	193. (C)	194. (D)	195. (A)
196. (A)	197. (A)	198. (D)	199. (C)	200. (B)

101. 모든 팀원들은 그들의 예정된 비행 시간 두 시간 전에 게이트에 도착해야 한다.

해설 대명사의 격을 판단하는 문제에서 명사 앞에 빈칸이 있으므로 소유격 대명사인 (A) their가 정답이다.

어휘 expect 기대하다 | scheduled 예정된

102. 마케팅 보고서 최종안을 이번 금요일까지 받아야 한다.

해설 draft 앞에는 first, second, final 같은 회차를 나타내는 표현이 자주 어울려 사용된다는 것을 알아 두고 (A) final을 정답으로 선택해야 한다. blank draft는 의미상 사용할 수 없는 표현이고, various 뒤에는 복수명사가 오게 되어 있으므로 여기서는 정답이 될 수 없다.

어휘 final draft 최종 원고 | blank 빈

103. Mr. Lee는 환자들에게 건강 상담과 보험금 청구 지원을 모두 제공한다.

해설 보기를 보면 상관접속사 문제임을 짐작할 수 있다. 상관접속사 문제는 짝을 지어서 외워 두면 해결된다. 빈칸 뒤에 있는 and의 짝은 both이다. 따라서 정답은 (D) both이다.

어휘 health consultation 건강 상담 | insurance claim 보험금 청구

ACTUAL

TEST

104. Jeremy Struker가 새로운 광고 캠페인을 이끌도록 이사회에 의해 선출되었다.

해설 동사가 없는 이 문장의 빈칸에는 반드시 동사가 들어가야 하므로 일단 준동사인 (A)는 제외한다. 선택지의 나머지 동사들이 능동태와 수동태로 구성되어 있는데, 빈칸 뒤에 목적어가 없으므로 수동태인 (D) was selected가 정답이다.

어휘 board of directors 이사회

105. Cornwall Music 사는 손으로 만든 악기들의 현 수요를 감당하기 위해 숙련된 장인들을 고용할 계획이다.

해설 문맥상 '~에 대한 수요를 처리하기 위해'라는 의미가 적합하므로, '수요, 요구'의 의미를 지닌 (A) demand 가 정답이다. 명사 demand가 전치사 for와 함께 쓰인다는 점도 정답의 단서가 된다.

어휘 hire 고용하다 | skilled 숙련된 | artisan 장인, 기능 보유자 | address (어려운 문제를) 다루다, 처리하다 | demand for ~에 대한 수요 | denial 부인 | claim 주장

106. Vonex 의류는 지난달 새 코트 제품군을 출시한 이후 판매량이 증가했다.

해설 빈칸 뒤에 절이 이어지고 있으므로 전치사인 (A)와 (C)는 일단 제외한다. 그리고 새 코트 제품군을 출시한 이후 판매량이 증가했다는 의미의 문장이 자연스러우므로 (D) since를 선택한다. 접속사나 전치사 어휘 문제에서 주절의 시제가 현재완료인 경우 보기 중 since나 for가 보이면 십중팔구 정답이다. since와 for가 모두 있는 경우 빈칸 뒤에 절이 나오거나 과거 시점을 나타내는 표현이 있으면 since, 기간 표현이 있으면 for가 정답이다.

어휘 see 장소를 주어로 써서 그 장소에서 어떤 일이 행해짐을 나타냄 | introduce (상품 따위를 시장에) 내놓다 | line 제품군

107. 물품이 일정보다 빨리 배송되었으므로, 그 제품은 처음 예상한 것보다 더 일찍 제작될 것이다.

해설 빈칸 뒤에 than이 있으므로 그 앞에는 당연히 비교급 형용사나 부사가 있어야 한다. 그러므로 정답은 (D) earlier이다.

어휘 supplies 비품 | deliver 운송하다, 배송하다 | ahead of schedule 일정보다 앞서 | project 예상하다

108. 업데이트된 시간표에 기초하여, 교육 워크숍은 오후 3시가 아닌 오후 4시에 시작될 것이다.

해설 일단 빈칸에 (A)가 들어가면 '오후 3시 이후 오후 4시'라는 의미가 되므로 당연히 정답이 될 수 없고, (C)와 (D)는 모두 접속사이므로 빈칸 뒤에 「주어 + 동사」 구조의 절이 있어야 한다. 문법적으로나 의미상 적절한 것은 (B) instead of이다.

어휘 update 갱신하다 | timetable 시간표 | instead of ~대신에

109. 역에서 개조 공사가 진행되고 있기 때문에 이 열차는 정차 없이 토피카를 지나갈 것이다.

해설 자동사 proceed는 뒤에 명사 Topeka를 취하기 위해 전치사가 필요하므로, 빈칸에는 전치사가 와야 하며, 문맥상 '토피카를 통과하여 간다'는 의미가 되어야 하므로 정답은 (A) through이다.

어휘 renovation 개조, 수리 | proceed 계속 진행하다, 앞으로 나아가다 | through ~을 통해서 | swiftly 재빨리

110. 비영리 기구인 Meteorologists International은 리야드 주변의 사막 지역에서 대기의 샘플을 채취할 것이다.

해설 빈칸 앞뒤 몇 단어만 읽어보면 리야드 주변의 사막 지역에서 대기의 샘플을 채취할 것이라는 의미를 파악할 수 있으므로 정답으로 (B) around를 선택해야 한다.

어휘 non-profit organization 비영리 기구 | air sample 공기 샘플

111. 지원서에 대한 최종 결정이 내려지면 후보자들은 연락을 받을 것이다.

해설 빈칸 뒤에 「주어 + 동사」 구조의 절이 왔으므로, 두 문장을 연결하는 접속사 (C), (D) 중에서 의미상 어울리는 정답을 선택해야 한다. '최종 결정이 나게 되면 후보자들이 연락을 받게 된다'는 문맥에 따라, '~하면, 하자마자'라는 의미를 지닌 접속사 (C) once가 정답이다.

어휘 candidate 후보자, 지원자 | make a decision on ~에 대한 결정을 내리다

112. Nitussa 자동차의 이사회는 Ms. Suarez가 다른 어떤 직원보다 훨씬 경험이 많다는 점을 확신하여 그녀를 부장으로 승진시켰다.

해설 비교급을 수식할 때는 '훨씬'이라는 뜻으로 much, still, even, far, a lot 같은 부사를 사용한다는 것을 기억하고 (B) much를 정답으로 선택해야 한다.

어휘 assure 확언하다, 확신하다 | experienced 경험이 많은 | executive board 이사회 | promote 승진시키다

113. Clint's 사진관은 오직 전문가에 의해 가공된 이미지만을 제공한다는 것을 자랑스럽게 생각합니다.

해설 빈칸 앞에 동사 offer가 있으므로 '------- processed images'가 offer의 목적어가 되는데, 이렇게 빈칸 뒤에 「형용사 + 명사」의 구조가 있을 때는 빈칸에 부사를 넣어서 부사가 형용사를, 형용사가 명사를 수식하는 구조로 만들어주면 되므로 (C) professionally가 정답이 된다.

어휘 process 가공[처리]하다 | profession 직업 | professionally 전문가에 의해, 전문적으로 | professional 전문적인, 전문가

114. Art Three Medias의 모든 디자이너는 최소 5년 이상 그래픽 아트 분야에서 일해왔다.

해설 빈칸 앞에 명사의 소유격이 있으므로 빈칸에는 명사가 들어가야 하는데, 빈칸 뒤의 동사 have worked가 복수형이므로 주어로 복수명사를 사용해야 한다. 그러므로 정답은 (B)와 (C) 중에서 선택해야 한다. 의미상 '그래픽 아트 분야에서 근무했다'라는 문장이 자연스러우므로 사람을 나타내는 명사인 (B) designers가 정답이다.

어휘 graphic arts 그래픽 아트

115. 〈Tampa Daily News〉의 음악 평론가는 Rod Oliver의 새로운 앨범의 노래들이 독창성이 떨어진다고 말했다.

해설 describe A as B(A를 B하다고 묘사하다[말하다])를 기억해두고 'Rod Oliver의 새로운 앨범의 노래들은 독창성이 떨어진다고 말했다'

라는 의미가 되도록 (D) described를 정답으로 선택해야 한다. (A) listened는 우리말로 바꿨을 때 의미가 통하는 것 같지만 뒤에 to를 함께 사용해야 하므로 정답이 될 수 없다.

어휘 **unoriginal** 독창성이 떨어지는 I **describe** 묘사하다, 말하다

116. 공연 예술 극장의 건설은 처음 예산을 훨씬 웃돌았지만, 결과는 그 비용을 들일 가치가 충분했다.

해설 빈칸 앞 문장에서 예산을 의미하는 budget을 단서로, 문맥상 비용을 의미하는 (A) expense가 정답이다.

어휘 **performing arts theater** 공연 예술 극장 I **well over** ~보다 훨씬 더 I **initial** 처음의, 최초의 I **budget** 예산 I **well worth** 가치가 충분한 I **expense** 비용 I **tariff** 관세 I **fare** (교통 수단의) 요금

117. Wakano 전자는 전 미대륙으로 시장을 확장하기 위해 Bergo 전자 매장 체인의 매입을 완결지었다.

해설 빈칸 앞의 in order to부터 빈칸 뒤의 South America까지를 보면 정답을 알 수 있다. 회사를 확장해서 미대륙으로 진출한다는 의미가 되어야 자연스러운 문장이므로 이동과 방향의 전치사 (D) into가 정답이다.

어휘 **finalize** 마무리 짓다 I **purchase** 구매 I **store chain** 매장 체인

118. 품질은 좋으면서도 비싸지 않은 건축 자재들의 사용이 Takata 건설사를 위해 비용 감소로 이어졌다.

해설 반대되는 내용을 연결하는 yet과 빈칸 뒷부분의 비용절감(a decrease in costs)을 단서로 (A) inexpensive가 정답이다.

어휘 **inexpensive** 비싸지 않은 I **incomplete** 불완전한 I **undecided** 결정하지 못한

119. 스스로도 베테랑 골퍼인 Ms. Mayweather는 전국에서 수입이 가장 많은 골퍼 Bishop Duarte의 멘토이기도 했다.

해설 빈칸 앞의 A veteran golfer와 빈칸 뒤의 Ms. Mayweather는 동격이므로 이 부분의 문장 구조는 이미 완성되어 있는 상태. 매달 출제되는 대명사의 격을 판단하는 문제에서 이미 완성된 문장 구조에 빈칸이 들어있을 때는 부사 역할을 할 수 있는 재귀대명사를 정답으로 선택해야 한다. 그러므로 (C) herself가 정답이다.

어휘 **veteran** 베테랑, 전문가 I **mentor** 멘토

120. Orion 주택 소유주 협회는 주거 지역에서의 자동차 속도 제한 상향에 반대하는 단체이다.

해설 be동사 뒤에 들어갈 수 있는 것은 능동을 의미하는 현재분사 (A)와 수동을 의미하는 과거분사 (B)이다. 협회가 자동차 속도 제한 상향에 반대하는 주체이기에 능동태가 되어야 하며, 문법적으로도 타동사 oppose 뒤에 목적어를 수반했으므로 능동태를 완성하는 현재분사 (A) opposing이 정답이다.

어휘 **homeowner** 주택 보유자 I **association** 협회 I **speed limit** 속도 제한 I **residential** 거주의 I **oppose** 반대하다

121. 어제 일자 〈Dallas Metro Times〉의 한 흥미로운 사설은 취업 시장의 점점 심해지는 경쟁이 부동산 가격에 영향을 미칠 것이라고 주장했다.

해설 빈칸 앞 An intriguing부터 빈칸 뒤 argued that까지만 살펴보면 정답을 알 수 있다. 어제 일자 신문의 '흥미로운 ~이 ~라고 주장했다'라는 문장이므로 신문의 여러 가지 글 중에서 주장을 펼치는 것으로 (D) editorial을 선택해야 한다.

어휘 **intriguing** 흥미로운 I **argue** 주장하다 I **affect** 영향을 미치다 I **real estate** 부동산 I **index** 색인 I **editorial** 사설

122. Mr. Pelt는 15년 전 입사한 이후로 노동 계약과 분쟁을 담당하는 수석 교섭관으로 근무해왔다.

해설 품사 문제에서 명사 뒤에 빈칸이 있을 때는 명사를 한 번 더 써서 복합 명사를 만들어주면 정답이 된다. 이 문장에서는 빈칸에 명사를 넣으면 the lead ------가 has been의 보어가 된다. 그러므로 빈칸에는 명사 (C)나 (D)를 넣어야 하는데, '수석'이라는 뜻의 lead는 직함 앞에 붙여야 하므로 사람명사인 (D) negotiator가 정답이다.

어휘 **labor contract** 노동 계약 I **dispute** 분쟁 I **negotiate** 협상하다

123. Ware 철물점은 지난달의 큰 폭풍의 영향을 받은 회사 중 하나였다.

해설 문법적으로는 네 개의 전치사가 모두 빈칸에 들어갈 수 있지만 문장의 의미상 Ware Hardware는 폭풍의 영향을 받은 회사 중 하나였다가 자연스러우므로 (A) among을 정답으로 선택해야 한다.

어휘 **affect** 영향을 미치다 I **storm** 폭풍

124. 급여에 관한 문의 사항이 있을 때 직원들은 저나 Ms. Singh에게 직접 연락하기 바랍니다.

해설 빈칸은 동사 contact의 목적어가 들어갈 자리이므로 목적격 대명사인 (A) me와 소유대명사인 (D) mine이 들어갈 수 있다. 문장 앞 부분을 읽어봤을 때 mine으로 바꿀 만한 '소유격 + 명사'에 해당하는 표현이 없으므로 목적격 대명사인 (A) me가 정답이다.

어휘 **inquiry** 문의 사항 I **directly** 직접

125. 그 이사는 애초에 이번 분기의 수익이 높을 것이라고 예상했지만, 나중에는 전망이 그리 좋지 않다고 보고했다.

해설 부사절이 접속사 While로 시작하고 있으므로 주절에는 부사절과 상반되는 내용이 나와야 한다. 그러므로 부사절의 initially projected(애초에 예상했다)와 주절의 later reported(나중에 보고했다), revenue to be high(수익이 높을 것으로)와 the outlook was not so great(전망이 그리 좋지 않다)가 서로 대조를 이루도록 (C) initially를 정답으로 선택하는 것이 적절하다.

어휘 **project** 예상하다 I **quarter** 분기 I **outlook** 전망 I **eventually** 결국 I **initially** 초기에

126. Tusco는 최근 매출 성장 및 생산 증가 덕분에 최고의 철강 제조업체로 꼽혔다.

해설 빈칸 앞에 명사 sales가 있으므로 빈칸에는 명사를 한 번 더 넣어서 복합명사를 만들어 앞에 있는 전치사 due to의 목적어가 되면서 소유격 대명사 their와 형용사 recent의 수식을 받도록 해주면 된다. 그러

므로 빈칸에는 명사인 (A)와 (B)가 들어갈 수 있는데, 빈칸 뒤에 등위 접속사 and가 있으므로 그 뒤에 있는 production increases와 병렬 구조가 되어야 한다. increases라는 추상명사와 병렬 구조가 되어야 한다면 빈칸에도 역시 사람이 아닌 추상명사가 들어가야 하므로 (A) growth가 정답이다.

어휘 list 명단에 올리다 | manufacturer 제조업체 | growth 성장

127. 영업 시간에 관한 불만사항 때문에, Mavin 의류회사는 오후 10시까지 문을 열기로 결정했다.

해설 선택지에 있는 네 개의 명사 '제품', '자원', '불만사항', '도전자' 중 빈칸 앞의 Due to, 빈칸 뒤의 concerning its operating hours와 어울려 쓸 수 있는 것은 '영업 시간에 관한 불만사항 때문에'라는 의미가 되는 (C) complaints밖에 없다.

어휘 operating hour 영업 시간 | resources 자원 | complaint 불만사항

128. 일단 주문을 하고 나면 수정할 수 없으므로 사무용품 신청서를 반드시 세심하게 검토해 주세요.

해설 because로 시작하는 절의 구성을 살펴보면 빈칸 앞의 you cannot make any revision이라는 주절과 '-------- the order is placed'라는 부사절로 이루어진다는 것을 알 수 있다. 빈칸에는 접속사가 필요하므로 보기 중 유일하게 접속사로 사용할 수 있는 (A) once가 정답이다.

어휘 office supply 사무용품 | revision 수정 | once 일단 ~하기만 하면 | immediately 즉시

129. 학교는 학생들이 사용할 수 있는 다양한 상품과 할인권을 포함하는 선물 세트를 8월 내내 나눠주었다.

해설 문장 속에 동사 gave away가 이미 존재하고 빈칸 앞에서 새로운 절이 시작되는 것도 아니므로 빈칸에는 다시 동사가 들어갈 수 없다. 따라서 동사인 (A)와 (B)를 제외하면 분사인 (C)와 (D) 중 정답을 선택해야 한다. 빈칸 뒤에 목적어 an assortment of items and vouchers가 있으므로 능동의 의미가 있는 현재분사 (C) containing이 정답이다.

어휘 give away 공짜로 나눠주다 | throughout ~ 내내 | an assortment of 여러 가지의 | voucher 쿠폰 | contain 포함하다

130. 소설 발간의 지연과 관계없이, Stephen Brodard는 예정대로 전국 투어를 시작해 모든 책 사인회에 참석할 것이다.

해설 빈칸 뒤에 delays to the novel's publication이라는 명사구와 쉼표가 나온 후에 주절이 이어지고 있으므로 빈칸에는 전치사가 들어가서 쉼표 앞부분을 부사구로 만들어줘야 한다. 그러므로 일단 접속부사인 (A)와 (C)는 정답이 될 수 없다. 주절에서 Stephen Brodard가 예정대로 전국 투어를 시작할 것이라는 내용이 나오고 있으므로 부사구는 '소설 발간의 지연과 관계없이'라고 나오는 것이 자연스럽다. 따라서 정답은 (D) Regardless of이다.

어휘 country-wide 전국의 | attend 참석하다 | book signing event 책사인회 | regardless of ~에 상관없이

[131-134] 다음 편지에 관한 문제입니다.

Ms. Morimoto께,

저는 귀하께서 승무원이 되기 위한 세 번째이자 마지막 관문인 면접을 보시게 되었음을 **131** 알려드리기 위해 이 편지를 드립니다. 귀하의 면접 일정은 5월 18일, 월요일 11시 15분으로 잡혀 있습니다. 그 날짜 **132** 이전에 영어 말하기 연습을 하시길 권합니다. 면접 때 항공사 대표들 중 두 분이 저희 캐나다 본사에서 와주실 예정입니다. 그분들은 일본어로 질문하지 않을 것이며 귀하께서도 일본어로 답하실 수 없습니다. **133** 대신에, 귀하께서는 항공사 대표분들이 사용하는 언어로 그분들과 대화를 하셔야 합니다. 저희는 귀하가 이 자리에 충분한 자질을 갖추고 있다는 점을 이미 **134** 알고 있으므로 이제 귀하가 그들에게 좋은 인상을 남기는 데 주안점을 두어야 합니다. 행운을 빕니다.

진심으로,

Robin Turner 드림
채용 담당
Canadian 항공

어휘 reach ~에 이르다 | present 제시하다 | announce 알리다 | admit 인정하다 | notify 공지[통지]하다 | representative 대표자, 대리인 | corporate 회사의 | headquarters 본사 | be qualified for ~에 대한 자격[자질]을 갖추다 | main 주요한 | focus 초점, 역점 | impress ~에 깊은 인상을 주다 | recruiter 채용 담당자

131. 해설 문맥상 'that 이하의 내용을 알려드린다'라는 의미의 동사가 적절하므로 정답은 (D) notify이다. (B) announce는 뒤에 사람이 올 경우 전치사 to가 와야 하므로 적절하지 않다.

132. 해설 빈칸 뒤에 시간을 나타내는 명사 that date(그 날짜)가 제시된 것으로 보아 문맥상 '면접일 전에' 말하기 연습을 해두라는 의미가 적절하므로 (B) Before가 정답이다. (C) Onto는 '~위로'라는 의미로 공간적 개념을 나타내고, (A) Since는 전치사로 쓰일 때 '~이래 줄곧, ~이후에'라는 의미이므로 부적절하다.

132. (A) 대신에, 귀하께서는 항공사 대표분들이 사용하는 언어로 그분들과 대화를 하셔야 합니다.

(B) 결과적으로, 귀하께서는 불어와 영어에 대한 지식을 테스트 받게 되실 것입니다.

(C) 그러므로 귀하는 그 시험의 일본어 부분을 성공적으로 통과하셨습니다.

(D) 그 동안, 일하는 데 사용할 언어 기술을 향상시킬 필요가 있습니다.

해설 앞 내용에서 영어 말하기 연습을 권장하고, 일본어에 대한 사용을 금지한다고 했으므로 문맥의 흐름상 (A) Instead, you need to speak to them in the language they use with you.가 적절하다. 아직 면접을 보지 않았고, 영어로 면접을 며칠 후에 진행할 예정이므로 (C)는 어색한 답변이다. 불어에 대한 언급이 없고, 아직 합격을 한 상황이 아니므로 (B), (D)도 어색하다.

134. **해설** 빈칸 앞에 시간을 나타내는 부사 already가 쓰인 것으로 보아 미래형인 (C)는 답이 될 수 없으며, 수동태인 (A) was learned는 사물이 주어가 되어야 하며, V-ing 형태인 (D)도 동사 자리에 올 수 없으므로 답이 될 수 없다. 문맥상 두 차례 면접을 통해 상대방의 자질을 인지하고 있는 상태를 나타내므로 (B) have learned가 정답이다.

여름 음악 시리즈의 귀환

Turlington 대학 심포니 오케스트라가 여름 연주회의 두 번째 시리즈를 공연할 것이라고 공식적으로 발표했다. 지난해 첫 번째 행사에 대한 엄청난 반응 **135** 때문에, 공연은 Caner 극장에서 열릴 것이다. 그보다 작은 Grimm 극장은 너무 협소해서 지난해에는 공연표를 원한 인원수를 수용할 수 없었던 것으로 드러났다.

프로그램 자체도 8주가 아닌 10주의 주말 프로그램들을 망라할 수 있도록 **136** 확장되었다. **137** 이는 오케스트라가 지난번보다 훨씬 더 많은 작품을 연주할 수 있게 해 줄 것이다. 그들은 성악가가 필요한 곡을 연주할 예정이므로 Turlington 대학 합창단도 이 무대에 합류할 **138** 예정이다.

만약 올해가 그들이 기대한 대로 성공적이면 여름 음악회 시리즈를 연례 행사화할 계획이다.

어휘 officially 공식적으로 | announce 발표하다 | perform 공연하다 | performance 공연 | response to ~에 대한 반응 | inaugural 개시의, 첫 | moreover 게다가 | therefore 그러므로 | take place 개최되다 | prove ~으로 판명되다 | accommodate 수용하다 | expand 확장시키다 | encompass ~을 망라하다 | annual 연례의

---

135. **해설** 빈칸 뒤에 명사구만 제시되어 있고 쉼표 뒤에는 주어와 동사로 이루어진 절이 이어지므로 전치사구 (B) Because of가 정답이다. 접속사구인 (A) So that과 접속부사인 (C) Moreover, (D) Therefore 모두 완전한 절을 이끈다.

---

136. **해설** 빈칸 앞에 제시된 has been으로 보아 현재완료의 수동태형임을 알 수 있으므로 과거분사형인 (A) expanded가 정답이다.

---

137. (A) 그들은 이와 같이 일정을 짧게 줄인 것에 대하여 사과했다.
(B) 이 모든 공연들은 오후 9시에 Grimm 극장에서 있을 것이다.
(C) 모든 공연은 오케스트라에 의하여 연주되는 음악만으로 구성되어 있다.
(D) 이는 오케스트라가 지난번보다 훨씬 더 많은 작품을 연주할 수 있게 해 줄 것이다.

해설 지난번 공연에 Grimm 극장이 협소했기 때문에 이번 공연에는 Caner 극장에서 8주보다 2주 늘린 10주의 프로그램으로 구성된다고 하였으므로 반대되는 내용인 (A), (B)는 오답이다. 또한 빈칸 다음 문장에서 합창단 또한 무대에 합류를 한다고 하였으므로 (C) 또한 오답이다. 따라서 정답은 (D) This will permit the orchestra to play even more pieces than before.이다.

---

138. **해설** 주어가 단수이고 빈칸 뒤에 V-ing형이 이어지고 있으므로 (A), (B)는 답이 될 수 없다. 바로 앞에 제시된 절에서 미래형 시제가 쓰였으므로, 이어지는 절에서도 역시 미래형을 써야 한다. 따라서 (D) will be가 정답이다.

Office Organizers 청소 용역업체는 올해 11월 2일에 브리즈번에 다섯 번째 사무실을 **139** 열 것입니다. **140** 그에 따라, 저희는 15명에서 20명으로 구성된 팀을 관리할 10명의 경력이 있는 청소부를 찾고 있습니다. 경영진 및 사업체들은 정기적으로 자신들의 사무실을 청소하기 위해 저희 팀들과 계약을 맺고 있습니다.

팀 관리자로서 귀하의 **141** 책무는 물품을 주문하고, 청소인력을 관리하고, 저희 고객들과 직접 소통하는 일이 될 것입니다. 지원자들은 적어도 2년의 건물관리 경험이 있고, 대형 청소 장비에 대해 잘 알고 있어야 합니다.

지원하시려면 자기소개서와 함께 이력서를 Jacqueline Carter에게 Jacqicarter@oohrmail.com으로 보내주십시오. **142** 만약 자격 요건을 갖추셨다면, 그녀가 면접을 잡기 위하여 귀하에게 연락할 것입니다.

어휘 expand 확장시키다 | inspect 점검하다, 시찰하다 | experienced 경력 있는 | individual 개인 | consequent ~의 결과로 나타나는 | consequence 결과 | executive 경영진, 임원 | contract 계약하다 | on a regular basis 정기적으로 | supplies 물품 | interact with ~와 소통하다 | description 설명서, 시술, 기술 | responsibility 책임, 책무 | client 의뢰인, 고객 | applicant 지원자 | janitorial 수위의, 관리인의 | heavy-duty 튼튼한, 잘 손상되지 않는; (장비가) 크고 무거운 | machinery 기계류 | apply 지원하다

---

139. **해설** 문맥상 가장 적절한 동사를 찾는 문제이다. 청소 서비스 업체의 다섯 번째 지사에 대해 언급했고, 이어서 인원 확충을 공고한 것으로 보아 사업 확장에 따른 사무소 개소에 관한 내용임을 알 수 있으므로 (B) open이 정답이다.

---

140. **해설** 빈칸 뒤에 쉼표가 제시되었고, 빈칸 앞의 문장과 뒤의 문장을 연결해 주는 말이 필요하므로 접속부사인 (A) Consequently가 정답이다.

---

141. **해설** 문맥상 가장 적절한 명사를 찾는 문제이다. include 이하의 내용들이 직무들을 나열하고 있으므로 이를 포괄하는 어휘인 (D) responsibilities가 정답이다.

---

142. (A) 지원하실 때 아무런 서류 제출도 필요 없습니다.
(B) 만약 자격 요건을 갖추셨다면, 그녀가 면접을 잡기 위하여 귀하에게 연락할 것입니다.
(C) 고객들이 귀하의 업무를 어떻게 생각하는지에 따라 귀하의 재고용을 결정할 것입니다.
(D) Ms. Carter는 기꺼이 귀하와 귀하의 회사를 위하여 열심히 일할 것입니다.

해설 Office Organizers 청소 용역업체의 새 지점 확장과 그로 인한 팀을 관리할 경력 청소부를 모집하고, 그에 대한 자격 요건에 대하여 설명하는 모집 글이므로 (B) If you are qualified, she will contact you to set up an interview.가 정답이다. 따라서 (C), (D)는 오답이다. 앞 문장에서 자기소개서와 이력서를 보내라고 하였으므로 반대되는 (A)도 오답이다.

[143-146] 다음 공지에 관한 문제입니다.

Montressor 교통 당국은 신규 노란색 노선인 5호선 지하철 공사가 완성 단계에 있다고 오늘 발표했다. 이 노선이 **143** 운행되는 곳으로는 Montressor 미술관, Smith 대학교, 그리고 Merrick 공원을 포함한다. **144** 이 노선은 Hazel 공원에서 Westborough 인근 지역까지 운행된다. 노선이 **145** 운행을 시작하기만 하면 이 노선의 대다수 인근 지역 교통 체증이 감소할 것으로 예상된다. 승객들은 구 교통카드를 사용할 수 있지만, 몇몇 정거장에서는 환승시 개찰구를 통과해야 할 것이다. **146** 하지만 환승시 부과되는 추가요금은 없을 것이다. 5호선은 10월 17일에 개통될 예정이다. 첫 차량이 출발하기 전에 Merrick 공원 역에서 개통식이 있을 예정이다. 개통식에서는 시장이 연설할 계획이다.

어휘 transit 수송, 통행 | authority 당국, 공단 | construction 공사 | near ~에 가까이 가다 | service 서비스를 제공하다 | once ~하기만 하면 | propose 제안하다 | modify 수정하다 | operate 운행하다 | collect 수집하다 | congestion 교통 혼잡 | neighborhood 인근 지역 | transit card 교통카드 | pass through ~을 통과하다 | transfer 갈아 타다 | likewise 또한 | indeed 참으로 | extra fee 추가 요금 | charge 부과하다 | ribbon cutting ceremony 개관식, 개통식 | give a speech 연설하다

143. **해설** 빈칸이 주어 Locations와 동사 include 사이에 있는 것으로 보아 주어를 수식하는 성분이 와야 한다. 따라서 동사인 (C)와 (D)는 답이 될 수 없다. Locations는 서비스를 받는 대상이므로 동작의 주체가 될 수 없다. 따라서 수동태형인 (B) to be serviced가 정답이다.

144. (A) 승객들이 타고 내릴 수 있는 위치는 3군데 밖에 없다.
 (B) 이 노선은 Hazel 공원에서 Westborough 인근 지역까지 운행된다.
 (C) 지하철 공사는 11월 중에는 완공되어야만 한다.
 (D) 최근에 예상했던 것보다 더 많은 승객들이 새로운 노선을 이용하고 있다.
 해설 5호선 지하철 공사가 거의 완료되었고, 10월 17일에 개통될 예정이라 하였으므로 (C), (D)는 오답이다. 신설 노선으로 서비스될 곳은 앞에 언급한 Montressor 미술관, Smith 대학교, Merrick 공원을 포함한다고 언급했으므로 이 장소에서만 승객들이 타고 내릴 수 있는 것은 아니다. 따라서 (B) The line will start at Hazel Park and end in the Westborough neighborhood.가 정답이다.

145. **해설** 문맥상 가장 적절한 동명사를 찾는 문제이다. 빈칸 뒤에 노선 운행 후의 결과에 대한 내용이 이어지는 것으로 보아 '노선이 운행을 시작하기만 하면'이라는 의미가 적절하므로 (C) operating이 정답이다.

146. **해설** 빈칸 앞 문장에서 환승 시 일부 정류장에서는 개찰구를 통과해야 한다는 내용이 제시되고 빈칸 뒤에서는 이 환승에 추가 요금이 부과되지는 않을 것이라고 했으므로 반대되는 내용을 잇는 접속부사인 (A) However가 정답이다.

[147-148] 다음 초대장에 관한 문제입니다.

Minton 가의
147 **La Fayette 아파트 단지 개장 행사**

6월 10일 수요일
West Side 부동산
Mavon 시 University 가, Suite 200
토론토 ONM5G,

기막히게 멋진 집들을 보러 오시는
여러분 모두를 환영합니다.
즉시 임대 가능합니다!

방문은 오후 3시부터 7시까지이며
음식과 음료가 제공될 것입니다.

148 임대 계약과 임대료에 관해서는
J. M. Stanton에게 (416) 555-1245로 연락 주세요.

어휘 grand opening 개장, 개점 | courteously 예의 바르게, 공손하게 | property 재산, 소유물 | immediate 즉각적인 | rent 임차 세를 놓다, 임차하다 | serve (상품·서비스를) 제공하다 | lease 세내다, 임차하다

147. 행사는 왜 열리는가?
 (A) 회사 채용 인터뷰 일정을 잡기 위해
 (B) 그 지역의 새로운 주택을 보여주기 위해
 (C) 주민들에게 건축 계획을 알리기 위해
 (D) 다시 단장된 본사를 축하하기 위해
 해설 문두의 La Fayette Apartment Complex Grand Opening on Minton Road를 통하여 아파트 개장식 행사임을 확인 할 수 있으므로 정답은 (B) To display new housing in the area이다.

148. J. M. Stanton의 직업은 무엇이겠는가?
 (A) 실내 장식가
 (B) 출장 요리업 관리자
 (C) 시내 관광 안내인
 (D) 판매 중개인
 해설 J. M. Stanton에 대한 언급이 되어 있는 부분을 주목해야 한다. 지문의 마지막 부분에서 임대 계약과 임대료에 관한 정보를 얻기 위해 J. M. Stanton에게 전화하라고 했으므로 부동산 판매 중개인으로 유추를 할 수 있다. 따라서 정답은 (D) Sales agent이다.

[149-150] 다음 문자 메시지에 관한 문제입니다.

발신: Maria Bertoni

수신: Rosaria Ducia

149 150 제 고객과의 점심 약속이 생각보다 오래 걸리니 저를 빼고 먼저 회의를 시작해 주시기 바랍니다. **149** 지난 분기 매출 보고서로 시작한 후 다음 분기를 예측하는 걸로 진행해 주시면 됩니다. 저는 그곳에 30분 후에 도착할 수 있을 것입니다.

어휘 appointment 약속 I take (시간이) 걸리다 I expect 예상하다 I go ahead (일 등을) 진행[추진]하다 I quarter 분기 I sales report 매출[판매] 보고서 I go on (말 등을) 계속하다 I prediction 예측, 예견 I get (장소에) 도착하다

149. 메시지는 왜 보내졌는가?

(A) 도움을 요청하기 위해

(B) 지침들을 주기 위해

(C) 몇 가지 정보를 확인하기 위해

(D) 점심 회의를 일정을 잡기 위해

해설 문두에서 고객과의 점심 약속이 예상보다 길어지므로 회의 시간에 늦을 예정이라고 하고, 회의 진행을 하되 지난 분기 매출로 시작해 다음 분기 매출 예측으로 진행하라고 진행 방식에 관한 지침들을 주고 있다. 따라서 정답은 (B) To provide instructions이다.

150. Ms. Bertoni에 관하여 언급된 것은 무엇인가?

(A) 영업 회의에 늦게 도착할 것이다.

(B) 새로운 프로젝트를 시작하고 싶어 한다.

(C) 매출이 감소할 것으로 예상한다.

(D) 새로운 고객을 얻었다.

해설 Ms. Bertoni는 메시지의 발신임을 확인할 수 있다. 서두에 Ms. Bertoni가 고객과의 약속이 예상보다 늦게 끝나니, 본인 없이 회의를 먼저 시작하라고 하고 있으므로 정답은 (A) She will arrive late to the sales meeting.이다.

[151-152] 다음 이메일에 관한 문제입니다.

수신: Jan Ling

발신: Elias Namora

날짜: 9월 12일

제목: Slater의 요청

안녕하세요 Jan,

Carrie Slater라는 고객이 오늘 일찍 오셔서 Avonlea 상업 구역의 개조 공사 프로젝트에 관해 문의하셨습니다. 그분은 올해 그 프로젝트에 관해 발행된 신문 기사들이 있는지를 알고 싶어 하셨습니다. 그분은 다른 약속이 있어서 오늘 늦게 기사를 위해 다시 올 거라고 말했습니다. 저는 **151** 저희 도서관 기록 보관소에서 많은 기사들을 찾았고, 그것들을 출력하여 그 위에 Ms. Slater의 성함을 써서 안내 데스크 위에 두었습니다. 이후 당신이 교대 근무하실 때, **152** 기록 보관소를 올해 것부터 찾아보시고, 당신이 찾은 그 밖의 다른 기사들을 출력해 놓으실 수 있으신지요? Ms. Slater께서는 오늘밤 늦게 우리가 찾아 놓은 자료들을 가지러 온다고 하셨습니다.

감사합니다.

Elias Namora

어휘 request 요청 I inquire 묻다, 알아보다 I renovation 개조, 보수 I relevant 적절한, 관련 있는 I a number of 많은 I archive 기록 보관소 I shift 교대 근무 I print out 출력하다 I search 찾다, 수색하다

151. Mr. Namora는 누구이겠는가?

(A) 신문 편집자

(B) 연구원

(C) 건설 근로자

(D) 도서관 사서

해설 Mr. Namora는 이메일 발신인이며, 'in our library's archives'와 자료를 찾아달라는 고객, Carrie Slater의 요청을 받은 것으로 미루어 도서관 사서로 유추할 수 있으므로 정답은 (D) A librarian이다.

152. Mr. Namora는 Ms. Ling에게 무엇을 해달라고 요청하는가?

(A) 이메일로 파일을 전송한다

(B) 데이터베이스에 이름을 추가한다

(C) 정보를 찾는다

(D) 기사를 검토한다

해설 지문 하단부에서 기록 보관실에서 기사를 찾아 인쇄해달라고 요청하고 있으므로 정답은 searching the archives를 바꿔 표현한 (C) Locate some information이다.

[153-154] 다음 문자 메시지에 관한 문제입니다.

Kate Lim

저 마닐라 국제 공항이에요. 근데 날씨가 안 좋아서 모든 비행기가 연착됐어요.

오후 7:42

Kate Lim

153 탑승 수속대에서 새벽 2시 5분에 블라디보스톡에 도착하는 비행기를 배정받았어요.

오후 7:43

Nate Sokolovska

걱정하지 말아요. 그래도 택시 잡을 수 있을 거예요.

오후 7:46

Kate Lim

제가 엄청 늦게 도착해도, 호텔 예약은 괜찮은 걸까요?

오후 7:50

Nate Sokolovska

제가 호텔에 전화해서 알아볼게요. 그나저나, **153** 내일 오후에 사무실에서 발표하는 건 준비됐어요?

오후 7:51

181

Kate Lim

거의 다 됐어요. **154** 제 방에 무선 인터넷이 되도록 좀 해 줄 수 있나요?

오후 7:52

Nate Sokolovska

154 물론이죠. 돈이 더 들 것 같긴 한데, 문제되진 않을 거예요.

오후 7:53

Kate Lim

고마워요. 내일 봐요! 오후 7:55

어휘 delay 지연되다 | due to ~때문에 | make sure ~을 확실히 하다

지하는 데 꼭 필요하므로, 편리하신 때에 저희에게 연락을 하셔서 방문 일정을 잡아 주십시오.

157 저희 병원은 최근에 Coastal 쇼핑몰에서 마이애미 시내의 새로운 사무소로 이전했습니다. **156** 이 이전을 기념하기 위해, 6월 26일까지 모든 치아 미백 치료에 대하여 30퍼센트 할인을 제공하고 있습니다. 더 많은 세부사항을 확인하시려면 동봉된 홍보 전단을 확인해 주십시오.

영업 시간은 전과 같습니다.
월요일에서 금요일, 오전 9시부터 오후 6시
토요일, 오전 9시부터 오후 3시

곧 뵐 수 있기를 기대합니다.

Manny Buck

Manny Buck
사무실 관리자
동봉물 재중

어휘 record 기록 | annual check-up 연례 건강 검진 | necessary 필요한 | maintain 유지하다 | dental 치아의 | hygiene 위생 | arrange a visit 방문 예약을 잡다 | at one's convenience 편리한 때에 | move 이사하다, 이동하다 | whitening treatment 미백 치료 | promotional 홍보의, 판촉의 | operating hours 영업 시간

---

153. Ms. Lim에 대해 알 수 있는 것은 무엇인가?

(A) 전에 마닐라를 방문해 본 적이 있다.
(B) 블라디보스톡에서 근무하고 있다.
(C) 출장 중이다.
(D) 탑승 수속 담당 직원이다.

해설 (A), (B), (D)는 모두 지문에 언급되지 않은 것들이다. 7시 51분의 대사를 보면 Ms. Lim이 내일 프레젠테이션을 한다고 했으므로 출장 목적으로 블라디보스톡에 가고 있다는 것을 알 수 있다. 그러므로 (C) She is traveling for business.가 정답이다.

---

154. 오후 7시 35분에 Mr. Sokolovska가 "물론이죠"라고 말한 의미는?

(A) Ms. Lim의 비행 스케줄을 확인해 줄 것이다.
(B) 방에 인터넷 서비스가 되도록 확실히 해 줄 것이다.
(C) 공항에서 Ms. Lim을 태워 올 것이다.
(D) 택시 서비스를 준비해 줄 것이다.

해설 해당 문장의 바로 앞 문장 Do you mind making sure that there is wireless Internet in my room?에 대한 응답이므로 무선 인터넷 사용이 가능하도록 하겠다는 의미이다. 그러므로 정답은 (B) He will ensure a room has Internet service.이다.

[155-157] 다음 편지에 관한 문제입니다.

Ellis 치과
High Beach 쇼핑 센터
5830 Round 가, 마이애미 33195
(305) 555-3758
www.ellisdentistry.com

6월 3일

Mr. Chuck Lom
21 Ranch 가
마이애미 33195

Mr. Lom께,

저희 기록에 따르면, **155** 귀하께서 연례 검진을 받으셔야 할 때입니다. 잘 알고 계신 것처럼, 정기 검진은 청결한 치아 위생 상태를 유

---

155. Mr. Buck은 왜 Mr. Lom에게 편지를 썼는가?

(A) 주문 구매를 확인시켜 주려고
(B) 지불을 요청하려고
(C) 그의 검진 결과를 알려주려고
(D) 진료 일정을 잡을 것을 상기시켜 주려고

해설 편지 첫머리의 you are due for your annual check-up을 통하여 연례 검진 시기인 것을 알리고 있고 이어지는 말에서 편할 때에 연락하여 방문 일정을 잡으라고 하고 있기 때문에 정답은 (D) To remind him to schedule an appointment이다.

---

156. 편지와 함께 무엇이 보내졌는가?

(A) 할인권
(B) 건강 보험업체의 명단
(C) 치아 제품 카탈로그
(D) 청구서

해설 편지에 동봉된 것에 관하여 언급된 내용을 찾아야 한다. 두 번째 문단의 두 번째 문장을 보면 매장 이전을 기념하여 홍보 행사가 있으며 홍보 전단이 동봉되어 있다고 설명한다. 동봉된 홍보 전단이 치아 미백 관련 치료의 30퍼센트 할인권임을 확인할 수 있다. 정답은 (A) A discount offer이다.

---

157. 편지에 따르면, Ellis 치과는 무엇을 바꾸었는가?

(A) 웹사이트 레이아웃
(B) 영업 시간
(C) 결제 방법
(D) 병원 위치

해설 편지를 발신하는 기업이 Elis 치과이고, 두 번째 단락의 첫 문장을 통해 최근에 Coastal Mall에서 마이애미 시내의 새로운 사무소로 이전한 것을 알 수 있다. 그러므로 정답은 (D) Its office location이다.

[158-160] 다음 기사에 관한 문제입니다.

Endura 배터리가 주목받다
Jared Mendoza 작성

뉴욕 (1월 13일) — 배터리 제조업체 Endura는 기록적인 3/4분기 수익을 발표함으로써 주주들의 기립박수를 받았다. 1년 전만 하더라도 거의 알려져 있지 않았었지만, Endura의 최신 제품군은 DENSE라는 신기술을 사용한다. **160** Endura의 새 배터리는 많은 언론 매체들에 의해 믿기 어려울 정도라는 평가를 받고 있다. **158** 이러한 모든 평판이 Endura의 주가를 치솟게 하고 있다.

수백 개의 회사들이 Endura의 제품을 사용하는 데 관심을 보이고 있다. **159** Endura 배터리는 전화기부터 전기 자동차까지 모든 것에서 경쟁 브랜드보다 수백 배 더 오래 가기 때문에 Vexon 같은 업계의 핵심 업체들이 따라잡느라 애를 쓰고 있다. 분석가들은 Endura의 기술이 장차 대부분의 전자기기에 들어갈 것으로 예상한다.

Hildreth 대학교 화공학 교수인 Vera Lincoln 박사는 "Endura의 제품은 기업들로 하여금 매우 짧은 기간에 걸쳐 제품을 혁신하도록 해줄 것입니다"라고 말했다. "Endura의 DENSE 기술은 배터리의 에너지 출력을 늘려주어서, 기존 제품의 더 작은 모델이라는 결과를 낳습니다."

회사 대변인은 오늘 아침 분기 수익을 발표한 후, 그들이 지금까지 보아온 수요에 근거해서 앞으로 여러 분기 동안 흑자를 보게 될 것이라고 전망했다.

어휘 **make one's mark** 주목받다 | **record-breaking** 신기록의 | **quarter** 분기 | **profit** 수익 | **to a standing ovation** 기립박수를 받으며 | **shareholder** 주주 | **stock price** 주가 | **scramble to** 앞을 다투어 (~하려고) 애쓰다 | **spokesperson** 대변인 | **news outlet** 언론매체

---

158. Endura에 대해 언급된 것은 무엇인가?
(A) 3분기 연속으로 흑자를 냈다.
(B) Vexon과 계약을 체결할 것이다.
(C) 1년 전에 설립되었다.
(D) 많은 투자자들을 끌어 모으고 있다.

해설 첫 번째 단락에서 좋은 평판으로 인해 주가가 올라가고 있다고 했는데 이것은 많은 투자를 유치하고 있다는 말이므로 (D) It is attracting many investors.가 정답이다.

---

159. Endura 배터리에 대해 보도된 것은 무엇인가?
(A) 대부분의 전자기기에서 발견된다.
(B) 다른 어떤 경쟁 브랜드보다도 작다.
(C) 장시간 에너지를 생산한다.
(D) Vera Lincoln 박사에 의해 개발되었다.

해설 두 번째 문단에서 경쟁 브랜드보다 수백 배 오래 간다라고 했으므로 이것을 바꿔 표현한 (C) They produce energy for a long time.이 정답이다.

---

160. [1], [2], [3], [4]로 표시된 곳 중에서 다음 문장이 들어가기에 가장 적절한 곳은 어디인가?

"Endura의 새 배터리는 많은 언론 매체들에 의해 믿기 어려울 정도라는 평가를 받고 있다."

(A) [1]
(B) [2]
(C) [3]
(D) [4]

해설 주어진 문장은 제품이 언론으로부터 매우 좋은 평가를 받았다는 내용인데, [1]에 이 문장을 삽입하면 바로 뒤 문장에서 이러한 언론의 평가를 'publicity(언론의 주목, 평판)'라는 단어로 바꿔 표현하고 있고, 언론의 좋은 평가로 인해 회사의 주가가 상승하고 있다는 내용이 되기 때문에 문맥상 자연스러워진다. 따라서 정답은 (A) [1]이다.

[161-163] 다음 잡지 목차에 관한 문제입니다.

목차
6월 421호

10 자연 건강 Mary Southwood가 **161** 식용 꽃 재배에 대한 몇 가지 조언을 드립니다.	**32 감상** **162** Maya Sandifer가 그녀의 최근 해외 여행에서의 유리 온실 사진들을 공유해드립니다.
19 맛이 좋은 나무 저희 작가들은 **161** 다양한 종류의 과실 나무를 선택하는 것에 관한 식견을 제공합니다.	**36 요리사** *Katie Simmons* Katie's 식당 주인이 가정에서 재배한 야채를 사용해 **163** 맛있는 샐러드를 준비하는 방법을 알려드립니다.
22 조언 Alana Han이 **161** 영양분이 많은 흙의 이점에 대해 설명해 드립니다.	**38 예산 맞추기** Paul Mason은 저렴하고 멋진 테라스를 디자인하는 방법을 알려드립니다.
26 필수 요소 Dominic Levin은 **161** 당신의 잔디를 아름답게 관리할 수 있는 몇 가지 방법에 대해서 이야기합니다.	**44 다음 호** 7월 호에 대한 간단한 소개

어휘 **contents** 목차, 내용물 | **tip** 조언, 정보 | **cultivate** 경작하다, 일구다 | **edible** 먹을 수 있는, 식용의 | **rich soil** 영양분이 많은 흙[토양] | **discuss** 토론하다 | **lawn** 잔디 | **share** 공유하다, 나누다 | **glass greenhouse** 유리 온실 | **overseas** 해외의 | **chef** 주방장, 요리사 | **describe** 묘사하다 | **prepare** 준비하다 | **homegrown** 국내산의, 그 지방산의, 가정에서 키운 | **design** 디자인하다 | **affordable** 줄 수 있는, (가격이) 알맞은 | **attractive** 매력적인, 멋진 | **patio** 야외 테라스 | **issue** (발행) 호; 사안 | **preview** 간단소개, 미리보기

161. 이 잡지의 초점은 무엇인가?

(A) 여행

(B) 식당

(C) 정원 가꾸기

(D) 건강 관리

해설 잡지 목차에 관한 지문이므로 각 컨텐츠 내의 키워드를 주목한다. cultivating edible flowers, fruit trees, rich soil, lawn, glass greenhouses, homegrown vegetables, design ~ patios를 통하여 원예, 화초 재배, 경작 등에 관한 주제들임을 알 수 있기 때문에 정답은 (C) Gardening이다.

---

162. 내용 목차에 따르면, 최근에 누가 해외 여행을 했는가?

(A) Ms. Sandifer

(B) Mr. Levin

(C) Ms. Southwood

(D) Ms. Han

해설 32 Reflections 항목에서 Maya Sandifer가 최근에 해외여행에 다녀왔음을 알 수 있으므로 정답은 (A) Ms. Sandifer이다.

---

163. 잡지의 어디에서 요리법을 찾을 수 있겠는가?

(A) 10페이지에서

(B) 22페이지에서

(C) 36페이지에서

(D) 44페이지에서

해설 요리와 관련된 키워드에 주목을 해야 한다. 36 Chef Katie Simmons 에서 Katie's 식당 주인이 맛있는 샐러드 요리법을 알려준다고 한다. 요리법에 관한 설명이므로 정답은 (C) On page 36이다.

[164-167] 다음 온라인 채팅 대화문에 관한 문제입니다.

Izumi Lane [오전 10:05]
모두들 안녕하세요. **164** 피드백 좀 필요합니다. Betsy Allen이 방금 Hardigan 운송사의 Carrie Moss와 전화 통화를 끝냈는데, **164** **165 167** 이번 주말 파티에 사용할 모든 물품의 양을 두 배로 늘려주기를 원합니다. 이거 가능한가요?

Marie Schupe [오전 10:06]
165 직원들이 야근을 한다면 그 정도 양의 음식은 이틀이면 준비할 수 있어요.

Lynn Kim [오전 10:08]
사람이 모자라지만 하루 시간을 주신다면 제가 임시직원을 좀 모집할 수 있습니다.

Andy Jansen [오전 10:09]
166 무엇보다도 먼저 메뉴를 확정해야 해요. 저희 팀이 오늘 오전 중에 확정 짓겠습니다.

Izumi Lane [오전 10:12]
이 일은 잘될 것 같군요. 목요일 퇴근시간 전까지 모든 것이 준비되고 행사를 위한 직원도 충분히 있게 될 겁니다. 그런데 배달은 어떻게 하죠?

Marie Schupe [오전 10:13]
승인해주신다면 추가로 트럭 두 대를 빌릴 수 있습니다.

Izumi Lane [오전 10:14]
좋아요. 그건 승인할 수 있어요. Gavin, 테이블 위에 놓을 좌석표를 전부 인쇄하는 데 얼마나 걸리겠어요?

Gavin Wong [오전 10:16]
금요일 퇴근 전에 해놓겠습니다.

Izumi Lane [오전 10:17]
좋아요. **167** Betsy에게 고객과 다시 통화해서 소식을 전해주라고 해야겠네요.

어휘 **set** 정하다, 결정하다 | **crew** 팀, 반, 조 | **work** (계획 따위가) 잘 되어 나가다 | **sign off on** ~을 승인하다 | **place card** 좌석 표(연회에서 사람 이름을 적어 앉을 탁자 위치에 얹어 놓는 표)

---

164. 오전 10시 5분에 Ms. Lane은 "피드백이 좀 필요합니다"라고 썼을 때 무엇을 의미하는가?

(A) 승인을 요청한다.

(B) 추가로 손님을 초대하고 싶다.

(C) 의견을 요청한다.

(D) 신제품에 대해 의논하고 싶다.

해설 주어진 문장에서 이어지는 문장을 보면 고객이 주문량을 두 배로 늘리고 싶어한다는 소식을 전하면서 이것이 가능하다고 생각하는지(Is this possible?) 직원들에게 묻고 있으므로 주어진 문장은 의견을 구한다는 뜻이다. 따라서 정답으로 (C) She is asking for some opinions. 를 선택해야 한다.

---

165. Ms. Lane은 어떤 종류의 사업체에서 근무하겠는가?

(A) 카센터

(B) 출장뷔페 업체

(C) 인쇄소

(D) 운송회사

해설 고객으로부터 주말 파티에 사용할 용품의 양을 두 배로 늘려달라는 요청을 받았고 이어지는 문장에서 직원들이 야근을 한다면 그 정도 양의 음식은 이틀이면 준비할 수 있다고 했으므로 Ms. Lane은 파티에 음식을 조달하는 회사에서 일한다는 것을 유추할 수 있다. 따라서 정답으로 (B) A catering company를 선택해야 한다.

---

166. 대화문에 따르면, 어느 팀이 다른 곳보다 먼저 일을 완료해야 하는가?

(A) Ms. Schupe의 팀

(B) Ms. Kim의 팀

(C) Mr. Wong의 팀

(D) Mr. Jansen의 팀

해설 Mr. Jansen이 무엇보다도 먼저 메뉴를 정해야 하고 자신의 팀이 조속히 그 일을 하도록 하겠다고 했으므로 가장 먼저 일을 완료할 팀은 Mr. Jansen의 팀이다. 따라서 정답은 (D) Mr. Jansen's team이다.

---

167. Ms. Allen은 Ms. Moss에게 무엇이라고 말하겠는가?

  (A) 행사의 비용이 절감될 거라고

  (B) 주문량을 늘려줄 수 있을 거라고

  (C) 배달은 수요일에 있을 거라고

  (D) 목요일에 Ms. Moss를 방문할 거라고

해설 첫 문장에서 Ms. Moss는 Ms. Allen을 통해 주문량을 늘려달라는 요청을 했는데 이어지는 내용은 몇 가지 조치를 취해 이것이 가능하다는 내용의 대화. 그리고 마지막 문장에서 Ms. Allen으로 하여금 고객에게 이 소식을 전하도록 하겠다고 했으므로 Ms. Allen은 Ms. Moss에게 요청대로 주문량을 늘려주겠다는 말을 할 것이라고 유추할 수 있다. 그러므로 정답은 (B) That she can increase an order이다.

[168-171] 다음 이메일에 관한 문제입니다.

수신: wso@ganttech.com
발신: xhuang@XPSenterprises.com
날짜: 8월 29일
제목: 귀하의 문의

Mr. So께,

168 XPS 사에 연락을 주셔서 감사합니다. **169** 온라인 상에서 귀사인 Gant 전자의 제품을 홍보하기 위해 저희 서비스를 고려하고 계신다니 매우 기쁩니다.

XPS 사는 15년 이상 운영되어 왔습니다. **170** 저희는 국내와 해외 모두에서 다양한 주요 업체들을 위한 마케팅 컨설턴트로 일해 왔습니다. 우리의 고객들 중 일부로는 마닐라의 CFC 제조사, 뉴욕의 Frasier 사와 런던의 UK 자동차가 있습니다. 저희와 함께 일하시면, 업체들은 인터넷 상으로 전 세계로 더 널리 알려지게 되어 혜택을 얻으실 수 있습니다.

XPS 사와 함께 일하기로 결정하신다면, 저희는 귀하께서 실망하시지 않으리라고 **171** 장담할 수 있습니다. XPS 사는 시간에 맞춰 주어진 예산 내에서 프로젝트를 끝내는 것으로 명성이 자자합니다. 귀하께서는 그 결과에 만족하실 거라 확신합니다.

귀하의 필요 사항들에 대해 더 자세히 논의하기 위한 회의를 잡고자 하신다면, 864-555-5142로 제게 직접 연락 주십시오. 곧 연락 받기를 바랍니다.

진심으로,

Xiao Huang
고객 상담부 매니저, XPS 사

어휘 contact 연락하다 I promote 홍보하다 I serve 근무하다, 봉사하다 I consultant 상담가, 자문위원 I domestically 국내에서; 가정적으로 I abroad 해외에 I benefit from ~로부터 이익을 얻다 I global 전 세계적인 I exposure 알려짐, 노출 I budget 예산 I hear from ~로부터 소식을 듣다

168. Ms. Huang은 왜 이메일을 보냈는가?

  (A) Gant 전자에서 있을 추후 회의를 확정하기 위해

  (B) 웹사이트를 설계하는 방법을 설명하기 위해

  (C) 새로운 프로젝트 시작일에 관한 정보를 제공하기 위해

  (D) 회사가 사업 관계를 맺도록 권하기 위해

해설 이메일 서두를 통하여, 온라인 제품 홍보에 관한 문의에 답변하기 위한 메일임을 확인할 수 있고, 두 번째 단락 마지막 부분에서 일하면 얻을 수 있는 혜택들에 대하여 설명하고 있다. 따라서 정답은 (D) To encourage a company to pursue a business relationship이다.

---

169. Gant 전자는 무엇을 원하겠는가?

  (A) 제품을 인터넷에 광고하는 것

  (B) 새로운 시설을 짓는 것

  (C) 서비스의 가격을 인상하는 것

  (D) 직원 수를 늘리는 것

해설 Gant 전자는 편지의 수신이다. 문두의 두 번째 문장을 통하여 온라인 제품 홍보에 관한 것에 대하여 XPS Enterprises를 고려하고 있다는 것을 알 수 있기 때문에 정답은 (A) Advertise its products on the Internet이다.

---

170. XPS 사에 관하여 언급되는 것은 무엇인가?

  (A) 최근에 새로운 직원들을 고용했다.

  (B) 수수료가 다른 컨설팅 회사들보다 더 저렴하다.

  (C) 하나 이상의 국가에서 사업을 한다.

  (D) 본사가 마닐라에 있다.

해설 대형 업체의 마케팅 컨설턴트로 국내와 해외를 포함, 최소 두 곳 이상에서 일을 한다는 것을 확인할 수 있기 때문에 정답은 (C) It does business in more than one country.이다.

---

171. 세 번째 단락, 첫 번째 줄의 단어 "assure"와 의미상 가장 가까운 것은

  (A) 확신시키다

  (B) 확보하다

  (C) 촉진하다

  (D) 약속하다

해설 지문의 we assure you that you won't be disappointed에서 assure와 의미가 비슷한 단어를 찾는 문제이다. 이 지문에서는 문맥상 '실망시키지 않을 것을 보장한다'는 내용이므로 바꿔 쓸 수 있는 말은 '약속하다'의 의미가 있는 (D) promise이다.

[172-175] 다음 정보에 관한 문제입니다.

공동체 게시판 광고 공간 이용 가능

Carvier 대학교는 레크리에이션 센터 북편의 동문 광장 서쪽에 있는 대형 게시대에 광고를 게재할 학생들을 초대합니다. 캠퍼스 소식을 위한 공간을 남겨둬야 하기 때문에 게시대의 공간은 제한되어 있으므로 **172** 공고문은 일주일 동안만 게시할 수 있습니다.

173 모든 자료는 검토를 위해 Carvier 커뮤니케이션 사무국에 communications@carvier.edu로 이메일을 보내야 합니다. **173** 학교 규정이나 기준을 준수하지 않은 모든 내용은 거부될 것입니다. **173** 광고는 반드시 A3 혹은 A4 용지 크기의 인쇄물에 적합하도록 해주시기 바랍니다. 이메일에, 당신의 광고가 게시되기를 원하는 정확한 날짜를 명시하기 바랍니다. 전화번호와 연락 가능한 시간도 포함시켜 주십시오.

174 승인이 나면, 기념 회관에 위치한 교무처에 직접 방문해서 **172** 70달러를 지불해야 합니다. 학생은 현금 또는 신용카드로 지불이 가능합니다. **175** 그렇지 않으면, Carvier 대학교로 송금하는 것도 가능합니다. 광고가 승인되는 데는 보통 1~3 영업일이 소요됩니다.

Carvier 커뮤니케이션 사무국
www.carvier.edu

어휘 kiosk 키오스크(신문, 음료 등을 파는 매점), 판매대 | room 공간, 자리 | notice 안내문, 공고문 | adhere to ~을 고수하다, 충실히 지키다 | reject 거부하다, 불합격시키다 | suitable 적합한, 적절한 | indicate 나타내다, 보여주다 | approval 인정, 승인 | in person 직접, 몸소

172. Carvier 대학교 게시판에 있는 광고에 대해 알 수 있는 것은 무엇인가?
(A) 컬러로 인쇄되어야 한다.
(B) 주당 70달러의 비용이 든다.
(C) 내용은 본인이 직접 전달해야 한다.
(D) 3일 동안만 게재할 수 있다.

해설 첫 번째 단락에서 공지사항은 일주일만 게시할 수 있다고 했고 마지막 단락을 보면 광고를 게재하는 비용이 70달러임을 알 수 있다. 두 부분을 종합해보면 광고를 일주일 게재하는 데 70달러가 든다고 했으므로 (B) It costs $70 per week.가 정답이 된다.

173. 게시판에 게재될 광고의 필수 요건으로 언급되지 않은 것은 무엇인가?
(A) 사전에 승인을 받아야 한다.
(B) 특정 규격에 맞아야 한다.
(C) 우편 주소를 포함해야 한다.
(D) 학교 규칙을 준수해야 한다.

해설 우선 보기 (A)는 모든 자료를 Carvier 커뮤니케이션 사무국에 보내어 사전 승인을 받아야 한다. 또한 (B)는 A3 or A4 규격으로 광고물을 인쇄해야 한다. (D)는 학교 규정이나 기준을 준수하지 않으면 거부된다고 하였다. 따라서 지문에 언급되지 않은 내용인 (C) It should include a mailing address.가 정답이다.

174. 결제는 어디에서 해야 하는가?
(A) 기념 회관에서
(B) 커뮤니케이션 사무국에서
(C) 동문 광장에서
(D) 레크리에이션 센터에서

해설 문제에 있는 the payment have to be made라는 키워드가 마지막 단락에 그대로 보이므로 Upon approval, a payment of $70 must be made in person at the University Registrar's Office located in the Memorial Union을 통해 Memorial Union에 있는 교무처에서 결제가 이루어져야 한다는 것을 알 수 있다. 따라서 (A) At the Memorial Union이 정답이다.

175. [1], [2], [3], [4]로 표시된 곳 중에서 다음 문장이 들어가기에 가장 적절한 곳은 어디인가?

"그렇지 않으면, Carvier 대학교로 송금하는 것도 가능합니다."

(A) [1]
(B) [2]
(C) [3]
(D) [4]

해설 주어진 문장이 지불 수단에 관련된 내용인데, 접속부사 Alternatively(그렇지 않으면)로 시작하고 있으므로 바로 앞 문장에는 wire transfer 외의 다른 수단을 언급하는 내용이 오는 것이 자연스럽다. 따라서 주어진 문장은 [4]에 들어가야 한다. 따라서 정답은 (D) [4]이다.

[176-180] 다음 광고와 웹페이지에 관한 문제입니다.

La Roche 과수원
당신을 위한 신선한 과일의 최고 공급처!

여러분의 가족을 데리고 오셔서, 100에이커의 과수원에서 여러분이 원하는 과일은 무엇이든 따 가세요. 몇 시간 동안만이라도 또는 하루 종일이라도 좋습니다. 단체도 환영합니다. 여러분의 편의를 위해 바구니도 제공하고, **176** 부지의 무료 주차도 제공하고 있습니다. **176** 소형 버스가 주차장에서 과수원으로 여러분들을 모셔다 드릴 것입니다.

일반 수확 시즌 (모든 과일은 무게를 따져 판매됨):
179 6월~7월
179 배, 체리, 블루베리, 포도
8월~10월
사과(세 가지 종류), 호박, 파인애플

176 집에서 직접 만든 잼과 파이뿐 아니라 현지에서 재배된 과일과 채소도 살 수 있는 우리 농장의 가게를 둘러보세요.

La Roche Trailblazer 산책로를 걸으며, 저희의 야생동물과 식물들을 구경하세요. 4킬로미터 길이의 **177** 산책로는 6월부터 10월까지 모든 방문객에게 개방됩니다.

어휘 source 원천, 근원 | acre 에이커(약 4,046 제곱미터) | orchard 과수원 | convenience 편리, 편의 | on-site 현장의 | harvest 수확, 추수 | browse 둘러보다, 훑어보다 | locally grown 현지에서 길러진/자란 | homemade 집에서 만든, 손으로 만든 | wildlife 야생동물 | trail 오솔길, 산책로

---

http://www.larocheorchard.com

뉴스	방문	매장	연락처

La Roche 고객님들께서는 주목해 주세요.

178 올해 계절에 맞지 않게 더운 기온 때문에, 우리 농작물이 예정보다 몇 주 더 빨리 준비가 될 것입니다. 이로 인해, **179** 과수원은 5월 28일부터 이용객 여러분께 개방됩니다.

186

5월 28일부터 La Roche 과수원의 개방 시간:

177 월요일 ~ 목요일 오전 11시부터 오후 5시
177 토요일 오전 11시부터 오후 6시
177 일요일 오전 11시부터 오후 4시

비가 많이 올 경우, 저희는 과수원 문을 닫을 것입니다. **180** 행사 종료에 대한 정보는 웹사이트를 체크하시거나 이메일로 공지를 받으시려면 이곳을 클릭하셔서 등록해 주세요.

어휘 unseasonally 계절에 맞지 않게 I crop 농작물 I ahead of schedule 예정보다 빨리 I as a result of ~의 결과로서 I closure 폐쇄 I notification 공지

---

176. 광고가 La Roche 과수원에 관하여 언급하지 않는 것은 무엇인가?
　(A) 지역 상품 판매
　(B) 과수원으로 가는 교통수단
　(C) 무료 주차
　(D) 피크닉 구역

해설 사실 확인 문제 유형이니 보기를 하나씩 지문과 대조해서 언급되어 있는지의 여부를 확인해야 한다. (A)는 you can buy locally grown fruits and vegetables as well as homemade jams and pies에서 확인할 수 있고, (B)도 Small buses will take you from the parking lot to the orchard에서 언급됨을 확인할 수 있다. (C)도 free on-site parking에서 알 수 있고, 피크닉 구역에 대한 언급은 없으므로 (D) Picnic areas가 정답이다.

---

177. 산책로에 관하여 알 수 있는 것은 무엇인가?
　(A) 겨울에 길이가 연장될 것이다.
　(B) La Roche 과수원의 인기 있는 관광 명소이다.
　(C) 경험이 많은 등산객들만 이용할 수 있다.
　(D) 금요일에는 문을 닫는다.

해설 광고 지문에서 산책로에 관한 언급을 찾아야 한다. 마지막 단락에서 La Roche Trailblazer Walk가 6월부터 10월까지만 대중에게 공개되는 것을 확인할 수 있다. 또한, 웹페이지 지문에서 Trailblazer Walk가 있는 포도원 개장 시간을 찾으면 Monday - Thursday, Saturday, Sunday에만 개장되는 것을 알 수 있다. 따라서 산책로 또한 금요일에는 폐장되어 있다는 것을 유추할 수 있다. 따라서 정답은 (D) It will be closed on Fridays.이다.

---

178. 웹 페이지에서 La Roche 과수원에 관하여 언급된 것은 무엇인가?
　(A) 이례적인 재배 시기를 겪고 있다.
　(B) 영업 시간이 단축되었다.
　(C) 수확으로 인해 더 많은 고용 기회가 창출됐다.
　(D) 가족 경영 사업체이다.

해설 웹페이지 서두에서 이상 기온으로 농작물 수확 일정이 앞당겨진다는 것을 확인할 수 있기 때문에 (A) It has had an unusual growing season.이 정답이다.

---

179. 이번 시즌에는 몇 월에 포도를 따는 것이 처음으로 가능해지겠는가?
　(A) 5월에
　(B) 6월에
　(C) 7월에
　(D) 9월에

해설 웹페이지 지문의 서두에 비정상적인 기온으로 인하여 과수원에 입장은 5월 28일로 일찍 개장하는 것을 알 수 있다. 광고 지문 첫머리에서 가족들과 함께 과수원에서는 6월부터 포도를 따는 것이 가능하다고 했기 때문에 과수원이 열리는 시점인 올해에는 5월 28일부터 포도 수확이 가능하다는 것을 알 수 있다. 따라서 정답은 (A) In May이다.

---

180. 웹페이지에 따르면, 고객들은 등록해서 무엇을 받을 수 있는가?
　(A) 버스 승차권
　(B) 잼과 파이의 요리법
　(C) 5월 28일 오프닝 행사 초대
　(D) 과수원 행사 종료에 대한 공지

해설 웹페이지의 마지막 부분에서 종료에 관한 정보를 이메일로 받으려면 웹사이트를 방문해 등록하라고 명시되어 있다. 그러므로 정답은 (D) Announcements of the orchard closing이다.

[181-185] 다음 웹사이트 게시글들에 관한 문제입니다.

Landon 컴퓨터 커뮤니티 포럼

181 Landon FN2 Slimline이 무선 접속 상태 유지가 안 됩니다.
Daniel Palmer 작성
8월 10일, 오전 10시 32분

Landon FNT 모델을 거의 4년 동안 쓴 후, 사흘 전 저는 새 모델인 Landon FN2 Slimline 노트북을 구입하기로 결정했습니다. 전반적으로 저는 이 새로운 모델에 매우 만족하지만, **181** 집에서 무선 인터넷 네트워크 접속을 유지하는 데 계속 어려움을 겪고 있습니다. 노트북은 처음에 네트워크로 연결이 되기는 하지만, 10분이 지난 후에는 접속이 끊깁니다. **183** 저의 FN2 Slimline을 다시 시작하거나 집의 네트워크에 다시 연결하는 것을 포함하여 몇 가지 해결책을 시도해 보았습니다. 그 어느 것도 소용이 없는 것 같습니다.

이 문제에 직면했던 다른 분들은 안 계십니까? 저는 이 문제가 모든 FN2 노트북에서 발생하는 것인지, 아니면 제 것만 그런지 잘 모르겠습니다. **182** 저는 제 네트워크에는 이상이 없다는 것을 장담합니다. 다른 브랜드의 노트북을 사용하고 있는 제 룸메이트들은 인터넷 접속에 문제가 없습니다.

어휘 wireless 무선의 I connectivity 연결(성) I post by ~에 의해 게재된 게시물 I overall 전반적으로, 전반적인 I initially 처음에 I disconnect 연결[접속]을 끊다 I solution 해결, 해결책 I restart 다시 시작하다, 재개하다 I reconnect 다시 연결하다 I encounter (위험·곤란 등에) 부닥치다, 접하다 I occur 발생하다

ACTUAL TEST

Landon 컴퓨터 커뮤니티 포럼

회신: Landon FN2 Slimline이 무선 접속 상태 유지가 안 됩니다.
Amira Mirelli 작성
8월 10일, 오후 12시 17분

안녕하세요 Daniel,

저도 최근에 당신과 같은 노트북을 Landon 컴퓨터에서 구매했고, 몇몇 동료들과 제가 비슷한 문제를 겪었습니다. 저는 네트워크 박스를 재설정하거나, **183** 노트북을 재부팅하고, 전원 케이블도 확인해서 다시 끼워봤지만 아무런 성과도 없었습니다. 그리고 나서 **184** 저는 Landon 컴퓨터의 지원 센터에 전화하기로 결정했습니다. 기술자는 즉시 제가 그 문제를 해결하도록 도와주었습니다. 그녀는 저에게 그 문제를 바로 해결해 줄 소프트웨어 업데이트의 링크 주소를 보내주었습니다. **185** 업데이트를 간단하게 다운로드 받아서 설치하세요(약 5분밖에 걸리지 않습니다). 소프트웨어 업데이트는 Landon 컴퓨터 웹사이트의 '다운로드' 섹션에서 찾을 수 있습니다. 일단 그 업데이트가 설치되면, 당신은 네트워크 접속 유지에 더 이상 문제를 겪지 않을 것입니다.

어휘 coworker 동료 I experience 겪다, 경험하다 I similar 흡사한 I reset 재설정하다 I technician 기술자 I immediately 즉시 I resolve 해결하다 I fix 고치다 I once 일단 ~하면 I install 설치하다

181. 첫 번째 게시글의 주제는 무엇인가?
(A) 새 노트북의 기술적 문제
(B) 노트북 컴퓨터 사용 설명서의 오류
(C) 지연된 수리 서비스
(D) 웹사이트의 끊어진 링크

해설 첫 번째 게시글의 제목이 Landon FN2 Slimline의 무선 인터넷 접속 유지가 계속 안 된다는 것이고, 본문도 집에서 계속 그 문제로 어려움을 겪고 있다는 내용인 것으로 보아 Landon FN2 Slimline 노트북에 전반적으로 기술적인 문제가 있다는 내용의 글이다. 따라서 정답은 (A) A technical problem with a new laptop이다.

182. Mr. Palmer의 무선 네트워크에 관하여 알 수 있는 것은 무엇인가?
(A) 교체될 필요가 있다.
(B) 룸메이트에 의해 컴퓨터 환경이 설정되었다.
(C) 제대로 작동한다.
(D) 거의 사용되지 않는다.

해설 첫 번째 지문의 두 번째 단락에서 Mr. Palmer는 자신의 노트북 컴퓨터에서 네트워크 접속이 안될 뿐 자신의 네트워크에는 이상이 없다고 확인하고 있으므로 정답이 (C) It is functioning properly.임을 확인할 수 있다.

183. Mr. Palmer와 Ms. Mirelli는 문제를 해결하기 위해 어떻게 노력했는가?
(A) 인터넷 설정을 조정함으로써
(B) 손상된 부품을 교체함으로써
(C) 전원 케이블을 점검함으로써
(D) 노트북을 다시 시작함으로써

해설 첫 번째 지문의 Mr. Palmer와 두 번째 지문의 Ms. Mirelli가 공통적으로 시도한 행동을 찾아야 한다. 첫 번째 지문에서 재부팅을 했다고 이야기하고 있고, 두 번째 게시글을 통하여 Ms. Mirelli 또한 컴퓨터 재부팅을 했다고 이야기하고 있으므로 정답은 (D) By restarting the laptop이다.

184. Ms. Mirelli에 관하여 언급된 것은 무엇인가?
(A) Landon 컴퓨터의 오랜 고객이다.
(B) Mr. Palmer에게 전에 이메일을 보냈다.
(C) Landon 컴퓨터에 근무한다.
(D) Landon 컴퓨터의 담당자에게 연락했다.

해설 두 번째 지문인 Ms. Mirelli의 게시글에서 문제 해결을 위해 Ms. Mirelli가 지원 센터에 전화하기로 결정했다는 것을 확인할 수 있으므로 (D) She contacted a Landon Computers' representative. 가 정답이다.

185. Ms. Mirelli는 무엇을 권하는가?
(A) Landon 컴퓨터에 제품을 반품할 것
(B) 소프트웨어 업데이트를 설치할 것
(C) 기술자와 회의를 잡을 것
(D) 취급 설명서를 구할 것

해설 두 번째 지문에서 Ms. Mirelli의 경험담을 살펴보면 기술자가 링크에서 소프트웨어 업데이트 링크 주소를 알려주어서 기술적인 문제를 바로 해결했다고 하고 있기 때문에 Ms. Mirelli가 권하고 있는 것은 소프트웨어 업데이트를 설치하는 것이다. 따라서 정답은 (B) Installing a software update임을 알 수 있다.

[186-190] 다음 제품 정보와 온라인 사용 후기, 답장에 관한 문제입니다.

https://www.gosunwraps.com/x_treme

홈	제품	홍보	계정	지원

SunWraps

유형 (회색)	가격
어린이용	150달러
어린이용 (맞춤제작)	250달러
성인용	250달러
성인용 (맞춤제작)	350달러

알림: **188** 밝은 남색 옵션도 곧 이용 가능합니다!

세부사항:
새로 나온 SunWraps X-Treme 선글라스는 당신의 활동적인 라이프스타일로 인해 생기는 마모에 대비하여 디자인되었습니다.

• 긁힘 방지 렌즈
• 견고한 테
• 미끄러짐을 방지하기 위한 특별한 무게

어휘 tint 색조, 옅은 색 I wear and tear 마모 I generate 발생시키다, 만들어 내다 I indestructible 파괴할 수 없는 I scratch 긁힘 I slippage 미끄러짐

https://www.gosunwraps.com/review_x-treme

1월 10일 Ramesh Khalsa 작성

친구들과 스키를 타러 자주 가는데, 갈 때마다 선글라스를 잃어버리거나 깨뜨리거나 긁히는 것 같습니다. 제가 소유했던 대부분의 안경은 스포츠의 모험적인 속성을 견디지 못했기에 **186** 오랜 기간동안 사용이 가능한 것을 하나 찾아냈다는 것은 큰 기쁨이었습니다. SunWraps가 정말 마음에 들지만 정말 많은 사람들이 저와 같은 색을 착용하더군요. 더 많은 옵션을 제공해주시면 좋겠습니다.

또한, 더 튼튼한 보호 케이스 제공에 관한 **187** 의견을 제시하고자 합니다. 안경과 같이 딸려오는 케이스는 너무 엉성해 보여서 너무 빨리 닳을 것 같습니다. 안경이 튼튼하지만, 케이스로 인해 이동 중 훼손될 수도 있을 겁니다.

어휘 adventurous 모험적인 I state 진술하다 I case 의견, 입장 I protective 보호하는 I flimsy 엉성하게 만든 I wear out 닳다 I damage 훼손하다

Mr. Khalsa께,

저희 선글라스를 즐겁게 사용하고 계시다니 기쁩니다. 그리고 기쁜 소식을 전해드립니다. 고객님의 요청도 있었고 그와 유사한 많은 요청이 있었기 때문에 저희 제품을 두 가지 유형으로 이용하실 수 있게 하겠습니다. b.herman@gosunwraps로 이메일을 보내셔서 **188** 아름다운 새 색상으로 나온 무료 표준형 X-Treme 선글라스를 하나 받으세요. **189** 이 선물을 보내드리기 전에 포스팅을 하신 후에 받으신 확인 이메일을 먼저 전달해주셔야 합니다.

또한, 케이스의 내구성에 관해 걱정하신다는 걸 알고 있습니다. 비록 얇지만, 저희가 사용하는 최신 소재는 여행 가방 안에서 아무렇게나 던지거나 깔고 앉아도 그 압력을 견디어낼 수 있으니 안심하셔도 됩니다. **190** 연구실에서 철저한 실험을 거쳤으며, 얇은 버전이 특별히 견고하고 오래간다는 것을 입증했습니다.

Bob Herman
SunWraps 총괄 부장

어휘 confirmation e-mail 확인 메일 I durability 내구성 I reassure 안심시키다 I slim 얇은 I state-of-the-art 최신식의 I material 소재 I withstand 견디 내다 I stress 압력 I toss 던지다 I thoroughly 철저히 I exceptionally 특별히 I sturdy 견고한 I long-lasting 오래 가는, 오래 지속될 수 있는

---

186. Mr. Khalsa는 자신의 선글라스에 대해 무엇을 썼는가?
(A) 현재 사용하는 테의 다른 사이즈를 갖고 싶다.
(B) 렌즈가 너무 두껍다.
(C) 여가 활동을 하는 동안 손상되지 않는다.
(D) 최근에 구입했다.

해설 이전에 사용했던 선글라스들은 스포츠 활동을 하는 동안 쉽게 망가졌는데, 오래 가는 것을 찾아서 기쁘다고 말했으므로 스포츠를 즐길 때도 손상되지 않는다고 말하는 (C) They do not get damaged during recreational activities.가 정답이다.

---

187. 사용 후기에서 두 번째 단락, 첫 번째 줄의 단어 "case"와 의미상 가장 가까운 것은
(A) 물품 목록
(B) 외양
(C) 입장, 견해
(D) 용기

해설 지문에서 사용한 case는 어떤 사안에 대한 자신의 입장이나 주장을 나타내므로 '입장, 견해'라는 의미가 있는 (C) position이 정답이다.

---

188. Mr. Herman은 Mr. Khalsa에게 무엇을 제공하는가?
(A) 표준형 회색 선글라스
(B) 표준형 남색 선글라스
(C) 맞춤 회색 선글라스
(D) 맞춤 남색 선글라스

해설 이메일에서 Mr. Herman은 Mr. Khalsa에게 이메일을 보내주면, 새로운 색상의 표준형 선글라스를 무료로 주겠다고 했는데, 웹사이트의 제품 소개에서 남색도 곧 출시된다고 했으므로 이 새로운 색상은 남색이라는 것을 알 수 있으므로 (B) Standard navy sunglasses를 정답으로 선택해야 한다.

---

189. Mr. Khalsa는 SunWraps로부터 선물을 받기 위해 무엇을 해야 하는가?
(A) 신제품에 대한 간단한 설문지를 작성한다
(B) 웹사이트에 올린 부정적인 후기를 삭제한다
(C) 결함이 있는 일부 선글라스를 반품한다
(D) 그가 사용 후기를 썼다는 것을 증명할 서류를 보낸다

해설 문제의 to receive a gift from SunWraps가 키워드인데 이 부분은 이메일에서 Before we mail this gift to you로 바뀌어 있다. 사용 후기를 쓴 후 받은 확인 이메일을 다시 회사로 보내달라고 했으므로 이 부분을 paraphrasing한 (D) Send a document proving he wrote a review가 정답이다.

---

190. Mr. Herman이 보호 케이스에 관하여 언급한 것은?
(A) 엄격한 실험이 진행되었다.
(B) 이전 버전보다 더 엉성하다.
(C) 다른 종류보다 가볍다.
(D) 더 유연하게 만들어졌다.

해설 사용 후기의 두 번째 단락을 보면 Mr. Khalsa는 선글라스 케이스의 내구성이 더 좋아지기를 바란다는 것을 알 수 있다. 사용 후기에 대한 답장에서 제품의 내구성에 대한 우려에 대한 응답으로 케이스에 사용된 최신 소재는 연구실에서 철저한 실험을 거쳐 견고하고 오래 간다는 것이 입증되었다고 했으므로 정답은 (A) It underwent rigorous tests.이다.

알림: 금요일에 책상의 짐을 꾸리세요!

아실지도 모르겠지만, Agro-Gene 직원들은 주말 동안 Sonoma Plaza 건너편에 있는 새로운 연구소 건물로 이전할 것입니다. **191** 이삿짐 회사가 모든 것을 새 건물로 가져가기 위해 금요일에 야근하는 것에 대해 동의했고 오후 5시 정각에 시작할 것입니다.

192 퇴근 시간 30분 전에 중요한 서류를 서랍에 넣어서 잠그고 모든 연구 장비를 치워 실험실의 보안을 유지하는 것이 중요합니다.

월요일에 새 건물에서 모두 만나기를 기대하며 즐거운 주말 되기 바랍니다.

어휘   pack 짐을 싸다 | brand-new 새로운 | lock 잠그다 | drawer 서랍 | put away 치우다 | equipment 장비

수신: **191** Caleb McCleod ⟨cmc@agro-gene.com⟩
발신: Sheena Estes ⟨s.estes@mechtransporters.com⟩
날짜: 9월 3일
제목: 이전 일정

Mr. McCleod께,

192 이것은 9월 3일 금요일 및 9월 4일 토요일 일정을 확인해드리기 위한 이메일입니다. **191** 귀하가 요청하신 대로, 저희 직원들이 금요일 저녁 오후 5시부터 모든 가구와 전자 장비를 건물에서 꺼낼 것입니다. **193** 중장비들은 모두 지하로 옮겨야 하고 그곳에 실험실 기술자들이 있을 것이라고 하셨습니다. 엘리베이터가 장비가 들어갈 만큼 크기가 충분한지 확인하겠습니다. 모든 작업은 토요일 오후 3시까지 완료될 것입니다.

문의나 특이사항이 있으시면 언제든지 물류부서의 Gabriel에게 연락주시기 바랍니다.

Sheena Estes
Mech 운송회사

어휘   confirm 확인하다 | machinery 기기 | basement 지하층 | logistics department 물류 부서

Agro-Gene 본사 이전

Jennifer D'Amato 작성

외관을 봐서는 알 수 없겠지만 19세기 Tempero Tower는 멋지게 단장을 했다. "건물이 역사적으로 유명한 외관은 유지하고 있지만, **193** Agro-Gene의 새 본사가 위치할 일층과 지하에는 많은 변화가 있었습니다"라고 Agro-Gene 회장 Caleb McCleod가 말한다.

이 벤처기업은 포도와 포도덩굴에 대한 연구를 개척해왔다. 특히 포도덩굴이 물을 덜 필요로 하도록 만들기 위한 연구를 하고 있다. 수석 과학자 Kim Scotts는 "기온의 변화로 인해 **194** 전통적인 와인 생산 지역의 연강수량이 줄고 있기 때문에 저희는 더 건조한 환경에서 잘 자라는 덩굴을 만들고 있습니다"라고 설명한다.

기자들은 최근 새 시설에서 진행된 프로모션 투어에서 Agro-Gene의 발전된 실험실을 들여다볼 수 있었다. **195** "이 새 공간은 어떠한 위험 화학물질도 공기 중으로 스며들지 못하도록 해줍니다"라고 Agro-Gene의 대변인 Howard Ruiz가 말했다.

Agro-Gene은 또한 매달 첫째, 셋째 토요일에 유전자 변형 식품의 현황에 대해 대중들을 대상으로 한 세미나를 제공한다. 이 모임은 변형식품의 위험성을 둘러싼 잘못된 믿음에 대해 알려주고 이를 타파하도록 의도되었다. 누구나 참가할 수 있다.

어휘   facade 건물 앞면 | startup 벤처기업, 신생기업 | peek into ~을 엿보다 | thrive 잘 자라다 | dispel (믿음, 느낌 등을) 떨쳐버리다 | myth 잘못된 믿음 | genetically engineered food 유전자 조작 식품

---

191. 공지사항은 누가 썼겠는가?

(A) Mr. Ruiz

(B) Mr. McCleod

(C) Ms. Scotts

(D) Ms. Estes

해설   공지사항에서 알려주기를 이삿짐 회사가 금요일 오후 5시부터 모든 물건을 옮겨 주기로 동의했다고 했는데 이것은 누군가의 요청이 있었음을 암시한다. 그런데 이메일을 읽어보면 '당신의 요청에 따라' 작업을 진행한다고 나와 있으므로 이삿짐 회사에 서비스를 의뢰한 사람은 이메일을 받는 사람인 Mr. McCleod이고 이 사람이 공지사항도 썼음을 유추할 수 있다. 따라서 정답은 (B) Mr. McCleod이다.

---

192. 9월 3일에 직원들이 하도록 지시하는 것은 무엇인가?

(A) 업무공간을 정돈한다

(B) 컴퓨터의 비밀번호를 만든다

(C) Sonoma Plaza에서 만난다

(D) 프로젝트 예산을 검토한다

해설   문제의 on September 3가 키워드이므로 먼저 지문을 훑어봐서 이것을 찾아내야 한다. 이메일의 첫 문장에 등장하는데, 이 날은 금요일이다. 그리고 나서 공지사항을 보면 이 날 해야 할 일을 지시하는 내용이 나오는데, 퇴근 시간 30분 전에 중요한 서류를 서랍에 넣어서 잠그고 모든 연구 장비를 치워 실험실의 보안을 유지하는 것이 중요하다고 했으므로 지시하는 사항은 실험실의 정돈이다. 그러므로 정답으로 (A) Organize a workspace를 선택해야 한다.

---

193. 실험실 기술자들에 대해 나타나 있는 것은 무엇인가?

(A) 금요일 오후 5시까지 근무할 것이다.

(B) 동물을 연구한다.

(C) 지하에서 일할 것이다.

(D) 사막 환경을 연구할 것이다.

해설   먼저 문제의 키워드 lab technicians를 지문에서 찾아내야 하는데, 이메일의 You mentioned that all of the heavy machinery goes in the basement where your lab technicians will be에서 발견할 수 있으며, 이 문장에 따르면 이들은 건물의 '지하층'에서 근무할 예정이다. 그리고 기사로 옮겨가 보면 Argo-Gene이 건물의 지하와 1층

을 사용할 것이라고 했으므로 (C) They will work underground.가 정답이다.

194. Agro-Gene에 대해 사실인 것은 무엇인가?
(A) 최근 새 사장을 임명했다.
(B) 토요일에는 폐점한다.
(C) 다양한 와인을 제조한다.
(D) 새로운 종류의 식물을 개발한다.

해설 기사에서 인용한 수석 과학자 Kim Scotts의 설명에서 정답을 알아낼 수 있는데, 기후 변화에 따라 강수량이 감소했기 때문에 더 건조한 환경에서도 잘 자랄 수 있는 식물을 개발한다고 했으므로 (D) It develops new kinds of plants.가 정답이다.

195. Mr. Ruiz는 새 시설에 대해 무엇이라고 말하는가?
(A) 해로운 요소로부터 환경을 보호한다.
(B) 임대 비용이 매우 저렴하다.
(C) 외부 방문자를 허용하지 않는다.
(D) 실험을 실시할 공간이 더 많다.

해설 문제의 키워드는 Mr. Ruiz say이며 이것은 기사에서 stated Howard Ruiz로 바뀌어 있다. 이 사람이 한 말을 읽어보면 정답을 알 수 있는데, 이 새 공간은 어떠한 위험 화학물질도 공기 중으로 스며들지 못하도록 해준다고 했으므로 이 부분을 Paraphrasing한 (A) They protect the environment from harmful elements.가 정답이 된다.

[196-200] 다음 공지사항과 평가, 기사에 관한 문제입니다.

A-Z Music

친애하는 고객님께,

A-Z 음반은 9월 1일 Santa Costa로 이전합니다. Downtown Miravalle에서의 마지막 주 8월 25~31일에 오셔서 모든 음악 제품에 대한 파격 세일을 이용하세요. 오시는 모든 분들께 가까운 저희 Santa Costa 매장에서 첫 구입에 사용하실 수 있는 20퍼센트 할인 쿠폰을 드립니다.

197 애석하게도 오랜 세월 함께한 매니저 Mark Appleton에게도 작별을 고하게 되었습니다. 더 이상 매장에서 그의 추천음악을 들을 수는 없겠지만, KZAJ 102.5 FM 〈After Hours〉라는 프로그램을 진행하면서 새로운 경력을 시작하오니 꼭 한 번 들어보시기 바랍니다.

애용해주셔서 감사드리며 Santa Costa에서도 뵙기를 기대합니다!

진심을 담아,

196 Angie Ernst
점주

어휘 **great deal** 매우 싼 거래 | **good for** (금전 등 면에서) ~의 가치가 있는; ~동안 유효한 | **check out** 살펴보다 | **patronage** (특정 상점·식당 등에 대한 고객의) 애용, 후원

---

https://www.KZAJ1025.com/comments

| 홈 | 프로그램 | 피드백 | 연락처 |

A-Z 음반이 Santa Costa로 옮겨갔을 때는 실망스러웠습니다. **197** 그러나 전 매니저가 이제 라디오에 나온다는 것을 알고는 기뻤습니다. 매주 청취자들이 지역의 콘서트 티켓을 받을 수 있는 콘테스트를 **198** 진행하더군요. 저와 제 동료들은 〈After Hours〉의 애청자들이며 프로그램이 앞으로 여러 해 동안 계속 방송되었으면 좋겠습니다.

Dagny Caroll

어휘 **delighted** 기쁜

시 중심부의 재활성화

Miravalle 시의회는 시내 개조의 두 번째 단계가 거의 완료되어 간다고 발표했다. 가장 낡은 건물들은 대규모 복원작업을 했다. Nevardo Flores 시장은 공사 때문에 일부 기존 상점들이 이전해야만 했지만 **199** 이러한 변화로 더 많은 관광객들을 유치하여 분명 시에 도움이 될 것이라고 믿는다. 계획을 검토한 금융 분석가들은 이러한 면에 있어서 Flores 시장의 견해에 동의한다.

많은 사람들이 시내 중심가의 이미지의 변화를 반기는 반면, 지역에서 오래 운영해온 일부 사업체들은 이웃 도시로 떠나고 있다. 주민들은 분명 Hermosa 꽃집이나 Gabby's 패션, **196** A-Z 음반과 같은 오랫동안 가장 사랑받던 업체들을 그리워할 것이다. 이들은 모두 임대료를 최대 40퍼센트까지 인상하려는 시의 계획을 이유로 들어 이전했다.

그러나 **200** 시 공무원 Jeff Gary는 일단 도심 개조가 완료되면 시에 대한 효과는 긍정적일 것이라고 말한다. "Gabby's 패션 같은 일부 업체들이 이 기간 동안 이전해야만 한다는 점은 안타깝습니다. 그러나 우리는 이러한 방식으로 변화하는 것이 더 많은 수익성 좋은 사업체들을 끌어들이고 **200** 우리 시민들을 위한 더 많은 일자리를 창출할 것이라는 점에 관하여 낙관합니다"라고 이 시의원은 말했다.

어휘 **revitalize** 새로운 활력을 주다, 재활성화시키다 | **existing** 기존의 | **attract** (공장 따위를) 유치하다 | **view** 견해, 생각, 의견, 태도 | **cite** (이유·예를) 들다, 끌어 대다 | **councilman** (지방 의회) 의원

196. Ms. Ernst는 왜 매장을 옮기겠는가?
(A) 부동산 가격이 너무 높기 때문에
(B) 직업을 바꾸기 때문에
(C) 매장에 공간이 더 필요하기 때문에
(D) 더 편리한 자리를 찾았기 때문에

해설 **이중지문 연계 추론** 일단 공지사항 마지막에 보낸 사람의 이름이 Angie Ernst인데, 이 사람은 A-Z 음반의 소유주(Owner)이다. 그리고 기사를 읽어보면 A-Z 음반이 최대 40퍼센트까지 임대료를 올리려는 시의 계획을 이유로 들면서 이전했다는 내용이 나오므로 이 부분을 패러프레이징한 (A) Because property prices are too high가 정답이다.

197. Mr. Appleton의 프로그램에 관하여 나타나 있는 점은 무엇인가?

(A) 상품을 나누어준다.

(B) 전에는 Ms. Ernst가 진행했다.

(C) 여러 해 동안 방송되었다.

(D) 지역 사업체들에게 할인을 제공한다.

해설　우선 Mr. Appleton's program이 문제의 키워드인데, 공지사항에서 Appleton이라는 이름이 나오는 부분을 읽어보면, 오랫동안 A-Z 음반에서 근무한 매니저인데 사임 후 라디오 프로그램을 진행할 것이라는 내용이다. 그리고 라디오 방송국 홈페이지의 고객 평가를 읽어보면 A-Z 음반의 전 매니저가 진행하는 라디오 프로그램에서 콘서트 티켓을 상품으로 주는 콘테스트를 진행한다는 내용이 나오므로 여기서 정답을 알아낼 수 있다. 상품을 나누어준다는 뜻의 문장인 (A) It gives out prizes.가 정답이다.

198. 평가에서 첫 번째 단락, 두 번째 줄의 단어 "runs"와 의미상 가장 가까운 것은

(A) 운전하다

(B) 작동시키다

(C) 경주[경쟁]하다

(D) (계획, 행사 등을) 준비[조직]하다

해설　주어진 단어의 사전적 의미를 보면 보기에 있는 네 개의 동사가 모두 동의어가 될 수 있으므로 문맥을 통해 정답을 파악해야 한다. He runs a weekly contest에서 runs는 라디오 프로그램의 한 코너를 '운영한다'는 뜻이므로 (D) organizes가 정답이다.

199. Downtown Miravalle에 관하여 무엇이 시사되고 있는가?

(A) 여러 유적지가 있다.

(B) 시의회 건물이 그곳으로 옮겨갈 것이다.

(C) 더 많은 관광객들을 불러모을 것이다.

(D) Mr. Gary의 사무실이 있다.

해설　기사문에서 Miravalle의 시장 Nevardo Flores가 관광객의 유치로 시가 이득을 볼 것이라고 믿고 있고, 금융 분석가들도 이 견해에 동의한다는 내용의 문장에서 정답이 (C) It will probably draw more visitors.임을 유추할 수 있다.

200. 기사에 따르면, Mr. Gary는 왜 개조 프로젝트에 관한 긍정적인 견해를 갖고 있는가?

(A) 대중교통 확충이라는 결과를 낳을 것이기 때문에

(B) 고용을 증대시킬 것이기 때문에

(C) 패션 지구를 형성할 것이기 때문에

(D) 조기에 마무리될 것이기 때문에

해설　문제의 키워드 Mr. Gary have a positive view를 찾기 위해 기사를 훑어가다 보면 키워드가 그대로 들어 있는 However, Jeff Gary, a city official, says that once the downtown renovation is complete, the effect on the town will be positive를 발견할 수 있다. 이어지는 내용을 읽어보면 개조 프로젝트로 인해 수익성을 갖춘 사업체들을 지역에 유치할 것이고 이것으로 인해 일자리가 창출된다고 말하고 있으므로 create more jobs를 패러프레이징한 (B) Because it will increase employment가 정답이다.

토익 개념&실전 종합서

파고다토익

실력 완성 RC